BUSINESS ANALYSIS & VALUATION

USING FINANCIAL STATEMENTS

Fourth Edition — Text & Cases

Krishna G. Palepu, PhD

Ross Graham Walker Professor of Business Administration
Harvard University

Paul M. Healy, PhD, ACA

James R. Williston Professor of Business Administration
Harvard University

SOUTH-WESTERN
CENGAGE Learning

Australia • Brazil • Japan • Korea • Mexico • Singapore • Spain • United Kingdom • United States

SOUTH-WESTERN
CENGAGE Learning

Business Analysis & Valuation: Using Financial Statements, 4th edition
Krishna G. Palepu, Paul M. Healy

VP/Editorial Director:
Jack W. Calhoun

VP/Editor-in-Chief:
Rob Dewey

Acquisitions Editor:
Matt Filimonov

Developmental Editor:
Craig Avery

Marketing Manager:
Kristen Hurd

Content Project Manager:
Diane Bowdler

Manager of Technology, Editorial:
Matt McKinney

Technology Project Manager:
Robin Browning

Website Project Manager:
Brian Courter

Manufacturing Coordinator:
Doug Wilke

Production House:
Integra Software Services
Pvt. Ltd.

Printer:
Transcontinental Gagne
Louiseville, QC

Art Director:
Linda Helcher

Internal Designer:
Ke Design

Cover Designer:
Paul Neff

Cover Image:
Jerry Alexander/Stone/
(c) Getty Images

Library of Congress Control
Number: 2007924488

For more information about
our products, contact us at:

Cengage Learning
Customer & Sales Support
1-800-354-9706

South-Western
Cengage Learning
5191 Natorp Boulevard
Mason, OH 45040
USA

PREFACE

Financial statements are the basis for a wide range of business analysis. Managers use them to monitor and judge their firms' performance relative to competitors, to communicate with external investors, to help judge what financial policies they should pursue, and to evaluate potential new businesses to acquire as part of their investment strategy. Securities analysts use financial statements to rate and value companies they recommend to clients. Bankers use them in deciding whether to extend a loan to a client and to determine the loan's terms. Investment bankers use them as a basis for valuing and analyzing prospective buyouts, mergers, and acquisitions. And consultants use them as a basis for competitive analysis for their clients. Not surprisingly, therefore, we find that there is a strong demand among business students for a course that provides a framework for using financial statement data in a variety of business analysis and valuation contexts. The purpose of this book is to provide such a framework for business students and practitioners. The first three editions of this book have succeeded far beyond our expectations in equipping readers with this useful framework, and the book has gained proponents in accounting and finance departments in business schools in the U.S. and around the world.

CHANGES FROM THE THIRD EDITION

Colleagues and reviewers have made suggestions and comments that led us to incorporate the following changes in the fourth edition:

- Data, analyses, and issues have been thoroughly updated in the fourth edition.
- The financial analysis and valuation chapters (chapters 6–8) have been updated with a focus on firms in the U.S. discount retail sector, primarily Wal-Mart and Dell.
- Chapter 6 on forecasting has been enhanced with an expanded discussion of business strategy analysis.
- We have increased conciseness by incorporating key elements of the chapter in the third edition on debt financing into this edition's chapters on credit analysis (Chapter 10) and corporate governance (Chapter 12).
- In our Text and Cases edition, we have included new and updated Harvard Business School cases, both to accompany the individual chapters as well as in Section 4 containing additional cases. In all, we include 29 cases in the fourth edition.
- We have enhanced the usability of the BAV software tool, including, most importantly, the ability to automatically download data from the Compustat database of the Wharton Research Data Services. This comprehensive software model, the **BAV Tool**, implements the analytical framework and techniques discussed in this book. BAV allows students to import a company's reported financial statements from any source, as long as they are in a Microsoft Excel spreadsheet format, and analyze them. The tool allows the analyst to import financial statements of a company from any database into an excel-based workbook, create a set of financial statements in a standardized format to facilitate analysis, and implement the key steps of analysis

discussed in the book – accounting adjustments, ratio and cash flow analysis, preparation of pro forma financial statements for a chosen forecast horizon (up to fifteen years), and estimate the intrinsic value of the company using a variety of valuation techniques. User-friendly interface and drop down menus allow the analyst to navigate through the tool with ease. Built-in databases of historical financial ratios allow students to compare their forecasting assumptions with historical trends.

The tool facilitates the following activities: (1) recasting the reported financial statements in a standard format for analysis; (2) performing accounting analysis as discussed in Chapters 3 and 4, making desired accounting adjustments, and producing restated financials; (3) computing ratios and free cash flows presented in Chapter 5; (4) producing forecasted income statement, balance sheet, and cash flow statements for as many as 15 years into the future, using the approach discussed in Chapter 6; and (5) valuing a company (either assets or equity) from these forecasts and preparing a terminal value forecast using the abnormal earnings, the abnormal returns, and discounted cash flow methods discussed in Chapters 7 and 8. The tool also allows students to graph their assumptions and compare them with the historical performance of a large group of U.S. companies that are in the same performance range at the beginning of the forecasting period. This comparison is facilitated by a database consisting of key ratios for a comprehensive set of U.S. public companies listed on Standard & Poor's Compustat. We think that the BAV Tool will make it significantly easier for students to apply the framework and techniques discussed in the book in a real-world context.

KEY FEATURES

This book differs from other texts in business and financial analysis in a number of important ways. We introduce and develop a **four-part framework for business analysis and valuation** using financial statement data. We then show how this framework can be applied to a variety of decision contexts.

Framework for Analysis

We begin the book with a discussion of the role of accounting information and intermediaries in the economy, and how financial analysis can create value in well functioning markets (Chapter 1). We identify four key components, or steps, of effective financial statement analysis:

- Business strategy analysis
- Accounting analysis
- Financial analysis
- Prospective analysis

The first step, **business strategy analysis** (Chapter 2), involves developing an understanding of the business and competitive strategy of the firm being analyzed. Incorporating business strategy into financial statement analysis is one of the distinctive features of this book. Traditionally, this step has been ignored by other financial statement analysis books. However, we believe that it is critical to begin financial statement analysis with a company's strategy because it provides an important foundation for the subsequent analysis. The strategy analysis section discusses contemporary tools for analyzing a company's industry, its competitive position and sustainability within an industry, and the company's corporate strategy.

Accounting analysis (Chapters 3 and 4) involves examining how accounting rules and conventions represent a firm's business economics and strategy in its financial statements, and, if necessary, developing adjusted accounting measures of perform-ance. In the accounting analysis section, we do not emphasize accounting rules. Instead we develop general approaches to analyzing assets, liabilities, entities, revenues, and expenses. We believe that such an approach enables students to effectively evaluate a company's accounting choices and accrual estimates, even if students have only a basic knowledge of accounting rules and standards. The material is also designed to allow students to make accounting adjustments rather than merely identify questionable accounting practices.

Financial analysis (Chapter 5) involves analyzing financial ratio and cash flow measures of the operating, financing, and investing performance of a company rela-tive to either key competitors or historical performance. Our distinctive approach focuses on using financial analysis to evaluate the effectiveness of a company's strategy and to make sound financial forecasts.

Finally, in **prospective analysis** (Chapters 6–8) we show how to develop fore-casted financial statements and how to use these to make estimates of a firm's value. Our discussion of valuation includes traditional discounted cash flow models as well as techniques that link value directly to accounting numbers. In discussing accounting-based valuation models, we integrate the latest academic research with traditional approaches such as earnings and book value multiples that are widely used in practice.

Although we cover all four steps of business analysis and valuation in the book, we recognize that the extent of their use depends on the user's decision context. For example, bankers are likely to use business strategy analysis, accounting analysis, financial analysis, and the forecasting portion of prospective analysis. They are less likely to be interested in formally valuing a prospective client.

Application of the Framework to Decision Contexts

The next section of the book shows how our business analysis and valuation frame-work can be applied to a variety of decision contexts:

- Equity securities analysis (Chapter 9)
- Credit analysis and distress prediction (Chapter 10)
- Merger and acquisition analysis (Chapter 11)
- Communication and governance (Chapter 12)

For each of these topics we present an overview to provide a foundation for the class discussions. Where possible we discuss relevant institutional details and the results of academic research that are useful in applying the analysis concepts developed earlier in the book. For example, the chapter on credit analysis shows how banks and rating agencies use financial statement data to develop analysis for lending decisions and to rate public debt issues. This chapter also presents academic research on how to determine whether a company is financially distressed.

Thomson ONE: Business School Edition

The fourth edition also includes access to *Thomson ONE: Business School Edition*, a web-based portal product that provides Thomson Financial content for the purpose of financial analysis. Access to Thomson ONE Business School Edition provides the capability of doing supplemental financial research that is independent of the text and its BAV Software. This application delivers powerful and flexible tools for turning critical market data into actionable intelligence for educational purposes. *Thomson ONE Business School Edition* is an educational version of the same financial resources used by Wall Street analysts on a daily basis. It includes the following content sets:

Worldscope® Includes company profiles, financials and accounting results, market per-share data, annual information, and monthly prices going back to 1980.

I/B/E/S Consensus Estimates Includes consensus estimates, analyst-by-analyst earnings coverage, and analysts' forecasts.

Disclosure SEC Database Includes company profiles, annual and quarterly company financials, pricing information, and earnings.

The analytical framework provided in the text—together with the Harvard Business School cases in the Text and Cases edition, the latest version of the BAV Software, Tool, and access to Thomson ONE: Business School Edition—help provide users with business and financial analysis tools needed for successful financial leadership in today's strategic business environment.

USING THE BOOK

We designed the book so that it is flexible for courses in financial statement analysis for a variety of student audiences—MBA students, master's in accounting students, executive program participants, and undergraduates in accounting or finance. Depending upon the audience, the instructor can vary the manner in which the conceptual materials in the chapters and end-of-chapter questions are used. To get the most out of the book, students should have completed basic courses in financial accounting, finance, and either business strategy or business economics. The text provides a concise overview of some of these topics. But it would probably be difficult for students with no prior knowledge in these fields to use the chapters as stand-alone coverage of them.

If the book is used for students with prior working experience or for executives, the instructor can use almost a pure case approach, adding relevant lecture sections as needed. When teaching students with little work experience, a lecture class can be presented first, followed by an appropriate case or other assignment material. Alternatively, lectures can be used as a follow-up to cases to more clearly lay out the conceptual issues raised in the case discussions. This may be appropriate when the book is used in undergraduate capstone courses. In such a context, cases can be used in course projects that can be assigned to student teams.

ACKNOWLEDGMENTS

The first edition of this book was co-authored with our colleague and friend, Victor Bernard. Vic was the Price Waterhouse Professor of Accounting and Director of the Paton Accounting Center at the University of Michigan. He passed away unexpectedly on November 14, 1995. We are indebted to Vic for his contributions to the ideas reflected in the book. Over the years, we have continued to include Vic as a co-author since the initial project was such a team effort and many of his early contributions continued to be reflected in the text. We wish to acknowledge Vic's enduring contributions to our own views on financial analysis and valuation. However, we have decided that in the twelve years since Vic's passing, it is time to recognize the sad reality that almost all of Vic's material has been updated to reflect the changes that have occurred in the field.

We also wish to thank Arjuna Costa for his tireless research assistance in the revision of the text chapters; Jonathan Barnett for his work as a research assistant on prior editions of the book and especially for his help in developing the BAV Model; Keith MacKay (Village Software) and HBS Publishing for building and enhancing the BAV Model; Chris Allen for assistance with data on financial ratios for U.S. companies; the Division of Research at the Harvard Business School for assistance in developing materials for this book; and our past and present MBA students for stimulating our thinking and challenging us to continually improve our ideas and presentation.

We especially thank the following colleagues who gave us feedback as we wrote this edition: Randolph Coyner (Florida Atlantic University), John Hand (University of North Carolina, Chapel Hill), Mary Fox Luquette (University of Louisiana at Lafayette), Amin Mawani (York University), Laurel Bond Mitchell (University of Redlands and Pomona College), Partha Mohanram (Columbia University), Jay Rich (Illinois State University), Michael Sandretto (University of Illinois, Urbana-Champaign), William Salatka (Wilfred Laurier University), and Linda Thorne (York University).

We are also very grateful to Laurie Palepu and Deborah Marlino for their help and assistance throughout this project. Special gratitude goes to Rob Dewey and Matt Filimonov for their publishing leadership on this edition, to our colleagues, and to Craig Avery, Kristen Hurd, and Diane Bowdler for their developmental, marketing, and production help. Michael Sandretto deserves great credit for his careful reading of each chapter in page proof and for his numerous insights. We would like to thank our parents and families for their strong support and encouragement throughout this project.

Krishna G. Palepu
Paul M. Healy

AUTHORS

Krishna G. Palepu is the Ross Graham Walker Professor of Business Administration and Senior Associate Dean for International Development, at the Harvard Business School, Harvard University. Prior to assuming his current administrative position, Professor Palepu held other positions at the School, including Senior Associate Dean, Director of Research, and Chair, Accounting and Control Unit.

Professor Palepu's current research and teaching activities focus on strategy and governance. In the area of strategy, his recent focus has been on the globalization of emerging markets. In the area of corporate governance, Professor Palepu's work focuses on how to make corporate boards more effective, and on improving corporate disclosure. Professor Palepu teaches these topics in several HBS programs aimed at members of corporate boards: "How to make corporate boards more effective," "Audit Committees in the new era of governance," "Compensation Committees: Preparing the challenges ahead." He also co-led Harvard Business School's Corporate Governance, Leadership, and Values initiative, launched in response to the recent wave of corporate scandals and governance failures.

Professor Palepu serves on a number of public company and non-profit Boards. He has been on the Editorial Boards of leading academic journals, and has served as a consultant to a wide variety of businesses. He is also a frequent commentator in the news media on issues related to emerging markets and corporate governance. Professor Palepu has a doctorate from the Massachusetts Institute of Technology, and an Honorary Doctorate from the Helsinki School of Economics and Business Administration.

Paul M. Healy is James R. Williston Professor of Business Administration and Chair of the Accounting and Management Unit at Harvard Business School, Harvard University. Professor Healy joined Harvard Business School as a Professor of Business Administration in 1997. His primary teaching and research interests include corporate financial reporting, financial analysis, corporate governance, and corporate finance. Professor Healy received his B.C.A. Honors (1st Class) in Accounting and Finance from Victoria University, New Zealand in 1977, his M.S. in Economics from the University of Rochester in 1981, his Ph.D. in Business from the University of Rochester in 1983, and is a New Zealand CPA. In New Zealand, Professor Healy worked for Arthur Young and ICI. Prior to joining Harvard, Professor Healy spent fourteen years on the faculty at the M.I.T. Sloan School of Management, where he received awards for teaching excellence in 1991, 1992, and 1997.

In 1993–94 he served as Deputy Dean at the Sloan School, and in 1994–95 he visited London Business School and Harvard Business School.

Professor Healy's research has focused on the performance of financial analysts, the effectiveness of management disclosure strategies, post-merger performance, and earnings management. His work has been published in leading journals in accounting and finance. In 1990, his article 'The Effect of Bonus Schemes on Accounting Decisions,' published in *Journal of Accounting and Economics*, was awarded the AICPA/AAA Notable Contribution Award. His text *Business Analysis and Valuation* was awarded the AICPA/AAA's Wildman Medal for contributions to the practice in 1997, and the AICPA/AAA Notable Contribution Award in 1998.

CONTENTS

3: Overview of Accounting Analysis   *3-1*

4: Implementing Accounting Analysis   *4-1*

PART THREE
BUSINESS ANALYSIS AND VALUATION APPLICATIONS

PART FOUR:
ADDITIONAL CASES

PART ONE

FRAMEWORK

Chapter 1

A Framework for Business Analysis and Valuation Using Financial Statements

Thi chapter outlines a comprehensive framework for financial statement analysis. Because financial statements provide the most widely available data on public corporations' economic activities, investors and other stakeholders rely on financial reports to assess the plans and performance of firms and corporate managers.

A variety of questions can be addressed by business analysis using financial statements, as shown in the following examples:

- A security analyst may be interested in asking: "How well is the firm I am following performing? Did the firm meet my performance expectations? If not, why not? What is the value of the firm's stock given my assessment of the firm's current and future performance?"
- A loan officer may need to ask: "What is the credit risk involved in lending a certain amount of money to this firm? How well is the firm managing its liquidity and solvency? What is the firm's business risk? What is the additional risk created by the firm's financing and dividend policies?"
- A management consultant might ask: "What is the structure of the industry in which the firm is operating? What are the strategies pursued by various players in the industry? What is the relative performance of different firms in the industry?"
- A corporate manager may ask: "Is my firm properly valued by investors? Is our investor communication program adequate to facilitate this process?" or "Is this firm a potential takeover target? How much value can be added if we acquire this firm? How can we finance the acquisition?"
- An independent auditor would want to ask: "Are the accounting policies and accrual estimates in this company's financial statements consistent with my understanding of this business and its recent performance? Do these financial reports communicate the current status and significant risks of the business?"

The industrial age has been dominated by two distinct and broad ideologies for channeling savings into business investments—capitalism and central planning. The capitalist market model broadly relies on the market mechanism to govern economic activity, and decisions regarding investments are made privately. Centrally planned economies have used central planning and government agencies to pool national savings and to direct investments in business enterprises. The failure of this model is evident from the fact that most of these economies have abandoned it in favor of the market model. In almost all countries in the world today, capital markets play an important role in channeling financial resources from savers to business enterprises that need capital.

Financial statement analysis is a valuable activity when managers have in-depth information on a firm's strategies and performance and a variety of institutional factors make it unlikely that they fully disclose this information. In this setting, outside analysts attempt to create "inside information" from analyzing financial statement data, thereby gaining valuable insights about the firm's current performance and future prospects.

To understand the contribution that financial statement analysis can make, it is important to understand the role of financial reporting in the functioning of capital markets and the institutional forces that shape financial statements. Therefore, we first present a brief description of these forces followed by a discussion of the steps that an analyst must perform to extract information from financial statements and provide valuable forecasts.

THE ROLE OF FINANCIAL REPORTING IN CAPITAL MARKETS

A critical challenge for any economy is the allocation of savings to investment opportunities. Economies that do this well can exploit new business ideas to spur innovation and create jobs and wealth at a rapid pace. In contrast, economies that manage this process poorly tend to dissipate their wealth and fail to support business opportunities.

Figure 1-1 provides a schematic representation of how capital markets typically work. Savings in any economy are widely distributed among households. There are usually many new entrepreneurs and existing companies that would like to attract these savings to fund their business ideas. While both savers and entrepreneurs would like to do business with each other, matching savings to business investment opportunities is complicated for at least three reasons. First, entrepreneurs typically have better information than savers on the value of business investment opportunities. Second, communication by entrepreneurs to investors is not completely credible because investors know entrepreneurs have an incentive to inflate the value of their ideas. Third, savers generally lack the financial sophistication needed to analyze and differentiate between the various business opportunities.

The information and incentive problems lead to what economists call the "lemons" problem, which can potentially break down the functioning of capital markets.[1] It works like this: Consider a situation where half the business ideas are "good" and the other half are "bad." If investors cannot distinguish between the two types of business ideas, entrepreneurs with bad ideas will try to claim that their ideas are as valuable as the

FIGURE 1-1   Capital Markets

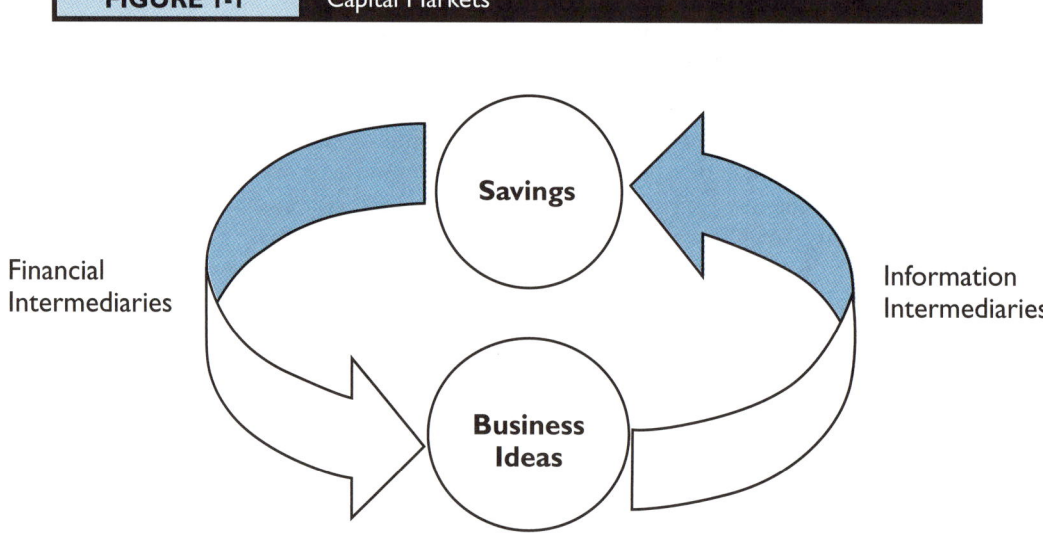

good ideas. Realizing this possibility, investors value both good and bad ideas at an average level. Unfortunately, this penalizes good ideas, and entrepreneurs with good ideas find the terms on which they can get financing to be unattractive. As these entrepreneurs leave the capital market, the proportion of bad ideas in the market increases. Over time, bad ideas "crowd out" good ideas, and investors lose confidence in this market.

The emergence of intermediaries can prevent such a market breakdown. Intermediaries are like a car mechanic who provides an independent certification of a used car's quality to help a buyer and seller agree on a price. There are two types of intermediaries in the capital markets. Financial intermediaries, such as venture capital firms, banks, mutual funds, and insurance companies, focus on aggregating funds from individual investors and analyzing different investment alternatives to make investment decisions. Information intermediaries, such as auditors, financial analysts, bond-rating agencies, and the financial press, focus on providing information to investors (and to the financial intermediaries who represent them) on the quality of various business investment opportunities. Both these types of intermediaries add value by helping investors distinguish good investment opportunities from the bad ones.

Financial reporting plays a critical role in the functioning of both the information intermediaries and financial intermediaries. Information intermediaries add value by either enhancing the credibility of financial reports (as auditors do), or by analyzing the information in financial statements (as analysts and the rating agencies do). Financial intermediaries rely on the information in financial statements to analyze investment opportunities, and they supplement this with information from other sources.

Ideally, the different intermediaries serve as a system of checks and balances to ensure the efficient functioning of the capital markets system. However, this is not always the case as on occasion the intermediaries tend to mutually reinforce rather than counterbalance each other. A number of problems can arise as a result of incentive issues, governance issues within the intermediary organizations themselves, and conflicts of interest, as evidenced by the spectacular failures of companies such as Enron and WorldCom.[2] However, in general this market mechanism functions efficiently and prices reflect all available information on a particular investment. Despite this overall market efficiency, individual securities may still be mispriced, thereby justifying the need for financial statement analysis.

In the following section, we discuss key aspects of the financial reporting system design that enable it to effectively play this vital role in the functioning of the capital markets.

FROM BUSINESS ACTIVITIES TO FINANCIAL STATEMENTS

Corporate managers are responsible for acquiring physical and financial resources from the firm's environment and using them to create value for the firm's investors. Value is created when the firm earns a return on its investment in excess of the cost of capital. Managers formulate business strategies to achieve this goal, and they implement them through business activities. A firm's business activities are influenced by its economic environment and its own business strategy. The economic environment includes the firm's industry, its input and output markets, and the regulations under which the firm operates. The firm's business strategy determines how the firm positions itself in its environment to achieve a competitive advantage.

As shown in Figure 1-2, a firm's financial statements summarize the economic consequences of its business activities. The firm's business activities in any time period are

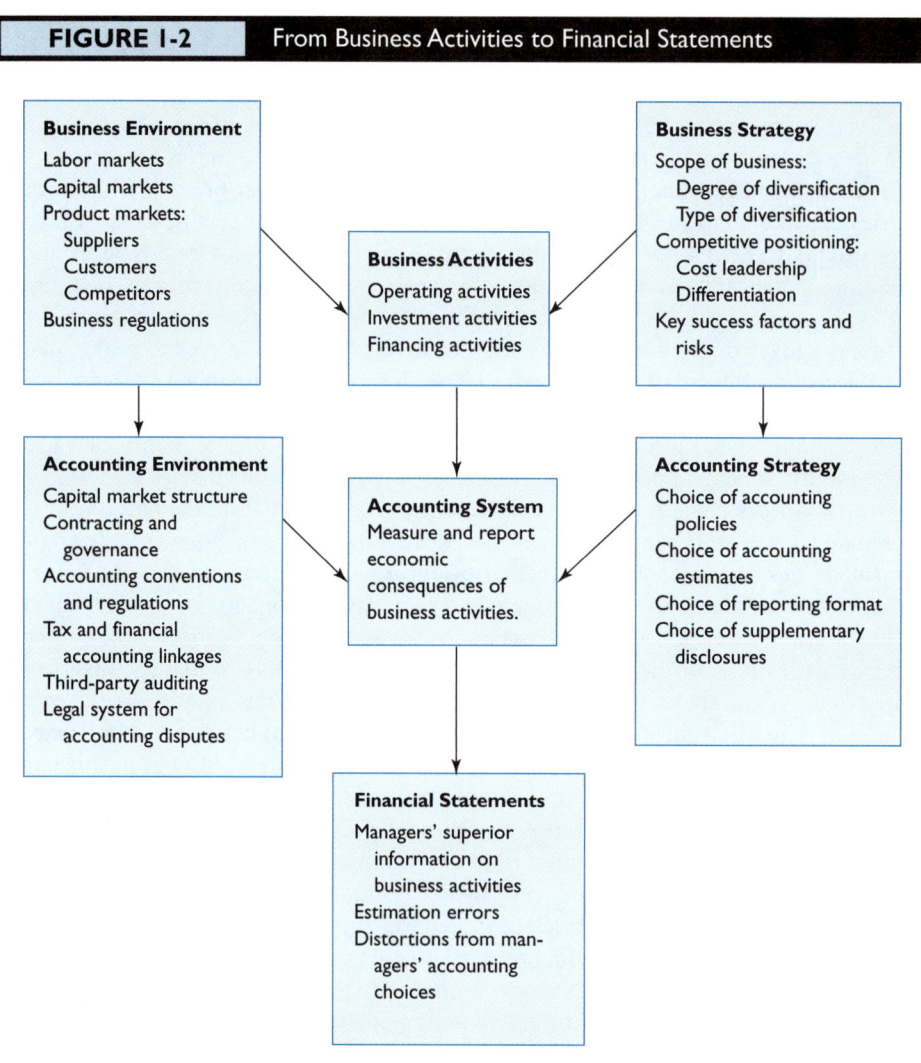

FIGURE 1-2   From Business Activities to Financial Statements

Business Environment
Labor markets
Capital markets
Product markets:
  Suppliers
  Customers
  Competitors
Business regulations

Business Activities
Operating activities
Investment activities
Financing activities

Business Strategy
Scope of business:
  Degree of diversification
  Type of diversification
Competitive positioning:
  Cost leadership
  Differentiation
Key success factors and
  risks

Accounting Environment
Capital market structure
Contracting and
  governance
Accounting conventions
  and regulations
Tax and financial
  accounting linkages
Third-party auditing
Legal system for
  accounting disputes

Accounting System
Measure and report
economic
consequences of
business activities.

Accounting Strategy
Choice of accounting
  policies
Choice of accounting
  estimates
Choice of reporting format
Choice of supplementary
  disclosures

Financial Statements
Managers' superior
  information on
  business activities
Estimation errors
Distortions from man-
  agers' accounting
  choices

too numerous to be reported individually to outsiders. Further, some of the activities undertaken by the firm are proprietary in nature, and disclosing these activities in detail could be a detriment to the firm's competitive position. The firm's accounting system provides a mechanism through which business activities are selected, measured, and aggregated into financial statement data.

INFLUENCES OF THE ACCOUNTING SYSTEM ON INFORMATION QUALITY

Intermediaries using financial statement data to do business analysis have to be aware that financial reports are influenced both by the firm's business activities and by its accounting system. A key aspect of financial statement analysis, therefore, involves understanding the influence of the accounting system on the quality of the financial statement data being used in the analysis. The institutional features of accounting systems discussed below determine the extent of that influence.

Feature 1: Accrual Accounting

One of the fundamental features of corporate financial reports is that they are prepared using accrual rather than cash accounting. Unlike cash accounting, accrual accounting distinguishes between the recording of costs and benefits associated with economic activities and the actual payment and receipt of cash. Net income is the primary periodic performance index under accrual accounting. To compute net income, the effects of economic transactions are recorded on the basis of *expected,* not necessarily *actual,* cash receipts and payments. Expected cash receipts from the delivery of products or services are recognized as revenues, and expected cash outflows associated with these revenues are recognized as expenses.

The need for accrual accounting arises from investors' demand for financial reports on a periodic basis. Because firms undertake economic transactions on a continual basis, the arbitrary closing of accounting books at the end of a reporting period leads to a fundamental measurement problem. Since cash accounting does not report the full economic consequence of the transactions undertaken in a given period, accrual accounting is designed to provide more complete information on a firm's periodic performance.

Feature 2: Accounting Conventions and Standards

The use of accrual accounting lies at the center of many important complexities in corporate financial reporting. Because accrual accounting deals with *expectations* of future cash consequences of current events, it is subjective and relies on a variety of assumptions. Who should be charged with the primary responsibility of making these assumptions? In the current system, a firm's managers are entrusted with the task of making the appropriate estimates and assumptions to prepare the financial statements because they have intimate knowledge of their firm's business.

The accounting discretion granted to managers is potentially valuable because it allows them to reflect inside information in reported financial statements. However, since investors view profits as a measure of managers' performance, managers have incentives to use their accounting discretion to distort reported profits by making biased assumptions. Further, the use of accounting numbers in contracts between the firm and outsiders provides another motivation for management manipulation of accounting numbers. Income management distorts financial accounting data, making them less valuable to external users of financial statements. Therefore, the delegation of financial reporting decisions to corporate managers has both costs and benefits.

A number of accounting conventions have evolved to ensure that managers use their accounting flexibility to summarize their knowledge of the firm's business activities and not disguise reality for self-serving purposes. For example, the measurability and conservatism conventions are accounting responses to concerns about distortions from managers' potentially optimistic bias. Both these conventions attempt to limit managers' optimistic bias by imposing their own pessimistic bias.

Accounting standards, promulgated by the Financial Accounting Standards Board (FASB) in the U.S. and similar standard-setting bodies in other countries, also limit potential distortions that managers can introduce into reported numbers. These uniform standards, such as the Generally Accepted Accounting Principles (GAAP) in the U.S. and the International Financial Reporting Standards (IFRS) internationally, attempt to reduce managers' ability to record similar economic transactions in dissimilar ways, either over time or across firms.

Increased uniformity from accounting standards, however, comes at the expense of reduced flexibility for managers to reflect genuine business differences in their firms' financial statements. Rigid accounting standards work best for economic transactions whose accounting treatment is not predicated on managers' proprietary information. However, when there is significant business judgment involved in assessing a transaction's economic consequences, rigid standards which prevent managers from using their superior business knowledge would be counterproductive. Further, if accounting standards are too rigid, they may induce managers to expend economic resources to restructure business transactions to achieve a desired accounting result.

Feature 3: Managers' Reporting Strategy

Because the mechanisms that limit managers' ability to distort accounting data add noise, it is not optimal to use accounting regulation to eliminate managerial flexibility completely. Therefore, real-world accounting systems leave considerable room for managers to influence financial statement data. A firm's reporting strategy, i.e., the manner in which managers use their accounting discretion, has an important influence on the firm's financial statements.

Corporate managers can choose accounting and disclosure policies that make it more or less difficult for external users of financial reports to understand the true economic picture of their businesses. Accounting rules often provide a broad set of alternatives from which managers can choose. Further, managers are entrusted with making a range of estimates in implementing these accounting policies. Accounting regulations usually prescribe *minimum* disclosure requirements, but they do not restrict managers from *voluntarily* providing additional disclosures.

A superior disclosure strategy will enable managers to communicate the underlying business reality to outside investors. One important constraint on a firm's disclosure strategy is the competitive dynamics in product markets. Disclosure of proprietary information about business strategies and their expected economic consequences may hurt the firm's competitive position. Subject to this constraint, managers can use financial statements to provide information useful to investors in assessing their firm's true economic performance.

Managers can also use financial reporting strategies to manipulate investors' perceptions. Using the discretion granted to them, managers can make it difficult for investors to identify poor performance on a timely basis. For example, managers can choose accounting policies and estimates to provide an optimistic assessment of the firm's true performance. They can also make it costly for investors to understand the true performance by controlling the extent of information that is disclosed voluntarily.

The extent to which financial statements reveal the underlying business reality varies across firms and across time for a given firm. This variation in accounting quality provides both an important opportunity and a challenge in doing business analysis. The process through which analysts can separate noise from information in financial statements, and gain valuable business insights from financial statement analysis, is discussed in the following section.

Feature 4: Auditing

Auditing, broadly defined as a verification of the integrity of the reported financial statements by someone other than the preparer, ensures that managers use accounting rules and conventions consistently over time, and that their accounting estimates are reasonable. Therefore, auditing improves the quality of accounting data.

Third-party auditing may also reduce the quality of financial reporting because it constrains the kind of accounting rules and conventions that evolve over time. For example, the FASB considers the views of auditors in the standard-setting process. Auditors are likely to argue against accounting standards producing numbers that are difficult to audit, even if the proposed rules produce relevant information for investors.

The legal environment in which accounting disputes between managers, auditors, and investors are adjudicated can also have a significant effect on the quality of reported numbers. The threat of lawsuits and resulting penalties has the beneficial effect of improving the accuracy of disclosure. However, the potential for a significant legal liability might also discourage managers and auditors from supporting accounting proposals requiring risky forecasts, such as forward-looking disclosures.

The governance structure of firms includes an audit committee of the board of directors. The audit committee is expected to be independent of management and its key roles include overseeing the work of the auditor and ensuring that financial statements are properly prepared. This governance mechanism further serves to enhance the quality and accountability of financial reporting.

The Impact of the Sarbanes-Oxley Act on Financial Reporting and Auditing

In the aftermath of the collapse of the dot-com bubble and high-profile accounting scandals such as Enron and WorldCom, the U.S. Congress passed the bipartisan Sarbanes-Oxley Act (the Act) in July 2002. The margin by which the bill was enacted—it passed by a vote of 424 to 3 in the House of Representatives and a vote of 99 to 0 in the Senate—and the far-reaching nature of the reforms reflected the degree to which the public's confidence in the quality of corporate financial reporting had been undermined.

The Act mandated certain fundamental changes to corporate governance as related to financial reporting and altered the relationship between a firm and its auditor. Some of the highlights of the Act include

- Creating a not-for-profit accounting oversight board, the Public Company Accounting Oversight Board (PCAOB), to ensure standards for auditing and the ethics and independence of public accounting firms;
- Mandating stricter guidelines for the composition and role of the audit committee of the Board of Directors, including director independence and financial expertise;
- Enhancing corporate responsibility for financial reporting by requiring the CEO and CFO to personally certify the appropriateness of periodic reports;
- Requiring management to assess and report on the adequacy of internal controls, which then needs to be certified by the auditor;
- Providing greater whistleblower protection;
- Allowing for the imposition of stiffer penalties, including prison terms and fines, for securities fraud;
- Prohibiting accounting firms from providing certain non-audit services contemporaneously with an audit and mandating audit partner rotation;
- Prescribing conflict of interest rules for equity research analysts; and
- Increasing the funding available to the Securities and Exchange Commission to ensure compliance.

While the Act does improve the quality of financial reporting and create a stronger regulatory environment, its detractors argue that in attempting to reduce information risk, the Act could have unintended consequences such as higher business costs (arising from higher audit fees, greater compliance costs, and potential litigation) and a disincentive for firms to take on business activities that entail complex or ambiguous accounting issues. Empirical evidence shows that the cost of compliance with the Act has had an impact on the decision of public companies to go private, perhaps in an attempt to avoid these costs.[3]

FROM FINANCIAL STATEMENTS TO BUSINESS ANALYSIS

Because managers' insider knowledge is a source of both value and distortion in accounting data, it is difficult for outside users of financial statements to separate true information from distortion and noise. Not being able to undo accounting distortions completely, investors "discount" a firm's reported accounting performance. In doing so, they make a probabilistic assessment of the extent to which a firm's reported numbers reflect economic reality. As a result, investors can have only an imprecise assessment of an individual firm's performance. Financial and information intermediaries can add value by improving investors' understanding of a firm's current performance and its future prospects.

Effective financial statement analysis is valuable because it attempts to get at managers' inside information from public financial statement data. Since intermediaries do not have direct or complete access to this inside information, they rely on their knowledge of the firm's industry and its competitive strategies to interpret financial statements. Successful intermediaries have at least as good an understanding of the industry economics as the firm's managers do, as well as a reasonably good understanding of the firm's competitive strategy. Although outside analysts have an information disadvantage relative to the firm's managers, they are more objective in evaluating the economic consequences of the firm's investment and operating decisions. Figure 1-3 provides a schematic overview of how business intermediaries use financial statements to accomplish four key steps: (1) business strategy analysis, (2) accounting analysis, (3) financial analysis, and (4) prospective analysis.

Analysis Step 1: Business Strategy Analysis

The purpose of business strategy analysis is to identify key profit drivers and business risks, and to assess the company's profit potential at a qualitative level. Business strategy analysis involves analyzing a firm's industry and its strategy to create a sustainable competitive advantage. This qualitative analysis is an essential first step because it enables the analyst to frame the subsequent accounting and financial analysis better. For example, identifying the key success factors and key business risks allows the identification of key accounting policies. Assessment of a firm's competitive strategy facilitates evaluating whether current profitability is sustainable. Finally, business analysis enables the analyst to make sound assumptions in forecasting a firm's future performance.

Analysis Step 2: Accounting Analysis

The purpose of accounting analysis is to evaluate the degree to which a firm's accounting captures the underlying business reality. By identifying places where there

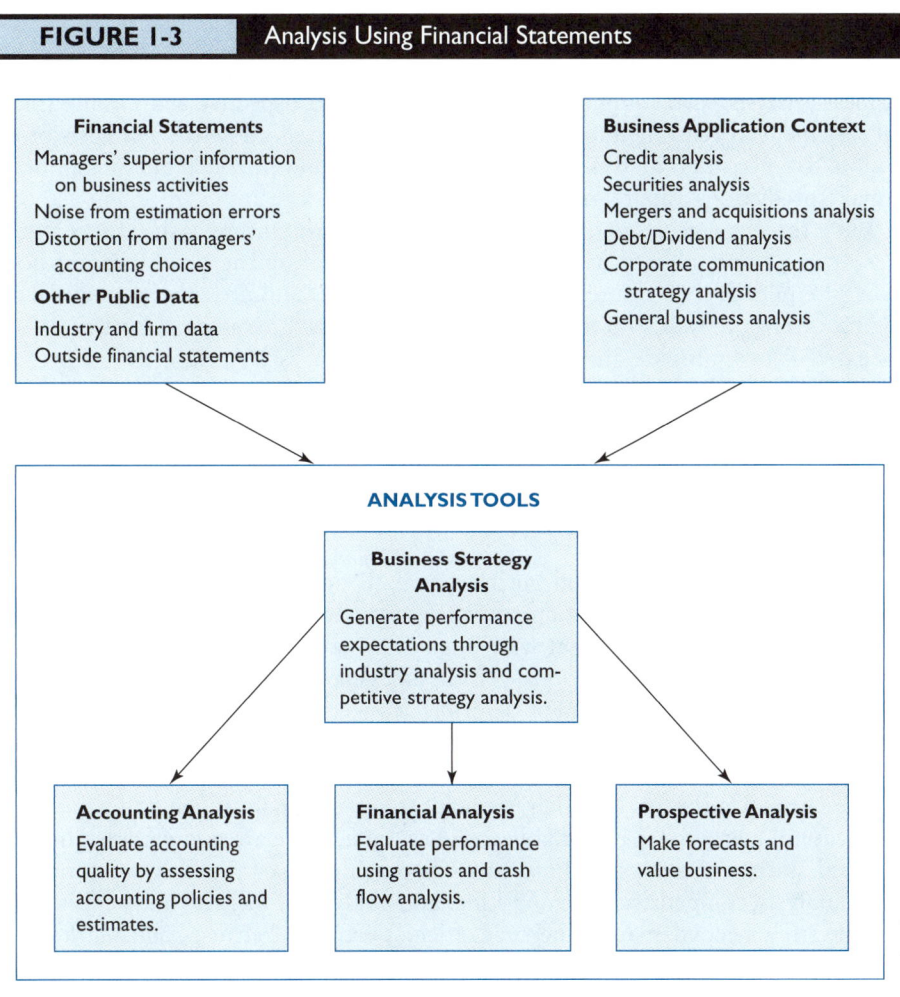

FIGURE 1-3   Analysis Using Financial Statements

Financial Statements
Managers' superior information
  on business activities
Noise from estimation errors
Distortion from managers'
  accounting choices

Other Public Data
Industry and firm data
Outside financial statements

Business Application Context
Credit analysis
Securities analysis
Mergers and acquisitions analysis
Debt/Dividend analysis
Corporate communication
  strategy analysis
General business analysis

ANALYSIS TOOLS

Business Strategy Analysis
Generate performance
expectations through
industry analysis and competitive strategy analysis.

Accounting Analysis
Evaluate accounting
quality by assessing
accounting policies and
estimates.

Financial Analysis
Evaluate performance
using ratios and cash
flow analysis.

Prospective Analysis
Make forecasts and
value business.

is accounting flexibility, and by evaluating the appropriateness of the firm's account-ing policies and estimates, analysts can assess the degree of distortion in a firm's reported numbers. Another important step in accounting analysis is to "undo" any distortions by recasting a firm's accounting numbers to create unbiased accounting data. Sound accounting analysis improves the reliability of conclusions from financial analysis, the next step in financial statement analysis.

Analysis Step 3: Financial Analysis

The goal of financial analysis is to use financial data to evaluate the current and past performance of a firm and to assess its sustainability. There are two important skills related to financial analysis. First, the analysis should be systematic and efficient. Sec-ond, the analysis should allow the analyst to use financial data to explore business issues. Ratio analysis and cash flow analysis are the two most commonly used finan-cial tools. Ratio analysis focuses on evaluating a firm's product market performance and financial policies while cash flow analysis focuses on a firm's liquidity and finan-cial flexibility.

Analysis Step 4: Prospective Analysis

Prospective analysis, which focuses on forecasting a firm's future, is the final step in business analysis. Two commonly used techniques in prospective analysis are financial statement forecasting and valuation. Both these tools allow the synthesis of the insights from business analysis, accounting analysis, and financial analysis in order to make predictions about a firm's future.

While the intrinsic value of a firm is a function of its future cash flow performance, it is also possible to assess a firm's value based on the firm's current book value of equity and its future return on equity (ROE) and growth. Strategy analysis, accounting analysis, and financial analysis, the first three steps in the framework discussed above, provide an excellent foundation for estimating a firm's intrinsic value. Strategy analysis, in addition to enabling sound accounting and financial analysis, also helps in assessing potential changes in a firm's competitive advantage and their implications for the firm's future ROE and growth. Accounting analysis provides an unbiased estimate of a firm's current book value and ROE. Financial analysis allows you to gain an in-depth understanding of what drives the firm's current ROE.

The predictions from a sound business analysis are useful to a variety of parties and can be applied in various contexts. The exact nature of the analysis will depend on the context. The contexts that we will examine include securities analysis, credit evaluation, mergers and acquisitions, and the assessment of corporate communication strategies. The four analytical steps described above are useful in each of these contexts. Appropriate use of these tools, however, requires a familiarity with the economic theories and institutional factors relevant to the context.

There are several ways in which financial statement analysis can add value, even when capital markets are reasonably efficient. First, there are many applications of financial statement analysis whose focus is outside the capital market context—credit analysis, competitive benchmarking, and analysis of mergers and acquisitions, to name a few. Second, markets become efficient precisely because some market participants rely on analytical tools such as the ones we discuss in this book to analyze information and make investment decisions. This in turn imposes greater discipline on corporate managers to develop an appropriate disclosure and communication strategy.

SUMMARY

Financial statements provide the most widely available data on public corporations' economic activities; investors and other stakeholders rely on them to assess the plans and performance of firms and corporate managers. Accrual accounting data in financial statements are noisy, and unsophisticated investors can assess firms' performance only imprecisely. Financial analysts who understand managers' disclosure strategies have an opportunity to create inside information from public data, and they play a valuable role in enabling outside parties to evaluate a firm's current and prospective performance.

This chapter has outlined the framework for business analysis with financial statements, using four key steps: business strategy analysis, accounting analysis, financial analysis, and prospective analysis. The remaining chapters in this book describe these steps in greater detail and discuss how they can be used in a variety of business contexts.

DISCUSSION QUESTIONS

1. John, who has just completed his first finance course, is unsure whether he should take a course in business analysis and valuation using financial statements since he believes that financial analysis adds little value, given the efficiency of capital markets. Explain to John when financial analysis can add value, even if capital markets are efficient.

2. Accounting statements rarely report financial performance without error. List three types of errors that can arise in financial reporting.

3. Joe Smith argues that "learning how to do business analysis and valuation using financial statements is not very useful, unless you are interested in becoming a financial analyst." Comment.

4. Four steps for business analysis are discussed in the chapter (strategy analysis, accounting analysis, financial analysis, and prospective analysis). As a financial analyst, explain why each of these steps is a critical part of your job and how they relate to one another.

NOTES

1. See G. Akerlof, "The Market for 'Lemons': Quality Uncertainty and the Market Mechanism," *Quarterly Journal of Economics* (August 1970): 488–500. Akerlof recognized that the seller of a used car knew more about the car's value than the buyer. This meant that the buyer was likely to end up overpaying, since the seller would accept any offer that exceeded the car's true value and reject any lower offer. Car buyers recognized this problem and would respond by only making low-ball offers for used cars, leading sellers with high quality cars to exit the market. As a result, only the lowest quality cars (the "lemons") would remain in the market. Akerlof pointed out that qualified independent mechanics could correct this market breakdown by providing buyers with reliable information on a used car's true value.

2. See P. Healy and K. Palepu, "How the Quest for Efficiency Undermined the Market," *Harvard Business Review* (July 2003): 76–85.

3. See, for example, E. Engel, R. Hayes, and X. Wang, "The Sarbanes-Oxley Act and Firms' Going-Private Decisions" (working paper, University of Chicago, 2004). Research evidence also points to the impact of Sarbanes-Oxley on firms' decision to "go dark" (cease filing with the SEC by deregistering their securities without changing shareholders). See, for example, A. Marosi and N. Massoud, "Why Do Firms Go Dark?" (working paper, University of Alberta, 2004); and C. Leuz, A. Triantis, and T. Wang, "Why Do Firms Go Dark? Causes and Economic Consequences of Voluntary SEC Deregistrations," (working paper, University of Pennsylvania, 2004).

The Role of Capital Market Intermediaries in the Dot-Com Crash of 2000

THE RISE AND FALL OF THE INTERNET CONSULTANTS

In the summer of 1999, a host of Internet consulting firms made their debut on the Nasdaq. Scient Corporation, which had been founded less than two years earlier in March 1997, went public in May 1999 at an IPO price of $20 per share ($10 on a pre-split basis). Its close on the first day of trading was $32.63. Other Internet consulting companies that went public that year included Viant Corporation, IXL Enterprises, and US Interactive (see **Exhibit 1**).

The main value proposition of these companies was that they would be able to usher in the new Internet era by lending their information technology and web expertise to traditional "old economy" companies that wanted to gain Web-based technology, as well as to the emerging dot-com sector. Other companies like Sapient Corporation and Cambridge Technology Partners had been doing IT consulting for years, but this new breed of companies was able to capitalize on the burgeoning demand for Internet expertise.

Over the following months, the stock prices of the Internet consultants rose dramatically. Scient traded at a high of $133.75 in March 2000. However, this was after a 2-1 split, so each share was actually worth twice this amount on a pre-split basis. This stock level represented a 1238% increase from its IPO price and a valuation of 62 times the company's revenues for the fiscal year 2000. Similar performances were put in by the other companies in this group. However, these valuation levels proved to be unsustainable. The stock prices of web consulting firms dropped sharply in April 2000 along with many others in the Internet sector, following what was afterwards seen as a general "correction" in the Nasdaq. The prices of the web consultants seemed to stabilize for a while, and many analysts continued to write favorably about their prospects and maintained buy ratings on their stocks. But starting early in September 2000, after some bad news from Viant Corporation and many subsequent analyst downgrades, the stocks went into a free-fall. All were trading in the single digits by February of 2001, representing a greater than 95% drop from their peak valuations (see **Exhibit 2**).

Gillian Elcock, MBA'01, prepared this case from published sources under the supervision of Professor Krishna Palepu. HBS cases are developed solely as the basis for class discussion. Cases are not intended to serve as endorsements, sources of primary data, or illustrations of effective or ineffective management.

The dramatic rise and fall of the stock prices of the Web consultants, along with many others in the Internet sector, caused industry observers to wonder how this could have happened in a relatively sophisticated capital market like that of the United States. Several well-respected venture capitalists, investment banks, accounting firms, financial analysts, and money management companies were involved in bringing these companies to market and rating and trading their shares (see **Exhibit 3**). Who, if anyone, caused the Internet stock price bubble? What, if anything, could be done to avoid the recurrence of such stock market bubbles?

Context: The Technology Bull Market

The 1980s and 1990s marked the beginning of a global technology revolution that started with the personal computer (PC) and led to the Internet era. Companies like Apple, Microsoft, Intel, and Dell Computer were at the forefront of this new wave of technology that promised to enhance productivity and efficiency through the computerization and automation of many processes.

The capital markets recognized the value that was being created by these companies. Microsoft, which was founded in 1975, had a market capitalization of over $600 billion by the beginning of 2000, making it the world's most valuable company, and its founder, Bill Gates, one of the richest men in the world. High values were also given to many of the other blue-chip technology firms such as Intel and Dell (**Exhibit 4**).

The 1990s ushered in a new group of companies that were based on information networks. These included AOL, Netscape, and Cisco. Netscape was a visible symbol of the emerging importance of the Internet: its browser gave regular users access to the World Wide Web, whereas previously the Internet had been mostly the domain of academics and experts. In March 2000, Cisco Systems, which made the devices that routed information across the Internet, overtook Microsoft as the world's most valuable company (based on market capitalization). This seemed further evidence of the value shift that was taking place from PC-focused technologies and companies to those that were based on the global information network.

It appeared obvious that the Internet was going to profoundly change the world through greater computing power, ease of communication, and the host of technologies that could be built upon it. Opportunities to build new services and technologies were boundless, and they were global in scale. The benefits of the Internet were expected to translate into greater economic productivity through the lowering of communication and transaction costs. It also seemed obvious that someone would be able to capitalize upon these market opportunities and that "the next Microsoft" would soon appear. No one who missed out on the original Microsoft wanted to do so the second time around.

A phrase that became popularized during this time was the "new economy." New economy companies, as opposed to old economy ones (exemplified by companies in traditional manufacturing, retail, and commodities), based their business models around exploiting the Internet. They were usually small compared to their old economy counterparts, with little need for their real-world "bricks and mortar" structures, preferring to outsource much of the capital intensive parts of the business and concentrate on the higher value-added, information-intensive elements. Traditional companies, finding their market shares and business models attacked by a host of nimble, specialized dot-com start-ups, lived in danger of "being Amazoned." To many, the new economy was the future and old economy companies would become less and less relevant.

The capital markets seemed to think similarly. From July 1999 to February 2000, as the Nasdaq Composite Index (which was heavily weighted with technology and Internet stocks) rose by 74.4%, the Dow Jones Industrial Average (which was composed mainly of old economy stocks) fell by 7.7%. Investors no longer seemed interested in anything that was not new economy.

Internet gurus and economists predicted the far-reaching effects of the Internet. The following excerpts represent the mood of the time:

> *Follow the personal computer and you can reach the pot of gold. Follow anything else and you will end up in a backwater. What the Model T was to the industrial era . . . the PC is to the information age. Just as people who rode the wave of automobile technology—from tire makers to fast food franchisers—prevailed in the industrial era, so the firms that prey on the passion and feed on the force of the computer community will predominate in the information era.*[1]

—George Gilder, 1992

* * * * *

> *Due to technological advances in PC-based communications, a new medium—with the Internet, the World Wide Web, and TCP/IP at its core—is emerging rapidly. The market for Internet-related products and services appears to be growing more rapidly than the early emerging markets for print publishing, telephony, film, radio, recorded music, television, and personal computers. . . . Based on our market growth estimates, we are still at the very early stages of a powerful secular growth cycle.*[2] *. . .*

—Mary Meeker, Morgan Stanley Dean Witter, February 1996

* * * * *

> *The easy availability of smart capital—the ability of entrepreneurs to launch potentially world-beating companies on a shoestring, and of investors to intelligently spread risk—may be the new economy's most devastating innovation. At the same time, onrushing technological change requires lumbering dinosaurs to turn themselves into clever mammals overnight. Some will. But for many others, the only thing left to talk about is the terms of surrender.*[3]

—*The Wall Street Journal*, April 17, 2000

In the new economy, gaining market share was considered key because of the benefits of network effects. In addition, a large customer base was needed to cover the high fixed costs often associated with doing business. Profitability was of a secondary concern, and Netscape was one of the first of many Internet companies to go public without positive earnings. Some companies deliberately operated at losses because it was essential to spend a lot early to gain market share, which would

---

1. Mary Meeker, Chris DePuy, "U.S. Investment Research, Technology/New Media, The Internet Report (Excerpt from Life After Television by George Gilder, 1992)," Morgan Stanley (February 1996).

2. Mary Meeker, Chris DePuy, "U.S. Investment Research, Technology/New Media, The Internet Report," Morgan Stanley (February 1996).

3. John Browning, Spencer Reiss, "For the New Economy, the End of the Beginning," The Wall Street Journal (Copyright 2000 Dow Jones & Company, Inc.).

presumably translate at a later point into profitability. This meant that revenue growth was the true measure of success for many Internet companies. Of course there were some dissenting voices, warning that this was just a period of irrational exuberance and the making of a classic stock market bubble. But for the most part, investors seemed to buy into the concept, as evidenced by the values given to several loss-making dot-coms (**Exhibit 5**).

Scient Corporation

The history of Scient, considered a leader in the Internet consulting space, is representative of what happened to the entire industry. The firm was founded in November 1997. Its venture capital backers included several leading firms such as Sequioa Capital and Benchmark Capital (see **Exhibit 3**).

Scient described itself as "a leading provider of a new category of professional services called eBusiness systems innovation" that would "rapidly improve a client's competitive position through the development of innovative business strategies enabled by the integration of emerging and existing technologies."[4] Its aim was to provide services in information technology and systems design as well as high-level strategy consulting, previously the domain of companies such as McKinsey and The Boston Consulting Group.

The company grew quickly to almost 2,000 people within 3 years, primarily organically. Its client list included AT&T, Chase Manhattan, Johnson & Johnson, and Homestore.com.[5] As with any consulting firm, its ability to attract and retain talented employees was crucial, since they were its main assets.

By the fiscal year ending in March 2000, Scient had a net loss of $16 million on revenues of $156 million (see financial statements in **Exhibit 6**). These revenues represented an increase of 653% over the previous year. Analysts wrote glowingly about the firm's prospects. In February 2000 when the stock was trading at around $87.25, a Deutsche Banc Alex Brown report stated:

> We have initiated research coverage of Scient with a BUY investment rating on the shares. In our view Scient possesses several key comparative advantages: (1) an outstanding management team; (2) a highly scalable and leverageable operating model; (3) a strong culture, which attracts the best and the brightest; (4) a private equity portfolio, which enhances long-term relationships and improves retention; and (5) an exclusive focus on the high-end systems innovation market with eBusiness and industry expertise, rapid time-to-market and an integrated approach. . . . Scient shares are currently trading at roughly 27x projected CY00 revenues, modestly ahead of pure play leaders like Viant (24x) and Proxicom (25x), and ahead of our interactive integrator peer group average of just over 16x. Our 12-month price target is $120. It is a stock we would want to own.[6]

And in March 2000, when the stock was at $77.75, Morgan Stanley, which had an "outperform" rating wrote:

> All said we believe Scient continue [sic] to effectively execute on what is a very aggressive business plan. . . . While shares of SCNT trade at a premium

---

4. Scient Corporation Prospectus, May 1999. Available from Edgar Online.

5. Scient Corporation website, <http://www.scient.com/non/content/clients/client_list/index.asp>.

6. F. Mark D'Annolfo, William S. Zinsmeister, Jeffrey A. Buchbinder, "Scient Corporation Premier Builder of eBusinesses," Deutsche Banc Alex Brown (February 14, 2000).

valuation to its peer group, we continue to believe that such level is warranted given the company's high-end market focus, short but impressive record of execution, and deep/experienced management team. As well, in our view there is a high probability of meaningful upward revisions to Scient's model.[7]

Scient's stock reached a high of $133.75 in March 2000 but fell to $44 by June as part of the overall drop in valuation of most of the technology sector. In September the company announced it had authorized a stock repurchase of $25 million. But in December 2000 it lowered its revenue and earnings expectations for the fourth quarter due to the slowdown in demand for Internet consulting services. The company also announced plans to lay off 460 positions worldwide (over 20% of its workforce) as well as close two of its offices, and an associated $40-$45 million restructuring charge. By February 2001 the stock was trading at $2.94.

Most of the analysts that covered Scient had buy or strong buy ratings on the company as its stock rose to its peak and even after the Nasdaq correction in April 2000. Then in September, a warning by Viant Corporation of results that would come in below expectations due to a slowdown in e-business spending from large corporate clients, prompted many analysts to downgrade most of the companies in the sector, including Scient (see **Exhibit 7**). Several large mutual fund companies were holders of Scient as its stock rose, peaked, and fell (see **Exhibit 8**).

As the major technology indices continued their slump during late 2000 and early 2001, and the stock prices of the Internet consulting firms floundered in the single digits, they received increasing attention from the press:

Examining the downfall of the eConsultants provides an excellent case study of failed business models. Rose-colored glasses, a lack of a sustainable competitive advantage, and a "me too" mentality are just some of the mistakes these companies made. . . . The eConsultants failed to do the one thing that they were supposed to be helping their clients do—build a sustainable business model . . . many eConsultants popped up and expected to be able to take on the McKinseys and Booz-Allens of the world. Now they are discovering that the relationships firmly established by these old economy consultants are integral to building a sustainable competitive advantage.[8]

Seems like everything dot-com is being shunned by investors these days. But perhaps no other group has experienced quite the brutality that Web consultancies have. Once the sweethearts of Wall Street, their stocks are now high-tech whipping boys. Even financial analysts, who usually strive to be positive about companies they cover, seem to have given up on the sector. . . . Many of these firms were built on the back of the dot-com boom. Now these clients are gone. At the same time, pressure on bricks-and-mortar companies to build online businesses has lifted, leading to the cancellation or delay of Web projects.[9]

---

7. Michael A. Sherrick, Mary Meeker, "Scient Corporation Quarter Update," Morgan Stanley Dean Witter (March 2, 2000).

8. Todd N. Lebor, "The Downfall of Internet Consultants," Fool's Den, Fool.com (December 11, 2000).

9. Amey Stone, "Streetwise—Who'll Help the Web Consultants?" BusinessWeek Online (New York, February 15, 2001). From www.businessweek.com.

The analysts who were formerly excited about Scient's prospects and had recommended the stock when it was trading at almost $80 per share now seemed much less enthusiastic. In January 2001, with the stock around $3.44, Morgan Stanley wrote:

> *We maintain our Neutral rating due to greater than anticipated market weakness, accelerating pricing pressure, the potential for increased turnover and management credibility issues. While shares of SCNT trade at a depressed valuation, we continute [sic] to believe that turnover and pricing pressure could prove greater than management's assumptions. While management indicated it would be "aggressive" to maintain its people, we still believe it will be difficult to maintain top-tier talent in the current market and company specific environment.*[10]

Performance of the Nasdaq

The performance of the stock prices of Scient and its peers mirrored that of many companies in the Internet sector. So dramatic was the drop in valuation of these companies, that this period was subsequently often referred to as the "Dot-com crash."

In the months following the crash, the equity markets essentially closed their doors to the Internet firms. Several once high-flying dot-coms, operating at losses and starved for cash, filed for bankruptcy or closed down their operations (see **Exhibit 9**).

The Nasdaq, which had reached a high of 5,132.52 in March of 2000 closed at 2470.52 in December 2000, a drop of 52% from its high. As of February 2001 it had not recovered, closing at 2151.83.

THE ROLE OF INTERMEDIARIES IN A WELL-FUNCTIONING MARKET

In a capitalist economy, individuals and institutions have savings that they want to invest, and companies need capital to finance and grow their businesses. The capital markets provide a way for this to occur efficiently. Companies issue debt or equity to investors who are willing to part with their cash now because they expect to earn an adequate return in the future for the risk they are taking.

However, there is an information gap between investors and companies. Investors usually do not have enough information or expertise to determine the good investments from the bad ones. And companies do not usually have the infrastructure and know-how to directly receive capital from investors. Therefore, both parties rely on intermediaries to help them make these decisions. These intermediaries include accountants, lawyers, regulatory bodies (such as the SEC in the United States), investment banks, venture capitalists, money management firms, and even the media (see **Exhibit 10**). The focus of this case is on the equity markets in the United States.

In a well-functioning system, with the incentives of intermediaries fully aligned in accordance with their fiduciary responsibility, public markets will correctly value companies such that investors earn a normal "required" rate of return. In particular, companies that go public will do so at a value which will give investors this fair rate of investment.

The public market valuation will have a trickle down effect on all intermediaries in the investment chain. Venture capitalists, who typically demand a very high return

---

10. Michael A. Sherrick, Mary Meeker, Douglas Levine, "Scient Corporation. Outlook Remains Cloudy, Adjusting Forecasts," Morgan Stanley Dean Witter (January 18, 2001).

on investment, and usually exit their portfolio companies through an IPO, will do their best to ensure these companies have good management teams and a sustainable business model that will stand the test of time. Otherwise, the capital markets will put too low a value on the companies when they try to go public. Investment bankers will provide their expertise in helping companies to go public or to make subsequent offerings, and introducing them to investors.

On the other side of the process, portfolio managers, acting on behalf of investors will only buy companies that are fairly priced, and will sell companies if they become overvalued, since buying or holding an overvalued stock will inevitably result in a loss. Sell-side analysts, whose clients include portfolio managers and therefore investors, will objectively monitor the performance of public companies and determine whether or not their stocks are good or bad investment at any point in time. Accountants audit the financial statements of companies, ensuring that they comply with established standards and represent the true states of the firms. This gives investors and analysts the confidence to make decisions based on these financial documents.

The integrity of this process is critical in an economy because it gives investors the confidence they need to invest their money into the system. Without this confidence, they would not plough their money back into the economy, but instead keep it under the proverbial mattress.

What Happened During the Dot-Com Bubble?

Many observers believed that something went wrong with the system during the dot-com bubble. In April 2001, *BusinessWeek* wrote about "The Great Internet Money Game. How America's top financial firms reaped billions from the Net boom, while investors got burned."[11] The following month, *Fortune* magazine's cover asked "Can we ever trust Wall Street again?"[12] referring to the way in which, in some people's opinions, Wall Street firms had led investors and companies astray before and after the dot-com debacle.

The implications of the Internet crash were far reaching. Many companies that needed to raise capital for investment found the capital markets suddenly shut to them. Millions of investors saw a large portion of their savings evaporate. This phenomenon was a likely contributor to the sharp drop in consumer confidence that took place in late 2000 and early 2001. In addition, the actual decrease in wealth threatened to dampen consumer spending. These factors, along with an overall slowing of the U.S. economy, threatened to put the United States into recession for the first time in over 10 years.

On a more macro level, the dot-coms used up valuable resources that could have been more efficiently allocated within the economy. The people who worked at failed Internet firms could have spent their time and energy creating lasting value in other endeavors, and the capital that funded the dot-coms could have been ploughed into viable, lasting companies that would have benefited the overall economy. However, it could be argued that there were benefits as well, and that the large investment in the technology sector positioned the United States to be a world leader in the future.

11. Peter Elstrom, "The Great Internet Money Game. How America's top financial firms reaped billions from the Net boom while investors got burned," BusinessWeek e.biz (April 16, 2001).

12. Fortune, May 14, 2001.

Nevertheless, the question remained: how could the dot-com bubble occur in a sophisticated capital market system like that of the United States? Why did the market allow the valuations of many Internet companies to go so high? What was the role of the intermediaries in the process that gave rise to the stock market bubble?

THE INTERMEDIARIES

One way to try to answer some of these questions is to look more closely at some of the key players in the investing chain. Much of the material in the following section is derived from interviews with representatives from each sector.

Venture Capitalists

Venture capitalists (VCs) provided capital for companies in their early stages of development. They sought to provide a very high rate of return to their investors for the associated risk. This was typically accomplished by selling their stake in their portfolio companies either to the public through an IPO, or to another company in a trade sale.

The partners in a VC firm typically had a substantial percentage of their net worth tied up in their funds, which aligned their interests with their investors. Their main form of compensation was a large share of profits (typically 20%) in addition to a relatively low fee based on the assets under management.

A large part of a VC's job was to screen good business ideas and entrepreneurial teams from bad ones. Partners at a VC firm were typically very experienced, savvy business people who worked closely with their portfolio companies to both monitor and guide them to a point where they have turned a business idea into a well-managed, fully functional company that could stand on its own. In a sense, their role was to nurture the companies until they reached a point where they were ready to face the scrutiny of the public capital markets after an IPO. Typically, companies would not go public until they had shown profits for at least three quarters.[13]

After the dot-com crash, some investors and the media started pointing fingers at the venture capitalists that had invested in many of the failed dot-coms. They blamed them for being unduly influenced by the euphoria of the market, and knowingly investing in and bringing public companies with questionable business models, or that had not yet proven themselves operationally. Indeed, many of the dot-coms went public within record time of receiving VC funding—a study of venture-backed initial public offerings showed that companies averaged 5.4 years in age when they went public in 1999, compared with 8 years in 1995.[14]

Did the venture capital investing process change in a way that contributed to the Internet bubble of 2000? According to a partner at a venture capital firm that invested in one of the Internet consulting companies, the public markets had a tremendous impact on the way VCs invested during the late 1990s.[15] He felt that, because of expectations of high stock market valuations, VC firms invested in companies during late 1990s that they would not have invested in under ordinary circumstances.

---

13. Peter Elstrom, "The Great Internet Money Game. How America's top financial firms reaped billions from the Net boom while investors got burned," BusinessWeek e.biz (April 16, 2001).

14. Shawn Neidorf, "Venture-Backed IPOs Make a Comeback," Venture Capital Journal (Wellesley Hills, Aug 1, 1999).

15. Limited partners are the investors in a venture capital fund; the venture capital firm itself usually serves as the general partner.

He also believed that the ready availability of money affected the business strategies and attitudes of the Internet companies: "If the [management] team knows $50 million is available, it acts differently e.g. 'go for market share'."

The VC partner acknowledged that VCs took many Internet companies public very early, but he felt that the responsibility of scrutinizing these companies lay largely with the investors that subscribed to the IPOs: "If a mutual find wants to invest in the IPO of a company that has no track record, profitability, etc but sees it as a liquidity event, it has made a decision to become a VC. Lots of mutual funds thought 'VC is easy, I want a piece of it.' "

Investment Bank Underwriters

Entrepreneurs relied on investment banks (such as Goldman Sachs, Morgan Stanley Dean Witter and Credit Suisse First Boston) in the actual process of doing an initial public offering, or "going public." Investment banks provided advisory financial services, helped the companies price their offerings, underwrite the shares, and introduce them to investors, often in the form of a road show.

Investment banks were paid a commission based on the amount of money that the company manages to raise in its offering, typically on the order of 7%.[16] Several blue-chip firms were involved in the capital-raising process of the Internet consultants (see **Exhibit 3**), and they also received a share of the blame for the dot-com crash in the months that followed it. In an article entitled *Just Who Brought Those Duds to Market?* the *New York Times* wrote:

> . . . *many Wall Street investment banks, from top-tier firms like Goldman, Sachs . . . to newer entrants like Thomas Weisel Partners . . . have reason to blush. In one blindingly fast riches-to-rags story, Pets.com filed for bankruptcy just nine months after Merrill Lynch took it public.*
>
> *Of course, investment banks that took these underperforming companies public may not care. They bagged enormous fees, a total of more than $600 million directly related to initial public offerings involving just the companies whose stocks are now under $1.*
>
> . . . *How did investment banks, paid for their expert advice, pick such lemons?*[17]

Sell-Side Analysts

Sell-side analysts worked at investment banks and brokerage houses. One of their main functions was to publish research on public companies. Each analyst typically followed 15 to 30 companies in a particular industry, and his or her job involved forming relationships with and talking to the managements of the companies, following trends in the industry, and ultimately making buy or sell recommendations on the stocks. The recommendations analysts made could be very influential with investors. If a well-respected analyst downgraded a stock, the reaction from the market could be severe and swift, resulting in a same-day drop in the stock price. Sell-side analysts typically interacted with buy-side analysts and portfolio managers at money

---

16. Source: casewriter interview.

17. Andrew Ross Sorkin, "Just Who Brought Those Duds to Market?" NYTimes.com (Copyright 2001 The New York Times Company).

management companies (the buy-side) to market or "sell" their ideas. In addition, they usually provided support during a company's IPO process, providing research to the buy-side before the company actually went public. Sell-side analysts were usually partly compensated based on the amount of trading fees and investment banking revenue they help the firm to generate through their research.

In the months following the dot-com crash, sell-side technology and Internet analysts found themselves the target of criticism for having buy ratings on companies that had subsequently fallen drastically in price. Financial cable TV channel CNBC ran a report called "Analyzing the Analysts," addressing the issue of whether or not they were to blame for their recommendations of tech stocks. A March 2001 article in *The Wall Street Journal* raised similar issues after it was reported that J.P. Morgan Chase's head of European research sent out a memo requiring all the company's analysts to show their stock recommendation changes to the company involved and to the investment banking division.[18] The previously mentioned issue of *Forbes* featured an article criticizing Mary Meeker, a prominent Internet analyst.[19] And a *Financial Times* article entitled "Shoot all the analysts" made a sweeping criticism of their role in the market bubble:

> ... *instead of forecasting earnings per share, they were now in the business of forecasting share prices themselves. And those prices were almost always very optimistic. Now, at last, they have had their comeuppance. Much of what many of them have done in the past several years has turned out to be worthless. High-flying stocks that a year ago were going to be cheap at twice the price have halved or worse—and some analysts have been putting out buy recommendations all the way down. . . . They should learn a little humility and get back to analysis.*[20]

Responding to the media criticism of financial analysts, Karl Keirstead, a Lehman Brothers analyst who followed Internet consulting firms, stated:

> *It is too easy as they do on CNBC to slam the analysts for recommending stocks when they were very expensive. In the case of the Internet consulting firms, looking back before the correction in April 2000, the fundamentals were "nothing short of pristine." The companies were growing at astronomical rates, and it looked as though they would continue to do so for quite a while. Under these assumptions, if you modeled out the financials for these companies and discounted them back at a reasonable rate, they did not seem all that highly valued.*[21]

Keirstead also pointed out that there were times when it was legitimate to have a buy rating on a stock that was "overvalued" based on fundamentals:

> *The future price of a stock is not always tied to the discounted value of cash flow or earnings, it is equal to what someone is willing to pay. This is especially true in periods of tremendous market liquidity and huge interest in young companies with illiquid stocks and steep growth curves that are difficult to*

18. Wade Lambert, Jathon Sapsford, "J.P. Morgan Memo to Analysts Raises Eyebrows," The Wall Street Journal (Thursday, March 22, 2001).

19. Peter Elkind, "Where Mary Meeker Went Wrong," Fortune (May 14, 2001).

20. "Shoot all the analysts," Financial Times (Tuesday, March 20, 2001).

21. Source: casewriter interview.

project. The valuation may seem too high, but if the fundamentals are improving and Street psychology and hype are building, the stock is likely to rally. Stock pickers must pay as much attention to these factors as the company and industry fundamentals.

When asked his view on why the buy-side institutions went along with the high valuations that these companies were trading for, Keirstead commented that, "A lot of buy-side analysts and portfolio managers became momentum investors in disguise. They claimed in their mutual fund prospectus that they made decisions based on fundamental analysis. Truth is, they played the momentum game as well."

Keirstead also commented on the criticism analysts had received for being too heavily influenced by the possibility of banking deals when making stock recommendations. He stated that this claim was "completely over-rated." Though there was some legitimacy to the argument and some of analysts' compensation did come from investment banking fees, it was a limited component. Analysts also got significant fees from the trading revenue they generated and the published rankings.[22] He pointed out that critics' arguments were ludicrous because if analysts only made decisions based on banking fees, it would jeopardize their rankings and credibility with their buy-side clients. However, he did note that the potential deal flow could have distorted the view of some technology analysts during the boom.

Finally, Keirstead described the bias that was present on the sell-side to be bullish:

To be negative when you are a sell-side analyst is to be a contrarian, to stick your neck out. You take a lot of heat, it's tough. And it would have been the wrong call for the last four years. Had I turned short in 1999 when these stocks seemed overvalued, I would have missed a 200% increase in the stocks. My view was: I can't be too valuation-sensitive. The stocks are likely to rise as long as the fundamentals hold and that's the position a lot of analysts took.

Consistent with this optimistic bias, there were very few sell recommendations from analysts during the peak of the Internet stock bubble. According to financial information company First Call, more than 70% of the 27,000 plus recommendations outstanding on some 6,000 stocks in November 2000 were strong buys or buys, while fewer than 1% were sells or strong sells.[23]

Buy-Side Analysts and Portfolio Managers

The "buy-side" refers to institutions that do the actual buying and selling of public securities, such as mutual fund companies, insurance companies, hedge funds, and other asset managers.

There were two main roles on the buy side: analysts and portfolio managers. Buy-side analysts had some of the same duties as their sell-side counterparts. They were usually assigned to a group of companies within a certain industry and were responsible for doing industry research, talking to the companies' management teams, coming up with earning estimates, doing valuation analysis, and ultimately rating the stock prices of the companies as either "buys" or "sells." The analyst's job

---

22. *Several financial journals published analyst rankings. The most prominent ranking was by* Institutional Investor *magazine which published annual rankings of sell-side analysts by industry. These rankings were very influential in the analyst and investment community.*

23. *Walter Updegrave, "The ratings game,"* Money *(New York, January 2001).*

was not yet complete, however. Though they did not publish their research, buy-side analysts needed to convince the portfolio managers within their company to follow their recommendations.

Portfolio managers were the ones who actually managed money, whether it was a retail mutual fund or an institutional account. Though they listened to the recommendations of the analysts, they were the ones who were ultimately responsible for buying or selling securities.

The compensation of the buy-side analysts was often linked to how well their stock recommendations do, and in the case of portfolio managers, compensation was determined by the performance of their funds relative to an appropriate benchmark return. These compensation schemes were designed to align the incentives of buy-side analysts and portfolio managers with the interests of investors.

Why then, did so may buy-side firms buy and hold on to the Internet consulting firms during the market bubble? Did they really believe the companies were worth what they were trading for? Or did they know they were overvalued, but invest in them anyway for other reasons?

According to a former associate at a large mutual fund company, many people within his company knew that most of the Internet companies were overvalued before the market correction, but they felt pressure to invest anyway:

> *My previous employer is known as a value investor, growth at a reasonable price. At first the general impression in the firm was that a lot of the Internet firms would blow up, that they didn't deserve these valuations. But articles were written about my company . . . that it was being left behind because it was not willing to invest in the Internet companies. Some of the analysts at the firm began to recommend companies simply because they knew that the stock prices would go up, even though they were clearly overvalued. And portfolio managers felt that if they didn't buy the stocks, they would lag their benchmarks and their competitors—they are rewarded on a one-year term horizon and three-year horizon. It is very important to meet their benchmark, it makes up a material part of their compensation. In addition, they compare against the performance of their peers for marketing purposes.*[24]

THE ROLE OF INFORMATION

The Accounting Profession

Independent accountants audited the financial statements of public companies to verify their accuracy and freedom from fraud. If they were reasonably satisfied, they provided an unqualified opinion statement which was attached to the company's public filings. If auditors were not fully satisfied, this is noted as well. Investors usually took heed of the auditor's opinion as it provided an additional level of assurance of the quality of the information they were receiving from companies.

In the year 2000, the accounting profession in the United States was dominated by five major accounting firms, collectively referred to as "The Big Five" (PriceWaterhouseCoopers, Deloitte & Touche, KPMG, Ernst & Young and Arthur Andersen). The top 100 accounting firms had roughly a 50% share of the market

---

24. *Source: casewriter interview.*

and the Big Five account for about 84% of the revenues of the top 100.[25] However, the Big Five made up an even larger percentage of the auditing activity of Internet IPOs. Of the 410 Internet services and software IPOs between January 1998 and December 2000, 373 of them, or 91% were audited by one of the Big Five accountants.[26]

During the aftermath of the dot-com crash, these firms came under some criticism for not adequately warning investors about the precarious financial position of some of the companies. The *Wall Street Journal* wrote an article addressing the fact that many dot-coms that went bankrupt were not given "going concern" clauses by their auditors. A going concern clause was included by an auditor if it had a substantial doubt that the company would be able to remain in operation for another 12 months:

> *In retrospect, critics say, there were early signs that the businesses weren't sustainable, including their reliance on external financing, rather than money generated by their own operations, to stay afloat. You wonder where some of the skepticism was . . . critics say many auditors appear to have presumed the capital markets would remain buoyant. For anybody to have assumed a continuation of those aberrant, irrational conditions was in itself irrational and unjustifiable whether it was an auditor, a board member or an investor. . . .[27]*

However, in the same article, accountants defended their actions by noting that going concern judgments were subjective, and that they were not able to predict the future any better than the capital markets.

Dr. Howard Schilit, founder and CEO of CFRA, an independent financial research organization,[28] believed that accountants certainly had to take a part of the blame for what happened. In his opinion, they "looked the other way when they could have been more rigorous in doing their work."[29] However, he noted that the outcome may not have been materially different even if they did.

One particular criticism he had was that many accountants didn't look closely enough at the substance of transactions and didn't do enough questioning of the circumstances surrounding sales contracts. His hope was that accountants "go back and learn what the basic rules are of when revenues should be booked. The rules haven't changed whether this is the new economy or old economy."

FASB—A Regulator

The Financial Accounting Standards Boards (FASB) was an independent regulatory body in the United States whose mission was to "establish and improve standards of financial accounting and reporting for the guidance and education of the public, including issuers, auditors, and users of financial information."[30] FASB standards

25. "Accounting Today Top 100 Survey Shows All is Well," The CPA Journal (May 1999).

26. Information extracted from IPO.com website <http://www.ipo.com>.

27. Johnathan Weil, "'Going Concerns': Did Accountants Fail to Flag Problems at Dot-Com Casualties?" The Wall Street Journal (February 9, 2001).

28. CFRA's mission is to warn investors and creditors about companies experiencing operational problems and particularly those that employ unusual or aggressive accounting practices to camouflage such problems.

29. Source: casewriter interview.

30. FASB website: <http://accounting.rutgers.edu/raw/fasb/>.

were recognized by the Securities and Exchange Commission (SEC), which regulates the financial reporting of public companies in the United States.

The accounting practices of some new economy firms posed challenges for auditors and investors, and though some observers felt that the accountants were not doing a good enough job, others thought that the accounting rules themselves were too ambiguous, and this fact lent itself to exploitation by the companies.

Specific examples included the treatment of barter revenues in the case of companies that exchanged on-line advertising space, the practice of booking gross rather than net revenues in commission-based businesses (e.g., Priceline.com), and the issue of when to recognize revenues from long-term contracts (e.g., MicroStrategy Inc.) Given that the valuations of many Internet firms were driven by how quickly they grew revenues, there was a lot of incentive to inflate this number. In fact, the accounting practices of dot-coms became so aggressive that the SEC had to step in:

> *The Securities & Exchange Commission's crackdown on the aggressive accounting practices that have taken off among many dot-com firms really began . . . when it quietly issued new guidelines to refocus corporate management and investors. . . . To rein in what it saw as an alarming trend in inflated revenue reports, the SEC required companies using lax accounting practices to restate financial results by the end of their next fiscal year's quarter. . . .*
>
> *The SEC has also directed the Financial Accounting Standards Board to review a range of Internet company accounting practices that could boost revenues or reduce costs unfairly. Under the scrutiny, more companies are likely to issue restatements of financial results. . . .*[31]

In another spin on the issue, some questioned whether the accounting rules set out by the regulatory bodies had in fact become obsolete for the new economy. In July 2000, leaders in the accounting community told a Senate Banking subcommittee that the United States needed "a new accounting model for the New Economy." A major concern of theirs was that the current rules did not allow companies to report the value of intangible assets on their balance sheets, such as customers, employees, suppliers and organization.[32] Others argued that the accounting rules caused Internet firms to appear unprofitable when they were actually making money. This was because old economy firms were allowed to capitalize their major investments such as factories, plants and equipment, whereas the rules did not allow capitalization of expenditures on R&D and marketing, which created value for many dot-com companies:

> *While Internet stocks may not be worth what they are selling for, the movement in their prices may not be as crazy as it seems. Many of these companies reporting losses actually make money—lots of it. It all has to do with accounting. Old-economy companies get to capitalize their most important investments, while new economy ones do not. While Amazon.com announces a loss almost every quarter, when it capitalizes its investments in intangibles that loss turns into a $400-million profit.*[33]

---

31. Catherine Yang, "Earth to Dot-Com Accountants," BusinessWeek (New York, April 3, 2000).

32. Stephen Barlas, "New accounting model demanded," Strategic Finance (Montvale, September 2000).

33. Geoffrey Colvin, "The Net's hidden profits," Fortune (New York, April 17, 2000).

RETAIL INVESTORS

The role of the general public in the dot-com craze cannot be ignored. In addition to the people who poured money into mutual funds, many retail investors began trading on their own, often electronically. A group of avid day traders grew up, some of whom quit their regular jobs to devote all their time and energy to trading stocks. Analysts estimated that they made up almost 18% of the trading volume of the NYSE and Nasdaq in 2000.[34] Sites such as Yahoo Finance grew in popularity, while chat rooms devoted to stocks and trading proliferated.

The number of accounts of Internet stock brokers like Etrade and Ameritrade grew rapidly (Etrade grew from 544 thousand brokerage accounts in 1998 to 3 million in 2000 and Ameritrade grew from 98 thousand accounts in 1997 to 1.2 million in 2000) as they slashed their commissions, some to as low as $8/trade compared to the $50-$300[35] charged by traditional brokerage firms. These companies were dot-coms themselves and they were able to slash prices partly because they were operating at losses that they were not penalized for by the capital markets. This gave rise to an interesting positive feedback loop: the Etrades of the world, funded by the dot-com frenzied capital markets slashed their prices and therefore encouraged more trading, which continued to fuel the enthusiasm of investors for the markets.

The financial press also became increasingly visible during this period. Several publications like *Barrons* and *The Wall Street Journal* had always been very influential in the financial community. However, a host of other information sources, often on the web, sprang up to support the new demand for information. CNBC and CNNfn, major network channels devoted to the markets, often featured analysts and portfolio managers making stock recommendations or giving their views on the market.

Many of the retail investors did not know much about finance or valuation, and often didn't understand much about the companies whose shares they were buying. They were therefore likely to be heavily influenced by some of the intermediaries previously described, especially the financial press, and the sell-side analysts that publicly upgraded and downgraded companies.

These investors were pointed to by some as having had a large role in driving Internet valuations to the levels they went to. The reasoning was that other more sophisticated buyers such as the institutional money managers, may have bought overvalued companies because they thought they could easily sell them later at even higher valuations to "dumb retail investors."

THE COMPANIES THEMSELVES

The entrepreneurs who founded the Internet consulting companies, and the management teams who ran them, could almost be described as bystanders to the process that took the stock prices of their companies to such lofty highs and then punishing lows. However, they were profoundly affected by these changes in almost every aspect of their businesses.

---

34. Amy S. Butte, "Day Trading and Beyond. A New Niche Is Emerging," Bear Stearns Equity Research, April 2000.

35. Lee Patterson, "If you can't beat 'em …," Forbes (New York, August 23, 1999).

Obviously there were many benefits to having a high stock price. According to a managing director (MD) at one of the Internet consultants, the company was facing a very competitive labor market while trying to grow organically, and having a stock that was doing well helped with recruiting people since the option part of the compensation package was attractive.[36] He also explained that people were proud to be a part of the firm, partly because the stock was doing so well.

As the stock price of the company continued to rise higher and higher, the MD admitted that he did become afraid that the market was overvaluing the company, and that this doubt probably went all the way up to the CEO. As he put it "we were trading at just absurd levels."

When asked about his thoughts on his firm's current stock price, the MD thought that the market had over-reacted and gone to the other extreme. He remarked that investors were worried that the Internet consulting firms were facing renewed competition from companies like IBM, the Big Five accounting firms and the strategy consulting firms. Overall, though the rise and fall of the company's stock price was in many ways a painful experience, this MD thought that the market bubble presented a good opportunity that the company was able to capitalize upon. It was able to do a secondary offering at a high price and now had lots of cash on its balance sheet. His view was that "If you look at competitive sustainability [in this business], it could boil down to the company with the best balance sheet wins."

THE BLAME GAME

In the aftermath of the dot-com crash, many tried to pinpoint whose fault it was that the whole bubble occurred in the first place. As mentioned previously, sell-side analysts, often the most visible group in the investment community, came under frequent attack in the media, as did, to some extent, venture capitalists, investment bankers, and even the accounting industry. Company insiders (including the founder of Scient) were also scrutinized for selling large blocks of shares when the stock prices of their companies were near their peaks.[37]

A *Wall Street Journal* article entitled "Investors, Entrepreneurs All Play the Blame Game," described how these various players were trying to blame each other for what happened:

> *With the tech-heavy Nasdaq Composite Index dancing close to the 2,000 mark—down from over 5,000—Internet entrepreneurs and venture capitalists have stepped up their finger-pointing about just who's at fault for the technology meltdown, which continues to topple businesses and once-cushy lifestyles. . . . Fingers pointed right and left—from entrepreneurs to venture capitalists, from analysts to day traders to shareholders—and back around again.*[38]

The Internet stock market bubble was certainly not the first one to occur. Other notables include the Tulip Craze of the seventeenth century and the Nifty

---

36. Source: casewriter interview.

37. Mark Maremont, John Hechinger, "If Only You'd Sold Some Stock Earlier—Say $100 Million Worth," The Wall Street Journal (March 22, 2001).

38. Rebecca Buckman, "Investors, Entrepreneurs All Play the Blame Game," The Wall Street Journal (March 5, 2001).

Fifty boom of the 1970s. In all cases market valuations went to unsustainably high levels and ended with a sharp decrease in valuation that left many investors empty-handed.

But the question of what happened in this latest bubble remained: who, if anyone, could be blamed for the dot-com rise and crash? How did the various intermediaries described here affect or cause what happened? Was there really a misalignment of incentives in the system? If so, could it be fixed so that this sort of thing did not happen in the future? Or were market bubbles an inevitable part of the way the economy functioned?

QUESTIONS

1. What is the intended role of each of the institutions and intermediaries discussed in the case for the effective functioning of capital markets?

2. Are their incentives aligned properly with their intended role? Whose incentives are most misaligned?

3. Who, if anyone, was primarily responsible for the Internet stock bubble?

4. What are the costs of such a stock market bubble? As a future business professional, what lessons do you draw from the bubble?

EXHIBIT I

Timeline of the Internet Consultants—Founding and IPO

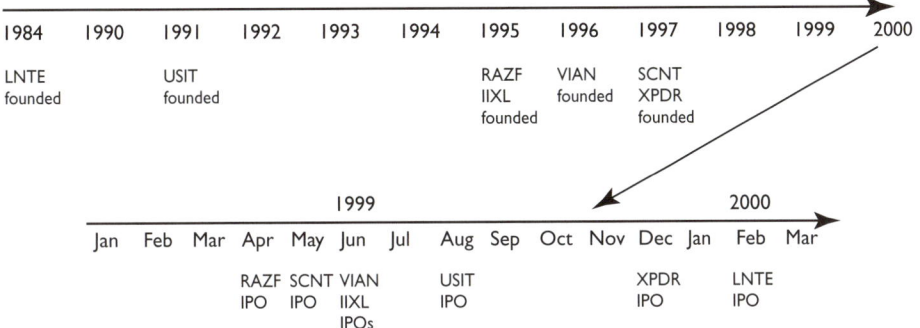

Source: Edgar Online, Marketguide.com.

EXHIBIT 2

Internet Consultants—Stock Price Highs and Lows

Company	IPO Price[a]	Peak Price	% Change IPO to Peak	Date of Peak	Price at End of Feb 2001	% Change from Peak
Scient	10	133.75	1,238%	10-Mar-00	2.94	−97.8%
Viant	8	63.56	695%	14-Dec-99	3.06	−95.2%
IXL Enterprises	12	58.75	390%	20-Jan-00	1.25	−97.9%
Lante	20	87.50	338%	29-Feb-00	1.81	−97.9%
Razorfish	8	56.94	612%	14-Feb-00	1.16	−98.0%
US Interactive	10	83.75	738%	4-Jan-00	0.56[b]	−99.3%
Xpedior	19	34.75	83%	10-Jan-00	0.69	−98.0%

Source: Bloomberg LP, The Center for Research in Security Prices (accessed via Wharton Research Database Services), Marketguide.com.

a. Split adjusted.

b. Last trade on January 11, 2001. Filed for bankruptcy under Chapter 11 in January 2001.

The Dot-Com Crash

EXHIBIT 3

Intermediaries in the Capital-raising Process of the Internet Consultants

Company	Venture Capital Stage Investors	Investment Bank Underwriters	Auditors[a]	Analyst Coverage	Selected Institutional Holders	Venture Funding ($M)	IPO Amount Raised ($M)[b]	IPO Underwriting Fee ($M)	% Institutional Ownership[c]
Scient	Sequoia Capital, Benchmark Capital, Stanford Univ., Capital Research, Morgan Stanley Venture Partners, Amerindo Investment Advisors, Palantir Capital	Morgan Stanley Dean Witter, Hambrecht & Quist, Thomas Weisel Partners	PWC	Merrill Lynch, Morgan Stanley Dean Witter, CSFB, Lehman Brothers, UBS Warburg, SG Cowen, others	Capital Research, Putnam, Janus Vanguard, Wellingon, State Street	31.2	60	4.2	34% (66% of float)
Viant	Kleiner Perkins Caufield & Byers, Mohr Davidow Ventures, Information Associates, Trident Capital, BancBoston Capital, General Motors, Technology Crossover Ventures	Goldman Sachs, Credit Suisse First Boston, WIT Capital Corporation	PWC	Goldman Sachs, Merrill Lynch, Lehman Brothers, CSFB, Wasserstein Perella, Bear Stearns, others	Fidelity, T Rowe Price, Putnam, Franklin, State Street, Vanguard, American Century, Goldman Sachs Asset Management	32.2	48	3.4	34% (67% of float)
IXL	Greylock Mgmt., Chase Capital Partners, Flatiron Partners, GE Capital, Kelso & Co., TTC Ventures, CB Capital, Portage Venture Partners, Transamerica Technology Finance	Merrill Lynch, BancBoston Robertson Stephens, DLJ, SG Cowen	PWC	Merrill Lynch, Robinson Humphrey, First Union Capital, others	Capital Research, State Street, Vanguard, Goldman Sachs Asset Management, GE Asset Management	91.0	72	5.0	29% (108% of float)
Lante	Frontenac Co., Dell Ventures, MSD Capital	Credit Suisse First Deutsche Bank Alex Brown, Thomas Weisel Partners	PWC	CSFB, Deutsche Bank, Thomas Weisel Partners, others	Fidelity, State Street, Vanguard, Goldman Sachs Asset Management	26.8	80	5.6	3% (21% of float)
Razorfish	N/A	Credit Suisse First Boston, BancBoston Robertson Stephens, BT Alex. Brown, Lehman Brothers	AA, PWC	CSFB, Lehman Brothers, SG Cowen, others	Janus, Capital Research, Fidelity, Vanguard, Goldman Sachs Asset Management	N/A	48	3.4	8% (14% of float)
US Interactive	Safeguard Scientific, Technology Leaders	Lehman Brothers, Hambrecht & Quist, Adams Harkness & Hill	KPMG	Lehman Brothers, Hambrecht & Quist, Deutsche Bank Alex Brown, others	T Rowe Price, Prudential, JP Morgan Investment Management, Credit Suisse Asset Mgmt.	N/A	46	2.0	4% (6% of float)
Xpedior	N/A	DLJ, First Union Securities, JP Morgan, The Robinson-Humphrey Group	E&Y	DLJ, First Union Securities, Robinson-Humphrey, others	Capital Research, T Rowe Price, Franklin, Vanguard, John Hancock	N/A	162	11.4	2% (10% of float)

Sources: Compiled by casewriter.

a. PW stands for PriceWaterhouseCoopers; AA for Arthur Anderson; E&Y for Ernst & Young.

b. Includes underwriting fee.

c. As of April 2001.

EXHIBIT 4

Market Capitalization of Major Technology Companies, January 2000

Company	Market Capitalization ($ billions)[a]	Stock Price (January 3, 2000)
Microsoft	603	116.56
Intel	290	87.00
IBM	218	116.00
Dell Computer	131	50.88
Helwett Packard	117	117.44
Compaq Computer	53	31.00
Apple Computer	18	111.94

Sources: Bloomberg LP, The Center for Research in Security Prices (accessed via Wharton Research Database Services), Edgar Online.

a. Based on share price close on January 3, 2000 and reported shares outstanding.

EXHIBIT 5

Market Valuations Given to Loss-making Dot-coms

Company	Net Income ('99/'00)[a] ($ millions)	Market Capitalization ($ billions)[b]	Stock Price (January 3, 2000)
Amazon.com	−720	30.8	89.38
DoubleClick	−56	30.1	268.00
Akamai Technologies	−58	29.7	321.25
VerticalNet	−53	12.4	172.63
Priceline.com	−1,055	8.4	51.25
E*Trade	−57	7.1	28.06
EarthLink	−174	5.2	44.75
Drugstore.com	−116	1.6	37.13

Sources: Bloomberg LP, The Center for Research in Security Prices (accessed via Wharton Research Database Services), Edgar Online.

a. As of end of 1999 or early 2000, depending on fiscal year end.

b. Based on share price close on January 3, 2000 and reported shares outstanding.

EXHIBIT 6

Scient—Consolidated Financial Statements

INCOME STATEMENT
(in thousands except per-share amounts)

	November 7, 1997 (inception) through March 31, 1998	Year Ended March 31, 1999	2000
Revenues	$179	$20,675	$155,729
Operating expenses:			
Professional services	102	10,028	70,207
Selling, general and administrative	1,228	15,315	90,854
Stock compensation	64	7,679	15,636
Total operating expenses	1,394	22,022	176,697
Loss from operations	(1,215)	(12,347)	(20,968)
Interest income and other, net	56	646	4,953
Net loss	$(1,159)	$(11,701)	$(16,015)
Net loss per share:			
Basic and diluted	$(0.10)	$(0.89)	$(0.29)
Weighted average shares	11,894	13,198	54,590

BALANCE SHEET
(in thousands except per-share amounts)

	March 31, 1999	March 31, 2000
ASSETS		
Current Assets:		
Cash and cash equivalents	$11,261	$108,102
Short-term investments	16,868	121,046
Accounts receivable, net	5,876	56,021
Prepaid expenses	811	4,929
Other	318	4,228
Total Current Assets	35,134	294,326
Long-term investments	—	3,146
Property and equipment, net	3,410	16,063
Other	268	219
	$38,812	$313,754
LIABILITIES AND STOCKHOLDERS' EQUITY		
Current Liabilities:		
Bank borrowings, current	$413	$1,334
Accounts payable	832	5,023
Accrued compensation and benefits	2,554	33,976
Accrued expenses	2,078	9,265
Deferred revenue	524	6,579
Capital lease obligations, current	625	2,624
Total Current Liabilities	7,026	58,801
Capital lease obligations, long-term	680	2,052
	8,835	61,718
Commitments and contingencies (Note 5)		
Stockholders' equity:		
Convertible preferred stock; issuable in series, $.0001 par value; 10,000 shares authorized; 9,012 and no shares issued and outstanding, respectively	1	—
Common stock: $.0001 par value; 125,000 shares authorized; 33,134 and 72,491 shares issues and outstanding, respectively	3	7
Additional paid-in capital	70,055	297,735
Accumulated other comprehensive loss	—	(47)
Unearned compensation	(27,222)	(16,784)
Accumulated deficit	(12,860)	(28,875)
Total Stockholders' Equity	29,977	252,036
	$38,812	$313,754

Sources: Scient Corporation 10-K; Edgar Online *http://www.freedgar.com* (May 11, 2001).

EXHIBIT 7

Analyst Downgrades of the Internet Consultants

Company	Number of Analysts that Downgraded during August 30–September 8, 2000
Viant	13
Scient	7
IXL Enterprises	7
US Interactive	5
Xpedior	3
Lante	1
Razorfish	0

Analyst Downgrades of Scient Corporation, August 30–September 8, 2000

Institution	Previous Recommendation	New Recommendation	Date of Downgrade
Merrill Lynch	LT Buy	LT Accumulate	1-Sep-2000
Lehman Brothers	Buy	Outperform	1-Sep-2000
ING Barings	Buy	Hold	1-Sep-2000
SG Cowen	Buy	Neutral	1-Sep-2000
Legg Mason	Buy	Market Perform	1-Sep-2000
BB&T Capital Markets	Hold	Source of Funds	1-Sep-2000
First Union Securities	Strong Buy	Buy	31-Aug-2000

Source: I/B/E/S (accessed via Wharton Research Database Services).

EXHIBIT 8

Selected Institutional Holders of Scient Corporation, 1999–2000

Institution	Quarter Ended:						
	June 1999	September 1999	December 1999	March 2000	June 2000	September 2000	December 2000
Capital Research	—	—	—	265	1,079,911	586,442	586,706
Putnam Investments	5,000	—	625,900	2,209,200	4,800,800	5,749,200	—
Wellington Management	—	—	—	—	—	—	803,000
State Street	—	12,450	38,167	52,867	89,667	180,668	672,352
Janus	267,300	273,915	483,730	775,085	1,359,700	4,382,250	—

Source: Edgar (SEC).

EXHIBIT 9

Dot-coms that Filed for Bankruptcy or Closed Operations (*Selected List*)

August 2000
Auctions.com
Hardware.com
Living.com
SaviShopper.com
GreatCoffee

September 2000
Clickmango.com
Pop.com
FreeScholarships.com
RedLadder.com
DomainAuction.com
Gazoontite.com
Surfing2Cash.com
Affinia.com

October 2000
FreeInternet.com
Chipshot.com
Stockpower.com
The Dental Store
More.com
WebHouse
UrbanFetch.com
Boxman.com
RedGorilla.com
Eve.com
MyLackey.com
BigWords.com
Mortgage.com
MotherNature.com
Ivendor
TeliSmart.com

November 2000
Pets.com
Caredata.com
Streamline.com
Garden.com
Furniture.com
TheMan.com
Ibelieve.com
eSociety
UrbanDesign.com
HalfthePlanet.com
Productopia.com
BeautyJungle.com
ICanBuy.com
Bike.com
Mambo.com
Babystripes.com
Thirsty.com
Checkout.com

December 2000
Quepasa.com
Finance.com
BizBuyer.com
Desktop.com
E-pods.com
Clickabid.com
HeavenlyDoor.com
ShoppingList.com
Babygear.com
HotOffice.com
Goldsauction.com
AntEye.com
EZBid
Admart
I-US.com
Riffage.com

January 2000
MusicMaker.com
Mercata
Send.com
CompanyLeader.com
Zap.com
Savvio.com
News Digital Media
TravelNow.com
Foodline.com
LetsBuyIt.com
e7th.cm
CountryCool.com
Ibetcha.com
Fibermarket.com
Dotcomix
New Digital Media
GreatEntertaining.com
AndysGarage.com
Lucy.com
US Interactive

Sources: Johnathan Weil, " 'Going Concerns': Did Accountants Fail to Flag Problems at Dot-Com Casualties?" *Wall Street Journal*, February 2001; Jim Battey, "Dot-com details: The numbers behind the year's e-commerce shake-out," *Infoworld*, March 2001.

EXHIBIT 10

Capital Flows from Investors to Companies

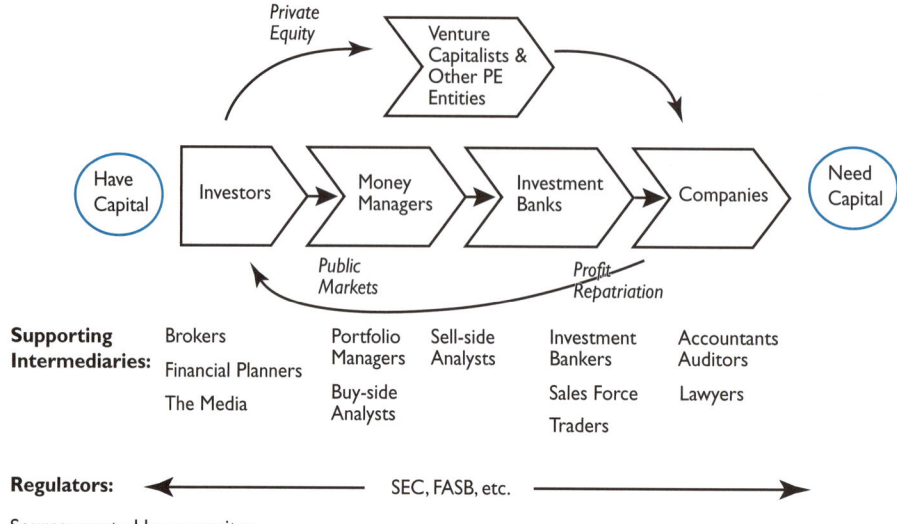

Source: created by casewriter.

PART TWO

BUSINESS ANALYSIS AND VALUATION TOOLS

Chapter 2
Strategy Analysis

S trategy analysis is an important starting point for the analysis of financial statements. Strategy analysis allows the analyst to probe the economics of a firm at a qualitative level so that the subsequent accounting and financial analysis is grounded in business reality. Strategy analysis also allows the identification of the firm's profit drivers and key risks. This in turn enables the analyst to assess the sustainability of the firm's current performance and make realistic forecasts of future performance.

A firm's value is determined by its ability to earn a return on its capital in excess of the cost of capital. What determines whether or not a firm is able to accomplish this goal? While a firm's cost of capital is determined by the capital markets, its profit potential is determined by its own strategic choices: (1) the choice of an industry or a set of industries in which the firm operates (industry choice), (2) the manner in which the firm intends to compete with other firms in its chosen industry or industries (competitive positioning), and (3) the way in which the firm expects to create and exploit synergies across the range of businesses in which it operates (corporate strategy). Strategy analysis, therefore, involves industry analysis, competitive strategy analysis, and corporate strategy analysis.[1] In this chapter, we will briefly discuss these three steps and use the personal computer industry, Dell Inc., and General Electric, respectively, to illustrate the application of the steps.

INDUSTRY ANALYSIS

In analyzing a firm's profit potential, an analyst has to first assess the profit potential of each of the industries in which the firm is competing because the profitability of various industries differs systematically and predictably over time. For example, the ratio of earnings before interest and taxes to the book value of assets for all U.S. companies between 1981 and 1997 was 8.8 percent. However, the average returns varied widely across specific industries: for the bakery products industry, the profitability ratio was 43 percentage points greater than the population average, and for the silver ore mining industry it was 23 percentage points less than the population average.[2] What causes these profitability differences?

There is a vast body of research in industrial organization on the influence of industry structure on profitability.[3] Relying on this research, strategy literature suggests that the average profitability of an industry is influenced by the "five forces" shown in Figure 2-1.[4] According to this framework, the intensity of competition determines the potential for creating abnormal profits by the firms in an industry. Whether or not the potential profits are kept by the industry is determined by the relative bargaining power of the firms in the industry and their customers and suppliers. We will discuss each of these industry profit drivers in more detail below.

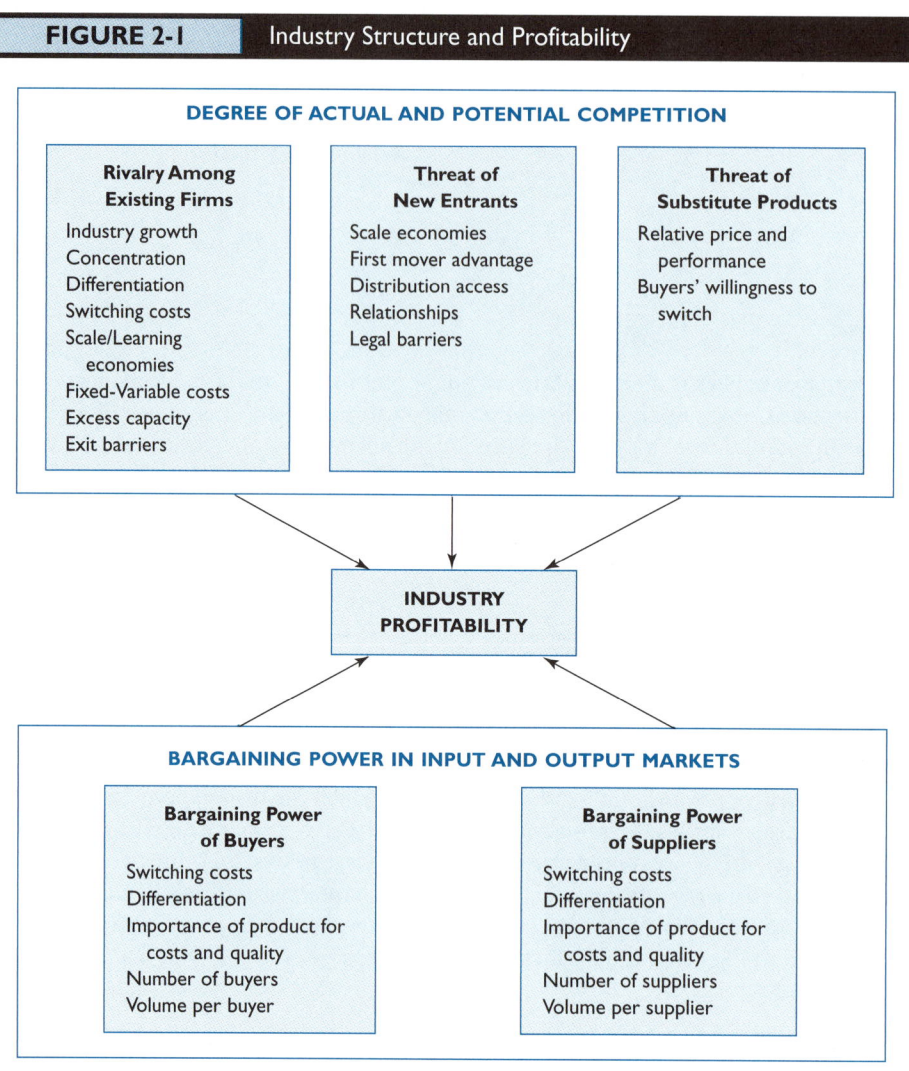

FIGURE 2-1   Industry Structure and Profitability

DEGREE OF ACTUAL AND POTENTIAL COMPETITION

**Rivalry Among
Existing Firms**

Industry growth
Concentration
Differentiation
Switching costs
Scale/Learning
  economies
Fixed-Variable costs
Excess capacity
Exit barriers

**Threat of
New Entrants**

Scale economies
First mover advantage
Distribution access
Relationships
Legal barriers

**Threat of
Substitute Products**

Relative price and
  performance
Buyers' willingness to
  switch

**INDUSTRY
PROFITABILITY**

BARGAINING POWER IN INPUT AND OUTPUT MARKETS

**Bargaining Power
of Buyers**

Switching costs
Differentiation
Importance of product for
  costs and quality
Number of buyers
Volume per buyer

**Bargaining Power
of Suppliers**

Switching costs
Differentiation
Importance of product for
  costs and quality
Number of suppliers
Volume per supplier

Degree of Actual and Potential Competition

At the most basic level, the profits in an industry are a function of the maximum price that customers are willing to pay for the industry's product or service. One of the key determinants of the price is the degree to which there is competition among suppliers of the same or similar products. At one extreme, if there is a state of perfect competition in the industry, micro-economic theory predicts that prices will be equal to marginal cost, and there will be few opportunities to earn supernormal profits. At the other extreme, if the industry is dominated by a single firm, there will be potential to earn monopoly profits. In reality, the degree of competition in most industries is somewhere in between perfect competition and monopoly.

There are three potential sources of competition in an industry: (1) rivalry between existing firms, (2) threat of entry of new firms, and (3) threat of substitute products or services. We discuss each of these competitive forces in the following paragraphs.

Competitive Force 1: Rivalry Among Existing Firms

In most industries the average level of profitability is primarily influenced by the nature of rivalry among existing firms in the industry. In some industries firms compete aggressively, pushing prices close to (and sometimes below) the marginal cost. In other industries firms do not compete aggressively on price. Instead, they find ways to coordinate their pricing, or compete on non-price dimensions such as innovation or brand image. Several factors determine the intensity of competition between existing players in an industry:

Industry Growth Rate If an industry is growing very rapidly, incumbent firms need not grab market share from each other to grow. In contrast, in stagnant industries the only way existing firms can grow is by taking share away from the other players. In this situation one can expect price wars among firms in the industry.

Concentration and Balance of Competitors The number of firms in an industry and their relative sizes determine the degree of concentration in an industry.[5] The degree of concentration influences the extent to which firms in an industry can coordinate their pricing and other competitive moves. For example, if there is one dominant firm in an industry (such as IBM in the mainframe computer industry in the 1970s), it can set and enforce the rules of competition. Similarly, if there are only two or three equal-sized players (such as Coca-Cola and Pepsi in the U.S. soft drink industry), they can implicitly cooperate with each other to avoid destructive price competition. If an industry is fragmented, price competition is likely to be severe.

Degree of Differentiation and Switching Costs The extent to which firms in an industry can avoid head-on competition depends on the extent to which they can differentiate their products and services. If the products in an industry are very similar, customers are ready to switch from one competitor to another purely on the basis of price. Switching costs also determine customers' propensity to move from one product to another. When switching costs are low, there is a greater incentive for firms in an industry to engage in price competition. The PC industry, where the standardization of the software and microprocessor has led to relatively low switching costs, is extremely price competitive.

Scale/Learning Economies and the Ratio of Fixed to Variable Costs If there is a steep learning curve or there are other types of scale economies in an industry, size becomes an important factor for firms in the industry. In such situations, there are incentives to engage in aggressive competition for market share. Similarly, if the ratio of fixed to variable costs is high, firms have an incentive to reduce prices to utilize installed capacity. The airline industry, where price wars are quite common, is an example of this type of situation.

Excess Capacity and Exit Barriers If capacity in an industry is larger than customer demand, there is a strong incentive for firms to cut prices to fill capacity. The problem of excess capacity is likely to be exacerbated if there are significant barriers for firms to exit the industry. Exit barriers are high when the assets are specialized or if there are regulations which make exit costly. The competitive dynamics of the steel industry demonstrates these forces at play.

Competitive Force 2: Threat of New Entrants

The potential for earning abnormal profits will attract new entrants to an industry. The very threat of new firms entering an industry potentially constrains the pricing of existing firms within it. Therefore, the ease with which new firms can enter an industry is a key determinant of its profitability. Several factors determine the height of barriers to entry in an industry:

Economies of Scale When there are large economies of scale, new entrants face the choice of having either to invest in large capacity which might not be utilized right away or to enter with less than the optimum capacity. Either way, new entrants will at least initially suffer from a cost disadvantage in competing with existing firms. Economies of scale might arise from large investments in research and development (the pharmaceutical or jet engine industries), in brand advertising (soft drink industry), or in physical plant and equipment (telecommunications industry).

First Mover Advantage Early entrants in an industry may deter future entrants if there are first mover advantages. For example, first movers might be able to set industry standards, or enter into exclusive arrangements with suppliers of cheap raw materials. They may also acquire scarce government licenses to operate in regulated industries. Finally, if there are learning economies, early firms will have an absolute cost advantage over new entrants. First mover advantages are also likely to be large when there are significant switching costs for customers once they start using existing products. For example, switching costs faced by the users of Microsoft's Windows operating system make it difficult for software companies to market a new operating system.

Access to Channels of Distribution and Relationships Limited capacity in the existing distribution channels and high costs of developing new channels can act as powerful barriers to entry. For example, a new entrant into the domestic auto industry in the U.S. is likely to face formidable barriers because of the difficulty of developing a dealer network. Similarly, new consumer goods manufacturers find it difficult to obtain supermarket shelf space for their products. Existing relationships between firms and customers in an industry also make it difficult for new firms to enter an industry. Industry examples of this include auditing and investment banking.

Legal Barriers There are many industries in which legal barriers such as patents and copyrights in research-intensive industries limit entry. Similarly, licensing regulations limit entry into taxi services, medical services, broadcasting, and telecommunications industries.

Competitive Force 3: Threat of Substitute Products

The third dimension of competition in an industry is the threat of substitute products or services. Relevant substitutes are not necessarily those that have the same form as the existing products but those that perform the same function. For example, airlines and car rental services might be substitutes for each other when it comes to travel over medium distances. Similarly, plastic bottles and metal cans substitute for each other as packaging in the beverage industry. In some cases, threat of substitution comes not from customers' switching to another product but from utilizing technologies that allow them to do without, or use less of, the existing products. For example, energy-conserving technologies allow customers to reduce their consumption of electricity and fossil fuels.

The threat of substitutes depends on the relative price and performance of the competing products or services and on customers' willingness to substitute. Customers' perception of whether two products are substitutes depends to some extent on whether they perform the same function for a similar price. If two products perform an identical function, then it would be difficult for them to differ from each other in price. However, customers' willingness to switch is often the critical factor in making this competitive dynamic work. For example, even when tap water and bottled water serve the same function, many customers may be unwilling to substitute the former for the latter, enabling bottlers to charge a price premium. Similarly, designer label clothing commands a price premium even if it is not superior in terms of basic functionality because customers place a value on the image or style offered by designer labels.

Bargaining Power in Input and Output Markets

While the degree of competition in an industry determines whether there is *potential* to earn abnormal profits, the *actual profits* are influenced by the industry's bargaining power with its suppliers and customers. On the input side, firms enter into transactions with suppliers of labor, raw materials and components, and finances. On the output side, firms either sell directly to the final customers or enter into contracts with intermediaries in the distribution chain. In all these transactions, the relative economic power of the two sides is important to the overall profitability of the industry firms.

Competitive Force 4: Bargaining Power of Buyers

Two factors determine the power of buyers: price sensitivity and relative bargaining power. Price sensitivity determines the extent to which buyers care to bargain on price; relative bargaining power determines the extent to which they will succeed in forcing the price down.[6]

Price Sensitivity Buyers are more price sensitive when the product is undifferentiated and there are few switching costs. The sensitivity of buyers to price also depends on the importance of the product to their own cost structure. When the product represents a large fraction of the buyers' cost (for example, the packaging material for soft drink producers), the buyer is likely to expend the resources necessary to shop for a lower cost alternative. In contrast, if the product is a small fraction of the buyers' cost (for example, windshield wipers for automobile manufacturers), it may not pay to expend resources to search for lower-cost alternatives. Further, the importance of the product to the buyers' own product quality also determines whether or not price becomes the most important determinant of the buying decision.

Relative Bargaining Power Even if buyers are price sensitive, they may not be able to achieve low prices unless they have a strong bargaining position. Relative bargaining power in a transaction depends, ultimately, on the cost to each party of not doing business with the other party. The buyers' bargaining power is determined by the number of buyers relative to the number of suppliers, volume of purchases by a single buyer, number of alternative products available to the buyer, buyers' costs of switching from one product to another, and the threat of backward integration by the buyers. For example, in the automobile industry, car manufacturers have considerable power over component manufacturers because auto companies are large buyers with several alternative suppliers to choose from, and switching costs are relatively low. In contrast, in the personal computer industry, computer makers have low bargaining power relative to the operating system software producers because of high switching costs.

Competitive Force 5: Bargaining Power of Suppliers

The analysis of the relative power of suppliers is a mirror image of the analysis of the buyer's power in an industry. Suppliers are powerful when there are only a few companies and few substitutes available to their customers. For example, in the soft drink industry, Coke and Pepsi are very powerful relative to the bottlers. In contrast, metal can suppliers to the soft drink industry are not very powerful because of intense competition among can producers and the threat of substitution by plastic bottles. Suppliers also have a lot of power over buyers when the suppliers' product or service is critical to buyers' business. For example, airline pilots have a strong bargaining power in the airline industry. Suppliers also tend to be powerful when they pose a credible threat of forward integration. For example, IBM is powerful relative to mainframe computer leasing companies because of its unique position as a mainframe supplier and its own presence in the computer leasing business.

APPLYING INDUSTRY ANALYSIS: THE PERSONAL COMPUTER INDUSTRY

Let us consider the above concepts of industry analysis in the context of the personal computer (PC) industry.[7] The industry began in 1981 when IBM announced its PC with Intel's microprocessor and Microsoft's DOS operating system, and it has seen spectacular growth since then. Now personal computers are almost ubiquitous—an estimated 208 million units were shipped worldwide in 2005 alone. Despite this growth in the sales volume, the industry is characterized by low profitability. The largest and best known companies in the industry, including IBM, Compaq, Dell and Hewlett-Packard, have been trying to improve performance since the early 1990s through internal restructuring and mergers. What accounts for this low profitability? What is the computer industry's future profit potential?

Competition in the Personal Computer Industry

Competition continues to be very intense for a number of reasons:

- The industry is fragmented, with many firms producing virtually identical products. Even though the computer market continues to become increasingly concentrated with a series of high-profile transactions, such as the mergers of Compaq with Hewlett-Packard and Gateway with eMachines and the sale of IBM's PC business to Lenovo, competition is intense—there are routine price cuts on a monthly basis. The top five vendors in 2005 controlled less than 50 percent of worldwide PC sales.
- Component costs account for more than 60 percent of total hardware costs of a personal computer, and volume purchases of components reduce these costs. While prices for critical components such as microprocessors and disk drives continue to decline, customers in turn expect lower prices, contributing to the increasing reliance on volume growth. Therefore, there is intense competition for market share among competing manufacturers.
- PCs produced by different firms in the industry are virtually identical, and there are few opportunities to differentiate the products. While brand name and service were dimensions that customers valued in the early years of the industry, they have become less important as PC buyers are more informed about the technology. Companies are attempting to differentiate themselves through innovative design and high-end performance, but this remains a small niche in the industry.
- Switching costs across different brands of PCs are relatively low because a vast majority of PCs use Intel microprocessors and Microsoft Windows operating systems.
- Access to distribution has not been a significant barrier, as demonstrated by Dell, which distributed its computers by direct mail through the 1980s and introduced Internet-based sales in the mid-1990s. In recent years, all the major PC manufacturers have adopted some elements of Dell's direct sales model, a

process that has accelerated with the popularity of Internet commerce. The advent of computer superstores like CompUSA also mitigated this constraint, since these stores were willing to carry several brands.

- Since virtually all the components needed to produce a personal computer were available for purchase, there were very few barriers to entering the industry. In fact, Michael Dell started Dell Computer Company in the early 1980s by assembling PCs in his University of Texas dormitory room.
- Apple's line of computers continues to offer competition as a substitute product. Workstations produced by Sun and other vendors are also potential substitutes at the higher end of the personal computer market though most PC manufacturers now offer more powerful machines as well.

The Power of Suppliers and Buyers

Suppliers and buyers have significant power over firms in the industry for these reasons:

- Essential hardware and software components for PCs are controlled by firms with a virtual monopoly and consequently manufacturers return a large portion of their net profits to the component makers. Intel continues to dominate microprocessor production for the personal computer industry with market share of close to 80 percent, though smaller rival AMD has made inroads on Intel's dominance, which could lead to greater price competition in the near future. Microsoft's control over the operating system market with its DOS and Windows operating systems persists, with between 85 and 90 percent of PCs worldwide using its software. While open source alternatives such as Linux remain a threat to Microsoft's dominance of the PC industry, pirated software in emerging economies is the real threat to Microsoft's revenue model. Software piracy is likely to lead to two simultaneous responses—low-cost versions of Windows in the emerging markets because of lower purchasing power, and price increases in the developed markets, neither of which will alleviate the margin pressure on PC manufacturers.[8]
- Buyers have gained more and more power as the PC industry has matured over the last two decades. Corporate buyers, who represent a significant portion of the customer base, are highly price sensitive since the expenditure on PCs represents a significant cost to their operations. Further, as penetration of the home market has increased, customers are less influenced by brand name. Except for a small, high-end market niche, buyers increasingly view PCs as commodities and use price as the most important consideration in their purchase decisions.

As a result of the intense rivalry and low barriers to entry in the personal computer industry, there is severe price competition among different manufacturers. Further, there is tremendous pressure on firms to spend large sums of money to introduce new products rapidly, maintain high quality, and provide excellent customer support. Both these factors have led to a low profit potential in the industry. The power of suppliers and buyers has reduced profit potential further. Thus, while the personal computer industry represents a technologically dynamic industry, its profit potential continues to be poor.

There are few indications of change in the basic structure of the personal computer industry, and there is little likelihood in the near term of viable competition emerging to unseat the domination of Microsoft and Intel in the input markets. Attempts by industry leaders like IBM to create alternative proprietary technologies have not succeeded. Desktop replacement cycles are lengthening, slowing demand. The PC industry is under further threat from the mobile device market. Although at an early stage, advanced mobile communication, Internet access, and multimedia entertainment technologies could replace the PC for some users. While many in the industry pin their hopes on the digital home with a media-centric PC to drive sales growth and improve margins, experience in the U.S. market to date has fallen short of expectations.[9] As a result, the profitability of the PC industry may not improve significantly any time in the near future.

Limitations of Industry Analysis

A potential limitation of the industry analysis framework discussed in this chapter is the assumption that industries have clear boundaries. In reality, it is often not easy to demarcate industry boundaries. For example, in analyzing Dell's industry, should one focus on the IBM-compatible personal computer industry or the personal computer industry as a whole? Should one include workstations in the industry definition? Should one consider only the domestic manufacturers of personal computers or also manufacturers abroad? Inappropriate industry definition will result in incomplete analysis and inaccurate forecasts.

COMPETITIVE STRATEGY ANALYSIS

The profitability of a firm is influenced not only by its industry structure but also by the strategic choices it makes in positioning itself in the industry. While there are many ways to characterize a firm's business strategy, as Figure 2-2 shows, there are two generic competitive strategies: (1) cost leadership and (2) differentiation.[10] Both these strategies can potentially allow a firm to build a sustainable competitive

FIGURE 2-2	Strategies for Creating Competitive Advantage

Cost Leadership

Supply same product or service at a lower cost.

Economies of scale and scope
Efficient production
Simpler product designs
Lower input costs
Low-cost distribution
Little research and development or
  brand advertising
Tight cost control system

Differentiation

Supply a unique product or service at a cost lower than the price premium customers will pay.

Superior product quality
Superior product variety
Superior customer service
More flexible delivery
Investment in brand image
Investment in research and
  development
Control system focus on creativity
  and innovation

Competitive Advantage

- Match between firm's core competencies and key success factors to execute strategy
- Match between firm's value chain and activities required to execute strategy
- Sustainability of competitive advantage

advantage. Strategy researchers have traditionally viewed cost leadership and differentiation as mutually exclusive strategies. Firms that straddle the two strategies are considered to be "stuck in the middle" and are expected to earn low profitability.[11] These firms run the risk of not being able to attract price conscious customers because their costs are too high; they are also unable to provide adequate differentiation to attract premium price customers.[12]

Sources of Competitive Advantage

Cost leadership enables a firm to supply the same product or service offered by its competitors at a lower cost. Differentiation strategy involves providing a product or service that is distinct in some important respect valued by the customer. As an example in retailing, Nordstrom has succeeded on the basis of differentiation by emphasizing exceptionally high customer service. In contrast, Filene's Basement is a discount retailer competing purely on a low-cost basis.

Competitive Strategy 1: Cost Leadership

Cost leadership is often the clearest way to achieve competitive advantage. In industries where the basic product or service is a commodity, cost leadership might be the only way to achieve superior performance. There are many ways to achieve cost leadership, including economies of scale and scope, economies of learning, efficient production, simpler product design, better sourcing and lower input costs, and efficient organizational processes. If a firm can achieve cost leadership, then it will be able to earn above-average profitability by merely charging the same price as its rivals. Conversely, a cost leader can force its competitors to cut prices and accept lower returns or to exit the industry.

Firms that achieve cost leadership focus on tight cost controls. They make investments in efficient scale plants, focus on product designs that reduce manufacturing costs, minimize overhead costs, capitalize on global sourcing opportunities, make little investment in risky research and development, and avoid serving marginal customers. They have organizational structures and control systems that focus on cost control.

Competitive Strategy 2: Differentiation

A firm following the differentiation strategy seeks to be unique in its industry along some dimension that is highly valued by customers. For differentiation to be successful, the firm has to accomplish three things. First, it needs to identify one or more attributes of a product or service that customers value. Second, it has to position itself to meet the chosen customer need in a unique manner. Finally, the firm has to achieve differentiation at a cost that is lower than the price the customer is willing to pay for the differentiated product or service.

Drivers of differentiation include providing superior intrinsic value via product quality, product variety, bundled services, or delivery timing. Differentiation can also be achieved by investing in signals of value such as brand image, product appearance, or reputation. Differentiated strategies require investments in research and development, engineering skills, and marketing capabilities. The organizational structures and control systems in firms with differentiation strategies need to foster creativity and innovation.

While successful firms choose between cost leadership and differentiation, they cannot completely ignore the dimension on which they are not primarily competing. Firms that target differentiation still need to focus on costs so that the differentiation can be achieved at an acceptable cost. Similarly, cost leaders cannot compete unless they achieve at least a minimum level on key dimensions on which competitors might differentiate, such as quality and service.

Achieving and Sustaining Competitive Advantage

The choice of competitive strategy does not automatically lead to the achievement of competitive advantage. To achieve competitive advantage, the firm has to have the capabilities needed to implement and sustain the chosen strategy. Both cost leadership and differentiation strategy require that the firm make the necessary commitments to acquire the core competencies needed and structure its value chain in an appropriate way. Core competencies are the economic assets that the firm possesses, whereas the value chain is the set of activities that the firm performs to convert inputs into outputs. The uniqueness of a firm's core competencies and its value chain and the extent to which it is difficult for competitors to imitate them determine the sustainability of a firm's competitive advantage.[13]

To evaluate whether a firm is likely to achieve its intended competitive advantage, the analyst should ask the following questions:

- What are the key success factors and risks associated with the firm's chosen competitive strategy?
- Does the firm currently have the resources and capabilities to deal with the key success factors and risks?
- Has the firm made irreversible commitments to bridge the gap between its current capabilities and the requirements to achieve its competitive advantage?
- Has the firm structured its activities (such as research and development, design, manufacturing, marketing and distribution, and support activities) in a way that is consistent with its competitive strategy?
- Is the company's competitive advantage sustainable? Are there any barriers that make imitation of the firm's strategy difficult?
- Are there any potential changes in the firm's industry structure (such as new technologies, foreign competition, changes in regulation, changes in customer requirements) that might dissipate the firm's competitive advantage? Is the company flexible enough to address these changes?

Applying Competitive Strategy Analysis

Let's consider the concepts of competitive strategy analysis in the context of Dell Inc., based in Round Rock, Texas. The company, founded by Michael Dell in his University of Texas dorm room, started selling "IBM clone" personal computers in 1984. From the beginning Dell sold its machines directly to end users rather than through retail outlets, at a significantly lower price than its competitors.

After rapid growth and some management hiccups, Dell firmly established itself in the PC industry by following a low-cost strategy. Within ten years of its founding, Dell was among the five largest PC vendors, and by 1999 Dell was the leading seller of PCs in the U.S. For the fiscal year ending February 3, 2006, Dell achieved $55.9 billion in revenues and $3.6 billion in net income, up from $49.2 billion and $3.0 billion, respectively, for the prior year. Dell's growth rates continue to outpace the market, and in 2005 it increased its market share in every region around the world. Dell's stellar performance over its first two decades made it one of the most profitable personal computer makers in a highly competitive industry. How did Dell achieve such performance?

Dell's superior performance was based on a low-cost competitive strategy that consisted of the following key elements:

- *Direct selling*. Dell sold most of its computers directly to its customers, thus saving on retail markups. As computer users become sophisticated, and as computers become standardized on the Windows-Intel platform, the value of distribution through retailers declined. Dell was the first company to capitalize on this trend. In 1996 Dell began selling computers through its Internet web site. In 2005 the company was generating a significant amount of its sales through on-line orders.
- *Made-to-order manufacturing*. Dell developed a system of flexible manufacturing that allowed the company to assemble and ship computers very quickly, usually within five days of receiving an order. This allowed the company to avoid large inventories of parts and assembled computers. Low inventories allowed Dell to save on working capital costs and also reduced costly write-offs of obsolete inventories, a significant risk in the fast-changing computer industry.
- *Third-party service*. Dell used two low-cost approaches to after-sales service: telephone-based service and third-party maintenance service. Dell had several hundred technical support representatives accessible to customers by phone any time of the day. Using a comprehensive electronic maintenance system, the service representatives could diagnose problems and help customers to resolve them in the vast majority of cases. In the rare instance where on-site maintenance was required, Dell used third-party maintenance contracts with office equipment companies such as Xerox. Through this service strategy, Dell was able to avoid investing in an expensive field service network without compromising on service quality.
- *Low accounts receivable*. Dell was able to reduce its accounts receivable days to an industry minimum by encouraging its customers to pay by credit card at the time of the purchase or through electronic payment immediately after the purchase.
- *Focused investment in R&D*. Dell recognized that most of the basic innovations in the personal computer industry were led by the component suppliers and software producers. For example, two key suppliers, Intel and Microsoft, invested billions of dollars in developing new generation processors and software, respectively. Dell's innovations were primarily in creating a low-cost, high velocity organization that could respond quickly to these changes. By focusing its R&D innovations, Dell was able to minimize these costs and get high returns on its investments.

As a result of the above strategy, Dell achieved a significant cost advantage over its competitors in the PC industry. This advantage resulted in a consistent pattern of rapid growth, increasing market share, and very high profitability in an industry that is characterized by rapid technological changes, significant supplier and buyer power, and intense competition. Further, because the strategy involved activities that are highly interrelated and involved continuous organizational innovations, Dell's business model was difficult to replicate.

However, there are signs that Dell's dominance is being challenged. The company missed its profit estimates and saw quarter over quarter profit declines in 2005 and 2006. On the commoditized PC front, competitors such as Hewlett-Packard have narrowed the productivity and price gap with Dell, further driving down profit margins. With the proliferation of new digital gear, consumers are increasingly seeking unique design features, which requires innovation, greater R&D spending, and often a retail presence. Dell's stock, which once traded at extraordinarily high earnings and book value multiples, has underperformed competitors such as Apple and Hewlett-Packard.

Dell's management has responded to the challenges of slowing growth. Dell is focusing on growing its international sales, especially in fast-growing consumer markets in China and India. To ensure that its direct model will work in these new geographies, Dell is shifting manufacturing overseas to be closer to its customers. Dell is also increasing its focus on the consumer market in the U.S. To help consumer market penetration, the firm is showing a willingness to break with its traditional direct-sales model and opened its first full store in Dallas in July 2006. It also announced plans to simplify its current pricing and rebate structure for consumers. In a departure from its belief in stressing internal growth, in May 2006 Dell acquired Alienware, a high-end PC manufacturer that offers Dell stronger branding and more stylish design in the niche gaming market. It will be interesting to see whether Dell's plans, dubbed Dell 2.0, are able to sustain the competitive advantage that led to its dominance as the PC industry continues to evolve.

CORPORATE STRATEGY ANALYSIS

So far in this chapter we have focused on strategies at the individual business level. While some companies focus on only one business, many companies operate in multiple businesses. For example, the average number of business segments operated by the top 500 U.S. companies in 1992 was eleven industries.[14] In recent years, there has been an attempt by U.S. companies to reduce the diversity of their operations and focus on a relatively few "core" businesses. However, multi-business organizations continue to dominate the economic activity in most countries in the world.

When analyzing a multi-business organization, an analyst has to evaluate not only the industries and strategies of the individual business units but also the economic consequences—either positive or negative—of managing all the different businesses under one corporate umbrella. For example, General Electric has been very successful in creating significant value by managing a highly diversified set of businesses ranging from aircraft engines to light bulbs. In contrast, Sears has not been very successful in managing retailing together with financial services, divesting itself of Allstate Insurance, Dean Witter, Coldwell Banker Residential Services, and its credit card business in the past 15 years to focus on retailing activities.

Sources of Value Creation at the Corporate Level

Economists and strategy researchers have identified several factors that influence an organization's ability to create value through a broad corporate scope. Economic theory suggests that the optimal scope of activity of a firm depends on the relative transaction cost of performing a set of activities inside the firm versus using the market mechanism.[15] Transaction cost economics implies that the multi-product firm is an efficient choice of organizational form when coordination among independent, focused firms is costly due to market transaction costs.

Transaction costs can arise out of several sources. They may arise if the production process involves specialized assets such as human capital skills, proprietary technology, or other organizational know-how that is not easily available in the marketplace. Transaction costs also may arise from market imperfections such as information and incentive problems. If buyers and sellers cannot solve these problems through standard mechanisms such as enforceable contracts, it will be costly to conduct transactions through market mechanisms.

For example, as discussed in Chapter 1, public capital markets may not work well when there are significant information and incentive problems, making it difficult for entrepreneurs to raise capital from investors. Similarly, if buyers cannot ascertain the quality of products being sold because of lack of information, or cannot enforce warranties because of poor legal infrastructure, entrepreneurs will find it difficult to break into new markets. Finally, if employers cannot assess the quality of applicants for new positions, they will have to rely more on internal promotions rather than external recruiting to fill higher positions in an organization. Emerging economies often suffer from these types of transaction costs because of poorly developed intermediation infrastructure.[16] Even in many advanced economies, examples of high transaction costs can be found. For example, in most countries other than the U.S., the venture capital industry is not highly developed, making it costly for new businesses in high technology industries to attract financing. Even in the U.S., transaction costs may vary across economic sectors. For example, until recently, electronic commerce was hampered by consumer concerns regarding the security of credit card information sent over the Internet.

Transactions inside an organization may be less costly than market-based transactions for several reasons. First, communication costs inside an organization are reduced because confidentiality can be protected and credibility can be assured through internal mechanisms. Second, the head office can play a critical role in reducing costs of enforcing agreements between organizational subunits. Third, organizational subunits can share valuable nontradable assets (such as organizational skills, systems, and processes) or nondivisible assets (such as brand names, distribution channels, and reputation).

There are also forces that increase transaction costs inside organizations. Top management of an organization may lack the specialized information and skills necessary to manage businesses across several different industries. This lack of expertise reduces the possibility of actually realizing economies of scope, even when there is potential for such economies. This problem can be remedied by creating a decentralized organization, hiring specialist managers to run each business unit, and providing these managers with proper incentives. However, decentralization will also potentially decrease goal congruence among subunit managers, making it difficult to realize economies of scope.

Whether or not a multi-business organization creates more value than a comparable collection of focused firms is, therefore, context dependent.[17] Analysts should ask the following questions to assess whether an organization's corporate strategy has the potential to create value:

- Are there significant imperfections in the product, labor, or financial markets in the industries (or countries) in which a company is operating? Is it likely that transaction costs in these markets are higher than the costs of similar activities inside a well managed organization?
- Does the organization have special resources such as brand names, proprietary know-how, access to scarce distribution channels, and special organizational processes that have the potential to create economies of scope?
- Is there a good fit between the company's specialized resources and the portfolio of businesses in which the company is operating?
- Does the company allocate decision rights between the headquarters office and the business units optimally to realize all the potential economies of scope?
- Does the company have internal measurement, information, and incentive systems to reduce agency costs and increase coordination across business units?

Empirical evidence suggests that creating value through a multi-business corporate strategy is difficult in practice. Several researchers have documented that diversified U.S. companies trade at a discount in the stock market relative to a comparable portfolio of focused companies.[18] Studies also show that acquisitions of one company by another, especially when the two are in unrelated businesses, often fail to create value for the acquiring companies.[19] Finally, there is considerable evidence that value is created when multi-business companies increase corporate focus through divisional spin-offs and asset sales.[20]

There are several potential explanations for this diversification discount. First, managers' decisions to diversify and expand are frequently driven by a desire to maximize the size of their organization rather than to maximize shareholder value. Second, diversified companies often suffer from incentive misalignment problems leading to suboptimal investment decisions and poor operating performance. Third, capital markets find it difficult to monitor and value multi-business organizations because of inadequate disclosure about the performance of individual business segments.

In summary, while companies can theoretically create value through innovative corporate strategies, there are many ways in which this potential fails to get realized in practice. Therefore, it pays to be skeptical when evaluating companies' corporate strategies.

Applying Corporate Strategy Analysis

Let's apply the concepts of corporate strategy analysis to General Electric (GE), one of the world's leading diversified businesses. GE has had a storied history since it was founded by Thomas Edison in 1878, and it is consistently one of the world's most admired companies. In May 2006, GE was the second largest corporation in the world as measured by its market capitalization, and it consistently ranks in the top ten in *Fortune* magazine's Global 500 rankings. GE has a portfolio of world class businesses that dominate their respective industries. GE sees itself not as a conglomerate built through a series of add-on acquisitions but as a group of diverse businesses that are closely integrated through a tradition of sharing talent and best practices and a culture of unwavering integrity.[21] The GE business mix, which management believes to be aligned with the prevailing demographic trends, is managed along six broad segments:

- *Infrastructure:* In 2005 Infrastructure represented about 35 percent of GE's profits. GE competes in all the major infrastructure markets including energy, aviation, rail, oil and gas, and water. GE generates more than 60 percent of its orders from outside the U.S. and is well positioned to benefit from the significant investments in infrastructure that is expected in the developing world. Long-term service agreements and the financial services components of the aviation and energy businesses provide a high-margin and diversified source of revenue.
- *Commercial Finance:* Commercial Finance contributes about 20 percent of the firm's profits. GE's franchise includes an extremely profitable real estate business and a variety of high-margin lending businesses in industry verticals such as healthcare and entertainment. Commercial Finance leverages a combination of strong origination, low cost of funds, and prudent risk management to deliver strong earnings growth.
- *Consumer Finance:* Consumer Finance produced approximately 15 percent of the profits, with over 70 percent of the earnings in this business unit coming from outside the U.S. GE has built significant capability in the developing

markets and is benefiting from rising incomes in these geographies. GE offers a wide suite of products ranging from personal and auto loans to mortgages and private-label credit cards.

- *Healthcare:* The Healthcare business represents about 10 percent of profits and its strong performance has been driven by favorable demographic trends, strong growth in service revenue, and a successful acquisition strategy. GE's diagnostic imaging equipment and patient monitoring systems are used in hospitals worldwide. Bio-sciences and drug discovery systems are a growing source of revenue within the Healthcare unit. GE is also using partnerships with firms such as Eli Lilly and Roche to expand its product development capabilities.
- *NBC Universal:* NBC Universal was created through the merger of the NBC network with Vivendi Universal's entertainment assets. Its television assets include NBC network, Spanish language network Telemundo, and cable channels such as Bravo and USA Network. Other properties include the Universal Pictures movie studio and Universal Parks and Resorts. While the segment contributed to 10 percent of earnings and includes stellar brands, the unit's performance has lagged as the NBC network has struggled of late.
- *Industrial:* Industrial encompasses a broad range of products and services that includes the pioneering lighting division, home appliances, residential security systems, and high-performance polymers used by electronics and automotive manufacturers. Industrial represents about 10 percent of the profits at GE. Industrial has capitalized on outsourcing trends and is cost competitive due to a strategy of sourcing products from China and Mexico.

Given the breadth of its business interests and the sheer size of the company, GE is able to enjoy tremendous benefits from common sourcing, consolidated IT platforms, and research synergies. The firm is able to scale ideas quickly and impose GE competencies such as process discipline, global distribution, and customer relationships on new ideas and acquisitions. In addition, there are certain core, overarching themes that influence the way GE is run that have contributed to its superior performance over a prolonged period:

- GE has been able to attract and develop talent on a sustained basis. Senior executives have spent time at multiple business units, have a first-hand knowledge of the drivers of the different businesses, and are positioned to identify synergies between them. Throughout its history, GE's top leaders have come from within the firm's executive ranks and personify the GE culture and values.
- GE is constantly optimizing the mix of businesses to exploit new growth opportunities. Since Jeff Immelt took over as CEO from Jack Welch in 2001, GE has divested $30 billion of slow-growth divisions and spent $65 billion on acquisitions to push into high-growth areas such as healthcare.
- GE is willing to continually reinvent itself to align better with the evolving needs of its customers and markets. This relentless push for re-evaluation and improvement is not limited to its business portfolio but extends to its processes, management capabilities, focus on innovation, and measures of success as well.
- GE has embraced globalization, and hence each of its businesses is focused on diversifying the geographic sources of revenues. GE's breadth of offerings allows the firm to adopt a "company to country" approach to business development in many emerging economies by providing infrastructure, financing, and partnership.[22]

However, GE's stock price has languished in recent times relative to the major U.S. market indices. Over the five-year period through the end of 2006, GE's stock has significantly underperformed the S&P 500 Index. While the Index has gained 24 percent, GE stock lost almost 8 percent of its value. Though some fund managers claim that they prefer to allocate assets among sectors themselves rather than leave it to the management of diversified companies, GE management has repeatedly stressed that it is not going to break up the business. It will be interesting to see whether GE can deliver stellar returns for its shareholders in the near and medium term or whether activist investors, who have successfully pushed companies such as Tyco and Cendant to break up, will seek to break up the company.

SUMMARY

Strategy analysis is an important starting point for the analysis of financial statements because it allows the analyst to probe the economics of the firm at a qualitative level. Strategy analysis also allows the identification of the firm's profit drivers and key risks, enabling the analyst to assess the sustainability of the firm's performance and make realistic forecasts of future performance.

Whether a firm is able to earn a return on its capital in excess of its cost of capital is determined by its own strategic choices: (1) the choice of an industry or a set of industries in which the firm operates (industry choice), (2) the manner in which the firm intends to compete with other firms in its chosen industry or industries (competitive positioning), and (3) the way in which the firm expects to create and exploit synergies across the range of businesses in which it operates (corporate strategy). Strategy analysis involves analyzing all three choices.

Industry analysis consists of identifying the economic factors which drive industry profitability. In general, an industry's average profit potential is influenced by the degree of rivalry among existing competitors, the ease with which new firms can enter the industry, the availability of substitute products, the power of buyers, and the power of suppliers. To perform industry analysis, the analyst has to assess the current strength of each of these forces in an industry and make forecasts of any likely future changes.

Competitive strategy analysis involves identifying the basis on which the firm intends to compete in its industry. In general, there are two potential strategies that could provide a firm with a competitive advantage: cost leadership and differentiation. Cost leadership involves offering at a lower cost the same product or service that other firms offer. Differentiation involves satisfying a chosen dimension of customer need better than the competition, at an incremental cost that is less than the price premium that customers are willing to pay. To perform strategy analysis, the analyst has to identify the firm's intended strategy, assess whether the firm possesses the competencies required to execute the strategy, and recognize the key risks that the firm has to guard against. The analyst also has to evaluate the sustainability of the firm's strategy.

Corporate strategy analysis involves examining whether a company is able to create value by being in multiple businesses at the same time. A well crafted corporate strategy reduces costs or increases revenues from running several businesses in one firm relative to the same businesses operating independently and transacting with each other in the marketplace. These cost savings or revenue increases come from specialized resources that the firm has to exploit synergies across these businesses. For these resources to be valuable, they must be nontradable, not easily imitated by competition, and nondivisible. Even when a firm has such resources, it can create value through a multi-business organization only when it is managed so that the information and agency costs inside the organization are smaller than the market transaction costs.

The insights gained from strategy analysis can be useful in performing the remainder of the financial statement analysis. In accounting analysis, the analyst can examine whether a firm's accounting policies and estimates are consistent with its stated strategy. For example, a firm's choice of functional currency in accounting for its international operations should be consistent with the level of integration between domestic and international operations that the business strategy calls for. Similarly, a firm that mainly sells housing to high-risk customers should have higher than average bad debts expenses and a higher than average allowance for loan losses.

Strategy analysis is also useful in guiding financial analysis. For example, in a cross-sectional analysis, the analyst should expect firms with cost leadership strategy to have lower gross margins and higher asset turnover than firms that follow differentiated strategies. In a time series analysis, the analyst should closely monitor any increases in expense ratios and asset turnover ratios for low-cost firms, and any decreases in investments critical to differentiation for firms that follow differentiation strategy.

Business strategy analysis also helps in prospective analysis and valuation. First, it allows the analyst to assess whether, and for how long, differences between the firm's performance and its industry's (or industries') performance are likely to persist. Second, strategy analysis facilitates forecasting investment outlays the firm has to make to maintain its competitive advantage.

DISCUSSION QUESTIONS

1. Judith, an accounting major, states, "Strategy analysis seems to be an unnecessary detour in doing financial statement analysis. Why can't we just get straight to the accounting issues?" Explain to Judith why she might be wrong.

2. What are the critical drivers of industry profitability?

3. One of the fastest growing industries in the last twenty years is the memory chip industry, which supplies memory chips for personal computers and other electronic devices. Yet the average profitability for this industry has been very low. Using the industry analysis framework, list all the potential factors that might explain this apparent contradiction.

4. Rate the pharmaceutical and lumber industries as high, medium, or low on the following dimensions of industry structure:

	Pharmaceutical Industry	Lumber Industry
Rivalry		
Threat of new entrants		
Threat of substitute products		
Bargaining power of buyers		
Bargaining power of suppliers		

Given your ratings, which industry would you expect to earn the highest returns?

5. Joe Smith argues, "Your analysis of the five forces that affect industry profitability is incomplete. For example, in the banking industry, I can think of at least three other factors

that are also important; namely, government regulation, demographic trends, and cultural factors." His classmate Jane Brown disagrees and says, "These three factors are important only to the extent that they influence one of the five forces." Explain how, if at all, the three factors discussed by Joe affect the five forces in the banking industry.

6. Coca-Cola and Pepsi are both very profitable soft drinks. Inputs for these products include corn syrup bottles/cans, and soft drink syrup. Coca-Cola and Pepsi produce the syrup themselves and purchase the other inputs. They then enter into exclusive contracts with independent bottlers to produce their products. Use the five forces framework and your knowledge of the soft drink industry to explain how Coca-Cola and Pepsi are able to retain most of the profits in this industry.

7. In the early 1980s, United, Delta, and American Airlines each started frequent flier programs as a way to differentiate themselves in response to excess capacity in the industry. Many industry analysts, however, believe that this move had only mixed success. Use the competitive advantage concepts to explain why.

8. What are the ways that a firm can create barriers to entry to deter competition in its business? What factors determine whether these barriers are likely to be enduring?

9. Explain why you agree or disagree with each of the following statements:
   a. It's better to be a differentiator than a cost leader, since you can then charge premium prices.
   b. It's more profitable to be in a high technology industry than a low technology one.
   c. The reason why industries with large investments have high barriers to entry is because it is costly to raise capital.

10. There are very few companies that are able to be both cost leaders and differentiators. Why? Can you think of a company that has been successful at both?

11. Many consultants are advising diversified companies in emerging markets such as India, South Korea, Mexico, and Turkey to adopt corporate strategies proven to be of value in advanced economies such as the U.S. and the U.K. What are the pros and cons of this advice?

NOTES

1. The discussion presented here is intended to provide a basic background in strategy analysis. For a more complete discussion of the strategy concepts, see, for example, *Contemporary Strategy Analysis* by Robert M. Grant (Cambridge, MA: Blackwell Publishers, 1991); *Economics of Strategy* by David Besanko, David Dranove, and Mark Shanley (New York: John Wiley & Sons, 1996); *Strategy and the Business Landscape* by Pankaj Ghemawat (Reading, MA: Addison Wesley Longman, 1999); and *Corporate Strategy: Resources and the Scope of the Firm* by David J. Collis and Cynthia Montgomery (Burr Ridge, IL: Irwin/McGraw-Hill, 1997).

2. These data are taken from "Do Competitors Perform Better When They Pursue Different Strategies?" by Anita M. McGahan (working paper, Harvard Business School, May 12, 1999).

3. For a summary of this research, see *Industrial Market Structure and Economic Performance,* second edition, by F. M. Scherer (Chicago: Rand McNally College Publishing Co., 1980).

4. See *Competitive Strategy* by Michael E. Porter (New York: The Free Press, 1980).

5. The U.S. Department of Justice and the Federal Trade Commission use the Herfindahl-Hirschman Index (HHI) to measure concentration when evaluating horizontal mergers. The HHI is calculated by summing the squares of the individual market shares of all the participants. The Department of Justice considers a market with a result of less than 1,000 to be a competitive marketplace; a result of 1,000 to 1,800 to be a moderately concentrated marketplace; and a result of 1,800 or greater to be a highly concentrated marketplace. The four-firm concentration ratio is another commonly used measure of industry concentration; it refers to the market share of the four largest firms in an industry.

6. While the discussion here uses *buyer* to connote industrial buyers, the same concepts also apply to buyers of consumer products. Throughout this chapter we use the terms *buyers* and *customers* interchangeably.

7. The data on Dell and the PC industry discussed here and elsewhere in this chapter were primarily drawn from "Dell Computer Corporation" by Das Narayandas and V. Kasturi Rangan, Harvard Business School Publishing Division, Case 9-596-058, and "Dell Online" by V. Kasturi Rangan and Marie Bell, Harvard Business School Publishing Division, Case 9-598-116, updated as appropriate for recent changes in the firm and industry.

8. Brian Gammage, Charles Smulders, and Martin Reynolds, "PC Market Realities Will Force Changes on Intel and Microsoft," Gartner, Inc., September 20, 2005.

9. Mikako Kitagawa, "Digital Home is Not a Mass PC Market," Gartner, Inc., May 10, 2005.

10. For a more detailed discussion of these two sources of competitive advantage, see Michael E. Porter, *Competitive Advantage: Creating and Sustaining Superior Performance* (New York: The Free Press, 1985).

11. Ibid.

12. In recent years one of the strategic challenges faced by corporations is having to deal with competitors who achieve differentiation with low cost. For example, Japanese auto manufacturers have successfully demonstrated that there is no necessary trade-off between quality and cost. Similarly, in recent years several highly successful retailers like Wal-Mart and Home Depot have been able to combine high quality, high service, and low prices. These examples suggest that combining low cost and differentiation strategies is possible when a firm introduces a significant technical or business innovation. However, such cost advantage and differentiation will be sustainable only if there are significant barriers to imitation by competitors.

13. See *Competing for the Future* by Gary Hamel and C. K. Prahalad (Boston: Harvard Business School Press, 1994) for a more detailed discussion of the concept of core competencies and their critical role in corporate strategy.

14. C. Montgomery, "Corporate Diversification," *Journal of Economic Perspectives,* Summer 1994.

15. The following works are seminal to transaction cost economics: R. Coase, "The Nature of the Firm," *Economica* 4 (1937): 386–405; *Markets and Hierarchies: Analysis and Antitrust Implications* by Oliver Williamson (New York: The Free Press, 1975); and D. Teece, "Toward an Economic Theory of the Multi-product Firm," *Journal of Economic Behavior and Organization* 3 (1982): 39–63.

16. For a more complete discussion of these issues, see T. Khanna and K. Palepu, "Building Institutional Infrastructure in Emerging Markets," *Brown Journal of World Affairs,* Winter/Spring 1998, and T. Khanna and K. Palepu, "Why Focused Strategies May Be Wrong for Emerging Markets," *Harvard Business Review,* July/August 1997.

17. For an empirical study which illustrates this point, see T. Khanna and K. Palepu, "Is Group Affiliation Profitable in Emerging Markets? An Analysis of Diversified Indian Business Groups," *Journal of Finance* (April 2000): 867–91.

18. See L. Lang and R. Stulz, "Tobin's q, diversification, and firm performance," *Journal of Political Economy* 102 (1994): 1248–80, and P. Berger and E. Ofek, "Diversification's Effect on Firm Value," *Journal of Financial Economics* 37 (1994): 39–65.

19. See P. Healy, K. Palepu, and R. Ruback, "Which Takeovers Are Profitable: Strategic or Financial?" *Sloan Management Review* 38 (Summer 1997): 45–57.

20. See K. Schipper and A. Smith, "Effects of Recontracting on Shareholder Wealth: The Case of Voluntary Spinoffs," *Journal of Financial Economics* 12 (December 1983): 437–67, and L. Lang, A. Poulsen, and R. Stulz, "Asset Sales, Firm Performance, and the Agency Costs of Managerial Discretion," *Journal of Financial Economics* 37 (January 1995): 3–37.

21. General Electric Company, 2001 Annual Report (Fairfield, CT, 2002), p. 6.

22. General Electric Company, 2005 Annual Report (Fairfield, CT, 2006), p. 10.

Inventec Corporation

Whoever owns the distribution channel owns the business. We are just the guys behind the scenes.

—Inventec executive Louis Woo

In Inventec Corp.'s gleaming new manufacturing compound on the outskirts of Shanghai's Pudong district, six automated assembly lines hummed with state of the art equipment. Hermetically sealed machines dispensed adhesive onto tiny boards. Next, high speed machines picked micro chip components off tapes and placed them onto the boards. Other machines soldered, cleaned and tested, until the guts of a notebook personal computer (PC) popped out to be encased in black plastic or metallic silver by human hands. Each line produced a new notebook computer every 16 seconds, for a combined output of 13,500 PCs per day. However, none of these PCs carried the Inventec name. Instead, the notebooks produced in this Chinese factory bore the brand logos of three competing multinational computer companies. Each PC was packaged in a brand manufacturer box, and shipped to client distribution centers around the world. Some were shipped via UPS from the Shanghai factory directly to consumers in the United States, with return address labels bearing the name and U.S. address of the brand company.

Inventec, with annual revenues topping 150 billion New Taiwan Dollars (NT$)[a] and market capitalization valued at over $1 billion, was one of Taiwan's leading Original Design Manufacturers (ODM). ODMs designed and manufactured electronic products such as computers, servers, MP3 players, PDAs and cellular telephones for client companies that marketed the products globally. In early 2005, scenes like the one above were taking place simultaneously in at least 10 Taiwanese ODM PC factories in and around Shanghai. Taiwan's four major notebook PC manufacturers were expected to account for nearly 60% of world production in 2005.[1]

Inventec had been one of the first Taiwanese ODMs to open plants in mainland China, beginning with a software development firm in 1991. More than 10 years

---

a. Between 2000 and 2005, the average exchange rate was NT$33.5 per U.S. dollar ($), ranging from NT$30.7 to NT$36.7.

Professor Krishna Palepu and Global Research Group Senior Researcher Ingrid Vargas prepared this case. HBS cases are developed solely as the basis for class discussion. Cases are not intended to serve as endorsements, sources of primary data, or illustrations of effective or ineffective management.

later, Inventec embarked on construction of the Pudong compound located between Shanghai's two major airports, and with easy access to Luchao Harbor and Yangshan Deep Water Harbor. When completed in 2006, the 500,000 square meter site would contain seven plants, an R&D center, an administrative building, a warehouse, and an on-site government customs office. About 35,000 employees, including 4,000 R&D engineers would occupy over 750,000 square meters of floor space. (See **Exhibit 1**.)

Since the 2001 easing of Taiwan government restrictions of high tech investment in China, all the major ODMs had opened notebook PC plants on the mainland to take advantage of lower operating costs, which could be as low as one seventh the cost in Taiwan. Lowering costs was essential in the brutally competitive industry where the players had to constantly underbid each other to win design and manufacturing contracts from a handful of branded PC firms.

Net margins on notebook computers, the single largest ODM product among all types of electronics, had dropped from about 10% in 2001 to just 3% to 4% for leading firms, and below 1% for second tier ODMs.[2] "Our customers have been squeezed left and right," said Louis Woo, senior advisor for Inventec. "The only way they can do business is to squeeze us." Industry-wide PC price and margin erosion was expected in continue through 2005.

Concerns about underutilization of Inventec's China plants pushed Inventec's stock price down in mid 2005.[3] Just a year earlier, analysts had been recommending Inventec stock due to the firm's exclusive production of the hugely successful Apple iPods.[4] But in late 2004, Apple split its iPod contracts among three competing ODMs.[5] Inventec also lost some of Cisco's VOIP phone business to a competing ODM, further shaking investor confidence. (See **Exhibit 2** for Inventec Corp. stock price movement.)

On the plus side, Inventec expected its Pudong complex to break even by 2006, and industry observers expected worldwide demand for notebook PCs along with outsourcing to ODMs to grow rapidly in coming years. Inventec also had more product diversity than most Taiwanese ODMs, and was particularly strong in the server market, an area with higher margins than notebooks. (See **Exhibit 3**.) But experience told Inventec's leaders that today's high margin products would be tomorrow's commodities. Could they find a way to get off the treadmill?

CONTRACT MANUFACTURING INDUSTRY

The $190 billion contract manufacturing industry produced about 40% of the world's consumer electronic products for Original Equipment Manufacturer (OEM)[b] clients such as Hewlett-Packard (HP), Dell, Apple and Palm, which marketed the finished products.[6] The industry comprised two segments: Electronics Manufacturing Services (EMS) and Original Design Manufacturing (ODM), respectively accounting for 61% and 39% of contract manufacturing revenue in 2004. In addition to manufacturing, both sectors provided clients with sourcing, procurement, and inventory management.

b. There was much confusion around the use of the term OEM. Media reports sometimes referred to contract manufacturers as OEMs because they worked on an "OEM basis." Industry analysts and specialized journals used OEM to refer to the brand firms who were the original manufacturers prior to outsourcing. In this case, OEM and "client" are used interchangeably.

The key distinction between EMS and ODM companies was their level of involvement in product design. Traditionally, an EMS provider manufactured a product based on a client's design, while an ODM firm designed, manufactured, and often shipped products directly to clients' customers. ODMs usually owned the intellectual property (IP) rights to their designs. As of 2004, Inventec had 1,700 patents awarded in Taiwan, nearly 1,600 in China and 180 in the United States, mostly for hardware and software product designs, but also some for processes. EMS firms that had ventured into design usually did so in close collaboration with clients, and did not retain IP rights. ODMs were also more likely to hold a client's inventory, taking on an additional risk.

Some industry observers defined ODMs as product companies and EMS providers as service companies. However, the line between the two sectors was blurring as ODMs broadened their product scope beyond their base in motherboards and notebook PCs (**Exhibit 4**), and more and more EMS firms incorporated design capabilities to move into the higher margin ODM sector. For example, EMS market leader Flextronics broke into the design business in 1996 when it won a manufacturing contract with Palm Inc. that included making substantial design updates to new generations of the Palm Pilot PDA. However, in 2001, Flextronics lost the Palm business to Inventec which offered a lower bid for more extensive design capacity.[7]

Revenue for the top 50 EMS providers had declined 10% between 2001 and 2002, and grew just 3% in 2003, but achieved 16% growth in 2004.[8] The smaller ODM sector had grown more steadily, and expanded by 27% between 2003 and 2004.[9] Predictions for 2008 placed global EMS revenue at $164 billion by 2008, and ODM revenue at $134 billion, based on expected five-year compound annual growth rates of 9.5% for EMS and 21.2% for ODM.[10]

ODM sector   Inventec was part of the ODM industry that started with the proliferation of motherboard companies in Taiwan during the 1980s. Over time, manufacturers added design staff so they could add more value and increase margins. Eventually the motherboard firms were designing and producing entire computers (some specializing in either desktops or laptops), and later moved into computer peripherals, servers, cameras and cellular telephones. By 2004, about 70% of the world's notebook computers were being produced by Taiwanese ODMs. ODMs also designed and manufactured about 70% of the world's PDAs, 65% of MP3 players, 30% of digital cameras and 20% of the nearly 700 million mobile phones sold annually.[11] (See **Exhibit 5** on the leading ODM firms.)

Originally, ODMs offered mainly "off the shelf" products to client companies that could purchase the finished product with slight customizations of exterior features and addition of the client logo. Outsourcing design could save a client up to 70% on development costs. For example, with the development of a typical cell phone running $10 million and taking up to 150 engineers, the savings could be significant.[12] But while cutting costs, OEMs might also forgo offering a unique product, sometimes leading to embarrassing situations. In 2002, for instance, news media reported that Gateway and Dell were selling the same ODM-made laptop, each with its own brand stamped on it.[13] Increasingly, client firms took product specifications and design requirements to several ODMs and had them bid competitively for the deal. By 2005, many clients worked closely with their ODM designers in a collaborative approach to new product development.

Client companies tended to limit ODM use to highly commoditized products with widely available designs. Personal computers, whether desktop or laptop, lent themselves to the ODM model because the technology was in the processor and operating system which could be readily purchased from companies such as Intel and

Microsoft. ODMs therefore tended to specialize in a few product lines such as laptops, cell phones and servers, though product offerings were expanding. (**Exhibit 6** shows EMS and ODM product categories.)

EMS sector   Electronics firms began turning to EMS providers in the 1980s when they needed extra manufacturing capacity. EMS facilities tended to be located in low-wage developing countries, and large volumes of business gave them leverage with suppliers. EMS firms passed most of the savings from their huge scale on to their clients, and sustained increasingly low margins. Some of the largest EMS firms were vertically integrated, producing many of their own component parts and sometimes earning larger margins from the provision of components than from the finished products. (See **Exhibit 7** on the leading EMS firms.)

EMS companies generally had more sophisticated production engineering and greater manufacturing capacity than ODMs. With operations spread across North and South America, Europe and Asia, they offered production sites closer to the final markets, plus global logistics and integrated IT services. By 2004, most of the leading EMS firms had leveraged their global footprints and extensive client lists to break into the ODM sector. Stung by the repeated loss of contracts to Taiwan's ODMs, EMS firms created in-house design teams and acquired second and third tier ODMs as subsidiaries.

In 2003, for example, Flextronics purchased handset ODM Microcell, with design centers in Finland and Denmark and launched a manufacturing joint venture in Nanjing, China. The following year Flextronics moved on to India, setting its sights on the lucrative software design industry. The EMS giant acquired and combined three telecom-focused design firms into a new Indian subsidiary called Flextronics Software Systems.[14] The firm designed software for telecommunications equipment including wireless data systems and cellular handsets for clients such as Lucent, Nokia, and Motorola. In fiscal year 2005, the new firm earned $17 million in profit on sales of $80 million, just a small fraction of Flextronics' $16 billion global revenue. But the subsidiary's 23.5% operating margin and 21.1% net margin, typical for Indian software firms, dwarfed Flextronics' overall margins of 3.2% and 2.4% respectively.[15]

Marketing themselves as the safer design solution, Celestica, Sanmina and other EMS firms also announced the creation of ODM divisions specializing in multiple products including handsets, servers and printers.[16] Most EMS design work was done exclusively to meet a particular client's needs. Selectron's vice president of strategic marketing explained that while many OEM clients relied on Selectron for the full product design, just like an ODM, "the difference is, we say we are not going to retain the IP and compete with the OEM. It's an important distinction and it's a line we are not going to cross. We believe if we start to compete with our customers, it poses a significant risk to our overall business model."[17]

OEM clients   As OEM R&D budgets shrank and product life cycles shortened, more and more OEMs looked to outsource aspects of design along with manufacturing. This meant that EMS and ODM firms were increasingly competing for the same client base. An OEM's decision to outsource to an EMS or ODM firm depended primarily on the type of product, the kind of technology, and the price. Many firms followed a policy of keeping cutting edge technology in-house, while outsourcing older technologies as they became commoditized. "You have to draw a line," said Motorola's CEO. At Motorola, "core intellectual property is above it, and commodity technology is below."[18] A Lucent executive put it this way: "You have to figure out what is core and what is context." Outsourcing some design made sense so that in-house engineers could focus on next-generation technologies, explained the executive. Design outsourcing was "about the flexibility to put resources in the right places at the right time," he added.[19]

Many OEMs worried that too much outsourcing, especially in the product design phase, risked their brand reputations. OEMs tended to be reticent about their ODM use, often requiring confidentiality clauses in contracts. OEMs also feared losing control over IP and giving up part of their profit in the form of licensing fees. Another danger was that ODMs could become direct competitors. Motorola saw this happen when BenQ, a leading Taiwanese ODM that designed and manufactured millions of mobile phones for Motorola, decided to enter the lucrative China market with its own brand of cell phone. Motorola responded by pulling its contract.[20]

Following the upset of ODM supply channels by Taiwan's September 1999 earthquake, OEMs moved to diversify contract manufacturing partnerships.[21] Before 1998, 80% of Dell's ODM use was exclusively with Quanta, and Compaq had used only two ODMs: Inventec and Arima. These and other OEMs started dividing their business among the five leading Taiwanese ODMs, and even some second-tier ODMs, thereby reducing their reliance on a single partnership and increasing their negotiating strength.[22] (See **Exhibit 8** for ODM client distribution.)

Consolidation among computer OEMs had also given OEMs greater bargaining power over the fragmented ODMs. For example, following the 2002 HP-Compaq merger, Compaq ODM partner Arima was losing money on each notebook it produced. Arima chose not to bid on new HP model production in 2003, cutting its notebook business in half. HP's business went to rival ODM Compal Electronics. Arima posted a net loss of $26.7 million in 2003.[23]

INVENTEC OVERVIEW

Inventec began as a contract manufacturer of telephones and calculators in 1975, with Texas Instruments as its biggest client. After diversifying into several new product lines during the 1990s, and a 1996 IPO on Taiwan's stock exchange, in 1999 Inventec decided to spin-off its business groups into separate subsidiary companies. Production of notebook PCs, servers and software stayed with Inventec Corp., the original and only publicly listed company. Inventec Corp. held equity stakes in each of its four subsidiaries: Inventec Appliances (49.1%); Inventec Multimedia and Telecom (54.1%); Inventec Micro-Electronics (70.5%) and electronic dictionary manufacturer Inventec Besta (38.7%). Together, the five companies had nearly 27,000 employees worldwide (74% in China), and revenue exceeding $6 billion in 2004. Inventec Corp. reported over $4 billion revenue in 2004, and was expected to reach $5 billion in 2005 (**Exhibit 9**). Over 70% of Inventec Corp.'s equity income from its subsidiaries derived from Inventec Appliances' PDA, cell phone and MP3 player product lines.[24]

Software

Since the early 1990s, Inventec had developed and marketed software under its own brands. Inventec's major software product was the Dr. Eye translation program, popular in mainland China and in Taiwan. Inventec made an important addition to its software offerings with the 2002 introduction of One Touch XP, a program used to simplify use of Microsoft's Windows XP. Developed by about 600 Inventec engineers working in China, One Touch XP practically eliminated the use of a mouse, allowing users to access almost any function with the press of a single key. Inventec sold about one million copies of the NT$399 standard and NT$699 premium versions of the program in the first six months, about 70% in China and 30% in Taiwan.[25]

Inventec engineers also developed software that was embedded into the hardware produced for OEM clients. Most of Inventec's patents were for software solutions, and this offered a way to add unique value for clients. Proprietary software was integrated into newer technology products such as servers, PDAs and cellular handsets. "Software is our strength," said Inventec executive C.W. Lin. "The core of our products is the software that provides differentiation." Predicting that the hardware sector would see only one more decade of growth, Inventec leaders believed the future lay in software, and planned to add about 10,000 new engineers between 2002 and 2007. "We believe the software business will give another shot to Inventec's sales as the PC hardware sector is weakening," said Inventec Vice Chairman Sayling Wen.[26]

Notebook PCs

Inventec started to manufacture laptops and word processors in 1989. In 1995, Inventec signed a deal with Compaq to help develop and manufacture a new multimedia notebook computer.[27] Since then, notebook PCs became the mainstay of Inventec's business, accounting for about 80% of Inventec Corp. revenue in 2004 when annual production reached seven million notebooks. Most notebook production took place in Shanghai's Hongqao and Pudong factories, both equipped with the latest computerized systems for manufacturing, testing and logistics. Volume production of notebooks was expected to grow by 50% in 2005, but Inventec's gross margins for this product had dropped below 4%.[28] "The notebook business is no longer about adding value—it's based on how fast you can deliver the lowest cost product," said Woo. Industry analysts believed Inventec's notebook margins were lower than that of other first tier ODMs because of its principal client's aggressive pricing strategy and Inventec's relatively small scale.[29]

Servers

Inventec was the first Taiwanese notebook manufacturer to produce servers and server components beginning in 1998, with the acquisition of the Taiwan assets of Digital Equipment Corporation's (DEC), then owned by Compaq. By 2000, Inventec revenues from servers reached NT$9.1 billion, four times the previous year's sales, but still less than 10% of total revenue.[30] In 2004, servers accounted for about 19% of total revenue.[31] Other ODMs began producing the higher margin servers too, but with annual output reaching about two million servers in 2004, Inventec remained Taiwan's largest server producer. However, in 2005, competitors Hon Hai, Quanta and Wistron were encroaching on the server market.

Consumer Electronics

Since the late 1990s, Inventec began designing and manufacturing a number of consumer electronics products, such as PDAs, mobile telephones, MP3 players, and digital cameras with significantly higher margins than for notebook production. Analysts considered consumer electronics, grouped under the Inventec Appliance (IAC) subsidiary, to be the most lucrative of Inventec's businesses, with gross margins estimated 14.3% for 2003. Inventec Corp. held a 51.3% stake in IAC, which had revenues of over NT$79 billion and net income exceeding NT$2 billion in 2004.[32] Palm, Apple, and Texas Instruments were IACs main clients, together accounting for about 75% of the subsidiary's sales.[33] About 20% of revenue was from the sale of own-brand products, largely cell phone handsets. IAC was planning an IPO on the Taiwan Stock Exchange in November 2005.[34]

PDAs   Building on is success with electronic dictionaries, Inventec introduced its own-brand Besta PDA in Taiwan in 1999, before international heavyweights like Palm and Compaq launched on the island in 2000. Soon, Inventec was making PDAs for OEM clients Psion of the United Kingdom, and Siemens of Germany.[35] In 2001 Inventec began co-developing PDAs with Palm Inc.[36] That same year, Inventec was selling its own-brand PDA, called the i-note, for NT$3900 in Taiwan, compared with the new Palm m105's selling price of NT$7,990.[37]

MP3 players   In 2001, in the midst of a depressed notebook market, Inventec landed a contract with Apple Computer to co-develop new generations of the Apple iPod MP3 Player. Apple engineers reportedly worked closely with Inventec, flying back and forth between Taipei and Silicon Valley to work out project details.[38] Inventec shipped an estimated 1.5 million iPod units in 2003, or 14% of the global MP3 market.[39] However, market share dropped dramatically when Apple divided its iPod orders among Inventec and competitors Hon Hai and Asustek in late 2004.[40]

Mobile telephones   Inventec was expecting to produce about 10 million mobile phones in 2005, about 30% bearing its own OKWAP brand.[41] Inventec created the OKWAP handsets with proprietary software that incorporated an electronic Chinese/English dictionary. Special features created for the local market such as unique ring tones helped make OKWAP one of the top four handset brands in Taiwan, with a 13% market share in 2003, and estimated at 20% for 2004. With the OKWAP brand directed at the high-end of the market, industry analysts estimated 30% to 35% gross margins for the handsets.[42]

Client Base

Client contracts were signed for each individual product line, and usually lasted for the life of a single model. Inventec's clients included the top computer and electronics brands. "Our strategy is to choose the best companies in the world to work with so we can learn from them. Having the number one or number two company in each product category as our client also ensures us a large market share for every product line," said Lin. But in its main product line, notebook PCs, Inventec had a narrower client base than most of its competitors. (Please refer back to **Exhibit 5**.)

Until 2002, when Inventec won a contract to build high-end notebooks for Toshiba, Compaq had been Inventec's only notebook client.[43] In 2004, HP-Compaq still accounted for about 75% of Inventec's notebook production. Inventec's relationship with Compaq was so important that decisions for expansion such as establishing the assembly plants in Scotland and Houston, Texas, Compaq's home base, were often dictated by the partnership. Inventec's 1998 acquisition of DEC from Compaq cemented ties with its principal client and led to desktop PC and server production for Compaq.[44] In 1999, Compaq announced it was transferring orders with its manufacturers in Singapore and South Korea's LG group to Inventec.[45] The same year Inventec invested NT$400 million to develop a global distributing system for notebook PCs manufactured for Compaq.[46]

Compaq had long been the Taiwan ODM industry's single largest customer, purchasing more than $10 billion from Taiwan firms in 2001, nearly twice as much as HP. Following the announcement of HP's acquisition of Compaq in 2001, stocks of Compaq ODM partners plummeted amid speculation that Compaq's former partnerships would be eliminated in favor of HP partners. This would have been particularly detrimental to Inventec which then produced notebooks and servers exclusively for Compaq. Other Compaq partners, such as Quanta and Compal, supplied to HP and other OEMs as well.[47] But HP retained Compaq's partnerships, buying \$14.5 billion in computers, notebooks and servers from several of Taiwan's top ODMs, amounting to nearly 10% of Taiwan's total exports for 2002.[48] Still, the newly expanded HP was determined to cut costs, and after the merger was in an even stronger position to squeeze its ODM suppliers.

MOVE TO MAINLAND CHINA

Software Development

Inventec was among the first Taiwanese ODMs to venture into mainland China, starting with a Shanghai software development center in 1991. Two years later, Inventec expanded its software business with satellites in Nanjing, Beijing, Tianjin and Xi'an. "We came to China because reforms in education had resulted in good quality engineers. They spoke the same language as Taiwan engineers, but cost a fraction of the salary," said Lin. Inventec software was focused on multimedia educational programs specializing in language training. By 1994 Inventec had invested \$15 million on the mainland, and its electronic dictionary was a best-seller in the local market.[49] In the late 1990s, Inventec stepped up its software investment to develop systems for MP3 players and palmtop PCs in Xi'an, one of China's ancient capitals located in central Shaanxi province where salaries were about half the level of Shanghai's.[50] Eventually, Inventec produced internal use software systems for the integration of R&D, manufacturing, global logistics and service in the company's own manufacturing plants.

In 2005, Inventec had about 1,500 software engineers working on the mainland, with software production centered in Tianjin (about 80 miles southeast of Beijing). Ten universities in the Tianjin area provided a steady supply of well-qualified R&D engineers. Another group of Inventec engineers in Beijing specialized in developing language and geographic guide software and interactive educational websites. Engineers in Beijing and Shanghai cost significantly more than in other parts of China because of the high demand from the firms centered in the large cities, noted an Inventec executive. Earning about \$10,000 annually in the major cities, software engineers in China cost about half as much as those in Taiwan, but Chinese salaries were rising rapidly.

Manufacturing Base

Inventec began ODM manufacturing in China when the company established a plant in Shanghai in 1999 to produce desktop PCs in alliance with Compaq. Compaq wanted to boost sales of its computers in Asia, including mainland China.[51] Inventec had not produced desktops before, but group chairman Yeh Kou-yi justified the move, noting that desktop PC sales were growing faster than notebooks, component prices had come down, and China offered a huge potential market. The desktops would be sold under the Compaq brand "because brand names of large manufacturers such as Compaq will be more easily accepted by customers in mainland China," said Yeh.[52]

Foreign multinationals had long pressed ODM partners to move production to the mainland to cut manufacturing costs and import duties and facilitate access to a growing market.[53] Taiwan's destructive 1999 Earthquake had hastened calls to move production to the mainland.[54] Inventec's move was followed by Acer and Mitac, which established desktop production lines in Guangdong and opened sales outlets in Beijing and Shanghai.[55] By 2000, most of the leading Taiwanese ODMs were manufacturing in mainland China where they made 42% of their desktop PC output, up from 28% a year earlier.[56]

Large scale investment began in 2000, in anticipation of a relaxation of Taiwan regulations that prohibited domestic IT firms from investing in China in the manufacture of newer technologies, including high-end desktops and notebook PCs.[57] Quanta, the last hold out in the ODM migration to China, announced a NT$600 million investment in notebook, motherboard and mobile phone production facilities in the Shanghai area. "We can't swim against the tide any longer," said the company's general manager. "Quanta has to accept the truth, for the sake of the company's future and the shareholders' profit, that investment in China is an important factor in sharpening competitiveness."[58]

In December 2000, Inventec's board approved a $29.5 million investment to establish a notebook PC plant in Shanghai with production capacity of 200,000 units per month, to be devoted mainly to orders from Compaq.[59] In 2001 Inventec invested another $10 million for a second China plant on a 6,061 square meter site at the Kunshan Industrial Zone in Jiangsu province, about 90 minutes from downtown Shanghai, where Compal and First International had also established notebook PC plants.[60] The Chinese government granted Inventec and several other foreign manufacturers expedited customs service permitting imported materials to clear customs in 3.5 hours and exports within one day.[61] By 2002, Inventec had three factories in the Shanghai area accounting for about 25% of the company's total output, with another 25% made in Malaysia, and 50% in Taiwan. Inventec invested $18 million to establish a research, development and production center for servers in Shanghai, and spent another $33.5 million to expand the Puxi, Shanghai plant in 2003, allowing output of 300,000 units per month. Inventec's Pudong campus was located within one of the central government's Export Processing Zones, which meant that Inventec was exempt from paying taxes on imports or goods purchased from Chinese companies, as long as the goods were used for the manufacture of products to be exported out of China.[62]

Though only about 10% of Inventec's mainland production was consumed in the local market, Inventec continued to move production into China to lower operating costs.[63] In 2005, about 90% of Inventec's notebook production was made in China. Quanta produced about 95% of its notebooks in China, and Compal had 100% notebook production in China.[64] An Inventec competitor with 18 factories in China noted that "The abundance of capacity in China is causing our average selling price to continue to erode. . . . What's so scary is now, since everybody has moved over there, China is no longer a low-cost area, because everyone has the same cost structure."[65]

China's Notebook PC Market

Notebook PC sales, expected to triple by 2008, accounted for about 37% of China's $5.7 billion PC market in 2004.[66] Nationwide, about 25 Chinese firms were manufacturing notebook PCs in late 2004, and they were rapidly losing market share to multinational players like Dell and HP.[67] Foreign brands already accounted for about 60% of China's notebook PC sales.[68] Initially aimed at the higher end of the Chinese market, foreign PC brands had moved to lower cost models. In 2003, HP cut into the Chinese brand market share with a PC model priced at RMB 4,999 ($603).[69] The foreign companies could compete on price because of their extensive use of Taiwanese ODMs—not even Chinese manufacturers could beat ODM scale efficiency.

Only one Chinese PC firm, Beijing-based Lenovo Group, was large enough to command ODMs to design and build PCs to its own specifications. Other Chinese firms could only buy off-the-shelf ODM products, or manufacture their own at a higher cost and lower level of quality.[70] Lenovo was already China's largest PC manufacturer when it began producing notebooks in 2000. Lenovo underpriced Toshiba, which had been China's number one notebook brand throughout the late 1990s. Toshiba maintained its high prices and never recovered. By 2004, it had slipped to fifth place behind Lenovo, Dell, IBM, and HP. Toshiba had been slow to outsource production to Taiwan's ODMs, and allowed its exclusive Chinese distributor to handle all marketing along with after sales service. In contrast, IBM and HP closely managed the sales channels and marketing in China. Instead of relying on a single Chinese distributor, they selected different distributors for each product line and handled strategic planning and brand management themselves.[71]

In 2004 Lenovo's 25% share of China's PC market share began to slip, and the company adjusted its strategy with a new a sales force dedicated to large business clients and government agencies and lower priced models targeting the rural market. "The growth of the whole PC market is lackluster. But the township market remains largely untapped," explained Lenovo's CEO.[72] China's PC penetration rate was estimated at just 5% in 2004, compared with 60% for the United States and 30% in Europe.[73] But with China's urban PC penetration at 50%, the real opportunity lay in the rural areas where 80% of the population lived. Lenovo began targeting households, schools and internet cafes in rural areas. By the end of 2004, sales of Lenovo's RMB 2,999 desktop PCs (about $363, or half the price of its pervious models) made up 20% of the company's China sales. Lenovo's market share was back up, but analysts estimated gross margins for the new models at about 8%, compared with nearly 15% for Lenovo's past PC sales.[74] Lenovo's move also launched a price war that lowered margins market-wide. Lenovo's net margins had dropped to 5.4% in late 2004, while the company's CFO estimated domestic competitors' net margins at 4%.[75]

Lenovo's May 2005 purchase of IBM's PC unit made it the world's third-largest PC maker, and the largest PC seller to Asia. But China would continue to be a very significant market for Lenovo, accounting for more than one fourth of the company's $13 billion in global sales.[76] The expanded Lenovo dominated China's PC market, with a 33% share overall, and 36% of notebook PC sales, flowed by Dell's 10% and HP's 8% notebook market shares.[77] Lenovo was pushing for an even larger piece of the market with a new budget notebook model introduced early in 2005. At RMB 6,499 ($786) it was the lowest laptop price in the company's history. HP followed with an RMB 6,999 ($847) model, half the price of its mainstream notebooks.[78]

NEXT STEPS

With margins expected to continue their downward trend in the foreseeable future, Inventec sought new strategies to capture more of the value produced by the company. Two possibilities that appeared promising were to increase the company's proportion of branded sales and to better leverage the company's expertise in software development.

Brand Development Option

Inventec had a number of own-brand products including notebooks PCs and PDAs that sold in Taiwan. Inventec's language learning software programs were best sellers in both Taiwan and mainland China. But like other Taiwan ODMs, Inventec focused its branded efforts on cellular handsets. In Taiwan, Inventec's OKWAP cell phone's 12% market share tied with another Taiwanese ODM, BenQ, for third place behind Nokia and Motorola. The global brands were struggling in Taiwan, but they were more interested in breaking Chinese manufacturers hold on the mainland handset market, and they needed ODM help to do it. As a McKinsey study advised, global handset brands could compete with the Chinese firms by outsourcing all but their sensitive high-end models to ODMs. Taiwan's ODMs could design Chinese-language handsets tailored to local tastes and produce them at a lower cost, all within China.[79]

But Taiwan's ODMs wanted the Chinese market for themselves. Both Inventec and BenQ won licenses from the Chinese government in May 2005 to market their handsets on the mainland. Inventec set up a marketing company in China with the goal of selling two million handsets on the mainland in 2005, for a 3% market share nationwide. About 500,000 OKWAP phones sold in China during 1Q05, securing about a 4% share of the eastern Chinese market.[80] "Although competition is intensifying in China, we will seek ways to lower our cost through building our own independent distributors," said an Inventec executive.[81] Inventec would soon be producing all of its cell phones on the mainland, he added, up from about 85% made in China in 2005.

Industry observers wondered if Taiwan's ODMs could do the same thing with their main product line. Could a company like Inventec market-own brand notebook PCs on the mainland in direct competition with its major clients? Another question was whether Inventec had the internal resources to become a major brand. Building a brand was very costly, said Woo. "It's a completely different game. Inventec is not a marketing company. We have been very comfortable working for others."

The BenQ model   BenQ was among the few Taiwan firms to climb up from contract manufacturing to branded sales. A subsidiary of Taiwan's Acer Computer for two decades, BenQ had spun-off in 2001 and added own-brand products to its ODM consumer electronics and computer peripherals business. The firm's branded products included LCD-TVs, computer monitors, and DVD players, and cellular handsets. Margins on its branded business were three to four percentage points higher than margins on ODM sales, said BenQ.[82] Investing 2%–3% annually on each of marketing and R&D, BenQ's branded sales rose steadily from 24% of the total in 2002, to 29% in 2003 and 37% of 2004's NT$165 billion.[83]

BenQ's CEO explained that the company avoided potential conflicts with its clients by making its branded products clearly different from those supplied to OEMs.[84] However, BenQ's success in taking market share as a branded manufacturer from its ODM clients had severe consequences. Motorola, which had a 50% share of Taiwan's handset sales, dropped BenQ as a mobile handset supplier in December 2004. Nokia cut its orders for clamshell handsets from BenQ three months later, transferring them to a Chinese manufacturer instead. However, in 2005, BenQ began supplying its high-end mobile handsets to telecom operators Italia Mobile and Britain's mm02. Industry observers noted that cellular operators such as Verizon and Sprint could follow suit and opt to bypass global handset brands and buy directly from the ODMs.

Could Inventec risk alienating its own clients by promoting branded sales? Was there a way to keep its top clients while developing its own notebook brand? The EMS companies had decided that they wanted nothing to do with branding. As Flextronics CEO Michael Marks commented, "I'm not going to compete with my customers. If we made an acquisition of a company with its own product line, we would kill it. We wouldn't want it as part of our company."[85] Were the EMS firms right to hold onto their customer base at the cost of flattening margins?

Software Development Option

Inventec had been developing software solutions for over two decades. Some observers believed the company had the expertise, resources, and local talent to go after a much larger software-centered market than electronic dictionaries. Inventec considered its software capability to be a major differentiator from the other Taiwan ODMs. Inventec had far more software patents than its competitors, but until now, Inventec's most sophisticated software was embedded in its hardware products. As part of a low-margin product line, the added value of the software was lost to Inventec.

Woo wondered if things could have turned out differently for Inventec:

Sometimes I ask myself whether we went down the wrong path. I look at India where companies that started in the same way that Inventec did in China could not go into the hardware business because of lack of infrastructure. They went into software because it was easier. And now they are serving the same companies we are: they serve HP and Toshiba. We are two sides of the same coin. But on their side of the coin gross margins are 40%, while on our side margins are 5%. The top three Indian software companies are making net margins above 20%, while we have 1% margins. Something is wrong here.

The India model   As Woo had noted, India's poor transportation infrastructure, much less developed than China's, had hindered computer hardware manufacturing because the transport and warehousing of parts and finished products could not be done efficiently. What India did have was world-class technological education and an abundance of highly–skilled engineers. Until around 2000, many of India's best educated professionals had left the country to work abroad, mainly in the United States. But when the U.S. economy slowed, more engineers began staying in India, and the country's IT service industry took off.

In 2005, India's IT services and software industry was estimated at $12 billion in annual revenues and was growing at 30% annually.[86] A few publicly traded companies led the industry. (See **Exhibit 10**.) These companies served the global IT outsourcing market, with most business coming from the United States. Widespread English skills among India's educated workforce facilitated the industry's growth. The largest industry segment was custom application development and maintenance, in which the Indian IT firms created software solutions for business process needs unmet by packaged software.

Indian R&D services and software product exports were valued at $2.3 billion in 2004. Other service areas included IT consulting and network infrastructure management. Only Wipro among the top Indian software firms also manufactured hardware, marketing a line of PCs in the domestic market. In 2005 the top Indian IT firms were moving further up the value chain to providing complete turnkey solutions for Fortune 500 companies. The industry's net margins had hovered at around 20% since 2002.

The same global computer companies that outsourced hardware production to Taiwan's ODMs often looked to India for software solutions. For example, Wipro had developed several projects for Toshiba, such as creating embedded drivers, utilities and web technologies for computer peripherals.[87] In July 2005, HP announced that it would extend its systems integration alliance with Wipro to HPs entire portfolio of open-view software. The partnership would deliver remote management services, systems integration and IT infrastructure consulting using HP's IT management software to global customers.[88] Could Inventec follow a similar model and use its software expertise to offer higher end services to its OEM clients?

CONCLUSION

As Inventec executives saw it, the company's greatest dilemma was being at the mercy of powerful clients. "If we complained about the low margins, our clients would just take their business to one of our competitors," said Woo. "It might take them three weeks or three months maximum to switch, but they could do it, and they would survive." But could Inventec survive if it lost a major client?

If Inventec launched its own line of notebooks in China, could the company compete with the likes of Lenovo, Toshiba or HP-Compaq on the mainland? Alternatively, could Inventec separate its proprietary software from its hardware products and have the added value recognized by the market? Was there any way out of the commodity trap for a company like Inventec?

QUESTIONS

1. Despite its growth and size, why is Inventec not very profitable?

2. What are the drivers of the average profitability of the Original Design and Manufacturing industry?

3. What are the key factors that a company like Inventec needs to manage to earn above-average profits in this industry?

4. Why is the Indian software industry, on average, so much more profitable than the Chinese ODM industry?

5. What strategic advice will you give Inventec to improve its profitability?

EXHIBIT 1A

Inventec's Pudong Compound as Planned for Completion in 2006

EXHIBIT 1B

Inventec Factory Building in Shanghai

Source: Company documents.

EXHIBIT 2

Inventec Corporation Stock Price vs. Taiwan SE 100 (2000–2005)

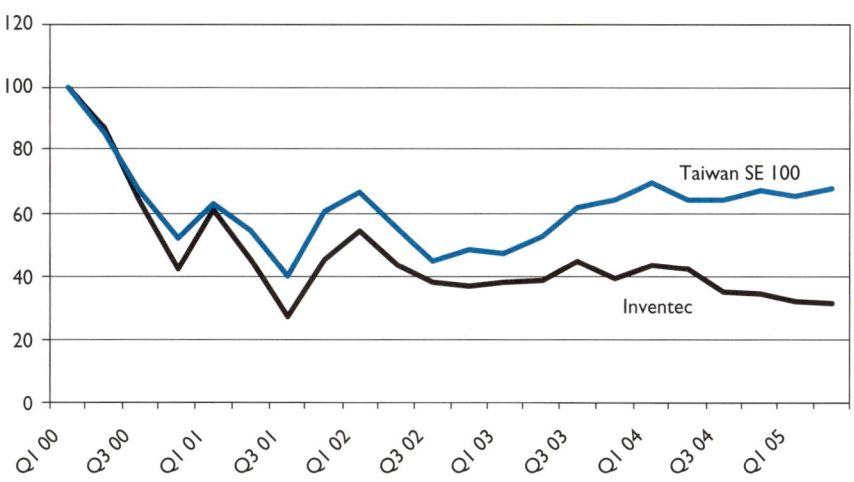

Source: Thomson Financial Datastream, July 20, 2005.

EXHIBIT 3

Inventec Corporation Product Line Estimates

	2002	2003	2004	F2005	F2006
Sales Breakdown (%)					
Notebook PCs	61	75	84	82	81
Servers	16	20	16	17	18
LAN & PDA	23	5	1	1	1
YoY Growth (%)					
Notebook PCs	−6	30	78	7	9
Servers	29	35	22	19	18
LAN & PDA	3	−75	−83	9	12
Gross Margins (%)					
Notebook PCs	5.7	6.9	5.2	5.0	5.0
Servers	11.3	14.0	7.8	7.5	8.5
LAN & PDA	7.0	5.3	2.0	4.0	4.8
Total gross margins	6.9	8.3	5.6	5.4	5.6

Source: Kevin Y. Chang, Pauline Chen., Credit Suisse First Boston, "Taiwan PC Hardware: Upside in All the Right Places," June 23, 2005, available from Investext, Thomson Research, http://research.thomsonib.com.

Note: These figures are only for products made directly by Inventec Corp. Data relating to consumer electronics and other products by Inventec subsidiary companies are not included.

EXHIBIT 4

Evolution of Taiwan ODM Business Models

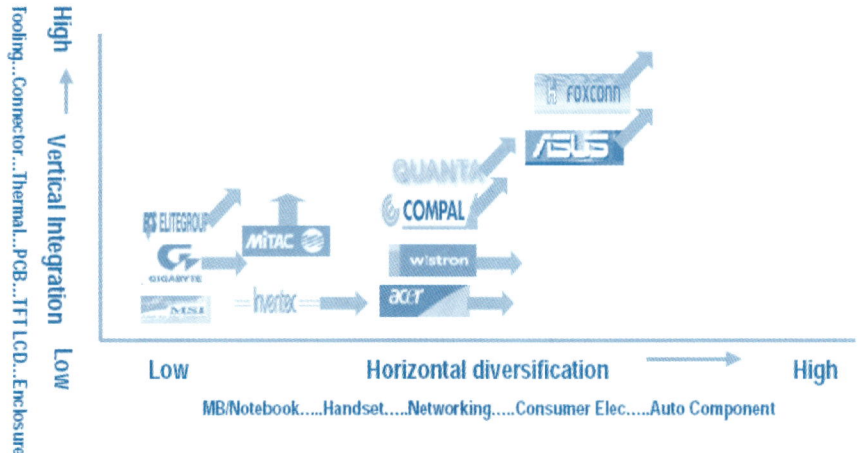

Source: Kevin Y. Chang, et al., Credit Suisse Equity Research, "Taiwan PC Hardware: Upside in All the Right Places," June 23, 2005, p. 13, available from Investext, Thomson Research, http://research.thomsonib.com.

EXHIBIT 5

Leading Taiwan Original Design Manufacturer (ODM) Financial Estimates for 2005

(US $ millions)	Asustek	Compal	Inventec	Quanta	Wistron
Revenue	10,889	7,251	4,751	11,967	4,097
Revenue growth YoY	39%	10%	16%	18%	12%
Net Income	656	251	59	409	58
Net income growth YoY	39%	22%	−25%	9%	12%
Gross margins (%)	10.4	5.7	5.4	5.8	5.2
Operating margins (%)	6.0	3.5	1.2	2.8	1.4
Net margins (%)	6.0	3.5	1.2	3.4	1.4
Return on assets (%)	11.0	7.5	3.2	8.1	4.6
Return on equity (%)	19.2	10.9	8.6	18.8	−5.2
P/E ratio (%)	12.2	14.0	13.3	13.8	12.9
EPS growth	26%	25%	3%	10%	NM
Market capitalization	7,454	3,370	1,020	6,103	742
OEM products	NB PC (32%)	NB PC (79%)	NB PC (80%)	NB PC (91%)	NB PC (67%)
(% contribution to revenue)	Desk PC (42%)	LCD TV (8%)	Servers (19%)	Servers (5%)	Servers (11%)
	Gaming (11%)	LCD monitor (7%)		Handsets (3%)	Desk PC (9%)
		Handsets (5%)			Gaming (9%)

Source: Compiled from Kevin Y. Chang, et al., Credit Suisse First Boston, "Taiwan PC Hardware: Upside in All the Right Places," June 23, 2005, available from Investext, Thomson Research, http://research.thomsonib.com.

EXHIBIT 6

Contract Manufacturing 2003 Revenue Breakdown by Segment

	ODM	EMS
Computer systems	44	20
Computer peripherals	25	19
Consumer electronics	13	9
Wireless telecom	12	14
Wired telecom	5	18
Automotive	1	2
Industrial	—	9
Medical	—	6
Military/aerospace	—	3
	100%	100%
Total revenue ($US bil)	51.7	94.7

Source: Adapted from Dennis Normile, "These Slim Margins are Not by Design," *Electronic Business*, September 2004, p. 50, available from ProQuest, ABI/Inform, http://www.proquest.com.

EXHIBIT 7

Leading Electronic Manufacture Service (EMS) Firms' Financial Estimates for 2005

(US$ millions)	Celestica	Flextronics	Jabil Circuit	Sanmina-SCI	Solectron
Revenue	8,801	15,908	7,538	11,791	10,643
Revenue growth YoY	0%	10%	21%	–4%	–9%
Net Income	119	388	226	119	168
Net income growth YoY	59%	65%	32%	1%	1231%
Gross margins	6.0	6.8	8.4	5.5	5.8
Operating margins	2.5	3.2	4.3	2.2	1.9
Net margins	1.4	2.4	3.0	1.0	1.6
Return on assets (%)	2.3	3.2	6.0	1.8	3.0
Return on equity (%)	4.8	7.0	11.1	4.5	6.6
P/E ratio (%)	27.0	22.0	26.8	NM	25.8
EPS growth (%)	NM	56	25	0	NM
Market capitalization	2,814	7,626	6,078	2,458	3,527
HQ Location	Canada	Singapore	Florida	California	California
Manufacturing and assembly sites (partial lists)	US, Canada, Brazil, Mexico, China, Thailand, Philippines, Malaysia, France, Singapore, Spain, Czech Republic	US, Canada, Brazil, Mexico, China, Japan, Malaysia, India, England, Ireland, Scotland, Finland, Denmark, France, Hungary, Sweden	US, Brazil, Mexico, China, Malaysia, Japan, India, England, Ireland, Scotland, France, Hungary, Italy, Netherlands,	US, Canada, Brazil, Mexico, China, Malaysia, Japan, Singapore, Australia, Israel, Hungary, France, Scotland, Sweden	US, Canada, Brazil, Mexico, China, Malaysia, Japan, Singapore, Taiwan, Germany, Netherlands, UK, Sweden, Turkey

Source: Compiled from company websites; OneSource Information Services, Inc., http://www.onesource.com and; David Pescherine, Kin Duncan, Citigroup Research, "EMS Model Book," August 15, 2005, available from Investext, Thomson Research, http://research.thomsonib.com.

Note: Companies had differing fiscal years. Data is for the fiscal year ending in calendar year 2005.

EXHIBIT 8

Leading Notebook ODM's Approximate Client Mix (% Notebook Revenue) in 2004

PC OEMs	Arima	Asustek	Compal	Inventec	Quanta	Wistron
Acer			8		8	33
Apple		39	5		6	
Dell			42		34	20
Fujitsu Siemens			2		1	5
HPQ			24	75	25	7
IBM			4		4	20
NEC	25		6		6	
Sony		25	8		8	
Toshiba			18	19		
Others	75	36	1	7	8	15
Total	100%	100%	100%	100%	100%	100%

Source: Ellen Tseng, et al., Morgan Stanley Equity Research, "Full Gear," Inventec Corp., April 8, 2004, p. 4, available from Investext, Thomson Research, http://research.thomsonib.com.

EXHIBIT 9

Inventec Corporation Financials in New Taiwan Dollars (millions), 2001–2005

Year Ended December 31st	2001	2002	2003	2004	F2005
Income Statement					
Revenue	62,298	68,300	81,578	131,370	152,028
Gross profit	4,648	5,742	5,821	7,100	8,196
Operating expense	3,430	3,851	4,822	5,194	6,315
Operating income	1,218	1,891	999	1,906	1,881
Nonoperating income	3,381	2,083	3,296	957	−72
Net Income	3,777	3,350	4,248	2,424	1,822
Balance Sheet					
Current assets	24,908	27,699	38,084	40,472	44,523
Total assets	34,910	42,180	52,184	54,226	60,529
Current liabilities	9,985	15,877	22,825	25,713	na
Total liabilities	10,879	16,637	23,673	26,170	31,803
Total equity	24,031	25,543	28,510	28,056	28,726
Cash Flows					
Operating activities	8,924	3,797	553	−733	13,055
Investing activities	−1,295	−4,438	1,853	−1,461	−1,650
Financing activities	−687	−1,669	−1,144	−2,702	−1,314
Net change in cash	6,772	−2,603	1,268	−4,887	10,091
Cash beginning balance	3,558	10,329	7,726	8,993	4,106
Cash ending balance	10,329	7,726	8,993	4,106	na

Source: Inventec Corporation Financial Statements for 2001–2004. Forecast figures are from Ellen Tseng, Morgan Stanley Equity Research, "2005 Remains a Tough Year," *Inventec Corp.*, May 11, 2005, available from Investext, Thomson Research, http://research.thomsonib.com.

Note: Revenue and operating figures refer to the PC related businesses held directly by Inventec Corp. Other business units such as consumer electronics and software belonged to subsidiary companies in which Inventec Corp. held equity shares. Investment income from these businesses was reported as part of "non-operating income."

EXHIBIT 10

Leading Indian Software Firms in FY2005

Fiscal Year Ended March 31, 2005	Infosys	Satyam	TCS	Wipro
Revenue (US$ mil)	1,592	794	2,168	1,856
Revenue growth YoY	47%	38%	40%	41%
Net income (US$ mil)	419	154	457	363
Net income growth YoY	48%	39%	38%	60%
Gross margins (%)	43.3	36.1	44.6	33.9
Operating margins (%)	28.6	20.5	23.7	22.8
Net margins (%)	26.3	19.5	21.1	19.5
Return on assets (%)	32.4	19.2	47.6	24.6
Return on equity (%)	37.3	21.5	82.3	35.0
P/E ratio (%)	33.3	23.8	27.4	32.0
EPS growth YoY (%)	47%	37%	31%	57%
Market capitalization (US$ mil)	14,289	3,856	14,182	11,721
Client industries	telecom, retail, transportation, aerospace, auto, banking, insurance, manufacturing	manufacturing, telecom, banking, insurance, retail, healthcare	banking, telecom, manufacturing, media, retail, transport, energy, utilities, healthcare	financial services, telecom, retail, manufacturing, utilities, healthcare
Major clients	Airbus, Boeing, Nortel, Cisco, Lucent, ING, JC Penny, Nordstrom	GE, State Farm, Microsoft	GE, GE Capital, Dell, HP, IBM, Lucent, Nortel, Nokia, Microsoft	Microsoft, Sun, NCR, HP, Toshiba, Alcatel, Cisco, Ericsson, Fujitsu, Lucent, Nokia

Source: Compiled from OneSource Information Services, Inc., http://www.onesource.com and; Anantha Narayan and Parag Gupta, Morgan Stanley Equity Research, "India Software," August 8, 2005, available from Investext, Thomson Research, http://research.thomsonib.com.

Note: Full company names—Infosys Technologies; Satyam Computer Services; Tata Consultancy Services; Wipro Technologies.

Inventec Corporation

ENDNOTES

1. Jaime Wang, "Market Focus: Original Design Manufacturers in the Notebook PC Market, Worldwide, 2004," Gartner Report No. G00129805, July 14, 2005, available from Gartner Inc, http://www.gartner.com, accessed July 20, 2005.

2. Dennis Normile, "These Slim Margins are Not by Design," *Electronic Business,* September 2004, p. 48, available from ProQuest, ABI/Inform, http://www.proquest.com, accessed July 25, 2005.

3. Ellen Tseng, Morgan Stanley Equity Research, "2005 Remains a Tough Year," *Inventec Corp.,* May 11, 2005, pp. 1–4, available from Investext, Thomson Research, http://research.thomsonib.com, accessed June 20, 2005.

4. Ellen Tseng, et al., Morgan Stanley Equity Research, "Full Gear," *Inventec Corp.,* April 8, 2004, p. 4, available from Investext, Thomson Research, http://research.thomsonib.com, accessed May 18, 2005.

5. Ines Ke, "Apple Computer Enlarges Procurement Business in Taiwan," *Taiwan Business News,* December 7, 2004, available from Factiva, http://www.factiva.com, accessed June 30, 2005.

6. Adam Pick, iSuppli Corporation, "The EMS/ODM Monitor," available from iSuppli website, http://www.isuppli.com, accessed May 10, 2005.

7. Robert S. Huckman and Gary P. Pisano, "Flextronics International, Ltd.," HBS Case No. 604-063, March 29, 2005, Harvard Business School Publishing, 2005, pp. 5–6.

8. James Carbone, "Targeting Design," *Purchasing,* October 21, 2004, p. 30, available from ProQuest, ABI/Inform, http://www.proquest.com, accessed April 10, 2005.

9. iSuppli market data reported in "Contract Manufacturing to Reach $298B by 2008," *Electronic News,* March 7, 2005, available from Factiva, http://www.factiva.com, accessed June 30, 2005.

10. Ibid.

11. Pete Engardio, et al. "Outsourcing Innovation," *BusinessWeek,* March 21, 2005, available from Factiva, http://www.factiva.com, accessed June 30, 2005.

12. For example, in 2001 PalmOne switched from using EMS providers to contracting a Taiwan ODM to design the hardware for its Treo smartphones. PalmOne still determined the look of the product, collaborating with the ODM on the design, but focused on the software. The new policy saved months of development time, cut defects by 50% and increased gross margins by about 20%. Pete Engardio, et al. "Outsourcing Innovation."

13. Stephan H. Wildstrom, "Don't be Fooled by the Name on the Box," *BusinessWeek,* June 17, 2002, available from ProQuest, ABI/Inform, http://www.proquest.com, accessed July 25, 2005); and Lee Gomes, "PCs Aren't Just Made in Asia Now: Many are Designed

There," *The Wall Street Journal*, July 19, 2004, available from Factiva, http://www.factiva.com, accessed June 30, 2005.

14. Rebecca Buckman, "Flextronics to Meld Indian Units," *The Asian Wall Street Journal,* December 13, 2004, available from Factiva, http://www.factiva.com, accessed June 30, 2005.

15. Anantha Narayan and Parag Gupta, Morgan Stanley Equity Research, "India Software," August 8, 2005, available from Investext, Thomson Research, http://research.thomsonib.com, accessed June 20, 2005.

16. Barbara Jorgensen, "But What About ODM," *Electronic Business,* December 2004, available from ProQuest, ABI/Inform, http://www.proquest.com, accessed April 10, 2005.

17. Kevin Sachs, vice president of strategic marketing for Selectron, quoted in James Carbone, "Targeting Design," p. 34.

18. Pete Engardio, et al. "Outsourcing Innovation."

19. Ibid.

20. Ibid.

21. "Compaq to Solicit New Notebook PC OEM Partners in Taiwan," *Taiwan Economic News,* November 16, 1999, available from Factiva, http://www.factiva.com, accessed June 30, 2005.

22. "Compaq and Dell to Diversify Sources of OEM PCs," *Taiwan Business News,* September 16, 1998, available from Factiva, http://www.factiva.com, accessed June 30, 2005.

23. Dennis Normile, "These Slim Margins are Not by Design," p. 48.

24. Ellen Tseng, et al., Morgan Stanley Equity Research, "Full Gear," p. 5.

25. "Inventec Corp. Launches Software to Enhance Computer Experience," *China Post,* August 21, 2002, available from Factiva, http://www.factiva.com, accessed June 30, 2005.

26. "Inventec Ventures from Notebook PC Manufacturing to Software Development," *Taiwan News,* August 21, 2002, available from Factiva, http://www.factiva.com, accessed June 30, 2005.

27. Dwight Silverman, Compaq, Taiwan Firm Plan Notebook," *Houston Chronicle,* February 3, 1995, available from Factiva, http://www.factiva.com, accessed June 30, 2005.

28. Ellen Tseng, Morgan Stanley Equity Research, "2005 Remains a Tough Year," p. 3.

29. Kent W.B. Chan, Ellen Tyan, Citigroup Smith Barney, "Taiwan Notebook ODMs: Out of the Frying Pan, Into the Fire?" April 23, 2004, pp. 28–29, available from Investext, Thomson Research, http://research.thomsonib.com, accessed June 20, 2005.

30. "Notebook Makers Enter Servers' Battlefield," *China Post,* May 5, 2001, available from Factiva, http://www.factiva.com, accessed June 30, 2005.

31. Ellen Tseng, Morgan Stanley Equity Research, "2005 Remains a Tough Year," p. 3.

32. Sabrina Kuo, "Taiwan Inventec Appliances to List Shares by November," *Dow Jones International News,* June 2, 2005, available from Factiva, http://www.factiva.com, accessed June 30, 2005.

33. Ellen Tseng, et al., Morgan Stanley Equity Research, "Full Gear," p. 4.

34. Sabrina Kuo, "Taiwan Inventec Appliances to List Shares by November."

35. "Local Notebook PC Makers Expanding into PDA Production," *Taiwan Economic News,* September 25, 2000, available from Factiva, http://www.factiva.com, accessed June 30, 2005.

36. "Palm Orders PDAs From Inventec Appliance and Asustek," *Taiwan Economic News,* July 11, 2002, available from Factiva, http://www.factiva.com, accessed June 30, 2005.

37. "New Palm m105 Sparks Fears of PDA Price War," *China Post,* March 15, 2001, available from Factiva, http://www.factiva.com, accessed June 30, 2005.

38. "Taiwan Press: Inventec Unit Lands Apple iPod Order," *Dow Jones International News,* November 1, 2001, and; Tim Culpan, "MP3 Not Just Another Pea in a Pod," *South China Morning Post,* July 24, 2002, both available from Factiva, http://www.factiva.com, accessed June 30, 2005.

39. Ellen Tseng, et al., Morgan Stanley Equity Research, "Full Gear," p. 14.

40. Ellen Tseng, Morgan Stanley Equity Research, "2005 Remains a Tough Year," p. 3.

41. Sabrina Kuo, "Taiwan Inventec Appliances to List Shares by November."

42. Ellen Tseng, et al., Morgan Stanley Equity Research, "Full Gear," p. 14.

43. "Inventec to Deliver High-End Notebook PCs to Toshiba," *Taiwan Economic News,* January 15, 2002, available from Factiva, http://www.factiva.com, accessed June 30, 2005.

44. "Inventec Takes Over Former DEC Plant," *Taiwan Business News,* September 15, 1998, available from Factiva, http://www.factiva.com, accessed June 30, 2005.

45. "Inventec's Revenue to Jump 30% on Compaq's New Notebook OC Orders," *Taiwan Economic News,* October 13, 1999, available from Factiva, http://www.factiva.com, accessed June 30, 2005.

46. "Inventec Sets up Global Distributing System," *Taiwan Economic News,* October 14, 1999, available from Factiva, http://www.factiva.com, accessed June 30, 2005.

47. "HP to Take Control of Procurement From Compaq in Taiwan," *China Post,* September 11, 2001, available from Factiva, http://www.factiva.com, accessed June 30, 2005.

48. Dan Nystedt, "HP to Stick With Local Suppliers," *Taipei Times,* July 4, 2002, available from Factiva, http://www.factiva.com, accessed June 30, 2005.

49. Xiao Wang, "Inventec to Expand Investment," *China Daily,* September 10, 1994, available from Factiva, http://www.factiva.com, accessed June 30, 2005.

50. "Software Firms Shift Mainland Investment into High Gear," *Taiwan Economic News,* April 12, 2000, available from Factiva, http://www.factiva.com, accessed June 30, 2005.

51. "Notebook Maker Inventec to Venture into Desktop Computers," *Taiwan Economic News,* January 12, 1998, available from Factiva, http://www.factiva.com, accessed June 30, 2005.

52. "Inventec to Venture Into Desktop PC Market," *Taiwan Economic News,* October 11, 1998, available from Factiva, http://www.factiva.com, accessed June 30, 2005.

53. See, for example, "Inventec's Shanghai Notebook PC Plant to be Completed in October," *Taiwan Economic News,* August 7, 2001, available from Factiva, http://www.factiva.com, accessed June 30, 2005.

54. "Quanta Finally Moves to Mainland," *Taiwan Business News,* September 5, 2000, available from Factiva, http://www.factiva.com, accessed June 30, 2005.

55. "Tatung to Set Up Information R&D Center in Jiangsu of Mainland," *Taiwan Economic News,* February 28, 2000, available from Factiva, http://www.factiva.com, accessed June 30, 2005.

56. "Half of Taiwanese Desktop PCs Sold From Mainland China," *Taiwan Economic News,* August 10, 2000, available from Factiva, http://www.factiva.com, accessed June 30, 2005.

57. The regulations prohibited Taiwanese manufacturers from investing in the production of level 586 or higher PCs in China.

58. "Quanta Finally Moves to Mainland," *Taiwan Business News,* September 5, 2000, available from Factiva, http://www.factiva.com, accessed June 30, 2005.

59. Alice Liu, "Inventec to Set up Notebook Plant in Shanghai," *Taiwan Business News,* December 22, 2000, and "Taiwan Inventec Considering Second China Plant in Kunshan," *Dow Jones International News,* January 29, 2001, both available from Factiva, http://www.factiva.com, accessed June 30, 2005.

60. "Inventec to Build Second Plant in Kunshan in 2001," *Taiwan Economic News,* January 30, 2001, and "Inventec to Invest a Further US$10million in Mainland China," both available from Factiva, http://www.factiva.com, accessed June 30, 2005.

61. "Inventec Shanghai Wins Customs Clearance Privilege," *Taiwan Economic News,* December 4, 2001, available from Factiva, http://www.factiva.com, accessed June 30, 2005.

62. Economist Intelligence Unit, "China: Trade Regulations," *EIU ViewsWire,* March 10, 2005, available from Factiva, http://www.factiva.com, accessed June 30, 2005.

63. Helen Ubels, "Taiwan Inventec Mulls More Expansion in China," *Dow Jones International News,* May 16, 2002, available from Factiva, http://www.factiva.com, accessed June 30, 2005.

64. Ben Lee, Nomura Asian Equity Research, "Wistron Corp," June 24, 2005, p. 13, available from Investext, Thomson Research, http://research.thomsonib.com, accessed June 20, 2005.

65. Lite-On CFO Ignatius Wei, quoted in Jason Dean, "Taiwan Industry: Right On, Lite-On," *Far Eastern Economic Review,* March 27, 2003, available from Factiva, http://www.factiva.com, accessed June 30, 2005.

66. Chinese PC market data available from Global Market Information Database, http://www.euromonitor.com, accessed June 14, 2005.

67. Euromonitor International, "Portable Personal Computers in China," October 2004, available from Global Markets Information Database, http://www.euromonitor.com, accessed June 14, 2005.

68. "Chinese PC Makers Undergo Frequent Personnel Changes," *SinoCast China IT Watch,* July 29, 2004, available from Factiva, http://www.factiva.com, accessed June 30, 2005.

69. Li Weitao, "Lenovo Nose-Diving into Rural Market," *Business Weekly,* August 10, 2004, available from Factiva, http://www.factiva.com, accessed June 30, 2005.

70. "Chinese PC Makers Undergo Frequent Personnel Changes."

71. "Toshiba Notebooks Mired in Trouble," *SinoCast China IT Watch,* January 31, 2005, available from Factiva, http://www.factiva.com, accessed June 30, 2005.

72. Yang Yuanqing, quoted in Li Weitao, "Lenovo Nose-Diving into Rural Market," *Business Weekly,* August 10, 2004, available from Factiva, http://www.factiva.com, accessed June 30, 2005.

73. "Competition in Lower-End PC Market Intensifying," *SinoCast China IT Watch,* August 23, 2004, available from Factiva, http://www.factiva.com, accessed June 30, 2005.

74. Li Weitao, "Lenovo Nose-Diving into Rural Market."

75. Justine Lau, "Lenovo Blames Poor Results on Price War," *Financial Times,* November 17, 2004, available from Factiva, http://www.factiva.com, accessed June 30, 2005.

76. "China Still Key for Lenovo PC Sales," *Cbnet,* May 20, 2005, available from ISI Emerging Markets, http://www.securities.com, accessed July 13, 2005.

77. Jeannie Cheung and Stanley Wong, Credit Suisse First Boston, "Lenovo Group: Don't Log Off," March 7, 2005, http://www.factiva.com, accessed June 30, 2005.

78. "Laptop Prices Ready to Crash," *Shanghai Daily,* January 27, 2005, available from Factiva, http://www.factiva.com, accessed June 30, 2005.

79. Bram J. Bout, Vincent Chang, and Sarena Lin, "China's Market for Mobile Phones," *The McKinsey Quarterly* (2004, No. 2) available from, http://www.mckinseyquarterly.com, accessed June 20, 2005.

Inventec Corporation

80. "Inventec Appliance Strives to Boost Sales in Mainland Market," *Taiwan Economic News,* May 18, 2005, available from Factiva, http://www.factiva.com, accessed June 30, 2005.

81. Sabrina Kuo, "Taiwan Inventec Appliances to List Shares by November."

82. "Survey; Moving On," *The Economist,* January 15, 2005, available from ProQuest ABI/Inform, http://www.proquest.com, accessed April 10, 2005.

83. Economist Intelligence Unit, "Taiwan Consumer Goods: Born Identity?" *EIU Executive Briefing,* available from Factiva, http://www.factiva.com, accessed June 30, 2005.

84. "Survey; Moving On," *The Economist.*

85. Claire Serant and Faith Hung, "EMS Industry's Next Investment: Taiwan ODMs," *EBN Manhasset,* April 8, 2002, available from ProQuest ABI/Inform, http://www.proquest.com, accessed April 10, 2005.

86. National Association of Software and Service Companies (India), NASSCOM website, http://www.nasscom.org, accessed August 20, 2005.

87. "Wipro-Toshiba TEC Open a New Chapter," June, 10, 2002, available from the Wipro website, http://www.wipro.com/newsroom, accessed August 20, 2005.

88. "India Industry: HP, Wipro to Strengthen Alliance," *The Economist Intelligence Unit–Viewswire,* July 21, 2005, available from Factiva, http://www.factiva.com, accessed June 30, 2005.

Inventec Corporation

Chapter 3

Overview of Accounting Analysis

T he purpose of accounting analysis is to evaluate the degree to which a firm's accounting captures its underlying business reality.[1] By identifying places where there is accounting flexibility, and by evaluating the appropriateness of the firm's accounting policies and estimates, analysts can assess the degree of distortion in a firm's accounting numbers. Having identified accounting distortions, analysts can then adjust a firm's accounting numbers using cash flow and footnote information to "undo" the distortions. Sound accounting analysis improves the reliability of conclusions from financial analysis, the next step in financial statement analysis.

THE INSTITUTIONAL FRAMEWORK FOR FINANCIAL REPORTING

There is typically a separation between ownership and management in public corporations. Financial statements serve as the vehicle through which owners keep track of their firms' financial situation. On a periodic basis, firms typically produce three primary financial reports: (1) an income statement that describes the operating performance during a time period, (2) a balance sheet that states the firm's assets and how they are financed, and (3) a cash flow statement (or in some countries, a funds flow statement) that summarizes the cash (or fund) flows of the firm. These statements are accompanied by footnotes that provide additional details on the financial statement line items, as well as by management's narrative discussion of the firm's performance in the Management Discussion and Analysis section.

To evaluate effectively the quality of a firm's financial statement data, the analyst needs to first understand the basic features of financial reporting and the institutional framework that governs them, as discussed in the following sections.

Accrual Accounting

One of the fundamental features of corporate financial reports is that they are prepared using accrual rather than cash accounting. Unlike cash accounting, accrual accounting distinguishes between the recording of costs and benefits associated with economic activities and the actual payment and receipt of cash. Net income is the primary periodic performance index under accrual accounting. To compute net income, the effects of economic transactions are recorded on the basis of *expected*, not necessarily *actual*, cash receipts and payments. Expected cash receipts from the delivery of products or services are recognized as revenues, and expected cash outflows associated with these revenues are recognized as expenses.

While there are many rules and conventions that govern a firm's preparation of financial statements, there are only a few conceptual building blocks that form the foundation of accrual accounting. The following definitions are critical to the income statement, which summarizes a firm's revenues and expenses[2]:

- **Revenues** are economic resources earned during a time period. Revenue recognition is governed by the realization principle, which proposes that revenues should be recognized when (a) the firm has provided all, or substantially all, the goods or services to be delivered to the customer and (b) the customer has paid cash or is expected to pay cash with a reasonable degree of certainty.[3]
- **Expenses** are economic resources used up in a time period. Expense recognition is governed by the matching and the conservatism principles. Under these principles, expenses are resource costs (a) directly associated with revenues recognized in the same period, (b) associated with benefits that are consumed in this time period, or (c) whose future benefits are not reasonably certain.
- **Profit** is the difference between a firm's revenues and expenses in a time period.[4]

The following fundamental relationship is therefore reflected in a firm's income statement:

$$Profit = Revenues - Expenses$$

In contrast, the balance sheet is a summary at one point in time. The principles that define a firm's assets, liabilities, and equity are as follows:

- **Assets** are economic resources owned by a firm that are (a) likely to produce future economic benefits and (b) measurable with a reasonable degree of certainty.
- **Liabilities** are economic obligations of a firm arising from benefits received in the past that (a) are required to be met with a reasonable degree of certainty and (b) whose timing is reasonably well defined.
- **Equity** is the difference between a firm's assets and its liabilities.

The definitions of assets, liabilities, and equity lead to the fundamental relationship that governs a firm's balance sheet:

$$Assets = Liabilities + Equity$$

Delegation of Reporting to Management

While the basic definitions of the elements of a firm's financial statements are simple, their application in practice often involves complex judgments. For example, how should revenues be recognized when a firm sells land to customers and also provides customer financing? If revenue is recognized before cash is collected, how should potential defaults be estimated? Are the outlays associated with research and development activities, whose payoffs are uncertain, assets or expenses when incurred? Are contractual commitments under lease arrangements or post-retirement plans liabilities? If so, how should they be valued?

Because corporate managers have intimate knowledge of their firms' businesses, they are entrusted with the primary task of making the appropriate judgments in portraying myriad business transactions using the basic accrual accounting framework. The accounting discretion granted to managers is potentially valuable because it allows them to reflect inside information in reported financial statements. However, since investors view profits as a measure of managers' performance, managers have an incentive to use their accounting discretion to distort reported profits by making biased assumptions. Further, the use of accounting numbers in contracts between the firm and outsiders provides a motivation for management manipulation of accounting numbers.

This earnings management distorts financial accounting data, making it less valuable to external users of financial statements. Therefore, the delegation of financial reporting decisions to managers has both costs and benefits. Accounting rules and auditing are mechanisms designed to reduce the cost and preserve the benefit of delegating financial reporting to corporate managers. The Sarbanes-Oxley Act increased the involvement of the audit committee of a firm's board of directors and required the personal certification of the CEO and CFO as to the appropriateness of financial reports as a way of reducing the costs of this delegation. The legal system is used to adjudicate disputes between managers, auditors, and investors.

Generally Accepted Accounting Principles

Given that it is difficult for outside investors to determine whether managers have used accounting flexibility to signal their proprietary information or merely to disguise reality, a number of accounting conventions have evolved to mitigate the problem. For example, in most countries financial statements are prepared using the historical cost convention, where assets and liabilities are recorded at historical exchange prices rather than fair values, replacement values, or values in use. This reduces managers' ability to overstate the value of the assets that they have acquired or developed, or to understate the value of liabilities. Of course, historical cost also limits the information that is available to investors about the potential of the firm's assets, since exchange prices are usually different from fair values or values in use.[5]

Accounting standards and rules also limit management's ability to misuse accounting judgment by regulating how particular types of transactions are recorded. For example, accounting standards for leases stipulate how firms are to record contractual arrangements to lease resources. Similarly, pension and other post-employment benefit standards describe how firms are to record commitments to provide pensions and other retirement benefits for employees. These accounting standards, which are designed to convey quantitative information on a firm's performance, are complemented by a set of disclosure principles. The disclosure principles guide the amount and kinds of information that is disclosed and require a firm to provide qualitative information related to the assumptions, policies, and uncertainties that underlie the quantitative data presented.

In the United States, the Securities and Exchange Commission (SEC) has the legal authority to set accounting standards. The SEC typically relies on private sector accounting bodies to undertake this task. Since 1973 accounting standards in the United States have been set by the Financial Accounting Standards Board (FASB); and Generally Accepted Accounting Principles (GAAP) denotes the standards, conventions, rules, and procedures that FASB requires firms to apply in preparing their financial statements. There are similar private sector or public sector accounting standard-setting bodies in many other countries. More recently, the International Accounting Standards Board (IASB) and its predecessor, the International Accounting Standards Committee (IASC), have been attempting to set worldwide accounting standards. Those standards, the International Financial Reporting Standards (IFRS), are gaining increasing acceptance throughout Europe and in many developed and emerging markets across the globe. While IFRS is not applicable to U.S. companies, experts anticipate that GAAP and IFRS are likely to ultimately converge. At present, foreign companies registered with the SEC have to file a Form 20-F, which shows a reconciliation between the company's IFRS or local accounts and U.S. GAAP.

Uniform accounting standards attempt to reduce managers' ability to record similar economic transactions in dissimilar ways, either over time or across firms. Thus they create a uniform accounting language and increase the credibility of financial statements by limiting a firm's ability to distort them. Increased uniformity from accounting standards, however, comes at the expense of reduced flexibility for managers to reflect genuine business differences in a firm's accounting decisions. Rigid accounting standards work best for economic transactions whose accounting treatment is not predicated on managers' proprietary information. However, when there is significant business judgment involved in assessing a transaction's economic consequences, rigid standards are likely to be dysfunctional for some companies because they prevent managers from using their superior knowledge of the business to determine how best to report the economics of key business events. Further, if accounting standards are too rigid, they may induce managers to expend economic resources to restructure business transactions to achieve a desired accounting result or to forego transactions that may be difficult to report on.

External Auditing

External auditing, broadly defined as a verification of the integrity of the reported financial statements by someone other than the preparer, ensures that managers use accounting rules and conventions consistently over time, and that their accounting estimates are reasonable. In the U.S., all listed companies are required to have their financial statements audited by an independent public accountant. The standards and procedures to be followed by independent auditors are known as Generally Accepted Auditing Standards (GAAS). Under the Sarbanes-Oxley Act, the responsibility for overseeing audit firms and for ensuring that they are complying with GAAS resides with the Public Company Accounting Oversight Board (PCAOB), a new U.S. regulatory body. All public accounting firms are required to register with the PCAOB, which has the power to inspect and investigate audit work, and if needed to discipline auditors.

The Sarbanes-Oxley Act also specifies the relationship between a company and its external auditor, requiring auditors to report to, and be overseen by, a company's audit committee rather than its management. In addition, the Act prohibits public accounting firms from providing non-audit services, such as bookkeeping, information systems design and implementation, valuation and a range of other consulting services, to a company that it audits. Finally, the Act requires that audit firms rotate the lead and reviewing audit partner every five years. These changes are expected to affect the economics of audit firms and to increase the cost of audits.

While auditors issue an opinion on published financial statements, it is important to remember that the primary responsibility for the statements still rests with corporate managers. Auditing improves the quality and credibility of accounting data by limiting a firm's ability to distort financial statements to suit its own purposes. However, as recent audit failures at companies such as Enron and WorldCom show, auditing is imperfect. Audits cannot review all of a firm's transactions. They can also fail because of lapses in quality, or because of lapses in judgment by auditors who fail to challenge management for fear of losing future business.

Third-party auditing may also reduce the quality of financial reporting because it constrains the kind of accounting rules and conventions that evolve over time. For example, the FASB considers the views of auditors in the standard-setting process. Auditors are likely to argue against accounting standards that produce numbers which are difficult to audit, even if the proposed rules produce relevant information for investors.

Legal Liability

The legal environment in which accounting disputes between managers, auditors, and investors are adjudicated can also have a significant effect on the quality of reported numbers. The threat of lawsuits and resulting penalties has the beneficial effect of improving the accuracy of disclosure. However, the potential for significant legal liability might also discourage managers and auditors from supporting accounting proposals requiring risky forecasts, for example, forward-looking disclosures. The U.S. auditing community often expresses this type of concern.

FACTORS INFLUENCING ACCOUNTING QUALITY

Because the mechanisms that limit managers' ability to distort accounting data themselves add noise, it is not optimal to use accounting regulation to completely eliminate managerial flexibility. Therefore, real-world accounting systems leave considerable room for managers to influence financial statement data. The net result is that information in corporate financial reports is noisy and biased, even in the presence of accounting regulation and external auditing.[6] The objective of accounting analysis is to evaluate the degree to which a firm's accounting captures its underlying business reality and to "undo" any accounting distortions. When potential distortions are large, accounting analysis can add considerable value.[7]

There are three potential sources of noise and bias in accounting data: (1) that introduced by rigidity in accounting rules, (2) random forecast errors, and (3) systematic reporting choices made by corporate managers to achieve specific objectives. Each of these factors is discussed below.

Noise from Accounting Rules

Accounting rules introduce noise and bias because it is often difficult to restrict management discretion without reducing the information content of accounting data. For example, the Statement of Financial Accounting Standards (SFAS) No. 2 issued by the FASB requires firms to expense research outlays when they are incurred. Clearly, some research expenditures have future value while others do not. However, because SFAS 2 does not allow firms to distinguish between the two types of expenditures, it leads to a systematic distortion of reported accounting numbers. Broadly speaking, the degree of distortion introduced by accounting standards depends on how well uniform accounting standards capture the nature of a firm's transactions.

Forecast Errors

Another source of noise in accounting data arises from pure forecast error, because managers cannot predict future consequences of current transactions perfectly. For example, when a firm sells products on credit, accrual accounting requires managers to make a judgment about the probability of collecting payments from customers. If payments are deemed "reasonably certain," the firm treats the transactions as sales, creating accounts receivable on its balance sheet. Managers then make an estimate of the proportion of receivables that will not be collected. Because managers do not have perfect foresight, actual customer defaults are likely to be different from estimated defaults, leading to a forecast error. The extent of errors in managers' accounting forecasts depends on a variety of factors including the complexity of the business transactions, the predictability of the firm's environment, and unforeseen economy-wide changes.

Managers' Accounting Choices

Corporate managers also introduce noise and bias into accounting data through their own accounting decisions. Managers have a variety of incentives to exercise their accounting discretion to achieve certain objectives[8]:

- *Accounting-based debt covenants.* Managers may make accounting decisions to meet certain contractual obligations in their debt covenants. For example, firms' lending agreements with banks and other debt holders require them to meet covenants related to interest coverage, working capital ratios, and net worth, all defined in terms of accounting numbers. Violation of these agreements may be costly because lenders can trigger penalties including demanding immediate repayment of their loans. Managers of firms close to violating debt covenants have an incentive to select accounting policies and estimates to reduce the probability of covenant violation. The debt covenant motivation for managers' accounting decisions has been analyzed by a number of accounting researchers.[9]
- *Management compensation.* Another motivation for managers' accounting choice comes from the fact that their compensation and job security are often tied to reported profits. For example, many top managers receive bonus compensation if they exceed certain prespecified profit targets. This provides motivation for managers to choose accounting policies and estimates to maximize their expected compensation.[10] Stock option awards can also potentially induce managers to manage earnings. Options provide managers with incentives to understate earnings prior to option grants to lower the firm's current stock price and hence the option exercise price, and to inflate earnings and stock prices at the time of option exercise.[11]
- *Corporate control contests.* In corporate control contests, including hostile takeovers and proxy fights, competing management groups attempt to win over the firm's shareholders. Accounting numbers are used extensively in debating managers' performance in these contests. Therefore, managers may make accounting decisions to influence investor perceptions in corporate control contests.[12]
- *Tax considerations.* Managers may also make reporting choices to trade off between financial reporting and tax considerations. For example, U.S. firms are required to use LIFO inventory accounting for shareholder reporting in order to use it for tax reporting. Under LIFO, when prices are rising, firms report lower profits, thereby reducing tax payments. Some firms may forgo the tax reduction in order to report higher profits in their financial statements.[13]
- *Regulatory considerations.* Since accounting numbers are used by regulators in a variety of contexts, managers of some firms may make accounting decisions to influence regulatory outcomes. Examples of regulatory situations where accounting numbers are used include antitrust actions, import tariffs to protect domestic industries, and tax policies.[14]
- *Capital market considerations.* Managers may make accounting decisions to influence the perceptions of capital markets. When there are information asymmetries between managers and outsiders, this strategy may succeed in influencing investor perceptions, at least temporarily.[15]
- *Stakeholder considerations.* Managers may also make accounting decisions to influence the perception of important stakeholders in the firm. For example, since labor unions can use healthy profits as a basis for demanding wage

increases, managers may make accounting decisions to decrease income when they are facing union contract negotiations. In countries like Germany, where labor unions are strong, these considerations appear to play an important role in firms' accounting policy. Other important stakeholders that firms may wish to influence through their financial reports include suppliers and customers.[16]

- *Competitive considerations.* The dynamics of competition in an industry might also influence a firm's reporting choices. For example, a firm's segment disclosure decisions may be influenced by its concern that disaggregated disclosure may help competitors in their business decisions. Similarly, firms may not disclose data on their margins by product line for fear of giving away proprietary information. Finally, firms may discourage new entrants by making income-decreasing accounting choices.

In addition to accounting policy choices and estimates, the level of disclosure is also an important determinant of a firm's accounting quality. Corporate managers can choose disclosure policies that make it more or less costly for external users of financial reports to understand the true economic picture of their businesses. Accounting regulations usually prescribe minimum disclosure requirements, but they do not restrict managers from voluntarily providing additional disclosures. Managers can use various parts of the financial reports, including the Letter to the Shareholders, Management Discussion and Analysis, and footnotes, to describe the company's strategy, its accounting policies, and its current performance. There is wide variation across firms in how managers use their disclosure flexibility.[17]

STEPS IN PERFORMING ACCOUNTING ANALYSIS

In this section we discuss a series of steps that an analyst can follow to evaluate a firm's accounting quality.

Step 1: Identify Principal Accounting Policies

As discussed in the chapter on business strategy analysis, a firm's industry characteristics and its own competitive strategy determine its key success factors and risks. One of the goals of financial statement analysis is to evaluate how well these success factors and risks are being managed by the firm. In accounting analysis, therefore, the analyst should identify and evaluate the policies and the estimates the firm uses to measure its critical factors and risks.

Key success factors in the banking industry include interest rate and credit risk management; in the retail industry, inventory management is important; and for a manufacturer competing on product quality and innovation, research and development, and product defects after sale are major areas of concern. A significant success factor in the leasing business is to make accurate forecasts of residual values of the leased equipment at the end of the lease terms. In each of these cases, the analyst has to identify the accounting measures the firm uses to capture these business constructs, the policies that determine how the measures are implemented, and the important estimates embedded in these policies. For example, the accounting measure a bank uses to capture credit risk is its loan loss reserves, and the accounting measure that captures product quality for a manufacturer is its warranty expenses and reserves. For a firm in the equipment leasing industry, one of the most important accounting policies is the way residual values are recorded. Residual values influence the company's reported profits and its asset base. If residual values are overestimated, the firm runs the risk of having to take large write-offs in the future.

Step 2: Assess Accounting Flexibility

Not all firms have equal flexibility in choosing their accounting policies and estimates. Some firms' accounting choice is severely constrained by accounting standards and conventions. For example, even though research and development is a key success factor for biotechnology companies, managers have no accounting discretion in reporting on this activity. Similarly, even though marketing and brand building are essential to the success of consumer goods firms, they are required to expense all their marketing outlays. In contrast, managing credit risk is one of the critical success factors for banks, and bank managers have the freedom to estimate expected defaults on their loans. Similarly, software developers have the flexibility to decide at what points in their development cycles the outlays can be capitalized.

If managers have little flexibility in choosing accounting policies and estimates related to their key success factors (as in the case of biotechnology firms), accounting data are likely to be less informative for understanding the firm's economics. In contrast, if managers have considerable flexibility in choosing the policies and estimates (as in the case of software developers), accounting numbers have the potential to be informative, depending upon how managers exercise this flexibility.

Regardless of the degree of accounting flexibility a firm's managers have in measuring their key success factors and risks, they have some flexibility with respect to several other accounting policies. For example, all firms have to make choices with respect to depreciation policy (straight-line or accelerated methods), inventory accounting policy (LIFO, FIFO, or Average Cost), and policies regarding the estimation of pension and other post-employment benefits (expected return on plan assets, discount rate for liabilities, and rate of increase in wages and health care costs). Since all these policy choices can have a significant impact on the reported performance of a firm, they offer an opportunity for the firm to manage its reported numbers and should be the focus of analysis in this step.

Step 3: Evaluate Accounting Strategy

When managers have accounting flexibility, they can use it either to communicate their firm's economic situation or to hide true performance. Some of the strategy questions one could ask in examining how managers exercise their accounting flexibility include the following:

- How do the firm's accounting policies compare to the norms in the industry? If they are dissimilar, is it because the firm's competitive strategy is unique? For example, consider a firm that reports a lower warranty allowance than the industry average. One explanation is that the firm competes on the basis of high quality and has invested considerable resources to reduce the rate of product failure. An alternative explanation is that the firm is merely understating its warranty liabilities.
- Do managers face strong incentives to use accounting discretion to manage earnings? For example, is the firm close to violating bond covenants? Or are the managers having difficulty meeting accounting-based bonus targets? Does management own significant stock? Is the firm in the middle of a proxy fight or union negotiations? Managers may also make accounting decisions to reduce tax payments or to influence the perceptions of the firm's competitors.
- Has the firm changed any of its policies or estimates? What is the justification? What is the impact of these changes? For example, if warranty expenses decreased, is it because the firm made significant investments to improve quality?
- Have the company's policies and estimates been realistic in the past? For example, firms may overstate their revenues and understate their expenses during the year

by manipulating quarterly reports, which are not subject to a full-blown external audit. However, the auditing process at the end of the fiscal year forces such companies to make large fourth-quarter adjustments, providing an opportunity for the analyst to assess the quality of the firm's interim reporting. Similarly, firms that depreciate fixed assets too slowly will be forced to take a large write-off later. A history of write-offs may be, therefore, a sign of prior earnings management.

- Does the firm structure any significant business transactions so that it can achieve certain accounting objectives? For example, leasing firms can alter lease terms (the length of the lease or the bargain purchase option at the end of the lease term) so that the transactions qualify as sales-type leases for the lessors. Enron structured acquisitions of joint venture interests and hedging transactions with special purpose entities to avoid having to show joint venture liabilities, and to avoid reporting investment losses in its financial statements.[18] Such behavior may suggest that the firm's managers are willing to expend economic resources merely to achieve an accounting objective.

Step 4: Evaluate the Quality of Disclosure

Managers can make it more or less easy for an analyst to assess the firm's accounting quality and to use its financial statements to understand business reality. While accounting rules require a certain amount of minimum disclosure, managers have considerable choice in the matter. Disclosure quality, therefore, is an important dimension of a firm's accounting quality.

In assessing a firm's disclosure quality, an analyst could ask the following questions:

- Does the company provide adequate disclosures to assess the firm's business strategy and its economic consequences? For example, some firms use the Letter to the Shareholders in their annual report to clearly lay out the firm's industry conditions, its competitive position, and management's plans for the future. Others use the letter to puff up the firm's financial performance and gloss over any competitive difficulties the firm might be facing.
- Do the footnotes adequately explain the key accounting policies and assumptions and their logic? For example, if a firm's revenue and expense recognition policies differ from industry norms, the firm can explain its choices in a footnote. Similarly, when there are significant changes in a firm's policies, footnotes can be used to disclose the reasons.
- Does the firm adequately explain its current performance? The Management Discussion and Analysis (MD&A) section of the annual report provides an opportunity to help analysts understand the reasons behind a firm's performance changes. Some firms use this section to link financial performance to business conditions. For example, if profit margins went down in a period, was it because of price competition or because of increases in manufacturing costs? If the selling and general administrative expenses went up, was it because the firm is investing in a differentiation strategy, or because unproductive overhead expenses were creeping up? Based on a review of the Fortune 500 companies, the SEC released in 2003 a circular indicating that companies should provide more discussion in MD&A about their critical accounting policies.[19] Companies were encouraged to disclose the most difficult and judgmental estimates and accounting policies they used, among other guidance.
- If accounting rules and conventions restrict the firm from measuring its key success factors appropriately, does the firm provide adequate additional disclosure to help outsiders understand how these factors are being managed? For example, if a firm invests in product quality and customer service, accounting rules do not allow the management to capitalize these outlays, even when the future benefits are certain. The firm's MD&A can be used to highlight how

these outlays are being managed and their performance consequences. For example, the firm can disclose physical indexes of defect rates and customer satisfaction so that outsiders can assess the progress being made in these areas and the future cash flow consequences of these actions.

- If a firm is in multiple business segments, what is the quality of segment disclosure? Some firms provide excellent discussion of their performance by product segments and geographic segments. Others lump many different businesses into one broad segment. The level of competition in an industry and management's willingness to share desegregated performance data influence a firm's quality of segment disclosure.

- How forthcoming is the management with respect to bad news? A firm's disclosure quality is most clearly revealed by the way management deals with bad news. Does it adequately explain the reasons for poor performance? Does the company clearly articulate its strategy, if any, to address the company's performance problems?

- How good is the firm's investor relations program? Does the firm provide fact books with detailed data on the firm's business and performance? Is management accessible to analysts?

Step 5: Identify Potential Red Flags

In addition to the preceding steps, a common approach to accounting quality analysis is to look for "red flags" pointing to questionable accounting. These indicators suggest that the analyst should examine certain items more closely or gather more information on them. Some common red flags are the following:

- *Unexplained changes in accounting, especially when performance is poor.* This may suggest that managers are using their accounting discretion to "dress up" their financial statements.[20]

- *Unexplained transactions that boost profits.* For example, firms might undertake balance sheet transactions, such as asset sales or debt for equity swaps, to realize gains in periods when operating performance is poor.[21]

- *Unusual increases in accounts receivable in relation to sales increases.* This may suggest that the company is relaxing its credit policies or artificially loading up its distribution channels to record revenues during the current period, a practice commonly referred to as "channel stuffing." If credit policies are relaxed unduly, the firm may face receivable write-offs in subsequent periods as a result of customer defaults. If the firm accelerates shipments to its distributors, it may face either product returns or reduced shipments in subsequent periods.

- *Unusual increases in inventories in relation to sales increases.* If the inventory build-up is due to an increase in finished goods inventory, it could be a sign that demand for the firm's products is slowing down, suggesting that the firm may be forced to cut prices (and hence earn lower margins) or write down its inventory. A build-up in work-in-progress inventory tends to be good news on average, probably signaling that managers expect an increase in sales. If the build-up is in raw materials, it could suggest manufacturing or procurement inefficiencies, leading to an increase in cost of goods sold (and hence lower margins).[22]

- *An increasing gap between a firm's reported income and its cash flow from operating activities.* While it is legitimate for accrual accounting numbers to differ from cash flows, there is usually a steady relationship between the two if the company's accounting policies remain the same. Therefore, any *change* in the relationship between reported profits and operating cash flows might indicate subtle changes in the firm's accrual estimates. For example, a firm undertaking large construction contracts might use the percentage-of-completion method to record revenues. While earnings and operating cash flows are likely to differ for such a firm, they should bear a steady relationship to each other. Now suppose the firm increases revenues in a period through an aggressive application of the percentage-of-completion method. Then its earnings will go up, but its cash flow remains unaffected. This change in the firm's accounting quality will be manifested by a *change* in the relationship between the firm's earnings and cash flows.

- *An increasing gap between a firm's reported income and its tax income.* Once again, it is quite legitimate for a firm to follow different accounting policies for financial reporting and tax accounting as long as the tax law allows it.[23] However, the relationship between a firm's book and tax accounting is likely to remain stable over time unless there are significant changes in tax rules or accounting standards. Thus, an increasing gap between a firm's reported income and its tax income may indicate that financial reporting to shareholders has become more aggressive. For example, warranty expenses are estimated on an accrual basis for financial reporting, but they are recorded on a cash basis for tax reporting. Unless there is a big change in the firm's product quality, these two numbers bear a consistent relationship to each other. Therefore, a change in this relationship can be an indication either that product quality is changing significantly or that financial reporting estimates are changing.

- *A tendency to use financing mechanisms such as research and development partnerships, special-purpose entities, and the sale of receivables with recourse.* While these arrangements may have a sound business logic, they can also provide management with an opportunity to understate the firm's liabilities and/or overstate its assets.[24]

- *Unexpected large asset write-offs.* This may suggest that management is slow to incorporate changing business circumstances into its accounting estimates. Asset write-offs may also be a result of unexpected changes in business circumstances.[25]

- *Large fourth-quarter adjustments.* A firm's annual reports are audited by the external auditors, but its interim financial statements are usually only reviewed. If a firm's management is reluctant to make appropriate accounting estimates (such as provisions for uncollectible receivables) in its interim statements, it could be forced to make adjustments at the end of the year as a result of pressure from its external auditors. A consistent pattern of fourth-quarter adjustments, therefore, may indicate aggressive management of interim reporting.[26]

- *Qualified audit opinions or changes in independent auditors that are not well justified.* These may indicate a firm's aggressive attitude or a tendency to "opinion shop."

- *Related-party transactions or transactions between related entities.* These transactions may lack the objectivity of the marketplace, and managers' accounting estimates related to these transactions are likely to be more subjective and potentially self-serving.[27]

While the preceding list provides a number of red flags for potentially poor accounting quality, it is important to do further analysis before reaching final conclusions. Each of the red flags has multiple interpretations; some interpretations are based on sound business reasons, and others indicate questionable accounting. It is, therefore, best to use the red flag analysis as a starting point for further probing, not as an end point in itself.[28]

Step 6: Undo Accounting Distortions

If the accounting analysis suggests that the firm's reported numbers are misleading, analysts should attempt to restate the reported numbers to reduce the distortion to the extent possible. It is, of course, virtually impossible to perfectly undo the distortion using outside information alone. However, some progress can be made in this direction by using the cash flow statement and the financial statement footnotes.

A firm's cash flow statement provides a reconciliation of its performance based on accrual accounting and cash accounting. If the analyst is unsure of the quality of the firm's accrual accounting, the cash flow statement provides an alternative benchmark of its performance. The cash flow statement also provides information on how individual line items in the income statement diverge from the underlying cash flows. For example, if an analyst is concerned that the firm is aggressively capitalizing certain costs that should be expensed, the information in the cash flow statement provides a basis to make the necessary adjustment.

Financial statement footnotes also provide information that is potentially useful in restating reported accounting numbers. For example, when a firm changes its accounting policies, it provides a footnote indicating the effect of that change if it is material. Similarly, some firms provide information on the details of accrual estimates such as the allowance for bad debts. The tax footnote usually provides information on the differences between a firm's accounting policies for shareholder reporting and tax reporting. Since tax reporting is often more conservative than shareholder reporting, the information in the tax footnote can be used to estimate what the earnings reported to shareholders would be under more conservative policies.

In Chapter 4, we show how to make accounting adjustments for some of the most common types of accounting distortions.

ACCOUNTING ANALYSIS PITFALLS

There are several potential pitfalls and common misconceptions in accounting analysis that an analyst should avoid.

1. Conservative accounting is not "good" accounting.

Some firms take the approach that it pays to be conservative in financial reporting and to set aside as much as possible for contingencies. This logic is commonly used to justify the expensing of R&D and advertising, and the rapid write-down of intangible assets. It is also used to support large loss reserves for insurance companies, for merger expenses, and for restructuring charges.

From the standpoint of a financial statement user, it is important to recognize that conservative accounting is not the same as "good" accounting. Financial statement users want to evaluate how well a firm's accounting captures business reality in an unbiased manner, and conservative accounting can be as misleading as aggressive accounting in this respect.

It is certainly true that it can be difficult to estimate the economic benefits from many intangibles. However, the intangible nature of some assets does not mean that they do not have value. Indeed, for many firms these types of assets are their most valued. For example, the two most valued assets for the pharmaceutical company Pfizer are its research capabilities that permit it to generate new drugs, and its sales force that enables it to sell those drugs to doctors. Yet neither is recorded on Pfizer's balance sheet. From the investors' point of view, accountants' reluctance to value intangible assets does not diminish their importance. If they are not included in financial statements, investors must look to alternative sources of information on these assets.

Further, conservative accounting often provides managers with opportunities for "income smoothing," which may prevent analysts from recognizing poor performance in a timely fashion. Finally, over time investors are likely to figure out which firms are conservative and may discount their management's disclosures and communications.

2. Not all unusual accounting is questionable.

It is easy to confuse unusual accounting with questionable accounting. While unusual accounting choices might make a firm's performance difficult to compare with other firms' performance, such an accounting choice might be justified if the company's business is unusual. For example, firms that follow differentiated strategies or firms that structure their business in an innovative manner to take advantage of particular market situations may make unusual accounting choices to properly reflect their business. Therefore, it is important to evaluate a company's accounting choices in the context of its business strategy.

Similarly, it is important not to automatically attribute all changes in a firm's accounting policies and accruals to earnings management motives.[29] Accounting changes can also reflect changed business circumstances. For example, as already discussed, a firm that shows unusual increases in its inventory might be preparing for a new product introduction. Similarly, unusual increases in receivables might merely be due to changes in a firm's sales strategy. Unusual decreases in the allowance for uncollectible receivables might reflect a firm's changed customer focus. It is therefore important for an analyst to consider all possible explanations for accounting changes and investigate them using the qualitative information available in a firm's financial statements.

VALUE OF ACCOUNTING DATA AND ACCOUNTING ANALYSIS

What is the value of accounting information and accounting analysis? Given the incentives and opportunities for managers to affect their firms' reported accounting numbers, some have argued that accounting data and accounting analysis are not likely to be useful for investors.

Researchers have examined the value of earnings and return on equity (ROE) by comparing stock returns that could be earned by a hypothetical investor who has perfect foresight of firms' earnings, return on equity (ROE), and cash flows for the following year.[30]To assess the importance of earnings, the hypothetical investor is assumed to buy stocks of firms that have earnings increases for the subsequent year and to sell stocks of firms with subsequent earnings decreases. If this strategy is followed each year during the period 1954 to 1996, the hypothetical investor would have earned an average return of 37.5 percent per year. If a similar investment strategy is followed using ROE, buying stocks with subsequent increases in ROE and selling stocks with ROE decreases, an even higher annual return, 43 percent, would be earned. In contrast, cash flow data appear to be considerably less valuable than earnings or ROE information. Annual returns generated from buying stocks with increased subsequent cash flows from operations and selling stocks with cash flow decreases would be only 9 percent. This suggests that next period's earnings and ROE performance are more relevant information for investors than cash flow performance.

Overall, this research suggests that the institutional arrangements and conventions created to mitigate potential misuse of accounting by managers are effective in providing assurance to investors. The research indicates that investors do not view earnings management as so pervasive as to make earnings data unreliable.

A number of research studies have examined whether accounting analysis is a valuable activity. By and large, this evidence indicates that there are opportunities for superior analysts to earn positive stock returns. Studies show that companies criticized in the financial press for misleading financial reporting subsequently suffered an average stock price drop of 8 percent.[31] Firms where managers appeared to inflate reported earnings prior to an equity issue and subsequently reported poor earnings performance had more negative stock performance after the offer than firms with no apparent earnings management.[32] Finally, firms subject to SEC investigation for earnings management showed an average stock price decline of 9 percent when the earnings management was first announced, and they continued to have poor stock performance for up to two years.[33]

These findings imply that analysts who are able to identify firms with misleading accounting are able to create value for investors. The findings also indicate that the stock market ultimately sees through earnings management. In most cases, earnings management is eventually uncovered and the stock price responds negatively to evidence that firms have inflated prior earnings through misleading accounting.

SUMMARY

In summary, accounting analysis is an important step in the process of analyzing corporate financial reports. The purpose of accounting analysis is to evaluate the degree to which a firm's accounting captures the underlying business reality. Sound accounting analysis improves the reliability of conclusions from financial analysis, the next step in financial statement analysis.

There are six principal steps in accounting analysis. The analyst begins by identifying the key accounting policies and estimates, given the firm's industry and its business strategy. The second step is to evaluate the degree of flexibility available to managers, given the accounting rules and conventions. Next, the analyst evaluates how managers exercise their accounting flexibility and the likely motivations behind managers' accounting strategy. The fourth step involves assessing the depth and quality of a firm's disclosures. The analyst should next identify any red flags needing further investigation. The final step in accounting analysis is to restate accounting numbers to remove any noise and bias introduced by the accounting rules and management decisions.

The next chapter discusses how to implement these concepts and shows how to make some of the most common types of adjustments.

DISCUSSION QUESTIONS

1. A finance student states, "I don't understand why anyone pays any attention to accounting earnings numbers, given that a 'clean' number like cash from operations is readily available." Do you agree? Why or why not?

2. Fred argues, "The standards that I like most are the ones that eliminate all management discretion in reporting—that way I get uniform numbers across all companies and don't have to worry about doing accounting analysis." Do you agree? Why or why not?

3. Bill Simon says, "We should get rid of the FASB and SEC since free market forces will make sure that companies report reliable information." Do you agree? Why or why not?

4. Many firms recognize revenues at the point of shipment. This provides an incentive to accelerate revenues by shipping goods at the end of the quarter. Consider two

companies, one of which ships its product evenly throughout the quarter, and the second which ships all its products in the last two weeks of the quarter. Each company's customers pay thirty days after receiving shipment. Using accounting ratios, how can you distinguish these companies?

5. a. If management reports truthfully, what economic events are likely to prompt the following accounting changes?
    *   Increase in the estimated life of depreciable assets
    *   Decrease in the uncollectible allowance as a percentage of gross receivables
    *   Recognition of revenues at the point of delivery rather than at the point cash is received
    *   Capitalization of a higher proportion of software R&D costs

    b. What features of accounting, if any, would make it costly for dishonest managers to make the same changes without any corresponding economic changes?

6. The conservatism principle arises because of concerns about management's incentives to overstate the firm's performance. Joe Banks argues, "We could get rid of conservatism and make accounting numbers more useful if we delegated financial reporting to independent auditors rather than to corporate managers." Do you agree? Why or why not?

7. A fund manager states, "I refuse to buy any company that makes a voluntary accounting change, since it's certainly a case of management trying to hide bad news." Can you think of any alternative interpretation?

NOTES

1. Accounting analysis is sometimes also called "quality of earnings analysis." We prefer to use the term *accounting analysis* since we are discussing a broader concept than merely a firm's earnings quality.

2. These definitions paraphrase those of the Financial Accounting Standards Board (FASB), Statement of Financial Accounting Concepts No. 6, "Elements of Financial Statements" (1985). Our intent is to present the definitions at a conceptual, not technical, level. For more complete discussion of these and related concepts, see the FASB's Statements of Financial Accounting Concepts.

3. SEC rules state that these criteria are satisfied when (i) there is persuasive evidence that an arrangement exists, (ii) delivery has occurred or services have been rendered, (iii) the selling price is fixed or determinable, and (iv) collectibility is reasonably assured. (see SAB 104).

4. Strictly speaking, the comprehensive net income of a firm also includes gains and losses from increases and decreases in equity from nonoperating activities or extraordinary items.

5. Both U.S. and international standard setters are placing increased emphasis on fair value as a basis for accounting valuation. See for example recent U.S. standards on derivatives and most marketable securities.

6. Thus, although accrual accounting is theoretically superior to cash accounting in measuring a firm's periodic performance, the distortions it introduces can make accounting data less valuable to users. If these distortions are large enough, current cash flows may measure a firm's periodic performance better than accounting profits. The relative usefulness of cash flows and accounting profits in measuring performance, therefore, varies from firm to firm. For empirical evidence on this issue, see P. Dechow, "Accounting Earnings and Cash Flows as Measures of Firm Performance: The Role of Accounting Accruals," *Journal of Accounting and Economics* 18 (July 1994): 3–42.

7. For example, Abraham Briloff wrote a series of accounting analyses of public companies in *Barron's* over several years. On average, the stock prices of the analyzed companies changed by about 8 percent on the day these articles were published, indicating the potential value of performing such analysis. For a more complete discussion of this evidence, see G. Foster, "Briloff and the Capital Market," *Journal of Accounting Research* 17 (Spring 1979): 262–74.

8. For a complete discussion of these motivations, see *Positive Accounting Theory*, by R. Watts and J. Zimmerman, (Englewood Cliffs, NJ: Prentice-Hall, 1986). A summary of this research is provided by T. Fields, T. Lys, and L. Vincent in "Empirical Research on Accounting Choice," *Journal of Accounting & Economics* 31 (September 2001): 255–307.

9. The most convincing evidence supporting the covenant hypothesis is reported in a study of the accounting decisions by firms in financial distress: A. Sweeney, "Debt-Covenant Violations and Managers' Accounting Responses," *Journal of Accounting and Economics* 17 (May 1994): 281–308.

10. Studies that examine the bonus hypothesis generally report evidence supporting the view that managers' accounting decisions are influenced by compensation considerations. See, for example, P. Healy, "The Effect of Bonus Schemes on Accounting Decisions," *Journal of Accounting and Economics* 7 (April 1985): 85–107; R. Holthausen, D. Larcker, and R. Sloan, "Annual Bonus Schemes and the Manipulation of Earnings," *Journal of Accounting and Economics* 19 (February 1995): 29–74; and F. Guidry, A. Leone, and S. Rock, "Earnings-Based Bonus Plans and Earnings Management by Business Unit Managers," *Journal of Accounting and Economics* 26 (January 1999): 113–42.

11. For empirical evidence that CEOs of firms with scheduled awards make opportunistic voluntary disclosures to maximize stock award compensation, see D. Aboody and R. Kasznik, "CEO Stock Option Awards and the timing of corporate voluntary disclosures, *Journal of Accounting and Economics* 29 (February 2000): 73–100.

12. L. DeAngelo, "Managerial Competition, Information Costs, and Corporate Governance: The Use of Accounting Performance Measures in Proxy Contests," *Journal of Accounting and Economics* 10 (January 1988): 3–36.

13. The trade-off between taxes and financial reporting in the context of managers' accounting decisions is discussed in detail in *Taxes and Business Strategy* by M. Scholes and M. Wolfson (Englewood Cliffs, NJ: Prentice-Hall, 1992). Many empirical studies have examined firms' LIFO/FIFO choices.

14. Several researchers have documented that firms affected by such situations have a motivation to influence regulators' perceptions through accounting decisions. For example, J. Jones documents that firms seeking import protections make income-decreasing accounting decisions in "Earnings Management During Import Relief Investigations," *Journal of Accounting Research* 29, no. 2 (Autumn 1991): 193–228. A number of studies find that banks that are close to minimum capital requirements overstate loan loss provisions, understate loan write-offs, and recognize abnormal realized gains on securities portfolios. See S. Moyer, "Capital Adequacy Ratio Regulations and Accounting Choices in Commercial Banks," *Journal of Accounting and Economics* 12 (July 1990): 123–54; M. Scholes, G. P. Wilson, and M. Wolfson, "Tax Planning, Regulatory Capital Planning, and Financial Reporting Strategy for Commercial Banks," *Review of Financial Studies* 3 (1990): 625–50; A. Beatty, S. Chamberlain, and J. Magliolo, "Managing Financial Reports of Commercial Banks: The Influence of Taxes, Regulatory Capital and Earnings," *Journal of Accounting Research* 33, no. 2 (1995): 231–61; and J. Collins, D. Shackelford, and J. Wahlen, "Bank Differences in the Coordination of Regulatory Capital, Earnings and Taxes," *Journal of Accounting Research* 33, no. 2 (Autumn 1995): 263–91. Finally, Kathy Petroni finds that financially weak property-casualty insurers that risk regulatory attention understate claim loss reserves: K. Petroni, "Optimistic Reporting in the Property Casualty Insurance Industry," *Journal of Accounting and Economics* 15 (December 1992): 485–508.

15. P. Healy and K. Palepu, "The Effect of Firms' Financial Disclosure Strategies on Stock Prices," *Accounting Horizons* 7 (March 1993): 1–11. For a summary of the empirical evidence, see P. Healy and J. Wahlen, "A Review of the Earnings Management Literature and Its Implications for Standard Setting," *Accounting Horizons* 13 (December 1999): 365–84.

16. R. Bowen, L. DuCharme, and D. Shores, "Stakeholders' Implicit Claims and Accounting Method Choice," *Journal of Accounting and Economics* 20 (December 1995): 255–295, argue that, based on theory and anecdotal evidence, managers choose long-run income-increasing accounting methods as a result of ongoing implicit claims between a firm and its customers, suppliers, employees, and short-term creditors.

17. Financial analysts pay close attention to managers' disclosure strategies; the Association for Investment Management and Research publishes an annual report evaluating them for U.S. firms. For a discussion of these ratings, see M. Lang and R. Lundholm, "Cross-sectional Determinants of Analysts' Ratings of Corporate Disclosures," *Journal of Accounting Research* 31 (Autumn 1993): 246–71.

18. See P. Healy and K. Palepu, "The Fall of Enron," *Journal of Economic Perspectives* 17, no. 2 (Spring 2003): 3–26.

19. Securities and Exchange Commission, "Summary by the Division of Corporation Finance of Significant Issues Addressed in the Review of the Periodic Reports of the Fortune 500 Companies," SEC Web site (accessed May 8, 2006).

20. For a detailed analysis of a company that made such changes, see "Anatomy of an Accounting Change" by K. Palepu in *Accounting & Management: Field Study Perspectives*, edited by W. Bruns, Jr. and R. Kaplan (Boston: Harvard Business School Press, 1987).

21. An example of this type of behavior is documented by John Hand in his study, "Did Firms Undertake Debt-Equity Swaps for an Accounting Paper Profit or True Financial Gain?" *The Accounting Review* 64 (October 1989): 587–623.

22. For an empirical analysis of inventory build-ups, see V. Bernard and J. Noel, "Do Inventory Disclosures Predict Sales and Earnings?" *Journal of Accounting, Auditing, and Finance* (Fall 1991).

23. This is true by and large in the United States and in several other countries. However, in some countries such as Germany and Japan, tax accounting and financial reporting have historically been closely tied together, so this particular red flag has not been very meaningful. With the adoption of international accounting standards and the development of public capital markets, financial reporting and tax accounting in these countries have begun to diverge.

24. For research on accounting and economic incentives in the formation of R&D partnerships, see A. Beatty, P. Berger, and J. Magliolo, "Motives for Forming Research and Development Financing Organizations," *Journal of Accounting and Economics* 19 (April 1995): 411–42. An overview of Enron's use of special purpose entities to manage earnings and window-dress its balance sheet is provided by P. Healy and K. Palepu, "The Fall of Enron," *Journal of Economic Perspectives* 17, no. 2 (Spring 2003): 3–26.

25. For an empirical examination of asset write-offs, see J. Elliott and W. Shaw, "Write-offs as Accounting Procedures to Manage Perceptions," *Journal of Accounting Research* 26, 1988: 91–119.

26. R. Mendenhall and W. Nichols report evidence consistent with managers taking advantage of their discretion to postpone reporting bad news until the fourth quarter. See R. Mendenhall and W. Nichols, "Bad News and Differential Market Reactions to Announcements of Earlier-Quarter versus Fourth-Quarter Earnings," *Journal of Accounting Research*, Supplement (1988): 63–86.

27. The role of insider transactions in the collapse of Enron are discussed by P. Healy and K. Palepu, "The Fall of Enron," *Journal of Economic Perspectives* 17, no. 2 (Spring 2003): 3–26.

28. This type of analysis is presented in the context of provisions for bad debts by M. McNichols and P. Wilson in their study, "Evidence of Earnings Management from the Provisions for Bad Debts," *Journal of Accounting Research*, Supplement (1988): 1–31.

29. This point has been made by several accounting researchers. For a summary of research on earnings management, see K. Schipper, "Earnings Management," *Accounting Horizons* (December 1989): 91–102.

30. See J. Chang, "The Decline in Value Relevance of Earnings and Book Values" (dissertation, Harvard University, 1998). Evidence is also reported by J. Francis and K. Schipper, "Have Financial Statements Lost Their Relevance?" *Journal of Accounting Research* 37, no. 2 (Autumn 1999): 319–52, and W. E. Collins, E. Maydew, and I. Weiss, "Changes in the Value-Relevance of Earnings and Book Value over the Past Forty Years, *Journal of Accounting and Economics* 24 (1997): 39–67.

31. See G. Foster, "Briloff and the Capital Market," *Journal of Accounting Research* 17, no. 1 (Spring 1979): 262–74.

32. See S. H. Teoh, I. Welch, and T. J. Wong, "Earnings Management and the Long-Run Market Performance of Initial Public Offerings," *Journal of Finance* 53 (December 1998a): 1935–74; S. H. Teoh, I. Welch, and T. J. Wong, "Earnings Management and the Post-Issue Underperformance of Seasoned Equity Offerings," *Journal of Financial Economics* 50 (October 1998): 63–99; and S. Teoh, T. Wong, and G. Rao, "Are Accruals During Initial Public Offerings Opportunistic?" *Review of Accounting Studies* 3, no. 1–2 (1998): 175–208.

33. See P. Dechow, R. Sloan, and A. Sweeney, "Causes and Consequences of Earnings Manipulation: An Analysis of Firms Subject to Enforcement Actions by the SEC," *Contemporary Accounting Research* 13, no. 1 (1996): 1–36, and M. D. Beneish, "Detecting GAAP Violation: Implications for Assessing Earnings Management among Firms with Extreme Financial Performance," *Journal of Accounting and Public Policy* 16 (1997): 271–309.

Harnischfeger Corporation

In February 1985, Peter Roberts, the research director of Exeter Group, a small Boston-based investment advisory service specializing in turnaround stocks, was reviewing the 1984 annual report of Harnischfeger Corporation (**Exhibit 4**). His attention was drawn by the $1.28 per share net profit Harnischfeger reported for 1984. He knew that barely three years earlier the company had faced a severe financial crisis. Harnischfeger had defaulted on its debt and stopped dividend payments after reporting a hefty $7.64 per share net loss in fiscal 1982. The company's poor performance continued in 1983, leading to a net loss of $3.49 per share. Roberts was intrigued by Harnischfeger's rapid turnaround and wondered whether he should recommend the purchase of the company's stock (see **Exhibit 3** for selected data on Harnischfeger's stock).

COMPANY BUSINESS AND PRODUCTS

Harnischfeger Corporation was a machinery company based in Milwaukee, Wisconsin. The company had originally been started as a partnership in 1884 and was incorporated in Wisconsin in 1910 under the name Pawling and Harnischfeger. Its name was changed to the present one in 1924. The company went public in 1929 and was listed on the New York Stock Exchange.

The company's two major segments were the P&H Heavy Equipment Group, consisting of the Construction Equipment and the Mining and Electrical Equipment divisions, and the Industrial Technologies Group, consisting of the Material Handling Equipment and the Harnischfeger Engineers divisions. The sales mix of the company in 1983 consisted of Construction Equipment, 32%; Mining and Electrical Equipment, 33%; Material Handling Equipment, 29%; and Harnischfeger Engineers, 6%.

Harnischfeger was a leading producer of construction equipment. Its products, bearing the widely recognized brand name P&H, included hydraulic cranes and lattice boom cranes. These were used in bridge and highway construction and for cargo and other material handling applications. Harnischfeger had market shares of about 20% in hydraulic cranes and about 30% in lattice boom cranes. In the 1980s the construction equipment industry in general was experiencing declining margins.

Electric mining shovels and excavators constituted the principal products of the Mining and Electrical Equipment Division of Harnischfeger. The company had a dominant share of the mining machinery market. The company's products were used in coal,

Professor Krishna Palepu prepared this case. The case is intended solely as the basis for class discussion and is not intended to serve as an endorsement, source of primary data, or illustration of effective or ineffective management. Copyright © 1985 by the President and Fellows of Harvard College. HBS Case 9-186-160.

copper, and iron mining. A significant part of the division's sales were from the sale of spare parts. Because of its large market share and the lucrative spare parts sales, the division was traditionally very profitable. Most of the company's future mining product sales were expected to occur outside the United States, principally in developing countries.

The Material Handling Equipment Division of Harnischfeger was the fourth-largest supplier of automated material handling equipment with a 9% market share. The division's products included overhead cranes, portal cranes, hoists, monorails, and components and parts. The demand for this equipment was expected to grow in the coming years as an increasing number of manufacturing firms emphasized cost reduction programs. Harnischfeger believed that the material handling equipment business would be a major source of its future growth.

Harnischfeger Engineers was an engineering services division engaged in design, custom software development, and project management for factory and distribution automation projects. The division engineered and installed complete automated material handling systems for a wide variety of applications on a fee basis. The company expected such automated storage and retrieval systems to play an increasingly important role in the "factory of the future."

Harnischfeger had a number of subsidiaries, affiliated companies, and licensees in a number of countries. Export and foreign sales constituted more than 50% of the total revenues of the company.

FINANCIAL DIFFICULTIES OF 1982

The machinery industry experienced a period of explosive growth during the 1970s. Harnischfeger expanded rapidly during this period, growing from $205 million in revenues in 1973 to $644 million in 1980. To fund this growth, the company relied increasingly on debt financing, and the firm's debt/equity ratio rose from 0.88 in 1973 to 1.26 in 1980. The worldwide recession in the early 1980s caused a significant drop in demand for the company's products starting in 1981 and culminated in a series of events that shook the financial stability of Harnischfeger.

Reduced sales and the high interest payments resulted in poor profit performance leading to a reported loss in 1982 of $77 million. The management of Harnischfeger commented on its financial difficulties:

> There is a persistent weakness in the basic industries, both in the United States and overseas, which have been large, traditional markets for P&H products. Energy-related projects, which had been a major source of business of our Construction Equipment Division, have slowed significantly in the last year as a result of lower oil demand and subsequent price decline, not only in the U.S. but throughout the world. Lack of demand for such basic minerals as iron ore, copper and bauxite have decreased worldwide mining activity, causing reduced sales for mining equipment, although coal mining remains relatively strong worldwide. Difficult economic conditions have caused many of our normal customers to cut capital expenditures dramatically, especially in such depressed sectors as the steel industry, which has always been a major source of sales for all P&H products.

The significant operating losses recorded in 1982 and the credit losses experienced by its finance subsidiary caused Harnischfeger to default on certain covenants of its loan agreements. The most restrictive provisions of the company's loan agreements required it to maintain a minimum working capital of $175 million, consolidated net worth of $180 million, and a ratio of current assets to current liabilities of 1.75. On

October 31, 1982, the company's working capital (after reclassification of about $115 million long-term debt as a current liability) was $29.3 million, the consolidated net worth was $142.2 million, and the ratio of current assets to current liabilities was 1.12. Harnischfeger Credit Corporation, an unconsolidated finance subsidiary, also defaulted on certain covenants of its loan agreements, largely due to significant credit losses relating to the financing of construction equipment sold to a large distributor. As a result of these covenant violations, the company's long-term debt of $124.3 million became due on demand, the unused portion of the bank revolving credit line of $25.0 million became unavailable, and the unused short-term bank credit lines of $12.0 million were canceled. In addition, the $25.1 million debt of Harnischfeger Credit Corporation also became immediately due. The company was forced to stop paying dividends and began negotiations with its lenders to restructure its debt to permit operations to continue. Price Waterhouse, the company's audit firm, qualified its audit opinion on Harnischfeger's 1982 annual report with respect to the outcome of the company's negotiations with its lenders.

CORPORATE RECOVERY PLAN

Harnischfeger responded to the financial crisis facing the firm by developing a corporate recovery plan. The plan consisted of four elements: (1) changes in the top management, (2) cost reductions to lower the break-even point, (3) reorientation of the company's business, and (4) debt restructuring and recapitalization. The actions taken in each of these four areas are described below.

To deal effectively with the financial crisis, Henry Harnischfeger, then chairman and chief executive officer of the company, created the position of chief operating officer. After an extensive search, the position was offered in August 1982 to William Goessel, who had considerable experience in the machinery industry. Another addition to the management team was Jeffrey Grade, who joined the company in 1983 as senior vice president of finance and administration and chief financial officer. Grade's appointment was necessitated by the early retirement of the previous vice president of finance in 1982. The engineering, manufacturing, and marketing functions were also restructured to streamline the company's operations (see **Exhibits 1** and **2** for additional information on Harnischfeger's current management).

To deal with the short-term liquidity squeeze, the company initiated a number of cost reduction measures. These included (1) reducing the workforce from 6,900 to 3,800; (2) eliminating management bonuses and reducing of benefits and freezing wages of salaried and hourly employees; (3) liquidating excess inventories and stretching payments to creditors; and (4) permanent closure of the construction equipment plant at Escanaba, Michigan. These and other related measures improved the company's cash position and helped to reduce the rate of loss during fiscal 1983.

Concurrent with the above cost reduction measures, the new management made some strategic decisions to reorient Harnischfeger's business. First, the company entered into a long-term agreement with Kobe Steel, Ltd., of Japan. Under this agreement, Kobe agreed to supply Harnischfeger's requirements for construction cranes for sale in the United States as Harnischfeger phased out its own manufacture of cranes. This step was expected to significantly reduce the manufacturing costs of Harnischfeger's construction equipment, enabling it to compete effectively in the domestic market. Second, the company decided to emphasize the high technology part of its business by targeting for future growth the material-handling equipment and systems business. To facilitate this strategy, the Industrial Technologies Group was created. As part of the reorientation, the company stated that it would develop and acquire new products, technology, and equipment, and would expand its abilities to provide computer-integrated solutions to handling, storing, and retrieval in areas hitherto not pursued—industries such as distribution warehousing, food, pharmaceuticals, and aerospace.

While Harnischfeger was implementing its turnaround strategy, it was engaged at the same time in complex and difficult negotiations with its bankers. On January 6, 1984, the company entered into agreements with its lenders to restructure its debt obligations into three-year term loans secured by fixed as well as other assets, with a one-year extension option. This agreement required, among other things, specified minimum levels of cash and unpledged receivables, working capital, and net worth.

> *The company reported a net loss of $35 million in 1983, down from the $77 million loss the year before. Based on the above developments during the year, in the 1983 annual report the management expressed confidence that the company would return to profitability soon.*
>
> *We approach our second century with optimism, knowing that the negative events of the last three years are behind us, and with a firm belief that positive achievements will be recorded in 1984. By the time the corporation celebrates its 100th birthday on December 1, we are confident it will be operating profitably and attaining new levels of market strength and leadership.*

During 1984 the company reported profits during each of the four quarters, ending the year with a pre-tax operating profit of $5.7 million, and a net income after tax and extraordinary credits of $15 million (see **Exhibit 4**). It also raised substantial new capital through a public offering of debentures and common stock. Net proceeds from the offering, which totaled $150 million, were used to pay off all of the company's restructured debt. In the 1984 annual report the management commented on the company's performance as follows:

> *1984 was the Corporation's Centennial year and we marked the occasion by rededicating ourselves to excellence through market leadership, customer service and improved operating performance and profitability.*
>
> * * * * *
>
> *We look back with pride. We move ahead with confidence and optimism. Our major markets have never been more competitive; however, we will strive to take advantage of any and all opportunities for growth and to attain satisfactory profitability. Collectively, we will do what has to be done to ensure that the future will be rewarding to all who have a part in our success.*

QUESTIONS

1. Identify all the accounting policy changes and accounting estimates that Harnischfeger made during 1984. Estimate, as accurately as possible, the effect of these on the company's 1984 reported profits.

2. What do you think are the motives of Harnischfeger's management in making the changes in its financial reporting policies? Do you think investors will see through these changes?

3. Assess the company's future prospects, given your insights from questions 1 and 2 and the information in the case about the company's turnaround strategy.

Harnischfeger Corporation

EXHIBIT 1

Board of Directors, Harnischfeger Corporation, 1984

	Director Since	Current Term	Shares Owned
Edward W. Duffy — Chairman of the Board and Chief Executive of United States Gypsum Company, manufacturer of building materials and products used in industrial processes, since 1983. Former Vice Chairman from 1981 to 1983; President and Chief Operating Officer from 1971 to 1981. Director American National Bank and Trust Company of Chicago, Walter E. Heller International Corporation, W. W. Grainger, Inc., and UNR Industries, Inc. Age 64.	1981	1985	100
Herbert V. Kohler, Jr. — Chairman, Chief Executive Officer, and Director of Kohler Company, manufacturer of plumbing and specialty products, engines and generators, since 1972; President since 1974. Age 44.	1973	1985	700
Taisuke Mori — Executive Vice Chairman and Director of Kobe Steel, Ltd., a Japanese manufacturer of steel and steel products, industrial machinery, construction equipment, aluminum, copper and alloy products, and welding equipment and consumables. Age 63.	1981	1985	None
William W. Goessel — President and Chief Operating Officer of the Corporation since 1982. Executive Vice President of Beloit Corporation from 1978, Director to 1982. Goulds Pumps, Inc. Age 56.	1982	1986	15,000
Henry Harnischfeger — Chairman of the Board and Chief Executive Officer of the Corporation since 1970; President from 1959 to 1982. Director, First Wisconsin Corporation and First Wisconsin National Bank of Milwaukee. Age 60.	1945	1986	611,362
Karl F. Nygren — Partner in Kirkland & Ellis, attorneys, since 1959. Age 56.	1964	1986	2,000
John P. Gallagher — Senior lecturer, Graduate School of Business, University of Chicago. Director, IC Industries, Inc., Stone Container Corporation, UNR Industries, Inc., American National Bank and Trust Company of Chicago, and Walter E. Heller International Corporation. Age 67.	1979	1987	500

(continued)

		Director Since	Current Term	Shares Owned
Jeffrey T. Grade	Senior Vice President Finance and Administration and Chief Financial Officer of the Corporation since August 1, 1983. Vice President Corporate of IC Industries from 1981 to 1983; Assistant Vice President from 1976 to 1981. Age 40.	1983	1987	3,750
Donald Taylor	President, Chief Operating Officer, and Director of Rexnord, Inc., a major manufacturer of industrial components and machinery, since 1978. Director, Johnson Controls, Inc., Marine Corporation, and Marine Bank, N.A. Age 56.	1979	1987	100
Frank A. Lee	Director of Foster Wheeler Corporation since 1971; Chairman of the Board from 1981 to 1982; President and Chief Executive from 1978 to 1981. Director, Belco Pollution Control Corporation, International General Industries, Inc., and Banker's Life Insurance Co. Age 59.	1983	1987	None

EXHIBIT 2

Executive Compensation, Harnischfeger Corporation

The following table sets forth all cash compensation paid to each of the Corporation's five most highly compensated executive officers and to all executive officers as a group for services rendered to the Corporation and its subsidiaries during fiscal 1984.

		Cash Compensation
Henry Harnischfeger	Chairman of the Board and Chief Executive Officer	$364,004
William W. Goessel	President and Chief Operating Officer	280,000
C. P. Cousland	Senior Vice President and group executive, P&H Heavy Equipment	210,000
Jeffrey T. Grade	Senior Vice President Finance and Administration and Chief Financial Officer	205,336
Douglas E. Holt	President, Harnischfeger Engineers, Inc.	152,839
All persons who were executive officers during the fiscal year as a group (14 persons)		2,159,066

1985 Executive Incentive Plan

In December 1984, the board of directors established an Executive Incentive Plan for fiscal 1985 which provides an incentive compensation opportunity of 40% of annual salary for 11 senior executive officers only if the Corporation reaches a specific net after-tax profit objective and it provides an additional incentive compensation of up to 40% of annual salary for seven of those officers if the corporation exceeds the objective. The Plan covered the chairman, president, senior vice presidents; president, Harnischfeger Engineers, Inc.; vice president, P&H World Services; vice president, material Handling Equipment; and secretary. Awards made regarding fiscal year 1984 are included in the Compensation Table above.

EXHIBIT 3
Selected Stock Price and Market Data

A. Stock Prices

	Harnischfeger's Stock Price			S&P 400 Industrials Index		
	High	Low	Close	High	Low	Close
January 4, 1985	9 1/8	8 6/8	9	186.4	181.8	182.2
January 11, 1985	10 6/8	8 7/8	10 5/8	188.2	182.2	182.8
January 18, 1985	11	10	10 4/8	191.9	186.9	191.3
January 25, 1985	11 2/8	10 1/8	11	199.7	191.3	198.6
February 1, 1985	11 5/8	10 7/8	11 2/8	201.8	198.6	200.0

Harnischfeger's stock beta = 0.95 (Value Line estimate)

B. Market Data

	February 1985
Median P/E ratio of Dow Jones Industrials	10.9
Median P/E ratio of Value Line stocks	11.3
Median P/E ratio of machinery industry (construction and mining equipment)	10.0
Prime rate	10.5%
91-day Treasury bill rate	8.4%
30-year Treasury bond yield	11.4%
Moody's Aaa corporate bond yield	12.0%

Harnischfeger Corporation

EXHIBIT 4

1984 Annual Report—Edited

TO OUR SHAREHOLDERS

The Corporation recorded gains in each quarter during fiscal 1984, returning to profitability despite the continued depressed demand and intense price competition in the world markets it serves.

For the year ended October 31, net income was $15,176,000 or $1.28 per common share, which included $11,005,000 or 93¢ per share from the cumulative effect of a change in depreciation accounting. In 1983, the Corporation reported a loss of $34,630,000 or $3.49 per share.

Sales for 1984 improved 24% over the preceding year, rising to $398.7 million from $321 million a year ago. New orders totaled $451 million, a $101 million increase over 1983. We entered fiscal 1985 with a backlog of $193 million, which compared to $141 million a year earlier.

All Divisions Improved

All product divisions recorded sales and operating improvements during 1984.

Mining equipment was the strongest performer with sales up over 60%, including major orders from Turkey and the People's Republic of China. During the year we began the implementation of the training, engineering and manufacturing license agreement concluded in November, 1983 with the People's Republic of China, which offers the Corporation long-term potential in modernizing and mechanizing this vast and rapidly developing mining market.

Sales of material handling equipment and systems were up 10% for the year and the increasingly stronger bookings recorded during the latter part of the year are continuing into the first quarter of 1985.

Sales on construction equipment products showed some signs of selective improvement. In the fourth quarter, bookings more than doubled from the very depressed levels in the same period a year ago, although the current level is still far below what is needed to achieve acceptable operating results for this product line.

Financial Stability Restored

In April, the financial stability of the Corporation was improved through a public offering of 2.15 million shares of common stock, $50 million of 15% notes due April 15, 1994, and $100 million of 12% subordinated debentures due April 15, 2004, with two million common stock purchase warrants.

Net proceeds from the offering totaled $149 million, to which we added an additional $23 million in cash, enabling us to pay off all of our long-term debt. As a result of the refinancing, the Corporation gained permanent long-term capital with minimal annual cash flow requirements to service it. We now have the financial resources and flexibility to pursue new opportunities to grow and diversify.

Furthermore, should we require additional funds, they will be available through a $52 million unsecured three-year revolving credit agreement concluded in June with ten U.S. and Canadian banks. An $80 million product financing capability was also arranged through a major U.S. bank to provide financing to customers purchasing P&H products.

Outlook

Throughout 1985 we believe we will see gradual improvements in most of our U.S. and world markets.

For our mining excavator product line, coal and certain metals mining are expected to show a more favorable long-term outlook in selected foreign requirements and our capability to source equipment from the U.S., Japan or Europe places us in a strong marketing position. In the U.S., we see only a moderate strengthening in machinery requirements for coal, while metals mining will remain weak.

Continuing shipments of the Turkish order throughout 1985 will help to stabilize our plant utilization levels and improve our operating results for this product line.

In our material handling and systems markets, particularly in the U.S., we are experiencing a moderately strong continuation of the improved bookings which we began to see in the third and fourth quarters of last year.

In construction lifting equipment markets, we expect modest overall economic improvement in the U.S., which should help to absorb the large numbers of idle lifting equipment that have been manufacturer, distributor and customer inventories for the last three years. As this overhang on the market is reduced we will see gradual improvement in new sales. Harnischfeger traditionally exports half of its U.S.-produced lifting products. However, as with mining equipment, the continued strength of the U.S. dollar severely restricts our ability to sell U.S.-built products in world markets.

In addition to the strong dollar and economic instability in many foreign nations, overcapacity in worldwide heavy equipment manufacturing remains a serious problem in spite of some exits from the market as well as consolidations within the industry.

The Corporation continues to respond to severe price competition through systematic cost reduction programs and through expanded sourcing of P&H equipment from our European operation and, most importantly, through our 30-year association with our Japanese partner, Kobe Steel, Ltd. P&H engineering and technology have established world standards for quality and performance for construction cranes and mining equipment, which customers can expect from every P&H machine regardless of its source. More than a dozen new models of foreign – sourced P&H construction cranes will be made available for the first time in the U.S. during 1985, broadening our existing product lines and giving competitive pricing to our U.S. distributors and customers.

To improve our future operating results, we restructured our three operating divisions into two groups. All construction and mining related activities are in the new "P&H Heavy Equipment Group." All material handling equipment and systems activities are now merged into the "Industrial Technologies Group." More

information on these Groups is reported in their respective sections.

We are pleased to announce that John P. Moran was elected Senior Vice President and Group Executive, Industrial Technologies Group, and John R. Teitgen was elected Secretary and General Counsel.

In September Robert F. Schnoes became a member of our Board of Directors. He is President and Chief Executive Officer of Burgess, Inc. and of Ultrasonic Power Corporation, and a member of the Board of Signode Industries, Inc.

Beginning Our Second Century

1984 was the Corporation's Centennial year and we marked the occasion by rededicating ourselves to excellence through market leadership, customer service and improved operating performance and profitability.

Our first century of achievement resulted from the dedicated effort, support and cooperation of our employees, distributors, suppliers, lenders, and shareholders, and we thank all of them.

We look back with pride. We move ahead with confidence and optimism. Our major markets have never been more competitive; however, we will strive to take advantage of any and all opportunities for growth and to attain satisfactory profitability. Collectively, we will do what has to be done to ensure that the future will be rewarding to all who have a part in our success.

Henry Harnischfeger
Chairman of the Board

William W. Goessel
President

January 31, 1985

Harnischfeger Corporation

MANAGEMENT'S DISCUSSION & ANALYSIS

Results of Operation

1984 Compared to 1983

Consolidated net sales of $399 million in fiscal 1984 increased $78 million or 24% over 1983. Sales increases were 62% in the Mining and Electrical Equipment Segment, and 10% in the Industrial Technologies Segment. Sales in the Construction Equipment Segment were virtually unchanged reflecting the continued low demand for construction equipment world-wide.

Effective at the beginning of fiscal 1984, net sales include the full sales price of construction and mining equipment purchased from Kobe Steel, Ltd. and sold by the Corporation, in order to reflect more effectively the nature of the Corporation's transactions with Kobe. Such sales aggregated $28.0 million in 1984.

The $4.0 million increase in Other Income reflected a recovery of certain claims and higher license and technical service fees.

Cost of Sales was equal to 79.1% of net sales in 1984 and 81.4% in 1983; which together with the increase in net sales resulted in a $23.9 million increase in gross profit (net sales less cost of sales). Contributing to this increase were improved sales of higher-margin replacement parts in the Mining Equipment and Industrial Technologies Segments and a reduction in excess manufacturing costs through greater utilization of domestic manufacturing capacity and economies in total manufacturing costs including a reduction in pension expense. Reductions of certain LIFO inventories increased gross profit by $2.4 million in 1984 and $15.6 million in 1983.

Product development selling and administrative expenses were reduced, due to the funding of R&D expenses in the Construction Equipment Segment pursuant to the October 1983 Agreement with Kobe Steel, Ltd., to reductions in pension expenses and provision for credit losses, and to the absence of the corporate financial restructuring expenses incurred in 1983.

Net interest expense in 1984 increased $2.9 million due to higher interest rates on the outstanding funded debt and a reduction in interest income.

Equity in Earnings (Loss) of Unconsolidated Companies included 1984 income of $1.2 million of Harnischfeger Credit Corporation, an unconsolidated finance subsidiary, reflecting an income tax benefit of $1.4 million not previously recorded.

The preceding items, together with the cumulative effect of the change in depreciation method described in Financial Note 2, were included in net income of $15.2 million or $1.28 per common share, compared with net loss of $34.6 million or $3.49 per share in 1983.

The sales orders booked and unshipped backlogs of orders of the Corporation's three segments are summarized as follows (in million of dollars):

Orders Booked	1984	1983
Industrial Technologies	$132	$106
Mining and Electrical Equipment	210	135
Construction Equipment	109	109
	$451	$350
Backlogs at October 31		
Industrial Technologies	$ 79	$ 71
Mining and Electrical Equipment	91	50
Construction Equipment	23	20
	$193	$ 141

1983 Compared to 1982

Consolidated net sales of $321 million in fiscal 1983 were $126 million or 28% below 1982. This decline reflected, for the second consecutive year, the continued low demand in all markets served by the Corporation's products, with exports even more severely depressed due to the strength of the dollar. The largest decline was reported in the Construction Equipment Segment down 34%; Mining and Electrical Equipment Segment, shipments were down 27%, and the Industrial Technologies Segment, 23%.

Cost of Sales was equal to 81.4% of net sales in 1983 and 81.9% in 1982. The resulting gross profit was $60 million in 1983 and $81 million in 1982, a reduction equal to the rate of sales decrease.

The benefits of reduced manufacturing capacity and economies in total manufacturing costs were offset by reduced selling prices in the highly competitive markets. Reductions of certain LIFO inventories increased gross profits by $15.6 million in 1983 and $7.2 million in 1982.

Product development, selling and administrative expenses were reduced as a result of expense reduction measures in response to the lower volume of business and undertaken in connection with the Corporation's corporate recovery program, and reduced provisions for credit losses, which in 1982 included $4.0 million in income support for Harnischfeger Credit Corporation.

Net interest expense was reduced $9.1 million from 1982 to 1983, due primarily to increased interest income from short-term cash investments and an accrual of $4.7 million in interest income on refundable income taxes not previously recorded.

The Credit for Income Taxes included a federal income tax benefit of $5 million, based upon the recent examination of the Corporation's income tax returns and refund claims. No income tax benefits were available for the losses of the U.S. operations in 1983.

The losses from unconsolidated companies recorded in 1983 included $0.5 million in Harnischfeger Credit Corporation; $2.1 million in Cranatex, Inc., a Corporation-owned distributorship in Texas; and $0.8 million in ASEA Industrial Systems Inc., then a 49%-owned joint venture between the Corporation and ASEA AB and now 19%-owned with the investment accounted for on the cost method.

The preceding items were reflected in a net loss of $34.6 million or $3.49 per share.

Liquidity and Financial Resources

In April 1984, the Corporation issued in public offerings 2,150,000 shares of Common Stock, $50 million principal amount of 15% Senior Notes due in 1994, and 100,000 Units consisting of $100 million principal amount of 12% Subordinated Debentures due in 2004 and 2,000,000 Common Stock Purchase Warrants.

The net proceeds from the sales of the securities of $149 million were used to prepay substantially all of the outstanding debt of the Corporation and certain of its subsidiaries.

During the year ended October 31, 1984, the consolidated cash balances increased $32 million to a balance of $96 million, with the cash activity summarized as follows (in million of dollars):

Funds provided by operations	$10
Funds returned to the Corporation upon restructuring of the Salaried Employees' Pension Plan	39
Debt repayment less the proceeds of sales of securities	(9)
Plant and equipment additions	(6)
All other changes – net	(2)
	$32

In the third quarter of fiscal 1984 the Corporation entered into a $52 million three-year revolving credit agreement with ten U.S. and Canadian banks. While the Corporation has adequate liquidity to meet its current working capital requirements, the revolver represents another step in the Corporation's program to strengthen its financial position and provide the required financial resources to respond to opportunities as they arise.

CONSOLIDATED STATEMENT OF OPERATIONS

(Dollar amounts in thousands except per share figures)

	Year Ended October 31		
	1984	1983	1982
Revenues			
Net sales	$398,708	$321,010	$447,461
Other income, including license and technical service fees	7,067	3,111	5,209
	405,775	324,121	452,670
Cost of sales	315,216	261,384	366,297
Operating Income	90,559	62,737	86,373
Less:			
Product development, selling and administrative expenses	72,196	85,795	113,457
Interest expense – net	12,625	9,745	18,873
Provision for plant closing	—	—	23,700
Income (Loss) before provision (credit) for income taxes, equity items and cumulative effect of accounting change	5,738	(32,803)	(69,657)
Provision (Credit) for income taxes	2,425	(1,400)	(1,600)
Income (Loss) before equity items and cumulative effect of accounting change	3,313	(31,403)	(68,057)
Equity items			
Equity in earnings (loss) of unconsolidated companies	993	(3,397)	(7,891)
Minority interest in (earnings) loss of consolidated subsidiaries	(135)	170	(583)
Income (loss) before cumulative effect of accounting change	4,171	(34,630)	(76,531)
Cumulative effect of change in depreciation method	11,005	—	—
Net income (loss)	$15,176	$(34,630)	$(76,531)
Earnings (loss) per common and common equivalent share:			
Income (loss) before cumulative effect of accounting change	$.35	$(3.49)	$(7.64)
Cumulative effect of change in depreciation method	.93	—	—
Net income (loss)	$1.28	$(3.49)	$(7.64)
Pro forma amounts assuming the changed depreciation method had been applied respectively:			
Net (loss)		$(33,918)	$(76,695)
(Loss) per common share		$(3.42)	$(7.65)

CONSOLIDATED BALANCE SHEET

(Dollar amounts in thousands except per share figures)

	October 31,	
	1984	1983
Assets		
Current Assets		
Cash and temporary investments	$96,007	$64,275
Accounts receivable	87,648	63,740
Inventories	144,312	153,594
Refundable income taxes and related interest	1,296	12,585
Other current assets	5,502	6,023
Prepaid income taxes	14,494	14,232
	349,259	314,449
Investments and Other Assets		
Investments in and advances to:		
Finance subsidiary, at equity in net assets	8,849	6,704
Other companies	4,445	2,514
Other assets	13,959	6,411
	27,253	15,629
Operating Plants		
Land and improvements	9,419	10,370
Buildings	59,083	60,377
Machinery and equipment	120,949	122,154
	189,451	192,901
Accumulated depreciation	(93,259)	(107,577)
	96,192	85,324
	$472,704	$415,402

(continued)

Harnischfeger Corporation

Harnischfeger Corporation

CONSOLIDATED BALANCE SHEET *(continued)*

(Dollar amounts in thousands except per share figures)

	October 31,	
	1984	1983
Liabilities and Shareholders' Equity		
Current Liabilities		
Short-term notes payable to banks by subsidiaries	$9,090	$8,155
Long-term debt and capitalized lease obligations		
payable within one year	973	18,265
Trade accounts payable	37,716	21,228
Employee compensation and benefits	15,041	14,343
Accrued plant closing costs	2,460	6,348
Advance payments and progress billings	20,619	15,886
Income taxes payable	1,645	3,463
Account payable to finance subsidiary	—	3,436
Other current liabilities and accruals	29,673	32,333
	117,217	123,457
Long-Term Obligations		
Long-term debt payable to:		
Unaffiliated lenders	128,550	139,092
Finance subsidiary	—	5,400
Capitalized lease obligations	7,870	8,120
	136,420	152,612
Deferred Liabilities and Income Taxes		
Accrued pension costs	57,611	19,098
Other deferred liabilities	5,299	7,777
Deferred income taxes	6,385	134
	69,295	27,009
Minority Interest	2,400	2,405
Shareholders' equity		
Preferred stock $100 par value – authorized 250,000 shares:		
Series A $7.00 cumulative convertible preferred shares: authorized, issued and outstanding 117,500 shares in 1984 and 100,000 shares in 1983	11,750	10,000
Common stock, $1 par value – authorized 25,000,000 shares: issued and outstanding 12,283,563 shares in 1984 and 10,133,563 shares in 1983	12,284	10,134
Capital in excess of par value of shares	114,333	88,332
Retained earnings	19,901	6,475
Cumulative translation adjustments	(10,896)	(5,022)
	147,372	109,919
	$472,704	$415,402

CONSOLIDATED STATEMENT OF CHANGES IN FINANCIAL POSITION

(Dollar amounts in thousands)

	Year Ended October 31,		
	1984	1983	1982
Funds Were Provided by (Applied to):			
Operations:			
Income (loss) before cumulative effect of accounting change	$4,171	$(34,630)	$(76,531)
Cumulative effect of change in depreciation method	11,005	—	—
Net income (loss)	15,176	(34,630)	(76,531)
Add (deduct) items included not affecting funds:			
Depreciation	8,077	13,552	15,241
Unremitted (earnings) loss of unconsolidated companies	(993)	3,397	7,891
Deferred pension contributions	(500)	4,834	—
Deferred income taxes	6,583	(3,178)	1,406
Reduction in accumulated depreciation resulting from change in depreciation method	(17,205)	—	—
Other – net	(2,168)	(67)	2,034
Decrease in operating working capital (see below)	7,039	11,605	72,172
Add (deduct) the effects on operating working capital of:			
Conversion of export and factored receivable sales to debt	—	23,919	—
Reclassification to deferred liabilities:			
Accrued pension costs	—	14,264	—
Other liabilities	—	5,510	—
Foreign currency translation adjustments	(6,009)	(1,919)	(5,943)
Funds provided by operations	10,000	37,287	16,270
Financing, Investment and Other Activities:			
Transactions in debt and capitalized lease obligations–Long-Term debt and capitalized lease obligations: Proceeds from sale of 15% Senior Notes and 12% subordinated debentures, net of issue costs	120,530	—	—
Other increases	1,474	—	25,698
Repayments	(161,500)	(760)	(9,409)
Restructured debt	—	158,058	—
Debt replaced, including conversion of receivable sales of $23,919, and short-term bank notes payable of $9,028	—	(158,058)	—
	(39,496)	(760)	16,289
Net increase (repayment) in short-term bank notes payable	2,107	(3,982)	(2,016)
Net increase (repayment) in debt and capitalized lease obligations	(37,389)	(4,742)	14,273
Issuance of:			
Common stock	21,310	—	449
Common stock purchase warrants	6,663	—	—
Salaried pension assets reversion	39,307	—	—

(continued)

Harnischfeger Corporation

CONSOLIDATED STATEMENT OF CHANGES IN FINANCIAL POSITION

(Dollar amounts in thousands)

	Year Ended October 31,		
	1984	1983	1982
Plant and equipment additions	(5,546)	(1,871)	(10,819)
Advances to unconsolidated companies	(2,882)	—	—
Other – net	269	1,531	848
Funds provided by (applied to) financing, investment and other activities	21,732	(5,082)	4,751
Increase in cash and temporary investments	$31,732	$32,205	$21,021
Cash Dividends	—	—	(2,369)
Increase in Cash and Temporary Investments	$31,732	$32,205	$18,652
Decrease (increase) in operating working capital (excluding cash items, debt and capitalized lease obligations):			
Accounts receivable	$(23,908)	$(5,327)	$42,293
Inventories	9,282	56,904	26,124
Refundable income taxes and related interest	11,289	(2,584)	(6,268)
Other current assets	259	10,008	(439)
Trade accounts payable	16,488	(1,757)	(3,302)
Employee compensation and benefits	698	(15,564)	(3,702)
Accrued plant closing costs	(3,888)	(14,148)	20,496
Other current liabilities	(3,181)	(15,927)	(3,030)
Decrease in operating working capital	$7,039	$11,605	$72,172

CONSOLIDATED STATEMENT OF SHAREHOLDERS' EQUITY

(Dollar amounts in thousands except per share figures)

	Preferred Stock	Common Stock	Capital in Excess of Par Value of Shares	Retained Earnings	Cumulative Translation Adjustments	Total
Balance at October 31, 1981	$10,000	$10,085	$87,932	$120,005	$ —	$228,022
Cumulative translation adjustments through October 31, 1981					$(1,195)	$(1,195)
Issuance of Common Stock: 10,000 shares to Kobe Steel, Ltd.		10	91			101
38,161 shares under stock purchase and dividend reinvestment plans		39	309			348
Net (loss)				(76,531)		(76,531)
Cash dividends paid on: Preferred stock				(350)		(350)
Common stock $.20 per share				(2,019)		(2,019)
Translation adjustments, net of deferred income taxes of $128					(2,928)	(2,928)
Balance at October 31, 1982	10,000	10,134	88,332	41,105	(4,123)	145,448
Net (loss)				(34,630)		(34,630)
Translation adjustments, including deferred income taxes of $33					(899)	(899)
Balance at October 31, 1983	10,000	10,134	88,332	6,475	(5,022)	109,919
Issuance of:						
2,150,00 shares of common stock		2,150	19,160			21,310
2,000,000 common stock purchase warrants			6,663			6,663
17,500 shares of Series A $7.00 cumulative convertible preferred stock in discharge of dividends payable on preferred stock	1,750			(1,750)		—
Net income				15,176		15,176
Translation adjustments, net of deferred income taxes of $300					(5,874)	(5,874)
Other			178			178
Balance at October 31, 1984	$11,750	$12,284	$114,333	$19,901	$(10,896)	$147,372

Harnischfeger Corporation

FINANCIAL NOTES

Note I

Summary of Significant Accounting Policies

Consolidation—The consolidated financial statements include the accounts of all majority-owned subsidiaries except a wholly-owned domestic finance subsidiary, a subsidiary organized in 1982 as a temporary successor to a distributor, both of which are accounted for under the equity method, and a wholly-owned Brazilian subsidiary, which is carried at estimated net realizable value due to economic uncertainty. All related significant intercompany balances and transactions have been eliminated in consolidation.

Financial statements of certain consolidated subsidiaries, principally foreign, are included, effective in fiscal year 1984, on the basis of their fiscal years ending September 30; previously, certain of such subsidiaries had fiscal years ending July (see Note 2). Such fiscal periods have been adopted by the subsidiaries in order to provide for a more timely consolidation with the Corporation.

Inventories—The Corporation values its inventories at the lower of cost or market. Cost is determined by the last-in, first-out (LIFO) method for inventories located principally in the United States, and by the first-in, first-out (FIFO) method for inventories of foreign subsidiaries.

Operating Plants, Equipment and Depreciation—Properties are stated at cost. Maintenance and repairs are charged to expense as incurred and expenditures for betterments and renewals are capitalized. Effective in 1981, interest is capitalized for qualifying assets during their acquisition period. Capitalized interest is amortized on the same basis as the related asset. When properties are sold or otherwise disposed of, the cost and accumulated depreciation are removed from the accounts and any gain or loss is included in income.

Depreciation of plants and equipment is provided over the estimated useful lives of the related assets, or over the lease terms of capital leases, using, effective in fiscal year 1984, the straight-line method for financial reporting, and principally accelerated methods for tax reporting purposes. Previously, accelerated methods, where applicable, were also used for financial reporting purposes (see Note 2). For

U.S. income tax purposes, depreciation lives are based principally on the Class Life Asset Depreciation Range for additions, other than buildings, in the years 1973 through 1980, and on the Accelerated Cost Recovery System for all additions after 1980.

Discontinued facilities held for sale are carried at the lower of cost less accumulated depreciation or estimated realizable value, which aggregated $4.9 million and $3.6 million at October 31, 1984 and 1983, respectively, and were included in Other Assets in the accompanying Balance Sheet.

Pension Plans—The Corporation has pension plans covering substantially all of its employees. Pension expenses of the principal defined benefit plans consist of current service costs of such plans and amortization of the prior service costs and actuarial gains and losses over periods ranging from 10 to 30 years. The Corporation's policy is to fund at a minimum the amount required under the Employee Retirement Income Security Act of 1974.

Income Taxes—The consolidated tax provision is computed based on income and expenses recorded in the Statement of Operations. Prepaid or deferred taxes are recorded for the difference between such taxes and taxes computed for tax returns. The Corporation and its domestic subsidiaries file a consolidated federal income tax return. The operating results of Harnischfeger GmbH are included in the Corporation's U.S. income tax returns.

Additional taxes are provided on the earnings of foreign subsidiaries which are intended to be remitted to the Corporation. Such taxes are not provided on subsidiaries' unremitted earnings which are intended to be permanently reinvested.

Investment tax credits are accounted for under the flow-through method as a reduction of the income tax provision, if applicable, in the year the related asset is placed in service.

Reporting Format—Certain previously reported items have been conformed to the current year's presentation.

Note 2

Accounting Changes:

Effective November 1, 1983, the Corporation includes in its net sales products purchased from Kobe Steel, Ltd. and sold by the Corporation, to reflect more effectively the nature of the Corporation's transactions with Kobe. Previously only the gross margin on Kobe-originated equipment was included. During fiscal year 1984 such sales aggregated $28.0 million. Also, effective November 1, 1983, the financial statements of certain foreign subsidiaries are included on the basis of their fiscal years ended July 31. This change had the effect of increasing net sales by $5.4 million for the year ended October 31, 1984. The impact of these changes on net income was insignificant.

In 1984, the Corporation has computed depreciation expense on plants, machinery and equipment using the straight-line method for financial reporting purposes. Prior to 1984, the Corporation used principally accelerated methods for its U.S. operating plants. The cumulative effect of this change, which was applied retroactively to all assets previously subjected to accelerated depreciation, increased net income for 1984 by $11.0 million or $.93 per common and common equivalent share. The impact of the new method on income for the year 1984 before the cumulative effect was insignificant.

As a result of the review of its depreciation policy, the Corporation, effective November 1, 1983, has changed its estimated depreciation lives on certain U.S. plants, machinery and equipment and residual values on certain machinery and equipment, which increased net income for 1984 by $3.2 million or $.27 per share. No income tax effect was applied to this change.

The changes in accounting for depreciation were made to conform the Corporation's depreciation policy to those used by manufacturers in the Corporation's and similar industries and to provide a more equitable allocation of the cost of plants, machinery and equipment over their useful lives.

Note 3

Cash and Temporary Investments

Cash and temporary investments consisted of the following (in thousands of dollars):

| | October 31, | |
	1984	1983
Cash–in demand deposits	$2,155	$11,910
Cash–in special accounts principally to support letters of credit	4,516	—
Temporary investments	89,336	52,365
	$96,007	$64,275

Temporary investments consisted of short-term U.S. and Canadian treasury bills, money market funds, time and certificates of deposit, commercial paper and bank repurchase agreements and bankers' acceptances. Temporary investments are stated at cost plus accrued interest, which approximates market value.

Note 4

Long-Term Debt, Bank Credit Lines and Interest Expense

Outstanding long-term debt payable to unaffiliated lenders was as follows (in thousands of dollars):

| | October 31, | |
	1984	1983
Parent Company:		
15% Senior Notes due April 15, 1994	$47,700	$ —
12% Subordinated Debentures, with an effective interest rate of 16.3%; sinking fund redemption payments of $7,500 due annually on April 15 in 1994–2003, and final payment of $25,000 in 2004	100,000	—
Term Obligations – Insurance company debt:		
9% Notes	—	20,000
9 7/8 Notes	—	38,750
8 7/8 Notes	—	40,500
Bank debt, at 105% of prime	—	25,000
Paper purchase debt, at prime or LIBOR, plus 1 1/4%	—	18,519
9.23% Mortgage Note due monthly to April, 1998	4,327	4,481
	152,027	147,250
Consolidated Subsidiaries		
Notes payable to banks in German marks	—	9,889
Contract payable in 1985–1989, in South African rands, with imputed interest rate of 12%	1,024	—
Other	—	36
	153,051	157,175
Less: Amounts payable within one year	644	17,799
Unamortized discounts	23,857	284
Long-Term Debt – excluding amounts payable within one year	$128,550	$139,092

Note 5

Harnischfeger Credit Corporation and Cranetex, Inc.

Condensed financial information of Harnischfeger Credit Corporation ("Credit"), an unconsolidated wholly-owned finance subsidiary, accounted for under the equity method, was as follows (in thousands of dollars):

Balance Sheet	October 31, 1984	1983
Assets		
Cash and temporary investments	$404	$19,824
Finance receivables – net	4,335	11,412
Factored account note and current account receivable from parent company	—	8,836
Other assets	4,181	661
	$8,920	$40,733
Liabilities and Shareholders' Equity		
Debt payable	$ —	$32,600
Advances from parent company	950	—
Other liabilities	71	1,429
	1,021	34,029
Shareholders' equity	7,899	6,704
	$8,920	$40,733

Statement of Operations	Year Ended October 31, 1984	1983	1982
Revenues	$1,165	$2,662	$9,978
Less:			
Operating Expenses	1,530	3,386	14,613
Provision (credit) for income taxes	(1,560)	(222)	180
Net income (loss)	$1,195	$(502)	$(4,815)

Credit's purchases of finance receivables from the Corporation aggregated $1.1 million in 1984, $46.7 million in 1983 and $50.4 million in 1982. In 1982, Credit received income support of $4.0 million from the Corporation.

In 1982, the Corporation organized Cranetex, Inc. to assume certain assets and liabilities transferred by a former distributor of construction equipment, in settlement of the Corporation's and Credit's claims against the distributor and to continue the business on an interim basis until the franchise can be trans-ferred to a new distributor. The Corporation recorded provisions of $2.5 million in 1983 and $2.3 million in 1982 and Credit recorded a provision of $6.7 million in 1982, for credit losses incurred in the financing of equipment sold to the former distributor.

The condensed balance sheet of Cranetex, Inc. was as follows (in thousand of dollars):

	October 31, 1984	1983
Assets		
Cash	$143	$49
Accounts receivables	566	428
Inventory	2,314	3,464
Property and equipment	1,547	1,674
	$4,570	$5,615
Liabilities & Deficit		
Loans payable	$4,325	$6,682
Other liabilities	338	620
	4,663	7,302
Shareholders' (deficit), net of accounts and advances payable to parent company	(93)	(1,687)
	$4,570	$5,615

The net losses at Cranetex, Inc. of $.2 million in 1984, $2.1 million in 1983 and $1.0 million in 1982 were included in Equity in Earnings (loss) of Unconsolidated Companies in the Corporation's Statement of Operations.

Note 6

Transactions with Kobe Steel, Ltd. and ASEA Industrial Systems Inc.

Kobe Steel, Ltd. of Japan ("Kobe"), has been a licensee for certain of the Corporation's products since 1955, and has owned certain Harnischfeger Japanese construction equipment patents and technology since 1981. As of October 31, 1984, Kobe held 1,030,000 shares or 8.4% of the Corporation's outstanding Common Stock (see Note 13). Kobe also owns 25% of the capital stock of Harnischfeger of Australia Pty. Ltd., a subsidiary of the Corporation. This ownership appears as the minority interest on the Corporation's balance sheet.

Under agreements expiring in December, 1990 Kobe pays technical service fees on P&H mining equipment produced and sold under license from the Corporation, and trademark and marketing fees on sales of construction equipment outside of Japan. Net fee income received from Kobe was $4.3 million in 1984, $3.1 million in 1983, and $3.9 million in 1982; this income is included in Other Income in the accompanying Statement of Operations.

In October 1983, the Corporation entered into a ten-year agreement with Kobe under which Kobe agreed to supply the Corporation's requirements for construction cranes for sale in the United States as it phases out its own manufacture of cranes over the next several years, and to make the Corporation the exclusive distributor of Kobe-built cranes in the United States. The Agreement also involves a joint research and development program for construction equipment under which the Corporation agreed to spend at least $17 million over a three-year period and provided it does so, Kobe agreed to pay this amount to the Corporation. Sales of cranes outside the United States continue under the contract terms described in the preceding paragraph.

The Corporation's sales to Kobe, principally components for mining and construction equipment, excluding the R&D expenses discussed in the preceding paragraph, approximated $5.2 million, $10.5 million and $7.0 million during the three years ended October 31, 1984, 1983 and 1982, respectively. The purchases from Kobe of mining and construction equipment and components amounted to approximately $33.7 million, $15.5 million and $29.9 million during the three years ended October 31, 1984, 1983 and 1982, respectively, most of which were resold to customers (see Note 2).

The Corporation owns 19% of ASEA Industrial Systems Inc. ("AIS"), an electrical equipment company controlled by ASEA AB of Sweden. The Corporation's purchases of electrical components from AIS aggregated $11.2 million in 1984 and $6.1 million in 1983 and its sales to AIS approximated $2.6 million in 1984 and $3.8 million in 1983.

The Corporation believes that its transactions with Kobe and AIS were competitive with alternative sources of supply for each party involved.

Note 7

Inventories

Consolidated inventories consisted of the following (in thousand of dollars);

| | October 31, | |
	1984	1983
At lower of cost or market (FIFO method):		
Raw materials	$11,003	$11,904
Work in process and purchased parts	88,279	72,956
Finished goods	79,111	105,923
	178,393	190,783
Allowance to reduce inventories to cost on the LIFO method	(34,081)	(37,189)
	$144,312	$153,594

Inventories valued on the LIFO method represented approximately 82% of total inventories at both October 31, 1984 and 1983.

Inventory reductions in 1984, 1983 and 1982 resulted in a liquidation of LIFO inventory quantities carried at lower costs compared with the current cost of their acquisitions. The effect of these liquidations was to increase net income by 2.4 million or $.20 per common share in fiscal 1984, and to reduce the net loss by approximately $15.6 million or $1.54 per share in 1983, and by $6.7 million or $.66 per share in 1982; no income tax effect applied to the adjustment in 1984 and 1983.

Note 8

Accounts Receivable

Accounts receivable were net of allowances for doubtful accounts of $5.9 million and $6.4 million at October 31, 1984 and 1983, respectively.

Note 9

Research and Development Expense

Research and development expense incurred in the development of new products or significant improvements to existing products was $5.1 million in 1984 (net of amounts funded by Kobe Steel, Ltd.) $12.1 million in 1983 and $14.1 million in 1982.

Note 10

Foreign Operations

The net sales, net income (loss) and net assets of subsidiaries located in countries outside the United States and Canada and included in the consolidated financial statements were as follows (in thousands of dollars):

| | Year Ended October 31, | | |
	1984	1983	1982
Net sales	$78,074	$45,912	$69,216
Net income (loss) after minority interests	828	(1,191)	3,080
Corporation's equity in total net assets	17,734	7,716	7,287

Foreign currency transaction losses included in Cost of Sales were $2.7 million in 1984, $1.2 million in 1983 and $1.3 million in 1982.

Note 11

Pension Plans and Other Postretirement Benefits

Pension expense for all plans of the Corporation and its consolidated subsidiaries was $1.9 million in 1984, $6.5 million in 1983 and $12.2 million in 1982.

Accumulated plan benefits and plan net assets for the Corporation's U.S. defined benefit plans, at the beginning of the fiscal years 1984 and 1983, with the data for the Salaried Employees' Retirement Plan as in effect on August 1, 1984, were as follows (in thousands of dollars):

	1984	1983
Actuarial present value of accumulated plan benefits:		
Vested	$52,639	$108,123
Nonvested	2,363	5,227
	$55,002	$113,350
Net assets available for benefits:		
Assets of the Pension Trusts	$45,331	$112,075
Accrued contributions not paid to the Trusts	16,717	12,167
	$62,048	$124,242

The Salaried Employees' Retirement Plan, which covers substantially all salaried employees in the U.S., was restructured during 1984 due to overfunding of the Plan. Effective August 1, 1984, the Corporation terminated the existing plan and established a new plan which is substantially identical to the prior plan except for an improvement in the minimum pension benefit. All participants in the prior plan became fully vested upon its termination. All vested benefits earned through August 1, 1984 were covered through the purchase of individual annuities at a cost aggregating $36.7 million. The remaining plan assets, which totaled $39.3 million, reverted to the Corporation in cash upon receipt of regulatory approval of the prior plan termination from the Pension Benefit Guaranty Corporation. For financial reporting purposes, the new plan is considered to be a continuation of the terminated plan. Accordingly, the $39.3 million actuarial gain which resulted from the restructuring is included in Accrued Pension Costs in the accompanying Balance Sheet and is being amortized to income over a ten-year period commencing in 1984. For tax reporting purposes, the asset reversion will be treated as a fiscal 1985 transaction. The initial unfunded actuarial liability of the new plan, computed as of November 1, 1983, of $10.3 million is also included in Accrued Pension Costs.

In 1982 and 1983, the Pension Trusts purchased certain securities with effective yields of 13% and 12%, respectively, and dedicated these assets to the plan benefits of a substantial portion of the retired employees and certain terminated employees with deferred vested rights. These rates, together with 9% for active employees in 1984, 8% in 1983 and 7 1/4% in 1982, were the assumed rates of return used in determining the annual pension expense and the actuarial present value of accumulated plan benefits for the U.S. plans.

The effect of the changes in the investment return assumption rates for all U.S. plans, together with the 1984 restructuring of the U.S. Salaried Employees' Plan, was to reduce pension expense by approximately $4.0 million in 1984 and $2.0 million in 1983, and the actuarial present value of accumulated plan benefits by approximately $60.0 million in 1984. Pension expense in 1983 was also reduced $2.1 million from the lower level of active employees. Other actuarial gains, including higher than anticipated investment results, more than offset the additional pension costs resulting from plan changes and interest charges on balance sheet accruals in 1984 and 1983.

The Corporation's foreign pension plans do not determine the actuarial value of accumulated benefits or net assets available for retirement benefits as calculated and disclosed above. For those plans, the total of the plans' pension funds and balance sheet accruals approximated the actuarially computed value of vested benefits at both October 31, 1984 and 1983.

The Corporation generally provides certain health care and life insurance benefits for U.S. retired employees. Substantially all of the Corporation's current U.S. employees may become eligible for such benefits upon retirement. Life insurance benefits are provided either through the pension plans or separate group insurance arrangements. The cost of retiree health care and life insurance benefits, other than the benefits provided by the pension plans, is expensed as incurred; such costs approximated $2.6 million in 1984 and $1.7 million in 1983.

Note 12

Income Taxes

Domestic and foreign income (loss) before income tax effects was as follows (in thousands of dollars):

| | Year Ended October 31, | | |
	1984	1983	1982
Domestic	$1,578	$(35,412)	$(77,600)
Foreign			
Harnischfeger GmbH	432	(2,159)	(475)
All other	3,728	4,768	8,418
	4,160	2,609	7,943
Total income (loss) before income tax effects, equity items and cumulative effect of accounting change	$5,738	$(32,803)	$(69,657)

Provision (credit) for income taxes, on income (loss) before income tax effects, equity items and cumulative effect of accounting change, consisted of (in thousands of dollars):

	1984	1983	1982
Currently payable (refundable):			
Federal	$ —	$(7,957)	$(9,736)
State	136	297	70
Foreign	2,518	3,379	5,376
	2,654	(4,281)	(4,290)
Deferred (prepaid):			
Federal	—	2,955	2,713
State and foreign	(229)	(74)	(23)
	(229)	2,881	2,690
Provision (credit) for income taxes	$2,425	$(1,400)	$(1,600)

Unremitted earnings of foreign subsidiaries which have been or are intended to be permanently reinvested were $19.1 million at October 31, 1984. Such earnings, if distributed, would incur income tax expense of substantially less than the U.S. income tax rate as a result of previously paid foreign income taxes, provided that such foreign taxes would become deductible as foreign tax credits. No income tax provision was made in respect of the tax-deferred income of a consolidated subsidiary that has elected to be taxed as a domestic international sales corporation. The Deficit Reduction Act of 1984 provides for such income to become nontaxable effective December 31, 1984.

At October 31, 1984, the Corporation had federal tax operating loss carry-forwards of approximately $70.0 million, expiring in 1998 and 1999, for tax return purposes, and $88.0 million for book purposes. In addition, the Corporation had for tax purposes, foreign tax credit carry-forwards of $3.0 million (expiring in 1985 through 1989), and investment tax credit carry-forwards of $1.0 million (expiring in 1997 through 1999). For book purposes, tax credit carry-forwards approximately $8.0 million. The carry-forward will be available for the reduction of future income tax provisions, the extent and timing of which are not determinable.

Differences in income (loss) before income taxes for financial and tax purposes arise from timing differences between financial and tax reporting and relate to depreciation, consolidating eliminations for inter-company profits in inventories, and provisions, principally, for warranty, pension, compensated absences, product liability and plant closing costs.

During 1983 an examination of the Corporation's 1977–1981 federal income tax returns and certain refund claims was completed by the Internal Revenue Service, and as a result, a current credit for federal income taxes of $8.0 million was recorded in 1983, $3.0 million of which was applied to the reduction of prepaid income taxes.

In 1984, tax credits fully offset any federal income tax otherwise applicable to the year's income, and in 1983 and 1982, the relationship of the tax benefit to the pre-tax loss differed substantially from the U.S. statutory tax rate due principally to losses from the domestic operations for which only a partial federal tax benefit was available in 1982. Consequently, an analysis of deferred income taxes and variance from the U.S. statutory rate is not presented.

REPORT OF INDEPENDENT ACCOUNTANTS

Price Waterhouse
Milwaukee, Wisconsin
November 29, 1984

To the Directors and Shareholders of Harnischfeger Corporation

In our opinion, the financial statements, which appear on pages 18 to 34 of this report, present fairly the consolidated financial position of Harnischfeger Corporation and its subsidiaries at October 31, 1984 and 1983, and the results of their operations and the changes in their financial position for each of the three years in the period ended October 31, 1984, in conformity with generally accepted accounting principles consistently applied during the period except for the change, with which we concur, in the method of accounting for depreciation expense as described in Note 2 of this report. Our examinations of these statements were made in accordance with generally accepted auditing standards and accordingly included such tests of the accounting records and such other auditing procedures as we considered necessary in the circumstances.

Price Waterhouse

Chapter 4
Implementing Accounting Analysis

We learned in Chapter 3 that accounting analysis requires the analyst to adjust a firm's accounting numbers using cash flow and footnote information to "undo" any accounting distortions. This entails recasting a firm's financial statements using standard reporting nomenclature and formats. Firms frequently use somewhat different formats and terminology for presenting their financial results. Recasting the financial statements using a standard template, therefore, helps ensure that performance metrics used for financial analysis are calculated using comparable definitions across companies and over time.

Once the financial statements have been standardized, the analyst is ready to identify any distortions in financial statements. The analyst's primary focus should be on those accounting estimates and methods that the firm uses to measure its key success factors and risks. If there are differences in estimates and methods between firms or for the same firm over time, the analyst's job is to assess whether they reflect legitimate business differences or differences in managerial judgment or bias. Differences arising from managerial bias will require adjustment. In addition, even if accounting rules are adhered to consistently, accounting distortions can arise because accounting rules themselves do a poor job of capturing firm economics, creating opportunities for the analyst to adjust a firm's financials in a way that presents a more realistic picture of its performance.

This chapter shows how to recast the firm's financial statements into a template that uses standard terminology and classifications, discusses the most common types of accounting distortions that can arise, and shows how to make adjustments to the standardized financial statements to undo these distortions.

A balance sheet approach is used to identify whether there have been any distortions to assets, liabilities, or owners' equity. Once an asset and liability misstatement has been identified, the analyst can make adjustments to the balance sheet at the beginning and/or end of the current year, as well as any needed adjustments to revenues and expenses in the latest income statement. This approach ensures that the financial ratios used to evaluate a firm's most recent results and forecast its future performance are based on financial data that appropriately reflect its business economics.

In some instances, information taken from a firm's footnotes and cash flow statement enables the analyst to make a precise adjustment for an accounting distortion. However, for many types of accounting adjustments, the company does not disclose all of the information needed to perfectly undo the distortion, requiring the analyst to make an approximate adjustment to the financial statements.

RECASTING FINANCIAL STATEMENTS

Firms sometimes use different nomenclature and formats to present their financial results. For example, the asset goodwill can be reported separately using such titles as Goodwill, Excess of Cost Over Net Assets of Acquired Companies, and Cost in Excess of Fair Value, or it can be included in the line item Other Intangible Assets. Interest Income can be reported either as a subcategory of Revenues, shown lower down the income statement as part of Other Income and Expenses, or sometimes as Interest Expense, Net of Interest Income.

These differences in financial statement terminology, classifications, and formats can make it difficult to compare performance across firms, and sometimes to compare performance for the same firm over time. The first task for the analyst in accounting analysis is, therefore, to recast the financial statements into a common format. This involves designing a template for the balance sheet, income statement, and cash flow statement that can be used to standardize financial statements for any company. Tables 4-1, 4-2, and 4-3 present the format used throughout the book to standardize the income statement, balance sheet, and cash flow statement, respectively.

To create standardized financials for a particular company, the analyst classifies each line item in that firm's financial statements using the appropriate account name from

TABLE 4-1	Standardized Income Statement Format
Standard Income Statement Accounts	**Sample Line Items in Reported Accounts**
Sales	Revenues Membership fees Commissions Licenses
Cost of Sales	Cost of merchandise sold Cost of products sold Cost of revenues Cost of services Depreciation on manufacturing facilities
SG&A	General and administrative Marketing & sales Salaries and benefits Servicing and maintenance Depreciation on selling and administrative facilities
Other Operating Expense	Amortization of intangibles Product development Research & development Provision for losses on credit sales Pre-opening costs Special charges

Net Interest Expense (Income)
  Interest Income
  Interest Expense
	
	Interest income
	Interest expense

(continued)

Standard Income Statement Accounts	Sample Line Items in Reported Accounts
Investment Income	Equity income (from associates) Dividend income Rental income[1]
Other Income	Gains on sale of investments/long-term assets Foreign exchange gains Pre-tax gains from accounting changes
Other Expense	Losses on sale of investments/long-term assets Foreign exchange losses Pre-tax losses from accounting changes Restructuring charges Merger expenses Asset impairments
Minority Interest	Minority interest
Tax Expense	Provision for taxes
Unusual Items (after tax)	Any gains or losses reported on an after-tax basis, such as Extraordinary items Non-recurring charges Effect of accounting changes

the above templates. This may require using information from the footnotes to ensure that accounts are classified appropriately. An example, applying the above template to standardize the financial statements for the year ending January 2006 for discount retailer Wal-Mart Stores, Inc., is shown in the appendix at the end of this chapter.

Once the financials have been standardized, the analyst can evaluate whether accounting adjustments are needed to correct any distortions in assets, liabilities, or equity, as discussed below.

ASSET DISTORTIONS

Accountants define assets as resources that a firm owns or controls as a result of past business transactions, and which are expected to produce future economic benefits that can be measured with a reasonable degree of certainty. Assets can take a variety of forms, including cash, marketable securities, receivables from customers, inventory, fixed assets, long-term investments in other companies, and intangibles.

Distortions in asset values generally arise because there is ambiguity about whether

- The firm owns or controls the economic resources in question,
- The economic resources are likely to provide future economic benefits that can be measured with reasonable certainty, or
- The fair values of assets are lower or higher than their book values.

TABLE 4-2   Standardized Balance Sheet Format

Assets

Standard Balance Sheet Accounts	Sample Line Items in Reported Accounts
Cash and Marketable Securities	Cash Short-term investments Time deposits
Accounts Receivable	Accounts/trade receivables (net) Trade debtors
Inventory	Inventory Finished goods Raw materials Work-in-process Stocks
Deferred Taxes – Current Asset	Deferred income taxes – current
Other Current Assets	Prepaid expenses Taxes refundable Current assets of discontinued operations Due from affiliates Due from employees
Long-Term Tangible Assets	Plant, property & equipment Land Non-current assets of discontinued operations

Liabilities and Equity

Standard Balance Sheet Accounts	Sample Line Items in Reported Accounts
Short-Term Debt	Notes payable Current portion of long-term debt Current portion of capital lease obligation
Accounts Payable	Accounts/trade payables Trade creditors
Other Current Liabilities	Accrued expenses Accrued liabilities Taxes payable Dividends payable Deferred (unearned) revenue Customer advances
Deferred Taxes – Current Liability	Deferred income taxes – current
Long-Term Debt	Long-term debt Senior term notes Subordinated debt Capital lease obligations Convertible debt Pension/post-retirement benefit obligation
Deferred Taxes – Long-Term Liability	Deferred income taxes – long-term

(continued)

Standard Balance Sheet Accounts	Sample Line Items in Reported Accounts
Long-Term Intangible Assets	Goodwill Software development costs Deferred financing costs Deferred subscriber acquisition costs Deferred charges Trademarks License rights
Deferred Taxes – LT Asset	Deferred income taxes – long-term
Other Long-Term Assets	Long-term investments Long-term receivables Investment in sales-type or direct-financing leases
Other Long-Term Liabilities (non-interest bearing)	Non-current deferred (unearned) revenues Other non-current liabilities
Minority Interest	Minority interest
Preferred Stock	Preferred stock Preferred convertible stock
Common Shareholders' Equity	Common stock Additional paid-in capital Capital in excess of par Treasury stock Retained earnings Cumulative foreign currency gains and losses Accumulated other comprehensive income

| TABLE 4-3 | Standardized Cash Flow Statement Format |

Standard Cash Flow Statement Accounts	Sample Line Items in Reported Accounts
Net Income	
Non-operating Gains (Losses)	Gain (loss) on sale of investments/non-current assets Cumulative effect of accounting changes Gain (loss) on foreign exchange Extraordinary gains (losses)
Long-Term Operating Accruals	Depreciation and amortization Deferred revenues/costs Deferred income taxes Impairment of non-current assets Other non-cash charges to operations Equity earnings of affiliates/unconsolidated subs, net of cash received Minority interest Stock bonus awards

Net (Investments in) or Liquidation of Operating Working Capital	Changes in:
	    Trade accounts receivable
	    Other receivables
	    Prepaid expenses
	    Trade accounts payable
	    Accrued expenses (liabilities)
	    Due from affiliates
	    Accounts payable and accrued expenses
	    Refundable/payable income taxes
	    Inventories
	    Provision for doubtful accounts and bad debts
	    Other current liabilities
	    Other current assets

Net (Investment in) or Liquidation of Operating Long-Term Assets	Purchase/sale of non-current assets Acquisition of research and development Acquisition/sale of business Capital expenditures Equity investments Acquisition of subsidiary stock Capitalization of computer software development costs Cost in excess of the fair value of net assets acquired Investment in sales-type and direct financing leases
Net Debt (Repayment) or Issuance	Principal payments on debt Borrowings (repayments) under credit facility Issuance (repayment) of long-term debt Net increase (decrease) in short-term borrowings Notes payable

(continued)

Standard Cash Flow Statement Accounts	Sample Line Items in Reported Accounts
Dividend (Payments)	Cash dividends paid on common stock Cash dividends paid on preferred stock Distributions
Net Stock (Repurchase) or Issuance	Proceeds from issuance of common stock Issue of common stock for services Issue (redemption) of preferred securities Issue of subsidiary equity Purchase (issue) of treasury stock

Who owns or controls resources?

For most resources used by a firm, ownership or control is relatively straightforward—the firm using the resource owns the asset. However, some types of transactions make it difficult to assess who owns a resource. For example, does the lessor or the lessee own or control a resource that has been leased? Or consider a firm that discounts a customer receivable with a bank. If the bank has recourse against the firm should the customer default, is the real owner of the receivable the bank or the company?

Accountants frequently use mechanical rules to determine whether a company owns or controls an asset. While these rules make it easy for accountants to implement accounting standards, they also permit managers to "groom" transactions to satisfy their own financial reporting objectives. For example, U.S. rules on lease accounting permit essentially the same lease transaction to be structured in such a way that the leased asset is reported on the balance sheet of the lessee, the lessor, or on neither party's balance sheet. Accounting analysis, therefore, involves assessing whether a firm's reported assets adequately reflect the key resources that are under its control, and whether adjustments are required to compare its performance with that of competitors.

Asset ownership issues also arise indirectly from the application of rules for revenue recognition. Firms are permitted to recognize revenues only when their product has been shipped or their service has been provided to the customer. Revenues are then considered "earned," and the customer has a legal commitment to pay for the product or service. As a result, for the seller, recognition of revenue frequently coincides with "ownership" of a receivable that is shown as an asset on its balance sheet. Therefore, accounting analysis that raises questions about whether or not revenues have been earned often affects the valuation of assets.

Ambiguity over whether a company owns an asset creates a number of opportunities for accounting analysis:

- Despite management's best intentions, financial statements sometimes do a poor job of reflecting the firm's economic assets since it is difficult for accounting rules to capture all of the subtleties associated with ownership and control.
- Because accounting rules on ownership and control permit managers to groom transactions such that essentially similar transactions are reported in very different ways, important assets may be omitted from the balance sheet even though the firm bears many of the economic risks of ownership.
- There may be legitimate differences in opinion between managers and analysts over residual ownership risks borne by the company, leading to differences in opinion over reporting for these assets.
- Aggressive revenue recognition, which boosts reported earnings, is likely to affect asset values.

Can economic benefits be measured with reasonable certainty?

It is almost always difficult to accurately forecast the future benefits associated with capital outlays because the world is uncertain. A company does not know whether a competitor will offer a new product or service that makes its own offering obsolete. It does not know whether the products manufactured at a new plant will be the type that customers want to buy. A company does not know whether changes in oil prices will make the oil drilling equipment that it manufactures less valuable.

Accounting rules deal with these challenges by stipulating the types of resources that can be recorded as assets and those that cannot. For example, the economic benefits from research and development (R&D) are generally considered highly uncertain—research projects may never deliver promised new products, the products they generate may not be economically viable, or products may be made obsolete by competitors' research. Accounting rules in most countries, therefore, require that R&D outlays be expensed.[2] In contrast, the economic benefits from plant acquisitions are considered less uncertain and are required to be capitalized.

Rules that require the immediate expensing of outlays for some key resources may be good accounting, but they create a challenge for the analyst—they make it more difficult to infer financial performance from the financial statements. If all firms expense R&D, financial statements will reflect differences in R&D success only when new products are commercialized rather than during the development process. The analyst may attempt to correct for this distortion by capitalizing key R&D outlays and adjusting the value of the intangible asset based on R&D updates.[3]

Have fair values of assets declined below book value?

An asset is impaired when its fair value falls below its book value. Of course, markets for many long-term operating assets are illiquid and incomplete, making it highly subjective to infer their fair values. Consequently, considerable management judgment is involved in deciding whether an asset is impaired and determining the value of any impairment loss.

For the analyst, this raises the possibility that asset values are misstated. In most countries, accounting rules require that a loss be recorded for permanent asset impairments. However, U.S. accounting rules (SFAS 144) permit a certain amount of asset overstatement since the test for asset impairment compares the asset's book value to the expected value of *undiscounted* (rather than *discounted*) future cash flows expected to be generated from future use and sale of the asset. This can create situations where no financial statement loss is reported for an asset that is economically impaired.

In addition, the task of determining whether there has been an asset impairment and valuing the impairment is delegated to management, with oversight by the firm's auditors. This leaves opportunities for potential management bias in valuing assets and for legitimate differences in opinion between managers and analysts over asset valuations. In most cases, management bias will lead to overstated assets since managers will prefer not to recognize an impairment. However, managers can also bias asset values downward by overstating the current level of impairment, thereby reducing future expenses and increasing future earnings.

Opportunities for accounting adjustments can therefore arise in the situations discussed above if

- Accounting rules do not do a good job of capturing the firm's economics,
- Managers use their discretion to distort the firm's performance, or
- There are legitimate differences in opinion between managers and analysts about economic uncertainties facing the firm that are reflected in asset values.

OVERSTATED ASSETS

Asset overstatements are likely to arise when managers have incentives to increase reported earnings. Thus, adjustments to assets also typically require adjustments to the income statement in the form of either increased expenses or reduced revenues. The most common forms of asset (and earnings) overstatement are the following:

1. *Delayed write-downs of current assets.* If current assets become impaired, that is, their realizable values fall below their book values, accounting rules generally require that they be written down to their fair values. Current asset impairments also affect earnings since write-offs are charged directly to earnings. Deferring current asset write-downs is, therefore, one way for managers to boost reported profits.[4] Analysts that cover firms where management of inventories and receivables is a key success factor (e.g., the fashion retail and consumer electronics industries) need to be particularly cognizant of this form of earnings management. If managers over-buy or over-produce in the current period, they are likely to have to offer customers discounts to get rid of surplus inventories. In addition, providing customers with credit carries risks of default. Warning signs for delays in current asset write-downs include growing days' inventory and days' receivable, write-downs by competitors, and business downturns for a firm's major customers.

2. *Underestimated reserves (e.g., allowances for bad debts or loan losses).* Managers make estimates of expected customer defaults on accounts receivable and loans and create reserves to cover these anticipated costs. If managers underestimate the value of these reserves, assets and earnings will be overstated. Warning signs of inadequate allowances include growing days' receivable, business downturns for a firm's major clients, and growing loan delinquencies.

3. *Accelerated recognition of revenues (increasing receivables).* Managers typically have the best information on the uncertainties governing revenue recognition—whether a product or service has been provided to customers and whether cash collection is reasonably likely. However, managers may also have incentives to accelerate the recognition of revenues, boosting reported earnings for the period. Accounts receivable and earnings will then be overstated. Aggressive revenue recognition is one of the most popular forms of earnings management cited by the SEC. Warning signs include growth in receivables outpacing sales growth, and increasing days' receivable.

4. *Delayed write-downs of long-term assets.* Deteriorating industry or firm economic conditions can affect the value of long-term assets as well as current assets. Firms are required to recognize impairments in the values of long-term assets when they arise. However, since second-hand markets for long-term assets are typically illiquid and incomplete, estimates of asset valuations and impairment are inherently subjective. This is particularly true for intangible assets such as goodwill. As a result, managers can use their reporting judgment to delay write-downs on the balance sheet and avoid showing impairment charges in the income statement.[5] This issue is likely to be particularly critical for asset-intensive firms in volatile markets (e.g., airlines) or for firms that follow a strategy of aggressive growth through acquisitions.[6] Warning signs of impairments in long-term assets include declining long-term asset turnover, declines in return on assets to levels lower than the weighted average cost of capital, write-downs by other firms in the same industry that have also suffered deteriorating asset use, and overpayment for or unsuccessful integration of key acquisitions.

5. *Understated depreciation/amortization on long-term assets.* Managers make estimates of asset lives, salvage values, and amortization schedules for depreciable

long-term assets. If these estimates are optimistic, long-term assets and earnings will be overstated. This issue is likely to be most pertinent for firms in asset-intensive businesses (e.g., airlines, utilities). A comparison of the firm's policies to those of its industry competitors with a similar asset base and strategy will help an analyst identify potential overstatements.

Examples of How to Correct for Asset Overstatement

We illustrate some of the distortions that lead to overstated assets and the types of corrections that the analyst can make to reduce bias in the financial statements.

Delayed Write-Downs of Current Assets

In recent years, the popularity of portable MP3 players has increased tremendously. Apple has dominated the market with its iPod player and managed to maintain a U.S. market share of over 75 percent. Rivals such as Creative Technology, Sony, Microsoft, and Samsung have entered the market aggressively in an attempt to grab a share of the market. Key risks facing these firms include rapid changes in MP3 player technology and inventory management in the face of both relentless competition and potential technological obsolescence.

Singapore-based Creative Technology posted impressive revenue growth from the second half of 2003 through the first quarter of 2005, with predictable spikes in holiday season sales in both 2003 and 2004. However, gross margins steadily declined from 35 percent to 23 percent over this period. A more worrying trend was the firm's inventory management. Growth in inventory far outpaced growth in sales, leading to a 58 percent increase in days' inventory, from 100 days for the quarter ending September 30, 2003, to 158 days for the quarter ending March 31, 2005. Inventory at the end of March 2006 was valued at $451.2 million, up from $183.9 million nine months prior. This increase in inventory raises questions for analysts about Creative Technology's inventory value and potential obsolescence.

An analyst can assess whether inventory is impaired by talking with suppliers and customers, observing the speed of new product launches for MP3 players and the performance of other firms in the industry, and understanding the general sentiment about expected market growth. Based on this research, an analyst can judge whether Creative Technology's slowdown in inventory turnover is likely to persist, whether there are serious technological risks for the current inventory and, if so, whether and how large an impairment charge is appropriate. Prior to the release of earnings for the June 31, 2005, quarter, several analysts raised questions about the growth in Creative Technology's inventory and anticipated that the company would be forced to record future inventory impairment charges.

Once an analyst concludes that inventory is overstated, the challenge is to estimate the magnitude of the write-down. For Creative Technology, this depends on the price discounts that are required to move slow-moving products. The after-tax cost of the impairment will reduce current and retained earnings. In addition, the tax effect of the impairment will lower the Tax Expense and reduce the Deferred Tax Liability since the inventory write-down is not recorded for tax purposes until the inventory is subsequently sold. Creative Technology enjoys a special status in Singapore that exempts certain elements of revenues from income tax. However, for illustrative purposes, using the local statutory tax rate of 20 percent, the financial statements could be modified as follows for an assumed inventory overstatement of $25 million:

		Adjustment
($ Millions)	Assets	Liabilities & Equity
Balance Sheet		
Inventory	−25.0	
Deferred Tax Liability		−8.8
Common Shareholders' Equity		−16.2
Income Statement		
Cost of Sales		+25.0
Tax Expense		−8.8
Net Income		−16.2

In August 2005, Creative Technology announced that it would take a $20 million charge against inventory to reflect a decline in prices of certain components used to manufacture MP3 players. In the quarter ending March 31, 2006, the company took another inventory write-down due to a steep drop in the price of components such as flash memory and hard drives. Not surprisingly, Creative Technology's share price tumbled in response to news of the write-downs—from a high of close to $17 per share in early 2005, the stock traded down to below $5 per share in mid-2006.

Underestimated Reserves

In late 2006, Community Health Systems (CHS) was the leading operator of general and acute care hospitals in nonurban communities in the U.S. The company owned 77 hospitals in 22 states, had a dominant market share in more than 85 percent of the markets it served, and in fiscal 2005 generated $3.7 billion in revenues.

CHS received payments for its services from governmental agencies, private insurers, and directly from the patients it served. Medicare was the single largest revenue provider, accounting for approximately 33 percent of net operating revenue in the quarter ended June 30, 2006. Managed care provided a further 25 percent of revenues, 10 percent came from Medicaid, and 13 percent was from self-pay sources (uninsured patients, patient deductibles, co-insurance payments not covered by the insurer, and patients whose insurance providers had failed to pay).

To estimate receivable allowances, CHS used an aging analysis which did not differentiate between risk characteristics of different classes of patients. For example, it failed to reflect that collection rates were lowest for self-pay accounts. As a result, in the 12-month period from June 2005 to June 2006, the company held the allowance for doubtful accounts as a percentage of gross receivables steady at 33 percent, even though there was an increase in the proportion of revenues and receivables from self-pay patients.

If an analyst decides that receivable allowances are understated, balance sheet adjustments are made to Accounts Receivable (for the gross change in reserve), to the Deferred Tax Liability (for the tax impact of the increased expense), and to Retained Earnings (for the net effect). For example, if an analyst decided that allowances for doubtful accounts for Community Health should be 36 percent rather than 33 percent, Accounts Receivable would have to be reduced by $37.5 million. Given the company's effective tax rate of 39 percent, this would reduce earnings and equity by $22.9 million and the Deferred Tax Liability by 14.6 million. The adjustment to the June 30, 2006, financial statements would, therefore, be as follows:

($ Millions)	Adjustment	
	Assets	Liabilities & Equity
Balance Sheet		
Accounts Receivable	−37.5	
Deferred Tax Liability		−14.6
Common Shareholders' Equity		−22.9
Income Statement		
Provision for Doubtful Accounts		+37.5
Tax Expense		−14.6
Net Income		−22.9

At the end of October 2006, CHS announced its results for the quarter ending September 30, 2006. The financial results included a $65 million increase in the allowance for bad debts and a change in methodology for estimating the allowance. Under the new method, CHS reserved a percentage of all self-pay accounts receivable based on their collection history. The company reported that the new methodology would better reflect changes in payor mix and historical collection patterns and allow it to respond to changes in trends. The share price declined 10 percent on the day the earnings were announced.

Accelerated Recognition of Revenues

In November 1999 and January 2000, analysts at the Center for Financial Research and Analysis (CFRA) raised questions about the propriety of revenue recognition for MicroStrategy, a software company. MicroStrategy recognized revenues from the sale of licenses "after execution of a licensing agreement and shipment of the product, provided that no significant Company obligations remain and the resulting receivable is deemed collectible by management."[7] CFRA analysts were concerned about MicroStrategy's booking two contracts worth $27 million as quarterly revenues when the contracts were not announced until several days after the quarter's end. If the analysts decided to adjust for these distortions, the following changes would have to be made to MicroStrategy's financial reports:
1. In the quarter that the contracts were booked, Sales and Accounts Receivable would both decline by $27 million.
2. Cost of Sales would decline and Inventory would increase to reflect the reduction in sales. The value of the Cost of Sales/Inventory adjustment can be estimated by multiplying the sales adjustment by the ratio of cost of sales to sales. For MicroStrategy, cost of license revenues is only 3 percent of license revenues, indicating that the adjustment would be modest ($0.8 m). Also, since MicroStrategy does not report any inventory, the balance sheet adjustment would be to prepaid expenses, which are included in Other Current Assets on the standardized balance sheet.

3. The decline in pretax income would result in a lower Tax Expense in the company's financial reporting books (but presumably not in its tax books). Consequently, the Deferred Tax Liability would have to be reduced. MicroStrategy's marginal tax rate was 35 percent, implying that the decline in the Tax Expense and Deferred Tax Liability would be \$9.2 million [(\$27 − 0.8) × .35].

The full effect of the adjustment on the quarterly financial statements would therefore be as follows:

	Adjustment	
(\$ millions)	Assets	Liabilities & Equity
Balance Sheet		
Accounts Receivable	−27.0	
Other Current Assets	+0.8	
Deferred Tax Liability		−9.2
Common Shareholders' Equity		−17.0
Income Statement		
Sales		−27.0
Cost of Sales		−0.8
Tax Expense		−9.2
Net Income		−17.0

Of course, provided the contracts were legitimate transactions, the above adjustments imply that forecasts of next quarter's revenues should include the \$27 million worth of contracts.

In March 2000, MicroStrategy confirmed that the CFRA analysts' suspicions about aggressive revenue recognition were legitimate. The company announced that it had "recorded revenue on certain contracts in one reporting period where customer signature and delivery had been completed, but where the contract may not have been fully executed by the Company in that reporting period."[8] After reviewing all licensing contracts near the end of the prior three years, MicroStrategy was forced to restate its financial statements to correct for the improprieties. The outcome was that accounts receivable for 1999 were reduced from \$61.1 million to \$37.6 million, leading to a dramatic drop in the company's stock price.

Delayed Write-Downs of Long-Term Assets

Consider the widely acclaimed merger between AOL and Time Warner. The combination of the two companies was justified as enabling AOL to cross-sell Time Warner's content (film, news, etc.) to its large subscriber base, a win for both companies. Careful strategic analysis, however, would raise some questions about the merits of the deal. Earlier combinations of content providers and distributors in the entertainment industry (e.g., Disney's acquisition of ABC) had faced difficulties in realizing their potential. Why would the outcome of an AOL–Time Warner merger be any different? Also, it was not clear why AOL had to buy Time Warner to access its content. Why couldn't AOL simply sign a long-term licensing agreement for content with Time Warner? Finally, the merger raised questions about the relationships AOL and Time Warner had with existing customers and suppliers. For example, would Time Warner still be able to sell its content to AOL's competitors (e.g., Microsoft), or would its own market be narrowed? Would AOL still be able to negotiate content deals with Time Warner's competitors? If Time Warner's content became stale, would AOL be committed to continue supplying it to its subscribers, leading to a decline in the value of both firms?

The questions about the economic benefits from the merger were quickly answered when Internet sector stocks crashed in mid-2000. AOL subsequently struggled to retain and grow its subscriber base and encountered more difficulty than expected in developing a successful business model to take advantage of Time Warner's content. As a result, in its December 31, 2001, report, the new company was forced to recognize that the $128 billion of goodwill recorded under the merger was impaired and would have to be written down by $54 billion at the end of the following quarter (March 2002).

This raised several issues for analyzing AOL Time Warner. First, given the questionable strategic rationale for the merger in the first place, did the initial $128 billion of goodwill ever represent a true economic asset? If not, when would it make sense to recognize the impairment of goodwill—prior to December 31, 2001, in the December 31 financials, or when the company subsequently reported the decline in value (March 2002)? Second, was the $54 billion write-down adequate given the magnitude of the Internet stock market crash, which indicated that investors as a whole had radically lowered their expectations for Internet stocks such as AOL?

If an analyst decided to record the $54 billion write-down in the December 2001 financials, it would be necessary to make the following balance sheet adjustments:

1. Reduce Long-term Intangible Assets by $54 billion.
2. Reduce the Deferred Tax Liability for the tax effect of the write-down. Assuming a 35 percent tax rate, this amounts to $19 billion.
3. Reduce Common Shareholders' Equity for the after-tax effect of the write-down ($35 billion).

| | Adjustment | |
($ billions)	Assets	Liabilities & Equity
Balance Sheet		
Long-Term Intangible Assets	−54	
Deferred Tax Liability		−19
Common Shareholders' Equity		−35
Income Statement		
Other Expenses		+54
Tax Expense		−19
Net Income		−35

Note that the write-down of depreciable assets at the beginning of the year requires the analyst to also estimate the write-down's impact on depreciation and amortization expense for the year, impacting net income. For AOL Time Warner, since the asset was goodwill, which was no longer amortized (see SFAS 142), no such expense adjustment was required.

At the end of 2002, AOL announced the write-down of a further $45.5 billion of goodwill, and many of the top AOL managers that had advocated the merger in the first place were no longer with the company.

UNDERSTATED ASSETS

Asset understatements typically arise when managers have incentives to deflate reported earnings. This may occur when the firm is performing exceptionally well and managers decide to store away some of the current strong earnings for a rainy day. Income smoothing, as it has come to be known, can be implemented by over-stating current period expenses (and understating the value of assets) during good times. Asset (and expense) understatements can also arise in a particularly bad year, when managers decide to "take a bath" by understating current period earnings to create the appearance of a turnaround in following years. Accounting analysis involves judging whether managers have understated assets (and also income) and, if necessary, adjusting the balance sheet and income statement accordingly.

Asset understatements can also arise because of accounting rules themselves. In many countries, accounting standards require firms to expense outlays for R&D and advertising because, even though they may create future value for owners, their outcomes are highly uncertain. Asset understatements can also arise when managers have incentives to understate liabilities. For example, if a firm records lease trans-actions as operating leases or if it discounts receivables with recourse, neither the assets nor the accompanying obligations are shown on its balance sheet. Yet, in some instances, this accounting treatment does not reflect the underlying economics of the transactions—the lessee may effectively own the leased assets, and the firm that sells receivables may still bear all of the risks associated with ownership. The ana-lyst will then want to adjust the balance sheet (and also the income statement) for these effects.

The most common forms of asset (and earnings) understatement arise when there are the following:

1. *Overstated write-downs of current assets.* Managers potentially have an incen-tive to overstate current asset write-downs either during years of exceptionally strong performance, or when the firm is financially distressed. By overstating current asset impairments and overstating expenses in the current period, man-agers can show lower future expenses, boosting earnings in years of sub-par performance or when a turnaround is needed. Overstated current asset write-downs can also arise when managers are less optimistic about the firm's future prospects than the analyst.

2. *Overestimated reserves (e.g., allowances for bad debts or loan losses).* If man-agers overestimate reserves for bad debts or loan losses, accounts receivable and loans will be understated.

3. *Overstated write-downs of long-term assets.* Overly pessimistic management estimates of long-term asset impairments reduce current period earnings and boost earnings in future periods.

4. *Overstated depreciation/amortization on long-term assets.* Firms that use tax depreciation estimates of asset lives, salvage values, or amortization rates are likely to amortize assets more rapidly than justifiable given the assets' economic usefulness, leading to long-term asset understatements.

5. *Lease assets off balance sheet.* Assessing whether a lease arrangement should be considered a rental contract (and hence recorded using the operating method) or equivalent to a purchase (and hence shown as a capital lease) is subjective. It depends on whether the lessee has effectively accepted most of the risks of ownership, such as obsolescence and physical deterioration. To standardize the reporting of lease transactions, U.S. accounting standards have created clear criteria for distinguishing between the two types. Under SFAS 13, a lease

transaction is equivalent to an asset purchase if any of the following conditions hold: (1) ownership of the asset is transferred to the lessee at the end of the lease term, (2) the lessee has the option to purchase the asset for a bargain price at the end of the lease term, (3) the lease term is 75 percent or more of the asset's expected useful life, and (4) the present value of the lease payments is 90 percent or more of the fair value of the asset. However, although the criteria for reporting leases are objective, they create opportunities for management to circumvent the spirit of the distinction between capital and operating leases, potentially leading to the understatement of lease assets.[9] This is likely to be an important issue for the analysis of asset-intensive industries where there are options for leasing (e.g., airlines and retail chains).[10]

6. *Discounted receivables off balance sheet even though the firm still retains considerable collection risk.* Under current U.S. accounting rules (SFAS 140), receivables that are discounted with a financial institution are considered "sold" if the "seller" cedes control over the receivables to the financier. Control is surrendered if the receivables are beyond the reach of the seller's creditors should the seller file for bankruptcy, if the financier has the right to pledge or sell the receivables, and if the seller has no commitment to repurchase the receivables. The seller can then record the discount transaction as an asset sale. Otherwise it is viewed as a financing transaction that generates a liability for the seller. However, just because a firm has "sold" receivables for financial reporting purposes does not necessarily mean that it is off the hook for credit risks. Financial institutions that discount receivables often have recourse against the seller, requiring the seller to continue to estimate bad debt losses. In this event, U.S. rules permit the transaction to be reported as an asset sale only when the seller satisfies the above conditions for surrendering control of the receivables and has experience in estimating the value of the recourse liability (i.e., allowances for credit and refinancing risks). In extreme cases, where there is significant uncertainty about the value of the recourse liability, the analyst has to decide whether to restate the firm's financial statements by returning the "sold" receivables to the balance sheet. As discussed later in this chapter, this will also increase the firm's liabilities, and it will affect its income statement since any gains and losses on the sale need to be excluded, and interest income on the notes receivables and interest expense on the loan need to be recorded each year.

7. *Key intangible assets, such as R&D and trademarked brands, not reported on the balance sheet.* Some firms' most important assets are excluded from the balance sheet. Examples include investments in R&D, software development outlays, and brands and membership bases that are created through advertising and promotions. Accounting rules in most countries specifically prohibit the capitalization of R&D outlays and membership acquisition costs, primarily because it is believed that the benefits associated with such outlays are too uncertain.[11] New products may never reach the market due to technological infeasibility or to the introduction of superior products by competitors; and new members that sign up for a service as a result of a promotions campaign may subsequently quit. Expensing the cost of intangibles has two implications for analysts. First, the omission of intangible assets from the balance sheet inflates measured rates of return on capital (either return on assets or return on equity).[12] For firms with key omitted intangible assets, this omission has important implications for forecasting long-term performance; unlike firms with no intangibles, competitive forces will not cause their rates of return to fully revert to the cost of capital over time. For example, pharmaceutical firms have shown very high rates of return over many decades, in part because of the impact of R&D accounting. A second effect of expensing outlays for intangibles is that it makes it more difficult for the analyst to assess whether the firm's

business model works. Under the matching concept, operating profit is a meaningful indicator of the success of a firm's business model since it compares revenues and the expenses required to generate them. Immediately expensing outlays for intangible assets runs counter to matching and, therefore, makes it more difficult to judge a firm's operating performance. Consistent with this, research shows that investors view R&D and advertising outlays as assets rather than expenses.[13] Understated intangible assets are likely to be important for firms in pharmaceutical, software, branded consumer products, and subscription businesses.

Examples of How to Correct for Asset Understatement

We illustrate some of the types of distortions that understate assets, and show corrections that the analyst can make to ensure that assets are reflected appropriately.

Overstated Depreciation for Long-Term Assets

In 2005 Lufthansa, the German national airline, reported that it depreciated its aircraft over 12 years on a straight-line basis, with an estimated residual value of 15 percent of initial cost. Air France-KLM, an airline formed by the merger of the French airline Air France and the Dutch airline KLM, is one of Lufthansa's main competitors. In contrast to Lufthansa, Air France-KLM reported that its aircraft depreciation was also estimated using the straight-line method but assuming an average life of 20 years and no salvage value.[14]

For the analyst, these differences raise several questions. Do Lufthansa and Air France-KLM fly different types of routes, potentially explaining the differences in their depreciation policies? Alternatively, do they have different asset management strategies? For example, does Lufthansa use newer planes to attract more business travelers, to lower maintenance costs, or to lower fuel costs? If there do not appear to be operating differences that explain the differences in the two firms' depreciation rates, the analyst may well decide that it is necessary to adjust the depreciation rates for one or both firms to ensure that their performance is comparable.

To adjust for this effect, the analyst could choose to decrease Lufthansa's depreciation rates to match those of Air France-KLM. The following financial statement adjustments would then be required in Lufthansa's financial statements:
1. Increase the book value of the fleet at the beginning of the year to adjust for the relatively high depreciation rates that had been used in the past. This will also require an offsetting increase in equity (retained earnings) and in the deferred tax liability.
2. Reduce the depreciation expense (and increase the book value of the fleet) to reflect the lower depreciation for the current year, and increase the tax expense (in 2005, Lufthansa's marginal tax rate was 35 percent.) On the balance sheet, show an increase in equity and deferred tax liability.

Note that these changes are designed to show Lufthansa's results as if it had always used the same depreciation assumptions as Air France-KLM rather than to reflect a change in the assumptions for the current year going forward. This enables the analyst to compare ratios that use assets (e.g., return on assets) for the two companies.

At the beginning of 2005, Lufthansa reported in its footnotes that its fleet of aircraft had originally cost €15,350 m, and that accumulated depreciation was €8,399 m. This implies that the average life of Lufthansa's fleet was 7.72 years, calculated as follows:

€ Millions (unless otherwise noted)		
Aircraft cost, 01/01/05	15,350	Reported
Depreciable cost	13,048	Cost × (1 − .15)
Accumulated depreciation, 01/01/05	8,399	Reported
Accumulated depreciation/Depreciable cost	64.4%	
Depreciable life	12 years	Reported
Average age of aircraft	7.72	12 × .644 years

If Lufthansa used the same useful life and salvage estimates as Air France-KLM, Accumulated Depreciation would have been only €5,929 m, thereby increasing the company's Long-term Tangible Assets by €2,470 m and Common Shareholders' Equity by €1,606 m.

€ Millions (unless otherwise noted)		
Aircraft cost, 01/01/05 date	15,350	Reported
Depreciable cost	15,350	No residual value
Depreciable life	20 years	Air France-KLM
Accumulated depreciation, 01/01/05	5,929	Over 7.72 years
Increase in Long-Term Tangible Assets	2,470	
Marginal Tax Rate	35.0%	Reported
Increase in Deferred Tax Liability	864	
Increase in Common Shareholders Equity	1,606	

Since Lufthansa made a net investment of €657 m in new aircraft in 2005, the depreciation expense for 2005 (included in Cost of Sales) would have been €784 m [(15,350 − 657/2)/20] versus the €871 m reported by the company.[15] Thus, Cost of Sales would decline by €87 m, increasing the Tax Expense for the year by €30 m. On the balance sheet, these changes would increase Long-Term Tangible Assets by €87 m, increase Deferred Tax Liability by €30 m, and increase Common Shareholders' Equity by €57 m.

In summary, if Lufthansa were using the same depreciation method as Air France-KLM, its financial statements for the years ended December 31, 2000 and 2001, would have to be modified as follows:

(€ Millions)	Adjustment December 31, 2005		Adjustment December 31, 2004	
	Assets	Liabilities & Equity	Assets	Liabilities & Equity
Balance Sheet				
Long-Term Tangible Assets	+2,470 + 87		+2,470	

(continued)

(€ Millions)	Adjustment December 31, 2005		Adjustment December 31, 2004	
	Assets	Liabilities & Equity	Assets	Liabilities & Equity
Deferred Tax Liability		+864 + 30		+864
Common Shareholders' Equity		+1,606 + 57		+1,606
Total Impact	+2,557	+2,557	+2,470	+2,470
Income Statement				
Cost of Sales		−87		
Tax Expense		+30		
Net Income		+57		

Lease Assets Off Balance Sheet

Japan Airlines (JAL) leases part of its flight equipment and reports for these transactions using the operating method. These leased resources are therefore excluded from JAL's balance sheet, making it difficult for an analyst to compare JAL's financial performance to that of other airlines that either own their equipment or record leased resources using the capital method, and hence show their value on their balance sheet.

JAL discloses that, even though it uses the operating method to report for leases, its leases actually qualify as capital leases.[16] To correct this accounting, the analyst can use information on lease commitments presented in JAL's lease footnote to estimate the value of the assets and liabilities that are omitted from the balance sheet. The leased equipment is then depreciated over the life of the lease, and the lease payments are treated as interest and debt repayment. JAL estimates the present value of its future lease commitments for the years ended March 31, 2005 and 2006, as follows[17]:

(¥ Millions)	March 31, 2006	March 31, 2005
Within 1 year	51,839	51,004
Over 1 year	347,488	345,002
	399,327	396,006

In addition, JAL reported a lease expense of ¥58,155 million in 2006, and the average interest rate on its outstanding debt was 1.7 percent. The weighted-average lease term is estimated to be 8 years. Given this information, the analyst can make the following adjustments to JAL's beginning and ending balance sheets, and to its income statement for the year ended March 31, 2006:

1. Capitalize the present value of the lease commitments for March 31, 2005, increasing Long-Term Tangible Assets and Long-Term Debt by ¥396,006 million.[18]
2. Calculate the value of any change in lease assets and lease liabilities during the year from new lease transactions or the return of leased equipment prior to the end of the contracted lease term. On March 31, 2005, JAL's liability for lease commitments in 2007 and beyond was ¥345,002 million. If there had been no changes in these commitments, one year later (on March 31, 2006)

they would have been valued at ¥350,867 million (¥345,002 m × 1.017). Yet JAL's actual lease commitment on March 31, 2006, was ¥399,327 million, indicating that the company increased its leased aircraft equipment capacity by ¥48,398 million. JAL's Long-Term Tangible Assets and Long-Term Debt therefore increased by ¥48,460 million during 2006 as a result of new lease commitments.

3. Reflect the change in lease asset value and expense from the depreciation during the year. The depreciation expense for 2006 (included in Cost of Sales) is the depreciation rate (1/8) multiplied by the beginning cost of leased equipment (¥396,006 million) plus depreciation on new lease commitments (¥48,460 million), prorated throughout the year. The depreciation expense for 2006 is therefore ¥52,530 million {[¥396,006 m + (¥48,460 m/2)]/8}.

4. Add back the lease expense in the income statement, included in Cost of Sales, and apportion the payment between Interest Expense and repayment of Long-Term Debt. As previously mentioned, the lease expense is ¥58,155 million. The portion of this that is shown as Interest Expense is calculated as follows:

Interest on beginning lease obligation (.017 × 396,006)	¥6,803
Plus: interest on 2006 net new lease commitments (.017 × 48,460/2)	412
Interest expense on lease debt	¥7,215

The Long-Term Debt repayment portion is then the remainder of the total lease payment, ¥50,940 million.

5. Make any needed changes to the Deferred Tax Liability to reflect differences in earnings under the capital and operating methods. JAL's expenses under the capital lease method are ¥59,745 million (¥52,940 million depreciation expense plus ¥7,215 million interest expense) versus ¥58,155 million under the operating method. JAL will not change its tax books, but for financial reporting purposes it will show higher earnings before tax and thus a higher Tax Expense through deferred taxes. In fiscal year 2006, JAL lost money as a result of which it paid no taxes. However, the statutory tax rate for the year was 40.7 percent. Given this tax rate, the Tax Expense will decrease by ¥647 million [0.407 × (¥59,745 m − ¥58,155 m)] and the Deferred Tax Liability will decrease by the same amount.

In summary, the adjustments to JAL's financial statements on March 31, 2005 and 2006 are as follows:

(¥ Millions)	Adjustment March 31, 2006		Adjustment March 31, 2005	
	Assets	Liabilities & Equity	Assets	Liabilities & Equity
Balance Sheet				
Long-Term Tangible Assets				
(1) Beginning capitalization	+396,006		+396,006	
(2) Net new lease commitments	+48,460			
(3) Annual depreciation	−52,530			

(continued)

(¥ Millions)	Adjustment March 31, 2006		Adjustment March 31, 2005	
	Assets	Liabilities & Equity	Assets	Liabilities & Equity
Long-Term Debt				
(1) Beginning debt		+396,006		+396,006
(2) Net new lease commitments		+48,460		
(4) Debt Repayment		−50,940		
(5) Deferred Tax Liability		−647		
Common Shareholders' Equity		−943		
Income Statement				
Cost of Sales				
(4) Lease expense		−58,155		
(3) Depreciation expense		+52,530		
(4) Interest Expense		+7,215		
(5) Tax Expense		−647		
Total Expenses		+943		
Net Income		−943		

These adjustments increase JAL's fixed assets by 18 percent in 2005 and 19 percent in 2006, reducing the company's asset turnover (sales/assets) from the reported value of 0.98 to 0.83 in 2005, and from 1.02 to 0.86 in 2006.

Key Intangible Assets Off Balance Sheet

How should the analyst approach the omission of intangibles? One way is to leave the accounting as is but to recognize that forecasts of long-term rates of return will have to reflect the inherent biases that arise from this accounting method. A second approach is to capitalize intangibles and amortize them over their expected lives.

For example, consider the case of Microsoft, the most valuable software company in the world. Microsoft capitalizes only a small portion of its software R&D costs, arguing that most of the costs are incurred before technological feasibility is reached, as required under U.S. standards. What adjustment would be required if the analyst decided to capitalize all of Microsoft's software R&D and to amortize the intangible asset using the straight-line method over the expected life of software (approximately three years)? Assume that R&D spending occurs evenly throughout the year and that only half a year's amortization is taken on the latest year's spending. Given R&D outlays for the years 2003 to 2006, the R&D asset at the end of fiscal year 2006 is $9.9 billion, calculated as follows:

Year	R&D Outlay	Proportion Capitalized 06/30/06	Asset 06/30/06	Proportion Capitalized 06/30/05	Asset 06/30/05
2006	$6.6 b	(1 − .33/2)	$5.5 b		
2005	6.1	(1 − .33/2 − .33)	3.1	(1 − .33/2)	$5.1 b
2004	7.7	(1 − .33/2 − .67)	1.3	(1 − .33/2 − .33)	3.9
2003	6.6			(1 − .33/2 − .67)	1.0
Total			$9.9 b		$10.0 b

The R&D amortization expense (included in Other Operating Expenses) for 2005 and 2006 are $6.7 billion and $6.8 billion, respectively, and are calculated as follows:

Year	R&D Outlay	Proportion Amortized 06/30/06	Expense 06/30/06	Proportion Amortized 06/30/05	Expense 06/30/05
2006	$6.6 b	.33/2	$1.1 b		
2005	6.1	.33	2.0	.33/2	$1.0 b
2004	7.7	.33	2.6	.33	2.6
2003	6.6	.33/2	1.1	.33	2.2
2002	6.3			.33/2	1.0
Total			$6.7 b		$6.8 b

Since Microsoft will continue to expense software R&D immediately for tax purposes, the change in reporting method will give rise to a Deferred Tax Liability. Given a marginal tax rate of 35 percent, this liability will equal 35 percent of the value of the Long-Term Intangible Assets reported, with the balance increasing Common Shareholders' Equity.

In summary, the adjustments required to capitalize software R&D for Microsoft for the years 2005 and 2006 are as follows:

($ Billions)	Adjustment June 30, 2006 Assets	Adjustment June 30, 2006 Liabilities & Equity	Adjustment June 30, 2005 Assets	Adjustment June 30, 2005 Liabilities & Equity
Balance Sheet				
Long-Term Intangible Assets	+9.9		+10.0	
Deferred Tax Liability		+3.4		+3.5
Common Shareholders' Equity		+6.5		+6.5
Income Statement				
Research and Development		−6.6		−6.1
Other Operating Expenses		+6.7		+6.8
Tax Expense		−0.1		−0.2
Total Expenses		0.0		+0.5
Net Income		0.0		−0.5

LIABILITY DISTORTIONS

Liabilities are defined as economic obligations arising from benefits received in the past, and for which the amount and timing is known with reasonable certainty. Liabilities include obligations to customers that have paid in advance for products or services; commitments to public and private providers of debt financing; obligations to federal and local governments for taxes; commitments to employees for unpaid wages, pensions, and other retirement benefits; and obligations from court or government fines or environmental cleanup orders.

Distortions in liabilities generally arise because there is ambiguity about whether (1) an obligation has really been incurred and/or (2) the obligation can be measured.

Has an obligation been incurred?

For most liabilities there is little ambiguity about whether an obligation has been incurred. For example, when a firm buys supplies on credit, it has incurred an obligation to the supplier. However, for some transactions it is more difficult to decide whether there is any such obligation. For example, if a firm announces a plan to restructure its business by laying off employees, has it made a commitment that would justify recording a liability? Or, if a software firm receives cash from its customers for a five-year software license, should the firm report the full cash inflow as revenues, or should some of it represent the ongoing commitment to the customer for servicing and supporting the license agreement?

Can the obligation be measured?

Many liabilities specify the amount and timing of obligations precisely. For example, a 20-year, $100 million bond issue with an 8 percent coupon payable semi-annually specifies that the issuer will pay the holders $100 million in 20 years, and it will pay out interest of $4 million every six months for the duration of the loan. However, for some liabilities it is difficult to estimate the amount of the obligation. For example, a firm that is responsible for an environmental cleanup clearly has incurred an obligation, but the amount is highly uncertain.[19] Similarly, firms that provide pension and post-retirement benefits for employees have incurred commitments that depend on uncertain future events, such as employee mortality rates and future inflation rates, making valuation of the obligation subjective. Future warranty and insurance claim obligations fall into the same category—the commitment is clear but the amount depends on uncertain future events.

Accounting rules frequently specify when a commitment has been incurred and how to measure the amount of the commitment. However, as discussed earlier, accounting rules are imperfect—they cannot cover all contractual possibilities and reflect all of the complexities of a firm's business relationships. They also require managers to make subjective estimates of future events to value the firm's commitments. Thus the analyst may decide that some important obligations are omitted from the financial statements or, if included, are understated, either because of management bias or because there are legitimate differences in opinion between managers and analysts over future risks and commitments. As a result, analysis of liabilities is usually with an eye to assessing whether the firm's financial commitments and risks are understated and/or its earnings overstated.

UNDERSTATED LIABILITIES

Liabilities are likely to be understated when the firm has key commitments that are difficult to value and therefore not considered liabilities for financial reporting purposes. Understatements are also likely to occur when managers have strong incentives to overstate the soundness of the firm's financial position or to boost reported earnings. By understating leverage, managers present investors with a rosy picture of the firm's financial risks. Earnings management also understates liabilities (namely deferred or unearned revenues) when revenues are recognized upon receipt of cash, even though not all services have been provided.

The most common forms of liabilities understatements arise when the following conditions exist:

1. *Unearned revenues are understated through aggressive revenue recognition.* If cash has already been received but the product or service has yet to be provided, unearned or deferred revenues are created. This liability reflects the company's

commitment to provide the service or product to the customer and is extinguished once that is accomplished. Firms that recognize revenues prematurely—after the receipt of cash but prior to fulfilling their product or service commitments to customers—understate deferred revenue liabilities and overstate earnings. Firms that bundle service contracts with the sale of a product are particularly prone to deferred revenue liability understatement since separating the price of the product from the price of the service is subjective.

2. *Loans from discounted receivables are off balance sheet.* As discussed earlier, receivables that are discounted with a financial institution are considered "sold" if the "seller" cedes control over the receivables to the financier. Yet if the sale permits the buyer to have recourse against the seller in the event of default, the seller continues to face collection risk. Given the management judgment involved in forecasting default and refinancing costs, as well as the incentives faced by managers to keep debt off the balance sheet, it is important for the analyst to evaluate the firm's estimates for default as well as the inherent commitments that it has for discounted receivables. Are the firm's estimates reasonable? Is it straightforward to forecast the costs of the default and prepayment risks? If not, does the analyst need to increase the value of the recourse liability? Or, in the extreme, does the analyst need to undo the sale and recognize a loan from the financial institution for the discounted value of the receivables.

3. *Long-term liabilities for leases are off balance sheet.* As discussed earlier in the chapter, key lease assets and liabilities can be excluded from the balance sheet if the company structures lease transactions to fit the accounting definition of an operating lease. Firms that groom transactions to avoid showing lease assets and obligations will have very different balance sheets from firms with virtually identical economics but which either use capital leases or borrow from the bank to actually purchase the equivalent resources. For firms that choose to structure lease transactions to fit the definition of an operating lease, the analyst can restate the leases as capital leases, as discussed in the Asset Understatement section. This will ensure that the firm's true financial commitments and risks will be reflected on its balance sheet, enabling comparison with peer firms.

4. *Pension and post-retirement obligations are not fully recorded.* Many firms make commitments to their employees under defined benefit pension plans and post-retirement benefit plans. Accounting rules require managers to estimate and report the present value of the commitments that have been earned by employees over their years of working for the firm. This obligation is offset by any assets that the firm has committed to pension/retirement plans to fund future plan benefits. If the funds set aside in the retirement plan are greater (less) than the plan commitments, the plan is overfunded (underfunded). Several important issues arise for analyzing pension/post-retirement plan obligations. First, estimating the obligations themselves is subjective—managers have to make forecasts of future wage and benefit rates, worker attrition rates, the expected lives of retirees, and the discount rate.[20] If these forecasts are too low, the firm's benefit obligations (as well as the annual expenses for benefits reported in the income statement) will be understated.[21] Second, accounting rules require that incremental benefit commitments that arise from changes to a plan, and changes in plan funding status that arise from abnormal investment returns on plan assets, are smoothed over time rather than reflected immediately. As a result, for labor-intensive firms that offer attractive retirement benefits to employees, it is important that the analyst assess whether reported pension and retirement plan liabilities reflect the firms' true commitments.

Examples of How to Correct for Liability Understatement

We illustrate some of these types of liability understatements and the corrections that the analyst can make to reduce bias in the financial statements.

Unearned Revenues Understated

Consider the case of MicroStrategy, the software company discussed earlier, which bundles customer support and software updates with its initial licensing agreements. This raises questions about how much of the contract price should be allocated to the initial license versus the company's future commitments. In March 2000, MicroStrategy conceded that it had incorrectly overstated revenues on contracts that involved significant future customization and consulting by $54.5 million. As a result, it would have to restate its financial statements for 1999 as well as for several earlier years. To undo the distortion to 1999 financials, the following adjustments would have to be made:

1. In the quarter that the contracts were booked by the company, Sales would decline and unearned revenues (included in Other Current Liabilities) would increase by $54.5 million.
2. Cost of Sales would decline and prepaid expenses (inventory for companies selling physical products) would increase to reflect the lower sales. As noted earlier, MicroStrategy's cost of license revenues is only 3 percent of license revenues, implying that the adjustment to prepaid expenses (included in Other Current Assets) and Cost of Sales is modest ($1.6 m).
3. The decline in pretax income would result in a lower Tax Expense in the company's financial reporting books (but presumably not in its tax books). Given MicroStrategy's marginal tax rate of 35 percent, the decline in the Tax Expense as well as in the Deferred Tax Liability is $18.5 million [($54.5 − 1.6) · .35].

The full effect of the adjustment on the quarterly financial statements would therefore be as follows:

($ millions)	Adjustment	
	Assets	Liabilities & Equity
Balance Sheet		
Other Current Assets	+1.6	
Other Current Liabilities		+54.5
Deferred Tax Liability		−18.5
Common Shareholders' Equity		−34.4
Income Statement		
Sales		−54.5
Cost of Sales		−1.6
Tax Expense		−18.5
Net Income		−34.4

MicroStrategy's announcement on March 10, 2000, that it had overstated revenues prompted the SEC to investigate the company. In the period when it announced its overstatements, MicroStrategy's stock price plummeted 94 percent, compared to the 37 percent drop by the NASDAQ in the same period.

Discounted Receivables Off Balance Sheet

Prior to 2000, Computer Associates (CA) discounted notes receivable from its long-term licensing contracts. In 2002 it reported a contingent liability of $218 million for receivables that had been discounted with recourse. The company did not provide information on the value of the recourse liability for these notes receivable, making it difficult to judge the adequacy of the allowance for credit and refinancing losses that potentially could arise on the discounted receivables. One way for the analyst to assess the impact of the financing is to reverse the sale and include a liability for the full $218 million on CA's balance sheet. This would require the following adjustments:

1. CA's Other Long-Term Assets would be increased by the receivable commitment ($218 million). In turn, Long-Term Debt would be recorded to reflect the value of the cash advanced to CA under the discount transaction. CA appears to charge its customers an annual interest rate of roughly 9 percent. Assuming customers repay the receivables in equal monthly installments over the next four years and the bank charges a 10 percent interest rate, the receivable loan would be valued at $214.1 million.
2. The after-tax difference between the face value of the receivables and the loan, which would have been shown as a loss on sale under the reported accounting, needs to be reversed, increasing equity. Given the above assumptions and CA's 35 percent marginal tax rate, the adjustment would increase Common Shareholders' Equity by $2.5 million [$3.9 \cdot (1 - .35)$].
3. The impact of the tax deduction from reporting a loss on sale, which would have reduced the Deferred Tax Liability, needs to be reversed. For CA this amount would have resulted in a roughly $1.4 million ($3.9 \cdot .35$) increase in the Deferred Tax Liability.
4. During the year ended March 31, 2003, customers are scheduled to make monthly payments on the discounted receivables, reducing the value of notes receivable under the adjusted accounting. For CA these amounted to $54.5 million ($218 million $\cdot$ .25). Notes receivable would increase if any additional notes were discounted during the year. For CA no new receivable discounts were undertaken since the company changed its sales strategy.
5. For 2003 CA's income statement would include Interest Income from notes receivable for $17.2 million $\{(218.0 \cdot .09) - [(54.5 \cdot .09) \cdot .5]\}$ and Interest Expense from the loan for roughly $18.7 million $\{(214.0 \cdot .10) - [(54.5 \cdot .10) \cdot .5]\}$ along with any tax effects.[22] The loan would decline by a smaller amount, since $1.6 million of the receivable repayments are allocated to covering the higher interest charged on the loan (exactly offsetting the spread between the Interest Income and the Interest Expense for the year).
6. The value of the loan increases by the amount of any additional discounts undertaken during the year ($0) and declines by the value of receivable repayments by customers ($54.5 million) net of the portion of the repayment that represents incremental interest charged by the bank relative to the rate CA charged its customers ($1.5 million, or $18.7 million − $17.2 million).

The overall effect of these adjustments on CA's financial statements would therefore be as follows:

($ millions)	Adjustment for March 31, 2002		Adjustment for March 31, 2003	
	Assets	Liabilities & Equity	Assets	Liabilities & Equity
Balance Sheet				
Other Long-Term Assets	+218.0		+218.0	
			−54.5	
Long-Term Debt		+214.1		+214.1
				−54.5
				+1.5
Balance Sheet				
Deferred Tax Liability		+1.4		+1.4
				−0.5
Common Shareholders' Equity		+2.5		+2.5
				−1.0
Income Statement				
Interest Income				+17.2
Interest Expense				+18.7
Tax Expense				−0.5
Net Income				−1.0

Pension/Post-Retirement Obligations Not Fully Recorded

Accounting rules require that firms estimate the value of defined benefit pension and post-retirement commitments as the present value of future expected payouts under the plans. The obligation under defined benefit pension plans is referred to as the Projected Benefit Obligation, and is the present value of plan commitments factoring in the impact of future increases in wage rates on projected payouts.[23] For post-retirement benefits such as health care costs and health insurance premiums, the firm's obligation is called the Projected Post-Retirement Benefit Obligation and is calculated as the present value of expected future benefits for employees and their beneficiaries.

Each year the firm's pension and post-retirement obligations are adjusted to reflect the following factors:

- *Service Cost:* Defined benefit plans typically provide additional benefits for each additional year of service with the company. The present value of incremental benefits earned from another year of service is called the service cost, and it increases the firm's obligation each year.
- *Interest Cost:* An interest cost is recorded to reflect the effective interest that accrues each year on the company's obligations to the pension and/or post-retirement plans. This cost is calculated by multiplying the Projected Post Retirement Benefit Obligation at the beginning of the year by the discount rate.
- *Actuarial Gains and Losses:* Each year the actuarial assumptions used to estimate the firm's commitments are reviewed and, if appropriate, changes are made. The effect of these changes is shown as Actuarial Gains and Losses.
- *Benefits Paid:* The plan commitments are reduced as the plan makes payments to retirees each year.

For example, in its financial statement footnotes, General Motors (GM) provided the following information on its projected obligation under its U.S. Other Benefits Plan (primarily representing future commitments for health benefits) for the years ended December 31, 2005 and 2004:

($ Millions)	2005	2004
U.S. Other Benefits Obligation		
Benefit obligation at beginning of year	$73,772	$64,547
Service cost	702	566
Interest cost	4,107	3,726
Plan participants' contributions	88	85
Actuarial losses	6,720	8,527
Benefits paid	(4,208)	(3,690)
Other	–	11
Benefit obligation at end of year	**$81,181**	**$73,772**

GM's obligation at the end of 2005 was $81.2 billion, a 10 percent increase over the prior year.

To meet their commitments under pension and other post-retirement plans, firms make contributions to the plans. These contributions are then invested in equities, debt, and other assets. Plan assets are therefore increased each year by new company contributions. They are also increased or decreased by the returns generated each year from plan investments. Finally, plan assets decline when the plan pays out benefits to retirees. For the years ended December 31, 2005 and 2004, GM reported the following assets for post-retirement plans:

($ Millions)	2005	2004
Plan Assets		
Fair value of plan assets at beginning of year	$16,016	$9,998
Actual return on plan assets	2,258	981
Employer contributions	2,008	5,037
Plan participants' contributions	–	–
Benefits paid	–	–
Fair value of plan assets at end of year	**$20,282**	**$16,016**

In 2005 GM's plan assets were $20.3 billion, an increase of over 25 percent from the previous year. The difference between GM's post-retirement plan obligations and the plan assets, $60.9 billion, represents the company's unfunded obligation to employees under the plan.

Of course, estimating pension and post-retirement obligations is highly subjective. It requires managers to forecast the future payouts under the plans, which in turn involves making projections of employees' service with the firm, retirement ages, and life expectancies, as well as future wage rates and health insurance costs. It also requires managers to select an interest rate to estimate the present value of the future benefits. For example, GM projected that health care costs would initially grow at 10 percent per year and then decline to a trend rate of 5 percent per year over the next 6 years. It also assumed that the appropriate discount rate was 5.0 percent. GM reports that a 1 percent increase in the health care cost trend rate would increase the post-retirement obligation by $9.3 billion. Given the management judgment involved in making these forecasts and assumptions, analysts should question whether reported obligations adequately reflect the firm's true commitments.

Since GM's unfunded post-retirement benefit obligation is $60.9 billion, it would seem reasonable to expect that the company will report a liability on its balance sheet for $60.9 billion. From December 31, 2006 onwards, SFAS 158 requires U.S. firms to recognize the full unfunded liability in the balance sheet. However, as discussed below, prior to this date, pension and post-retirement accounting was more complex. SFAS 87 required firms to smooth out shocks to plan obligations and assets. For example, under the former rules, if GM agrees to increase its post-retirement or pension benefits for current workers, the value of its obligation will increase, but it amortized this "prior period service obligation" over employees' average expected remaining years of service rather than right away. Also, if the value of plan assets increases or decreases unexpectedly in a given year, or there needs to be an adjustment in the actuarial assumptions made to estimate the obligation, the financial statement impact under SFAS 87 was reflected gradually rather than immediately. Thus, even though the actual gap between GM's post-retirement obligation and plan assets is $60.9 billion, this is not the value of the liability recorded on its 2005 balance sheet[24]. GM provides a separate disclosure that reconciles the actual and the reported obligation:

($ Millions)	2005	2004
Funded status	$(60,899)	$(57,756)
Unrecognized actuarial losses	30,592	27,345
Unrecognized prior service cost	(714)	(445)
Employer net contributions in the fourth quarter	(1,176)	4,000
Benefits paid in the fourth quarter	846	999
Net amount recognized	$(31,351)	$(25,857)

The unrecognized actuarial losses reported in these years arises because GM's earlier actuarial assumptions about parameters such as future health care costs, retirement rates, and assumed rates of return on plan assets have proven to be optimistic. These effects were recognized over time rather than right away. Similarly, prior service costs represent additional commitments from post-retirement plan changes that are recognized over time. Consequently, GM's 2005 reported post-retirement liability understated its real commitment by 29.5 billion ($60.9 billion less $31.4 billion).[25]

What does pension and post-retirement accounting imply for financial analysis? It is reasonable for the analyst to raise several questions about a firm's pension and post-retirement obligations, particularly for firms in labor-intensive industries.

1. Are the assumptions made by the firm to estimate its pension and post-retirement obligations realistic? These include assumptions about the discount rate, which is supposed to represent the current market interest rate on benefit obligations, as well as assumptions about increases in wage and benefit costs. If these assumptions are optimistic, the obligations recorded on the books understate the firm's real economic commitment. As discussed above, GM notes that a 1 percent increase in expected health care costs increases its obligation by $9.3 billion. The analyst can use this information to adjust for any optimism in management's assumptions. For example, if the analyst decided that GM's forecasts of future healthcare costs were too low and needed to increase by 1 percent, the post-retirement obligation would have to be increased by $9.3 billion, with offsetting declines to equity (for the after-tax effect) and to the deferred tax

liability. The adjustment to GM's 2005 balance sheet, assuming a 35 percent tax rate, would be as follows:

($ Millions)	Assets	Adjustment — Liabilities & Equity
Balance Sheet		
Benefit Obligations		+9,300
Deferred Tax Liability		−3,255
Common Shareholders' Equity		−6,045

2. For financial statements dated prior to December 31, 2006, the process of smoothing prior service costs and differences between actual and forecasted parameters for pension and other benefit plans affected the recognized obligation. For GM these factors have led to a substantial understatement of the reported liability. As noted above, GM reported a liability for unfunded post-retirement benefits that was $29.5 billion less than the actual obligations. The analyst can adjust for this distortion by increasing the firm's Benefit Obligations, and making offsetting adjustments to the Deferred Tax Liability (since the change would not affect the company's taxable income) and to Common Shareholders' Equity. Assuming a 35 percent tax rate, the adjustment to GM's 2005 balance sheet would be as follows:

($ Millions)	Assets	Adjustment — Liabilities & Equity
Balance Sheet		
Benefit Obligations		+29,548
Deferred Tax Liability		−10,342
Common Shareholders' Equity		−19,206

3. What effect do pension assumptions play in the income statement? The pension cost each year comprises (a) Service cost, plus (b) Interest cost, plus (c) Amortization of any prior period service costs, plus or minus (d) Amortization of actuarial gains and losses, minus (e) Expected return on plan assets (the expected long-term return multiplied by beginning assets under management). For example, GM shows that its post-retirement expenses for 2005 and 2004 are as follows:

($ Millions)	2005	2004
Service cost	$702	$566
Interest cost	4,107	3,726
Expected return on plan assets	(1,684)	(1,095)
Amortization of prior service cost	(70)	(87)
Recognized net actuarial loss/(gain)	2,250	1,138
Net expense	**$5,305**	**$4,248**

This expense reflects the effect of smoothing actual asset returns, prior period service costs, and revisions in actuarial assumptions discussed earlier. If these effects are reflected in the pension/benefit obligation in full (as discussed above), their amortization can be excluded from the current year expense. However, the revised expense will need to be adjusted to include the actual return on plan assets for the current year rather than the expected return. Let's see how this would affect the expense reported by GM. The benefit expense for 2005 would decline by $2.18 billion, representing the amortization of recognized net actuarial losses ($2.25 billion) and prior period service cost (−$0.07 billion). In addition, the actual return on post-retirement plan assets in 2005 was $0.574 billion higher than the expected return reflected in the expense. The net effect of these adjustments would be to reduce the benefit expense by $2.754 billion. Since this adjustment would not change the firm's tax books, it would increase the Tax Expense by $0.964 billion (.35 · $2.754 m). The full income statement adjustment would therefore be as follows:

($ Millions)	Adjustment
Income Statement	
SG&A Expense	(2,754)
Tax Expense	+964
Net Income	+1,790

4. Once the analyst is satisfied that the financial statements reflect realistic assumptions about pension/post-retirement costs and obligations, it is possible to assess the overall impact of these arrangements on a firm's cost structure relative to its competitors. For GM, this could lead the analyst to assess how GM is positioned relative to other U.S. manufacturers (such as Ford) and to non-U.S. competitors (such as Toyota, Honda, and Volkswagon).

EQUITY DISTORTIONS

Accounting treats stockholders' equity as a residual claim on the firm's assets after paying off the other claimholders. Consequently, equity distortions arise primarily from distortions in assets and liabilities. For example, distortions in assets or liabilities that affect earnings also lead to distortions in equity. However, equity distortions can also arise that are not captured in an asset and liability analysis. One such distortion is for hybrid securities.

Hybrid securities include convertible debt and debt with warrants attached. These securities are partially pure debt and partially equity. Current accounting rules do not separate these components, typically implying that the balance sheet overstates firm debt and understates its equity. Without adjusting for this distortion, it can be difficult to understand the real financial risks and returns for firms with different types of hybrids. New accounting rules proposed by the FASB are likely to address this issue by requiring securities such as convertible debt to be separated into two components on the balance sheet, a debt component and an equity component. Each would be valued at its fair value at the date of issue. This approach could be adopted by the analyst.

Examples of How to Correct for Equity Distortions

We illustrate the equity distortion arising from the issuance of hybrid securities and the corrections that the analyst can make to reduce bias in the financial statements.

Hybrid Securities

On February 3, 1999, Amazon.com completed an offering of $1.25 billion of 4.75 percent Convertible Subordinated Notes due in 2009. Several months earlier Amazon had issued senior notes with an annual interest rate of 10 percent. The conversion premium was therefore significant—if the notes had not included a conversion option, Amazon would probably have had to pay a coupon rate in excess of 10 percent. The value of the $1.25 billion convertible issue at a 10 percent discount rate is only $0.87 billion, implying that the convertibility premium was worth roughly $0.38 billion. One way to adjust for this effect is to record the debt component at $0.87 billion and to show the $0.38 billion conversion premium as part of Common Shareholders' Equity. Interest on the debt would then be based on the 10 percent coupon rate rather than the 4.75 percent (which reflects the conversion premium).

The effect of this adjustment on Amazon's financial statements at March 31, 2002, would be as follows:

($ billions)	Adjustment for March 31, 2002	
	Assets	Liabilities & Equity
Balance Sheet		
Long-Term Debt		−0.38
Common Shareholders Equity		+0.38

SUMMARY

To implement accounting analysis, the analyst must first recast the financial statements into a common format so that financial statement terminology and formatting is comparable between firms and across time. A standard template for recasting the financials, presented in this chapter, is used throughout the remainder of the book.

Once the financial statements are standardized, the analyst can determine what accounting distortions exist in the firm's assets, liabilities, and equity. Common distortions that overstate assets include delays in recognizing asset impairments, underestimated reserves, aggressive revenue recognition leading to overstated receivables, and optimistic assumptions on long-term asset depreciation. Asset understatements can arise if managers overstate asset write-offs, use operating leases to keep assets off the balance sheet, or make conservative assumptions for asset depreciation. They can also arise because accounting rules require outlays for key assets (e.g., R&D and brands) to be immediately expensed. For liabilities, the primary concern for the analyst is whether the firm understates its real commitments. This can arise from off-balance liabilities (e.g., operating lease obligations), from questionable management judgment and limitations in accounting rules for estimating pension and benefit plan liabilities, and from aggressive revenue recognition that understates unearned revenue obligations. Equity distortions frequently arise when there are distortions in assets and liabilities. However, they can also arise if firms issue hybrid securities.

Adjustments for distortions can, therefore, arise because accounting standards, although applied appropriately, do not reflect a firm's economic reality. They can also arise if the analyst has a different point of view than management about the estimates and assumptions made in preparing the financial statements. Once distortions have been identified, the analyst can use footnote and cash flow statement information to make adjustments to the balance sheet at the beginning and/or end of the current year, as well as any needed adjustments to revenues and expenses in the latest income statement. This ensures that the most recent financial ratios used to evaluate a firm's performance and to forecast its future results are based on financial data that appropriately reflect its business economics.

Several points are worth remembering when doing accounting analysis. First, the bulk of the analyst's time and energy should be focused on evaluating and adjusting accounting policies and estimates that describe the firm's key strategic value drivers. Of course, this does not mean that management bias is not reflected in other accounting estimates and policies, and the analyst should certainly examine these. But given the importance of evaluating how the firm is managing its key success factors and risks, the bulk of the accounting analysis should be spent examining those policies that represent these key factors and risks.

It is also important to recognize that many accounting adjustments can only be approximations rather than precise calculations since much of the information necessary for making precise adjustments is not disclosed. The analyst should therefore try to avoid worrying about being overly precise in making accounting adjustments. By making even crude adjustments, it is usually possible to mitigate some of the limitations of accounting standards and problems of management bias in financial reporting.

DISCUSSION QUESTIONS

1. Use the templates shown in Tables 4-1, 4-2, and 4-3 to recast the following financial statements for Dell Inc.

Dell Inc. Consolidated Statements of Financial Position
(in millions)

	February 3, 2006	January 28, 2005
ASSETS		
Current assets:		
Cash and cash equivalents	$7,042	$4,747
Short-term investments	2,016	5,060
Accounts receivable, net	4,089	3,563
Financing receivables, net	1,363	985
Inventories	576	459
Other	2,620	2,083
Total current assets	17,706	16,897
Property, plant, and equipment, net	2,005	1,691
Investments	2,691	4,294
Long-term financing receivables, net	325	199
Other non-current assets	382	134
Total assets	$23,109	$23,215

(continued)

Dell Inc. Consolidated Statements of Financial Position
(in millions)

	February 3, 2006	January 28, 2005
LIABILITIES AND STOCKHOLDERS' DEFICIT		
Current liabilities:		
Accounts payable	$9,840	$8,895
Accrued and other	6,087	5,241
Total current liabilities	15,927	14,136
Long-term debt	504	505
Other non-current liabilities	2,549	2,089
Total Liabilities	18,980	16,730
Commitments and contingent liabilities	–	–
Stockholders' equity:		
Preferred stock and capital in excess of $.01 par value; shares issued and outstanding: none	–	–
Common stock and capital in excess of $.01 par value; shares authorized: 7,000; shares issued: 2,818 and 2,769, respectively	9,540	8,195
Treasury stock, at cost; 488 and 284 shares, respectively	(18,007)	(10,758)
Retained earnings	12,746	9,174
Other comprehensive loss	(103)	(82)
Other	(47)	(44)
Total stockholders' equity	4,129	6,485
Total liabilities and stockholders' equity	$23,109	$23,215

Dell Inc. Consolidated Statements of Income
(in millions)

	February 3, 2006	January 28, 2005	January 30, 2004
Net revenue	$55,908	$49,205	$41,444
Cost of revenue	45,958	40,190	33,892
Gross margin	9,950	9,015	7,552
Operating expenses:			
Selling, general, and administrative	5,140	4,298	3,544
Research, development, and engineering	463	463	464
Total operating expenses	5,603	4,761	4,008
Operating income	4,347	4,254	3,544
Investment and other income, net	227	191	180
Income before income taxes	4,574	4,445	3,724
Income tax provision	1,002	1,402	1,079
Net income	$3,572	$3,043	$2,645

Dell Inc. Consolidated Statements of Cash Flows (in millions)

	February 3, 2006	January 28, 2005	January 30, 2004
CASH FLOWS FROM OPERATING ACTIVITIES:			
Net income	$3,572	$3,043	$2,645
Adjustments to reconcile net income to net cash provided by operating activities:			
Depreciation and amortization	393	334	263
Tax benefits of employee stock plans	261	249	181
LIABILITIES denominated in foreign currencies	70	(602)	(677)
Other	188	78	113
Changes in:			
Operating working capital	(67)	1,755	872
Non-current assets and liabilities	422	453	273
Net cash provided by operating activities	4,839	5,310	3,670
CASH FLOWS FROM INVESTING ACTIVITIES:			
Investments:			
Purchases	(7,562)	(12,261)	(12,099)
Maturities and sales	12,168	10,469	10,078
Capital expenditures	(728)	(525)	(329)
Purchase of assets held in master lease facilities	–	–	(636)
Cash assumed in consolidation of Dell Financial Services L.P.	–	–	172
Net cash provided by (used in) investing activities	3,878	(2,317)	(2,814)
CASH FLOWS FROM FINANCING ACTIVITIES:			
Repurchase of common stock	(7,249)	(4,219)	(2,000)
Issuance of common stock under employee plans and other	1,023	1,091	617
Net cash used in financing activities	(6,226)	(3,128)	(1,383)
Effect of exchange-rate changes on cash and cashequivalents	(196)	565	612
Net increase in cash and cash equivalents	$2,295	$430	$85

2. Refer to the Creative Technology example on delaying write-downs of current assets. How much excess inventory do you estimate Creative Technology is holding in March 2005 if the firm's optimal days' inventory is 100 days? Calculate the inventory impairment charge for Creative Technology if 50 percent of this excess inventory is deemed worthless? Record the changes to Creative Technology's financial statements from adjusting for this impairment.

3. Acceptance Insurance Companies Inc. underwrites and sells specialty property and casualty insurance. The company is the third largest writer of crop insurance products

in the United States. In its 1998 10-K report to the SEC, it discloses the following information on the loss reserves created for claims originating in 1990:

Percentage of claim liability arising in 1990 paid as of:	
One year later	40.6%
Two years later	70.8
Three years later	88.5
Four years later	101.2
Five years later	107.5
Six years later	109.7
Seven years later	111.4
Eight years later	111.8

Net reserves for 1990 obligations re-estimated as of:	
One year later	100.3%
Two years later	102.3
Three years later	107.4
Four years later	110.7
Five years later	112.7
Six years later	112.0
Seven years later	112.5
Eight years later	113.4
Net cumulative deficiency	−13.4

Was the initial estimate for loss reserves originating in 1990 too low or too high? How has the firm updated its estimate of this obligation over time? What percentage of the original liability remains outstanding for 1990 claims at the end of 1998? As a financial analyst, what questions would you have for the CFO on its 1990 liability?

4. AMR, the parent of American Airlines, provides the following footnote information on its capital and operating leases:

AMR's subsidiaries lease various types of equipment and property, primarily aircraft and airport facilities. The future minimum lease payments required under capital leases, together with the present value of such payments, and future minimum lease payments required under operating leases that have initial or remaining noncancelable lease terms in excess of one year as of December 31, 2005, were (in millions):

Year Ending December 31,	Capital Leases	Operating Leases
2006	$263	$1,065
2007	196	1,039
2008	236	973
2009	175	872
2010	140	815
2011 and thereafter	794	7,453
	$1,804	$12,217
Less amount representing interest	716	
Present value of net minimum lease payments	$1,088	

AMR further disclosed that "lease terms vary but are generally 10 to 25 years for aircraft and seven to 40 years for other leased property and equipment." Assuming that all leases are for aircraft with an average lease term of 15 years, what interest rate does AMR use to capitalize its capital leases? Use this rate to capitalize AMR's operating leases at December 31, 2005. Record the adjustment to AMR's balance sheet to reflect the capitalization of operating leases. How would this reporting change affect AMR's Income Statement in 2006?

5. What approaches would you use to estimate the value of brands? What assumptions underlie these approaches? As a financial analyst, what would you use to assess whether the brand value of £1.575 billion reported by Cadbury Schweppes in 1997 was a reasonable reflection of the future benefits from these brands? What questions would you raise with the firm's CFO about the firm's brand assets?

6. As the CFO of a company, what indicators would you look at to assess whether your firm's long-term assets were impaired? What approaches could be used, either by management or an independent valuation firm, to assess the dollar value of any asset impairment? As a financial analyst, what indicators would you look at to assess whether a firm's long-term assets were impaired? What questions would you raise with the firm's CFO about any charges taken for asset impairment?

7. The cigarette industry is subject to litigation for health hazards posed by its products. The industry has been in an ongoing process of negotiating a settlement of these claims with state and federal governments. As the CFO for Altria Group, the parent company of Philip Morris, one of the larger firms in the industry, what information would you report to investors in the annual report on the firm's litigation risks? How would you assess whether the firm should record a liability for this risk, and if so, what approach would you use to assess the value of this liability? As a financial analyst following Altria, what questions would you raise with the CEO over the firm's litigation liability?

8. Refer to the General Motors example on post-retirement benefits. Show the adjustments that would be required to record the full amount of the unfunded post-retirement benefit on December 31, 2004. What factors account for the difference between the adjustments to Common Shareholders' Equity on December 31, 2004 and 2005?

9. Refer to the Lufthansa example on asset depreciation estimates. What adjustments would be required if Lufthansa's aircraft depreciation were computed using an average life of 25 years and salvage value of 5 percent (instead of the reported values of 12 years and 15 percent)? Show the adjustments to the 2004 and 2005 balance sheets, and to the 2005 income statement.

10. In early 2003 Bristol-Myers Squibb announced that it would have to restate its financial statements as a result of stuffing as much as $3.35 billion worth of products into wholesalers' warehouses from 1999 through 2001. The company's sales and cost of sales during this period was as follows:

	2001	2000	1999
Net sales	$18,139	$17,695	$16,502
Cost of products sold	5,454	4,729	4,458

The company's marginal tax rate during the three years was 35 percent. What adjustments are required to correct Bristol-Myers Squibb's balance sheet for December 31, 2001? What assumptions underlie your adjustments? How would you expect the adjustments to affect Bristol-Myers Squibb's performance in the coming few years?

NOTES

1. If a firm's primary business income is from rentals, rental income will be classified as Sales, rather than Investment Income.

2. A notable exception in the U.S. is the requirement that software development costs be capitalized once the software reaches the stage of technological feasibility (see SFAS 86).

3. See P. Healy, S. Myers, and C. Howe, "R&D Accounting and the Tradeoff Between Relevance and Objectivity," *Journal of Accounting Research* 40 (June 2002): 677–711, for an analysis of the value of capitalizing R&D and then annually assessing impairment.

4. J. Elliott and D. Hanna find that the market anticipates large write-downs by about one quarter, consistent with managers' reluctance to take write-downs on a timely basis. See "Repeated Accounting Write-Offs and the Information Content of Earnings," *Journal of Accounting Research* 34, Supplement, 1996.

5. J. Francis, D. Hanna, and L. Vincent find that management is more likely to exercise judgment in its self-interest for goodwill write-offs and restructuring charges than for inventory or PP&E write-offs. See "Causes and Effects of Discretionary Asset Write-Offs," *Journal of Accounting Research* 34, Supplement, 1996.

6. P. Healy, K. Palepu, and R. Ruback find that acquisitions added value for only one third of the 50 largest acquisitions during the early 1980s, suggesting that acquirers frequently do not recover goodwill. See "Which Takeovers Are Profitable—Strategic or Financial?" *Sloan Management Review*, Summer 1997.

7. MicroStrategy 1998 10-K, Footnote 1–Organization and Summary of Significant Accounting Policies.

8. MicroStrategy 1999 10-K, Footnote 3–Restatement of Financial Statements.

9. Managers can avoid capitalizing leases by assuming long asset lives (that get around the 75% of asset life rule) and high discount rates (to avoid violating the 90% of present value rule). Research indicates that some firms responded to the adoption of SFAS 13, which changed the rules for lease capitalization, by grooming transactions to avoid having to capitalize leases. See E. Imhoff and J. Thomas, "Economic Consequences of Accounting Standards: The Lease Disclosure Rule Change," *Journal of Accounting & Economics* 10 (December 1988): 277–311, and S. El-Gazzar, S. Lilien, and V. Pastena, "Accounting for Leases by Lessees," *Journal of Accounting & Economics* 8 (October 1986): 217–238. FASB has responded by issuing ten standards on leases, five interpretations, ten technical bulletins, and 27 EITFs, many designed to reduce managers' ability to avoid capitalizing leases.

10. E. Imhoff, R. Lipe, and D. Wright show that adjustments to capitalize operating leases have a significant impact on leverage and other key financial ratios. See "Operating Leases: Impact of Constructive Capitalization," *Accounting Horizons* 5 (March 1991): 51–64.

11. Accounting rules in the U.S., the U.K., Canada, and Germany require expensing R&D outlays. Expensing is the norm in Japan and France, even though capitalization is permitted.

12. P. Healy, S. Myers, and C. Howe, "R&D Accounting and the Tradeoff Between Relevance and Objectivity," *Journal of Accounting Research* 40 (June 2002): 677–711, show that the magnitude of this bias is sizable.

13. See B. Bublitz and M. Ettredge, "The Information in Discretionary Outlays: Advertising, Research and Development," *The Accounting Review* 64 (1989): 108–124; S. Chan, J. Martin, and J. Kensinger, "Corporate Research and Development Expenditures and Share Value," *Journal of Financial Economics* 26 (1990): 255–276; R. Dukes, "An Investigation of the Effects of Expensing Research and Development Costs on Security Prices," in proceedings of the conference on topical research in accounting (New York University, 1976); J. Elliott, G. Richardson, T. Dyckman, and R. Dukes, "The Impact of SFAS No. 2 on Firm Expenditures on Research and Development: Replications and Extensions," *Journal of Accounting* 22 (1984): 85–102; M. Hirschey and J. Weygandt, "Amortization Policy for Advertising and Research and Development Expenditures," *Journal of Accounting Research* 23 (1985): 326–335; C. Wasley and T. Linsmeier, "A Further Examination of the Economic Consequences of SFAS No. 2," *Journal of Accounting Research* 30 (1992): 156–164; E. Eccher, "Discussion of the Value Relevance of Intangibles: The Case of Software Capitalization," *Journal of Accounting Research* 36 (1998): 193–198; B. Lev and T. Sougiannis, "The Capitalization, Amortization, and Value-Relevance of R&D," *Journal of Accounting and Economics* 21 (1996): 107–138; and D. Aboody and B. Lev, "The Value-Relevance of Intangibles: The Case of Software Capitalization" (working paper, University of California, 1998).

14. See Lufthansa, Annual Report 2005 (Cologne, Germany: Deutsche Lufthansa AG, 2006) and Air France-KLM 2005–06 Reference Document (Paris, France: Air France-KLM, 2006).

15. It is interesting to note that Lufthansa's depreciation expense for the year 2005 is significantly lower than expected given its 12-year life and 15 percent salvage estimates. The reported depreciation under these assumptions would have been €1,110 m ({13,048 + [(657 · .85)/2]}/12). The company provides no explanation for the difference.

16. See Japan Airlines, Annual Report 2006, Footnote 10.

17. JAL actually shows the present value of its lease commitments. However, most companies report the value of future lease payments for the next five years and then show a lump sum value for all payments beyond five years. To estimate the value of the lease liability, the analyst must decide how to allocate this lump sum over year six and beyond, and estimate a suitable interest rate on the lease debt. It is then possible to compute the present value of the lease payments.

18. When a firm records a capital lease, the Long-Term Tangible Asset equals the Long-Term Debt only at inception. Thereafter, the two numbers are unequal because the asset is reduced by depreciation expense while the debt is reduced by the lease payment net of interest expense. For most companies it is not possible to learn the book value of the asset, requiring the analyst to record the asset at the same value as the debt. However, JAL's annual report shows that, had it capitalized the leased assets, their net book value on March 31, 2005 would have been ¥388,896, while the liability would have been ¥396,006. Since this information is typically not available, we have chosen not to use it in our analysis.

19. M. Barth and M. McNichols discuss ways for investors to estimate the value of environmental liabilities. See "Estimation and Market Valuation of Environmental Liabilities Relating to Superfund Sites," *Journal of Accounting Research* 32, Supplement, 1994.

20. Defined contribution plans, where companies agree to contribute fixed amounts today to cover future benefits, require very little forecasting to estimate their annual cost since the firm's obligation is limited to its annual obligation to contribute to the employees' retirement funds.

21. E. Amir and E. Gordon show that firms with larger post-retirement benefit obligations and more leverage tend to make more aggressive estimates of post-retirement obligation parameters. See "A Firm's Choice of Estimation Parameters: Empirical Evidence from SFAS No. 106," *Journal of Accounting, Auditing & Finance* 11, no. 3, Summer 1996.

22. The interest expense is only a rough approximation of the amount that would be reported by CA since it does not adjust for the portion of the customer payments that were effectively interest for the bank given the premium rate charged.

23. In their footnotes, firms also report the Accumulated Benefit Obligation for the pension plan, which is the present value of plan commitments using current wage rates and salary scales.

24. In its 2006 financial statements, reported using SFAS 158, GM does record the full value of its U.S. post-retirement obligation as a Long-Term Liability. During 2006, GM amended its post-retirement plan to eliminate $15.1 billion of its obligation leaving its unfunded liability at $46.4 billion.

25. M. Barth finds that investors regard these footnote disclosures as more useful than the liability reported in the financial statements. See "Relative Measurement Errors Among Alternative Pension Asset and Liability Measures," *The Accounting Review* 66, no. 3, 1991.

APPENDIX: RECASTING FINANCIAL STATEMENTS INTO STANDARDIZED TEMPLATES

The following tables show the financial statements for Wal-Mart Stores, Inc., for the year ended January 2006, both as reported by the company and as standardized using the classifications discussed in this chapter. The first column in each reported financial statement presents the classifications that are used for each line item to standardize the statements. Note that the classifications are not applied to subtotal lines such as Total current assets or Net income. The recast financial statements for Wal-Mart are prepared by simply totaling the balances of line items with the same standard classifications. For example, on the balance sheet there are two line items classified as Other Current Liabilities – Accrued liabilities and Accrued income taxes.

Wal-Mart Reported Consolidated Balance Sheet
(in millions)

Fiscal Year Ended January 31		2006	2005	2004
	Assets			
	Current assets:			
Cash and Marketable Securities	Cash and cash equivalents	6,414	5,488	5,199
Accounts Receivable	Receivables	2,662	1,715	1,254
Inventory	Inventories	32,191	29,762	26,612
Other Current Assets	Prepaid expenses and other	2,557	1,889	1,356
	Total current assets	$43,824	$38,854	$34,421
	Property and equipment, at cost:			
Long-Term Tangible Assets	Land	16,643	14,472	12,699
Long-Term Tangible Assets	Buildings and improvements	56,163	46,574	40,192
Long-Term Tangible Assets	Fixtures and equipment	22,750	21,461	17,934
Long-Term Tangible Assets	Transportation equipment	1,746	1,530	1,269
	Property and equipment, at cost	$97,302	$84,037	$72,094
Long-Term Tangible Assets	Less accumulated depreciation	21,427	18,637	15,684
	Property and equipment, net	$75,875	$65,400	$56,410
	Property under capital lease:			
Other Long-Term Assets	Property under capital lease	5,578	4,556	4,286
Other Long-Term Assets	Less accumulated amortization	2,163	1,838	1,673
	Property under capital lease, net	$3,415	$2,718	$2,613
Long-Term Intangible Assets	Goodwill	12,188	10,803	9,882
Other Long-Term Assets	Other assets and deferred charges	2,885	2,379	2,079
	Total assets	$138,187	$120,154	$105,405

(continued)

**Wal-Mart Reported Consolidated Balance Sheet
(in millions) (*continued*)**

Fiscal Year Ended January 31		2006	2005	2004
	Liabilities and shareholders' equity			
	Current liabilities:			
Short-Term Debt	Commercial paper	3,754	3,812	3,267
Accounts Payable	Accounts payable	25,373	21,987	19,425
Other Current Liabilities	Accrued liabilities	13,465	12,120	10,671
Other Current Liabilities	Accrued income taxes	1,340	1,281	1,377
Short-Term Debt	Long-term debt due within one year	4,595	3,759	2,904
Short-Term Debt	Obligations under capital leases due within one year	299	223	196
	Total current liabilities	$48,826	$43,182	$37,840
Long-Term Debt	Long-term debt	26,429	20,087	17,102
Long-Term Debt	Long-term obligations under capital leases	3,742	3,171	2,997
Deferred Taxes– Long-Term Liability	Deferred income taxes and other	4,552	2,978	2,359
Minority Interest	Minority interest	1,467	1,340	1,484
	Shareholders' equity:			
Preferred Stock	Preferred stock ($0.10 par value; 100 shares authorized, none issued)	–	–	–
Common Shareholders' Equity	Common stock ($0.10 par value; 11,000 shares authorized, 4,165 and 4,234 issued and outstanding at January 31, 2006 and January 31, 2005, respectively)	417	423	431
Common Shareholders' Equity	Capital in excess of par value	2,596	2,425	2,135
Common Shareholders' Equity	Accumulated other comprehensive income	1,053	2,694	851
Common Shareholders' Equity	Retained earnings	49,105	43,854	40,206
	Total shareholders' equity	$53,171	$49,396	$43,623
	Total liabilities and shareholders' equity	138,187	120,154	105,405

Source: SEC 10-K filings.

Wal-Mart Reported Consolidated Statements of Income
(in millions except per share amounts)

Fiscal Year Ended January 31		2006	2005	2004
	Revenues:			
Sales	Net sales	312,427	285,222	256,329
Other Income	Other income, net	3,227	2,910	2,352
		$315,654	$288,132	$258,681
	Costs and expenses:			
Cost of Sales	Cost of sales	240,391	219,793	198,747
SG&A	Operating, selling, general and administrative expenses	56,733	51,248	44,909
	Operating income	$18,530	$17,091	$15,025
	Interest:			
Interest Expense	Debt	1,171	934	729
Interest Expense	Capital leases	249	253	267
Interest Income	Interest income	(248)	(201)	(164)
	Interest, net	$1,172	$986	$832
	Income from continuing operations before income taxes and minority interest	17,358	16,105	14,193
	Provision for income taxes:			
Tax Expense	Current	5,932	5,326	4,941
Tax Expense	Deferred	(129)	263	177
		$5,803	$5,589	$5,118
	Income from continuing operations before minority interest	11,555	10,516	9,075
Minority Interest	Minority interest	(324)	(249)	(214)
	Income from continuing operations	$11,231	$10,267	$8,861
Unusual Items (after tax)	Income from discontinued operation, net of tax	–	–	193
	Net income	$11,231	$10,267	$9,054
	Basic net income per common share	2.68	2.41	2.08
	Diluted net income per common share	2.68	2.41	2.07
	Dividends per common share	0.60	0.52	0.36

Source: SEC 10-K filings.

Wal-Mart Reported Consolidated Statements of Cash Flows (in millions)

Fiscal Year Ended January 31		2006	2005	2004
	Cash flows from operating activities			
Net Income	Income from continuing operations	11,231	10,267	8,861
	Adjustments to reconcile net income to net cash provided by operating activities:			
Long-Term Operating Accruals	Depreciation and amortization	4,717	4,264	3,852
Long-Term Operating Accruals	Deferred income taxes	(129)	263	177
Long-Term Operating Accruals	Other operating activities	620	378	173
	Changes in certain assets and liabilities, net of effects of acquisitions:			
Net (Inv.) Liquidation of Op. WC	Decrease (increase) in accounts receivable	(456)	(304)	373
Net (Inv.) Liquidation of Op. WC	Increase in inventories	(1,733)	(2,494)	(1,973)
Net (Inv.) Liquidation of Op. WC	Increase in accounts payable	2,390	1,694	2,587
Net (Inv.) Liquidation of Op. WC	Increase in accrued liabilities	993	976	1,896
	Net cash provided by operating activities of continuing operations	$17,633	$15,044	$15,946
Net Income **	Net cash provided by operating activities of discontinued operation	–	–	50
	Net cash provided by operating activities	$17,633	$15,044	$15,996
	Cash flows from investing activities			
Net (Inv.) Liquidation of Op. L-T Assets	Payments for property and equipment	(14,563)	(12,893)	(10,308)
Net (Inv.) Liquidation of Op. L-T Assets	Investment in international operations, net of cash acquired	(601)	(315)	(38)
Net (Inv.) Liquidation of Op. L-T Assets	Proceeds from the disposal of fixed assets	1,049	953	481
Net (Inv.) Liquidation of Op. L-T Assets	Proceeds from the sale of McLane	–	–	1,500
Net (Inv.) Liquidation of Op. L-T Assets	Other investing activities	(68)	(96)	78
	Net cash used in investing activities of continuing operations	(14,183)	(12,351)	$(8,287)
Net (Inv.) Liquidation of Op. L-T Assets	Net cash used in investing activities of discontinued operation	–	–	(25)
	Net cash used in investing activities	$(14,183)	$(12,351)	$(8,312)

(continued)

Fiscal Year Ended January 31		**2006**	**2005**	**2004**
	Cash flows from financing activities			
Net Debt (Repayment) or Issuance	Increase (decrease) in commercial paper	(704)	544	688
Net Debt (Repayment) or Issuance	Proceeds from issuance of long-term debt	7,691	5,832	4,099
Net Stock (Repayment) or Issuance	Purchase of Company stock	(3,580)	(4,549)	(5,046)
Dividend (Payments)	Dividends paid	(2,511)	(2,214)	(1,569)
Net Debt (Repayment) or Issuance	Payment of long-term debt	(2,724)	(2,131)	(3,541)
Net Debt (Repayment) or Issuance	Payment of capital lease obligations	(245)	(204)	(305)
Net Stock (Repayment) or Issuance	Other financing activities	(349)	113	111
	Net cash used in financing activities	$(2,422)	$(2,609)	$(5,563)
Non-Operating Gains (Losses)	Effect of exchange rate changes on cash	(102)	205	320
	Net increase in cash and cash equivalents	$926	$289	$2,441
	Cash and cash equivalents at beginning of year	5,488	5,199	2,758
	Cash and cash equivalents at end of year	6,414	5,488	5,199

Source: SEC 10-K filings.

** *Wal-Mart separately reports cash from discontinued operations in its consolidated financial statements at a value of $50. We have included this as part of Net Income, rather than showing the full income effect of $193 million and including −$143 million of accruals for discontinued operations.*

The standardized financial statements for Wal-Mart are as follows:

Wal-Mart Standardized Consolidated Balance Sheet (in millions)

Fiscal Year Ended January 31	2006	2005	2004
ASSETS			
Cash and Marketable Securities	$6,414	$5,488	$5,199
Accounts Receivable	2,662	1,715	1,254
Inventory	32,191	29,762	26,612
Other Current Assets	2,557	1,889	1,356
Total Current Assets	43,824	38,854	34,421
Long-Term Tangible Assets	75,875	65,400	56,410
Long-Term Intangible Assets	12,188	10,803	9,882
Other Long-Term Assets	6,300	5,097	4,692
Total Long-Term Assets	94,363	81,300	70,984
Total Assets	$138,187	$120,154	$105,405
LIABILITIES			
Accounts Payable	$25,373	$21,987	$19,425
Short-Term Debt	8,648	7,794	6,367
Other Current Liabilities	14,805	13,401	12,048
Total Current Liabilities	48,826	43,182	37,840
Long-Term Debt	30,171	23,258	20,099
Deferred Taxes	4,552	2,978	2,359
Other Long-Term Liabilities (non-interest bearing)	–	–	–
Total Long-Term Liabilities	34,723	26,236	22,458
Total Liabilities	83,549	69,418	60,298
Minority Interest	1,467	1,340	1,484
SHAREHOLDERS' EQUITY			
Preferred Stock	–	–	–
Common Shareholders' Equity	53,171	49,396	43,623
Total Shareholders' Equity	53,171	49,396	43,623
Total Liabilities and Shareholders' Equity	$138,187	$120,154	$105,405

**Wal-Mart Standardized Consolidated Statements of Income
(in millions except per share amounts)**

Fiscal Year Ended January 31	2006	2005	2004
Sales	$ 312,427	$ 285,222	$ 256,329
Cost of Sales	240,391	219,793	198,747
Gross Profit	72,036	65,429	57,582
SG&A	56,733	51,248	44,909
Other Operating Expense	–	–	–
Operating Income	15,303	14,181	12,673
Investment Income	–	–	–
Other Income, net of Other Expense	3,227	2,910	2,352
Other Income	3,227	2,910	2,352
Other Expense	–	–	–
Net Interest Expense (Income)	1,172	986	832
Interest Income	248	201	164
Interest Expense	1,420	1,187	996
Minority Interest	(324)	(249)	(214)
Pre-Tax Income	17,034	15,856	13,979
Tax Expense	5,803	5,589	5,118
Unusual Gains, Net of Unusual Losses (after tax)	–	–	–
Net Income	$ 11,231	$ 10,267	$ 8,861
Preferred Dividends	–	–	–
Net Income to Common	$ 11,231	$ 10,267	$ 8,861

Wal-Mart Standardized Consolidated Statements of Cash Flows (in millions)

Fiscal Year Ended January 31	January 29, 2006	January 30, 2005	February 1, 2004
Net Income	$ 11,231	$ 10,267	$ 8,911
After-tax net interest expense (income)	773	638	527
Non-operating losses (gains)	102	(205)	(320)
Long-term operating accruals	5,208	4,905	4,202
Depreciation and amortization	4,717	4,264	3,852
Other	491	641	350
Operating cash flow before working capital investments	17,110	16,015	13,960
Net (investment in) or liquidation of operating working capital	1,194	(128)	2,883
Operating cash flow before investment in long-term assets	18,304	15,887	16,843
Net (investment in) or liquidation of operating long-term assets	(14,183)	(12,351)	(8,312)
Free cash flow available to debt and equity	4,121	3,536	8,531
After-tax net interest income (expense)	(773)	(638)	(527)
Net debt (repayment) or issuance	4,018	4,041	941
Free cash flow available to equity	7,366	6,939	8,945
Dividend (payments)	(2,511)	(2,214)	(1,569)
Net stock issuance (repurchase), and other equity changes	(3,929)	(4,436)	(4,935)
Net increase (decrease) in cash balance	$ 926	$ 289	$ 2,441

Revenue Recognition Problems in the Communications Equipment Industry

O n November 21, 2000, Lucent Technologies announced that it was revising its fourth quarter results as a result of revenue recognition problems discovered by its auditors during the year-end financial review. The revision lowered revenues by $125 million and earnings per share by 2 cents from 18 cents. In response, Lucent's stock price fell by 16% to $17.56.

One month later, on December 22, Lucent announced that after a more comprehensive review, revenues for the fourth quarter would need to be adjusted downward by $679 million to $8.7 billion, and that earnings per share would be revised from the initially predicted 18 cents to 10 cents. The stock plummeted by a further 19% to $13.625 (see Exhibit 1 for a graph of Lucent's stock price during 2000). Finally, on December 29, the company reported that it was increasing its provision for customer bad debts to $252 million for the fiscal year ended September 30, 2000.

As he reflected on Lucent's revisions and revenue recognition problems, John O'Connor, a communications equipment industry analyst at Dana Katz Inc., a mid-tier investment bank, wondered whether other companies in the industry faced similar risks. To be sure, Lucent's revenue recognition issues arose partially from its own internal control and management problems. However, they also appeared to be exacerbated by industry-wide challenges arising from excess capacity in the telecommunications sector and the declining fortunes of internet businesses. O'Connor decided that it would be worth spending time examining the potential for revenue recognition problems at Lucent's major competitors.

LUCENT'S PROBLEMS

Lucent Technologies provided communications systems and software for large wire and wireless communications network operators and service providers. More than 75% of the company's sales were to large service providers. Its two largest customers, Verizon and AT&T, accounted for 13% and 10% of sales, respectively. Lucent provided medium- to long-term financing and financing guarantees to its customers.

Professor Paul Healy and Research Associate Arjuna Costa (MBA 2001) prepared this case. This case was developed from published sources. HBS cases are developed solely as the basis for class discussion. Cases are not intended to serve as endorsements, sources of primary data, or illustrations of effective or ineffective management.

Many of these loans, however, were not included on its balance sheet, since they had been sold to financial institutions. By December 31, 2000, Lucent had made agreements to extend credit to customers for $5.7 billion, $1.8 billion of had been used, and was finalizing an agreement with a customer to extend an additional $1.6 billion of credit. Lucent had also made commitments to guarantee customer debt of about $1.8 billion, $740 million of which had been used.

Even before the discovery of its accounting problems, the year 2000 had been a challenging one for Lucent. In product development it had failed to foresee the rapid switch to fiber-optic networks, enabling competitors such as Nortel Networks Inc. to capture market share. As a result, after meeting earnings projections for 15 consecutive quarters, at the end of 2000 the company reported earnings declines for two consecutive quarters leading to a series of layoffs and restructurings. In October, Richard McGinn, its chairman and CEO, was replaced by former CEO Henry Schacht. Exhibit 2 shows key news events for Lucent during 2000.

Lucent attributed the revenue revisions affecting fiscal 2000 (its fiscal year ended on September 30) to a variety of factors. The initial $125 million adjustment was due to "misleading documentation and incomplete communications between a sales team and the financial organization with respect to offering a customer credits in connection with a software license."[1] The company stated that the recorded sale did not meet its revenue recognition rules. As a result, one employee was fired and disciplinary action was taken against several others.

In subsequent revisions announced on December 22, Lucent took back $452 million in equipment that had been sold to systems integrators and distributors but not been passed on to customers because of their weakened financial condition. Lucent noted that in "verbal agreements" it had agreed to take back the equipment, and it resolved to fulfill this commitment to preserve customer relationships. Also, the company discovered that sales teams had verbally offered credits to customers for use at a later date to help secure fourth-quarter sales. It decided to reflect the credits as expenses in the fourth quarter, reducing revenues by $74 million. Finally, revenue had been recognized on the sale of a system that had not been completely shipped, lowering fourth-quarter revenues by an additional $28 million.[2]

One week later, on December 29, Lucent reported that it had almost doubled its provision for bad debts.

Not surprisingly, most analysts responded negatively to the announcements of Lucent's revenue recognition problems. Michael Ching, an analyst with Merrill Lynch, lowered his rating of the company from long-term buy to long-term accumulate and lowered his 2001 earnings expectations from 65 cents a share to 20 cents a share after the November announcement (and to nil after the December announcement). In supporting his revision, Ching argued "it's very dangerous to assume some of those revenue recognition issues won't impact revenue figures going forward. That's why we're being so cautious."[3] Paul Sagawa, at Sanford C. Bernstein, commented: "Over the last two or three years, lax financial controls have resulted in sales force pulling orders ahead into the last weeks of a quarter, often with the aid

---

1. "Lucent Revises Its Revenues Downward-Total of $679 Million Is Cut For Fiscal 4th Quarter; 1st-Period Loss Is Seen," Shawn Young, Wall Street Journal, December 22, 2000.

2. Source of information on reasons for restatements: "Lucent Revises Its Revenues Downward-Total of $679 Million Is Cut For Fiscal 4th Quarter; 1st-Period Loss Is Seen," Shawn Young, Wall Street Journal, December 22, 2000.

3. Michael Ching, Lengthening List of Questions: Lowering Long-Term Rating, Merrill Lynch, November 21, 2000.

of customer discounts, in order to post quota-beating results"[4] but remained optimistic ". . . Debbie Hopkins, CFO is spearheading the implementation of strong financial controls and information systems."[5]

CHANGES IN COMMUNICATIONS EQUIPMENT INDUSTRY

Two important changes drove the spectacular growth experienced by firms in the communications equipment industry in the 1990s. The first was the less restrictive regulatory environment in the U.S. telecommunications industry. Prior to the 1996 Telecommunications Act, when telecommunications services were a regulated monopoly, regulation provided a floor for service prices in long distance and wireless services, enabling service providers to recover the costs of any capacity-increasing investments. The new legislation changed this arrangement, leading industry observers to anticipate greater price competition among providers, as well as rapid growth in demand for core network services and opportunities to provide new information services to subscribers.

The second major driver of growth in the communications equipment industry arose from rapid technological advances, particularly the explosion in applications and use of the Internet, the promise of development of a broadband network, and changes in wireless technology. The changes in wireless technology "simultaneously vastly improved service quality and vastly reduced the average cost of capacity in a wireless network. Moreover, intense competition among numerous carriers led to falling prices, so that the price premium for wireless shrank—and for some users essentially disappeared."[6]

As a result of these regulatory and technology changes, the late 1990s witnessed "massive investments to expand the capacity of both wireless and wire line networks as well as to facilitate the expected boom in high-speed data transmission."[7] Firms that supplied this network capacity included Lucent Technologies, Nortel Networks, Alcatel, Siemens, Motorola, Cisco Systems, and Juniper Networks, all of whom reported explosive revenue growth. The systems, services and software provided by these firms enabled wired and wireless telecommunications companies and cable and satellite TV service providers to deliver integrated voice, data, video and multimedia services to their subscribers. In addition, firms in the communications equipment industry supplied businesses and governments with the hardware, software and services needed to create networks through the internet. As shown in Exhibit 3, worldwide revenues for the communications equipment market grew at an annual rate of 23% per year from 1994 to 1999, from $104 billion to $290 billion.

By the end of 2000, however, the technology boom had lost momentum, leading to excess capacity within the telecommunications sector, increased price competition from both wire and wireless firms, the first ever decline in local wire access company customers, and decreased demand for internet networking equipment, software and services.

---

4. Paul Sagawa and Matthew Nagle, Lucent: Clearing the Air; Reducing Estimates, *Sanford C. Bernstein & Co., December 2000.*

5. Ibid.

6. Robert E. Litan and Roger G. Noll, "The Uncertain Future of the Telecommunications Industry," January 2004, Brookings Institution, Policy Brief No. 129.

7. Ibid.

POTENTIAL REVENUE RECOGNITION PROBLEMS AT LUCENT'S COMPETITORS

Under US GAAP, revenues cannot be recognized until they were earned and realizable. Accounting standards defined revenues as being earned "when the entity has substantially accomplished what it must do to be entitled to the benefits represented by the revenues."[8] Revenues were considered to be realizable when "the assets received . . . are readily converted into known amounts of cash or claims to cash."[9] Companies for which revenues had yet to be collected were required to estimate a reserve or provision for bad debts to reflect expected losses on customer collections.

In his discussion of earnings management, former SEC Chairman Arthur Levitt noted that managers were frequently permitted to exercise business judgment in deciding when to recognize revenue. As a result, he argued, premature recognition of revenue had become a popular way to manage earnings.[10] Consistent with Levitt's allegation, in the period 1998 to 2000, 21% of company financial restatements were attributable to improper revenue recognition, the most common restatement reason.[11]

Given the prevalence of revenue recognition restatements and Lucent's recent problems, in early 2001 John O'Connor decided to judge whether revenue recognition problems were likely to arise at the following key Lucent competitors:

Cisco Systems[12]   Cisco Systems was a leading provider of networking hardware, software, and services that connected computing devices to networks and computer networks to each other. In 2000, routers and switches made up 80% of revenues. The company's diverse customer base included large enterprises, service providers, small/medium-sized businesses and consumers. No single customer accounted for more than 10% of sales. Cisco's multi-channel approach to sales and marketing included a direct sales force to distributors, value-added resellers, and systems integrators. Cisco provided lease financing to customers and channel partners. On January 27, 2001 (quarter end), these were valued at $516 million and were included on the balance sheet as non-current long-term lease receivables.

Juniper Networks[13]   Juniper Networks provided high performance routers and software for Internet and other telecommunications service providers that built infrastructure for the Internet. Its target market was major service providers. In 2000, one firm, WorldCom, Inc., accounted for approximately 18% of its revenues. Juniper's marketing and sales strategy included the use of a direct sales force, value-added reseller relationships with Alcatel and Nortel, among others, and an original equipment manufacturer partnership through a strategic distribution relationship with Ericsson, which enabled it to outsource manufacturing and avoid carrying inventory. Juniper typically did not provide financing for its customers.

Nortel Networks[14]   Nortel was a leading global supplier of networking solutions for the Internet as well as other data, voice and video networks using both wire and

8. "Recognition and Measurement in Financial Statements of Business Enterprises," Statement of Financial Accounting Concepts No. 5 (Stamford, CT, FASB 1984), para. 83.

9. Ibid.

10. See "The Numbers Game," Remarks by Arthur Levitt at NYU Center for Law and Business, September 28, 1998.

11. See "An Analysis of Restatement Matters: Rules, Errors, Ethics for the Five Years Ended December 2002," Huron Consulting Group.

12. Source: Cisco Systems, Inc., July 29, 2000 10-K (San Jose: Cisco Systems, Inc., 2000).

13. Source: Juniper Networks, Inc., December 31, 2000 10-K (Sunnyvale: Juniper Networks, Inc., 2000).

14. Source: Nortel Networks Inc., December 31, 2000 10-K (Brampton, Ontario: Nortel Networks Inc., 2000).

wireless technologies. In 2000, services accounted for 82% of revenues. Although 60% of its revenues were from the U.S., Nortel was not dependent on any single client. Its sales were primarily made through a direct sales force, but it also used distributors and licensees. Nortel provided significant medium- and long-term financing to its customers. At December 31, 2000, Nortel had entered into agreements to provide $5.6 billion of credit to its customers, $1.5 billion of which had been used.

For each company O'Connor collected quarterly financial statement data for 1998 to 2000 (shown in **Exhibits 4** to **7**). To judge managers' financial reporting pressures, he also assembled data on management stock options outstanding (**Exhibit 8**), trading by insiders (**Exhibit 9**), and company bond ratings (**Exhibit 10**). As he reviewed this information, O'Connor wondered what measures provided the best early warnings of revenue recognition problems? Did Lucent exhibit any early warning signs? And based on these measures, what risks were faced by Lucent's competitors?

QUESTIONS

1. In late 2000, Lucent announced that revenues would be adjusted downwards by $679 million as a result of revenue recognition problems. Yet the firm's market capitalization plummeted by $24.7 billion. Why do you think the market reacted so negatively to Lucent's announcements of the problems?

2. What financial statement adjustments will Lucent have to make to correct the revenue recognition problems announced in late 2000?

3. How would you judge whether a firm is likely to face revenue recognition problems?

4. Assess whether any of Lucent's competitors are likely to face revenue recognition problems in the coming quarters.

EXHIBIT I

Stock Price Performance for Lucent Technologies, January 1, 2000 to December 31, 2000

Source: Price-Data.com.

EXHIBIT 2

Time line of significant events for Lucent Technologies for 2000

Date	Event
January 9, 2000	Announced major shortfall in first quarter profits relative to analyst expectations
May 4, 2000	To sell slow-growing power-systems business
June 1, 2000	To acquire optical networking firm, Chromatis Networks, for $4.5 billion in stock
June 12, 2000	Lehman analyst lowers profit forecasts
June 15, 2000	Considering spinning-off microelectronics unit
June 16, 2000	Signed $1.5 billion contract to supply Verizon with equipment
July 21, 2000	Announced $301 million loss for third quarter, and warned of weaker fourth quarter revenues and profits. To spin-off microelectronics unit
July 27, 2000	Head of optical unit to resign
August 4, 2000	To split optical networking division into two units to refocus business
August 7, 2000	Hired new CFO, Deborah Hopkins, with large signing bonus
October 6, 2000	Signed 5-year contract to supply SBC Communications with more than $1 billion of equipment
October 11, 2000	Warns of fourth quarter profit decline
October 12, 2000	S&P and Moody's lowered outlook ratings
October 24, 2000	Richard McGinn ousted as Chairman/CEO. Reappointed former CEO Henry Schacht as interim replacement
November 8, 2000	Plans to cut work force by as much as 10%
November 22, 2000	Announced restating fourth quarter results, reducing revenues by $125 million and earnings per share by 2 cents
December 22, 2000	Announced operating loss of 25 to 30 cents per share for first quarter, and erased $679 million of revenues from earlier fourth quarter
December 29, 2000	Increased bad debt reserve for fiscal year 2000 by $252 million

Source: Compiled by the casewriters.

EXHIBIT 3

Worldwide Revenues for the Communications Equipment Market for 1994 to 1999 (in USD millions)

	1994	1995	1996	1997	1998	1999
Networking Communications Equipment	$13,505	$19,403	$26,328	$33,777	$36,716	$42,823
Remote LAN and Internet Access Equipment	3,098	5,950	8,849	8,885	8,724	11,377
Voice Communications Equipment	16,857	19,319	20,886	20,320	22,274	24,769
Mobile Communications	16,061	21,242	28,266	38,125	53,444	63,185
Public Network Equipment	7,322	10,304	11,149	13,539	16,250	18,043
Total Telecommunications Equipment	$104,028	$139,007	$173,489	$208,007	$253,680	$290,400

Source: Adapted by HBS from Gartner, Inc., "Global Telecom Market Take, Second Quarter 2000," by William L. Hahn, July 24, 2000.

EXHIBIT 4

Summary Quarterly Financial Information for Lucent Technologies Inc. for 1998 to 2000 (in USD millions)

CONSOLIDATED INCOME STATEMENTS

	Dec-00	Sep-00	Jun-00	Mar-00	Dec-99	Sep-99	Jun-99	Mar-99	Dec-98	Sep-98	Jun-98	Mar-98
Revenues	5,841	4,939	8,713	10,256	9,905	11,564	9,315	8,220	9,204	8,038	7,228	6,157
Cost of sales	4,530	3,418	4,923	5,939	5,259	6,141	4,834	4,327	4,386	4,255	3,949	3,433
SG&A expenses	2,137	773	1,494	2,030	1,969	2,678	2,063	1,902	1,774	1,828	1,566	1,487
R&D expenses	1,285	1,057	1,878	1,110	978	1,547	1,141	1,157	947	1,137	1,615	1,086
Operating income	(2,111)	(309)	418	1,177	1,699	1,198	1,277	834	2,097	818	98	151
Other income and expenses – net[a]	(147)	(111)	40	(68)	157	273	(100)	(160)	24	(126)	(86)	(27)
Earnings before taxes	(2,258)	(420)	458	1,109	1,856	1,471	1,177	674	2,121	692	12	124
Income taxes	(679)	(111)	472	355	606	605	427	232	721	304	245	101
Income from continuing operations	(1,579)	(309)	(14)	754	1,250	866	750	442	1,400	388	(233)	23
Income from discontinued operations	—	(175)	(287)	—	—	—	—	—	—	—	—	—
Extraordinary gain	1,154	—	—	—	—	—	—	—	—	—	—	—
Cumulative effect of accounting change	30	—	—	—	—	—	—	—	1,308	—	—	—
Net income	(395)	(484)	(301)	754	1,250	866	750	442	2,708	388	(233)	23

Source: Company reports and regulatory filings from company website, SEC website and Thomson Research (accessed August 2006).

a. Includes interest income and expense.

Revenue Recognition Problems

Revenue Recognition Problems

CONSOLIDATED BALANCE SHEETS

	Dec-00	Sep-00	Jun-00	Mar-00	Dec-99	Sep-99	Jun-99	Mar-99	Dec-98	Sep-98	Jun-98	Mar-98
Assets												
Cash and cash equivalents	3,814	1,467	710	1,709	2,219	1,816	1,495	792	940	685	1,099	969
Accounts receivables	7,837	10,059	10,431	10,918	10,524	10,800	9,879	9,101	9,531	7,329	6,166	5,945
Less: Allowances	551	501	330	345	381	362	393	349	346	390	374	369
Accounts receivables – net	7,286	9,558	10,101	10,573	10,143	10,438	9,486	8,752	9,185	6,939	5,792	5,576
Completed goods	3,543	2,976	2,568	3,024	3,062	2,946	2,917	2,281	1,777	1,578	1,594	1,463
Works in progress	3,336	2,701	2,368	2,297	2,318	2,102	2,262	2,051	2,001	1,503	1,379	1,411
Inventories	6,879	5,677	4,936	5,321	5,380	5,048	5,179	4,332	3,778	3,081	2,973	2,874
Contracts in process – net	1,691	1,881	1,758	1,416	1,164	1,103	1,338	1,106	1,060	1,259	1,405	1,332
Other current assets – net	3,239	2,907	3,076	3,395	2,672	3,526	3,312	2,792	2,388	2,114	2,036	1,958
Total current assets	22,909	21,490	20,581	22,414	21,578	21,931	20,810	17,774	17,351	14,078	13,305	12,709
Total long-term assets	27,132	27,302	25,759	17,583	17,056	16,844	16,346	15,066	14,290	12,642	11,974	11,955
Total assets	**50,041**	**48,792**	**46,340**	**39,997**	**38,634**	**38,775**	**37,156**	**32,840**	**31,641**	**26,720**	**25,279**	**24,664**
Liabilities and equity												
Current liabilities	12,473	10,877	8,187	9,292	9,917	11,778	11,956	11,562	12,441	10,428	10,196	9,418
Long-term debt	3,099	3,076	3,842	3,833	3,832	4,162	3,712	3,716	2,404	2,409	1,899	1,918
Other long-term liabilities	8,721	8,667	8,181	9,290	8,806	9,251	9,085	8,511	8,359	8,349	8,262	8,292
Total liabilities	24,293	22,620	20,210	22,415	22,555	25,191	24,753	23,789	23,204	21,186	20,357	19,628
Shareholders' equity	25,748	26,172	26,130	17,582	16,079	13,584	12,403	9,051	8,437	5,534	4,922	5,036
Total liabilities and equity	**50,041**	**48,792**	**46,340**	**39,997**	**38,634**	**38,775**	**37,156**	**32,840**	**31,641**	**26,720**	**25,279**	**24,664**

Source: Company reports and regulatory filings from company website, SEC website and Thomson Research (accessed August 2006).

CONSOLIDATED STATEMENTS OF CASH FLOWS

	Dec-00	Sep-00	Jun-00	Mar-00	Dec-99	Sep-99	Jun-99	Mar-99	Dec-98	Sep-98	Jun-98	Mar-98
Net cash provided by operating activities	(1,104)	682	(846)	344	124	996	195	(366)	(1,101)	(95)	1,161	(85)
Net cash provided by investing activities	1,909	(1,114)	(1,013)	(376)	23	(650)	(107)	(663)	(367)	(831)	(1,579)	(388)
Net cash from debt holders/ leases	1,576	1,475	605	(766)	(292)	90	(111)	744	1,528	303	500	130
Net cash from equity/ preferred holders	1	214	199	281	495	(162)	270	141	185	207	69	107
Net cash provided by financing activities	1,577	1,689	804	(485)	203	(72)	159	885	1,713	510	569	237
Effect of exchange rates on cash	(35)	48	(34)	7	(11)	47	14	(31)	10	2	(21)	(20)
Net increase in cash and equivalents (continuing operations)	2,347	1,305	(1,089)	(510)	339	321	261	(175)	255	(414)	130	(256)

Source: Company reports and regulatory filings from company website, SEC website and Thomson Research (accessed August 2006).

Revenue Recognition Problems

EXHIBIT 5

Summary Quarterly Financial Information for Cisco Systems, Inc. for 1998 to 2000 (in USD millions)

CONSOLIDATED INCOME STATEMENTS

	Jan-01	Oct-00	Jul-00	Apr-00	Jan-00	Oct-99	Jul-99	Apr-99	Jan-99	Oct-98	Jul-98	Apr-98
Revenues	6,748	6,519	5,782	4,919	4,350	3,877	3,592	3,147	2,827	2,588	2,390	2,184
Cost of sales	2,581	2,378	2,098	1,748	1,536	1,364	1,259	1,102	985	894	819	750
SG&A expenses	1,886	1,788	1,608	1,220	1,114	928	855	752	660	598	532	480
R&D expenses	1,249	1,451	1,329	1,207	641	900	573	418	706	368	342	682
Operating income	1,032	902	747	744	1,059	685	905	875	476	728	697	273
Other income and expenses – net[a]	275	420	538	313	151	106	97	90	80	65	60	52
Earnings before taxes	1,307	1,322	1,285	1,057	1,210	791	1,002	965	556	793	756	325
Income taxes	433	524	542	395	385	353	358	319	268	275	265	260
Net income	874	798	743	662	825	438	644	646	288	518	492	65

Source: Company reports and regulatory filings from company website, SEC website and Thomson Research (accessed August 2006).

a. Includes interest income and expense.

EXHIBIT 5

CONSOLIDATED BALANCE SHEETS

	Jan-01	Oct-00	Jul-00	Apr-00	Jan-00	Oct-99	Jul-99	Apr-99	Jan-99	Oct-98	Jul-98	Apr-98
Assets												
Cash and cash equivalents	4,782	6,391	5,525	4,653	3,968	1,765	2,016	1,851	2,307	1,881	1,692	2,113
Accounts receivables	3,601	2,944	2,342	1,960	1,740	1,418	1,269	1,305	1,514	1,372	1,338	1,304
Less: Allowances	89	57	43	38	29	27	27	30	37	39	40	31
Accounts receivables – net	3,512	2,887	2,299	1,922	1,711	1,391	1,242	1,275	1,477	1,333	1,298	1,273
Completed goods	690	704	615	466	341	313	311	271	201	169	143	117
Works in progress	1,843	1,252	617	412	354	342	341	350	271	206	219	192
Inventories	2,533	1,956	1,232	878	695	655	652	621	472	375	362	308
Lease receivables	454	459	588	N/A	N/A	N/A	80	N/A	N/A	N/A	N/A	N/A
Other current assets – net	1,631	1,366	1,466	1,627	1,348	1,081	625	579	552	409	411	448
Total current assets	12,912	13,059	11,110	9,080	7,722	4,892	4,615	4,326	4,808	3,998	3,762	4,143
Long-term lease receivables	516	550	527	N/A	N/A	N/A	500	N/A	N/A	N/A	N/A	N/A
Other long-term assets	22,453	20,543	21,223	17,005	13,669	12,515	9,610	8,382	6,626	5,867	5,155	3,755
Total assets	**35,881**	**34,152**	**32,870**	**26,085**	**21,391**	**17,407**	**14,725**	**12,708**	**11,434**	**9,865**	**8,917**	**7,898**
Liabilities and equity												
Current liabilities	6,335	5,802	5,196	5,099	3,778	3,029	3,003	2,412	2,234	1,869	1,767	1,547
Long-term debt	—	—	—	—	—	—	—	—	—	—	—	—
Other long-term liabilities		664	1,132	915	1,045	452	—	—	—	—	—	—
Total liabilities	6,335	6,466	6,328	6,014	4,823	3,481	3,003	2,412	2,234	1,869	1,767	1,547
Minority Interest	48	45	45	45	45	44	44	44	44	43	43	43
Shareholders' equity	29,498	27,641	26,497	20,026	16,523	13,882	11,678	10,252	9,156	7,953	7,107	6,308
Total liabilities and equity	**35,881**	**34,152**	**32,870**	**26,085**	**21,391**	**17,407**	**14,725**	**12,708**	**11,434**	**9,865**	**8,917**	**7,898**

Source: Company reports and regulatory filings from company website, SEC website and Thomson Research (accessed August 2006).

N/A: Not available.

Revenue Recognition Problems

CONSOLIDATED STATEMENTS OF CASH FLOWS

	Jan-01	Oct-00	Jul-00	Apr-00	Jan-00	Oct-99	Jul-99	Apr-99	Jan-99	Oct-98	Jul-98	Apr-98
Net cash provided by operating activities	1,463	1,363	1,621	1,805	1,539	1,176	1,482	1,241	865	850	896	817
Net cash provided by investing activities	(3,384)	(378)	(1,510)	(2,337)	508	(1,038)	(1,612)	(2,170)	(592)	(563)	(1,672)	(267)
Net cash from debt holders/leases	17	(19)	(5)	(8)	—	6	1	(6)	—	11	(5)	(0)
Net cash from equity holders	360	338	559	363	373	269	221	204	187	128	145	144
Net cash provided by financing activities	377	319	554	355	373	275	222	198	187	139	140	144
Net increase in cash and equivalents (continuing operations)	(1,544)	1,304	665	(177)	2,420	413	92	(731)	460	426	(636)	694

Source: Company reports and regulatory filings from company website, SEC website and Thomson Research (accessed August 2006).

EXHIBIT 6

Summary Quarterly Financial Information for Juniper Networks for 1998 to 2000 (in USD millions)

CONSOLIDATED INCOME STATEMENTS

	Dec-00	Sep-00	Jun-00	Mar-00	Dec-99	Sep-99	Jun-99	Mar-99	Dec-98	Sep-98	Jun-98	Mar-98
Revenues	295.4	201.2	113.0	63.9	45.4	29.6	17.6	10.0	3.8	—	—	—
Cost of sales	101.4	70.3	40.8	25.1	18.4	12.5	8.0	6.3	3.8	0.4	0.2	—
SG&A expenses	62.3	31.1	33.7	16.9	12.3	8.1	5.7	4.3	3.2	2.2	1.4	0.9
R&D expenses	40.2	23.6	18.0	16.0	15.8	11.5	8.0	6.2	6.1	8.3	6.1	3.5
Operating income	91.5	76.2	20.5	5.9	(1.1)	(2.5)	(4.2)	(6.8)	(9.4)	(10.8)	(7.6)	(4.4)
Other income and expenses — net[a]	8.1	11.6	9.9	6.6	6.1	1.4	0.4	0.1	0.1	0.2	0.4	0.5
Earnings before taxes	99.6	87.9	30.4	12.5	5.0	(1.2)	(3.8)	(6.7)	(9.3)	(10.6)	(7.2)	(3.9)
Income taxes	37.4	29.8	10.8	4.5	1.9	0.4	0.1	—	—	—	—	—
Net income	62.2	58.1	19.6	8.1	3.1	(1.6)	(3.9)	(6.7)	(9.3)	(10.6)	(7.2)	(3.9)

Source: Company reports, prospectuses, and regulatory filings from company website, SEC website and Thomson Research (accessed August 2006).

a. Includes interest income and expense.

Revenue Recognition Problems

CONSOLIDATED BALANCE SHEETS[a]

	Dec-98	Mar-99	Jun-99	Sep-99	Dec-99	Mar-00	Jun-00	Sep-00	Dec-00
Assets									
Cash and cash equivalents	20.1	49.4	107.8	84.6	346.0	1,350.0	1,181.9	1,138.9	1,144.7
Accounts receivables	8.1	8.6	17.3	13.6	24.6	30.0	60.7	116.3	180.3
Less: Allowances	—	—	—	—	0.6	—	—	—	3.7
Accounts receivables – net	8.1	8.6	17.3	13.6	24.0	30.0	60.7	116.3	176.5
Other current assets – net	0.7	0.8	0.9	3.5	7.9	11.8	15.8	20.8	27.3
Total current assets	28.8	58.9	126.0	101.7	377.8	1,391.8	1,258.4	1,276.0	1,348.5
Total long-term assets	7.8	8.2	17.1	45.9	135.5	303.1	571.9	669.4	754.6
Total assets	**36.7**	**67.1**	**143.1**	**147.6**	**513.4**	**1,694.9**	**1,830.4**	**1,945.4**	**2,103.1**
Liabilities and equity									
Current liabilities	14.4	17.2	26.6	34.4	55.7	74.5	135.8	191.3	216.4
Long-term debt	—	—	—	—	—	1,150.0	1,150.0	1,150.0	1,150.0
Other long-term liabilities	5.2	2.8	2.5	0.0	—	—	15.7	11.1	6.7
Total liabilities	19.6	20.0	29.2	34.4	55.7	1,224.5	1,301.6	1,352.4	1,373.1
Shareholders' equity	17.1	47.1	114.0	113.2	457.7	470.4	528.8	593.0	730.0
Total liabilities and equity	**36.7**	**67.1**	**143.1**	**147.6**	**513.4**	**1,694.9**	**1,830.4**	**1,945.4**	**2,103.1**

Source: Company reports, prospectuses, and regulatory filings from company website, SEC website and Thomson Research (accessed August 2006).

a. *Quarterly data for quarters ending March 1998, June 1998, and September 1998, not disclosed as company was privately held.*

CONSOLIDATED STATEMENTS OF CASH FLOWS

	Dec-00	Sep-00	Jun-00	Mar-00	Dec-99	Sep-99	Jun-99	Mar-99	Dec-98	Sep-98	Jun-98	Mar-98
Net cash provided by operating activities	128.6	58.4	60.9	21.2	12.6	10.7	(1.2)	(1.7)	(8.8)	(6.3)	(6.0)	(3.7)
Net cash provided by investing activities	(30.7)	(294.4)	(334.6)	(234.5)	(215.7)	(63.1)	(24.7)	(1.9)	(2.6)	1.5	4.7	5.7
Net cash from debt holders/leases	0.0	0.0	0.0	1,123.3	0.0	(3.7)	(0.3)	(3.4)	1.0	1.9	1.1	0.6
Net cash from equity holders[a]	(106.1)	10.2	2.2	0.4	324.6	0.1	69.7	35.8	0.5	0.2	—	—
Net cash provided by financing activities	(106.1)	10.2	2.2	1,123.7	324.6	(3.5)	69.4	32.4	1.4	2.1	1.1	0.6
Net increase in cash and equivalents (continuing operations)	(8.2)	(225.9)	(271.4)	910.5	121.6	(56.0)	43.5	28.8	(10.0)	(2.8)	(0.2)	2.6

Source: Company reports, prospectuses, and regulatory filings from company website, SEC website and Thomson Research (accessed August 2006).

a. Includes preferred stock.

Revenue Recognition Problems

Revenue Recognition Problems

EXHIBIT 7

Summary Quarterly Financial Information for Nortel Networks for 1998 to 2000 (in USD millions)

CONSOLIDATED INCOME STATEMENTS

	Dec-00	Sep-00	Jun-00	Mar-00	Dec-99	Sep-99	Jun-99	Mar-99	Dec-98	Sep-98	Jun-98	Mar-98
Revenues	8,818	7,314	7,821	6,322	6,993	5,393	5,413	4,418	5,768	4,141	4,156	3,510
Cost of sales	4,804	4,096	4,485	3,718	3,928	3,099	3,075	2,495	3,239	2,346	2,419	2,046
SG&A expenses	3,570	2,722	2,326	1,852	1,629	1,383	1,569	1,568	1,869	1,282	1,025	626
R&D expenses	1,556	1,038	1,378	1,524	786	755	701	666	448	616	610	779
Restructuring Charges	9	—	67	195	44	103	62	—	27	388	32	—
Operating income	(1,121)	(542)	(435)	(967)	606	53	6	(311)	185	(491)	70	59
Other income and expenses – net[a]	(25)	181	16	501	67	105	27	(27)	(44)	326	(9)	(32)
Earnings before taxes	(1,146)	(361)	(419)	(466)	673	158	33	(338)	141	(165)	61	27
Income taxes	271	225	326	256	250	150	171	125	263	133	123	82
Net income	(1,417)	(586)	(745)	(722)	423	8	(138)	(463)	(122)	(298)	(62)	(55)

Source: Company reports and regulatory filings from company website, SEC website and Thomson Research (accessed August 2006).

a. Includes interest income and expense.

CONSOLIDATED BALANCE SHEETS

	Dec-00	Sep-00	Jun-00	Mar-00	Dec-99	Sep-99	Jun-99	Mar-99	Dec-98	Sep-98	Jun-98	Mar-98
Assets												
Cash and cash equivalents	1,644	1,758	3,331	2,060	2,257	1,213	927	1,520	2,281	1,879	495	538
Accounts receivables	8,598	7,737	7,345	7,634	7,114	7,286	6,830	5,883	5,722	5,727	5,314	4,722
Less: Allowances	400	400	406	375	328	374	367	287	260	237	226	—
Accounts receivables – net	8,198	7,337	6,939	7,259	6,786	6,912	6,463	5,596	5,462	5,490	5,088	4,722
Completed goods	2,572	2,443	1,901	1,677	1,381	1,168	987	882	768	—	—	—
Works in progress	1,764	1,616	1,463	1,948	1,575	1,414	1,225	1,113	919	—	—	—
Inventories	4,336	4,059	3,364	3,625	2,956	2,582	2,212	1,995	1,687	2,017	1,886	2,022
Other current assets – net	2,352	2,057	1,925	1,259	1,069	966	896	881	887	1,004	627	599
Total current assets	16,530	15,211	15,559	14,203	13,068	11,673	10,498	9,992	10,317	10,390	8,096	7,881
Long-term receivables	1,911	1,538	1,307	1,506	1,853	1,195	1,062	803	688	408	380	347
Less: Allowances	383	310	286	288	286	199	140	83	115	67	56	—
Long-term receivables – net	1,528	1,228	1,021	1,218	1,567	996	922	720	573	341	324	347
Other long-term assets	24,122	17,464	17,455	14,532	7,962	8,056	8,257	8,051	8,842	9,329	3,942	3,836
Total assets	**42,180**	**33,903**	**34,035**	**29,953**	**22,597**	**20,725**	**19,677**	**18,763**	**19,732**	**20,060**	**12,362**	**12,064**
Liabilities and equity												
Current liabilities	9,058	7,727	8,157	7,524	7,790	7,019	6,090	5,344	5,893	6,042	4,720	4,334
Long-term debt	1,178	1,243	1,222	1,484	1,624	1,470	1,513	1,596	1,648	1,673	1,561	1,566
Other long-term liabilities	2,031	1,804	1,899	1,926	573	640	555	675	537	420	478	512
Total liabilities	12,267	10,774	11,278	10,934	9,987	9,129	8,158	7,615	8,078	8,135	6,759	6,412
Minority Interest	804	797	788	164	92	134	87	87	89	104	74	137
Shareholders' equity	29,109	22,332	21,969	18,855	12,518	11,462	11,432	11,061	11,565	11,821	5,529	5,515
Total liabilities and equity	**42,180**	**33,903**	**34,035**	**29,953**	**22,597**	**20,725**	**19,677**	**18,763**	**19,732**	**20,060**	**12,362**	**12,064**

Source: Company reports and regulatory filings from company website, SEC website and Thomson Research (accessed August 2006).

Revenue Recognition Problems

Revenue Recognition Problems

CONSOLIDATED STATEMENTS OF CASH FLOWS

	Dec-00	Sep-00	Jun-00	Mar-00	Dec-99	Sep-99	Jun-99	Mar-99	Dec-98	Sep-98	Jun-98	Mar-98
Net cash provided by operating activities	961	(956)	642	(607)	1,292	38	120	(477)	1,347	320	140	(221)
Net cash provided by investing activities	(1,184)	(700)	586	377	(399)	99	(830)	(281)	(691)	1,123	(244)	(293)
Net cash from debt holders/leases	87	49	(20)	25	92	110	23	(85)	(130)	8	105	(205)
Net cash from equity holders	12	57	65	122	64	33	95	84	(84)	(67)	(44)	(114)
Net cash provided by financing activities	99	106	45	147	156	143	118	(1)	(214)	(59)	61	(319)
Effect of exchange rates on cash	10	(23)	(2)	(10)	—	6	(1)	(2)	(40)	—	—	—
Net increase in cash and equivalents (continuing operations)	(114)	(1,573)	1,271	(93)	1,044	286	(593)	(761)	402	1,384	(43)	(833)

Source: Company reports and regulatory filings from company website, SEC website and Thomson Research (accessed August 2006).

EXHIBIT 8

Management Stock Options Outstanding (in 000) for Communications Equipment Firms for Years 1997 to 2000

	2000	1999	1998	1997
Lucent Technologies, Inc. (year ended 9/30)				
Common shares – basic (in millions)	3,384.3	3,071.8	3,022.4	2,894.6
Stock options outstanding (in millions)	431.5	266.5	251.8	183.2
Weighted Average Exercise Price (USD)	39.34	26.06	19.84	12.26
Stock Price at Fiscal Year End (USD)	25.20	49.85	26.60	15.63
Cisco Systems (year ended 7/31)				
Common shares – basic (in millions)	7,138.0	6,821.0	6,304.0	6,037.0
Stock options outstanding (in millions)	971.0	889.0	876.0	810.0
Weighted Average Exercise Price (USD)	24.19	11.22	6.25	4.05
Stock Price at Fiscal Year End (USD)	65.44	31.06	16.42	8.83
Juniper Networks (year ended 12/31)				
Common shares – basic (in millions)	318.1	311.8	123.4	114.7
Stock options outstanding (in millions)	52.9	44.5	21.6	10.3
Weighted Average Exercise Price (USD)	39.96	12.56	0.28	0.03
Stock Price at Fiscal Year End (USD)	126.06	56.67	<– Privately held –>	
Nortel Networks (year ended 12/31)				
Common shares – basic (in millions)	3,095.8	2,754.3	2,652.4	2,075.5
Stock options outstanding (in millions)	331.6	234.5	220.1	100.3
Weighted Average Exercise Price (USD)	32.37	15.25	9.02	7.08
Stock Price at Fiscal Year End (USD)	32.06	50.50	12.50	11.09

Source: Company reports and regulatory filings from company website, SEC website and Thomson Research (accessed August 2006); historic stock price information from Bloomberg (accessed August 2006).

Revenue Recognition Problems

Revenue Recognition Problems

EXHIBIT 9

Quarterly Net Sales of Shares by Insiders at Communications Equipment Firms from 1998 to 2000[a]

	2000, Q4	2000, Q3	2000, Q2	2000, Q1	1999, Q4	1999, Q3	1999, Q2	1999, Q1	1998, Q4	1998, Q3	1998, Q2	1998, Q1
Lucent Technologies	—	—	812	—	576	193	157	—	—	1,402	255	337
Cisco Systems	180	2,885	—	8,910	101	5,419	312	5,774	6,902	8,077	—	3,448
Juniper Networks	708	1,240	234	1,488	—	(960)	—	—	—	—	—	—
Nortel Networks	(77)	—	—	314	—	—	—	—	—	—	—	—

Source: Thomson Financial (TFN) Insider Filing Data, accessed via Wharton Research Data Services, August 2006.

a. Sale of shares less purchase of shares, not including shares purchased as a result of an exercise of options.

EXHIBIT 10

Standard & Poor's Debt Rating History for Communications Equipment Firms from 1998 to 2000

Date	Long-Term Debt Rating	Outlook	Closing Stock Price
Lucent Technologies			
Month prior to ratings action	A	Stable	Average: 26.19
Oct. 11, 2000	A	Negative	17.27
Oct. 23, 2000	A	Watch Negative	17.93
Dec. 21, 2000	BBB+	Watch Negative	11.53
Feb. 12, 2001	BBB−	Negative	12.03
Juniper Networks			
Throughout period	B+	Positive	
Nortel Networks			
Throughout period	A+	Negative	

Notes: Cisco Systems, Inc. had no rated debt outstanding.

Source: Standard & Poor's Ratings Direct, accessed August 2006. Stock price information from Bloomberg, accessed August 2006.

Chapter 5
Financial Analysis

The goal of financial analysis is to assess the performance of a firm in the context of its stated goals and strategy. There are two principal tools of financial analysis: ratio analysis and cash flow analysis. Ratio analysis involves an assessment of how various line items in a firm's financial statements relate to one another. Cash flow analysis allows the analyst to examine the firm's liquidity and to assess the management of operating, investment, and financing cash flows.

Financial analysis is used in a variety of contexts. Ratio analysis that compares a company's present performance to its past performance and/or to the performance of its peers provides the foundation for making forecasts of future performance. As we will discuss in later chapters, financial forecasting is useful in company valuation, credit evaluation, financial distress prediction, security analysis, and mergers and acquisitions analysis.

RATIO ANALYSIS

The value of a firm is determined by its profitability and growth. As shown in Figure 5-1, the firm's growth and profitability are influenced by its product market and financial market strategies. The product market strategy is implemented through the firm's competitive strategy, operating policies, and investment decisions. Financial market strategies are implemented through financing and dividend policies.

Thus, the four levers managers can use to achieve their growth and profit targets are (1) operating management, (2) investment management, (3) financing strategy, and (4) dividend policy. The objective of ratio analysis is to evaluate the effectiveness of the firm's policies in each of these areas. Effective ratio analysis involves relating the financial numbers to the underlying business factors in as much detail as possible. While ratio analysis may not give an analyst all the answers regarding the firm's performance, it will help the analyst frame questions for further probing.

In ratio analysis, the analyst can (1) compare ratios for a firm over several years (a time-series comparison), (2) compare ratios for the firm and other firms in the industry (cross-sectional comparison), and/or (3) compare ratios to some absolute benchmark. In a time-series comparison, the analyst can hold firm-specific factors constant and examine the effectiveness of a firm's strategy over time. Cross-sectional comparison facilitates examining the relative performance of a firm within its industry, holding industry-level factors constant. For most ratios there are no absolute benchmarks. The exceptions are measures of rates of return, which can be compared to the cost of the capital associated with the investment. For example, subject to distortions caused by accounting, the rate of return on equity (ROE) can be compared to the cost of equity capital.

In the discussion below, we will illustrate these approaches using the example of Wal-Mart Stores, Inc., the largest U.S. retailer. We will compare Wal-Mart's ratios for

FIGURE 5-1	Drivers of a Firm's Profitability and Growth

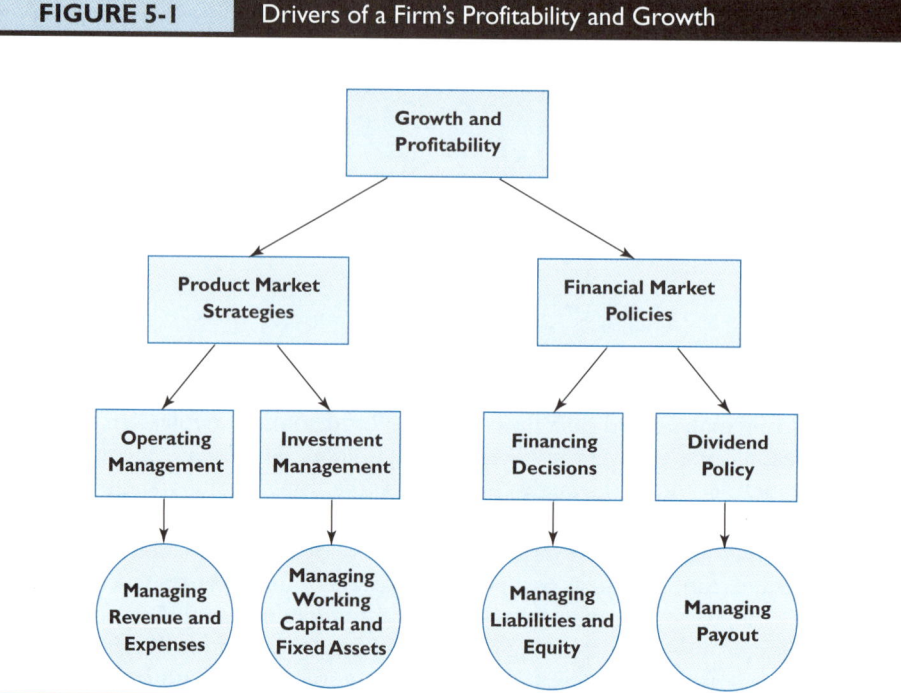

the fiscal year ending January 31, 2006, with its own ratios for the fiscal year ending January 31, 2005, and with the ratios for Target Corporation, another U.S. retailer and one of Wal-Mart's principal competitors, for the fiscal year ending January 28, 2006.[1]

Wal-Mart has dominated, and continues to dominate, the retailing landscape in the U.S. As the second largest corporation in the U.S. when measured by revenue in 2005 (second only to Exxon Mobil), Wal-Mart has created a brand that is synonymous with low prices and value. Wal-Mart is known for effectively managing all aspects of its operating, investing, and financing activities, creating one of the pre-eminent global corporations. On the other hand, Target has, in many ways, reinvented itself over the past decade to successfully position itself as the discount retailer for the fashion conscious consumer. This has enabled Target to distinguish itself from Wal-Mart and carve out a market niche at the higher end of the discount retail market. We will examine whether this strategy has been successful for Target and how it compares to Wal-Mart across the various measures of financial performance that will be described in this chapter. We will also try to see which strategy is delivering better performance for shareholders.

In order to facilitate replication of the ratio calculations presented below, we present in the appendix to this chapter three versions of the financial statements of both these companies. The first version is the one reported by the two companies in their SEC filings. The second set of financial statements is presented in the standardized format described in Chapter 4. These "standardized financial statements" put both companies' financials in one standard format to facilitate direct comparison. The data is taken from Standard & Poor's Compustat database, which generally follows the format used by the companies in their own SEC filings, with minor modifications to make the data comparable across companies. A third format, labeled "Condensed Financial Statements," recasts the standardized financial statements to facilitate the calculation of several ratios discussed in the chapter. We will discuss later in the chapter how this recasting process works.

It is important to ensure that the financial statements of the company being analyzed do not include any data that will distort the analysis. Since the purpose of financial statement analysis is to better understand the performance of the firm as it relates to its strategy, care needs to be taken that any operations and events that are extraneous to that strategy do not change the picture that the analyst forms of the firm. The major categories of such distortions include one-time write-offs of assets and results from discontinued operations, including the gain or loss on the disposal of such operations. In such instances, it is useful to look at financial results of the core operations of the firm by adjusting the presented financial statements to exclude the impact of one-time effects. For example, in 2004 Target divested its interest in Marshall Field's and Mervyn's. Its 2004 results therefore reflected a partial year of revenues and earnings from those operations. In addition, its earnings were boosted by the gain on the sale of the discontinued operations. Without adjusting for these effects it is difficult to meaningfully use Target's 2004 results as a benchmark for performance in 2005 and beyond.

Background Information on Wal-Mart and Target

Wal-Mart Stores, Inc.

Wal-Mart is the number one retailer in the world, dwarfing its rivals in terms of both sales and earnings. Wal-Mart's success originates largely from its retailing philosophy, reflected in its slogan "every day low prices" (EDLP). EDLP entails offering a broad array of quality merchandise at low prices every day, giving customers the confidence that prices will not fluctuate as a result of promotional activity. This retailing proposition is delivered through more than 6,000 retail stores worldwide. While nearly two-thirds of its stores are located in the U.S., Wal-Mart has been expanding internationally and has grown to be the largest retailer in Canada, Mexico, and Puerto Rico. Wal-Mart reported a record $312.4 billion in net sales during the year ended January 31, 2006, and net income was a record $11.2 billion.

Wal-Mart offers its customers the full complement of products ranging from discount staples such as food and clothing to electronics, toys and entertainment, sporting goods, and prescription drugs. While generating impressive returns for its shareholders, Wal-Mart, through its breadth of affordable merchandise, has had a positive impact on the standard of living of its customers. According to a recently published study, Wal-Mart's lower prices and its impact on other retailers' prices saved consumers in the U.S. an estimated $263 billion in 2004, which translates into $2,329 per household.[a]

Wal-Mart's business is divided into three segments:

(1) Wal-Mart Stores, the primary U.S. retail business, accounts for 67 percent of the fiscal 2005[b] revenues from three retail store formats—supercenters, discount stores, and neighborhood markets. In addition, Wal-Mart operates an online retail store;

(2) SAM'S CLUB, which are membership warehouse clubs (and online retail) that account for 12.7 percent of fiscal 2005 sales. Members include both individuals and small and large businesses; and

(3) International operations, which account for 20.1 percent of fiscal 2005 sales through a variety of retail formats and restaurants including supercenters, discount stores, and SAM'S CLUB stores. As of January 31, 2006, Wal-Mart

had a presence in nine foreign countries and Puerto Rico. Subsequently, Wal-Mart increased its stake in CARHCO, a Central American retailer, giving it majority control over a retailer with a presence in five countries in the region.

While Wal-Mart has in many ways perfected the large discount retail model in the U.S., it is constantly improving on its strategy and operations and looking for innovative growth opportunities. Wal-Mart is currently opening stores in urban locations, which is a shift from its roots. It is also trying to replicate Target's success in catering to a higher-income customer with a selection of better designed and fashionable merchandise. In this attempt to appeal to a more affluent customer, Wal-Mart is remodeling a number of its stores, increasing the selection of designer apparel and organic foods, and is actively courting a class it terms "selective" shoppers. These customers come to the store for certain basic commodities but do not believe that Wal-Mart can cater to their quality and style requirements when it comes to apparel and home furnishings.

Wal-Mart has been looking increasingly to its international operations to drive profitable growth in the future. It has chosen a strategy of greenfield operations, joint ventures, and acquisitions to expand overseas, often leveraging a partner's local market knowledge while bringing its expertise in merchandising, supply chain management, and other facets of operations and finance. Two of Wal-Mart's earliest and most successful international operations were in neighboring Canada and Mexico. Wal-Mart was one of the early entrants into the Chinese market, establishing a presence there in 1996. Large acquisitions followed over the rest of the nineties in Germany, Brazil, and the UK, which were followed by acquisitions in Japan and Central America. Wal-Mart has also been lobbying to gain access to the high-growth Indian market. Wal-Mart has shown a willingness to rationalize international operations by disposing of underperforming assets as evidenced by recent exits from the highly competitive South Korean and German markets.

For all its successes, Wal-Mart attracts its fair share of criticism—from the media, its employees, politicians, and the community at large. Wal-Mart has long been vilified for what some have deemed unfair labor practices and poor benefits compensation, and it is the subject of numerous lawsuits alleging discrimination and violations of other wage-and-hour labor laws. Wal-Mart's attempts to address these claims, such as by improving health insurance for employees, will impact future profitability. Wal-Mart has also encountered resistance from community members and local governments as it has pursued expansion opportunities. For instance, some communities in California, a lucrative market for the retailer, have resisted planned Wal-Mart stores because of the perceived increase in traffic and a loss of open space in their neighborhoods. This opposition to Wal-Mart's expansion could limit its domestic growth prospects.

Wal-Mart clearly faces significant challenges and will rely on its seasoned executive team to continue to innovate and drive growth and profitability. In mid 2006, the sell side analyst community had mixed views about Wal-Mart's future success. Citigroup was positive on the stock and expected it to appreciate by 25 percent as a result of improved earnings per share growth from product mix enhancements.[c] On the other hand, JP Morgan's analysts gave the stock a "Neutral" rating, citing, among other reasons, an "augmented risk profile" due to factors such as "merchandise makeovers, international expansion, and field level management changes."[d]

Target Corporation

Target is the second largest discount chain in the U.S. behind Wal-Mart and operates close to 1,400 large-format, general merchandise discount stores. In the competitive world of retailing, Target seems to have identified a profitable market niche and created a sustainable position in the short and medium term. The company markets itself to discount store consumers who are more affluent, by appealing to their design sense and fashion consciousness. Target's brand promise, "Expect More. Pay Less," captures both its upscale appeal and its discount prices—the firm is widely recognized as having identified and successfully capitalized on a market for "cheap chic" goods. To augment this differentiated retailing strategy, Target has created a clever, trendy, and often non-traditional approach to its marketing campaigns. For the most recent fiscal year ended January 28, 2006, the company posted record core operating earnings ($2.4 billion) and record sales ($52.6 billion).

Target strives to create emotional ties with its customers, referred to as "guests," through superior design. Target's merchandising focuses on exclusive private-label collections from prominent designers while continuing to deliver the convenience and low prices that are central to its discount store heritage. Given Target's reliance on changing fashion trends, time to market is crucial. As a result, the company relies heavily on direct sourcing of merchandise and has invested in strengthening its supply chain. It has also invested in building Target.com, the online store which provides it with an integrated, multichannel approach to retailing.

Target's focus on design spills over to the stores themselves, as it experiments with different store design prototypes to refine its customers' shopping experience. In January 2006, Target operated 1,397 stores in the U.S. (compared to Wal-Mart's more than 3,200 domestic stores.) Target management expected to open more than 100 new stores in 2006 with a goal of 2,000 locations by 2010 and an ultimate vision of 3,000, implying an aggressive growth strategy. Management stressed that most of this expansion would come from within the U.S.—it was not yet looking to international growth.[e] Consistent with its focus on the core discount store business, in 2004 Target divested its stakes in Marshall Field's and Mervyn's department store chains.

Given Target's market niche, some analysts have expressed concern that its expansion could come at the expense of profitability. A February 2004 study by Morgan Stanley showed that Target already had a strong presence in California and the northeast corridor, two of the more affluent regions of the country where its value proposition had most traction. Expansion into less wealthy regions could mean a gradual reduction in both per store productivity and same store sales growth over time. This pressure could be offset by a general increase in living standards that would enable people to move up from being purely price-driven Wal-Mart shoppers to becoming style-driven Target shoppers.

Target National Bank, a wholly owned subsidiary of Target, has a credit card business which consists of both proprietary credit cards (usable either at Target stores or Target.com) and Target VISA cards. In fiscal 2005, credit cards contributed 2.6 percent of revenues. While there has been some concern that a credit card business could distract management from its core retailing operations, the customer information gathered from the card allows Target to better respond to its customer shopping needs and contributes to its ability to retain its margin on sales.

Although Target's strategy has paid off handsomely in recent years, it faces significant competitive threats. Wal-Mart is not likely to allow Target to solidify its market niche uncontested and is considering two competitive responses—to increase the appeal of its merchandise through better design and to widen the price gap with Target on commodity products to entice more shoppers to its stores. The other threat to Target is that customers begin splitting their shopping between two locations—for instance, shopping at Wal-Mart for consumables and commodities, which is essentially a price conscious decision, and then at another large retailer such as Kohl's for the purely fashion driven purchases.

Wall Street's view of Target was generally positive in mid 2006, with most analysts expecting price appreciation on Target's stock. Morgan Stanley, for instance, had a bullish outlook for the stock and expected its price to increase 25 percent.[f] Deutsche Bank, which expected a price rise of 20 percent, noted their confidence in Target management's "ability to execute against its long-term strategic plans, despite our expectations for a macro slowdown" and in the firm's ability to sustain 8–10 percent square foot growth for the next 12 years.[g]

a. Global Insight. *The Economic Impact of Wal-Mart,* November 2, 2005.
b. Wal-Mart refers to its fiscal year ended January 31, 2006, as fiscal 2006. However, for the sake of consistency, this book will refer to it as fiscal 2005.
c. Deborah Weinswig and Charmaine Tang, *Wal-Mart Stores, Inc.,* Citigroup, July 2, 2006, via Thomson Research/Investext (accessed July 2006).
d. Charles Grom, Matthew Boss, and Paul Trussel, *Wal-Mart Stores, Inc.,* JP Morgan, July 3, 2006, via Thomson Research/Investext (accessed July 2006).
e. Target Corporation, 2005 Annual Report (Minneapolis: Target Corporation, 2006), p. 8.
f. Gregory Melich, *Target Corp.,* Morgan Stanley, July 18, 2006, via Thomson Research/Investext (accessed July 2006).
g. William A. Dreher Jr., Vin Chao, and Shane Higgins, *Target,* Deutsche Bank, July 12, 2006, via Thomson Research/Investext (accessed July 2006).

Measuring Overall Profitability

The starting point for a systematic analysis of a firm's performance is its return on equity (ROE), defined as

$$\text{ROE} = \frac{\text{Net income}}{\text{Shareholder's equity}}$$

ROE is a comprehensive indicator of a firm's performance because it provides an indication of how well managers are employing the funds invested by the firm's shareholders to generate returns. On average over long periods, large publicly traded firms in the U.S. generate ROEs in the range of 11 to 13 percent.

In the long run, the value of the firm's equity is determined by the relationship between its ROE and its cost of equity capital.[2] That is, those firms that are expected over the long run to generate ROEs in excess of the cost of equity capital should have market values in excess of book value, and vice versa. (We will return to this point in more detail in the chapter on valuation.)

A comparison of ROE with the cost of capital is useful not only for analyzing the value of the firm but also in considering the path of future profitability. The generation of consistent supernormal profitability will, absent significant barriers to entry, attract competition. For that reason ROEs tend over time to be driven by competitive forces toward a "normal" level—the cost of equity capital. Thus, one can think of the cost of equity capital as establishing a benchmark for the ROE that would be observed in a long-run competitive equilibrium. Deviations from this level arise for two general reasons. One is the industry conditions and competitive strategy that cause a firm to generate supernormal (or subnormal) economic profits, at least over the short run. The second is distortions due to accounting.

Table 5-1 shows the ROE based on reported earnings for Wal-Mart and Target.

	Wal-Mart	**Wal-Mart**	**Target**
Ratio	**FY2005**	**FY2004**	**FY2005**
Return on equity	22.7%	23.5%	18.5%

TABLE 5-1   Return on Equity for Wal-Mart and Target

Wal-Mart outperformed Target in 2005, despite the fact that Wal-Mart failed to sustain the level of profitability that it achieved in the prior year. Target's ROE of 18.5 percent trails the 22.7 percent earned by Wal-Mart in 2005. The performance of both companies over the past two years has exceeded both historical trends of ROE in the economy and reasonable estimates of the cost of equity capital for the firms.[3]

Wal-Mart's superior profitability performance relative to Target is reflected in the difference between the market value of equity to book value ratios for the two firms. As we will discuss in Chapter 7, ROE is a key determinant of a company's market to book ratio. As of early April 2006, when both companies had released their 2006 year-end results, Wal-Mart's market to book ratio was 3.6 and Target's ratio was 3.2. This differential in market valuation could be an indication that investors expected Wal-Mart to continue to outperform Target in the coming years and earn a superior return for its shareholders.

Decomposing Profitability: Traditional Approach

A company's ROE is affected by two factors: how profitably it employs its assets and how big the firm's asset base is relative to shareholders' investment. To understand the effect of these two factors, ROE can be decomposed into return on assets (ROA) and a measure of financial leverage, as follows:

$$\text{ROE} = \text{ROA} \times \text{Financial leverage}$$

$$= \frac{\text{Net income}}{\text{Assets}} \times \frac{\text{Assets}}{\text{Shareholders' equity}}$$

ROA tells us how much profit a company is able to generate for each dollar of assets invested. Financial leverage indicates how many dollars of assets the firm is able to deploy for each dollar invested by its shareholders.

The return on assets itself can be decomposed into a product of two factors:

$$ROA = \frac{\text{Net income}}{\text{Sales}} \times \frac{\text{Sales}}{\text{Assets}}$$

The ratio of net income to sales is called net profit margin or return on sales (ROS); the ratio of sales to assets is known as asset turnover. The profit margin ratio indicates how much the company is able to keep as profits for each dollar of sales it makes. Asset turnover indicates how many sales dollars the firm is able to generate for each dollar of its assets.

Table 5-2 displays the three drivers of ROE for our retail firms: net profit margins, asset turnover, and financial leverage. The small decline in Wal-Mart's ROE in 2005 was driven by a drop in asset utilization, from 2.73 to 2.61. Profit margins for Wal-Mart were steady and financial leverage increased modestly. Given its strategy, it is not surprising that Target had higher profit margins and lower asset turnover than Wal-Mart, However, the higher margins did not offset the lower turnover, resulting in a lower ROA for Target. Financial management of the two firms is similar. Consequently, Target's lower operating performance was also reflected in a lower ROE.

TABLE 5-2	Traditional Decomposition of ROE		
Ratio	Wal-Mart FY2005	Wal-Mart FY2004	Target FY2005
Net profit margin (ROS)	3.6%	3.6%	4.6%
× Asset turnover	2.61	2.73	1.63
= Return on assets (ROA)	9.3%	9.8%	7.5%
× Financial leverage	2.43	2.40	2.48
= Return on equity (ROE)	22.7%	23.5%	18.5%

Decomposing Profitability: Alternative Approach

Even though the above approach is popularly used to decompose a firm's ROE, it has several limitations. In the computation of ROA, the denominator includes the assets claimed by all providers of capital to the firm, but the numerator includes only the earnings available to equity holders. The assets themselves include both operating assets and financial assets such as cash and short-term investments. Further, net income includes income from operating activities as well as interest income and expense, which are consequences of financing decisions. Often it is useful to distinguish between these two drivers of performance. Finally, the financial leverage ratio used above does not recognize the fact that a firm's cash and short-term investments are in essence "negative debt" because they can be used to pay down the debt on the company's balance sheet.[4] These issues are addressed by an alternative approach to decomposing ROE.[5]

Before discussing this alternative ROE decomposition approach, we define in Table 5-3 some terminology used in this section as well as in the rest of this chapter.

TABLE 5-3	Definitions of Accounting Items Used in Ratio Analysis

Item	Definition
Net interest expense after tax	(Interest expense − Interest income) × (1 − Tax rate)[a]
Net operating profit after taxes (NOPAT)	Net income + Net interest expense after tax
Operating working capital	(Current assets − Cash and marketable securities) − (Current liabilities − Short-term debt and current portion of long-term debt)
Net long-term assets	Total long-term assets − Non-interest-bearing long-term liabilities
Net debt	Total interest bearing liabilities − Cash and marketable securities
Net assets	Operating working capital + Net long-term assets
Net capital	Net debt + Shareholders' equity

[a] *The calculation of net interest expense treats interest expense and interest income as absolute values, independent of how these figures are reported in the income statement.*

We use the terms defined above to recast the financial statements of Wal-Mart and Target. These recasted financial statements, which are shown in the appendix as condensed statements, are used to decompose ROE in the following manner:

$$\text{ROE} = \frac{\text{NOPAT}}{\text{Equity}} - \frac{(\text{Net interest expense after tax})}{\text{Equity}}$$

$$= \frac{\text{NOPAT}}{\text{Net assets}} \times \frac{\text{Net assets}}{\text{Equity}} - \frac{\text{Net interest expense after tax}}{\text{Net debt}} \times \frac{\text{Net debt}}{\text{Equity}}$$

$$= \frac{\text{NOPAT}}{\text{Net assets}} \times \left(1 + \frac{\text{Net debt}}{\text{Equity}}\right) - \frac{\text{Net interest expense after tax}}{\text{Net debt}} \times \frac{\text{Net debt}}{\text{Equity}}$$

$$= \text{Operating ROA} + (\text{Operating ROA} - \text{Effective interest rate after tax}) \times \text{Net financial leverage}$$

$$= \text{Operating ROA} + \text{Spread} \times \text{Net financial leverage}$$

Operating ROA is a measure of how profitably a company is able to deploy its operating assets to generate operating profits. This would be a company's ROE if it were financed entirely with equity. Spread is the incremental economic effect from introducing debt into the capital structure. This economic effect of borrowing is positive as long as the return on operating assets is greater than the cost of borrowing. Firms that do not earn adequate operating returns to pay for interest cost reduce their ROE by borrowing. Both the positive and negative effect is magnified by the extent to which a firm borrows relative to its equity base. The ratio of net debt to equity provides a measure of this net financial leverage. A firm's spread times its net financial leverage, therefore, provides a measure of the financial leverage gain to the shareholders.

Operating ROA can be further decomposed into NOPAT margin and operating asset turnover as follows:

$$\text{Operating ROA} \; = \; \frac{\text{NOPAT}}{\text{Sales}} \times \frac{\text{Sales}}{\text{Net assets}}$$

NOPAT margin is a measure of how profitable a company's sales are from an operating perspective. Operating asset turnover measures the extent to which a company is able to use its operating assets to generate sales.

Table 5-4 presents the alternative decomposition of ROE for Wal-Mart and Target. The ratios in this table show that Wal-Mart's operating ROA was nearly 75 percent higher than its traditional ROA. In 2005 for example, operating ROA (based on earnings before net interest expense) was 16.1 percent, whereas traditional ROA (based on earnings after net interest expense) was only 9.3 percent. Despite improved NOPAT margins in 2005, Wal-Mart's operating ROA declined during the year. This was attributable to declining net asset turnover, reflecting faster growth in net operating assets (stores) than in sales.

TABLE 5-4	Distinguishing Operating and Financing Components in ROE Decomposition		
Ratio	**Wal-Mart FY2005**	**Wal-Mart FY2004**	**Target FY2005**
Net operating profit margin	3.9%	3.8%	5.2%
× Net operating asset turnover	4.16	4.41	2.59
= Operating ROA	16.1%	16.9%	13.4%
Spread	12.7%	13.6%	9.1%
× Net financial leverage	0.53	0.49	0.56
= Financial leverage gain	6.7%	6.6%	5.1%
ROE = Operating ROA + Financial leverage gain	22.7%	23.5%	18.5%

The difference in ROA and operating ROA is equally pronounced for Target: its ROA in 2005 was 7.5 percent whereas the operating ROA was 13.3 percent. Like Wal-Mart, Target's NOPAT margin, which excludes the impact of its financing choices, was higher than its traditional return on sales ratio shown in Table 5-2. As Target is able to finance a portion of its net operating assets through non-interest-bearing long-term liabilities, its net operating asset turnover is significantly higher than its traditionally defined asset turnover shown in Table 5-2.

Both Wal-Mart and Target benefit from their financial management decisions as both show gains from financial leverage. However, the difference between the traditional ROA and its alternative operating ROA for both firms underscores the importance of distinguishing the operating performance of firms from the impact of its financial management to gain valuable insight into firm strategy and performance.

The key elements of operating ROA illustrate the different strategies pursued by the two firms. Wal-Mart dominates the low-end retail market, and its business model is dependent on high sales volumes of relatively low margin goods. Its

NOPAT margins of 3.9 percent combined with high asset turnover of over four demonstrates its ability to successfully execute that strategy, leading to a healthy operating ROA of over 16 percent in both 2004 and 2005. In contrast, Target has attempted to differentiate itself from its discount retail competitors by adding an element of design and fashion to its product offerings. This ensured that Target earned a higher NOPAT margin of 5.2 percent in 2005 versus 3.9 percent for Wal-Mart. Not surprisingly, however, it had a markedly lower operating asset turnover when compared to Wal-Mart. Overall, Wal-Mart's approach to discount retailing seems to be more successful than Target's, though it will be interesting to see how increased competition from Target will affect Wal-Mart's performance. One possibility is that Target's strategy to position itself at the higher end of the market is a defensible niche that is starting to pay off and Wal-Mart is beginning to lose ground to its design-centric rival. Another likely scenario is that Wal-Mart has not made its competitive response yet and that Target's margin performance is not sustainable in the face of a direct challenge by its larger rival.

Both firms are able to create shareholder value through their respective financing strategies. Given the financial strength of both firms—Wal-Mart is rated AA and Target has an A rating from S&P—both firms have a relatively low cost of debt. As a result, the spread between Wal-Mart's operating ROA and its after-tax interest cost was 12.7 percent in 2005. Wal-Mart's financing choices resulted in a net debt to equity ratio of around 50 percent. The combination of spread and leverage contributed to a net increment of 6.7 percent to Wal-Mart's ROE in 2005. Target's spread of 13.3 percent in 2005 is lower than Wal-Mart's, reflecting both its lower operating ROA and marginally higher cost of debt. Target's ROE in 2005 was enhanced by 5.2 percent as a result of its financing policies.

The appropriate benchmark for evaluating operating ROA is the weighted average cost of debt and equity capital, or WACC. In the long run, the value of a firm's assets is determined by how its operating ROA compares to this norm. Moreover, over the long run and absent some barrier to competitive forces, operating ROA will tend to be pushed toward the weighted average cost of capital. Since the WACC is typically lower than the cost of equity capital, operating ROA tends to be pushed to a level lower than that to which ROE tends.

The average operating ROA for large firms in the U.S. over long periods of time is in the range of 9 to 11 percent. In both 2004 and 2005, Wal-Mart comfortably exceeded these benchmarks. In addition, Target's performance in 2005 beat the long-run averages. This impressive operating performance of both firms would have been obscured by using the simple ROA measure.[6]

Assessing Operating Management: Decomposing Net Profit Margins

A firm's net profit margin or return on sales (ROS) shows the profitability of the company's operating activities. Further decomposition of a firm's ROS allows an analyst to assess the efficiency of the firm's operating management. A popular tool used in this analysis is the common-sized income statement in which all the line items are expressed as a percentage of sales revenues.

Common-sized income statements make it possible to compare trends in income statement relationships over time for the firm, and trends across different firms in the industry. To illustrate how the income statement analysis can be used, common-sized income statements for Wal-Mart and Target are shown in Table 5-5. The table also shows some commonly used profitability ratios. We will use the information in

TABLE 5-5	Common-Sized Income Statement and Profitability Ratios		
Ratio	**Wal-Mart FY2005**	**Wal-Mart FY2004**	**Target FY2005**
Line Items as a Percent of Sales			
Sales	100.0%	100.0%	100.0%
Cost of sales	75.2%	75.3%	66.4%
Selling, general & admin. expenses	18.1%	17.9%	22.8%
Other income/expense	0.6%	0.7%	2.7%
Net interest expense/income	0.4%	0.4%	1.0%
Income taxes	1.9%	2.0%	2.8%
Unusual gains/loss, net of taxes	0.0%	0.0%	0.0%
Net income	3.8%	3.8%	4.4%
Key Profitability Ratios			
Gross profit margin	24.8%	24.7%	33.6%
EBITDA margin	7.4%	7.5%	11.0%
NOPAT margin	3.9%	3.8%	5.2%
Recurring NOPAT margin	3.3%	3.4%	5.1%

Table 5-5 to investigate why Wal-Mart has had a steady net income margin (or return on sales) of 3.8 percent in both 2005 and 2004, while Target posted margins of 4.4 percent in 2005.

Gross Profit Margins

The difference between a firm's sales and cost of sales is gross profit. Gross profit margin is an indication of the extent to which revenues exceed direct costs associated with sales, and it is computed as

$$\text{Gross profit margin} = \frac{\text{Sales} - \text{Cost of sales}}{\text{Sales}}$$

Gross margin is influenced by two factors: (1) the price premium that a firm's products or services command in the marketplace and (2) the efficiency of the firm's procurement and production process. The price premium a firm's products or services can command is influenced by the degree of competition and the extent to which its products are unique. The firm's cost of sales can be low when it can purchase its inputs at a lower cost than competitors and/or run its production processes more efficiently. This is generally the case when a firm has a low-cost strategy.

Table 5-5 indicates that Wal-Mart's gross margin of 24.8 percent in 2005 was virtually unchanged from 2004, reflecting a relatively stable macroeconomic environment and no radical shift in the competitive environment or the firm's own strategy. As a consequence, Wal-Mart was able to maintain its prices and margins without having to resort to deep discounting to spur sales. Wal-Mart did not make any major changes to its strategy and product mix and continued to execute on its efficient sourcing systems.

Consistent with Target's premium product and price strategy relative to Wal-Mart, its gross margin in 2005 was significantly higher than Wal-Mart's gross margins in the same period. Target's impressive gross margin of 33.6 percent in 2005 reflects a combination of factors including an increased market acceptance for its premium, design-oriented discount strategy, better product mix and pricing, and strong sourcing and distribution capabilities.

Selling, General, and Administrative Expenses

A company's selling, general, and administrative (SG&A) expenses are influenced by the operating activities it has to undertake to implement its competitive strategy. As discussed in Chapter 2, firms with differentiation strategies have to undertake activities to achieve it. A company competing on the basis of quality and rapid introduction of new products is likely to have higher R&D costs relative to a company competing purely on a cost basis. Similarly, a company that attempts to build a brand image, distribute its products through full-service retailers, and provide significant customer service is likely to have higher selling and administration costs relative to a company that sells through warehouse retailers or direct mail and does not provide much customer support.

A company's SG&A expenses are also influenced by the efficiency with which it manages its overhead activities. The control of operating expenses is likely to be especially important for firms competing on the basis of low cost. However, even for differentiators, it is important to assess whether the cost of differentiation is commensurate with the price premium earned in the marketplace.

Several ratios in Table 5-5 allow us to evaluate the effectiveness with which Wal-Mart and Target managed their SG&A expenses. First, the ratio of SG&A expense to sales shows how much a company is spending to generate each sales dollar. Wal-Mart definitely had the edge in terms of a cost management strategy as demonstrated by its lower ratio of SG&A to sales. In 2005 Wal-Mart's SG&A expenses as a percent of sales was 18.1 percent compared to 22.8 percent for Target. It is interesting to note that Wal-Mart showed a small increases in its cost structure from 2004 to 2005.

Wal-Mart's lower gross margins and lower SG&A to sales are not surprising given its low cost strategy. In contrast, by catering to a slightly more affluent consumer, with higher prices, merchandising and service costs, Target had higher margins and also higher SG&A expenses. A key question is, when both these costs are netted out, which company performed better? Two ratios provide useful signals here: net operating profit margin (NOPAT margin) and EBITDA margin:

$$\text{NOPAT margin} = \frac{\text{NOPAT}}{\text{Sales}}$$

$$\text{EBITDA margin} = \frac{\text{Earnings before interest, taxes, depreciation, and amortization}}{\text{Sales}}$$

NOPAT margin provides a comprehensive indication of the operating performance of a company because it reflects all operating costs and eliminates the effects of debt policy. EBITDA margin provides similar information, except that it excludes depreciation and amortization expense, a significant non-cash operating expense. Some analysts prefer to use EBITDA margin because they believe that it focuses on "cash" operating items. While this is to some extent true, it can be potentially misleading for two reasons. EBITDA is not a strictly cash concept because sales, cost of sales, and SG&A expenses often include non-cash items. Also, depreciation is a real operating expense, and it reflects to some extent the consumption of resources. Therefore, ignoring it can be misleading.

Table 5-5 shows that Wal-Mart made a marginal improvement to its NOPAT margins from 2004 to 2005. Despite this improvement, Wal-Mart was able to earn only 3.9 cents in net operating profits out of every dollar of sales it generated, whereas Target earned 5.2 cents per sales dollar.

Recall that in Table 5-3 we define NOPAT as net income plus net interest expense. Therefore, NOPAT is influenced by any unusual or nonoperating income (expense) items included in net income. We can calculate a "recurring" NOPAT margin by eliminating these items. For both Wal-Mart and Target the major portion of their profits came from their core businesses. Wal-Mart's recurring NOPAT is lower than its NOPAT margin— 3.3 percent versus 3.9 percent in 2005—due to other income reported by the company, most likely a result of investment income. While Target divested itself of its Marshall Field's and Mervyn's subsidiaries in 2004, the impact of this change was not reflected in the 2005 results. As a result, its recurring NOPAT very closely approximated the regular NOPAT margin. In general, recurring NOPAT may be a better benchmark to use when extrapolating current performance into the future since it reflects margins from the core business activities of a firm, especially if in the particular years analyzed the firm generated income from non-core or discontinued operations.

Target also has a better EBITDA margin than Wal-Mart. Care needs to be taken when examining this ratio, especially in sectors such as retailing. Certain retailers choose to own both the land and the buildings for the stores that they operate, while others choose to enter into off-balance-sheet leases. As a result, the depreciation expenses can vary widely between firms choosing different strategies, and can lead to results that may be misleading. For Wal-Mart and Target, these differences appear to be modest: nearly 17 percent of Target's stores are either leased or built on leased land versus more than 21 percent for Wal-Mart's U.S. stores and 23 percent for SAM'S CLUB stores.

Tax Expense

Taxes are an important element of a firm's total expenses. Through a wide variety of tax planning techniques, firms can attempt to reduce their tax expenses.[7] There are two measures one can use to evaluate a firm's tax expense. One is the ratio of tax expense to sales, and the other is the ratio of tax expense to earnings before taxes (also known as the average tax rate). The firm's tax footnote provides a detailed account of why its average tax rate differs from the statutory tax rate.

Table 5-5 shows that Wal-Mart's income tax expenses as a percent of sales were lower than Target's. This was due in part to the fact that Target had higher pre-tax profits as a percent of sales. However, Wal-Mart's tax rate in 2005 was also lower than Target's— 33.4 percent versus 37.6 percent. This was a result of two factors: (1) Wal-Mart benefited from international operations, since its effective tax rate was lower on international operations than on domestic profits, and (2) Wal-Mart's mix of locations within the U.S. resulted in a lower state income tax liability. As Wal-Mart continues its domestic expansion, it will enter states with higher tax rates, leading to a gradual increase in its local tax liability. This is likely to be offset by the growing importance of the international operations and the lower tax rates on those earnings.

In summary, an examination of common-sized income statement ratios can illuminate strategic and operational differences among competitors. Wal-Mart's profitability is driven by a tight control over its expenses, which helps it compensate for lower gross margin when compared to Target.

Key Analysis Questions

A number of business questions will be useful to an analyst assessing the various elements of operating management:

- Are the company's margins consistent with its stated competitive strategy? For example, a differentiation strategy should usually lead to higher gross margins than a low-cost strategy.
- Are the company's margins changing? Why? What are the underlying business causes—changes in competition, changes in input costs, or poor overhead cost management?
- Is the company managing its overhead and administrative costs well? What are the business activities driving these costs? Are these activities necessary?
- Are the company's tax policies sustainable, or is the current tax rate influenced by one-time tax credits?
- Do the firm's tax planning strategies lead to other business costs? For example, if the operations are located in tax havens, how does this affect the company's profit margins and asset utilization? Are the benefits of tax planning strategies (reduced taxes) greater than the increased business costs?

Evaluating Investment Management: Decomposing Asset Turnover

Asset turnover is the second driver of a company's return on equity. Since firms invest considerable resources in their assets, using them productively is critical to overall profitability. A detailed analysis of asset turnover allows the analyst to evaluate the effectiveness of a firm's investment management. There are two primary areas of investment management: (1) working capital management and (2) management of long-term assets, both of which are discussed in further detail below.

Working Capital Management

Working capital is defined as the difference between a firm's current assets and current liabilities. However, this definition does not distinguish between operating components (such as accounts receivable, inventory, and accounts payable) and financing components (such as cash, marketable securities, and notes payable). An alternative measure that makes this distinction is operating working capital, defined in Table 5-3 as

$$\text{Operating working capital} = (\text{Current assets} - \text{cash and marketable securities}) \\ - (\text{Current liabilities} - \text{Short-term and current portion of long-term debt})$$

The components of operating working capital that analysts primarily focus on are accounts receivable, inventory, and accounts payable. A certain amount of investment in working capital is generally necessary for the firm to run its normal operations. For example, a firm's credit policies and distribution policies determine its optimal level of accounts receivable. The nature of the production process and the need for buffer stocks determine the optimal level of inventory. Finally, accounts payable is a routine source of financing for the firm's working capital, and payment practices in an industry determine the normal level of accounts payable.

The following ratios are useful in analyzing a firm's working capital management: operating working capital as a percent of sales, operating working capital turnover, accounts receivable turnover, inventory turnover, and accounts payable turnover. The turnover ratios can also be expressed in number of days of activity that the operating working capital (and its components) can support. These ratios are defined below:

$$\text{Operating working capital to sales ratio} = \frac{\text{Operating working capital}}{\text{Sales}}$$

$$\text{Operating working capital turnover} = \frac{\text{Sales}}{\text{Operating working capital}}$$

$$\text{Accounts receivable turnover} = \frac{\text{Sales}}{\text{Accounts receivable}}$$

$$\text{Inventory turnover} = \frac{\text{Cost of goods sold}^8}{\text{Inventory}}$$

$$\text{Accounts payable turnover} = \frac{\text{Purchases}}{\text{Accounts payable}} \ or \ \frac{\text{Cost of goods sold}}{\text{Accounts payable}}$$

$$\text{Days' receivables} = \frac{\text{Accounts receivable}}{\text{Average sales per day}}$$

$$\text{Days' inventory} = \frac{\text{Inventory}}{\text{Average cost of goods sold per day}}$$

$$\text{Days' payables} = \frac{\text{Accounts payable}}{\text{Average purchases (or cost of goods sold) per day}}$$

Operating working capital turnover indicates how many dollars of sales a firm is able to generate for each dollar invested in operating working capital. Accounts receivable turnover, inventory turnover, and accounts payable turnover allow the analyst to examine how productively the three principal components of working capital are being used. Days' receivables, days' inventory, and days' payables are another way to evaluate the efficiency of a firm's working capital management.[9]

Long-Term Assets Management

Another area of investment management concerns the utilization of a firm's long-term assets. It is useful to define again a firm's investment in long-term assets:

$$\text{Net long-term assets} = (\text{Total long-term assets} - \text{Non-interest-bearing long-term liabilities})$$

Long-term assets generally consist of net property, plant, and equipment (PP&E), intangible assets such as goodwill, and other assets. Non-interest-bearing long-term liabilities include items such as deferred taxes. We define net long-term assets and net working capital in such a way that their sum, net operating assets, is equal to the sum of net debt and equity, or net capital. This is consistent with the way we defined operating ROA earlier in the chapter.

The efficiency with which a firm uses its net long-term assets is measured by the following two ratios: net long-term assets as a percent of sales and net long-term asset turnover, defined as

$$\text{Net long-term asset turnover} = \frac{\text{Sales}}{\text{Net long-term assets}}$$

Property plant and equipment (PP&E) is the most important long-term asset in a firm's balance sheet. The efficiency with which a firm's PP&E is used is measured either by the ratio of PP&E to sales or by the PP&E turnover ratio:

$$\text{PP\&E turnover} = \frac{\text{Sales}}{\text{Net property, plant, and equipment}}$$

Key Analysis Questions

The ratios discussed in the two preceding sections allow the analyst to explore a number of business questions:

- How well does the company manage its inventory? Does the company use modern manufacturing techniques? Does it have good vendor and logistics management systems? If inventory ratios are changing, what is the underlying business reason? Are new products being planned? Is there a mismatch between the demand forecasts and actual sales?
- How well does the company manage its credit policies? Are these policies consistent with its marketing strategy? Is the company artificially increasing sales by loading the distribution channels?
- Is the company taking advantage of trade credit? Is it relying too much on trade credit? If so, what are the implicit costs?
- Is the company's investment in plant and equipment consistent with its competitive strategy? Does the company have a sound policy of acquisitions and divestitures?

Table 5-6 shows the asset turnover ratios for Wal-Mart and Target. Wal-Mart is extremely efficient at managing its working capital needs. Its negative operating working capital turnover ratio indicates that it finances its accounts receivable, inventory, and other operating current assets through accounts payable and other accrued liabilities. This is due to a combination of its efficient supply chain management, the fact that it does not have credit card operations that lead to large receivables, and its negotiating power based on its size, which results in favorable trade credit terms from its vendors. Wal-Mart's working capital management has been relatively stable for 2004 and 2005, though its long-term asset utilization deteriorated slightly, as both net long-term asset turnover and PP&E turnover declined.

Target's working capital management trails that of Wal-Mart by a significant margin. Target still has a large portion of its asset base tied up in operating working capital. Target's strategy of financing its customers through its in-house credit card operations leads to large accounts receivables and lengthy days' accounts receivable—38 days in 2005 compared to two days for Wal-Mart. In addition, its customer focus and higher margins lead to slower-turning inventory and long-term assets.

TABLE 5-6	Asset Management Ratios		
Ratio	Wal-Mart FY2005	Wal-Mart FY2004	Target FY2005
Operating working capital/Sales	−0.7%	−0.6%	7.5%
Net long-term assets/Sales	24.7%	23.3%	31.1%
PP&E/Sales	21.9%	20.5%	32.0%
Operating working capital turnover	−148.9	−156.4	13.3
Net long-term assets turnover	4.0	4.3	3.2
PP&E turnover	4.6	4.9	3.1
Accounts receivable turnover	182.7	228.2	9.6
Inventory turnover	8.0	8.1	6.5
Accounts payable turnover	10.9	11.1	6.0
Days' accounts receivable	2.0	1.6	38.1
Days' inventory	45.6	45.1	56.3
Days' account payable	33.6	32.7	60.4

Evaluating Financial Management: Analyzing Financial Leverage

Financial leverage enables a firm to have an asset base larger than its equity. The firm can augment its equity through borrowing and the creation of other liabilities such as accounts payable, accrued liabilities, and deferred taxes. Financial leverage increases a firm's ROE as long as the cost of the liabilities is less than the return from investing these funds. In this respect, it is important to distinguish between interest-bearing liabilities such as notes payable, other forms of short-term and long-term debt that carry an explicit interest charge, and other liabilities. Some of these other forms of liability, such as accounts payable or deferred taxes, do not carry any interest charge at all. Others, such as capital lease obligations and pension obligations, carry an implicit interest charge. Finally, some firms carry large cash balances or investments in marketable securities. These balances reduce a firm's net debt because conceptually the firm can pay down its debt using its cash and short-term investments.

While financial leverage can potentially benefit a firm's shareholders, it can also increase their risk. Unlike equity, liabilities have predefined payment terms, and the firm faces risk of financial distress if it fails to meet these commitments. There are a number of ratios to evaluate the degree of risk arising from a firm's financial leverage.

Current Liabilities and Short-Term Liquidity

The following ratios are useful in evaluating the risk related to a firm's current liabilities:

$$\text{Current ratio} = \frac{\text{Current assets}}{\text{Current liabilities}}$$

$$\text{Quick ratio} = \frac{\text{Cash} + \text{Short-term investments} + \text{Accounts receivable}}{\text{Current liabilities}}$$

$$\text{Cash ratio} = \frac{\text{Cash} + \text{Marketable securities}}{\text{Current liabilities}}$$

$$\text{Operating cash flow ratio} = \frac{\text{Cash flow from operations}}{\text{Current liabilities}}$$

All the above ratios attempt to measure the firm's ability to repay its current liabilities. The first three compare a firm's current liabilities with its short-term assets that can be used to repay those liabilities. The fourth ratio focuses on the ability of the firm's operations to generate the resources needed to repay its current liabilities.

Since both current assets and current liabilities have comparable duration, the current ratio is a key index of a firm's short-term liquidity. Analysts view a current ratio of more than one to be an indication that the firm can cover its current liabilities from the cash realized from its current assets. However, the firm can face a short-term liquidity problem even with a current ratio exceeding one when some of its current assets are not easy to liquidate. Quick ratio and cash ratio capture the firm's ability to cover its current liabilities from liquid assets. Quick ratio assumes that the firm's accounts receivable are liquid. This is true in industries where the credit-worthiness of the customers is beyond dispute, or when receivables are collected in a very short period. When these conditions do not prevail, cash ratio, which considers only cash and marketable securities, is a better indication of a firm's ability to cover its current liabilities in an emergency. Operating cash flow is another measure of the firm's ability to cover its current liabilities from cash generated from operations of the firm.

The liquidity ratios for Wal-Mart and Target are shown in Table 5-7. On all dimensions of liquidity, Target has a greater cushion than Wal-Mart. None of Wal-Mart's liquidity ratios were higher than one in either 2004 or 2005. Wal-Mart's lower level of liquidity reflects its tight working capital management. Given its financial strength and stability, Wal-Mart's short-term creditors are probably not very concerned about its ability to fulfill its obligations in a timely manner. Target's creditors are also likely to be very comfortable with the firm's liquidity situation.

TABLE 5-7   Liquidity Ratios

Ratio	Wal-Mart FY2005	Wal-Mart FY2004	Target FY2005
Current ratio	0.90	0.92	1.69
Quick ratio	0.17	0.17	0.94
Cash ratio	0.13	0.14	0.27
Operating cash flow ratio	0.43	0.42	0.58

Debt and Long-Term Solvency

A company's financial leverage is also influenced by its debt financing policy. There are several potential benefits from debt financing. First, debt is typically cheaper than equity because the firm promises predefined payment terms to debt holders. Second, in most countries interest on debt financing is tax deductible whereas dividends to shareholders are not tax deductible. Third, debt financing can impose discipline on the firm's management and motivate it to reduce wasteful expenditures. Fourth, for non-public debt, it is likely to be easier for management to communicate their proprietary information on the firm's strategies and prospects to private lenders than to public capital markets. Such communication can potentially reduce a firm's cost of capital. For all these reasons, it is advantageous for firms to use at least some debt in their capital structure. Too much reliance on debt financing, however, is potentially costly to the firm's shareholders. The firm will face financial distress if it defaults on the interest and principal payments. Debt holders also impose covenants on the firm, restricting the firm's operating, investment, and financing decisions.

The optimal capital structure for a firm is determined primarily by its business risk. A firm's cash flows are highly predictable when there is little competition or there is little threat of technological changes. Such firms have low business risk and hence they can rely heavily on debt financing. In contrast, if a firm's operating cash flows are highly volatile and its capital expenditure needs are unpredictable, it may have to rely primarily on equity financing. Managers' attitude towards risk and financial flexibility also often determine a firm's debt policies.

There are a number of ratios which help the analyst in this area. To evaluate the mix of debt and equity in a firm's capital structure, the following ratios are useful:

$$\text{Liabilities-to-equity ratio} = \frac{\text{Total liabilities}}{\text{Shareholders' equity}}$$

$$\text{Debt-to-equity ratio} = \frac{\text{Short-term debt} + \text{Long-term debt}}{\text{Shareholders' equity}}$$

$$\text{Net-debt-to-equity ratio}$$
$$= \frac{\text{Short-term debt} + \text{Long-term debt} - \text{Cash and marketable securities}}{\text{Shareholders' equity}}$$

$$\text{Debt-to-capital ratio} =$$
$$\frac{\text{Short-term debt} + \text{Long-term debt}}{\text{Short-term debt} + \text{Long-term debt} + \text{Shareholders' equity}}$$

$$\text{Net-debt-to-net-capital ratio} =$$
$$\frac{\text{Interest bearing liabilities} - \text{Cash and marketable securities}}{\text{Interest bearing liabilities} - \text{Cash and marketable securities} + \text{Shareholders' equity}}$$

The first ratio reformulates one of the three primary ratios underlying ROE, the assets-to-equity ratio (it is the assets-to-equity ratio minus one). The second ratio provides an indication of how many dollars of debt financing the firm is using for each dollar invested by its shareholders. The third ratio uses net debt, which is total debt minus cash and marketable securities, as the measure of a firm's borrowings. The fourth and fifth ratios measure debt as a proportion of total capital. In calculating all the above ratios, it is important to include all interest-bearing obligations, whether the interest charge is explicit or implicit. Recall that examples of line items which carry an implicit interest charge include capital lease obligations and pension obligations.

Analysts sometimes include any potential off-balance-sheet obligations that a firm may have, such as non-cancellable operating leases, in the definition of a firm's debt.

The ease with which a firm can meet its interest payments is an indication of the degree of risk associated with its debt policy. The interest coverage ratio provides a measure of this construct:

$$\text{Interest coverage (earnings basis)} = \frac{\text{Net income} + \text{Interest expense} + \text{Tax expense}}{\text{Interest expense}}$$

Interest coverage (cash flow basis)

$$= \frac{\text{Cash flow from operations} + \text{Interest expense} + \text{Taxes paid}}{\text{Interest expense}}$$

One can also calculate coverage ratios that measure a firm's ability to measure all fixed financial obligations, such as interest payment, lease payments, and debt repayments, by appropriately redefining the numerator and denominator in the above ratios. In doing so it is important to remember that some fixed charge payments, such as interest and lease rentals, are paid with pretax dollars while others, such as debt repayments, are made with after-tax dollars.

The earnings-based coverage ratio indicates the dollars of earnings available for each dollar of required interest payment; the cash-flow-based coverage ratio indicates the dollars of cash generated by operations for each dollar of required interest payment. In both these ratios, the denominator is the interest expense. In the numerator we add taxes back because taxes are computed only after interest expense is deducted. A coverage ratio of one implies that the firm is barely covering its interest expense through its operating activities, which is a very risky situation. The larger the coverage ratio, the greater the cushion the firm has to meet interest obligations.

Key Analysis Questions

Some of the business questions to ask when the analyst is examining a firm's debt policies follow:

- Does the company have enough debt? Is it exploiting the potential benefits of debt—interest tax shields, management discipline, and easier communication?
- Does the company have too much debt given its business risk? What type of debt covenant restrictions does the firm face? Is it bearing the costs of too much debt, risking potential financial distress and reduced business flexibility?
- What is the company doing with the borrowed funds? Investing in working capital? Investing in fixed assets? Are these investments profitable?
- Is the company borrowing money to pay dividends? If so, what is the justification?

We show debt and coverage ratios for Wal-Mart and Target in Table 5-8.

Wal-Mart's net debt to equity ratios in 2004 and 2005 were close to 50 percent, implying it financed its net assets conservatively with an equal mix of debt and equity. Target's leverage ratios in 2005 were very similar to those of Wal-Mart.

TABLE 5-8	Debt and Coverage Ratios		
Ratio	Wal-Mart FY2005	Wal-Mart FY2004	Target FY2005
Liabilities to equity	1.41	1.37	1.48
Debt to equity	0.64	0.61	0.73
Net debt to equity	0.53	0.49	0.56
Debt to capital	0.39	0.38	0.42
Net debt to net capital	0.34	0.33	0.36
Net debt to equity, including operating lease obligations[a]	0.61	0.58	0.65
Interest coverage (earnings based)	11.80	13.13	8.26
Interest coverage (cash flow based)	15.86	16.79	12.10
Fixed charges coverage, including lease payments (earnings based)	6.92	7.32	6.63
Fixed charges coverage, including lease payments (cash flow based)	9.15	9.23	9.60

[a] Present value of leases estimated using the cost of debt and an approximation of average life

Given that both companies rely on operating leases for about one-fifth of their stores, it is important to estimate the impact of the operating lease obligations on the firms' leverage and interest coverage. Using the respective costs of debt and an estimate of average life of the operating leases, it is possible to form an estimate of the implicit leverage on the balance sheet of both firms. As Table 5-8 shows, the net debt to equity ratio goes from 0.53 to 0.61 for Wal-Mart if the impact of operating leases is included. The ratio for Target increases from 0.56 to 0.65 for the year 2005.

In general, both companies are in an extremely comfortable situation relative to their fixed obligations, even after factoring in operating leases commitments. Wal-Mart's coverage ratios are consistently superior to those of Target, primarily as a result of its higher profitability.

Ratios of Disaggregated Data

So far we have discussed how to compute ratios using information in the financial statements. Analysts often probe the above ratios further by using disaggregated financial and physical data. For example, for a multibusiness company, one could analyze the information by individual business segments. Such an analysis can reveal potential differences in the performance of each business unit, allowing the analyst to pinpoint areas where a company's strategy is working and where it is not. It is also possible to probe financial ratios further by computing ratios of physical data pertaining to a company's operations. The appropriate physical data to look at varies from industry to industry. As an example in retailing, one could compute productivity statistics such as sales per store, sales per square foot, customer transactions per store, and average amount of sale per customer transaction. In the hotel industry, room occupancy rates provide important information; in the cellular telephone industry, acquisition cost per new subscriber and subscriber retention rate are important. These disaggregated ratios are particularly useful for young firms and young industries such as Internet firms, where accounting data may not fully capture the business economics due to conservative accounting rules.

Putting It All Together: Assessing Sustainable Growth Rate

Analysts often use the concept of sustainable growth as a way to evaluate a firm's ratios in a comprehensive manner. A firm's sustainable growth rate is defined as

$$\text{Sustainable growth rate} = \text{ROE} \times (1 - \text{Dividend payout ratio})$$

We already discussed the analysis of ROE in the previous four sections. The dividend payout ratio is defined as

$$\text{Divided payout ratio} = \frac{\text{Cash dividends paid}}{\text{Net income}}$$

A firm's dividend payout ratio is a measure of its dividend policy. Firms pay dividends for several reasons. They provide a way to return to shareholders any cash generated in excess of the firm's operating and investment needs. When there are information asymmetries between a firm's managers and its shareholders, dividend payments can serve as a signal to shareholders about managers' expectation of the firm's future prospects. Firms may also pay dividends to attract a certain type of shareholder base.

Sustainable growth rate is the rate at which a firm can grow while keeping its profitability and financial policies unchanged. A firm's return on equity and its dividend payout policy determine the pool of funds available for growth. Of course the firm can grow at a rate different from its sustainable growth rate if its profitability, payout policy, or financial leverage changes. Therefore, the sustainable growth rate provides a benchmark against which a firm's growth plans can be evaluated. Figure 5-2 shows how a firm's sustainable growth rate can be linked to all the ratios discussed in this chapter. These linkages allow an analyst to examine the drivers of a firm's current sustainable growth rate. If the firm intends to grow at a higher rate than its sustainable growth rate, one could assess which of the ratios are likely to change in the process.

Key Analysis Questions

Analysis of sustainable growth can lead to asking the following types of business questions:

- How quickly can the firm grow its business by keeping its profitability and financial policies unchanged?
- If it intends growing faster, where is the growth going to come from? Is management expecting profitability to increase? Or asset productivity to improve? Are these expectations realistic? Is the firm planning for these changes?
- If the firm is planning to increase its financial leverage or cut dividends, what is the likely impact of these financial policy changes?

FIGURE 5-2 Sustainable Growth Rate Framework for Financial Ratio Analysis

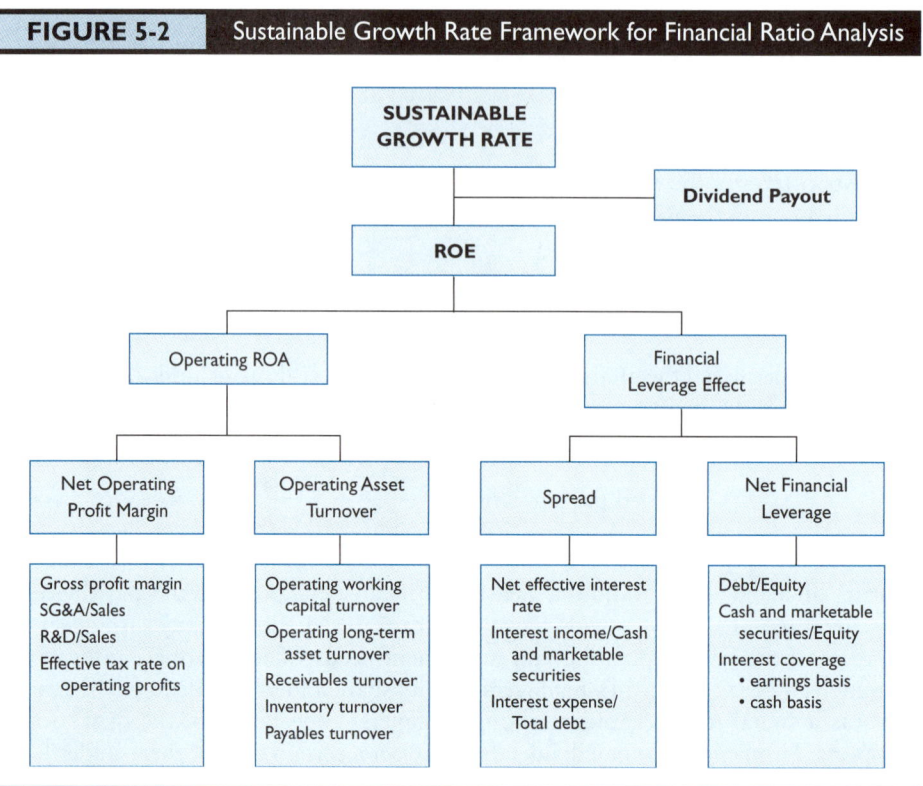

Table 5-9 shows the sustainable growth rate and its components for Wal-Mart and Target. Recall that Wal-Mart was considerably more profitable than Target in 2005. Despite its higher return on equity, Wal-Mart's higher dividend payout ratio narrows the sustainable growth rate gap between Target and itself. Wal-Mart's actual sales and asset growth rates in 2005 were lower than implied by its 2004 sustainable growth rate due to a number of factors including a drop in operating asset turnover and a share repurchase program. Wal-Mart grew sales by only 9.5 percent and its operating ROA declined while its leverage increased marginally.

TABLE 5-9 Sustainable Growth Rate

Ratio	Wal-Mart FY2005	Wal-Mart FY2004	Target FY2005
Return on equity	22.7%	23.5%	18.5%
Dividend payout ratio	22.4%	21.6%	13.2%
Sustainable growth rate	17.7%	18.5%	16.0%

In 2005 it appears that Wal-Mart's and Target's sustainable growth rates are converging. This implies that growth rates for the two firms are about the same if they choose to maintain their current operating and financing policies.

Historical Patterns of Ratios for U.S. Firms

To provide a benchmark for analysis, Table 5-10 reports historical values of the key ratios discussed in this chapter. These ratios are calculated using financial statement data for all publicly listed U.S. companies. The table shows the values of ROE, its key components, and the sustainable growth rate for each of the years 1988 to 2005, and the average for this period. The data show that the average ROE over this time frame has been 10.5 percent, average operating ROA has been 8.5 percent, and the average spread between operating ROA and net borrowing costs after tax has been 2.1 percent. The average sustainable growth rate for U.S. companies during this period has been 4.9 percent. Of course, an individual company's ratios might depart from these economy-wide averages for a number of reasons, such as industry effects, company strategies, and management effectiveness. Nonetheless, the average values in the table serve as useful benchmarks in financial analysis.

| **TABLE 5-10** | Historical Values of Key Financial Ratios |

Year	ROE	NOPAT Margin	Operating Asset Turnover	Operating ROA	Spread	Net Financial Leverage	Sustainable Growth Rate
1988	13.1%	7.7%	1.73	12.0%	2.7%	0.88	6.3%
1989	11.5%	7.8%	1.65	10.8%	2.6%	1.11	5.1%
1990	9.7%	6.9%	1.64	10.1%	1.5%	1.21	3.5%
1991	6.8%	6.3%	1.56	7.4%	0.0%	1.22	0.7%
1992	4.4%	4.3%	1.60	6.1%	−0.6%	1.17	−1.6%
1993	9.1%	5.0%	1.67	6.6%	0.9%	1.19	2.9%
1994	13.9%	7.2%	1.76	10.8%	3.8%	1.19	7.9%
1995	13.8%	6.1%	1.82	8.3%	6.8%	1.15	7.4%
1996	14.7%	6.7%	1.82	9.3%	7.5%	1.18	8.7%
1997	13.9%	7.6%	1.82	10.4%	3.7%	1.16	8.3%
1998	13.1%	8.1%	1.76	9.7%	2.3%	1.28	7.4%
1999	13.6%	8.0%	1.69	9.9%	3.8%	1.29	8.5%
2000	10.1%	7.3%	1.71	8.0%	1.8%	1.35	5.4%
2001	1.3%	3.9%	1.47	2.8%	−3.3%	1.29	−2.7%
2002	−0.3%	2.4%	1.35	−1.1%	−6.4%	1.35	−4.4%
2003	13.2%	8.2%	1.58	9.4%	3.3%	1.46	8.6%
2004	13.2%	8.0%	1.70	10.0%	3.2%	1.36	8.3%
2005	13.9%	9.1%	1.78	12.1%	3.5%	1.12	8.3%
Average	**10.5%**	**6.7%**	**1.67**	**8.5%**	**2.1%**	**1.22**	**4.9%**

Ratios are based on beginning balance sheet data.

Source: Financial statement data for all publicly traded U.S. companies between 1987 and 2005, listed in Standard & Poor's Compustat database.

CASH FLOW ANALYSIS

The ratio analysis discussion focused on analyzing a firm's income statement (net profit margin analysis) or its balance sheet (asset turnover and financial leverage). The analyst can get further insights into the firm's operating, investing, and financing policies by examining its cash flows. Cash flow analysis also provides an indication of the quality of the information in the firm's income statement and balance sheet. As before, we will illustrate the concepts discussed in this section using Wal-Mart's and Target's cash flows.

Cash Flow and Funds Flow Statements

All U.S. companies are required to include a statement of cash flows in their financial statements under Statement of Financial Accounts Standard No. 95 (SFAS 95). In the cash flow statement, firms report their cash flows in three categories: cash flow from operations, cash flow related to investments, and cash flow related to financing activities. Cash flow from operations is the cash generated by the firm from the sale of goods and services after paying for the cost of inputs and operations. Cash flow related to investment activities shows the cash paid for capital expenditures, intercorporate investments, acquisitions, and cash received from the sales of long-term assets. Cash flow related to financing activities shows the cash raised from (or paid to) the firm's stockholders and debt holders.

Firms use two cash flow statement formats: the direct format and the indirect format. The key difference between the two formats is the way they report cash flow from operating activities. In the direct cash flow format, which is used by only a small number of firms, operating cash receipts and disbursements are reported directly. In the indirect format, firms derive their operating cash flows by making adjustments to net income. Because the indirect format links the cash flow statement with the firm's income statement and balance sheet, many analysts and managers find this format more useful. As a result, the FASB required firms using the direct format to report operating cash flows in the indirect format as well.

Recall from Chapter 3 that net income differs from operating cash flows because revenues and expenses are measured on an accrual basis. There are two types of accruals embedded in net income. First, there are current accruals like credit sales and unpaid expenses. Current accruals result in changes in a firm's current assets (such as accounts receivable, inventory, prepaid expenses) and current liabilities (such as accounts payable and accrued liabilities). The second type of accruals included in the income statement is noncurrent accruals such as depreciation, deferred taxes, and equity income from unconsolidated subsidiaries. To derive cash flow from operations from net income, adjustments have to be made for both these types of accruals. In addition, adjustments have to be made for nonoperating gains included in net income such as profits from asset sales.

Some firms outside the U.S. report a funds flow statement rather than a cash flow statement of the type described above. Prior to SFAS 95, U.S. firms also reported a similar statement. Funds flow statements show working capital flows, not cash flows. It is useful for analysts to know how to convert a funds flow statement into a cash flow statement.

Funds flow statements typically provide information on a firm's working capital from operations, defined as net income adjusted for noncurrent accruals, and gains from the sale of long-term assets. As discussed above, cash flow from operations essentially involves a third adjustment, the adjustment for current accruals. Thus it is relatively straightforward to convert working capital from operations to cash flow from operations by making the relevant adjustments for current accruals related to operations.

Information on current accruals can be obtained by examining changes in a firm's current assets and current liabilities. Typically, operating accruals represent changes in all the current asset accounts other than cash and cash equivalents, and changes in all the current liabilities other than notes payable and the current portion of long-term debt.[10] Cash from operations can be calculated as follows:

Working capital from operations
- Increase (or + decrease) in accounts receivable
- Increase (or + decrease) in inventory
- Increase (or + decrease) in other current assets excluding cash and cash equivalents
+ Increase (or − decrease) in accounts payable
+ Increase (or − decrease) in other current liabilities excluding debt.

Funds flow statements also often do not classify investment and financing flows. In such a case, the analyst has to classify the line items in the funds flow statement into these two categories by evaluating the nature of the business transactions that give rise to the flow represented by the line items.

Analyzing Cash Flow Information

Cash flow analysis can be used to address a variety of questions regarding a firm's cash flow dynamics:

- How strong is the firm's internal cash flow generation? Is the cash flow from operations positive or negative? If it is negative, why? Is it because the company is growing? Is it because its operations are unprofitable? Or is it having difficulty managing its working capital properly?
- Does the company have the ability to meet its short-term financial obligations, such as interest payments, from its operating cash flow? Can it continue to meet these obligations without reducing its operating flexibility?
- How much cash did the company invest in growth? Are these investments consistent with its business strategy? Did the company use internal cash flow to finance growth, or did it rely on external financing?
- Did the company pay dividends from internal free cash flow, or did it have to rely on external financing? If the company had to fund its dividends from external sources, is the company's dividend policy sustainable?
- What type of external financing does the company rely on? Equity, short-term debt, or long-term debt? Is the financing consistent with the company's overall business risk?
- Does the company have excess cash flow after making capital investments? Is it a long-term trend? What plans does management have to deploy the free cash flow?

While the information in reported cash flow statements can be used to answer the above questions directly in the case of some firms, it may not be easy to always do so for a number of reasons. First, even though SFAS 95 provides broad guidelines on the format of a cash flow statement, there is still significant variation across firms in how cash flow data are disclosed. Therefore, to facilitate a systematic analysis and comparison across firms, analysts often recast the information in the cash flow statement using their own cash flow model. Second, firms include interest expense and interest income in computing their cash flow from operating activities. However, these two items are not strictly related to a firm's operations. Interest expense is a function of financial leverage, and interest income is derived from financial assets rather than operating assets. Therefore it is useful to restate the cash flow statement to take this into account.

Analysts use a number of different approaches to restate the cash flow data. One such model is shown in Table 5-11. This presents cash flow from operations in two stages. The first step computes cash flow from operations before operating working capital investments. In computing this cash flow, the model excludes interest expense and interest income. To compute this number starting with a firm's net income, an analyst adds back three types of items: (1) after-tax net interest expense because this is a financing item that will be considered later; (2) nonoperating gains or losses typically arising out of asset disposals or asset write-offs because these items are investment related and will be considered later; and (3) long-term operating accruals such as depreciation and deferred taxes because these are non-cash operating charges.

TABLE 5-11	Cash Flow Analysis		
Ratio	**Wal-Mart FY2005**	**Wal-Mart FY2004**	**Target FY2005**
Net Income	11,231.0	10,267.0	2,408.0
After-tax net interest expense (income)	876.2	716.2	315.0
Non-operating losses (gains)	0.0	0.0	70.0
Long-term operating accruals	5,208.0	5,046.0	1,813.0
Operating cash flow before working capital investments	**17,315.2**	**16,029.2**	**4,606.0**
Net (investments in) or liquidation of operating working capital	1,194.0	(269.0)	160.0
Operating cash flow before investment in long-term assets	**18,509.2**	**15,760.2**	**4,766.0**
Net (investment in) or liquidation of operating long-term assets	**(14,183.0)**	**(12,351.0)**	**(4,149.0)**
Free cash flow available to debt and equity	4,326.2	3,409.2	617.0
After-tax net interest income (expense)	(876.2)	(716.2)	(315.0)
Net debt (repayment) or issuance	4,018.0	4,041.0	386.0
Free cash flow available to equity	**7,468.0**	**6,734.0**	**688.0**
Dividend (payments)	(2,511.0)	(2,214.0)	(318.0)
Net stock issuance (repurchase), and other equity changes	(4,031.0)	(4,231.0)	(1,026.0)
Net increase (decrease) in cash balance	**926.0**	**289.0**	**(656.0)**
Cash flow from Discontinued Operations	0.0	0.0	0.0
Net increase (decrease) in cash balance – As reported	**926.0**	**289.0**	**(656.0)**

Several factors affect a firm's ability to generate positive cash flow from operations. Healthy firms that are in a steady state should generate more cash from their customers than they spend on operating expenses. In contrast, growing firms—especially those with heavy outlays for research and development, advertising and marketing, or building an organization to sustain future growth—may experience negative operating cash flow. Firms' working capital management also affects whether they generate positive cash flow from operations. Firms in the growing stage typically use cash flow for operating working capital items such as funding customers (accounts receivable) and purchasing inventories (net of accounts payable financing from suppliers). Net investments in working capital are a function of firms' credit policies (accounts receivable), payment policies (payables, prepaid expenses, and accrued liabilities), and expected growth in sales (inventories). Thus, in interpreting firms' cash flow from operations after working capital, it is important to keep in mind their growth strategy, industry characteristics, and credit policies.

The cash flow analysis model next focuses on cash flows related to long-term investments. These investments take the form of capital expenditures, intercorporate investments, and mergers and acquisitions. Any positive operating cash flow after making operating working capital investments allows the firm to pursue long-term growth opportunities. If the firm's operating cash flows after working capital investments are not sufficient to finance its long-term investments, it has to rely on external financing to fund its growth. Such firms have less flexibility to pursue long-term investments than those that can fund their growth internally. There are both costs and benefits from being able to fund growth internally. The cost is that managers can use the internally generated free cash flow to fund unprofitable investments. Such wasteful capital expenditures are less likely if managers are forced to rely on external capital suppliers. However, reliance on external capital markets may make it difficult for managers to undertake long-term risky investments if it is not easy to communicate to the capital markets the benefits from such investments.

Any excess cash flow after these long-term investments is free cash flow that is available for both debt holders and equity holders. Debt cash transactions include interest payments and principal payments as well as new borrowing. Cash flow after payments to debt holders is free cash flow available to equity holders. Cash transactions involving shareholders include dividend payments and stock repurchases, as well as issues of new equity.

Firms with negative free cash flow to both debt and equity have to borrow additional funds to meet their interest and debt repayment obligations, cut dividend payments, or issue additional equity. Managers of firms in this situation are often reluctant to cut dividends for fear that it will be viewed negatively by investors. While this may be feasible in the short term, it is not prudent for a firm to continue to pay dividends to equity holders unless it has a positive free cash flow on a sustained basis. In contrast, firms with large positive free cash flow to debt and equity run the risk of making unproductive investments to pursue growth for its own sake. An analyst, therefore, should carefully examine the investment plans of such firms.

The model in Table 5-11 suggests that the analyst should focus on a number of cash flow measures: (1) cash flow from operations before investment in working capital and interest payments, to examine whether or not the firm is able to generate a cash surplus from operations; (2) cash flow from operations after investment in working capital, to assess how the firm's working capital is being managed and whether or not it has the flexibility to invest in long-term assets for future growth; (3) free cash flow available to debt and equity holders, to assess a firm's ability to meet its interest and principal payments; and (4) free cash flow available to equity holders, to assess the firm's financial ability to sustain its dividend policy and to identify potential agency problems from excess free cash flow. These measures have to be evaluated in the context of the company's business, its growth strategy, and its financial policies. Further, changes in these measures from year to year provide valuable information on the stability of the cash flow dynamics of the firm.

Key Analysis Questions

The cash flow model in Table 5-11 can be also used to assess a firm's earnings quality. The reconciliation of a firm's net income with its cash flow from operations facilitates this exercise. Following are some of the questions an analyst can probe in this respect:

- Are there significant differences between a firm's net income and its operating cash flow? Is it possible to clearly identify the sources of this difference? Which accounting policies contribute to this difference? Are there any one-time events contributing to this difference?
- Is the relationship between cash flow and net income changing over time? Why? Is it because of changes in business conditions or because of changes in the firm's accounting policies and estimates?
- What is the time lag between the recognition of revenues and expenses and the receipt and disbursement of cash flows? What type of uncertainties need to be resolved in between?
- Are the changes in receivables, inventories, and payables normal? If not, is there adequate explanation for the changes?

Finally, as we will discuss in Chapter 7, free cash flow available to debt and equity and free cash flow available to equity are critical inputs into the cash-flow-based valuation of firms' assets and equity, respectively.

Analysis of Wal-Mart's and Target's Cash Flow

Both Wal-Mart and Target reported their cash flows using the indirect cash flow statement. Table 5-11 recasts these statements using the approach discussed above so that we can analyze the two companies' cash flow dynamics.

The cash flow analysis presented in Table 5-11 shows that Wal-Mart had an operating cash flow before working capital investments of $17.3 billion in 2005. The difference between its earnings and this cash flow is attributable primarily to depreciation and amortization charges, which is a non-cash expense that is included in the company's income statement.

In 2005 Wal-Mart was able to generate a further $1.2 billion from the liquidation of operating working capital, due in large part to an increase in its accounts payable. As mentioned before, Wal-Mart's size and the volume of its purchases make it an attractive client to most suppliers, enabling it to manage its relations with suppliers to generate additional cash flow. As a result of this improved working capital management, Wal-Mart had an operating cash flow before investment in long-term assets of $18.5 billion. In 2004 Wal-Mart also generated significant cash flows from its operations despite making a small net investment in operating working capital.

In both years Wal-Mart was able to finance substantial investments in long-term assets from cash flow from operations. The firm invested $12.4 billion and $14.2 billion in long-term assets in 2004 and 2005, respectively, still leaving positive cash flow for its debt and equity holders. Since Wal-Mart was a net borrower during this period, free cash flow available to its equity holders exceeded that available to debt and equity. The company utilized this free cash flow to pay regular dividends, to buy back company shares, and to build up its cash balance.

Like Wal-Mart, Target's non-cash operating charges had a significant impact on the firm's net income. Operating cash flow before working capital investments was 70 percent higher than net income in 2005. Despite increases in accounts receivables and inventory, Target was able to reduce its working capital investments in 2005 by increasing use of supplier credit through accounts payable and other accrued liabilities.

In 2005 Target used $4.1 billion of its operating cash flow to invest in long-term assets, primarily to open new stores and refurbish existing ones, leaving $617.0 million available to debt and equity holders. The company was also a net borrower, with a modest increase in outstanding debt. As a result, $688 million was available for stockholders. Dividends and stock buybacks were $1,344 million, leading to a decline in the cash balance in 2005.

SUMMARY

This chapter presents two key tools of financial analysis: ratio analysis and cash flow analysis. Both these tools allow the analyst to examine a firm's performance and its financial condition given its strategy and goals. Ratio analysis involves assessing the firm's income statement and balance sheet data. Cash flow analysis relies on the firm's cash flow statement.

The starting point for ratio analysis is the company's ROE. The next step is to evaluate the three drivers of ROE, which are net profit margin, asset turnover, and financial leverage. Net profit margin reflects a firm's operating management, asset turnover reflects its investment management, and financial leverage reflects its financing policies. Each of these areas can be further probed by examining a number of ratios. For example, common-sized income statement analysis allows a detailed examination of a firm's net margins. Similarly, turnover of key working capital accounts such as accounts receivable, inventory, and accounts payable, and turnover of the firm's fixed assets allow further examination of a firm's asset utilization. Finally, short-term liquidity ratios, debt policy ratios, and coverage ratios provide a means of examining a firm's financial leverage.

A firm's sustainable growth rate—the rate at which it can grow without altering its operating, investment, and financing policies—is determined by its ROE and its dividend policy. The concept of sustainable growth provides a way to integrate the different elements of ratio analysis and to evaluate whether or not a firm's growth strategy is sustainable. If a firm's plans call for growing at a rate above its current sustainable rate, then one can analyze which of the firm's ratios is likely to change in the future.

Cash flow analysis supplements ratio analysis in examining a firm's operating activities, investment management, and financial risks. Firms in the U.S. are currently required to report a cash flow statement summarizing their operating, investment, and financing cash flows. Firms in other countries typically report working capital flows, but it is possible to use this information to create a cash flow statement.

Since there are wide variations across firms in the way cash flow data are reported, analysts often use a standard format to recast cash flow data. We discussed one such cash flow model in this chapter. This model allows the analyst to assess whether a firm's operations generate cash flow before investments in operating working capital, and how much cash is being invested in the firm's working capital. It also enables the analyst to calculate the firm's free cash flow after making long-term investments, which is an indication of the firm's ability to meet its debt and dividend payments. Finally, the cash flow analysis shows how the firm is financing itself, and whether its financing patterns are too risky.

The insights gained from analyzing a firm's financial ratios and its cash flows are valuable in forecasts of the firm's future prospects.

DISCUSSION QUESTIONS

1. Which of the following types of firms do you expect to have particularly high or low asset turnover? Explain why.
   - a supermarket
   - a pharmaceutical company
   - a jewelry retailer
   - a steel company

2. Which of the following types of firms do you expect to have high or low sales margins? Why?
   - a supermarket
   - a pharmaceutical company
   - a jewelry retailer
   - a software company

3. James Broker, an analyst with an established brokerage firm, comments: "The critical number I look at for any company is operating cash flow. If cash flows are less than earnings, I consider a company to be a poor performer and a poor investment prospect." Do you agree with this assessment? Why or why not?

4. In 2005 IBM had a return on equity of 26.7 percent, whereas Hewlett-Packard's return was only 6.4 percent. Use the decomposed ROE framework to provide possible reasons for this difference based on the data below:

	IBM	HP
NOPAT/Sales	9.0%	2.7%
Sales/Net Assets	2.16	2.73
Effective After Tax Interest Rate	2.4%	1.1%
Net Financial Leverage	0.42	−0.16

5. Joe Investor asserts, "A company cannot grow faster than its sustainable growth rate." True or false? Explain why.

6. What are the reasons for a firm having lower cash from operations than working capital from operations? What are the possible interpretations of these reasons?

7. ABC Company recognizes revenue at the point of shipment. Management decides to increase sales for the current quarter by filling all customer orders. Explain what impact this decision will have on
   - Days' receivable for the current quarter
   - Days' receivable for the next quarter
   - Sales growth for the current quarter
   - Sales growth for the next quarter
   - Return on sales for the current quarter
   - Return on sales for the next quarter

8. What ratios would you use to evaluate operating leverage for a firm?

9. What are the potential benchmarks that you could use to compare a company's financial ratios? What are the pros and cons of these alternatives?

10. In a period of rising prices, how would the following ratios be affected by the accounting decision to select LIFO, rather than FIFO, for inventory valuation?
    - Gross margin
    - Current ratio
    - Asset turnover
    - Debt-to-equity ratio
    - Average tax rate

NOTES

1. We will call the fiscal year ending January 31, 2006, as the year 2005, and the fiscal year ending January 31, 2005, as the year 2004.

2. In computing ROE, one can either use the beginning equity, ending equity, or an average of the two. Conceptually, the average equity is appropriate, particularly for rapidly growing companies. However, for most companies, this computational choice makes little difference as long as the analyst is consistent. Therefore, in practice most analysts use ending balances for simplicity. This comment applies to all ratios discussed in this chapter where one of the items in the ratio is a flow variable (items in the income statement or cash flow statement) and the other item is a stock variable (items in the balance sheet). Throughout this chapter we use the beginning balances of the stock variables.

3. We discuss in greater detail in Chapter 8 how to estimate a company's cost of equity capital. The cost of equity for Wal-Mart and Target is in the 10 to 12 percent range.

4. Strictly speaking, part of a cash balance is needed to run the firm's operations, so only the excess cash balance should be viewed as negative debt. However, firms do not provide

information on excess cash, so we subtract all cash balances in our definitions and computations. An alternative possibility is to subtract only short-term investments and ignore the cash balance completely.

5. See D. Nissim and S. Penman, "Ratio Analysis and Valuation: From Research to Practice," *Review of Accounting Studies* 6 (2001): 109–154, for a more detailed description of this approach.

6. Both Wal-Mart and Target have a solid credit rating and a relatively low cost of debt. Given the level of leverage, the weighted average cost of capital will be lower than the cost of equity. We will discuss in Chapter 8 how to estimate a company's weighted average cost of capital.

7. See *Taxes and Business Strategy* by Myron Scholes and Mark Wolfson (Englewood Cliffs, NJ: Prentice-Hall, 1992).

8. If firms that are analyzed use different inventory methods, the analyst can adjust to a common method for computing inventory turnover and days inventory. This can be accomplished by adjusting LIFO inventory and LIFO cost of sales to FIFO values using disclosures on the effect of LIFO inventory valuation in the inventory footnote disclosure.

9. There are a number of issues related to the calculation of these ratios in practice. First, in calculating all the turnover ratios, the assets used in the calculations can either be beginning of the year values, year-end values, or an average of the beginning and ending balances in a year. We use the beginning of the year values in our calculations. Second, strictly speaking, one should use credit sales to calculate accounts receivable turnover and days' receivables. But since it is usually difficult to obtain data on credit sales, total sales are used instead. Similarly, in calculating accounts payable turnover or days' payables, cost of goods sold is substituted for purchases for data availability reasons.

10. Changes in cash and marketable securities are excluded because this is the amount being explained by the cash flow statement. Changes in short-term debt and the current portion of long-term debt are excluded because these accounts represent financing flows, not operating flows.

APPENDIX
PART A: WAL-MART STORES, INC. FINANCIAL STATEMENTS

Wal-Mart's financial statements as reported by the firm are shown in the appendix to Chapter 4.

Note: The standardized statements shown below are generated by the BAV software tool and based on data reported by the Standard & Poor's Compustat database, which makes minor modifications to the data as reported by the firm. As a consequence, the standardized statements shown below will not be an exact match to the standardized statements shown in the appendix to Chapter 4.

Wal-Mart Stores, Inc.
Standardized Statements of Income ($ millions)

Fiscal Year Ended January 31	2006	2005	2004
Sales	**313,335**	**286,103**	**257,157**
Cost of Sales	235,691	215,493	195,247
Gross Profit	**77,644**	**70,610**	**61,910**
SG&A	56,733	51,105	44,909
Other Operating Expense	4,700	4,300	3,500
Operating Income	**16,211**	**15,205**	**13,501**
Investment Income	–	–	–
Other Income, net of Other Expense	2,476	2,006	1,668
Other Income	2,476	2,006	1,668
Other Expense	–	–	–
Net Interest Expense (Income)	1,329	1,106	976
Interest Income	248	201	164
Interest Expense	1,577	1,307	1,140
Minority Interest	324	249	214
Pre-Tax Income	**17,034**	**15,856**	**13,979**
Tax Expense	5,803	5,589	5,118
Unusual Gains, Net of Unusual Losses (after tax)	–	–	193
Net Income	**11,231**	**10,267**	**9,054**
Preferred Dividends	–	–	–
Net Income to Common	**11,231**	**10,267**	**9,054**

Source: Standard & Poor's Compustat database and BAV Model v4.3.

Wal-Mart Stores, Inc.
Standardized Balance Sheet ($ millions)

Year Beginning February 1	2006	2005	2004
Assets			
Cash and Marketable Securities	6,414	5,488	5,199
Accounts Receivable	2,662	1,715	1,254
Inventory	32,191	29,447	26,612
Other Current Assets	2,557	1,841	1,356
Total Current Assets	**43,824**	**38,491**	**34,421**
Long-Term Tangible Assets	79,290	68,567	58,530
Long-Term Intangible Assets	12,188	10,803	9,882
Other Long-Term Assets	2,885	2,362	2,079
Total Long-Term Assets	**94,363**	**81,732**	**70,491**
Total Assets	**138,187**	**120,223**	**104,912**
Liabilities			
Accounts Payable	25,373	21,671	19,332
Short-Term Debt	8,648	7,781	6,367
Other Current Liabilities	14,805	13,436	11,719
Total Current Liabilities	**48,826**	**42,888**	**37,418**
Long-Term Debt	30,171	23,669	20,099
Deferred Taxes	–	–	–
Other Long-Term Liabilities (non-interest bearing)	4,552	2,947	2,288
Total Long-Term Liabilities	**34,723**	**26,616**	**22,387**
Total Liabilities	**83,549**	**69,504**	**59,805**
Minority Interest	1,467	1,323	1,484
Shareholders' Equity			
Preferred Stock	–	–	–
Common Shareholders' Equity	53,171	49,396	43,623
Total Shareholders' Equity	**53,171**	**49,396**	**43,623**
Total Liabilities and Shareholders' Equity	**138,187**	**120,223**	**104,912**

Source: Standard & Poor's Compustat database and BAV Model v4.3.

Wal-Mart Stores, Inc.
Standardized Statements of Cash Flows ($ millions)

Year Ended January 31	2006	2005	2004
Net Income	11,231	10,267	9,054
After-tax net interest expense (income)	876	716	619
Non-operating losses (gains)	–	–	–
Long-term operating accruals	5,208	5,046	4,084
Depreciation and amortization	4,717	4,405	3,852
Other	491	641	232
Operating cash flow before working **capital investments**	**17,315**	**16,029**	**13,757**
Net (investments in) or liquidation of operating working capital	1,194	(269)	2,858
Operating cash flow before investment **in long-term assets**	**18,509**	**15,760**	**16,615**
Net (investment in) or liquidation of operating long-term assets	(14,183)	(12,351)	(8,312)
Free cash flow available to debt and **equity**	**4,326**	**3,409**	**8,303**
After-tax net interest income (expense)	(876)	(716)	(619)
Net debt (repayment) or issuance	4,018	4,041	941
Free cash flow available to equity	**7,468**	**6,734**	**8,625**
Dividend (payments)	(2,511)	(2,214)	(1,569)
Net stock issuance (repurchase), and other equity changes	(4,031)	(4,231)	(4,615)
Net increase (decrease) in cash balance	**926**	**289**	**2,441**

Source: Standard & Poor's Compustat database and BAV Model v4.3.

Wal-Mart Stores, Inc.
Condensed Statements of Income ($ millions)

Year Ended January 31	2006	2005	2004
Sales	313,335	286,103	257,157
Net Operating Profit after Tax	12,107	10,983	9,673
Net Income	11,231	10,267	9,054
+ Net Interest Expense after Tax	876	716	619
= **Net Operating Profit after Tax**	12,107	10,983	9,673
− Net Interest Expense after Tax	876	716	619
Interest Expense	1,577	1,307	1,140
− Interest Income	248	201	164
= Net Interest Expense (Income)	1,329	1,106	976
× (1−Tax Expense/Pre-Tax Income)	0.659	0.648	0.634
= **Net Interest Expense after Tax**	876	716	619
= **Net Income**	11,231	10,267	9,054
− Preferred Stock Dividends	–	–	–
= **Net Income to Common**	11,231	10,267	9,054

Source: BAV Model v4.3.

Wal-Mart Stores, Inc.
Condensed Balance Sheet ($ millions)

Year Beginning February 1	2006	2005	2004
Beginning Net Working Capital	(2,768)	(2,104)	(1,829)
Accounts Receivable	2,662	1,715	1,254
+ Inventory	32,191	29,447	26,612
+ Other Current Assets	2,557	1,841	1,356
− Accounts Payable	25,373	21,671	19,332
− Other Current Liabilities	14,805	13,436	11,719
= **Beginning Net Working Capital**	(2,768)	(2,104)	(1,829)
+ **Beginning Net Long-Term Assets**	88,344	77,462	66,719
Long-Term Tangible Assets	79,290	68,567	58,530
+ Long-Term Intangible Assets	12,188	10,803	9,882
+ Other Long-Term Assets	2,885	2,362	2,079
− Minority Interest	1,467	1,323	1,484
− Deferred Taxes	–	–	–
− Other Long-Term Liabilities (non-interest bearing)	4,552	2,947	2,288
= **Beginning Net Long-Term Assets**	88,344	77,462	66,719
= **Total Assets**	85,576	75,358	64,890
Beginning Net Debt	32,405	25,962	21,267
Short-Term Debt	8,648	7,781	6,367
+ Long-Term Debt	30,171	23,669	20,099
− Cash	6,414	5,488	5,199
= **Beginning Net Debt**	32,405	25,962	21,267
+ **Beginning Preferred Stock**	–	–	–
+ **Beginning Shareholders' Equity**	53,171	49,396	43,623
= **Total Net Capital**	85,576	75,358	64,890

Source: BAV Model v4.3.

APPENDIX
PART B: TARGET CORPORATION FINANCIAL STATEMENTS

Note: The standardized statements shown below are generated by the BAV software tool and based on data reported by the Standard & Poor's Compustat database, which makes minor modifications to the data as reported by the firm. As a consequence, the standardized statements shown below will not be an exact match to the standardized statements that would result from the preceding manual standardization exercise.

Target Corporation
Standardized Statements of Income ($ millions)

Fiscal Year Ended January	2006	2005	2004
Sales	52,620	46,839	48,163
Cost of Sales	34,927	31,445	31,790
Gross Profit	17,693	15,394	16,373
SG&A	11,988	10,534	11,534
Other Operating Expense	1,409	1,259	1,320
Operating Income	4,296	3,601	3,519
Investment Income	–	–	–
Other Income, net of Other Expense	69	(89)	–
Other Income	69	(89)	–
Other Expense	–	–	–
Net Interest Expense (Income)	505	481	559
Interest Income	27	–	–
Interest Expense	532	481	559
Minority Interest	–	–	–
Pre-Tax Income	3,860	3,031	2,960
Tax Expense	1,452	1,146	1,119
Unusual Gains, Net of Unusual Losses (after tax)	–	1,313	–
Net Income	2,408	3,198	1,841
Preferred Dividends	–	–	–
Net Income to Common	2,408	3,198	1,841

Source: Standard & Poor's Compustat database and BAV Model v4.3.

Target Corporation
Standardized Balance Sheet ($ millions)

Year Beginning February	2006	2005	2004
Assets			
Cash and Marketable Securities	1,648	2,245	716
Accounts Receivable	6,226	5,497	5,776
Inventory	5,838	5,384	5,343
Other Current Assets	693	796	1,093
Total Current Assets	**14,405**	**13,922**	**12,928**
Long-Term Tangible Assets	19,038	16,860	16,969
Long-Term Intangible Assets	183	206	364
Other Long-Term Assets	1,369	1,305	1,131
Total Long-Term Assets	**20,590**	**18,371**	**18,464**
Total Assets	**34,995**	**32,293**	**31,392**
Liabilities			
Accounts Payable	6,268	5,779	5,448
Short-Term Debt	753	504	866
Other Current Liabilities	2,567	1,937	2,000
Total Current Liabilities	**9,588**	**8,220**	**8,314**
Long-Term Debt	9,119	9,034	10,217
Deferred Taxes	851	973	–
Other Long-Term Liabilities (non-interest bearing)	1,232	1,037	1,796
Total Long-Term Liabilities	**11,202**	**11,044**	**12,013**
Total Liabilities	**20,790**	**19,264**	**20,327**
Minority Interest	–	–	–
Shareholders' Equity			
Preferred Stock	–	–	–
Common Shareholders' Equity	14,205	13,029	11,065
Total Shareholders' Equity	**14,205**	**13,029**	**11,065**
Total Liabilities and Shareholders' Equity	**34,995**	**32,293**	**31,392**

Source: Standard & Poor's Compustat database and BAV Model v4.3.

Target Corporation
Standardized Statements of Cash Flows ($ millions)

Year Ended January	2006	2005	2004
Net Income	**2,408**	**3,198**	**1,841**
After-tax net interest expense (income)	315	299	348
Non-operating losses (gains)	70	59	54
Long-term operating accruals	1,813	120	2,131
Depreciation and amortization	1,409	1,259	1,320
Other	404	(1,139)	811
Operating cash flow before working capital investments	**4,606**	**3,676**	**4,374**
Net (investments in) or liquidation of operating working capital	160	(182)	(866)
Operating cash flow before investment in long-term assets	**4,766**	**3,494**	**3,508**
Net (investment in) or liquidation of operating long-term assets	(4,149)	1,179	(2,919)
Free cash flow available to debt and equity	**617**	**4,673**	**589**
After-tax net interest income (expense)	(315)	(299)	(348)
Net debt (repayment) or issuance	386	(1,477)	(72)
Free cash flow available to equity	**688**	**2,897**	**169**
Dividend (payments)	(318)	(272)	(237)
Net stock issuance (repurchase), and other equity changes	(1,026)	(1,088)	26
Net increase (decrease) in cash balance	**(656)**	**1,537**	**(42)**

Source: Standard & Poor's Compustat database and BAV Model v4.3.

Target Corporation
Condensed Statements of Income ($ millions)

Year Ended January	2006	2005	2004
Sales	**52,620**	**46,839**	**48,163**
Net Operating Profit after Tax	**2,723**	**3,497**	**2,189**
Net Income	2,408	3,198	1,841
+ Net Interest Expense after Tax	315	299	348
= Net Operating Profit after Tax	**2,723**	**3,497**	**2,189**
− Net Interest Expense after Tax	315	299	348
Interest Expense	532	481	559
− Interest Income	27	–	–
= Net Interest Expense (Income)	505	481	559
× (1 − Tax Expense/Pre-Tax Income)	0.624	0.622	0.622
= Net Interest Expense after Tax	**315**	**299**	**348**
= Net Income	**2,408**	**3,198**	**1,841**
− Preferred Stock Dividends	–	–	–
= Net Income to Common	**2,408**	**3,198**	**1,841**

Source: BAV Model v4.3.

Target Corporation
Condensed Balance Sheet ($ millions)

Year Beginning February	2006	2005	2004
Beginning Net Working Capital	3,922	3,961	4,764
Accounts Receivable	6,226	5,497	5,776
+ Inventory	5,838	5,384	5,343
+ Other Current Assets	693		1,093
− Accounts Payable	6,268	5,779	5,448
− Other Current Liabilities	2,567	1,937	2,000
= **Beginning Net Working Capital**	3,922	3,961	4,764
+ **Beginning Net Long-Term Assets**	18,507	16,361	16,668
Long-Term Tangible Assets	19,038	16,860	16,969
+ Long-Term Intangible Assets	183	206	364
+ Other Long-Term Assets	1,369	1,305	1,131
− Minority Interest	−	−	−
− Deferred Taxes	851	973	−
− Other Long-Term Liabilities (non-interest bearing)	1,232	1,037	1,796
= **Beginning Net Long-Term Assets**	18,507	16,361	16,668
= **Total Assets**	22,429	20,322	21,432
Beginning Net Debt	8,224	7,293	10,367
Short-Term Debt	753	504	866
+ Long-Term Debt	9,119	9,034	10,217
− Cash	1,648	2,245	716
= **Beginning Net Debt**	8,224	7,293	10,367
+ **Beginning Preferred Stock**	−	−	−
+ **Beginning Shareholders' Equity**	14,205	13,029	11,065
= **Total Net Capital**	22,429	20,322	21,432

Source: BAV Model v4.3.

United Parcel Service's IPO

This is an historic step for UPS. We intend to remain the pre-eminent company in our industry and expand our role as an enabler of global commerce. A publicly traded stock will build on our financial strength as a triple-A rated company and give us more flexibility to pursue strategic opportunities around the world. This will allow us to better meet the changing needs of our customers for innovative new products and services.

— James Kelly, UPS Chairman and CEO, July 21, 1999

In July of 1999, United Parcel Service (UPS) surprised both Wall Street and Main Street with the announcement that, after more than 90 years as a private, employee-owned operation, it was planning an initial public offering that would transform "Big Brown" into a publicly traded company. UPS was a company with $1.7 billion of net income and almost a century-long track record of financial performance, a marked contrast to the Internet and technology-related IPOs launched in the late 1990s. Although pricing for the shares had yet to be announced, the offering looked likely to be the largest IPO in U.S. history.

Determining an appropriate price for the new shares was a central concern of the joint Morgan Stanley Dean Witter & Co.-UPS deal team that had been charged with launching the offering. The actual price per share would be set only hours before the first trading day for the new stock. In the weeks before the listing the deal team would be expected to consider a variety of factors in fixing the offer price, including current and future trends in the package delivery industry, UPS's strengths and weaknesses relative to other competitors, UPS's recent financial performance, and the valuation of comparable companies.

The Package Delivery Industry

In 1999, package delivery in the United States was a $43 billion industry serving a broad array of distinct customer segments—individuals sending overnight letters, small-to-medium-sized enterprises demanding affordable shipment of time-critical parcels, and large corporations moving heavy freight between facilities.

Professor Paul Healy and Brett Laschinger and Ajay Shroff (MBAs'02) prepared this case. HBS cases are developed solely as the basis for class discussion. Cases are not intended to serve as endorsements, sources of primary data, or illustrations of effective or ineffective management.

The industry offered two basic products—air and ground. Ground traditionally referred to deliveries made within one to six business days using surface transportation such as cars, vans, trucks, and trains. For much of the century, ground was the only reliable option for moving letters and parcels. Air delivery enabled customers to request overnight service, which was expedited using complex air networks. Two- and three-day air products, a segment that rapidly expanded in the 1980s and 1990s given its substantially lower price compared to overnight products and faster delivery time relative to traditional ground services, was often referred to as "time-deferred" or "deferred" service. Although the lines between air express and ground had blurred somewhat as ground networks improved to the point where overnight and "two-day air" deliveries could be made on the ground, industry analysts continued to segment the market in these terms. As of 1999, the domestic air industry (including overnight and deferred) comprised 60% of the market by revenue and 46% by volume, compared with 40% of revenue and 54% of volume for ground.[1] (See **Exhibits 1** to **3** for historical market size and growth data.)

The asset-intensive and highly complex nature of both the domestic air and ground industries had resulted in intense competition among three very large competitors: Atlanta-based UPS (51% share of market by revenue), Memphis-based Federal Express (26%), and the U.S. Postal Service (17%).[2] See **Exhibit 4** for overnight, deferred, and ground market share data. UPS was the market leader in the $17 billion ground segment, with competition coming from FedEx and USPS as well as private delivery fleets of individual companies, courier services, regional delivery services, LTL trucking firms and third-party logistics companies. UPS was the number two player to the USPS in the deferred segment, and number two to FedEx in the overnight express market.

U.S. Postal Service

The U.S. Postal Service (USPS) was a quasi-government entity which moved more than four times as many deliveries each day as UPS and FedEx combined,[3] and operated a delivery network that reached every household and commercial address in the country, six days a week. The USPS offered a number of delivery products that competed directly with UPS's offerings. The most prominent of these was Priority Mail, which offered ground shipment of packages in 1 to 3 business days to any destination in the United States. Priority Mail was generally considered to be less expensive but also less reliable than either UPS's or FedEx's two- and three-day offerings. The USPS also lacked the premier logistics and package tracking information systems that both FedEx and UPS had developed. However, rumor had it that Lockheed Martin had been hired to help the Postal Service create a comparable tracking system to be completed in 2001.[4]

Observers pointed out that with e-mail and other forms of electronic communication cutting deeply into the USPS's traditional regular mail monopoly, the Service

1. *SJ Consulting estimates.*

2. *SJ Consulting estimates.*

3. *USPS web site. Includes first-class mail in addition to parcel volume. First-class mail represents about 90% of USPS's total shipment volume.*

4. *Brian O'Reilly, "UPS vs. FedEx: They've Got Mail," Fortune, February 7, 2000.*

was especially eager to allocate resources to other segments of the package delivery market, which would mean more frequent competition with UPS and FedEx.[5]

FedEx

FedEx, a $17 billion global transportation and logistics enterprise, was credited with single-handedly pioneering the concept of overnight delivery in the early 1970s. By the late 1990s, FedEx moved over 3 million packages each day, with the ability to reach virtually every business address in the United States and almost every country around the world within 24 hours. Federal Express, the overnight delivery arm of FedEx Corp., was by far its largest and most important operating unit, accounting for 84% of total revenues and 83% of operating income in 1998. FedEx also controlled a variety of other related businesses. FedEx Custom Critical was a time-critical carrier, FedEx Logistics provided logistics solutions and assistance to other businesses, and Viking Freight operated as a less-than-truckload West Coast regional carrier. FedEx's operating philosophy with respect to these various companies was to "operate independently, compete collectively,"[6] and hence each operating company remained a separate operating entity with discrete management and its own trucks, sorting hubs and other assets.

With the 1998 acquisition of Roadway Package System (RPS), the second-largest ground delivery business-to-business small-package shipper in the nation (after UPS), FedEx also developed a presence in the ground business. Prior to the acquisition, RPS employed 22,000 direct and contract employees, operated 365 sorting and other facilities in North America, and reported revenues of $1.3 billion. It was estimated that RPS served 10%–12% of the U.S. B2B ground delivery market in 1998.[7] RPS had achieved its considerable success in part by selectively targeting some of UPS's most valuable accounts—high-volume customers in high-density locations. RPS had also developed the premier package logistics and tracking software in the ground delivery industry. Following the acquisition, FedEx renamed RPS as FedEx Ground to take advantage of its own strong brand.

Other Competitors

Smaller players in the U.S. market included Airborne Freight, CNF, and DHL. Airborne Freight, with 1998 revenues of just over $3 billion, was the third-largest U.S. express delivery carrier, and had achieved significant growth over the 1990s by positioning itself as the low-cost overnight delivery alternative for business-to-business customers. CNF focused on ground delivery and heavyweight airfreight. DHL, a European international express-mail carrier, was active in U.S. international shipping. In 1998, the German government-backed Deutsche Post AG acquired a 25% stake in DHL and was expected to compete more aggressively for U.S. domestic business.

Industry Outlook

In July 1999, the outlook for the package industry was mixed. Robust GDP growth and ever-increasing demands for faster delivery suggested continued strong growth

---

5. *Deutsche Bank Alex Brown, UPS Equity Research Report, December 1, 1999.*

6. *FedEx Web site.*

7. *"RPS Adopts a New Name as Parent FedEx Shifts its Marketing Strategy,"* Pittsburgh Business Times Journal, *January 21, 2000.*

potential for the air express segment, which had enjoyed double-digit expansion through the 1980s and high single-digit growth in the 1990s. However, the digitization of documents and emergence of electronic signatures threatened the significant overnight letter business. As for the ground industry, which had grown at a rate somewhat in excess of U.S. GDP, the rapid expansion of Internet shopping hinted at a potential boost for the B2C ground business, while industry rivalry threatened intense price competition.[8]

In terms of international delivery, the large integrated carriers had constructed global delivery networks that could reach over 90% of the world's population. International revenue was derived from the export needs of U.S.-based customers as well as intra-country operations in other parts of the world. As saturation occurred in the U.S. market, industry observers anticipated that this market would provide an attractive growth opportunity.

UNITED PARCEL SERVICE (UPS)

With over 340,000 employees, 149,000 delivery vehicles, 500 planes, and $25 billion in annual revenues, UPS was the largest parcel delivery company in the world. The company delivered nearly 13 million packages each business day (9,000 packages every minute) to over 200 countries worldwide. Each year UPS moved some 6% of the United States' Gross Domestic Product (GDP). In addition to air and ground package delivery, UPS helped its customers with supply chain management, logistics, and financial services. The company had daily contact with 1.8 million customers (including every company in the *Fortune* 1000) and made deliveries to 6 million business and residential addresses. In 1999, *Fortune* magazine recognized UPS as the "World's Most Admired Global Mail, Package and Freight Delivery Company" and *Forbes* magazine named UPS "Company of the Year."[9]

History

Using $100 borrowed from a friend, 19-year old James "Jim" Casey founded the American Messenger Company in Seattle, Washington, in 1907. The company provided private messenger and delivery services—such as the transportation of letters, hand-baggage, and trays of food—by bicycle, foot, and streetcar.[10]

In the 1920s, the company, renamed the United Parcel Service, shifted its focus to package delivery for retailers who sought to outsource that function. UPS grew quietly alongside the retail industry for the next three decades, slowly expanding its geographical reach and breadth of services. During this period, the company pioneered the concept of consolidated delivery—combining packages for a particular neighborhood within one delivery vehicle—and developed the first-ever mechanical sorter and conveyor belt system.

Gradual innovation and expansion continued until the 1950s when UPS realized that its growth options would be limited if it remained solely focused on package delivery for retailers. As of 1954, UPS had operations in only 16 cities. To expand its geographic reach and scope of operations, UPS had to petition state and federal

8. *SJ Consulting estimates.*

9. *UPS 1999 Annual Report, filed March 30, 2000.*

10. *"United Parcel Service (A)," HBS Case No. 488-016 (Boston, MA: Harvard Business School Publishing, 1992), p. 3.*

authorities for broader business activity rights. Over the next 30 years, UPS fought dozens of legal and regulatory battles to gain the right to operate delivery vehicles within each state, and between any two states—known in the industry as "common carrier" rights. By 1980, UPS achieved national coverage and had become a direct and formidable competitor to the USPS. By the early 1980s, UPS's ground business had grown so rapidly that it quickly surpassed USPS's in terms of parcel (i.e., non-letter) volume. Over the next two decades UPS went on to become the largest player in the ground delivery segment.[11]

UPS grew its air network in parallel with its ground infrastructure. Blue Label Air, a two-day service between major cities, began in 1953 and reached national coverage by 1978. During the 1970s, despite the rapid growth of the overnight express market which newly formed Federal Express pioneered, UPS stuck to 2–3 day air service at a rate one-tenth that of FedEx's overnight service.[12] In August 1982, however, "in response to customer demand," UPS finally announced its entry into the next-day air express arena, nine years after FedEx.[13]

The 1980s and early 1990s were pivotal for UPS as it was forced to play "catch up" to FedEx in the air express segment and respond to market share gains by RPS and the USPS on the ground. The company's responses included a major technology upgrade, changes in pricing, and a change in marketing strategy. Between 1988 and 1999, UPS spent more than $1 billion per year upgrading its infrastructure to track packages precisely, deliver electronic proof of delivery, and manage shipments on-line. The new systems included electronic scanners, bar codes on packages, and computerized clipboards for all UPS drivers.[14] In addition, the company hired thousands of programmers and technicians to manage its information needs and develop innovative applications and services for its customers. By 1999, UPS could handle six times as many on-line tracking requests as FedEx,[15] leading *Forbes* magazine to declare, "UPS used to be a trucking company with technology. Now it's a technology company with trucks."[16]

UPS also responded to competitive challenges by changing its pricing and marketing strategies. It began transitioning away from using standard rates to allowing prices to vary across markets and customers based on cost differences. It also introduced a widely aired new ad campaign that touted "We run the tightest ship in the shipping business,"[17] a marked change from its prior policy of shying away from publicity.

Throughout the 1990s UPS steadily captured market share in the express arena, reaching an estimated 32% share by 1998, and its ground business returned to a pace of moderate growth despite cost-cutting and targeted sales efforts by competitors.[18]

---

11. John D. Williams, Staff Reporter for The Wall Street Journal (New York, NY), "The Brown Giant: UPS Delivers Profits By Expanding Its Area," August 25, 1980, p. 1.

12. John D. Williams, Staff Reporter for The Wall Street Journal (New York, NY), "The Brown Giant: UPS Delivers Profits By Expanding Its Area," August 25, 1980, p. 1.

13. Sharen Kindel, "When Elephants Dance," Financial World, June 9, 1992, p. 76.

14. Kenneth Labich, "Big Changes at Big Brown," Fortune, January 18, 1988, p. 60.

15. Fedex.com and UPS.com company Web sites.

16. From www.ups.com, "Speeches," Mike Eskew, March 29, 2000.

17. Kenneth Labich, "Big Changes at Big Brown," Fortune, January 18, 1988, p. 57.

18. SJ Consulting.

Reflecting on UPS's transformation during the 1990s, UPS CEO Jim Kelly proclaimed, "Truth is, we're not your father's UPS anymore!"[19]

UPS chose to expand the scope of its business in 1993 with the formation of UPS Logistics Group, which provided supply chain management solutions and consulting services to UPS's customer base. Typical service contracts included back-end fulfillment for Sprint PCS, the timely delivery of fresh ingredients to all Papa John's Pizza locations, and the distribution of vehicles from Ford's manufacturing plants to automobile dealerships nationwide. By 1999, the Logistics Group generated nearly $1 billion in incremental revenue for the company.[20]

Operations

UPS coordinated and managed the pickup of 13 million packages each day from 2 million addresses for delivery to over 6 million commercial and residential addresses worldwide. To do so, it relied on a carefully designed network of vehicles, sorting facilities, and hubs as well as the support of a sophisticated IT system. The system had been developed and refined over the last decade and was continually enhanced to ensure the highest levels of reliability, efficiency, and speed.

Drivers followed precisely defined routes to pickup packages from customers at pre-set times. Those packages were taken to hubs where they were consolidated and sorted at speeds of upwards of hundreds of thousands of packages per hour. Packages for the same zip code or delivery area were loaded onto the appropriate conveyor belt and then onto the familiar brown trucks in the order in which they would be delivered. This allowed drivers to deliver their packages in sequence, "from one address to the next-closest address . . . as quickly and productively as possible."[21]

Unlike FedEx, UPS made no distinction between the operating facilities for air and ground operations. All facilities were shared, including the single fleet of trucks that handled the pickup and delivery of all UPS shipments. The integration of its air and ground operations gave UPS the ability to optimize utilization of its assets while still meeting customer service requirements. For example, the same fleet of UPS trucks was used to pick up and deliver ground and air packages. Also, because the operations were integrated, a package marked for "Next Day Air" delivery could be transported by truck if that method of transportation was deemed less expensive and just as reliable (see **Exhibit 5**). UPS's sophisticated IT systems coordinated this process.[22]

Human Resource Management

Since its inception, UPS enjoyed a loyal workforce with an operational and service-excellence culture. Employees were recruited through part-time positions and educational assistance programs. They were trained in carefully studied work methods and educated about UPS's time-tested policies and procedures at a cost of over $300 million annually.[23] These educational programs, combined with on-the-job training and role

19. James Kelly, speech at the Robert C. Goizueta Global Leadership Award Breakfast, December 14, 2001 (available at www.ups.com, "Speeches").

20. 1999 UPS Annual Report.

21. www.pressroom.ups.com/about/history/0,1701,,00.html or www.ups.com, "Company History."

22. Ibid.

23. http://www.pressroom.ups.com/about/history/0,1701,,00.html or www.ups.com, "Company History."

modeling, helped UPS command one of the lowest turnover rates in the industry (less than 5% annually) and succeeded in developing a portion of its workforce for management positions each year. UPS took pride in this "promote from within" policy which was epitomized by the fact that James "Jim" Kelly, UPS's chairman and chief executive officer, started his career as a package delivery driver.

The company's unique culture emphasized accountability and efficient execution at every level of the organization. Operating employees adhered to fairly rigid operational guidelines developed by industrial engineers and rooted in time motion studies. Drivers, for example, were instructed on how to best perform their jobs from the moment they started work until the end of their day. A lengthy and detailed guide precisely defined how a driver should start the delivery vehicle's engine, greet customers, scan packages, and even buckle and unbuckle his or her safety belt between stops. Within corporate headquarters, employees faced similar policies that focused on efficiency, "such as no coffee at desks, and two 15-minute breaks during the work day."[24] These and other operating features were captured in the company's *Policy Book*, which had guided the company since 1929.

Since 1919, union issues were a way of life at UPS. Over 200,000 of UPS's 340,000 employees belonged to the International Brotherhood of Teamsters, making UPS the largest single constituency for that union. Labor relations had generally been harmonious. The only exception had arisen during a 15-day work stoppage in 1997 that cost UPS several hundred million in lost revenues and an immeasurable loss of goodwill among certain customers. Management and the unions were able to strike flexible work arrangements when needed to allow UPS to offer customers a greater range of services. In return, UPS drivers and other unionized personnel enjoyed the highest pay in the industry.

Experts believed UPS's combination of "controls, rules, a detailed union contract, and carefully studied work methods . . . helped guarantee the customer reliable, low-cost service."[25]

VALUATION BENCHMARKS

The IPO team considered several potential benchmarks for valuing UPS. The first potential benchmark was the trucking industry. Industry analysts typically included package delivery firms in the trucking industry, making it a natural comparison. However, the team decided that the fragmented trucking industry, with its low barriers to entry and poor profitability, was of limited value as a benchmark for UPS. Instead, the investment banking members of the team favored using Federal Express as a benchmark, whereas UPS's management argued that UPS was better compared to "best-of-breed" companies in other industries.

Federal Express

UPS's foremost publicly listed competitor, particularly in the overnight express segment of the market, was Tennessee-based FedEx Corporation. FedEx operated a fleet of 634 aircraft and 41,000 pickup and delivery vehicles, and employed 88,000

---

24. *"United Parcel Service (A),"* HBS Case No. 488-016 *(Boston, MA: Harvard Business School Publishing, 1992), p. 15.*

25. *David E. Bowen and Edward E. Lawler, "The Empowerment of Service Workers: What, Why, How, and When,"* Sloan Management Review, *Spring 1992: 32.*

permanent full-time and 50,000 permanent part-time employees. On November 1, 1999, FedEx's stock price closed at $41.50, representing a price-earnings multiple of 19.8 and a price-book value of 2.7 (see **Exhibit 6**).

Although FedEx had been created as an overnight air express carrier and UPS had focused on multi-day ground delivery, over time their business models had converged. This had been accelerated by FedEx's acquisition of RPS. FedEx Chairman Fred Smith noted the newly merged company transformed FedEx into a "global transportation and logistics powerhouse. Customers increasingly demand a complete, seamless solution to supply chain management needs on a global basis, and the [Federal Express] companies will be able to offer it."[26]

In an effort to keep ground delivery operating costs below those of UPS, FedEx was planning to utilize contracted drivers and trucks, which were significantly cheaper than their rival's Teamster-organized delivery workforce. FedEx also planned to invest in RPS's existing ground network to expand its reach and capacity,[27] and to increase RPS's customer service levels through enhancing technology and training.[28]

UPS and FedEx also both looked to the international delivery business as a key source of growth. In 1999, FedEx's international services represented 25% of total revenues and had been growing at an annual rate of almost 10%. For UPS, international operations for the nine months ended September 30, 1999, accounted for $2.56 billion (or 13%) of UPS's revenues and $147 million (or 5%) of operating profits.

However, there were also important differences between the two companies that could be relevant in using FedEx multiples for valuing UPS. UPS's recent financial performance was superior to FedEx's. Over the three years from 1997 to 1999, UPS reported average net profit margins of 6.5% and Return on Equity (ROE) of 25.2%, versus 2.8% and 10.6% respectively for FedEx. Financial statements for UPS and FedEx are shown in **Exhibits 7** and **8**.

The differences in FedEx and UPS's financial and non-financial performance reflected several underlying factors. UPS relied to a greater degree than FedEx on the ground delivery business, which had a different cost structure than the air-express delivery business (see **Exhibits 9** and **10**). Further, UPS's ground delivery business took advantage of much higher daily package volumes and customer density than FedEx's operations, which meant that UPS drivers would on average pick up and deliver significantly more packages per hour than FedEx drivers could. Finally, some observers believed that UPS's decision to operate their ground and express businesses as one integrated company sharing the same trucks and sorting centers gave it an operating advantage over FedEx, which maintained separate operating units for each of express and ground delivery.[29]

Superior customer service was one of the distinguishing hallmarks of FedEx, and for this reason FedEx was generally seen as competing most effectively at the higher-end, high-service segment of the package-delivery market. FedEx's commitment to high-customer service was reflected in its best-in-industry on-time reliability record, and the flexibility it offered customers in pickup and delivery times. For example, it had even been known to keep trucks idling outside a customer's business to help deliver an unforeseen order on time.

---

26. *"RPS Greets World with New Parent Federal Express,"* Pittsburgh Post-Gazette, January 29, 1998.

27. *"FedEx Hits the Ground Running,"* Modern Materials Handling, July 2001.

28. *"They've Got Mail,"* Fortune, February 7, 2000.

29. *Bear Stearns UPS Equity Research Report,* November 24, 1999.

Finally, there were differences in financial management policies at the two companies. UPS maintained a AAA credit rating, whereas FedEx's rating was BBB.[30] FedEx used operating leases to finance much of its aircraft fleet, whereas UPS financed its fleet with operating cash flow, public debt, or long-term capital leases. **Exhibits 11** and **12** present footnote information on lease obligations for the two companies.

Best-of-Breed Industry Leaders

UPS's management believed that the company's stock price should be valued at a premium to reflect its superior performance over other firms in the industry. It noted that there was support for this approach in the market, where other companies with comparable dominant positions in their industry commanded significant best-of-breed stock price premiums over their competitors. For example, Coca-Cola's price-to-earnings and market-to-book multiples were 39 and 15 respectively, versus 25 and 8 for PepsiCo. Wal-Mart commanded a price-to-earnings multiple of 46 and a market-to-book multiple of 11.6, versus 27 and 6 for Target. **Exhibit 13** presents a comparison of price premiums and financial performance for selected companies considered "best-of-breed" industry leaders.

UPS'S IPO

Industry Trends and Opportunities

UPS management had decided by the late 1990s to focus on three emerging trends that they believed would define the package delivery industry of the future, and which would present the company with opportunities for continued growth. These were the emerging trends of globalization, e-commerce, and supply-chain management.

Globalization   By the late 1990s, international trade represented over one-quarter of total U.S. GDP—up from only 11% in 1970. While UPS had not expanded globally as quickly or forcefully as other companies, by 1998 it was generating over $3 billion in global revenues, with 37,000 non-U.S. UPS employees delivering almost 1 million packages a day to, from and within over 200 countries. John Alden, vice-chairman of UPS, noted: "In the package delivery industry, globalization means that we must knit together worldwide distribution networks that match our customers' geographic operations. If we don't, our competitors will."[31] As a result, one of UPS's major strategic growth initiatives was building capacity in non-U.S. markets—first Europe and more recently Asia and Latin America.[32]

E-Commerce   UPS projected that by 2003 online B2C sales in the United States would surpass the $100 billion spent annually on catalog sales.[33] Already the preferred shipper for online commerce, UPS was moving to strengthen its position in this new market through a number of initiatives. For instance, it was aggressively pursuing partnerships with online retailers and other e-commerce players like e-Bay,

---

30. *On August 31, 1999, the yield for 20-year U.S. Treasury bonds was 6.5%, the yield for AAA-rated debt was 6.9%, and the yield for BBB-rated debt was 8.0%. Source: Standard & Poor's, Inc.*

31. *"What in the World Drives UPS?,"* International Business, *March/April 1998.*

32. *As of October 1999, UPS, unlike FedEx, had not received rights to fly to China.*

33. *Jim Kelly, speech to the Economic Club of Detroit, January 19, 1999.*

and by 1999 UPS functionality was being offered on over 10,000 business web sites.[34] The company was also working on UPS Returns on the Web, a service that, when unveiled, would allow customers to print a return label from their home PC to ease the process of customer returns of online purchases to the retailer of origin.[35]

Supply Chain Management   UPS managers likened the supply-chain of the future to a moving conveyor belt: "a supply chain in constant motion means minimal inventory, lower costs, and faster time-to-market. The inventory, if you could call it that, is always in transit."[36] Increasingly, UPS was forging partnerships with supplier companies, from auto manufacturer suppliers to electronic component producers, which involved UPS handling the continuous flow of shipments to down-market corporate customers. Additionally, through its UPS Logistics Group, UPS began offering suppliers a portfolio of financial services and logistics technology software applications designed to help them better manage their inventory and shipping logistics.

UPS's management anticipated that the company would be able to fund much of these growth opportunities through operating cash flows. The primary benefit from the IPO would, therefore, not be the funds raised from the stock offering; indeed management committed that it would use the IPO proceeds to repurchase its own stock. Instead, the IPO would provide UPS with publicly traded stock—an attractive tax-efficient medium of exchange—to fund any subsequent acquisitions. In explaining the change in strategy, management noted:

> As we enter the twenty-first century, we face a rapidly changing competitive and operating environment. The package-delivery industry is globalizing and consolidating at an unprecedented rate. We face new competitive challenges from postal monopolies, which have considerable resources and infrastructures. We believe that we should have a publicly traded equity security that we could use when appropriate for strategic alliances and acquisitions in order to maintain our pre-eminent position.[37]

Impact on Current Owners and UPS Culture

In 1999, approximately two-thirds of UPS's equity was held by current and retired employees; the remaining third was owned by founding families and foundations. Under the company's Management Incentive Plan, in place since the mid-1940s, 15% of profits were set aside each year for stock awards to supervisors and managers. Employees that received stock awards were encouraged to hold the stock as long as they remained with the company, and most chose to do so. For those employees that wished to sell, typically after retirement, the company would buy back the stock at a price set each quarter by the board of directors. In mid-1999, the price set by the board was $25.50.

UPS's employee ownership had served the company well. It had enabled the company to grow a capital-intensive business without needing to incur the costs of outside financing. Its employees were extremely loyal; many had joined the firm as part-time workers while at college, and then stayed after graduation. It was not uncommon for employees to spend their entire working career at UPS. Virtually all

---

34. Ibid.

35. UPS 2000 Annual Report.

36. Jim Kelly, speech to the Houston Forum, October 6, 1999.

37. UPS Form S-4 Registration Statement, July 21, 1999, p. 63.

of the seven executives that served on the firm's board began their careers "tossing boxes in the warehouse, driving trucks through the streets or handling paperwork in the back office."[38] As a result, experts on corporate culture and resource management observed that the company succeeded by "promoting a 'we all win together, we all fail together' kind of mentality. . . . The common experience of getting packages delivered creates tremendous loyalty among UPS employees. . . . Senior management understands what it means to be a regular person, because they once were that."[39]

To ensure that the IPO preserved the company's culture and control by employees, the offering created two classes of shares. Class A shares, for existing owners, would carry 10 votes each, whereas Class B shares, to be issued to the public, would carry only one vote each. The funds raised in the IPO would then be used to repurchase shares from Class A shareholders, enabling them to divest up to 10% of their holdings. For the following 18 months, Class A shares would gradually become available to be sold in the market, at which point they would become Class B shares. As a result of this arrangement, it was anticipated that after the IPO, current UPS shareowners would own 90% of the firm's equity and control about 99% of the vote. Considerable time at UPS was devoted to educating management owners about the reasons for becoming a public company, the details of the share changes, and company policy on employee share ownership and trading.

Offer Pricing

As the IPO date approached, Morgan Stanley Dean Witter & Co.-UPS deal team considered what price to recommend for the offer. What were UPS's future business and financial prospects, given its positioning in the package delivery industry? Were FedEx multiples reasonable benchmarks for valuing UPS stock? Or, given its consistently strong financial returns, should UPS be benchmarked relative to best-in-breed industry leaders?

QUESTIONS

1. What are the key success factors and risks for UPS given its business strategy?

2. How is UPS performing? What factors are driving this performance? Is the current performance likely to be sustained? Why or why not?

3. How is FedEx performing? How, if at all, do its performance and plans affect your assessment of the sustainability of UPS's current performance?

4. Given your assessment of the company's strategy and the sustainability of its performance, forecast the key factors for UPS's stock value.

5. What is your estimate of UPS's value and its multiples?

6. How do your estimates of UPS's PE and PB multiples compare with those for FedEx? How do they compare with those for the "best of breed" companies' multiples?

---

38. Jerry Knight, "Managers Are No Strangers To the Brown-Collar World," The Washington Post, August 13, 1997.

39. Ibid.

United Parcel Service's IPO

EXHIBIT 1

Size of U.S. Overnight, Deferred, and Ground Markets, 1990–1999

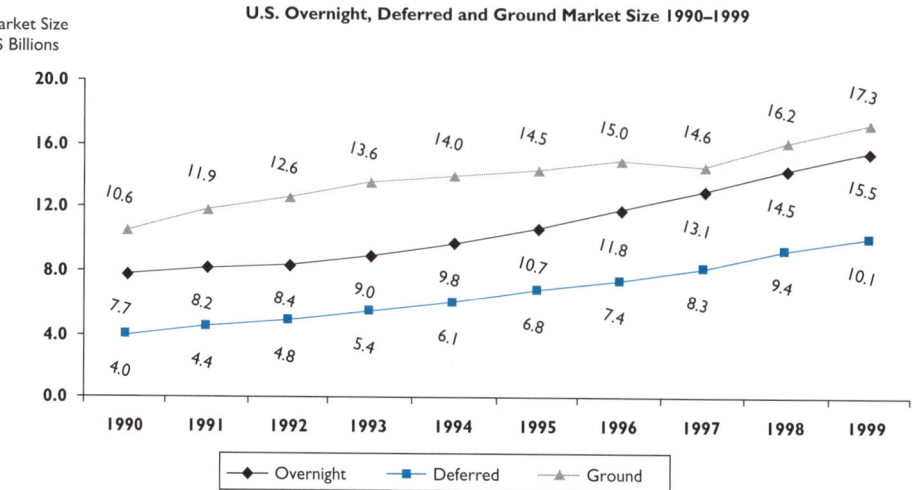

Source: SJ Consulting Group.

EXHIBIT 2

Package Volume in U.S. Overnight, Deferred, and Ground Markets, 1990–1999

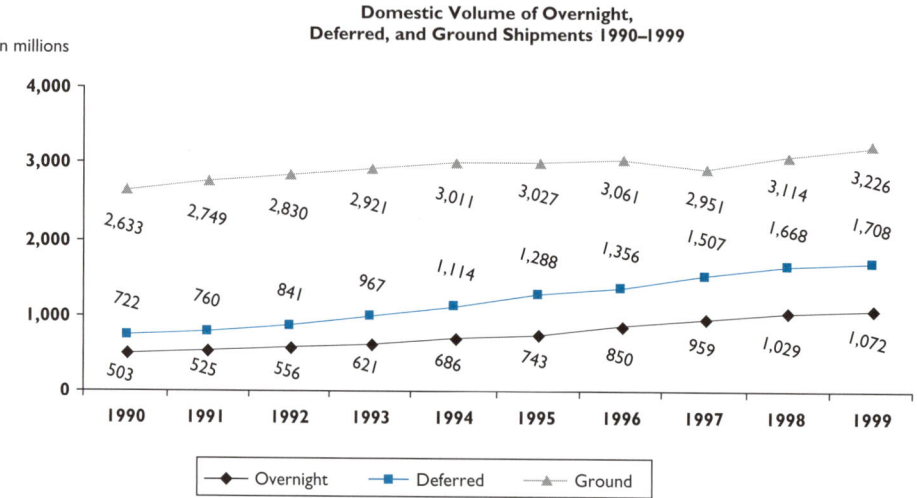

Source: SJ Consulting Group.

EXHIBIT 3

Air Express and Ground Market Growth Rates, 1990–2005E

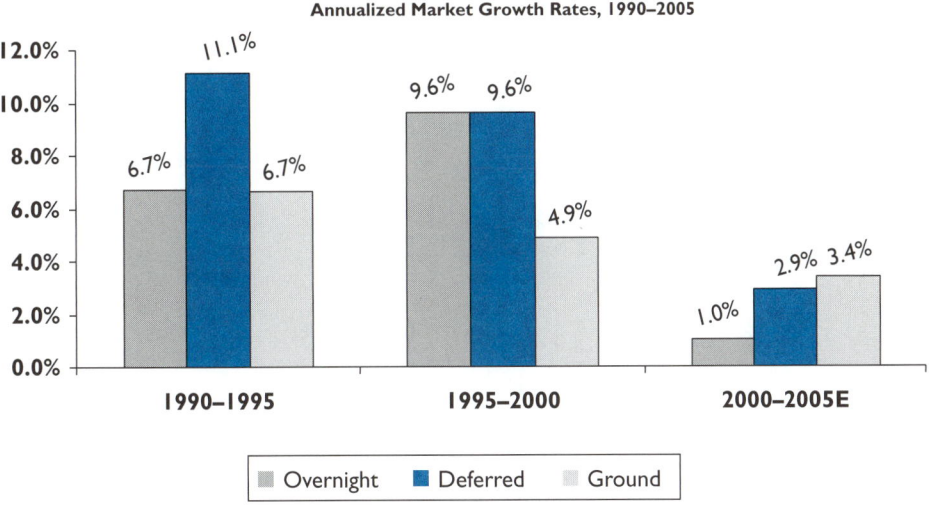

Source: SJ Consulting Group.

United Parcel Service's IPO

United Parcel Service's IPO

EXHIBIT 4

Overnight, Deferred, and Ground Market Shares, 1990–1999

Overnight					By Revenue						By Volume
	1990	1991	1992	1993	1994	1995	1996	1997	1998	1999	1999
UPS Next Day Air	31%	30%	30%	30%	30%	30%	32%	31%	32%	34%	25%
FDX Overnight	51%	51%	50%	50%	50%	49%	49%	48%	47%	46%	46%
ABF Next Day	10%	11%	12%	13%	13%	14%	13%	15%	15%	14%	23%
USPS Express Mail	8%	8%	8%	7%	7%	7%	6%	6%	6%	6%	6%
Deferred	1990	1991	1992	1993	1994	1995	1996	1997	1998	1999	1999
UPS Deferred	40%	38%	35%	34%	32%	30%	30%	28%	26%	27%	13%
FDX Deferred (E2, ES)	16%	17%	16%	18%	18%	19%	18%	20%	23%	22%	13%
ABF Second Day	5%	5%	6%	6%	6%	6%	7%	6%	6%	6%	4%
USPS Priority Mail	39%	40%	43%	42%	44%	45%	45%	46%	45%	45%	70%
Ground	1990	1991	1992	1993	1994	1995	1996	1997	1998	1999	1999
UPS Ground	87%	87%	85%	85%	83%	82%	82%	81%	80%	80%	79%
FedEx Ground without RPS	0%	0%	0%	0%	0%	0%	0%	0%	0%	0%	0%
with RPS*	5%	5%	6%	7%	8%	8%	8%	9%	10%	10%	11%
USPS Parcel Post	8%	8%	9%	8%	9%	10%	10%	10%	10%	10%	10%

* RPS acquired by FedEx in 10/97.

Note: Ground market shares are based on the revenues and volume of the largest providers in the industry. They do not include data for private delivery fleets of individual companies, courier services, regional delivery services, LTL trucking firms, and third-party logistics companies.

Source: SJ Consulting Group.

EXHIBIT 5

UPS vs. FedEx Process Flow Diagrams

With UPS . . .

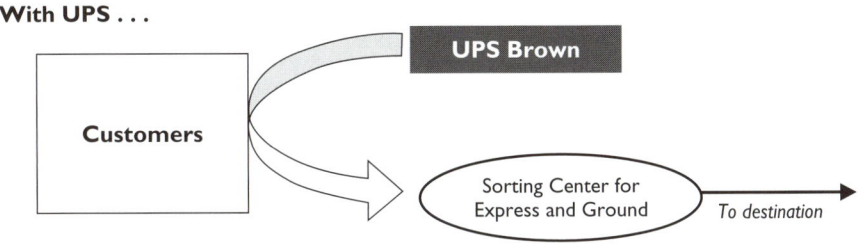

With FedEx . . .

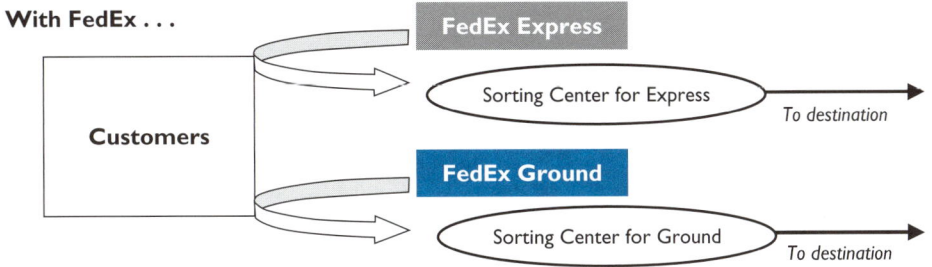

Source: Derived by casewriters.

EXHIBIT 6

FedEx Stock Price Performance and Valuation Multiples

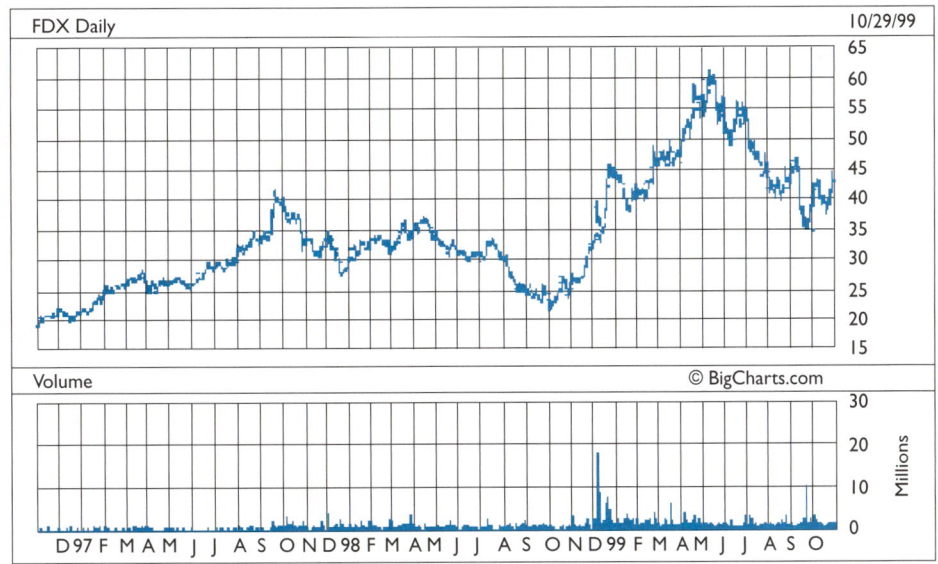

Source: BigCharts.com.

Market Data and Multiples—(November 1, 1999)

Shares outstanding (weighted average, diluted)	300.6 million
Share price	$41.50
Price/Earnings[a]	19.8
Price/Total revenue[b]	0.74
Market/Book value[c]	2.68
Equity Beta[d]	1.16

a. Total market capitalization/Net income.

b. Total market capitalization/Total revenue.

c. Total market capitalization/Shareholders' equity.

d. Salomon Smith Barney Equity Research report on FedEx, June 22, 1999.

Source: FedEx company filings.

EXHIBIT 7

UPS Financial Statements, 1994–1999

STATEMENT OF INCOME (year ended December 31)

(Financial data in millions, except per share amounts)	1994	1995	1996	1997	1998	Nine Months Ended September 30, 1998	Nine Months Ended September 30, 1999
REVENUE							
U.S. domestic package	16,943	17,773	18,881	18,868	20,650	15,129	16,239
International package	2,346	2,886	2,989	2,934	3,237	2,342	2,562
Non-package	287	386	498	656	901	653	805
TOTAL REVENUES	19,576	21,045	22,368	22,458	24,788	18,124	19,606
Operating expenses:							
Compensation and benefits	11,727	12,401	13,326	13,289	14,346	10,587	11,226
Other	6,293	6,478	7,013	7,461	7,352	5,315	5,522
Restructuring charge	—	372	—	—	—	—	—
TOTAL OPERATING EXPENSES	18,020	19,251	20,339	20,760	21,698	15,902	16,748
OPERATING PROFIT (LOSS)							
U.S. domestic package	1,821	1,937	2,181	1,654	2,899	2,098	2,522
International package	(390)	(250)	(281)	(67)	56	19	147
Non-package	125	107	129	111	135	105	85
Corporate	—	—	—	—	—	—	104
TOTAL OPERATING PROFIT	1,556	1,794	2,029	1,698	3,090	2,222	2,858
Other income (expense):							
Investment income	13	26	39	70	84	56	115
Interest expense	(29)	(77)	(95)	(187)	(227)	(169)	(170)
Tax assessment	—	—	—	—	—	—	(1,786)
Miscellaneous, net	35	(35)	(63)	(28)	(45)	(3)	(30)
INCOME BEFORE INCOME TAXES	1,575	1,708	1,910	1,553	2,902	2,106	987
Income taxes	632	665	764	644	1,161	847	765
NET INCOME	943	1,043	1,146	909	1,741	1,259	222
Per share amounts:							
Basic earnings per share	0.84	0.93	1.03	0.82	1.59	1.16	0.20
Diluted earnings per share	0.82	0.92	1.01	0.81	1.57	1.14	0.20
Dividends declared per share	0.28	0.32	0.34	0.35	0.43	0.20	0.28
Net income before impact of tax assessment	943	1,043	1,146	909	1,741	1,259	1,664
As a percentage of revenue	4.8%	5.0%	5.1%	4.0%	7.0%	7.0%	8.5%

Source: UPS Company Filings.

United Parcel Service's IPO

BALANCE SHEET

United Parcel Service

In millions, except where noted As of December 31,	1997	1998
ASSETS		
CURRENT ASSETS		
Cash and cash equivalents	460	1,240
Marketable securities and short-term investments	—	389
Accounts receivable	2,405	2,713
Prepaid employee benefit costs	669	703
Materials, supplies and other prepaid expenses	417	380
Common stock held for stock plans	526	—
Total Current Assets	4,477	5,425
PROPERTY, PLANT, AND EQUIPMENT		
Vehicles	3,519	3,482
Aircraft (including aircraft under capitalized leases)	6,771	7,739
Land	654	651
Buildings	1,433	1,478
Leasehold improvements	1,734	1,803
Plant equipment	4,063	4,144
Construction-in-progress	328	257
	18,502	19,554
Less accumulated depreciation and amortization	7,495	8,170
Net Property, Plant, and Equipment	11,007	11,384
Other Assets	428	258
TOTAL ASSETS	15,912	17,067
LIABILITIES AND SHAREOWNERS' EQUITY		
CURRENT LIABILITIES		
Accounts payable	1,207	1,322
Accrued wages and withholdings	1,194	1,092
Dividends payable	191	247
Deferred income taxes	140	—
Current maturities of long-term debt	41	410
Other current liabilities	625	646
Total Current Liabilities	3,398	3,717
Long-Term Debt (including capitalized lease obligations)	2,583	2,191
Accumulated Postretirement Benefit Obligation	911	969
Deferred Taxes, Credits and Other Liabilities	2,933	3,017
SHAREOWNERS' EQUITY		
Preferred stock, no par value, authorized 200,000,000 shares, none issued	—	—
Class A common stock, par value $.01 per share, authorized 4,600,000,000 shares, issued 1,101,295,534 and 1,118,000,000 in 1999 and 1998		
Class B common stock, par value $.01 per share, authorized 5,600,000,000 shares, issued 109,400,000 and -0- in 1999 and 1998	56	11
Additional paid-in capital	—	325
Retained earnings	6,112	7,325
Accumulated other comprehensive loss	(81)	(63)
Unrealized loss on marketable securities	—	—
	6,087	7,598
Treasury stock, at cost (-0- and 23,211,904 shares in 1997 and 1998)	—	(425)
	6,087	7,173
TOTAL LIABILITIES AND SHAREOWNERS' EQUITY	15,912	17,067

Source: UPS Company Filings.

Financial Data in Millions		Year Ended December 31				6 Months Ended
Balance Sheet Data (at end of period)	1994	1995	1996	1997	1998	June 30, 1999
Working capital	$ 120	$ 261	$ 1,097	$ 1,079	$ 1,708	$ 434
Long-term debt	$ 1,127	$ 1,729	$ 2,573	$ 2,583	$ 2,191	$ 2,138
Total assets	$11,182	$12,645	$14,954	$15,912	$17,067	$18,302
Shareowner's equity	$ 4,647	$ 5,151	$ 5,901	$ 6,087	$ 7,173	$ 6,122

Source: UPS Company Filings.

Excerpts from Management's Discussion and Analysis of Financial Condition and Results of Operations, June 30, 1999

1999 Compared to 1998

Net income for 1999 decreased by $858 million from 1998, resulting in a decrease in diluted earnings per share from $1.57 in 1998 to $0.77 in 1999. These results reflect the charge we recorded during the second quarter of 1999, resulting from an unfavorable ruling of the U.S. Tax Court. Excluding the impact of this one-time charge of $1.442 billion, our net income for 1999 would have been $2.325 billion, with an associated diluted earnings per share of $2.04.

On August 9, 1999, the U.S. Tax Court issued an opinion unfavorable to us regarding a Notice of Deficiency asserting that we are liable for additional tax for the 1983 and 1984 tax years. The Court held that we are liable for tax on income of Overseas Partners Ltd., a Bermuda company, which had reinsured excess value package insurance purchased by our customers beginning in 1984.

The Court held that for the 1984 tax year we are liable for taxes of $31 million on income reported by OPL, penalties and penalty interest of $93 million and interest for a total after-tax exposure estimated at approximately $246 million. In February 2000, the Court entered a decision in accord with its opinion.

In addition, during the first quarter of 1999, the IRS issued two Notices of Deficiency asserting that we are liable for additional tax for the 1985 through 1987 tax years, and the 1988 through 1990 tax years. The primary assertions by the IRS relate to the reinsurance of excess value package insurance, the issue raised for the 1984 tax year. The IRS has based its assertions on the same theories included in the 1983–1984 Notice of Deficiency.

We anticipate that the IRS will take similar positions for tax years subsequent to 1990. Based on the Tax Court opinion, we currently estimate that our total after-tax exposure for the tax years 1984 through 1999 could be as high as $2.353 billion. We believe that a number of aspects of the Tax Court decision are incorrect, and we intend to appeal the decision to the U.S. Court of Appeals for the Eleventh Circuit.

In the second quarter 1999 financial statements, we recorded a tax assessment charge of $1.786 billion, which included an amount for related state tax liabilities. The charge included taxes of $915 million and interest of $871 million. This assessment resulted in a tax benefit of $344 million related to the interest component of the assessment. As a result, our net charge to net income for the tax assessment was $1.442 billion, increasing our total after-tax reserve at that time with respect to these matters to $1.672 billion. The tax benefit of deductible interest is included in income taxes; however, since none of the income on which this tax assessment is based is our income, we have not classified the tax charge as income taxes.

We determined the size of our reserve with respect to these matters in accordance with generally accepted accounting principles based on our estimate of our most likely liability. In making this determination, we concluded that it was more likely that we would be required to pay taxes on income reported by OPL and interest, but that it was not probable that we would be required to pay any penalties and penalty interest. If penalties and penalty interest ultimately are determined to be payable, we would have to record an additional charge of up to $681 million.

On August 31, 1999, we deposited $1.349 billion with the IRS related to these matters for the 1984 through 1994 tax years. We included the profit of the excess value package insurance program, using the IRS's methodology for calculating these amounts, for both 1998 and 1999 in filings we made with the IRS in the fourth quarter of 1999. In February 2000, we deposited $339 million with the IRS related to these matters for the 1995 through 1997 tax years.

These deposits and filings were made in order to stop the accrual of interest, where applicable, on that amount of the IRS's claim, without conceding the IRS's position or giving up our right to appeal the Tax Court's decision.

1998 Compared to 1997

Net income increased by $832 million in 1998 over 1997. Approximately $496 million of this improvement was due primarily to higher revenue per piece on U.S. domestic products, improved product mix, improved international operating results and the containment of operating expense growth. The remaining increase of $336 million resulted from the change in net income for August 1998 as compared to August 1997, the period in which the Teamsters strike occurred.

Source: UPS Company Filings.

EXHIBIT 8

FedEx Financial Statements, 1996–1999

CONSOLIDATED STATEMENTS OF INCOME
FDX Corporation

In thousands, except Earnings Per Share	Years ended May 31	1996	1997*	1998	1999
Revenues		$10,273,619	$14,237,892	$15,872,810	$16,773,470
OPERATING EXPENSES:					
Salaries and employee benefits		4,619,990	6,150,247	6,647,140	7,087,728
Purchased transportation		370,650	1,252,901	1,481,590	1,537,785
Rentals and landing fees		959,055	1,138,690	1,304,296	1,396,694
Depreciation and amortization		719,609	928,833	963,732	1,035,118
Maintenance and repairs		617,657	773,765	874,400	958,873
Fuel		578,614	734,722	726,776	604,929
Merger expenses		—	—	88,000	—
Restructuring and impairment charges (credits)		—	225,036	(16,000)	—
Other		1,784,220	2,526,696	2,792,216	2,989,257
		9,649,795	13,730,890	14,862,150	15,610,384
OPERATING INCOME		623,824	507,002	1,010,660	1,163,086
OTHER INCOME (EXPENSE):					
Interest, net		(95,599)	(104,195)	(124,413)	(98,191)
Other, net		11,734	23,058	13,271	(3,831)
		(83,865)	(81,137)	(111,142)	(102,022)
INCOME FROM CONTINUING OPERATIONS BEFORE INCOME TAXES		539,959	425,865	899,518	1,061,064
PROVISION FOR INCOME TAXES		232,182	229,761	401,363	429,731
INCOME FROM CONTINUING OPERATIONS		307,777	196,104	498,155	631,333
INCOME FROM DISCONTINUED OPERATIONS, NET OF INCOME TAXES		—	—	4,875	—
NET INCOME		$307,777	$196,104	$503,030	$631,333
EARNINGS PER COMMON SHARE					
Continuing operations		$2.69	$.67	$1.70	$2.13
Discontinued operations		—	—	.02	—
		$2.69	$.67	$1.72	$2.13
EARNINGS PER COMMON SHARE, ASSUMING DILUTION					
Continuing operations		$2.69	$.67	$1.67	$2.10
Discontinued operations		—	—	.02	—
		$2.69	$.67	$1.69	$2.10

Source: FedEx Company Filings.

Financial results for 1997 and subsequent years are consolidated to include the acquisition of Caliber System Inc.

EXHIBIT 8

FedEx Corporation

CONSOLIDATED BALANCE SHEETS
FDX Corporation

May 31 In millions	1995	1996	1997*	1998	1999
ASSETS					
CURRENT ASSETS					
Cash and cash equivalents	357.6	93.5	160.9	229.6	325.3
Receivables, less allowances	1,130.3	1,271.6	1,878.0	1,943.4	2,153.2
Spare parts, supplies and fuel	193.3	222.1	339.4	364.7	291.9
Deferred income taxes	115.8	92.6	197.0	232.8	290.7
Prepaid expenses and other	72.2	48.5	68.6	109.6	79.9
Total current assets	1,869.1	1,728.3	2,643.7	2,880.1	3,141.0
PROPERTY AND EQUIPMENT, AT COST					
Flight equipment	3,006.7	3,372.6	3,741.4	4,056.5	4,556.7
Package handling and ground support					
equipment and vehicles	1,841.1	2,148.5	3,131.1	3,425.3	3,858.8
Computer and electronic equipment	1,224.0	1,439.9	1,957.9	2,162.6	2,363.6
Other	1,625.9	1,717.5	2,557.6	2,819.4	2,940.7
	7,697.7	8,678.5	11,387.9	12,463.9	13,719.9
Less accumulated depreciation and amortization	3,982.5	4,561.9	5,917.5	6,528.8	7,160.7
Net property and equipment	3,715.2	4,116.6	5,470.4	5,935.1	6,559.2
OTHER ASSETS					
Goodwill	397.3	380.7	370.3	356.3	344.0
Equipment deposits and other assets	451.8	473.4	559.8	514.6	604.0
Total other assets	849.0	854.1	930.2	870.9	948.0
	6,433.4	6,699.0	9,044.3	9,686.1	10,648.2
LIABILITIES AND STOCKHOLDERS' INVESTMENT					
CURRENT LIABILITIES					
Current portion of long-term debt	255.4	8.0	356.7	257.5	14.9
Accounts payable	618.6	705.5	999.8	1,145.4	1,134.0
Accrued expenses	904.5	904.9	1,223.0	1,400.9	895.4
Other Liabilities	—	—	—	—	740.5
Total current liabilities	1,778.5	1,618.4	2,579.5	2,803.8	2,784.8
LONG-TERM DEBT, LESS CURRENT PORTION	1,324.7	1,325.3	1,598.0	1,385.2	1,359.7
DEFERRED INCOME TAXES	56.0	64.0	181.8	274.1	293.5
OTHER LIABILITIES	1,028.6	1,115.1	1,183.9	1,261.7	1,546.6
COMMITMENTS AND CONTINGENCIES (NOTES 5, 13 and 14)					
COMMON STOCKHOLDERS' INVESTMENT					
Common Stock, $.10 par value	5.6	5.7	14.8	14.7	29.8
Additional paid-in capital	775.3	815.1	938.0	992.8	1,061.3
Retained earnings	1,466.4	1,766.6	2,621.5	2,999.4	3,615.8
Accumulated other comprehensive income	0.0	0.0	0.0	(27.3)	(24.7)
	2,247.3	2,587.4	3,574.3	3,979.6	4,682.2
Less treasury stock, at cost, and deferred compensation	1.7	11.3	73.1	18.4	18.5
Total common stockholders' investment	2,245.6	2,576.1	3,501.2	3,961.2	4,663.7
	6,433.4	6,699.0	9,044.3	9,686.1	10,648.2

Source: FedEx Company Filings.

*Note: Financial results for 1997 and subsequent years are consolidated to include the acquisition of Caliber System Inc.

The accompanying Notes to Consolidated Financial Statements are an integral part of these balance sheets.

EXHIBIT 9

Selected UPS Operating Statistics (financial data in millions)

	Year Ended December 31,			
	1995	1996	1997	1998
Operating Data:				
Delivery volume (in millions of packages)	3,094	3,153	3,038	3,137
Average daily package volume (in thousands)				
U.S. domestic:				
Next Day Air	668	760	822	938
Deferred	716	763	771	783
Ground	9,949	10,015	9,521	9,645
Total U.S. domestic	11,333	11,538	11,114	11,366
International				
Domestic	722	683	678	730
Export	175	194	217	256
Total International	897	877	895	986
Total average daily package volume	12,230	12,415	12,009	12,352
Average revenue per piece:				
U.S. domestic:				
Next Day Air	$19.34	$19.34	$19.49	$19.69
Deferred	11.27	11.39	11.86	12.39
Ground	4.95	5.09	5.19	5.51
Total U.S. domestic	6.20	6.44	6.71	7.15
International				
Domestic	6.22	6.10	5.36	5.14
Export	37.18	37.32	35.01	33.46
Total International	12.26	13.01	12.55	12.49
Total average revenue per piece	$6.64	$6.91	$7.15	$7.58
Revenue:				
U.S. domestic:				
Next Day Air	$3,269	$3,734	$4,054	$4,690
Deferred	2,041	2,207	2,314	2,464
Ground	12,463	12,940	12,500	13,496
Total U.S. domestic	17,773	18,881	18,868	20,650
International				
Domestic	1,136	1,058	919	953
Export	1,646	1,839	1,922	2,176
Cargo	176	177	226	270
Total International	2,958	3,074	3,067	3,399
Non-package	314	413	523	739
Total revenue	$21,045	$22,368	$22,458	$24,788
Operating weekdays	253	254	253	254
Capital expenditures (in millions)	$2,096	$2,333	$1,984	$1,645

Source: UPS Prospectus Filing, September 1999.

EXHIBIT 10

Summary of FedEx and UPS Operating Statistics

	UPS	FedEx
Calendar 1998 Average Daily Package Volume (thousands of packages)		
• U.S. Express	938	1,957
• U.S. Deferred	783	894
• U.S. Ground	9,645	1,385
• Total U.S.	11,366	4,236
• Total International	986	282
• Total packages	12,352	4,518
Calendar 1998 Average U.S. Revenue per package[a]		
• Express	$19.69	$14.34
• Deferred	$12.39	$9.93
• Ground	$5.51	$5.36
Number of Employees (full-time and contract positions)	340,000	156,386
Total on-balance sheet assets	$23.0 billion	$10.6 billion
Number of jet and small aircraft owned and leased	536	634
Number of vehicles	149,000	46,000

Source: Derived by casewriters using UPS and FedEx Company Filings.

a. Revenues per package (yield) is a function of both average package weight and distance.

EXHIBIT 11

FedEx Note on Leases

The company utilizes certain aircraft, land, facilities and equipment under capital and operating leases that expire at various dates through 2027. In addition, supplemental aircraft are leased under agreements that generally provide for cancellation upon 30 days' notice.

The components of property and equipment recorded under capital leases were as follows:

May 31, 1999 ($ thousands)

Package handling and ground support equipment and vehicles	$245,041
Facilities	134,442
Computer and electronic equipment and other	6,496
	385,979
Less accumulated depreciation	268,696
	$117,283

Rent expense under operating leases for the years ended May 31 was as follows:

($ thousands)

Minimum rentals	$1,246,259
Contingent rentals	59,839
	$1,306,098

Contingent rentals are based on hours flown under supplemental aircraft leases.

A summary of future minimum lease payments under capital leases and non-cancelable operating leases (principally aircraft and facilities) with an initial or remaining term in excess of one year at May 31, 1999 is as follows:

($ thousands)	Capital Leases	Operating Leases
2000	$15,023	$1,011,957
2001	15,023	933,339
2002	15,023	876,055
2003	15,023	809,770
2004	14,894	764,550
Thereafter	302,502	8,717,952
	$377,488	$13,113,623

At May 31, 1999, the present value of future minimum lease payments for capital lease obligations including certain tax exempt bonds was $200,077,000.

FedEx makes payments under certain leveraged operating leases that are sufficient to pay principal and interest on certain pass through certificates. The pass through certificates are not direct obligations of, or guaranteed by, the Company or FedEx.

Source: 1999 FedEx Annual Report, Notes to Consolidated Statements.

EXHIBIT 12

UPS Note on Leases

UPS has capitalized lease obligations for certain aircraft, which are included in Property, Plant, and Equipment at December 31 as follows:

1998 ($ millions)

Aircraft	$614
Accumulated amortization	(38)
	$576

UPS leases certain aircraft, facilities, equipment, and vehicles under operating leases, which expire at various dates through 2034. Total aggregate minimum lease payments under capitalized leases and under operating leases are as follows (in millions):

($ millions)	Capitalized Leases	Operating Leases
1999	$67	$211
2000	67	146
2001	67	115
2002	67	94
2003	67	77
After 2003	526	477
Total minimum lease payments	$861	$1,120
Less inputed interest	(263)	
Present value of minimum capitalized lease payments	598	
Less current portion	(39)	
Long-term capitalized lease obligations	$559	

Source: UPS Prospectus Filing, September 1999, Notes to Financial Statements.

EXHIBIT 13

Selected "Best-of-Breed" Ratios vs. Industrial Comparables

	Stock Price[a]	Market Cap (billions)	Net Income[b] (millions)	ROE	Price to Earnings	Market to Book
Home Depot	$68.50	100.8	1,979	25%	50.9	12.7
Lowes	$49.31	18.9	556	17%	34.1	5.8
Coca-Cola	$49.94	124.7	3,174	40%	39.3	15.6
PepsiCo	$32.19	48.9	1,921	31%	25.5	7.9
Wal-Mart	$50.81	227.4	4,927	25%	46.1	11.6
Target	$64.31	28.4	1,052	22%	27.0	6.0

Source: Derived by case writers using SEC filings and market data from bigcharts.com. accessed on 06/23/02.

a. As of close of trading October 15, 1999.

b. Latest 12 months.

United Parcel Service's IPO

Chapter 6

Prospective Analysis: Forecasting

Most financial statement analysis tasks are undertaken with a forward-looking decision in mind—and much of the time it is useful to summarize the view developed in the analysis with an explicit forecast. Managers need forecasts to formulate business plans and provide performance targets; analysts need forecasts to help communicate their views of the firm's prospects to investors; and bankers and debt market participants need forecasts to assess the likelihood of loan repayment. Moreover, there are a variety of contexts (including but not limited to security analysis) where the forecast is usefully summarized in the form of an estimate of the firm's value. This estimate can be viewed as an attempt to best reflect in a single summary statistic the manager's or analyst's view of the firm's prospects.

Prospective analysis includes two tasks—forecasting and valuation—that together represent approaches to explicitly summarizing the analyst's forward-looking views. In this chapter we focus on forecasting; valuation is the topic of the next two chapters. Forecasting is not so much a separate analysis as it is a way of summarizing what has been learned through business strategy analysis, accounting analysis, and financial analysis. However, there are certain techniques and knowledge that can help a manager or analyst to structure the best possible forecast, conditional on what has been learned in the previous steps. Below we summarize an approach to structuring the forecast, offer information useful in getting started, explore the relationship between the other analytical steps and forecasting, and give detailed steps to forecast earnings, balance sheet data, and cash flows. The key concepts discussed in this chapter are illustrated using a forecast for Wal-Mart, the discount retailer examined in Chapter 5.

THE OVERALL STRUCTURE OF THE FORECAST

The best way to forecast future performance is to do it comprehensively—producing not only an earnings forecast, but also a forecast of cash flows and the balance sheet. A comprehensive approach is useful, even in cases where one might be interested primarily in a single facet of performance, because it guards against unrealistic implicit assumptions. For example, if an analyst forecasts growth in sales and earnings for several years without explicitly considering the required increases in working capital and plant assets and the associated financing, the forecast might possibly imbed unreasonable assumptions about asset turnover, leverage, or equity capital infusions.

A comprehensive approach involves many forecasts, but in most cases they are all linked to the behavior of a few key "drivers." The drivers vary according to the type of business, but for businesses outside the financial services sector, the sales forecast is nearly always one of the key drivers; profit margin is another. When asset turnover is expected to remain stable—often a realistic assumption—working capital accounts and investment in plant should track the growth in sales closely. Most major expenses also track sales, subject to expected shifts in profit margins. By linking forecasts of such amounts to the sales forecast, one can avoid internal inconsistencies and unrealistic implicit assumptions.

In some contexts the manager or analyst is interested ultimately in a forecast of cash flows, not earnings per se. Nevertheless, in practice even forecasts of cash flows tend to be grounded on forecasts of accounting numbers, including sales, earnings, assets, and liabilities. Of course it would be possible in principle to move directly to forecasts of cash flows—inflows from customers, outflows to suppliers and laborers, and so forth—and in some businesses this is a convenient way to proceed. In most cases, however, the growth prospects, profitability, and investment and financing needs of the firm are more readily framed in terms of accrual-based sales, operating earnings, assets, and liabilities. These amounts can then be converted to cash flow measures by adjusting for the effects of non-cash expenses and expenditures for working capital and plant, property, and equipment.

A Practical Framework for Forecasting

The most practical approach to forecasting a company's financial statements is to focus on projecting "condensed" financial statements, as used in the ratio analysis in Chapter 5, rather than attempting to project detailed financial statements at the level that the company reports. There are several reasons for this recommendation. Forecasting condensed financial statements involves a relatively small set of assumptions about the future of the firm, so the analyst will have more ability to think about each of the assumptions carefully. A detailed line-item forecast is likely to be very tedious, and an analyst may not have a good basis to make all the assumptions necessary for such forecasts. Further, for most purposes, condensed financial statements are all that are needed for analysis and decision making. We therefore approach the task of financial forecasting with this framework.

Recall that the condensed income statement that we used in Chapter 5 consists of the following elements: sales, net operating profits after tax (NOPAT), net interest expense after tax, taxes, and net income. The condensed balance sheet consists of net operating working capital, net long-term assets, net debt, and equity. Also recall that we start with a balance sheet at the beginning of the forecasting period. Assumptions about how we use the beginning balance sheet and run the firm's operations will lead to the income statement for the forecasting period; assumptions about investment in working capital and long-term assets, and how we finance these assets, results in a balance sheet at the end of the forecasting period.

To forecast the condensed income statement, one needs to begin with an assumption about next period's sales. Beyond that, assumptions about NOPAT margin, interest rate on beginning debt, and tax rate are all that are needed to prepare the condensed income statement for the period.

To forecast the condensed balance sheet for the end of the period (or the equivalent, the beginning of the next period), we need to make the following additional assumptions: (1) the ratio of net operating working capital to sales, to estimate the level of working capital needed to support those sales; (2) the ratio of net operating long-term assets to the following year's sales, to calculate the expected level of net operating long-term assets; and (3) the ratio of net debt to capital to estimate the levels of debt and equity needed to finance the estimated amount of assets on the balance sheet.

Once we have the condensed income statement and balance sheet, it is relatively straightforward to compute the condensed cash flow statement, including cash flow from operations before working capital investments, cash flow from operations after working capital investments, free cash flow available to debt and equity, and free cash flow available to equity.

We discuss how best to make the necessary assumptions to forecast the condensed income statement, balance sheet, and cash flow statements below.

PERFORMANCE BEHAVIOR: A STARTING POINT

Every forecast has, at least implicitly, an initial benchmark—some notion of how a particular amount, such as sales or earnings, would be expected to behave in the absence of detailed information. For example, in beginning to contemplate fiscal 2006 profitability for Wal-Mart, 2005 performance might be a starting point. Another potential starting point might be 2005 performance adjusted for recent trends. A third possibility that might seem reasonable—but one that generally turns out not to be very useful—is the average performance over several prior years.

By the time one has completed a business strategy analysis, an accounting analysis, and a detailed financial analysis, the resulting forecast might differ significantly from the original point of departure. Nevertheless, for purposes of having a starting point that can help anchor the detailed analysis, it is also useful to know how certain financial statistics behave "on average" for all firms.

In the case of some key statistics, such as earnings, a point of departure based only on prior behavior of the number is more powerful than one might expect. Research demonstrates that some such benchmarks for earnings are almost as accurate as the forecasts of professional security analysts, who have access to a rich information set (we return to this point in more detail below). Thus, the benchmark is often not only a good starting point but also close to the amount forecast after detailed analysis. Large departures from the benchmark could be justified only in cases where the firm's situation is demonstrably unusual.

Reasonable points of departure for forecasts of key accounting numbers can be based on the evidence summarized below. Such evidence may also be useful for checking the reasonableness of a completed forecast.

Sales Growth Behavior

Sales growth rates tend to be "mean-reverting": firms with above-average or below-average rates of sales growth tend to revert over time to a "normal" level (historically in the range of 7 to 9 percent for U.S. firms) within three to ten years. Figure 6-1 documents this effect for 1988 through 2005 for all the publicly traded, nonfinancial services U.S. firms covered by the Compustat database. All firms are ranked in terms of their sales growth in 1988 (year 1) and formed into five portfolios based on the relative ranking of their sales growth in that year. Firms in portfolio 1 are in the top 20 percent of rankings in terms of their sales growth in 1988, those in portfolio 2 fall into the next 20 percent, while those in portfolio 5 are in the bottom 20 percent when ranked by sales growth. The sales growth rates of firms in each of these five portfolios are traced from 1988 through the subsequent nine years (years 2 to 10). The same experiment is repeated with 1992 and then 1996 as the base year (year 1). The results are averaged over the three experiments and the resulting sales growth rates of each of the five portfolios for years 1 through 10 are plotted in Figure 6-1.

| FIGURE 6-1 | Behavior of Sales Growth for U.S. Firms over Time, 1988–2005 |

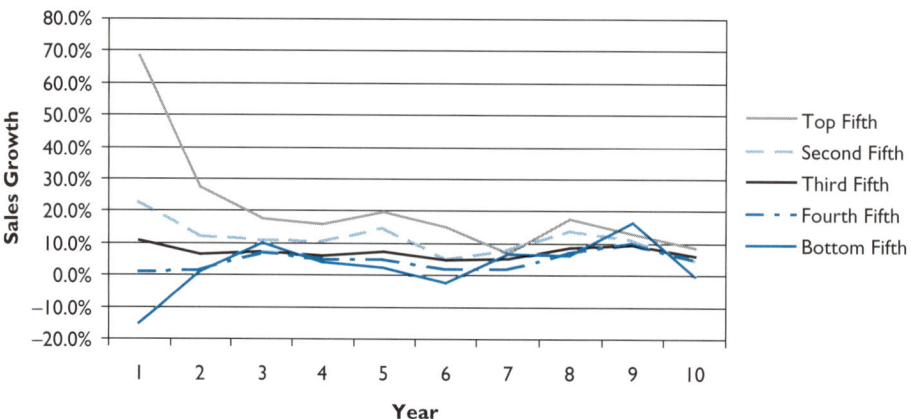

The figure shows that the group of firms with the highest growth initially—sales growth rates of close to 70 percent—experience a decline to about an 18 percent growth rate within two years and are never above 20 percent in the next seven years. Those with the lowest initial sales growth rates, negative 15 percent, improve immediately to a marginally positive sales growth in year 2. Over years 6 to 10 these firms average 7.5 percent growth annually. One explanation for the pattern of sales growth seen in Figure 6-1 is that as industries and companies mature, their growth rate slows down due to demand saturation and intra-industry competition. Therefore, even when a firm is growing rapidly at present, it is generally unrealistic to assume that the current high growth will persist indefinitely. Of course, how quickly a firm's growth rate reverts to the average depends on the characteristics of its industry and its own competitive position within an industry.

Earnings Behavior

Earnings have been shown on average to follow a process that can be approximated by a "random walk" or "random walk with drift." This implies that the prior year's earnings is a good starting point in considering future earnings potential. Even a simple random walk forecast—one that predicts next year's earnings will be equal to last year's earnings—is surprisingly useful. One study documents that professional analysts' year-ahead forecasts are only 22 percent more accurate, on average, than a simple random walk forecast.[1] Thus a final earnings forecast will usually not differ dramatically from a random walk benchmark. In addition, it is reasonable to adjust this simple benchmark for the earnings changes of the most recent quarter, i.e., changes relative to the comparable quarter of the prior year after controlling for the long-run trend in the series.

Although the average level of earnings over several prior years is not useful, long-term trends in earnings tend to be sustained on average, and so they are also worthy of consideration. If quarterly data are also included, then some consideration should usually be given to any departures from the long-run trend that occurred in the most recent quarter. For most firms, these most recent changes tend to be partially repeated in subsequent quarters.[2]

Return on Equity Behavior

Given that prior earnings serve as a useful benchmark for future earnings, one might expect the same to be true of measures of return on investment such as ROE. That, however, is not the case for two reasons. First, even though the average firm tends to sustain the current earnings level, this is not true of firms with unusual levels of ROE. Firms with abnormally high (low) ROE tend to experience earnings declines (increases).[3]

Second, firms with higher ROEs tend to expand their investment bases more quickly than others, which causes the denominator of the ROE to increase. Of course, if firms could earn returns on the new investments that match the returns on the old ones, then the level of ROE would be maintained. However, firms have difficulty continuing to generate those impressive ROEs. Firms with higher ROEs tend to find that, as time goes by, their earnings growth does not keep pace with growth in their investment base, and ROE ultimately falls.

The resulting behavior of ROE and other measures of return on investment is characterized as mean-reverting, a pattern similar to that observed for sales growth rates earlier. Firms with above-average or below-average rates of return tend to revert over time to a "normal" level (historically in the range of 10 to 15 percent for U.S. firms) within no more than ten years.[4] Figure 6-2 documents this effect for U.S. firms from 1988 through 2005. All firms are ranked in terms of their ROE in 1988 (year 1) and formed into five portfolios in a similar fashion to the sales growth analysis above. Firms in portfolio 1 have the top 20 percent ROE rankings in 1988, those in portfolio 2 fall into the next 20 percent, and those in portfolio 5 have the bottom 20 percent. The average ROE of firms in each of these five portfolios is then traced through nine subsequent years (years 2 to 10). The same experiment is repeated with 1992 and 1996 as the base year (year 1). Figure 6-2 plots the average ROE of each of the five portfolios in years 1 to 10 averaged across these three experiments.

Though the five portfolios start out in year 1 with a wide range of ROEs (−65 percent to +32 percent), by year 10 the pattern of mean-reversion is clear. The most profitable group of firms initially—with average ROEs of 32 percent—experience a decline to 23 percent within three years. By year 10 this group of firms has an ROE of 15 percent. Those with the lowest initial ROEs (−65 percent) experience a

| FIGURE 6-2 | Behavior of ROE for U.S. Firms over Time, 1988–2005 |

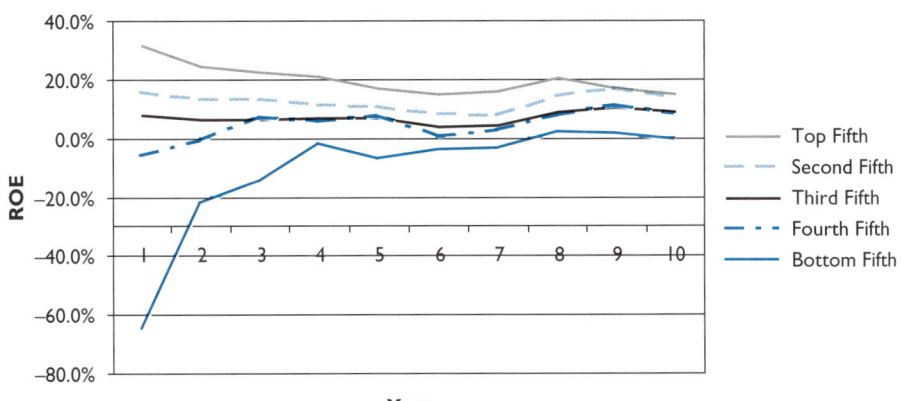

dramatic increase in ROE in the first four years and are marginally profitable or breakeven by the final three years.

The pattern in Figure 6-2 is not a coincidence—it is exactly what the economics of competition would predict. The tendency of high ROEs to fall is a reflection of high profitability attracting competition; the tendency of low ROEs to rise reflects the mobility of capital away from unproductive ventures toward more profitable ones.

Despite the general tendencies documented in Figure 6-2, there are some firms whose ROEs may remain above or below normal levels for long periods of time. In some cases the phenomenon reflects the strength of a sustainable competitive advantage (e.g., Wal-Mart), but in other cases it is purely an artifact of conservative accounting methods. A good example of the latter phenomenon in the U.S. is pharmaceutical firms, whose major economic asset, the intangible value of research and development, is not recorded on the balance sheet and is therefore excluded from the denominator of ROE. For these firms, one could reasonably expect high ROEs—in excess of 20 percent—over the long run, even in the face of strong competitive forces.

The Behavior of Components of ROE

The behavior of rates of return on equity can be analyzed further by looking at the behavior of its key components. Recall from Chapter 5 that ROEs and profit margins are linked as follows:

$$\begin{aligned}
\text{ROE} &= \text{Operating ROA} + (\text{Operating ROA} - \text{Net interest rate after tax}) \\
&\quad \times \text{Net financial leverage} \\
&= \text{NOPAT margin} \times \text{Operating asset turnover} + \text{Spread} \\
&\quad \times \text{Net financial leverage}
\end{aligned}$$

The time-series behavior of the primary components of ROE for U.S. companies for 1988 through 2005 are shown in a series of figures in the appendix to this chapter. Some major conclusions can be drawn from these figures:

(1) Operating asset turnover tends to be rather stable, in part because it is largely a function of the technology of the industry. The only exception to this is the set of firms with very high asset turnover, which tends to decline somewhat over time before stabilizing;

(2) Net financial leverage also tends to be stable, simply because management policies on capital structure aren't often changed; and

(3) NOPAT margin stands out as the most variable component of ROE. If the forces of competition drive abnormal ROEs toward more normal levels, the change is most likely to arrive in the form of changes in profit margins. The change in NOPAT margin will drive changes in the spread, since the cost of borrowing is likely to remain stable because leverage tends to be stable.

To summarize, profit margins and ROEs tend to be driven by competition to normal levels over time. What constitutes normal varies widely according to the technology employed within an industry and the corporate strategy pursued by the firm, both of which influence turnover and leverage.[5] In a fully competitive equilibrium, profit margins should remain high for firms that must operate with a low turnover, and vice versa.

The above discussion of rates of return and margins implies that a reasonable starting point for forecasting such statistics should consider more than just the most recent observation. One should also consider whether that rate or margin is above or below a normal level. If so, then absent detailed information to the contrary, one would expect some movement over time toward that norm. Of course this central tendency might be overcome in some cases—for example, where the firm has erected barriers to competition that can protect margins, even for extended periods. The lesson from the evidence, however, is that such cases are unusual.

In contrast to rates of return and margins, it is reasonable to assume that asset turnover, financial leverage, and net interest rate remain relatively constant over time. Unless there is an explicit change in technology or financial policy being contemplated for future periods, a reasonable starting point for assumptions for these variables is the current period level. The only exceptions to this appear to be firms with either very high asset turns that experience some decline in this ratio before stabilizing, or those firms with very low (usually negative) net debt to capital that appear to increase leverage before stabilizing. In addition, firms with very high levels of leverage tend to survive at a lower rate than more conservatively financed firms, driving down averages over time.

As we proceed with the steps involved in producing a detailed forecast, the reader will note that we draw on knowledge of the behavior of accounting numbers to some extent. However, it is important to keep in mind that a knowledge of average behavior will not fit all firms well. The art of financial statements analysis requires not only knowing what the "normal" patterns are but also having expertise in identifying those firms that will not follow the norm.

RELATIONSHIP OF FORECASTING TO THE OTHER ANALYSES

In general, the mean-reverting behavior of sales growth and return on equity that is demonstrated by the broader market should hold true. The starting point for any forecast should therefore be the time-series behavior of the various measures of firm performance, as discussed. However, the three levels of analysis that precede prospective analysis—strategy, accounting, and financial performance—can also lead to informed decisions by an analyst about expected performance, especially in the short and medium term.

We use the example of Wal-Mart, the discount retailer discussed in Chapter 5, to illustrate the strategic analysis that informs the forecast as well as the mechanics of forecasting. A projection of the future performance of Wal-Mart for year 2006[6] must be grounded in an understanding of questions such as these:

- From business strategy analysis: Has Wal-Mart been able to create a retailing infrastructure that will allow it to continue to dominate the U.S. market? Will Wal-Mart be able to replicate this market dominance internationally? At what rate will the company be able to grow its sales, both in the short term and the long term, without sacrificing its margins? Will competitors such as Target be able to replicate Wal-Mart's efficiency while competing with a differentiated product offering?
- From accounting analysis: Are there any aspects of Wal-Mart's accounting that suggest past earnings and assets are misstated, or expenses or liabilities are misstated? If so, what are the implications for future accounting statements?
- From financial analysis: What are the sources of Wal-Mart's superior performance? Is this performance sustainable? Is there any discernible pattern in Wal-Mart's past performance? If so, are there any reasons why this trend is likely to continue or to change?

The key challenge in building a forecast, therefore, is to predict whether Wal-Mart will be able to maintain its competitive advantage and current performance levels or whether competition will force Wal-Mart to follow the general mean-reverting trends discussed above.

Macroeconomic Factors

In the first half of 2006, the U.S. economy was in a period of relative stability. The economy had recovered from the low points in 2001 and 2002, and consumer spending had shown modest growth. Wal-Mart's proposition of a wide variety of dependable products at low prices continued to appeal to the millions of low-income shoppers that patronized the store.

However, several factors are worrying from the perspective of Wal-Mart's growth prospects and could lead to short-term profit concerns. High gas prices tend to temper consumer enthusiasm for driving to suburban stores in search of discounts, which could lead to a drop in Wal-Mart's sales outside of its limited urban presence. The spectacular increase in real estate values over the past decade, which fueled increases in consumer spending, was viewed by many market experts as susceptible to a market correction. Falling real estate prices, rising interest rates, and increased bank foreclosures could put pressure on discretionary spending, leading to a potential drop in Wal-Mart's sales. However, a loss in sales from traditional Wal-Mart shoppers could be counterbalanced by a widening of Wal-Mart's customer base, as higher income consumers turn to Wal-Mart stores in an effort to save money. Finally, Wal-Mart's business model, which is based on domestic sales of internationally sourced products, is susceptible to changes in the relative value of the U.S. dollar. If the dollar weakens relative to the Chinese yuan, for instance, the cost of Wal-Mart's imports from China could rise sharply, negatively impacting margins.

The impact of changing macro-economic conditions on Wal-Mart's performance in the short, medium, and long term cannot be forecast with a high degree of certainty. Consequently, it is advisable to focus on the firm's particular strategy and competitive position and assume that the impact of changes in the business cycle will even out in the long run.

Sales Growth

Despite the intense competition in retailing, the seasoned executive team at Wal-Mart has built an impressive track record of meeting and exceeding investor expectations, and it is reasonable to expect that they will continue to deliver the same strong growth that they have in the past. Wal-Mart has essentially two growth drivers—domestic sales in the U.S., which show signs of stagnating as a result of the intensity of competition and market saturation; and international sales, where the growth opportunities, especially in large emerging markets such as China, India, and Brazil seem extremely attractive.

Wal-Mart currently operates over 3,200 stores in the U.S. among its various Wal-Mart store formats. Sales for Wal-Mart Stores grew 9.4 percent in the year ending January 2006, compared to 10.1 and 10.9 percent in each of the previous two years. Comparable store sales grew by only 3 percent, a relatively low level that is likely to persist as Wal-Mart continues its new store expansion program. Given that Wal-Mart has a fairly comprehensive retail network, new store openings tend to cannibalize sales from existing stores in the same area, reducing growth in comparable store sales. New store openings are also likely to slow as unique attractive locations become increasingly scarce. At the same time, Wal-Mart is actively courting more affluent customers and working to make its product offerings more stylish and appealing. However, it is unclear whether this initiative will be successful in offsetting the slowdown in same store sales. Wal-Mart also faces a discount retail paradigm-shifting threat from Target that could erode its market leadership. Thus, it is reasonable to expect that Wal-Mart Stores' overall sales growth will trend downward, though probably at a slower pace than would be implied by the mean-reverting tendency of sales growth for the overall market.

SAM'S CLUB sales grew 7.2 percent during the year ended January 2006, and it has exhibited a slowing trend in sales growth over the last three years similar to that of Wal-Mart Stores. In fiscal year 2005, comparable club sales grew 5.0 percent and square footage grew 3.8 percent. SAM'S CLUB faces formidable competition from other wholesale club operators, primarily Costco and BJ's Wholesale Club. Though it is reasonable to expect that sales growth at SAM'S CLUB will slow, the slowdown is likely to be more gradual than at Wal-Mart Stores as its current comparable store sales growth remains robust and it has a smaller base of stores (fewer than 600 stores), giving it more expansion opportunities.

Wal-Mart's International operations present an interesting forecasting challenge. The subtleties of local tastes and bureaucratic complexities in local real estate markets have made it extremely challenging for nondomestic retailing companies to establish market leadership outside their home markets. Although Wal-Mart has achieved dominant positions in the Canadian and Mexican markets through a mixture of acquisitions and joint ventures, its ability to replicate this success in what are widely acknowledged to be the major growth markets—the emerging consumer economies in China, India, Brazil, and Russia—remains to be seen. Wal-Mart's value-oriented philosophy, which was extremely successful in the underserved and fragmented markets of suburban and rural America, may well be replicable in many of the key developing economies with similar market characteristics, implying that international sales are likely to outpace U.S. sales over the forecast horizon. Thus, the projections suggest that in ten years nearly 30 percent of Wal-Mart's sales will be generated by its overseas operations, compared to the current 20 percent. A key question is whether this growth will add value for Wal-Mart if the international expansion comes from acquisitions, which for many companies are zero net present value undertakings.

Overall, the projections in Table 6-1 show a gradual improvement in sales growth over the next couple of years, followed by a slow decline in growth. While this pattern is based on a mixture of business intelligence and a knowledge of long-term trends in the market, it is important to note that an analyst could capture much of the dynamics of the projections merely by assuming that Wal-Mart will not be immune to the long-run forces of competition and mean reversion.

TABLE 6-1	Forecasted Sales Growth for Wal-Mart									
Forecast year	**2006**	**2007**	**2008**	**2009**	**2010**	**2011**	**2012**	**2013**	**2014**	**2015**
Wal-Mart Stores	9.0%	9.0%	8.8%	8.5%	8.3%	8.0%	7.8%	7.5%	7.3%	7.0%
SAM'S CLUB	7.0%	7.0%	6.9%	6.8%	6.7%	6.5%	6.3%	6.1%	6.0%	6.0%
International	12.0%	13.0%	14.0%	14.0%	14.0%	13.0%	12.0%	11.0%	10.0%	10.0%
Overall Sales Growth	**9.3%**	**9.6%**	**9.6%**	**9.5%**	**9.4%**	**9.0%**	**8.6%**	**8.2%**	**7.8%**	**7.7%**

NOPAT Margins

In the highly competitive U.S. market, Wal-Mart Stores is likely to have to resort to deeper discounting to offset the threat of competition from other discount retailers such as Target. At the same time, Wal-Mart is trying to beat Target at its own game by increasing the design component of its product offerings and appealing to more affluent discount shopping consumers. This improved merchandising could lead to a narrowing of the margin gap seen in the comparison of Wal-Mart and Target in Chapter 5, at least on selective merchandise. However, Wal-Mart's shift in strategy away from its now synonymous "every day low prices" strategy could also lead to some short-term execution missteps, such as overstocked inventory and mispricing. Thus, there could be unexpected short-term disruptions to Wal-Mart's margin growth as a result of its strategy of pursuing higher-income consumers. Overall, it is likely that the competitive pressures will have a greater impact than the modifications to product strategy and sourcing that Wal-Mart expects to implement, leading to a gradual but steady decline in NOPAT margins.

International operations of Wal-Mart are expected to show higher growth but have relatively low margins, which will have an impact on overall margins for the firm. Several offsetting forces are likely to affect International margins in the medium-term. As transportation and general infrastructure improves in many of Wal-Mart's developing economy markets, and as Wal-Mart is able to impose its efficiency in supply chain management on its international operations, it is possible that International margins will show some improvement in the medium term. More direct sourcing and improved in-country distribution will also help improve margins. At the same time, as large economies such as China develop, competition is likely to heat up, leading to margin declines that mimic mean-reverting trends seen in the U.S. We predict that international margins are likely to improve in the medium term due to improvements in developing country infrastructure, but in the longer term there is likely to be mean reversion. As shown in Table 6-2, Wal-Mart's average NOPAT margins are expected to decline due to the increased importance of the faster growing, but lower margin, International business.

TABLE 6-2	Forecasted NOPAT Margins for Wal-Mart									
Forecast year	2006	2007	2008	2009	2010	2011	2012	2013	2014	2015
Wal-Mart Stores	4.4%	4.3%	4.2%	4.1%	4.0%	3.9%	3.8%	3.6%	3.4%	3.2%
SAM'S CLUB	2.1%	2.1%	2.1%	2.0%	2.0%	1.9%	1.9%	1.8%	1.8%	1.8%
International	3.2%	3.2%	3.3%	3.4%	3.4%	3.4%	3.4%	3.3%	3.3%	3.2%
Overall Margins	**3.9%**	**3.8%**	**3.8%**	**3.7%**	**3.7%**	**3.6%**	**3.5%**	**3.4%**	**3.2%**	**3.1%**

Working Capital to Sales

Wal-Mart's working capital management has consistently beaten that of its peers, and this dominance is likely to continue. Wal-Mart currently has a negative net operating working capital to sales ratio. This implies that Wal-Mart is able to fund its working capital needs—primarily for accounts receivable and inventory—through trade and other short-term creditors and accruals.

Wal-Mart continues to invest heavily in its logistics and distribution network, keeping inventory levels at a minimum. As the firm increases its reliance on direct sourcing, its working capital advantage is likely to increase further. Working capital needs are also likely to decline as it improves operations in its International business and takes advantage of its growing international presence to negotiate more favorable terms with its suppliers. Therefore, it is reasonable to expect that its net operating working capital to sales ratio will remain at or near zero as the firm's market power grows and it continues to invest in its supply chain.

Long-Term Assets to Sales

As the pace of Wal-Mart's new store openings in the U.S. slows, comparable store sales growth should improve as fewer new stores will open up near existing stores, reducing the risk of customer cannibalization. This should have a beneficial impact on the firm's long-term asset use in both Wal-Mart and SAM'S CLUB divisions. Counteracting this improvement is the fact that new store openings are likely to be more capital intensive than in the past for two reasons. First, real estate prices in the U.S. have risen sharply over the past decade. Additionally, Wal-Mart is moving away from its rural base into regions where average real estate prices are higher. This change in the cost structure of Wal-Mart's domestic long-term asset base could lead to a reduction in asset turns.

The International business is currently extremely asset intensive when compared to the firm's U.S. businesses. However, as Wal-Mart gains traction in many of its developing markets, same store sales growth is likely to improve. Additionally, as the firm's market power grows, its relationships with host countries could strengthen, giving it access to cheaper real estate and better locations. A combination of these factors should enhance asset utilization in International operations, though it will still trail the performance of U.S. stores.

Overall, as International sales growth outpaces that of the U.S. businesses, Wal-Mart's ratio of long-term assets to sales is likely to gradually deteriorate over the forecast horizon.

Capital Structure

Wal-Mart's Board of Directors authorized a $10.0 billion share repurchase program in September 2004. At the end of January 2006, approximately $6.1 billion of shares had yet to be purchased under this buyback authorization. There is no time limit within which the program needs to be completed, and decisions are made in light of the firm's overall leverage, among other factors. Thus, it is unlikely that the share repurchase will lead to any fundamental, long-term change in Wal-Mart's capital structure, and leverage should remain relatively stable. Given the financial strength of the firm, any short-term fluctuations in leverage should not have any impact on the cost of debt.

MAKING FORECASTS

The analysis of Wal-Mart's performance in Chapter 5, and the preceding discussions about general market behavior and Wal-Mart's strategic positioning, leads to the conclusion that while Wal-Mart consistently generated above-market returns for its shareholders, in the long run it is likely that a portion of the firm's abnormal profits will be competed away. The performance of the firm will revert towards the mean, as has been the general trend that we have seen earlier in the chapter.

Table 6-3 shows the forecasting assumptions for years 2006 to 2015. Table 6-4 shows the forecasted income statements for these same fiscal years, and beginning of the year balance sheets for years 2007 to 2016. Recall that the balance sheet at the beginning of fiscal 2006 is the same as the balance sheet reported by the company for the year ending January 31, 2006. We have chosen a ten-year forecasting period because we believe that the firm should reach a relatively steady state of performance by then (discussed in further detail in Chapter 8). We discuss below the forecasting assumptions, which are based on the foregoing discussion of the various elements that comprise the forecast.

The Overall One Year Ahead Forecast

As mentioned above, we have the actual balance sheet for the beginning of 2006, so there is no need to forecast this. Making a short-term income statement forecast, such as a one year ahead forecast, is usually a straightforward extrapolation of recent performance. This is a particularly valid approach for an established company such as Wal-Mart for several reasons. First, the company is unlikely to effect major changes to its operating and financing policies in the short term unless it is in the middle of a restructuring program. Second, the beginning of the year balance sheet for any given year will put constraints on operating activities during that fiscal year. For example, inventories at the beginning of the year will determine to some extent the sales activities during the year; stores in operation at the beginning of the year also determine to some extent the level of sales achievable during the year. To put it another way, since our discussion above shows that asset turns for a company do not usually change significantly in a short time, sales in any period are to some extent constrained by the beginning of the period assets in place in the company's balance sheet. Of course Wal-Mart is likely to achieve some flexibility in this regard as it has explicit plans to expand assets during the year through new store openings. Changes in the asset utilization could also be driven by increases in same store sales and changes to its product mix.

As shown below in Table 6-3, we assume that sales will grow at 9.3 percent. This is marginally lower than the 9.5 percent sales growth that the company achieved in

TABLE 6-3	Forecasting Assumptions for Wal-Mart									
Forecast year	2006	2007	2008	2009	2010	2011	2012	2013	2014	2015
Sales growth rate	9.3%	9.6%	9.6%	9.5%	9.4%	9.0%	8.6%	8.2%	7.8%	7.7%
NOPAT margin	3.9%	3.8%	3.8%	3.7%	3.7%	3.6%	3.5%	3.4%	3.2%	3.1%
Beginning net operating working capital/sales	−0.8%	0.0%	0.0%	0.0%	0.0%	0.0%	0.0%	0.0%	0.0%	0.0%
Beginning net operating long-term assets/sales	25.8%	25.2%	25.4%	25.6%	25.9%	26.0%	26.0%	26.3%	26.5%	26.8%
Beginning net debt to capital ratio	37.9%	37.9%	37.9%	37.9%	37.9%	37.9%	37.9%	37.9%	37.9%	37.9%
After tax cost of debt	3.3%	3.3%	3.3%	3.3%	3.3%	3.3%	3.3%	3.3%	3.3%	3.3%

2005. While the consensus among analysts that follow the stock is for higher growth, our strategic analysis led to an expectation of slowing growth in the U.S. market that offsets possible increases in international sales, leading to an overall slowdown. This growth rate leads to an expected sales level in 2006 of $342.6 billion, up from $313.3 billion in 2005 as Table 6-4 shows.

The next key assumption to be made about Wal-Mart's performance in 2006 is its NOPAT margin. We expect Wal-Mart to be able to maintain its margin of 3.9 percent from the previous year. Wal-Mart's market leadership in the U.S. should allow the firm to protect its margins in the domestic business. Furthermore, improvements in the International business should maintain Wal-Mart's overall margins in the short-term.

The next two forecast items—net operating working capital to sales and net operating long-term assets to sales—have already been determined by the balance sheet position at January 31, 2006. Therefore, we are starting with a given level of assets to work with. So we can either make an assumption about sales growth rate and check the implied ratio of beginning net assets to sales for reasonableness, or make an assumption of the beginning net assets to sales ratio for the year and check for the reasonableness of the implied sales growth rate. In other words, we are free to make only one of the two assumptions—either sales growth or net asset turns. In subsequent years in the forecast horizon, we relax this constraint because we can build up both a desired beginning balance sheet and income statement for the following years.

The third assumption we make to forecast Wal-Mart's income statement for 2006 relates to the after-tax cost of debt. The company's beginning level of debt and its beginning debt to capital ratio for 2006 are determined by its actual balance sheet at the start of the fiscal year. Although the firm is in the middle of completing a share repurchase program, the effect on leverage is not likely to affect its cost of debt (adjusting for any changes in overall market interest rates). As a result, it is reasonable to assume that the firm's relative cost of debt will be similar to its cost of borrowing in prior years as reflected in the yield on its intermediate term bonds. Given stable interest rates, the cost of borrowing is expected to remain stable at 5.15 percent, or 3.35 percent on an after-tax basis.

These assumptions together lead to a projected $12.2 billion net income in fiscal year compared with a reported net income of $11.2 billion in 2005.

Overall Forecasts for Years Two to Ten

In making longer-term forecasts, in this instance for years two to ten, we have relied on our analysis of the firm and its prospects as well as the time-series behavior of various performance ratios discussed earlier. Given our assumptions of increased growth in international markets, we assume that Wal-Mart will be able to increase its sales growth rate to 9.6 percent in years two and three. Thereafter, sales growth will gradually decline as the firm finds fewer locations in the U.S. in which to profitably expand, and comparable store domestic sales growth flatten out. While the International business is expected to maintain its high growth rate over the medium term, the relatively smaller scale of those operations leads to a gradual overall decline in sales growth.

The pattern of margins in Wal-Mart's domestic and foreign businesses is likely to diverge, as International operations initially show improvements in margins. For the firm overall, we assume a pattern of steady and then declining NOPAT margins over time. These assumptions are again consistent with the time-series trend we documented earlier in the chapter for firms with initially high NOPAT and with our

TABLE 6-4   Forecasted Financial Statements for Wal-Mart

Forecast year	2006	2007	2008	2009	2010	2011	2012	2013	2014	2015
Beginning Balance Sheet										
Beg. Net Working Capital	−2,768	0	0	0	0	0	0	0	0	0
+ Beg. Net Long-Term Assets	88,344	94,546	104,527	115,477	127,486	139,917	151,937	166,343	181,019	196,873
= **Net Operating Assets**	**85,576**	**94,546**	**104,527**	**115,477**	**127,486**	**139,917**	**151,937**	**166,343**	**181,019**	**196,873**
Net Debt	32,405	35,802	39,581	43,728	48,275	52,982	57,534	62,989	68,546	74,550
+ Preferred Stock	0	0	0	0	0	0	0	0	0	0
+ Shareholders' Equity	53,171	58,744	64,946	71,749	79,211	86,935	94,403	103,354	112,473	122,323
= **Net Capital**	**85,576**	**94,546**	**104,527**	**115,477**	**127,486**	**139,917**	**151,937**	**166,343**	**181,019**	**196,873**
Income Statement										
Sales	342,629	375,435	411,628	450,786	493,126	537,648	584,130	632,291	681,861	734,359
Net operating profits after tax	13,284	14,360	15,531	16,755	18,034	19,288	20,483	21,264	21,958	22,644
− Net interest expense after tax	1,085	1,198	1,325	1,464	1,616	1,774	1,926	2,109	2,295	2,496
= Net income	12,199	13,162	14,206	15,291	16,418	17,515	18,557	19,155	19,664	20,149
− Preferred dividends	0	0	0	0	0	0	0	0	0	0
= **Net income to common**	**12,199**	**13,162**	**14,206**	**15,291**	**16,418**	**17,515**	**18,557**	**19,155**	**19,664**	**20,149**
Operating Return on Assets	15.5%	15.2%	14.9%	14.5%	14.1%	13.8%	13.5%	12.8%	12.1%	11.5%
Return on Common Equity	22.9%	22.4%	21.9%	21.3%	20.7%	20.1%	19.7%	18.5%	17.5%	16.5%
Book Value of Assets Growth Rate	13.6%	10.5%	10.6%	10.5%	10.4%	9.8%	8.6%	9.5%	8.8%	8.8%
Book Value of Common Equity Growth Rate	7.6%	10.5%	10.6%	10.5%	10.4%	9.8%	8.6%	9.5%	8.8%	8.8%
Net Operating Asset Turnover	4.0	4.0	3.9	3.9	3.9	3.8	3.8	3.8	3.8	3.7
Net income	12,199	13,162	14,206	15,291	16,418	17,515	18,557	19,155	19,664	20,149
− Change in net working capital	(2,768)	-	-	-	-	-	-	-	-	-
− Change in net long-term assets	(6,202)	(9,981)	(10,950)	(12,009)	(12,431)	(12,020)	(14,406)	(14,676)	(15,854)	(15,089)
+ Change in net debt	3,397	3,779	4,147	4,547	4,707	4,552	5,455	5,557	6,004	4,349
= Free cash flow to equity	6,626	6,960	7,403	7,829	8,694	10,047	9,606	10,036	9,814	9,409
Net operating profit after tax	13,284	14,360	15,531	16,755	18,034	19,288	20,483	21,264	21,958	22,644
− Change in net working capital	(2,768)	-	-	-	-	-	-	-	-	-
− Change in net long-term assets	(6,202)	(9,981)	(10,950)	(12,009)	(12,431)	(12,020)	(14,406)	(14,676)	(15,854)	(15,089)
= Free cash flow to capital	4,314	4,379	4,581	4,746	5,603	7,268	6,077	6,588	6,104	5,359

assessment of the competitive response of the other players in Wal-Mart's industry. While Wal-Mart clearly has a significant competitive advantage over its rivals, it is prudent to assume, given the history of U.S. firms, that this advantage will decline over time. Wal-Mart Stores faces the greatest competitive threats, so we assume that its NOPAT margins decline steadily at the rate of 0.1 percent per year. SAM'S CLUB stores are assumed to maintain their margins for a period of three years, after which they decline gradually from 2.1 percent in year three to 1.8 percent by year 10. Wal-Mart International is able to increase its margins from years two through four and then hold them steady for a further period of three years. Eventually, even margins in the International business decline as competition heats up. Overall, we assume that the company's NOPAT margin is steady to declining and by year 10, Wal-Mart's NOPAT margins are expected to have dropped to 3.1 percent compared to the current margin of 3.9 percent.

Wal-Mart currently has a negative net working capital to sales ratio of -0.7 percent. Based on the sales growth assumption for year one, this is projected to be -0.8 percent at the beginning of year two. The forecast assumes that the situation deteriorates marginally until net working capital is zero at the beginning of year three, and this is maintained throughout the forecast horizon.

As discussed, Wal-Mart's International business is highly asset intensive when compared to domestic operations. As International sales growth outpaces domestic growth, asset turns firm-wide should deteriorate. Consequently, the ratio of net long-term assets to sales is expected to increase from 25.2 percent in year two to 26.8 by year 10.

The company's capital structure should remain relatively unchanged. Although the firm is in the midst of executing an authorized share repurchase, we do not expect leverage to be materially different from the past. As a result, the ratio of net debt to book value of net capital of 37.9 percent is maintained for the duration of the forecast horizon. This assumption of a constant capital structure policy is consistent with the general pattern observed in the historical data discussed earlier in the chapter. Consequently, the forecast assumes that Wal-Mart's cost of debt remains at 5.15 percent, or an after-tax cost of 3.35 percent. The cost of debt is expected to be equal to the yield on an intermediate-term bond issued by Wal-Mart.

Having made this set of key assumptions, it is a straightforward task to derive the forecasted income statements and beginning balance sheets for years 2006 through 2015 as shown in Table 6-4. Under these forecasts, Wal-Mart's sales will grow to $734.4 billion, more than double the level in 2005. By 2015, the firm will have a net operating asset base of $196.9 billion and shareholders' equity of $122.3 billion. Consistent with market-wide patterns of mean-reversion in returns, Wal-Mart's return on equity will decline steadily from the 22.7 percent reported in 2005 to 16.5 percent by 2015, and operating return on assets will show a similar pattern.

Cash Flow Forecasts

Once we have forecasted income statements and balance sheets, we can derive cash flows for the years 2006 through 2015. Note that we need to forecast the beginning balance sheet for 2016 to compute the cash flows for 2015. This balance sheet is not shown in Table 6-4. For the purpose of illustration, we assume that all the sales growth and the balance sheet ratios remain the same in 2016 as in 2015. Based on this, we project a beginning balance sheet for 2016 and compute the cash flows for 2015. Cash flow to capital is equal to NOPAT minus increases in net working capital and net long-term assets. Cash flow to equity is cash flow to capital minus net interest after tax plus increase in net debt. These two sets of forecasted cash flows are presented in Table 6-4. As the table shows, the free cash flow to all providers of capital increases from $4.3 billion to a high of $7.3 billion in 2011 before declining to $5.4 billion by 2015. In addition, the firm is expected to increase the free cash flow it generates to its equity holders from $6.6 billion in 2006 to $9.4 billion by 2015.

SENSITIVITY ANALYSIS

The projections discussed thus far represent nothing more than an estimation of a most likely scenario for Wal-Mart. Managers and analysts are typically interested in a broader range of possibilities. For example, an analyst estimating the value of Wal-Mart might consider the sensitivity of projections to the key assumptions about sales growth, profit margins, and asset utilization. What if Wal-Mart is able to retain more of its competitive advantage in the U.S. than assumed in the above forecasts? Alternatively, what if it is unable to improve its levels of asset utilization as assumed or to maintain its high growth rates in the International business division? It is wise to also generate projections based on a variety of assumptions to determine the sensitivity of the forecasts to these assumptions.

There is no limit to the number of possible scenarios that can be considered. One systematic approach to sensitivity analysis is to start with the key assumptions underlying a set of forecasts, and then examine the sensitivity to the assumptions with greatest uncertainty in a given situation. For example, if a company has experienced a variable pattern of gross margins in the past, it is important to make projections using a range of margins. Alternatively, if a company has announced a significant change in its expansion strategy, asset utilization assumptions might be more uncertain. In determining where to invest one's time in performing sensitivity analysis, it is therefore important to consider historical patterns of performance, changes in industry conditions, and changes in a company's competitive strategy.

In the case of Wal-Mart, two likely alternatives to the forecast can be readily envisioned. The forecast presented above expects that Wal-Mart's dominance of the U.S. market gradually wanes, while the International division contributes stellar growth and improvement in performance. An upside case for Wal-Mart would have the firm continuing to dominate the U.S. retail industry and resisting the mean-reverting trends that characterize the market in general, in addition to the increased contribution from international operations. On the downside, the projected boost from the International business could fail to materialize, hastening the decline in Wal-Mart's overall performance towards the market averages.

Seasonality and Interim Forecasts

Thus far, we have concerned ourselves with annual forecasts. However, especially for security analysts in the U.S., forecasting is very much a quarterly exercise. Forecasting quarter-by-quarter raises a new set of questions. How important is seasonality? What is a useful starting point—the most recent quarter's performance? The comparable quarter of the prior year? Some combination of the two? How should quarterly data be used in producing an annual forecast? Does the item-by-item approach to forecasting used for annual data apply equally well to quarterly data?

Full consideration of these questions lies outside the scope of this chapter, but we can begin to answer some of them.

Seasonality is a more important phenomenon in sales and earning behavior than one might guess. It is present for more than just the retail sector firms that benefit from holiday sales. Seasonality also results from weather-related phenomena (e.g., for electric and gas utilities, construction firms, and motorcycle manufacturers), new product introduction patterns (e.g., for the automobile industry), and other factors. Analysis of the time series behavior of earnings for U.S. firms suggests that at least some seasonality is present in nearly every major industry.

The implication for forecasting is that one cannot focus only on performance of the most recent quarter as a starting point. In fact, the evidence suggests that, in forecasting earnings, if one had to choose only one quarter's performance as a basis for forecasting, it would be the comparable quarter of the prior year, not the most recent quarter. Note how this finding is consistent with the reports of analysts or the financial press; when they discuss a quarterly earnings announcement, it is nearly always evaluated relative to the performance of the comparable quarter of the prior year, not the most recent quarter.

Research has produced models that forecast sales, earnings, or EPS based solely on prior quarters' observations. These models are not used by many analysts since they have access to much more information than such simple models contain. However, the models are useful for helping those unfamiliar with the behavior of earnings data to understand how it tends to evolve over time. Such an understanding can provide useful general background, a point of departure in forecasting that can be adjusted to reflect details not revealed in the history of earnings, or a "reasonableness" check on a detailed forecast.

One model of the earnings process that fits well across a variety of industries is the so-called Foster model.[7] Using Q_t to denote earnings (or EPS) for quarter t, and $E(Q_t)$ as its expected value, the Foster model predicts that

$$E(Q_t) = Q_{t-4} + \delta + \phi(Q_{t-1} - Q_{t-5})$$

Foster shows that a model of the same form also works well with quarterly sales data.

The form of the Foster model confirms the importance of seasonality because it shows that the starting point for a forecast for quarter t is the earnings four quarters ago, Q_{t-4}. It states that, when constrained to using only prior earnings data, a reasonable forecast of earnings for quarter t includes the following elements:

- the earnings of the comparable quarter of the prior year (Q_{t-4});
- a long-run trend in year-to-year quarterly earnings increases (δ); and
- a fraction (ϕ) of the year-to-year increase in quarterly earnings experienced most recently ($Q_{t-1} - Q_{t-5}$).

The parameters δ and ϕ can easily be estimated for a given firm with a simple linear regression model available in most spreadsheet software.[8] For most firms the parameter ϕ tends to be in the range of .25 to .50, indicating that 25 to 50 percent of an increase in quarterly earnings tends to persist in the form of another increase in the subsequent quarter. The parameter δ reflects in part the average year-to-year change in quarterly earnings over past years, and it varies considerably from firm to firm.

Research indicates that the Foster model produces one quarter ahead forecasts that vary from actual results by $.30 to $.35 per share, on average. Such a degree of accuracy stacks up surprisingly well with that of security analysts, who obviously have access to much information ignored in the model. As one would expect, most of the evidence supports analysts' being more accurate, but the models are good enough to be a reasonable approximation in most circumstances. While it would certainly be unwise to rely completely on such a mechanistic model, an understanding of the typical earnings behavior reflected by the model is useful.

SUMMARY

Forecasting represents the first step of prospective analysis and serves to summarize the forward-looking view that emanates from business strategy analysis, accounting analysis, and financial analysis. Although not every financial statement analysis is accompanied by such an explicit summarization of a view of the future, forecasting is still a key tool for managers, consultants, security analysts, investment bankers, commercial bankers and other credit analysts, among others.

The best approach to forecasting future performance is to do it comprehensively—producing not only an earnings forecast but also a forecast of cash flows and the balance sheet as well. Such a comprehensive approach provides a guard against internal inconsistencies and unrealistic implicit assumptions. The approach described here involves a condensed, line-by-line analysis, so as to recognize that different items on the income statement and balance sheet are influenced by different drivers. Nevertheless, it remains the case that a few key projections—such as sales growth and profit margin—usually drive most of the projected numbers.

The forecasting process should be embedded in an understanding of how various financial statistics tend to behave on average, and what might cause a firm to deviate from that average. Absent detailed information to the contrary, one would expect sales and earnings numbers to persist at their current levels, adjusted for overall trends of recent years. However, rates of return on investment (ROEs) tend, over several years, to move from abnormal to normal levels—close to the cost of equity capital—as the forces of competition come into play. Profit margins also tend to shift to normal levels, but for this statistic "normal" varies widely across firms and industries, depending on the levels of asset turnover and leverage. Some firms are capable of creating barriers to entry that enable them to fight these tendencies toward normal returns, even for many years, but such firms are the unusual cases.

Forecasting should be preceded by a comprehensive business strategy, accounting, and financial analysis. It is important to understand the dynamics of the industry in which the firm operates and its competitive positioning within that industry. Therefore, while general market trends provide a useful benchmark, it is critical that the analyst incorporate the views developed about the firm's prospects to guide the forecasting process.

For some purposes, including short-term planning and security analysis, forecasts for quarterly periods are desirable. One important feature of quarterly data is seasonality; at least some seasonality exists in the sales and earnings data of nearly every industry. An understanding of a firm's intra-year peaks and valleys is a necessary ingredient of a good forecast of performance on a quarterly basis.

Forecasts provide the input for estimating a firm's value, which can be viewed as the best attempt to reflect in a single summary statistic the manager's or analyst's view of the firm's prospects. The process of converting a forecast into a value estimate is labeled valuation and is discussed next.

DISCUSSION QUESTIONS

1. Merck is one of the largest pharmaceutical firms in the world, and over an extended period of time in the recent past, it consistently earned higher ROEs than the pharmaceutical industry as a whole. As a pharmaceutical analyst, what factors would you consider to be important in making projections of future ROEs for Merck? In particular, what factors would lead you to expect Merck to continue to be a superior performer in its industry, and what factors would lead you to expect Merck's future performance to revert to that of the industry as a whole?

2. John Right, an analyst with Stock Pickers Inc., claims, "It is not worth my time to develop detailed forecasts of sales growth, profit margins, etcetera, to make earnings projections. I can be almost as accurate, at virtually no cost, using the random walk model to forecast earnings." What is the random walk model? Do you agree or disagree with John Right's forecast strategy? Why or why not?

3. Which of the following types of businesses do you expect to show a high degree of seasonality in quarterly earnings? Explain why.
   - a supermarket
   - a pharmaceutical company
   - a software company
   - an auto manufacturer
   - a clothing retailer

4. What factors are likely to drive a firm's outlays for new capital (such as plant, property, and equipment) and for working capital (such as receivables and inventory)? What ratios would you use to help generate forecasts of these outlays?

5. How would the following events (reported this year) affect your forecasts of a firm's future net income?
   - an asset write-down
   - a merger or acquisition
   - the sale of a major division
   - the initiation of dividend payments

6. Consider the following two earnings forecasting models:

$$E(EPS_{t+1}) = EPS_t$$

Model 1:

$$E(EPS_{t+1}) = \frac{1}{5}\sum_{t=1}^{5} EPS_t$$

$E(EPS_{t+1})$ is the expected forecast of earnings per share for year $t + 1$, given information available at t. Model 1 is usually called a random walk model for earnings, whereas Model 2 is called a mean-reverting model. The earnings per share for Wal-Mart Stores for the fiscal years ending January 2001 (FY2000) through January 2005 (FY2004) are as follows:

Fiscal Year	2000	2001	2002	2003	2004
EPS	$1.41	$1.48	$1.80	$2.08	$2.41

a. What would the forecast for earnings per share in FY2005 be for each model?

b. Actual earnings per share for Wal-Mart in FY2005 were $2.68. Given this information, what would be the FY2006 forecast for earnings per share for each model? Why do the two models generate quite different forecasts? Which do you think would better describe earnings per share patterns? Why?

7. Joe Fatcat, an investment banker, states, "It is not worth my while to worry about detailed long-term forecasts. Instead, I use the following approach when forecasting cash flows beyond three years: I assume that sales grow at the rate of inflation, capital expenditures are equal to depreciation, and that net profit margins and working capital to sales ratios stay constant." What pattern of return on equity is implied by these assumptions? Is this reasonable?

NOTES

1. See P. O'Brien, "Analysts' Forecasts as Earnings Expectations," *Journal of Accounting and Economics* (January 1988): 53–83.

2. See G. Foster, "Quarterly Accounting Data: Time Series Properties and Predictive Ability Results," *The Accounting Review* (January 1977): 1–21.

3. See R. Freeman, J. Ohlson, and S. Penman, "Book Rate-of-Return and Prediction of Earnings Changes: An Empirical Investigation," *Journal of Accounting Research* (Autumn 1982): 639–53.

4. See S. Penman, "An Evaluation of Accounting Rate-of-Return," *Journal of Accounting, Auditing, and Finance* (Spring 1991): 233–56; E. Fama and K. French, "Size and Book-to-Market Factors in Earnings and Returns," *Journal of Finance* (March 1995): 131–56; and V. Bernard, "Accounting-Based Valuation Methods: Evidence on the Market-to-Book Anomaly and Implications for Financial Statements Analysis," (working paper, University of Michigan, 1994). Ignoring the effects of accounting artifacts, ROEs should be driven in a competitive equilibrium to a level approximating the cost of equity capital.

5. A "normal" profit margin is that which, when multiplied by the turnover achievable within an industry and with a viable corporate strategy, yields a return on investment that just covers the cost of capital. However, as mentioned above, accounting artifacts can cause returns on investment to deviate from the cost of capital for long periods, even in a competitive equilibrium.

6. Wal-Mart's fiscal year ends on January 31. Throughout the chapter we refer to the forecast for the year ended January 31, 2007 as the 2006 year, since eleven of the twelve months of operations occur in 2006.

7. See Foster, op. cit. A somewhat more accurate model is furnished by Brown and Rozeff, but it requires interactive statistical techniques for estimation. See L. Brown and M. Rozeff, "Univariate Time Series Models of Quarterly Accounting Earnings per Share," *Journal of Accounting Research* (Spring 1979): 179–89.

8. To estimate the model, we write in terms of realized earnings (as opposed to expected earnings) and move Q_{t-4} to the left-hand side:

$$Q_t - Q_{t-4} = \delta + \phi(Q_{t-1} - Q_{t-5}) + e_t$$

We now have a regression where $(Q_t - Q_{t-4})$ is the dependent variable, and its lagged value—$(Q_{t-1} - Q_{t-5})$—is the independent variable. Thus, to estimate the equation, prior earnings data must first be expressed in terms of year-to-year changes; the change for one quarter is then regressed against the change for the most recent quarter. The intercept provides an estimate of δ, and the slope is an estimate of ϕ. The equation is typically estimated using 24 to 40 quarters of prior earnings data.

9. See O'Brien, op. cit.

APPENDIX: THE BEHAVIOR OF COMPONENTS OF ROE

In Figure 6-2 we show that ROEs tend to be mean-reverting. In this appendix we show the behavior of the key components of ROE—operating ROA, operating margin, operating asset turnover, and net financial leverage. These ratios are computed using the same portfolio approach described in the chapter, based on the data for all publicly listed U.S. firms for the time period 1988 through 2005.

FIGURE A-1   Behavior of Operating ROA for U.S. Firms, 1988–2005

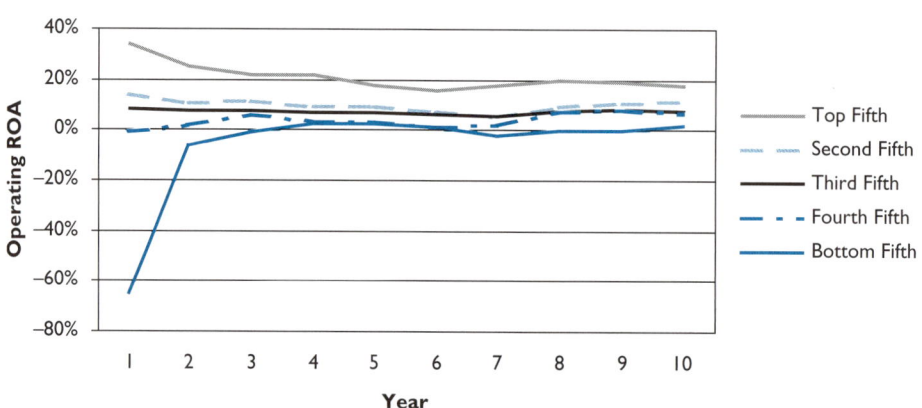

FIGURE A-2   Behavior of NOPAT Margin for U.S. Firms, 1988–2005

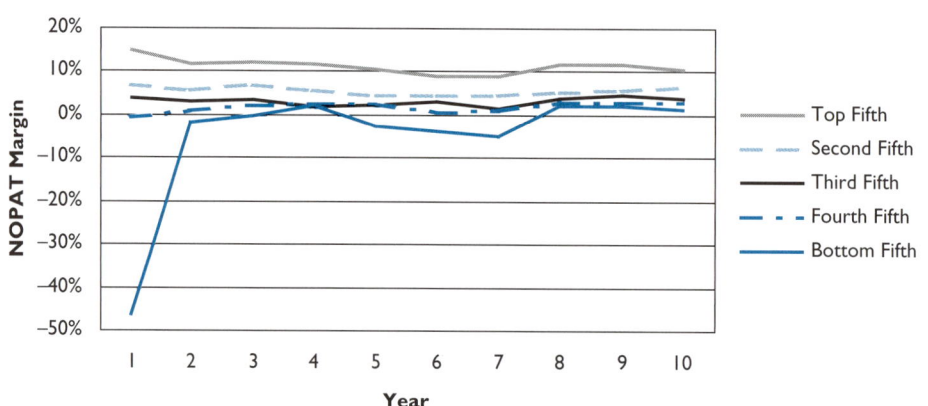

FIGURE A-3   Behavior of Operating Asset Turnover for U.S. Firms, 1988–2005

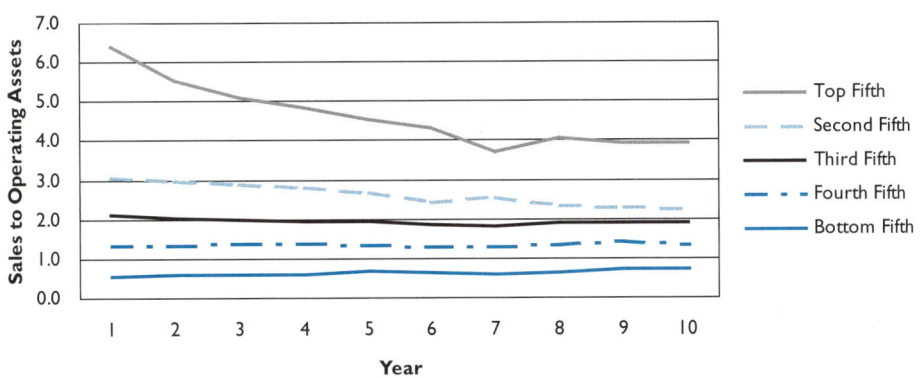

FIGURE A-4   Behavior of Net Financial Leverage for U.S. Firms, 1988–2005

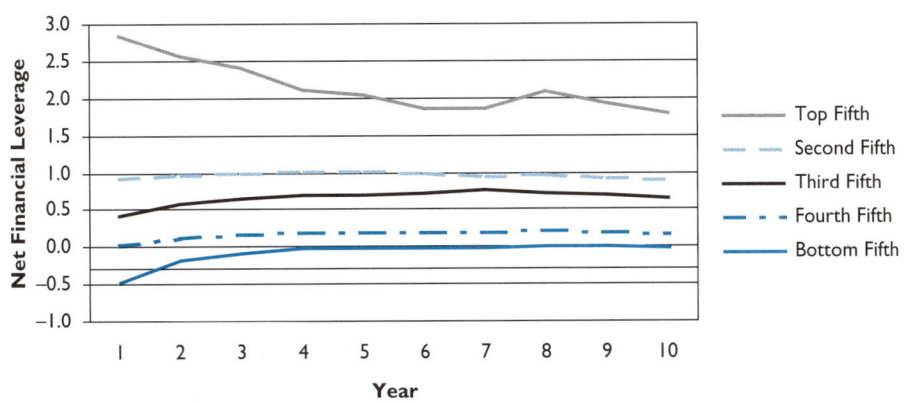

Krispy Kreme Doughnuts

Krispy Kreme is one of a kind phenomena, in our view, boasting a combination of a powerful consumer brand, a multi-channel distribution channel and a business model that produces best-in-class financial returns. . . . Krispy Kreme is still an attractive growth story, in our view, and represents a well-established brand still early in its growth trajectory.

—CIBC World Markets analysts John Glass and Jeffrey Farmer, June 3, 2002

Krispy Kreme Doughnuts completed its initial public offering on April 5, 2000. By the end of the first day of trading, its stock had soared 76% from the $5.50 offering price to $9.25 (adjusted for two 2-for-1 stock splits). In the following two years, Krispy Kreme's stock price reached a high of $45.66 (in late December 2001) and was trading at around $37 in late May 2002. (**Exhibit 1** shows Krispy Kreme's stock performance relative to the S&P 500 from the IPO date to May 30, 2002.)

During the two years following the IPO, Krispy Kreme reported strong growth and financial performance. For example, for the year ended February 3, 2002, revenue growth was 31%, earnings growth was 80%, and the company's return on beginning equity was 21%. (Financial statements for Krispy Kreme for the year ended February 3, 2002 and the first quarter of 2003 are shown in **Exhibit 2**.)

A key challenge for CIBC World Markets' John Glass and Jeffrey Farmer was to forecast the company's financial performance for the next few years. Would Krispy Kreme be able to sustain its recent revenue and earnings growth? What working capital and other resources would the company require? How would it finance its growth? To answer these questions, Glass and Farmer would have to understand Krispy Kreme's growth strategy, the basis for its recent financial performance, and the nature of competition in the doughnut industry.

KRISPY KREME'S BUSINESS[1]

In 1937 Vernon Rudolph purchased a secret recipe for yeast-raised doughnuts from a French chef from New Orleans, rented a building in Winston-Salem, North Carolina, and began selling Krispy Kreme doughnuts to local grocery stores. Within a year, he had knocked a hole in the wall of his production facility and begun selling "hot original glazed" doughnuts to customers directly.

The company's reputation for making tasty, high-quality doughnuts grew steadily throughout the southeastern United States in the 1960s and 1970s. New stores were added either as company-owned outlets or as franchise operations (known as franchise associates). In the mid-1990s the company's management decided to pursue a strategy of geographic expansion using a new area developer franchise model. Under this model, a developer for a metropolitan region was granted a license to develop a specified number of new Krispy Kreme stores. New area developer stores soon appeared in Washington and Baltimore. In 1996, the first New York City store was opened; in 1999, stores were opened in California; and in 2001, the first international store was added, in Toronto, Canada. In the years ended January 2001 and January 2002, area developer store openings accounted for 72% and 83% of systemwide store growth, respectively.

By April 2002, the Krispy Kreme network comprised 222 factory stores in 34 states and produced 5 million doughnuts a day, or 2 billion doughnuts a year. Systemwide sales were $621.7 million in the year ended February 3, 2002, and $183.1 million for the first quarter of 2002 (a 30.4% increase over the first quarter for the prior year). Comparable store sales grew by 11.7% in the year ended February 3, 2002, and 10.5% in the first quarter of 2002.

Krispy Kreme generated revenues from three sources. First, it owned and operated doughnut stores. Second, it received royalties from franchise associates and area developers. Finally, it received revenues from the sale of doughnut mixes and doughnut-making equipment to franchise associates and area developers.

In April 2002, 75 of the Krispy Kreme network stores were company owned, an increase of 12 over the prior year. These stores baked and sold doughnuts and complementary products on-site. They also sold to grocery stores and supermarkets under either the Krispy Kreme brand or under the retailer's label.

Franchise associates owned and operated 53 of the 222 network stores in April 2002. Associate agreements with Krispy Kreme were typically for 15 years and required franchise owners to pay royalties of 3% for on-premises sales and 1% for all other sales (excluding private-label sales). Associates were not required to contribute to company advertising. Krispy Kreme anticipated that it would not add any further stores under this model, preferring instead to use the new area developer model.

Area developers had opened 94 stores by April 2002. Under the terms of the area developer agreements, Krispy Kreme received a one-time franchise fee between $20,000 and $40,000 for each new store opening, a 4.5% royalty fee on all sales, and a 1% contribution toward company advertising. These agreements had a 15-year term and could be renewed at Krispy Kreme's discretion. Krispy Kreme typically did not provide financing to area developers.

Finally, Krispy Kreme received revenues from the sale of proprietary doughnut mixes and doughnut-making equipment, both produced in Winston-Salem, to

---

1. *Information on Krispy Kreme's history, operations, and financing strategy are from the company's 10-K statement for the fiscal year ended February 3, 2002.*

franchise associates and area developers. The revenues generated from these sales were attributed to Krispy Kreme Manufacturing and Distribution (KKM&D). (**Exhibit 3** shows the breakdown of revenues and operating expenses for KKM&D as well as for the company store and franchise business segments.)

COMPETITORS

The doughnut industry was highly fragmented. The second-largest retailer after Krispy Kreme, Dunkin Donuts, was owned by the British food and spirits conglomerate Allied Domecq. Dunkin Donuts operated 4,736 franchise stores in 43 states and 20 countries and sold 4.4 million doughnuts a day, or 1.6 billion doughnuts per year.[2] Other competitors were regional operators. Winchell's was located primarily on the West Coast and operated 200 stores;[3] Donut Connection had 140 stores in 13 states, primarily in the mid-Atlantic region;[4] and Honeydew Donuts operated 100 stores in New England.[5] Finally, there were hundreds of regional bakeries that sold doughnuts through supermarkets, convenience stores, restaurants, and retail stores.

GROWTH PLANS[6]

Krispy Kreme expected to open 62 new stores in 2003, mostly franchise stores. Area developers were contractually obligated to open 200 stores in the period 2003 to 2006. In addition to domestic growth, the company indicated that it was exploring long-term opportunities for growth in Japan, South Korea, Australia, Spain, and the United Kingdom.

On average, the development of a new store required an initial investment of $800,000 for a building of around 4,600 square feet, plus $625,000 for equipment, furniture, and fixtures. In February 2002, company-owned stores generated average weekly sales per store of $72,000 versus $53,000 for franchise stores. This difference reflected significantly lower sales for older associate stores. Area developer franchise stores showed similar sales patterns to those of company-owned stores. (Average weekly sales per store for company-owned and franchise stores in the period 1998 to 2002 are shown in **Exhibit 4**.)

In addition to growth through opening new stores, Krispy Kreme planned to increase the sale of complementary products through existing stores. In February 2001, it acquired Digital Java, a small Chicago-based coffee company, to enable the addition of enhanced espresso and coffee offerings at Krispy Kreme stores.

In fall 2000 Krispy Kreme announced the development of a smaller hot doughnut machine that produced the same quality doughnuts as existing larger machines. The

---

2. See Allied Domecq financial report for 2002.

3. See Winchell's Web site.

4. See Donut Connection's Web site.

5. See Honeydew Donuts Web site.

6. Information on Krispy Kreme's growth plans is from the company's 10-K statement for the fiscal year ended February 3, 2002.

new machine was being tested in three doughnut and coffee shops in 2002 and was to be added to 10 to 12 more stores in 2003. If successful, the smaller machine would enable Krispy Kreme to begin offering hot doughnuts in small coffee shops and malls, allowing it to expand into smaller markets and into dense urban areas that were more costly to reach under the larger factory store model.

The growth in franchise operations required Krispy Kreme to invest heavily in plants, property, and equipment. For example, in the year ended February 2002 the company spent $37 million to construct and equip new company-owned factory stores, to remodel older company stores, to acquire and upgrade equipment-manufacturing facilities, to install coffee-roasting operations in stores, and to construct doughnut and coffee shops. The company's management anticipated that to achieve its planned growth it would have to continue to invest aggressively in both long-term assets and working capital.

Krispy Kreme had historically used a combination of debt and equity to finance its growth. In 2002, it raised funds through a $17.2 million stock offering (for 10.4 million shares), increased its revolving credit facility from $28 million to $40 million, and agreed to a $35 million bank loan to fund the construction of a new mix and distribution facility.[7] Krispy Kreme's management anticipated that, as of February 2002, the company's capital needs for the next 24 months could be covered by "the proceeds from the initial public offering completed in April 2000 and our follow-on public offering completed in early February 2001, cash flow generated from operations and our borrowing capacity under lines of credit. . . . If additional capital is needed, we may raise such capital through public or private equity or debt financing."

ANALYST FORECASTS

An important function performed by the analysts who followed Krispy Kreme was to forecast the company's financial performance for the coming two years. As shown in **Exhibit 5**, which contains excerpts from their June 2, 2002 report on Krispy Kreme, Glass and Farmer approached this task by first forecasting system-wide revenues (for company-owned stores and stores owned by franchise associates and area developers). These forecasts reflected the company's plans for new store growth and growth in sales from existing stores given the company's business model and competitive pressures. From these forecasts, Glass and Farmer were able to forecast Krispy Kreme's revenues and margins for its three core businesses (store sales, franchise operations, and sales of mix and equipment). Based on this analysis, they predicted that Krispy Kreme would report earnings per share of $0.64 for the year ended January 2003 and $0.83 for the January 2004 year. These forecasts represented projected earnings growth of 42% and 33% for the next two years, respectively, virtually identical to consensus predictions for all analysts covering Krispy Kreme.[8]

---

7. Under the terms of the revolving credit agreement, the company would pay interest at the lower of the prime rates less 110 basis points and one-month LIBOR plus 100 basis points.

8. See *First Call* consensus earnings forecasts at June 1, 2002. A total of eight firms followed Krispy Kreme at the end of May 2002. In addition to CIBC World Markets, they included BB&T Capital Markets (Andrew Wolf), Brean Murray & Co. (Kathleen Heaney), Dain Rauscher Wessels (David Geraty), JP Morgan & Co. (John Ivankoe and David Linsen), Merrill Lynch (Peter Oakes), Thomas Weisel Partners (Skip Carpenter), and Deutsche Banc Alex Brown. Source: Krispy Kreme Doughnuts Investors Relations Web site.

QUESTIONS

1. Analysts are predicting that Krispy Kreme will be able to perform highly effectively and continue to grow rapidly in the coming two years. Do you agree with their analysis? If so, why? If not, why not?

2. What factors did the CIBC analysts examine to forecast sales growth for KKD in the years ended January 2003 and 2004? What assumptions did they implicitly make about number of new stores and weekly sales per store (for both company and franchise stores)? What are their implicit assumptions about revenue growth from franchise operations and KKM&D? Do you agree with these forecasts?

3. What are the NOPAT margins that the CIBC analysts have forecasted for KKD for the years ended January 2003 and 2004? What assumptions were made about specific expense items (e.g. margins, G&A, D&A, taxes)? Do you agree with these forecasts?

4. The CIBC analysts do not forecast KKD's balance sheet for the following year (ended January 2003). Make your own balance sheet forecasts.

5. In general, do you expect analysts' forecasts for a company like KKD to be optimistic, pessimistic, or unbiased? Why?

EXHIBIT 1

Stock Performance for Krispy Kreme and the S&P 500, April 2000 to May 2002

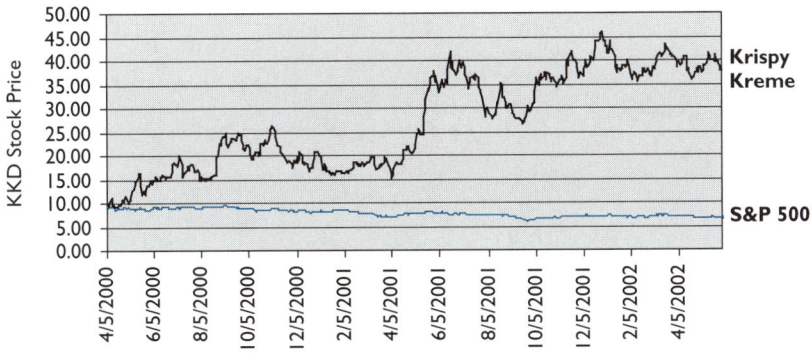

Source: Chart created from information found on Standard & Poor's Research Insight.

Note: Krispy Kreme's equity beta was 1.4 (source: SmartMoney.com). The long-term government bond rate on May 30, 2002 was 5.79% (source: Federal Reserve Statistical Release).

EXHIBIT 2

Financial Statements for Krispy Kreme Doughnuts for the Fiscal Years Ended January 30, 2000 to February 3, 2002, and for the Quarters Ended April 29, 2001 and May 5, 2002

CONSOLIDATED BALANCE SHEETS

	YEAR ENDED			QUARTER ENDED	
In thousands	JAN. 30, 2000	JAN. 28, 2001	FEB. 3, 2002	APR. 29, 2001	MAY 5, 2002
ASSETS					
CURRENT ASSETS:					
Cash and cash equivalents	$3,183	$7,026	$21,904	$21,326	$21,601
Short-term investments	—	18,103	15,292	24,738	22,073
Accounts receivable, net	17,965	19,855	26,894	20,202	29,232
Accounts receivable, affiliates	1,608	2,599	9,017	5,028	8,443
Other receivables	794	2,279	2,771	2,498	1,919
Inventories	9,979	12,031	16,159	11,511	21,118
Prepaid expenses	3,148	1,909	2,591	1,796	2,700
Income taxes refundable	861	—	2,534	34	—
Deferred income taxes	3,500	3,809	4,607	4,775	5,741
Total current assets	41,038	67,611	101,769	91,908	112,827
Property and equipment, net	60,584	78,340	112,577	85,464	151,152
Deferred income taxes	1,398	—	—	—	—
Long-term investments	—	17,877	12,700	11,319	6,058
Investment in unconsolidated joint ventures	—	2,827	3,400	4,921	4,382
Intangible assets	—	—	16,621	—	16,508
Other assets	1,938	4,838	8,309	6,578	7,387
Total assets	$104,958	$171,493	$255,376	$200,190	$298,314

(continued)

Krispy Kreme Doughnuts

CONSOLIDATED BALANCE SHEETS (continued)

In thousands	YEAR ENDED			QUARTER ENDED	
	JAN. 30, 2000	JAN. 28, 2001	FEB. 3, 2002	APR. 29, 2001	MAY 5, 2002
LIABILITIES AND SHAREHOLDERS' EQUITY					
CURRENT LIABILITIES:					
Accounts payable	$13,106	$8,211	$12,095	$15,671	$14,763
Book overdraft		5,147	9,107	—	8,074
Accrued expenses	14,080	21,243	26,729	16,941	20,832
Revolving line of credit	—	3,526	3,871	4,400	4,171
Current maturities of long-term debt	2,400	—	731	—	2,382
Income taxes payable	—	41	—	—	303
Total current liabilities	29,586	38,168	52,533	37,012	50,525
Deferred income taxes	—	579	3,930	2,113	727
Compensation deferred (unpaid)	990	1,106	727	954	35,133
Long-term debt, net of current portion	20,502	—	3,912	—	5,957
Accrued restructuring expenses	4,259	3,109	1,919	2,855	1,653
Other long-term obligations	1,866	1,735	2,197	1,641	2,883
Total long-term liabilities	27,617	6,529	12,685	7,563	46,353
Minority interest	—	1,117	2,491	1,059	2,703
SHAREHOLDERS' EQUITY:					
Common stock, no par value, 100,000 shares authorized; issued and outstanding – 51,832 (2001) and 54,271 (2002)	—	85,060	121,052	108,741	123,777
Common stock, $10 par value, 1,000 shares authorized; issued and outstanding – 467 (2000) and 0 (2001)	15,475	—	—	—	—
Unearned compensation	—	(188)	(186)	(176)	(169)
Notes receivable, employees	(2,547)	(2,349)	(2,580)	(2,958)	(2,556)
Nonqualified employee benefit plan assets	—	−126	−138	(126)	(339)
Nonqualified employee benefit plan liability	—	126	138	126	339
Accumulated other comprehensive income	—	609	456	683	(105)
Retained earnings	34,827	42,547	68,925	48,266	77,786
Total shareholders' equity	47,755	125,679	187,667	154,556	198,733
Total liabilities and shareholders' equity	$104,958	$171,493	$255,376	$200,190	$298,314

STATEMENT OF OPERATIONS

In thousands, except per share data	YEAR JAN. 30, 2000	JAN. 28, 2001	FEB. 3, 2002	THREE MONTHS APR. 29, 2001	MAY 5, 2002
Total revenues	$220,243	$300,715	$394,354	$87,921	$111,059
Operating expenses	190,003	250,690	316,946	71,195	86,362
General and administrative expenses	14,856	20,061	27,562	6,222	7,623
Depreciation and amortization expenses	4,546	6,457	7,959	1,872	2,546
Income (loss) from operations	10,838	23,507	41,887	8,632	14,528
Interest expense (income), net, and other	1,232	(1,698)	(2,408)	(976)	(495)
Equity loss in joint ventures	—	706	602	(171)	(198)
Minority interest	—	716	1,147	(175)	(533)
Loss on sale of property and equipment	—	—	—	(39)	—
Income (loss) before income taxes	9,606	23,783	42,546	9,223	14,292
Provision (benefit) for income taxes	3,650	9,058	16,168	3,504	5,431
Net income (loss)	$5,956	$14,725	$26,378	$5,719	$8,861
Net income (loss) per share:					
Basic	$0.16	$0.30	$0.49	$0.11	$0.16
Diluted	0.15	0.27	0.45	$0.10	$0.15
Shares used in calculation of net income (loss) per share:					
Basic	37,360	49,184	53,703	51,991	55,381
Diluted	39,280	53,656	58,443	57,190	59,073

CONSOLIDATED STATEMENTS OF CASH FLOWS

	YEAR ENDED			QUARTER ENDED	
In thousands	JAN. 30, 2000	JAN. 28, 2001	FEB. 3, 2002	APR. 29, 2001	MAY 5, 2002
CASH FLOW FROM OPERATING ACTIVITIES:					
Net income	$5,956	$14,725	$26,378	$5,719	$8,861
Items not requiring (providing) cash:					
Depreciation and amortization	4,546	6,457	7,959	1,872	2,546
Deferred income taxes	258	1,668	2,553	568	893
Loss on disposal of property and equipment, net	—	20	235	39	—
Compensation expense related to restricted stock awards	—	22	52	12	17
Tax benefit from exercise of nonqualified stock options	—	595	9,772	2,944	1,689
Provision for restructuring	(127)	—	—	—	—
Provision for store closings and impairment	1,139	318	—	—	—
Minority interest	—	716	1,147	175	533
Equity loss in joint ventures	—	706	602	171	198
Change in assets and liabilities:					
Receivables	(4,760)	(3,434)	(13,317)	(2,127)	(912)
Inventories	(93)	(2,052)	(3,977)	520	(4,846)
Prepaid expenses	(1,619)	1,239	(682)	113	(109)
Income taxes, net	(2,016)	902	(2,575)	(75)	2,837
Accounts payable	540	2,279	3,884	(450)	2,668
Accrued expenses	4,329	7,966	4,096	(3,165)	(6,255)
Deferred compensation and other long-term obligations	345	(15)	83	(246)	319
Net cash provided by operating activities	8,498	32,112	36,210	6,070	8,439
CASH FLOW FROM INVESTING ACTIVITIES:					
Purchase of property and equipment	(11,335)	(25,655)	(37,310)	(8,956)	(40,954)
Proceeds from disposal of property and equipment	—	1,419	3,196	9	—
Proceeds from disposal of assets held for sale	830	—	—	—	—
Acquisition of associate and area developer markets, net of cash acquired	—	—	(20,571)	—	—
Investments in unconsolidated joint ventures	—	(4,465)	(1,218)	(1,265)	(1,187)
(Increase) decrease in other assets	479	(3,216)	(4,237)	(3,696)	755
(Purchase) sale of investments, net	—	(35,371)	7,877	(3)	(235)
Net cash used for investing activities:	(10,026)	(67,288)	(52,263)	(13,911)	(41,621)

(continued)

CONSOLIDATED STATEMENTS OF CASH FLOWS *(continued)*

	YEAR ENDED			QUARTER ENDED	
In thousands	JAN. 30, 2000	JAN. 28, 2001	FEB. 3, 2002	APR. 29, 2001	MAY 5, 2002
CASH FLOW FROM FINANCING ACTIVITIES:					
Repayment of long-term debt	$(2,400)	$(3,600)	$ —	$ —	$(128)
Net (repayments) borrowings from revolving line of credit	—	(15,775)	345	874	300
Borrowings of long-term debt	4,282	—	4,643	—	33,000
Proceeds from stock offering	—	65,637	17,202	17,202	—
Proceeds from exercise of stock options	—	104	3,906	2,656	1,036
Minority interest	—	401	227	(233)	(321)
Book overdraft	482	(941)	3,960	1,372	(1,033
Cash dividends paid	(1,518)	(7,005)	—	—	—
Issuance of notes receivable	(674)	—	—	—	—
Collection of notes receivable	226	198	648	270	25
Net cash provided by financing activities:	398	39,019	30,931	22,141	32,879
Net increase (decrease) in cash and cash equivalents	(1,130)	3,843	14,878	14,300	(303)
Cash and cash equivalents at beginning of year	4,313	3,183	7,026	7,026	21,904
Cash and cash equivalents at end of year	$3,183	$7,026	$21,904	$21,326	$21,601
Supplemental schedule of non-cash investing and financing activities					
Issuance of stock to Krispy Kreme Profit-Sharing Stock Ownership Plan	—	$3,039	—	—	—
Issuance of restricted common shares	—	210	50	—	—
Issuance of stock in conjunction with acquisition of associate market	—	—	4,183	—	—
Issuance of stock in exchange for employee notes receivable	—	—	879	—	—
Unrealized gain (loss) on investments	—	609	(111)	74	(94)
Foreign currency translation adjustment	—	—	—	—	(8)
Change in fair value of cash flow hedge	—	—	—	—	459

Source: Krispy Kreme Doughnut's Annual Report for February 3, 2002 and the quarterly report for May 5, 2002.

EXHIBIT 3

Business Segment Data for Krispy Kreme Doughnuts for the Fiscal Years Ended
January 30, 2000 to February 3, 2002

	YEAR ENDED		
In thousands	JAN. 30, 2000	JAN. 28, 2001	FEB. 3, 2002
REVENUES BY BUSINESS SEGMENT			
Company Store Operations	$164,230	$213,677	$266,209
Franchise Operations	5,529	9,445	14,008
KKM&D	50,484	77,593	114,137
Total revenues	$220,243	$300,715	$394,354
OPERATING EXPENSES BY BUSINESS SEGMENT:			
Company Store Operations	$142,925	$181,470	$217,419
Franchise Operations	4,012	3,642	4,896
KKM&D	43,066	65,578	94,631
Total operating expenses	$190,003	$250,690	$316,946

Source: Krispy Kreme Doughnut's Annual Report, February 3, 2002.

EXHIBIT 4

Operating Data for Krispy Kreme Doughnuts for the Fiscal Years Ended February 1,
1998 to February 3, 2002

	FEB. 1, 1998	JAN. 31, 1999	JAN. 30, 2000	JAN. 28, 2001	FEB. 3, 2002
Systemwide sales ($000)	$203,439	$240,316	$318,854	$448,129	$621,665
Number of stores at end of period:					
Company	58	61	58	63	75
Franchised	62	70	86	111	143
Systemwide	120	131	144	174	218
Average weekly sales per store ($000)					
Company	$42	$47	$54	$69	$72
Franchised	23	28	38	43	53
Operating cash flow/store revenues	NA	20.3%	23.2%	26.1%	28.6%

Source: Krispy Kreme Doughnut's 10-K, February 3, 2002.

EXHIBIT 5

Excerpts from the CIBC World Markets Equity Research Report on Krispy Kreme Doughnuts, Inc., prepared by John S. Glass and Jeffery D. Farmer on June 3, 2002

COMPANY OVERVIEW

For both investors and consumers, Krispy Kreme is one of a kind phenomena, in our view, boasting a combination of a powerful consumer brand, a multi-channel distribution channel and a business model that produces best-in-class financial returns. What's more, the company is vertically integrated, not only retailing doughnuts, but also manufacturing and distributing high-margin doughnut mix as well as manufacturing proprietary doughnut-making equipment.

Krispy Kreme is still an attractive growth story, in our view, and represents a well-established brand still early in its growth trajectory. The company is just one-third of the way through the roll-out of their large-format factory stores—not including the substantial incremental growth prospects of its prototype smaller-format units.

These prospects have not gone unnoticed. Since its IPO in April 2000 priced at a split-adjusted $5.50, the stock has risen over 600% in the last 26 months, making it the most successful public offering in recent years. That performance has been fueled by substantial sales and earnings outper-formance—as well as a fair amount of publicity. The key components to the Krispy Kreme business model follow.

TABLE A

Company-Operated and Systemwide Unit Same-Store Sales (1999–2002E)

Company Stores	1999	2000	2001	2002
1Q	7.1%	23.3%	13.1%	10.5%
2Q	9.7%	24.4%	11.9%	10.0%E
3Q	14.0%	23.6%	11.1%	8.0%E
4Q	17.1%	20.6%	10.7%	8.0%E
Year	12.0%	22.9%	11.7%	9.0%E

Systemwide Stores	1999	2000	2001	2002
1Q	9.8%	19.1%	11.4%	12.9%
2Q	13.4%	19.4%	13.1%	10.5%E
3Q	15.9%	15.5%	13.6%	8.5%E
4Q	16.6%	14.9%	13.1%	8.5%E
Year	14.1%	17.1%	12.8%	10.0%E

Source: CIBC World Markets and company information.

Company-owned Retail Stores

Company-owned stores, most of which are in the Deep South, are referred to internally as the 'heritage markets,' representing about 60% of Krispy Kreme's profits. Although the company has focused most of its growth in franchised markets and has owned few new stores of its own, sales and profit trends have nonetheless been healthy due to a combination of strong comp store sales, driven by a combination of retail and wholesale business. While management has designated franchising in new markets as its primary growth driver, there is nonetheless substantial opportunity for growth in the heritage markets to develop underpenetrated markets as well as increase same-store sales through more efficient wholesale distribution and new wholesale accounts.

TABLE B

Systems and Operating Margin Leverage

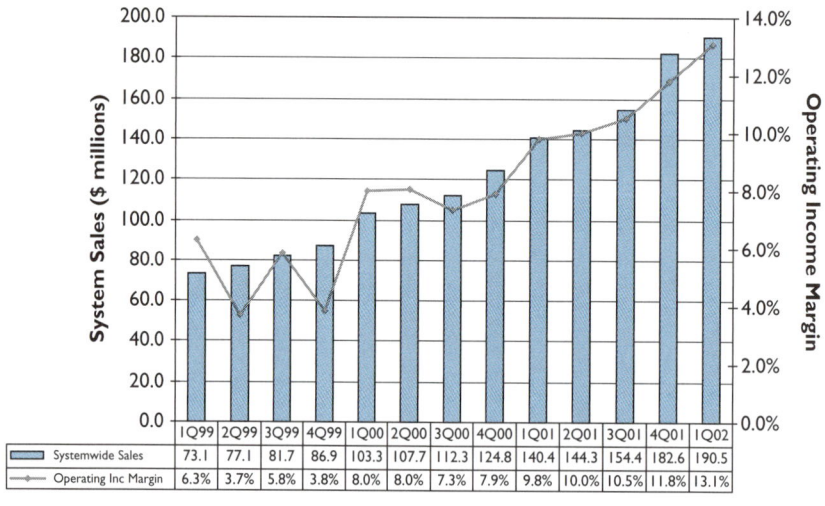

	1Q99	2Q99	3Q99	4Q99	1Q00	2Q00	3Q00	4Q00	1Q01	2Q01	3Q01	4Q01	1Q02
Systemwide Sales	73.1	77.1	81.7	86.9	103.3	107.7	112.3	124.8	140.4	144.3	154.4	182.6	190.5
Operating Inc Margin	6.3%	3.7%	5.8%	3.8%	8.0%	8.0%	7.3%	7.9%	9.8%	10.0%	10.5%	11.8%	13.1%

Source: CIBC World Markets and company information.

In addition, management has from time to time elected to repurchase older franchised markets—particularly those where there is still significant growth potential. Markets recently acquired include Charleston, SC, Savannah, GA, Cleveland and Akron, OH, and Baltimore, MD. In many cases, the company will resell a stake in these markets but retain the majority.

Margin expansion in the company-owned markets has been substantial, up 500 bp to 16% in 2001 as the company leveraged fixed costs through volume increases and focused on operation, particularly better labor cost management. Best-in-class store margins (including D&A) run into the high teens, particularly given that average weekly sales at company units were $72,000 in 2001, or $3.7 million annualized.

TABLE C

Average Weekly Sales per Store (1999–2001)

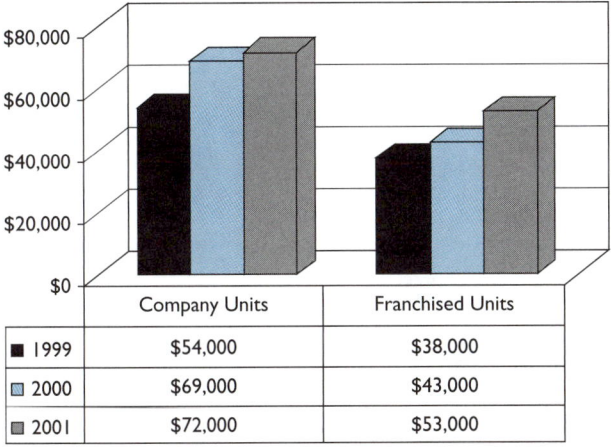

	Company Units	Franchised Units
■ 1999	$54,000	$38,000
▢ 2000	$69,000	$43,000
▣ 2001	$72,000	$53,000

Source: CIBC World Markets and company information.

Franchise Income

While the company has always had a close-knit group of original franchisees—known as the Associates—its real franchising growth came in the mid-1990s when the company began committing to area developer agreements outside its heritage markets. These new agreements are more profitable—4.5% royalties vs. 3% for Associates—and the income stream is much faster growing as the area developers rapidly roll out new units. In 2001, the area developer store base grew at a 68% clip to 143 units. Franchise income now represents 16% of profits, but given its inherent high-margin nature (current profit flow through is 65% on its way to 75% to 80%) and growth rate (franchise profits grew by nearly 60% in 2001) we expect the franchise income will continue to be a margin and earnings driver over the next several years as area developers continue to grow sales faster than the company-owned units.

In part, the growth in franchise income has been driven by massive new store openings as the company enters new markets. In fact, Krispy Kreme's new store openings follow an inverse store maturation curve, often producing peak volumes in a new store the first few weeks and then slowly settling over the next 12 months to a normalized level. *Typically, new stores retain about 40% of opening week sales. However, given the unusually strong first week sales recently, in some cases the retention rate is likely to be closer to 15% to 25%.* For example, new stores opened recently in Denver, Seattle, and Minneapolis have produced opening week volumes of $400,000 to $480,000. Over time, average weekly volume may settle around $75,000 to $100,000.

TABLE D

Krispy Kreme's Record Opening Week Sales

Date	Location	Opening Week Sales*
May 2002	Minneapolis, MN	$480,693
December 2001	Toronto, ONT	$465,003
November 2001	Seattle, WA	$454,125
April 2001	Denver, CO	$369,000

*Toronto opening in Canadian dollars

Source: CIBC World Markets and company information.

This honeymoon phenomenon could negatively impact systemwide comp store sales. If sales do not stabilize within 18 months (the point when stores enter the comp base), systemwide comp store sales will be negatively impacted—the magnitude depends on the number of units coming into the comp base, but could be as great as a 5% to 10% negative impact in some quarters. *Big-store openings also give rise to another phenomenon: 70% of franchisee sales are not in the comp base, so comp store sales are not yet a key driver of franchise income and KKM&D sales.* Since the company itself is not opening new stores, the above *has no impact* on company-owned comp store sales.

TABLE E

Hypothetical Weekly Sales Trends

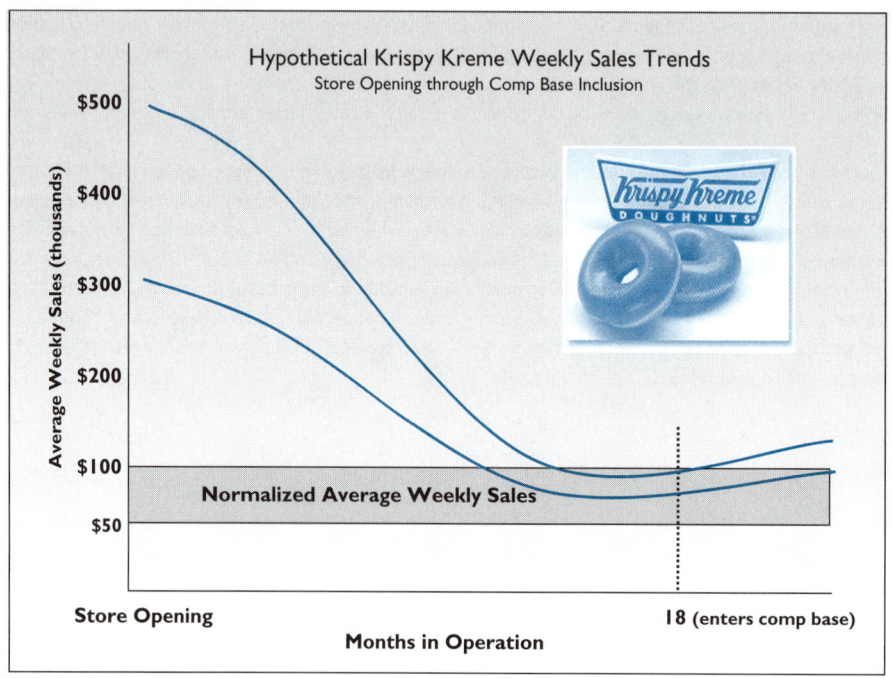

Source: CIBC World Markets and company information.

Krispy Kreme Manufacturing and Distribution (KKM&D)

KKM&D is the company's captive manufacturing and distribution arm. The manufacturing—primarily of doughnut mix which must be purchased by franchisees and machinery—is the higher-margin business, while the distribution margins are cost plus an estimated 2% to 3% markup. Blended margins for KKM&D run 16.6% of sales and are rising at a 100bp clip per year due to greater capacity utilization. The company opened a second distribution facility on the West Coast last year, and will open a second manufacturing facility in Effingham, IL shortly, helping to reduce shipping costs (both in and out) and raising margins. Sales growth for KKM&D should keep lock step with top-line growth of franchises.

Incremental Sales/Earnings Drivers

Embedded in each of these three lines, we think there are at least four incremental earnings drivers beyond the current base business. Those are:

1. **Hot Doughnut Shop**   Late in 2001, the company announced it had developed a prototype small-format unit (1,000–1,500 square feet), complete with a much smaller doughnut machine which reheats and glazes doughnuts. The implication on growth and unit potential is profound, in our view, allowing Krispy Kreme to enter urban centers, malls, and a variety of other locations that could not be reached through the factory store model. These small units also facilitate the sale of coffee, which has a much tighter draw radius than a traditional doughnut shop. Data on these new units is scare as only a handful exist. But, based on the number of Starbucks (4,000) and Dunkin Donuts (3,600) in the U.S., the opportunity for high-quality coffee and doughnuts given the Krispy Kreme brand is substantial. Unit sales potential for these smaller units could range from $750,000 to 1.5 million, in our view, based on what similar concepts are able to produce. We note that there is no empirical data at this time.

2. **Coffee sales**   Currently, beverage sales are a distant second to doughnuts at Krispy Kreme, running 10% of sales, and coffee just half of that. We think through a combination of more focus on the beverage program and the smaller more conventional markets, coffee sales are likely to grow in proportion to overall sales. Coffee is also where the repeat business is in this segment, in our view.

3. **Equity stakes in franchises**   In most new franchise agreements, Krispy has taken an equity stake—anywhere from 20% to 70%. As franchisees become profitable, these equity stakes will become profit contributors. Currently, they run at a modest loss.

4. **International**   We believe the brand has significant international potential and is natural in places such as the U.K., Japan, and potentially other European countries. International expansion is not currently in our forecast.

FINANCIAL OUTLOOK

Over the next three years, we expect Krispy Kreme to grow its earnings by 35%, driven by a combination of:

- Top-line growth of 25% to 30%, including systemwide square footage growth of 25% to 30% and mid-single digit comp sales.
- Margin expansion of 75 bp to 100 bp per year due to 1) mix shift toward higher margin KKM&D and franchise income, and 2) margin improvements in each of these categories.

The company's track record of exceeding earnings expectations is strong, with outperformance in each of the eight quarters since the company has come public. Earnings per share grew 65% in 2001. Our current forecast calls for 36% EPS growth in 2002.

An element for continued earnings growth at Krispy Kreme will be margin expansion. As **Table F** shows, the company now is already at its original long-term operating margin goal of 10%. Given the revenue mix shift toward higher profit income streams, operating efficiency improvements in company stores, and increased capacity utilization and lower shipping costs for the distribution and manufacturing operations, we believe operating profit margins can reach 15% over the next three to five years, well ahead of the original 10% goal.

TABLE F

Upward Revision of Margin Guidance

	CY 1998	CY 2001	Long-Term at IPO	Long-Term Today
Company Stores	9.0%	16.0%	13–14%	16–18%
Franchise Ops	13.5%	65.0%	70–75%	70–75%
Support Ops	13.0%	16.6%	16–17%	17–18%
G & A	6.0%	7.0%	6–7%	6–7%
EBIT	3.0%	10.6%	9–10%	14–16%

Source: CIBC World Markets and company information.

Financial Condition

Given the company's primary focus on the franchising and strong cash flow, to date the company has been able to fund its own expansion internally. In 2001, cash from operations of $30.5 million financed the company's $25.6 million cap-ex budget and $6.3 million in investments in joint ventures. However, Krispy Kreme's financing needs are likely to be greater in the near future given the addition of more manufacturing and distribution assets and more joint venture investment opportunities. In 2002, we expect that cap-ex will be $43 million plus an additional $35 million from the recently canceled synthetic lease program, which is likely now to be funded by debt. We expect cash from operations to be around $35 million to $40 million.

Recent Trends

Business trends for the last three quarters have been very consistent with systemwide comp store sales around 11% to 13% and company stores at about 10%; these results were achieved despite challenging comparisons from 2000 of 17% on a systemwide basis. In the F1Q, EPS grew 51%, driven by 26% top line and over 300 bp of operating margin expansion. Although store development was modest—a net of four units—the company is still committed to operating 62 new units, or 28% systemwide square footage growth.

Our current forecast for 2002 calls for 26% revenue growth, driven by 9% to 10% systemwide comps and 62 new units, as well as 100 bp of operating margin expansion (to 12+%).

RISK AND UNCERTAINTIES

- **Decelerating comp store sales** Decelerating comp store sales, particularly due to large new store openings entering the comp base, could negatively impact comp store sales—a metric widely used in valuing retail stocks. We note as before that 70% of franchisee revenues are still noncomp, therefore a comp deceleration in the franchise base would not materially impact earnings near term.

- **Increasing capital costs** Given the need for new production and distribution capacity, capital intensity is rising, as described earlier in this report. New unit costs have risen to $1.3 million to $1.5 million from an initial $1 million cost (ex-land) due to increased equipment and building costs. This primarily impacts franchisees as company new unit development has been limited.

- **Limited operating history with small-format units** While we are highly optimistic about the company's new smaller-format units, there is limited operating history to date and no public information on the unit economics.

- **Competition** Although we are less concerned about competition in the doughnut category, Krispy Kreme will encounter competition as it enters the coffee segment. Still, it is our view that its existing brand and customer loyalty will mitigate that risk.

Krispy Kreme Doughnuts

- **Fad risk** Although Krispy Kreme is about 65 years old, its initial reception in many markets is unlikely to be sustained over time. We expect some cannibalization as the brand becomes better established. Offsetting this, we believe, will be the positive impact of the more convenience-oriented small-format units.

TABLE G
Krispy Kreme Income Statement (FY01–FY04E)

Fiscal Year Ends: January	FY 2001A	FY 2002A	FY 2003E	FY 2004E
Company Stores	213,677	266,209	303,206	334,624
Franchised Stores	234,452	355,456	533,968	779,888
Systemwide Sales	$448,129	$621,655	$837,174	$1,114,512
Company Stores	213,677	266,209	303,206	334,624
Franchise Operations	9,445	14,963	22,615	32,128
Support Sales	77,516	114,137	169,507	239,445
Net Sales	$300,638	$394,354	$494,818	$606,197
Company Store Expenses	181,469	217,418	245,065	270,026
Franchise Expenses	3,643	4,896	6,771	9,780
Support Operations Expenses	65,512	94,631	138,413	194,058
Operating Expenses	250,624	316,946	390,249	473,864
D & A	6,458	7,959	10,121	12,081
General & Admin. Expense	20,061	27,562	33,959	40,918
Operating Profit	29,953	41,887	60,489	79,334
Interest/Other Expense (Income)	(1,593)	(2,408)	(1,395)	(1,400)
Joint Venture Income (Loss)	(600)	(602)	(198)	450
Minority Interest	(717)	(1,147)	(1,183)	(850)
Earnings Before Taxes	23,771	42,546	60,503	80,334
Income Taxes	9,058	16,168	22,991	30,527
Net Income	14,713	26,378	37,512	49,807
EPS	$0.27	$0.45	$0.63	$0.84
Avg. Shs. Outs. (FD)	53,656	58,434	59,174	59,574
Sales Ratios				
Operating Expenses	83.36%	80.37%	78.87%	78.17%
Contribution Profit (Bef. G & A)	16.64%	19.63%	21.13%	21.83%
D & A	2.15%	2.02%	2.05%	1.99%
General Administrative Exp.	6.67%	6.99%	6.86%	6.75%
Operating Income	9.96%	10.62%	12.22%	13.09%
Tax Rate	38.10%	38.00%	38.00%	38.00%
Net Income	4.89%	6.69%	7.58%	8.22%
Year-Over-Year % Change:				
Systemwide Sales	40.6%	38.7%	34.7%	33.1%
Company Sales	36.5%	31.2%	25.5%	22.5%
Operating Expenses	29.6%	26.5%	23.1%	21.4%
Selling General & Admin. Expense	27.5%	37.4%	23.2%	20.5%
Operating Profit	167.5%	39.8%	44.4%	31.2%
Net Income	147.0%	79.3%	42.2%	32.8%
EPS	81.1%	64.6%	40.4%	31.9%

Source: CIBC World Markets and company information.

TABLE H

Krispy Kreme Balance Sheet (FY2000–FY2002)

Fiscal Year Ended: January (dollars in millions)	FY 2000A	FY 2001A	FY2002A
Assets			
Cash/S-T investments	$3,183	$25,129	$37,196
Receivables (net)	20,367	24,733	38,682
Inventory	9,979	12,031	16,159
Other	7,509	5,718	9,732
Total Current Assets	41,038	67,611	101,769
Net Plant, Property, & Equipment	60,584	78,340	112,577
Other Assets	3,336	25,542	41,030
Total Long-term assets	63,920	103,882	153,607
Total Assets	**$104,958**	**$171,493**	**$255,376**
Liabilities & Stockholders' Equity			
Accounts Payable	$13,106	$14,697	$21,202
Accrued Liabilities	14,080	19,904	26,729
Current Mat. of Debt	2,400	0	0
Other		3,567	4,602
Total current liabilities	29,586	38,168	52,533
Long-term debt	20,502	0	3,912
Other long-term liabilities	7,115	6,529	8,773
Total long-term liabilities	27,617	6,529	12,685
Total liabilities	57,203	44,697	65,218
Minority interest		1,117	2,491
Total Stockholders' Equity	47,755	125,679	187,667
TOTAL LIABILITIES & EQUITY	**$104,958**	**$171,493**	**$255,376**

Chapter 7

Prospective Analysis: Valuation Theory and Concepts

The previous chapter introduced forecasting, the first stage of prospective analysis. In this and the following chapter we describe valuation, the second and final stage of prospective analysis. This chapter focuses on valuation theory and concepts, and the following chapter discusses implementation issues.

Valuation is the process of converting forecasts into an estimate of the value of the firm's assets or equity. At some level, nearly every business decision involves valuation, at least implicitly. Within the firm, capital budgeting involves considering how a particular project will affect firm value. Strategic planning focuses on how value is influenced by larger sets of actions. Outside the firm, security analysts conduct valuation to support their buy/sell decisions, and potential acquirers (often with the assistance of investment bankers) estimate the value of target firms and the synergies they might offer. Even credit analysts, who typically do not explicitly estimate firm value, must at least implicitly consider the value of the firm's equity "cushion" if they are to maintain a complete view of the risk associated with lending activity.

In practice a wide variety of valuation approaches are employed. For example, in evaluating the fairness of a takeover bid, investment bankers commonly use five to ten different methods of valuation. Among the available methods are the following:

- *Discounted dividends.* This approach expresses the value of the firm's equity as the present value of forecasted future dividends.
- *Discounted abnormal earnings.* Under this approach, the value of the firm's equity is expressed as the sum of its current book value and the present value of forecasted abnormal earnings.
- *Valuation based on price multiples.* Under this approach, a current measure of performance or single forecast of performance is converted into value by applying an appropriate price multiple derived from the value of comparable firms. For example, firm value can be estimated by applying a price-to-earnings ratio to a forecast of the firm's earnings for the coming year. Other commonly used multiples include price-to-book ratios and price-to-sales ratios.
- *Discounted cash flow (DCF) analysis.* This approach involves the production of detailed, multiple-year forecasts of cash flows. The forecasts are then discounted at the firm's estimated cost of capital to arrive at an estimated value.

These methods are developed throughout the chapter, and their pros and cons discussed. All of the approaches can be structured in two ways. The first is to directly value the equity of the firm, since this is usually the variable the analyst is interested in estimating. The second is to value the assets of the firm, that is, the claims of equity and net debt, and then to deduct the value of net debt to arrive at the final equity estimate. Theoretically, both approaches should generate the same values. However, as we will see in the next chapter, there are implementation issues in reconciling the approaches. In this chapter we illustrate valuation using an all-equity firm to simplify the discussion. A brief discussion of the theoretical issues in valuing a firm's assets is included in Appendix A.

THE DISCOUNTED DIVIDENDS VALUATION METHOD

How should shareholders think about the value of their equity claims on a firm? Finance theory holds that the value of any financial claim is simply the present value of the cash payoffs that its claimholders receive. Since shareholders receive cash payoffs from a company in the form of dividends, the value of their equity is the present value of future dividends (including any liquidating dividend).

$$Equity\ value = PV\ of\ expected\ future\ dividends$$

If we denote the expected future dividend for a given year as DIV and r_e as the cost of equity capital (the relevant discount rate), the stock value is as follows:

$$Equity\ value = \frac{DIV_1}{(1 + r_e)} + \frac{DIV_2}{(1 + r_e)^2} + \frac{DIV_3}{(1 + r_e)^3} + \ldots$$

Notice that the valuation formula views a firm as having an indefinite life. But in reality firms can go bankrupt or get taken over. In these situations shareholders effectively receive a terminating dividend on their stock.

If a firm had a constant dividend growth rate (g_d) indefinitely, its value would simplify to the following formula, which represents the present value of a growing perpetuity:

$$Equity\ value = \frac{DIV_1}{r_e - g_d}$$

To better understand how the discounted dividend approach works, consider the following example. At the beginning of year 1, Down Under Company raises $60 million of equity and uses the proceeds to buy a fixed asset. Operating profits before depreciation (all received in cash) are expected to be $40 million in year 1, $50 million in year 2, and $60 million in year 3. The firm pays out all operating profits as dividends and pays no taxes. At the end of year 3, the company terminates and has no residual value. If the cost of equity capital for this firm is 10 percent, the value of the firm's equity is computed as follows:

Year	Dividend	PV Factor	PV of Dividend
1	$40 m	0.909	$36.4 m
2	50 m	0.826	41.3 m
3	60 m	0.751	45.1 m
Equity value			$122.8 m

The above valuation method is called the dividend discount model. It forms the basis for most of the popular theoretical approaches to stock valuation. The remainder of the chapter discusses how this model can be recast to generate the discounted abnormal earnings, price multiple, and discounted cash flow models of value.

THE DISCOUNTED ABNORMAL EARNINGS VALUATION METHOD

There is a direct link between dividends and earnings. If all equity effects (other than capital transactions) flow through the income statement,[1] the expected book value of equity for existing shareholders at the end of year 1 (BVE_1) is simply the book value at the beginning of the year (BVE_0) plus expected net income (NI_1) less expected dividends (DIV_1).[2] This relation can be rewritten as follows:

$$DIV_1 = NI_1 + BVE_0 - BVE_1$$

By substituting this identity for dividends into the dividend discount formula and rearranging the terms, stock value can be rewritten as follows (Appendix B provides a simple proof of this formula):

Equity value = Book value of equity + PV of expected future abnormal earnings

Abnormal earnings are net income adjusted for a capital charge, which is computed as the discount rate multiplied by the beginning book value of equity. Abnormal earnings incorporate an adjustment to reflect the fact that accountants do not recognize any opportunity cost for equity funds used. Thus, the discounted abnormal earnings valuation formula is:

Equity value

$$= BVE_0 + \frac{NI_1 - r_e \cdot BVE_0}{(1 + r_e)} + \frac{NI_2 - r_e \cdot BVE_1}{(1 + r_e)^2} + \frac{NI_3 - r_e \cdot BVE_2}{(1 + r_e)^3} + \ldots$$

The earnings-based formulation has intuitive appeal. If a firm can earn only the required rate of return on its book value, then investors should be willing to pay no more than book value for the stock. Investors should pay more or less than book value if earnings are above or below this normal level. Thus, the deviation of a firm's market value from book value depends on its ability to generate "abnormal earnings." The formulation also implies that a firm's stock value reflects the cost of its existing net assets (i.e., its book equity) plus the present value of future growth options (represented by cumulative abnormal earnings).

To illustrate the earnings-based valuation approach, let's return to the Down Under Company example. Assuming the company depreciates its fixed assets using the straight-line method, its accounting-based earnings will be $20 million lower than dividends in each of the three years. The firm's beginning book equity, earnings, capital charges, abnormal earnings, and valuation will be as follows:

Year	Beginning Book Value	Earnings	Capital Charge	Abnormal Earnings	PV Factor	PV of Abnormal Earnings
1	$60 m	$20 m	$6 m	$14 m	0.909	$12.7 m
2	40 m	30 m	4 m	26 m	0.826	21.5 m
3	20 m	40 m	2 m	38 m	0.751	28.6 m
Cumulative PV of abnormal earnings						62.8 m
+ Beginning book value						60.0 m
= Equity value						$122.8 m

This stock valuation of $122.8 million is identical to the value estimated when the expected future dividends are discounted directly.

Key Analysis Questions

Valuation of equity under the discounted abnormal earnings method requires the analyst to answer the following questions:

- What are expected future net income and book values of equity (and therefore abnormal earnings) over a finite forecast horizon (usually five to ten years) given the firm's industry competitiveness and the firm's positioning?
- What is expected future abnormal net income beyond the final year of the forecast horizon (called the "terminal year") based on some simplifying assumptions? If abnormal returns are expected to persist, what are the barriers to entry that deter competition?
- What is the firm's cost of equity used to compute the present value of abnormal earnings?

Accounting Methods and Discounted Abnormal Earnings

One question that arises when valuation is based directly on earnings and book values is how the estimate is affected by managers' choice of accounting methods and accrual estimates. Would estimates of value differ for two otherwise identical firms if one used more conservative accounting methods than the other? We will see that, provided analysts recognize the impact of differences in accounting methods on future earnings (and hence their earnings forecasts), the accounting effects per se should have no influence on their value estimates. There are two reasons for this. First, accounting choices that affect a firm's current earnings also affect its book value, and therefore they affect the capital charges used to estimate future abnormal earnings. For example, conservative accounting not only lowers a firm's current earnings and book equity but also reduces future capital charges and inflates its future abnormal earnings. Second, double-entry bookkeeping is by nature self-correcting. Inflated earnings for one period have to ultimately be reversed in subsequent periods.

To understand how these two effects undo the effect of differences in accounting methods or accrual estimates, let's return to Down Under Company and see what happens if its managers choose to be conservative and expense some unusual costs that could have been capitalized as inventory in year 1. This accounting decision causes earnings and ending book value to be lower by $10 million. The inventory is then sold in year 2. For the time being, let's say the accounting choice has no influence on the analyst's view of the firm's real performance.

Management's choice reduces abnormal earnings in year 1 and book value at the beginning of year 2 by $10 million. However, future earnings will be higher, for two reasons. First, future earnings will be higher (by $10 million) when the inventory is sold in year 2. Second, the capital charge for normal earnings will be based on a book value of equity that is lower by $10 million. The $10 million decline in abnormal earnings in year 1 is perfectly offset (on a present value basis) by the $11 million higher abnormal earnings in year 2. As a result, the value of Down Under Company under conservative reporting is identical to the value under the earlier accounting method ($122.8 million).

Year	Beginning Book Value	Earnings	Abnormal Earnings	PV Factor	PV of Abnormal Earnings
1	$60 m	$10 m	$4 m	0.909	$3.6 m
2	30 m	40 m	37 m	0.826	30.6 m
3	20 m	40 m	38 m	0.751	28.6 m
Cumulative PV of abnormal earnings					62.8 m
+ Beginning book value					60.0 m
= Equity value					$122.8 m

Provided the analyst is aware of biases in accounting data that arise from managers' using aggressive or conservative accounting choices, abnormal earnings-based valuations are unaffected by variation in accounting decisions. This shows that strategic and accounting analyses are critical precursors to abnormal earnings valuation. The strategic and accounting analysis tools help the analyst to identify whether abnormal earnings arise from sustainable competitive advantage or from unsustainable accounting manipulations. For example, consider the implications of failing to understand the reasons for a decline in earnings from a change in inventory policy for Down Under Company. If an analyst mistakenly interpreted the decline as indicating that the firm was having difficulty moving its inventory, rather than that it had used conservative accounting, the analyst might reduce expectations of future earnings. The estimated value of the firm *would* then be lower than that reported in our example.

VALUATION USING PRICE MULTIPLES

Valuations based on price multiples are widely used by analysts. The primary reason for the popularity of this method is its simplicity. Unlike the discounted dividend, discounted abnormal earnings, and discounted cash flow methods, multiples-based valuations do not require detailed multiyear forecasts of a number of parameters such as growth, profitability, and cost of capital.

Valuation using multiples involves the following steps:

Step 1: Select a measure of performance or value (e.g., earnings, sales, cash flows, book equity, book assets) as the basis for multiple calculations. The two most commonly used metrics are based on earnings and book equity.

Step 2: Calculate price multiples for comparable firms, i.e., the ratio of the market value to the selected measure of performance or value.

Step 3: Apply the comparable firm multiple to the performance or value measure of the firm being analyzed.

Under this approach, the analyst relies on the market to undertake the difficult task of considering the short- and long-term prospects for growth and profitability and their implications for the values of the comparable firms. Then the analyst assumes that the pricing of the comparable firms is applicable to the firm at hand.

Main Issues with Multiples-Based Valuation

On the surface, using multiples seems straightforward. Unfortunately, in practice it is not as simple as it would appear. Identification of comparable firms is often quite difficult. There are also some choices to be made concerning how multiples will be calculated. Finally, understanding why multiples vary across firms, and how applicable another firm's multiple is to the one at hand, requires a sound knowledge of the determinants of each multiple.

Selecting Comparable Firms

Ideally, price multiples used in a comparable firm analysis are those for firms with similar operating and financial characteristics. Firms within the same industry are the most obvious candidates. But even within narrowly defined industries, it is often difficult to identify comparable firms. Many firms are in multiple industries, making it difficult to identify representative benchmarks. In addition, firms within the same industry frequently have different strategies, growth opportunities, and profitability, creating selection problems.

One way of dealing with these issues is to average across *all* firms in the industry. The analyst implicitly assumes that the various sources of noncomparability cancel each other out, so that the firm being valued is comparable to a "typical" industry member. Another approach is to focus on only those firms within the industry that are most similar.

For example, consider using multiples to value Wal-Mart. Business databases such as OneSource and Hoover's classify Wal-Mart as a discount and variety retailer in the nonapparel sector. Its closest competitors include Big Lots, BJ's Wholesale Club, Costco, Dollar General, Dollar Tree, Family Dollar, Sears, and Target. The average price–earnings ratio for these competitors was 22.19 and the average price-to-book ratio was 2.54. However, it is unclear whether these multiples are useful benchmarks for valuing Wal-Mart. Wal-Mart has a wider product offering than most of these competitors and operates on a significantly larger scale, both in terms of revenue and geographic reach. In addition, it competes in a variety of sectors against specialized retailers such as grocery stores and home improvement stores.

Multiples for Firms with Poor Performance

Price multiples can be affected when the denominator variable is temporarily performing poorly. This is especially common when the denominator is a flow measure, such as earnings or cash flows. For example, Big Lots, one of Wal-Mart's competitors, was unprofitable in the fiscal year ended January 2006 and marginally profitable in the twelve months ended July 2006. As a result, Big Lots had a price–earnings ratio of 51.54, well above the industry average.

Analysts have numerous options for handling the problems for multiples created by transitory shocks to the denominator. One option is to simply exclude firms with large transitory effects from the set of comparable firms. If Big Lots were excluded from Wal-Mart's peer group, the average price–earnings ratio for the industry declines from 22.19 to 17.53, which is much closer to the overall median ratio of 17.20. The magnitude of this effect illustrates how sensitive price–earnings multiples can be to transitory shocks. If poor performance is due to a one-time write-down or special item, analysts can simply exclude that effect from their computation of the comparable multiple. Finally, analysts can reduce the effect on multiples of temporary problems in past performance by using a denominator that is a forecast of future performance rather than the past measure itself. Multiples based on forecasts are termed *leading* multiples, whereas those based on historical data are called *trailing* multiples. Leading multiples are less likely to include one-time gains and losses in the denominator, simply because such items are difficult to anticipate.

Adjusting Multiples for Leverage

Price multiples should be calculated in a way that preserves consistency between the numerator and denominator. Consistency is an issue for those ratios where the denominator reflects performance *before* servicing debt. Examples include the price-to-sales multiple and any multiple of operating earnings or operating cash flows. When calculating these multiples, the numerator should include not just the market value of equity but the value of debt as well.

Determinants of Value-to-Book and Value–Earnings Multiples

Even across relatively closely related firms, price multiples can vary considerably. The abnormal earnings valuation method provides insight into factors that lead to differences in value-to-book and value–earnings multiples across firms.

If the abnormal earnings formula is scaled by book value, the left-hand side becomes the equity value-to-book ratio as opposed to the equity value itself. The right-hand side variables now reflect three multiple drivers: (1) earnings deflated by book value, or our old friend return on equity (ROE), discussed in Chapter 5, (2) the growth in equity book value over time, and (3) the firm's cost of equity. The actual valuation formula is as follows:

$$\text{Equity value-to-book ratio} = 1 + \frac{ROE_1 - r_e}{(1 + r_e)} + \frac{(ROE_2 - r_e)(1 + gbve_1)}{(1 + r_e)^2}$$

$$+ \frac{(ROE_3 - r_e)(1 + gbve_1)(1 + gbve_2)}{(1 + r_e)^3} + \dots$$

where $gbve_t$ = growth in book value (BVE) from year $t - 1$ to year t or

$$\frac{BVE_t - BVE_{t-1}}{BVE_{t-1}}$$

A firm's value-to-book ratio is largely driven by the magnitude of its future abnormal ROEs, defined as ROE less the cost of equity capital (ROE $- r_e$). Firms with positive abnormal ROEs are able to invest their net assets that create value for shareholders and will have price-to-book ratios greater than one. In contrast, firms with negative abnormal ROEs are unable to invest shareholder funds at a rate greater than their cost of capital and have ratios below one.

The magnitude of a firm's value-to-book multiple also depends on the amount of growth in book value. Firms can grow their equity base by issuing new equity or by reinvesting profits. If this new equity is invested in positive valued projects for shareholders, that is, projects with ROEs that exceed the cost of capital, the firm will boost its equity value-to-book multiple. Conversely, for firms with ROEs that are less than the cost of capital, equity growth further lowers the multiple.

The valuation task can now be framed in terms of the following essential questions about the firm's value drivers:

- Will the firm be able to generate ROEs that exceed its cost of equity capital? If so, for how long?
- How quickly will the firm's investment base (book value) grow?

If desired, the equation can be rewritten so that future ROEs are expressed as the product of their components: profit margins, sales turnover, and leverage. Thus the approach permits us to build directly on projections of the same accounting numbers utilized in financial analysis (see Chapter 5) without the need to convert projections of those numbers into cash flows. Yet in the end, the estimate of value should be the same as that from the dividend discount model.[3]

Returning to the Down Under Company example, the implied equity value-to-book multiple can be estimated as follows:

	Year 1	Year 2	Year 3
Beginning book value	$60 m	$40 m	$20 m
Earnings	$20 m	$30 m	$40 m
ROE	0.33	0.75	2.00
− Cost of capital	0.10	0.10	0.10
= Abnormal ROE	0.23	0.65	1.90
× (1 + compound book value growth)	1.00	0.67	0.33
= Abnormal ROE scaled by book value growth	0.23	0.43	0.63
× PV factor	0.909	0.826	0.751
= PV of abnormal ROE scaled by book value growth	0.212	0.358	0.476
Cumulative PV of abnormal ROE scaled by book value growth	1.046		
+ 1.00	1.000		
= Equity value-to-book multiple	2.046		

The equity value-to-book multiple for Down Under is therefore 2.046, and the implied stock value is $122.8 ($60 times 2.046), once again identical to the dividend discount model value.

The equity value-to-book formulation can also be used to construct the equity value–earnings multiple as follows:

$$\text{Equity value-to-earnings multiple} = \text{Equity value-to-book multiple} \times \frac{\text{Book value of equity}}{\text{Earnings}}$$

$$= \frac{\text{Equity value-to-book multiple}}{\text{ROE}}$$

In other words, the same factors that drive a firm's equity value-to-book multiple also explain its equity value–earnings multiple. The key difference between the two multiples is that the value–earnings multiple is affected by the firm's current level of ROE performance, whereas the value-to-book multiple is not. Firms with low current ROEs therefore have very high value–earnings multiples and vice versa. If a firm has a zero or negative ROE, its PE multiple is not defined. Value–earnings multiples are therefore more volatile than value-to-book multiples.

The following data for a subset of comparable firms in the discount and variety retail industry illustrate the relation between ROE, equity growth, the price-to-book ratio, and the price–earnings ratio:

Company	ROE	Book Value Growth	Price-to-Book Ratio	Price–Earnings Ratio
Wal-Mart	22.3%	18.1%	3.36	16.33
Sears	10.3%	2.7%	1.96	19.49
Target	18.2%	6.3%	2.92	16.96
Big Lots	4.0%	−9.3%	2.02	51.54

The price-to-book multiples indicate that investors expect that Wal-Mart will have the highest future abnormal ROEs, highest net asset growth, and/or lowest cost of capital combination of the four firms, followed by Target. Expectations for Sears and Big Lots are similar, but somewhat lower than for Wal-Mart or Target. In contrast, the price-to-earnings multiples are highest for Big Lots and Sears. Given their relatively low price-to-book multiples, the explanation for their price–earnings multiples rests in their low current ROEs. The price–earnings multiples imply that the market believes that Big Lots' current 4% ROE will improve substantially in the future, whereas Sears is expected to show modest improvement in its ROE.

Key Analysis Questions

To value a firm using multiples, an analyst must assess the quality of the variable used as the multiple basis and determine the appropriate peer firms to include in the benchmark multiple. Analysts are therefore likely to be interested in answering the following questions:

- How well does the denominator used in the multiple reflect the firm's performance? For example, if earnings or book equity are used as the denominator, has the firm made conservative or aggressive accounting choices that affect these variables and that are likely to unwind in the coming years? Is the firm likely to show strong growth in earnings or book equity? If earnings are the denominator, does the firm have temporarily poor or strong performance?
- What is the sustainability of the firm's growth and ROE based on the competitive dynamics of its industry and product market and its own competitive position?
- Which are the most suitable peer companies to include in the benchmark multiple computation? Have these firms had growth (earnings or book values), profitability, and quality of earnings comparable to the firm being analyzed? Do they have the same risk characteristics?

SHORTCUT FORMS OF EARNINGS-BASED VALUATION

The discounted abnormal earnings valuation formula can be simplified by making assumptions about the relation between a firm's current and future abnormal earnings. Similarly, the equity value-to-book formula can be simplified by making assumptions about long-term ROEs and growth.

Abnormal Earnings Simplification

Several assumptions about the relation between current and future net income are popular for simplifying the abnormal earnings model. First, abnormal earnings can be assumed to follow a random walk. The random walk model for abnormal earnings implies that an analyst's best guess about future expected abnormal earnings are current abnormal earnings. The model assumes that past shocks to abnormal earnings persist forever, but that future shocks are random or unpredictable. The random walk model can be written as follows:

$$\text{Forecasted } AE_1 = AE_0$$

Forecasted AE_1 is the forecast of next year's abnormal earnings and AE_0 is current period abnormal earnings. Under the model, forecasted abnormal earnings for two years ahead are simply abnormal earnings in year one, or once again current abnormal earnings. In other words, the best guess of abnormal earnings in any future year is just current abnormal earnings. It is also possible to include a drift term in the model, allowing earnings to grow by a constant amount, or at a constant rate in each period.

How does the above assumption about future abnormal earnings simplify the discounted abnormal earnings valuation model? If abnormal earnings follow a random walk, all future forecasts of abnormal earnings are simply current abnormal earnings. Consequently, the present value of future abnormal earnings can be calculated by valuing the current level of abnormal earnings as a perpetuity. It is then possible to rewrite value as follows:

$$\text{Stock value} = BVE_0 + \frac{AE_0}{r_e}$$

The stock value is the book value of equity at the end of the year plus current abnormal earnings divided by the cost of capital. The perpetuity formula can be adjusted to incorporate expectations of constant growth in future abnormal earnings.

In reality, shocks to abnormal earnings are unlikely to persist forever. Firms that have positive shocks are likely to attract competitors that will reduce opportunities for future abnormal performance. Firms with negative abnormal earnings shocks are likely to fail or to be acquired by other firms that can manage their resources more effectively. The persistence of abnormal performance will therefore depend on strategic factors such as barriers to entry and switching costs, discussed in Chapter 2. To reflect this, analysts frequently assume that current shocks to abnormal earnings decay over time. Under this assumption, abnormal earnings are said to follow an autoregressive model. Forecasted abnormal earnings are then

$$\text{Forecasted } AE_1 = \beta AE_0$$

β is a parameter that captures the speed with which abnormal earnings decay over time. If there is no decay, β is 1 and abnormal earnings follow a random walk. If β is 0, abnormal earnings decay completely within one year. Estimates of β using actual company data indicate that for a typical U.S. firm, β is approximately 0.6. However, it varies by industry and is smaller for firms with large accruals and one-time accounting charges.[4]

The autoregressive model implies that stock values can again be written as a function of current abnormal earnings and book values[5]:

$$\text{Stock value} = \text{BVE}_0 + \frac{\beta AE_0}{r_e + (1 - \beta)}$$

This formulation implies that stock values are simply the sum of current book value plus current abnormal earnings weighted by the cost of equity capital and persistence in abnormal earnings.

ROE and Growth Simplifications

It is also possible to make simplifications about long-term ROEs and equity growth to reduce forecast horizons for estimating the equity value-to-book multiple. Firms' long-term ROEs are affected by such factors as barriers to entry in their industries, change in production or delivery technologies, and quality of management. As discussed in Chapter 6, these factors tend to force abnormal ROEs to decay over time. One way to model this decay is to assume that ROEs revert to the mean. Forecasted ROE after one period then takes the following form:

$$\text{Forecasted } ROE_1 = ROE_0 + \beta(ROE_0 - \overline{ROE})$$

$\overline{ROE}$ is the steady state ROE (either the firm's cost of capital or the long-term industry ROE) and β is a "speed of adjustment factor" that reflects how quickly it takes the ROE to revert to its steady state.[6]

Growth rates in the book value of equity are driven by several factors. First, the size of the firm is important. Small firms can sustain very high growth rates for an extended period, whereas large firms find it more difficult to do so. Second, firms with high rates of growth are likely to attract competitors, which reduces their growth rates. As a result, steady-state rates of growth in book equity are likely to be similar to rates of growth in the overall economy, which in the U.S. have averaged 3–4 percent per year.

The long-term patterns in ROE and book equity growth rates imply that for most companies there is limited value in making forecasts for valuation beyond a relatively short horizon, generally five to ten years. Powerful economic forces tend to lead firms with superior or inferior performance early in the forecast horizon to revert to a level that is comparable to that of other firms in the industry or the economy. For a firm in steady state, that is, expected to have a stable ROE and book equity growth rate (*gbve*), the value-to-book multiple formula simplifies to the following:

$$\text{Equity value-to-book multiple} = 1 + \frac{ROE_0 - r_e}{r_e - gbve}$$

Consistent with this simplified model, there is a strong relation between price-to-book ratios and current ROEs. Figure 7-1 shows the relation between these variables for firms in the variety and discount retail industry we discussed earlier. The correlation between the two variables is 0.69.

FIGURE 7-1	Relationship Between ROE and Price-to-Book Multiples

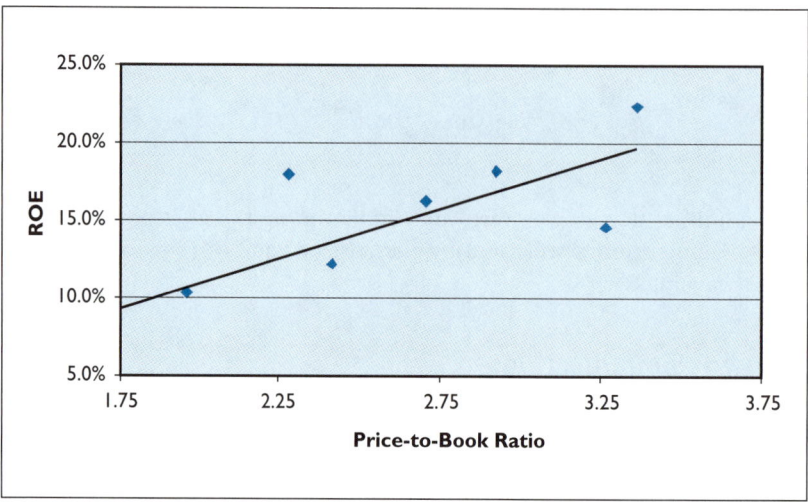

Of course, analysts can make a variety of simplifying assumptions about a firm's ROE and growth. For example, they can assume that they decay slowly or rapidly to the cost of capital and the growth rate for the economy. They can assume that the rates decay to the industry or economy average ROEs and book value growth rates. The valuation formula can easily be modified to accommodate these assumptions

THE DISCOUNTED CASH FLOW MODEL

The final valuation method discussed here is the discounted cash flow approach, the valuation method taught in most finance classes. Like the abnormal earnings approach, it is derived from the dividend discount model. It is based on the insight that dividends can be recast as free cash flows,[7] as follows:

$$\text{Dividends} = \text{Operating cash flow} - \text{Capital outlays} + \text{Net cash flows from debt owners}$$

As discussed in Chapter 5, operating cash flows to equity holders are simply net income plus depreciation less changes in working capital accruals. Capital outlays are capital expenditures less asset sales. Finally, net cash flows from debt owners are issues of new debt less retirements less the after-tax cost of interest. By rearranging these terms, the free cash flows to equity can be written as

$$\text{Dividends} = \text{Free cash flows to equity} = NI - \Delta BVA + \Delta BVND$$

where NI is net income, ΔBVA is the change in book value of net operating assets (including changes in working capital plus capital expenditures less depreciation expense), and $\Delta BVND$ is the change in book value of net debt (interest-bearing debt less excess cash).

The dividend discount model can therefore be written as the present value of free cash flows to equity. Under this formulation, value to shareholders is estimated as follows:

Equity value = PV of free cash flows to equity claim holders

$$= \frac{NI_1 - \Delta BVA_1 + \Delta BVND_1}{(1 + r_e)} + \frac{NI - \Delta BVA_2 + \Delta BVND_2}{(1 + r_e)^2} + \dots$$

Valuation under the discounted cash flow method therefore involves the following steps:

Step 1: Forecast free cash flows available to equity holders over a finite forecast horizon (usually five to ten years).

Step 2: Forecast free cash flows beyond the terminal year based on some simplifying assumption.

Step 3: Discount free cash flows to equity holders at the cost of equity. The discounted amount represents the estimated value of free cash flows available to equity.

Returning to the Down Under Company example, there is no debt, so the free cash flows to owners are simply the operating profits before depreciation. Since the company's cost of equity is assumed to be 10 percent, the present value of the free cash flows is calculated as follows:

Year	Free Cash Flows	PV Factor	PV of Free Cash Flows
1	$40 m	0.909	$36.4 m
2	50 m	0.826	41.3 m
3	60 m	0.751	45.1 m
Equity value			$122.8 m

Notice that the value of Down Under's equity is exactly the same as that estimated using the discounted abnormal earnings method. This should not be surprising. Both methods are derived from the dividend discount model. And in estimating value under the two approaches, we have used the same underlying assumptions to forecast earnings and cash flows.

COMPARING VALUATION METHODS

We have discussed three methods of valuation derived from the dividend discount model: discounted dividends, discounted abnormal earnings (or abnormal ROEs), and discounted cash flows. Since the methods are all derived from the same underlying model, no one version can be considered superior to the others. As long as analysts make the same assumptions about firm fundamentals, value estimates under all three methods will be identical. However, we discuss below important differences between the models.

Differences in Focus

The methods frame the valuation task differently and can in practice focus the analyst's attention on different issues. The earnings-based approaches frame the issues in terms of accounting data such as earnings and book values rather than cash flows. Analysts spend considerable time analyzing historical income statements and balance sheets, and their primary forecasts are typically for these accounting variables.

Defining values in terms of ROEs has the advantage that it focuses analysts' attention on ROE, the same key measure of performance that is decomposed in a standard financial analysis. Furthermore, because ROEs control for firm scale, it is likely to be easier for analysts to evaluate the reasonableness of their forecasts by benchmarking them with ROEs of other firms in the industry and in the broader economy. This type of benchmarking is more challenging for free cash flows and abnormal earnings.

Differences in Required Structure

The methods differ in the amount of analysis and structure required for valuation. The discounted abnormal earnings and ROE methods require analysts to construct both pro forma income statements and balance sheets to forecast future earnings and book values. In contrast, the discounted cash flow method requires analysts to forecast income statements and changes in working capital and long-term assets to generate free cash flows. Finally, the discounted dividend method requires analysts to forecast dividends.

The discounted abnormal earnings, ROE, and free cash flow models all require more structure for analysis than the discounted dividend approach. They therefore help analysts avoid structural inconsistencies in their forecasts of future dividends by specifically requiring a prediction of firms' future performance and investment opportunities. Similarly, the discounted abnormal earnings/ROE method requires more structure and work than the discounted cash flow method to build full pro forma balance sheets. This allows analysts to avoid inconsistencies in the firm's financial structure.

Differences in Terminal Value Implications

A third difference between the methods is in the effort required for estimating terminal values. Terminal value estimates for the abnormal earnings and ROE methods tend to represent a much smaller fraction of total value than under the discounted cash flow or dividend methods. On the surface, this would appear to mitigate concerns about the aspect of valuation that leaves the analyst most uncomfortable. Is this apparent advantage real? As explained below, the answer turns on how well value is already reflected in the accountant's book value.

The abnormal earnings valuation does not eliminate the discounted cash flow terminal value problem, but it does reframe it. Discounted cash flow terminal values include the present value of *all* expected cash flows beyond the forecast horizon. Under abnormal earnings valuation, that value is broken into two parts: the present values of *normal* earnings and *abnormal* earnings beyond the terminal year. The terminal value in the abnormal earnings technique includes only the *abnormal* earnings. The present value of *normal* earnings is already reflected in the original book value.

The abnormal earnings approach, then, recognizes that current book value and earnings over the forecast horizon already reflect many of the cash flows expected to arrive after the forecast horizon. The approach builds directly on accrual accounting. For example, under accrual accounting book equity can be thought of as the minimum recoverable future benefits attributable to the firm's net assets. In addition, revenues are typically realized when earned, not when cash is received. The discounted cash flow approach, on the other hand, "unravels" all of the accruals, spreads the resulting cash flows over longer horizons, and then reconstructs its own "accruals" in the form of discounted expectations of future cash flows. The essential difference between the two approaches is that abnormal earnings valuation recognizes that the accrual process may already have performed a portion of the valuation task, whereas the discounted cash flow approach ultimately moves back to the primitive cash flows underlying the accruals.

The usefulness of the accounting-based perspective thus hinges on how well the accrual process reflects future cash flows. The approach is most convenient when the accrual process is "unbiased," so that earnings can be abnormal only as the result of economic rents and not as a product of accounting itself.[8] The forecast horizon then extends to the point where the firm is expected to approach a competitive equilibrium and earn only normal earnings on its projects. Subsequent abnormal earnings would be zero, and the terminal value at that point would be zero. In this case, *all* of the firm's value is reflected in the book value and earnings projected over the forecast horizon.

Of course, accounting rarely works so well. For example, in most countries research and development costs are expensed, and book values fail to reflect any research and development assets. As a result, firms that spend heavily on research and development—such as pharmaceutical companies—tend, on average, to generate abnormally high earnings even in the face of stiff competition. Purely as an artifact of research and development accounting, abnormal earnings would be expected to remain positive indefinitely for such firms, and the terminal value could represent a substantial fraction of total value.

If desired, the analyst can alter the accounting approach used by the firm in his or her own projections. "Better" accounting would be viewed as that which reflects a larger fraction of the firm's value in book values and earnings over the forecast horizon.[9] This same view underlies analysts' attempts to "normalize" earnings; the adjusted numbers are intended to provide better indications of value, even though they reflect performance only over a short horizon.

Recent research has focused on the performance of earnings-based valuation relative to discounted cash flow and discounted dividend methods. The findings indicate that over relatively short forecast horizons, ten years or less, valuation estimates using the abnormal earnings approach generate more precise estimates of value than either the discounted dividend or discounted cash flow models. This advantage for the earnings-based approach persists for firms with conservative or aggressive accounting, indicating that accrual accounting in the U.S. does a reasonably good job of reflecting future cash flows.[10]

Research also indicates that abnormal earnings estimates of value outperform traditional multiples, such as price–earnings ratios, price-to-book ratios, and dividend yields, for predicting future stock movements.[11] Firms that have high abnormal earnings model estimates of value relative to their current price show positive abnormal future stock returns, whereas firms with low estimated value-to-price ratios have negative abnormal stock performance.

Key Analysis Questions

The above discussion on the trade-offs between different methods of valuing a company raises several questions for analysts about comparing methods and considering which is likely to be most reliable for their analysis:

- What are the key performance parameters that the analyst forecasts? Is more attention given to forecasting accounting variables, such as earnings and book values, or to forecasting cash flow variables?

- Has the analyst linked forecasted income statements and balance sheets? If not, is there any inconsistency between the two statements, or in the implications of the assumptions for future performance? If so, what is the source of this inconsistency and does it affect discounted earnings-based and discounted cash flow methods similarly?
- How well does the firm's accounting capture its underlying assets and obligations? Does it do a good enough job that we can rely on book values as the basis for long-term forecasts? Alternatively, does the firm rely heavily on off-balance-sheet assets, such as R&D, which make book values a poor lower bound on long-term performance?
- Has the analyst made very different assumptions about long-term performance in the terminal value computations under the different valuation methods? If so, which set of assumptions is more plausible given the firm's industry and its competitive positioning?

SUMMARY

Valuation is the process by which forecasts of performance are converted into estimates of price. A variety of valuation techniques are employed in practice, and there is no single method that clearly dominates others. In fact, since each technique involves different advantages and disadvantages, there are gains to considering several approaches simultaneously.

For shareholders, a stock's value is the present value of future dividends. This chapter described three valuation techniques directly based on this dividend discount definition of value: discounted dividends, discounted abnormal earnings/ROEs, and discounted free cash flows. The discounted dividend method attempts to forecast dividends directly. The abnormal earnings approach expresses the value of a firm's equity as book value plus discounted expectations of future abnormal earnings. Finally, the discounted cash flow method represents a firm's stock value through expected future free cash flows discounted at the cost of capital.

Although these three methods were derived from the same dividend discount model, they frame the valuation task differently. In practice they focus the analyst's attention on different issues and require different levels of structure in developing forecasts of the underlying primitive, future dividends.

Price-multiple valuation methods were also discussed. Under these approaches, analysts calculate ratios of current price to historical or forecasted measures of performance for comparable firms. The benchmarks are then used to value the performance of the firm being analyzed. Multiples have traditionally been popular, primarily because they do not require analysts to make multiyear forecasts of performance. However, it can be difficult to identify comparable firms to use as benchmarks. Even across highly related firms, there are differences in performance that are likely to affect their multiples.

The chapter discussed the relation between two popular multiples, value-to-book and value–earnings ratios, and the discounted abnormal earnings valuation. The resulting formulations indicate that value-to-book multiples are a function of future abnormal ROEs, book value growth, and the firm's cost of equity. The value–earnings multiple is a function of the same factors and the current ROE.

DISCUSSION QUESTIONS

1. Joe Watts, an analyst at EMH Securities, states: "I don't know why anyone would ever try to value earnings. Obviously, the market knows that earnings can be manipulated and only values cash flows." Discuss.

2. Explain why terminal values in accounting-based valuation are significantly lower than those for DCF valuation.

3. Manufactured Earnings is a "darling" of Wall Street analysts. Its current market price is $15 per share, and its book value is $5 per share. Analysts forecast that the firm's book value will grow by 10 percent per year indefinitely, and the cost of equity is 15 percent. Given these facts, what is the market's expectation of the firm's long-term average ROE?

4. Given the information in question 3, what will be Manufactured Earnings' stock price if the market revises its expectations of long-term average ROE to 20 percent?

5. Analysts reassess Manufactured Earnings' future performance as follows: growth in book value increases to 12 percent per year, but the ROE of the incremental book value is only 15 percent. What is the impact on the market-to-book ratio?

6. How can a company with a high ROE have a low PE ratio?

7. What types of companies have
   a. a high PE and a low market-to-book ratio?
   b. a high PE ratio and a high market-to-book ratio?
   c. a low PE and a high market-to-book ratio?
   d. a low PE and a low market-to-book ratio?

8. Free cash flows (FCF) used in DCF valuations discussed in the chapter are defined as follows:

   FCF to debt and equity = Earnings before interest and taxes × (1 − tax rate) + Depreciation and deferred taxes − Capital expenditures −/+ Increase/decrease in working capital

   FCF to equity = Net income + Depreciation and deferred taxes − Capital expenditures −/+ Increase/decrease in working capital +/− Increase/decrease in debt

   Which of the following items affect free cash flows to debt and equity holders? Which affect free cash flows to equity alone? Explain why and how.
   • An increase in accounts receivable
   • A decrease in gross margins
   • An increase in property, plant, and equipment
   • An increase in inventory
   • Interest expense
   • An increase in prepaid expenses
   • An increase in notes payable to the bank.

9. Starite Company is valued at $20 per share. Analysts expect that it will generate free cash flows to equity of $4 per share for the foreseeable future. What is the firm's implied cost of equity capital?

10. Janet Stringer argues that "the DCF valuation method has increased managers' focus on short-term rather than long-term performance, since the discounting process places much heavier weight on short-term cash flows than long-term ones." Comment.

NOTES

1. The incorporation of all noncapital equity transactions into income is called clean surplus accounting. It is analogous to comprehensive income, the concept defined in FAS 130.

2. Changes in book value also include new capital contributions. However, the dividend discount model assumes that new capital is issued at fair value. As a result, any incremental book value from capital issues is exactly offset by the discounted value of future dividends to new shareholders. Capital transactions, therefore, do not affect firm valuation.

3. It may seem surprising that one can estimate value with no explicit attention to two of the cash flow streams considered in DCF analysis, investments in working capital and capital expenditures. The accounting-based technique recognizes that these investments cannot possibly contribute to value without impacting abnormal earnings and, therefore, only their earnings impacts need be considered. For example, the benefit of an increase in inventory turnover surfaces in terms of its impact on ROE (and thus, abnormal earnings) without the need to consider explicitly the cash flow impacts involved.

4. See P. M. Dechow, A. P. Hutton, and R. G. Sloan, "An empirical assessment of the residual income valuation model," *Journal of Accounting and Economics* 23, January 1999.

5. This formulation is a variant of a model proposed by J. Ohlson, "Earnings, book values, and dividends in security valuation," *Contemporary Accounting Research* 11, Spring 1995. Ohlson includes in his forecasts of future abnormal earnings a variable that reflects relevant information other than current abnormal earnings. This variable then also appears in the stock valuation formula. Empirical research by Dechow, Hutton, and Sloan, "An empirical assessment of the residual income valuation model," *Journal of Accounting and Economics* 23, January 1999, indicates that financial analysts' forecasts of abnormal earnings do reflect considerable information other than current abnormal earnings, and that this information is useful for valuation.

6. This specification is similar to the model for dividends developed by J. Lintner, "Distribution of incomes of corporations among dividends, retained earnings, and taxes," *American Economic Review* 46 (May 1956): 97–113.

7. In practice, firms do not have to pay out all of their free cash flows as dividends; they can retain surplus cash in the business. The conditions under which a firm's dividend decision affects its value are discussed by M. H. Miller and F. Modigliani in "Dividend Policy, Growth and the Valuation of Shares," *Journal of Business* 34 (October 1961): 411–33.

8. Unbiased accounting is that which, in a competitive equilibrium, produces an expected ROE equal to the cost of capital. The actual ROE thus reveals the presence of economic rents. Market-value accounting is a special case of unbiased accounting that produces an expected ROE equal to the cost of capital, even when the firm is not in a competitive equilibrium. That is, market-value accounting reflects the present value of future economic rents in book value, driving the expected ROEs to a normal level. For a discussion of unbiased and biased accounting, see G. Feltham and J. Ohlson, "Valuation and Clean Surplus Accounting for Operating and Financial Activities," *Contemporary Accounting Research* 11, No. 2 (Spring 1995): 689–731.

9. In Bennett Stewart's book on EVA valuation, *The Quest for Value* (New York: HarperBusiness, 1999), he recommends a number of accounting adjustments including the capitalization of research and development.

10. S. Penman and T. Sougiannis, "A Comparison of Dividend, Cash Flow, and Earnings Approaches to Equity Valuation," *Contemporary Accounting Research* (Fall 1998): 343–83, compares the valuation methods using actual realizations of earnings, cash flows, and dividends to estimate prices. J. Francis, P. Olsson, and D. Oswald, "Comparing Accuracy and Explainability of Dividend, Free Cash Flow and Abnormal Earnings Equity Valuation Models," *Journal of Accounting Research* 38 (Spring 2000): 45–70, estimates values using *Value Line* forecasts.

11. See C. Lee, J. Myers, and B. Swaminathan, "What is the Intrinsic Value of the Dow?" *Journal of Finance* (October 1999): 1693–1741.

APPENDIX A: ASSET VALUATION METHODOLOGIES

All of the valuation approaches discussed in this chapter can also be structured to estimate the value of a firm's assets (or the combined debt and equity) rather than its equity. Switching from equity valuation to asset valuation is often as simple as substituting financial measures related to equity for financial measures related to the entire firm. For example, in the earnings-based valuation model, net income (the earnings flow to equity) is replaced by NOPAT (the earnings available for debt and equity), and book values of assets replace the book value of equity. Value multiples are based on ROEs for the equity formulation and on ROAs for valuing asset multiples. And the discount rate for equity models is the cost of equity compared to the weighted average cost of capital (or WACC) for asset valuation models.

The formulas used for asset valuation under the various approaches are presented below.

Abnormal Earnings Valuation

Under the earnings-based approach, the value of the assets is

Assets value

$$= BVA_0 + \frac{NOPAT_1 - WACC \cdot BVA_0}{(1 + WACC)} + \frac{NOPAT_2 - WACC \cdot BVA_1}{(1 + WACC)^2} + \cdots$$

BVA is the book value of the firm's assets, NOPAT is net operating profit (before interest) after tax, and WACC is the firm's weighted-average cost of debt and equity. From this asset value, the analyst can deduct the market value of net debt to generate an estimate of the value of equity.

Valuation Using Price Multiples

The multiple valuation can be structured as the debt plus equity value-to-book assets ratio by scaling the abnormal NOPAT formula by book value of net operating assets. The valuation formula then becomes

Debt plus equity value-to-book ratio

$$= 1 + \frac{ROA_1 - WACC}{(1 + WACC)} + \frac{(ROA_2 - WACC)(1 + gbva_1)}{(1 + WACC)^2}$$
$$+ \frac{(ROA_3 - WACC)(1 + gbva_1)(1 + gbva_2)}{(1 + WACC)^3} + \cdots$$

where ROA = operating return on asset = NOPAT/(Operating working capital + Net long-term assets)

WACC = weighted average cost of debt and equity

$gbva_t$ = growth in book value of assets (BVA) from year $t - 1$ to year t or

$$\frac{BVA_t - BVA_{t-1}}{BVA_{t-1}}$$

The value of a firm's debt and equity to net operating assets multiple therefore depends on its ability to generate asset returns that exceed its WACC, and on its ability to grow its asset base. The value of equity under this approach is then the estimated multiple times the current book value of assets less the market value of debt.

Discounted Cash Flow Model

The free cash flow formulation can be structured by estimating the value of claims to net debt and equity and then deducting the market value of net debt. This approach is more widely used in practice because it does not require explicit forecasts of changes in debt balances. The value of debt plus equity is computed as follows:

Debt plus equity value = PV of free cash flows to net debt and equity claim holders

$$= \frac{NOPAT_1 - \Delta BVA_1}{(1 + WACC)} + \frac{NOPAT_2 - \Delta BVA_2}{(1 + WACC)^2} + \cdots$$

The firm's asset valuation therefore depends on the expected free cash flows to debt and equity holders during the forecast horizon, the forecasted terminal value of free cash flows, and the weighted average cost of capital.

APPENDIX B: RECONCILING THE DISCOUNTED DIVIDENDS AND DISCOUNTED ABNORMAL EARNINGS MODELS

To derive the earnings-based valuation from the dividend discount model consider the following two-period valuation:

$$\text{Equity value} = \frac{DIV_1}{(1 + r_e)} + \frac{DIV_2}{(1 + r_e)^2}$$

With clean surplus accounting, dividends (DIV) can be expressed as a function of net income (NI) and the book value of equity (BVE):

$$DIV_t = NI_t + BVE_{t-1} - BVE_t$$

Substituting this expression into the dividend discount model yields the following:

$$\text{Equity value} = \frac{NI_1 + BVE_0 - BVE_1}{(1 + r_e)} + \frac{NI_2 + BVE_1 - BVE_2}{(1 + r_e)^2}$$

This can be rewritten as follows:

$$\text{Equity value} = \frac{NI_1 - r_e BVE_0 + BVE_0(1 + r_e) - BVE_1}{(1 + r_e)}$$

$$+ \frac{NI_2 - r_e BVE_1 + BVE_1(1 + r_e) - BVE_2}{(1 + r_e)^2}$$

$$= BVE_0 + \frac{NI_1 - r_e BVE_0}{(1 + r_e)} + \frac{NI_2 - r_e BVE_1}{(1 + r_e)^2} - \frac{BVE_2}{(1 + r_e)^2}$$

As the forecast horizon expands, the final term (the present value of liquidating book value) becomes inconsequential. The value of equity is therefore the current book value plus the present value of future abnormal earnings.

Valuation Ratios in the Restaurant Industry

Despite a stagnant U.S. economy, the restaurant industry in the period 2000–2002 continued to flourish. The pattern of 12 straight years of real growth was expected to continue in 2003, with real growth of 1.8%, up from 1.3% in 2002.[1] Underlying this growth was consumers' propensity to eat out. The percentage of food dollars spent away from the home had increased from 25% in 1955 to 46% in 2000 and was expected to grow to 53% by 2010.[2] As a result, many different restaurant companies had emerged to cater to the varying consumer demands. These ranged from fast-food restaurants, to casual dining facilities with varied menus, to upscale restaurants with more focused offerings. The following brief descriptions outline the strategies for four restaurant firms (with names concealed).[3] **Exhibit 1** presents key financial ratios for these same firms in the period 1999–2002.[4]

COMPANY A

Company A developed, franchised, and operated casual "bar and grill" restaurants under its own brand. At the end of 2002, there were 1,500 restaurants operating under the company name, 76% owned by franchisees and 24% by the company itself. These were located in 49 U.S. states and eight countries outside the U.S. Between 1993 and 2002, more than 100 new restaurants were opened each year.

The restaurants themselves were designed to appeal to all ages and to reflect the local neighborhood, with décor that included photographs and memorabilia highlighting hometown heroes, local schools, and area history. Each restaurant offered a diverse menu of moderately priced food and beverage items, including beef, chicken, pork, seafood, and pasta items prepared in a variety of cuisines, as well as appetizers, salads, sandwiches, specialty drinks, and desserts. Substantially all the

1. Nicole M. Miller, Sterne, Agee and Leach, Inc., Equity Research Report on the Restaurant Industry, August 25, 2003.

2. Ibid.

3. Business descriptions are taken from the firms' 10-K statements.

4. Financial statement data is taken from the companies' annual reports.

restaurants offered beer, wine, liquor, and premium specialty drinks. At the end of 2002, the average guest check in company restaurants was $10.25.

COMPANY B

Company B owned and operated a chain of primarily midpriced, full-service, casual steakhouse restaurants that were designed to appeal to a broad and diverse demographic and socioeconomic mix of diners aged from 25 to 54. At the end of 2002, it operated 249 restaurants in 39 states in the United States and 20 in Australia. The company added one new restaurant in 1999, one in 2000, 11 in 2001, and none in 2002.

The restaurants were designed to feature a Texas-style concept with Texas artifacts and music. Their "Texas roadhouse" ambience was enhanced by specially selected country western music and neon signs. The decor included planked wooden floors, dim lighting, flags, and other Texas memorabilia. Each restaurant served a limited menu, concentrating on high-quality USDA choice-grade steaks that were mesquite grilled, as well as offering ribs, chicken, and fish. Meals were served in generous "Texas-sized" portions, and full liquor and bar service was available. In 2001, the average check per customer was $17.50 at dinner and $12.50 at lunch.

In addition to its casual steakhouses, Company B owned and operated 20 upscale steakhouses where, in 2001, the average guest check for dinner was $76.

COMPANY C

Company C operated upscale full-service, casual-dining restaurants, primarily under its own name. In early 2003, it owned and operated 64 restaurants in 20 states. Twelve new restaurants were opened in 2002. Management announced that it planned to open 14 new restaurants in 2003 and anticipated that the market could accommodate as many as 200 restaurants.

Its restaurants offered approximately 200 menu items including appetizers, pizza, seafood, steaks, chicken, burgers, pasta, specialty items, salads, sandwiches, omelets, and desserts (including approximately 40 varieties of cheesecake and other baked desserts), as well as providing full liquor service. Substantially all menu items (except desserts manufactured at the company's bakery production facility) were prepared on the restaurant premises using fresh ingredients. The restaurants were recognized by consumers for offering exceptional value with generous food portions at moderate prices. For fiscal 2002, the average guest check was $15.78.

In addition, Company C operated a bakery production facility that produced approximately 40 varieties of cheesecake as well as other baked desserts for the company's restaurants. The bakery operation also produced and sold branded and private-label cheesecakes and other baked products to other leading food-service operators, retailers, and distributors.

COMPANY D

Company D owned and operated food, beverage, and other concessions at airports throughout the United States, often through cobranded arrangements with companies such as Carl's Jr., TCBY frozen yogurt, and Sam Adams Brewery. In early 2003, it operated 142 individual concessions in 28 airports, up from only 16 concessions in 1997. Contracts ranged from concessions to operate single and multiple food and beverage outlets to a master concession to operate all food and beverage, as well as news and gift and merchandise, locations at an airport.

Following its successful November 2000 acquisition of an airport concessions operator with a strong presence in the northeastern United States, Company D's management announced that the firm's strategy would be to consolidate small and medium-sized operators of concessions at airports throughout the country.

QUESTIONS

1. What do you expect to drive a company's price-to-book equity and price-to-earnings multiples?

2. Match the price-to-book equity valuation multiple below with each of the four restaurant businesses discussed above. What is your reasoning for the matches you selected?

Restaurant	Price/Book Value
	4.4
	3.9
	1.0
	1.0

Source: Table created by casewriters.

3. Match the price-to-earnings valuation multiples below with each of the four restaurant businesses discussed above. What is your reasoning for the matches you selected?

Restaurant	Price/Earnings
	34.5
	28.0
	20.0
	9.6

Source: Table created by casewriters.

EXHIBIT I

Financial Comparison for Four Restaurant Firms (beginning balance sheet values are used to compute ratios that use balance sheet items)

Company A

	1999	2000	2001	2002
DECOMPOSING PROFITABILITY: DUPONT ALTERNATIVE				
Net Operating Profit After tax Sales	9.0%	9.9%	9.1%	10.1%
× Sales/Net Assets	1.53	1.93	2.06	2.19
= Operating ROA	13.8%	19.0%	18.9%	22.1%
Spread (Operating ROA – Effective Interest Rate After Tax)	9.5%	14.3%	14.2%	21.3%
× Net Financial Leverage	0.47	0.41	0.28	0.16
= Financial Leverage Gain	4.5%	5.9%	4.0%	3.4%
ROE (Operating ROA + Spread * Net Financial Leverage)	18.3%	24.9%	22.9%	25.5%
EVALUATING OPERATING MANAGEMENT				
Key Growth Rates:				
Annual Sales Growth	3.4%	3.1%	7.8%	11.1%
Annual Net Income Growth	8.4%	16.6%	1.9%	28.9%
Key Profitability Ratios:				
Cost of Sales/Sales	46.5%	46.3%	46.0%	45.5%
Gross Margin	53.5%	53.7%	54.0%	54.5%
Investment Income/Sales	0.0%	0.0%	0.0%	0.0%
SG&A/Sales	37.6%	37.2%	37.9%	38.6%
Other Operating Expense/Sales	1.7%	1.0%	1.0%	0.2%
Other Income, Net of Other Expense/Sales	0.1%	0.1%	−0.6%	0.1%
EBIT Margin	14.2%	15.6%	14.5%	15.8%
Net Interest Expense (Income)/Sales	1.4%	1.1%	0.8%	0.1%
Pretax Income Margin	12.8%	14.5%	13.7%	15.7%
Taxes/Sales	4.7%	5.3%	5.0%	5.7%
Unusual Gains, Net of Unusual Losses (after tax)/Sales	0.0%	0.0%	0.0%	0.0%
Net Income Margin	8.1%	9.2%	8.7%	10.0%
Net Operating Profit After Tax	9.0%	9.9%	9.1%	10.1%
Recurring Net Operating Profit After Tax	9.0%	9.8%	9.5%	10.0%

Company B

	1999	2000	2001	2002
DECOMPOSING PROFITABILITY: DUPONT ALTERNATIVE				
Net Operating Profit After Tax Sales	−0.8%	1.2%	3.6%	6.2%
× Sales/Net Assets	1.24	1.31	1.45	1.57
= Operating ROA	−1.0%	1.6%	5.3%	9.7%
Spread (Operating ROA − Effective Interest Rate After Tax)	−1.0%	0.2%	0.8%	8.7%
× Net Financial Leverage	−0.16	−0.10	−0.07	−0.17
= Financial Leverage Gain	0.2%	0.0%	−0.1%	−1.5%
ROE (Operating ROA + Spread * Net Financial Leverage)	−0.9%	1.6%	5.2%	8.2%
EVALUATING OPERATING MANAGEMENT				
Key Growth Rates:				
Annual Sales Growth	−4.9%	−1.3%	4.1%	3.9%
Annual Net Income Growth[a]	n.m.	n.m.	193.6%	70.7%
Key Profitability Ratios:				
Cost of Sales/Sales	35.5%	35.0%	34.2%	32.8%
Gross Margin	64.5%	65.0%	65.8%	67.2%
Investment Income/Sales	0.0%	0.0%	0.0%	0.0%
SG&A/Sales	54.0%	57.6%	54.8%	53.3%
Other Operating Expense/Sales	11.8%	5.5%	5.2%	4.8%
Other Income, Net of Other Expense/Sales	0.4%	0.2%	0.4%	0.3%
EBIT Margin	−1.0%	2.1%	6.1%	9.5%
Net Interest Expense (Income)/Sales	0.0%	−0.2%	−0.3%	−0.2%
Pretax Income Margin	−1.0%	2.3%	6.4%	9.7%
Taxes/Sales	−0.3%	0.8%	2.2%	3.2%
Unusual Gains, Net of Unusual Losses (after tax)/Sales	−0.1%	−0.2%	−0.3%	−0.1%
Net Income Margin	−0.8%	1.4%	3.9%	6.4%
Net Operating Profit After Tax Margin	−0.8%	1.2%	3.6%	6.2%
Recurring Net Operating Profit After Tax Margin	−1.0%	1.3%	3.7%	6.1%

a. n.m. = not meaningful.

Valuation Ratios in the Restaurant Industry

Company C

	1999	2000	2001	2002
DECOMPOSING PROFITABILITY: DUPONT ALTERNATIVE				
Net Operating Profit After Tax Sales	5.8%	6.6%	6.8%	7.2%
× Sales/Net Assets	2.86	3.14	2.84	2.42
= Operating ROA	16.5%	20.8%	19.2%	17.3%
Spread (Operating ROA − Effective Interest Rate After Tax)	12.0%	14.3%	13.8%	5.0%
× Net Financial Leverage	−0.24	−0.25	−0.21	−0.07
= Financial Leverage Gain	−2.9%	−3.5%	−2.9%	−0.3%
ROE (Operating ROA + Spread * Net Financial Leverage)	13.6%	17.3%	16.3%	17.0%
EVALUATING OPERATING MANAGEMENT				
Key Growth Rates:				
Annual Sales Growth	31.0%	26.1%	23.0%	20.9%
Annual Net Income Growth	183.1%	47.2%	22.1%	25.5%
Key Profitability Ratios:				
Cost of Sales/Sales	27.4%	26.8%	27.1%	25.4%
Gross Margin	72.6%	73.2%	72.9%	74.6%
Investment Income/Sales	0.0%	0.0%	0.0%	0.0%
SG&A/Sales	38.4%	37.7%	37.0%	37.2%
Other Operating Expense/Sales	25.4%	25.0%	25.6%	26.6%
Other Income, Net of Other Expense/Sales	0.2%	−0.1%	0.3%	0.3%
EBIT Margin	9.1%	10.4%	10.6%	11.1%
Net Interest Expense (Income)/Sales	−0.8%	−1.1%	−0.8%	−0.6%
Pretax Income Margin	9.9%	11.5%	11.4%	11.7%
Taxes/Sales	3.6%	4.2%	4.1%	4.2%
Unusual Gains, Net of Unusual Losses (after tax)/Sales	0.0%	0.0%	0.0%	0.0%
Net Income Margin	6.3%	7.3%	7.3%	7.5%
Net Operating Profit After Tax Margin	5.8%	6.6%	6.8%	7.2%
Recurring Net Operating Profit After Tax Margin	5.7%	6.7%	6.6%	6.9%

Company D

	1999	2000	2001	2002
DECOMPOSING PROFITABILITY: DUPONT ALTERNATIVE				
Net Operating Profit After Tax Sales	2.2%	3.4%	3.9%	5.6%
× Sales/Net Assets	1.88	1.99	1.64	1.74
= Operating ROA	4.1%	6.7%	6.4%	9.8%
Spread (Operating ROA − Effective Interest Rate After Tax)	−17.6%	−9.6%	−15.5%	−8.3%
× Net Financial Leverage	0.88	0.86	0.21	0.22
= Financial Leverage Gain	−15.6%	−8.3%	−3.2%	−1.8%
ROE (Operating ROA + Spread * Net Financial Leverage)	−11.5%	−1.6%	3.2%	8.0%
EVALUATING OPERATING MANAGEMENT				
Key Growth Rates:				
Annual Sales Growth	23.8%	30.2%	29.5%	12.7%
Annual Net Income Growth	n.m.	n.m.	n.m.	160.0%
Key Profitability Ratios:				
Cost of Sales/Sales	31.9%	31.2%	28.3%	26.9%
Gross Margin	68.1%	68.8%	71.7%	73.1%
Investment Income/Sales	0.0%	0.0%	0.0%	0.0%
SG&A/Sales	44.5%	44.7%	45.3%	45.7%
Other Operating Expense/Sales	21.4%	20.7%	22.5%	21.7%
Other Income, Net of Other Expense/Sales	0.0%	0.0%	−0.3%	0.3%
EBIT Margin	2.2%	3.4%	3.6%	6.1%
Net Interest Expense (Income)/Sales	5.5%	3.8%	2.3%	2.0%
Pretax Income Margin	−3.3%	−0.4%	1.3%	4.0%
Taxes/Sales	0.0%	0.0%	0.0%	0.3%
Unusual Gains, Net of Unusual Losses (after tax)/Sales	0.0%	0.0%	0.3%	0.0%
Net Income Margin	−3.3%	−0.4%	1.6%	3.8%
Net Operating Profit After Tax Margin	2.2%	3.4%	3.9%	5.6%
Recurring Net Operating Profit After Tax Margin	2.2%	3.4%	3.9%	5.4%

Source: Created by casewriters.

Valuation Ratios in the Restaurant Industry

Chapter 8

Prospective Analysis: Valuation Implementation

To move from the valuation theory discussed in the previous chapter to the actual task of valuing a company, we have to deal with two key issues. First, we have to estimate the cost of capital to discount our forecasts. And second, we have to make forecasts of financial performance stated in terms of abnormal earnings and book values, or free cash flows, over the life of the firm. The forecasting task itself is divided into two subcomponents: (1) detailed forecasts over a finite number of years and (2) a forecast of terminal value, which represents a summary of performance beyond the detailed forecast horizon.

This chapter builds on the forecast developed in Chapter 6 and provides guidance on calculating cost of capital, computing a terminal value, and synthesizing the different pieces of the analytical process to estimate firm or equity value.

COMPUTING A DISCOUNT RATE

To value a company's assets, the analyst discounts abnormal NOPAT, abnormal operating ROA, or cash flows available to both debt and equity holders. The proper discount rate to use is, therefore, the weighted average cost of capital (WACC). The WACC is calculated by weighting the costs of debt and equity capital according to their respective market values:

WACC = Percent debt financing × Cost of debt (after tax) + Percent equity financing × Cost of equity capital

Weighting the Costs of Debt and Equity

The weights assigned to debt and equity represent their respective fractions of total capital provided, measured in terms of economic values. Computing an economic value for debt should not be difficult. It is reasonable to use book values if interest rates have not changed significantly since the time the debt was issued. Otherwise, the value of the debt can be estimated by discounting the future payouts at current market rates of interest applicable to the firm.

What is included in debt? Should short-term as well as long-term debt be included? Should payables and accruals be included? The answer is revealed by recalling that abnormal NOPAT and free cash flows to debt and equity are the earnings and cash flows *before* servicing short-term and long-term debt—indicating that both short-term and long-term debt should be considered a part of capital when computing the WACC. Servicing of other liabilities, such as accounts payable or accruals, should already have been considered as we computed abnormal NOPAT or free cash flows. Thus internal consistency requires that operating liabilities not be considered a part of capital when computing the WACC.

The tricky problem we face is assigning an economic value to equity. That is the very amount we are trying to estimate in the first place! How can the analyst possibly assign an economic value to equity at this intermediate stage, given that the estimate will not be known until all steps in the DCF analysis are completed?

One common approach to the problem is to insert at this point "target" ratios of debt to capital and equity to capital. For example, one might expect that a firm will, over the long run, maintain a capital structure that is 40 percent debt and 60 percent equity. The long-run focus is reasonable because we are discounting cash flows over a long horizon.

Another way around the problem is to start with book value of equity as a weight for purposes of calculating an initial estimate of the WACC, which in turn can be used in the discounting process to generate an initial estimate of the value of equity. That initial estimate can then be used in place of the book value to arrive at a new WACC, and a second estimate of the value of equity can be produced. This process can be repeated until the value used to calculate the WACC and the final estimated value converge. However, the analyst needs to be cautious in using this approach if the firm's economic leverage is likely to change over time.

Estimating the Cost of Debt

The cost of debt is the interest rate on the debt. If the assumed capital structure in future periods is the same as the historical structure, then the current interest rate on debt will be a good proxy for this. However, if the analyst assumes a change in capital structure, then it is important to estimate the expected interest rate given the new level of debt. One approach to this would be to estimate the expected credit rating of the company at the new level of debt and use the appropriate interest rates for that credit category.

It is also worth noting that the cost of debt will change over time if market interest rates are expected to change. This can arise if investors expect inflation to increase or decrease over the forecast horizon. Since we typically discount nominal earnings or cash flows, the cost of debt is a nominal rate, and will change over time to reflect changes in inflation. This can be handled by scaling the cost of debt up or down over time to reflect expected changes in interest rates each year. If interest rates are projected to rise by 3 percent as a result of expected inflation, the cost of debt for the firm we are analyzing should also increase by 3 percent. The yield curve, which shows how investors expect interest rates to change over time can be used to assess whether time-varying interest rates are likely to be important to include in the analysis.

Finally, the cost of debt should be expressed on a net-of-tax basis because it is after-tax cash flows that are being discounted. In most settings the market rate of interest can be converted to a net-of-tax basis by multiplying it by one minus the marginal corporate tax rate.

Estimating the Cost of Equity

Estimating the cost of equity can be difficult, and a full discussion of the topic lies beyond the scope of this chapter. At any rate, even an extended discussion would not supply answers to all the questions that might be raised in this area because the field of finance is in a state of flux over what constitutes an appropriate measure of the cost of equity.

One common approach is to use the capital asset pricing model (CAPM), which expresses the cost of equity as the sum of a required return on riskless assets plus a premium for beta or systematic risk:

Cost of equity = Riskless rate of return + Beta risk × Market risk premium

To estimate the required return on riskless assets, analysts often use the rate on intermediate-term treasury bonds, based on the observation that it is cash flows beyond the short term that are being discounted.[1]

The systematic or beta risk of a stock reflects the sensitivity of its cash flows and earnings (and hence stock price) to economy-wide market movements.[2] A firm whose performance increases or decreases at the same rate as changes in the economy as a whole will have a beta of one. Firms whose performance is highly sensitive to economy-wide changes, such as luxury goods producers, capital goods manufacturers, and construction firms, will have beta risks that exceed one. And firms whose earnings and cash flows are less sensitive to economic changes, such as regulated utilities or supermarkets, will have betas that are lower than one. Financial services firms, such as Standard & Poor's and Value Line, provide estimates of beta for publicly-listed companies that are based on the historical relation between the firm's stock returns and the returns on the market index. These estimates provide a useful way to assess publicly-traded firms' beta risks. For firms that are not publicly-traded, analysts can use betas for publicly-traded firms in the same industries, adjusting for any differences in financial leverage, as an indicator of their likely beta risks.

Finally, the market risk premium is the amount that investors demand as additional return for bearing beta risk. It is the excess of the expected return on the market index over the riskless rate. Over the 1926–2005 period, returns to the Standard and Poor's 500 index have exceeded the rate on intermediate-term treasury bonds by 6.8 percent.[3] As a result, many analysts assume that the market risk premium is around 7 percent. However, others argue that a variety of changes in the U.S. economy make the historical risk premium an invalid basis for forecasting expected risk premium going forward. Recent academic research suggests that the expected risk premium in the market in recent years has declined substantially to between 3 and 4 percent, leading some analysts to use these lower rates in their valuations.[4]

Although the above CAPM is often used to estimate the cost of capital, the evidence indicates that the model is incomplete. Assuming stocks are priced competitively, stock returns should be expected to compensate investors for just the cost of their capital. Thus, long-run average returns should be close to the cost of capital and should (according to the CAPM) vary across stocks according to their systematic risk. However, factors beyond just systematic risk seem to play some role in explaining variation in long-run average returns. The most important such factor is labeled the "size effect": smaller firms (as measured by market capitalization) tend to generate higher returns in subsequent periods. The reason for this size effect is unclear. It could mean either that smaller firms are riskier than indicated by the CAPM or that they are underpriced at the point their market capitalization is measured, or some combination of the two. Average stock returns for U.S. firms (including NYSE, AMEX, and NASDAQ firms) varied across size deciles from 1926 to 2005 as shown in Table 8-1.

The table shows that, historically, investors in firms in the top two deciles of the size distribution have realized returns of only 11.3 and 13.2 percent. In contrast, firms in the smallest two size deciles have realized significantly higher returns, ranging from 17.5 to 21.6 percent. Not surprisingly, however, the volatility of large stocks has been

| TABLE 8-1 | Stock Returns, Volatility, and Firm Size | | | |

Size Decile	Market value of largest company in decile in 2005 ($ millions)	Fraction of total market value represented by decile in 2005 (%)	Average annual stock return, 1926–2005 (%)	Beta, 1926–2005	Size Premium (return in excess of CAPM – %)
1–smallest	265.0	0.8	21.6	1.41	6.4
2	586.4	1.0	17.5	1.34	2.7
3	872.1	1.3	16.6	1.28	2.3
4	1,281.0	1.7	15.6	1.23	1.7
5	1,728.9	2.4	15.3	1.18	1.7
6	2,519.3	3.2	14.9	1.16	1.5
7	3,961.4	4.7	14.3	1.13	1.1
8	7,187.2	7.6	13.8	1.10	0.9
9	16,016.5	14.0	13.2	1.04	0.7
10–largest	367,495.1	63.3	11.3	0.91	−0.4

Source: Ibbotson and Associates, *Stocks, Bonds, Bills, and Inflation* (2006).

significantly lower than that of smaller stocks. Stocks in the largest decile have a beta of less than one compared to 1.41 for the smallest decile. Note, however, that if we use returns based on firm size as an indicator of the cost of capital, we are implicitly assuming that large size is indicative of lower risk. Firms in the smallest decile have earned an average of 6.4 percent above the theoretical CAPM return over time. Yet finance theorists have not developed a well accepted explanation for why that should be the case.

One method for estimating the cost of capital combines the CAPM and the "size effect." The approach calls for adjusting the CAPM-based cost of capital for the difference between the average return on the market index used in the CAPM (the Standard and Poor's 500) and the average return on firms of size comparable to the firm being evaluated. The resulting cost of capital is

$$\text{Cost of equity} = \text{Riskless rate of return} + \text{Beta risk} \times \text{Market risk premium} + \text{Size premium}$$

In light of the continuing debate on how to measure the cost of capital, it is not surprising that managers and analysts often consider a range of estimates. In addition to the question about whether or not the historical risk premium of approximately 7 percent is valid today, there is debate over whether beta is a relevant measure of risk, and whether other metrics such as size should be reflected in cost of capital estimates. Since these debates are still unresolved, it is prudent for analysts to use a range of risk premium estimates in computing a firm's cost of capital.

Adjusting Cost of Equity for Changes in Leverage

The cost of both debt and equity change as a function of a firm's economic leverage. As leverage increases, debt and equity become more risky and therefore more costly. If an analyst is contemplating changing capital structure during the forecasting time period, either relative to the historical capital structure of the firm or over time, it is important to re-estimate the cost of debt and equity to take these changes into account. We describe below a simple approach to this task.

We begin with the observation that the beta of a firm's assets is equal to the weighted average of its debt and equity betas, weighted by the economic values of debt and equity to total economic capital. As noted above, financial services firms report estimates of betas for publicly-traded firms based on the historical relation between their stock returns and returns on the market index. Debt betas can be inferred from the capital asset pricing model if we have information on the current interest rate and risk-free rate. The economic value of debt is typically estimated using the book value of debt whereas the economic value of equity is usually estimated using the firm's market equity capitalization. From these estimated equity and debt betas and the estimated economic capital structure, we can infer the firm's asset beta.

When the firm's economic capital structure changes, its equity and debt betas will change but its asset beta remains the same. We can take advantage of this fact to estimate the expected equity beta for the new capital structure. We first have to get an estimate of the interest rate on debt at the new capital structure level. Once we have this information, we can estimate the implied debt beta using the capital asset pricing model and the risk-free rate. Now we can estimate the equity beta for the new capital structure using the identity that the new equity beta and the new debt beta, weighted by the new economic capital structure weights, have to add up to the asset beta estimated earlier.

Estimating Wal-Mart's Cost of Capital

To estimate the cost of capital for Wal-Mart, we start with the assumption that its pre-tax cost of debt is 5.15 percent, based on the yield on its intermediate-term bonds at the beginning of fiscal 2006 (with an assumed tax rate of 35 percent, this translates into a after-tax cost of debt of 3.3 percent). The company's equity beta was calculated in February 2006 to be 0.90. The ten-year Treasury bond rate at that time was yielding 4.5 percent. Using the historical risk premium for equities of 6.8 percent, we can calculate its cost of equity to be 10.6 percent. Clearly this estimate is only a starting point, and the analyst can change the estimate by changing the assumed market risk premium or by adjusting for the size effect.

Wal-Mart's equity market value in February 2006, after the financial performance of the preceding fiscal year had been announced, was approximately $191 billion and its net book debt was $32.4 billion. Using these numbers we can calculate the "economic value" weights of debt and equity in the company's capital structure as 15 percent and 85 percent, respectively. Based on these weights and the above estimates of costs of equity and debt, our estimate of Wal-Mart's weighted average cost of capital (WACC) in February 2006 is 9.5 percent, as shown in Table 8-2. We keep Wal-Mart's book leverage constant throughout the forecasting period. But this does not necessarily ensure that economic leverage will be constant. Economic leverage will change if book debt grows at a different rate than the economic value of equity. Growth in future book debt is driven by the forecasted growth in Wal-Mart's sales and profitability. These factors are capitalized in Wal-Mart's current economic equity valuation. As a result, estimated future economic equity values for the firm are driven by its cost of capital and dividend

TABLE 8-2	Wal-Mart's Weighted Average Cost of Capital		
	Cost of Funds ×	**Economic Weighting** =	**Weighted Cost**
Debt	3.3%	15.0%	0.5%
Equity	10.6%	85.0%	9.0%
Capital			9.5%

policy. As we will see later in this chapter, if the economic capital structure is not stable, using the current weights to estimate WACC will result in economic asset valuations that do not reconcile with those for debt and equity.

These calculations imply that, as a starting point, we will use a 10.6 percent cost of equity to discount forecasts of abnormal earnings and cash flows available to Wal-Mart's equity holders, and the 9.5 percent WACC to discount forecasts of abnormal NOPAT and cash flows generated for all of its capital contributors (debt and equity).

DETAILED FORECASTS OF PERFORMANCE

The horizon over which detailed forecasts are made is itself a choice variable. We will discuss later in this chapter how the analyst might make this choice. Once it is made, the next step is to consider the set of assumptions regarding a firm's performance that are needed to arrive at the forecasts. We described in Chapter 6 the general framework of financial forecasting and illustrated the approach using Wal-Mart.

The key to sound forecasts is that the underlying assumptions are grounded in a company's business reality. Strategy analysis provides a critical understanding of a company's value proposition, and whether current performance is likely to be sustainable in future. Accounting analysis and ratio analysis provide a deep understanding of a company's current performance, and whether the ratios themselves are reliable indicators of performance. It is, therefore, important to see the valuation forecasts as a continuation of the earlier steps in business analysis rather than as a discrete exercise not connected to the rest of the analysis.

Since valuation involves forecasting over a long time horizon, it is not practical to forecast all the line items in a company's financial statements. Instead, the analyst has to focus on the important elements of a firm's performance. Specifically, we forecasted Wal-Mart's condensed income statement, beginning balance sheet, and free cash flows for a period of ten years starting in fiscal year 2006 (year beginning in February 2006). We will use these same forecasting assumptions and financial forecasts, which are repeated here in Tables 8-3 and 8-4, as a starting point to value Wal-Mart as of February 1, 2006.

TABLE 8-3 Forecasting Assumptions for Wal-Mart

For fiscal year	2006	2007	2008	2009	2010	2011	2012	2013	2014	2015
Sales growth rate	9.3%	9.6%	9.6%	9.5%	9.4%	9.0%	8.6%	8.2%	7.8%	7.7%
NOPAT margin	3.9%	3.8%	3.8%	3.7%	3.7%	3.6%	3.5%	3.4%	3.2%	3.1%
Beginning net operating working capital/sales	−0.8%	0.0%	0.0%	0.0%	0.0%	0.0%	0.0%	0.0%	0.0%	0.0%
Beginning net operating long-term assets/sales	25.8%	25.2%	25.4%	25.6%	25.9%	26.0%	26.0%	26.3%	26.5%	26.8%
Beginning net debt to capital ratio	37.9%	37.9%	37.9%	37.9%	37.9%	37.9%	37.9%	37.9%	37.9%	37.9%
After-tax cost of debt	3.3%	3.3%	3.3%	3.3%	3.3%	3.3%	3.3%	3.3%	3.3%	3.3%

TABLE 8-4   Forecasted Financial Statements for Wal-Mart

For fiscal year	2006	2007	2008	2009	2010	2011	2012	2013	2014	2015
Beginning Balance Sheet										
Beg. net working capital	−2,768	0	0	0	0	0	0	0	0	0
+ Beg. net long-term assets	88,344	94,546	104,527	115,477	127,486	139,917	151,937	166,343	181,019	196,873
= Net operating assets	**85,576**	**94,546**	**104,527**	**115,477**	**127,486**	**139,917**	**151,937**	**166,343**	**181,019**	**196,873**
Net debt	32,405	35,802	39,581	43,728	48,275	52,982	57,534	62,989	68,546	74,550
+ Preferred stock	0	0	0	0	0	0	0	0	0	0
+ Shareholders' equity	53,171	58,744	64,946	71,749	79,211	86,935	94,403	103,354	112,473	122,323
= Net capital	**85,576**	**94,546**	**104,527**	**115,477**	**127,486**	**139,917**	**151,937**	**166,343**	**181,019**	**196,873**
Income Statement										
Sales	342,629	375,435	411,628	450,786	493,126	537,648	584,130	632,291	681,861	734,359
Net operating profits after tax	13,284	14,360	15,531	16,755	18,034	19,288	20,483	21,264	21,958	22,644
− Net interest expense after tax	1,085	1,198	1,325	1,464	1,616	1,774	1,926	2,109	2,295	2,496
= Net income	12,199	13,162	14,206	15,291	16,418	17,515	18,557	19,155	19,664	20,149
− Preferred dividends	0	0	0	0	0	0	0	0	0	0
= Net income to common	**12,199**	**13,162**	**14,206**	**15,291**	**16,418**	**17,515**	**18,557**	**19,155**	**19,664**	**20,149**
Operating return on assets	15.5%	15.2%	14.9%	14.5%	14.1%	13.8%	13.5%	12.8%	12.1%	11.5%
Return on equity	22.9%	22.4%	21.9%	21.3%	20.7%	20.1%	19.7%	18.5%	17.5%	16.5%
Book value of assets growth rate	13.6%	10.5%	10.6%	10.5%	10.4%	9.8%	8.6%	9.5%	8.8%	8.8%
Book value of equity growth rate	7.6%	10.5%	10.6%	10.5%	10.4%	9.8%	8.6%	9.5%	8.8%	8.8%
Net operating asset turnover	4.0	4.0	3.9	3.9	3.9	3.8	3.8	3.8	3.8	3.7
Net income	12,199	13,162	14,206	15,291	16,418	17,515	18,557	19,155	19,664	20,149
− Change in net working capital	(2,768)	-	-	-	-	-	-	-	-	-
− Change in net long-term assets	(6,202)	(9,981)	(10,950)	(12,009)	(12,431)	(12,020)	(14,406)	(14,676)	(15,854)	(15,089)
+ Change in net debt	3,397	3,779	4,147	4,547	4,707	4,552	5,455	5,557	6,004	4,349
= Free cash flow to equity	6,626	6,960	7,403	7,829	8,694	10,047	9,606	10,036	9,814	9,409
Net operating profit after tax	13,284	14,360	15,531	16,755	18,034	19,288	20,483	21,264	21,958	22,644
− Change in net working capital	(2,768)	-	-	-	-	-	-	-	-	-
− Change in net long-term assets	(6,202)	(9,981)	(10,950)	(12,009)	(12,431)	(12,020)	(14,406)	(14,676)	(15,854)	(15,089)
= Free cash flow to capital	4,314	4,379	4,581	4,746	5,603	7,268	6,077	6,588	6,104	5,359

Making Performance Forecasts for Valuing Wal-Mart

As discussed in Chapter 7, the forecasts required to convert the financial forecasts shown above into estimates of value differ depending on whether we wish to value a firm's equity or its assets. To value equity, the essential inputs are

- Abnormal earnings: net income less shareholders' equity at the beginning of the year times cost of equity;
- Abnormal ROE: the difference between ROE and cost of equity; or
- Free cash flows to equity: net income less the increase in operating working capital less the increase in net long-term assets plus the increase in net debt.

Alternatively, to value a company's assets, the significant performance forecasts would be

- Abnormal NOPAT: NOPAT less total net capital at the beginning of the year times the weighted average cost of capital;
- Abnormal operating ROA: the difference between operating ROA and the weighted average cost of capital; or
- Free cash flows to capital: NOPAT less the increase in operating working capital less the increase in net long-term assets.

Table 8-5 shows Wal-Mart's performance forecasts for all six of these financial statement variables for the ten-year period 2006 to 2015.

TABLE 8-5	Performance Forecasts for Wal-Mart									
For fiscal year	2006	2007	2008	2009	2010	2011	2012	2013	2014	2015
Equity Valuation										
Abonormal earnings	6,552	6,923	7,308	7,671	8,006	8,282	8,532	8,179	7,719	7,158
Abnormal ROE	12.3%	11.8%	11.3%	10.7%	10.1%	9.5%	9.0%	7.9%	6.9%	5.9%
Free cash flow to equity	6,626	6,960	7,402	7,830	8,694	10,046	9,606	10,037	9,813	9,409
Asset Valuation										
Abnormal NOPAT	5,122	5,343	5,561	5,741	5,875	5,944	5,992	5,399	4,693	3,868
Abnormal Operating ROA	6.0%	5.7%	5.3%	5.0%	4.6%	4.2%	3.9%	3.2%	2.6%	2.0%
Free cash flow to capital	4,314	4,379	4,580	4,746	5,603	7,269	6,077	6,588	6,105	5,359
Discount factors:										
Equity	0.904	0.817	0.739	0.668	0.604	0.546	0.493	0.446	0.403	0.364
Assets	0.913	0.833	0.761	0.695	0.634	0.579	0.529	0.482	0.440	0.402
Growth factors*:										
Equity	1.00	1.10	1.22	1.35	1.49	1.64	1.78	1.94	2.12	2.30
Assets	1.00	1.10	1.22	1.35	1.49	1.64	1.78	1.94	2.12	2.30

* The growth factor is relevant only for calculating the present value for abnormal ROE and ROA.

As discussed earlier, to derive cash flows in 2015, we need to make assumptions about sales growth rate and balance sheet ratios in 2016. The cash flow forecasts shown in Table 8-5 are based on the simple assumption that the sales growth and beginning balance sheet ratios in 2016 remain the same as in 2015. We discuss the sensitivity of this assumption and the terminal value assumption later in the chapter.

Wal-Mart's projected abnormal ROE declines steadily over the forecast horizon, from 12.3 percent in 2006 to 5.9 percent in 2015. Abnormal Operating ROA also shows a similar trend, in keeping with the expected gradual attrition due to the forces of competition. A somewhat different pattern is shown for abnormal earnings and abnormal NOPAT, which both trend upward for the first six to seven years before declining. This pattern arises because Wal-Mart is able to increase the investment base on which it earns it abnormal profits for a period of time, leading to increasing abnormal earnings and NOPAT. However, after 2012 declining profitability drives even the absolute level of abnormal profits down.

TERMINAL VALUES

Explicit forecasts of the various elements of a firm's performance generally extend for a period of five to ten years. The final year of this forecast period is labeled the *terminal year* (selection of an appropriate terminal year is discussed later in this section). Terminal value is then the present value of either abnormal earnings or free cash flows occurring beyond the terminal year. Since this involves forecasting performance over the remainder of the firm's life, the analyst must adopt some assumption that simplifies the process of forecasting. A key question is whether it is reasonable to assume a continuation of the terminal year performance or whether some other pattern is expected.

Clearly, the continuation of a sales growth that is significantly greater than the average growth rate of the economy is unrealistic over a very long horizon. That rate would likely outstrip inflation in the dollar and the real growth rate of the world economy. Over many years, it would imply that the firm would grow to a size greater than that of all other firms in the world combined. But what would be a suitable alternative assumption? Should we expect the firm's sales growth rate to ultimately settle down to the rate of inflation? Or to a higher rate, such as the nominal GDP growth rate? And perhaps equally important, will a firm that earns abnormal profits continue to do so by maintaining its profit margins on a growing, or even existing, base of sales?

To answer these questions, we must consider how much longer the rate of growth in industry sales can outstrip overall economic growth, and how long a firm's competitive advantages can be sustained. Clearly, looking eleven or more years into the future, any forecast is likely to be subject to considerable error. Below we discuss a variety of alternative approaches to the task of calculating a terminal value.

Terminal Values with the Competitive Equilibrium Assumption

Fortunately, in many if not most situations, how we deal with the seemingly imponderable questions about long-range growth in sales simply *does not matter very much!* In fact, under plausible economic assumptions, there is no practical need to consider sales growth beyond the terminal year. Such growth may be *irrelevant* so far as the firm's current value is concerned.

How can long-range growth in sales *not* matter? The reasoning revolves around the forces of competition. One impact of competition is that it tends to constrain a firm's ability to identify, on a consistent basis, growth opportunities that generate supernormal profits. The other dimension that competition tends to impact is a firm's margins. Ultimately, we would expect high profits to attract enough competition to drive down a firm's margins, and therefore its returns, to a normal level. At this point, the firm will earn its cost of capital, with no abnormal returns or terminal value. (Recall the evidence in Chapter 6 concerning the reversion of ROEs to normal levels over a horizon of five to ten years.)

Certainly a firm may at a point in time maintain a competitive advantage that permits it to achieve returns in excess of the cost of capital. When that advantage is protected with patents or a strong brand name, the firm may even be able to maintain it for many years, perhaps indefinitely. With hindsight, we know that some such firms—Coca-Cola and Wal-Mart, for instance—were able not only to maintain their competitive edge but also to expand it across a dramatically increasing investment base. However, with a few exceptions, it is reasonable to assume that the terminal value of the firm will be zero under the competitive equilibrium assumption, obviating the need to make assumptions about long-term growth rates.

Competitive Equilibrium Assumption Only on Incremental Sales

An alternative version of the competitive equilibrium assumption is to assume that a firm will continue to earn abnormal earnings forever on the sales it had in the terminal year, but there will be no abnormal earnings on any incremental sales beyond that level. If we invoke the competitive equilibrium assumption on incremental sales beyond the terminal year, then it does not matter what sales growth rate we use beyond that year, and we may as well simplify our arithmetic by treating sales *as if* they will be constant at the terminal year level. Then operating ROA, ROE, NOPAT, net income, free cash flow to capital, and free cash flow to equity will all remain constant at the terminal year level.

For example, by treating Wal-Mart as if its competitive advantage can be maintained only on the *nominal* sales level achieved in the year 2015, we will be assuming that in *real* terms its competitive advantage will shrink. Under this scenario, it is simple to estimate the terminal value by dividing the 2015 level of each of the variables by the appropriate discount rate. As one would expect, terminal values in this scenario will be higher than those with no abnormal returns on all sales in years 2016 and beyond. This is entirely due to the fact that we are now assuming that Wal-Mart can retain indefinitely its superior performance on its existing base of sales.

Terminal Value with Persistent Abnormal Performance and Growth

Each of the approaches described above appeals in some way to the competitive equilibrium assumption. However, there are circumstances where the analyst is willing to assume that the firm may defy competitive forces and earn abnormal rates of return on new projects for many years. If the analyst believes supernormal profitability can be extended to larger markets for many years, it can be accommodated within the context of a valuation analysis.

One possibility is to project earnings and cash flows over a longer horizon, i.e., until the competitive equilibrium assumption can reasonably be invoked. In the case of

Wal-Mart, for example, we could assume that the supernormal profitability will continue for five years beyond 2015 (for a total forecasting horizon of 15 years from the beginning of the forecasting period), but after that period the firm's ROE and Operating ROA will be equal to its cost of equity and its weighted average cost of capital, respectively.

Another possibility is to project growth in abnormal earnings or cash flows at some constant rate. For instance, one could expect Wal-Mart to maintain its advantage on a sales base that remains constant in *real* terms, implying that sales grow beyond the year 2015 at the expected long-run U.S. inflation rate of 3.5 percent. Beyond our terminal year, 2015, as the sales growth rate remains constant at 3.5 percent, abnormal earnings, free cash flows, and book values of assets and equity also grow at a constant rate of 3.5 percent. This is simply because we held all other performance ratios constant in this period. As a result, abnormal operating ROA and abnormal ROE remain constant at the same level as in the terminal year.

This approach is more aggressive than the preceding assumptions about terminal value, but it may be more realistic. After all, there is no obvious reason why the *real* size of the investment base on which Wal-Mart earns abnormal returns should depend on inflation rates. The approach, however, still relies to some extent on the competitive equilibrium assumption. The assumption is now invoked to suggest that supernormal profitability can be extended only to an investment base that remains constant in real terms. In rare situations, if the company has established a market dominance that the analyst believes is immune to the threat of competition, the terminal value can be based on both positive real sales growth and abnormal profits. As mentioned earlier, Wal-Mart might be just such a company.

When we assume that the abnormal performance persists at the same level as in the terminal year, projecting abnormal earnings and free cash flows is a simple matter of growing them at the assumed sales growth rate. Since the rate of growth in abnormal earnings and cash flows is constant starting in the year after the terminal year, it is also straightforward to discount those flows. The present value of the flow stream is the flow at the end of the first year divided by the difference between the discount rate and steady-state growth rate, provided that the discount rate exceeds the growth rate. There is nothing about this valuation method that requires reliance on the competitive equilibrium assumption, so it could be used with *any* rate of growth in sales. The question is not whether the arithmetic is available to handle such an approach but rather how realistic it is.

Terminal Value Based on a Price Multiple

A popular approach to terminal value calculation is to apply a multiple to abnormal earnings, cash flows, or book values of the terminal period. The approach is not as ad hoc as it might first appear. Note that under the assumption of no sales growth, abnormal earnings or cash flows beyond the terminal year remain constant. Capitalizing these flows in perpetuity by dividing by the cost of capital is equivalent to multiplying them by the inverse of the cost of capital. For example, in the case of Wal-Mart, capitalizing free cash flows to equity at its cost of equity of 10.6 percent is equivalent to assuming a terminal cash flow multiple of 9.4. Thus, applying a multiple in this range to Wal-Mart is similar to discounting all free cash flows beyond 2015 while invoking the competitive equilibrium assumption on incremental sales.

The mistake to avoid here is to capitalize the future abnormal earnings or cash flows using a multiple that is too high. The earnings or cash flow multiples might be high currently because the market anticipates abnormally profitable growth. However, once that growth is realized, the price–earnings multiple should fall to a normal level. It is that normal price–earnings ratio, applicable to a stable firm or one that can grow only through zero net present value projects, that should be used in the terminal value calculation. Thus, multiples in the range of 7 to 10—close to the reciprocal of cost of equity and WACC—should be used here. Higher multiples are justifiable only when the terminal year is closer and there are still abnormally profitable growth opportunities beyond that point. A similar logic applies to the estimation of terminal values using book value multiples.

Selecting the Terminal Year

A critical question posed by the above discussion is how long to make the detailed forecast horizon. When the competitive equilibrium assumption is used, the answer is whatever time is required for the firm's returns on incremental investment projects to reach that equilibrium—an issue that turns on the sustainability of the firm's competitive advantage. As indicated in Chapter 6, historical evidence indicates that most firms in the U.S. should expect ROEs to revert to normal levels within five to ten years. But for the typical firm, we can justify ending the forecast horizon even earlier as the return on *incremental* investment can be normal even while the return on *total* investment (and therefore ROE) remains abnormal. Thus a five- to ten-year forecast horizon should be more than sufficient for most firms. Exceptions would include firms so well insulated from competition (perhaps due to the power of a brand name) that they can extend their investment base to new markets for many years and still expect to generate supernormal returns.

Estimates of Wal-Mart's Terminal Value

Choosing Terminal Year

In the case of Wal-Mart, the terminal year used is ten years beyond the current one. Table 8-4 shows that the ROE (and operating ROA) is forecasted to decline only gradually over these ten years, from 22.9 percent in 2006 to 16.5 percent by 2015. At this level the company will earn an abnormal return on equity of approximately 5.9 percent, since its cost of equity is estimated to be 10.6 percent.

Based on the foregoing strategic assessment of Wal-Mart, we believe that the firm has created a competitive advantage that should be sustainable in the long term. Consequently, we assume that the firm will have reached a steady state of performance in 2015 and extending the forecast horizon will not lead to further insights into how market dynamics will impact Wal-Mart's performance. The overall projection, therefore, expects that while Wal-Mart's current level of market dominance is not sustainable and that growth will slow and margins will get squeezed, the firm has created a market position that will allow it to make some level of abnormal earnings in the long term that drives its terminal value. Based on this logic, we will fix 2015 as the terminal year for Wal-Mart and attempt to estimate its terminal value at that time.

Terminal Value Under Varying Assumptions

Table 8-6 shows Wal-Mart's terminal value under the various theoretical approaches we discussed above. Scenario 1 of this table shows the terminal value if we assume that Wal-Mart will continue to grow its sales at 7.7 percent beyond fiscal year 2015, and that it will continue to earn the same level of abnormal returns as in 2015 (that is, we assume that all the other forecasting assumptions will be the same as in 2015). This scenario essentially summarizes Wal-Mart performance in perpetuity under the assumption that the firm will continue to make persistent abnormal returns and leads

TABLE 8-6		Terminal Values for Wal-Mart Under Various Assumptions (Using Abnormal Earnings Methodology)			
Scenario Number	Approach	Scenario	Terminal Sales Growth	Terminal NOPAT Margins	Value Beyond Forecast Horizon (Terminal Value)
1	Persistent Abnormal Performance	Sales growth and margins based on detailed analysis and forecast	7.7%	3.0%	87,108
2	Abnormal Returns on Constant Sales (Real Terms)	Sales grow at the rate of inflation, margins maintained	3.5%	3.0%	34,113
3	Abnormal Returns on Constant Sales (Nominal Terms)	Essentially zero sales growth, margins maintained	0.0%	3.0%	22,097
4	Competitive Equilibrium	Margins reduced so no abnormal earnings	7.7%	2.1%	0

to a terminal value of $87.1 billion. Scenario 2 assumes that Wal-Mart is able to maintain its abnormal returns only on a base of sales that is constant in real terms. Scenario 2 calculates the terminal value assuming that Wal-Mart will maintain its margins only on sales that grow at the long-run expected rate of inflation, assumed to be 3.5 percent, dropping the terminal value down to $34.1 billion. Scenario 3 shows the terminal value if we assume that the company's competitive advantage can be maintained only on the nominal sales level achieved in 2015. As a result, sales growth beyond the terminal year is assumed to be zero, which is equivalent to assuming that incremental sales do not produce any abnormal returns. The terminal value under this scenario drops to $22.1 billion. The final scenario invokes the competitive equilibrium assumption, i.e., margins will be eroded such that the firm will have no abnormal returns irrespective of the rate of sales growth, leading to no terminal value. For the sake of illustration, the expected sales growth of 7.7 percent is maintained. To portray the competitive equilibrium, margins are lowered to eliminate any competitive advantage that Wal-Mart will have.

COMPUTING ASSET AND EQUITY VALUES

Table 8-7 shows the estimated value of Wal-Mart's assets and equity, each using the three different methods discussed in Chapter 7. The value of assets is estimated using abnormal operating ROA, abnormal NOPAT, and free cash flows to debt and equity. The value of equity is estimated using operating ROE, abnormal NOPAT, and free cash flow to equity. These values are computed using the financial forecasts in Table 8-5 and the terminal value forecast using the persistent abnormal performance scenario.

In Table 8-7, present values of abnormal NOPAT and free cash flow to capital are computed using a WACC of 9.5 percent, and present values of abnormal earnings and free cash flow to equity are computed using a cost of equity of 10.6 percent. To calculate the present values of abnormal operating ROA and abnormal ROE, the

TABLE 8-7	Valuation Summary for Wal-Mart Using Various Methodologies

	Beginning Book Value	Value from Forecast Period 2006 to 2015	Value Beyond Forecast Horizon (Terminal Value)	Total Value	Value Per Share ($)
Equity Value					
Abnormal earnings	53,171	45,035	87,108	185,314	44.49
Abnormal ROE	53,171	45,035	87,108	185,314	44.49
Free cash flows to equity	N/A	49,708	135,606	185,314	44.49
Asset Value					
Abnormal NOPAT	85,576	33,910	74,179	193,665	N/A
Abnormal ROA	85,576	33,910	74,179	193,665	N/A
Free cash flow to capital	N/A	33,365	160,299	193,665	N/A

values for each year are first multiplied by the corresponding growth factor, as shown in the formulae in Chapter 7, and then they are discounted using the WACC and cost of equity, respectively. Under the assumptions and forecast we have made, Wal-Mart's estimated value per share is $44.49 and the total firm value is $193.7 billion.

Value estimates show that the abnormal returns method, abnormal earnings method, and the free cash flow method result in the same value, as claimed in Chapter 7. Note also that Wal-Mart's terminal value represents a significantly larger fraction of the total value of assets and equity under the free cash flow method relative to the other methods. As discussed, this is due to the fact that the abnormal returns and earnings methods rely on a company's book value of assets and equity, so the terminal value estimates are estimates of incremental values over book values. In contrast, the free cash flow approach ignores the book values, so the terminal value forecasts are estimates of total value during this period.

The primary calculations in the above estimates treat all flows as if they arrive at the end of the year. Of course, they are likely to arrive throughout the year. If we assume for the sake of simplicity that cash flows will arrive mid-year, then we should adjust adjust our value estimates upward by the amount $\left[1 + \left(\frac{r}{2}\right)\right]$, where r is the discount rate.

Finally, it is worth noting that the asset valuation ($193,665) and the equity valuation ($185,314) imply that the value of debt should be $8,315, which differs from the actual value of $32,405. This arises because Wal-Mart's economic leverage increases over the forecast horizon. The estimated WACC used to compute asset valuations is based on the beginning economic leverage and therefore does not correctly capture these changes. Given the difficulties of forecasting these subtle changes in economic leverage, we recommend valuing equity directly using abnormal earnings, abnormal ROEs, or equity free cash flows.

Value Estimates Versus Market Values

As the discussion above shows, valuation involves a substantial number of assumptions by analysts. Therefore, the estimates of value will vary from one analyst to the other. The only way to ensure that one's estimates are reliable is to make sure that the assumptions are grounded in the economics of the business being valued. It is also useful to check the assumptions against the time-series trends for performance ratios discussed in Chapter 6. While it is legitimate to make assumptions that differ markedly from these trends in any given case, it is important for the analyst to be able to articulate the business and strategy reasons for making such assumptions.

When a company being valued is publicly traded, it is possible to compare one's own estimated value with the market value of a company. When an estimated value differs substantially from a company's market value, it is useful for the analyst to understand why such differences arise. A way to do this is to redo the valuation exercise and figure out what valuation assumptions are needed to arrive at the observed stock price. One can then examine whether the market's assumptions are more or less valid relative to one's own assumptions. As we discuss in the next chapter, such an analysis can be invaluable in using valuation to make buy or sell decisions in the security analysis context.

In the case of Wal-Mart, our estimated value of the firm's equity is almost identical to the observed value at the end of February 2006, when the market had assimilated the announced results for the quarter and fiscal year ended January 31, 2006.

Sensitivity Analysis

Recall that in Chapter 6, we developed what we believed to be a reasonable assessment of Wal-Mart's expected future performance. The resulting valuation seems to be in line with the market's expectations, as the imputed value per share closely approximated the traded value per share at the time. However, we acknowledged that the company's future could play out in multiple ways and proposed two alternative scenarios. As shown in Table 8-8, if Wal-Mart is able to maintain higher growth rates and better NOPAT margins in its domestic business, its value per share would be $55.80. If, on the other hand, its international business fails to deliver the expected returns in conjunction with increased domestic competition, its stock would be worth only $38.10 per share. The changes in stock value in these scenarios are driven primarily by changes in sales growth and margins, performance measures that are most strongly affected by the forces of competition.

TABLE 8-8	Equity Valuation Under Various Scenarios Using Abnormal Earnings				
Scenario	**Beginning Book Value**	**Value from Forecast Period 2006 to 2015**	**Value Beyond Forecast Horizon (Terminal Value)**	**Total Value**	**Value Per Share ($)**
U.S. Market Slowdown Balanced by International Growth	53,171	45,035	87,108	185,314	44.49
Maintain U.S. Market Growth, Supplement with International Growth	53,171	47,408	131,809	232,389	55.80
Strong Competition on Both Domestic and International Fronts	53,171	43,748	61,788	158,707	38.10

SOME PRACTICAL ISSUES IN VALUATION

The above discussion provides a blueprint for doing valuation. In practice, the analyst has to deal with a number of other issues that have an important effect on the valuation task. We discuss below three frequently encountered complications—accounting distortions, negative book values, and excess cash.

Dealing with Accounting Distortions

We know from the discussion in Chapter 7 that accounting methods per se should have no influence on firm value, despite the fact that abnormal returns and earnings valuation approaches used here are based on numbers that vary with accounting method choices.

Since accounting choices must affect both earnings *and* book value, and because of the self-correcting nature of double-entry bookkeeping (all "distortions" of accounting must ultimately reverse), estimated values will not be affected by accounting choices *as long as the analyst recognizes the accounting distortions.*[5]

If accounting reliability is a concern, the analyst has to expend resources on accounting adjustments. When a company uses "biased" accounting—either conservative or aggressive—the analyst needs to recognize the bias to ensure that value estimates are not biased. If a thorough analysis is not performed, a firm's accounting choices can influence analysts' perceptions of the real performance of the firm and hence the forecasts of future performance. Accounting choice would affect expectations of future earnings and cash flows, and distort the valuation, regardless of whether the valuation is based on DCF or discounted abnormal earnings. For example, if a firm overstates current revenue growth through aggressive revenue recognition, failure to appreciate the effect is likely to lead the analyst to overstate future revenues, affecting both earnings and cash flow forecasts.

An analyst who encounters biased accounting has two choices—either to adjust current earnings and book values to eliminate managers' accounting biases, or to recognize these biases and adjust future forecasts accordingly. Whereas both approaches lead to the same estimated firm value, the choice will have an important impact on what fraction of the firm's value is captured within the forecast horizon, and what remains in the terminal value. Holding forecasting horizon and future growth opportunities constant, higher accounting quality allows a higher fraction of a firm's value to be captured by the current book value and the abnormal earnings within the forecasting horizon.

Dealing with Negative Book Values

A number of firms have negative earnings and/or negative values of book equity. Firms in the start-up phase have negative equity. These firms incur large investments whose payoff is uncertain. Accountants write off these investments as a matter of conservatism, leading to negative book equity. Examples of firms in this situation include biotechnology firms, Internet firms, telecommunication firms, and other high technology firms. A second category of firms with negative book equity are those that are performing poorly, resulting in cumulative losses exceeding the original investment by the shareholders.

Negative book equity makes it difficult to use the accounting-based approach to value a firm's equity. There are several possible ways to get around this problem. The first approach is to value the firm's assets (using, for example, abnormal operating ROA or abnormal NOPAT) rather than equity. Then, based on an estimate of the value of the firm's debt, one can estimate the equity value. Another alternative is to "undo" accountants' conservatism by capitalizing the investment expenditures written off. This is possible if the analyst is able to establish that these expenditures are value creating. A third alternative, feasible for publicly-traded firms, is to start from the observed stock price and work backwards. Using reasonable estimates of cost of equity and steady-state growth rate, the analyst can calculate the average long-term level of abnormal earnings needed to justify the observed stock price. Then the analytical task can be framed in terms of examining the feasibility of achieving this abnormal earnings "target."

It is important to note that the value of firms with negative book equity often consists of a significant option value. For example, the value of high-tech firms is driven not only by the expected earnings from their current technologies but also the payoff from technology options embedded in their research and development efforts. Similarly, the value of troubled companies is driven to some extent by the "abandonment option"—shareholders with limited liability can put the firm to debt holders and creditors. One can use the options theory framework to estimate the value of these "real options."

Dealing with Excess Cash and Excess Cash Flows

Firms with excess cash balances, or large free cash flows, also pose a valuation challenge. In our projections in Table 8-4, we implicitly assumed that cash beyond the level required to finance a company's operations will be paid out to the firm's shareholders. Excess cash flows are assumed to be paid out to shareholders either in the form of dividends or stock repurchases. Notice that these cash flows are already incorporated into the valuation process when they are earned, so there is no need to take them into account when they are paid out.

It is important to recognize that both the accounting-based valuation and the discounted cash flow valuation assume a dividend payout that can potentially vary from period to period. This dividend policy assumption is required as long as one wishes to assume a constant level of financial leverage, a constant cost of equity, and a constant level of weighted average cost of capital used in the valuation calculations. Firms rarely have such a variable dividend policy in practice. However, this in itself does not make the valuation approaches invalid, as long as a firm's dividend policy does not affect its value. That is, the valuation approaches assume that the well known Modigliani-Miller theorem regarding the irrelevance of dividends holds.

A firm's dividend policy can affect its value if managers do not invest free cash flows optimally. For example, if a firm's managers are likely to use excess cash to undertake value-destroying acquisitions, then our approach overestimates the firm's value. If the analyst has these types of concerns about a firm, one approach is to first estimate the firm according to the approach described earlier and then adjust the estimated value for whatever agency costs the firm's managers may impose on its investors. One way to evaluate whether or not a firm suffers from severe agency costs is to examine the effectiveness of its corporate governance processes.

SUMMARY

We illustrate in this chapter how to apply the valuation theory discussed in Chapter 7. The chapter explains the set of business and financial assumptions needed to complete the valuation exercise. We first discuss how to compute cost of equity and the weighted average cost of capital. We then build on the detailed forecasts developed in Chapter 6 and illustrate the mechanics of estimating terminal values of earnings, free cash flows, and accounting rates of return. Using a detailed example, we show how a firm's equity values and asset values can be computed using earnings, cash flows, and rates of return. The sensitivity of equity and firm value to the assumptions, both during the forecast horizon and for the terminal value, are highlighted. Finally, we offer ways to deal with some commonly encountered practical issues, including accounting distortions, negative book values, and excess cash balances.

DISCUSSION QUESTIONS

1. How would the forecasts in Table 8-4 change if Wal-Mart were to maintain a sales growth rate of 10 percent per year from 2006 to 2016 (and all the other assumptions are kept unchanged)?

2. Recalculate the forecasts in Table 8-4 assuming that the NOPAT profit margin is held steady for the first five years of the forecast and then declines by 0.1 percentage points per year thereafter (keeping all the other assumptions unchanged).

3. Recalculate the forecasts in Tables 8-4 and 8-5 assuming that the ratio of net operating working capital to sales is 3 percent, and the ratio of net long-term assets to sales is 30 percent for all the years from fiscal 2006 to fiscal 2015. Keep all the other assumptions unchanged.

4. Calculate Wal-Mart's cash payouts to its shareholders in the years 2006–2015 that are implicitly assumed in the projections in Table 8-4.

5. How would the abnormal earnings calculations in Table 8-5 change if the cost of equity assumption is changed to 12 percent?

6. How would the terminal values in Table 8-6 change if the sales growth in years 2016 and beyond is 10 percent, and the company keeps forever its abnormal returns at the same level as in fiscal 2015 (keeping all the other assumptions in the table unchanged)?

7. Calculate the proportion of terminal values to total estimated values of equity under the abnormal earnings method and the discounted cash flow method for the results shown in Table 8-7. Why are these proportions different?

8. What will Wal-Mart's cost of equity be if the equity market risk premium is 5 percent?

9. Assume that Wal-Mart changes its capital structure so that its market value weight of debt to capital increases to 20 percent, and its after-tax interest rate on debt at this new leverage level is 4 percent. Assume that the equity market risk premium is 7 percent. What will be the cost of equity at the new debt level? What will be the weighted average cost of capital?

10. Nancy Smith says she is uncomfortable making the assumption that Wal-Mart's dividend payout will vary from year to year. If she makes a constant dividend payout assumption, what changes does she have to make in her other valuation assumptions to make them internally consistent with each other?

NOTES

1. See T. Copeland, T. Koller, and J. Murrin, *Valuation: Measuring and Managing the Value of Companies,* 2nd edition (New York: John Wiley & Sons, 1994). Theory calls for the use of a short-term rate, but if that rate is used here, a difficult practical question rises: How does one reflect the premium required for expected inflation over long horizons? While the premium could, in principle, be treated as a portion of the term $[E(r_m) - r_f]$, it is probably easier to use an intermediate- or long-term riskless rate that presumably reflects expected inflation.

2. One way to estimate systematic risk is to regress the firm's stock returns over some recent time period against the returns on the market index. The slope coefficient represents an estimate of β. More fundamentally, systematic risk depends on how sensitive the firm's operating profits are to shifts in economy-wide activity and the firm's degree of leverage. Financial analysis that assesses these operating and financial risks should be useful in arriving at reasonable estimates of β. See W. Beaver, P. Kettler, and M. Scholes, "The Association Between Market Determined and Accounting Determined Risk Measures," *The Accounting Review,* Vol. XLV, No. 4 (1970), who develop a model for estimating beta using financial statement data.

3. The average return reported here is the arithmetic mean as opposed to the geometric mean. Ibbotson and Associates explain why this estimate is appropriate in this context (see *Stocks, Bonds, Bills, and Inflation,* 2006 Yearbook, Chicago).

4. See W. Gebhardt, C. Lee, and B. Swaminathan, "Toward an Implied Cost of Capital," *Journal of Accounting Research* 39, no. 1 (2001): 135–176, and J. Claus and J. Thomas, "The Equity Premium Is Much Lower Than You Think It Is: Empirical Estimates from a New Approach," *Journal of Finance* 56 (2001): 1629–1666.

5. Valuation based on discounted abnormal earnings does require one property of the forecasts: that they be consistent with "clean surplus accounting." Such accounting requires the following relation:

   End-of-period book value = Beginning book value · earnings − dividends ± capital contributions/withdrawals

   Clean surplus accounting rules out situations where some gain or loss is excluded from earnings but is still used to adjust the book value of equity. For example, under U.S. GAAP, gains and losses on foreign currency translations are handled this way. In applying the valuation technique described here, the analyst would need to deviate from GAAP in producing forecasts and treat such gains/losses as a part of earnings. However, the technique does *not* require that clean surplus accounting has been applied *in the past*—so the existing book value, based on U.S. GAAP or any other set of principles, can still serve as the starting point. All the analyst needs to do is apply clean surplus accounting in his/her forecasts. That is not only easy but also usually the natural thing to do anyway.

Home Depot, Inc. in the New Millennium

On October 12, 2000, Home Depot, the largest and fastest growing Do-It-Yourself (DIY) home improvement and building supply retailer, and the third-largest retailer of any sort in the United States, shocked many investors by announcing that earnings in the third and fourth quarters of 2000 would be a good deal lower than expected. In response, the company's stock price experienced its largest one-day drop, falling 28% (to $35), which erased $33 billion from its market value.

Arthur Blank, Home Depot's CEO, said that the earnings shortfall was primarily the result of a slowing economy. In fact, retail stocks generally had been down all year, and when Home Depot made its announcement, other retail stocks fell as well. To many analysts, however, Home Depot had competencies that very few other retailers had. It was one of the most successful retailers in American history. From the fall of 1981, when the company went public, to the end of 1999, its stock had risen at a compound annual rate of 52%. During the decade of the 1990s, its diluted earnings per share had risen at a compound annual rate of 29%. On October 12, however, the company said that it expected earnings for the third quarter (ending at the end of October) to be only $.28 per share, compared with $.25 in the third quarter of 1999. For the fourth quarter (ending in January), it expected earnings to be $.26 or $.25, compared with $.25 in the fourth quarter of the previous year. For the full year, it expected earnings to be $1.16 or $1.17, compared with $1.00 in 1999.

The U.S. economy had experienced uninterrupted growth since 1992. Between June 1999 and May 2000, however, the Federal Reserve had raised interest rates six times—or a total of 1.75 percentage points—in an effort to slow the economy, and economists had been noticing some softening of overall consumer demand.

Because of the nature of Home Depot's business, many observers regarded it as, if not recession proof, fairly protected from the vicissitudes of the economy. It was primarily involved in selling materials that ordinary people used for home improvement projects. The company was undertaking several significant growth initiatives, and it wasn't clear whether the decline in the company's stock price was primarily a function of a slowing economy, a reaction to an overvaluation of the stock, or a reflection of possible problems with the company's strategy for the future. Despite

Research Associates Jeremy Cott and Jonathan Barnett prepared this case under the supervision of Professor Krishna Palepu. HBS cases are developed solely as the basis for class discussion. Cases are not intended to serve as endorsements, sources of primary data, or illustrations of effective or ineffective management.

a fourth quarter that was deemed to be the most challenging in the company's history, during which earnings declined 20% compared to the prior year's quarter, by the time Home Depot released financial results for the current fiscal year (fiscal 2000, ended January 31, 2001), the company's stock price had rebounded to $48. **Exhibit 1** provides a graph of Home Depot's stock price from January 1, 2000 through January 31, 2001. **Exhibit 2** compares changes in Home Depot's stock to those of the S&P 500 and the S&P Retail Stores index (a composite of 35 retail stocks) during the same period.

HISTORY

Bernard Marcus and Arthur Blank founded Home Depot in 1978 in Atlanta, Georgia. They had been managing a chain of Handy Dan home improvement stores but thought that if they had to compete against a no-frills warehouse, they would be in trouble. So they started such a company themselves.

The company they founded revolutionized the do-it-yourself home improvement market in the United States. They opened stores that contained a huge assortment of building materials and home improvement products and targeted as customers both individual homeowners and small contractors. The stores *were* the warehouses, and they sold large volumes of goods at low prices. The really distinctive feature of Home Depot, however, was that it also provided knowledgeable customer service. Many salespeople had themselves worked in the building trades, and in any case they were all required to attend product knowledge training classes. Thus in 1988, *Fortune* magazine viewed Home Depot as "the only company that has successfully brought off the union of low prices and high service."[1] The company was thus able to make home improvement projects both less expensive and more understandable for many people.

Competitive Advantages

Not only did Home Depot introduce the "Big-Box" method of hardware merchandising, but the firm's successful strategic union of low price, high assortment, high service, and a quality guarantee, drew scores of customers from smaller hardware stores and home centers, leaving many competitors with no option but to go out of business. In the face of mounting pressure from the Big-Box model, remaining industry participants sought to adopt a similar format, yet Home Depot's rapid proliferation and operational efficiency was overwhelming, triggering industry-wide consolidation.

As Home Depot grew in size, it garnered significant buying power over its suppliers. For example, Home Depot gained concessions in pricing, exclusive merchandise, and other benefits that were not available to smaller chains, and which contributed further to the retrenchment or dissolution of other home center competitors. The company earned a reputation for pressuring its suppliers who, lured by the opportunity to secure a purchase order commitment from the giant retailer, often went the extra yard to secure the relationship.

Home Depot's low-price, high-service strategy put continuous pressure on management to minimize operating expenses. While management minimized the cost of goods sold through aggressive negotiations with suppliers, the firm's geographic clustering strategy (also referred to as a market saturation strategy) allowed the firm

---

1. Bill Saporito, "The Fix Is In at Home Depot," *Fortune, February 29, 1988.*

Home Depot, Inc. in the New Millennium

to realize economies of scale in logistics, supply chain management, and advertising. Focused primarily on large metropolitan areas, the store clustering strategy simultaneously prevented smaller would-be competitors from securing premium sites and realizing similar gains in operating efficiency. While other home improvement retailers struggled to identify alternative sources of cost savings in order to compete, economies of scale in Home Depot's aggressive advertising, in turn, further entrenched the firm's positioning in the minds' of consumers.

In addition to the competitive advantages associated with its bargaining power and its store location strategy, Home Depot was also proactive in identifying and implementing best-practices that aided the bottom line. For example, the company has consistently stayed at the forefront of information systems technology. As early as 1990, all stores were connected via a proprietary satellite data communications network that provided for a fast and accurate exchange of information, and which expedited the firm's ability to respond to market changes. A more recent example is Home Depot's Service Performance Improvement (SPI) program introduced in 2000. SPI is a series of programs designed to shift most of the handling of inventory to hours after the store is closed. As a result, the store is easier for customers to shop, products are more readily available, and Home Depot employees can focus all of their time on serving customers. Thus, SPI simultaneously increased sales productivity and customer satisfaction. In fiscal 2000, SPI milestones included a 28% increase in nighttime freight team productivity, and a 98% decrease in pallets left on the floor, creating a better shopping environment for customers.[2] As evidence of its commitment to rollout best practices as quickly as possible, Home Depot planned to implement the program in every store by year-end 2001.[3]

Home Depot's high-service offering was well received by customers and became an added source of competitive advantage. Met with a knowledgeable sales staff that included professional plumbers, electricians, carpenters, painters, and other experienced home improvement tradespeople, Home Depot customers who sought out advice at the start of a project often placed follow-up calls to that same advisor, as the store's policy encouraged, and were apt to make follow-on purchases from the same store. Home Depot's experience showed that high levels of customer satisfaction readily translated into high levels of customer loyalty, making it difficult for competitors to attract Home Depot's customers.

Financial and Operating Performance

Over the years the company's financial and operating performance had been extraordinary. **Exhibit 3** shows its return on book equity, and the decomposition of that return on equity, from 1986 through 2000. **Exhibit 4** shows various measures of operating performance over the same period.

The company's stock price had risen dramatically over the years. There were, however, significant variations in stock returns from year to year. **Exhibit 5** shows annual changes in returns on the company's stock for the past decade, along with comparable data for the S&P 500. It also shows annual figures for earnings per share figures and the number of common shares outstanding. Finally, **Exhibit 6** provides detailed income statements, balance sheets, and cash flow statements for the past few years. As of the end of 1999 the company was by far the largest home improvement retailer in the country. (The second-largest, Lowe's, was about half Home Depot's

---

2. Dabrowski, Ann F., Home Depot, Lehman Brothers Global Equity Research report, February 20, 2001.

3. Home Depot 2000 Annual Report, Letter to Shareholders, February 19, 2001.

size.) It operated 930 stores, almost all of them in the United States and Canada. The company was planning on 21%–22% annual growth in stores over the next several years, so that the number of stores by the end of 2003 would total over 1,900.

Macroeconomic Factors

During the period in which Home Depot had existed, the home improvement industry in the United States had grown at an annual rate of about 6%, or slightly slower than the U.S. economy as a whole. In 1998, however, it grew about 10.4% and in 1999 about 7.3%—which exceeded the economy as a whole. In June 2000, with the expectation of some slowing in the economy, the Home Improvement Research Institute projected average nominal growth in the industry of about 4.5% a year over the next several years (see **Exhibit** 7).

The home improvement industry was generally thought to have benefited in recent years from low interest rates, strong housing turnover, rising home ownership, and increases in discretionary income. During the recession of 1990–1991 Home Depot experienced only a small decline in same-store sales, but at that point it occupied a far smaller share of the market. In 1995 macroeconomic factors evidently had a greater impact. Between February 1994 and January 1995, 30-year mortgage interest rates increased from 7.15% to 9.15% (a 20% increase). By contrast, in full-year 1990, 1991, 1992, 1993, 1996, 1997, and 1998, they declined. In October 1998, they reached a 31-year low of 6.5%. In May 2000, however, they had climbed up to 8.6%, before falling a bit below 8% in the fall.

Management Changes

Over the years, Bernard Marcus and Arthur Blank had generally worked closely together. To some people they seemed, in terms of the decisions they made, almost interchangeable. In 1997, however, Blank succeeded Marcus as CEO of the company, with Marcus remaining as chairman. (Marcus was 68 years old in 1997; Blank was 13 years younger.) Blank commented in 1999: "My role is certainly very different than Bernie's was in the earlier days of our company. Back then, we were just trying to open the stores. Now the role is much more complex because we're thinking about how to drive deeper into the industry and how to serve customers differently in other segments of the industry."[4]

Fiscal 2000 witnessed yet another management succession. In a somewhat rare move in the retailing industry, Home Depot went outside the business in recruiting Robert Nardelli to succeed Arthur Blank as President and CEO. Nardelli was formerly the President and CEO of GE Power Systems, a division of General Electric. Blank, in turn, joined Marcus as Co-Chairman of the Board.

STYLE OF OPERATING

The company never seemed to regard the way it operated as settled. It spoke fairly often of "reexamining" or "reviewing" certain procedures and practices, and "testing" or "experimenting" with new ones. It would typically try out new products or procedures in a small number of stores, and only after it saw the results there would it extend them to many more stores.

Decision-making regarding the location of new stores also had a distinctive character. Stores existed in almost all states in the United States, as well as in all

---

4. Patti Bond, "Executive Pushes New Concepts," Cox News Service, August 9, 1999.

Canadian provinces. Some of the new stores the company opened were in new markets for the company (new regions or metropolitan areas). However, in recent years about two-thirds of new stores were opened in existing markets. Company management had specific reasons for this:

> *In existing markets, we believe a number of Home Depot stores are operating at or above their optimum capacity. To increase customer service levels and enhance long-term market penetration, we often open new stores near the edge of the market areas served by existing stores. While these openings may initially have a negative impact on comparable store-for-store sales, we believe this "cannibalization" strategy increases customer satisfaction and overall market share by reducing delays in shopping, increasing utilization by existing customers and attracting new customers to more convenient locations.[5]*

The company had for years offered special services in its stores closely related to the products it sold. For example, there were brief courses—"how-to clinics"—to help customers in carrying out projects (e.g., installing tile, organizing closets). There were also longer, four-week courses that were part of what the company called Home Depot University. (About 50,000 customers took these longer courses in 1999.) Through a closely related operation, customers could also rent trucks on an hourly basis if they had bulky purchases that they needed to transport. The company also offered proprietary credit cards, which accounted for 17% of all sales. (During 1999 it also began testing a program that would allow customers to apply for unsecured loans to make large purchases in its stores.)

COMPETITION

Among home improvement retailers that sold primarily to do-it-yourself customers, Home Depot's principal competitor was Lowe's, which had annual sales of $18.8 billion. Lowe's operated 650 stores at the end of 2000 and planned to add 115–120 new stores in 2001.[6] Lowe's began in 1946 with small stores in rural towns. In the mid-1990s, however, it began to copy Home Depot's model, opening huge, warehouse-type stores in metropolitan markets, complete with how-to clinics for its customers. Lowe's sold some product lines that Home Depot didn't and also tried to appeal more to women shoppers, with wider aisles and brighter lighting than Home Depot. In certain markets Lowe's and Home Depot went head to head with each other. Some of their stores were virtually within eyesight of each other. (**Exhibit 8** shows summary data for Lowe's for 1997–2000.)

The next largest competitors—Menards and HomeBase—were far smaller, but they were geographically more focused. Menards, which had annual sales of about $4 billion, operated solely in several midwestern states and was said to have a loyal customer base. In the greater Milwaukee area, for instance, Menards' share of the home improvement market in 1998 was 35%; Home Depot's was 15%. HomeBase, which had annual sales of about $1.5 billion, operated solely in several western states. Its stores were as large as Home Depot's—averaging over 100,000 square feet—and 50 of them were located in California (where Home Depot had 122 sites).

---

5. *1999 10-K.*

6. *Lowe's Companies 2000 Annual Report*

When Home Depot began growing in the 1980s its most important competitor was Hechinger, which was considered "the premium home-improvement chain by which Wall Street measured every other chain."[7] Hechinger had historically operated a chain of upscale community hardware and building-supply stores that were known for very good customer service, but when it tried to follow Home Depot into the "big box" warehouse format, it lost out in market after market. In 1999, after years of declining performance, it went out of business. A customer visiting one of its stores during the waning days of the company said: "It's obvious they don't put anything into employee training. There are good people there who are just not prepared. If I needed anything serious I'd go to Home Depot."[8]

REDEFINITION OF THE MARKET

Home Depot reports noted that the company's name was "synonymous" with home improvement. Total home improvement product sales in the United States totaled $159 billion in 1999. That would make Home Depot's market share close to 24%.

In 1997, however, the company engaged in what it called a "redefinition" of its industry. Most of its sales came from do-it-yourself customers. Product sales for that market, it said, totaled about $100 billion in the United States in 1997. However, product sales to professional customers (e.g., contractors, electricians, plumbers, landscapers, property maintenance managers) represented an even larger market. It totaled approximately $265 billion in the United States in 1997. Excluding the "heavy industrial" sector, which the company said it didn't serve, the professional market totaled about $215 billion. Of that market, the company said, its share was less than 4%.

Thereafter the company would refer to its relevant market as something a lot broader than the market with which it had historically been associated—residential home repair and remodeling by do-it-yourself customers. It now said its market consisted of "all sales of home improvement and other housing and building-related products for new and existing homes." And it said that it was developing long-term strategies with this view of the market in mind.[9]

At the end of 1998 the company said its total market was $365 billion. This included the "heavy industrial" sector. At the end of 1999 it said that, although it couldn't measure its market share precisely, it estimated it was about 8.9%. It also said that it expected to increase its North American market share to 18% by the end of 2003.[10]

GROWTH INITIATIVES

The company had a variety of growth initiatives in the works. It was pursuing growth in terms of customer groups, product categories, store formats, store location, and sales channels.

---

7. Erica Johnston, "The Region in Review," Washington Post, September 12, 1999.

8. Stephanie Stoughton, "Hechinger Files For Bankruptcy Protection," Washington Post, June 12, 1999.

9. Home Depot 1998 Annual Report.

10. Home Depot 1999 Annual Report.

Customer Groups

The customer group with which Home Depot had for years been associated was non-professional, do-it-yourself (DIY) customers. In recent years, however, it had shifted to a triple-customer strategy, which also included:

Buy-it-yourself customers   The company was making increased efforts to serve the needs of what it called buy-it-yourself (BIY) customers, people who wanted to select the materials that would go into their homes but who wanted someone else to actually install them. The company already offered a number of installation services and was in the process of adding new services of this sort for roofing, vinyl siding, and replacement windows. (The company arranged for these services through approximately 6,200 third-party contractors, from whom it collected a fee.) "As the population ages," the company said, "we expect more customers will want products installed for them." The total market for installation services in the United States was about $75 billion. The company said that it was about to surpass Sears Roebuck as the largest installer of home improvement products but that it still had less than 2% of the installation market. It therefore regarded this as a terrific opportunity. It expected its installation services to increase at least 40% a year over the next few years.

Professional customers   The company was also working hard on expanding its share of the market for professional customers (e.g., contractors, electricians, plumbers, landscapers, property maintenance managers). The market for professional customers was huge, and it also involved a greater propensity for repeat business. Thus, for example, the company was increasing the availability in its stores of products packaged in "job lot" quantities; it was providing customer service geared specifically to professionals through a "Pro Service Desk" in many of its stores; it was doing mass mailings of catalogues containing over 15,000 products of particular interest to facility maintenance managers and the building trades. In addition, in late 1999 it acquired a company named Apex Supply, which was a wholesaler of plumbing, air conditioning, and related products geared to professional customers. "Through this acquisition," the company said, "we believe we will increase our penetration of the professional plumbing trades and be able to handle special orders for plumbing products more efficiently in Home Depot stores."

Company management recognized that the needs of professional customers were quite different from the needs of its do-it-yourself customers. Thus it claimed that it "experimented" with certain changes geared to professional customers in its stores before fully implementing them in order "to ensure that the do-it-yourself customer is not disadvantaged."[11] National "rollout" of the "pro initiative" was expected to take place over the next three years. At the start of 2000 it was operating in 110 stores.

In 1999 the analyst at Deutsche Banc Alex Brown, Dan Wewer, thought, "the pro business will probably influence [Home Depot's] sales and profitability more than any of the other initiatives."[12] At the same time, the professional segment of the business was apt to be more cyclical than the DIY segment.

---

11. *1997 Annual Report.*

12. Patti Bond, "Executive Pushes New Concepts," *Cox News Service*, August 9, 1999.

Product Categories

The store was always in the process of reviewing and revising its product offerings. Occasionally, however, it made some significant changes. In 1999, for example, the company began selling major appliances (e.g., ovens, refrigerators, dishwashers) at 135 of its stores and said that it expected to be selling them in all of its stores by the end of 2000. (It actually stocked in the stores only "the more popular" items but provided computer kiosks at which customers could special-order many more items.) It said that it regarded appliances as a natural extension of the products and services it was already selling and a way of "extending the trusting relationship" it had with customers.

In 1999 Home Depot acquired a company named Georgia Lighting, a specialty lighting designer, distributor, and retailer. Management believed that the acquisition would "strengthen our sourcing, training, and merchandising in lighting" in its stores.

In an appeal to both do-it-yourself and professional customers, the company was also expanding a tool rental service. It already had 10 different categories of tools that it rented on an hourly, weekly, or monthly basis. Company management believed that this service "increased the sales of related merchandise without reducing the sales of equipment similar to that available for rental." This service was growing fast. At the end of 1998 the tool rental service existed in 46 stores; at the end of 1999, 150 stores; and the company expected the service to be available in 350 stores by the end of 2000. (It expected the service would ultimately exist in 60% of all of its stores.)

Store Formats

The store format with which Home Depot was primarily associated was the warehouse-type store that carried a huge assortment of home improvement products. The company was now, however, about to move forward with a very different store format. This was the Expo Design Center stores, which targeted customers interested in carrying out major home decorating projects.

Expo Design stores were often located right next to a warehouse store and were almost as large. Expo Design stores, however, sold higher-end products and services. They carried much less inventory than the warehouse stores. About 80% of the floor space consisted of sample displays of how different rooms (e.g., a kitchen or bedroom or bathroom) might look when remodeled. If a customer was interested in a major home decorating project, he or she would pay a retainer fee to get started, and store employees would work with the customer to handle every aspect of the remodeling process. The goal was for each project to generate $10,000 or more worth of products and services. As a business model, the Expo stores involved—compared with the warehouse stores—less inventory, higher gross margins, higher payroll expense, and probably a greater sensitivity to cyclical changes in discretionary income.

Home Depot opened its first Expo Design store in 1991 and added a few more in the next few years. They were initially treated as a kind of laboratory, and, over the years, the company made many changes in their size and format. By the end of 1998 there were 8 of these stores. Then in 1999 the company added 7 more, and it said it planned to be operating about 200 of them within 5 to 6 years.

The company had also begun testing a much smaller store format, one that was meant to satisfy customers' needs for smaller projects. These stores would be about one-third the size of the big stores, would be in more "convenient" locations, and would operate not under the Home Depot name but under the name Villager's Hardware. (They would compete with neighborhood hardware stores like TrueValue and Ace Hardware.) In 1999 the company opened two of these smaller stores in New Jersey and planned to open two more in 2000. Blank said that this store concept would be in "test mode" for an unspecified period of time.

International Growth

The company was beginning to expand internationally. In 1998 it opened two stores in Chile and one in Puerto Rico. In 1999 it added two more in Chile and another in Puerto Rico.[13] (The Chilean stores it operated as a joint venture with a Chilean department store. Home Depot controlled two-thirds of the equity.) Over the next few years it planned to open several additional stores in Chile and Argentina. "Every day," Blank said in March 1999, "we learn more about serving the diverse needs of customers in other areas of the world. We are also learning that the Home Depot culture is, indeed, transferable, and customer service is valued around the world."[14]

How far the company would go with international expansion, however, wasn't clear. In August 1999 Blank said that "international growth is going to be very important in the next 5 to 15 years. We'll be planting seeds in the next 5 years, maybe in the Far East, or it could be in Europe." He noted some potential problems with this, however. "There are challenges in all of our growth initiatives, but the international realm is the most complex because of real estate and the logistics of the supply chain. Obviously, there are language and cultural differences to overcome, too."[15]

Alternative Channel

The company was in the process of developing its Internet site. The site was meant primarily to provide people with information about home improvement projects (e.g., a calculator to estimate the amount of material a person would need). The company was also going to sell products over the Internet, but it was moving into this only gradually, and it regarded the Internet not as an alternative sales channel but as a sales channel that would be additional or complementary to its physical stores. So far its e-commerce was in operation only in a few metropolitan markets: orders placed over the Internet were being fulfilled from the company's physical stores, and customers could choose to pick them up at the stores or have them delivered. Arthur Blank claimed, however, that the web site would eventually be the "world's largest e-commerce site in our industry."[16]

POTENTIAL PROBLEMS

The company's growth plans involved some risks. The following describes a few of them.

Market saturation   One risk was the possibility of over saturation of certain big-city markets. Home Depot and Lowe's were both planning on opening a lot of new

---

13. For an extended account of Home Depot's considerations in opening its first stores in Chile, see Clifford Krauss, "Foreign Expansion: Well-Planned or Ill-Timed?" New York Times, September 6, 1998.

14. 1998 Annual Report.

15. Patti Bond, "Executive Pushes New Concepts," Cox News Service, August 9, 1999.

16. Debbie Howell, "Home Depot Touts Pro, E-Tail Initiatives," National Home Center News, June 19, 2000.

stores in the United States in the next few years, and many of them would be in markets that they were already in. These markets were seen as extremely attractive, but there was a question of how many stores they could support. In the Atlanta, Georgia, area, for example, there were 43 Home Depot, Lowe's, Ace Hardware, and True Value stores within 20 miles of each other. In Portland, Oregon, Home Depot was planning in 2000 to increase the number of stores it had from 7 to 13. Lowe's was in the process of constructing 2 large stores there. HomeBase wasn't planning any additions but already had 4 stores there. In the Dallas/Fort Worth area, Home Depot had 30 stores, while Lowe's had 14. Lowe's had been in the Dallas market for just a few years, and observers noted that when it moved in, prices at home improvement stores fell.

Different customer groups   Home Depot was a "category killer," but there were components of its product mix that other companies addressed in a more focused way. For example, national and regional wholesalers of electrical products, who sold to professional customers, believed that they could offer more than Home Depot—in terms of a broader and deeper inventory, more knowledgeable sales help with technical questions, and reliable delivery. In their view, "Home Depot, for all its high-profile positioning as a source of supply for professional contractors, still focuses primarily on the fastest-moving items." Some of these wholesalers found that "their customers still needed more than that."[17]

The example of one company demonstrated the problems in pursuing a "dual-customer" strategy. A regional seller of home improvement products named National Home Centers opened stores in the late 1970s that were geared primarily to professional contractors. In 1983 it began marketing to both professional contractors and do-it-yourself customers. In 1998, however, it shifted its focus back to professional contractors, saying that it couldn't adequately compete in both markets.

Appliances   Home Depot's chairman, Bernard Marcus, said that the company planned to eventually be number one in the retail market for major appliances. At the moment, Sears had about 30%, or $6 billion, of the market; it offered on its premises a broad product assortment; and it also maintained an extensive service network. Circuit City had recently given up on selling appliances, which freed up about 5% of the market. Wal-Mart, however, had announced that it was entering the market along with Home Depot, and both of those companies intended to sell most appliances through computer kiosks in their stores. (Home Depot's current market share was about 3%.)

Cross-selling   There was also a question of how much cross-selling, or bundling of products and services, Home Depot could successfully handle. Its big stores were already, in a sense, department stores (what people in the past might have bought at the lumber shop, the paint shop, the wallpaper shop, and so on), but the company was now taking this concept much farther (e.g., providing installation services, selling appliances). Huge financial corporations like Citicorp were basing much of their strategy on cross-selling. In order to be successful at cross-selling, however, companies had to be able to truly integrate different products within a given organizational structure. In addition, the increasing availability of information through the Internet made it easier for consumers to locate providers of different products and services on their own.

---

17. Jim Lucy, "The Super Influencials," *Broadcast Engineering*, May 1999.

Employees   Home Depot ended 1999 with 201,000 employees. It had long regarded high-quality customer service as one of the keys to its success. The company planned, however, on more than doubling the number of stores over the next four years. It claimed that attracting good "associates" wasn't difficult, but the challenges of maintaining high levels of customer service over a far larger market base could be substantial.

Macroeconomy   Naturally, the macroeconomy was a wild card. The company had historically claimed that its fortunes were relatively insulated from changes in the macroeconomy, but the record suggested that that might not be the case. (See **Exhibit 2** and information on pages 2–3.)

THE VIEW OF STOCK ANALYSTS

In the previous year or two, sell-side analysts had generally been supportive of Home Depot's various growth initiatives (e.g., going more after professional customers, expanding the Expo Design store format, adding to its product line, opening some sites in other countries, developing Internet business). There occasionally were expressions of concern about the possible saturation of certain big-city markets, particularly given the competition from Lowe's. However, large parts of the country weren't remotely near any Home Depot or Lowe's store, and analysts were aware that Home Depot and Lowe's generally took a certain amount of market share away from other businesses and that they helped to actually expand the market (by making home-improvement projects less expensive and more understandable for many people).[18]

In the previous 10 months, however, there had been very different views among analysts about the appropriate valuation of the company's stock. The following provide some examples.

- Raymond James report on 12/29/99, when the stock price had just reached its all-time high of $68. The price was at that point 70 times trailing earnings and 56 times the analyst's estimated earnings for the year 2000. He expected an earnings growth rate of 25% over the next several years. He said that, in his view, Home Depot was the best-managed retailer in the country, if not the world. It continued to have, he believed, great fundamentals. But at the current stock price, he essentially regarded it as overvalued. Interestingly, he also noted that company management had "conditioned the Street to expect it to beat [estimated] numbers."

- Credit Suisse/First Boston report on 2/25/00, when the stock was trading at $54. The analyst noted that the market had just had a "tepid" reaction to the company's announcement of fourth quarter results, even though they exceeded consensus estimates by a bit. He said that this reflected a general concern over interest rates and the Federal Reserve's intent to slow consumer spending, which would hurt most retailers. He thought that Home Depot's ability to continue to gain market share and increase margins would, however, offset some of the slowdown in consumer spending. He had positive comments about all of the company's growth initiatives. He regarded the "pro initiative" (the effort to increase sales to professional customers) as the company's

---

18. *SalomonSmithBarney's report on Home Depot, dated December 2, 1998, contains a detailed analysis of the possibility of market saturation.*

most important growth initiative, thought that it could eventually increase sales by 7% to 10% in each store where it was operating, but also believed that it wasn't yet operating in enough stores to have a material impact on earnings growth. He expected an earnings growth rate of 23% over the next several years, an EPS of $1.25 in 2000, and a 25% increase in the stock price over the next 12 months.

- Morgan Stanley Dean Witter report on 3/1/00, when the stock was trading at $55. The analyst expected earnings growth rate over the next several years of 22%. Her EPS estimate for 2000 was $1.25. She had positive comments on all of the company's growth initiatives. She thought that rising interest rates would have some impact on the company. Nevertheless, she thought the current P/E of 44 (relative to 2000 estimated earnings) would be maintained, and she expected an 18% increase in the stock price over the next 12 months.

- CIBC World Markets report on 4/12/00, when the stock was trading at $66. He noted that the stock was at that point trading at 66 times trailing earnings and 53 times his estimated earnings for the year 2000 (which was $1.25). He noted that the latter was twice the multiple for the S&P 500 (which was 26 times estimated earnings). He expected an earnings growth rate of 25% over the next few years—although, given the strength of the company's growth initiatives, he felt that it might exceed that. He noted that the Fed had been raising interest rates in an effort to slow the economy down. He disputed the analogy, however, to the last period of rising interests (1994–1995) and the negative impact that that evidently had on Home Depot's performance. Things were different now, in his view. For example, the company's growth initiatives had a lot of potential; consumer spending remained strong; the company's greater purchasing clout now would help it maintain gross margins; the company's competitive position had improved with the weakening of smaller competitors. Thus he was bullish on the stock, with a 12-month price target roughly 30% higher than its current price.

- Lehman Brothers report on 5/16/00, when the stock was trading at $56. Like other analysts, he expected an earnings growth rate of 25% over the next few years. He noted that the stock was currently trading at a 45 times his estimated EPS for 2000 (which was $1.25). He noted that the P/E multiple of 45 represented a 79% premium to the S&P 500 and a 81% premium to his long-term estimated growth rate for the company of 25%. He regarded this valuation as "attractive."

- A.G. Edwards report on 8/22/00, when the stock was trading at $50. This analyst was cautious about the stock, even though he regarded Home Depot as a great company. He noted that the annual growth rate in the company's earnings over the last 10 years had averaged about 30%, and he now expected a more moderate growth rate of about 25% a year. He therefore anticipated a contraction of the then-current P/E multiple of 41 (based on his estimated EPS for 2000, which was $1.25).

- SalomonSmithBarney report on 8/23/00, when the stock was trading at $50. This analyst was also cautious about the stock, even though he also regarded Home Depot as a great company. He expected a deceleration in the company's earnings growth to about 25% a year. He thought this would occur primarily because of the macroeconomic environment—higher interest rates and a slowing economy. He noted that the stock was currently trading at a P/E multiple of

Home Depot, Inc. in the New Millennium

41 (based on his estimated EPS for 2000, which was $1.25) but that the average multiple for the company during the 1990s had been about 32. He also noted that the company's P/E-to-growth ratio was currently about 1.5 (based on earnings for the next 12 months and assuming a long-term earnings growth rate of 25%) but that, over the last 10 years, the company's P/E-to-growth ratio had averaged about 1.2. The lowest such ratio for the company occurred in late 1995, when it was 0.7. He thought that the current economic environment for housing-oriented businesses like Home Depot was similar to that in 1995 (e.g., a lagging effect from rising mortgage interest rates), and he noted that in 1995 Home Depot experienced a sharp deceleration in same-store sales increases. He was confident that the stock would not move down to the valuation level reached in late 1995. The company's business was, in his view, too outstanding for that. Nevertheless, he was cautious about the stock's near-term prospects. He added that he wasn't downgrading Lowe's stock as well because Lowe's stock didn't have nearly as high a valuation.

PROSPECTS

Several months earlier, in the spring of 2000, Arthur Blank acknowledged that the company's share price had already suffered to some extent because of concerns about rising interest rates, but he said he wasn't concerned about these short-term dips. He continued to expect 23% to 25% growth in earnings per share over the next several years. "At the end of the day," he said, "we feel our prospects are very good. Essentially what we've done for the last 21 years is what we'll continue to do."[19]

QUESTIONS

1. What is your estimate of the intrinsic value of Home Depot's stock as of February 1, 2001?

2. What set of assumptions regarding Home Depot's future growth rate, return on equity, and cost of equity are consistent with its observed stock price of $48.20 on February 1, 2001?

---

19. Patti Bond, "Home Depot: Retailer Plans to Stick to Usual Winning Script," Atlanta Journal and Constitution, *May 21, 2000.*

EXHIBIT 1

Home Depot's Stock Price

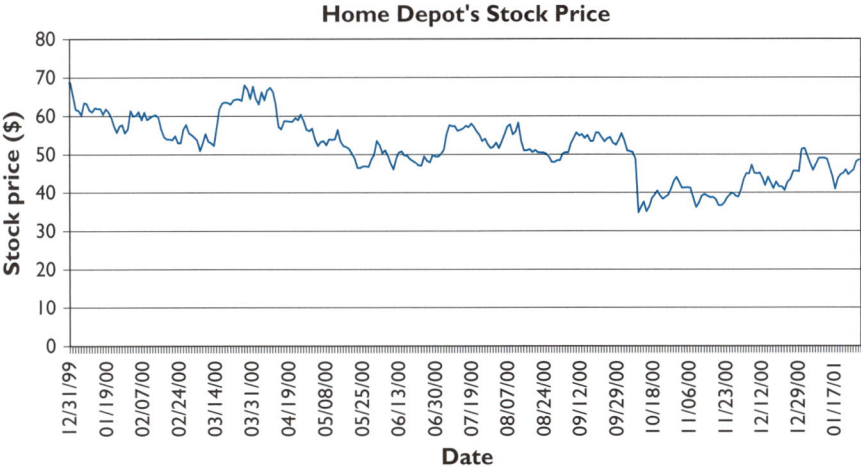

Source: Bloomberg; Federal Reserve; *The Wall Street Journal.*

Data as of early October 2000:

Home Depot's beta: 1.09

Yields on Treasury securities:

30-day: 6.00%; 90-day: 6.18%; 1-year: 6.13%; 10-year: 5.8%; 30-year: 5.83%.

EXHIBIT 2

Return on Home Depot's Stock Compared to S&P Retail Index and S&P 500

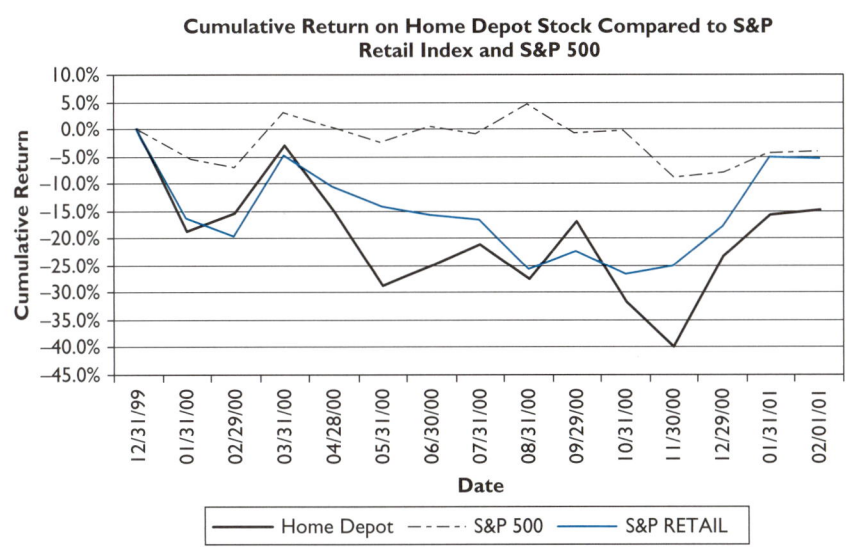

Source: Bloomberg.

Home Depot, Inc. in the New Millennium

Home Depot, Inc. in the New Millennium

EXHIBIT 3

Home Depot: Decomposition of ROE, 1986–2000

	1986	1987	1988	1989	1990	1991	1992	1993	1994	1995	1996	1997	1998	1999	2000	Average 1986–2000
ROE	26.8%	33.2%	23.9%	29.2%	31.9%	36.5%	21.5%	19.9%	21.5%	21.3%	18.8%	19.5%	22.7%	26.5%	20.9%	25.0%
Decomposition:																
NOPAT ($ millions)	30	56	77	114	167	240	346	439	609	722	932	1,159	1,618	2,315	2,565	N/A
NOPAT margin	2.9%	3.8%	3.9%	4.1%	4.4%	4.7%	4.8%	4.7%	4.9%	4.7%	4.8%	4.8%	5.4%	6.0%	5.6%	4.6%
Net assets ($ millions)	290	263	347	475	681	1,079	1,568	2,735	3,267	4,390	5,602	6,647	8,235	10,258	12,950	N/A
Operating asset turnover	3.5	5.5	5.8	5.8	5.6	4.8	4.6	3.4	3.8	3.5	3.5	3.6	3.7	3.7	3.5	4.3
Operating ROA	10.2%	21.1%	22.3%	24.0%	24.5%	22.2%	22.1%	16.1%	18.6%	16.4%	16.6%	17.4%	19.6%	22.6%	19.8%	19.6%
Net debt ($ millions)	201	100	27	92	169	395	(123)	431	413	968	614	691	1,137	1,518	609	N/A
Net financial leverage	225.0%	61.0%	8.0%	24.0%	33.0%	58.0%	−7.0%	19.0%	16.0%	28.0%	12.0%	12.0%	16.0%	17.0%	4.9%	35.1%
Net interest expense after tax ($ millions)	5.7	1.5	0.6	1.6	3.7	(9.1)	(16.7)	(18.7)	4.6	(9.5)	(5.8)	(1.2)	4.3	(5.5)	(15.9)	N/A
Net interest rate after tax	2.8%	1.5%	2.2%	1.8%	2.2%	−2.3%	13.6%	−4.3%	1.0%	−1.0%	−0.9%	−0.2%	0.4%	−0.4%	−2.6%	0.9%
Spread	7.4%	19.6%	20.1%	22.2%	22.4%	24.6%	8.4%	20.4%	17.6%	17.4%	17.6%	17.6%	19.3%	22.9%	22.4%	18.7%
Financial leverage effect	16.7%	12.0%	1.7%	5.3%	7.4%	14.3%	−0.6%	3.9%	2.8%	4.9%	2.1%	2.1%	3.1%	3.9%	1.1%	5.4%

(continued)

Source: Compustat and casewriter's calculations.

Notes: *Explanations of terms appears on following page.

*Years indicated end in January of the following year. Thus, 2000 data is for the 12-month period ending at the end of January 2001.
N/A, Not applicable.

Home Depot: Decomposition of ROE, 1986–2000 (continued)

Explanation of terms

ROE
= Net income/Equity
= Operating ROA + Financial leverage effect

NOPAT (net operating profit after taxes)
= Net income − Net interest expense after tax

NOPAT margin
= NOPAT/Sales

Net assets
= Operating working capital + Net long-term assets

Operating working capital = (Current assets − Cash and marketable securities) − (Current liabilities − Short-term debt and current portion of long-term debt)

Net long-term assets = Total long-term assets − Non-interest-bearing long-term liabilities

Operating asset turnover
= Sales/Net assets

Operating ROA
= NOPAT/Net assets
= NOPAT margin × Operating asset turnover

Net debt
= Total interest-bearing liabilities − Cash and marketable securities

Net financial leverage
= Net debt/Equity

Net interest expense after tax
= (Interest expense − Interest income) × (1 − effective tax rate)

Net interest rate after tax
= (Net interest expense after tax)/Net debt

Spread
= Operating ROA − Net interest rate after tax

Financial leverage effect
= Net financial leverage × Spread

Source: Palepu, Healy, and Bernard, *Business Analysis and Valuation* (2nd edition).

Home Depot, Inc. in the New Millennium

EXHIBIT 4
Home Depot: Operational Data, 1986–2000

	1986	1987	1988	1989	1990	1991	1992	1993	1994	1995	1996	1997	1998	1999	2000	Average 1986–2000
Sales ($ millions)	$1,011	$1,454	$2,000	$2,758	$3,815	$5,137	$7,148	$9,239	$12,477	$15,470	$19,535	$24,156	$30,219	$38,434	$45,738	N/A
Number of stores	60	75	96	118	145	174	214	264	340	423	512	624	761	930	1,134	N/A
Total square footage at year-end (000)	5,000	6,000	8,000	10,000	13,000	16,000	21,000	26,000	35,000	44,000	54,000	66,000	81,000	100,000	123,000	N/A
Increase in square footage	20.6%	27.6%	33.4%	26.9%	27.4%	24.1%	26.8%	26.3%	33.2%	26.3%	21.6%	23.1%	22.8%	23.5%	22.6%	26%
Average square footage per store (000)	80	82	86	88	92	95	98	100	103	105	105	106	107	108	108	N/A
Sales growth rate		44%	38%	38%	38%	35%	39%	29%	35%	24%	26%	24%	25%	27%	19%	31%
Same-store sales increase	7%	18%	13%	13%	10%	11%	15%	7%	8%	3%	7%	7%	7%	10%	4%	10%
Weekly sales per store (000)	$355	$418	$464	$515	$566	$633	$724	$764	$802	$787	$803	$829	$844	$876	$864	N/A
Sales per square foot	$230	$265	$282	$303	$322	$348	$387	$398	$404	$390	$398	$406	$410	$423	$415	N/A
Number of customer transactions (millions)	34	48	64	84	112	146	189	236	302	370	464	550	665	797	937	N/A
Average sale per transaction	$29.73	$30.24	$31.13	$32.65	$33.92	$35.13	$37.72	$39.13	$41.29	$41.78	$42.09	$43.63	$45.05	$47.87	$48.65	N/A
Working capital/Sales	10.6%	5.1%	4.3%	4.6%	3.7%	3.2%	3.2%	4.3%	4.5%	5.8%	5.9%	5.4%	6.1%	5.3%	5.7%	5%
Net long-term assets/Sales	18.1%	13.0%	13.1%	12.6%	14.2%	17.8%	18.7%	25.3%	21.3%	22.7%	22.8%	22.1%	21.2%	21.4%	22.6%	19%
Number of employees at year-end	6,600	9,100	13,000	17,500	21,500	28,000	38,900	50,600	67,300	80,800	98,100	124,400	156,700	201,400	227,300	N/A

Source: Company Annual Reports; Compustat; casewriter's calculations.

Notes: *Years indicated end in January of the following year. Thus, 2000 data is for the 12-month period ending at the end of January 2001.

*N/A, Not applicable.

EXHIBIT 5

Home Depot: EPS and Stock Data, 1990–2000

	1990	1991	1992	1993	1994	1995	1996	1997	1998	1999	2000
Diluted EPS	$0.10	$0.13	$0.18	$0.22	$0.29	$0.34	$0.43	$0.55	$0.71	$1.00	$1.10
Diluted EPS increase	43%	30%	38%	22%	32%	17%	26%	28%	29%	41%	10%
Weighted number of shares oustanding assuming dilution (millions)	1,824	1,985	2,096	2,132	2,142	2,151	2,195	2,287	2,320	2,342	2,352
Total return on stock											
Home Depot	54%	167%	48%	–20%	19%	6%	6%	81%	111%	77%	–21%
S&P 500	–5%	32%	8%	10%	2%	38%	22%	34%	28%	21%	–3%

Source: Company Annual Report; Bloomberg.

Home Depot, Inc. in the New Millennium

EXHIBIT 6A

Home Depot: Income Statements ($ millions, except earnings per share)

	Years Ending January			
	2001	2000	1999	1998
Net Sales	45,738	38,434	30,219	24,156
Cost of Merchandise Sold	32,057	27,023	21,614	17,375
Gross Profit	13,681	11,411	8,605	6,781
Operating Expenses				
Selling and Store Operating	8,513	6,832	5,341	4,303
Pre-Opening	142	113	88	65
General and Administrative	835	671	515	413
Non-Recurring Charge	—	—	—	104
Total Operating Expenses	9,490	7,616	5,944	4,885
Operating Income	4,191	3,795	2,661	1,896
Interest and Investment Income	47	37	30	44
Interest Expense	(21)	(28)	(37)	(42)
Interest, net	26	9	(7)	2
Earnings Before Income Taxes	4,217	3,804	2,654	1,898
Income Taxes	1,636	1,484	1,040	738
Net Earnings	2,581	2,320	1,614	1,160
Basic Earnings Per Share	1.11	1.03	0.73	0.53
Diluted Earnings Per Share	1.10	1.00	0.71	0.52

Source: Company 10-K.

Note: Cost of merchandise sold includes all of the company's depreciation and amortization expense, which totaled $463 million, $373 million, and $283 million in years ending January 2000, 1999, and 1998, respectively. By contrast, Lowe's does not include depreciation and amortizations in its cost of merchandise sold figures; it has a separate operating expense line for them.

EXHIBIT 6B

Home Depot: Balance Sheets ($ millions)

	Years Ending January		
	2001	2000	1999
Assets			
Cash and Cash Equivalents	167	168	62
Short-term Investments	10	2	—
Receivables, net	835	587	469
Merchandise Inventories	6,556	5,489	4,293
Other Current Assets	209	144	109
Total Current Assets	7,777	6,390	4,933
Property and Equipment			
Land	4,230	3,248	2,739
Buildings	6,167	4,834	3,757
Furniture, Fixtures and Equipment	2,877	2,279	1,761
Leasehold Improvements	665	493	419
Construction in Progress	1,032	791	540
Capital Leases	261	245	206
	15,232	11,890	9,422
Less Accumulated Depreciation and Amortization	2,164	1,663	1,262
Net Property and Equipment	13,068	10,227	8,160
Cost in Excess of the Fair Value of			
Net Assets Acquired	314	311	268
Other	226	153	104
Total Assets	21,385	17,081	13,465
Liabilities and Stockholders' Equity			
Accounts Payable	1,976	1,993	1,586
Accrued Salaries and Related Expenses	627	541	395
Sales Taxes Payable	298	269	176
Other Accrued Expenses	1,402	763	586
Income Taxes Payable	78	61	100
Current Installments of Long-Term Debt	4	29	14
Total Current Liabilities	4,385	3,656	2,857
Long-term Debt, excluding current installments	1,545	750	1,566
Other Long-Term Liabilities	245	237	208
Deferred Income Taxes	195	87	85
Minority Interest	11	10	9
Stockholders' Equity			
Common Stock	116	115	111
Paid-in Capital	4,810	4,319	2,817
Retained Earnings	10,151	7,941	5,876
Other	(73)	(34)	(64)
Total Stockholders' Equity	15,004	12,341	8,740
Total Liabilities and Stockholders' Equity	21,385	17,081	13,465

Source: Company 10-K.

Home Depot, Inc. in the New Millennium

EXHIBIT 6C

Home Depot: Cash Flow Statements ($ millions)

	Years Ending January			
	2001	2000	1999	1998
Cash Flows from Operating Activities				
Net Earnings	2,581	2,320	1,614	1,160
Depreciation and Amortization	601	463	373	283
(Increase) Decrease in Receivables, net	(246)	(85)	85	(166)
Increase in Merchandise Inventories	(1,075)	(1,142)	(698)	(885)
Increase in Accounts Payable and				
Accrued Expenses	754	820	423	577
Increase in Income Taxes Payable	151	93	59	83
Other	30	(23)	61	(23)
	2,796	2,446	1,917	1,029
Cash Flows from Investing Acquired				
Capital Expenditures	(3,558)	(2,581)	(2,053)	(1,420)
Purchase of Remaining Interest in				
The Home Depot Canada	—	—	(261)	—
Payments for Businesses Acquired, net	(26)	(101)	(6)	(61)
Proceeds from Sales of Property				
and Equipment	95	87	45	85
Purchases of Investments	(39)	(32)	(2)	(194)
Proceeds from Maturieties of Investments	30	30	4	599
Advances Secured by Real Estate, net	(32)	(25)	2	20
	(3,530)	(2,622)	(2,271)	(971)
Cash Flows from Financing Activities				
(Repayments) Issuance of Commercial				
Paper Obligations, net	754	(246)	246	—
Proceeds from Long-Term Borrowings, net	32	522	—	15
Repayments of Long-Term Debt	(29)	(14)	(8)	(40)
Proceeds from Sale of Common Stock, net	351	267	167	122
Cash Dividends Paid to Stockholders	(371)	(255)	(168)	(139)
Minority Interest Contributions				
to Partnership	—	7	11	10
	737	281	248	(32)
Effect of Exchange Rate Changes	(4)	1	(4)	—
Increase (Decrease) in Cash and				
Cash Equivalents	(1)	106	(110)	26
Cash and Cash Equivalents at				
Beginning of Year	168	62	172	146
Cash and Cash Equivalents at End of Year	167	168	62	172

Source: Company 10-K.

Note: At the end of 1999, the company said it owned 77% of its stores and leased 23% of them. In recent years it had increased the relative percentage of stores that were owned because it felt that doing so provided greater operating control and flexibility and generally lower occupancy costs. It noted that the cost of new stores to be constructed and owned by the company averaged $13.2 million. The cost to fix up stores to be leased averaged $4.3 million. The cost of inventory for new stores averaged $3.2 million, net of vendor financing.

EXHIBIT 7

Projected Growth in U.S. Market for Home Improvement Products, as of June 2000

Year	Percent Change over Previous Year
2000	6.30%
2001	3.20%
2002	4.00%
2003	4.40%
2004	4.60%

Source: Home Improvement Research Institute.

EXHIBIT 8

Summary Data for Lowe's ($ millions)

	2000	1999	1998	1997
Sales	$18,779	$15,905	$13,330	$11,108
NOPAT	$853	$727	$530	$398
NOPAT margin	4.5%	4.6%	4.0%	3.6%
Net assets	$8,029	$4,961	$3,545	$2,810
Operating ROA (NOPAT/Net assets)	10.6%	14.7%	15.0%	14.2%
Number of stores at year-end	650	576	520	477
Same-store sales increase	1.2%	6.0%	6.0%	4.0%
Sales per square foot	$277	$303	$273	$302

Source: Company Annual Report and 10-K; casewriter's calculations.

Home Depot, Inc. in the New Millennium

PART THREE

BUSINESS ANALYSIS AND VALUATION APPLICATIONS

Chapter 9
Equity Security Analysis

Equity security analysis is the evaluation of a firm and its prospects from the perspective of a current or potential investor in the firm's stock. Security analysis is, however, just one step in a larger investment process that involves (1) establishing the objectives of the investor, (2) forming expectations about the future returns and risks of individual securities, and then (3) combining individual securities into portfolios to maximize progress toward the investment objectives.

Security analysis is the foundation for the second step of projecting future returns and assessing risk. Security analysis is typically conducted with an eye toward identifying mispriced securities in the hopes of generating returns that more than compensate the investor for risk. However, that need not be the case. For analysts who do not have a comparative advantage in identifying mispriced securities, the focus should be on gaining an appreciation for how a security would affect the risk of a given portfolio, and whether it fits the profile that the portfolio is designed to maintain.

Security analysis is undertaken by individual investors, by analysts at brokerage houses and investment banks (sell-side analysts), and by analysts that work at the direction of fund managers for various institutions (buy-side analysts). The institutions employing buy-side analysts include mutual funds, hedge funds, insurance companies, universities, and others.

A variety of questions are dealt with in security analysis:

- A sell-side analyst asks: Is the industry I am covering attractive, and if so why? How do different firms within the industry position themselves? What are the implications for my earnings forecasts? Given my expectations for a firm, does its stock appear to be mispriced? Should I recommend this stock as a buy, a sell, or a hold?
- A buy-side analyst for a "value stock fund" asks: Does this stock possess the characteristics we seek in our fund, that is, does it have a relatively low ratio of price–earnings, low price-to-book value, and other fundamental indicators? Do its prospects for earnings improvement suggest good potential for high future returns on the stock?
- An individual investor asks: Does this stock present the risk profile that suits my investment objectives? Does it enhance my ability to diversify the risk of my portfolio? Is the firm's dividend payout rate low enough to minimize my tax liability while I continue to hold the stock?

As the above questions underscore, there is more to security analysis than estimating the value of stocks. Nevertheless, for most sell-side and buy-side analysts, the key goal remains the identification of mispriced stocks.

INVESTOR OBJECTIVES AND INVESTMENT VEHICLES

The investment objectives of individual savers in the economy are highly idiosyncratic. For any given saver they depend on factors such as income, age, wealth, tolerance for risk, and tax status. For example, savers with many years until retirement are likely to prefer to have a relatively large share of their portfolio invested in equities, which offer a higher expected return than fixed income (or debt) securities and higher short-term variability. Investors in high tax brackets are likely to prefer to have a large share of their portfolio in stocks that generate tax-deferred capital gains rather than stocks that pay dividends or interest-bearing securities.

Mutual funds (or unit trusts as they are termed in some countries) have become popular investment vehicles for savers to achieve their investment objectives. Mutual funds sell shares in professionally managed portfolios that invest in specific types of stocks and/or fixed income securities. They therefore provide a low-cost way for savers to invest in a portfolio of securities that reflects their particular appetite for risk.

The major classes of mutual fund include (1) money market funds that invest in CDs and treasury bills, (2) bond funds that invest in debt instruments, (3) equity funds that invest in equity securities, (4) balanced funds that hold money market, bond, and equity securities, and (5) real estate funds that invest in commercial real estate. Within the bond and equities classes of funds, however, there are wide ranges of fund types. For example, bond funds include

- *Corporate bond funds* that invest in investment-grade rated corporate debt instruments,
- *High yield funds* that invest in non-investment-grade rated corporate debt,
- *Mortgage funds* that invest in mortgage-backed securities, and
- *Municipal funds* that invest in municipal debt instruments, which generate income that can be exempt from federal and often state and local taxes.

Equity funds include

- *Income funds* that invest in stocks that are expected to generate dividend income,
- *Growth funds* that invest in stocks expected to generate long-term capital gains,
- *Income and growth funds* that invest in stocks that provide a balance of dividend income and capital gains,
- *Value funds* that invest in equities that are considered to be undervalued,
- *Short funds* that sell short equity securities that are considered to be overvalued,
- *Index funds* that invest in stocks that track a particular market index, such as the S&P 500,
- *Size-based funds* that invest based on the market capitalization of the company, such as large-cap and small-cap funds,
- *Sector funds* that invest in stocks in a particular industry segment, such as the technology or health sciences sectors, and
- *Regional funds* that invest in equities from a particular country or geographic region, such as Japan, Europe, or the Asia-Pacific region.

Since the 1990s, hedge funds have gained increased prominence and the assets controlled by these funds have grown significantly. While generally open only to institutional investors and certain qualified wealthy individuals, hedge funds are becoming an increasingly important force in the market. Hedge funds employ a variety of investment strategies including

- *Market neutral funds* that typically invest equal amounts of money in purchasing undervalued securities and shorting overvalued ones to neutralize market risk,
- *Short-selling funds,* which short sell the securities of companies that they believe are overvalued, and

- *Special situations funds* that invest in undervalued securities in anticipation of an increase in value resulting from a favorable turn of events.

These fund types employ very different strategies. But for many, fundamental analysis of companies is the critical task. This chapter focuses on applying the tools we have developed in Part 2 of the book to analyze equity securities.

EQUITY SECURITY ANALYSIS AND MARKET EFFICIENCY

How a security analyst should invest his or her time depends on how quickly and efficiently information flows through markets and becomes reflected in security prices. In the extreme, information would be reflected in security prices fully and immediately upon its release. This is essentially the condition posited by the *efficient markets hypothesis*. This hypothesis states that security prices reflect all available information, as if such information could be costlessly digested and translated immediately into demands for buys or sells without regard to frictions imposed by transactions costs. Under such conditions, it would be impossible to identify mispriced securities on the basis of public information.

In a world of efficient markets, the expected return on any equity security is just enough to compensate investors for the unavoidable risk the security involves. Unavoidable risk is that which cannot be "diversified away" simply by holding a portfolio of many securities. Given efficient markets, the investor's strategy shifts away from the search for mispriced securities and focuses instead on maintaining a well diversified portfolio. Aside from this, the investor must arrive at the desired balance between risky securities and risk-free short-term government bonds. The desired balance depends on how much risk the investor is willing to bear for a given increase in expected returns.

The above discussion implies that investors who accept that stock prices already reflect available information have no need for analysis involving a search for mispriced securities. If all investors adopted this attitude, of course no such analysis would be conducted, mispricing would go uncorrected, and markets would no longer be efficient![1] This is why the efficient markets hypothesis cannot represent an equilibrium in a strict sense. In equilibrium there must be just enough mispricing to provide incentives for the investment of resources in security analysis.

The existence of some mispricing, even in equilibrium, does not imply that it is sensible for just anyone to engage in security analysis. Instead, it suggests that securities analysis is subject to the same laws of supply and demand faced in all other competitive industries: It will be rewarding only for those with the strongest comparative advantage. How many analysts are in that category depends on a number of factors, including the liquidity of a firm's stock and investor interest in the company.[2] For the smallest publicly traded firms in the U.S., there is typically no formal following by analysts, and would-be investors and their advisors are left to form their own opinions on a stock. Recent research shows a trend of reduced sell-side analyst coverage following new regulations for investment banks following the scandals of the late 1990s.[3] Coverage of IBM, for example, has declined from about 40 sell-side professional analysts in March 2003 to 25 analysts in September 2006. This decline has been at least partially offset by an increase in the number of analysts employed on the buy-side.

Market Efficiency and the Role of Financial Statement Analysis

The degree of market efficiency that arises from competition among analysts and other market agents is an empirical issue addressed by a large body of research spanning the last three decades. Such research has important implications for the role of financial statements in security analysis. Consider for example the implications of an extremely efficient market, where information is fully impounded in prices within minutes of its revelation. In such a market, agents could profit from digesting financial statement information in two ways. First, the information would be useful to the select few who receive newly announced financial data, interpret it quickly, and trade on it within minutes. Second, and probably more important, the information would be useful for gaining an understanding of the firm, so as to place the analyst in a better position to interpret future news (from financial statements as well as other sources) as it arrives.

On the other hand, if securities prices fail to reflect financial statement data fully, even days or months after its public revelation, market agents could profit from such data by creating trading strategies designed to exploit any systematic ways in which the publicly available data are ignored or discounted in the price-setting process.

Market Efficiency and Managers' Financial Reporting Strategies

The degree to which markets are efficient also has implications for managers' approaches to communicating with their investment communities. The issue becomes most important when the firm pursues an unusual strategy, or when the usual interpretation of financial statements would be misleading in the firm's context. In such a case, the communication avenues managers can successfully pursue depend not only on management's credibility but also on the degree of understanding present in the investment community. We will return to the issue of management communications in more detail in Chapter 12.

Evidence of Market Efficiency

There is an abundance of evidence consistent with a high degree of efficiency in the primary U.S. securities markets.[4] In fact, during the 1960s and 1970s, the evidence was so one-sided that the efficient markets hypothesis gained widespread acceptance within the academic community and had a major impact on the practicing community as well.

Evidence pointing to very efficient securities markets comes in several forms:

- When information is announced publicly, the markets react *very* quickly.
- It is difficult to identify specific funds or analysts who have consistently generated abnormally high returns.
- A number of studies suggest that stock prices reflect a rather sophisticated level of fundamental analysis.

While a large body of evidence consistent with efficiency exists, recent years have witnessed a re-examination of the once widely accepted thinking. A sampling of the research includes the following:

- On the issue of the speed of stock price response to news, a number of studies suggest that even though prices react quickly, the initial reaction tends to be incomplete.[5]
- A number of studies point to trading strategies that could have been used to outperform market averages.[6]
- Related evidence—still subject to ongoing debate about its proper interpretation—suggests that even though market prices reflect some relatively sophisticated analysis, prices still do not fully reflect all the information that could be garnered from publicly available financial statements.[7]

The controversy over the efficiency of securities markets is unlikely to be resolved soon. However, there are some lessons that are accepted by most researchers. First, securities markets not only reflect publicly available information, but they also anticipate much of it before it is released. The open question is what fraction of the response remains to be impounded in price once the day of the public release comes to a close. Second, even in most studies that suggest inefficiency, the degree of mispricing is relatively small for large stocks.

Finally, even if some of the evidence is currently difficult to align with the efficient markets hypothesis, it remains a useful benchmark (at a minimum) for thinking about the behavior of security prices. The hypothesis will continue to play that role unless it can be replaced by a more complete theory. Some researchers are developing theories that encompass the existence of market agents who are forced to trade for unpredictable "liquidity" reasons, and prices that differ from so-called "fundamental values," even in equilibrium.[8] Also, behavioral finance models recognize that cognitive biases can affect investor behavior.[9]

APPROACHES TO FUND MANAGEMENT AND SECURITIES ANALYSIS

Approaches used in practice to analyze securities and manage funds are quite varied. One dimension of variation is the extent to which the investments are actively or passively managed. Another is whether a quantitative or a traditional fundamental approach is used. Security analysts also vary considerably in terms of whether they produce formal or informal valuations of the firm.

Active Versus Passive Management

Active portfolio management relies heavily on security analysis to identify mispriced securities. The passive portfolio manager serves as a price taker, avoiding the costs of security analysis and turnover while typically seeking to hold a portfolio designed to match some overall market index or sector performance. Combined approaches are also possible. For example, one may actively manage 20 percent of a fund balance while passively managing the remainder. The widespread growth of passively managed funds in the U.S. over the past 20 years serves as testimony to the growing belief that it is difficult to consistently earn returns that are superior to broad market indices such as the S&P 500 Index.

Quantitative Versus Traditional Fundamental Analysis

Actively managed funds must depend on some form of security analysis. Some funds employ *technical analysis,* which attempts to predict stock price movements on the basis of market indicators (prior stock price movements, volume of shares traded, etc.). In contrast, *fundamental analysis,* the primary approach for security analysis, attempts to evaluate the current market price relative to projections of the firm's future earnings and cash-flow generating potential. Fundamental analysis involves all the steps described in the previous chapters of this book: business strategy analysis, accounting analysis, financial analysis, and prospective analysis (forecasting and valuation). In recent years, some analysts have supplemented traditional fundamental analysis, which involves a substantial amount of subjective judgment, with more quantitative approaches.

The quantitative approaches themselves are quite varied. Some involve simply "screening" stocks on the basis of some set of factors, such as trends in analysts' earnings revisions, price–earnings ratios, price-to-book ratios, and so on. Whether such approaches are useful depends on the degree of market efficiency relative to the screens. Quantitative approaches can also involve implementation of some formal model to predict future stock returns. Longstanding statistical techniques such as regression analysis and probit analysis can be used, as can more recently developed, computer-intensive techniques such as neural network analysis. Again, the success of these approaches depends on the degree of market efficiency and whether the analysis can exploit information in ways not otherwise available to market agents as a group.

Quantitative approaches play a more important role in security analysis today than they did a decade or two ago. However, by and large, analysts still rely primarily on fundamental analysis involving complex human judgments.

Formal Versus Informal Valuation

Full-scale, formal valuations based on the methods described in Chapter 7 have become more common in recent years. However, less formal approaches are also popular. For example, an analyst can compare his or her long-term earnings projection with the consensus forecast to generate a buy or sell recommendation. Another possible approach, that might be labeled "marginalist," involves no attempt to value the firm. The analyst simply assumes that if he or she has unearthed favorable (or unfavorable) information believed not to be recognized by others, the stock should be bought (or sold).

Unlike many security analysts, investment bankers produce formal valuations as a matter of course. Investment bankers, who estimate values for the purpose of bringing a private firm to the public market, for evaluating a merger or buyout proposal, for issuing a fairness opinion or for making a periodic managerial review, must document their valuation in a way that can readily be communicated to management and, if necessary, to the courts.

THE PROCESS OF COMPREHENSIVE SECURITY ANALYSIS

Given the variety of approaches practiced in security analysis, it is impossible to summarize all of them here. Instead, we briefly outline steps to be included in a comprehensive security analysis. The amount of attention focused on any given step varies among analysts.

Selection of Candidates for Analysis

No analyst can effectively investigate more than a small fraction of the securities on a major exchange, and thus some approach to narrowing the focus must be employed. Sell-side analysts are often organized within an investment house by industry or sector. Thus they tend to be constrained in their choices of firms to follow. However, from the perspective of a fund manager or an investment firm as a whole, there is usually the freedom to focus on any firm or sector.

As noted earlier, funds typically specialize in investing in stocks with certain risk profiles or characteristics (e.g., growth stocks, "value" stocks, technology stocks, and cyclical stocks). Managers of these types of funds seek to focus the energies of their analysts on identifying stocks that fit their fund objective. In addition, individual investors who seek to maintain a well diversified portfolio without holding many stocks also need information about the nature of a firm's risks and how they fit with the risk profile of their overall portfolio.

An alternative approach to stock selection is to screen firms on the basis of some potential mispricing followed by a detailed analysis of only those stocks that meet the specified criteria. For example, one fund managed by a large U.S. insurance company screens stocks on the basis of recent "earnings momentum" as reflected in revisions in the earnings projections of sell-side and buy-side analysts. Upward revisions trigger investigations for possible purchase. The fund operates on the belief that earnings momentum is a positive signal of future price movements. Another fund complements the earnings momentum screen with one based on recent short-term stock price movements, in the hopes of identifying earnings revisions not yet reflected in stock prices.

Key Analysis Questions

Depending on whether fund managers follow a strategy of targeting stocks with specific types of characteristics, or of screening stocks that appear to be mispriced, the following types of questions are likely to be useful:

- What is the risk profile of a firm? How volatile is its earnings stream and stock price? What are the most likely bad outcomes in the future? What is the upside potential? How closely linked are the firm's risks to the health of the overall economy? Are the risks largely diversifiable, or are they systematic?
- Does the firm possess the characteristics of a growth stock? What is the expected pattern of sales and earnings growth for the coming years? Is the firm reinvesting most or all of its earnings?
- Does the firm match the characteristics desired by "income funds"? Is it a mature or maturing company, prepared to "harvest" profits and distribute them in the form of high dividends?
- Is the firm a candidate for a "value fund"? Does it offer measures of earnings, cash flow, and book value that are high relative to the price? What specific screening rules can be implemented to identify misvalued stocks?

Inferring Market Expectations

If the security analysis is conducted with an eye toward the identification of mispricing, it must ultimately involve a comparison of the analyst's expectations with those of "the market." One possibility is to view the observed stock price as the reflection of market expectations and to compare the analyst's own estimate of value with that price. However, a stock price is only a "summary statistic." It is useful to have a more detailed idea of the market's expectations about a firm's future performance, expressed in terms of sales, earnings, and other measures. For example, assume that an analyst has developed new insights about a firm's near-term sales. Whether those insights represent new information for the stock market, and whether they indicate that a "buy" recommendation is appropriate, can be easily determined if the analyst knows the market consensus sales forecast.

Around the world a number of agencies summarize analysts' forecasts of sales and earnings. Forecasts for the next year or two are commonly available, and for many firms, a "long-run" earnings growth projection is also available—typically for three to five years. Some financial information providers in the U.S provide continuous on-line updates to such data, so if an analyst revises a forecast, that can be made known to fund managers and other analysts within seconds.

As useful as analysts' forecasts of sales and earnings are, they do not represent a complete description of expectations about future performance, and there is no guarantee that consensus analyst forecasts are the same as those reflected in market prices. Further, financial analysts typically forecast performance for only a few years, so it is helpful to understand what types of long-term forecasts are reflected in stock prices. Armed with the model in Chapters 7 and 8 that expresses price as a function of future cash flows or earnings, an analyst can draw some educated inferences about the expectations embedded in stock prices.

For example, consider the valuation of Electronic Arts Inc. (EA), a developer of interactive software video games. On November 15, 2006, EA's stock price closed at $58.84, giving it a market capitalization of $18.1 billion. Through September 30, 2006, the company suffered eight consecutive quarters of year-over-year profit declines and reported a 53 percent decline in earnings for the fiscal year ended March 31, 2006. Earnings per share (EPS) declined from $1.87 in fiscal year 2004 to $0.75 in fiscal year 2006. The stock was trading at over 100 times trailing twelve months earnings, clearly indicating that the market was expecting earnings to rebound. Performance in the quarter ended September 30, 2006, showed early evidence of this rebound as the firm returned to profitability after two consecutive quarters of losses.

The decline in profitability was driven by a variety of reasons. The major video game hardware manufacturers such as Sony and Nintendo, for which EA published game software, were in the midst of releasing new and more powerful game consoles following the release of Microsoft's new game player. EA had been aggressively investing in the development of new video game titles for these new consoles. The company was also investing in games for the online market as well as handheld devices and cell phones. In addition to incurring these additional research and development costs, the company experienced declining sales in anticipation of the transition to the new hardware, lower margins as a result of price cuts to stimulate sales, and higher marketing and sales costs.

The market expected EA's financial downturn to continue through the fiscal year ending March 2007. Analysts expected EA to generate EPS of only $0.11 in 2007, an 85 percent decrease from the prior year. However, EPS were expected to rebound to $0.95 (an increase of 764 percent) and $2.03 (an increase of 114 percent) in the following two years. Most analysts projected earnings only over a three-year period.[10]

How do these forecasts by analysts reconcile with the actual market valuation of EA? What were the market's implicit assumptions about the short-term and long-term earnings growth for the company? By altering the amounts for key value drivers and arriving at combinations that generate an estimated value equal to the observed market price, the analyst can infer what the market might have been expecting for EA in November 2006.

A reasonable estimate of EA's cost of equity capital is in the range of 10 percent to 12 percent. As a result of strong revenue growth, the company's book value has grown at an average of 20 percent over the past five years, and it is likely that this growth will persist over the next five years. Focusing on earnings as the value driver, critical questions for judging the market valuation of EA are (1) how quickly the company's earnings will rebound to the levels of two years ago, (2) what the firm's near-term earnings growth prospects are, and (3) whether the company will continue to outperform the earnings growth rates of the average firms in the economy, which has historically been around 4 percent? The analysis in Table 9-1 shows different scenarios for EA's future performance that would justify its current stock price, assuming a cost of equity capital of 10 percent.

Table 9-1 shows the implications for EA's earnings growth using the three-year estimates of the various sell-side analysts covering the stock as well as scenarios if the expected short-term turnaround does not materialize as expected. The table also shows the implied EPS and ROEs that the various turnaround scenarios would imply. Even using the market's estimates for the first three years, EA would need to maintain an impressive rate of earnings growth through 2011. If the turnaround is faster than the market consensus, EA's earnings could show only a modest decline in 2007 and grow by 150 percent the following year as the firm's investments pay off. However, the company still needs to achieve impressively high average growth through 2011 to justify the $58 stock price. If, on the other hand, the turnaround in the current year's performance is slower than anticipated, the pressure on EA to produce superior earnings growth in the short term is intensified, with required growth rates of 100 percent even four years in the future. Critically, all three scenarios require strong earnings growth beyond the forecast horizon. For instance, in the scenario of a slow turnaround, EA would need to maintain an earnings growth rate of 7 percent in perpetuity, a rate that few companies have managed to maintain. In addition, any missteps could lead the stock to become more risky and volatile, implying a higher cost of capital. In this case, even higher rates of earnings growth would be needed to justify the current market price.

This type of scenario analysis provides the analyst with insights about investors' expectations for EA, and is useful for judging whether the stock is correctly valued. Security analysis need not involve such a detailed attempt to infer market

TABLE 9-1 Alternative Assumptions About Value Drivers for Electronic Arts Consistent with Observed Market Price of $58.84 (Assuming 10 Percent Cost of Equity Capital)

Analysts' Mean Earnings Forecast Through 2009	2007	2008	2009	2010	2011	Post 2011
Earnings Growth	−85%	764%	114%	75%	50%	6.0%
Earnings Per Share	0.11	0.95	2.03	3.56	5.34	
Return on Equity	1%	7%	13%	19%	24%	

Turnaround Faster Than Predicted	2007	2008	2009	2010	2011	Post 2011
Earnings Growth	−25%	150%	100%	60%	30%	5.0%
Earnings Per Share	0.56	1.41	2.82	4.51	5.86	
Return on Equity	5%	11%	18%	24%	26%	

Turnaround Slower Than Predicted	2007	2008	2009	2010	2011	Post 2011
Earnings Growth	−85%	350%	200%	100%	57%	7.0%
Earnings Per Share	0.11	0.50	1.49	2.98	4.67	
Return on Equity	1%	4%	10%	16%	21%	

expectations. However, whether or not an explicit analysis is made, a good analyst understands what economic scenarios could plausibly be reflected in the observed price.

Key Analysis Questions

By using the discounted abnormal earnings/ROE valuation model, analysts can infer the market's expectations for a firm's future performance. This permits analysts to ask whether the market is over- or undervaluing a company. Typical questions that analysts might ask from this analysis include the following:

- What are the market's assumptions about long-term ROE and growth? For example, is the market forecasting that the company can grow its earnings without a corresponding level of expansion in its asset base (and hence equity)? If so, how long can this persist?
- How do changes in the cost of capital affect the market's assessment of the firm's future performance? If the market's expectations seem to be unexpectedly high or low, has the market reassessed the company's risk? If so, is this change plausible?

Developing the Analyst's Expectations

Ultimately, a security analyst must compare his or her own view of a stock with the view embedded in the market price. The analyst's view is generated using the same analytical tools discussed in Chapters 2 through 8. The final product of this work is, of course, a forecast of the firm's future earnings and cash flows and an estimate of the firm's value. However, that final product is less important than the understanding of the business and its industry that the analysis provides. It is such understanding that enables the analyst to interpret new information as it arrives and to infer its implications.

Key Analysis Questions

In developing expectations about a firm's future performance using the financial analysis tools discussed throughout this book, the analyst is likely to ask the following types of questions:

- How profitable is the firm? In light of industry conditions, the firm's corporate strategy, and its barriers to competition, how sustainable is that rate of profitability?
- What are the opportunities for growth for this firm?
- How risky is this firm? How vulnerable are operations to general economic downturns? How highly levered is the firm? What does the riskiness of the firm imply about its cost of capital?
- How do answers to the above questions compare to the expectations embedded in the observed stock price?

The Final Product of Security Analysis

For financial analysts, the final product of security analysis is a recommendation to buy, sell, or hold the stock (or some more refined ranking). The recommendation is supported by a set of forecasts and a report summarizing the foundation for the recommendation. Analysts' reports often delve into significant detail and include an assessment of a firm's business as well as a line-by-line income statement, balance sheet, and cash flow forecasts for one or more years.

In making a recommendation to buy or sell a stock, the analyst has to consider the investment time horizon required to capitalize on the recommendation. Are anticipated improvements in performance likely to be confirmed in the near term, allowing investors to capitalize quickly on the recommendation? Or do expected performance improvements reflect long-term fundamentals that will take several years to play out? Longer investment horizons impose greater risk to investors that the company's performance will be affected by changes in economic conditions that cannot be anticipated by the analyst, reducing the value of the recommendation. Consequently, thorough analysis requires the ability not only to recognize whether a stock is misvalued, but also to anticipate when a price correction is likely to take place.

Because there are additional investment risks from following recommendations that require long-term commitments, security analysts tend to focus on making recommendations that are likely to pay off in the short term. This might explain why so few analysts recommended selling dot-com and technology stocks during the late 1990s when their prices would be difficult to justify on the basis of long-term fundamentals. It also explains why analysts recommended Enron's stock at its peak, even though the kind of analysis performed in this chapter would have shown that the future growth and ROE performance implied by this price would be extremely difficult to achieve. It also implies that to take advantage of long-term fundamental analysis can often require access to patient, long-term capital.

PERFORMANCE OF SECURITY ANALYSTS AND FUND MANAGERS

There has been extensive research on the performance of sell-side security analysts and fund managers during the last three decades. A few of the key findings are summarized below.

Performance of Sell-Side Analysts

Despite the recent failure of sell-side analysts to foresee the dramatic price declines for dot-com and telecommunications stocks, and to detect the financial shenanigans and overvaluation of companies such as Enron and WorldCom, research shows that analysts generally add value in the capital market. Analyst earnings forecasts are more accurate than those produced by time series models that use past earnings to predict future earnings.[11] Of course, this should not be too surprising since analysts can update their earnings forecasts between quarters to incorporate new firm and economy information, whereas time-series models cannot. In addition, stock prices tend to respond positively to upward revisions in analysts' earnings forecasts and recommendations, and negatively to downward revisions.[12] Further, recent research indicates that sell-side analysts' buy recommendations outperform the market index and risk benchmarks by 6.5 percent and 7.5 percent per year, respectively.[13] Finally, recent research finds that analysts play a valuable role in improving market efficiency.

For example, stock prices for firms with higher analyst following incorporate more rapidly information on accruals and cash flows than prices of less followed firms.[14]

Several factors seem to be important in explaining analysts' earnings forecast accuracy. Not surprisingly, forecasts of near-term earnings are much more accurate than those of long-term performance.[15] This probably explains why analysts typically make detailed forecasts for only one or two years ahead. Studies of differences in earnings forecast accuracy among analysts find that the more accurate ones tend to specialize by industry and work for large, well funded firms that employ other analysts who follow the same industry.[16]

Although analysts perform a valuable function in the capital market, research shows that their forecasts and recommendations tend to be biased. Early evidence on bias indicated that analyst earnings forecasts tended to be optimistic and that their recommendations were almost exclusively for buys.[17] Several factors potentially explain this finding. First, security analysts at brokerage houses are typically compensated on the basis of the trading volume that their reports generate. Given the costs of short selling and the restrictions on short selling by many institutions, brokerage analysts have incentives to issue optimistic reports that encourage investors to buy stocks rather than to issue negative reports that create selling pressure.[18] Second, until 2003 analysts that worked for investment banks were rewarded for promoting public issues by current clients and for attracting new banking clients, creating incentives for optimistic forecasts and recommendations. Studies show that analysts who work for lead underwriters make more optimistic long-term earnings forecasts and recommendations for firms raising equity capital than unaffiliated analysts.[19]

Evidence indicates that during the late 1990s there was a marked decline in analyst optimism in forecasts of near-term earnings.[20] One explanation offered for this change is that during this time analysts relied heavily on private discussions with top management to make their earnings forecasts. Management allegedly used these personal connections to manage analysts' short-term expectations downward so that the firm could subsequently report earnings that beat analysts' expectations. In response to concerns about this practice, in October 2000 the SEC approved Regulation Fair Disclosure, which prohibits management from making selective disclosures of nonpublic information. Studies show that this regulatory intervention has led to greater independence from management by analysts and an increased effort in independent information discovery.[21]

There has also been a general decline in sell-side analysts' optimistic recommendations during the past few years. Many large investment banks now require analysts to use a forced curve to rate stocks, leading to a greater number of the lowest ratings. Factors that underlie this change include a sharp rise in trading by hedge funds, which actively seek stocks to short-sell. In contrast, traditional money management firms are typically restricted from short-selling, and are more interested in analysts' buy recommendations than their sells. Second, regulatory changes in the U.S. under the Global Settlement require tight separation between investment banking and equity research at investment banks.

Performance of Fund Managers

Measuring whether mutual and pension fund managers earn superior returns is a difficult task for several reasons. First, there is no agreement about how to estimate benchmark performance for a fund. Studies have used a number of approaches—some have used the Capital Asset Pricing Model (CAPM) as a benchmark while others have used multifactor pricing models. For studies using the CAPM, there are questions about what type of market index to use. For example, should it be an equal- or value-weighted index, a NYSE index or a broader market index? Second, many of the traditional measures of fund performance abstract from market-wide performance, which understates fund abnormal performance if fund managers can time the market by reducing portfolio risk prior to market declines and increasing risks before a market run-up. Third, the overall volatility of stock returns stretches the limits of statistical power needed to measure fund performance. Finally, tests of fund performance are likely to be highly sensitive to the time period examined. Value or momentum investing could therefore appear to be profitable depending on when the tests are conducted.

Perhaps because of these challenges, there is no consistent evidence that actively managed mutual funds generate superior returns for investors. While some studies find evidence of positive abnormal returns for the industry, others conclude that returns are generally negative.[22] Of course even if mutual fund managers on average can only generate "normal" returns for investors, it is still possible for the best managers to show consistently strong performance. Some studies do in fact document that funds earning positive abnormal returns in one period continue to outperform in subsequent periods. However, more recent evidence suggests that these findings are caused by general momentum in stock returns or are offset by high fund expenses from management fees and/or trading costs.[23] Researchers have also examined which, if any, investment strategies are most successful. However, no clear consensus appears—several studies have found that momentum and high turnover strategies generate superior returns, whereas others conclude that value strategies are better.[24]

Finally, recent research has examined whether fund managers tend to buy and sell many of the same stocks at the same time. There is evidence of "herding" behavior, particularly by momentum fund managers.[25] This could arise because managers have access to common information, because they are affected by similar cognitive biases, or because they have incentives to follow the crowd.[26] For example, consider the rationale of a fund manager who holds a stock but who, through long-term fundamental analysis, estimates that it is misvalued. If the manager changes the fund's holdings accordingly and the stock price returns to its intrinsic value in the next quarter, the fund will show superior relative portfolio performance and will attract new capital. However, if the stock continues to be misvalued for several quarters, the informed fund manager will underperform the benchmark and capital will flow to other funds. In contrast, a risk-averse manager who simply follows the crowd will not be rewarded for detecting the misvaluation, but neither will this manager be blamed for a poor investment decision when the stock price ultimately corrects, since other funds made the same mistake.

There has been considerably less research on the performance of pension fund managers. Overall, the findings show little consistent evidence that pension fund managers either over- or under-perform traditional benchmarks.[27]

SUMMARY

Equity security analysis is the evaluation of a firm and its prospects from the perspective of a current or potential investor in the firm's stock. Security analysis is one component of a larger investment process that involves (1) establishing the objectives of the investor or fund, (2) forming expectations about the future returns and risks of individual securities, and then (3) combining individual securities into portfolios to maximize progress toward the investment objectives.

Some security analysis is devoted primarily to assuring that a stock possesses the proper risk profile and other desired characteristics prior to inclusion in an investor's portfolio. However, especially for many professional buy-side and sell-side security analysts, the analysis is also directed toward the identification of mispriced securities. In equilibrium, such activity will be rewarding for those with the strongest comparative advantage. They will be the ones able to identify any mispricing at the lowest cost and exert pressure on the price to correct the mispricing. What kinds of efforts are productive in this domain depends on the degree of market efficiency. A large body of evidence exists that is supportive of a high degree of efficiency in the U.S. market, but recent studies have reopened the debate on this issue.

In practice, a wide variety of approaches to fund management and security analysis are employed. However, at the core of the analyses are the same steps outlined in Chapters 2 through 8 of this book: business strategy analysis, accounting analysis, financial analysis, and prospective analysis (forecasting and valuation). For the professional analyst, the final product of the work is, of course, a forecast of the firm's future earnings and cash flows, and an estimate of the firm's value. But that final product is less important than the understanding of the business and its industry, which the analysis provides. It is such understanding that positions the analyst to interpret new information as it arrives and infer its implications.

Finally, the chapter summarizes some key findings of the research on the performance of both sell-side and buy-side security analysts.

DISCUSSION QUESTIONS

1. Despite many years of research, the evidence on market efficiency described in this chapter appears to be inconclusive. Some argue that this is because researchers have been unable to link company fundamentals to stock prices precisely. Comment.

2. Geoffrey Henley, a professor of finance, states, "The capital market is efficient. I don't know why anyone would bother devoting time to following individual stocks and doing fundamental analysis. The best approach is to buy and hold a well diversified portfolio of stocks." Do you agree? Why or why not?

3. What is the difference between fundamental and technical analysis? Can you think of any trading strategies that use technical analysis? What are the underlying assumptions made by these strategies?

4. Investment funds follow many different types of investment strategies. Income funds focus on stocks with high dividend yields, growth funds invest in stocks that are expected to have high capital appreciation, value funds follow stocks that are considered to be undervalued, and short funds bet against stocks they consider to be overvalued. What types of investors are likely to be attracted to each of these types of funds? Why?

5. Intergalactic Software Company went public three months ago. You are a sophisticated investor who devotes time to fundamental analysis as a way of identifying mispriced stocks. Which of the following characteristics would you focus on in deciding whether to follow this stock?
   • The market capitalization
   • The average number of shares traded per day
   • The bid–ask spread for the stock

- Whether the underwriter that brought the firm public is a Top Five investment banking firm
- Whether the firm's audit company is a Big Four firm
- Whether there are analysts from major brokerage firms following the company
- Whether the stock is held mostly by retail or by institutional investors

6. Intergalactic Software Company's stock has a market price of $20 per share and a book value of $12 per share. If its cost of equity capital is 15 percent and its book value is expected to grow at 5 percent per year indefinitely, what is the market's assessment of its steady state return on equity? If the stock price increases to $35 and the market does not expect the firm's growth rate to change, what is the revised steady state ROE? If instead the price increase was due to an increase in the market's assessments about long-term book value growth rather than long-term ROE, what would the price revision imply for the steady state growth rate?

7. There are two major types of financial analysts: buy-side and sell-side. Buy-side analysts work for investment firms and make stock recommendations that are available only to the management of funds within that firm. Sell-side analysts work for brokerage firms and make recommendations that are used to sell stock to the brokerage firms' clients, which include individual investors and managers of investment funds. What would be the differences in tasks and motivations of these two types of analysts?

8. Many market participants believe that sell-side analysts are too optimistic in their recommendations to buy stocks and too slow to recommend sells. What factors might explain this bias?

9. Joe Klein is an analyst for an investment banking firm that offers both underwriting and brokerage services. Joe sends you a highly favorable report on a stock that his firm recently helped go public and for which it currently makes the market. What are the potential advantages and disadvantages in relying on Joe's report in deciding whether to buy the stock?

10. Joe states, "I can see how ratio analysis and valuation help me do fundamental analysis, but I don't see the value of doing strategy analysis." Can you explain to him how strategy analysis could be potentially useful?

NOTES

1. P. Healy and K. Palepu, "The Fall of Enron," *Journal of Economic Perspectives* 17, no. 2 (Spring 2003): 3–26, discuss how weak money manager incentives and a lack of proper long-term analysis contributed to the stock price run-up and subsequent collapse of Enron. A similar discussion on factors affecting the rise and fall of dot-com stocks is provided in "The Role of Capital Market Intermediaries in the Dot-Com Crash of 2000," Harvard Business School Case 9-101–110, 2001.

2. See R. Bhushan, "Firm characteristics and analyst following," *Journal of Accounting and Economics* 11 (2/5), July 1989: 255–75, and P. O'Brien and R. Bhushan, "Analyst following and institutional ownership," *Journal of Accounting Research* 28, Supplement (1990): 55–76.

3. P. Mohanram and S. Sunder, "How Has Regulation FD Affected the Operations of Financial Analysts?" *Contemporary Accounting Research 23*, no. 2 (2006): 491–525.

4. Reviews of evidence on market efficiency are provided by E. Fama, "Efficient Capital Markets: II," *Journal of Finance* 46 (December 1991): 1575–1617; S. Kothari, "Capital Markets Research in Accounting," *Journal of Accounting and Economics* 31 (September 2001):105–231; and C. Lee, "Market Efficiency in Accounting Research," *Journal of Accounting and Economics* 31 (September 2001): 233–53.

5. For example, see V. Bernard and J. Thomas, "Evidence That Stock Prices Do Not Fully Reflect the Implications of Current Earnings for Future Earnings," *Journal of Accounting and Economics* 13 (December 1990): 305–41.

6. For example, the superior returns earned by pursuing a "value stock" strategy were examined by J. Lakonishok, A. Shleifer, and R. Vishny, "Contrarian Investment, Extrapolation, and Risk," *Journal of Finance* 49 (December 1994): 1541–78, and R. Frankel and C. Lee, "Accounting Valuation, Market Expectation, and Cross-Sectional Stock Returns," *Journal of Accounting and Economics* 25 (June 1998): 283–319.

7. For example, see J. Ou and S. Penman, "Financial Statement Analysis and the Prediction of Stock Returns," *Journal of Accounting and Economics* 11 (November 1989): 295–330; R. Holthausen and D. Larcker, "The Prediction of Stock Returns Using Financial Statement Information," *Journal of Accounting and Economics* 15 (June/September 1992): 373–412; and R. Sloan, "Do Stock Prices Fully Reflect Information in Accruals and Cash Flows about Future Earnings?" *The Accounting Review* 71 (July 1996): 298–325.

8. A. Shleifer, "Do Demand Curves for Stocks Slope Down," *Journal of Finance and Quantitative Analysis* 34 (March 1986): 579–90, argues that stocks show a positive abnormal returns immediately after entering the S&P 500 Index as a result of increased demand from index funds. While extensive research exists on the idea that trading as a result of investor preference creates short-term price pressure in spin-off transactions, J. Abarbanell, B. Bushee, and J. Raedy, "Institutional Investor Preferences and Price Pressure: The Case of Corporate Spin-Offs," *Journal of Business* 76 (2003): 233–61, finds that this trading is not associated with abnormal price movements for parents or subsidiaries around the spin-off.

9. For an overview of research in behavioral finance, see R. Thaler, *Advances in Behavioral Finance* (New York: Russell Sage Foundation, 1993), and A. Shleifer, *Inefficient Markets: An Introduction to Behavioral Finance* (Oxford: Oxford University Press, 2000). Numerous studies have documented the bias introduced by various elements of irrational behavior such as overconfidence, herding, regret, and loss aversion.

10. These forecasts were taken from Thomson One Analytics.

11. See L. Brown and M. Rozeff, "The Superiority of Analyst Forecasts as Measures of Expectations: Evidence from Earnings," *Journal of Finance* 33 (1978): 1–16; L. Brown, P. Griffin, R. Hagerman, and M. Zmijewski, "Security Analyst Superiority Relative to Univariate Time-Series Models in Forecasting Quarterly Earnings," *Journal of Accounting and Economics* 9 (1987): 61–87; and D. Givoly, "Financial Analysts' Forecasts of

Earnings: A Better Surrogate for Market Expectations," *Journal of Accounting and Economics* 4, no. 2 (1982): 85–108.

12. See D. Givoly and J. Lakonishok, "The Information Content of Financial Analysts' Forecasts of Earnings: Some Evidence on Semi-Strong Efficiency," *Journal of Accounting and Economics* 2 (1979): 165–86; T. Lys and S. Sohn, "The Association Between Revisions of Financial Analysts' Earnings Forecasts and Security Price Changes," *Journal of Accounting and Economics* 13 (1990): 341–64; and J. Francis and L. Soffer, "The Relative Informativeness of Analysts' Stock Recommendations and Earnings Forecast Revisions," *Journal of Accounting Research* 35, no. 2 (1997): 193–212.

13. See B. Groysberg, P. Healy, C. Chapman, and Y. Gui, "Do Buy-Side Analysts Out-Perform the Sell-Side?" (working paper, Harvard Business School, June 2006). The study also finds that buy-side analysts at a large money management firm make more optimistic earnings forecasts and less profitable buy recommendations than sell-side analysts.

14. See M. Brennan, N. Jegadeesh, and B. Swaminathan, "Investment Analysis and the Adjustment of Stock Prices to Common Information," *Review of Financial Studies* 6, no. 4 (1993): 799–824, and B. Ayers and R. Freeman, "Evidence That Analyst Following and Institutional Ownership Accelerate the Pricing of Future Earnings," *Review of Accounting Studies* 8, no. 1 (2003): 47–67.

15. See P. O'Brien, "Forecasts Accuracy of Individual Analysts in Nine Industries." *Journal of Accounting Research* 28 (1990): 286–304.

16. See M. Clement, "Analyst Forecast Accuracy: Do Ability, Resources, and Portfolio Complexity Matter?" *Journal of Accounting and Economics* 27 (1999): 285–304; J. Jacob, T. Lys, and M. Neale, "Experience in Forecasting Performance of Security Analysts." *Journal of Accounting and Economics* 28 (1999): 51–82; and S. Gilson, P. Healy, C. Noe, and K. Palepu, "Analyst Specialization and Conglomerate Stock Breakups," *Journal of Accounting Research* 39 (December 2001): 565–73.

17. See L. Brown, G. Foster, and E. Noreen, "Security Analyst Multi-Year Earnings Forecasts and the Capital Market," *Studies in Accounting Research*, no. 23, American Accounting Association (Sarasota, FL), 1985. In addition, M. McNichols and P. O'Brien, in "Self-Selection and Analyst Coverage," *Journal of Accounting Research*, Supplement (1997): 167–208, find that analyst bias arises primarily because analysts issue recommendations on firms for which they have favorable information and withhold recommending firms with unfavorable information.

18. See A. Cowen, B. Groysberg, and P. Healy, "Which Types of Analyst Firms Are More Optimistic?" *Journal of Accounting and Economics* 41 (2006): 119–146.

19. See H. Lin and M. McNichols, "Underwriting Relationships, Analysts' Earnings Forecasts and Investment Recommendations," *Journal of Accounting and Economics* 25, no. 1 (1998): 101–28; R. Michaely and K. Womack, "Conflict of Interest and the Credibility of Underwriter Analyst Recommendations," *Review of Financial Studies* 12, no. 4 (1999): 653–86; and P. Dechow, A. Hutton, and R. Sloan, "The Relation Between Analysts' Forecasts of Long-Term Earnings Growth and Stock Price Performance Following Equity Offerings," *Contemporary Accounting Research* 17, no. 1 (2000): 1–32.

20. See L. Brown, "Analyst Forecasting Errors: Additional Evidence," *Financial Analysts' Journal* (November/December 1997): 81–88, and D. Matsumoto, "Management's Incentives to Avoid Negative Earnings Surprises," *The Accounting Review* 77 (July 2002): 483–515.

21. See P. Mohanram and S. Sunder, "How Has Regulation FD Affected the Functioning of Financial Analysts?" *Contemporary Accounting Research* 23, no. 2 (2006): 491–525.

22. For example, evidence of superior fund performance is reported by M. Grinblatt and S. Titman, "Mutual Fund Performance: An Analysis of Quarterly Holdings, *Journal of Business* 62 (1994), and by D. Hendricks, J. Patel, and R. Zeckhauser, "Hot Hands in Mutual Funds: Short-Run Persistence of Relative Performance," *The Journal of Finance* 48 (1993): 93–130. In contrast, negative fund performance is shown by M. Jensen, "The Performance of Mutual Funds in the Period 1945–64," *The Journal of Finance* 23 (May 1968): 389–416, and B. Malkiel, "Returns from Investing in Equity Mutual Funds from 1971 to 1991," *Journal of Finance* 50 (June 1995): 549–73.

23. M. Grinblatt and S. Titman, "The Persistence of Mutual Fund Performance," *Journal of Finance* 47 (December 1992): 1977–86, and D. Hendricks, J. Patel, and R. Zeckhauser, "Hot Hands in Mutual Funds: Short-Run Persistence of Relative Performance," *Journal of Finance* 48 (March 1993): 93–130, find evidence of persistence in mutual fund returns. However, M. Carhart, "On Persistence in Mutual Fund Performance," *The Journal of Finance* 52 (March 1997): 57–83, shows that much of this is attributable to momentum in stock returns and to fund expenses; B. Malkiel, "Returns from Investing in Equity Mutual Funds from 1971 to 1991," *The Journal of Finance* 50 (June 1995): 549–73, shows that survivorship bias is also an important consideration.

24. See M. Grinblatt, S. Titman, and R. Wermers, "Momentum Investment Strategies, Portfolio Performance, and Herding: A Study of Mutual Fund Behavior," *The American Economic Review* 85 (December 1995): 1088–105.

25. For example, J. Lakonishok, A. Shleifer, and R. Vishny, "Contrarian Investment, Extrapolation, and Risk," *Journal of Finance* 49 (December 1994): 1541–79, find that value funds show superior performance, whereas M. Grinblatt, S. Titman, and R. Wermers, "Momentum Investment Strategies, Portfolio Performance, and Herding: A Study of Mutual Fund Behavior," *The American Economic Review* 85 (December 1995): 1088–105, find that momentum investing is profitable.

26. See D. Scharfstein and J. Stein, "Herd Behavior and Investment," *The American Economic Review* 80 (June 1990): 465–80, and P. Healy and K. Palepu, "The Fall of Enron," *Journal of Economic Perspectives* 17, no. 2 (Spring 2003): 3–26.

27. For evidence on performance by pension fund managers, see J. Lakonishok, A. Shleifer, and R. Vishny, "The Structure and Performance of the Money Management Industry," Brookings Papers on Economic Activity, Washington, DC (1992): 339–92; T. Coggin, F. Fabozzi, and S. Rahman, "The Investment Performance of U.S. Equity Pension Fund Managers: An Empirical Investigation," *The Journal of Finance* 48 (July 1993): 1039–56; and W. Ferson and K. Khang, "Conditional Performance Measurement Using Portfolio Weights: Evidence for Pension Funds," *Journal of Financial Economics* 65 (August 2002): 249–282.

Merrill Lynch in 2003: Sunny Skies Ahead?

In January 2003, Merrill Lynch, the world's biggest brokerage firm, reported that its pre-tax earnings were four times higher in 2002 ($2.5 billion) than in 2001 ($573 million). Public reaction to the news was mixed.

Some analysts were upbeat about Merrill's report. Several hailed Merrill's 51-year old CEO, Stanley O'Neal as a genius for having turned around the company's performance during a stagnant economy and a year of poor market conditions.[1] By cutting costs and focusing on profitable lines of business, these analysts claimed, O'Neal—the first African American ever to lead Merrill—was remaking the company into a leaner, more effective brokerage house and investment bank. They supported O'Neal's new strategic vision, which included reducing headcount, emphasizing wealth management services, and focusing on more profitable financial products and services.

Critics pointed out that Merrill's improved earnings came at a high cost. By reducing Merrill's corps of full-time employees—from a high of 72,600 in 2001 to 50,900 at the end of 2002—these critics claimed, O'Neal had diminished the traditional strength of the company: its brokerage arm. While acknowledging that some cutbacks were necessary, several analysts questioned whether the payroll reduction, especially the dismissal of 6,000 brokers, would hurt the company, when (and if) the economy began its recovery.[2]

In 2002, the entire financial services industry was becoming more competitive amidst dismal market conditions, scandal, and a sluggish economy. Equity markets suffered their sharpest declines since the 1970s.[3] Research analysts at several Wall Street investment banking firms, including Merrill, were indicted for producing flawed research to benefit their clients, and in some cases, themselves. Many individual investors who had lost their investments sued the brokerage firms in which they had placed their trust and savings. Industry profits fell from $21 billion in 2000 to about $7 billion in 2002.[4]

Professors Boris Groysberg and Paul Healy and Senior Researcher David Kiron, Global Research Group prepared this case. This case was developed from published sources. HBS cases are developed solely as the basis for class discussion. Cases are not intended to serve as endorsements, sources of primary data, or illustrations of effective or ineffective management.

1. David Rynecki, "Putting the Muscle Back in the Bull," Fortune, April 5, 2004, via Factiva. (Unless noted, all articles cited in this case were accessed through Factiva, www.factiva.com.)

2. Emily Thornton, "The New Merrill Lynch," BusinessWeek, May 5, 2003.

3. Merrill Lynch, 2002 Annual Report (New York: Merrill Lynch, 2003), p. 14.

4. Lynda M. Applegate, "Citigroup 2003: Testing the Limits of Convergence (A)," HBS Case No. 804-041 (Boston, Harvard Business School Publishing, June 4, 2004), p. 4.

Merrill Lynch in 2003

The U.S. economy contributed to the poor market conditions, or at a minimum, failed to stimulate the equities markets. In 2002, the U.S. Gross Domestic Product grew 2.4%; a sluggish growth rate that was expected to continue for at least two additional years.[5]

The scandals tarnished the credibility of financial services firms and the industry in general. Merrill, in particular, was hit hard by the Internet research scandals, and its involvement with the Enron and IMClone scandals. Its senior research analyst and group head for the Internet sector, Henry Blodget, was censured by the SEC for publicly recommending stocks that he privately derided and was permanently barred from the securities industry. Merrill was criticized for its complex and sometimes conflicting relationships as investor, lender, underwriter, and counterparty in energy-derivatives with Enron and its CFO, Andy Fastow. The total cost to the company of settlements with the SEC, New York attorney general, Eliot Spitzer, and developing an education program for its researchers had already reached $280 million.[6]

However, even with costly scandals, a tarnished reputation, a depressed market, and economic stagnation, Merrill's 2002 financial results were a marked improvement over its prior year (Merrill's summary financial statements are shown in **Exhibit 1**). The firm's 2002 performance also eclipsed that of industry peers. Morgan Stanley, the company that most closely mirrored Merrill's mix of investment banking, institutional trading, retail brokerage, financial advisory, and money management businesses, had 2002 pre-tax profits that were 18% lower than its own 2001 pre-tax profits. Summary financial information for Morgan Stanley is shown in **Exhibit 2**.

In its 2002 Annual report, Merrill Lynch wrote:

> *Over the past 12 months, we have built on the restructuring initiated at the end of 2001, aggressively controlled expenses, diversified revenues, and liberated resources to invest in our future. We have resized our company and reshaped it into a portfolio of diversified businesses to deliver superior client service and shareholder value across economic cycles. We have rededicated ourselves to a performance-based culture, grounded in excellence and integrity. . . .Personally, I feel confident that the story developing at Merrill Lynch will be not about cost cuts—but about opportunities created. We have redefined Merrill Lynch as a portfolio of diverse, nimble, high-performing businesses aimed at profitability and growth. Each business in the portfolio creates compelling opportunities to expand and enhance service to our clients and generate shareholder value.[7]*

5. Ibid.

6. $100 million to settle with Spitzer over questionable investment research; $100 million fine to pay for programs for independent research and investor education and $80 million to settle with SEC over questionable involvement of Merrill execs in the Enron scandal. From Press Releases, Office of New York State Attorney General Eliot Spitzer. "Spitzer, Merrill Lynch Reach Unprecedented Agreement to Reform Investment Practices," May 21, 2002: SEC, NY Attourney General, NASD, NASAA, NYSE and State Regulators Announce Historic Agreement to Reform Investment Practices, December 20th 2002; SEC Press Release, "SEC Charges Merrill Lynch, Four Merrill Lynch Executives with Aiding and Abetting Enron Accounting Fraud," March 17, 2003.

7. Merrill Lynch, 2002 Annual Report (New York: Merrill Lynch, 2003), pp. 1–2.

There was little doubt that O'Neal's efforts to overhaul the company had helped to increase Merrill's profitability. The issue was: would O'Neal's changes, whatever their appropriateness for the days passed, be appropriate for the days ahead?

HISTORY

From its inception in 1914, Merrill had had a succession of strong and visionary leaders. Founder Charles Merrill launched the company as an underwriting company, then partnered with his friend Edmund Lynch to form a retail brokerage firm that focused on small investors instead of the large institutional investors then the focus of other brokerage houses. With Merrill Lynch, individual investors received personal financial services for the first time. Charles Merrill became known as the man who brought Wall Street to Main Street.

During the 1970s, Donald Regan (Treasury Secretary under Ronald Reagan, 1980–1984) strengthened Merrill's investment banking division and oversaw the company's early globalization efforts. Merrill Lynch's consumer business was expanded in 1976 with the creation of Merrill Lynch Asset Management (MLAM). One year later, Merrill entered the consumer banking business, in effect, with the introduction of its cash management account, which combined a securities margin account with a money market account, a checking account and a VISA debit card.

Merrill continued to leverage its traditional strength in retail brokerage during the 1980s and 1990s to enhance its standing as an investment bank and to develop an international presence. In 1983, it became the first regular foreign member of the Tokyo Stock Exchange.[8] It was the first U.S. securities firm to open an office in the People's Republic of China (1993, Shanghai). A total of 33 new branch offices were opened in Japan. Operations were launched in India and dozens of smaller markets. Between 1997 and 2000, worldwide payroll jumped from 60,500 to 72,000. "By 1990 [Merrill] was the leading investment bank in the world, a crown it wore for 11 consecutive years. What it gave up were the thick profit margins enjoyed by its peers, said one business journalist."[9] Focus on revenues allowed Merrill Lynch to achieve top rankings in most underwriting tables.

Despite the growth, there were ominous signs that the company's focus on revenues, rather than profits, was leading to trouble.

By the late 1990s, Merrill bankers were taking on more low-margin deals to maintain the firm's ranking in the influential industry league tables but overlooking the ultimate need for profits. Revenues soared at a 15% annualized rate for the decade, but expenses were rising at an almost parallel pace. In 1996, Merrill's profit margins were five percentage points worse than those of its rivals, on average. Two years later the gap had swelled to ten points. In 2000, the best year for investment banking in the history of Wall Street, Merrill's underwriting and advisory business eked out a $200 million profit.

---

8. *Ibid.*

9. David Rynecki & Patricia Neering, "Can Stan O'Neal Save Merrill? He's ripping apart the securities firm, piece by piece. He's making enemies. He's not apologizing. It might just work," *Fortune*, September 30, 2002.

The hallmark of the firm's performance was "mediocrity," says Ahmass Fakahany, now Merrill's CFO, who remembers management meetings that dwelled on inane topics like dress-down days instead of profitability.[10]

A NEW COMPETITIVE LANDSCAPE

Full service investment banks, such as Merrill Lynch, typically generated revenues from a wide range of business activities, including underwriting, M&A advisory services, retail and institutional brokerage, asset management, and proprietary trading. **Exhibit 3** provides a breakdown of industry revenues for the investment banking sector across these business activities 1997 to 2002. **Exhibit 4** presents market shares for Merrill Lynch and three competing banks, again for different business activities, from 1998 to 2002.

Underwriting units at banks helped companies, local authorities and governments to issue debt or equity securities by selling these securities to investors. In return, the banks received a percentage of the funds raised as underwriting fees. M&A advisory services were offered to companies involved in mergers or acquisitions, and included help in finding the right purchaser or seller, arranging financing, and valuing the business or assets to be sold/purchased. Banks received a fee, typically a percentage of the value of the sales/purchase value, for providing these services. Brokerage units offered investment advice and trade execution to retail and institutional clients, generating commissions on the trades. Asset management units formed mutual funds to invest money received from investors (both individuals and institutions). Compensation for asset management was an annual fee, typically a percentage of the total assets under management. Finally, proprietary trading created profits (or losses) from the bank trading using its own capital (rather than that of its clients).

In 2002, significant changes in the competitive landscape were affecting many of these businesses. A changing regulatory environment was prompting mergers among financial service companies, with potential implications for underwriting and advisory businesses. The Internet continued to provide investors with new low-cost ways of trading securities and receiving investment advice. And an aging baby boomer population was increasing demand for wealth management services.

Universal Banks

In 1999, the U.S. congress repealed the 1933 Glass-Steagall Act, which had prohibited commercial banks from underwriting, insurance and other non-bank activities, and replaced it with new, more permissive regulations that permitted the formation of so-called Universal banks, i.e., financial holding companies that offered one-stop shopping for a variety of financial services. To their retail customers, these mega-banks offered banking, credit, insurance, wealth management advice, even mortgages. To corporate and institutional clients, they offered underwriting, investment research, credit, as well as merger and acquisition services. One observer described the impact of the new regulations on the industry:

The demarcations among investment banks, commercial banks, insurance companies, and other financial services firms grew fainter and fainter and largely disappeared with the repeal of Glass-Steagall. . . . Commercial banks were eager

---

10. Rynecki, "Putting the Muscle Back in the Bull."

to get the hefty returns on equity enjoyed by investment banks, investment banks wanted access to more reliable revenue streams derived from asset management, and everyone wanted a larger share of each client's wallet.[11]

The deregulation of the commercial and investment banking sectors was followed by several significant mergers. For example, in 1998, Citibank (a commercial bank) merged with Travellers Group (which included Salomon Smith Barney investment bank and Traveller's insurance company) to form Citigroup. In 2000, the investment bank J.P. Morgan combined with the commercial bank Chase Manhattan to create J.P. Morgan Chase.

Many observers contended that these Universal banks were meeting an explicit demand among banks' corporate clientele. "The corporate consolidation of the '90s has given us a lot of giant companies that used to have relationships with ten firms, but now they want only two or three, and they want them to be able to do anything, anywhere in the world, any size, any time,"[12] said James Lee Jr., vice chairman of J.P. Morgan in 2001. However, it was far from clear that the corporations demanding one-stop shopping reflected a corporate consensus. "In general I'm one of those people who does not really need one-stop shopping. I feel comfortable taking the best in breed for each transaction," said Lucent treasurer Hund-Mejean.[13]

Universal banks had several benefits in a slow moving economy. Universal banks could buy their way into lucrative, more traditional investment banking deals, such as bond issuances by offering credit lines at discounted rates. The banks were so big that they had in-house expertise to effectively conduct a multi-billion dollar bond issuance. In the past only investment banking firms had the necessary skills, but now that commercial banks had merged with investment firms, they had the talent and scale to gain share in this segment of the investment banking market. Investment banks, like Merrill, sometimes offered bridge loans or acquisition credits, but typically did not offer credit lines because of their low margins and high risk. However, with their larger loan portfolios, Universal banks could more easily absorb the risk associated with these credit lines and, unlike the investment banks, did not have to report their credit lines as loan commitments until the lines were actually used.

Increasingly, corporations began demanding loans and credit from all banks as a condition of participation in their debt offerings and underwritings. "If you're sitting in a company with a choice between giving the high-margin business to the people who supported you on the credit side and giving it to a group of competitors who are not necessarily going to do the job any better and who haven't made credit available to you, what are you going to choose?" said Michael Carpenter, CEO of Citigroup's investment banking unit.[14] A 2001 *Institutional Investor* survey of CFOs found that 40% of those surveyed had "demanded credit as a condition for giving investment banking business."[15]

For investment banks, the pressure to make such loans was so great, and represented such a great risk, that Standard & Poors in 2001 downgraded its outlook for Merrill, Goldman Sachs and Morgan Stanley from "stable" to "negative" on the grounds that they "would have to make risky loans to compete with commercial banks."[16]

---

11. *Futures International Competitive Intelligence Group, 2002,* as cited in Applegate, "Citigroup 2003: Testing the Limits of Convergence (A)," p. 4.

12. Justin Schack, "The New Battle for the Bulge," Institutional Investor, vol. 35, no. 8 (August 2001).

13. Schack, "The New Battle for the Bulge."

14. Ibid.

15. Ibid.

16. Ibid.

The Internet's Impact on Brokerage

Prior to the development of the Internet in the mid-1990s, the retail brokerage industry had been dominated by firms that provided full service investment advisory services to its clients, such as Merrill Lynch, and discount brokers like Charles Schwab. Schwab, which was created in 1975 following the deregulation of fixed commissions, had become a major player in the industry by providing investors with access to third party research, enabling it to have a lower cost structure and to offer investors lower trading costs. In contrast, Merrill Lynch provided its clients with access to its own research reports, the costs of which were covered through higher trading commissions. Over the years, deregulation and the growth of discount brokerage had led to a decline in commissions, from roughly 10.5 cents per share in 1985 to 7 cents in 1990 and to less than 6 cents by 2000.

The emergence of the Internet increased the downward pressure on commissions by providing brokerage firms with lower cost ways of interacting with clients wishing to trade and by providing investors with new independent sources of investment advice. Investors could access investment information and advice online from a wide range of sources at minimal cost. New companies, such as E-trade and Ameritrade emerged, providing investors with minimal investment advice, but significantly lower trading costs. Schwab responded quickly to the changes, adding new Internet-based services that it estimated reduced the costs of executing trades by as much as 80%.[17] Merrill Lynch followed in 1999, creating its own proprietary online trading platform.

Wealth Management

In the United States, an aging baby boomer population was expected to produce a historic generational transfer of wealth. Managing the build-up to this transfer was the focus of many financial services firms.

Much of the focus of these firms was on individuals with high net worth (defined by Merrill as individuals with $1 million or more in assets, excluding primary residential real estate). In 2000, the $8.8 trillion North American high net worth market was composed of 2.5 million individuals.[18] **Exhibit 5** shows high worth net assets for Merrill Lynch and several competitors. Analysts believed that this market would grow to $13 trillion by 2005. The number of households with more than $10 million in investable assets was expected to increase 25% by 2006. The number of households with between one and ten million dollars in investable assets was expected to increase 40% by 2006. The number of households with between $100,000 and $1,000,000 in investable assets was expected to increase 20% by 2006.[19]

Managing financial services to wealthy individuals had changed significantly from the 1970s. James P. Gorman, Merrill Lynch executive vice president and president of the firm's Global Private Client Group commented: "In the '70s and '80s, it was managing wealth trade by trade. By the '90s, it had evolved from transactional management to asset management. Now in the 21st century, wealth management goes beyond investments to embrace personal life goals such as education and retirement needs, and intergenerational wealth transfer."[20] He further explained, "Wealth management is the

17. See Lynda Applegate, F. Warren McFarlan, and Jamie Ladge, "Charles Schwab in 2002," HBS Case No. 803-70 (Boston, Harvard Business School Publishing, February 11, 2003).

18. Information in this paragraph is based on J. J. Hughes, "Brokerage and Asset Management Research: The Charles Schwab Corporation," Robertson Stephens, Inc., June 13, 2001.

19. Applegate, "Charles Schwab in 2002."

20. Jane Wollman Rusoff, "Whither wealth management? Merrill Lynch has been restructuring itself to provide high-end advisory services through highly trained advisors to wealthy clients. Will the rest of the industry follow?" Research 26: 81 (August 2003). © Copyright 2003 Gale Group Inc., Adams Business Media, 2003.

management of individuals' total net worth—both investments and liabilities. It's not just the investment side of their personal life—but the credit side too. Are you better off, for example, investing in some securities, or paying down some of your mortgage? It's a person's total wealth picture."[21]

Addressing the complex needs associated with the successful delivery of relevant financial services required a high level of costly technical expertise. Gorman described some of these costs:

> *Because wealth management is so wide-ranging, it takes greater technical knowledge to practice it properly—especially for very affluent or ultra-wealthy individuals—even though most services can be outsourced. The future is likely to bring only larger firms offering "true wealth management. . . . For most companies, the cost of training is too big and the technology, products and services required too many. So you'll see [industry] consolidation. The cost of serving this client segment properly is prohibitively high."[22]*

Despite the high costs of market entry, many financial service firms, both small and large, were jockeying for a piece of this market. Merrill Lynch already had a substantial position within this market: 60% of its clients had assets worth at least a million dollars. However, Merrill also faced significant and growing competition from Universal banks, from its investment banking peers and from other brokerages, such as Charles Schwab, which was trying to reposition itself as a service provider to high net worth individuals. By 2002, Schwab had purchased U.S. Trust, which had expertise managing high net worth individuals and was targeting fee-based services to customers based on their asset level.

The significance of wealth management as a future driver of growth, however, remained open to debate. Chris Poch, a senior manager at Smith Barney said, "Wealth management is not the wave of the future—it's the wave of today. We are mid-wave. There's no doubt about it. It's a long-term change."[23] But, money manager Kenneth L. Fisher, chairman and CIO of Fisher Investments in Woodside, California, was more cautious, "Wealth management's longevity hinges on the nation's baby boomers. If they end up embracing it, it's a material force for a very long time. If they choose not to, then Wealth management becomes a phrase you won't be hearing much about five to 10 years from now."[24]

O'NEAL'S TRANSFORMATION OF MERRILL LYNCH

Raised on his grandfather's Alabama farm, E. Stanley O'Neal moved with his family at the age of 12 to a housing project in Atlanta. Though it was tough to find work, his father successfully landed a position with a nearby General Motors plant. O'Neal later attended the General Motors Institute, which allowed him to study engineering and industrial management while working in the plant. The first college graduate in his family, he joined GM as a supervisor after graduating in the top 20% of his class. In 1978 he obtained his MBA from Harvard Business School with honors, on a full GM scholarship, and joined the treasurer's office at GM in New York. After eight years at GM, Merrill Lynch recruited O'Neal. His career then took him through various positions in

21. Rusoff, "Whither Wealth Management?"
22. Ibid.
23. Ibid.
24. Ibid.

financial services, global capital markets, investor strategies, corporate and institutional clients, and corporate services. In 2000, after serving for two years as the firm's Chief Financial Officer, O'Neal became the first-ever non-broker to head Merrill Lynch's U.S. Private Client Business.[25] In July 2001, O'Neal assumed the presidency.

Upon obtaining his new position, O'Neal focused on both long-term and short-term changes that would help Merrill compete more effectively inside the industry's new competitive landscape. The short-term changes began as soon as he became Merrill's president six weeks before the tragic events of September 11, 2001. In his role as president and then subsequently CEO, O'Neal's mission was to make a "meaner, leaner and more profitable" firm.

To achieve his objective, O'Neal began shifting the firm's heavy emphasis on booking revenue to a focus on profit. Expenses at Merrill's retail brokerage division were running out of control, its trust business was losing money, and its 401(K) unit had not turned a profit in 14 years. "Costs were moving at such a rapid pace," recalled O'Neal, "that they were going to overwhelm the speed at which revenues were moving and revenues were moving at a pace that we had never seen before. Unless you postulated that somehow costs would come down, or that revenues would continue to grow at [the same] rate or accelerate, it wasn't hard to figure out that [we] had a problem."[26] To cut costs, O'Neal began restructuring the company, cutting jobs, and instilling a new culture that rewarded accountability; effectively destroying the "Mother Merrill" culture that had for some time coddled underperforming staff.

O'Neal's cost-cutting initiatives encountered some fierce resistance within the firm. Some of his secret corporate communications were leaked not once but twice to newspapers by executives in-the-know. O'Neal, who had a reputation for being aloof and "ruthless,"[27] resisted back. With support from the company's board of directors, he eliminated the old guard on the company's senior team, removing nearly half of the 19 senior managers. He also began undoing the company's expansion across the globe and Internet, selling off or closing underperforming brokerage operations in South Africa, Canada, and Australia,[28] and cutting $35 million from the online commerce portal after determining that it was costing more to capture new customers than these customers would ever spend trading. He outsourced the troubled mortgage unit's customer service operation, which saved the company $50 million; set up SWAT teams to find savings, and began applying return-on-investment strategies to Merrill's technology investments.

In addition to cutting costs, O'Neal redirected the firm's three business divisions that were responsible for revenues (Global Private Client, Global Markets & Investment Banking Group, and Merrill Lynch Investment Managers) towards more profitable clients.

Global Private Client Group (GPC)

GPC provided retail investors with advice-based wealth management products and services from both proprietary and third-party sources. Financial information for the business unit is shown in **Exhibit 6. Exhibit 7** shows comparative data on private client assets, number of financial advisors and net asset flows for Merrill Lynch and several competitors.

---

25. Susan Young, "A Long Road of Learning: Merrill Lynch's Stan O'Neal," Harvard Business School Bulletin, June 2001, available from Harvard Business School Bulletin Online.

26. Charles Pretzlik and Gary Silverman, "The Fortunes of a Radical Traditionalist," Financial Times, October 31, 2003.

27. O'Neal once told a senior executive that "Ruthless... isn't always bad." From Rynecki, "Putting the Muscle Back in the Bull."

28. Rynecki, "Putting the Muscle Back in the Bull."

When O'Neal became president in 2001, many brokers were not generating enough fees to pay their own salary. "Few clients with less than $100,000 in assets generate enough fees to cover the $1,500 that industry mavens say it costs Merrill to assign an investor a personal broker. Wealthier, more profitable, customers had an estimated $140 billion with other financial firms. And Merrill was restructuring to serve these high clients."[29] Gorman explained GPC's approach:

> *You have to treat people according to their complexity. If you've got $20,000 to invest and want to talk 10 times a day about different aspects of the market, then you're going to be blocking the line for somebody who's got $200 million to invest. A person who wants basic account information can get that by calling up the call center. A client who wants to set up a trust for their children needs to sit down with a trust specialist and get real comprehensive advice?*[30]

To serve its high net worth clients, Merrill developed its own group of wealth management service providers. Management believed that investment products were increasingly undifferentiated, with many firms offering the same financial product through third-party relationships as they sold through their own brokers. New products were copied so rapidly that there was little first mover advantage. The key to success, O'Neal believed, was to provide top clients with outstanding service. "We [needed to strip] away some of the gloss and confusion and [go] back to the roots of the business, which is giving people good advice."[31] For clients with $1 million or more in investable assets, Merrill provided Wealth Management Advisors. For the highest net worth individuals, those with $10 million or more, Merrill cultivated a group of Private Wealth Advisors.

To improve the performance and customer focus of its financial advisors, Merrill invested heavily in training, reorganized many of its advisors into teams, and changed its compensation incentives. The Certified Financial Manager training program was extended to five years. Financial advisors who completed the program and one additional certification were offered a $100,000 bonus. Private Wealth Advisors had to pass even more rigorous tests. To enhance customer service, brokers were organized in teams. By 2002, 45% of the firm's advisors were in teams, with 80% being the ultimate goal. In addition, to better align the interests of the firm's financial advisors with that of its clients Merrill restructured its commission-based remuneration to focus advisors on "annuitized business and on the total financial needs of higher net worth clients."[32] Brokers' commissions for trades in accounts worth less than $100,000 were eliminated.

Merrill developed new products for its wealthier clients. In 2002, Merrill clients invested $3.1 billion in special hedge funds and other private equities. According to one observer, "O'Neal wants [these investments] to rise substantially, along with sales of sophisticated financial products such as futures and exchange traded funds and fancy derivatives. He is determined to coddle the very rich as much as necessary to keep current clients loyal and win over new ones."[33] O'Neal is reported to have told

29. Thornton, "The New Merrill Lynch."

30. Rusoff, "Whither Wealth Management?"

31. Ibid.

32. Stan O'Neal, "Merrill Lynch's Platform for Growth," speech given at Salomon Smith Barney Financial Services Conference, New York, January 31, 2002. www.ml.com (investor relations).

33. Thornton, "The New Merrill Lynch."

one group of analysts, "We do not even consider ourselves to be in the retail securities business anymore. We're in the wealth management business."[34]

To support and advise its clients with less than $100,000 in invested assets, Merrill created a telephone-based Financial Advisor Center, with call centers in New Jersey and Florida. Even within the new Financial Advisory Center, Merrill segmented its services. Clients with $20,000 in assets at the firm would receive two telephone calls a year to review their portfolios, whereas clients with $50,000 or more would receive service from a "dedicated team" of service reps.

Call center's clients were not happy with Merrill's segmentation strategy. "It was considered by some in the industry as being disrespectful to the smaller client," explains Gorman. "And initially we did lose clients, yes. But putting those with less than $100,000 into the call center was the honest thing to do in my opinion. If they have $20,000, don't pretend they are receiving high-touch financial advice. At least now there is some sort of structure as to the services and products they receive." And the loss of some clients, says Gorman, was inconsequential in the greater scheme.

> It received a lot of media attention, as, in figures, it was a lot of people who left. But putting it into perspective, it was not a lot of money. We have about $20 billion in our call-center business, which is 1.7% of all our clients' money. And in honesty, we would have lost clients anyway as they were not being served properly. Some of the smaller investors now have more contact with an advisor than before.[35]

Some Merrill brokers were also unhappy about the change. "The whole segmentation issue left a bad taste in the mouth of advisors as it was delivered like an order from the New York office," says an ex-employee. "It's a relationship business, and you cannot tell Mary Smith in Chicago that her clients of 20 years' standing are now to be put in a different segment and she can no longer deal with them. The powers in New York may well be correct that those products are better for Mary Smith's clients but it was considered unfair to have it forced upon them."[36] As a result, several financial advisors defected to competitors.

GPC's restructuring and segmentation of clients for the domestic market was also implemented aggressively in the international division. Much of this was necessitated by the unprofitable growth during the boom years. "From 1998 to 2000—the heady days—everything went extremely well," said Ausaf Abbas, head of EMEA GPC.

> In Canada we had bought Midland Walwyn, in Japan we had bought a lot of the assets of Yamaichi Securities, in Australia we had bought Macintosh Securities, we took 100% control of our business in South Africa and entered into a joint broking venture with HSBC. The number of advisors grew dramatically during this period and we shifted focus away from high-net-worth individuals to the mass affluent—clients with less than $500,000 in assets. We thought we could be like Merrill Lynch in the U.S., but with the benefit of hindsight that was a bad strategic move. We lost $900 million in Japan over four years.[37]

34. Rusoff, "Whither wealth management?"

35. Helen Avery, "Merrill shrugs off the herd mentality," Euromoney, August 1, 2004, www.euromoney.com. © Copyright 2004 Euromoney Institutional Investor plc.

36. Avery, "Merrill shrugs off the herd mentality."

37. Ibid.

In autumn 2001, O'Neal appointed Kelly Martin to run the international division of GPC. Kelly quickly sold the Canadian and South African businesses and restructured Japan. The international private-client business was segmented: clients with accounts for less than $1 million were served by a call center, and clients worth $1 million to $25 million were served by the wealth management division. However, the primary focus was on clients with more than $25 million in assets and institutional services.[38] Abbas noted that "as a strategy, this segmentation made sense, but in the early days our core business was the $1 million to $25 million range internationally, which was where the majority of revenue and almost all of the pre-tax profits came from. If you start neglecting the core business and focusing on two new areas you are trying to grow instead, that is dangerous."[39] As a result, the international business continued to lose money in 2001, worsening in 2002.

Despite the obvious ongoing challenges, management at GPC was optimistic about the future. Gorman noted:

> We've now completed the restructuring and, on a competitive set, we're the most profitable in the industry. We've improved our range of services, technology and training which have been expensive but we're big enough to absorb that. We have more people who are producing more, and our competitors will find it hard. And we've developed a different edge to our culture and management philosophy. . . . We have lots of products for which clients can pay a fee or have a wrap account type structure, so revenues are more stable, rather than being dependent on trading. . . . If you asked most people to guess what percentage of our revenue came from people buying and selling stocks, most would probably say 50%. It is in fact 13%. . . . We're not tied solely to the equity markets and can deliver a return to shareholders whether the market is up or down.[40]

Rejuvenating Investment Banking: GMI

GMI provided clients with underwriting, investment research, securities sales and trading, and mergers and acquisitions advice. When securities were sold to the public, Merrill Lynch acted as an underwriter, committing to purchasing the securities from the client at a predetermined price. Equity and debt salespeople and traders were responsible for executing the trade of these securities between the investment bank and the public. The salespeople provided investment advice, while the traders were responsible for executing the purchases and sales of securities. An investment research team provided periodic reports on companies with recent developments and stock recommendations. The mergers and acquisitions advisory group advised clients on the sale or purchase of assets of an entire company.

Under O'Neal's leadership, Merrill's investment banking began focusing on more profitable underwriting and advisory deals, typically for smaller clients, and paying less attention to the rankings, which were based on the size of the underwriting deals. In a series of meetings with analysts, O'Neal explained the firm's new strategy as follows:

> Although many people focus on the league tables, to me ranking by fees is a much more interesting measure because it focuses on the quality rather than the

---

38. *Ibid.*
39. *Ibid.*
40. *Ibid.*

quantity of deals.[41] *We will be placing greater emphasis on profitable market share. We're moving away from broad market share goals in highly-commoditized low margin businesses, but intensifying our focus on the markets, segments and products where we can create differentiated value for clients.*[42]

In 2002, GMI had a record year for net profits ($2.4 billion) and net operating margins (28.2%), even though the division's 2002 revenues were 18% lower than 2001 revenues. Financial information for GMI is shown in **Exhibit 8**. Merrill attributed GMI's 2002 success to strong expense management, which led to the reduction of non-interest costs by 19% or $1.4 billion. Arshad Zakaria, who headed GMI, merged five investment banking platforms in Princeton, London, Tokyo, Singapore and Sydney into just two (Princeton and London), saving 25% in head count and 30% on fixed expenses. In addition, the firm reported that it had benefited from a strong debt market business, which partially offset a reduction in equity investment banking revenues; and from its focus on higher margin investment banking.

Changing Asset Management Industry: MLIM

MLIM helped clients achieve their financial goals by providing a broad range of products for private, mutual fund and institutional investors. The firm charged a fixed percentage fee of the assets it managed. Asset management firms attempted to distinguish themselves from their competitors in a variety of ways. Investors were ultimately interested in earning superior investment returns. But, firms also competed through cost management, access to distribution channels, breadth of products offered, sales support strength, brand image, and use of technology. Many of these forms of competition had created pressure for consolidation in the industry.

Asset management emerged during the 1990s as an important activity for investment banks, as increased competition in their traditional businesses and the volatility of the global financial markets prompted them to seek out more stable earnings. **Exhibit 9** presents data on net asset flows over time into the U.S. money management industry. **Exhibit 10** shows assets under management for the 25 largest asset management firms. As one industry expert explained, "the thirst to get money management has come from a strong desire to dampen the cyclical amplitude of the investment-banking business."[43] In addition, asset management was considered to be attractive because "the larger a money manager gets, once all fixed costs are covered, it can realize up to 80% in margins on each dollar of revenue."[44]

Merrill Lynch's Investment Managers division was led by Bob Doll. At the end of 2002, it had $462 billion under management and served a globally diversified client base of mutual fund investors, high-net-worth individuals, pension funds, corporations, and governments. Financial information for MLIM is shown in **Exhibit 11**. Doll explained: "MLIM has an outstanding opportunity to increase sales through Merrill Lynch's own network of Financial Advisors and extensive institutional relationships. Sales coverage has been realigned to correspond to GPC's segmentation strategy, improving sales support. . . . *Merrill Lynch Consults Diversified Portfolios*

---

41. Stan O'Neal, Salomon Smith Barney Investor Conference, New York, January 29, 2003.

42. Stan O'Neal, "Merrill Lynch's Platform for Growth," Salomon Smith Barney Financial Services Conference, New York, January 31, 2002.

43. Rose Darby, "Courting Stability," Investment Dealers' Digest, September 7, 1998, pp. 18–23.

44. Ibid.

were created in partnership with GPC and are specifically tailored to meet our private clients' needs."[45]

Over the prior two years, Merrill's money management unit had suffered many cuts and voluntary defections, dropping in size from 4,000 to 3,000 people. To stabilize the situation, Doll imposed "a compensation package under which half of a fund manager's pay was based on one-, three- and five-year investment performance; 25% on assets and 25% on peer reviews such as the "partnership voting" scheme, under which managers have 100 "points" to award each other."[46] To streamline the operations, Doll also merged a lot of funds, down to 125 funds from 165 three years ago.[47]

CIBC Analysts, Ken Worthington and Niamh Guinan, argued that "while MLIM has done an excellent job at improving its fund performance, its financial advisors, like many of its competitors with captive asset managers, are having difficulty selling in-house funds because of perceived conflicts. Merrill is actively focusing on increasing distribution setting up third-party sub advisor and private label relationships. We think this will be difficult and take time. However, we believe that within the next year or two MER's financial advisors will again sell the MLIM funds if performance remains strong because they are incentivized through their ownership of MER stock."[48]

CONCLUSION

In mid 2002, Merrill Lynch was the subject of numerous takeover rumors as its stock price plummeted to a low of $28.43. By the end of the year, the rumors had all but ceased and its stock had recovered to reach $43 in mid-January 2003. **Exhibit 12** shows the company's stock price performance from December 1999 to December 2002. However, O'Neal made it clear that the company would continue to change. "Continuing to do business in exactly the same way is not a winning proposition,"[49] he said several months before he became Chairman.

Many industry observers viewed the changes positively and considered Merrill to be very well-positioned for any economic recovery. For example, Daniel Goldberg and Angel Lupercio, analysts at Bear Stearns, commented:

> We continue to believe Merrill Lynch represents one of the best leveraged plays to a recovery in the global equity markets among the major securities brokerage firms. . . . First, the firm has reduced overall headcount by 30% (or 21,700 people) since its peak of 72,600 in September 2000, compared with an average of 10% to 15% for most of its competitors. Based on the firm's current structure, new revenues could yield an incremental margin of 50%. Second, management continues to realign resources in order to pursue more profitable businesses. For example, the firm has transferred nearly 1.5 million client accounts and approximately $20 billion in assets to the financial advisory center for more efficient servicing.[50]

---

45. Merrill Lynch, 2002 Annual Report (New York: Merrill Lynch, 2003), p. 7.

46. Erin E. Arvedlund, "Merrill Redux: Will Doll stem turnover in the bull's pen? Plus proxy news," Barron's, January 27, 2003.

47. Ibid.

48. CIBC Analysts, Ken Worthington and Niamh Guinan, "MER Q2 Earnings Below Expectations – Boding Ill for Competitors," July 14, 2004, p. 4.

49. Rynecki, "Putting the Muscle Back in the Bull."

50. Daniel Goldberg and Angel Lupercio, "Merrill Lynch & Co.—Outperform," Bear Stearns analyst report, January 23, 2003.

However, other observers were more skeptical, questioning whether the restructurings had been too severe and would make it difficult for the firm to respond quickly to a market upturn, particularly in the all-important retail market. For example, Emily Thornton at *Business Week* noted that in the retail brokerage business, competitors such as Salomon Smith Barney and Morgan Stanley Dean Witter & Co. had been adding brokers at the same time that Merrill had cut reps. Merrill argued that its restructuring had enabled its brokers to become more productive than its rivals—they managed $1.2 trillion in client assets versus only $588 billion at Morgan Stanley. Yet Salomon Smith Barney's brokers managed roughly as many assets per head as brokers at Merrill, and Morgan Stanley anticipated that by rolling out new services it could boost productivity significantly. In addition, there were questions about whether Merrill's brokers would continue to be as effective in signing up new customers following the research scandals which had damaged the firm's credibility.[51] Also, others wondered if the fall in the league tables would have long-term reputational effects. Richard Strauss, an analyst at Deutsche Bank commented: "It's been a tough few years and you have to give the GPC business an A for effort, but it will all come down to how the retail environment develops. They need the retail market to pick up if they want more than lackluster profits. It is still mostly GMI that is driving the Merrill Lynch business."[52]

Going forward, O'Neal explained:

"We face an uncertain year from a position of strength: in our financial foundation, client relationships, diverse businesses and, most importantly, the extraordinary talent of our people. More than reacting to a changing world, we are committed to leading *change—setting new standards for the industry, creating a more disciplined, agile and accountable culture, and generating sustained, meaningful value for clients, shareholders and employees, now and in the future.*[53]

QUESTIONS:

As an equity analyst following the investment banking industry:

1. How would you rate Merrill Lynch's company performance relative to that of Morgan Stanely? What factors underlie Merrill's performance?

2. What are the key success factors and risks facing Merrill Lynch for each of its major business units (GPC, GMI, and MLIM)?

3. Evaluate the financial performance of each of Merrill's major business units. What changes would you be looking for management to make in the coming few years for each business unit? How would these changes affect the key financial metrics for each unit?

4. Would you recommend Merrill Lynch as a good investment?

---

51. Emily Thornton, "Merrill: Is Stan the Man?" BusinessWeek, June 17, 2002.
52. Richard Strauss, Deutsche Bank, Analyst Report.
53. Merrill Lynch, 2002 Annual Report (New York: Merrill Lynch, 2003), p. 4.

EXHIBIT I

Merrill Lynch Selected Financial Data

(dollars in millions; except per share amounts)

	Year Ended Last Friday in December				
	2002	2001	2000	1999	1998
Results of Operations					
Revenues					
Investment banking					
Underwriting	1,710	2,438	2,699	2,382	2,162
Strategic advisory	703	1,101	1,381	1,313	1,103
Principal transactions	2,340	3,930	5,964	4,671	2,850
Commissions	$4,657	$5,266	$6,977	6,355	5,814
Asset management and portfolio					
service fees	4,914	5,351	5,688	4,753	4,202
Other	751	528	967	746	650
Subtotal	15,075	18,614	23,676	20,220	16,781
Interest and dividend revenues	13,178	20,143	21,176	15,112	18,056
Less Interest Expense	9,645	16,877	18,086	13,019	17,038
Total Net Revenues	18,608	21,880	26,766	22,313	17,799
Non-Interest Expenses					
Compensation & benefits	9,425	11,269	13,730	11,337	9,308
Other	5,418	7,036	7,319	6,770	5,941
Restructuring & other charges	8	2,198			430
Total Non-Interest Expenses	14,851	20,503	21,049	18,107	15,679
Earnings before Income Taxes & Pref.					
Dividends	3,757	1,377	5,717	4,206	2,120
Income Tax Expense	1,053	609	1,738	1,319	725
Preferred Dividends on Subsidiaries'					
Securities	191	195	195	194	124
Net Earnings	$2,513	$573	$3,784	$2,693	$1,271
Net Earnings Available to Common					
Stockholders[a]	$2,475	$535	$3,745	$2,654	$1,233
Financial Position					
Total Assets	$447,928	$435,692	$423,831	$309,850	$286,446
Short-Term Borrowings[b]	$180,213	$178,154	$187,176	$115,409	$98,655
Long-Term Borrowings	$78,524	$76,572	$70,223	$54,043	$57,599
Preferred Securities Issued by Subsidiaries	$2,658	$2,695	$2,714	$2,725	$2,627
Common Stockholders Equity	$22,450	$19,583	$17,879	$12,579	$9,839
Preferred Equity	$425	$425	$425	$425	$425
Common Share Data[c] *(in 000, except*					
per share)					
Earnings Per Share:					
Basic	$2.87	$0.64	$4.69	$3.52	$1.69
Diluted	$2.63	$0.57	$4.11	$3.11	$1.49
Weighted-Average Shares Outstanding:					
Basic	862,318	838,683	798,273	754,672	728,929
Diluted	942,222	938,555	911,416	853,499	830,276
Shares Outstanding at Year-End[d]	867,291	843,474	807,955	752,501	729,981
Book Value Per Share	$25.69	$23.03	$21.95	$16.49	$13.31
Dividends Paid Per Share	$0.64	$0.64	$0.61	$0.53	$0.46

(continued)

Merrill Lynch in 2003

Merrill Lynch Selected Financial Data (*continued*)

	Year Ended Last Friday in December				
	2002	2001	2000	1999	1998
Financial Ratios					
Pre-tax Profit Margin[e]	20.20%	6.30%	21.40%	18.80%	11.90%
Common Dividend Payout Ratio	22.30%	100.00%	13.00%	15.10%	27.20%
Return on Average Assets	0.50%	0.10%	1.00%	0.80%	0.40%
Return on Average Common Stockholders' Equity	11.70%	2.70%	24.20%	23.80%	13.40%
Average Leverage Ratio[f]	19.0x	19.3x	19.8x	22.4x	30.9x
Average Adjusted Leverage Ratio[g]	13.2x	13.7x	14.0x	15.1x	20.0x
Other Statistics					
Full-Time Employees:					
U.S.	40,000	43,400	51,700	49,700	47,900
Non-U.S.	10,900	13,700	19,900	18,200	17,300
Total[h]	50,900	57,100	71,600	67,900	65,200
Private Client Financial Advisors	14,000	16,400	20,200	18,600	17,800
Client Assets (*dollars in billions*)	$1,288	$1,458	$1,681	$1,696	$1,446

Source: Merrill Lynch 10-K.

[a]*Net earnings less preferred stock dividends.*

[b]*Consists of Payables under repurchase agreements and securities loaned transactions, Commercial paper and other short-term borrowings, and Deposits.*

[c]*All share and per share data have been restated for the two-for-one common stock split paid in August 2000 (see Note 13 to the Consolidated Financial Statements).*

[d]*Does not include 3,911; 4,195; 4,654; 8,019; and 9,012 shares exchangeable into common stock (see Note 13 to the Consolidated Financial Statements) at year-end 2002, 2001, 2000, 1999, and 1998, respectively.*

[e]*Earnings before income taxes and dividends on Preferred securities issued by subsidiaries to Net revenues.*

[f]*Average total assets to average total stockholders' equity and Preferred securities issued by subsidiaries.*

[g]*Average total assets less average (i) Receivables under resale agreements, (ii) Receivables under securities borrowed transactions, and (iii) Securities received as collateral to average total stockholders' equity and Preferred securities issued by subsidiaries.*

[h]*Excludes 1,500 and 3,500 full-time employees on salary continuation severance at year-end 2002 and 2001, respectively.*

EXHIBIT 2

Morgan Stanley Financial Data

	2002	2001	2000	1999	1998
Financial Position					
Total Assets	$529,489	$482,628	$421,279	$366,967	$317,590
Consumer loans	23,404	$20,108	$21,743	$20,963	$16,412
Long-Term Borrowings	44,051	$40,917	$30,366	$22,685	$23,803
Common Stockholders Equity	21,885	$20,716	$19,271	$17,014	$14,119
Financial Ratios					
Net operating profit margin	34.7%	39.0%	38.5%	36.6%	39.6%
* Operating asset turnover	0.06	0.09	0.11	0.09	0.09
= Operating ROA	2.0%	3.5%	4.0%	3.4%	3.7%
Spread	0.5%	0.6%	1.2%	1.2%	0.9%
* Financial Leverage	23.19	22.30	20.86	20.57	21.49
= **Financial Leverage Gain**	11.6%	13.4%	24.1%	24.5%	19.1%
Return on Ending Equity = Operating ROA +					
Financial Leverage Gain	13.7%	16.8%	28.1%	27.9%	22.8%
Common Size Income Statement					
Revenues					
Investment banking	8.1%	8.0%	11.3%	13.2%	11.3%
Principal transactions	8.5%	12.1%	17.1%	19.1%	11.0%
Commissions	10.6%	7.4%	8.2%	8.1%	7.5%
Asset management, distribution & adm.	12.7%	9.8%	9.9%	10.1%	10.5%
Merchant & cardmember fees	4.6%	3.2%	2.8%	3.0%	4.2%
Servicing	6.7%	4.4%	3.4%	3.6%	3.2%
Interest and dividend revenues	51.1%	56.3%	47.9%	43.6%	55.4%
Other	2.0%	1.2%	1.2%	0.7%	0.9%
Subtotal	104.3%	102.5%	101.8%	101.5%	104.0%
Less: Consumer loan loss reserves	4.3%	2.5%	1.8%	1.5%	4.0%
Total Net Revenues	100.0%	100.0%	100.0%	100.0%	100.0%
Non-Interest Expenses					
Compensation & benefits	25.5%	21.9%	24.6%	24.5%	22.4%
Other	20.0%	16.3%	15.2%	16.2%	16.2%
Restructuring & other charges	0.8%	0.0%	0.0%	0.0%	0.0%
Total Non-Interest Expenses	46.3%	38.2%	39.8%	40.7%	38.6%
Interest Expense	38.5%	48.4%	41.0%	36.6%	45.5%
Income Tax Expense	5.3%	4.8%	6.9%	8.6%	6.7%
Dividends on Pref. Subs. Securities	0.3%	0.1%	0.1%	0.1%	0.1%
Extraordinary Item	0.0%	−0.1%	0.0%	0.0%	0.0%
Cumulative effect of accounting	0.0%	−0.1%	0.0%	0.0%	−0.4%
Net Earnings	9.6%	8.2%	12.3%	14.0%	11.1%
Earnings applicable to common shares	9.6%	8.1%	12.2%	13.9%	10.9%
Growth Rates					
Investment banking	−26%	−32%	11%	35%	
Principal transactions	−49%	−31%	16%	101%	
Commissions	4%	−13%	31%	26%	
Asset management, distribution & adm.	−6%	−4%	27%	11%	
Merchant & cardmember fees	5%	7%	22%	−17%	
Servicing	10%	28%	21%	32%	
Interest and dividend revenues	−34%	14%	43%	−9%	
Total Net Revenues	−27%	−3%	30%	15%	

Source: Morgan Stanley 10-K and casewriter computations.

EXHIBIT 3

Estimated Global Investment Banking Industry Revenues ($ in billions)

	1997	1998	1999	2000	2001	2002
Equity Underwriting	6.7	6.7	8.8	14.3	8.7	7.2
Equity Trading	26.2	29.2	30.8	52.7	38.2	28.5
Fixed Income Underwriting	13.0	14.9	13.9	13.3	19.9	19.1
Fixed Income Trading	36.1	24.4	34.7	39.9	48.7	55.2
Asset Management	67.8	77.0	91.0	98.8	95.2	90.3
M&A Advisory	6.2	11.0	13.2	16.1	12.6	9.0
Retail Brokerage	53.1	56.0	73.2	87.9	73.1	66.9
Clearing/Processing/Other	3.7	4.4	5.2	6.1	4.8	4.7
Total Industry Revenue	**212.8**	**223.5**	**270.8**	**329.2**	**301.2**	**280.9**
Change vs. Prior Year		5%	21%	22%	−9%	−7%

Source: Ruchi Madan, Robert Sobhani and Prashant Bhatia, "Brokers & Asset Managers: Initiative Coverage," August 1, 2003, p. 8.

EXHIBIT 4

Estimated Market Shares of Leading Investment Banks by Revenue Type

	1998	1999	2000	2001	2002
Share of Total Fees					
Morgan Stanley	5.6%	6.5%	6.7%	6.2%	5.4%
Goldman Sachs	3.4	4.3	4.7	4.9	4.6
Lehman	1.8	2.0	2.3	2.2	2.2
Merrill Lynch	7.9	8.0	7.9	7.1	6.4
Bear Stearns	1.5	1.5	1.2	1.3	1.5
Share of Total Equity Underwriting Fees					
Morgan Stanley	12.2%	14.4%	10.7%	8.9%	7.4%
Goldman Sachs	16.5	17.6	16.6	12.9	11.6
Lehman	4.6	5.2	5.7	5.1	5.8
Merrill Lynch	15.3	14.3	11.4	15.5	11.4
Bear Stearns	4.2	2.5	1.6	1.5	2.4
Share of Total Fixed Income Underwriting Fees					
Morgan Stanley	7.9%	9.1%	6.1%	4.5%	3.9%
Goldman Sachs	3.3	3.9	3.0	2.9	2.6
Lehman	3.9	5.1	4.4	4.5	4.6
Merrill Lynch	4.4	3.7	3.3	3.5	3.3
Bear Stearns	2.4	2.1	1.8	1.4	1.6
Share of Total M&A Advisory Fees					
Morgan Stanley	12.1%	14.4%	13.3%	11.3%	10.7%
Goldman Sachs	16.2	17.2	16.1	15.9	16.5
Lehman	4.7	3.8	4.8	4.7	4.8
Merrill Lynch	9.8	9.8	8.6	8.8	7.8
Bear Stearns	3.3	2.9	2.7	2.1	1.8
Share of Total Retail Brokerage Fees					
Morgan Stanley	6.3%	5.6%	6.4%	6.0%	5.7%
Goldman Sachs	1.3	1.5	1.3	1.2	1.0
Lehman	0.9	0.8	0.9	1.0	1.1
Merrill Lynch	13.5	14.2	13.6	13.4	12.7
Bear Stearns	0.7	0.6	0.5	0.5	0.5
Share of Total Institutional Equity Trading Fees					
Morgan Stanley	8.5%	11.8%	11.3%	12.1%	12.6%
Goldman Sachs	4.7	7.5	8.6	10.1	7.9
Lehman	2.5	4.6	5.0	4.7	3.5
Merrill Lynch	N/A	12.9	10.6	9.2	8.3
Bear Stearns	2.5	3.5	2.7	3.0	3.9
Share of Total Fixed-Income Trading Fees					
Morgan Stanley	6.3%	9.5%	7.2%	8.0%	5.9%
Goldman Sachs	6.2	8.4	7.8	10.1	10.3
Lehman	5.7	4.8	5.2	4.6	4.7
Merrill Lynch	2.7	6.4	6.9	6.5	6.2
Bear Stearns	4.3	4.0	2.7	3.3	3.5
Share of Total Asset Management Fees					
Morgan Stanley	2.3%	2.3%	3.0%	2.7%	2.6%
Goldman Sachs	0.9	1.0	1.4	1.5	1.8
Lehman	0.0	0.0	0.0	0.0	0.0
Merrill Lynch	2.4	2.3	2.1	2.0	1.7
Bear Stearns	0.1	0.2	0.2	0.2	0.2

Source: Ruchi Madan, Robert Sobhani and Prashant Bhatia, "Brokers & Asset Managers: Initiative Coverage," August 1, 2003, p. 28.

Merrill Lynch in 2003

EXHIBIT 5

Assets Invested (in $ billions) at Merrill Lynch and Competing Firms by High Net Worth Households (with assets greater than $1 million)

	Value of High Net Worth Assets	Percentage of Total Assets
Merrill Lynch	$730	67%
Charles Schwab	415	54%
Morgan Stanley, Prudential, UBS	each <300	

Source: Ruchi Madan, Robert Sobhani and Prashant Bhatia, "Brokers & Asset Managers: Initiative Coverage," August 1, 2003, p. 50.

EXHIBIT 6

Merrill Lynch Global Private Client Performance (in $ millions)

	2002	2001	2000	1999	1998
Commissions	$2,469	$3,045	$4,468	$4,132	$3,990
Principal transactions and net issue revenues	1,165	1,576	2,024	2,105	1,944
Asset management and portfolio service fees	3,532	3,676	3,911	3,075	2,679
Net interest profit	1,336	1,518	1,534	1,183	884
Other revenues	279	102	160	124	84
Total net revenues	8,781	9,917	12,097	10,619	9,581
Non-interest expenses before recoveries related to September 11 and restructuring and other charges	7,576	8,999	10,597	9,233	8,015
Pre-tax earnings before recoveries related to September 11 and restructuring and other charges	1,205	918	1,500	1,386	1,566
Recoveries related to September 11	25	—	—	—	—
Restructuring and other charges	66	(1,077)	—	—	—
Pre-tax earnings (loss)	$1,296	$(159)	$1,500	$1,386	1,566
Profitability trends					
Pre-tax profit margin before recoveries related to September 11 and restructuring and other charges	13.7%	9.3%	12.4%	13.1%	16.3
Pre-tax profit margin	14.8	N/M	12.4	13.1	16.3
Business unit detail (in $ billions)					
Assets in GPC accounts					
U.S.	$1,053	$1,185	$1,337	$1,338	$1,164
Non-U.S.	89	101	140	137	98
Total	$1,142	$1,286	$1,477	$1,475	$1,262
Total full-time employees	31,900	36,400	46,100	44,900	42,500
Total Financial Advisors	14,000	16,400	20,200	18,600	17,800

Source: Merrill Lynch Annual Report.
N/M–not meaningful.

EXHIBIT 7

Private Client Net Revenue ($ millions), Number of Financial Advisors, and Private Client Net Flows as a Percentage of Assets at Leading U.S. Firms for 2001 and 2002

Firm	Private Net Client Revenue		Number of Financial Advisors		Private Client Net Flows as % Assets	
	2001	2002	2001	2002	2001	2002
Merrill Lynch	9,867	8,774	16,400	14,000	4.5%	1.5%
Smith Barney	5,940	5,830	12,927	12,690	NA	4.3%
Morgan Stanley	4,455	4,069	13,690	12,546	NA	NA
Wachovia/Prudential[a]	4,622	4,658	13,923	12,840	NA	NA
UBS PaineWebber[b]	3,770	3,576	8,718	8,857	6.5%	5.0%
Charles Schwab[c]	3,177	2,996			8.8%	6.0%
AG Edwards[d]	2,399	2,259	7,317	7,279	NA	NA
E*Trade[e]	912	862			NA	NA
Ameritrade	432	504			NA	NA
Total	35,575	33,527	72,975	68,212		
% Change		−5.8%		−6.5%		

Source: Ruchi Madan and Prashant Bhatia, "Brokers & Asset Managers," Citigroup Smith Barney, June 10, 2004, p. 6.

NA = Not available.

[a]Wachovia/Prudential revenue includes services business. Deal to combined Wachovia/Prudential retail businesses closed in 3Q03, prior to that private client revenues are stated pro-forma. Wachovia/Prudential includes approximately 3,100 Series 6 advisors.

[b]UBS PaineWebber figures for all quarters translated into U.S. $ using the period average Swiss Franc/U.S. $ exchange rate. UBS PW 2Q03 revenue number excludes CHF161 gain on disposal of Correspondent Services Corporation.

[c]Charles Schwab revenue includes individual investor and U.S. Trusts segments.

[d]AG Edwards revenue figures include the company's small investment banking segment.

[e]E*Trade figures exclude traditional banking revenue.

Merrill Lynch in 2003

EXHIBIT 8

Merrill Lynch Global Markets and Investment Banking Performance (dollars in millions)

	2002	2001	2000	1999	1998
Commissions	$2,080	$2,111	$2,398	$2,034	$1,764
Principal transactions and net interest profit	3,714	4,562	6,133	4,309	1,757
Investment banking	2,148	3,135	3,449	2,952	2,746
Other revenues	488	467	809	497	494
Total net revenues	8,430	10,275	12,789	9,792	6,761
Non-interest expenses before recoveries related to September 11 and restructuring and other charges	6,054	7,465	8,698	7,094	5,715
Pre-tax earnings before recoveries related to September 11 and restructuring and other charges	2,376	2,810	4,091	2,698	1,046
Recoveries related to September 11	90	—	—	—	—
Restructuring and other charges	(51)	(833)	—	—	—
Pre-tax earnings	$2,415	$1,977	$4,091	2,698	1,046
Profitability trends					
Pre-tax profit margin before recoveries related to September 11 and restructuring and other charges	28.2%	27.3%	32.0%	27.6%	15.5%
Pre-tax profit margin	28.6	19.2	32.0	27.6%	15.5%
Business unit detail					
Debt underwriting	$622	$693	$439	$427	$656
Equity underwriting	824	1,343	1,632	1,256	1,019
Strategic advisory services	702	1,099	1,378	1,269	1,071
Total	$2,148	$3,135	$3,499	$2,952	$2,746
Total full-time employees	10,900	11,900	14,300	14,000	13,400

Source: Merrill Lynch Annual Report.

EXHIBIT 9

Annual Net Long-Term Fund Flows for U.S. Asset Management Industry (US $ billions)

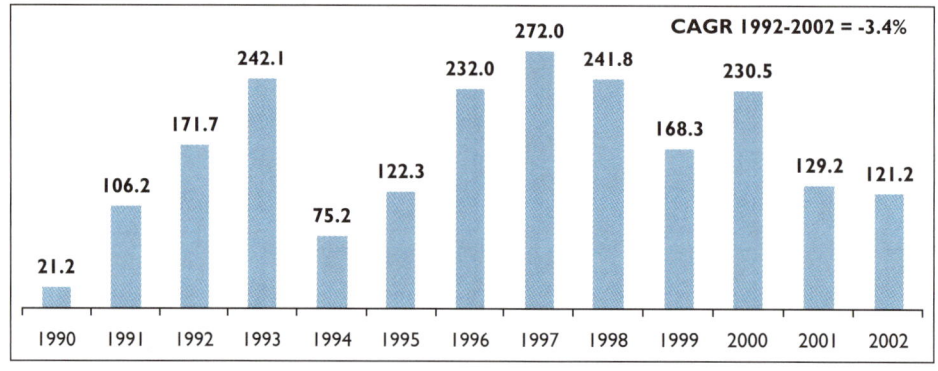

Source: Henry H. McVey, "U.S. Asset Management, Brokerage & Multinational Banks," Morgan-Stanley, October 24, 2003, p. 4.

EXHIBIT 10

Assets Under Management for the Largest Asset Management Firms ($ in millions)

Rank	Company Name	Worldwide Assets Under Management	Share of Assets
1	State Street Global	$766,548	5.95%
2	Barclays Global	715,100	5.55
3	Fidelity Investments	639,524	4.96
4	Deutsche Asset	511,126	3.97
5	JP Morgan	374,784	2.91
6	AIG Global	271,416	2.11
7	Vanguard Group	266,239	2.07
8	Merrill Lynch	266,046	2.06
9	TIAA-CREF	262,290	2.04
10	Alliance Capital	246,369	1.91
11	Prudential Financial	242,082	1.88
12	BlackRock	231,505	1.80
13	Goldman Sachs	226,323	1.76
14	Northern Trust	217,144	1.69
15	Credit Suisse Asset	211,663	1.64
16	PIMCO	203,886	1.58
17	Zurich Scudder	198,293	1.54
18	UBS Asset	192,910	1.50
19	Citigroup Asset	184,585	1.43
20	Banc of America	183,057	1.42
21	Morgan Stanley	176,704	1.37
22	Federated Investors	167,701	1.30
23	GE Asset	157,690	1.22
24	INVESCO	143,203	1.11
25	Legg Mason	135,797	1.05

Source: Ruchi Madan, Robert Sobhani and Prashant Bhatia, "Brokers & Asset Managers: Initiative Coverage," August 1, 2003, p. 53.

Merrill Lynch in 2003

EXHIBIT 11

Merrill Lynch Investment Managers Performance (in $ millions)

	2002	2001	2000	1999	1998
Commissions	$177	$249	$335	$383	$350
Asset management fees	1,368	1,639	1,761	1,664	1,514
Other revenues	8	44	113	198	128
Total net revenues	1,553	1,932	2,209	2,245	1,992
Non-interest expenses	1,209	1,630	1,754	1,763	1,565
Pre-tax earnings before restructuring and other charges	344	302	455	482	427
Restructuring and other charges	(23)	(283)	—		
Pre-tax earnings	$321	$19	$455	$482	$427
Profitability trends					
Pre-tax profit margin before restructuring and other charges	22.2%	15.6%	20.6%	21.5%	21.4%
Assets Under Management (in $ billions)					
Retail	$189	$220	$250	$300	$288
Institutional	235	266	262	255	221
Private investors	38	43	45	39	35
Total	$462	$529	$557	$594	$544
Equity	$195	$220	$295	$300	$270
Fixed income	100	100	100	100	100
Money market	135	175	110	170	140
Private investors	32	34	52	24	34
Total	$462	$529	$557	$594	$544
Full-time employees	2,800	3,100	4,000	3,500	3,200

Source: Merrill Lynch Annual Report.

EXHIBIT 12

Merrill Lynch Relative Stock Price Performance, December 1999–January 2004

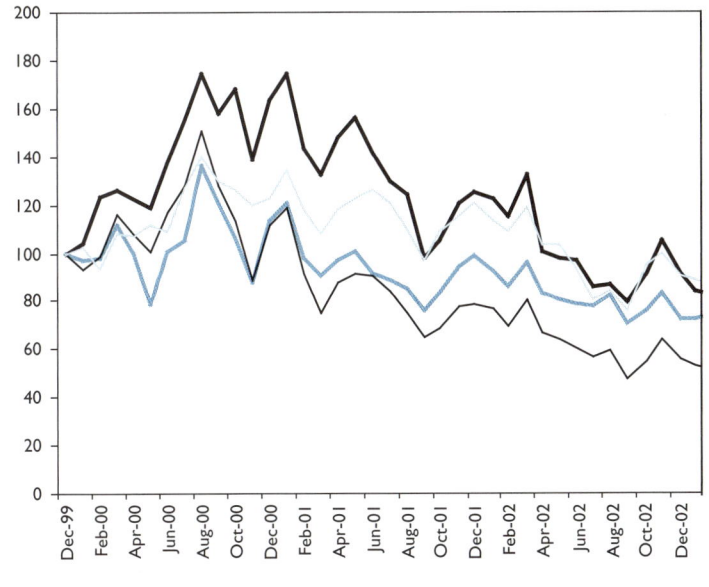

──── MERRILL LYNCH &.CO. ──── GOLDMAN SACHS GP. ──── MORGAN STANLEY ⋯⋯ CITIGROUP

Source: Thompson Datastream.

Merrill Lynch in 2003

Chapter 10

Credit Analysis and Distress Prediction

Credit analysis is the evaluation of a firm from the perspective of a holder or potential holder of its debt, which includes trade payables, loans, and public debt securities. A key element of credit analysis is the prediction of the likelihood a firm will face financial distress. Credit analysis is involved in a wide variety of decision contexts:

- A commercial banker asks: Should we extend a loan to this firm? If so, how should it be structured? How should it be priced?
- If the loan is granted, the banker must later ask: Are we still providing the services, including credit, that this firm needs? Is the firm still in compliance with the loan terms? If not, is there a need to restructure the loan, and if so, how? Is the situation serious enough to call for accelerating the repayment of the loan?
- A potential investor asks: Are these debt securities a sound investment? What is the probability that the firm will face distress and default on the debt? Does the yield provide adequate compensation for the default risk involved?
- An investor contemplating purchase of debt securities in default asks: How likely is it that this firm can be turned around? In light of the high yield on this debt relative to its current price, can I accept the risk that the debt will not be repaid in full?
- A potential supplier asks: Should I sell products or services to this firm? The associated credit will be extended only for a short period, but the amount is large and I should have some assurance that collection risks are manageable.

Finally, there are third parties—those other than borrowers and lenders—who are interested in the general issue of how likely it is that a firm will avoid financial distress:

- An auditor asks: How likely is it that this firm will survive beyond the short run? In evaluating the firm's financials, should I consider it a going concern?
- An actual or potential employee asks: How confident can I be that this firm will be able to offer employment over the long term?
- A potential customer asks: What assurance is there that this firm will survive to provide warranty services, replacement parts, product updates, and other services?
- A competitor asks: Will this firm survive the current industry shakeout? What are the implications of potential financial distress at this firm for my pricing and market share?

This chapter develops a framework to evaluate a firm's creditworthiness and assess the likelihood of financial distress.

WHY DO FIRMS USE DEBT FINANCING?

Before discussing the credit market and credit analysis, it is worth understanding why firms use debt financing. Debt financing is attractive to firms for two key reasons:

- *Corporate interest tax shields.* In many countries including the U.S., tax laws provide for the corporate tax deductibility of interest paid on debt. No such corporate tax shield is available for dividend payments or retained earnings. Therefore, corporate tax benefits should encourage firms with high effective tax rates and few forms of tax shields other than interest to favor debt financing.
- *Management incentives for value creation.* Firms with relatively high leverage face pressures to generate cash flows to meet payments of interest and principal, reducing resources available to fund unjustifiable expenses and investments that do not maximize shareholder value. Debt financing, therefore, focuses management on value creation, reducing conflicts of interest between managers and shareholders.

However, there are also costs of debt financing. As a firm increases its use of debt financing, it increases the likelihood of financial distress, where it is unable to meet interest or principal repayment obligations to creditors. This forces the firm to restructure its financial claims, either under formal bankruptcy proceedings or out of bankruptcy. Financial distress has multiple negative consequences for the firm:

- *Legal costs of financial distress.* Restructurings are likely to be costly, since the parties involved have to hire lawyers, bankers, and accountants to represent their interests, and to pay court costs if there are formal legal proceedings. These are often called the direct costs of financial distress.
- *Costs of foregone investment opportunities.* Distressed firms face significant challenges in raising capital as potential new investors and creditors will be wary of becoming embroiled in the firm's legal disputes. Thus, firms in distress are often unable to finance new investments even though they may be profitable for its owners.
- *Costs of conflicts between creditors and stockholders.* When faced with financial distress, creditors focus on the firm's ability to service its debt while shareholders worry that their equity will revert to the creditors if the firm defaults. Thus, managers face increased pressure to make decisions that typically serve the interests of the stockholders, and creditors react by increasing the costs of borrowing for the firm's stockholders.

Firms are more likely to fall into financial distress if they have high business risks and their assets are easily destroyed in financial distress. For example, firms with human capital and brand intangibles are particularly sensitive to financial distress since dissatisfied employees and customers can leave or seek alternative suppliers. In contrast, firms with tangible assets can sell their assets if they get into financial distress, providing additional security for lenders and lowering the costs of financial distress. Firms with intangible assets are therefore less likely to be highly leveraged than firms whose assets are mostly tangible.

The above discussion implies that a firm's long-term decisions on the use of debt financing reflects a trade-off between the corporate interest tax shield and incentive benefits of debt against the costs of financial distress. As the firm becomes more highly leveraged, the costs of leverage presumably begin to outweigh the tax and monitoring benefits of debt.

Table 10-1 shows median leverage ratios for all publicly-traded stocks in selected industries for the year ended December 31, 2005. Median debt-to-book equity ratios are highest for the water supply and electric services industries, which are typically not highly sensitive to economy risk and whose core assets are primarily physical equipment and property that are readily transferable to debt holders in the event

TABLE 10-1	Median Leverage in Selected Industries – Year-end 2005	
	Net Interest-Bearing Debt-to-Book Equity	
Industry	**All Listed Firms**	**NYSE Firms**
Prepackaged Computer Software	−54.5%	−41.6%
Pharmaceuticals	−60.9%	−11.8%
Petroleum Refining	−2.2%	−2.2%
Hotels & Motels	40.0%	45.9%
Water Supply	78.0%	78.0%
Electric Services	92.4%	95.1%

of financial distress. In contrast, the software and pharmaceutical industries' core assets are their research staffs. Ownership of these types of assets cannot be easily transferred to debt holders if the firm is in financial distress and researchers are sensitive to budget cuts. As a result, firms in these industries have relatively conservative capital structures. Petroleum refining and hotel firms have leverage in between these extremes, reflecting the need to balance the impact of having extensive physical assets and being subject to more volatile revenue streams.

It is also interesting to note that NYSE firms in general tend to have higher debt financing than non-NYSE firms in the same industries, with the difference most pronounced in pharmaceuticals. This probably reflects the fact that larger NYSE firms tend to have more product offerings and to be more diversified geographically, reducing their vulnerability to negative events for a single product or market, and enabling them to take on more debt.

THE MARKET FOR CREDIT

An understanding of credit analysis requires an appreciation for the various players in the market for credit. We briefly describe below the major suppliers of debt financing:

Commercial Banks

Commercial banks are important players in the market for credit. Since banks tend to provide a range of services to a client, and have intimate knowledge of the client and its operations, they have a comparative advantage in extending credit in settings where (1) knowledge gained through close contact with management reduces the perceived riskiness of the credit and (2) credit risk can be contained through careful monitoring of the firm.

Bank lending operations are constrained by a low tolerance for risk to ensure that the overall loan portfolio will be of acceptably high quality to bank regulators. Because of the importance of maintaining public confidence in the banking sector and the desire to shield government deposit insurance from risk, governments have incentives to constrain banks' exposure to credit risk. Banks also tend to shield themselves from the risk of shifts in interest rates by avoiding fixed-rate loans with long maturities. Since banks' capital comes mostly from short-term deposits, such long-term loans leave them exposed to increases in interest rates, unless the risk can be hedged with derivatives. Thus banks are less likely to play a role when a firm requires a very long-term commitment to financing. However, in some cases banks place the debt with investors looking for longer-term credit exposure.

Non-Bank Financial Institutions

Banks face competition in the commercial lending market from a variety of sources. In the U.S., there is competition from savings and loans institutions, though these firms tend to focus on financing mortgages. Finance companies compete with banks in the market for asset-based lending (i.e., the secured financing of specific assets such as receivables, inventory, or equipment). Insurance companies are also involved in a variety of lending activities. Since life insurance companies face obligations of a long-term nature, they often seek investments of long duration (e.g., long-term bonds or loans to support large, long-term commercial real estate and development projects). Investment bankers are prepared to place debt securities with private investors or in the public markets (discussed below). Various government agencies are also a source of credit.

Public Debt Markets

Some firms have the size, strength, and credibility necessary to bypass the banking sector and seek financing directly from investors, either through sales of commercial paper or through the issuance of bonds. Such debt issues are facilitated by the assignment of a debt rating, which measures the underlying credit strength of the firm and determines the yield that must be offered to investors.

Banks often provide financing in tandem with a public debt issue or other source of financing. In highly levered transactions, such as leveraged buyouts, banks commonly provide financing along with public debt that has a lower priority in case of bankruptcy. The bank's "senior financing" would typically be scheduled for earlier retirement than the public debt, and it would carry a lower yield. For smaller or start-up firms, banks often provide credit in conjunction with equity financing from venture capitalists. Note that in the case of both the leveraged buyout and the start-up company, the bank helps provide the cash needed to make the deal happen, but it does so in a way that shields it from risks that would be unacceptably high for the banking sector.

Sellers Who Provide Financing

Another sector of the market for credit is manufacturers and other suppliers of goods and services. As a matter of course, such firms tend to finance their customers' purchases on an unsecured basis for periods of 30 to 60 days. Suppliers will, on occasion, also agree to provide more extended financing, usually with the support of a secured note. A supplier may be willing to grant such a loan in the expectation that the creditor will survive a cash shortage and remain an important customer in the future. However, the customer would typically seek such an arrangement only if bank financing is unavailable because it could constrain flexibility in selecting among and/or negotiating with suppliers.

THE CREDIT ANALYSIS PROCESS IN PRIVATE DEBT MARKETS

Credit analysis is more than just establishing the creditworthiness of a firm, that is, its ability to pay its debts at the scheduled times. The decision to extend credit is not a binary one—the firm's exact value, its upside potential, and its distance from the threshold of creditworthiness are all equally important. There are ranges of credit-worthiness, and it is important for purposes of pricing and structuring a loan to understand where a firm lies within that range. While downside risk must be the primary consideration in credit analysis, a firm with growth potential offers opportunities for future income-generating financial services from a continued relationship.

This broader view of credit analysis involves most of the issues already discussed in the prior chapters on business strategy analysis, accounting analysis, financial analysis, and prospective analysis. Perhaps the greatest difference is that credit analysis rarely involves any explicit attempt to estimate the value of the firm's equity. However, the determinants of that value are relevant in credit analysis because a larger equity cushion translates into lower risk for the creditor.

Below we describe a representative but comprehensive series of steps that is used by commercial lenders in credit analysis. However, not all credit providers follow these guidelines. For example, when compared to a banker, manufacturers conduct a less extensive analysis on their customers since the credit is very short-term and the manufacturer is willing to bear some credit risk in the interest of generating a profit on the sale.

We present the steps in a particular order, but they are in fact all interdependent. Thus analysis at one step may need to be rethought depending on the analysis at some later step.

Step 1: Consider the Nature and Purpose of the Loan

Understanding the purpose of a loan is important not only for deciding whether it should be granted but also for structuring the loan based on duration, purpose, and size. Loans might be required for only a few months, for several years, or even as a permanent part of a firm's capital structure. Loans might be used for replacement of other financing, to support working capital needs, or to finance the acquisition of long-term assets or another firm.

The required amount of the loan must also be established. In the case of small and medium-sized companies, bankers typically prefer to be the sole financier of the business. This preference is not only to gain an advantage in providing a menu of financial services to the firm but also to maintain a superior interest in case of bankruptcy. If other creditors are willing to subordinate their positions to the bank, that would of course be acceptable as far as the bank is concerned.

Often the commercial lender deals with firms that may have parent-subsidiary relations, posing the question of the appropriate counterparty. In general, the entity that owns the assets that will serve as collateral (or that could serve as such if needed in the future) acts as the borrower. If this entity is the subsidiary and the parent presents some financial strength independent of the subsidiary, a guarantee of the parent could be considered.

Step 2: Consider the Type of Loan and Available Security

The type of loan is a function of not only its purpose but also the financial strength of the borrower. Thus, to some extent, the loan type will be dictated by the financial analysis described in Step 3. Some of the possible loan types are as follows:

- *Open line of credit.* An open line of credit permits the borrower to receive cash up to some specified maximum on an as-needed basis for a specified term, such as one year. To maintain this option, the borrower pays a fee (e.g., 3/8 of 1 percent) on the unused balance in addition to a market rate of interest on any used amount. An open line of credit is useful in cases where the borrower's cash needs are difficult to anticipate.

- *Revolving line of credit.* When it is clear that a firm will need credit beyond the short run, financing may be provided in the form of a "revolver." The terms of a revolver, which is sometimes used to support working capital needs, requires the borrower to make payments as the operating cycle proceeds and inventory and receivables are converted to cash. However, it is also expected that cash will continue to be advanced as long as the borrower remains in good standing. In addition to interest on amounts outstanding, a fee is charged on the unused line.
- *Working capital loan.* Such a loan is used to finance inventory and receivables, and it is usually secured. The maximum loan balance may be tied to the balance of the working capital accounts. For example, the loan may be allowed to rise to no more than 80 percent of receivables less than 60 days old.
- *Term loan.* Term loans are used for long-term needs and are often secured with long-term assets such as plant or equipment. Typically, the loan will be amortized, requiring periodic payments to reduce the loan balance.
- *Trade credit.* Trade credit generally takes two forms—an interim loan to an exporter to be repaid when the exports are paid for by the foreign importer, or credit extended by an exporter to an importer, allowing them to pay at some time after they take delivery.
- *Mortgage loan.* Mortgages support the financing of real estate, have long terms, and generally require periodic amortization of the loan balance.
- *Lease financing.* Lease financing can be used to facilitate the acquisition of any asset but is most commonly used for equipment, including vehicles, and buildings. Leases may be structured over periods of 1 to 15 years, depending on the life of the underlying asset.

Much bank lending is done on a secured basis, especially with smaller and more highly levered companies. Security will be required unless the loan is short-term and the borrower exposes the bank to only minimal default risk. When security is required, an important consideration is whether the amount of available security is sufficient to support the loan. The amount that a bank will lend based on given security involves business judgment and depends on a variety of factors that affect the liquidity of the security should the firm face financial distress. The following are some rules of thumb often applied in commercial lending to various categories of security:

- *Receivables.* Accounts receivable are usually considered the most desirable form of security because they are the most liquid. One large regional bank allows loans of 50 to 80 percent of the balance of nondelinquent accounts. The percentage applied is lower when (1) there are many small accounts that would be costly to collect in case the firm is distressed; (2) there are a few very large accounts, such that problems with a single customer could be serious; and/or (3) the customer's financial health is closely related to that of the borrower, so that collectibility is endangered just when the borrower is in default. On the latter score, banks often refuse to accept receivables from affiliates as effective security.
- *Inventory.* The desirability of inventory as security varies widely. The best-case scenario is inventory consisting of a common commodity that can easily be sold to other parties if the borrower defaults. More specialized inventory, with appeal to only a limited set of buyers or that is costly to store or transport, is less desirable. The large regional bank mentioned above lends up to 60 percent on raw materials, 50 percent on finished goods, and 20 percent on work in process.
- *Machinery and equipment.* Machinery and equipment is less desirable as collateral. It is likely to be used, and it must be stored, insured, and marketed. Keeping the costs of these activities in mind, banks typically will lend only up to 50 percent of the estimated value of such assets in a forced sale such as an auction.

- *Real estate*. The value of real estate as collateral varies considerably. Banks will often lend up to 80 percent of the appraised value of readily salable real estate. On the other hand, a factory designed for a unique purpose would be much less desirable.

Even when a loan is not secured initially, a bank can require a "negative pledge" on the firm's assets—a pledge that the firm will not use the assets as security for any other creditor. In that case, if the borrower begins to experience difficulty and defaults on the loan, and if there are no other creditors in the picture, the bank can demand the loan become secured if it is to remain outstanding.

Step 3: Conduct a Financial Analysis of the Potential Borrower

This portion of the analysis involves all the steps discussed in our chapters on business strategy analysis, accounting analysis, and financial analysis. The emphasis, however, is on the firm's ability to service the debt at the scheduled rate. All the factors that could impact that ability, such as the presence of off-balance-sheet lease obligations and the sustainability of the firm's operating profit stream, need to be carefully examined. The focus of the analysis depends on the type of financing under consideration. For example, if a short-term loan is needed to support seasonal fluctuations in inventory, the emphasis would be on the ability of the firm to convert the inventory into cash on a timely basis. In contrast, a term loan to support plant and equipment must be made with confidence in the long-run earnings prospects of the firm. This step incorporates both an assessment of the potential borrower's financial status using ratio analysis and a forecast to determine future payment prospects.

Ratio Analysis

Ultimately, since the key issue in the financial analysis is the likelihood that cash flows will be sufficient to repay the loan, lenders focus much attention on solvency ratios: the magnitude of various measures of profits and cash flows relative to debt service and other requirements. Therefore, ratio analysis from the perspective of a creditor differs somewhat from that of an owner. There is greater emphasis on cash flows and earnings available to *all* claimants (not just owners) *before* taxes (since interest is tax-deductible and paid out of pretax dollars). The *funds flow coverage ratio* illustrates the creditor's perspective:

$$\text{Funds flow coverage} = \frac{\text{EBIT} + \text{Depreciation}}{\text{Interest} + \dfrac{\text{Debt repayment}}{(1 - \text{tax rate})} + \dfrac{\text{Preferred dividends}}{(1 - \text{tax rate})}}$$

Earnings before both interest and taxes in the numerator is compared directly to the interest expense in the denominator, because interest expense is paid out of pre-tax dollars. In contrast, any payment of principal scheduled for a given year is non-deductible and must be made out of after-tax profits. In essence, with a 50 percent tax rate, one dollar of principal payment is "twice as expensive" as a one-dollar interest payment. Scaling the payment of principal by $(1 - \text{tax rate})$ accounts for this. The same idea applies to preferred dividends, which are not tax deductible.

The funds flow coverage ratio provides an indication of how comfortably the funds flow can cover unavoidable expenditures. The ratio excludes payments such as common dividends and capital expenditures on the premise that they could be reduced to zero to make debt payments if necessary.[1] Clearly, however, if the firm is to survive in the long run, funds flow must be sufficient to not only service debt but also maintain plant assets. Thus long-run survival requires a funds flow coverage ratio well in excess of 1.[2]

To the extent the ratio exceeds 1, it indicates the "margin of safety" the lender faces. When such a ratio is combined with an assessment of the variance in its numerator, it provides an indication of the probability of nonpayment. However, it would be overly simplistic to establish any particular threshold above which a ratio indicates a loan is justified. A creditor clearly wants to be in a position to be repaid on schedule, even when the borrower faces a reasonably foreseeable difficulty. That argues for lending only when the funds flow coverage is expected to exceed 1, even in a recession scenario—and higher if some allowance for capital expenditures is prudent.

The financial analysis should produce more than an assessment of the risk of nonpayment. It should also identify the nature of the significant risks. At many commercial banks it is standard operating procedure to summarize the analysis of the firm by listing the key risks that could lead to default and factors that could be used to control those risks if the loan were made. That information can be used in structuring the detailed terms of the loan so as to trigger default when problems arise, at a stage early enough to permit corrective action.

Forecasting

Implicit in the discussion of the ratio analysis is a forward-looking view of the firm's ability to service the loan. Good credit analysis should also be supported by explicit forecasts. The basis for such forecasts is usually management, though lenders perform their own tests as well. An essential element of this step is a sensitivity analysis to examine the ability of the borrower to service the debt under a variety of scenarios such as changes in the economy or in the firm's competitive position. Ideally, the firm should be strong enough to withstand downside risks such as a drop in sales or a decrease in profit margins.

At times it is possible to reconsider the structure of a loan so as to permit it to "cash flow." That is, the term of the loan might be extended or the amortization pattern changed. Often a bank will grant a loan with the expectation that it will be continually renewed, thus becoming a permanent part of the firm's financial structure (labeled an "evergreen" loan). In that case the loan will still be written as if it is due within the short term, and the bank must assure itself of a viable "exit strategy." However, the firm would be expected to service the loan by simply covering interest payments.

Step 4: Assemble the Detailed Loan Structure, Including Loan Covenants

If the analysis thus far indicates that a loan is in order, the final step is to assemble the detailed structure. Having previously determined the type of loan and repayment schedule, the focus shifts to the loan covenants and pricing.

Writing Loan Covenants

Loan covenants specify mutual expectations of the borrower and lender by specifying actions the borrower will and will not take. Covenants generally fall into three categories: (1) those that require certain actions such as regular provision of financial statements; (2) those that preclude certain actions such as undertaking an acquisition without the permission of the lender; and (3) those that require maintenance of certain financial ratios. Loan covenants must strike a balance between protecting the interests of the lender and providing the flexibility management needs to run the business. The covenants represent a mechanism for ensuring that the business will remain as strong as the two parties anticipated at the time the loan was granted.

The principal covenants that govern the management of the firm include restrictions on other borrowing, pledging assets to other lenders, selling substantial assets, engaging in mergers or acquisitions, and paying of dividends. The financial covenants should seek to address the significant risks identified in the financial analysis, or to at least provide early warning that such risks are surfacing. Some commonly used financial covenants follow:

- *Maintenance of minimum net worth.* This covenant assures that the firm will maintain an "equity cushion" to protect the lender. Covenants typically require a level of net worth rather than a particular level of income. In the final analysis, the lender may not care whether that net worth is maintained by generating income, cutting dividends, or issuing new equity. Tying the covenant to net worth offers the firm the flexibility to use any of these avenues to avoid default.
- *Minimum coverage ratio.* Especially in the case of a long-term loan, such as a term loan, the lender may want to supplement a net worth covenant with one based on coverage of interest or total debt service. The funds flow coverage ratio presented above would be an example. Maintenance of some minimum coverage helps ensure that the ability of the firm to generate funds internally is strong enough to justify the long-term nature of the loan.
- *Maximum ratio of total liabilities to net worth.* This ratio constrains the risk of high leverage and prevents growth without either retaining earnings or infusing equity.
- *Minimum net working capital balance or current ratio.* Constraints on this ratio force a firm to maintain its liquidity by using cash generated from operations to retire current liabilities (as opposed to acquiring long-lived assets).
- *Maximum ratio of capital expenditures to earnings before depreciation.* Constraints on this ratio help prevent the firm from investing in growth (including the illiquid assets necessary to support growth) unless such growth can be financed internally, with some margin remaining for debt service.

Required financial ratios are typically based on the levels that existed at the time that the agreement was executed, perhaps with some allowance for deterioration but often with some expected improvement over time. Violation of a covenant represents an event of default that could cause immediate acceleration of the debt payment, but in most cases the lender uses the default as an opportunity to re-examine the situation and either waive the violation or renegotiate the loan.

Covenants are included not only in private lending agreements but also in public debt agreements. However, public debt agreements tend to have less restrictive covenants for two reasons. First, since negotiations resulting from a violation of public debt covenants are costly (possibly involving not just the trustee, but bondholders as well), the covenants are written to be triggered only in serious circumstances. Second, public debt is usually issued by stronger, more credit-worthy firms, though there is a large market for high-yield debt. For the most financially healthy firms with strong debt ratings, very few covenants will be used, generally only those necessary to limit dramatic changes in the firm's operations, such as a major merger or acquisition.

Loan Pricing

A detailed discussion of loan pricing falls outside the scope of this text. The essence of pricing is to assure that the yield on the loan is sufficient to cover (1) the lender's cost of borrowed funds; (2) the lender's costs of administering and servicing the loan; (3) a premium for exposure to default risk; and (4) at least a normal return on the equity capital necessary to support the lending operation. The price is often stated in terms of a deviation from the bank's prime rate (the rate charged to stronger borrowers). For example, a loan might be granted at prime plus $1\frac{1}{2}$ percent. An alternative base is LIBOR, or the London Interbank Offer Rate, the rate at which large banks from various nations lend blocks of funds to each other.

Banks compete actively for commercial lending business, and it is rare that a yield includes more than 2 percentage points to cover the cost of default risk. If the spread to cover default risk is, say, 1 percent, and the bank recovers only 50 percent of amounts due on loans that turn out bad, then the bank can afford only 2 percent of their loans to fall into that category. This underscores how important it is for banks to conduct a thorough analysis and to contain the riskiness of their loan portfolio.

FINANCIAL STATEMENT ANALYSIS AND PUBLIC DEBT

Fundamentally, the issues involved in analysis of public debt are no different from those of bank loans and other private debt issues. Institutionally, however, the contexts are different. Bankers can maintain very close relations with clients so as to form an initial assessment of their credit risk and monitor their activities during the loan period. In the case of public debt, the investors are distanced from the issuer. To a large extent, they must depend on professional debt analysts, including debt raters, to assess the riskiness of the debt and monitor the firm's ongoing activities. Such analysts and debt raters thus serve an important function in closing the information gap between issuers and investors.

The Meaning of Debt Ratings

A firm's debt rating influences the yield that must be offered to sell the debt instruments. After the debt issue, the rating agencies continue to monitor the firm's financial condition. Changes in the rating are associated with fluctuation in the price of the securities. The two major debt rating agencies in the U.S. are Moody's and Standard and Poor's. Other rating agencies include Fitch Ratings, A.M. Best, and Dun & Bradstreet.

Using the Standard and Poor's labeling system, the highest possible rating is AAA. Proceeding downward from AAA, the ratings are AA, A, BBB, BB, B, CCC, CC, C, and D, where D indicates debt in default. Table 10-2 presents examples of firms in rating categories AAA through D, as well as average yields across all firms in each category. Less than 1 percent of the public nonfinancial companies rated by Standard & Poor's have the financial strength to merit a AAA rating. Among the few are General Electric, Johnson & Johnson, and Toyota—all among the largest, most profitable firms in the world. AA firms are also very strong and include Microsoft and Wal-Mart. Firms rated AAA and AA have the lowest costs of debt financing; at year-end 2005, their average yields were less than a quarter of a percent over the 12-month LIBOR rate.

To be considered investment grade, a firm must achieve a rating of BBB or higher, which is an important threshold as many funds are precluded by their charters from investing in any bonds below that grade. Even to achieve a grade of BBB is difficult. Daimler Chrysler, the automobile manufacturer and owner of Mercedes Benz, one of the world's most recognizable brands, was rated BBB, or barely investment grade in May 2006. Its large U.S. rivals, Ford and General Motors, were rated BB and B, respectively, at the same time. Some of the world's largest airlines, including British Airways and American Airlines, are also rated below investment grade.

Table 10-2 shows that the cost of debt financing rises markedly once firms' debt falls below investment grade. For example, at year-end 2005, yields for BBB rated debt issues were less than 1 percent over the 12 month LIBOR rate whereas yields for B rated issues were more than 3 percent above LIBOR rates. Yields for firms with CCC rated debt, which were close to bankruptcy, were more than 7 percent over LIBOR, and the debt securities of a few firms in default that were still traded yielded between 30 percent and 40 percent over the benchmark.

Table 10-3 shows median financial ratios for firms by debt rating category. Firms with AAA and AA ratings have very strong earnings and cash flow performance as

TABLE 10-2	Debt Ratings: Example Firms and Average Yields by Category			
S&P debt rating	**Example firms in 2006**	**Percentage of public industrials given same rating by S&P**	**Average yield, year-end 2005**	**Average spread over 12 month LIBOR rate**
AAA	General Electric Johnson & Johnson Toyota Motor Corporation	0.7%	4.92%	0.08%
AA	Home Depot Inc. GlaxoSmithKline Wal-Mart Stores, Inc.	2.4%	5.06%	0.22%
A	Coca-Cola Enterprises McDonald's Corp. Target Corporation	15.4%	5.21%	0.37%
BBB	Daimler Chrysler AG Best Buy Co. Duke Energy Corp.	25.4%	5.75%	0.91%
BB	Ford Motor Company Amazon.com British Airways	27.3%	7.60%	2.76%
B	General Motors Lucent Technologies American Airlines (AMR)	24.6%	7.88%	3.04%
CCC	XM Satellite Radio Silicon Graphics	3.3%	12.00%	7.16%
CC	Fedders Corporation	0.2%	16.81%[a]	11.97%
D	Northwest Airlines Calpine Corporation	0.8%	39.91%[a]	35.07%

a. Representative yields as most securities not actively traded.

Source: Standard and Poor's Compustat 2006.

well as minimal leverage. AAA rated firms often have large surpluses of cash such that net debt is negative. Firms in the BBB class are only moderately leveraged, with about 32 percent of net capitalization coming from net debt. Earnings tend to be relatively strong, as indicated by a pretax interest coverage (EBIT/interest) of 5.5 and a cash flow debt coverage (cash flow from operations/total debt) of nearly 38 percent. Firms at the bottom of the ratings spectrum, however, face significant risks: They typically report losses, have high leverage, and have interest coverage ratios less than 1.

TABLE 10-3	Debt Ratings: Median Financial Ratios by Category

Median ratios for overall category in January 2006 (excludes financial firms)

S&P debt rating	Earnings before interest and taxes to net capital	Pretax interest coverage	Cash flow from operations to total debt	Net debt to net capital
AAA	25.3%	31.4	118%	−3%
AA	32.2	16.7	85	14
A	20.2	9.2	52	27
BBB	16.5	5.5	38	32
BB	15.1	3.9	26	40
B	10.6	1.4	12	65
CCC	2.9	0.2	1	116
CC	−6.9	−1.2	−5	100
D	−18.1	−0.4	15	93

Source: Standard and Poor's Compustat 2006.

Factors That Drive Debt Ratings

Research using quantitative models of debt ratings demonstrates that some of the variation in ratings can be explained by selected financial statement ratios. Some debt rating agencies rely heavily on these types of quantitative models and they are also commonly used by insurance companies, banks, and others to assist in the evaluation of the riskiness of debt issues for which a public rating is not available.

Table 10-4 lists the factors used by three different firms in their quantitative debt-rating models. The firms include one insurance company and one bank, which use the models in their private placement activities, and an investment research firm, which employs the model in evaluating its own debt purchases and holdings. In each case, profitability and leverage play an important role in the rating. One firm also uses size as an indicator, with larger size associated with higher ratings.

Several researchers have developed quantitative models of debt ratings. Two of these models, both by Kaplan and Urwitz and shown in Table 10-5, highlight the relative importance of the different factors.[3] Model 1 has a greater ability to explain variation in bond ratings. However, it includes some factors based on stock

TABLE 10-4	Factors Used in Quantitative Models of Debt Ratings		
	Firm 1	**Firm 2**	**Firm 3**
Profitability measures	Return on long-term capital	Return on long-term capital	Return on long-term capital
Leverage measures	Long-term debt to capitalization	Long-term debt to capitalization Total debt to total capital	Long-term debt to capitalization
Profitability and leverage	Interest coverage Cash flow to long-term debt	Interest coverage Cash flow to long-term debt	Fixed charge coverage Coverage of short-term debt and fixed charges
Firm size	Sales	Total assets	
Other		Standard deviation of return Subordination status	

market data, which are not available for all firms. Model 2 is based solely on financial statement data.

The factors in Table 10-5 are listed in the order of their statistical significance in Model 1. An interesting feature is that the most important factor explaining debt ratings is not a financial ratio at all—it is simply firm size! Large firms tend to get better ratings than small firms. Whether the debt is subordinated or unsubordinated is next most important, followed by a leverage indicator. Profitability appears less important, but in part that reflects the presence in the model of multiple factors (ROA and interest coverage) that capture profitability. The explanatory power of profitability is then divided between these two variables.

When applied to a sample of bonds that were not used in the estimation process, the Kaplan-Urwitz Model 1 predicted the rating category correctly in 44 of 64 cases, or 63 percent of the time. Where it erred, the model was never off by more than one category, and in about half of those cases its prediction was more consistent with the market yield on the debt than was the actual debt rating. The discrepancies between actual ratings and those estimated using the Kaplan-Urwitz model indicate that rating agencies incorporate factors other than financial ratios in their analysis. These are likely to include the types of strategic, accounting, and prospective analyses discussed throughout this book.

Although debt ratings can be explained reasonably well in terms of a handful of financial ratios based on publicly available data, ratings changes have an important signaling effect. Debt rating downgrades are greeted with drops in both bond and stock prices,[4] even though the capital markets anticipate much of the information reflected in rating changes. This is due to the fact that changes often represent reactions to recent known events and the rating agencies typically indicate in advance that a change is being considered.

| TABLE 10-5 | Kaplan-Urwitz Models of Debt Ratings | | |

Firm or debt characteristic	Variable reflecting characteristic	Coefficients	
		Model 1	Model 2
	Model intercept	5.67	4.41
Firm size	Total assets[a]	.0010	.0013
Subordination status of debt	1 = subordinated; 0 = unsubordinated	−2.36	−2.56
Leverage	Long-term debt to total assets	−2.85	−2.72
Systematic risk	Market model beta, indicating sensitivity of stock price to market-wide movements (1 = average)[b]	−.87	—
Profitability	Net income to total assets	5.13	6.40
Unsystematic risk	Standard deviation of residual from market model (average = .10)[b]	−2.90	—
Riskiness of profit stream	Coefficient of variation in net income over five years (standard deviation/mean)	—	−.53
Interest coverage	Pretax funds flow before interest to interest expense	.007	.006

The score from the model is converted to a bond rating as follows:

If score > 6.76, predict AAA
   score > 5.19, predict AA
   score > 3.28, predict A
   score > 1.57, predict BBB
   score < 0.00, predict BB

a. *The coefficient in the Kaplan-Urwitz model was estimated at .005 (Model 1) and .006 (Model 2). Its scale has been adjusted to reflect that the estimates were based on assets measured in dollars from the early 1970s. Given that $1 from 1972 is approximately equivalent to $4.79 in 2006, the original coefficient estimate has been divided by 4.79.*

b. *Market model is estimated by regressing stock returns on the market index, using monthly data for the prior 5 years.*

PREDICTION OF DISTRESS AND TURNAROUND

The key task in credit analysis is assessing the probability that a firm will face financial distress and fail to repay a loan. A related analysis, relevant once a firm begins to face distress, involves considering whether it can be turned around. In this section, we consider evidence on the predictability of these states.

The prediction of either distress or turnaround is a complex, difficult, and subjective task that involves all of the steps of analysis discussed throughout this book: business strategy analysis, accounting analysis, financial analysis, and prospective analysis. Purely quantitative models of the process can rarely serve as substitutes for the hard work the analysis involves. However, research on such models does offer some insight into which financial indicators are most useful in the task. Moreover, there are some settings where extensive credit checks are too costly to justify, and where quantitative distress prediction models are useful.

Models for Distress Prediction

Several distress prediction models have been developed over the years.[5] They are similar to the debt rating models, but instead of predicting ratings, they predict whether a firm will face some state of distress, typically defined as bankruptcy, within a specified period such as one year. One study suggests that the factors most useful (on a stand-alone basis) in predicting bankruptcy one year in advance are the firm's level of profitability, the volatility of that profitability (as measured by the standard deviation of ROE), and its leverage.[6] Interestingly, liquidity measures turn out to be much less important. Current liquidity won't save an unhealthy firm if it is losing money at a fast pace.

A number of more robust, multifactor models have also been designed to predict financial distress. One such model, the Altman Z-score model, weights five variables to compute a bankruptcy score.[7] For public companies the model is as follows[8]:

$$Z = 1.2(X_1) + 1.4(X_2) + 3.3(X_3) + 0.6(X_4) + 1.0(X_5)$$

where
X_1 = net working capital/total assets (measure of liquidity)
X_2 = retained earnings/total assets (measure of cumulative profitability)
X_3 = EBIT/total assets (measure of return on assets)
X_4 = market value of equity/book value of total liabilities (measure of market leverage)
X_5 = sales/total assets (measure of sales generating potential of assets)

The model predicts bankruptcy when $Z < 1.81$. The range between 1.81 and 2.67 is labeled the "gray area."

The following table presents calculations for two companies, Wal-Mart and General Motors (GM), at the end of their respective 2005 fiscal years:

	Model Coefficient	Wal-Mart January 2006		General Motors December 2005	
		Ratios	Score	Ratios	Score
Net working capital/Total assets	1.2	−0.036	−0.04	−0.042	−0.05
Retained earnings/Total assets	1.4	0.363	0.51	−0.002	0.00
EBIT/Total assets	3.3	0.111	0.37	−0.023	−0.08
Market value of equity/Book value of total liabilities	0.6	2.299	1.38	0.027	0.02
Sales/Total assets	1.0	2.260	2.26	0.430	0.43
			4.47		0.32

The table shows the wide performance gap between two of America's most well known firms. Wal-Mart's Z score demonstrates its financial strength and reflects its AA rating.

Wal-Mart has delivered steady sales and earnings growth over the past ten years, and its liabilities are only 43 percent of its market capitalization, indicating relatively low financial leverage. GM's Z score, on the other hand, highlights its poor performance and is emblematic of the fragile state of the U.S. auto industry. GM's net income has declined steadily since 2003, with the losses in 2005 wiping out the firm's retained earnings. Even before servicing its debt, GM posted a loss in 2005. Finally, GM's liabilities are 37 times larger than its market capitalization, an indication of its precarious financial state. As a result, GM's debt was downgraded to B at the end of 2005.

Such models have some ability to predict failing and surviving firms. Altman reports that when the model was applied to a holdout sample containing 33 failed and 33 non-failed firms (the same proportion used to estimate the model), it correctly predicted the outcome in 63 of 66 cases. However, the performance of the model would degrade substantially if applied to a holdout sample where the proportion of failed and non-failed firms was not forced to be the same as that used to estimate the model.

The commercially available ZETA model, also developed by Altman, improves on the predictive power and accuracy of the Z-score model. The ZETA model incorporates seven variables and includes measures of the stability of earnings, debt service coverage, and firm size.[9] While distress prediction models cannot serve as a replacement for in-depth analysis of the kind discussed throughout this book, they do provide a useful reminder of the power of financial statement data to summarize important dimensions of a firm's performance. In addition, they can be useful for screening large numbers of firms prior to more in-depth analysis of corporate strategy, management expertise, market position, and financial ratio performance. The ZETA model, for instance, is used by some manufacturers and other firms to assess the creditworthiness of their customers.

Investment Opportunities in Distressed Companies

The debt securities of firms in financial distress trade at steep discounts to par value. Some hedge fund managers and investment advisors specialize in investing in these securities—even purchasing the debt of firms operating under bankruptcy protection. Investors in these securities can earn attractive returns if the firm recovers from its cash flow difficulties.[10]

Distressed debt investors assess whether the firm is likely to overcome its immediate cash flow problems and whether it has a viable long-run future. Two elements of the framework laid out in Part 2 of this book are particularly relevant to analyzing distressed opportunities. The first is a thorough analysis of the firm's industry and competitive positioning and an assessment of its business risks. This is followed by the construction of well reasoned forecasts of its future cash flow and earnings performance in light of the business analysis.

SUMMARY

Debt financing is attractive to firms with high marginal tax rates and few non-interest tax shields, making interest tax shields from debt valuable. Debt can can also help create value by deterring management of firms with high, stable income/cash flows and few new investment opportunities from over-investing in unprofitable new ventures.

However, debt financing also creates the risk of financial distress, which is likely to be particularly severe for firms with volatile earnings and cash flows, and intangible assets that are easily destroyed by financial distress.

Prospective providers of debt use credit analysis to evaluate the risks of financial distress for a firm. Credit analysis is important to a wide variety of economic agents—not only bankers and other financial intermediaries but also public debt analysts, industrial companies, service companies, and others.

At the heart of credit analysis lie the same techniques described in Chapters 2 through 8: business strategy analysis, accounting analysis, financial analysis, and portions of prospective analysis. The purpose of credit analysis in private debt markets goes beyond the assessment of the likelihood that a potential borrower will fail to repay the loan. It also serves to identify the nature of the main risks involved, and to guide how the loan might be structured to mitigate or control those risks. A well structured loan provides the lender with a viable "exit strategy," even in the case of default. Properly designed accounting-based covenants are essential to this structure.

Fundamentally, the issues involved in analysis of public debt are no different from those involved in evaluating bank loans or other private debt. Institutionally, however, the contexts are different. Investors in public debt are usually not close to the borrower and must rely on other agents, including debt raters and other analysts, to assess creditworthiness. Debt ratings, which depend heavily on firm size and financial measures of performance, have an important influence on the market yields that must be offered to issue debt.

The primary task in credit analysis is assessment of the probability of default. The task is complex, difficult, and to some extent, subjective. A few financial ratios can help predict financial distress with some accuracy. The most important indicators for this purpose are profitability, volatility of profits, and leverage. While there are a number of models that predict distress based on financial indicators, they cannot replace the in-depth forms of analysis discussed in this book.

DISCUSSION QUESTIONS

1. Financial analysts typically measure financial leverage as the ratio of debt to equity. However, there is less agreement on how to measure debt, or even equity. How would you treat the following items in computing this ratio? Justify your answers.
   - Revolving credit agreement with bank
   - Cash and marketable securities
   - Operating leases
   - Unrecorded pension commitments
   - Deferred tax liabilities
   - Preferred stock
   - Convertible debt

2. U.S. public companies with "low" leverage have an interest-bearing net debt-to-equity ratio of 0 percent or less, firms with "medium" leverage have a ratio between 1 and 62 percent, and "high" leverage firms have a ratio of 63 percent or more. Given these data, how would you classify the following firms in terms of their optimal debt-to-equity ratio (high, medium, or low)?
   - a successful pharmaceutical company
   - an electric utility
   - a manufacturer of consumer durables
   - a commercial bank
   - a start-up software company

3. What are the critical performance dimensions for (a) a retailer and (b) a financial services company that should be considered in credit analysis? What ratios would you suggest looking at for each of these dimensions?

4. Why would a company pay to have its public debt rated by a major rating agency (such as Moody's or Standard and Poor's)? Why might a firm decide not to have its debt rated?

5. Some have argued that the market for original-issue junk bonds developed in the late 1970s as a result of a failure in the rating process. Proponents of this argument suggest that rating agencies rated companies too harshly at the low end of the rating scale, denying investment grade status to some deserving companies. What are proponents of this argument effectively assuming were the incentives of rating agencies? What economic forces could give rise to this incentive?

6. Many debt agreements require borrowers to obtain the permission of the lender before undertaking a major acquisition or asset sale. Why would the lender want to include this type of restriction?

7. Betty Li, the CFO of a company applying for a new loan, states, "I will never agree to a debt covenant that restricts my ability to pay dividends to my shareholders because it reduces shareholder wealth." Do you agree with this argument?

8. Cambridge Construction Company follows the percentage-of-completion method for reporting long-term contract revenues. The percentage-of-completion is based on the cost of materials shipped to the project site as a percentage of total expected material costs. Cambridge's major debt agreement includes restrictions on net worth, interest coverage, and minimum working capital requirements. A leading analyst claims that "the company is buying its way out of these covenants by spending cash and buying materials, even when they are not needed." Explain how this might be possible.

9. Can Cambridge improve its Z score by behaving as the analyst claims in Question 8? Is this change consistent with economic reality?

10. A banker asserts, "I avoid lending to companies with negative cash from operations because they are too risky." Is this a sensible lending policy?

11. A leading retailer finds itself in a financial bind. It doesn't have sufficient cash flow from operations to finance its growth, and it is close to violating the maximum debt-to-assets ratio allowed by its covenants. The Vice-President for Marketing suggests, "We can raise cash for our growth by selling the existing stores and leasing them back. This source of financing is cheap since it avoids violating either the debt-to-assets or interest-coverage ratios in our covenants." Do you agree with his analysis? Why or why not? As the firm's banker, how would you view this arrangement?

NOTES

1. The same is true of preferred dividends. However, when preferred stock is cumulative, any dividends missed must be paid later, when and if the firm returns to profitability.

2. Other relevant coverage ratios are discussed in Chapter 5.

3. R. Kaplan and G. Urwitz, "Statistical Models of Bond Ratings: A Methodological Inquiry," *Journal of Business* (April 1979): 231–61.

4. See R. Holthausen and R. Leftwich, "The Effect of Bond Rating Changes on Common Stock Prices," *Journal of Financial Economics* (September 1986): 57–90, and J. Hand, R. Holthausen, and R. Leftwich, "The Effect of Bond Rating Announcements on Bond and Stock Prices," *Journal of Finance* (June 1992): 733–52.

5. See E. Altman, "Financial Ratios, Discriminant Analysis, and the Prediction of Corporate Bankruptcy," *Journal of Finance* (September 1968): 589–609; E. Altman, *Corporate Financial Distress* (New York: John Wiley, 1993); W. Beaver, "Financial Ratios as Predictors of Distress," *Journal of Accounting Research*, Supplement (1966): 71–111; J. Ohlson, "Financial Ratios and the Probabilistic Prediction of Bankruptcy," *Journal of Accounting Research* (Spring 1980): 109–131; and M. Zmijewski, "Predicting Corporate Bankruptcy: An Empirical Comparison of the Extant Financial Distress Models" (working paper, SUNY at Buffalo, 1983).

6. Zmijewski, op. cit.

7. Altman, *Corporate Financial Distress*, op. cit.

8. For private firms, Altman, ibid., adjusts the public model by changing the numerator for the variable X_4 from the market value of equity to the book value. The revised model follows:

$$Z = .717(X_1) + .847(X_2) + 3.11(X_3) + 0.420(X_4) + .998(X_5)$$

where
   X_1 = net working capital/total assets
   X_2 = retained earnings/total assets
   X_3 = EBIT/total assets
   X_4 = book value of equity/book value of total liabilities
   X_5 = sales/total assets

The model predicts bankruptcy when $Z < 1.23$. The range between 1.23 and 2.90 is labeled the "gray area."

9. See Altman, *Corporate Financial Distress*, op. cit.

10. In the period from January 1994 through April 30, 2006, distressed investing outperformed 10 out of 11 other strategies that were tracked by the Credit Suisse/Tremont Hedge Fund Index. The average annual return over that period was 13.60 percent versus a return of 11.3185 percent for the S&P 500 index (assuming dividends were reinvested in the index).

Amazon.com in the Year 2000

On June 22, 2000, Ravi Suria, a credit analyst at Lehman Brothers, issued a report sounding an alarm about the convertible debt of Amazon.com. When he looked at the company's financials, he saw a "weak balance sheet, poor working capital management, and massive negative operating cash flow." He regarded the debt as "extremely weak and deteriorating" and strongly advised investors to avoid it.

Amazon.com was, he noted, "the pioneering and best-established brand" among Internet retailers. Nevertheless, he was convinced that the company was going to run out of cash in less than a year because of its poor operating performance, reflecting basic weaknesses in its business model. Amazon, he said, had really evolved from a "virtual" retailer to something more like a "real world" retailer, and was encountering the same kinds of cash flow problems and problems related to management of working capital that had spelled disaster for many retailers in the past. In February 1999 the company had issued $1.25 billion in convertible debt. A year later, it completed a second offering of convertible debt, this time for $680 million. As Suria saw things, however, the company was burning cash up fast, and if it was not able to start generating positive free cash flows soon, it would be in dire straits. "The party is over," he said, "and the February round of financing seems to have been the last call."[1]

In response to Suria's report, the price of Amazon's convertible debt dropped 15%, and its stock price dropped 19%, in one day after the report became public.

BACKGROUND[2]

Jeff Bezos—Amazon's founder, chairman, and CEO—knew a good deal about the worlds of both technology and finance. After earning a degree in computer science and electrical engineering at Princeton, he worked for two years in commercial banking; then four years in investment banking in New York, managing a hedge fund.

Research Associate Jeremy Cott prepared this case under the supervision of Professor Krishna Palepu. This case was developed from published sources. HBS cases are developed solely as the basis for class discussion. Cases are not intended to serve as endorsements, sources of primary data, or illustrations of effective or ineffective management.

1. Ravi Suria (Lehman Brothers), "Amazon.com, Inc.: Credit Analysis of the Convertible Bonds," June 22, 2000.

2. For a detailed description of Amazon's business and its competitive strategy during its early years, see "Leadership Online: Barnes & Noble vs. Amazon.com" (HBS No. 798-063).

Then, fascinated by the possibilities of selling consumer goods over the Internet, he started Amazon.com. The company was founded in 1994, began selling books online in 1995, and went public in 1997.

Bezos initially considered a number of possible retailing businesses for the Internet. He regarded book selling as especially attractive for several reasons:

- The number of products that customers might want was far larger than any physical store could carry. There were over a million books in print—and many more that were out of print. (The largest physical book stores, so-called "superstores," carried about 150,000 titles. Mall stores and small independent stores carried a small fraction of that.)
- The existing market was large. Annual retail sales of books were about $25 billion in the United States and about $80 billion worldwide.
- The book publishing and retailing industries were relatively fragmented. No book publisher controlled more than 15% of the U.S. market, and the two largest land-based book retailers, Barnes & Noble and Borders, controlled about 25% of the market. (Barnes & Noble and Borders, however, had been expanding significantly in recent years.)

Bezos' decision to locate the company in Seattle, Washington was also deliberate. The Seattle area had a lot of computer-technical talent (e.g., Microsoft was located nearby); it was near one of the largest book wholesalers in the country; and it would provide, he felt, a time-zone advantage in making shipments to customers around the country.[3]

EVOLUTION OF CORPORATE STRATEGY

As the company developed, it made two major changes in strategy: (1) it began doing more self-distribution, and (2) it expanded the product line from books to other products.

Self-Distribution

During the first few years of its existence, Amazon pursued a "sell all, carry few" strategy. In the fall of 1997, for example, it billed itself as the world's largest bookstore, offering a selection of 2.5 million different titles. It actually stocked, however, only a few thousand. Generally, it ordered books from its suppliers (primarily wholesalers) only after making the sale to a customer. About 95% of Amazon's sales were handled that way.

Competition from Barnes & Noble, the largest land-based book retailer in the country, prompted a change in this approach. When Barnes & Noble opened its online store in May 1997, it said that it would use the distribution strength of its land-based operation to gain a competitive advantage in its online selling. Barnes & Noble operated a large distribution center in New Jersey where it stocked about 400,000 titles and from which it shipped books to its many physical stores around the country. Barnes & Noble said that it would also use this distribution center to fill many of the individual orders that it received from online customers.[4] There were two advantages to this approach:

- First, it reduced the cost of goods. Most of the books that Barnes & Noble stocked in its distribution center were ordered direct from publishers rather than wholesalers. Books ordered from publishers cost less than books ordered

---

3. *Ibid.*

4. *"Barnes & Noble Drops Names, Disses Amazon.com as Web Site Launches,"* Book Publishing Report, May 19, 1997.

Amazon.com in the Year 2000

from wholesalers. The difference was several additional percentage points in discount, which, in a low-margin business like book retailing, was significant. (The cost of holding inventory was of course an offsetting cost factor.) Amazon had been ordering most of its books from wholesalers because wholesalers delivered books much faster than publishers. In the fall of 1997, however, the Chief Operating Officer of Barnes & Noble, Steve Riggio, said, "The cost advantages of self-distribution are tremendous." He said that 40% of the books it sold were supplied by its own distribution complex, and he planned to get to 50% within a year. Jeff Bezos said, "The logistics of distribution are the iceberg below the waterline of online bookselling."[5]

- Second, having greater control over the order fulfillment process could provide greater assurance of the quality of a key element of customer service. In 1999, for example, Toys "R" Us, in planning to go online to challenge eToys, concluded that it needed to handle the fulfillment operation itself. "The minute you outsource," the CEO of Toys "R" Us said, "it's just something that's out of your hands. What happens at Christmas time when you're using [a certain third-party fulfillment operation]? They're servicing [someone else]. How do you get your service priorities to the top of the list?"[6]

The move to self-distribution changed the competitive landscape. When Barnes & Noble opened its online store in May 1997, it said that it would offer "the lowest everyday prices of any online bookseller."[7] It began by announcing discounts on a lot of books that were greater than what Amazon at that point was offering, and stiffer price competition was thus set in motion.

In response, in the fall of 1997 Amazon announced that it would enlarge its Seattle warehouse by 70%, open a new one on the East Coast, in Delaware, and buy a much larger portion of its books direct from publishers.

Then in 1999 Amazon made a dramatic move. It increased the number of distribution centers it had from two to ten, thus giving it over four million square feet of warehouse and distribution space. In its 1999 10-K it said that it carried "increased levels of inventory in order to be able to meet customer demand and ship products to customers on a timely basis," and that in 1999 it "increased our direct purchasing from manufacturers." It didn't disclose, however, what percentage of customer orders it filled from its own stock.

Selling Other Products

When Amazon first went online in 1995, it sold only books. When it went public in May 1997 it was selling books and a small number of tapes and CDs related to books.

5. Quotations come from Anthony Bianco, "Virtual Bookstores Start to Get Real," Business Week, October 27, 1997. The economics of order-fulfillment in e-tailing could take a few different forms. At one extreme, Buy.com—a multi-product e-tailer that opened for business in 1997—outsourced almost everything having to do with inventory: it didn't maintain any inventory on its balance sheet, and wholesalers fulfilled all of the orders that it received. Buy.com said that this was the most efficient way of handling things, but it paid the wholesalers' markup on the goods as well as a fee that wholesalers charged for carrying out the fulfillment function. Many e-tailers outsourced some, but not all, of its order fulfillment. When Musicland—the successful, land-based retailer of CDs, tapes, DVDs, and books—went online in 1999, it said that it would do its own order fulfillment. It claimed that, by using its existing distribution infrastructure, it would save 10% of sales compared with e-tailers who outsourced the order fulfillment function. It would save about 5%, it said, by ordering direct from manufacturers, thereby avoiding the wholesaler's markup; and about 5% by using its own distribution system, which was what it said other companies paid third-party distributors. (The source for the information about Musicland is Jim McCartney, "Launching Web Site Is More Than Defensive Strategy for Some Retailers," Saint Paul Pioneer Press, June 16, 1999.)

6. Abigail Goldman, "E-Commerce Gets an F Without the D Word," Los Angeles Times, July 25, 1999.

7. "Barnes & Noble Drops Names . . .," op. cit.

In 1998, however, Amazon began to significantly expand its product offerings, and by mid-2000 it had established, and was operating on its web site, businesses that sold not only books, but also music CDs, video tapes, DVDs, computer games, toys, software, consumer electronics, tools and hardware, lawn and patio products, and kitchen products. All of these products it sold itself: that is, it bought the actual inventory, and it sold it directly to customers. The company also set itself up as a middleman for, or strategic partner to, a number of other businesses that were allowed to use space on Amazon's web site to sell their own products to Amazon's customers.

"Marketplace Services"   In these arrangements the company provided space on its web site to auction businesses and thousands of small, non-auction businesses so that consumers could eventually come to the Amazon web site and—as Jeff Bezos put it— "find and discover anything they want to buy. That's anything with a capital 'A.' "[8] He ruled out only animals, porn, and contraband.

One auction business involved the famous art auction house Sothebys. The large assemblage of small, non-auction businesses was named "zShops." As Bezos said when announcing the zShops program in the fall of 1999, the "z" stands for zero. "What we're trying to do is create a shopping environment that has zero risk, zero hassles, and zero products you can't find." For example, he said that Amazon would guarantee up to $1,000 of any customer's purchase from these zShops. That is, the customer would get up to $1,000 of his or her money back if the merchant didn't fulfill the order.[9]

From these small, non-auction businesses Amazon would receive monthly subscription fees ($9.99) and sales commissions (up to 5% of the sale). Amazon wouldn't own or manage any of their inventories. Bezos characterized this as a low-top-line, high-margin business. When asked, however, whether he had any sense of how much of Amazon's revenue would come from this service, Bezos said he didn't.

"Strategic Partnerships"   Amazon was also making minority investments in many e-commerce companies.[10] These companies were given distinct, co-branded sections on the Amazon web site where they sold their products or services, and Amazon received advertising revenues from them for allowing them to do so. Thus, for example, the "health and beauty products" section was co-branded with the company Drugstore.com, in which Amazon had made a minority investment; the "pet products" section was co-branded with the company Pets.com, in which Amazon had also made a minority investment. Amazon considered these strategic partnerships (of which there were, in 2000, about a dozen) part of the "Amazon Commerce Network" (ACN). The company had high hopes for them. In a press release in February 2000, the company said that these equity-method partnerships/investments "represent more than $500 million in revenue commitments to Amazon.com over the next five years." In the first quarter of 2000, Amazon recorded $20 million of ACN revenues, and analysts believed that the direct cost of those revenues was negligible.

---

8. Helen Jung, "Amazon Opens Site to Other Merchants," Seattle Times, September 29, 1999.

9. Ibid.

10. Most of these companies were identified in Amazon's financial statements as "equity-method investees." Equity-method accounting applied to investments that gave the investor "significant influence," but not outright control, over an investee. (This was normally assumed to involve ownership of between 20% and 50% of the investee's common stock.) Once the investment was made, the investing company would record in its financial statements its proportional share of the investee's profit or loss.

These strategic partnerships had been attracting both admiration and skepticism from analysts. To some, Amazon was partly adopting the role of a venture capitalist, investing in various early-stage e-commerce companies that it viewed as especially promising. As a principal at Chase Capital Partners said, "If you can lock up the best of breed corporate partners, you can effectively block out the competition."[11] To other analysts, however, there was an illusory quality to these relationships. Amazon had begun to record high-margin advertising revenues from these companies, but the companies as a whole were losing a lot of money.[12] (As **Exhibit 1a** shows, Amazon's share of the losses of its equity-method investees in 1999 was $77 million; in the first quarter of 2000, $88 million.)

Rationale   What was the business rationale for this dramatic expansion in product offerings? Bezos said that it would allow the company to leverage its "Internet platform." By this he meant the company's growing customer base and brand name, the innovative technology it was developing, and its distribution capabilities. "We believe," the company's Annual Report stated, "that this platform allows us to launch new e-commerce businesses quickly, with a high quality of customer experience, economical incremental cost, and good prospects for success."

Implications of Amazon's Strategy

Bezos said repeatedly that he was committed to placing growth ahead of profitability during the first few years of the company's existence. The key to Amazon's appeal, he believed, would be the high level of customer service it provided, involving huge product selection, easy-to-use search and browse features, personalized shopping services, secure payment protection, and reliable and timely delivery.

Amazon's expansion was also geographic. It could ship products almost anywhere, but in 1999 it also established distinct web sites and distribution facilities in England and Germany.

Thus in mid-2000 Amazon was the largest Internet retailer in the world, with $1.9 billion in trailing twelve-month revenues and 20 million customers in over 150 countries. It claimed to offer for sale 18 million different products (SKUs). And its brand was very well known.

Some observers, however, believed that Amazon was badly over-extending itself. In trying to be all things to all people, some people felt, the company was taking on more than it could handle. Al Ries, the author of a book on Internet branding, said, "The most powerful brands in the world stand for something simple. Volvo stands for safety. Dell is a personal computer. Even Microsoft is software. Now Amazon is going to stand for books and charcoal grills. This makes no sense to me."[13]

Since the web was indifferent to distance and place, it was, in the view of some people, better suited to specialist retailers, to "category killers," than to generalists. (For example, eToys specialized in selling toys; CDNow specialized in selling CDs, Outpost.com specialized in selling computers and other electronic products.) Specialist retailers would, in this view, know more about particular categories of products

---

11. Stephen Lacey, "Amazon.com: Venture Capital on Steriods," IPO Reporter, March 27, 2000.

12. Gretchen Morgenson, "Bond Market Seems Wary of Amazon," New York Times, February 9, 2000; Herb Greenberg, "More on the Bear Case for Amazon," TheStreet.com, April 27, 2000.

13. Quoted in Robert Hof, "Can Amazon Make It?" Business Week, July 10, 2000.

and would be better able to develop the merchandising skills necessary to make their particular businesses successful.

Customer Service

In Jeff Bezos' view, however, what Amazon.com "stood for" was high-quality customer service. And part of the reason why it could provide that, he believed, was that people at Amazon knew more about e-commerce than anyone else. In 1998 the chairman of Putnam/Penguin, one of the largest book publishers in the world, said, "When you talk to Amazon, you realize it's a technology company, not a merchant."[14] Such was the sophistication of the company's software, Bezos claimed, that "coming to Amazon will not be like entering the halls of a huge, soulless department store. It will be more like stopping by at a local shop where your every taste and preference is known."[15] The company had in fact been developing many information-rich features for its web site—for example, product reviews by both outside experts and other Amazon customers, the customer's own purchasing history, "collaborative filtering" software that aimed to provide a kind of electronic word-of-mouth among people with similar tastes, e-mails to alert customers to the release of new products they had asked about, an ability given to customers to track the shipment of products they had ordered.

Pricing

An academic study, published in April 2000, seemed to support Bezos' view of things.[16] Amazon often engaged in aggressive pricing in order to attract customers, but the academic study found that pricing differences among Internet retail businesses, even for commodity-type products like books and CDs, were as pronounced as they were for conventional retailers and that Internet sites with the lowest prices didn't necessarily have the largest market shares. Amazon, for example, was the leader in online book and CD sales but, this study found, didn't necessarily have the lowest prices. The level of customer satisfaction and customer service it provided was evidently key to its ability to attract customers.

Amazon itself, however, regarded the pricing issue as a threat. "New and expanded web technologies," it said in its 1999 10-K, "may increase the competitive pressures on online retailers. For example, 'shopping agent' technologies permit customers to quickly compare our prices with those of our competitors. This increased competition may reduce our operating margins, diminish our market share, or impair the value of our brand."

A professor of operations and information management, Eric Clemons, writing in the *Financial Times* in June 2000 about particular kinds of risk in the e-commerce world, noted that Amazon, like most e-commerce businesses, was continuing to spend significant amounts of money to acquire new customers, but he wasn't at all sure that that made sense:

> *It is too early to determine if consumers will remain loyal to these sites, allowing these retailers time to harvest profits and cover the costs of their acquisition, or whether the web's empowerment of consumer choice will mean that customers constantly migrate to the lowest-cost online seller. If the web is as*

14. David Streitfeld, "Booking the Future," Washington Post, July 10, 1998.

15. "Amazon's Delta," The Economist, November 20, 1999.

16. Erik Brynjolfsson, "Frictionless Commerce?" Management Science, March 2000.

liberating and empowering as most accounts have led us to believe, all business models based on paying to acquire share are flawed.[17]

FINANCING STRATEGY

Amazon had started with private equity financing of about $1 million. It sold $8 million of convertible preferred in 1996 (which was converted to common the following year). The IPO in May 1997 brought in about $50 million. The company had also been receiving cash from employees when they exercised their stock options.

The company had issued debt on three occasions:

- In May 1998 the company sold 10% senior discount notes due in 2008. They were sold for $326 million, but their value at maturity would be $530 million. They accreted interest until 2003 and paid cash interest after that. (During 1999 the company repurchased $266 million principal amount of this issue [representing $178 million accreted value]. Thus as of year-end 1999, the accreted amount outstanding was $191 million.)
- In February 1999 the company sold $1.25 billion par value of 4.75% convertible subordinated notes due in 2009.
- In February 2000 the company sold €690 ($680 million) par value of 6.875% euro-denominated convertible subordinated notes due in 2010.

When this second set of convertibles was issued, observers noted the much-higher interest rate that Amazon had to offer compared to the 4.75% interest rate it offered on the convertibles it had sold just a year earlier. Some observers also suggested that Amazon had taken the offering to Europe because it had been a tough sell in the United States. The company denied this. It said that it sold this second set of convertibles in Europe because it wanted to broaden its market recognition there. It also said that it intended to use some of the proceeds from the issue to support growth in its European operations.

Thus at the end of the first quarter of 2000, Amazon had $2.15 billion in debt outstanding (including some capital leases), of which about $1.9 billion consisted of the convertibles. The convertibles were rated triple C by both Standard & Poor's and Moody's. A summary of the terms of the two convertible issues is provided in **Exhibit 5. Exhibit 6** shows the company's cash obligations, for interest and principal, for all of its debt securities over the next ten years.

FINANCIAL PERFORMANCE

Exhibits **1a, 1b,** and **1c** show Amazon.com's Income Statements, Balance Sheets, and Cash Flow Statements for the last few years. **Exhibit 2** shows some data about customers that analysts referred to a fair amount. **Exhibit 3** shows segment information for the company for the last three years and for the first quarter of 2000. **Exhibit 4** provides information about its fixed assets.

Since its inception, the company had recorded total sales of about $3 billion and total losses of $1.2 billion (of which about $350 million was amortization of goodwill and other intangibles). Total cash flows from operations had been a negative $380 million. The stock went public in May 1997 at about $2 a share (split adjusted), peaked at $106 in late 1999, and had declined to $42 just before the Lehman analyst issued his critical report.

---

17. Eric Clemons, "Managing Risk," Financial Times, June 13, 2000.

Some of the components of the Income Statement involved accounting policies or had meanings that were somewhat different from what one would expect in most businesses.

Sales

Most of Amazon's sales were product sales. The sales figures also included, however, revenue that the company had begun to record from its "Amazon Commerce Network" partners. Most of the revenue from these companies wasn't coming in the form of cash, however; it was coming in the form of the companies' stock. (As **Exhibit 1c** shows, $18 million of the $20 million of ACN revenues that Amazon recorded during the first quarter of 2000 was non-cash.) What happened essentially was that Amazon would receive a certain amount of these companies' stock when the partnership agreements were signed. The stock would be valued as of that date, recorded initially as unearned revenue, and then later credited to revenue as Amazon provided the related services (space on its web site). If the value of the stock declined, that would be reflected in Amazon's financial statements only when Amazon marked it down as a "permanent impairment."

Marketing and Sales Expense

This included not only standard kinds of marketing and sales expense (e.g., advertising and promotional expenditures and payroll for those functions) but also fulfillment expense. Fulfillment expense, the company said, represented "those costs incurred in operating and staffing distribution and customer service centers, including costs attributable to receiving, inspecting, and warehousing inventories; picking, packaging and preparing customers' orders for shipment; and responding to inquiries from customers." All of the company's distribution centers were leased, and almost all of them were accounted for as operating leases.

Another key component of Amazon's marketing expenses was what it called its "Associates Program." Many companies were agreeing to place on their web sites a link to Amazon.com—involving, say, a product recommendation—and for every sale that Amazon made as a result of that link, Amazon would pay a referral fee of between 5% and 15%. Many Internet businesses were developing this kind of "associate" or "affiliate" marketing, but Amazon had the largest such program, involving (as of early 2000) 430,000 web sites.

Technology and Content

Technology and content expenses consisted primarily of payroll and related expenses for the development of computer software and telecommunications systems, as well as for the acquisition of certain editorial content such as freelance reviews. Technology and content costs, it said, "are generally expensed as incurred, except for certain costs relating to the development of internal-use software that are capitalized and depreciated over estimated useful lives."

In Bezos' view, certain expenditures on technology could reduce fulfillment costs. For example, he said that a lot of customers had been calling its customer service department regarding problems that the company had now enabled them to handle themselves by means of an online software tool.[18]

---

18. "Newsmaker Q&A," BusinessWeek Online: Daily Briefing, <http / www.businessweek.com>, June 30, 2000.

Amortization of Goodwill and Other Intangibles

Amazon had acquired a number of companies; the acquisitions were generally accounted for as "purchases"; and most of the purchase prices had been allocated to goodwill and other intangible assets. Amazon said that it was amortizing those assets over a period of only two to four years.

Stock Options

Amazon didn't record the cost of stock options in its income statements—which was acceptable under generally accepted accounting standards. However, it disclosed that, had it recorded the fair value of stock options granted (using the Black-Scholes option pricing model), its net profit in 1999 and 1998 would have been $312 million and $70 lower, respectively.

BUSINESS MODEL

Amazon's business plan, of course, was premised on the expectation that it would ultimately perform better than comparable land-based retailers. **Exhibit 7a** shows some key operating data for Barnes & Noble and Borders, the two largest land-based book retailers in the United States. (Both of these companies were involved in online bookselling businesses, but those businesses were structured as separate entities. Therefore the data in **Exhibit 7a** should reasonably represent the performance of their land-based bookselling operations.) Amazon's aggressive pricing resulted in relatively low gross margins, and **Exhibit 7b** shows some key operating data for two very successful, land-based retailers that operated with low gross margins. (Wal-Mart was the largest retailer in the world. Costco was the largest operator of discount warehouse stores in the United States.)

COMPANY GUIDANCE

In April, when it reported first quarter 2000 results, the company told analysts that it expected to have positive cash flows from operations for the balance of the calendar year. It said it also expected that its cash flows from operations would fully cover its planned capital expenditures of approximately $250–$300 million and that its cash balance at the end of the calendar year would be about $1 billion. It said that it hoped to reduce fulfillment expense as a percentage of sales from 17% in the 1st quarter to the low teens by the fourth quarter. It also said it expected its operating margin loss (excluding amortization, stock-based compensation, and other special charges) to fall from 21% in 1999 to single digits for all of 2000. In addition, Bezos reiterated his intention to continue to invest in new product lines and to expand further in international markets.

ANALYSTS' ASSESSMENT OF AMAZON'S STOCK AND DEBT

During the first few years of Amazon's existence, stock analysts had been groping for ways to value the company's stock. Some analysts assumed certain multiples of sales or earnings for a company of this sort, forecasted sales or earnings figures for Amazon a number of years down the road, and then discounted those values back to the present. Some analysts attempted to calculate the present value of each of Amazon's customers (which involved an extraordinary array of assumptions). Most analysts gave very little attention to cash flows.[19]

An equity analyst at Prudential Securities, however, argued in February 1999 that "one of the appeals of Amazon.com's business model is its cash flow." She pointed out that, since its inception, the company had generated positive cash flow from operations of $30 million, had spent $37 million on capital expenditures, and therefore had had cumulative cash outflow of under $10 million. Thus, she said, the company "has essentially built its business with a net cash outlay of less than $10 million."[20]

Lehman Brothers Report

When the Lehman Brothers analyst, Ravi Suria, sounded his alarm about the company's debt in June 2000, he focused almost exclusively on cash flows. He was a debt analyst, and although the upside potential of the debt securities he was dealing with was tied to their convertibility into common stock, he focused his analysis on the company's credit risk.[21]

"In a best-case scenario," he said, "we believe that the current cash balances will last the company through the first quarter of 2001." "Despite [the company's] much-touted brand identity, first mover advantage, virtual storefronts, hits and visits," he said he found the company "woefully lacking from an operational aspect."

He noted that the company, since it opened for business, had recorded $1.2 billion in accounting losses. More important from his point of view, however, was the fact that its operating cash flows had been negative almost every quarter. Add its capital expenditures to that, he said, and total free cash flows from the fourth quarter of 1997 through the first quarter of 2000 had been a minus $718 million. (**Exhibit 8** shows information that he put together.)

So far the company had been supported, in his view, by an extremely forgiving capital market. For every $1 of revenue that the company had generated from the start of 1997 through the first quarter of 2000, he claimed, it had raised $.95 from the capital markets. The total figures he cited were $2.9 billion in revenue during that period and $2.8 billion raised from the capital markets. He defined money raised from the capital markets as consisting of money from the IPO in 1997, cash received from the three debt securities, and cash received from employees' exercise of stock options.

The component of Amazon's financial performance that Suria emphasized more than anything else in his report was what he called "cash flow per unit of product sold." He said, "We believe that the fundamental problem with the operations lies in the fact that Amazon does not generate positive net cash flow per unit of product it sells." The first few times he referred to this he didn't define what he meant, but then later in his report he said, "Our favorite metric for measuring success of a company is to look at its operating cash flow. . . . It is the best measurement of the ability of a

---

19. For example, in her first report on Amazon in September 1997, Mary Meeker, the soon-to-be very influential analyst of Internet stocks at Morgan Stanley Dean Witter, recommended the stock, but more or less said that it was almost impossible to do a valuation of it. She put together a matrix indicating a whole range of possible valuations based on a variety of assumptions about price-to-sales ratios, net margins, discount rates, and sales figures for the year 2001. She stated, "We have learned that too much focus on valuation can often lead to short-sighted investment errors." (Mary Meeker [Morgan Stanley Dean Witter], "Amazon.com: Initiating Coverage," September 22, 1997.)

20. Amy Ryan (Prudential Securities), "Amazon.com," February 1, 1999.

21. Ravi Suria (Lehman Brothers), op. cit.

retailing business to make money per unit sold." By this measurement, he said, Amazon's performance had been getting worse as time went on. There was, he said, "a clear correlation between [Amazon's] cash outflows and [its] revenues—indicating operational inefficiencies at the unit sales level."

From his point of view, the most important ingredient in Amazon's cash flow was its management of working capital. Thus he focused on accounts receivable, accounts payable, and inventory.

- **Accounts receivable**. Amazon didn't have any (because customers paid with credit cards). This, he said, was the strongest operating characteristic of the company.
- **Accounts payable**. Amazon, he thought, had become fairly savvy in stretching payables. However, payment of accounts payable in the first quarter of 2000 increased cash outflow by $207 million, and he thought that payables flexibility was likely to decrease for the company.
- **Inventory**. Suria thought this was the biggest problem Amazon faced. The critical period for most retailers, he said, was the fourth and first quarters, the periods tied to peak seasonal sales. Suria calculated Amazon's inventory turnover quarter by quarter, and he also used sales in the numerator (rather than cost of goods) because, he said, of the different accounting conventions used by companies to determine expense classifications. **Exhibit 9** shows the inventory turnover figures that he calculated. They had decreased steadily, he said, from 8.5 in the first quarter of 1998 to a low of 2.9 in the first quarter of 2000. More important than the absolute level of inventory turnover, he said, was its steady deterioration. This showed that the company wasn't managing its sales growth well.

Then there were, in his view, other problems on the horizon as well: the fact that the company was now selling greater numbers of toys and electronics, which he said were logistically more difficult to handle than books; the presence of an increasing number of old-world retailers in the e-tailing space; Amazon's intention to continue to establish new businesses; a probable slowdown in the economy.

His pessimistic view of Amazon's prospects had to do largely with its business model:

> *As the e-tailing model begins to look more and more like standard retailers, the cash flow cycle of the business will track that of an Old Economy retailer. Thus, depending upon the season, working capital either sucks in cash or spins out cash. But, net-net for a successful retailer, the annualized operating cash flow should be consistently positive, especially when the operating costs are not burdened by startup costs that many expanding retailers face in opening new physical locations.*[22]

Finally, he pointed out, Amazon had very little financial flexibility. As of the end of the first quarter of 2000, the company's debt to capital ratio was 99%. The ratio of debt to tangible capital, however—that is, netting out the large amount of goodwill and other intangibles—was 141%. "Going into what is arguably its most challenging holiday season," he said, "we believe that the combination of negative cash flow, poor working capital management, and high debt load in a hyper competitive environment will put the company under extremely high risk."

The company, he said, had to do either one of two things—start becoming cash sufficient, or keep raising capital until it became cash sufficient. He was doubtful about the prospects for either of these two things.

---

22. *Ibid.*

Reactions

The financial markets reacted immediately to the Lehman Brothers report. The day after it was issued, the prices of the two convertible debt securities dropped 15%. The common stock dropped 19%, thus losing about $2.8 billion of its market value. **Exhibit 10** shows graphs of the prices of Amazon's two convertible debt issues from their issue date through the end of June 2000. **Exhibit 11** shows, for the period from the beginning of 1999 through the end of June 2000, the return on Amazon's stock compared to the return on the Nasdaq index.

Amazon's Reaction   A company spokesperson called the Lehman Brothers report "pure hogwash," although he didn't identify any specific facts or assumptions that were wrong. "We are nowhere near running out of cash," he said, "and anybody who understands the cash flow dynamics of our company understands that."[23]

Bezos said the report was "baloney." When asked why the company, then, wasn't profitable, Bezos said that the books, music, and video segment was now showing an operating profit but that, at the same time, the company was investing in a lot of young businesses. "It would have been easy to make the business profitable at much lower revenue levels," he said, "but we wouldn't have had the opportunity to build an important and lasting company." Bazos said the argument had been made innumerable times that the company was buying products for a dollar and selling them for 90 cents. He said that wasn't the case. He said the company was selling dollar bills for $1.20 but that the reason it wasn't profitable was that it was investing in a lot of new things.[24]

Barron's   Alan Abelson, in his "Up and Down Wall Street" column in *Barron's* on June 26, called the Lehman Brothers report "brilliant, thorough, and very well crafted." He also said it was "miraculously free of the gibberish and webbygook that ooze from virtually all the brokerage stuff churned out on anything tech and everything Internet." Abelson noted that "Amazon has inspired comment in [*Barron's*] on a number of occasions in the past few years, and we have been consistently underwhelmed by the company and its prospects. . . . Indeed, the first truly penetrating dissection of Amazon appeared in [*Barron's*] in January 1999." (The article was entitled "Bubble Trouble" and the byline for it was "Alan Abelson and Rhonda Brammer.") He said that the thrust of that article was that "the company's fabled business plan had been anticipated by the pig farmer who lost 50 bucks on every pig he sold but was confident of making it up in volume." The article, he said, had essentially argued that "it was a reasonably safe bet that Amazon would never make any money." And he said that that, in a sense, was the core of the Lehman Brothers report.[25]

Business Week   *Business Week* ran a long article providing a more mixed reaction.[26] It restated the key arguments and figures that the Lehman analyst had presented, said that this was "scary stuff," and noted that timing now was critical. The sharp downturn that had occurred in the stocks of many Internet companies

---

23. *"Irrational Over-reaction,"* Business Line, July 5, 2000.

24. *"Newsmaker Q&A,"* BusinessWeek Online: Daily Briefing, <http//www.businessweek.com>, June 30, 2000.

25. *Alan Abelson, "Virtual Disaster,"* Barron's, June 26, 2000.

26. *Robert Hof, op. cit.*

"means that Amazon's access to new capital will likely be cut off now, so the clock is ticking." The article also raised questions about Amazon's whole "one-stop shopping mentality" (selling everything from books to charcoal grills) and what some people considered the over-extension of its brand.

On the other hand, it pointed out various positive trends. The company's operating losses (excluding special items like amortization and stock-based compensation) declined from 26% in the fourth quarter of 1999 to 17% in the first quarter of 2000. The company, it said, was evidently able to move customers quickly to new product offerings—for example, the company became the largest seller of CDs after only four months—and both its repeat business as a percentage of total business and the average dollar sale per customer were increasing (see **Exhibit 2**). It also noted the view of some people that the Lehman analyst made the mistake of "focusing on the one year of Amazon's greatest expansion and projecting those costs forward into the future."

Other Analysts   Mary Meeker, the influential analyst of Internet stocks at Morgan Stanley Dean Witter, reiterated her "buy" recommendation but sounded a note of caution. She said she thought the year-end holiday season could be a make-or-break time for the company.[27] Most stock analysts reiterated their "buy" recommendation. That included the equity analyst at Lehman Brothers.

The analyst at Salomon Smith Barney, Tim Albright, said he thought the concerns about Amazon's running out of cash were way overblown. He projected revenues for the company of $3.0 billion in 2000 and $4.9 billion in 2001. He also expected the company to lose $342 in cash from March 2000 through March 2001 but to generate $93 million in cash flow from March 2001 through March 2002, thus ending the March 2001 and 2002 quarters with $666 million and $757 million in cash, respectively. He said that even when he stress-tested his cash flow model for lower inventory turnover and higher payables turnover, the company would still have plenty of cash on hand at the end of both periods.[28]

The chief executive of an e-commerce company based in Seattle said in early July that he thought Amazon had the best chance of surviving the e-tailing shakeout but that it might have to drastically revise its business model in the face of competition from real-world retailers like Wal-Mart. "The economics haven't proven their way out yet," he said. "It's a tough issue. I come down on either side of it on any given day. It's going to be a wait and see thing."[29]

LATER DEVELOPMENTS

Exhibit 12 shows Amazon's income statements, balance sheets, and cash flow statements through the first quarter of 2001. Ravi Suria's claim in June 2000 that "in a best-case scenario . . . the current cash balances will last the company through the first quarter of 2001" didn't pan out. At the end of the first quarter of 2001, Amazon had total cash and marketable securities of $643 million.

In August 2000 Amazon transferred much of the management and risk of its toys business to Toys "R" Us—an established bricks and mortar retailer that had entered the online world the previous year. Amazon sold all of its toys inventory to Toys "R"

---

27. Frances Katz, "Fear Spurs Amazon Drop," Atlanta Journal and Constitution, June 24, 2000.

28. Tim Albright (Salomon Smith Barney), "Amazon.com," July 13, 2000.

29. Scott Hillis, "Amazon Turns 5, But Some Doubt It Will Survive," Toronto Star, July 17, 2000.

Us (for $29 million). The web site for Toys "R" Us, however, became part of Amazon's web site. Per an agreement that the two companies reached, Toys "R" Us would purchase and own all of the inventory for the toys business, and Amazon would provide the necessary customer service, order fulfillment, and warehousing, for which it would receive from Toys "R" Us a combination of fixed payments and variable payments related to sales volume.

In the second half of 2000, two of the online retailers with which Amazon had had "strategic relationships" closed down. One was Living.com, which had been selling furniture and other home products and in which Amazon had invested about $10 million. The other was Pets.com, which had been selling pet supplies and in which Amazon had invested $58 million. Both companies had attempted to raise additional capital to keep going but were unable to do so.

In January 2001 Amazon indicated that although 2000 sales were 68% higher than prior year's sales, they had fallen short of expectations, and it announced the closure of one of its distribution facilities in the United States and the partial closure of another. (Prior to the announcement the company had been operating eight distribution centers in the U.S.) It also announced the streamlining of various departments, which involved laying off about 1,300 employees. (At the end of 2000 it had employed about 9,000 people.) These moves produced restructuring charges in the first quarter of 2001 of $114 million (classified as "Impairment-related and other" in its income statement).

The company's securities continued to decline. From the end of June 2000 to the end of April 2001, its stock price fell about 58%, and the prices of its convertible debt issues fell about 20% (to about 50% of par). Market analysts were divided on whether Amazon would fall prey to the ongoing Internet retailing shakeout, or would be an exception to the trend and emerge as a winner.

QUESTIONS

1. What is your assessment of the long-term viability of Amazon's business model?

2. Do you agree with Ravi Suria's analysis of the credit risks associated with Amazon's bonds?

3. Why did the markets (both bond and stock) react so significantly to Suria's report?

EXHIBIT 1A

Amazon.com: Income Statements ($ millions)

	1997 Full Year	1998 Full Year	1999 Full Year	2000 1st qtr.
Sales[a]	148	610	1,640	574
Cost of sales[b]	(119)	(476)	(1,349)	(446)
Gross profit	29	134	291	128
Operating expenses				
Marketing and sales[c]	(40)	(133)	(413)	(140)
Technology & content	(14)	(46)	(160)	(61)
General & administrative	(7)	(16)	(70)	(26)
Stock-based compensation	(1)	(2)	(31)	(14)
Amortization of goodwill & other intangibles	0	(42)	(215)	(83)
Merger, acquisition, & investment-related costs	0	(4)	(8)	(2)
Operating loss	(33)	(109)	(606)	(198)
Interest expense	—	(27)	(84)	(27)
Interest income	2	14	45	10
Other income (expense), net	0	0	2	(5)
	(31)	(122)	(643)	(220)
Equity in losses of equity-method investees	—	(3)	(77)	(88)
Net loss	(31)	(125)	(720)	(308)
Average # of shares o/s (millions)	261	296	327	344

Source: Company 10-Ks and 10-Qs.

a. Revenues consisted primarily of sales to customers. However, beginning in 2000 a portion represented advertising revenue from the Amazon.com Commerce Network (ACN) ($20 million in the first quarter of 2000).

b. "Cost of sales" consisted of the cost of merchandise sold, the cost of inbound and outbound shipping charges, and the cost of packaging materials. One special charge was an inventory writedown of $39 million in the 4th quarter of 1999.

c. The two largest components were advertising and fulfillment expenses. Advertising expense in full-year 1999, 1998, and 1997 was $141 million, $60 million, and $21 million, respectively. Fulfillment expense in full-year 1999, 1998, and 1997 was $188 million, $50 million, and $12 million, respectively. During the first quarters of 2000 and 1999 it was $100 million and $34 million, respectively.

EXHIBIT IB

Amazon.com: Balance Sheets ($ millions)

	1997 31-Dec	1998 31-Dec	1999 31-Dec	2000 31-Mar
Current assets				
Cash & marketable securities	125	373	706	1,009
Inventories	9	30	221	172
Prepaid expenses, etc.	3	21	85	90
	137	424	1,012	1,271
Fixed assets	10	30	318	335
Goodwill & other purchased intangibles		179	730	647
Investments		7	371	422
Other	2	8	40	55
Total assets	149	648	2,471	2,730
Current liabilities				
Accounts payable	33	113	463	256
Accrued expenses & other current liabilities	10	48	207	161
Unearned revenue	—	—	55	134
Current portion of long-term debt	1	1	14	16
	44	162	739	567
Long-term debt	77	348	1,466	2,137
Stockholders' equity				
Common stock	66	300	1,148	1,216
Accumulated deficit	(38)	(162)	(882)	(1,190)
	28	138	266	26
Total liabilities & stockholders equity	149	648	2,471	2,730

Source: Company 10-Ks and 10-Qs.

EXHIBIT 1C

Amazon.com: Cash Flow Statements ($ millions)

	1997	1998	1999		2000
	Full Year	Full Year	4th qtr.	Full Year	1st qtr.
Operating activities					
Net loss	(31)	(125)	(324)	(720)	(308)
Depreciation & amortization of fixed assets	3	10		37	18
Amort. of deferred stock-based compensation	2	2		31	14
Equity in losses of equity-method investees	—	3		77	88
Amortization of goodwill & other intangibles	—	43		215	83
Non-cash interest expense	—	24		29	6
Non-cash revenue for advertising & promotional services	—	—		(6)	(18)
Other	—	2		17	(1)
	(26)	(41)	(171)	(320)	(118)
Changes in operating assets & liabilities, net of effects from acquisitions					
Inventories	(8)	(21)	(83)	(172)	48
Prepaid expenses & other current assets	(3)	(17)	(27)	(60)	3
Accounts payable	30	79	208	330	(207)
Accrued expenses & other current liabilities	8	31	90	107	(37)
Interest payable	—	—	15	25	(9)
	27	72	203	230	(202)
Net cash provided (used) in operating activities	1	31	31	(90)	(320)
Investing activities					
Sales of marketable securities	4	332		4,025	1,014
Purchases of marketable securities	(122)	(547)		(4,290)	(1,333)
Purchase of fixed assets	(8)	(28)		(287)	(27)
Acquisitions and investments in businesses, net of cash acquired	—	(19)		(370)	(47)
Net cash used in investing activities	(126)	(262)		(922)	(393)
Financing activities					
Proceeds from long-term debt	75	326		1,264	679
Repayment of long-term debt	—	(78)		(189)	(4)
Financing costs & other	(2)	(8)		(35)	(16)
Proceeds from issuance of capital stock and exercise of stock options[a]	53	14		64	21
Net cash provided by financing activities	126	254		1,104	680
Net increase (decrease) in cash	1	23		92	(33)
Cash at beginning of period	1	2		25	117
Cash at end of period	2	25		117	84

(*continued*)

Amazon.com: Cash Flow Statements ($ millions) (*continued*)

	1997 Full Year	1998 Full Year	1999 4th qtr.	1999 Full Year	2000 1st qtr.
Supplemental cash flow information					
Stock issued in connection with business acquisitions	—	217		774	—
Equity securities for unearned Amazon **Commerce Network services**	—	—		54	98
Cash paid for interest	—	27		60	—

Source: Company 10-Ks and 10-Qs.

a. Proceeds from the exercise of stock options were $68 million and $6 million in 1999 and 1998, respectively. In 1997 the company received approximately $50 million through its IPO.

Amazon.com in the Year 2000

Amazon.com in the Year 2000

EXHIBIT 2

Amazon.com: Customer Data

	1997 Full Year	1998 Full Year	1999 1st qtr.	1999 2nd qtr.	1999 3rd qtr.	1999 4th qtr.	1999 Full Year	2000 1st qtr.
No. of customer accounts	1,510,000	6,200,000	8,400,000	10,700,000	13,100,000	16,900,000	16,900,000	20,000,000.
No. of new customers	1,375,000	4,690,000	2,200,000	2,300,000	2,400,000	3,800,000	10,700,000	3,100,000
Average sale per customer in trailing 12-month period			$108			$116		$121
Orders from repeat customers as % of all orders			66%			73%		76%
Customer acquisition cost[a]			$13	$19	$14	$19		$13

Source: Company reports; estimates by Morgan Stanley Dean Witter, Merrill Lynch, Robertson Stephens; various press reports.

a. "Customer acquisition cost" was a metric used by a good many analysts of e-commerce businesses. For Amazon, analysts calculated it by dividing total sales and marketing costs (excluding fulfillment costs) by the number of new customers acquired during a given period of time. (This assumes that sales and marketing costs relate solely to new customers.) Studies done by the Boston Consulting Group and Forrester Research concluded that the average "customer acquisition cost" in the e-commerce world in 1999 was about $40.

EXHIBIT 3

Amazon.com: Segment Information ($ millions)

	U.S. Books, Music, and DVD/Video	Inter- national	Early-Stage Businesses & Other	Con- solidated
2000 (first quarter)				
Revenues from external customers	401	75	97	574
Gross profit (loss)	83	16	29	128
Segment loss	(2)	(27)	(69)	(99)
Other operating expenses	—	—	—	(99)
Net interest expense and other	—	—	—	(22)
Equity in losses of equity-method investees	—	—	—	(88)
Net loss				(308)
1999				
Revenues from external customers	1,308	168	164	1,640
Gross profit (loss)	263	35	(8)	291
Segment loss	(31)	(79)	(242)	(352)
Other operating expenses	—	—	—	(253)
Net interest expense and other	—	—	—	(38)
Equity in losses of equity-method investees	—	—	—	(77)
Net loss				(720)
1998				
Revenues from external customers	588	22	—	610
Gross profit	129	5	—	134
Segment loss	(35)	(25)	—	(61)
Other operating expenses	—	—	—	(48)
Interest expense, net	—	—	—	(12)
Equity in losses of equity-method investees	—	—	—	(3)
Net loss				(125)
1997				
Revenues from external customers	148	—	—	148
Gross profit	29	—	—	29
Segment loss	(31)	—	—	(31)
Other operating expenses	(1)	—	—	(1)
Interest income, net	1	—	—	1
Equity in losses of equity-method investees	—	—	—	—
Net loss				(31)

Source: Company 10-K and 10-Q.

Notes:

* "Other operating expenses" include amortization of goodwill and other intangibles, acquisition- and investment-related costs, and stock-based compensation.

* "Early-stage businesses" includes electronics, software, video games, toys, home improvement products, "marketplace services," and the "Amazon Commerce Network."

EXHIBIT 4

Amazon.com: Fixed Assets ($ millions)

	Dec. 31	
	1999	1998
Computers, equipment and software[a]	187	36
Leasehold improvements	44	6
Leased assets	52	—
Construction in progress	83	2
	366	44
Less accumulated depreciation and amortization	(49)	(14)
Fixed assets, net	317	30

Source: Company 10-K.

a. Consists mostly of servers, storage, and telecom systems.

EXHIBIT 5

Summary of Terms of Amazon's Convertible Notes

Terms common to both issues

- Rank equally, but are subordinate to all existing and future senior debt, including trade payables of subsidiaries. "As of December 31, 1999, we had approximately $901 million of indebtedness that constituted senior indebtedness."
- Unsecured.
- "The indenture does not contain any financial covenants and does not restrict us from paying dividends, incurring indebtedness, or issuing or repurchasing our other securities. The indenture does not protect you in the event of a highly leveraged transaction or a change in control except in limited circumstances."
- "We may from time to time reduce the conversion price [by any amount] . . . if our board of directors has made a determination that this reduction would be in our best interests."

Terms specific to 4.75% convertible notes

- Pay interest semi-annually.
- Convertible to 12.816 common shares; the conversion price was therefore $78.03.
- Redeemable by the company after 2002 at fairly standard redemption prices, involving small premiums. Prior to 2002 the company could redeem them at par if the company's average stock price for a certain number of days exceeded 150% of the conversion price. If the company did so, however, it would have to pay a significant penalty (approximately $208 for every $1,000 note).

(continued)

Summary of Terms of Amazon's Convertible Notes (*continued*)

Terms specific to 6.875% convertible notes

- Pay interest annually.
- Convertible to 9.529 common shares; the conversion price was therefore €104.94. Include a sweetener—reset provisions that would lower the conversion price in February 2001 and February 2002 if the company's stock price fell. (Specifically, the conversion price would be lowered if the euro-equivalent of the average stock price for a certain number of days was below €104.94. The conversion price couldn't, however, be reset below €84.883.)
- Redeemable by the company after 2003 at par. Prior to 2003 the company could withdraw the conversion rights altogether if the company's average stock price for a certain number of days exceeded 160% of the initially stated conversion price (thus €167.92). If the company did so, however, it would have to pay a significant penalty (approximately €200 for every €1,000 note).
- Exchange ratio between the euro and the dollar not fixed.

Source: Form S-3, dated 3/15/99; Form 8-K, dated 2/14/00.

EXHIBIT 6

Cash Obligations for Debt: Interest plus Repayment of Principal ($ millions)

Year	10% Discount Notes Due 2008	4.75% Convertible Notes Due 2009	6.875% Convertible Notes Due 2010	Total
2000	0	59	0	59
2001	0	59	47	106
2002	0	59	47	106
2003	26	59	47	132
2004	26	59	47	132
2005	26	59	47	132
2006	26	59	47	132
2007	26	59	47	132
2008	290	59	47	396
2009		1,309	47	1,356
2010			727	727

Source: 10-K and 10-Qs.

Note: The 6.875% notes are euro-denominated. Dollar proceeds from the issue in 2000 were $680, and the above interest and repayment amounts assume that the exchange rate between the euro and dollar is unchanged. The indenture of the issue, however, doesn't fix the exchange rate.

EXHIBIT 7A

Comparison With the Two Largest Land-Based Book Retailers

	1999	1998	1997
Barnes & Noble			
Total sales (billions)	$3.5	$3.0	$2.8
Total selling space in retail stores (millions of square feet)	15.1	13.8	
Gross margin	39%	39%	39%
Ordinary overhead exps. as % of sales	33%	33%	33%
ROE	16%	15%	
ROE excluding goodwill	22%	18%	
Inventory turnover	2.1	2.0	
Ratio of inventory to accounts payable (year-end)	1.8	1.9	
Borders			
Total sales (billions)	$3.0	$2.6	$2.3
Total selling space in retail stores (millions of square feet)	11.6	9.5	
Gross margin	39%	39%	39%
Ordinary overhead exps. as % of sales	34%	33%	33%
ROE	12%	14%	
ROE excluding goodwill	14%	16%	
Inventory turnover	1.7	1.7	
Ratio of inventory to accounts payable (year-end)	1.9	1.7	

Source: Company 10-Ks.

Notes:

* Inventory turnover is an annualized figure calculated in the customary way: cost of goods sold divided by the average of beginning and ending inventory balances.

* Gross margin, overhead expense, and inventory turnover involve estimates made by the casewriter to make those figures comparable to Amazon. The problem is that Barnes & Noble and Borders include "occupancy costs" (i.e., rent, CAM charges, etc.) with cost of goods sold, and the estimates reassign occupancy costs to ordinary overhead expense.

* In addition to selling space in retail stores, Barnes & Noble and Borders each had about 1 million square feet of space in its distribution centers (from which it shipped merchandise to retail stores).

EXHIBIT 7B

Comparison with Financially Successful Companies with Low Gross Margins

	1999	1998	1997
Wal-Mart			
Total sales (billions)	$165	$138	$118
Gross margin	21%	21%	21%
Ordinary overhead exps. as % of sales	16%	16%	16%
ROE	24%	22%	
Inventory turnover	7	6	
Ratio of inventory to accounts payable (year-end)	1.5	1.7	
Costco			
Total sales (billions)	$27	$24	$22
Gross margin	12%	12%	12%
Ordinary overhead exps. as % of sales	9%	9%	9%
ROE	16%	17%	
Inventory turnover	12	12	
Ratio of inventory to accounts payable (year-end)	1.2	1.2	

Source: Company 10-Ks.

Notes:

* Inventory turnover is an annualized figure calculated in the customary way: cost of goods sold divided by the average of beginning and ending inventory balances.

* Neither of these companies had any significant amount of goodwill on their balance sheets.

EXHIBIT 8

Lehman Brothers Information: Amazon's Cash Flows ($ millions)

Quarter	Operating Cash Flow	Capital Expenditures	Free Cash Flows
Dec-97	7	(3)	4
Mar-98	(7)	(2)	(9)
Jun-98	2	(6)	(4)
Sep-98	(3)	(11)	(14)
Dec-98	39	(10)	29
Mar-99	(17)	(19)	(36)
Jun-99	(30)	(92)	(122)
Sep-99	(75)	(71)	(146)
Dec-99	31	(105)	(74)
Mar-00	(320)	(27)	(347)
	(373)	(346)	(719)

Source: Ravi Suria (Lehman Brothers), op. cit.

EXHIBIT 9

Lehman Brothers Information: Amazon's Inventory Turnover

Quarter	Inventory Turnover
Mar-98	8.5
Jun-98	8.1
Sep-98	8.3
Dec-98	10.3
Mar-99	7.9
Jun-99	6.0
Sep-99	4.0
Dec-99	4.0
Mar-00	2.9

Source: Ravi Suria (Lehman Brothers), op. cit.

EXHIBIT 10A

Amazon's 4.75% Convertible Note

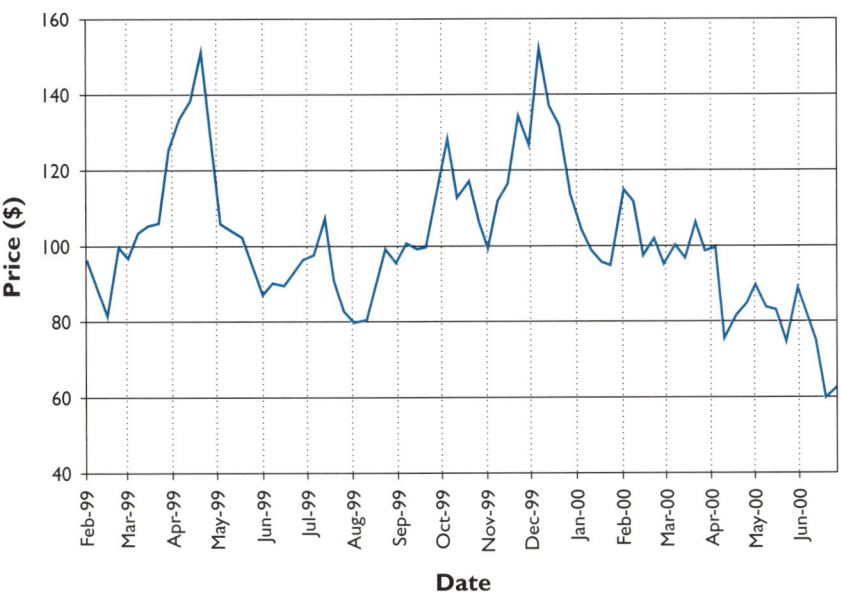

Source: Bloomberg.

EXHIBIT 10B

Amazon's 6.875% Convertible Note

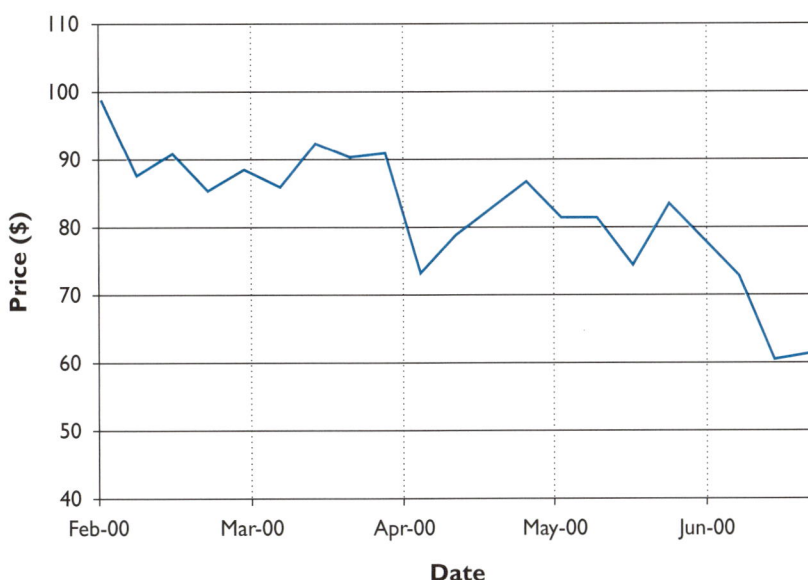

Source: Bloomberg.

EXHIBIT 11

Return on Amazon's Stock Compared to Nasdaq Index

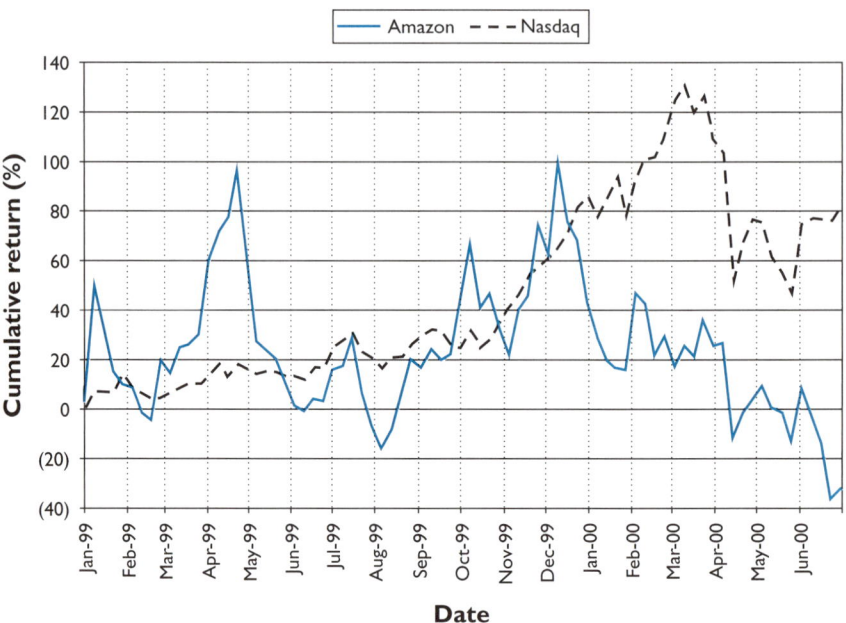

Source: Bloomberg.

EXHIBIT 12A

Amazon.com: Income Statements ($ millions)

	2000 Full Year	2001 1st qtr.
Sales	2,762	700
Cost of sales	(2,106)	(518)
Gross profit	656	182
Operating expenses		
Fulfillment	(415)	(98)
Marketing	(180)	(37)
Technology & content	(269)	(70)
General & administrative	(109)	(26)
Stock-based compensation	(25)	(3)
Amortization of goodwill & other intangibles	(322)	(51)
Impairment-related and other	(200)	(114)
Operating loss	(864)	(217)
Interest expense	(131)	(34)
Interest income	41	10
Other income (expense), net	(10)	(4)
Non-cash gains and losses, net	(142)	34
Net interest expense and other	(242)	6
Loss before equity in losses of equity-method investees	(1,106)	(211)
Equity in losses of equity-method investees	(305)	(13)
Loss before change in accounting	(1,411)	(224)
Cumulative effect of change in accounting principle	—	(10)
Net loss	(1,411)	(234)
Average number of shares o/s (millions)	351	357

Source: Company 10-Ks and 10-Qs.

EXHIBIT 12B

Amazon.com: Balance Sheets ($ millions)

	2000 Dec. 31	2001 31-Mar
Current assets		
Cash	823	447
Marketable securities	278	196
Inventories	174	156
Prepaid expenses, etc.	86	57
	1,361	856
Fixed assets	367	304
Goodwill & other purchased intangibles	255	204
Investments in equity-method investees	52	23
Other equity investments	40	29
Other	60	54
Total assets	2,135	1,470
Current liabilities		
Accounts payble	485	257
Accrued expenses & other current liabilities	342	234
Unearned revenue	131	94
Current portion of long-term debt	17	19
	975	604
Long-term debt	2,127	2,119
Stockholders' equity		
Common stock	1,326	1,274
Accumulated deficit	(2,293)	(2,527)
	(967)	(1,253)
Total liabilities & stockholders equity	2,135	1,470

Source: Company 10-Ks and 10-Qs.

EXHIBIT 12C

Amazon.com: Cash Flow Statements ($ millions)

	2000 Full Year	2001 1st qtr.
Operating activities		
Net loss	(1,411)	(234)
Depreciation & amortization of fixed assets	84	23
Amort. of deferred stock-based compensation	25	3
Equity in losses of equity-method investees	305	13
Amortization of goodwill & other intangibles	322	51
Impairment-related and other	200	62
Amortization of previously unearned revenue	(108)	(33)
Non-cash investment gains and losses, net	143	(34)
Non-cash interest expense and other	25	7
Cumulative effect of change in accounting principle	—	10
	(415)	(132)
Changes in operating assets & liabilities		
Inventories	46	20
Prepaid expenses & other current assets	(9)	27
Accounts payable	22	(230)
Accrued expenses & other current liabilities	94	(58)
Unearned revenue	98	18
Interest payable	34	(52)
	285	(275)
Net cash provided (used) in operating activities	(130)	(407)
Investing activities		
Sales of marketable securities	546	94
Purchases of marketable securities	(184)	(30)
Purchase of fixed assets	(135)	(19)
Investments in equity-method investees and other investments	(63)	—
Net cash used in investing activities	164	45
Financing activities		
Proceeds from long-term debt	681	10
Repayment of long-term debt	(17)	(5)
Financing costs & other	(16)	—
Proceeds from issuance of capital stock and exercise of stock options	45	6
Net cash provided by financing activities	693	11
Effect of exchange-rate changes on cash	(38)	(24)
Net increase (decrease) in cash	689	(375)
Cash at beginning of period	133	822
Cash at end of period	822	447
Supplemental cash flow information		
Stock issued in connection with business acqs.	32	—
Fixed assets acquired under financing agreements	9	2
Equity securities received for commercial agreements	107	—
Cash paid for interest	92	86

Source: Company 10-Ks and 10-Qs.

Chapter 11
Mergers and Acquisitions

Mergers and acquisitions have long been a popular form of corporate investment, particularly in countries with Anglo-American forms of capital markets. There is no question that these transactions provide a healthy return to target stockholders. However, their value to acquiring shareholders is less understood. Many skeptics point out that given the hefty premiums paid to target stockholders, acquisitions tend to be negative-valued investments for acquiring stockholders.[1]

A number of questions can be examined using financial analysis for mergers and acquisitions:

- Securities analysts can ask: Does a proposed acquisition create value for the acquiring firm's stockholders?
- Risk arbitrageurs can ask: What is the likelihood that a hostile takeover offer will ultimately succeed, and are there other potential acquirers likely to enter the bidding?
- Acquiring management can ask: Does this target fit our business strategy? If so, what is it worth to us and how can we make an offer that can be successful?
- Target management can ask: Is the acquirer's offer a reasonable one for our stockholders? Are there other potential acquirers that would value our company more than the current bidder?
- Investment bankers can ask: How can we identify potential targets that are likely to be a good match for our clients? And how should we value target firms when we are asked to issue fairness opinions?

In this chapter we focus primarily on the use of financial statement data and analysis directed at evaluating whether a merger creates value for the acquiring firm's stockholders. However, our discussion can also be applied to these other merger analysis contexts. The topic of whether acquisitions create value for acquirers focuses on evaluating the (1) motivations for acquisitions, (2) pricing of offers, (3) forms of payment, and (4) likelihood that an offer will be successful. Throughout the chapter we use Exxon's merger with Mobil in 1999 to illustrate how financial analysis can be used in a merger context.[2]

MOTIVATION FOR MERGER OR ACQUISITION

There are a variety of reasons that firms merge or acquire other firms. Some acquiring managers may want to increase their own power and prestige. Others, however, realize that business combinations provide an opportunity to create new economic value for their stockholders. New value can be created in the following ways:

1. *Taking advantage of economies of scale.* Mergers are often justified as a means of providing the two participating firms with increased economies of scale. Economies of scale arise when one large firm can perform a function more

efficiently than two smaller firms. For example, Exxon and Mobil are both major oil firms with considerable overlap in production and administrative facilities. The merger was expected to provide operating synergies from eliminating duplicate facilities and excess capacity, and from reducing general and administrative costs.

2. *Improving target management.* Another common motivation for acquisition is to improve target management. A firm is likely to be a target if it has systematically underperformed its industry. Historical poor performance could be due to bad luck, but it could also be due to the firm's managers making poor investment and operating decisions, or deliberately pursuing goals which increase their personal power but cost stockholders.

3. *Combining complementary resources.* Firms may decide that a merger will create value by combining complementary resources of the two partners. For example, a firm with a strong research and development unit could benefit from merging with a firm that has a strong distribution unit.

4. *Capturing tax benefits.* In the U.S. the 1986 Tax Reform Act eliminated many of the tax benefits from mergers and acquisitions. However, several merger tax benefits remain. The major benefit is the acquisition of operating tax losses. If a firm does not expect to earn sufficient profits to fully utilize operating tax loss carryforward benefits, it may decide to buy another firm which is earning profits. The operating losses and loss carryforwards of the acquirer can then be offset against the target's taxable income.[3] A second tax benefit often attributed to mergers is the tax shield that comes from increasing leverage for the target firm. This was particularly relevant for leveraged buyouts in the 1980s.[4]

5. *Providing low-cost financing to a financially constrained target.* If capital markets are imperfect, perhaps because of information asymmetries between management and outside investors, firms can face capital constraints. Information problems are likely to be especially severe for newly formed, high-growth firms. These firms can be difficult for outside investors to value since they have short track records and their financial statements provide little insight into the value of their growth opportunities. Further, since they typically have to rely on external funds to finance their growth, capital market constraints for high-growth firms are likely to affect their ability to undertake profitable new projects. Public capital markets are therefore likely to be costly sources of funds for these types of firms. An acquirer that understands the business and is willing to provide a steady source of finance may therefore be able to add value.[5]

6. *Creating value through restructuring and break-ups.* Acquisitions are often pursued by financial investors such as leveraged buy-out firms that expect to create value by breaking up the firm. The break-up value is expected to be larger than the aggregate worth of the entire firm. Often, a consortium of financial investors will acquire a firm with a view of unlocking value from various components of the firm's asset base. For example, two private equity firms, Kohlberg, Kravis and Roberts and Bain Capital, partnered with real estate company Vornado Realty Trust, to purchase the retailer Toys "R" Us. The consortium was widely expected to close down numerous retail locations to monetize the value of the real estate.

7. *Penetrating new geographies.* Cross-border acquisitions are pursued by firms to expand product markets, to capitalize on new technologies, and to capture labor cost advantages which presumably could not have been achieved through joint ventures or supplier contracts. In the 25-year period between 1981 and 2005, over 10 percent of all acquisitions in the U.S. were led by foreign buyers, with close to 1,500 such deals announced in 2005 alone.[6]

8. *Increasing product-market rents.* Firms can also have incentives to merge to increase product-market rents. By merging and becoming a dominant firm in the industry, two smaller firms can collude to restrict their output and raise prices, thereby increasing their profits. This circumvents problems that arise in

cartels of independent firms, where firms have incentives to cheat on the cartel and increase their output.

While product-market rents make sense for firms as a motive for merging, the two partners are unlikely to announce their intentions when they explain the merger to their investors, since most countries have antitrust laws which regulate mergers between two firms in the same industry. For example, in the U.S. there are three major antitrust statutes—The Sherman Act of 1890, The Clayton Act of 1914, and The Hart Scott Rodino Act of 1976.

Anti-competitive concerns were significant for the Exxon-Mobil merger since Exxon and Mobil were the largest and second largest U.S. oil producers, respectively. Merger approval was required by both the U.S. Federal Trade Commission (FTC) and the European Commission. Both did eventually approve the merger but required the new firm to sell assets in certain businesses and regions to preserve competition.

While many of the motivations for acquisitions are likely to create new economic value for shareholders, some are not. Firms that are flush with cash but have few new profitable investment opportunities are particularly prone to using their surplus cash to make acquisitions. Stockholders of these firms would probably prefer that managers pay out any surplus cash flows as dividends, or use the funds to repurchase the firm's stock. However, these options reduce the size of the firm and the assets under management's control. Management may therefore prefer to invest the free cash flows to buy new companies, even if they do not create value for stockholders. Of course, managers will never announce that they are buying a firm because they are reluctant to pay out funds to stockholders. They may explain the merger using one of the motivations discussed above, or they may argue that they are buying the target at a bargain price.

Another motivation for mergers that is valued by managers but not stockholders is diversification. Diversification was a popular motivation for acquisitions in the 1960s and early 1970s. Acquirers sought to dampen their earnings volatility by buying firms in unrelated businesses. Diversification as a motive for acquisitions has since been widely discredited. Modern finance theorists point out that in a well functioning capital market, investors can diversify for themselves and do not need managers to do so for them. In addition, diversification has been criticized when leading firms lose sight of their major competitive strengths and expand into businesses where they do not have expertise.[7] These firms eventually recognize that diversification-motivated acquisitions do not create value, leading to divestitures of business units. Divestitures have been the source of over a third of all acquisitions over the past 25 years, and in 2005 alone, close to 3,600 deals were a result of corporate divestitures.[8]

Key Analysis Questions

In evaluating a proposed merger, analysts are interested in determining whether the merger creates new wealth for acquiring and target stockholders, or whether it is motivated by managers' desires to increase their own power and prestige. Key questions for financial analysis are likely to include:

- *What is the motivation(s) for an acquisition and the anticipated benefits disclosed by acquirers or targets?*
- *What are the industries of the target and acquirer?* Are the firms related horizontally or vertically? How close are the business relations between

them? If the businesses are unrelated, is the acquirer cash-rich and reluctant to return free cash flows to stockholders?

- *What are the key operational strengths of the target and the acquirer?* Are these strengths complementary? For example, does one firm have a renowned research group and the other a strong distribution network?
- *Is the acquisition a friendly one, supported by target management, or hostile?* In the case of a hostile takeover, which is more likely to occur for targets with poor-performing management, will the transaction go through despite the opposition of management who will want to preserve its jobs? Will the hostile acquirer have sufficient access to information to mitigate the risk of overpayment?
- *What is the premerger performance of the two firms?* Performance metrics are likely to include ROE, gross margins, general and administrative expenses to sales, and working capital management ratios. On the basis of these measures, is the target a poor performer in its industry, implying that there are opportunities for improved management? Is the acquirer in a declining industry and searching for new directions?
- *What is the tax position of both firms?* What are the average and marginal current tax rates for the target and the acquirer? Does the acquirer have operating loss carryforwards and the target taxable profits?

This analysis should help the analyst understand what specific benefits, if any, the merger is likely to generate.

Motivation for the Exxon-Mobil Merger

Several industry factors influenced Exxon and Mobil to merge. Since the OPEC oil embargo of 1973, the oil industry had been subjected to wide price fluctuations that increased exploration risks. For example, real prices per barrel increased from $11.83 in 1973 to $50.94 in 1981 and then declined precipitously to $16.61 per barrel in 1986. Between 1987 and 1998, prices continued to fluctuate wildly, with a low of $10.53 in 1998 and a high of $23.15 in 1990. In addition to pricing risks, oil companies faced significant political risks in exploration since much of their reserves were located in politically volatile countries, where private property rights were subject to change.

The industry responded to these challenges by adopting cost reduction programs. From 1980 to 1992, employment at eight major oil companies declined by 63 percent, from 800,000 to 300,000. Headquarters staff at six of the largest firms declined from 3,000 to 800 in the period 1988 to 1992. In addition, companies sought to increase flexibility by leasing rather than owning tankers. But as prices continued to plummet in the late 1990s, oil companies sought other ways to increase efficiency.

The outcome was a series of large mergers and acquisitions that transformed the industry: BP merged with Amoco in 1998 and acquired Arco the following year; Total, a French oil firm, acquired the large Belgian oil firm Petrofina in late 1998 and subsequently purchased Elf Aquitaine in a $49 billion hostile takeover; Texaco was acquired by Chevron in 2000; and Phillips Petroleum acquired Tosco in early 2001, and late during the same year agreed to merge with Conoco.

The management of Exxon and Mobil argued that a merger would provide the new company with three significant benefits. First, the merger would facilitate efficiency improvements such as streamlining administrative overhead, eliminating excess capacity and duplicate facilities, using purchasing power to reduce raw material costs, and coordinating exploration in regions where the two firms operated separately. At the time of the merger, management estimated that it would save $730 million by cutting roughly 9,000 jobs and closing offices, an additional $1.2 billion by trimming business overlap, and another $780 million by sharing exploration, procurement budgets, and technology. All told, management stated that it could realize cost savings of about $2.8 billion per year through the merger. These savings were expected to be fully realized by the third year after the merger. Second, management noted that the two companies had complementary strengths and assets that would help increase productivity. While Exxon was financially conservative and had been growing its oil reserves only modestly, with an average five-year reserve replacement ratio of only 102 percent, Mobil was touted as one of the leading exploration firms, with a five-year reserve replacement ratio of 147 percent. Exxon was a leader in deepwater exploration in West Africa, which complemented Mobil's production and exploration activities in Nigeria and Equatorial Guinea. In the Caspian, Exxon's presence in Azerbaijan complemented Mobil's strength in Kazakhstan, including a significant interest in the Tengiz field and its presence in Turkmenistan. Complementary exploration and production operations also existed in South America, Russia, and Eastern Canada. Finally, management argued that the merger provided the company with the scale required to manage the risks associated with very sizeable investments involved in new exploration projects.

Analysts and the financial media concurred with management's assessments of the economic benefits that potentially would be derived from the merger. Some analysts nevertheless expressed concern that differences in the cultures of the two companies might make it difficult for them to actually achieve these synergies. Exxon had a reputation for being "tight-lipped and conservative" whereas Mobil was viewed as "more open, both to the public and to new ideas."[9]

ACQUISITION PRICING

A well thought-out economic motivation for a merger or acquisition is a necessary but not sufficient condition for it to create value for acquiring stockholders. The acquirer must be careful to avoid overpaying for the target. Overpayment makes the transaction highly desirable and profitable for target stockholders, but it diminishes the value of the deal to acquiring stockholders. A financial analyst can use the following methods to assess whether the acquiring firm is overpaying for the target.

Analyzing Premium Offered to Target Stockholders

One popular way to assess whether the acquirer is overpaying for a target is to compare the premium offered to target stockholders to premiums offered in similar transactions. If the acquirer offers a relatively high premium, the analyst is typically led to conclude that the transaction is less likely to create value for acquiring stockholders.

Premiums differ significantly for friendly and hostile acquisitions. Premiums tend to be about 30 percent higher for hostile deals than for friendly offers, implying that hostile acquirers are more likely to overpay for a target.[10] There are several reasons for this. First, a friendly acquirer has access to the internal records of the target, improving the accuracy in valuing the target and making it less likely that it will be surprised by hidden liabilities or problems once it has completed the deal. In contrast, a hostile acquirer does not have this advantage in valuing the target during negotiations and is more likely to overpay. Second, the delays that typically accompany a hostile acquisition often provide opportunities for competing bidders to make an offer for the target, leading to a bidding war.

Comparing a target's premium to values for similar types of transactions is straightforward, but has several practical problems. First, it is not obvious how to define a comparable transaction. Figure 11-1 shows the mean and median premiums paid for U.S. targets over a 25-year period between 1981 and 2005. Average premiums rose from around 40 percent through the mid-1990s to between 50 and 60 percent in 1999–2001. Median premiums also increased during this period, from around 30 percent to 40 percent. Despite the increase in M&A activity in 2004 and 2005, median premiums dropped significantly from the highs of 1999–2001 to only 23 to 24 percent. However, mean and median premiums have to be interpreted with caution since there is considerable variation across transactions, making it difficult to use these estimates as a benchmark.

A second problem in using premiums offered to target stockholders to assess whether an acquirer overpaid is that measured premiums can be misleading if an offer is anticipated by investors. The stock price run-up for the target will then tend to make estimates of the premium appear relatively low. This limitation can be partially offset by using target stock prices one month prior to the acquisition offer as the basis for calculating premiums. However, in some cases offers may have been anticipated for even longer than one month.

FIGURE 11-1	Merger Activity and Premium Paid: 1981–2005

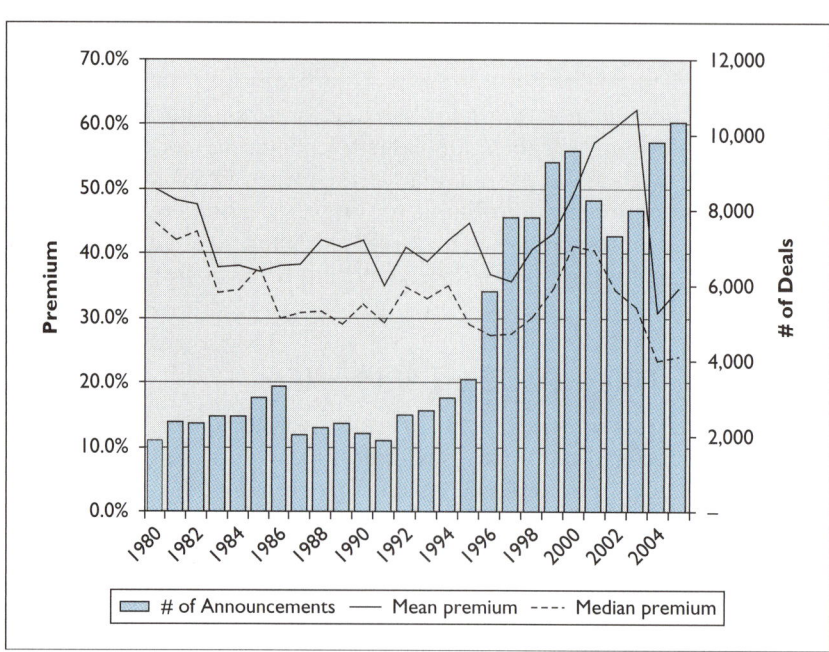

Source: Mergerstat Review 2006 (FactSet Mergerstat, LLC).

Finally, using target premiums to assess whether an acquirer overpaid ignores the value of the target to the acquirer after the acquisition. The acquirer expects to benefit from the merger by improving the target firm's operating performance through a combination of economies of scale, improved management, tax benefits, and spillover effects derived from the acquisition. Clearly, acquirers will be willing to pay higher premiums for targets that are expected to generate higher merger benefits. Thus, examining the premium alone cannot determine whether the acquisition creates value for acquiring stockholders.

Analyzing Value of the Target to the Acquirer

A second and more reliable way of assessing whether the acquirer has overpaid for the target is to compare the offer price to the estimated value of the target to the acquirer. This latter value can be computed using the valuation techniques discussed in Chapters 7 and 8. The most popular methods of valuation used for mergers and acquisitions are earnings multiples and discounted cash flows. Since a comprehensive discussion of these techniques is provided earlier in the book, we focus here on implementation issues that arise for valuing targets in mergers and acquisitions.

We recommend first computing the value of the target as an independent firm. This provides a way of checking whether the valuation assumptions are reasonable, since for publicly listed targets we can compare our estimate with premerger market prices. It also provides a useful benchmark for thinking about how the target's performance, and hence its value, is likely to change once it is acquired.

Earnings Multiples

To estimate the value of a target to an acquirer using earnings multiples, we have to forecast earnings for the target and decide on an appropriate earnings multiple, as follows:

Step 1: Forecasting earnings Earnings forecasts are usually made by first forecasting next year's net income for the target assuming no acquisition. Historical sales growth rates, gross margins, and average tax rates are useful in building a pro forma income model. Once we have forecasted the income for the target as an independent firm, we can incorporate into the pro forma model any improvements in earnings performance that we expect to result from the acquisition. Performance improvements can be modeled on numerous dimensions including

- Higher operating margins through economies of scale in purchasing, or increased market power;
- Reductions in expenses as a result of consolidating research and development staffs, sales forces, and/or administration; or
- Lower average tax rates from taking advantage of operating tax loss carryforwards.

Step 2: Determining the price-earnings multiple How do we determine the earnings multiple to be applied to our earnings forecasts? If the target firm is listed, it may be tempting to use the preacquisition price-earnings multiple to value postmerger earnings. However, there are several limitations to this approach. First, for many targets, earnings growth expectations are likely to change after a merger, implying that there will be a difference between the pre- and postmerger price-earnings multiples. Postmerger earnings should then be valued using a multiple for firms with comparable growth and risk characteristics. (See discussion in Chapter 7.) A second problem is that premerger price-earnings multiples are unavailable for unlisted targets. Once again it becomes necessary to decide which types of listed firms are likely to be good comparables. In addition, since the earnings being valued are the projected earnings for the next 12 months or the next full fiscal year, the appropriate benchmark ratio should be a *forward* price-earnings ratio. Finally, if a premerger price-earnings multiple is appropriate for valuing postmerger earnings, care is required to ensure that the multiple is calculated prior to any acquisition announcement since the price will increase in anticipation of the premium to be paid to target stockholders.

The following table summarizes how price-earnings multiples are used to value a target firm before an acquisition (assuming it will remain an independent entity) and to estimate the value of a target to a potential acquirer:

Summary of Price-Earnings Valuation for Targets

Value of target as an independent firm	Target earnings forecast for the next year, assuming no change in ownership, multiplied by its *premerger* forward PE multiple.
Value of target to potential acquirer	Target *revised* earnings forecast for the next year, incorporating the effect of any operational changes made by the acquirer, multiplied by its *postmerger* forward PE multiple.

Limitations of Price-Earnings Valuation As explained in Chapter 7, there are serious limitations to using earnings multiples for valuation. In addition to these limitations, the method has two more that are specific to merger valuations:

1. PE multiples assume that merger performance improvements come either from an immediate increase in earnings or from an increase in earnings growth (and hence an increase in the postmerger PE ratio). In reality, improvements and savings can come in many forms—gradual increases in earnings from implementing new operating policies, eliminating overinvestment, managing working capital better, or paying out excess cash to stockholders. These types of improvements are not naturally reflected in PE multiples.
2. PE models do not easily incorporate any spillover benefits from an acquisition for the acquirer since they focus on valuing the earnings of the target.

Discounted Abnormal Earnings or Cash Flows

As discussed in Chapters 7 and 8, we can also value a company using the discounted abnormal earnings and discounted free cash flow methods. These require us to first forecast the abnormal earnings or free cash flows for the firm and then discount them at the cost of capital, as follows.

Step 1: Forecasting abnormal earnings/free cash flows A pro forma model of expected future income and cash flows for the firm provides the basis for forecasting abnormal earnings/free cash flows. As a starting point, the model should be constructed under the assumption that the target remains an independent firm. The model should reflect the best estimates of future sales growth, cost structures, working capital needs, investment and research and development needs, and cash requirements for known debt retirements, developed from a financial analysis of the target. The abnormal earnings method requires that we forecast abnormal earnings or net operating profit after tax (NOPAT) for as long as the firm expects new investment projects to earn more than their cost of capital. Under the free cash flow approach, the pro forma model will forecast free cash flows to either the firm or to equity, typically for a period of five to ten years. Once we have a model of the abnormal earnings or free cash flows, we can incorporate any improvements in earnings/free cash flows that we expect to result from the acquisition. These will include the cost savings, cash received from asset sales, benefits from eliminating overinvestment, improved working capital management, and excess cash paid out to stockholders.

Step 2: Compute the discount rate If we are valuing the target's postacquisition abnormal NOPAT or cash flows to the firm, the appropriate discount rate is the weighted average cost of capital (WACC) for the target, using its expected *postacquisition* capital structure. Alternatively, if the target's equity cash flows are being valued directly or if we are valuing abnormal earnings, the appropriate discount rate is the target's *postacquisition cost of equity* rather than its WACC. Two common mistakes are to use the acquirer's cost of capital or the target's *preacquisition* cost of capital to value the postmerger abnormal earnings/cash flows from the target.

The computation of the target's postacquisition cost of capital can be complicated if the acquirer plans to make a change to the target's capital structure after the acquisition, since the target's costs of debt and equity will change. As discussed in Chapter 8, this involves estimating the asset beta for the target, calculating the new equity and debt betas under the modified capital structure, and finally computing the revised cost of equity capital or WACC. As a practical matter, the effect of these changes on the WACC is likely to be quite small unless the revision in leverage has a significant effect on the target's interest tax shields or its likelihood of financial distress.

The following table summarizes how the discounted abnormal earnings/cash flow methods can be used to value a target before an acquisition (assuming it will remain an independent entity) and to estimate the value of a target firm to a potential acquirer.

Summary of Discounted Abnormal Earnings/Cash Flow Valuation for Targets

Value of target as an independent firm	(a) Present value of abnormal earnings/free cash flows to target equity assuming no acquisition, discounted at *premerger* cost of equity, or
	(b) Present value of abnormal NOPAT/free cash flows to target debt and equity assuming no acquisition, discounted at *premerger* WACC, less value of debt.
Value of target to potential acquirer	(a) Present value of abnormal earnings/free cash flows to target equity, *including benefits from merger,* discounted at *postmerger* cost of equity, or
	(b) Present value of abnormal NOPAT/free cash flows to target debt and equity, *including benefits from merger,* discounted at *postmerger* WACC, less value of debt.

Step 3: Analyze sensitivity Once we have estimated the expected value of a target, we will want to examine the sensitivity of our estimate to changes in the model assumptions. For example, answering the following questions can help the analyst assess the risks associated with an acquisition:

- What happens to the value of the target if it takes longer than expected for the benefits of the acquisition to materialize?
- What happens to the value of the target if the acquisition prompts its primary competitors to respond by also making an acquisition? Will potential changes in industry dynamics affect the firm's plans and estimates?

Key Analysis Questions

To analyze the pricing of an acquisition, the analyst is interested in assessing the value of the acquisition benefits to be generated by the acquirer relative to the price paid to target stockholders. Analysts are therefore likely to be interested in answers to the following questions:

- What is the premium that the acquirer paid for the target's stock? What does this premium imply for the acquirer in terms of future performance improvements to justify the premium?
- What are the likely performance improvements that management expects to generate from the acquisition? For example, are there likely to be increases in the revenues for the merged firm from new products, increased prices, or better distribution of existing products? Alternatively, are there cost savings as a result of taking advantage of economies of scale, improved efficiency, or a lower cost of capital for the target?
- What is the value of any performance improvements? Values can be estimated using multiples or discounted abnormal earnings/cash flow methods.

Exxon's Pricing of Mobil

Exxon's $74.2 billion price for Mobil represented a 26.4 percent premium to target stockholders over the market value on November 20, 1998, when rumors of a merger first reached Wall Street. This was below the mean and median premiums reported for all acquisitions during that year (41 percent and 30 percent, respectively). However, it was toward the high end of estimates made by J. P. Morgan, Exxon's financial advisor, who reviewed 38 large comparable acquisitions and concluded that a 15–25 percent premium was justified. In comparison, BP had paid a 35 percent premium for Amoco during the same period.

In terms of traditional multiples-based forms of valuation, Exxon's pricing of Mobil appears to be reasonable. For example, at the time of the announcement of Exxon's offer, the PE multiple for other firms in the oil industry that were comparable to Mobil ranged from 19.3 to 23.8. Exxon's offer valued Mobil at 22.7 times current earnings.

The market reaction to the acquisition announcement suggests that analysts initially believed that the deal was marginal for Exxon's stockholders—Exxon's stock price dropped by 1.5 percent (adjusted for market-wide changes), or $2.6 billion, during the 11 days prior to the announcement through to the actual announcement day. However, by the tenth trading day after the announcement, Exxon's stock was up 3.6 percent (also adjusted for market-wide changes), or $6.3 billion. Given the $15.5 billion premium that Exxon paid for Mobil, investors believed that the merger would create value of $21.8 billion.

Subsequent short-term financial results for Exxon-Mobil support the market's optimism about the merger synergies. In August 2000, Exxon-Mobil announced that merger synergies had reached $4.6 billion, far ahead of projections at the time of the merger. Analysts projected that they would reach $7.0 billion by 2002.

ACQUISITION FINANCING AND FORM OF PAYMENT

Even if an acquisition is undertaken to create new economic value and is priced judiciously, it may still destroy shareholder value if it is inappropriately financed. Several financing options are available to acquirers, including issuing stock or warrants to target stockholders, or acquiring target stock using surplus cash or proceeds from new debt. The trade-offs between these alternatives from the standpoint of target stockholders usually hinge on their tax and transaction cost implications. For acquirers, they can affect the firm's capital structure and provide new information to investors.

As we discuss below, the financing preferences of acquiring and target stockholders can diverge. Financing arrangements can therefore increase or reduce the attractiveness of an acquisition from the standpoint of acquiring stockholders. As a result, a complete analysis of an acquisition will include an examination of the implications of the financing arrangements for the acquirer.

Effect of Form of Payment on Acquiring Stockholders

From the perspective of the acquirer, the form of payment is essentially a financing decision. As discussed in Chapter 10, in the long term firms choose whether to use debt or equity financing to balance the tax and incentive benefits of debt against the risks of financial distress. For acquiring stockholders, the costs and benefits of different financing alternatives therefore usually depend on three factors described below: how the offer affects their firm's capital structure, any information effects associated with different forms of financing, and control issues arising from the form of payment.

Capital Structure Effects of Form of Financing

In acquisitions where debt financing or surplus cash are the primary form of consideration for target shares, the acquisition increases the net financial leverage of the acquirer. This increase in leverage may be part of the acquisition strategy, since one way an acquirer can add value to an inefficient firm is to lower its taxes by increasing interest tax shields. However, in many acquisitions an increase in postacquisition leverage is a side effect of the method of financing and not part of a deliberate tax-minimizing strategy. Demands by target shareholders for consideration in cash could lead the acquirer to have a postacquisition capital structure that can potentially reduce shareholder value for the acquirer by increasing the risk of financial distress.

To assess whether an acquisition leads an acquirer to have too much leverage, financial analysts can assess the acquirer's financial risk following the proposed acquisition by these methods:

- Analyze the business risks and the volatility of the combined, postacquisition cash flows against the level of debt in the new capital structure, and the implications for possible financial distress.
- Assess the pro forma financial risks for the acquirer under the proposed financing plan. Popular measures of financial risk include debt-to-equity and interest-coverage ratios, as well as projections of cash flows available to meet debt repayments. The ratios can be compared to similar performance metrics for the acquiring and target firms' industries to determine whether postmerger ratios indicate that the firm's probability of financial distress has increased significantly.
- Examine whether there are important off-balance-sheet liabilities for the target and/or acquirer that are not included in the pro forma ratio and cash flow analysis of postacquisition financial risk.

- Determine whether the pro forma assets for the acquirer are largely intangible and therefore sensitive to financial distress. Measures of intangible assets include such ratios as market to book equity and tangible assets to the market value of equity.

Information Problems and the Form of Financing

In the short term, information asymmetries between managers and external investors can make managers reluctant to raise equity to finance new projects. Managers' reluctance arises from their fear that investors will interpret the decision as an indication that the firm's stock is overvalued. In the short term, this effect can lead managers to deviate from the firm's long-term optimal mix of debt and equity. As a result, acquirers are likely to prefer to use internal funds or debt to finance an acquisition since these forms of consideration are less likely to be interpreted negatively by investors.[11]

The information effects imply that firms forced to use stock financing are likely to face a stock price decline when investors learn of the method of financing.[12] From the viewpoint of financial analysts, the financing announcement may, therefore, provide valuable news about the acquiring managers' views of their own company's value prior to the acquisition. On the other hand, it should have no implications for analysis of whether the acquisition creates value for acquiring shareholders since the news reflected in the financing announcement is about the *preacquisition* value of the acquirer and not about the *postacquisition* value of the target to the acquirer.

A second information problem arises if the acquiring management does not have good information about the target. Stock financing then provides a way for acquiring stockholders to share the information risks with target shareholders. If the acquirer finds out after the acquisition that the value of the target is less than previously anticipated, the accompanying decline in the acquirer's equity price will be partially borne by target stockholders who continue to hold the acquirer's stock. In contrast, if the target's shares were acquired in a cash offer, any postacquisition loss would be fully borne by the acquirer's original stockholders. The risk-sharing benefits from using stock financing appears to be widely recognized for acquisitions of private companies, where public information on the target is largely unavailable.[13] In practice it appears to be considered less important for acquisitions of large public corporations.

Control and the Form of Payment

There is a significant difference between the use of cash and stock in terms of its impact on the voting control of the combined firm postacquisition. Financing an acquisition with cash allows the acquirer to retain the structure and composition of its equity ownership. On the other hand, depending on the size of the target firm relative to the acquirer, an acquisition financed with stock could have a significant impact on the ownership and control of the firm postacquisition. This could be particularly relevant to a family-controlled acquirer. Therefore, the effects of control need to be balanced against the other costs and benefits when determining the form of payment.

Over the last 25 years, offers that are 100 percent cash have comprised 42 percent of all acquisitions, exceeding all-stock offers (30 percent) and mixed stock and cash offers (28 percent). The popularity of all-cash offers has increased since 2000, rising to 54 percent of all deals in 2005 whereas the use of all-stock offers has declined to only 21 percent.

Effect of Form of Payment on Target Stockholders

The key payment considerations for target stockholders are the tax and transaction cost implications of the acquirer's offer.

Tax Effects of Different Forms of Consideration

Target stockholders care about the after-tax value of any offer they receive for their shares. In the U.S., whenever target stockholders receive cash for their shares, they are required to pay capital gains tax on the difference between the takeover offer price and their original purchase price. Alternatively, if they receive shares in the acquirer as consideration and the acquisition is undertaken as a tax-free reorganization, they can defer any taxes on the capital gain until they sell the new shares.

As a result, U.S. tax laws appear to cause target stockholders to prefer a stock offer to a cash one. This is certainly likely to be the case for a target founder who still has a significant stake in the company. If the company's stock price has appreciated over its life, the founder will face a substantial capital gains tax on a cash offer and will therefore probably prefer to receive stock in the acquiring firm. However, cash and stock offers can be tax-neutral for some groups of stockholders. For example, consider the tax implications for risk arbitrageurs, who take a short-term position in a company that is a takeover candidate in the hope that other bidders will emerge and increase the takeover price. They have no intention of holding stock in the acquirer once the takeover is completed and will pay ordinary income tax on any short-term trading gain. Cash and stock offers therefore have identical after-tax values for risk arbitrageurs. Similarly, tax-exempt institutions are likely to be indifferent to whether an offer is in cash or stock.

Transaction Costs and the Form of Payment

Transaction costs are another factor related to the form of payment that can be relevant to target stockholders. Transaction costs are incurred when target stockholders sell any stock received as consideration for their shares in the target. These costs will not be faced by target stockholders if the bidder offers them cash. Transaction costs are unlikely to be significant for investors who intend to hold the acquirer's stock following a stock acquisition. However, they may be relevant for investors who intend to sell, such as risk arbitrageurs.

Key Analysis Questions

For an analyst focused on the acquiring firm, it is important to assess how the method of financing affects the acquirer's capital structure and its risks of financial distress by asking the following questions:

- What is the leverage for the newly created firm? How does this compare to leverage for comparable firms in the industry?
- What are the projected future cash flows for the merged firm? Are these sufficient to meet the firm's debt commitments? How much of a cushion does the firm have if future cash flows are lower than expected? Is the firm's debt level likely to impair its ability to finance profitable future investments if future cash flows are below expectations?

Exxon's Financing of Mobil

Exxon offered Mobil shareholders 1.32 Exxon shares for each Mobil share. Given Mobil's 780 million shares outstanding, Exxon issued 1,030 million shares, which at $72 per share implied a total offer of $74.2 billion. While the premerger equity value of Exxon represented 75 percent of the combined market value, the premium paid for Mobil's shares caused the postmerger proportion of ownership to drop to about 70 percent for Exxon and rise to 30 percent for Mobil.

The merger was structured as a "tax-free reorganization" for federal income tax purposes. This implied that Mobil shareholders would not recognize any gain or loss for federal income tax purposes from exchanging their Mobil stock for Exxon-Mobil stock in the merger.

By using stock to finance the acquisition, Exxon actually reduced its financial leverage. Initially the market reacted negatively to the offer, lowering Exxon's stock price by 1.5 percent (adjusting for marketwide returns) on the announcement date (December 1, 1998). This reaction could have occurred because investors interpreted Exxon's stock offer as indicating that its own managers considered its stock to be overvalued. Yet in the following ten days, Exxon's stock staged a recovery, increasing by 3.6 percent.

ACQUISITION OUTCOME

The final question of interest to the analyst evaluating a potential acquisition is whether it will indeed be completed. If an acquisition has a clear value-based motive, the target is priced appropriately, and its proposed financing does not create unnecessary financial risks for the acquirer, it may still fail because the target receives a higher competing bid, there is opposition from entrenched target management, or the transaction fails to receive necessary regulatory approval. Therefore, to evaluate the likelihood that an offer will be accepted, the financial analyst has to understand whether there are potential competing bidders who could pay an even higher premium to target stockholders than is currently offered. They also have to consider whether target managers are entrenched and likely to oppose an offer to protect their jobs, as well as the political and regulatory environment in which the target and the acquirer operate.

Other Potential Acquirers

If there are other potential bidders for a target, especially ones who place a higher value on the target, there is a strong possibility that the bidder in question will be unsuccessful. Target management and stockholders have an incentive to delay accepting the initial offer to give potential competitors time to also submit a bid. From the perspective of the initial bidder, this means that the offer could potentially reduce stockholder value by the cost of making the offer (including substantial investment banking and legal fees). In practice, a losing bidder can usually recoup these losses and sometimes even make healthy profits from selling to the successful acquirer any shares it has accumulated in the target.

On some occasions, the original bidder includes a break-up fee in the acquisition contract which is payable should the target company choose to be acquired by a different partner. For example, in late 2005 Johnson & Johnson signed an agreement to acquire Guidant Corporation for about $21 billion. A takeover battle for Guidant resulted when Boston Scientific made a higher offer. Over the ensuing seven weeks (from December 2005 to January 2006), both Johnson & Johnson and Boston Scientific increased their bids on multiple occasions. Eventually, Boston Scientific won with a $27 billion offer. However, in addition to the purchase price, Boston Scientific had to reimburse Guidant the termination fee of $705 million payable to Johnson & Johnson.

Key Analysis Questions

The financial analyst can determine whether there are other potential acquirers for a target and how they value the target by asking the following questions:

- Who are the acquirer's major competitors? Could any of these firms provide an even better fit for the target?
- Are there other firms that could also implement the initial bidder's acquisition strategy? For example, if this strategy relies on developing benefits from complementary assets, look for potential bidders who also have assets complementary to the target. If the goal of the acquisition is to replace inefficient management, what other firms in the target's industry could provide management expertise?

Target Management Entrenchment

If target managers are entrenched and fearful for their jobs, it is likely that they will oppose a bidder's offer. Some firms have implemented "golden parachutes" for top managers to allay their concerns about job security at the time of an offer. Golden parachutes provide top managers of a target firm with attractive compensation rewards should the firm get taken over.[14] However, many firms do not have such schemes, and opposition to an offer from entrenched management is a very real possibility.

More generally, there are a variety of structural impediments know as takeover defense mechanisms that provide a disincentive to acquiring firms. Many such defenses were used during the turbulent 1980s, when hostile acquisitions were at their peak. Some of the most widely adopted include poison pills, staggered boards, super-majority rules, dual-class recapitalizations, fair-price provisions, ESOP plans, and changes in states of incorporation to states with more restrictive anti-takeover laws. While the existence of takeover defenses for a target indicates that its management is likely to fight a bidding firm's offer, defenses have typically not prevented an acquisition from taking place. Instead, they tend to cause delays, which increase the likelihood that there will be competing offers made for the target, including offers by friendly parties solicited by target management, called "white knights." Takeover defenses, therefore, increase the likelihood that the bidder in question will be outbid for the target, or that it will have to increase its offer significantly to win a bidding contest. Given these risks, some have argued that acquirers are now less likely to embark on a potentially hostile acquisition.

Key Analysis Questions

To assess whether the target firm's management is entrenched and therefore likely to oppose an acquisition, analysts can ask the following questions:

- Does the target firm have takeover defenses designed to protect management?

- Has the target been a poor performer relative to other firms in its industry? If so, management's job security is likely to be threatened by a takeover, leading it to oppose any offers.
- Is there a golden parachute plan in place for target management? Golden parachutes provide attractive compensation for management in order to deter opposition to a takeover for job security reasons.

Antitrust and Security Issues

Regulators such as the Federal Trade Commission in the U.S. and the European Competition Commission assess the effects of an acquisition on the competitive dynamics of the industry in which the firms operate. The objective is to ensure that no one firm, through mergers and acquisitions, creates a dominant position that can impede effective competition in specific geographies or product markets. For instance, in July 2001 the European Competition Commission rejected GE's proposed $41 billion purchase of Honeywell International on the grounds that the merger would have severely reduced competition in the aerospace industry and resulted in higher prices for customers, particularly airlines.

In addition, political concerns around firms that have an impact on the national and economic security of a country come under the scrutiny of local lawmakers, whose opposition can often derail cross-border acquisition efforts. The U.S., for instance, has a specific inter-agency committee that vets foreign takeovers of U.S. assets on national security grounds. Two recent high profile cases—China's CNOOC oil company's proposed acquisition of California-based Unocal in mid-2005 and Dubai Ports World's acquisition of U.S. port terminals in March 2006—underscore the importance of assessing this risk. Chevron, another interested bidder for Unocal, used CNOOC's links to the Chinese government to generate political opposition to the CNOOC bid, which eventually led CNOOC to drop its offer. Similarly, political opposition based on the United Arab Emirates government's control of Dubai Ports World and the national security concerns over port infrastructure forced the company to sell the U.S. operations as part of its acquisition of British port operator P&O.

Key Analysis Questions

To assess whether the regulators and/or government is likely to oppose an acquisition, analysts can ask the following questions:

- What proportion of industry sales do the two firms control? Is this likely to be of concern to regulators in countries in which the firms operate? Are the combined firms likely to be able to reduce regulatory opposition by selling certain business units?
- Is the target firm or the industry in which it operates of strategic importance or in the national interest of the country in which it is located? Is the ownership structure of the acquirer likely to create political opposition to the deal?

Analysis of Outcome of Exxon's Offer for Mobil

Analysts covering Mobil had little reason to question whether Mobil would be sold to Exxon. The offer was a friendly one that had received the approval of Mobil's management and board of directors. There probably was some risk of another major oil company entering the bidding for Mobil. For example, BP had shown an appetite for making major acquisitions with its purchase of Amoco in August 1998. In early 1999 BP also acquired Arco in a second mega-deal. Chevron was also rumored to be open to an acquisition, and in October 2000 it acquired Texaco. In the end, none of these competitors made a bid for Mobil.

Despite the spate of mergers in the petroleum industry starting in 1997, the concentration level in the overall industry was well below the threshold at which the U.S. regulatory agencies would raise antitrust concerns. While this test applied to the global exploration and production markets, the refining and distribution markets were more segmented. Consequently, regulators required Exxon-Mobil to divest its wholesale distribution facilities. The European Commission, after a series of probes of the merger, mandated the sale of numerous assets and business lines as a pre-requisite of its approval for the merger. The acquisition was completed on December 1, 1999, twelve months after announcement of the initial agreement.

SUMMARY

This chapter summarizes how financial statement data and analysis can be used by financial analysts interested in evaluating whether an acquisition creates value for an acquiring firm's stockholders. Obviously, much of this discussion is also likely to be relevant to other merger participants, including target and acquiring management and their investment banks.

For the external analyst, the first task is to identify the acquirer's acquisition strategy. We discuss a number of strategies. Some of these are consistent with maximizing acquirer value, including acquisitions to take advantage of economies of scale, improve target management, combine complementary resources, capture tax benefits, provide low-cost financing to financially constrained targets, and increase product-market rents.

Other strategies appear to benefit managers more than stockholders. For example, some unprofitable acquisitions are made because managers are reluctant to return free cash flows to shareholders, or because managers want to lower the firm's earnings volatility by diversifying into unrelated businesses.

The financial analyst's second task is to assess whether the acquirer is offering a reasonable price for the target. Even if the acquirer's strategy is based on increasing shareholder value, it can overpay for the target. Target stockholders will then be well rewarded but at the expense of acquiring stockholders. We show how the ratio analysis, forecasting, and valuation techniques discussed earlier in the book can all be used to assess the worth of the target to the acquirer.

The method of financing an offer is also relevant to a financial analyst's review of an acquisition proposal. If a proposed acquisition is financed with surplus cash or new debt, it increases the acquirer's financial risk. Financial analysts can use ratio analysis of the acquirer's postacquisition balance sheet and pro forma estimates of cash flow volatility and interest coverage to assess whether demands by target stockholders for consideration in cash lead the acquirer to increase its risk of financial distress.

Finally, the financial analyst is interested in assessing whether a merger is likely to be completed once the initial offer is made, and at what price. This requires the analyst to determine whether there are other potential bidders, whether target management is entrenched and likely to oppose a bidder's offer, or whether the deal could fail due to antitrust or security concerns.

DISCUSSION QUESTIONS

1. Since the year 2000, there has been a noticeable increase in mergers and acquisitions between firms in different countries (termed cross-border acquisitions). What factors could explain this increase? What special issues can arise in executing a cross-border acquisition and in ultimately meeting your objectives for a successful combination?

2. Private equity firms have become an important player in the acquisition market. These private investment groups offer to buy a target firm, often with the cooperation of management, and then take the firm private. Private equity buyouts rose from just 2 percent of U.S. merger and acquisition activity in 2000 to 15 percent as of December 2005. Private equity buyers tend to finance a significant portion of the acquisition with debt.

   a. What types of firms would make ideal candidates for a private equity buyout? Why?

   b. How might the buyout firm add sufficient value to the target to justify a high buyout premium?

3. Kim Silverman, CFO of the First Public Bank Company, notes, "We are fortunate to have a cost of capital of only 10 percent. We want to leverage this advantage by acquiring other banks that have a higher cost of funds. I believe that we can add significant value to these banks by using our lower cost financing." Do you agree with Silverman's analysis? Why or why not?

4. The Boston Tea Company plans to acquire Hi Flavor Soda Co. for $60 per share, a 50 percent premium over current market price. John E. Grey, the CFO of Boston Tea, argues that this valuation can easily be justified using a price-earnings analysis: "Boston Tea has a price-earnings ratio of 15, and we expect that we will be able to generate long-term earnings for Hi Flavor Soda of $5 per share. This implies that Hi Flavor is worth $75 to us, well below our $60 offer price." Do you agree with this analysis? What are Grey's key assumptions?

5. You have been hired by GT Investment Bank to work in the merger department. The analysis required for all potential acquisitions includes an examination of the target for any off-balance-sheet assets or liabilities that have to be factored into the valuation. Prepare a checklist for your examination.

6. A target company is currently valued at $50 in the market. A potential acquirer believes that it can add value in two ways: $15 of value can be added through better working capital management, and an additional $10 of value can be generated by making available a unique technology to expand the target's new product offerings. In a competitive bidding contest, how much of this additional value will the acquirer have to pay out to the target's shareholders to emerge as the winner?

7. In 1995 Disney acquired ABC television at a significant premium. Disney's management justified much of this premium by arguing that the acquisition would guarantee access for Disney's programs on ABC's television stations. Evaluate the economic merits of this claim.

8. A leading oil exploration company decides to acquire an Internet company at a 50 percent premium. The acquirer argues that this move creates value for its own stockholders because it can use its excess cash flows from the oil business to help finance growth in the new Internet segment. Evaluate the economic merits of this claim.

9. Under current U.S. accounting standards, acquirers are required to capitalize goodwill and report any subsequent declines in value as an impairment charge. What performance metrics would you use to judge whether goodwill is impaired?

10. As an external adviser to the U.S. Government's interagency committee that vets foreign takeovers, you have been asked to provide expert testimony on the proposed takeover of a major U.S. airport by a Dutch airport management services company. Would you recommend that the acquisition be granted regulatory approval? What are the different issues you will examine and present to the committee?

NOTES

1. In a review of studies of merger returns, Michael Jensen and Richard Ruback conclude that target shareholders earn positive returns from takeovers, but that acquiring shareholders only break even. See M. Jensen and R. Ruback, "The Market for Corporate Control: The Scientific Evidence," *Journal of Financial Economics* 11 (April 1983): 5–50.

2. Much of our discussion is based on the analysis of the acquisition presented by F. Weston, "The Exxon-Mobil Merger: An Archetype," *Journal of Applied Finance* 12, no. 1, Spring/Summer 2002.

3. Of course, another possibility is for the profitable firm to acquire the unprofitable one. However, in the U.S. the IRS will disallow the use of tax loss carryforwards by an acquirer if it appears that an acquisition was tax-motivated.

4. See S. Kaplan, "Management Buyouts: Evidence on Taxes as a Source of Value," *Journal of Finance* 44 (1989): 611–632.

5. K. Palepu, "Predicting Takeover Targets: A Methodological and Empirical Analysis," *Journal of Accounting and Economics* 8 (March 1986): 3–36.

6. FactSet Mergerstat, LLC, *Mergerstat Review 2006* (Santa Monica, CA, 2006), pp. 248–249.

7. Chapter 2 discusses the pros and cons of corporate diversification and evidence on its implications for firm performance.

8. FactSet Mergerstat, LLC, *Mergerstat Review 2006* (Santa Monica, CA, 2006), pp. 248–249.

9. See S. Liesman and A. Sullivan, "Tight-Lipped Exxon, Outspoken Mobil Face Major Image, Cultural Differences," *Wall Street Journal*, December 2, 1998.

10. See P. Healy, K. Palepu, and R. Ruback, "Which Mergers Are Profitable—Strategic or Financial?," *Sloan Management Review* 38, no. 4 (Summer 1997): 45–58.

11. See S. Myers and N. Majluf, "Corporate Financing and Investment Decisions When Firms Have Information That Investors Do Not," *Journal of Financial Economics* (June 1984): 187–221.

12. For evidence see N. Travlos, "Corporate Takeover Bids, Methods of Payments, and Bidding Firms' Stock Returns," *Journal of Finance* 42 (1987): 943–963.

13. See S. Datar, R. Frankel, and M. Wolfson, "Earnouts: The Effects of Adverse Selection and Agency Costs on Acquisition Techniques," *Journal of Law, Economics, and Organization* 17 (2001): 201–238.

14. H. Singh and F. Harianto, "Management–Board Relationships, Takeover Risk, and the Adoption of Golden Parachutes," *Academy of Management Journal* 32 (1989): 7–24, find that entrenched managers create golden parachute contracts to avoid the disciplinary effect of corporate takeovers. J. Machlin, H. Choe, and J. Miles, "The Effects of Golden Parachutes on Takeover Activity," *Journal of Law and Economics* 36 (1993): 861–876, find that golden parachutes increase the likelihood of an acquisition.

I n late January 1991, Didier Pineau-Valencienne, CEO and Chairman of the French firm Groupe Schneider, was frustrated at his lack of success in building a closer working relationship between his company and Square D, Schneider's American counterpart in the electrical equipment industry. Convinced that a global market was developing for electrical equipment, Pineau-Valencienne believed that Schneider needed to become a major player in the U.S. market to maintain its future competitive position. Given the lack of success in partnering with Square D, he was considering the option of acquiring the company.[1]

THE ELECTRICAL EQUIPMENT INDUSTRY

The electrical equipment industry generated revenue from new construction as well as from the maintenance of existing equipment. Demand for both closely followed general economic conditions. The 1990 economic slump hit the electrical manufacturing segment in the United States severely. However, by early 1991 analysts expected prospects for the industry to brighten with the predicted upturn in the economy and the construction market.

Two related trends dominated the industry in 1990: globalization and industry concentration. The first of these had led many U.S. firms to expand internationally to take advantage of market growth in Western Europe and Pacific Rim countries. These international opportunities had been enhanced by the globalization of product standards in the industry. The most widely accepted standards in the U.S. were developed by the National Electrical Manufacturers Association (NEMA). European products conformed to a different set of standards, developed by the International Electrical Commission (IEC) in Geneva. However, many in the industry expected that the move toward a unified Europe, set for 1992, would ultimately lead IEC standards to become dominant in the world.

The second major trend in the industry, concentration of manufacturing and research capabilities, resulted from increasing costs of development and production as well as from globalization. The development of a new product line cost between $46 million and $74 million (FF 250 million to FF 400 million). Globalization of markets and product standards enabled firms to take advantage of economies of scale, using their expertise and technologies to create common products for domestic and international markets.

1. Edouard De Vitry D'Avaucourt prepared this case under the supervision of Professor Paul Healy. Additional comments and information were provided by Professors Paul Asquith from the MIT Sloan School of Management and Anant Sundaram from the Amos Tuck School. The case is intended solely as the basis for class discussion and is not intended to serve as an endorsement, source of primary data, or illustration of effective or ineffective management.

SQUARE D COMPANY

Square D was a major supplier of electrical equipment, services, and systems in the U.S. (see Exhibit 1 for Square D's U.S. market shares). The company was incorporated in 1903 and had grown steadily since then. It owned and operated 18 manufacturing plants in 11 foreign countries. Operations were concentrated in two segments: electrical distribution and industrial control. The electrical distribution segment manufactured products and systems used to transmit electricity from power lines to outlets for residential, commercial, industrial, or other types of buildings. The industrial control segment manufactured products and provided services to control power used by electrical devices or processes.

One of Square D's strengths was its network of independent electrical distributors, or wholesalers, which marketed its products. Individual distributors, selected by Square D, provided products and services to all types of clients (contractors, utilities, industrial users, and original equipment manufacturers). This extensive network was the result of many years of relationship building, and was the envy of most of Square D's competitors.

Square D's major competitors included ABB, Westinghouse, Siemens, Allen Bradley, General Electric, and Schneider (through its subsidiaries Télémécanique and Merlin Gerin). These companies competed across a number of segments. In late 1990 *US Industrial Outlook* ranked Square D second in the U.S. industrial control business after Allen Bradley. In electrical distribution, the company ranked third in the U.S. market behind Westinghouse and General Electric.

Square D had an impressive financial track record—it had been profitable for each of the last 59 years. In the mid-1980s, however, company performance indicators deteriorated, prompting the Board to make a change in top management. Jerre Stead joined Square D as president and COO in 1987, was elected CEO in 1988, and was appointed Chairman of the Board in 1989. Stead led a revitalization plan to restore the company's performance and help it face the new industry challenges. Under the plan the following restructuring changes were made:

- Some facilities in the U.S. and Canada were closed, and others were consolidated.
- The firm's businesses were reorganized into three externally focused sectors serving industrial control, electrical distribution, and international markets.
- The resources generated by redeployments and disposal of operations not closely related to the core were used to strengthen core businesses.

Thanks to these efforts, Square D weathered the 1990 recession better than many of its competitors. In 1990 Square D's sales were $1.7 billion (see Exhibit 2 for financial statements), 71% in the electrical distribution segment (85% of operating earnings) and 29% in the industrial control segment (15% of operating earnings). By early 1991 analysts were expressing optimism about the industry's prospects for late 1991 and 1992, especially those for Square D. *Value Line* noted that "a stronger economy, a rebound in housing, and positive operating leverage . . . could enable earnings per share to surge to $5.50 or so in 1992 (from $4.73 in 1990)."

GROUPE SCHNEIDER

Schneider was founded in October 1886 as a partnership and was transformed into a corporation (*société anonyme*) in 1966. It was one of the largest industrial groups in France and ranked 184 in Fortune's 500 (worldwide ranking).

In 1981, with the arrival of Pineau-Valencienne as chairman and CEO of the group, Schneider embarked on an ambitious restructuring program. The first stage of the program was to divest all loss-making businesses (shipbuilding, railways, and telephone equipment), which had historically generated much of the firm's sales. Selling these businesses allowed the group to simplify its operational structure and to strengthen its finances. In the second stage of the restructuring Schneider focused on two core businesses:

- Electrical equipment manufacturing for power distribution and automation of industrial complexes (56% of sales, 85% of operating profits in 1990).
- Electrical building contracting (44% of sales, 15% of operating profits in 1990).

As a result of the restructuring efforts, Schneider transformed itself from a diversified holding company into an industrial group focused on electrical equipment, engineering, and contracting. The company was organized around four major industrial subsidiaries:

- *Merlin Gerin*—Manufacturer of high-, medium-, and low-voltage equipment, as well as process control systems.
- *Télémécanique*—Manufacturer of automation systems and equipment.
- *Jeumont Schneider*—Manufacturer of electrical and electronic engineering equipment.
- *Spie Batignolles*—Provider of electrical contracting and civil engineering services.

With sales of 51 billion francs (financial statements are presented in Exhibit 3) and 85,000 employees throughout the world in 1990, Schneider ranked second or third in most segments of the global electrical equipment industry.

In the late 1980s, Pineau-Valencienne became convinced that the industry was moving more toward a global industry. In his communications with analysts, he emphasized that IEC standards would gain influence in the U.S. and would become the worldwide standard. In addition, he believed that increasing R&D and manufacturing costs would encourage international concentration. Consequently, Schneider began a third restructuring stage—geographical diversification. This move was initiated with two major acquisitions in 1989:

- Spie Batignolles acquired 15% of DAVY, the leading British engineering company.
- Schneider acquired a controlling interest in Federal Pioneer, the leading Canadian electrical equipment manufacturer.

The Relationship Between Schneider and Square D

Schneider became interested in Square D in 1988. In September 1988, Pineau-Valencienne arranged a meeting between the top executives of the two companies, during which Schneider presented its vision of a possible joint venture. After this presentation, operational meetings were scheduled from fall 1988 to spring 1989 to determine the product lines most suitable for such a joint venture. To protect the information exchanged, the companies entered into a confidentiality agreement in late October 1988. This restricted the use and public disclosure of confidential information received during the discussions, but it did not contain any "standstill" provisions limiting purchase of securities or business combination proposals.

Very early in the negotiations it became clear that the two CEOs diverged in their understanding of the nature of the relationship. Pineau-Valencienne had hoped that

Schneider would acquire an equity position in Square D to cement the relationship. Stead, however, made it very clear that he did not welcome this, and requested that Square D's independence be respected. In correspondence on September 25, 1989, Pineau-Valencienne made his views very clear, connecting the future of the joint venture discussions to Square D's agreeing to Schneider acquiring a 20% interest in Square D. As a result, joint venture discussions between the two firms terminated. Frustrated over this standstill, in September 1990 Pineau-Valencienne indicated to Stead that Schneider's interests in Square D had changed from a joint venture to a "friendly cash merger transaction." Square D's Board subsequently became increasingly hostile to Schneider's proposals.

At the same time that Schneider was making overtures to Square D, Square D was organizing legal defenses against hostile takeovers. In 1989 it moved to Delaware, where state laws require hostile bidders to have a minimum of 85% of the shares tendered to effect a takeover. In addition, it created poison pill amendments to fight potential unsolicited bids, including a Common Stock Purchase Plan (see Exhibit 4 for details).

During November 1990, unusual activity was noticeable in Square D's stock. Rumors of a takeover led to a jump in volume and increased the share price from $36.50 on October 22 to $49.75 on November 7 (see Exhibit 5). On November 6, 1990, Stead discussed the unusual activity in a phone conversation with Pineau-Valencienne, who expressed an interest in having the opportunity to propose a transaction to Square D if any other parties were given such an opportunity.

On February 1, 1991, *Value Line Investments Survey* made the following comments:

> *Square D stock is trading on takeover speculation, as it has for the past three months. Square D has several attractions (including positions in selected electrical equipment markets), and could well be a tempting takeover target, especially to a foreign company trying to establish or to enlarge a market presence in the U.S. An acquirer might be willing to pay $70 a share or more for the company. But after three months of unusually heavy trading in the stock, during which time all of its outstanding shares theoretically have changed hands, no evidence of a pending buyout attempt has appeared. If none is eventually forthcoming, we'd expect the stock to gradually drift lower, perhaps to the range of $40–$45 a share. At this juncture, only speculative investors should be holding these shares.*

Potential Acquisition of Square D

One option that Pineau-Valencienne was considering was to make a bid for Square D. After two years of contacts with Square D, he had a number of ideas for synergies and sources of value that could result from a full combination of the two companies. These included:

- Rationalizing R&D efforts between the two companies and sharing the benefits of existing technologies;
- Providing access to larger distribution channels for both companies;
- Rationalizing manufacturing capabilities; and
- Expanding Square D's product lines by selling products developed by Télémécanique or Merlin Gerin.

Lazard Frères, the financial advisor of Schneider, was asked to analyze the stand-alone value of Square D as well as its value to Schneider. To determine Square D's standalone value, Lazard Frères prepared a set of base assumptions for the firm's future performance as an independent entity. They projected that (a) sales would grow 3.5% in 1991 and 7% per year thereafter; (b) EBIT would be 15–16% of sales; (c) net working capital would continue to be 11–13% of sales; (d) projected capital expenditures would be 5% of sales; and (e) depreciation expenses would remain at 4% of sales between 1991 and 1997, and 4.3% thereafter. Based on the synergies between Schneider and Square D, Lazard Frères estimated that Square D could save approximately $60 million per year in expenses (after tax) if it were combined with Schneider. In addition, the disposal of some of Square D's unrelated assets could generate $150 million in cash. Other data relevant to the valuation of Square D is presented in Exhibit 6.

One other issue that Pineau-Valencienne was concerned about in a possible acquisition of Square D was its effect on Schneider's income. Under French accounting, Schneider would have to amortize goodwill, regardless of whether the offer was cash or stock-financed. Lazard Frères estimated that asset and liability revaluations under an acquisition would be minimal, implying that there would be significant goodwill amortization charges, even if the maximum period of 40 years was chosen. Pineau-Valencienne expected that many analysts would react negatively to the resulting dilution of earnings.

Didier Pineau-Valencienne felt he had to make a quick decision. There were rumors that Square D already had been approached by a number of other companies about a business combination. Pineau-Valencienne was very concerned that other competitors could gain control of Square D, leaving Schneider with few opportunities to gain access to the U.S. market.

QUESTIONS

1. Assess and discuss the strategic fit between Square D and Schneider. What are the economic pros and cons of a combination?

2. Evaluate the base assumptions Lazard Frères made for valuing Square D. What is the company worth to Schneider under these assumptions?

3. Use your own assumptions to estimate the value of Square D as an independent company. What is the company worth to Schneider?

4. What would be the effect of the acquisition on Schneider's future earnings, assuming that it was forced to pay the full value of Square D? Should Schneider be concerned about this effect?

5. If you were Mr. Pineau-Valencienne in late January 1991, what would you do? Would you offer a bid for Square D? If so, how much would you bid, and would you make your offer friendly or hostile?

EXHIBIT 1

Schneider and Square D Market Shares, U.S. and Europe

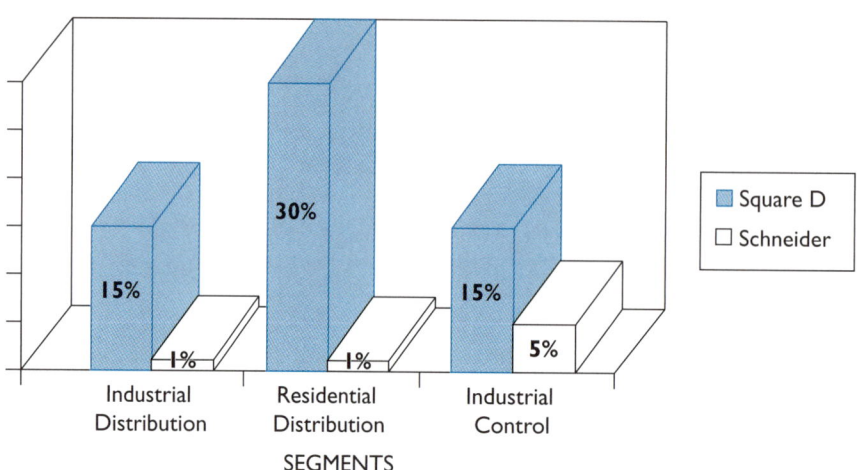

U.S. Market Shares

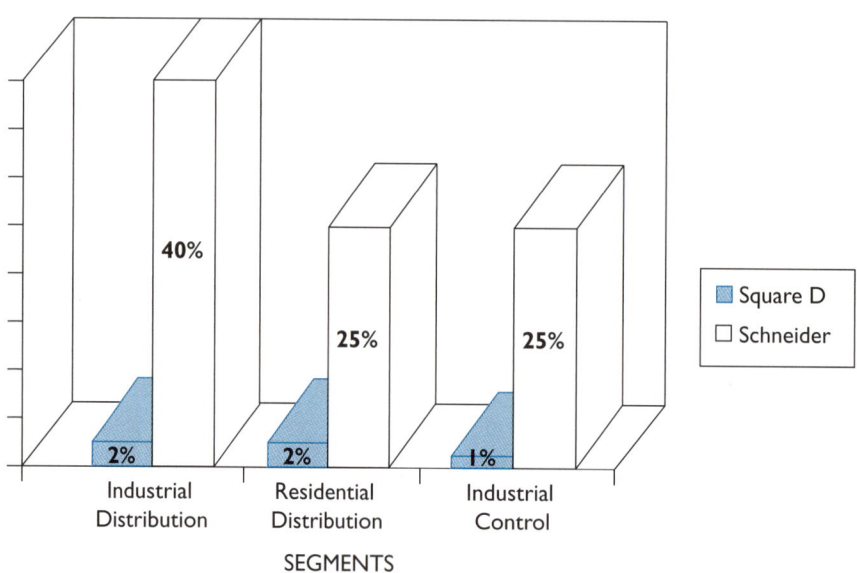

European Market Shares

EXHIBIT 2

Selected Pages from Square D's 1990 Annual Report

CONSOLIDATED FINANCIAL STATEMENTS

CONSOLIDATED STATEMENTS OF NET EARNINGS

(Amounts in thousands, except per share)	Year Ended December 31		
	1990	1989	1988
Net Sales	$1,653,319	$1,598,688	$1,497,772
Costs and Expenses:			
Cost of products sold	1,088,977	1,027,348	979,591
Selling, administrative and general	385,903	369,726	338,962
Restructuring charge	—	26,320	—
Operating Earnings	178,439	175,294	179,219
Non-Operating Income	34,740	17,106	17,255
Interest Expense	(28,760)	(31,438)	(22,082)
Earnings from Continuing Operations before Income Taxes	184,419	160,962	174,392
Provision for Income Taxes	67,773	59,856	63,310
Earnings from Continuing Operations	116,646	101,106	111,082
Discontinued Operations:			
(Loss) earnings from operations, net of income tax (benefit) expense: 1990—$(1,188); 1989—$(1,086); 1988—$3,831	(312)	798	7,852
Gain on disposal, net of other provisions; net of income taxes of $1,865	4,391	—	—
Earnings from Discontinued Operations	4,079	798	7,852
Net Earnings	120,725	101,904	118,934
Preferred Dividend, Net of Income Taxes	6,176	3,300	—
Net Earnings Available for Common Shareholders	$114,549	$98,604	$118,934
Earnings per Common Share:			
Primary:			
Continuing operations	$4.76	$3.95	$4.15
Discontinued operations	.18	.03	.29
Net Earnings	$4.94	$3.98	$4.44
Fully Diluted:			
Continuing operations	$4.57	$3.88	$4.13
Discontinued operations	.16	.03	.29
Net Earnings	$4.73	$3.91	$4.42
Weighted Average Number of Common Shares Outstanding:			
Primary	23,181	24,763	26,776
Fully diluted	25,088	25,809	27,016

CONSOLIDATED BALANCE SHEETS

	December 31,	
(Dollars in thousands, except per share)	1990	1989
ASSETS		
Current Assets:		
Cash and short-term investments	$244,933	$66,348
Receivables, less allowances (1990—$23,759; 1989—$18,556)	305,241	314,123
Inventories	159,109	151,316
Prepaid expenses	12,664	15,206
Prepaid income taxes	4,714	—
Deferred income tax benefit	34,988	26,459
Net assets of discontinued operation	—	117,116
Total Current Assets	761,649	690,568
Investment in Leveraged Leases	137,182	133,344
Property, Plant and Equipment:		
Land	24,477	22,216
Buildings and improvements	222,105	212,992
Equipment	552,785	501,531
Property, Plant and Equipment—at cost	799,367	736,739
Less accumulated depreciation	349,265	318,261
Property, Plant and Equipment—net	450,102	418,478
Net Assets of Discontinued Operations	36,681	52,949
Excess of Purchase Price Over Net Assets of Businesses		
Acquired, Less Amortization (1990—$13,769; 1989—$12,978)	51,391	50,528
Other Assets	22,744	26,718
Total Assets	$1,459,749	$1,372,585

LIABILITIES AND COMMON SHAREHOLDERS' EQUITY

	1990	1989
Current Liabilities:		
Short-term debt	$123,871	$263,730
Current maturities of long-term debt	15,067	10,174
Accounts payable and accrued expenses	220,575	200,686
Income taxes	—	10,327
Dividends payable	12,633	11,893
Total Current Liabilities	372,146	496,810
Long-Term Debt	244,820	123,420
Deferred Income Taxes	82,381	74,464
Deferred Income Taxes—Leveraged Leases	127,699	112,473
Other Liabilities	14,000	—
Minority Interest	10,941	9,295
Preferred Stock, No Par Value, Authorized 6,000,000 Shares;		
Issued 1,709,402 Shares, Outstanding 1,701,822 Shares,		
Cumulative Series A ESOP Convertible Preferred Stock	$124,568	$125,000
Note Receivable from ESOP Trust	(25,000)	(125,000)
Unearned ESOP Compensation	(95,400)	—
Common Shareholders' Equity:		
Common stock, par value $1.66²/₃, authorized		
100,000,000 shares	49,601	49,409
Additional paid-in capital	130,401	120,211

(continued)

CONSOLIDATED BALANCE SHEETS (*continued*)

(Dollars in thousands, except per share)	December 31, 1990	1989
Retained earnings	773,126	713,225
Cumulative translation adjustments	3,262	(8,788)
Treasury stock—at cost	(352,796)	(317,934)
Total Common Shareholders' Equity	603,594	556,123
Total Liabilities and Common Shareholders' Equity	$1,459,749	$1,372,585

CONSOLIDATED STATEMENTS OF CASH FLOWS

(Dollars in thousands)	Year Ended December 31, 1990	1989	1988
Cash and Short-Term Investments at January 1	$66,348	$65,855	$94,488
Cash and Short-Term Investments were Provided from (Used for):			
Operating Activities:			
Earnings from Continuing Operations	116,646	101,106	111,082
Add (deduct) non-cash items included in earnings from continuing operations:			
Depreciation and amortization	59,300	49,443	45,174
Deferred income taxes	1,707	(25,147)	(8,506)
Deferred income taxes—leveraged leases	15,226	23,445	25,683
(Gain) loss on sale of property, plant and equipment	(1,011)	1,936	657
(Gain) loss on foreign exchange	(2,222)	964	(52)
Minority interest	1,646	985	1,047
Other credits to earnings—net	—	(15)	(63)
Current Items (net of effects of purchase of businesses):			
Receivables	13,501	(58,515)	(20,789)
Inventories	(1,285)	26,568	(52,795)
Prepaid expenses	2,769	12,027	1,635
Accounts payable and accrued expenses	(7,312)	16,736	20,316
Income taxes	(15,253)	(3,319)	8,243
Net cash provided from continuing operations	183,712	146,214	131,632
Net cash (used for) provided from discontinued operations	(484)	2,971	721
Net cash provided from operating activities	183,228	149,185	132,353
Investing Activities:			
Increase in investment in leveraged leases	$(3,838)	$(2,876)	$(4,829)
Purchase of businesses, net of $103 of cash acquired	—	(9,271)	—
Property additions	(83,117)	(80,024)	(70,419)
Proceeds from sale of business	175,476	—	—

(*continued*)

Schneider and Square D

CONSOLIDATED STATEMENTS OF CASH FLOWS (*continued*)

	Year Ended December 31,		
(Dollars in thousands)	1990	1989	1988
Proceeds from sale of property, plant and equipment	21,774	6,186	14,222
Decrease (increase) in other investments	1,281	(12,794)	24,692
Net cash provided from (used for) investing activities	111,576	(98,779)	(36,334)
Financing Activities:			
Net (decrease) increase in short-term debt	(143,983)	142,262	44,430
Increase in long-term debt	27,883	614	11,066
Reductions in long-term debt	(14,412)	(21,580)	(17,910)
Proceeds of note receivable from ESOP trust	125,000	—	—
Loan to ESOP trust	(25,000)	—	—
Cash dividends paid on common stock	(50,128)	(50,590)	(54,601)
Cash dividends paid on preferred stock	(9,956)	(5,000)	—
Common stock issued	6,602	8,929	6,349
Purchase of treasury stock	(34,916)	(126,778)	(111,394)
Redemption of preferred stock	(432)	—	—
Treasury stock issued	54	114	256
Net cash used for financing activities	(119,288)	(52,029)	(121,804)
Effect of exchange rate changes on cash	3,069	2,116	(2,848)
Net Increase (Decrease) in Cash and Short-Term Investments	178,585	493	(28,633)
Cash and Short-Term Investments at December 31[2]	$244,933	$66,348	$65,855

2. See accompanying notes to consolidated financial statements.

NOTES TO CONSOLIDATED FINANCIAL STATEMENTS
(Dollars in thousands, except per share)

A. Summary of Significant Accounting Policies

Principles of Consolidation

The financial statements include the accounts of the company and all majority-owned subsidiaries. Investments in unconsolidated affiliates are accounted for by the equity method. All significant intercompany accounts and transactions have been eliminated. The statements are based on years ended December 31, except for substantially all international subsidiaries whose fiscal years end November 30.

Cash and Short-Term Investments

Cash consists of cash in banks and time deposits. Short-term investments consist of a variety of highly liquid short-term instruments with purchased maturities of generally three months or less. Short-term investments are carried at cost, which approximates market.

Inventories

Inventories are stated at the lower of cost or market. Cost of inventories is determined using the last-in, first-out (LIFO) method for substantially all domestic inventories and certain international inventories. The first-in, first-out (FIFO) method is used for substantially all international inventories.

Property, Plant and Equipment

Depreciation of property, plant and equipment is provided on a straight-line basis over the estimated useful lives of the assets. Accelerated methods are used for income tax purposes.

Businesses Acquired

The excess of purchase price over net assets of businesses acquired is amortized on a straight-line basis over not more than forty years.

Income Taxes

Income taxes are accounted for in accordance with APB No. 11. The Financial Accounting Standards Board has issued Statement No. 96, which will change the accounting for income taxes; the company will adopt this statement no later than January 1, 1992.

Off-Balance Sheet Financial Instruments

The company enters into a variety of financial instruments in the management of its exposure to changes in interest rates and foreign currency rates. These instruments include interest rate swap agreements and foreign exchange contracts. These financial instruments do not represent a material off-balance sheet risk in relation to the financial statements.

Earnings per Common Share

Primary earnings per common share are determined by dividing the weighted average number of common shares outstanding during the year into net earnings after deducting after-tax dividends attributable to preferred shares. Common share equivalents in the form of stock options and convertible debt are excluded from the calculation since they do not have a material dilutive effect on per share figures. Fully diluted earnings per share reflect the conversion of all convertible preferred stock and common stock equivalents into common stock.

Reclassifications

Certain amounts in the 1989 and 1988 financial statements have been reclassified to conform to the current year's financial statement presentation.

B. Discontinued Operations

As of June 30, 1990, the company reported its General Semiconductor Industries (GSI) business as a discontinued operation, and as of September 30, 1989, the company reported its Yates Industries (Yates) copper foil business as a discontinued operation. Accordingly, the consolidated financial statements of the company have been reclassified to report separately the net assets and operating results of these discontinued operations. Financial results for periods prior to the dates of discontinuance have been restated to reflect continuing operations.

In January 1990, the company concluded the sale of its Yates operations in Europe and its 50% joint venture interest in Japan. In April 1990, the company completed the sale of its Yates operation in Bordentown, N.J. Total gross proceeds from the sale of all Yates operations were $175,476. The proceeds from the sale of Yates operations and the associated costs approximated management's original estimates. Management is actively pursuing the sale of the GSI business.

A gain from the sale of Yates, offset by provisions for a loss on the prospective sale of GSI and costs associated with other previously discontinued businesses, resulted in a gain of $4,391, net of income taxes, in the second quarter of 1990 from discontinued operations. The gain on the sale of Yates is net of a $14,000 provision for long-term environmental costs. The gain from the sale of Yates' foreign locations included a gain of $6,895 from the recognition of cumulative translation adjustments.

Net assets of discontinued operations were $36,681 and $170,065 at December 31, 1990 and 1989, respectively. These amounts consist of current assets; property, plant and equipment; other noncurrent assets; and current and concurrent liabilities.

Sales applicable to the discontinued operations prior to the dates of discontinuance were $16,158, $124,121, and $159,000 in 1990, 1989, and 1988, respectively. Interest expense of $249, $2,730 and $2,246, net of income taxes, was allocated to the discontinued operations prior to dates of discontinuance based on net assets for 1990, 1989, and 1988, respectively. The operating results of GSI from the date of discontinuance to December 31, 1990 were immaterial.

C. Restructuring Charge

In 1989, a restructuring charge of $17,511 net of taxes, or $.71 per share, was incurred by the company as a part of a plan to rationalize and improve profitability of several businesses and product lines both in the United States and abroad. The charge is principally comprised of costs associated with product, facility and organizational rationalization of the electrical distribution segment; product rationalization of the industrial control segment; plant consolidation and organizational restructuring in Canada; reorganization in Europe; and marketing restructuring.

D. Acquisitions

In 1989, the company acquired Crisp Automation, Inc. of Dublin, Ohio. Crisp Automation is a designer of process controls and factory automation systems and operates as part of the Square D Automation Products business. Also in 1989, the company acquired Electrical Specialty Products (ESP) of Montevallo, Alabama. ESP is a manufacturer of electrical connectors and operates as part of the Square D Connectors business. These acquisitions were accounted for as purchases; their sales and net earnings for the periods prior to the dates of acquisition were not material.

G. Inventories

Inventories valued by the last-in, first-out (LIFO) method aggregated $83,941 and $65,017 at December 31, 1990 and 1989, respectively. If the first-in, first-out (FIFO) method had been used, inventories would have been $138,120 and $140,076 higher than reported in the accompanying consolidated balance sheets at December 31, 1990 and 1989, respectively.

Inventories are maintained by element of cost; therefore, it is not practical to determine major classes such as finished goods, work in process and raw materials.

H. Lease Commitments

The company rents various warehouse and office facilities and certain equipment, principally computers and vehicles, under lease arrangements classified as operating leases.

Future minimum rental payments under noncancelable operating leases with initial terms of one year or more as of December 31, 1990 are:

1991	$10,160
1992	7,266
1993	5,520
1994	4,473
1995	975
Remainder	1,224
Total	$29,618

J. Debt

Long-term debt consists of:

	1990	1989
ESOP Notes, 7.7%, due on various dates to 2004	$120,400	$—
Senior Notes, 10.0%, due 1995	75,000	75,000
Industrial Revenue Bonds, 5.6% to 8.8%, due on various dates to 2004	25,715	26,610
First Mortgage Notes, 9.0% to 9.2%, due on various dates to 2009	10,825	11,119
Subordinated Convertible Notes, 9.0%, due 1992 (net of unamortized discount at 13.0%: 1990—$220, 1989—$376)	2,787	4,096
Payable to banks; average rate 1990—13.8%, 1989—10.3%; due on various dates to 1996	1,114	2,423
Other debt: average rate 1990—14.4%, 1989—12.7%; due on various dates to 2000	24,046	14,346
Subtotal	259,887	133,594
Less current maturities	15,067	10,174
Total	$244,820	$123,420

The aggregate annual maturities of long-term debt for the years 1991 through 1995 are $15,067, $14,642, $14,968, $13,877, and $82,187, respectively.

The Employee Stock Ownership Plan (ESOP) Notes include $25,000 of direct borrowings by the company, the proceeds from which have been advanced in the form of a loan to the company's ESOP. Direct borrowings of the ESOP, aggregating $95,400 as of December 31, 1990, have been guaranteed by the company and accordingly, are reported as long-term debt of the company. See Note Q for further discussion.

Industrial Revenue Bonds of $9,115 and the First Mortgage Notes are secured by the property and equipment acquired with the proceeds of the financings.

The Subordinated Convertible Notes are convertible at a rate of 28.57 shares for each one thousand dollars of principal. The company has reserved 85,934 shares of common stock for the conversion.

The company has entered into revolving credit agreements in which twelve of its principal banks participate. The agreements provide for up to $180,000 of revolving credit through 1994. The credit is available in both the domestic and euro markets.

Short-term debt includes bank borrowings of $33,611 and $19,438 and commercial paper of $70,260 and $214,292 at December 31, 1990 and 1989, respectively. Additionally, short-term debt includes a master note agreement of $20,000 and $30,000 at December 31, 1990 and 1989, respectively.

The company has additional unused short-term lines of credit which aggregated $69,501 at December 31, 1990.

K. Income Taxes

Pre-tax income from continuing operations is as follows:

	1990	1989	1988
United States	$163,674	$142,855	$155,453
International	20,745	18,107	18,939
Total	$184,419	$160,962	$174.392

Income tax provisions for continuing operations are as follows:

	1990	1989	1988
Current:			
U.S. Federal	$33,452	$46,784	$35,261
International	7,999	4,752	3,989
State	9,037	9,902	6,625
	50,488	61,438	45,875
Deferred:			
U.S. Federal	17,189	(1,375)	17,475
International	(869)	1,479	228
State	965	(1,686)	(268)
	17,285	(1,582)	17,435
Total	$67,773	$59,856	$63,310

The components of the deferred income tax provision are as follows:

	1990	1989	1988
Leasing subsidiary income	$17,077	$22,502	$25,256
401(k) contributions	4,383	—	—
State tax	965	(1,686)	(268)
Tax over book depreciation	2,535	1,301	751
Deferred taxable income on installment sales	—	(13,006)	(5,615)

(continued)

	1990	1989	1988
Alternative minimum tax	—	8,484	1,634
Funding of group health insurance trust	—	(6,863)	(11,634)
Restructuring charge	—	(4,510)	—
Other	(7,675)	(7,804)	7,311
Deferred Income Tax Expense (Benefit)	$17,285	$(1,582)	$17,435

A reconciliation between the statutory and effective tax rates for continuing operations is as follows:

	1990	1989	1988
U.S. Federal statutory rate	34.0%	34.0%	34.0%
State income taxes, net of Federal benefit	3.6	3.4	2.4
Rate reduction	—	—	(2.5)
U.S. tax on international dividend	0.4	0.3	4.2
International rate differential	0.1	(0.9)	(2.6)
Leasing subsidiary	(0.1)	(0.2)	(0.8)
Restructuring charge	—	0.6	—
Other	(1.3)	—	1.6
Effective tax rate	36.7%	37.2%	36.3%

No provisions have been made for possible international withholding and U.S. income taxes payable on the distribution of approximately $120,009 of undistributed earnings which have been or will be reinvested abroad or are expected to be returned to the United States in tax-free distributions. Provisions for taxes have been made for all earnings which the company presently plans to repatriate.

L. Supplementary Earnings Statement Information

	1990	1989	1988
Non-Operating Income:			
Interest income	$25,501	$14,497	$9,666
Settlement of lawsuit	5,695	—	—
Income from leveraged leases	5,273	6,694	8,219
Gain (loss) on sale of property, plant and equipment	1,005	(1,933)	(673)
Other non-operating (expense) income	(2,734)	(2,152)	43
Total	$34,740	$17,106	$17,255
Research and Development	$55,384	$44,720	$46,533
Maintenance and Repairs	47,328	49,572	47,131
Advertising	26,584	25,933	19,586
Rents	22,857	23,238	19,958
Foreign Currency Transaction (Loss) Gain	(1,423)	292	2,343

Schneider and Square D

O. Pension Plans

The company's domestic operations maintain several pension plans, primarily defined benefit pension plans covering substantially all employees for normal retirement benefits at age 65. Defined benefits for salaried employees are based on a final average compensation formula and hourly plans are based on an amount per year of service formula. The company makes annual contributions to the plans in accordance with ERISA and IRS regulations, including amortization of past service cost over the average remaining service life of active employees.

In 1989 the company adopted SFAS No. 87 for its significant international pension plans. For the company's international pension plans that have not adopted SFAS No. 87, the excess of vested benefits over fund assets is insignificant. The company makes annual contributions to the plans in accordance with the laws and regulations of the respective international taxing jurisdictions in which the company operates.

Components of net periodic pension cost for the company's domestic and international pension plans consist of the following:

	1990	1989	1988
Service cost—benefits earned during period	$12,409	$11,039	$9,515
Net deferral and amortization	(42,253)	24,976	(11,621)
Interest on projected benefit obligation	28,547	25,796	25,414
Actual return on plan assets	10,809	(55,795)	(14,388)
Net periodic pension cost	$9,512	$6,016	$8,920

The net periodic pension cost attributable to the company's significant international pension plans was $843 and $1,000 in 1990 and 1989, respectively.

The following tables set forth the company's domestic and international pension plans' funded status and amounts recognized in the company's balance sheet at December 31:

	Overfunded Plans		Underfunded Plans	
	1990	1989	1990	1989
Actuarial present value of benefit obligations:				
Vested employees	$(193,615)	$(194,793)	$(96,325)	$(90,466)
Non-vested employees	(12,169)	(6,073)	(15,407)	(3,251)
Total accumulated benefit obligation	(205,784)	(200,866)	(111,732)	(93,717)
Additional amounts related to projected salary increases	(35,705)	(45,637)	(3,949)	(3,095)
Projected benefit obligation	(241,489)	(246,503)	(115,681)	(96,812)
Fair value of plan assets (primarily common equities and fixed income instruments)	245,953	267,184	75,493	68,884
Projected benefit obligation less than (in excess of) plan assets	4,464	20,681	(40,188)	(27,928)
Unrecognized net (gain) loss	(7,583)	(15,018)	9,451	8,442
Unrecognized prior service cost	(6,374)	(6,934)	17,281	4,673
Unrecognized net liability existing at the date of initial adoption of SFAS No. 87	6,604	1,682	1,378	4,569
(Accrued) Prepaid Pension Cost	$(2,889)	$411	$(12,078)	$(10,244)

The economic assumptions used in determining the actuarial present value of the projected benefit obligation of the domestic plans were:

	1990	1989
Weighted average discount rate	9.0%	8.3%
Rate of increase in future compensation levels	5.3	5.3
Rate of return on plan assets	10.0	10.0

The assumed rates for the company's international plans, which reflect the economic conditions of each plan, generally varied from U.S. rates by 1.0% to 2.0%.

Total pension expense for all plans was $10,914, $8,073, and $12,962 for 1990, 1989, and 1988, respectively. Actuarial assumptions were revised in 1990, 1989 and 1988 principally to update the investment return and rates of pay increase to levels more reflective of current economic conditions. These and other changes increased pension expense in 1990 by approximately $920 and reduced pension expense in 1989 and 1988 by approximately $5,838 and $1,218, respectively.

P. Post-Retirement Benefits

The company provides health plan coverage and life insurance benefits for retired employees of substantially all of its domestic operations. Substantially all of the company's employees may become eligible for these benefits when they retire from active employment with the company. The cost of retiree health coverage is recognized as an expense when claims are paid. The cost of life insurance benefits is recognized as an expense as premiums are paid. These costs totaled $6,165 in 1990, $5,075 in 1989, and $3,982 in 1988.

The Financial Accounting Standards Board has issued Statement of Financial Accounting Standards No. 106, "Employers' Accounting for Post-Retirement Benefits Other Than Pensions." This Statement will require accrual of post-retirement benefits during the years an employee provides services. While the impact of this new standard has not been fully determined, the change will result in significantly greater expense being recognized for these benefits. The company plans to adopt this Statement in 1993.

T. Segment and Geographic Information

The company is engaged in the manufacture and sale of electrical distribution products, systems and services and industrial control products, systems and services, and operates in virtually every major marketing area in the world. Major manufacturing plants are located throughout the United States and in Europe, Latin America, Canada, Australia and Thailand.

The electrical distribution segment primarily consists of the manufacture and sale of products, systems and services used in the distribution of electricity. Distribution equipment is used principally in distributing electricity from the end of transmission lines to points of utilization within residential, commercial, industrial or other types of buildings. Distribution products include industrial molded case circuit breakers, miniature circuit breakers, load centers, safety switches, metering devices, switchboards, panelboards, motor control centers, low and medium voltage switchgear, busways and raceways, dry type transformers and power and cast resin transformers.

The industrial control segment mainly consists of the manufacture and sale of control products, systems and services that control the electricity used in the operation of power utilization devices or processes. Control equipment includes motor starters, contactors, push buttons, adjustable frequency motor controllers and sensors. Other products in this segment include programmable controllers, cell controllers, electronic computerized control and data-gathering systems, uninterruptible power systems, power protection equipment, infrared radiation thermometers and pyrometers and snap dome switches and keyboards.

Substantially all products of the electrical distribution and industrial control segments are marketed through the company's own marketing organization and distributed through a system of strategically located warehouses. The majority of all sales are made directly to authorized electrical distributors who, in turn, market the products to electrical contractors, electrical utilities, large industrial plants and other classes of trade.

Sales between geographic areas and industry segments are based on prices approximating current market values. Net sales to a group of customers under common control, for both industry segments, were $161,015 in 1990, $161,156 in 1989, and, $176,700 in 1988.

Financial information by industry segment for the three years ended December 31, 1990 is summarized as follows:

Industry Segments	1990	1989	1988
Sales			
Electrical Distribution:			
Unaffiliated customers	$1,170,420	$1,117,619	$1,057,359
Intercompany	18,203	13,083	10,484
	1,188,623	1,130,702	1,067,843
Industrial Control:			
Unaffiliated customers	482,899	481,069	440,413
Intercompany	63,919	51,923	49,244
	546,818	532,992	489,657
Eliminations	(82,122)	(65,006)	(59,728)
Consolidated	$1,653,319	$1,598,688	$1,497,772
Operating Earnings			
Electrical Distribution	$152,280	$143,541	$138,229
Industrial Control	26,302	31,614	40,046
Eliminations	(143)	139	944
Consolidated	$178,439	$175,294	$179,219
Identifiable Assets			
Electrical Distribution	$920,781	$755,253	$701,973
Industrial Control	503,079	447,913	418,247
Eliminations	(792)	(646)	(835)
Identifiable Assets of Continuing Operations	$1,423,068	$1,202,520	$1,119,385
Net Assets of Discontinued Operations	36,681	170,065	181,338
Consolidated	$1,459,749	$1,372,585	$1,300,723
Depreciation and Amortization Expense			
Electrical Distribution	$36,688	$29,815	$26,345
Industrial Control	22,612	19,628	18,829
Capital Additions			
Electrical Distribution	$54,763	$50,323	$43,980
Industrial Control	39,125	30,125	27,975

Effective September 30, 1989, the company changed its reportable segments from Electrical Equipment and Electronic Products to Electrical Distribution Products, Systems and Services and Industrial Control Products, Systems and Services.

Financial information by geographic area for the three years ended December 31, 1990, is summarized as follows:

Geographic Areas	1990	1989	1988
Sales			
United States:			
Unaffiliated customers	$1,332,390	$1,321,769	$1,256,009
Intercompany	73,646	62,253	47,479
	1,406,036	1,384,022	1,303,488
Europe:			
Unaffiliated customers	138,836	115,678	105,471
Intercompany	22,617	23,691	25,207
	161,453	139,369	130,678
Latin America:			
Unaffiliated customers	78,867	68,178	53,242
Intercompany	1,300	1,217	1,761
	80,167	69,395	55,003
Other International:			
Unaffiliated customers	103,226	93,063	83,050
Intercompany	447	256	620
	103,673	93,319	83,670
Eliminations	(98,010)	(87,417)	(75,067)
Consolidated	$1,653,319	$1,598,688	$1,497,772
Operating Earnings			
United States	$164,155	$163,202	$156,791
Europe	3,555	212	4,098
Latin America	10,445	12,547	11,212
Other International	650	(463)	3,942
Eliminations	(366)	(204)	3,176
Consolidated	$178,439	$175,294	$179,219
Identifiable Assets			
United States	$1,131,085	$952,865	$883,334
Europe	158,637	120,483	109,297
Latin America	65,847	62,171	62,924
Other International	70,203	69,357	64,886
Eliminations	(2,704)	(2,356)	(1,056)
Identifiable Assets of Continuing Operations	1,423,068	1,202,520	1,119,385
Net Assets of Discontinued			
Operations	36,681	170,065	181,338
Consolidated	$1,459,749	$1,372,585	$1,300,723

(continued)

Schneider and Square D

Schneider and Square D

SELECTED FINANCIAL DATA (continued)

	1990	1989	1988	1987	1986	1985
Summary of Operations						
Net sales	$1,653,319	$1,598,688	$1,497,772	$1,330,784	$1,274,932	$1,223,193
Cost of products sold	1,088,977	1,027,348	979,591	838,749	820,457	787,310
Selling, administrative, and general expenses	385,903	369,726	338,962	287,386	267,066	237,790
Restructuring charge	—	26,320	—	11,192	—	—
Non-operating income	34,740	17,106	17,255	17,590	26,670	14,486
Interest expense	28,760	31,438	22,082	19,699	24,977	21,191
Earnings from continuing operations before income taxes	184,419	160,962	174,392	191,348	189,102	191,388
Provision for income taxes	67,773	59,856	63,310	75,736	85,191	89,465
Earnings from continuing operations	116,646	101,106	111,082	115,612	103,911	101,923
Earnings (loss) from discontinued operations, net of income taxes	4,079	798	7,852	(5,611)	(4,983)	(14,735)
Net earnings	120,725	101,904	118,934	110,001	98,928	87,188
Financial Information						
Working capital	$ 389,503	$ 193,758	$ 178,399	$ 192,693	$ 204,083	$ 202,076
Property, plant and equipment—at cost	799,367	736,739	673,946	630,754	606,757	570,538
Total assets	1,459,749	1,372,585	1,300,723	1,252,819	1,178,826	1,118,473
Long-term debt	244,820	123,420	135,467	141,085	166,389	201,028
Common shareholders' equity	603,594	556,123	636,029	679,711	670,789	606,139
Capital additions	93,888	80,448	71,955	35,356	71,617	61,880
Depreciation and amortization	59,300	49,443	45,174	42,277	38,548	32,430
Share Data						
Earnings per common share:						
Primary:						
Continuing operations	$4.76	$3.95	$4.15	$4.01	$3.59	$3.53
Discontinued operations	.18	.03	.29	(.19)	(.17)	(.51)
Net earnings	4.94	3.98	4.44	3.82	3.42	3.02
Fully diluted:						
Continuing operations	4.57	3.88	4.13	3.98	3.56	3.50
Discontinued operations	.16	.03	.29	(.19)	(.17)	(.50)
Net earnings	4.73	3.91	4.42	3.79	3.39	3.00
Cash dividends declared per common share	2.20	2.00	1.94	1.86	1.84	1.84
Common shares outstanding at December 31	22,886	23,489	25,691	27,660	28,966	28,864
Common shareholders' equity per share	$26.37	$23.68	$24.76	$24.57	$23.16	$21.00

SELECTED FINANCIAL DATA (*continued*)

	1990	1989	1988	1987	1986	1985
Key Financial Relationships						
Gross profit	34.1%	35.7%	34.6%	37.0%	35.6%	35.6%
Current ratio	2.0:1%	1.4:1%	1.5:1%	1.7:1%	1.9:1%	1.8:1%
Average total debt to average total equity	66.2%	55.7%	38.2%	29.0%	39.2%	40.5%
Average long-term debt to average capital[3]	23.3%	13.6%	15.6%	16.7%	22.0%	19.8%

EXHIBIT 3

Schneider Financial Statements and Accounting Policies

STATEMENT OF INCOME

(in FF million for the year ended December 31)	1990	1989	1988
Net sales	**49,884**	**45,127**	**40,493**
Cost of goods sold, personnel and administrative expenses	(44,978)	(41,008)	(36,766)
Depreciation and amortization	(1,565)	(1,166)	(1,272)
Operating expenses	**(46,543)**	**(42,174)**	**(38,038)**
Operating income	**3,341**	**2,953**	**2,455**
Interest expense – net	(832)	(757)	(182)
Income before non-recurring items, amortization of goodwill, taxes and minority interest	**2,509**	**2,196**	**2,273**
Non-recurring items:			
Gains on disposition of assets – net	419	550	484
Other non-recurring income and expense – net	(367)	(343)	(642)
Income before taxes, employee profit-sharing, amortization of goodwill and minority interests	**2,561**	**2,403**	**2,115**
Employee profit-sharing	(158)	(130)	(126)
Income taxes	(802)	(912)	(701)
Net income of fully consolidated companies before amortization of goodwill	**1,601**	**1,361**	**1,288**
Amortization of goodwill	(236)	(235)	(345)
Net income of fully consolidated companies	**1,365**	**1,126**	**943**
Group's share of income of companies accounted for by the equity method	**4**	**17**	**(53)**
Minority interests	(445)	(266)	(330)
Net income (Schneider SA share)	**924**	**877**	**560**
Net income (Schneider SA share) per share – in FF 48.85	62.96	63.06	
Net income (Schneider SA share) per share after dilution – in FF	61.65	60.53	N/A

3. All financial data for the periods prior to 1990 have been restated for discontinued operations.

All financial data for the periods prior to 1988 have been restated for the consolidation of a majority-owned subsidiary.

Schneider and Square D

BALANCE SHEET

(in FF million for the year ended December 31)	1990	1989	1988
ASSETS			
Current Assets			
Cash and equivalents	1,841.3	3,400.3	1,579.6
Marketable securities	3,020.9	1,924.3	1,243.7
Accounts receivable – trade	14,597.4	14,987.3	13,998.5
Other receivables and prepaid expenses	4,738.1	3,876.5	4,054.9
Deferred taxes	407.5	290.2	236.9
Inventories and work in process	7,712.6	7,159.0	29,715.3
Total current assets	**32,317.8**	**31,637.6**	**50,828.9**
Non-Current Assets			
Property, plant and equipment	14,293.9	13,107.5	12,019.7
Accumulated depreciation	(6,691.5)	(6,365.6)	(6,409.5)
Property, plant and equipment – net	7,602.4	6,741.9	5,610.2
Investments accounted for by the equity method	175.9	135.7	244.9
Other equity investments	1,727.9	571.3	684.6
Other investments	573.0	618.3	909.8
Total investments	2,476.8	1,325.3	1,839.3
Intangible assets – net	147.5	153.5	115.0
Goodwill – net	7,032.8	6,087.8	5,596.8
Total non-current assets	**17,259.5**	**14,308.5**	**13,161.3**
Total assets	**49,577.3**	**45,946.1**	**63,990.2**
LIABILITIES AND SHAREHOLDERS' EQUITY			
Current Liabilities			
Accounts payable – trade	9,867.9	9,614.6	8,440.8
Taxes and benefits payable	4,822.5	4,795.8	3,748.4
Other payables and accrued liabilities	5,230.4	4,332.2	3,405.5
Short-term debt	3,120.5	3,165.8	3,081.3
Customer prepayments	2,505.9	3,848.3	27,606.1
Total current liabilities	**25,547.2**	**25,756.7**	**46,282.1**
Long-term debt	9,958.4	7,345.9	7,712.1
Provisions for contingencies	3,942.6	3,890.0	3,758.8
Shareholder's Equity			
Capital stock	1,414.4	1,397.2	1,146.3
Retained earnings	6,091.1	5,344.6	3,046.6
Total Shareholders' Equity	**7,505.5**	**6,741.8**	**4,192.9**
Minority interests	2,623.6	2,211.7	2,044.3
Total shareholders' equity and minority interests	**10,129.1**	**8,953.5**	**6,237.2**
Total liabilities and shareholders' equity	**49,577.3**	**45,946.1**	**63,990.2**

STATEMENT OF CASH FLOWS

(in FF million for the year ended December 31)	1990	1989
I. Operating activities		
Net income of fully consolidated companies	1,368.5	1,143.7
Depreciation, amortization and provisions, net of recoveries	2,164.0	2,283.0
(Gains) on disposals of assets	(418.7)	(550.1)
Others	(0.8)	(28.7)
Net cash provided by operating activities before changes in operating assets and liabilities	**3,113.0**	**2,847.9**
Decrease (increase) in accounts receivable	(944.4)	1,170.4
Inventories and work in process	675.4	(1,708.6)
Increase (decrease) in accounts payable	578.7	(16.3)
Other current assets and liabilities	(1,681.4)	736.0
Net change in operating assets and liabilities	**(1,371.7)**	**181.5**
Net cash provided by operating activities	**1,741.3**	**3,029.4**
II. Investing activities		
Disposals of fixed assets	712.9	1,394.8
Purchases of property, plant and equipment and intangible assets	(2,589.5)	(2,154.3)
Financial investments	(2,788.2)	(1,068.8)
Other long-term investments	125.5	13.4
Net cash used in investing activities	**(4,539.3)**	
(1,814.9)		
III. Financing activities		
Reduction in long-term debt	(1,626.4)	(3,045.2)
New borrowings	1,508.7	2,435.1
Convertible bonds issued	2,655.6	634.7
Common stock issued	71.9	1,877.0
Dividends paid:		
Schneider SA shareholders	(174.6)	(126.1)
Minority interests	(116.5)	(69.7)
Net cash provided by financing activities	**2,318.7**	**1,705.8**
IV. Net effect of exchange rate and other changes	**13.8**	**178.5**
Net increase (decrease) in cash and cash equivalents (I + II + III + IV)	**(465.5)**	**3,098.8**
Cash and cash equivalents at beginning of year	**3,424.9**	**326.1**
at end of year	**2,959.4**	**3,424.9**

The following notes are an integral part of these financial statements.

Schneider and Square D

SELECTED NOTES TO FINANCIAL STATEMENTS

1. Accounting Principles

The consolidated financial statements of Schneider SA have been prepared in accordance with French generally accepted accounting principles and with the international accounting principles recommended by the International Accounting Standards Committee (I.A.S.C.). The differences between these principles and U.S. GAAP are explained in Note l.m), below.

The financial statements of consolidated subsidiaries, which are prepared in accordance with accounting principles generally accepted in the countries in which they operate, have been restated in accordance with the principles applied by the Group.

a) Consolidation principles

All significant companies that are controlled directly or indirectly by Schneider SA have been fully consolidated.

Companies over which Schneider SA exercises significant influence have been accounted for by the equity method.

As an exception to the above principles, Banque Morhange, in which the Group holds a majority interest but whose operations are not material in relation to the Group as a whole, has also been consolidated by the equity method.

In accordance with French generally accepted accounting principles, joint ventures in which the Group is the managing partner are fully consolidated by Schneider SA, after deducting the other partners' share in the income or loss of the joint venture. In cases where the Group is not the managing shareholder, only Schneider SA's share of the income or loss is accounted for, except for two contracts which are consolidated by the proportional method.

Goodwill is amortized out of income over a maximum of forty years based on estimated useful life.

b) Translation of the financial statements of foreign subsidiaries

The financial statements of foreign subsidiaries are translated into French francs as follows:

—Assets and liabilities are translated at year-end exchange rates;

—Income statement and cash flow items are translated at average exchange rates.

Differences arising on translation are recorded under shareholders' equity.

c) Translation of foreign currency transactions

With the exception of the transactions described below, foreign currency debts and receivables are translated into French francs at year-end exchange rates. As allowed under French law, translation differences are recorded in the income statement under interest income and expense.

Exchange gains as well as carrybacks and carryforwards related to forward purchases and sales of foreign currency used to hedge the Group's trading commitments are deferred and recognized at the same time as the gain or loss on the underlying transaction.

Gains and losses on unhedged forward currency transactions are credited or charged to income. The gain or loss corresponds to the difference between the forward exchange rate provided for in the contract and the exchange rate prevailing at year end for purchases and sales made in the same currency and according to the same term.

In cases where a speculative currency position is considered to exist due to the future interest on fixed to variable currency swaps, the interest is discounted on the basis of the fixed rate and stated at the exchange rate prevailing at year end for cash transactions. The translation difference is credited or charged to income.

d) Financial instruments based on exchange and interest rates

The Group uses financial instruments based on exchange and interest rates. The methods used to account for these instruments are described above.

e) Long-term contracts

Income from long-term contracts is recognized by the percentage-of-completion method, based on the financial status of the contract. Probable losses upon completion of a given contract are provided for in full as soon as they become known. The cost of work in process includes costs relating directly to the contracts and a percentage of overheads.

The estimated cost of the remaining work on contracts expected to generate a loss does not take account of any income from claims, except where such claims have been accepted by the customer and the latter has no major financing problems. Contracts in progress are therefore stated at the lower of cost or realizable value.

In accordance with the logic underlying the percentage-of-completion method, work in process is matched with customer prepayments received upon presentation of a schedule of work performed to date. However, prepayments in connection with the work in process include:

—Prepayments to finance production;

—Prepayments for work in process on contracts which are still in the early stages and for which it is not possible to make any estimate of probable income or losses; and

—Contracts scheduled to last less than twelve months.

f) Research and development expenditures

Internally-financed research and development expenditures are charged to income for the period.

g) Deferred taxes

Deferred taxes corresponding to timing differences between the recognition of income and expenses in the consolidated financial statements and for tax purposes are accounted for by the liability method.

h) Provisions for retirement bonuses

The Group's liability for retirement bonuses is calculated taking into account projected future compensation levels. The method used is in accordance with the Financial Accounting Standards Board (FASB) Statement of Financial Accounting Standards No. 87.

Part of the Group's liability for retirement bonuses is provided for and part is funded by an insured plan. The provisions are calculated for all eligible employees and the same discount and indexation rates are used for all Group companies that have adopted this method. For the insured plan, the current value of the plan assets has been calculated and provision has been made for any unfunded liability.

i) Marketable securities

Almost all marketable securities represent conventional short-term instruments (commercial paper, mutual funds and related securities). They are stated at cost. In the case of bonds and other debt instruments, cost includes accrued interest.

j) Inventories and work in process

Inventories and work in process are stated at weighted average cost. Any difference between cost and realizable value is provided for.

The cost of work in process, semi-finished and finished products includes direct materials and labor costs, sub-contracting costs incurred up to the balance sheet date and a percentage of production overheads

k) Property, plant and equipment

Land, buildings and equipment are stated at cost. Assets held at the time of a legal revaluation are stated at revalued cost. An equivalent amount is recorded in shareholders' equity, under retained earnings or revaluation reserve, and is written back to income in an amount matching the corresponding depreciation and disposals, so that the revaluation has no impact on income.

In the case of subsidiaries operating in high-inflation countries, the impact of legal revaluations is eliminated on consolidation and the resulting translation differences are recorded in retained earnings.

Property, plant and equipment is depreciated on a straight-line basis over the estimated useful lives of the assets.

Property, plant and equipment acquired under a capital lease is capitalized on the basis of the cost of the asset concerned and depreciated in accordance with the above principles. An obligation in the same amount is recorded on the liabilities side of the balance sheet.

l) Non-consolidated equity investments and other investments

Non-consolidated equity investments and other investments are stated at cost, except for investments held at the time of the 1977 legal revaluation. Each year, the carrying value is compared to fair value and any difference is provided for. Fair value is determined by reference to the Group's share in the underlying net assets, the expected future profitability and business prospects of the investee company, and – in the case of listed securities – the market value of the stock.

m) Differences between Schneider SA accounting principles and U.S. GAAP

The main differences between the accounting principles described above and U.S. GAAP are as follows:

Write-ups

As mentioned in Note I.k. above, the Company has performed certain write-ups which are contrary to U.S. GAAP. The write-ups have no impact on income but do affect shareholders' equity.

Schneider and Square D

Consolidation

As indicated in Note a, Banque Morhange, whose operations are not material in relation to the Group as a whole, has been accounted for by the equity method.

Provisions for contingencies

In U.S. GAAP, the part of these provisions related to operating cycles would be considered as accrued liabilities.

Customer prepayments

In the consolidated financial statements, customer prepayments are recorded as a separate component of current liabilities. Under U.S. GAAP, work in process in an amount equal to the cost of the work performed for which no income or loss has been recognized.

Deferred taxes

In December 1987, the FASB issued a new standard concerning the accounting treatment of deferred taxes. The application of this standard is not compulsory in 1990. The Company has not yet decided the date at which it will start applying this standard and, in view of the complexity of the new rules, has not determined the impact that its application would have had on the 1990 financial statements as presented.

Non-recurring income and expense

Non-recurring income and expense includes items that the Company considers to be non-recurring but that would be treated as operating income and expense under U.S. GAAP. In addition, under U.S. GAAP, the amortization of goodwill would have been accounted for under income from continuing operations.

These reclassifications would have the following impact on income from continuing operations:

(in FF million)	1990	1989
Income from continuing operations, before tax	2,509	2,196
Non-recurring income other than extraordinary items	(237)	85
Amortization of goodwill	(236)	(235)
Income from continuing operations, before tax, according to U.S. GAAP	2,036	2,046

EXHIBIT 4

Square D Common Stock Purchase Plan

The firm's Articles of Incorporation were modified in August 1988 as follows:

The Company adopted a new Share Purchase Rights Plan and declared a dividend distribution of one new common purchase right on each outstanding share of Square D common stock. The rights are exercisable only if someone acquires 20% or more of the company's common stock or announces a tender offer. At any time a person or group acquires 20% or more of the company's outstanding common stock and prior to that person acquiring 50% or more of the company's common stock, the company may exchange the rights (other than rights owned by such 20% or greater shareholder) in whole or in part for one share of common stock per right. If a person or group acquires 20% or more of the common stock, or certain events occur, each right not owned by the 20% or greater shareholder becomes exercisable for the number of shares of the company having a market value of twice the exercise price of the right. If the company is acquired in a merger or other business combination transaction or 50% or more of its assets or earning power are sold at any time after the rights become exercisable, the rights entitle a holder to buy a number of shares of common stock of the acquiring company having a market value of twice the exercise price of each right.

Schneider and Square D

EXHIBIT 5

Selected Square D Stock Data for the Fourth Quarter 1990[a]

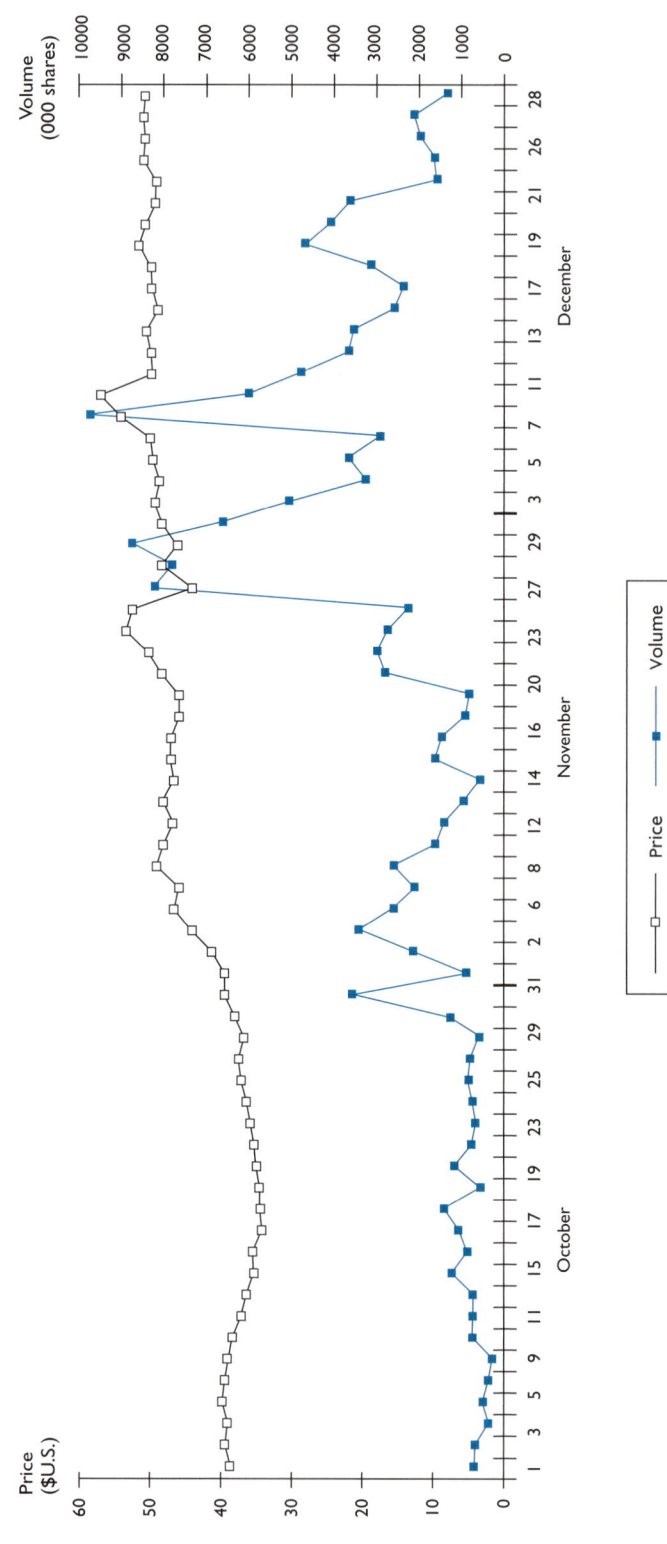

a. In late 1990, approximately 23 million shares were outstanding.

EXHIBIT 6

Valuation Data for Square D

Square D equity beta	0.95
Moody's corporate bond average yield in February 1991 for major ratings:	
Aaa	8.83%
Aa	9.16%
A	9.38%
Ba	10.07%
Prime rate in February 1991	8.8%
Treasury bills rates in February 1991 (3 months)	6.0%
Government 30-year treasuries rates in February 1991	8.25%
Square D commercial paper rating in February 1991	
(on a scale from P3 to P1, P1 being the best rating)	P1
Square D corporate bonds rating in February 1991	Aa3
U.S. federal statutory tax rate in 1990	34.0%
State income tax rate, net of federal benefit in 1990	3.6%

Chapter 12
Communication and Governance

Corporate governance has become an increasingly important issue in capital markets throughout the world following financial market meltdowns in Asia and the U.S. These market collapses exposed problems of accounting misstatements and lack of corporate transparency, as well as governance problems and conflicts of interest among the intermediaries charged with monitoring management and corporate disclosures.

The breakdowns have increased the challenge for managers in communicating credibly with skeptical outside investors, making it more difficult for new (and in some cases even established) firms to raise capital. Financial reports, the traditional platform for management to communicate with investors, were viewed with increased skepticism following a number of widely publicized audit failures and the demise of Arthur Andersen.

The market crashes have also raised questions about improving the quality of governance by information and financial intermediaries. New regulations, such as the Sarbanes-Oxley Act in the U.S., attempt to increase accountability and financial competence for audit committees and external auditors, who are charged with reviewing the financial reporting and disclosure process, and accountability for the CEO and CFO who are required to certify the validity of both financial statements and internal controls.

This chapter discusses how many of the financial analysis tools developed in Chapters 2 through 8 can be used by managers to develop a coherent disclosure strategy, and by corporate board members and external auditors to improve the quality of their work. The following types of questions are dealt with:

- Managers ask: Is our current communication policy effective in helping investors understand the firm's business strategy and expected future performance, thereby ensuring that our stock price is not seriously over- or undervalued?
- Audit committee members ask: What are the firm's key business risks? Are they reflected appropriately in the financial statements? How is management communicating on important risks that cannot be reflected in the financial statements? Is information on the firm's performance as presented to the board consistent with that provided to investors in the financial report and firm disclosures?
- External auditors ask: What are the firm's key business risks, and how are they reflected in the financial statements? Where should we focus our audit tests? Is our assessment of the firm's performance consistent with that of external investors and analysts? If not, are we overlooking something, or is management misrepresenting the firm's true performance in disclosures?

Throughout this book we have focused primarily on showing how financial statement data can be helpful for analysts and outside investors in making a variety of decisions. In this chapter we change our emphasis and focus primarily on management and governance agents. Of course an understanding of the management communication process and corporate governance is also important for security analysts and investors. The approach taken here, however, is more germane to insiders since most of the types of analyses we discuss are not available to outsiders.

GOVERNANCE OVERVIEW

As we discuss throughout this book, outside investors require access to reliable information on firm performance, both to value their debt and equity claims and to monitor the performance of management. When investors agree to provide capital to the firm, they require that managers provide information on their company's performance and future plans.

However, left to their own devices, managers are likely to paint a rosy picture of the firm's performance in their disclosures. There are three reasons for manager optimism in reporting. First, most managers are genuinely positive about their firms' prospects, leading them to unwittingly emphasize the positive and downplay the negative.

A second reason for management optimism in reporting arises because firm disclosures play an important role in mitigating "agency" problems between managers and investors.[1] Investors use firm disclosures to judge whether managers have either run the firm in investors' best interests or abused their authority and control over firm resources. Reporting consistently poor earnings increases the likelihood that top management will be replaced, either by the board of directors or by an acquirer who takes over the firm to improve its management.[2] Of course, managers are aware of this and have incentives to show positive performance.

Finally, managers are also likely to make optimistic disclosures prior to issuing new equity. Recent evidence indicates that entrepreneurs tend to take their firms public after disclosure of strong reported, but frequently unsustainable, earnings performance. Also, seasoned equity offers typically follow strong, but again unsustainable, stock and earnings performance. The strong earnings performance prior to IPOs and seasoned offers appears to be at least partially due to earnings management.[3] Rational outside investors recognize management's incentives to manage earnings and inflate expectations prior to a new issue. They respond by discounting the stock, demanding a hefty new issue discount, and in extreme cases refusing to purchase the new stock. This raises the cost of capital and potentially leaves some of the best new ventures and projects unfunded.[4]

As discussed in Chapter 1, financial and information intermediaries help reduce agency and information problems faced by outside investors. These intermediaries evaluate the quality of management representation in the firm's disclosures, provide their own analysis of firms' (and managers') performance, and make investment recommendations and decisions on behalf of investors. As presented in Figure 12-1, these intermediaries include internal governance agents, assurance professionals, information analyzers, and professional investors. The importance of these intermediaries is underscored by the magnitude of the fees that they collectively receive from investors and entrepreneurs.

Internal governance agents, such as corporate boards, are responsible for monitoring a firm's management. Their functions include reviewing business strategy, evaluating and rewarding top management, and assuring the flow of credible information to external parties. Assurance professionals, such as external auditors, enhance the credibility of financial information prepared by managers. Information analyzers, such as financial analysts and ratings agencies, are responsible for gathering and analyzing

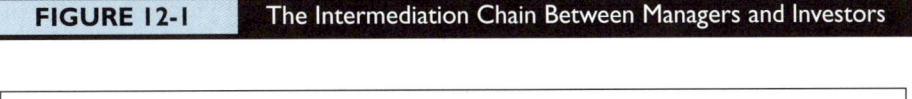

FIGURE 12-1   The Intermediation Chain Between Managers and Investors

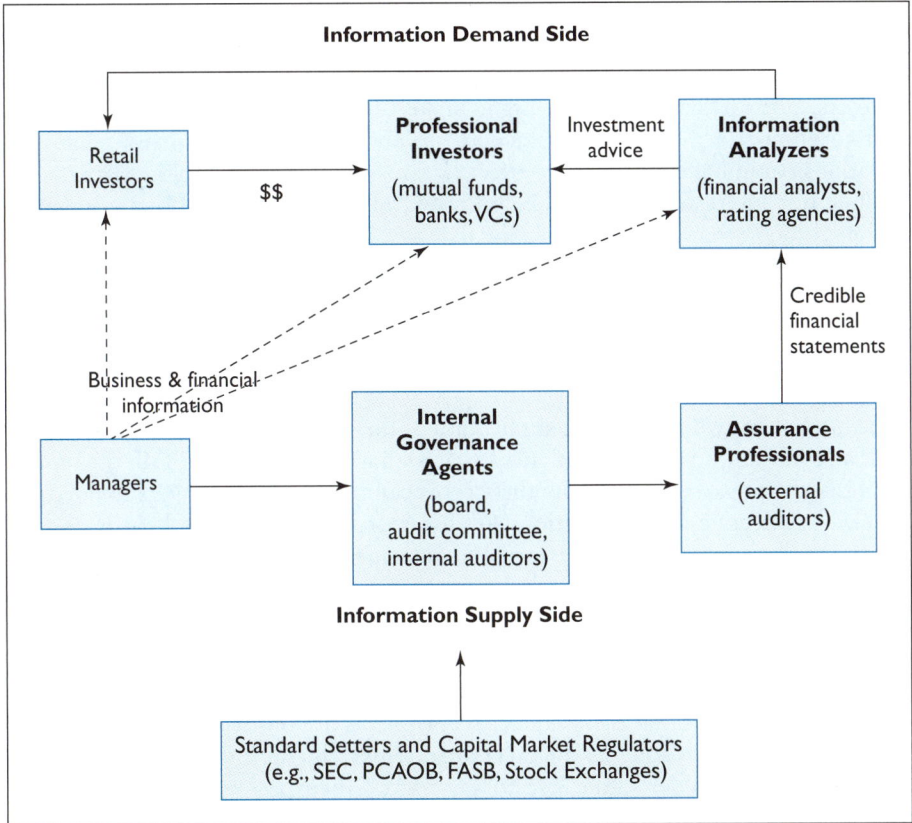

information to provide performance forecasts and investment recommendations to both professional and retail individual investors. Finally, professional investors (such as banks, investment advisors, private equity firms, hedge funds, mutual funds, insurance companies, and venture capital firms) make investment decisions on behalf of dispersed investors. They are therefore responsible for valuing and selecting investment opportunities in the economy.

In this framework, management, internal governance agents, and assurance professionals are charged with supplying information. The demand for information comes from individual and professional investors and information analyzers. Both the supply and demand sides are governed by a variety of regulatory institutions. These include public regulators, such as the Securities and Exchange Commission (SEC), the Public Company Accounting Oversight Board (PCAOB), and bank regulators, as well as private sector bodies such as the Financial Accounting Standards Board (FASB), the American Institute of Certified Public Accountants (AICPA), and stock exchanges.

The level and quality of information and residual information and agency problems in capital markets are determined by the organizational design of these intermediaries and regulatory institutions. Key organizational design questions include: What are the optimal incentive schemes for rewarding top managers? What should be the composition and charter of corporate boards? Should auditors assure that financial reports comply with accounting standards or represent a firm's underlying economics? Should there be detailed accounting standards or a few broad accounting principles? What should be the organizational form and business scope of auditors and analysts? What incentive schemes should be used for professional investors to align their interests with individual investors?

A variety of economic and institutional factors are likely to influence the answers to these design questions. Examples include the ability to write and enforce optimal contracts, proprietary costs that might make disclosure costly for investors, and regulatory imperfections. The spectacular rise and fall of Enron suggests that these limitations could have a first-order effect on the functioning of capital markets.

While it is interesting to speculate on how to improve the functioning of capital markets through changes in organizational design, that issue goes beyond the scope of this chapter. Instead, we discuss how the financial analysis tools developed in Chapters 2 through 8 can be used to improve the performance of some of the information intermediaries who have been widely criticized following revelations of financial reporting fraud and misstatements at companies such as Enron, WorldCom, Tyco, Xerox, Global Crossing, and Lucent.[5]

We have already discussed the application of financial analysis tools to equity and credit analysts and to professional investors in Chapters 9 through 11. In the remainder of this chapter, we discuss how these tools can be used by managers to develop a strategy for effective communication with investors, by members of boards of directors and audit committees in overseeing management and the audit process, and by audit professionals.

MANAGEMENT COMMUNICATION WITH INVESTORS

Some managers argue that communication problems are not worth worrying about. They maintain that as long as managers make investment and operating decisions that enhance shareholder value, investors will value their performance and the firm's stock accordingly. While this is true in the long run, since all information is eventually public, it may not hold in the short or even medium term. If investors do not have access to the same information as management, they will probably find it difficult to value new and innovative investments. In an efficient capital market, they will not consistently over- or undervalue these new investments, but their valuations will tend to be noisy. This can make stock prices relatively noisy, leading management at various times to consider their firms to be either seriously over- or undervalued.

Does it matter if a firm's stock is over- or undervalued for a period? Most managers would prefer to not have their stock undervalued, since it makes it more costly to raise new financing. They may also worry that undervaluation is likely to increase the chance of a takeover by a hostile acquirer, with an accompanying reduction in their job security. Managers of firms that are overvalued may also be concerned about the market's assessment, since they are legally liable for failing to disclose information relevant to investors.[6] They may therefore not wish to see their stock seriously overvalued, even though overvaluation provides opportunities to issue new equity at favorable rates.

A Word of Caution

As noted above, it is natural that many managers believe that firms are undervalued by the capital market. This frequently occurs because it is difficult for managers to be objective about their company's future performance. After all, it is part of their job to sell the company to new employees, customers, suppliers, and investors. In addition, forecasting the firm's future performance objectively requires them to judge their own capabilities as managers. Thus, many managers may argue that investors are uninformed and that their firm is undervalued. Only some can back that up with solid evidence.

If management decides that the firm does face a genuine information problem, it can begin to consider whether and how this could be redressed. Is the problem potentially serious enough that it is worth doing something to alter investors' perceptions? Or is the problem likely to resolve itself within a short period? Does the firm have plans to raise new equity or to use equity to acquire another company? Is management's job security threatened? As we discuss below, management has a wide range of options in this situation.

Key Analysis Questions

We recommend that before jumping to the conclusion that their firms are under-valued, managers should analyze their firms' performance and compare their own forecasts of future performance with those of analysts, using the following approach:

- *Is there a significant difference between internal management forecasts of future earnings and cash flows and those of outside analysts?*
- *Do any differences between managers' and analysts' forecasts arise because of different expectations about economy-wide performance?* Managers may understand their own businesses better than analysts, but they may not be any better at forecasting macroeconomic conditions.
- *Can managers identify any factors that might explain a difference between analysts' and managers' forecasts of future performance?* For example, are analysts unaware of positive new R&D results, do they have different information about customer responses to new products and marketing campaigns, etc.? These types of differences could indicate that the firm faces an information problem.

Example: Communication Issues for FPIC Insurance Group

In 1999 FPIC Insurance Group Inc. was the largest provider of liability insurance for doctors and hospitals in Florida. In the period 1996 to 1998, FPIC reported stable returns on equity of 17 percent, average growth in revenues, net income, and book equity of 25 percent. On December 31, 1998, the firm had a book value per share of $15.85, a price-to-book value of 2.23, a price to earnings multiple of 15.9, and an equity beta of 1.57.

In August 1999, the firm's stock price declined from $45.25 to $14.25. The stock decline began on August 10, the day the company reported a 48 percent jump in second-quarter profits to $7.4 million. The earnings increase was in part attributable to FPIC's Florida Physicians unit releasing $8.1 million in reserves it had set aside against future claims, compared with $4 million in the year-ago quarter. In addition, the company reported higher-than-expected claims in a health insurance plan offered to Florida Dental Association members.

Reuters reported that the stock price decline reflected investors' concern about the quality of the firm's earnings. In response, FPIC spokeswoman Amy D. Ryan stated, "As far as we're concerned, we had a great quarter." The company's chief operating officer, John Byers, argued that the company's decision to release the unit's reserves was normal business practice and based on its expectations of future claims. In response to the higher than expected dental claims, the company announced that it had increased its rates for this insurance.

The sharp decline in its price raises questions about the valuation of the company's stock. On September 9, 1999, the price-to-book ratio was less than 1, and the price-to-earnings multiple was 6.0. The market, therefore, expected that the company would generate a return on equity somewhat lower than its cost of capital. FPIC's management appeared to be puzzled by the sharp drop in price and argued that the market was undervaluing the firm. However, before reaching this conclusion, a number of questions need to be answered:

- Was the firm previously overvalued? If so, what forces were behind the market's high valuation of the company? Had management been painting too rosy a picture for the company's future in its meetings with analysts?
- What events explain the company's sudden drop in stock value? As noted above, the primary question for analysts was the quality of the firm's earnings. However, management needed to have a deeper understanding of these issues.
- If management believed that the firm was actually undervalued, what options were available to correct the market's view of the company?

COMMUNICATION THROUGH FINANCIAL REPORTING

Financial reports are the most popular format for management communication. Below we discuss the role of financial reporting as a means of investor communication, the institutions that make accounting information credible, and the situations in which the reporting is likely to be ineffective.

Accounting as a Means of Management Communication

As we discussed in Chapters 3 and 4, financial reports are an important medium for management communication with external investors. Reports provide investors with an explanation of how their money has been invested, a summary of the performance of those investments, and a discussion of how current performance fits within the firm's overall philosophy and strategy.

Accounting reports not only provide a record of past transactions but also reflect management estimates and forecasts of the future. For example, they include estimates of bad debts, forecasts of the lives of tangible assets, and implicit forecasts that outlays will generate future cash flow benefits that exceed their cost. Since management is likely to be in a position to make forecasts of these future events that are more accurate than those of external investors, financial reports are a potentially useful way of communicating with investors. However, as discussed, investors are also likely to be skeptical of reports prepared by management. The Sarbanes-Oxley Act requires the CEO and CFO to certify that the financials fairly represent the financial performance of the company and that internal controls are adequate to support those financial statements. This requirement increases the accountability of senior management and mitigates some of the investors' skepticism.

Factors That Increase the Credibility of Accounting Communication

A number of mechanisms mitigate conflicts of interest in financial reporting and increase the credibility of accounting information that is communicated to stockholders. These include accounting standards, auditing, monitoring of management by financial analysts, and management reputation.

Accounting Standards and Auditing

Accounting standards, such as those promulgated by the FASB and the SEC in the U.S., provide guidelines for managers on how to make accounting decisions and provide outside investors with a way of interpreting these decisions. Uniform accounting standards attempt to reduce managers' ability to record similar economic transactions in different ways, either over time or across firms. Compliance with these standards is enforced by external auditors who attempt to ensure that managers' estimates are reasonable. Auditors, therefore, reduce the likelihood of earnings management.

Monitoring by Financial Analysts

Financial intermediaries such as analysts also limit management's ability to manage earnings. Financial analysts specialize in developing firm- and industry-specific knowledge, enabling them to assess the quality of a firm's reported numbers and to make any necessary adjustments. Analysts evaluate the appropriateness of management's forecasts implicit in accounting method choices and reported accruals. This requires a thorough understanding of the firm's business and the relevant accounting rules used in the preparation of its financial reports. Superior analysts adjust reported accrual numbers, if necessary, to reflect economic reality, perhaps by using the cash flow statement and the footnote disclosures.

Analysts' business and technical expertise as well as their legal liability and incentives differ from those of auditors. Consequently, analyst reports can provide information to investors on whether the firm's accounting decisions are appropriate or whether managers are overstating the firm's economic performance to protect their jobs.[7]

Management Reputation

A third factor that can counteract external investors' natural skepticism about financial reporting is management reputation. Managers that expect to have an ongoing relation with external investors and financial intermediaries may be able to build a track record for unbiased financial reporting. By making accounting estimates and judgments that are supported by subsequent performance, managers can demonstrate their competence and reliability to investors and analysts. As a result, managers' future judgments and accounting estimates are more likely to be viewed as credible.

Limitations of Financial Reporting for Investor Communication

While accounting standards, auditing, monitoring of management by financial analysts, and management concerns about its reputation increase the credibility and informativeness of financial reports, these mechanisms are far from perfect. Consequently, there are times when financial reporting breaks down as a means for management to communicate with external investors. These breakdowns can arise when (1) there are no accounting rules to guide practice or the existing rules do not distinguish between poor and successful performers, (2) auditors and analysts do not have the expertise to judge new products or business opportunities, or (3) management faces credibility problems.

Accounting Rule Limitations

Despite the rapid increase in new accounting standards, accounting rules frequently do not distinguish between good and poor performers. For example, current accounting rules do not permit managers to show on their balance sheets in a timely fashion the benefits of investments in quality improvements, human resource development programs, research and development (with the exception of software development costs), and customer service.

Some of the problems with accounting standards arise because it takes time for standard setters to develop appropriate standards for many new types of economic transactions. Other difficulties arise because standards are the result of compromises between different interest groups (e.g., auditors, investors, corporate managers, and regulators).

Auditor and Analyst Limitations

While auditors and analysts have access to proprietary information, they do not have the same understanding of the firm's business as managers. The discrepancy between managers' and auditors'/analysts' business assessments is likely to be most severe for firms with distinctive business strategies, or firms that operate in emerging industries. In addition, auditors' decisions in these circumstances are likely to be dominated by concerns about legal liability, hampering management's ability to use financial reports to communicate effectively with investors.

Finally, conflicts of interest faced by auditors and analysts make their analysis imperfect. Conflicts can potentially induce auditors to side with management to retain the firm as an audit client. They can also arise for analysts who provide favorable ratings and research on companies to increase their firm's investment banking business and trading volume among less informed investors. New regulations that increase oversight of audit firms by the Public Company Accounting Oversight Board, and limit the impact of investment banking on financial analysts' incentives, have been put in place to reduce auditor and analyst conflicts of interest.

Management Credibility Problems

There is limited evidence on when management is likely to face credibility problems with investors. However, managers of new firms, firms with volatile earnings, firms in financial distress, and firms with poor track records in communicating with investors should expect to find it difficult to be seen as credible reporters.

If management has a credibility problem, financial reports are likely to be viewed with considerable skepticism. Investors will view financial reporting estimates that increase income as evidence that management is padding earnings. This makes it very difficult for management to use financial reports to communicate positive news about current or future performance.

Example: Accounting Communication for FPIC Insurance Group

FPIC Insurance Group's key financial reporting estimates are for loss reserves for insurance claims using actuarial analyses of its own and other insurers' claims histories. At the end of fiscal year 1998, FPIC reported a loss reserve of $242.3 million. In its 10-K, management warned that "the uncertainties inherent in estimating ultimate losses on the basis of past experience have grown significantly in recent years, principally as a result of judicial expansion of liability standards and expansive interpretations of insurance contracts. These uncertainties may be further affected by, among other factors, changes in the rate of inflation and changes in the propensities of individuals to file claims. The inherent uncertainty of establishing reserves is relatively greater for companies writing long-tail casualty insurance."

To help investors assess its track record in making loss estimates, FPIC is required to provide a detailed breakdown of changes in loss estimates from prior years given actual claim losses. These data indicate that FPIC has actually been quite conservative in prior years' forecasts and has historically incurred fewer losses than it had initially predicted.

It is interesting to note that the area that raised questions for investors about FPIC's record was precisely its conservative estimation of loss reserves and their subsequent reversal. By being conservative, management may have raised questions about its ability to forecast losses reliably in the future, or given investors the impression that it had been managing earnings.

Key Analysis Questions

For management interested in understanding how effectively the firm's financial reports help it communicate with outside investors, the following questions are likely to provide a useful starting point:

- What are the primary business risks that have to be managed effectively? What processes and controls are in place to manage the business risks? How are these risks reflected in the financial statements? For example, credit risks are reflected in the bad debt allowance, and product quality risks are reflected in allowances for product returns and the method of revenue recognition. For these types of risks, what message is the firm sending on the management of these risks through its estimates or choices of accounting methods? Has the firm been unable to deliver on the forecasts underlying these choices? Alternatively, does the market seem to be ignoring the message underlying the firm's financial reporting choices, indicating a lack of credibility?
- How does the firm communicate about important risks that cannot be reflected in accounting estimates or methods? For example, a company's management of its technological innovation risk through research and development is difficult to reflect in its financial statements, and investors will still have questions about this business issue.

COMMUNICATION THROUGH FINANCIAL POLICIES

Managers can also use financing policies to communicate effectively with external investors. One important difference between this type of communication and additional disclosure is that the firm does not provide potentially proprietary information to competitors. Financial policies that are useful in this respect include dividend payouts, stock repurchases, financing choices, and hedging strategies.

Dividend Payout Policies

A firm's dividend payout decisions can provide information to investors on managers' assessments of the firm's future prospects. Dividend payout, defined as cash dividends as a percentage of income available to common shareholders, reflects the extent to which a company pays out profits or retains them for reinvestment. Because paying dividends reduces financial slack and is thus costly, a firm's dividend policy can help management communicate effectively with external investors. Investors recognize that managers will only increase their firm's dividend rate if they anticipate that the payout will not have a serious effect on the firm's future financing options. Thus, the decision to increase dividends can help investors appreciate management's optimism about the firm's future performance and ability to finance growth. This arises because dividend payouts tend to be sticky as managers are reluctant to cut dividend payouts. Managers will only increase dividends when they are confident that they will be able to sustain the increased payout rate in future years. Consequently, investors interpret dividend increases as signals of managers' confidence in the quality of current and future earnings.[8]

As a result, managers in high-growth firms tend to set low dividend payout policies and retain their internally generated funds for reinvestment to minimize any costs from capital market constraints on financing growth options. On the other hand, firms with high and stable operating cash flows and few investment opportunities have high dividend payouts to reduce managers' incentives to reinvest free cash flows in unprofitable ventures.

Stock Repurchases

In some countries, such as the U.S. and the U.K., managers can use stock repurchases to communicate with external investors. Under a stock repurchase, the firm buys back its own stock, either through a purchase on the open market, through a tender offer, or through a negotiated purchase with a large stockholder. Of course a stock repurchase, particularly a tender offer repurchase, is an expensive way for management to communicate with outside investors that they believe that the firm is undervalued. Firms typically pay a hefty premium to acquire their shares in tender offer repurchases, potentially diluting the value of the shares that are not tendered or not accepted for tender. In addition, the fees to investment banks and lawyers, and for share solicitation, are not trivial. Given these costs, it is not surprising that research findings indicate that stock repurchases are effective signals to investors about the level and risk of future earnings performance.[9] Research findings also suggest that firms that use stock repurchases to communicate with investors have accounting assets that are less reflective of firm value and have high general information asymmetry.[10]

Financing Choices

Firms that have problems communicating with external investors may be able to use financing choices to reduce them. For example, a firm that is unwilling to provide proprietary information to help dispersed public investors value it appropriately may be willing to provide such information to a knowledgeable private investor, which can become a large stockholder/creditor, or to a bank that agrees to provide the company with a significant new loan. A firm with credibility problems in financial reporting can also sell stock or issue debt to an informed private investor such as a large customer who has superior information about the quality of its product or service.

Such changes in financing and ownership can mitigate communication problems in two ways. First, the terms of the new financing arrangement and the credibility of the new lender or stockholder can provide investors with information to reassess the value of the firm. Second, the accompanying increased concentration of ownership and the role of large block holders in corporate governance can have a positive effect on valuation. If investors are concerned about management's incentives to increase shareholder value, the presence of a new block shareholder or significant creditor on the board can be reassuring. This type of monitoring arises in leveraged buyouts, startups backed by venture capital firms, and firms with equity partnership investments. In Japanese and German corporations, it may also arise because large banks own both debt and equity and have close working relationships with firms' managers.

Of course, in the extreme, management can decide that the best option for a firm is to no longer operate as a public company. This can be accomplished by a management buyout, where a buyout group (including management) leverages its own investment (using bank or public debt finance), buys the firm, and takes it private. The buyout group hopes to run the firm for several years and then take the company public again, hopefully with a track record of improved performance that enables investors to value the firm more effectively.

Hedging

An important source of mispricing arises if investors are unable to distinguish between unexpected changes in reported earnings due to management performance and transitory shocks that are beyond managers' control (e.g., foreign currency translation gains and losses). Managers can counteract these effects by hedging such "accounting" risks. Even though hedging may be costly, it is valuable if it reduces information problems that potentially lead to misvaluation.

Example: Stock Buybacks at FPIC Insurance Group

On August 12, 1999, FPIC Insurance Group announced that it would immediately begin purchasing shares of its common stock. As many as 429,000 shares were to be repurchased under the program. The company argued that the dramatic drop in its stock price was unwarranted and that its stock was now greatly undervalued. William R. Russell, president and chief executive officer of FPIC stated:

> We believe the recent drop in our stock price may be linked to certain changes in our reserving policy that were described in our earnings release. We believe that our reserving policy is now and has always been appropriate. We believe that the market has overreacted and that FPIC continues to be an excellent long-term investment. Our repurchases . . . reflect our commitment to enhance shareholder value. (Reuters, August 12, 1999)

The repurchase temporarily arrested FPIC's stock price slide. The price recovered from $21 to around $26 during the period surrounding the announcement. However this effect was temporary, and the price subsequently fell further to $14.25. On November 9, 1999, with the stock trading at $15.75, the Board of Directors approved an additional stock buyback program, authorizing the repurchase of an additional 500,000 shares. The announcement, which came in conjunction with the release of third quarter earnings, received a favorable market reaction, and the stock closed the day at $17.31, a gain of almost 10 percent.

Key Analysis Questions

For management considering whether to use financing policies to communicate more effectively with investors, the following questions are likely to provide a useful starting point for analysis:

- Have other potentially less costly actions, such as expanded disclosure or accounting communication, been considered? If not, would these alternatives provide a lower cost means of communication? Alternatively, if management is concerned about providing proprietary

> information to competitors, or has low credibility, these options may not be effective.
> - Does the firm have sufficient free cash flow to be able to implement a share repurchase program or to increase dividends? If the firm has excess cash available today but expects to be constrained in the future, a stock repurchase may be more effective. Alternatively, if management expects to have some excess cash available each year, a dividend increase may be in order.
> - Is the firm cash constrained and unable to increase disclosure for proprietary reasons? If so, management may want to consider changing the mix of owners as a way of indicating to investors that another informed outsider is bullish on the company. Of course, another possibility is for management itself to increase its stake in the company.

ALTERNATE FORMS OF INVESTOR COMMUNICATION

Given the limitations of accounting standards, auditing, and monitoring by financial analysts, as well as the reporting credibility problems faced by management, firms that wish to communicate effectively with external investors are often forced to use alternative methods. We discuss two additional ways that managers can communicate with external investors and analysts below.

Analyst Meetings

One popular way for managers to help mitigate communication problems is to meet regularly with financial analysts that follow the firm. At these meetings, management will field questions about the firm's current financial performance and discuss its future business plans. In addition to holding analyst meetings, many firms appoint a director of public relations, who provides further regular contact with analysts seeking more information on the firm.

In the last ten years, conference calls have become a popular forum for management to communicate with financial analysts. Recent research finds that firms are more likely to host calls if they are in industries where financial statement data fail to capture key business fundamentals on a timely basis.[11] In addition, conference calls themselves appear to provide new information to analysts about a firm's performance and future prospects.[12] Smaller and less heavily traded firms in particular benefit from initiating investor conference calls.[13]

While firms continue to meet with analysts, new SEC rules, called Regulation Fair Disclosure (or Reg FD), have changed the nature of these interactions. Under these new rules, which became effective in the U.S. in October 2000, firms that provide material nonpublic information to security analysts or professional investors must simultaneously (or promptly thereafter) disclose the information to the public. While Reg FD has reduced the information that managers disclose in private meetings, recent research shows that the regulation has enhanced the conference call's ability to improve analyst forecast accuracy and consensus by eliminating selective disclosure.[14]

Voluntary Disclosure

Another way for managers to improve the credibility of their financial reporting is through voluntary disclosure. Accounting rules usually prescribe minimum disclosure requirements, but they do not restrict managers from voluntarily providing additional information. These could include an articulation of the company's long-term strategy, specification of nonfinancial leading indicators that are useful in judging the effectiveness of the strategy implementation, explanation of the relation between the leading indicators and future profits, and forecasts of future performance. Voluntary disclosures can be reported in the firm's annual report, in brochures created to describe the firm to investors, in management meetings with analysts, or in investor relations responses to information requests.[15]

One constraint on expanded disclosure is the competitive dynamics in product markets. Disclosure of proprietary information on strategies and their expected economic consequences may hurt the firm's competitive position. Managers then face a trade-off between providing information that is useful to investors in assessing the firm's economic performance and withholding information to maximize the firm's product market advantage.

A second constraint in providing voluntary disclosure is management's legal liability. Forecasts and voluntary disclosures can potentially be used by dissatisfied shareholders to bring civil action against management for providing misleading information. This seems ironic, since voluntary disclosures should provide investors with additional information. Unfortunately, it can be difficult for courts to decide whether managers' disclosures were good-faith estimates of uncertain future events which later did not materialize, or whether management manipulated the market. Consequently many corporate legal departments recommend against management providing much voluntary disclosure. One aspect of voluntary disclosure, earnings guidance, has been particularly controversial. There is growing evidence that the guidance provided by management plays an important role in leading analysts' expectations towards achievable earnings targets, and that management guidance is more likely when analysts' initial forecasts are overly optimistic.[16]

Finally, management credibility can limit a firm's incentives to provide voluntary disclosures. If management faces a credibility problem in financial reporting, any voluntary disclosure it provides is also likely to be viewed skeptically. In particular, investors may be concerned about what management is not telling them, particularly since such disclosures are not audited.

Example: Other Forms of Communication at FPIC Insurance Group

In the months subsequent to the earnings announcement and the precipitous drop in stock price, the board and management of FPIC Insurance Group made a series of moves to regain investor confidence. On August 23, 1999, in a high level management shake-up, the company's chief financial officer and the president of FPIC's Physicians Insurance subsidiary were fired. According to a statement by FPIC Chairman Robert Baratta, ". . . the board of directors felt the company could benefit from changes at this time in its senior management structure." (Reuters, August 24, 1999)

In addition, over the three-month period from August through October 1999, insiders were active buyers of the stock. During that time, nine different insiders purchased additional shares in contrast to no sellers. This sent a strong signal to investors that those people with a close understanding of the firm were believers in its business prospects and confident that the stock performance would eventually reflect that.

In a move to address investor concerns regarding its reserve policy, the company commissioned a reserve study by a nationally recognized independent actuarial adviser that performed no other services for FPIC. The study analyzed the net loss and allocated loss adjustment expense reserves as of June 30, 1999. According to CEO Russell, "We are happy to report that this study confirms our belief that our reserves with respect to this business are adequate. This study should eliminate the concerns that have been raised." However, the voluntary study and added disclosure did not do much to address investors' concerns, and the stock price lost 12 percent in the two days following the announcement. FPIC was hit by the general economic downturn from 2000 to 2002. In the fourth quarter of 2000, the company increased its loss reserves dramatically in response to unfavorable trends in claims data. In 2000, it barely broke even and in 2001 it reported a sizable loss. Performance improved in 2002, and by 2004 it earned a 14.4% ROE and had 19% sales growth. The stock price steadily recovered and in May 2007 was $44.50.

THE ROLE OF THE AUDITOR

In the U.S. the auditor is responsible for providing investors with assurance that the financial statements are prepared in accordance with Generally Accepted Accounting Principles, or GAAP. This requires the auditor to evaluate whether transactions are recorded in a way that is consistent with the rules produced by regulators (including the FASB, PCAOB, and SEC) and whether management estimates reflected in the financial statements are reasonable. The results of the audit are disclosed in the audit report, which is part of the financial statements. The auditor issues an unqualified report if (a) the firm's financial statements conform to GAAP, (b) the accounting methods are applied consistently throughout the prior three years, (c) the internal controls are adequate, and (d) there is no substantial doubt about the firm's ability to survive. If the financials do not conform to GAAP, the auditor is required to issue a qualified or an adverse report that provides information to investors on the discrepancies. If the auditor is uncertain about whether the firm can survive during the coming year, a going concern report is issued that points out the firm's survival risks.

In contrast, in the U.K. and countries that have adopted the U.K. system, such as Australia, New Zealand, Singapore, Hong Kong, and India, auditors undertake a broader review than their U.S. counterparts. U.K. audits are required to not only assess whether the financial statements are prepared in accordance with U.K. GAAP, but also to judge whether they fairly reflect the client's underlying economic performance. This additional assurance requires more judgment on the part of the auditor and increases the value of the audit to outside investors.

The essential procedures involved in a typical audit include (1) understand the client's business and industry to identify key risks for the audit, (2) evaluate the firm's internal control system to assess whether it is likely to produce reliable information, (3) perform preliminary analytic procedures to identify unusual events and possible errors, and (4) collect specific evidence on controls, transactions, and account balance details to form the basis for the auditor's opinion. In most cases client management is willing to respond to issues raised by the audit to ensure that the company receives an unqualified audit opinion. Once the audit is completed, the auditor presents a summary of audit scope and findings to the Audit Committee of the firm's board of directors.

It is worth noting that in both the U.S. and U.K. systems, the audit is not intended to detect fraud. Of course in some cases it may do so, but that is not its purpose. The detection of fraud is the domain of the internal audit department of the firm itself.

Challenges Facing Audit Industry

To understand the current problems facing the audit industry, it is necessary to go back to the mid-1970s, when two critical events created pressures on audit firms to cut costs and seek other revenue sources. The first of these was a decision by the Federal Trade Commission, concerned with a potential oligopoly by the large audit firms, to pressure the major firms to compete aggressively with each other for clients. The second was a shift in legal standards that enabled investors of companies with accounting problems to seek legal redress against the auditor without having to show that they had specifically relied on questionable accounting information in making their investment decisions. Instead, they could assert that they had relied on the stock price itself, which was affected by the misleading disclosures. This change, along with increasing litigiousness, dramatically increased the lawsuit risk for auditors.

Audit firms responded to the new business environment in several ways. They lobbied for mechanical accounting and auditing standards and developed standard operating procedures to reduce the variability in audits. This approach reduced the cost of audits and provided a defense in the case of litigation. But it also meant that auditors were more likely to view their role narrowly rather than exercise broader business judgment.

Furthermore, while mechanical standards make auditing easier, they do not necessarily increase corporate transparency.[17] Audit firms decided that profit margins would be thin in a world of mechanized, standardized audits, and they responded in two ways. One way was by aggressively pursuing a high volume strategy, and so audit partner compensation and promotion became more closely linked to a cordial relationship with top management that attracted new audit clients and retained existing clients. This made it difficult for partners to be effective watchdogs. The large audit firms also responded to challenges to their core business by developing new consulting services, which were higher margin and higher growth. This diversification strategy deflected top management energy and partner talent from the audit side of the business to the more profitable consulting part.

The Enron debacle dramatically illustrated many of the problems facing the industry.[18] The use of mechanical, standardized audits encouraged Enron's auditors to take a narrow perspective on their role as financial report watchdogs. Even though they may have believed that Enron's reports met GAAP, they failed to ask big-picture questions about their client's strategy, core risks, and the company's overall transparency. Mechanical standards made it easier for Enron's unscrupulous managers not only to meet the letter of GAAP (although in the end they did not even do that) but also to skirt their spirit, concealing important obligations and overstating profits. Finally, the pressure on Enron's auditors to retain their clients and to grow their firms' consulting businesses reduced their independence, leading them to approve questionable accounting decisions and to work closely with management to meet Enron's financial reporting objectives.

The Sarbanes-Oxley Act was designed to correct some of the structural problems facing the industry. The Act has banned audit firms from providing certain types of consulting services to their audit clients and mandates that the audit partner be rotated every five years. The Act requires the Audit Committee of the Board of Directors to become more active in appointing the auditor and reviewing the audit. While these actions are widely expected to improve governance and the audit process, they have been a boon to audit firm profitability, with the added costs becoming a point of controversy in the business community.

Role of Financial Analysis Tools in Auditing

How can the financial analysis tools discussed in this book be used by audit professionals? The relevance to the audit of the four steps in financial analysis—strategy analysis, accounting analysis, financial analysis, and prospective analysis—is discussed briefly below.

Strategy Analysis Strategy analysis is critical to the first stage of the audit, understanding the client's business and industry. It is important that the auditor develop the expertise to be able to identify the chief risks facing its client. Given the sheer volume of activity, it is impossible to review all the transactions of the firm during the audit. Time and attention should be focused on the areas that investors need in order to evaluate the firm's value proposition and how well it is managing key success factors. These are also likely to be the areas worth further testing and analysis by the auditor, to assess their impact on the financial statements.

Accounting Analysis For the auditor, accounting analysis involves two steps. First, the auditor must understand how the key success factors and risks are reflected in the financial statements. The second step in accounting analysis is for the auditor to evaluate management judgment reflected in the critical financial statements items.

Financial Analysis Financial ratios help auditors judge whether there are any unusual performance changes for their client, either relative to past performance or relative to their competitors. Any such changes merit further investigation to ensure that the reasons for the change can be fully explained and to determine what additional tests are required to satisfy the auditor that the reported changes in performance are justified. Careful ratio analysis can also reveal whether clients are facing business problems that might induce management to conceal losses or keep significant obligations off the balance sheet. Such information should alert auditors that extra care and additional detailed tests are likely to be required to reach a conclusion on the client's financial statements.

Prospective Analysis Auditors use prospective analysis to assess whether estimates and forecasts made by management are consistent with the firm's economic position. In addition, the market's perception of a client's future performance provides a useful benchmark for affirming or questioning the auditor's assessment of the client's prospects. If the auditor concludes that the market is either overly optimistic or pessimistic about a client, he or she can determine whether additional disclosure will help investors develop a more realistic view of the company's prospects.

Key Analysis Questions

The following questions are likely to provide a useful starting point for auditors in their analysis of a client's financial statements:

- What are the chief business risks facing the firm? How well are these risks managed?
- What are the accounting policies and estimates that reflect the firm's principal risks? What tests and evidence are required to evaluate management judgment that is reflected in these accounting decisions?
- Do the critical ratios indicate any unusual changes in client performance? What tests and evidence are required to understand the causes of such changes?
- Has firm performance deteriorated, creating pressure on management to manage earnings or record off-balance-sheet transactions? If so, what additional tests and evidence are required to provide assurance that the financial statements are consistent with GAAP?
- How is the market assessing the client's prospects? If different from the auditor, what is the reason for the difference? If the market is overly optimistic or pessimistic, are there implications for client disclosure or accounting estimates?

Example: Auditing FPIC Insurance Group

For FPIC Insurance Group, how well the company manages claim risk is its most critical success factor. Not surprisingly, the stock price volatility appears to be largely driven by changing perceptions of this risk. In the financial statements, claim risk is reflected in the reserves set aside for future claims. This should be a principal focus of the audit.

Questions for the auditor include the following:

- Why did the company change its reserve policy this period? Does the change reflect a change in its business model, such as an attempt to reduce insurance sales to more risky customers? If so, is there evidence of a change in customer demographics and claim patterns?
- Does the change reflect excessive over-reserving by the client in earlier periods? If so, why did the auditors approve this earlier policy? Why did management select this year to release those reserves?
- Is the change in reserve policy justifiable, or is management simply responding to pressure to meet unrealistic market expectations?
- What information is available about a representative sample of outstanding claims? Are estimates of the cost of settling these claims realistic given prior settlements and experiences for other firms in the same industry?
- If the change in claim reserves appears to be reasonable, what additional information can the firm provide to investors to address their concerns? Will this information need to be audited?

THE ROLE OF THE AUDIT COMMITTEE

Audit committees are responsible for overseeing the work of the auditor, for ensuring that the financial statements are properly prepared, and for reviewing the internal controls at the company. Audit committees, which are mandated by many stock exchanges and by the SEC, typically comprise three to four outside directors who meet regularly before or after the full board meetings.

In the last few years, requirements for audit committee have been expanded and formalized. In December 1999, the SEC, the national stock exchange(s), and the Auditing Standards Board issued new audit committee rules based largely on recommendations of the Blue Ribbon Committee (BRC) on Improving the Effectiveness of Corporate Audit Committees. The new rules defined best practices for judging audit committee members' independence and qualifications.

Following the collapse of Enron, additional audit committee requirements were created under the Sarbanes-Oxley Act. The Act requires that audit committees take formal responsibility for appointing, overseeing, and negotiating fees with external auditors. Audit committee members are required to be independent directors with no consulting or other potentially compromising relation to management. It is recommended that at least one member of the committee have financial expertise, such as being a CFO, CEO, or retired audit partner.

The audit committee is expected to be independent of management and to take an active role in reviewing the propriety of the firm's financial statements. Committee members are expected to question management and the auditors about the quality of the firm's financial reporting, the scope and findings of the external audit, and the quality of internal controls.

In reality, however, the audit committee has to rely extensively on information from management as well as internal and external auditors. Given the ground that it has to cover, its limited available time, and the technical nature of accounting standards, audit committees are not in a position to catch management fraud or auditors' failures on a timely basis.

How then can the audit committee add value?[19] We believe that many of the financial analysis tools discussed in this book can provide a useful way for audit committees to approach their tasks. Many of the applications of the financial analysis steps discussed for auditors also apply for audit committees.

In its scrutiny of financial statements, the committee should use the 80–20 rule, devoting most of its time to assessing the effectiveness of those *few* policies and decisions that have the *most* impact on investors' perceptions of the company's critical performance indicators. This should not require any additional work for committee members, since they should already have a good understanding of the firm's key success factors and risks from discussions of the full board.

Audit committee members should also have sufficient financial background to identify where in the financial statements the important risks are reflected. Their discussions with management and external auditors should focus on these risks. How well are they being managed? How are the auditors planning their work to focus on these areas? What evidence have they gathered to judge the adequacy of the financial statement estimates?

The audit committee also receives regular reviews of company performance from management as part of their board duties. Committee members should be especially proactive in requesting information that helps them evaluate how the firm is managing its key risks, since this information can also help them judge the quality of the financial statements. Audit committee members need to ask: Is information on company performance we are receiving in our regular board meetings consistent with the picture portrayed in the financial statements? If not, what is missing? Are additional disclosures required to ensure that investors are well informed about the firm's operations and performance?

Finally, audit committees need to focus on capital market expectations, not just statutory financial reports. In today's capital markets, the game begins when companies set expectations via analyst meetings, press releases, and other forms of investor communications. Indeed, the pressure to manage earnings is often a direct consequence of Wall Street's unrealistic expectations, either deliberately created by management or sustained by their inaction. Thus, it is also important for audit committees to oversee the firm's investor relations strategy and ensure that management sets realistic expectations for both the short and long term.

Key Analysis Questions

The following questions are likely to provide a useful starting point for audit committees in their discussions with management and auditors about the firm's financial statements:

- How are the critical business risks facing the firm being managed?
- How are these risks reflected by accounting policies and estimates in the financial statements? What was the basis for the external auditor's assessment of these items?
- Is information on the critical value drivers and firm performance presented to the full board consistent with the picture of the firm reflected in the financial statements and MD&A?
- What expectations is management creating in the capital market? Are these likely to cause undue pressure to manage earnings?

SUMMARY

This chapter discussed how many of the financial analysis tools developed in Chapters 2 through 8 can be used by managers to develop a coherent disclosure strategy, and by corporate board members and external auditors to improve the quality of their work.

By communicating effectively with investors, management can potentially reduce information problems for outside investors, lowering the likelihood that the stock will be mispriced or unnecessarily volatile. This can be important for firms that wish to raise new capital or avoid takeovers, or whose management is concerned that its true job performance is not reflected in the firm's stock price.

The typical way for firms to communicate with investors is through financial reporting. Accounting standards and auditing make the reporting process a way for managers to not only provide information about the firm's current performance but also indicate, through accounting estimates, where they believe the firm is headed in the future. However, financial reports are not always able to convey the type of forward-looking information that investors need. Accounting standards often do not permit firms to capitalize outlays, such as R&D, that provide significant future benefits to the firm.

A second way that management can communicate with investors is through non-accounting means. We discussed several such mechanisms, including using financial policies (such as stock repurchases, dividend increases, and hedging) to help signal management's optimism about the firm's future performance; meeting with financial analysts to explain the firm's strategy, current performance, and outlook; and disclosing additional information, both quantitative and qualitative, to provide investors with similar information as management has.

In this chapter we have stressed the importance of communicating effectively with investors. But firms also have to communicate with other stakeholders, including employees, customers, suppliers, and regulatory bodies. Many of the same principles discussed here can also be applied to management communication with these other stakeholders.

Finally, we examined the capital market role of governance agents, such as external auditors and audit committees. Both have recently faced considerable public scrutiny following a spate of financial reporting meltdowns in the U.S. Much has been done to improve the governance and independence of these intermediaries. We focus on how the financial analysis tools developed in the book can be used to improve the quality of audit and audit committee work. The tools of strategy analysis, accounting analysis, financial analysis, and prospective analysis can help auditors and audit committee members to identify the key issues in the financial statements to focus on and provide commonsense ways of assessing whether there are potential reporting problems that merit additional testing and analysis.

DISCUSSION QUESTIONS

1. Apple's inventory increased from $1 billion on December 29, 1994, to $1.95 billion one year later. In contrast, sales for the fourth quarter in each of these years increased from $2 billion to $2.6 billion. What is the implied annualized inventory turnover for Apple for these years? What different interpretations about future performance could a financial analyst infer from this change? What information could Apple's management provide to investors to clarify the change in inventory turnover? What are the costs and benefits to Apple from disclosing this information?

What issues does this change raise for the auditor? What additional tests would you want to conduct as Apple's auditor?

2. a. What are likely to be the long-term critical success factors for the following types of firms?
   - a high technology company such as Microsoft
   - a large low-cost retailer such as Wal-Mart

   b. How useful is financial accounting data for evaluating how well these two companies are managing their critical success factors? What other types of information would be useful in your evaluation? What are the costs and benefits to these companies from disclosing this type of information to investors?

3. Management frequently objects to disclosing additional information on the grounds that it is proprietary. For instance, when the FASB proposed to expand disclosures on (a) accounting for stock-based employee compensation (issued in December 2002) and (b) business segment performance (issued in June 1997), many corporate managers expressed strong opposition to both proposals. What are the potential proprietary costs from expanded disclosures in each of these areas? If you conclude that proprietary costs are relatively low for either, what alternative explanations do you have for management's opposition?

4. Financial reporting rules in many countries outside the U.S. (e.g., the U.K., Australia, New Zealand, and France) permit management to revalue fixed assets (and in some cases even intangible assets) which have increased in value. Revaluations are typically based on estimates of realizable value made by management or independent valuers. Do you expect that these accounting standards will make earnings and book values more or less useful to investors? Explain why or why not. How can management make these types of disclosures more credible?

5. Under a management buyout, the top management of a firm offers to buy the company from its stockholders, usually at a premium over its current stock price. The management team puts up its own capital to finance the acquisition, with additional financing typically coming from a private buyout firm and private debt. If management is interested in making such an offer for its firm in the near future, what are its financial reporting incentives? How do these differ from the incentives of management that are not interested in a buyout? How would you respond to a proposed management buyout if you were the firm's auditor? What about if you were a member of the audit committee?

6. You are approached by the management of a small start-up company that is planning to go public. The founders are unsure about how aggressive they should be in their accounting decisions as they come to the market. John Smith, the CEO, asserts, "We might as well take full advantage of any discretion offered by accounting rules, since the market will be expecting us to do so." What are the pros and cons of this strategy? As the partner of a major audit firm, what type of analysis would you perform before deciding to take on a start-up that is planning to go public?

7. Two years after a successful public offering, the CEO of a biotechnology company is concerned about stock market uncertainty surrounding the potential of new drugs in the development pipeline. In his discussion with you, the CEO notes that even though they have recently made significant progress in their internal R&D efforts, the stock has

performed poorly. What options does he have to help convince investors of the value of the new products? Which of these alternatives are likely to be feasible?

8. Why might the CEO of the biotechnology firm discussed in Question 7 be concerned about the firm being undervalued? Would the CEO be equally concerned if the stock were overvalued? Do you believe that the CEO would attempt to correct the market's perception in this overvaluation case? How would you react to company concern about market under- or overvaluation if you were the firm's auditor? Or if you were a member of the audit committee?

9. When companies decide to shift from private to public financing by making an initial public offering for their stock, they are likely to face increased costs of investor communications. Given this additional cost, why would firms opt to go public?

10. German firms are traditionally financed by banks, which have representatives on the companies' boards. How would communication challenges differ for these firms relative to U.S. firms, which rely more on public financing?

NOTES

1. M. Jensen and W. Meckling, "Theory of the Firm: Managerial Behavior, Agency Costs, and Capital Structure," *Journal of Financial Economics* 3 (October 1976): 305–360, analyzed agency problems between managers and outside investors. Subsequent work by Bengt Holmstrom and others examined how contracts between managers and outside investors could mitigate the agency problem.

2. K. Murphy and J. Zimmerman, "Financial Performance Surrounding CEO Turnover," *Journal of Accounting and Economics* 16 (January/April/July 1993): 273–315, find a strong relation between CEO turnover and earnings-based performance.

3. See S. Teoh, I. Welch, and T. Wong, "Earnings Management and the Long-Run Market Performance of Initial Public Offerings," *The Journal of Finance* 63 (December 1998): 1935–1974, and S. Teoh, I. Welch, and T. Wong, "Earnings Management and the Underperformance of Seasoned Equity Offerings," *Journal of Financial Economics* 50 (October 1998): 63–99.

4. This market imperfection often referred to as a "lemons" or "information" problem, is also discussed in Chapter 1. It was first studied by George Akerlof in relation to the used car market in "The Market for 'Lemons': Quality Uncertainty and the Market Mechanism," *Quarterly Journal of Economics* 90 (1970): 629–650.

5. Of course improved analysis alone is unlikely to be sufficient to improve market intermediation if the structural reforms implemented by the Sarbanes-Oxley Act and the stock exchanges fail to correct the serious conflicts of interest for intermediaries that we have witnessed in the last few years.

6. D. Skinner, "Earnings Disclosures and Stockholder Lawsuits," *Journal of Accounting and Economics* (November 1997): 249–283, finds that firms with bad earnings news tend to predisclose this information, perhaps to reduce the cost of litigation that inevitably follows bad news quarters.

7. For example, G. Foster, "Briloff and the Capital Market," *Journal of Accounting Research* 17, no. 1 (Spring 1979): 262–274, finds firms that are criticized for their accounting by Abraham J. Briloff in *Barron's* on average suffer an 8 percent decline in their stock price around the article publication date. H. Desai and P. Jain, "Long-Run Stock Returns Following Briloff's Analyses," *Financial Analysts Journal* 60, no. 2 (March/April 2004): 47–56, find significant declines in one- and two-year performance of the firms that Briloff criticized.

8. Findings by P. Healy and K. Palepu in "Earnings Information Conveyed by Dividend Initiations and Omissions," *Journal of Financial Economics* 21 (September 1988): 149–175, indicate that investors interpret announcements of dividends initiations and omissions as managers' forecasts of future earnings performance.

9. See L. Dann, R. Masulis, and D. Mayers, "Repurchase Tender Offers and Earnings Information," *Journal of Accounting and Economics* (September 1991): 217–252, and M. Hertzel and P. Jain, "Earnings and Risk Changes Around Stock Repurchases," *Journal of Accounting and Economics* (September 1991): 253–276.

10. See M. Barth and R. Kasznik, "Share Repurchases and Intangible Assets," *Journal of Accounting and Economics* 28 (December 1999): 211–241.

11. See S. Tasker, "Bridging the Information Gap: Quarterly Conference Calls as a Medium for Voluntary Disclosure." *Review of Accounting Studies* 3, no. 1–2 (1998): 137–167.

12. See R. Frankel, M. Johnson, and D. Skinner, "An Empirical Examination of Conference Calls as a Voluntary Disclosure Medium," *Journal of Accounting Research* 37, no. 1 (Spring 1999): 133–150.

13. See M. Kimbrough, "The Effect of Conference Calls on Analyst and Market Underreaction to Earnings Announcements," *The Accounting Review* 80, no. 1 (January 2005): 189–219.

14. See A. Irani, "The Effect of Regulation Fair Disclosure on the Relevance of Conference Calls to Financial Analysts," *Review of Quantitative Finance and Accounting* 22, no. 1 (January 2004): 15–28.

15. Recent research on voluntary disclosure includes M. Lang and R. Lundholm, "Cross-Sectional Determinants of Analysts' Ratings of Corporate Disclosures," *Journal of Accounting Research* 31 (Autumn 1993): 246–271; M. Lang and R. Lundholm, "Corporate Disclosure Policy and Analysts," *The Accounting Review* 71 (October 1996): 467–492; M. Welker, "Disclosure Policy, Information Asymmetry and Liquidity in Equity Markets," *Contemporary Accounting Research* (Spring 1995): 801–827; C. Botosan, "The Impact of Annual Report Disclosure Level on Investor Base and the Cost of Capital," *The Accounting Review* (July 1997): 323–350; and P. Healy, A. Hutton, and K. Palepu, "Stock Performance and Intermediation Changes Surrounding Sustained Increases in Disclosure," *Contemporary Accounting Research* 16, no. 3 (Fall 1999): 485–521. This research finds that firms are more likely to provide high levels of disclosure if they have strong earnings performance, issue securities, have more analyst following, and have less dispersion in analyst forecasts. In addition, firms with high levels of disclosure policies tend to have a lower cost of capital and bid–ask spread. Finally, firms that increase disclosure

have accompanying increases in stock returns, institutional ownership, analyst following, and stock liquidity. In addition, in "The Role of Supplementary Statements with Management Earnings Forecasts," *Journal of Accounting Research* 41 (December 2003): 867–890, A. Hutton, G. Miller, and D. Skinner examine the market response to management earnings forecasts and find that bad news forecasts are always informative but that good news forecasts are informative only when they are supported by verifiable forward-looking statements.

16. See J. Cotter, I. Tuna, and P. Wysocki, "Expectations Management and Beatable Targets: How do Analysts React to Explicit Earnings Guidance?" *Contemporary Accounting Research* 23, no. 3 (Autumn 2006): 593–628.

17. For example, M. Nelson, J. Elliott, and R. Tarpley, in "Evidence from Auditors About Managers' and Auditors' Earnings Management Decisions," *The Accounting Review* 77 (2002 Supplement): 175–202, show that mechanical accounting rules for structured finance transactions lead to more earnings management.

18. See P. Healy and K. Palepu, "The Fall of Enron," *Journal of Economic Perspectives* 17, no. 2 (Spring 2003): 3–26, and P. Healy and K. Palepu, "How the Quest for Efficiency Undermined the Market," *Harvard Business Review* (July 2003): 76–85.

19. See P. Healy and K. Palepu, "Audit the Audit Committees: After Enron Boards Must Change the Focus and Provide Greater Financial Transparency," *Financial Times*, June 10, 2002, p. 14.

Financial Reporting Problems at Molex, Inc. (A)

In mid-November 2004, Molex's Board of Directors met to decide the future of Joe King and Diane Bullock, the company's CEO and CFO respectively. Molex's external auditors, Deloitte & Touche, had accused both of failing to disclose an $8 million pre-tax inventory valuation error in a recent letter of representation to the auditors. In response, King and Bullock argued that at the time of their letter they had determined that the financial impact of the error was immaterial. Despite an inquiry by the Audit Committee, which concluded that management had not deliberately withheld information from the auditors, Deloitte & Touche was not satisfied. The audit firm insisted that it could no longer rely on Bullock's and King's representations, and would be unable to complete its review of the first quarter results until representations were received from a new CFO and in all likelihood a new CEO.

MOLEX BACKGROUND AND MANAGEMENT

Founded in Lisle, Illinois in 1938 by Frederick Krehbiel, Molex Inc. designed, manufactured and distributed electronic connectors that were used by a wide range of industries.[1] For example, in the computer industry its connectors were used to produce computers, servers and printers; in the telecommunications industry they were used to produce mobile phones and networking equipment; the consumer products industry used Molex connectors to manufacture CD and DVD players, cameras, plasma and LCD televisions; and the automotive industry used them for the production of engine control units and adaptive breaking systems. In 2003, Molex was the second largest firm in the connector industry, with a worldwide share of 6.9%, and production and distribution facilities located throughout the world.[2]

---

1. *The Krehbiel family continued to have a controlling interest in Molex. Brothers Frederick A. Krehbiel and John H. Krehbiel, Jr. were Co-Chairs of the Board of Directors and former CEOs, and Fred L. Krehbiel, the son of John H. Krehbiel, Jr. was a member of the board.*

2. *The number one firm in the industry was Tyco Electronics, with a 19.7% market share. See "Top 100 Connector Manufacturers," Market Research Report, Bishop & Associates, September 2004.*

In July 2001, Molex's board of directors appointed Joe King as vice chairman and chief executive officer. Trained as an engineer in Ireland, King had joined Molex as a quality control manager in 1975. Initially responsible for overseeing manufacturing quality at the company's Shannon plant and for working with customers on technical issues, he soon took over material management, including planning, purchasing and inventory control. King was subsequently promoted to assistant head of international operations, which covered the U.S. Export Group and Computer Systems, and then to vice president of operations, where he oversaw most of the company's technical systems and was in charge of developing and implementing a strategic plan for international operations. From 1985 to 1988, as corporate vice president and president of the Far East south region, he opened an operating facility in Malaysia, initiated discussions on operations that would later open in Thailand and China, and developed the region's marketing and engineering capabilities. As competition in the region intensified during the late 1980's, King stressed customer service, quality, and new product development as ways for Molex to compete more effectively. In 1988, he was appointed group vice president-international, responsible for sales and manufacturing operations in Europe, the Far East and new international ventures. Eight years later, King became executive vice president for functional groups worldwide, where he played a key role in integrating domestic and international operations, consolidating global staff functions, and assigning all regions to report to one person, the president and chief operating officer.[3]

In contrast, Molex's chief financial officer, Diane Bullock, had a very brief history with the firm. She had been hired in October of 2003 to replace Bob Mahoney as CFO effective January 1, 2004. Bullock had previously held a variety of global financial positions in the automotive components industry and in public accounting.

MOLEX FINANCIAL PERFORMANCE

2002 and 2003 were challenging years for Molex. The company experienced a sharp downturn in demand for its products, particularly from technology customers. Molex management reacted by reducing its workforce and expenses, and by directing investment into products less affected by recession. Management's task was further complicated by heavy short selling of Molex's stock during the downturn. For example, during 2003, average short-interest was 8 million shares, roughly 12.5 days of average daily share volume.[4]

The first sign of a recovery came during the quarter ended December 31, 2003 (the second quarter of the June 30, 2004 fiscal year), when sales and earnings increased by 21% and 46% respectively over the same quarter one year earlier. In response, Molex's stock price jumped by 6% relative to the Nasdaq Composite Index.

However, the stock price increase proved to be temporary. On February 17, an online research firm, CashFlowNews.com, observed that Molex's free cash flow (defined as cash flow from operations minus capital expenditures) had declined 52% for the twelve months ended December 31, 2003, from $240 million to a six-year low of $114 million. Following publication of the report, Molex's stock fell by 8% relative to the Nasdaq Composite Index (see **Exhibit 1** for a graph of Molex's stock price performance).

---

3. Source: Joseph King Bio on http://www.ttiinc.com/object/ME_ExecIntKing.html.

4. Source: Bloomberg.

Molex showed steady financial improvement during the first six months of 2004. Revenues for the year ended June 30, 2004 increased by almost 22%, and net income more than doubled from $84.9 million to $176.0 million (see **Exhibit 2** for a ten year summary of Molex's financial performance). The company reported fourth quarter earnings per share of $0.30, exceeding its own prior estimates of $0.27 to $0.29, and analyst estimates of $0.28.[5]

In a July 27, 2004 press release and in the 2004 10-K filed on September 10, 2004, management estimated that earnings per share for the first quarter of the following year would be between $0.26 and $0.29, compared to analyst forecasts of $0.29. In discussing the company's future prospects, management noted that:

> *The outlook in the majority of the Company's global markets remains strong. . . . The Company expects revenue growth of 16 percent to 19 percent during fiscal 2005 and net income is expected to grow faster than revenues due to leverage from the higher volume. Earnings per share are expected in the range of $1.24 to $1.34, an increase of 35 to 45 percent.*

Yet despite increased sales and earnings for 2004, and management's expectation of continued sales and earnings growth, Molex's stock price lagged the market and short interest in its stock remained high (8 million shares in August 2004).

AUDIT INDUSTRY CHALLENGES

2002 and 2003 were also challenging years for the audit industry. Its reputation for independence and high quality audits plunged following a wave of corporate accounting scandals that included Enron, Worldcom, Adelphia, Global Crossing and Freddie Mac in the US, and Ahold and Parmalat in Europe.

In mid-2002, Enron's auditor, Arthur Andersen, the fifth largest auditing firm, was convicted of obstruction of justice for shredding documents related to its Enron audit. Since *U.S. Securities and Exchange Commission* (SEC) rules prohibited convicted felons from auditing public companies, Arthur Andersen was forced to surrender its licenses and its right to practice before the SEC, leaving only four large accounting firms (in order of size, Deloitte & Touche, PriceWaterhouseCooper, Ernst & Young, and KPMG).

Although Arthur Andersen was the audit firm most closely identified with the accounting scandals, many of the other leading firms were also affected. For example, several of Deloitte & Touche's largest clients (notably Adelphia, Fortress Re, Parmalat, and Ahold) were hit with fraud and accounting problems, leading the accounting firm to face a string of law suits claiming billions of dollars in potential damages.

Following the scandals and the collapse of Arthur Andersen, new regulations were adopted to improve the independence and quality of audits. For example, the Sarbannes Oxley Act of 2003 created a new oversight board (the Public Company Accounting Oversight Board) that was assigned responsibility for reviewing and disciplining accounting firms' audit quality, ethical standards, and independence. In addition, the act required audit partners to be rotated every five years. Audit firms, which had developed large consulting practices during the 1980s and 1990s, were prohibited from selling many of these services (including information systems design and implementation; appraisals, valuation, and actuarial services; and internal audit services) to their audit clients. Finally, audit committees, rather than management, were assigned

---

5. *Analyst estimates are from Thomson First Call.*

responsibility for appointing and overseeing the external auditor, and for pre-approving the purchase of any material non-banned consulting services.

MOLEX'S ACCOUNTING PROBLEM

In mid-July 2004, Molex's corporate finance group identified a potential problem with inventory that had affected results for several years. Profits on inventory sales between Molex subsidiaries (but which had not been sold to an external customer by period-end) had not been excluded in computing the consolidated firm's earnings and inventory. Consequently, earnings, inventory and retained earnings were most likely overstated.

After the discovery, disclosure of the misstatements to top management, the auditors, the audit committee, and investors took place as follows:

July 21, 2004: Diane Bullock (the company's CFO) brought the matter to the attention of other top management at a meeting that included Joe King (the Vice-Chairman of the Board and CEO). A decision was made to investigate the matter further to assess whether and to what extent there was a problem. But based on subsequently gathered information, management concluded that the amounts involved were not material.[6]

July 27, 2004: Fourth quarter results were released with no mention of the problem.

September 10, 2004: The management representation letter for the annual financial statements and 10-K, dated August 20, 2004 and signed by King and Bullock, was delivered to the external auditors (Deloitte & Touche LLP).[7] The letter made no mention of the inventory error.

October 15, 2004: Prior to releasing results for the first quarter ending September 30, 2004, Molex's management discussed the error for the first time with Deloitte & Touche and proposed recognizing $2 million of the adjustment during the current quarter with additional amounts recognized in subsequent quarters throughout the year.

October 19, 2004: At an Audit Committee meeting where the issue was discussed, Deloitte & Touche disagreed with management's October 15 proposal and argued that the entire error amount should be recorded in the first quarter. At the meeting, the Audit Committee asked the auditors whether the error was material and Deloitte & Touche responded that it was not. The Audit Committee then requested that management and Deloitte & Touche work to determine the appropriate accounting.

October 20, 2004: Molex announced its first quarter results: revenues $640 million, net income $55.6 million, and earnings per share $0.29. The full amount of the accounting error ($8 million before-tax and $5.8 million after-tax, of which approximately $3.0 million before-tax and $2.2 million after-tax was related to the year ended June 30, 2004) was included as an adjustment to current operating results, but the error was considered immaterial and not disclosed (see **Exhibit 4** for a summary of the first quarter results).

October 21, 2004: The Audit Committee met again. Deloitte & Touche reiterated that the accounting error was not material. However, after the meeting was adjourned, the engagement partner from Deloitte & Touche questioned Diane Bullock

---

6. For financial reporting purposes, materiality was defined as "the magnitude of an omission or misstatement in the financial statements that makes it probable that a reasonable person relying on those statements would have been influenced by the information or made a different judgment if the correct information had been known" (FASB Concept Statement Number 2). Interpreting this definition frequently involved the exercise of professional judgment.

7. A management representation letter is required as part of the audit engagement. The letter is drafted by the auditor, given to the client's management to print on its letterhead, and signed by the CEO and CFO. In the letter, management acknowledges that it is responsible for the financial statements, and commits in writing to prior oral representations made to the auditor that were relied on in conducting the audit. The representations are intended to reduce any misunderstandings between the auditors and management. **Exhibit 3** provides a sample representation letter.

as to whether she was aware of the inventory error before signing the September 10, 2004 representation letter. When she confirmed that she had been aware of the problem at that time, Deloitte & Touche expressed concern about the significance of the omission to the Audit Committee. Bullock and King responded that, since the error's effect on the firm's financial performance was deemed immaterial, they did not think that it needed to be addressed in the letter.

In an attempt to resolve the dispute, the Audit Committee held an inquiry with the help of independent legal and accounting advisors. The inquiry revealed no additional adjustments were required and that management had not deliberately withheld information from the auditors.

THE BOARD'S CHALLENGE

Deloitte & Touche continued to express dissatisfaction over top management's representations. It argued that management had known about the magnitude of the error as early as July 21 and had expressly decided not to inform Deloitte & Touche at that time. Because of this belief, the auditors concluded that they were no longer willing to rely on Bullock and King's representations.

In an attempt to satisfy Deloitte & Touche, Molex removed Bullock as CFO and installed an acting CFO; however, she remained an executive officer of the company having responsibilities in the finance area. Subsequently, Deloitte & Touche advised Molex that it would only be able to complete its review of the first quarter results in connection with the company's 10-Q filing when representations were received from the new CFO and a new CEO and if both King and Bullock were removed as executive officers having no influence over financial reporting or internal controls.

In November, Molex's Board convened to discuss the situation (see **Exhibit 5** for information on the Board of Directors). It appeared to face three options. (1) It could accede to the auditor's request to remove Bullock and King as executive officers so that they would not have any influence over financial reporting or internal controls. (2) It could ignore Deloitte & Touche's demand, forcing the auditor to either refuse to review the quarterly financial statements or to resign. In either case, Molex would be unable to file its quarterly results on time with the SEC and NASDAQ, violating the Exchange's listing requirements.[8] (3) It could dismiss Deloitte & Touche and hire a new auditor, in which case an 8-K would have to be filed with the SEC to explain the change.

QUESTIONS:

1. What was the financial reporting problem at Molex? How would the correction of the problem be recorded in Molex's financial statements?

2. What is the role of top management, the board, the audit committee, and the external auditors in financial reporting?

3. Why were the auditors so concerned about the problem? If you were a member of the board, would you agree with their concerns? How would you respond to the auditor's request that the CFO (and possibly the CEO) be replaced?

---

8. When NASDAQ determined that a company was delinquent in meeting its listing requirements, it notified the company that it had seven days to issue a press release announcing the delinquency and to file for a hearing with the NASDAQ Hearing Panel. At the hearing, the company was required to present a plan for how it intended to regain and subsequently maintain compliance. If the Panel found the plan convincing, it granted the company a conditional listing (called a limited-duration exception) and added an identifying letter "E" after the company's ticker. If the Panel decided not to grant an exception, the company's securities were delisted or transferred to The NASDAQ SmallCap Market.

EXHIBIT I

Molex Stock Price Performance Relative to NASDAQ from Jan.1, 2004 to Nov. 15, 2004

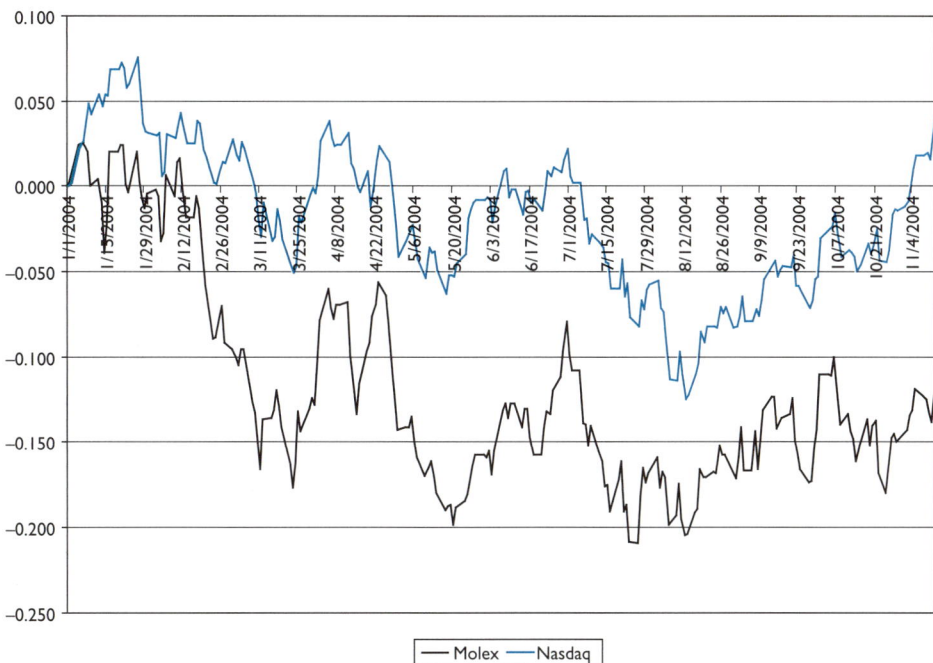

Source: Thomson Financial's Datastream.

Financial Reporting Problems at Molex, Inc.

Financial Reporting Problems at Molex, Inc.

EXHIBIT 2

Molex Incorporated, Ten-Year Financial Highlights Summary (in thousands, except per share data)

	2004	2003	2002	2001	2000	1999	1998	1997	1996	1995
Operations										
Net revenue	$2,246,715	$1,843,098	$1,711,497	$2,365,549	$2,217,096	$1,711,649	$1,622,975	$1,539,712	$1,382,673	$1,197,747
Gross profit	776,746	579,248	536,551	859,610	853,892	668,125	670,266	640,895	562,731	512,498
Income before income taxes	239,892	110,042	93,221	291,416	323,694	230,214	274,823	262,369	228,953	214,492
Income taxes	63,571	24,762	16,684	87,424	100,810	52,363	92,490	95,581	83,300	90,273
Net income[a]	175,950	84,918	76,479	203,919	222,454	178,029	182,243	166,716	145,586	124,035
Earnings per share:[b]										
Basic	0.93	0.44	0.39	1.04	1.13	0.92	0.93	0.85	0.74	0.63
Diluted	0.92	0.44	0.39	1.03	1.12	0.91	0.92	0.84	0.74	0.63
Net income – percent of net revenue	7.8%	4.6%	4.5%	8.6%	10.0%	10.4%	11.2%	10.8%	10.5%	10.4%
Financial Position										
Current assets	1,168,644	962,113	915,343	891,865	1,023,009	881,338	867,791	873,614	734,589	773,036
Current liabilities	428,464	356,148	359,593	374,106	475,449	342,441	336,275	342,026	275,182	278,046
Working capital	740,180	605,965	555,750	517,759	547,560	538,897	531,516	531,588	459,407	494,990
Current ratio	2.7	2.7	2.5	2.4	2.2	2.6	2.6	2.6	2.7	2.8
Property, plant and equipment, net	1,022,378	1,007,948	1,067,590	1,092,567	980,775	809,602	676,161	665,468	613,125	567,303
Total assets	2,572,346	2,329,870	2,253,920	2,213,627	2,247,106	1,902,012	1,639,634	1,636,931	1,460,999	1,441,020
Long-term debt	10,243	13,137	14,223	19,351	21,593	20,148	5,566	7,350	7,450	8,122
Capital leases	3,796	3,731	3,626	6,114	—	—	—	—	—	—
Shareholders' equity	2,065,994	1,896,568	1,827,652	1,765,640	1,705,804	1,500,537	1,261,570	1,235,912	1,131,271	1,107,268
Return on beginning equity	9.3%	4.6%	4.3%	12.0%	14.8%	14.1%	14.7%	14.7%	13.1%	14.1%
Dividends per share[b]	0.1	0.1	0.1	0.1	0.09	0.05	0.05	0.04	0.03	0.02
Average common shares:[b]										
Basic	190,207	191,873	194,327	195,471	196,060	194,340	195,750	196,389	196,768	195,343
Diluted	192,186	193,229	195,986	197,633	198,208	195,631	197,971	198,349	198,819	197,414

Source: Company 10-K, September 10, 2004.

a. Fiscal 2003 results include a charge of $35.0 million ($24.8 million after-tax) for restructuring costs and $5.1 million ($3.8 million after-tax) for write-down of investments. Fiscal 2002 results included a restructuring charge of $24.2 million ($18.8 million after-tax) and a charge for investment impairment of $10.0 million ($6.5 million after-tax). Fiscal 2001 results included a restructuring charge of $30.8 million ($21.4 million after-tax) and a charge for excess and slow moving inventory of $12.7 million ($8.9 million after-tax).

b. Restated for the following stock dividends: 25% –January 2000; 25% –November 1997; 25% –February 1997; 25% –August 1995; 25% –November 1994.

EXHIBIT 3

Sample Management Representation Letter, written on client letterhead

(Date)
(To the Auditor)

We are providing this letter in connection with your review of the financial statements of (name of entity) as of (dates) and for the (periods of review e.g. for the years then ended) for the purpose of expressing limited assurance that there are no material modifications that should be made to the statements in order for them to be in conformity with generally accepted accounting principles. We confirm that we are responsible for the fair presentation in the financial statements of financial position, results of operations, and cash flows in conformity with generally accepted accounting principles.

Certain representations in this letter are described as being limited to matters that are material. Items are considered material, regardless of size, if they involve an omission or misstatement of accounting information that, in the light of surrounding circumstances, makes it probable that the judgment of a reasonable person relying on the information would be changed or influenced by the omission or misstatement.

1. We confirm, to the best of our knowledge and belief [as of (the date of the auditor's review report)] the following representations made to you during your review.
2. The financial statements referred to above are fairly presented in conformity with generally accepted accounting principles.

    We have made available to you all:

    a. Financial records and related data.
    b. Minutes of the meetings of stockholders, directors, and committees of directors, or summaries of actions of recent meetings for which minutes have not yet been prepared.
3. There are no material transactions that have not been properly recorded in the accounting records underlying the financial statements.[9]
4. We acknowledge our responsibility to prevent and detect fraud.
5. We have no knowledge of any fraud or suspected fraud affecting the entity involving management or others where the fraud could have a material effect on the financial statements, including any communications received from employees, former employees or others.
6. We have no plans or intentions that may materially affect the carrying amounts or classification of assets and liabilities.
7. There are no material losses (such as from obsolete inventory or purchase or sales commitments) that have not been properly accrued or disclosed in the financial statements.
8. There are no:

    a. Violations or possible violations of laws or regulations, whose effects should be considered for disclosure in the financial statements or as a basis for recording a loss contingency.
    b. Unasserted claims or assessments that our lawyer has advised us are probable of assertion that must be disclosed in accordance with Financial Accounting Standards Board (FASB) Statement No. 5 [AC section C59], Accounting for Contingencies.

(continued)

9. *A substantially lower materiality threshold is used for determining the materiality of a transaction for the management representation letter than is applied for financial reporting purposes.*

EXHIBIT 3 (*continued*)

    c. Other material liabilities or gain or loss contingencies that are required to be accrued or disclosed by FASB Statement No. 5.

9. The company has satisfactory title to all owned assets, and there are no liens or encumbrances on such assets, nor has any asset been pledged as collateral.

10. We have complied with all aspects of contractual agreements that would have a material effect on the financial statements in the event of noncompliance.

11. The following have been properly recorded or disclosed in the financial statements:

    a. Related party transactions, including sales, purchases, loans, transfers, leasing arrangements, and guarantees, and amounts receivable from or payable to related parties.

    b. Guarantees, whether written or oral, under which the company is contingently liable.

    c. Significant estimates and material concentrations known to management that are required to be disclosed in accordance with the AICPA's Statement of Position 94–6, Disclosure of Certain Significant Risks and Uncertainties. [Significant estimates are estimates at the balance sheet date that could change materially within the next year. Concentrations refer to volumes of business, revenues, available sources of supply, or markets or geographic areas for which events could occur that would significantly disrupt normal finances within the next year.]

[Add additional representations that are unique to the entity's business or industry]

12. We are in agreement with the adjusting journal entries you have recommended, and they have been posted to the company's accounts. (if applicable)

13. To the best of our knowledge and belief, no events have occurred subsequent to the balance-sheet date and through the date of this letter that would require adjustment to or disclosure in the aforementioned financial statements.

14. We have responded fully and truthfully to all inquiries made to us by you during your review.

_____

(Name of Owner or Chief Executive Officer and Title)

_____

(Name of Chief Financial Officer and Title, where applicable)

Source: AICPA website, aicpa.org.

EXHIBIT 4

Molex First Quarter Financial Results for September 30, 2004

Fiscal First Quarter Results

Revenue of $640.2 million increased 29 percent from last year's first quarter of $496.8 million. Revenue in local currencies increased 25 percent, as currency translation increased net revenue by approximately $19 million when compared with last year's first quarter. Revenue for the first quarter included $18 million from the automotive acquisition in Europe that was completed on April 2, 2004. Excluding the acquisition, revenue increased 25 percent from last year's first quarter. Net income was $55.6 million compared with last year's first quarter of $32.1 million, an increase of 74 percent. Earnings per share of $0.29 increased 71 percent, compared with $0.17 reported for the first quarter a year ago.

    Joe King, Vice-Chairman and Chief Executive Officer, said, "Revenue growth compared with last year's first quarter revenue was very strong. Revenue also increased sequentially, an excellent result in this seasonally challenging quarter. We believe we are growing significantly faster than the overall connector market, primarily due to our ongoing investment in new products and our global capabilities. We were also pleased with the strong growth in earnings after absorbing higher costs for many of our raw materials."

Regional Results

Revenue in the Far East South region was $190 million, an increase of 33 percent, primarily driven by the digital consumer, PC, and mobile communication markets. In this region, we continue to gain market share, based on our many new products and increased penetration into our global customers who continue to transfer production to the region. Revenue in the Far East North region (Japan and Korea) was $132 million, an increase of 13 percent in dollars and 6 percent in local currencies. This growth was primarily due to new products for the digital consumer and communication markets. Revenue in the Americas region was $177 million, an increase of 17 percent, due to stronger demand for high-speed, industrial and medical electronics products, which more than offset lower demand in automotive. Revenue in Europe was $128 million, an increase of 73 percent in dollars and 61 percent in local currencies. Excluding the previously mentioned automotive acquisition, revenue increased 49 percent in dollars, as the region recovers from recession.

Operating Results

Gross profit margin was 35.7 percent compared with last year's first quarter margin of 33.8 percent. Pretax return on sales was 12 percent compared with 8.9 percent in the year ago quarter. The effective tax rate for the first quarter was 27 percent, the same rate as last year's first quarter. The Company now anticipates an effective tax rate of 27 percent for the 2005 fiscal year, compared with previous guidance of 27.5 percent and a 2004 fiscal year rate of 26.5 percent. Net return on sales was 8.7 percent compared with 6.5 percent in last year's first quarter. Cash and marketable securities were $331.4 million at September 30, 2004.

The Company's order backlog on September 30, 2004 stood at $313.6 million, a 51 percent increase compared with $208 million for the same period last year. Without the impact of changes in currency rates, the order backlog would have increased 48 percent. New orders for the first quarter were $622.4 million, an increase of 21 percent compared with last year's first quarter. This was a reasonable result, considering an estimated $25 million in orders were advanced by customers into the June quarter, as discussed in the June 30, 2004 earnings release.

Research and Development Expenditures and Capital Spending

Research and development expenditures for the first quarter were $33.4 million, an increase of 24 percent when compared with the same period last year. Capital expenditures were $48.4 million for the quarter versus $45.3 million last year.

Fiscal Second Quarter Outlook

King continued, "Our operations in the Far East continue to drive our results. We expect this trend to continue, based on the magnitude of production transferred by our global customers to the region and supported by our technical capabilities and long term history of working in the region."

It is apparent that many of our customers in the Americas are in the process of adjusting their finished goods inventory to more conservative levels. However, we believe that the amount of actual connector inventory within these channels is reasonable, and therefore the outlook in the majority of our markets remains encouraging. In addition, we expect to gain market share based on our positions within key market segments – such as digital consumer, mobile communication and mobile computing – that are growing faster than the overall connector market, as well as our focus on the emerging medical electronics market.

Based on these facts, the Company expects that revenue for the fiscal second quarter ending December 31, 2004, will be in a range of $635–$650 million. This represents an increase of 16–18 percent over last year's fiscal second quarter. The Company expects that earnings per share will be in a range of $0.29–$0.31, an increase of 38–48 percent over last year's fiscal second quarter earnings per share.

Stock Buyback Actions

During the quarter, the Company purchased 875,000 shares of MOLXA common stock, at a total cost of $21.9 million. These purchases were done under a $100 million Board authorization for the full fiscal year ending June 30, 2005.

CONSOLIDATED BALANCE SHEET
(unaudited, in thousands)

	Sept. 30, 2004	June 30, 2004
ASSETS		
Current assets:		
Cash and cash equivalents	$238,292	$234,431
Marketable securities	93,153	104,223
Accounts receivable, net	544,736	529,630
Inventories	283,417	265,344
Other current assets	40,027	35,016
Total current assets	1,199,625	1,168,644
Property, plant and equipment, net	1,009,163	1,022,378
Goodwill	164,969	164,915
Other assets	194,930	216,409
Total assets	$2,568,687	$2,572,346
LIABILITIES AND SHAREHOLDERS' EQUITY		
Current liabilities:		
Accounts payable	$225,731	$234,823
Accrued expenses	132,625	143,160
Other current liabilities	47,508	50,481
Total current liabilities	405,864	428,464
Other non-current liabilities	9,361	10,487
Accrued pension and postretirement benefits	51,435	52,151
Long-term debt	10,075	10,243
Obligations under capital leases	3,143	3,796
Minority interest in subsidiaries	3,383	1,211
Shareholders' equity:		
Common Stock	10,747	10,734
Paid-in capital	376,518	369,660
Retained earnings	2,209,211	2,160,368
Treasury stock	−532,216	−509,161
Deferred unearned compensation	−32,722	−32,180
Accumulated other comprehensive income	53,888	66,573
Total shareholders' equity	2,085,426	2,065,994
Total liabilities and shareholders' equity	$2,568,687	$2,572,346

EXHIBIT 4

CONSOLIDATED INCOME STATEMENT
(unaudited, in thousands, except per share data)

	September 30	
	2004	2003
Net Revenue	$640,230	$496,763
Cost of sales	411,558	328,739
GROSS PROFIT	228,672	168,024
Selling, general and administrative expenses:		
Selling	54,020	44,416
General and administrative	102,192	83,048
Total selling, general and administrative expenses	156,212	127,464
INCOME FROM OPERATIONS	72,460	40,560
Other (income) expense:		
Equity income	(2,029)	(2,183)
(Gain)/loss on investments	(1,152)	
Interest, net	(925)	(1,235)
Total other (income) expense	(4,106)	(3,418)
INCOME BEFORE INCOME TAXES AND MINORITY INTEREST	76,566	43,978
Income taxes and minority interest	20,924	11,916
NET INCOME	$55,642	$32,062
EARNINGS PER SHARE:		
Basic	$0.29	$0.17
Diluted	$0.29	$0.17
AVERAGE COMMON SHARES OUTSTANDING:		
Basic	188,763	190,679
Diluted	190,617	192,372
CASH DIVIDENDS PER SHARE	$0.04	$0.03

Source: Company Press Release, 20 October 2004.

Financial Reporting Problems at Molex, Inc.

Michael J. Birck   Director since 1995. Member of the Audit Committee[10] and the Executive Committee. Age 66. Founder and Chairman of the Board of Tellabs, Inc. (telecommunications equipment). Also served on the board of Illinois Tool Works Inc.

Douglas K. Carnahan   Director since 1997 and Chairman of the Audit Committee. Age 63. Retired former executive of Hewlett-Packard Company (computers, computer peripherals and instrumentation).

Michelle L. Collins   Director since 2003 and member of the Nominating and Corporate Governance Committee. Age 44. Co-founder and Managing Director of Svoboda, Collins LLC (private equity firm), and former partner of William Blair & Company, LLC (1992–1997). Also served on the board of CDW Corporation.

Edgar D. Jannotta   Director since 1986. Chairman of the Nominating and Corporate Governance Committee and member of the Executive Committee. Age 73. Investment banker and Chairman of William Blair & Company, LLC (securities and investment banking). Also served on the boards of Bandag, Incorporated, Aon Corporation, and Exelon Corporation.

J. Joseph King   Vice Chairman of the Board and Chief Executive Officer of Molex. Director since 1999 and member of the Executive Committee. Age 60. Owned 0.2% of voting common stock, and 201,293 stock options. Also served on the board of Cabot Microelectronics Corporation.

EXHIBIT 5
Molex Board of Directors

Frederick A. Krehbiel   Co-Chairman of the Board of Molex. Director since 1972 and member of the Executive Committee. Age 63. Elected Vice Chairman and Chief Executive Officer in 1988 and Chairman of the Board of Directors in 1993. Became Co-Chairman in 1999 and served as Co-Chief Executive Officer from 1999–2001. Owned 28.0% of voting common stock. Also served on the boards of Tellabs, Inc., W.W. Grainger, Inc. and DeVry Inc.

John H. Krehbiel, Jr.   Co-Chairman of the Board of Molex. Director since 1966 and member of the Executive Committee. Age 67. President of Molex 1975–1999 and Chief Operating Officer 1996–1999. Became Co-Chairman in 1999 and served as Co-Chief Executive Officer from 1999–2001. Owned 32.8% of voting common stock.

Fred L. Krehbiel   Director since 1993. Age 39. President of Molex Connector Products Division (Americas). Worked at Molex since 1988 in various engineering, marketing, and managerial capacities. Previously served as Assistant to the Regional President (Americas) for the Global Desktop Business (1998–2000) and President of the Automotive Division (Americas) (2000–2003). Owned 1.0% of voting common stock and 6,250 stock options.

Joe W. Laymon   Director since 2002 and member of the Compensation Committee. Age 51. Group Vice President, Corporate Human Resources & Labor Affairs of Ford Motor Company (automobile manufacturer). Previously worked for U.S. State Department—Agency for International Development, Human Resource at Xerox Corporation (1979–1996), and Eastman Kodak Company (1996–2000).

Donald G. Lubin   Director since 1994 and member of the Nominating and Corporate Governance Committee. Age 70. Partner of Sonnenschein Nath & Rosenthal (private law practice). Also served on the board of McDonald's Corporation.

Masahisa Naitoh   Director since 1995 and member of the Compensation Committee. Age 66. Chairman and CEO of The Institute of Energy Economics, Japan (private think tank). Previously held senior positions at The Institute of Energy Economics and Itochu Corporation (a Japanese global trading firm). Also served on the board of E.I. DuPont de Nemours and Company.

---

10. *Molex's Audit Committee does not have a "Financial Expert" as defined (but not required) by the applicable SEC Rules. In its Proxy Statement, the company explained that "given the level of financial sophistication and business experience of the Audit Committee members, the board of directors believes that the Audit Committee members can perform the audit committee functions as required."*

Robert J. Potter   Director since 1981. Chairman of the Compensation Committee and member of the Audit Committee. Age 71. President and Chief Executive Officer of R. J. Potter Company (consulting business). Also served on the boards of Cree, Inc. and Zebra Technologies Corporation.

Martin P. Slark   Director since 2000 and member of the Executive Committee. Age 49. President and Chief Operating Officer of Molex. Worked at Molex since 1976 filling various administrative, operational, and executive positions both internationally and domestically. Served as Executive Vice President from 1999–2001, and assumed the post of President and Chief Operating Officer on July 1, 2001. Owned 0.1% of voting common stock and 137,623 stock options. Also served on the board of directors of Hub Group, Inc.

Source: Company Proxy Statement, September 15, 2004.

Financial Reporting Problems at Molex, Inc.

PART FOUR

ADDITIONAL CASES

America Online, Inc.

When it comes to technology companies, the stock market's current mania, it's hard to top America Online, Inc. Technology stocks are hot, up about 50 percent on average this year, but AOL is positively scalding, up about 135 percent. In fact, AOL's stock has soared more than 2,000 percent from its initial public offering, in 1992. The Vienna-based company has 35 times the customers and 20 times the revenue it had five years ago. It's the nation's biggest on-line company and is building a recognized brand.

But look closely and you see that AOL is as much about accounting technology as it is about computer technology. So make sure you understand the numbers before rushing out to buy AOL, which is valued at about $4 billion.

The above report written by Allan Sloan appeared on October 24, 1995, in *Newsweek's* business section.[1]

COMPANY BACKGROUND

Founded in Vienna, VA, America Online, Inc. (AOL) was a leader in the development of a new mass medium that encompassed online services, the Internet, multimedia, and other interactive technologies. Through its America Online service the company offered members a broad range of features including real-time talk, electronic mail, electronic magazines and newspapers, online classes and shopping, and Internet access. In addition to its online service, AOL's business had expanded during 1995 to include access software for the Internet, production and distribution of original content, interactive marketing and transactions capabilities, and networks to support the transmission of data.

AOL generated revenues principally from consumers through membership fees, as well as from content providers and merchandisers through advertising, commissions on merchandise sales and other transactions, and from other businesses through the sale of network and production services. Through continued investment in the growth of its existing online service, the pursuit of related business opportunities, its ability to provide a full range of interactive services, and its technological flexibility, the company positioned itself to lead the development of the evolving mass medium for interactive services.

Stephen Case and James Kimsey founded America Online's predecessor, Quantum Computer Services, in 1985. Quantum offered its Q-Link service for Commodore computers. In 1989, the service was extended to Apple computers. The company changed its name to America Online in 1991 and went public

---

1. "Look Beyond the High-Tech Accounting To Measure America Online's Market Risk," Allan Sloan, Newsweek, October 24, 1995.

in 1992. That same year, AOL licensed its on-line technology to Apple for use in eWorld and NewtonMail services for which AOL continues to receive a usage-based royalty. In 1993, the company expanded its market with a Windows version of its software and began developing a version for palmtop computer. In 1994, AOL's subscription base surpassed those of CompuServe and Prodigy, two rival online service providers, making AOL the number one consumer online service in the United States. By the end of October 1995, AOL had a subscriber base of more than four million members.

AOL's Products

The broad range of features offered by the America Online service was designed to meet the varied needs of its four million members. A key feature of the online service was the ease with which members with related interests could communicate through real-time conferences, e-mail, and bulletin boards. Members used the interactive communications facilities to share information and ideas, exchange advice, and socialize. It was America Online's goal to continue developing and adding new sources of information and content in support of these member activities. The range of features offered by America Online included the following:

- *Online Community.* In addition to its e-mail service, AOL promoted real-time online communications by scheduling conferences and discussions on specific topics, offering interactive areas that served as "meeting rooms" for members to participate in lively interactive discussions with other members, and providing public bulletin boards on which members could share information and opinions on subjects of general or specialized interest.
- *Computing.* AOL provided its members access to tens of thousands of public domain and "shareware" software programs, to online help from 300 hardware and software developers, and to online computer shopping and online computer magazines such as *MacWorld, PC World* and *Computer Life.*
- *Education and References.* AOL's online educational services allowed adults and children to learn without leaving their homes. AOL contracted with professional instructors to teach real-time interactive classes in subjects of both general academic interest and adult education (such as creative writing and gourmet cooking). Regular tutoring sessions were offered in English, biology and math. Education and reference services included the Library of Congress, College Board, CNN, Smithsonian, *Consumer Reports,* and *Compton's Encyclopedia.*
- *News and Personal Finance.* AOL offered a broad range of information services, including domestic and international news, weather, sports, stock market prices, and personalized portfolio tracking. Members could search news wires for stories of interest, access mutual fund information through Fidelity Online and Morningstar, and execute brokered trades online through PC Financial Network. Subscribers had access to over 70 magazines, newspapers, and wire services including *The New York Times, Chicago Tribune, San Jose Mercury News, Time, Scientific American,* and *Reuters.*
- *Travel and Shopping.* AOL member, also had access to travel and shopping reference materials and transaction services. Subscribers could send customized greeting cards through Hallmark Corporation, send flowers through 1-800-Flowers, shop for CDs and tapes online at Tower Records, book vacation packages with Preview Vacations, and access account data and travel information and services with American ExpressNet. Additionally, AOL had introduced its own interactive shopping service, 2Market, which featured goods and services from numerous catalogs and retailers.

- *Entertainment and Children's Programming.* AOL provided various clubs and forums for games and sports, multi-player games, and other related content for both adults and children. Specialized content was provided by such organizations as MusicSpace, the Games Channel, Disney Adventures, Comedy Clubs, Nintendo Power Source, Kids Only, Hollywood Online, Warner-Reprise Records, American Association for Retired Persons, MTV, Cooking Club, Environment Club, and Baby Boomers' Forum.

Customer Acquisition and Retention

AOL's biggest expenditure was the cost of attracting new subscribers. AOL aggressively marketed its online service using both independent marketing efforts, such as direct mail packets with AOL software disks and television and print advertising featuring a toll-free telephone number for ordering the AOL software, as well as co-marketing efforts with computer magazine publishers and personal computer hardware and software producers. These companies bundled the AOL software with their computer products, facilitating easy trial use by their customers. With the AOL software in hand, the customer needed only a personal computer, a telephone line, and a computer modem to gain access to AOL's online service. Accompanying each program disk was a unique registration number and password that could be used to generate a new AOL account. Customers could activate their accounts by providing AOL with their credit card account number. The first ten hours of access by this new account were free, after which AOL automatically billed the customer's credit card account the standard monthly rate until the customer canceled the AOL account.

These types of promotions were expensive, costing more than $40 per new subscriber in 1994. Thus, to retain these new subscribers and increase customer loyalty and satisfaction, AOL invested in specialized retention programs including regularly scheduled online events and conferences, online promotions of upcoming events and new features, and the regular addition of new content, services, and software programs. AOL's goal was to maximize customer subscription life.

Critical to customer retention and usage rates was the content available on AOL. To build and create unique content America Online participated in numerous joint ventures. During 1995 its alliances grew to include American Express, ABC, Reuters, Shoppers Express, Business Week, Fidelity, Vanguard, and the National Education Association. Also important to AOL were the newest stars of cyberspace, special-interest sites created by entrepreneurs such as Tom and David Gardner, who created Motley Fool and Follywood, two of the most popular sites offered on America Online. These hot special-interest sites kept customers on line, running up metered time and revenues. Traditionally, AOL had kept 80 percent or more of the revenues generated by these sites and had demanded exclusive contracts with the entrepreneurs creating them. However, content providers now had the option of setting up sites on the Internet World Wide Web. While they could not yet collect fees from Web browsers, this new distribution channel was changing the balance of power between AOL and its content providers.[2]

Compared to its competitors, AOL's rate structure was the easiest for consumers to understand and anticipate. A monthly fee of $9.95 provided access to all of America Online's services for up to five hours each month. Each additional hour was $2.95 and

---

2. "On-Line Stars Hear Siren Calls to Free Agency," Steven Lohr, New York Times, November 25, 1995.

no additional downloading fees were charged. CompuServe and Prodigy offered the same standard pricing but charged additional fees for premium services and downloading. Microsoft Network (MSN), the newest entrant into the online services industry, offered a standard monthly plan of up to three hours for $4.95, with each additional hour costing $2.50. Content providers on MSN also applied charges to customers based on usage rates. The additional fees charged by AOL's competitors made it more difficult for their customers to anticipate their monthly spending.

Strategy for Future Growth

Through a tapestry of alliances and subsidiaries, AOL's goal was to establish a central and defining leadership position in the worldwide market for interactive services. Toward this end, AOL had signed new strategic partnerships with American Express, Business Week Online, and NTN Communications; shipped the 2Market CD-ROM shopping service with an online connection; and completed its acquisitions of Internet software developers BookLink Technologies, Inc., NaviSoft, Inc., and Internet backbone developer Advanced Network & Services (ANS). These deals, along with AOL's growing membership base, its enhanced look and feel, and its ability to program content to appeal to users, uniquely positioned America Online to lead the development of the new interactive services industry. In implementing its strategy, AOL pursued a number of initiatives:

- *Invest in Growth of Existing Service.* America Online planned to continue to invest in the rapid growth of its existing online service. AOL believed it could attract and retain new members by expanding the range of content and services it offers, continuing to improve the engaging multimedia context of its service and building a sense of community online. At the same time, by offering access to a large, growing, and demographically attractive audience, together with software tools and services to develop content and programming for that audience, AOL believed it would continue to appeal to content and service providers.
- *Exploit New Business Opportunities.* AOL intended to leverage its technology, management skills, and content packaging skills to identify and exploit new business opportunities, such as electronic commerce, entry into international markets, and the "consumerization" of the Internet with its highly graphical interface software and its World Wide Web browser, which used high-speed compression technology to improve access speed and graphic display performance.
- *Provide a Full Range of Interactive Services.* Through acquisitions and internal development, AOL had assembled content development, distribution capabilities, access software, and its own communications network to become a full service, vertically integrated provider of interactive services. As a result, AOL believed it was well positioned to influence the evolution of the interactive services market.
- *Maintain Technological Flexibility.* AOL recognized the need to provide its services over a diverse set of platforms. Its software worked on different types of personal computers and operating systems (including Macintosh, Windows 3.xx and Windows 95) and supported a variety of different media, including online services, the Internet, and CD-ROM. AOL intended to adapt its products and services as new technologies become available.

While AOL currently generated revenues largely from membership fees, AOL's management believed that these initiatives would allow the company to increase the proportion of its revenues generated from other sources, such as advertising fees, commissions on merchandise sales to consumers, and revenues from the sale of production and network services to other enterprises.

INDUSTRY COMPETITION AND OUTLOOK

The online consumer services industry represented $1.1 billion in revenues in 1994 and was expected to grow by 30 percent to $1.4 billion in 1995. Eleven million customers subscribed to commercial online services worldwide and this number was expected to explode in the next five years. Industry leaders America Online, CompuServe, and Prodigy served about 8.5 million of the existing subscribers (4.0 million, 2.8 million, and 1.6 million, respectively). This oligopoly had very successfully acted as middlemen between thousands of content providers and millions of customers. They were the publishers, closely controlling the product and paying content providers, the writers, only modest royalties. However, with the advent of the Internet World Wide Web and the entrance of Microsoft Network, content providers now had alternative distribution channels that offered greater control over their products and potentially higher revenues.

Forbes discussed this topic in its August 28, 1995 issue:

> *Until recently the only way to reach cyberspace browsers was through one of the big three on-line services, America Online, CompuServe and Prodigy. That oligopoly is set to fade fast, and it's not just Microsoft that threatens. It's the whole Internet, the pulsating, undisciplined and rapidly expanding network of World Wide Web computers that contain public data bases.[3]*

While the big three acted as publishers, Microsoft had decided to act more like a bookstore, one in which every author (content provider) was his/her own publisher. Customers of MSN paid $4.95 per month for up to three hours (each additional hour was $2.50). Then, each content provider charged whatever it wanted for its material, so much per hour, per page, or per picture. Microsoft kept a 30 percent commission out of the provider's fee and passed along the rest to the content provider. In addition to offering content providers a larger share of the revenues, MSN also offered content providers greater control over their own products. In contrast to the standardized screen displays and icons of the big three, MSN permitted content providers to use any font and format they wished. Thus, while Microsoft still acted as a middleman, it played a very limited and passive role in determining content and fees charged for that content.

Beyond Microsoft lurked the vast potential of the Internet World Wide Web, where the middleman's role was shrunk still further. On the Internet, everyone with a computer was his/her own publisher. Customers would sign up for an Internet on-ramp service, of the sort offered by PST, Netcom, or MCI. Once on the net, the subscriber used browsing software like Netscape or Spyglass to roam the world's databases. While it remained difficult for self-publishers on the Internet to collect fees from browsers who read their pages, that was expected to change quickly as banks, Microsoft, and other intermediaries worked on systems to provide on-line currency.

Many content providers were beginning to take advantage of these alternative distribution channels. For example, *Wired* magazine, unwilling to settle for just 20 percent of the revenues from subscribers spending time on its pages on AOL, created HotWired on the Internet. Andrew Anker, chief technologist at *Wired*, believed that HotWired would soon be more lucrative than the America Online venture and he noted that on the Internet his firm had greater control of its own product.

---

3. "Who Needs the Middleman?," Nikhil Hutheesing, Forbes, August 28, 1995.

General Electric's NBC decided to switch from AOL to Microsoft Network. "While we had many users visiting us on America Online, we weren't making much revenue," explained Martin Yudkovitz, a senior vice-president at NBC.[4]

With the migration of proprietary services and content to Web sites, the unique offerings of the big three services were declining. However, the online services were still better for interactive communications with full-fledged message boards and live chat. The Web, on the other hand, was mainly a publication environment for reading. The question remained, what would be the role of online service providers in the future? Would they become just another Internet access provider with their own look and browsers or could they continue to offer something unique to users?

Some analysts were projecting that the U.S. online services market would grow 30–35 percent annually through the year 2000, and that the Internet market would grow even faster. These analysts expected America Online to retain about a 20 percent market share.[5] On the other hand, Forrester Research of Cambridge Mass., predicted that the big three, America Online, CompuServe, and Prodigy, would continue to add subscribers only through 1997. After that, Forrester predicted, it would be all downhill for the big three.[6]

AOL'S RECENT PERFORMANCE

For the fourth quarter ended June 30, 1995, America Online announced that its earnings were $0.16, excluding $0.01 merger expenses and $0.02 amortization of goodwill. This was a significant improvement over 1994's fourth-quarter earnings, $0.02, and above analysts' estimate, $0.14. Service revenues surged to $139 million, versus analysts' estimate of $132 million, and total revenues rose to $152 million versus $40.4 in the fourth quarter of 1994. For the fiscal year ended June 30, 1995, AOL reported a loss of $33.6 million on revenues of $394 million compared with a profit of $2.5 million on revenues of $116 million a year earlier. New charges recorded for the first time in 1995 included $50.3 million for acquired R&D, $1.7 million amortization of goodwill, and $2.2 million in merger expenses. See Exhibit 3, America Online's 1995 Abridged Annual Report.

New subscriber momentum continued to be strong, increasing 233 percent year-over-year and adding 691,000 new net subscribers during the fourth quarter. All major metrics used by analysts to evaluate AOL's franchise and gauge the "health" of its rapidly growing subscriber base also improved during the quarter: projected retention rates rose to 41 months from 39 months; paid usage grew to 2.93 hours from 2.73, and projected lifetime revenues per subscriber increased to $714 from $667. See Exhibit 2 for the history of America Online's User Metrics. However, analysts were projecting lower gross margins in the future as subscribers continued to transition to higher-speed access and as AOL introduced a heavy-usage pricing plan in response to Microsoft's lower per hour pricing.

On November 8, 1995, America Online announced its results for the first quarter of fiscal 1996 ended September 30, 1995. Even though revenues rose to $197.9 million from $56 million a year earlier, America Online reported a loss of $10.3 million

4. *Ibid.*

5. "America Online, Inc. – Company Report," A. Pooley, The Chicago Corporation, April 18, 1995.

6. Op. cit. Forbes, August 28, 1995.

compared with a profit of $1.5 million a year earlier. America Online took a $16.9 million charge to reflect research and development taking place at Ubique, a company it acquired on September 21, 1995, as well as to pay off other recently acquired assets. It took another charge of $1.7 million for amortization of goodwill. These charges were partially offset by AOL's decision to increase the period over which it amortized subscriber acquisition costs. Effective July 1, 1995, these costs would be amortized over 24 months rather than 12–18 months. The effect of the change in accounting estimates for the three months ended September 30, 1995, was to decrease the reported loss by $1.95 million. AOL also announced that it added 711,000 subscribers in the first quarter of 1996, bringing its total subscriber base to four million.[7]

America Online's stock price had been on the move since the company's initial public offering (IPO) in March 1992. The stock price appreciated from the IPO price of $2.90 to $7.31, $14.63, and $28.00 at calendar year end 1992, 1993, and 1994, respectively. At its current price of $81.63 dated November 8, 1995, the company's market value was around $4.0 billion. See Exhibit 1 for the stock price history of America Online, its equity beta, and additional market-based data.

THE CONTROVERSY SURROUNDING AOL

America Online's stock was one of the most controversial of this period. Some analysts promoted the stock's potential for price appreciation, while others recommended selling the shares short to profit from a decline in price. Bulls saw America Online as part of a revolution in communication, like cellular phones and cable television in the early days. They considered AOL's graphical interface software, its high-speed Web browser, and Mr. Case's marketing genius (subscribership had quadrupled to over four million in a little over a year) to be major competitive advantages. Bears, on the other hand, anticipating new entrants competing in the online services industry and a migration of subscribers to the Internet, questioned whether AOL would continue to experience high growth in its subscriber base or be able to retain existing subscribers.

Shortsellers had sold around seven million America Online shares, betting that the stock's price would not go up forever. Shortsellers pointed to the recent hedging activities by Apple Computer to lock in profits on its 5.7 percent stake as an indication that AOL's stock was overvalued. Adding fuel to the shortsellers' fire, corporate insiders at AOL had sold some of their shareholdings. Between March 9 and March 15 of 1995, seventeen insiders sold approximately 200,000 shares, including the company founders, President Steven Case (25,000 shares for $2.1 million) and Chairman James Kimsey (40,000 shares for $3.3 million).[8]

Adding to the controversy, some analysts labeled AOL's accounting "aggressive." AOL amortized its software development costs over five years, a long time in the fast-changing, uncertain online services industry, and AOL capitalized subscriber acquisition costs when its number one competitor, CompuServe, did not. Furthermore, effective July 1, 1995, AOL extended the amortization period for its subscriber acquisition costs from about 15 months to 24 months. Given the uncertainties surrounding AOL's

---

7. *"America Online Posts $10.3 Million Loss But Says Revenue Rose 250% in Quarter,"* The Washington Post, *November 8, 1995.*

8. *As of August 15, 1995 all executive officers and directors as a group continued to own 3,729,547 shares, Steven Case owned 1,036,790 shares and James Kimsey owned 679,616 shares.*

subscriber retention rates and revenue growth as competition emerged in the young industry, analysts questioned the wisdom of AOL's accounting decisions. The big risk AOL faced was that eventually customers could switch on-line services as frequently as they now move among long-distance carriers.

While America Online expensed the free trial expenses (i.e., those charges incurred from the ten free hours given away in the initial month), it capitalized the marketing costs associated with acquiring a customer including direct mail, advertising, start-up kits, and bundling costs. As indicated in its annual report, prior to July 1, 1995, the capitalization had occurred on two schedules depending on the acquisition method. Costs for subscribers acquired through direct marketing programs were amortized over a 12-month period. Costs for subscribers acquired through co-marketing efforts with personal computer producers and magazine publishers were amortized over an 18-month period, as these bundling campaigns had historically shown a longer response time. However, effective July 1, 1995, AOL increased the period over which it amortized subscriber acquisition costs to 24 months for both acquisition methods.

Defending AOL's accounting choices, Lennert Leader, the Chief Financial Officer of America Online, Inc., said that the company was following standard accounting procedures in matching the timing of expenses with the period over which the revenues would be received. He argued that the company's marketing and software development expenses produced customer accounts that last a long time. Thus, he said, it was appropriate to write off the costs over a period of years, even though AOL had spent the cash.[9]

However, some analysts raised red flags about AOL's accounting choices. As noted in the October 24, 1995 *Newsweek* article:

> One of AOL's hidden assets is the brilliant accounting decision it made to treat its marketing and research and development costs as capital items rather than expenses.
>
> AOL charges R&D expenses over a five-year period, a very long time in the on-line biz. In July, AOL began charging off marketing expenses over two years, up from about 15 months.
>
> Why change to 24 months from 15? Leader said it's because the average life of an AOL account has climbed to 41 months from 25 months in 1992. How many AOL customers have been around for 41 months? Almost none, as Leader concedes. That's understandable, considering that AOL has added virtually all its customers in the past 36 months. Leader says the 41-month average live number comes from projections. Of course, it will take years to find out if he's right.[10]

Analysts were also concerned about AOL's cash flow situation and the signal sent by the timing of its latest equity offering. The *Newsweek* article continued:

> Accounting is terribly important to AOL. The better the numbers look, the more Wall Street loves it and the easier AOL can sell new shares to raise cash to pay its bills. On October 10 [AOL] raised about $100 million by selling new shares. AOL sold the stock even though its shares had fallen to $58.37 from about $72 in September, when the sale plans were announced. Most companies would have delayed the offering, waiting for the price to snap back. AOL didn't, prompting cynics to think the company really needed the money.

---

9. Op. cit., *Newsweek*, October 24, 1995.

10. Op. cit., *Newsweek*, October 24, 1995.

Some analysts believed that AOL issued shares when its stock price was low because the company needed the cash immediately. Others argued that AOL was building a war chest needed because deep-pocketed rivals such as Microsoft were about to start an online price war and because increasingly information providers were going directly to the Internet, rather than using middlemen such as AOL. Some analysts interpreted CompuServe's recent adoption of more aggressive accounting techniques as a sign that it too was readying for war. Beginning the first quarter of fiscal 1996, CompuServe would capitalize direct response advertising costs associated with customer acquisition activity.[11]

While AOL's stock price rebounded to $81.63 by November 8, 1995, there were many questions concerning AOL's future. How would the demand for AOL's services be affected by the entry of Microsoft Network and the growth of Internet? Would AOL's accounting choices stand the test of time? What if AOL's subscription growth rates slowed or subscriber renewal rates fell? Did AOL have the financial flexibility to face these competitive pressures and accounting risks?

QUESTIONS

1. Prior to 1995, why was America Online (AOL) so successful in the commercial online industry relative to its competitors CompuServe and Prodigy?

2. As of 1995, what are the key changes taking place in the commercial online industry? How are they likely to affect AOL's future prospects?

3. Was AOL's policy to capitalize subscriber acquisition costs justified prior to 1995?

4. Given the changes discussed in question 2, do you think AOL should change its accounting policy as of 1995? Is the company's response consistent with your view?

5. What would be the effect on AOL's 1994 and 1995 ending balance sheets if the company had followed the policy of expensing subscriber acquisition outlays instead of capitalizing them? What would be the effect of expensing subscriber acquisition costs on AOL's 1995 income statement?

---

11. *Op. cit., Newsweek, October 24, 1995.*

America Online, Inc.

EXHIBIT 1
Stock Price History for America Online, Inc.

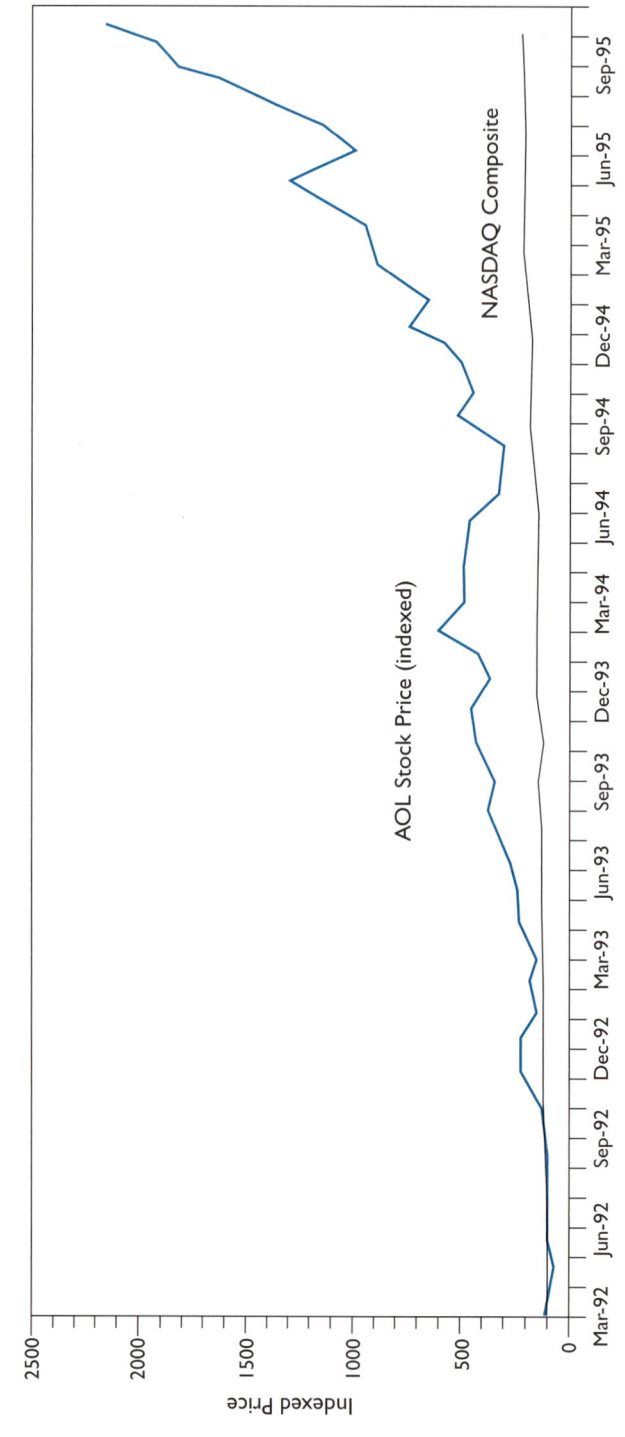

Additional market-based data:

America Online's equity beta	1.4
Moody's AAA corporate debt in November 1995 (%)	7.02
Treasury bills rate in November 1995 (%)	5.35
Government 30-year treasury rates in November 1995 (%)	6.26

Sources: Datastream International, Standard and Poor's Compustat, and the Wall Street Journal.

EXHIBIT 2

America Online, Inc. User Metrics to June 30, 1995

	Dec-93	Mar-94	Jun-94	Sep-94	Dec-94	Mar-95	Jun-95
Paid usage (hours)	1.85	2	2.1	2.27	2.46	2.73	2.93
Projected average months' retention	30	32	32+	34	36	39	41
Projected average lifetime revenue	$443	$496	$496	$551	$612	$667	$714
Internet usage (% time)		1%	3%	4%	5%	6%	9%

Source: Alex Brown & Sons, Inc., August 24, 1995.

America Online, Inc.

EXHIBIT 3

America Online 1995 Abridged Annual Report

REPORT OF INDEPENDENT AUDITORS

Board of Directors and Stockholders
America Online, Inc.

We have audited the accompanying consolidated balance sheets of America Online, Inc., as of June 30, 1995 and 1994, and the related consolidated statements of operations, changes in stockholders' equity and cash flows for each of the three years in the period ended June 30, 1995. These financial statements are the responsibility of the Company's management. Our responsibility is to express an opinion on these financial statements based on our audits.

We conducted our audits in accordance with generally accepted auditing standards. Those standards require that we plan and perform the audit to obtain reasonable assurance about whether the financial statements are free of material misstatement. An audit includes examining, on a test basis, evidence supporting the amounts and disclosures in the financial statements. An audit also includes assessing the accounting principles used and significant estimates made by management, as well as evaluating the overall financial statement presentation. We believe that our audits provide a reasonable basis for our opinion.

In our opinion, the financial statements referred to above present fairly, in all material respects, the consolidated financial position of America Online, Inc. at June 30, 1995 and 1994, and the consolidated results of their operations and their cash flows for each of the three years in the period ended June 30, 1995, in conformity with generally accepted accounting principles.

As discussed in Note 9 to the consolidated financial statements, in fiscal 1994 the Company changed its method of accounting for income taxes. As discussed in Note 2 to the consolidated financial statements, in fiscal 1995 the Company changed its method of accounting for short-term investments in certain debt and equity securities.

Ernst & Young LLP

Vienna, Virginia
August 25, 1995

America Online, Inc.

SELECTED CONSOLIDATED FINANCIAL AND OTHER DATA

	Year Ended June 30,				
	1995	1994	1993	1992	1991
	(In Thousands, Except Per Share Data)				
Statements of Operations Data:					
Online service revenues	$358,498	$100,993	$38,462	$26,226	$19,515
Other revenues	35,792	14,729	13,522	12,527	10,646
Total Revenues	394,290	115,722	51,984	38,753	30,161
Income (loss) from operations	(19,294)	4,608	1,925	3,685	1,341
Income (loss) before extraordinary items	(33,647)	2,550	399	2,344	1,100
Net income (loss) (1)	(33,647)	2,550	1,532	3,768	1,761
Income (loss) per common share:					
Income (loss) before extraordinary item	$(0.99)	$0.07	$0.01	$0.10	$0.06
Net income (loss)	$(0.99)	$0.07	$0.05	$0.17	$0.09
Weighted average shares outstanding	33,986	34,208	29,286	22,828	19,304

	As of June 30,				
	1995	1994	1993	1992	1991
	(in thousands)				
Balance Sheet Data:					
Working capital (deficiency)	$(456)	$47,890	$10,498	$12,363	$(966)
Total assets	406,464	154,584	39,279	31,144	11,534
Total debt	21,810	9,302	2,959	2,672	1,865
Stockholders' equity (deficiency)	217,944	98,297	23,785	21,611	(8,623)
Other data (at fiscal year end):					
Subscribers	3,005	903	303	182	131

(1) Net loss in the fiscal year ended June 30, 1995, includes charges of $50.3 million for acquired research and development and $2.2 million for merger expenses. See Note 3 of the Notes to Consolidated Financial Statements.

MANAGEMENT'S DISCUSSION AND ANALYSIS OF FINANCIAL CONDITIONS AND RESULTS OF OPERATIONS

Overview

The Company has experienced a significant increase in revenues over the past three fiscal years. The higher revenues have been principally produced by increases in the Company's subscriber base resulting from growth of the online services market, the introduction of a Windows version of America Online in the middle of fiscal 1993, which greatly increased the available market for the Company's service, as well as the expansion of its services and content. Additionally, revenues have increased as the average monthly revenue per subscriber has risen steadily during the past three years, primarily as a result of an increase in the average monthly paid hours of use per subscriber.

The Company's online service revenues are generated primarily from subscribers paying a monthly member's fee and hourly charges based on usage in excess of the number of hours of usage provided as part of the monthly fee. Through December 31, 1994, the Company's standard monthly membership fee, which includes five hours of service, was $9.95, with a $3.50 hourly fee for usage in excess of five hours per month. Effective January 1, 1995, the hourly fee for usage in excess of five hours per month decreased from $3.50 to $2.95, while the monthly membership fee remained unchanged at $9.95.

The Company's other revenues are generated primarily from providing new media and interactive marketing services, data network services, and multimedia and CD-ROM production services. Additionally, the Company generates revenues related to online transactions and advertising, as well as development and licensing fees.

In fiscal 1995 the Company acquired RCC, NaviSoft, BookLink, ANS, WAIS, Medior and Global Network Navigator, Inc. Additionally, in August 1995, the Company entered into an agreement to acquire Ubique. For additional information relating to these acquisitions, refer to Notes 3 and 13 of the Notes to Consolidated Financial Statements.

The online services market is highly competitive. The Company believes that existing competitors, which include, among others, CompuServe, Prodigy and MSN, are likely to enhance their service offerings. In addition, new competitors have announced plans to enter the online services market, resulting in greater competition for the Company. The competitive environment could require new pricing programs and increased spending on marketing, content procurement and product development; limit the Company's opportunities to enter into and/or renew agreements with content providers and distribution partners; limit the Company's ability to grow its subscriber base; and result in increased attrition in the Company's subscriber base. Any of the foregoing events could result in an increase in costs as a percentage of revenues, and may have a material adverse effect on the Company's financial condition and operating results.

During September 1995, the Company modified the components of subscriber acquisition costs deferred and will be expensing certain subscriber acquisition cost as incurred, effective July 1, 1995. All costs capitalized before this change will continue to be amortized. The effect of this change for the year ended June 30, 1995 (including the amortization of amounts capitalized as of June 30, 1994) would have been to increase marketing costs by approximately $8 million. This change will have a greater impact on the Company's marketing costs in fiscal 1996, as the Company expects to significantly increase subscriber acquisition activity, including those subscriber acquisition expenditures which the Company will be expensing as incurred.

In addition, effective July 1, 1995, the Company changed the period over which it amortizes subscriber acquisition cost from twelve and eighteen months to twenty-four months. Based on the Company's historical average customer life experience, the change in amortization period is being made to more appropriately match subscriber acquisition costs with associated online service revenues. The effect of this change in accounting estimate for the year ended June 30, 1995 would have been to decrease the amount of the amortization of subscriber acquisition costs by approximately $27 million. While this change will thereby positively impact operating margins, the Company expects that any such positive impact will be partially offset by increased investments in marketing and other business activities during fiscal 1996 and the decision, effective July 1, 1995, to expense certain subscriber acquisition costs as incurred.

Results of Operations

Fiscal 1995 Compared to Fiscal 1994

Online Service Revenues.   For fiscal 1995, online service revenues increased from $100,993,000 to $358,498,000, or 255%, over fiscal 1994. This increase was primarily attributable to a 289% increase in revenues from IBM-compatible subscribes and a 196% increase in revenues from Macintosh subscribers as a result of a 273% increase in the number of IBM-compatible subscribers and a 143% increase in the number of Macintosh subscribers. The percentage increase in online service revenues in fiscal 1995 was greater than the percentage increase in subscribers principally due to an increase in the average monthly online service revenue per subscriber, which increased from $15.00 in fiscal 1994 to $17.10 in fiscal 1995.

Other Revenues.   Other revenues, consisting principally of new media and interactive marketing services, data network services, multimedia and CD-ROM production services, and development and licensing fees, increased from $14,729,000 in fiscal 1994 to $35,792,000 in fiscal 1995. This increase was primarily attributable to data network revenues and multimedia and CD-ROM production service revenues from companies acquired during fiscal 1995.

Cost of Revenues.   Cost of revenues includes network-related costs, consisting primarily of data and voice communication costs, costs associated with operating the data center and providing customer support, royalties paid to information and service providers and other expenses related to marketing and production services. For fiscal 1995, cost of revenues increased from $69,043,000 to $229,724,000, or 233%, over fiscal 1994, and decreased as a percentage of total revenues from 59.7% to 58.3%.

The increase in cost of revenues was primarily attributable to an increase in data communication costs, customer support costs and royalties paid to information and service providers. Data communication costs increased primarily as a result of the larger customer base and more usage by customers. Customer support costs, which include personnel and telephone costs associated with providing customer support, were higher as a result of the larger customer base and a large number of new subscriber registrations. Royalties paid to information and service providers

increased as a result of a larger customer base and more usage and the Company's addition of more service content to broaden the appeal of the America Online service.

The decrease in cost of revenues as a percentage of total revenues is primarily attributable to a decrease in expenses related to marketing services and personnel related costs as a percentage of total revenues, partially offset by an increase in data communication costs as a percentage of total revenues, primarily resulting from an increase in higher baud speed usage at a higher variable rate as well as lower hourly pricing for online service revenue which became effective January 1, 1995.

Marketing.   Marketing expenses include the costs to acquire and retain subscribers and other general marketing expenses. Subscriber acquisition costs are deferred and charged to operations over a twelve or eighteen month period, using the straight-line method, beginning the month after such costs are incurred. For additional information regarding the accounting for deferred subscriber acquisition costs, refer to Note 2 of the Notes to Consolidated Financial Statements. For fiscal 1995, marketing expenses increased from $23,548,000 to $77,064,000, or 227%, over fiscal 1994, and decreased as a percentage of total revenues from 20.3% to 19.5%. The increase in marketing expenses was primarily due to an increase in the number and size of marketing programs to expand the Company's subscriber base. The decrease in marketing expenses as a percentage of total revenues is primarily attributable to a decrease as a percentage of total revenues in personnel related costs.

Product Development.   Product development costs include research and development expenses, other product development costs and the amortization of software costs. For fiscal 1995, product development expenses increased from $4,961,000 to $12,842,000, or 159%, over fiscal 1994, and decreased as a percentage of total revenues from 4.3% to 3.3%. The increase in product development costs was primarily attributable to an increase in personnel costs related to an increase in the number of technical employees. The decrease in product development costs as a percentage of total revenues was principally a result of the substantial growth in revenues, which more than offset the additional product development costs. Product development costs,

America Online, Inc.

before capitalization and amortization, increased by 126% in fiscal 1995.

General and Administrative. Fiscal 1995 general and administrative costs increased from $13,562,000 to $41,966,000, or 209%, over fiscal 1994, and decreased as a percentage of total revenues from 11.7% to 10.6%. The increase in general and administrative expenses was principally attributable to higher office and personnel expenses related to an increase in the number of employees. The decrease in general and administrative costs as a percentage of total revenues was a result of the substantial growth in revenues, which more than offset the additional general and administrative costs, combined with the semi-variable nature of many of the general and administrative costs.

Acquired Research and Development. Acquired research and development costs, totaling $50,335,000, relate to in-process research and development purchased pursuant to the Company's acquisition of two early-stage Internet technology companies, BookLink and NaviSoft. The purchased research and development relating to the BookLink and NaviSoft acquisitions was the foundation of the development of the Company's Internet related products.

Amortization of Goodwill. Amortization of goodwill relates to the Company's acquisition of ANS, which resulted in approximately $44 million in goodwill. The goodwill related to the ANS acquisition is being amortized on a straight-line basis over a ten-year period.

Other Income. Other income consists primarily of investment and rental income net of interest expense. For fiscal 1995, other income increased from $1,774,000 to $3,023,000. This increase was primarily attributable to an increase in interest income generated by higher levels of cash available for investment, partially offset by a decrease in rental income and an increase in interest expense.

Merger Expenses. Non-recurring merger expenses totaling $2,207,000 were recognized in fiscal 1995 in connection with the mergers of the Company with RCC, WAIS and Medior.

Provisions for Income Taxes. The provision for income taxes was $3,832,000 and $15,169,000 in fiscal year 1994 and fiscal 1995, respectively. For additional information regarding income taxes, refer to Note 9 of the Notes to Consolidated Financial Statements.

Net Loss. The net loss in fiscal 1995 totaled $33,647,000. The net loss in fiscal 1995 included charges of $50,335,000 for acquired research and development and $2,207,000 for merger expenses.

Liquidity and Capital Resources

The Company has financed its operations through cash generated from operations, sale of its common stock and funding by third parties for certain product development activities. Net cash provided by operating activities was $2,205,000, $1,884,000 and $15,891,000 for fiscal 1993, fiscal 1994 and fiscal 1995, respectively. Included in operating activities were expenditures for deferred subscriber acquisition costs of $10,685,000, $37,424,000 and $111,761,000 in fiscal 1993, fiscal 1994 and fiscal 1995, respectively. Net cash used in investing activities was $8,915,000, $41,870,000 and $85,725,000 in fiscal 1993, fiscal 1994 and fiscal 1995, respectively. Investing activities included $20,523,000 in fiscal 1995 related to business acquisitions, substantially all of which were related to the acquisition of ANS.

In December 1993 the Company completed a public stock offering of 4,000,000 shares of common stock which generated net cash proceeds of approximately $62.7 million.

In April 1995 the company entered into a joint venture with Bertelsmann to offer interactive online services in Europe. In connection with the agreement, the Company received approximately $54 million through the sale of approximately 5% of its common stock to Bertelsmann.

The Company leases the majority of its equipment under noncancelable operating leases, and as part of its network portfolio strategy is building AOLnet, its data communications network. The buildout of this network requires a substantial investment in telecommunication equipment, which the Company plans to finance principally though leasing. In addition, the Company has guaranteed minimum commitments under certain data and voice communication agreements. The Company's future lease commitments and guaranteed minimums are discussed in Note 6 of the Notes to Consolidated Financial Statements.

The Company uses its working capital to finance ongoing operations and to fund marketing and content programs and the development of its products and services. The Company plans to continue to invest aggressively in acquisition marketing and content programs to expand its subscriber base, as well as in computing and support infrastructure. Additionally, the Company expects to use a portion of its cash for the acquisition and subsequent funding of technologies, products or businesses complementary to the Company's current business. Apart from its agreement to acquire Ubique, as discussed below, the Company has no agreements or understandings to acquire any businesses. The Company anticipates that available cash and cash provided by operating activities will be sufficient to fund its operations for the next fiscal year.

Various legal proceedings have arisen against the Company in the ordinary course of business. In the opinion of management, these proceedings will not have a material effect on the financial position of the Company.

The Company believes that inflation has not had a material effect on its results of operations.

On August 23, 1995, the Company entered into a stock purchase agreement to purchase Ubique, an Israeli company. The Company has agreed to pay approximately $15 million ($1.5 million in cash and $13.5 million in common stock) in the transaction, which is to be accounted for as a purchase. Subject to the results of an in-process valuation, a substantial portion of the purchase price may be allocated to in-process research and development and charged to the Company's operations in the first quarter of fiscal 1996.

CONSOLIDATED STATEMENTS OF OPERATIONS
(Amounts in Thousands, Except Per Share Data)

| | Year ended June 30, | | |
	1995	1994	1993
Revenues:			
Online service revenues	$358,498	$100,993	$ 38,462
Other revenues	35,792	14,729	13,522
Total revenues	394,290	115,722	51,984
Costs and expenses:			
Cost of revenues	229,724	69,043	28,820
Marketing	77,064	23,548	9,745
Product development	12,842	4,961	2,913
General and administrative	41,966	13,562	8,581
Acquired research and development	50,335	—	—
Amortization of goodwill	1,653	—	—
Total costs and expenses	413,584	111,114	50,059
Income (loss) from operations	(19,294)	4,608	1,925
Other income, net	3,023	1,774	371
Merger expenses	(2,207)	—	—
Income (loss) before provision for income taxes and extraordinary item	(18,478)	6,382	2,296
Provision for income taxes	(15,169)	(3,832)	(1,897)
Income (loss) before extraordinary item	(33,647)	2,550	399
Extraordinary item – tax benefit arising from net operating loss carryforward	—	—	1,133
Net income (loss)	$(33,647)	$2,550	$1,532
Earnings (loss) per share:			
Income (loss) before extraordinary item	$ (0.99)	$ 0.07	$ 0.01
Net income (loss)	$ (0.99)	$ 0.07	$ 0.05
Weighted average shares outstanding	33,986	34,208	29,286

See accompanying notes.

America Online, Inc.

CONSOLIDATED BALANCE SHEETS
(Amounts in Thousands, Except Per Share Data)

	June 30,	
	1995	1994
Assets		
Current assets:		
Cash and cash equivalents	$ 45,378	$ 43,891
Short-term investments	18,672	24,052
Trade accounts receivable	32,176	8,547
Other receivables	11,103	2,036
Prepaid expenses and other current assets	25,527	5,753
Total current assets	132,856	84,279
Property and equipment at cost, net	70,466	20,306
Other assets:		
Product development costs, net	18,914	7,912
Deferred subscriber acquisition costs, net	77,229	26,392
License rights, net	5,537	53
Other assets	11,479	2,800
Deferred income taxes	35,627	12,842
Goodwill, net	54,356	—
	$406,464	$154,584
Liabilities and Stockholders' Equity		
Current liabilities:		
Trade accounts payable	$ 84,639	$ 15,642
Accrued personnel costs	2,829	896
Other accrued expenses and liabilities	23,509	13,076
Deferred revenue	20,021	4,488
Line of credit	484	1,690
Current portion of long-term debt and capital lease obligations	1,830	597
Total current liabilities	133,312	36,389
Long-term liabilities:		
Notes payable	17,369	5,836
Capital lease obligations	2,127	1,179
Deferred income taxes	35,627	12,842
Deferred rent	85	41
Total liabilities	188,520	56,287
Stockholders' equity:		
Preferred stock, $.01 par value; 5,000,000 shares authorized, none issued	—	—
Common stock, $.01 par value; 100,000,000 shares authorized, 37,554,849 and 30,771,212 shares issued and outstanding at June 30, 1995 and 1994, respectively	375	308
Additional paid-in capital	251,539	98,836
Accumulated deficit	(33,970)	(847)
Total stockholders' equity	217,944	98,297
	$406,464	$154,584

See accompanying notes.

America Online, Inc.

CONSOLIDATED STATEMENTS OF CASH FLOWS
(Amounts in Thousands)

	Year ended June 30,		
	1995	1994	1993
Cash flows from operating activities:			
Net income (loss)	$ (33,647)	$ 2,550	$ 1,532
Adjustments to reconcile net income to net cash provided by operating activities:			
Depreciation and amortization	11,136	2,965	1,957
Amortization of subscriber acquisition costs	60,924	17,922	7,038
Loss/(Gain) on sale of property and equipment	37	5	(39)
Charge for acquired research and development	50,335	—	—
Changes in assets and liabilities:			
Trade accounts receivable	(14,373)	(4,266)	(936)
Other receivables	(9,057)	(681)	(966)
Prepaid expenses and other current assets	(19,641)	(2,867)	(1,494)
Deferred subscriber acquisition costs	(111,761)	(37,424)	(10,685)
Other assets	(8,432)	(2,519)	(89)
Trade accounts payable	60,824	10,204	2,119
Accrued personnel costs	1,846	367	336
Other accrued expenses and liabilities	5,703	9,526	1,492
Deferred revenue	7,190	2,322	1,381
Deferred income taxes	14,763	3,832	759
Deferred rent	44	(52)	(200)
Total adjustments	49,538	(666)	673
Net cash provided by operating activities	15,891	1,884	2,205
Cash flows from investing activities:			
Short-term investments	5,380	(18,947)	(5,105)
Purchase of property and equipment	(57,751)	(17,886)	(2,041)
Product development costs	(13,011)	(5,132)	(1,831)
Sale of property and equipment	180	95	62
Purchase costs of acquired businesses	(20,523)	—	—
Net cash used in investing activities	(85,725)	(41,870)	(8,915)
Cash flows from financing activities:			
Proceeds from issuance of common stock, net	61,253	67,372	609
Principal and accrued interest payments on line of credit and long-term debt	(3,298)	(7,716)	(6,924)
Proceeds from line of credit and issuance of long-term debt	13,741	14,200	7,181
Tax benefit from stock option exercises	—	—	6
Principal payments under capital lease obligations	(375)	(142)	(112)
Net cash provided by financing activities	71,321	73,714	760
Net increase (decrease) in cash and cash equivalents	1,487	33,728	(5,950)
Cash and cash equivalents at beginning of period	43,891	10,163	16,113
Cash and cash equivalents at end of period	$ 45,378	$ 43,891	$ 10,163
Supplemental cash flow information			
Cash paid during the period for:			
Interest	1,067	575	193
Income taxes	—	—	15

See accompanying notes.

NOTES TO CONSOLIDATED FINANCIAL STATEMENTS

1. Organization

America Online, Inc. ("the Company") was incorporated in the State of Delaware in May 1985. The Company, based in Vienna, Virginia, is a leading provider of online services, offering its subscribers a wide variety of services, including e-mail, online conferences, entertainment, software, computing support, interactive magazines and newspapers, and online classes, as well as easy and affordable access to services of the Internet. In addition, the Company is a provider of data network services, new media and interactive marketing services, and multimedia and CD-ROM production services.

2. Summary of Significant Accounting Policies

Principles of consolidation – The consolidated financial statements include the accounts of the Company and its subsidiaries. All significant intercompany accounts and transactions have been eliminated. Investments in affiliates owned twenty percent or more and corporate joint ventures are accounted for under the equity method. Other securities in companies owned less than twenty percent are accounted for under the cost method.

Business combinations – Business combinations which have been accounted for under the purchase method of accounting include the results of operations of the acquired business from the date of acquisition. Net assets of the companies acquired are recorded at their fair value to the Company at the date of acquisition.

Other business combinations have been accounted for under the pooling of interests method of accounting. In such cases, the assets, liabilities, and stockholders' equity of the acquired entities were combined with the Company's respective accounts at recorded values. Prior period financial statements have been restated to give effect to the merger unless the effect of the business combination is not material to the financial statements of the Company.

Revenue and cost recognition – Online service revenue is recognized over the period services are provided. Other revenue, consisting principally of marketing, data network and multimedia production services, as well as development and royalty revenues, are recognized as services are rendered. Deferred revenue consists principally of third-party development funding not yet recognized and monthly subscription fees billed in advance.

Property and equipment – Property and equipment are depreciated or amortized using the straight-line method over the estimated useful life of the asset, which ranges from 5 to 40 years, or over the life of the lease.

Property and equipment under capital leases are stated at the lower of the present value of minimum lease payments at the beginning of the lease term or fair value at inception of the lease.

Deferred subscriber acquisition costs – Subscriber acquisition costs are deferred and charged to operations over a twelve or eighteen month period (straight-line method) beginning the month after such costs are incurred. These costs, which relate directly to subscriber solicitations, principally include printing, production and shipping of starter kits and the costs of obtaining qualified prospects by various targeted direct marketing programs (i.e., direct marketing response cards, mailing lists) and from third parties, and are recorded separately from ordinary operating expenses. No indirect costs are included in subscriber acquisition costs. To date, all subscriber acquisition costs have been incurred for the solicitation of specific identifiable prospects. Costs incurred for other than those targeted at specific identifiable prospects for the Company's services, and general marketing, are expensed as incurred.

The Company's services are sold on a monthly subscription basis. Subscriber acquisition costs incurred to obtain new subscribers are recoverable from revenues generated by such subscribers within a short period of time after such costs are incurred.

Effective July 1, 1992, the Company changed, from twelve months to eighteen months, the period over which it amortizes the cost of deferred subscriber acquisition costs relating to marketing activities in which the Company's starter kit is bundled and distributed by a third-party marketing company. The change in accounting estimate was made to more accurately match revenues and expenses. Based on the Company's experience and the distribution channels used in such marketing activities, there is a greater time lag between the time the Company incurs the cost for the starter kits and the time the starter kits begin to generate new customers than with direct marketing activities. Also, the period over which new subscribers (and related revenues) are generated is longer than that experienced with the use of traditional independent, direct marketing activities. The effect of this change in accounting estimate for the year ended June 30, 1993 was to increase income before extraordinary item and net income by $264,000 ($.01 per share).

In the first quarter of fiscal 1995 the Company adopted the provisions of Statement of Position ("SOP") 93–7 "Reporting on Advertising Costs," which provides guidance on financial reporting on advertising costs. The adoption of SOP 93–7 had no effect on the Company's financial position or results of operations.

Product development costs – The Company capitalizes cost incurred for the production of computer software used in the sale of its services. Costs capitalized include direct labor and related overhead for software produced by the Company and the costs of software purchased from third parties. All costs in the software development process which are classified as research and development are expensed as incurred until technological feasibility has been established. Once technological feasibility has been established, such costs are capitalized until the software is commercially available. To the extent the Company retains the rights to software development funded by third parties, such costs are capitalized in accordance with the Company's normal accounting policies. Amortization is provided on a product-by-product basis, using the greater of the straight-line method or current year revenue as a percent of total revenue estimates for the related software product not to exceed five years, commencing the month after the date of product release.

Product development costs consist of the following:

	Year ended June 30,	
	1995	1994
	(in thousands)	
Balance, beginning of year	$ 7,912	$ 3,915
Cost capitalized	13,011	5,132
Cost amortized	(2,009)	(1,135)
Balance, end of year	$18,914	$ 7,912

The accumulated amortization of product development costs related to the production of computer software totaled $7,894,000, and $5,885,000 at June 30, 1995 and 1994, respectively.

Included in product development costs are research and development costs totaling $3,856,000, $2,126,000, and $1,130,000 and other product development costs totaling $6,977,000, $1,050,000 and $579,000 in the years ended June 30, 1995, 1994 and 1993, respectively.

License rights – The cost of acquired license rights is amortized using the straight-line method over the term of the agreement for such license rights, ranging from one to three years.

Goodwill – Goodwill consists of the excess of cost over the fair value of net assets acquired and certain other intangible assets relating to purchase transactions. Goodwilll and intangible assets are amortized over periods ranging from 5–10 years.

Operating lease costs – Rent expense for operating leases is recognized on a straight-line basis over the lease term. The difference between rent expense incurred and rental payments is charged or credited to deferred rent.

Cash, cash equivalents and short-term investments – The Company considers all highly liquid investments with an original maturity of three months or less to be cash equivalents. In fiscal 1995, the Company adopted Statement of Financial Accounting Standards No. 115 ("SFAS 115"), "Accounting for Certain Investments in Debt and Equity Securities." The adoption was not material to the Company's financial position or results of operations. The Company has classified all debt and equity securities as available-for-sale. Available-for-sale securities are carried at fair value, with unrealized gains and losses reported as a separate component of stockholders' equity. Realized gains and losses and declines in value judged to be other-than-temporary on available-for-sale securities are included in other income. Available-for-sale securities at June 30, 1995, consisted of U.S. Treasury Bills and other - obligations of U.S. Government agencies totaling $7,579,000 and U.S. corporate debt obligations totaling $11,093,000. At June 20, 1995, the estimated fair value of these securities approximated cost.

Net income (loss) per common share – Net income (loss) per share is calculated by dividing income (loss) before extraordinary item and net income (loss) by the weighted average number of common and, when dilutive, common equivalent shares outstanding during the period.

Reclassification – Certain amounts in prior years' consolidated financial statements have been reclassified to conform to the current year presentation.

3. Business Combination

Pooling Transactions

On August 19, 1994, Redgate Communications Corporation ("RCC") was merged with and into a subsidiary of the Company. The Company exchanged 1,789,300 shares of common stock for all of the outstanding common and preferred stock and warrants of RCC. Additionally, 401,148 shares of the Company's common stock were reserved for outstanding stock options issued by RCC and assumed by the Company. The merger was accounted for under the pooling of interests method of accounting, and accordingly, the accompanying consolidated financial statements have been restated for all periods prior to the acquisition to include the financial position, results of operations and cash flows of RCC. Effective August 1994, RCC's fiscal year-end has been changed from December 31 to June 30 to conform to the Company's fiscal year-end.

Revenues and net earnings (loss) for the individual entities are as follows:

	Three months ended September 30, 1994	Year ended June 30,	
	(unaudited)	1994	1993
	(in thousands)		
Total revenues:			
AOL	$50,783	$104,410	$40,019
RCC	3,813	11,312	11,965
Less intercompany sales	(173)	—	—
	$54,423	$115,722	$51,984
Net income (loss):			
AOL	$3,018	$6,210	$4,210
RCC	(42)	(3,660)	(2,678)
Merger expenses	(1,710)	—	—
	$1,266	$2,550	$1,532

In connection with the merger of the Company and RCC, merger expenses of $1,710,000 were recognized during 1995.

During fiscal 1995, Medior, Inc. and Wide Area Information Servers, Inc. were merged into subsidiaries of the Company. The Company issued 1,082,019 shares of its common stock in the transactions. The transactions were accounted for under the pooling of interests method of accounting. Prior year financial statements have not been restated for the transactions because the effect would not be material to the operations of the Company.

Purchase Transactions

During fiscal 1995, the Company acquired NaviSoft, Inc. ("NaviSoft"), BookLink Technologies, Inc. ("BookLink"), Advanced Network & Services, Inc. ("ANS") and Global Network Navigator, Inc., in transactions accounted for under the purchase method of accounting. The Company paid a total of $97,669,000, of which $75,697,000 was in stock and $21,972,000 was in cash for the acquisitions. Of the aggregate purchase price, approximately $50,335,000 was allocated to in-process research and development and $55,314,000 was allocated to goodwill and other intangible assets.

The following unaudited pro forma information relating to the BookLink and ANS acquisitions is not necessarily an indication of the combined results that would have occurred had the acquisitions taken place at the beginning of the period, nor is necessarily an indication of the results that may occur in the future. Pro forma information for NaviSoft and Global Network Navigator, Inc. is immaterial to the operations of the consolidated entity. The amount of the aggregate purchase price allocated to in-process research and development for both the NaviSoft and BookLink acquisitions has been excluded from the pro forma information as it is a non-recurring item.

	Year ended June 30,	
	1995	1994
	(in thousands except per share data)	
Revenues	$410,147	$135,785
Income (loss) from operations	23,117	(5,465)
Pro forma income (loss)	11,205	(4,694)
Pro forma income (loss) per share	$0.25	$(0.16)

4. Property and Equipment

Property and equipment consist of the following:

	June 30,	
	1995	1994
	(in thousands)	
Computer equipment	$49,167	$12,418
Furniture and fixtures	4,992	1,398
Buildings	13,800	5,648
Land	6,075	2,052
Building improvements	6,284	1,343
Property under capital leases	8,486	2,686
Leasehold improvements	3,059	306
	91,863	25,851
Less accumulated depreciation and amortization	(21,397)	(5,545)
Net property and equipment	$70,466	$20,306

5. License Rights

License rights consist of the following:

	June 30,	
	1995	1994
	(in thousands)	
License rights	$7,484	$954
Less accumulated amortization	(1,947)	(901)
	$5,537	$53

6. Commitments and Contingencies

The Company leases equipment under several long-term capital and operating leases. Future minimum payments under capital leases and noncancelable operating leases with initial terms of one year or more consist of the following:

	Capital Leases	Operating Leases
	(in thousands)	
Year ending June 30,		
1996	$1,654	$20,997
1997	1,236	21,264
1998	641	19,450
1999	310	8,711
2000	103	3,511
Thereafter	—	2,636
Total minimum lease payments	3,944	$76,569
Less amount representing interest	(402)	
Present value of net minimum capital lease payments, including current portion of $1,415	$3,542	

The Company's rental expense under operating leases in the years ended June 30, 1995, 1994 and 1993 totaled approximately $10,001,000, $2,889,000, and $2,155,000, respectively.

Communication networks – The Company has guaranteed monthly usage levels of data and voice communications with one of its vendors. The remaining commitments are $113,400,000, $59,000,000, $9,000,000 and $6,750,000 for the years ending June 30, 1996, 1997, 1998 and 1999, respectively. The related expense for the years ended June 30, 1995, 1994 and 1993 was $138,793,000, $40,315,000 and $11,226,000, respectively.

Contingencies – Various legal proceedings have arisen against the Company in the ordinary course of business. In the opinion of management, these proceedings will not have a material effect on the financial position of the Company.

7. Notes Payable

Notes payable at June 30, 1995 totaled approximately $18 million and consist primarily of amounts borrowed to finance the purchases of two office buildings. The notes are collateralized by the respective properties. The notes have a variable interest rate equal to 105 basis points above the 30 day London Interbank Offered Rate and a fixed interest rate of 8.48% per annum at June 30, 1995. Aggregate maturities of notes payable for the years ended June 30, 1996, 1997, 1998, 1999, 2000 and thereafter are $415,000, $429,000, $445,000, $462,000, $480,000 and $15,553,000, respectively.

8. Other Income

The following table summarizes the components of other income:

	Year ended June 30,		
	1995	1994	1993
	(in thousands)		
Interest income	$3,920	$1,646	$572
Interest expense	(1,054)	(575)	(172)
Other	157	703	(29)
	$3,023	$1,774	$371

9. Income Taxes

The provision for income taxes is attributable to:

| | Year ended June 30, | | |
	1995	1994	1993
	(in thousands)		
Income before extraordinary item	$15,169	$3,832	$1,897
Tax benefit arising from net operating loss carryforward	—	—	(1,133)
	$15,169	$3,832	$764
Current	$—	$—	$ 5
Deferred	15,169	3,832	759
	$15,169	$3,832	$764

The provision for income taxes differs from the amount computed by applying the statutory federal income tax rate to income before provision for income taxes and extraordinary item. The sources and tax effects of the differences are as follows:

| | Year ended June 30, | | |
	1995	1994	1993
	(in thousands)		
Income tax at the federal statutory rate of 34%	$(6,283)	$2,170	$781
State income tax, net of federal benefit	1,597	403	200
Losses relating to RCC	—	1,259	916
Nondeductible merger expenses	750	—	—
Nondeductible charge for purchased research and development	17,114	—	—
Loss, for which no tax benefit was derived	1,632	—	—
Other	359	—	—
	$15,169	$ 3,832	$ 1,897

Deferred income taxes arise because of differences in the treatment of income and expense items for financial reporting and income tax purposes, primarily relating to deferred subscriber acquisition and product development costs.

As of June 30, 1995, the Company has net operating loss carryforwards of approximately $109 million for tax purposes which will be available, subject to certain annual limitations, to offset future taxable income. If not used, these loss carryforwards will expire between 2001 and 2010. To the extent that net operating loss carryforwards, when realized, relate to stock option deductions, the resulting benefits will be credited to stockholders' equity.

The Company's income tax provision was computed on the federal statutory rate and the average state statutory rates, net of the related federal benefit.

Effective July 1, 1993 the Company changed its method of accounting for income taxes from the deferred method to the liability method required by FASB Statement No. 109, "Accounting for Income Taxes." As permitted under the new rules, prior years' financial statements have not been restated.

No increase to net income resulted from the cumulative effect of adopting Statement No. 109 as of July 1, 1993. The deferred tax asset increased by approximately $5,965,000 as a result of the adoption. Similarly, the deferred tax liability, stockholders' equity and the valuation allowance increased by approximately $3,173,000, $759,000 and $2,033,000, respectively.

Deferred income taxes reflect the net tax effects of temporary differences between the carrying amounts of assets and liabilities for financial reporting purposes and the amounts used for income tax purposes. Significant components of the Company's deferred tax liabilities and assets are as follows:

| | June 30, | |
	1995	1994
	(in thousands)	
Deferred tax liabilities:		
Capitalized software costs	$7,008	$2,962
Deferred member acquisition costs	28,619	9,880
Net deferred tax liabilities	$35,627	$12,842
Deferred tax assets:		
Net operating loss carryforwards	$39,000	$17,510
Total deferred tax assets	39,000	17,510
Valuation allowance for deferred assets	(3,373)	(4,668)
Net deferred tax assets	$35,627	$12,842

13. Subsequent Event

On August 23, 1995, the Company entered into a stock purchase agreement to purchase Ubique, Ltd., an Israeli company. The Company has agreed to pay approximately $15 million ($1.5 million in cash and $13.5 million in common stock) in the transaction, which is to be accounted for under the purchase method of accounting. Subject to the results of an in-process valuation, a substantial portion of the purchase price may be allocated to in-process research and development and charged to the Company's operations in the first quarter of fiscal 1996.

QUARTERLY INFORMATION (UNAUDITED)

	Quarter Ended				
	September 30	December 31	March 31	June 30	Total
Fiscal 1995[a]					
Online service revenues	$50,056	$69,712	$99,814	$138,916	$358,498
Other revenues	6,880	6,683	9,290	12,939	35,792
Total revenues	56,936	76,395	109,104	151,855	394,290
Income (loss) from operations	4,623	(35,258)	233	11,108	(19,294)
Net income (loss)	1,481	(38,730)	(2,587)	6,189	(33,647)
Net income (loss) per share[b]	$ 0.04	$(0.20)	$(0.07)	$0.13	$(0.99)
Fiscal 1994					
Online service revenues	$14,299	$20,292	$28,853	$37,549	$100,993
Other revenues	4,780	4,239	2,836	2,874	14,729
Total revenues	19,079	24,531	31,689	40,423	115,722
Income from operations	531	520	1,931	1,626	4,608
Net income	303	70	1,272	905	2,550
Net income per share[b]	$ 0.01	$—	$ 0.03	$0.02	$0.07

a. Historical financial information for amounts previously reported in fiscal 1995 has been adjusted to account for pooling of interest transactions.

b. The sum of per-share earnings (loss) does not equal earnings (loss) per share for the year due to equivalent share calculations which are impacted by the Company's loss in 1995 and by fluctuations in the Company's common stock market prices.

Anacomp, Inc.

O n September 10, 1982, Anacomp, a computer software company, released its first annual report after being listed on the New York Stock Exchange. Prior to 1982, the company's stock was traded on the over-the-counter market. In the annual report, Anacomp's management outlined the company's strategy for new software systems development:

Anacomp is committed to being the world's leading supplier of software and services to the banking industry. Anacomp and its subsidiaries have licensed software products, sold data processing services, or entered into software consulting agreements with more than 200 billion-dollar financial institutions around the world. But the bank marketplace is changing rapidly. Regulatory and technological changes are blurring the distinctions between banks and other financial institutions. Bank customers – both retail and wholesale – are becoming more sophisticated and more demanding. Bankers require computer systems which encourage total customer relationships, adapt quickly to product changes, and meet requirements of round-the-clock banking.

Since 1979, Anacomp has been developing a totally new generation of banking computer software systems to serve those evolving needs. Anacomp's software development effort is one the most substantial ever undertaken by an independent computer services vendor. It is based on an Anacomp innovation – the software R&D partnership – and on the philosophy of getting prospective customers involved in developing the software products they will eventually use.

In 1979, when its net worth was $10 million, Anacomp recognized the opportunity to develop at a cost of $12 million a major new IBM-based real-time retail banking system. The development was expected to take several years to complete. Anacomp selected the limited partnership alternative to buffer the company's stockholders from the financial risks involved. To help assure the development of a superior product, Anacomp also sought the participation of a cross-section of major financial institutions – the ultimate users of the bank product. To induce these banks to become co-developers, it was necessary to

---

show that the required funding was in place and that Anacomp's commitment was firmly established. A limited partnership was the best way to induce four "primary development banks" to contribute collectively $6 million and 24 software development people for two years to the project.

The same considerations were present in each of the four subsequent partnerships – BANKSERV 10000, CEFT, CDA, and CIBS. Each partnership assumed development risks; except for BANKSERV 10000, each project involved several major banks acting as co-developers with Anacomp. Any product developed becomes the property of the partnership. Anacomp has the option to purchase the products but is under no obligation to exercise this option; Anacomp did purchase the CIS and BANKSERV 10000 systems in 1982. In total, more than $60 million has been raised since 1979 for investment in the development of new wholesale and retail banking software products.

COMPANY BACKGROUND

Anacomp, Inc., based in Indianapolis, Indiana, began as a computer and data services company in 1969. The company was founded by Ronald Palamara, a Ph.D. in computer sciences. Among the computer services offered by the company were the design and implementation of computer software systems and the management of customers' computer facilities. The company also operated customers' data centers, offered data processing and microfilming services, and sold micrographic equipment. The company viewed that its future growth would primarily come from the design and development of software for the banking industry.

Prior to 1980, the company's principal proprietary software system for commercial banks and thrift institutions was the Customer Integrated/Reference File (CI/RF) system. CI/RF integrated a customer's banking relationships, such as checking, savings, loans, etc. and incorporated them into a single record. The system was utilized by banks in 20 states throughout the United States, including Manufacturers Hanover Trust and Sumitomo Bank of California. The system and software primarily used a computer language designed for computers manufactured by NCR Corporation.

Beginning in 1980 Anacomp announced plans to develop a number of new software systems for the banking and financial services industry. For the retail banking industry the company was developing two new products: the Continuous Integrated System (CIS) and the BANKSERVE 10000 system. CIS was claimed to be the first on-line real-time retail banking transactions processing system designed for IBM computers. The BANKSERVE 10000 system would allow banks to share networks of point-of-sale terminals or automated teller machines on a national or regional basis.

Anacomp had also announced plans to develop a full line of software systems to help banks deal more efficiently with their wholesale customers/companies, institutions, and other banks. The Corporate Electronic Funds Transfer (CEFT) system was expected to combine three banking functions: an electronic funds transfer mechanism that would take payments from external sources, a money transfer component which would automate the bank's internal paying and receiving functions, and a corporate funds control component which would allows the bank to monitor its own cash position and the cash position of each customer. The Corporate Deposit and Analysis

(CDA) system, another wholesale banking product that Anacomp targeted for development, was expected to automate the bank's depository relationships with large corporations and other banks.

In August 1982 the company announced that it was initiating the development of yet another new software system, Corporate International Banking System (CIBS). CIBS was the most complex system the company planned to date, and was intended to help a large international bank automate certain internal treasury operations, generate complete information on the bank's foreign currency positions, and automate the processing of letters of credit and documentary credit collections.

Anacomp's management believed that the above software systems, if successfully developed and implemented, would enable the company to become a leading supplier of software and services to the banking industry.

INDUSTRY AND COMPETITION[1]

The computer services industry was marked by very rapid growth. In 1981, computer service revenues totaled $18.9 billion, up 23% from $15.4 billion a year, according to INPUT, a leading international consulting firm. INPUT had estimated that the industry growth rate between 1981 and 1986 would be approximately 23% per annum.

There were three major segments of the computer services industry: processing services, professional services, and software products. The companies in the processing area offered customers access to a large computer facility in which batch processing, remote computing services, and facilities management services were performed. This segment accounted for 57% of total computer services revenues in 1981 and was expected to grow at a compound annual rate of 17% between 1981 and 1986. The companies in the professional services segment provided customers alternatives to in-house data processing. These services included custom-made computer systems and programming to perform specialized tasks, as well as the management of data processing facilities. The professional services segment, which accounted for 23% of total computer services industry revenues in 1981, was expected to grow 29% annually from 1981 to 1986. Software products, the third segment of the software services industry, was the fastest-growing sector. Software products consist of instructions that guide computer equipment through tasks. This segment was expected to grow at an annual compound growth rate of 33% between 1981 and 1986.

The high growth rates of the computer services industry were being fueled by the large number of computers installed and customers' realization of the value computer services can have in lifting their productivity. Hardware, the premiere growth area of the 1960s and 1970s, had since taken on a commodity-like status as a result of progressively lower manufacturing costs. Computer services, on the other hand, increased in value and in price.

The computer services industry in 1982 consisted of some 5,000 companies ranging from small software operations to giants such as IBM. Smaller companies in the industry generally concentrated on serving particular market niches; their performance depended on factors influencing these small sectors.

There was active competition in each of the areas of services provided by Anacomp. In the computer service area, Anacomp competed with other computer service

---

1. *Material in this section is drawn from Standard & Poor's industry surveys on office equipment systems and services, October 21, 1982.*

Anacomp, Inc.

companies, manufacturers of mainframe computers, and companies developing in-house computer service capabilities. In the data center service business, Anacomp competed with other data processing and micrographic service companies. Anacomp believed that the services performed by it represented only a small portion of the market in each of the fields it operated.

The computer services industry was subject to rapid technological change requiring constant adaptation to provide competitive service. Competition in the computer services industry was based primarily on technical capability and expertise, pricing, quality of work, and ability to meet system development deadlines. In the other areas of Anacomp's business, competition was based upon the reliability and timeliness of the services and products provided.

TOP MANAGEMENT

The names, ages, and current and former positions of Anacomp's executive officers in September 1982 were as follows:

Ronald D. Palamara, Ph.D., age 42, served as Chairman and President for more than the past five years.

Stanley E. Hirschfeld, age 47, became Senior Vice President of Corporate Development during 1981. For more than the prior five years, he served as Vice President – Finance and Secretary of Anacomp.

Ralph C. McAuley, age 47, became President of Anacomp's Computer Services group during 1981. For more than the five prior years, he served as Vice President of Data Processing Services.

John J. Flanigan, age 42, became Group Vice President of Data Services during 1981. During the prior five-year period, he served as Vice President of Data Processing Services.

Christopher Duffy, age 44, became Vice President and Chief Administrative Officer during 1981. For more than the five prior years, he served as Vice President and General Manager of an Indianapolis television station.

Myles Hannan, age 44, became Vice President – Finance, General Counsel and Secretary during 1981. During 1979 and 1980, he served as Vice President-Law and Administration for Delaware North Companies, Incorporated. For more than the prior two years he served as a Vice President-Legal and Staff Divisions of the Stop & Shop Companies, Inc.

William C. Ater, age 40, became Vice President of Administration during 1981. During 1979 and 1980, he served as Anacomp's Vice President of Bank Data Processing. For more than the prior two years, he served in various computer management positions with NCR Corporation.

As of the end of fiscal 1981, all officers and directors as a group owned 15.1% of Anacomp's common stock and were paid $2.9 million in cash and cash equivalent forms of remuneration during the year.

NEW SOFTWARE SYSTEMS DEVELOPMENT

Anacomp organized and financed its new software development in a unique manner. During the fiscal year ended June 30, 1980, Anacomp initiated the development of a major new computer software system called Continuous Integrated System (CIS) to be marketed to major financial institutions. According to Anacomp's management, CIS would represent a major advance over the company's current CI/RF system.

The company stated that, in view of the anticipated significant development expenditure for the CIS system, Anacomp entered into an agreement in November 1979 with a limited partnership, RTS Associates. Under this agreement, Anacomp agreed to develop the CIS system on behalf of the partnership. In return, RTS agreed to pay a development fee of $6 million, of which $2.2 million was paid in 1980. Upon completion of the development of the CIS system, Anacomp agreed to market CIS for five years on a commission basis. Anacomp also had the option to acquire all rights to the CIS system at the greater of its appraised fair market value or RTS's investment plus a fixed profit. RTS had the right to extend Anacomp's five-year marketing agreement an additional five years or to cancel it if Anacomp did not use its best efforts to market CIS.

RTS Associates' payments for the CIS development expenses were financed by (1) an investment of $1.444 million by the partners, (2) a $3.25 million bank loan to RTS, secured by bank letters of credit and personal guarantees of the limited partners, and (3) a $2.2 million loan to RTS, personally guaranteed by the limited partners, from Anacomp, with interest at 11% per annum payable quarterly through December 31, 1981, and with principal and interest payable thereafter in 84 equal monthly installments. In addition, if the CIS development expenses exceeded $6 million and therefore RTS was required to pay further development fees, Anacomp agreed to loan RTS, without recourse to the limited partners, up to $1.5 million to complete the CIS system.

Several officers and directors of Anacomp were affiliated with the corporate general partner of RTS, and were also investors in the limited partnership arrangement. Ronald Palamara, the Chairman of the Board and President of Anacomp, and three other directors of Anacomp, were also directors and officers of the corporate general partner of RTS. The ownership interest of Anacomp's officers and directors in the limited partnership amounted to 38.5% of the total.

During the fiscal year 1981, thirteen major banks, including the National Bank of North America in New York, the Shawmut National Bank in Boston, Provident National Bank in Philadelphia, and the First National Bank in Kansas City, contracted with Anacomp to participate as advisory banks in the CIS project for a nonrefundable fee of $150,000 each. The arrangement permitted each bank to review the project during development and provide input regarding changes to enhance the ultimate marketability of CIS.

In June 1982, Anacomp announced that the CIS system development was completed. The company also announced that it purchased the system from RTS Associates for $16 million.

FINANCIAL PERFORMANCE

After reporting a strong increase in revenues and profits from 1978 to 1981, Anacomp reported a slower revenue growth and a decline in profits in fiscal 1982. Dr. Palamara, commented that the 1982 performance was a short-term aberration, and that the company's long-term strategy and prospects were sound:

Fiscal 1982 marked the beginning of one era and the end of another for Anacomp. A new era began with five events having tremendous long-term significance for Anacomp: the purchase of two major software products, the completion of our most significant acquisition, an offering of $50 million in convertible debentures, the formation of history's largest software research *and development partnership, and Anacomp's listing on the New York Stock Exchange. Thus, despite a difficult fourth quarter which was affected by several non-recurring items and resulted in lower earnings for the year, fiscal 1982 was perhaps the most significant year of achievements in Anacomp's history.*

Judged solely by the numbers, of course, 1982 does not seem especially memorable. . . . In terms of positioning the company for future growth, however, 1982 may well be remembered as the most significant year in Anacomp's history. . . .

We believe that Anacomp's performance in future years will demonstrate that the company is well along in its evolution from a small, explosive-growth firm to a nationally recognized market leader.

Dr. Palamara projected record financial results in fiscal 1983. He also assured investors that Anacomp would place renewed emphasis on improving the company's profitability and reducing its financial leverage.

Exhibit 1 shows Anacomp's stock price data around the time of its 1982 results. An abridged version of the company's annual report is presented in Exhibit 2.

QUESTIONS

1. Evaluate Anacomp's new product development strategy. What are the risks and benefits of this strategy for Anacomp's shareholders?

2. How is Anacomp's accounting influenced by the way the company organizes and finances its new product development?

3. Compare Anacomp's cash flow performance with its accounting performance. What is your evaluation of the company's financial condition?

4. What is your assessment of Anacomp's future?

EXHIBIT I

Anacomp—Stock Price and Trading Volume Data

Trading	Anacomp Trading Volume (thousands)	Anacomp Closing Price (dollars)	S&P 500 Composite Closing
9/1/82	109	10.875	118.25
9/2/82	92	10.875	120.38
9/3/82	437	11.125	122.68
9/7/82	120	10.875	121.37
9/8/82	231	11.000	122.20
9/9/82	230	10.750	121.97
9/10/82	417	10.625	120.97
9/13/82	284	10.375	122.24

Anacomp's common stock beta=1.3 (Value Line estimate).

Stock Trading Information

| | Stock Price | | Cash |
	High	Low	Dividends
Fiscal Year 1981:			
First quarter	$15.63	$10.63	$.026
Second quarter	19.88	13.75	.026
Third quarter	16.50	12.75	.026
Fourth quarter	18.38	15.13	.030
Fiscal Year 1982:			
First quarter	16.63	11.25	.030
Second quarter	14.00	11.88	.030
Third quarter	12.25	10.00	.030
Fourth quarter	13.38	10.88	.030

Other Information

Interest rate on 3-month Treasury bills:	8.2%
Interest rate on 20-year Government bonds:	12.2%
P/E ratio for Standard & Poor's 400 Industrials:	23.2

EXHIBIT 2

ANACOMP, INC.—1982 Annual Report (edited)

To our Shareholders

Fiscal 1982 marked the beginning of one era and the end of another for Anacomp.

A new era began with five events having tremendous long-term significance for Anacomp: the purchase of two major software products, the completion of our most significant acquisition, an offering of $50 million in convertible debentures, the formation of history's largest software research and development partnership and Anacomp's listing on the New York Stock Exchange. Thus, despite a difficult fourth quarter which was affected by several non-recurring items and resulted in lower earnings for the year, fiscal 1982 was perhaps the most significant year of achievements in Anacomp's history.

Judged solely by the numbers, of course, 1982 does not seem especially memorable. Although revenues rose slightly over 1981, earnings per share declined due to the impact of fourth quarter results, which reflected several one-time changes and short-term factors. These factors are described in detail in our fourth quarter report.

In terms of positioning the company for future growth, however, 1982 may well be remembered as the most significant year in Anacomp's history.

- In January, Anacomp completed a $50 million offering of 13⅞% convertible subordinated debentures which, after an original issue discount, increased the company's working capital position by $41 million.
- Listing on the New York Stock Exchange in April recognized Anacomp's stature in the computer services industry and provided the opportunity for greater visibility as the computer reaches out to new, worldwide markets.
- During June of the year, Anacomp purchased two major retail banking software systems which we had been developing for investment partnerships. CIS, a totally integrated system that we believe will revolutionize retail banking in the 1980s, was purchased for nearly $16 million, CIS has already attracted a financial commitment from nearly 35 banks, seven of which had signed substantial license agreements by the end of the year. BANKSERV® 10000, a system to provide banks with a new level of electronic transaction switching and processing capabilities, was purchased for $2.3 million.
- Also during June, Anacomp signed an agreement with IBM Corporation which gives us the capability to be a primary source of supply for a bank's branch automation requirements.
- The acquisition of 24 micrographic data imaging centers from DSI Corporation and Kalvar Corporation in May provided the ability to deliver Anacomp services to an even broader base or regular, repetitive customers, and the opportunity to offer new services through an expanded delivery system.
- After the close of the fiscal year, funding for the CIBS research and development partnership was completed with the closing of the final portion of $26.25 million in partnership interests. The partnership will contract with Anacomp to develop CIBS, the Corporate International Banking System, a complex software system for use by large banks and other financial institutions engaged in international business.

We believe Anacomp's performance in future years will demonstrate that the company is well along in its evolution from a small, explosive-growth firm to a nationally recognized market leader.

To ensure that Anacomp's evolution will result in a stable company, with performance attractive to investors, Anacomp will be placing renewed emphasis in several areas. These areas will include our rate of return, where we anticipate achieving a superior return on investment from the maturation of software projects, existing operations, plus the addition of quality investments.

We also expect to reduce our leverage ratio over the next few years by calling our convertible debt, when this becomes practical, and by taking other appropriate measures. We will continue to employ strategic planning approaches in all our business units. Lastly, we will seek out those acquisitions which blend with our long-term goals.

We have projected record financial results in fiscal 1983 as the company asserts its leadership in bank software and micrographic data imaging. We appreciate the continued support of our stockholders and employees which makes that goal achievable.

Sincerely,

Ronald D. Palamara, Ph.D.
President and Chairman of the Board
September 10, 1982

MANAGEMENT'S DISCUSSION AND ANALYSIS OF FINANCIAL CONDITION AND RESULTS OF OPERATIONS

Anacomp, Inc. and Subsidiaries

General

In September 1980, Anacomp completed a public offering of $30,000,000 of 9½% Convertible Subordinated Debentures due 2000. In January 1981, Anacomp completed an offering outside the United States of $12,500,000 of 9% Convertible Subordinated Debentures due 1996, with warrants to purchase a like amount of debentures. In January 1982, Anacomp completed the public offering of $50,000,000 of 13⅞% Convertible Subordinated Debentures due 2002. The Debentures were offered at an original issue discount of 15%, with net proceeds of $41,125,000, and carry an effective cost of 16.6%. The cash from these offerings has been used to finance the expansion of receivables and unbilled revenues, to retire long-term debt, to provide funds for acquisitions, and to increase working capital. During the past three years, Anacomp has completed the acquisition of eleven business entities. The acquisitions and the debenture offerings accounted for the major changes in Anacomp's financial condition and results of operations.

Financial Condition and Liquidity

During 1982, working capital increased $1,949,000. The major source of working capital, other than operations, was the increase in long-term debt, primarily the result of the January offering of $50,000,000 of debentures and to a lesser extent the exercise of warrants to purchase $1,289,000 of additional 9% debentures. The major use of working capital was the purchase of computer software systems from limited partnerships. Other major uses of working capital were the purchase of marketable securities held as long-term investments, the retirement of long-term debt, and additions of fixed assets. During the year, cash was used to finance the increase in unbilled revenues, to purchase 92% of the shares of DSI Corporation, and to pay certain software development costs. As a result, the current ratio at June 30, 1982, is 2.40, compared to 3.84 at June 30, 1981. At June 30, 1982, Anacomp had $35,000,000 of available but unused lines of credit that could be used if needed to provide short-term financing. Negotiations are currently being held with a group of banks to establish a revolving credit arrangement which will replace the existing lines of credit.

At the present time, Anacomp has no major commitments to acquire assets or facilities which will require a substantial outlay of working capital. It is anticipated that the current acquisition program will continue in the future as opportunities present themselves.

Anacomp currently expects to incur approximately $6,000,000 during 1983 on enhancements to a computer software system, of which approximately $3,000,000 is expected to be funded by others. The project is being undertaken because the results will yield a product with improved marketability, which at the same time will meet commitments to certain customers.

Operations—Fiscal 1982 Compared to 1981

Revenues for 1982 increased only 3% over fiscal 1981, with the increase being generated primarily by internal growth and the addition of internally generated projects. Software development projects, especially two new projects contracted for by major banks and limited partnerships, and higher levels of sales of minicomputers and microcomputers and related software, contributed the largest portion of the increase. Revenues were also increased by certain data centers. These increases, along with smaller increases in other areas, were largely offset by reduced revenue being generated by other data centers as a result of a consolidation of certain operations.

Total operating costs and expenses increased 10.4% during fiscal 1982. Personnel costs and outside services costs associated with the increased software development activity were the major factors in the increase. Other contributors to the increase were higher supply costs, equipment-related costs, and the cost of computer hardware sales, each caused by higher levels of activity. Also, amortization of purchased software added to the overall increase, along with generally higher prices for all purchased goods and services. These increases were partially offset by cost reductions from the synergism obtained from prior acquisitions, a reduction in costs as a result of consolidating certain administrative functions and, in the third quarter, from the recovery of previously recorded expenses.

Margins for the current periods were substantially lower than the prior year due to the emphasis on completing large systems development projects as opposed to generating new license fees for other products. Margins earned on development work have typically been less than those earned from software licensing and related activities. The reduction in revenue in certain data centers has also tended to reduce margins, as the revenue losses have preceded to some extent the current cost reduction and consolidation efforts.

Interest expense increased in the convertible year as a result of the interest on the 9½% Convertible Subordinated Debentures offered during fiscal 1981 and the 13⅞% Convertible Subordinated Debentures offered in January 1982. Interest income was derived from investing the proceeds from these offerings not otherwise utilized. Due to the uses of cash mentioned previously and a lowering of interest rates on investments, interest income decreased throughout the current period.

The extraordinary credit arose from the sale of a branch office which had been acquired in 1981 in a transaction accounted for as a pooling of interests. The amount of the credit is the gain realized, net of related income taxes.

The provision for income taxes reflects the normal tax relating to the income reported for financial statement purposes after recognizing the impact of investment tax credits, non-deductible expenses, and the effect of interest due from the under-depositing of tax payments as a result of the denial of a request for a change in certain reporting policies for tax purposes.

Fiscal 1981 Compared to 1980

Of the $34,725,000 increase in revenue, the major portion was attributable to acquisitions included for the first time in 1981, or for the full period in 1981, plus internal growth generated by those acquisitions. Other changes in revenue for the year resulted primarily from new software development sales and non-recurring licensing agreements (especially from new software systems for banks, financed in part by limited partnerships), offset in part by reduced revenues due to declining activity in certain data centers and the completion of certain non-repetitive software projects.

Direct costs of service and equipment increased 54%, primarily from the costs associated with the recent acquisitions plus increased expenses required to support increased software development, and rising costs for personnel and other services. Selling, general and administrative expenses increased 17% from the costs associated with the recent acquisitions plus the expenses necessary to manage the rapidly growing company and from rising personnel costs. The increases in other direct operating and selling, general and administrative costs were offset in part by a savings of approximately $1,255,000 being realized during 1981 due to a change in the funding of Anacomp's contribution to the Thrift Plan for Employees.

Interest income increased from interest earned by cash investment programs and from the interest earned on notes receivable.

Interest expense increased primarily from the interest on the recently issued 9% and 9½% Convertible Subordinated Debentures, with other increases from debt incurred to finance acquisitions and interest on short-term borrowings, offset somewhat by lower interest on the 10% Convertible Subordinated Debentures due to conversions to equity.

Other income included the gain from a transaction with Kalvar which resulted from an agreement whereby Anacomp sold to Kalvar its Kalvar preferred stock for Kalvar common stock and sold its option to acquire additional Kalvar common stock in exchange for a promissory note from Kalvar.

The provision for income taxes reflects the normal tax relating to the income reported for financial statement purposes after giving effect to the benefits obtained from investment tax credits and from the exclusion of dividend income. The expected tax rate for fiscal 1981 was revised downward during the fourth quarter as a result of a large capital gain arising primarily from the transaction with Kalvar.

SELECTED FINANCIAL DATA

Anacomp, Inc., and Subsidiaries

(dollars in thousands, except per share amounts)	1982	1981	1980	1979	1978
For the year ended June 30:					
Revenues	$109,599	$106,368	$71,643	$41,662	$23,433
Income before provision for income taxes and extraordinary credit	$3,622	$13,997	$7,787	$5,045	$3,154
Income before extraordinary credit	$2,779	$7,938	$4,627	$2,704	$1,542
Net income	$4,609	$7,938	$4,627	$2,704	$1,542
Earnings per common and common equivalent share:					
Income before extraordinary credit	.30	$.87	$.70	$.57	$.39
Net income	.50	$.87	$.70	$.57	$.39
Earnings per common share assuming full dilution:					
Income before extraordinary credit	.29	$.83	$.66	$.51	$.32
Net income	.48	$.83	$.66	$.51	$.32
Cash dividends declared per common share	$.12	$.11	$.10	$.09	$.06
As of June 30:					
Current assets	$99,044	$75,453	$33,453	$16,200	$9,869
Current liabilities	$41,276	$19,634	$22,079	$11,452	$3,561
Working capital	$57,768	$55,819	$11,374	$4,748	$6,308
Total assets	$211,660	$130,798	$76,950	$30,069	$14,182
Long-term debt	$105,208	$50,591	$10,608	$8,162	$3,993
Stockholders' equity	$61,035	$55,891	$44,077	$10,211	$6,639
Book value per common share	$6.59	$6.18	$5.56	$2.14	$1.55
Number of employees	2,300	2,000	1,800	895	430
Number of holders of common stock	7,930	5,575	3,810	1,955	1,225

Anacomp, Inc.

CONSOLIDATED BALANCE SHEET

	June 30,	
(dollars in thousands, except per share amounts)	1982	1981
Assets		
Current assets		
Cash (including temporary investments)	$34,519	$29,392
Accounts and notes receivable, less allowances for doubtful		
accounts of $1,915 and $1,210, respectively	25,284	23,216
Unbilled revenues	18,534	15,863
Inventories	4,469	3,014
Deferred CIBS development costs (Note 3)	5,647	—
Prepaid expenses (including income taxes of $3,018 and		
$1,242, respectively)	10,591	3,968
Total current assets	99,044	75,453
Property and equipment, at cost less accumulated depreciation		
and amortization of $10,189 and $8,660, respectively	25,112	14,930
Cost of computer software systems purchased, less		
accumulated depreciation of $1,584 and $186, respectively	20,363	1,747
Excess of purchase price over net assets of businesses		
acquired, less accumulated amortization of $2,319 and		
$1,285, respectively	42,646	24,291
Other assets	24,495	14,377
	$211,660	$130,798
Liabilities and Stockholders' Equity		
Current liabilities		
Notes payable, banks	$14,000	$—
Current portion of long-term debt	2,907	2,359
Accounts payable	8,151	8,787
Accrued salaries, wages and bonuses	4,604	3,863
Accrued interest payable	5,129	1,747
Income taxes	—	419
Other accrued liabilities	6,485	2,459
Total current liabilities	41,276	19,634
Long-term debt, net of current portion:		
Convertible subordinated debentures	86,274	43,340
Other long-term debt	18,934	7,251
Total long-term debt	105,208	50,591
Deferred income taxes	3,177	4,015
Minority interest	964	667
Stockholder's equity		
Preferred stock – $1 par value, authorized 1,000,000 shares,		
none issued	—	—
Common stock – $1 par value, authorized 25,000,000 shares,		
9,256,544 and 9,042,722 issued, respectively	9,257	9,043
Capital in excess of par value of common stock	37,305	35,207
Unrealized losses on marketable securities	(899)	(233)
Retained earnings	15,372	11,874
Total stockholders' equity	61,035	55,891
	$211,660	$130,798

CONSOLIDATED STATEMENT OF INCOME

(dollars in thousands, except per share amounts)	Year Ended June 30		
	1982	1981	1980
Revenues:			
Services provided	$88,045	$87,304	$58,781
Equipment sold	21,554	19,064	12,862
	109,599	106,368	71,643
Operating costs and expenses:			
Costs of services provided	67,302	62,464	40,342
Costs of equipment sold	16,764	13,900	9,172
Selling, general and administrative expenses	19,888	17,821	15,284
	103,954	94,185	64,798
	5,645	12,183	6,845
Interest income	5,525	3,204	485
Interest expense	(8,158)	(4,090)	(1,381)
Other, net	610	2,700	1,838
	(2,023)	1,814	942
Income before provision for income taxes and extraordinary credit	3,622	13,997	7,787
Provision for income taxes	843	6,059	3,160
Income before extraordinary credit	2,779	7,938	4,627
Extraordinary credit, net of related tax	1,830	—	—
Net income	$4,609	$7,938	$4,627
Earnings per common and common equivalant share:			
Income before extraordinary credit	$.30	$.87	$.70
Extraordinary credit	.20	—	—
Net income	$.50	$.87	$.70
Earnings per common share assuming full dilution:			
Income before extraordinary credit	$.29	$.83	$.66
Extraordinary credit	.19	—	—
Net income	$.48	$.83	$.66
Cash dividends declared per share	$.12	$.11	$.10

Anacomp, Inc.

CONSOLIDATED STATEMENT OF CHANGES IN FINANCIAL POSITION

(dollars in thousands)	Year ended June 30		
	1982	1981	1980
Working capital was provided by:			
Income before extraordinary credit	$2,779	$7,938	$4,627
Charges to income not requiring an outlay of working capital:			
Depreciation and amortization	6,708	4,368	3,026
Deferred income taxes	(1,314)	3,951	2
Other	143	416	331
Working capital provided by operations	8,316	16,673	7,986
Working capital provided by extraordinary credit	742	—	—
Dispositions of property and equipment	702	218	2,001
Decrease in investment in Computer Micrographics, Inc.	—	—	1,733
Long-term debt incurred	55,680	43,636	7,158
Issuances of common stock	2,236	4,813	28,371
Other	3,224	1,024	(84)
	70,900	66,364	47,165
Working capital was applied to:			
Additions to property and equipment	11,172	3,533	5,171
Excess of purchase price over net assets of businesses acquired	19,791	4,172	18,900
Noncurrent assets of companies acquired in purchase transactions	5,315	1,088	4,593
Noncurrent liabilities of businesses acquired in purchase transactions	(2,892)	(1,040)	(2,199)
Purchase of computer software systems	20,014	1,734	—
Increase in investments	6,099	4,806	2,027
Increase in other assets	4,441	1,977	4,443
Reduction of long-term debt	3,900	4,693	6,911
Cash dividends declared	1,111	956	693
	68,951	21,919	40,539
	$1,949	$44,445	$6,626
Increase in working capital represented by:			
Increase (decrease) in current assets:			
Cash (including temporary investments)	$5,127	$24,649	$1,484
Accounts and notes receivable	2,068	6,841	8,333
Unbilled revenues	2,671	7,283	5,605
Inventories	1,455	513	1,383
Deferred CIBS development costs	5,647	—	—
Prepaid expenses	6,623	2,714	448
Decrease (increase) in current liabilities:			
Notes payable	(14,000)	4,000	(3,250)
Current portion of long-term debt	(548)	791	(315)
Accounts payable	636	(1,022)	(4,716)
Accrued salaries, wages and bonuses	(741)	(1,185)	(683)
Accrued interest payable	(3,382)	(1,639)	(48)
Income taxes	419	1,162	286
Other accrued liabilities	(4,026)	338	(1,901)
Increase in working capital	$1,949	$ 44,445	$6,626

The accompanying notes are an integral part of the consolidated financial statements.

NOTES TO CONSOLIDATED FINANCIAL STATEMENTS
(dollars in thousands, except per share amounts)

Note 1. Summary of Significant Accounting Policies

Consolidation

The consolidated financial statements include the accounts of Anacomp, Inc. ("Anacomp") and its majority-owned subsidiaries except Anacomp Leasing Company, Inc., an immaterial wholly-owned subsidiary, which is reflected in the equity method in the accompanying financial statements. Intercompany transactions have been eliminated. Certain amounts in the 1981 and 1980 financial statements have been reclassified to conform to the 1982 presentation.

Revenue Recognition

Revenues are generally recognized as follows:

(1) Data preparation, data processing, facility management and computer output microfilm ("COM") services and sales are recognized as the services are performed or products are shipped.

(2) Revenues from granting perpetual licenses of existing software systems which do not require substantial modification are recognized at the time the license agreement is executed, if collectibility is reasonably assured and the software system is delivered to the customer.

(3) Revenues from contracts for development and/or modifications to existing software systems are recognized under methods which approximate the percentage-of-completion method, except for revenues from development contracts with certain limited partnerships which are reported on the completed contract method, other than immaterial amounts reported for 1980 (see Note 3). Losses on such contracts are recognized when identified.

Revenue recognized under items (2) and (3) may precede the date at which the customer may be billed pursuant to the contract terms. Substantially all unbilled revenue is collected in the year subsequent to the year revenue is recognized.

The subject of revenue recognition for development contracts with limited partnerships including certain arrangements described in (3) above is presently under review by the Financial Accounting Standards Board (FASB). Anacomp will comply with any Statement of Financial Standards issued by the FASB. In April, 1982, the FASB issued an exposure draft entitled "Research and Development Arrangements." Anacomp believes that it is in substantial compliance with the exposure draft, and that approval of the draft by the FASB would not result in an adjustment to the amounts presented in the financial statements.

Inventories

Inventories are stated at the lower of cost or market, cost being determined primarily on the specific identification basis.

The cost of the inventories is distributed as follows:

| | June 30 | | |
	1982	1981	1980
Equipment held for resale	$3,084	$1,899	$1,315
Operating supplies	1,385	1,115	1,186
	$4,469	$3,014	$2,501

Purchased Computer Software Systems

Purchased computer software systems held for licensing to others are earned at cost less accumulated depreciation. Depreciation is recorded over the estimated marketing lives of the software, and is computed based on the greater of the amount calculated using either a percent-of-revenue or the straight-line method. The percent-of-revenue method is based on the total estimated future revenues expected to be derived from sales of the software, while straight-line depreciation is provided using estimated marketing lives of five to ten years.

Amortization of Excess Purchase Price over Net Assets

Excess of purchase price over net assets of business acquired is amortized on the straight-line method over the estimated useful life, currently ranging from five to twenty years, if determined, and over 40 years if life is indeterminate.

Earnings per Share

The computation of earnings per common and common equivalent share is based upon the weighted average number of common shares outstanding during the year plus (in years in which they have a dilutive effect) the effect of common shares contingently issuable, primarily from stock options, conversion of subordinated debentures issued during fiscal 1981 and, for 1980, common shares purchased in July 1980, in connection with an employment agreement (see Note 13). Interest expense, net of taxes, on the subordinated debentures is added to net income in the computation of earnings per common and common equivalent share.

The fully diluted per share computation reflects the effect of common shares contingently issuable upon conversion of each convertible subordinated debenture outstanding in years in which such conversions would cause dilution. Interest expense, net of income taxes, on the debentures assumed to be converted is added to net income in the computation of fully diluted earnings per share. Fully diluted earnings per share also reflects additional dilution related to stock options due to the use of the year-end market price, when higher than the average price for the year.

The weighted average number of common and common equivalent shares used to compute earnings per share is 9,281,640, 9,425,788, and 6,624,955 for 1982, 1981, and 1980, respectively. The average number of shares used to compute earnings per common share assuming full dilution is 9,667,794, 11,457,335 and 7,149,132 for the respective years. The numbers of shares for all years are adjusted for all stock splits and stock dividends declared.

Vacation Pay

In November 1980, the Financial Accounting Standards Board issued Statement of Financial Accounting Standards No. 43 (SFAS No. 43), "Accounting for Compensated Absences," which requires the accrual of vacation pay earned but not taken. The provisions of SFAS No. 43 require the restatement of prior periods and therefore the cumulative effect as of July 1, 1979, is shown as an adjustment to retained earnings at that date. The effect of this change was to reduce net income by $97 ($.01 per share) in 1982, $72 ($.01 per share) in 1981, and $273 ($.03 per share) in 1980.

Note 3. Major Software Products and Related Party Transactions

CIS

In June 1982, Anacomp purchased for $16,000 a major new computer software system called CIS (Continuous Integrated System) developed by Anacomp for RTS Associates ("RTS"), a limited partnership formed in 1979. Several officers and directors of Anacomp who are affiliated with RTS's general partner are also investors in RTS, aggregating approximately 39% of the combined general and limited partnership units. The remaining partnership interests are owned by persons not affiliated with Anacomp. Anacomp contracted to develop the system on a best efforts basis, and RTS agreed to pay a development fee of $6,000, of which $4,750 was paid through 1981, and an additional $1,250 during 1982. RTS paid Anacomp an additional $1,500 after actual costs to Anacomp exceeded $6,000. Anacomp had previously loaned $2,200 to RTS, personally guaranteed by the limited partners, and loaned the additional $1,500 as provided for in the development agreement. RTS paid all such loans in full out of the proceeds of the sale of the CIS system.

Concurrent with the development of CIS for the RTS partnership, a complimentary project was being developed for four CIS Primary Development Banks. Each bank committed $1,500 to fund modifications of the CIS project to conform to their specific requirements and thereby obtained a nonexclusive license to CIS as so modified. Under the terms of the Primary Development Bank agreements, 10% of any revenue from licensing CIS to others will accrue to each of the banks until such time as their entire $1,500 development fee has been recovered. At June 30, 1982, seven other banks had entered into, or committed to enter into, license agreements for CIS.

During 1981 and 1982, twenty major banks contracted with Anacomp to participate as Advisory Development Banks on the CIS project for a nonrefundable fee of $150. The fee permits each bank to review the project during development and provide input, which is not binding to Anacomp, regarding changes which would enhance the marketability of CIS. Anacomp defers a portion of this fee which will be recognized as services are provided to the participating banks throughout the terms of their contracts.

EFT

During fiscal 1981, Anacomp initiated and completed development of a new computer software switching system called H-10000 to be marketed to major financial institutions. Anacomp entered into an agreement with EFT Partners, Ltd. ("EFT"), a limited partnership formed in the fall of 1980. Several officers and directors of Anacomp purchased limited partnership units in EFT, aggregating approximately 31% of the partnership units, and Kranzley & Co., a wholly-owned subsidiary of Anacomp, was the general partner. The remaining limited partnership interests were owned by persons not affiliated with Anacomp. Anacomp agreed to develop and market the system, and EFT agreed to pay a development fee of $1,000, of which $910 was paid during 1981 and an additional $90 during 1982. The contract was reported on the completed contract basis; revenue and profits were recognized upon completion during the fourth quarter of 1981. In June 1982, Kranzley & Co. exercised its right under the purchase option to buy the interests of the limited partners at the appraised fair market value for the H-10000 system of $2,300.

CEFT

During fiscal 1981, Anacomp entered into an agreement with CEFT Partners, Ltd. ("CEFT"), a limited partnership formed in December, 1980, and primary development banks to jointly develop a new computer funds transfer software system to be marketed to major financial institutions. Certain officers, directors and employees of Anacomp purchased limited partnership units in CEFT aggregating approximately 9% of the limited partnership units. The remaining partnership interest and the general partnership interest are owned by persons not affiliated with Anacomp.

Under the development agreement, Anacomp agreed to develop the new system on a best effort basis. The agreement permits Anacomp to contract with primary development banks to provide development fees up to $1,000 in addition to the $2,100 development fee to be paid by the partnership. In June 1981, the general partner agreed to permit Anacomp to increase the bank fees allowable to $2,000 on this project. Contracts with five banks aggregating $2,000 have been completed.

Anacomp has acquired rights to a system owned by a major bank at a cost of $500 to assist and expedite the completion of the system. A portion of this cost has been charged to expense as a system development cost and the remainder is being amortized over the expected marketing life of the purchased system in its unmodified form.

The system was certified as being complete in July 1982, and Anacomp has agreed to market it for seven years on an exclusive commission basis. Anacomp has the option to acquire all rights to the system at the greater of (a) fair market value or (b) $3,000 to $5,000, depending on the date the option is exercised. Revenues earned on this software development project were $3,150 and $942 during fiscal 1981 and 1982.

CBS

During fiscal 1981, Anacomp entered into an agreement with CBS Partners, Ltd. ("CBS"), a limited partnership formed in April 1981, and primary development banks to jointly develop a wholesale banking computer software system to be marketed to major financial institutions. Certain officers, directors and employees of Anacomp purchased limited partnership units in the partnership aggregating approximately 20% of the limited partnership units. The remaining limited partnership interest and the general partnership interest are owned by persons not affiliated with Anacomp. Under the development agreement, Anacomp agreed to develop the new system on a best efforts basis. The agreement permits Anacomp to contract with primary development banks to provide development fees up to $3,750 in addition to the $4,500 development fee to be paid by the partnership. Contracts with three banks aggregating $3,750 have been completed.

Anacomp has acquired rights to a wholesale banking system owned by a major bank at a cost of $1,350 to assist and expedite the completion of the system. A portion of this cost is being charged to expense as a system development cost and the remainder is being amortized over the expected marketing life of the purchased system in its unmodified form.

Upon completion of the system, Anacomp has agreed to market it for seven years on an exclusive commission basis. Anacomp has the option to acquire all rights to CBS at the greater of (a) fair market value or (b) $7,000 to $9,000, depending on the date the option is exercised. Revenues earned on this software development project were $2,620 and $4,319 during 1981 and 1982.

CIBS

Subsequent to June 30, 1982, Anacomp entered into an agreement with CIBS Partners, Limited ("CIBS"), a limited partnership formed in April 1981, to develop new software systems for large banks engaged in international business. Certain officers, directors and employees of Anacomp purchased limited partnership units in CIBS aggregating approximately 6.5% of the limited partnership units. The remaining limited partnership interests are owned by persons not affiliated with Anacomp. Anacomp is the sole holder of $400 of the non-voting preferred stock of the corporate general partner. The partnership payments under the development agreements are to be funded with $26,250 of partners' capital investment.

Under the development agreement, Anacomp has agreed to develop the new systems on a best efforts basis. The agreement permits Anacomp to contract with primary development banks to provide development fees up to $12,000 in addition to the $23,000 development fee to be paid by the partnership. A contract with one bank for $500 has been completed.

Upon completion of the systems, Anacomp has agreed to lease the systems for five years on an exclusive basis at rental based on a percentage of license fees generated. Anacomp has the option to acquire all rights to the systems during the three-year period commencing one year after completion of the systems at total prices ranging from $46,400 to $59,700, plus a share of licensing fees generated thereafter, depending on the year in which the option is exercised.

At June 30, 1982, the Company considered the funding for this project to be imminent. Accordingly, costs of $5,647, including $2,750 to acquire rights to certain software incurred in commencing the development of CIBS, were deferred until such time as project funding became available in August 1982. Such costs will be charged to operations in fiscal 1983.

Other

During fiscal 1980, a group of officers and directors of Anacomp formed a limited partnership which purchased a computer system and leased it to Anacomp at a competitive rental rate. In May 1982, the Company purchased the computer equipment from the partnership for $1,167, which was its appraised value.

Note 5. Cash, Cash Investments and Short-Term Borrowings:

Cash balances at June 30, 1982 and 1981, include temporary investments of $34,380 and $26,550, respectively, at costs which approximate market value. Of the amounts invested at June 20, 1982, $10,000 is pledged as collateral for the short-term borrowings from banks of $10,000 and is restricted as to withdrawal.

At June 20, 1982, Anacomp has short-term lines of credit from banks in the amount of $39,000, of which $35,000 is unused. Anacomp has agreed to maintain compensating balances, not restricted as to withdrawal, on certain of these lines. The average of compensating balances on these lines was approximately 5% of the available lines during fiscal 1982.

Note 7. Other Assets:

The following comprise other assets:

	June 30	
	1982	1981
Investment in Kalvar Corporation, including $1,028 note receivable in both years and income bond and preferred stock in 1982 and preferred stock in 1982	$6,428	$3,398
Marketable securities valued at the lower of cost or market	6,068	3,665
Notes receivable, RTS Associates	—	2,095
Notes receivable, other	4,132	400
Employment and non-compete agreements, less accumulated amortization of $1,297 and $848, respectively	491	737
Deferred debenture costs, less accumulated amortization of $313 and $152, respectively	3,470	2,026
Deferred charges, other	3,906	2,056
	$24,495	$14,377

Note 8. Long-Term Debt:

Long-term debt is comprised of the following:

	June 30	
	1982	1981
10% Convertible Subordinated Debentures due November 1, 1988	$758	$915
9½% Convertible Subordinated Debentures due September 1, 2000	29,925	29,295
9% Convertible Subordinated Debentures due January 15, 1996	13,789	12,500
13⅞% Convertible Subordinated Debentures due January 15, 2002 (net of unamortized original issue discount of $7,440)	42,560	—
Notes payable to banks at an average rate of 15.5% at June 30, 1982 due in installments to 1985	12,880	1,436
Other	8,203	8,174
	108,115	52,950
Less current portion	2,907	2,359
	$105,208	$50,591

Other debt includes equipment purchase notes, debtor to finance acquisitions, mortgages and obligations under capitalized financial leases. These items have effective costs of 9¾% to 15% and are payable in installments over varying periods extending to 2006. Shares representing substantially all of the operations of DSI are pledged as collateral for a note with a discounted balance of $2,793 at June 30, 1982. At June 30, 1982, processing equipment with an aggregate book value of approximately $3,600 is pledged as collateral under certain of the debt agreements.

Anacomp is guarantor of a bank loan to Anacomp's wholly-owned leasing subsidiary. At June 30, 1982, the balance of the debt being guaranteed is $480.

At June 30, 1982, the aggregate maturities of long-term debt through fiscal year 1987 are: 1983, $2,907; 1984, $12,972; 1985, $3,482; 1986, $347; and 1987, $219.

Note 9. Capital Stock:

Stock Dividends and Stock Splits

The Board of Directors declared the following stock dividends and stock splits during the three years ended June 30, 1982:

    January, 1980 – five-for-four stock split
    March, 1981 – five-for-four stock split

All applicable share and per share amounts have been restated to reflect the stock dividends and stock splits. All conversion prices and stock option data have also been adjusted to give effect to the stock dividends and stock split.

Note 10. Segment Information:

Anacomp operates in two business segments—data center services and computer services. Data center services consist of providing computer output microfilm ("COM") and computer processing for banks and credit unions through a network of branch offices, where Anacomp's equipment and personnel process data for numerous customers at each branch site. Computer services consist or providing computer software, primarily to large financial institutions, and managing computer facilities for large customers, primarily state and local governments.

	Consolidated	Data Center Services	Computer Services	Consolidated	Data Center Services	Computer Services
		Year Ended June 30, 1982			Year Ended June 30, 1981	
Revenues	$109,599	$67,418	$42,181	$106,368	$67,899	$38,469
Operating profit	$12,451	$8,504	$3,947	$18,191	$7,294	$10,897
Income before taxes	$3,622			$13,997		
Depreciation and amortization	$6,054	$3,636	$2,418	$3,859	$2,527	$1,332
Corporate depreciation and amortization	$654			$509		
		June 30, 1982			June 30, 1981	
Identifiable assets	$155,039	$84,785	$70,254	$93,737	$57,332	$36,405
Corporate assets	56,621			37,061		
	$211,660			$130,798		

Approximately 19% of Anacomp's fiscal 1982 consolidated revenues were provided by major computer services contracts which extend beyond one year, including those contracts in process discussed in Note 3. Contracts of this type provided 18% of the 1981 and 20% of the 1980 revenues. This included system licensing and modification contracts, which accounted for 13% of revenues in 1982, 11% in 1981 and 1980, and facility management arrangements, which accounted for 6% of revenues in 1982, 7% in 1981 and 9% in 1980.

Revenues from various federal, state and local government agencies amounted to approximately 11% of revenues in 1982 and 1981, and 14% in 1980.

Note 11. Income Taxes:

Deferred taxes are provided where differences exist between the period in which transactions affect taxable income and the period in which they enter into the determination of income for financial reporting purposes. Investment tax credits are reflected in income in the year realized by reducing the current provision for federal taxes on income.

The following table sets forth the components of the provision for income taxes:

Year Ended June 30	1982	1981	1980
Charge equivalent to realized tax benefits of preacquisition losses of acquired companies	$67	$164	$250
Charge equivalent to realized tax benefits from early disposition of shares issued under qualified stock option and stock purchase plans	76	252	81
Charge equivalent to realized tax benefits from certain acquisition expenditures	276	—	—
Taxes currently payable:			
Federal	2,536	1,034	2,263
State	889	602	377
Deferred	(3,001)	4,007	189
	$843	$6,059	$3,160

The deferred income tax effects of timing differences are as follows:

Year Ended June 30	1982	1981	1980
Excess of tax over book depreciation	$1,906	$265	$189
Use of cash basis accounting for tax purposes	(3,830)	3,830	—
Accrued interest on convertible debentures	(1,282)	(436)	—
Election of installment sale for tax purposes	506	(8)	—
Deferred income of foreign subsidiary	109	187	—
Deferred income of DISC	(156)	140	—
Transfer from deferred to currently payable	(264)	—	—
Other	10	29	—
	$(3,001)	$4,007	$189

The following is a reconciliation of income taxes calculated at the United States federal statutory rate to the provision for income taxes:

Year Ended June 30	1982	1981	1980
Provision for taxes on income at statutory rate	$1,666	$6,439	$3,582
Investment tax credit	(1,950)	(333)	(377)
State income taxes, net of federal income tax benefit	569	325	204
Nondeductible amortization of intangible assets	474	332	169
Difference between capital gain and statutory tax rates	—	(316)	(269)
Dividend deduction of 85% of dividend income	(119)	(179)	—
Interest on tax deposits, net of federal income tax benefit	302	—	—
Other	(99)	(209)	(149)
	$843	$6,059	$3,160

At June 30, 1982, certain subsidiaries of Anacomp have net operating loss carryforwards of approximately $1,997. The carryforwards pertain to preacquisition losses of the subsidiaries and therefore can be utilized only to the extent that the subsidiaries produce taxable income in the future. Any tax benefit resulting from the utilization of these carryforwards will reduce the intangible assets recorded at the time of purchase of the subsidiaries. The carryforwards expire in the following fiscal years: 1992, $357; 1993, $774; 1994, $514; and 1995, $352.

Note 12. Other Income and Extraordinary Credit

Year Ended June 30	1982	1981	1980
Gain (loss) on transaction with Kalvar	$(725)	$898	$1,567
Gain on sale of certain assets	630	855	25
Other	705	947	246
	$610	$2,700	$1,838

The extraordinary credit in 1982 arose from the sale of a branch office which had been acquired in 1981 as part of an acquisition accounted for as a pooling of interests. The gain was $2,541 before income taxes, determined at the capital gains rate of $711.

Note 13. Lease and Other Commitments:

Anacomp has commitments under long-term operating leases, principally for building space, covering periods generally up to five years. The following summarizes by year the future minimum lease payments due within the next five years and under all noncancellable operating lease obligations which extend beyond one year.

Fiscal	As of June 30, 1982
1983	$3,933
1984	3,159
1985	2,362
1986	1,605
1987	565
1988 and thereafter	626
Total minimum payments required	$12,250

Anacomp and Dr. Ronald D. Palamara, president and chairman of Anacomp, are parties to a March 27, 1980, employment and noncompetition agreement pursuant to which Anacomp agreed (a) to pay Dr. Palamara commencing July 1, 1980, a base annual salary of $125 plus an amount equal to 3.54% of Anacomp's annual income before income taxes in excess of $1,000, (b) to make a one-time payment of $430 in July, 1980, to Dr. Palamara for his agreement not to compete with Anacomp for three years following any termination of service with Anacomp and (c) to sell Dr. Palamara, in July, 1980, 428,688 shares of Anacomp common stock for a consideration of $6.08 per share, that being the per share market price on the date of the agreement. Of the $6.08 per share consideration, Dr. Palamara agreed to pay $1.22 per share and granted Anacomp a right of first refusal to purchase such shares upon any resale by Dr. Palamara or subsequent holders at $4.86 below the sale price, $4.86 being the balance of the $6.08 per share consideration.

Note 15. Supplementary Income Statement Information

Supplementary income statement information follows:

Year Ended June 30,	1982	1981	1980
Maintenance and repairs	$4,475	$3,738	$2,271
Depreciation and amortization of property, equipment and purchased computer software systems	$4,789	$2,938	$2,246
Amortization of intangible assets	$1,919	$1,430	$780
Taxes other than payroll and income taxes	$1,000	$507	$410
Rents	$7,503	$8,084	$4,819

REPORT OF INDEPENDENT ACCOUNTANTS

To the Board of Directors and Stockholders of Anacomp, Inc.

We have examined the consolidated balance sheet of Anacomp, Inc. and Subsidiaries as of June 30, 1982 and 1981, and the related consolidated statements of income, stockholders' equity, and changes in financial position for each of the three years in the period ended June 30, 1982. Our examinations were made in accordance with generally accepted auditing standards and, accordingly, included such tests of the accounting records and such other auditing procedures as we considered necessary in the circumstances.

In our opinion, the financial statements referred to above present fairly the consolidated financial position of Anacomp, Inc. and Subsidiaries as of June 30, 1982 and 1981, and the consolidated results of their operations and changes in financial position for each of the three years in the period ended June 30, 1982, in conformity with generally accepted accounting principles applied on a consistent basis, after restatement for the change, with which we concur, in the method of accounting for vacation pay as described in Note 1 to the financial statements.

Coopers & Lybrand

Indianapolis, Indiana
September 1982

Boston Chicken, Inc.

Perhaps no company better captures the spirit of the new economy than Boston Chicken Inc., which aims to do for the rotisserie what Colonel Sanders did for the deep fryer. . . . There is nothing particularly new about rotisserie chicken—those birds have been turning succulently in delicatessen windows for generations. But Boston Chicken is not really about poultry—it is about developing a market-winning formula for picking real estate, designing stores, organizing a franchise operation and analyzing data. These are Boston Chicken's innovations—trade secrets that can be every bit as valuable as a new drug or computer chip design. With them, Boston Chicken has not only developed the secret for delivering generous quantities of home-cooking at affordable prices, but also transformed what had been a mom-and-pop business into a new national category—take-out home-cooked food—that potentially can draw business away from both supermarkets and restaurants.

—*The Washington Post,* July 4, 1994

Boston Chicken was founded in 1989 by Scott Beck to operate and franchise food service stores that sold meals featuring rotisserie-cooked chicken, fresh vegetables, salads, and other side dishes. The firm's concept was to combine fresh, flavorful, and appealing meals associated with traditional home cooking with a high level of convenience and value. Meals cost less than $5 per person, were sold in bright, inviting retail stores, and were available for take-out or for on-site consumption. "Our strategy," Beck noted, "is to be a home meal replacement. Our number one competitor is pizza."[1]

To help operationalize his vision, Beck assembled a management team with considerable prior experience in both the fast-food business and franchising operations. Beck himself became one of the first and largest franchisees for Blockbuster Video while still in his 20s. He later sold his franchises back to the parent company for $120 million. Other top executives included the former president of Kentucky Fried Chicken, and former vice-presidents of Bennigan's, Taco Bell, Red Lobster, Chili's, and Baker's Square.

Professor Paul M. Healy prepared this case as the basis for class discussion rather than to illustrate either effective or ineffective handling of an administrative situation.

1. The Washington Post, *July 4, 1994.*

COMPANY STRUCTURE AND GROWTH STRATEGY

By the end of 1994, the Boston Chicken system operated 534 stores, compared to only 34 stores at the end of 1991. This translated to an annual rate of growth of almost 500% per year, with a new store being opened on average every two days. As reported in the financial statements presented in **Exhibit 1**, revenues for this period increased dramatically, from $5.2 million in 1991 to $96.2 million in 1994 and net income rose to $16.2 million (from a loss of $2.6 million). This growth continued throughout 1995; by the third quarter there were more than 750 stores in operation and quarterly sales had reached $38 million (see **Exhibit 2** for a summary of quarterly results). The company was voted "America's Favorite Chicken Chain" in a 1995 survey published by *Restaurant and Institutions* magazine.

To provide financing for its rapid growth, Boston Chicken went public in November 1993. The offering, for 1.9 million shares, was highly successful, as the stock price soared from the initial offering price of $10 to a high of $26.50. However, within months of the offer the stock had fallen back to $18. Nonetheless, a second offering for two million shares at $18.50 in August 1994 was oversubscribed. The company responded by increasing the offer to six million shares, raising $105 million of new capital (after issue costs).

Competition in the $200 billion restaurant industry was fierce, and several other companies were quick to take advantage of Boston Chicken's success. For example, in mid-1993 Pepsico's Kentucky Fried Chicken (KFC) introduced "rotisserie-gold" roasted chicken in most of its 5,100 restaurants. Within four months KFC reported that sales of the new chicken had topped $160 million, making KFC the world's largest rotisserie chicken chain. KFC spent $100 million to launch the new product, including a national network advertising campaign. However, some analysts believed that Boston Chicken's biggest challenge would not come from other competitors, but on how well the company met its goals.[2]

In its 1994 Annual Report, Boston Chicken described its main goals as strengthening its area developer organizations, creating communications infrastructure to support area developers, building an organization to continue new market development, and continuing operational improvements to ensure that the retail concept kept pace with changes in consumer tastes.

Area Developer Organizations

The company's franchising strategy was different from that of most other successful franchisers. Instead of selling store franchises to a large number of small franchisees, Boston Chicken focused on franchising to large regional developers. It established a network of 22 regional franchises, which targeted the 60 largest U.S. metropolitan markets. Each franchise was expected to have the scale necessary to ensure operational efficiency and marketing clout. The typical franchisee was an independent businessman with 15–20 years of relevant management experience, strong financial resources, and a mandate to open 50 to 100 new stores in the region. This structure was intended to provide the entrepreneurial energy of a franchise operation with the control and economies of scale of company-owned operations.

Under typical franchise agreements, developers paid Boston Chicken a one-time $35,000 per store franchise fee, a $10,000 fee to cover grand opening expenses, and an annual 5% royalty on gross revenues. In addition, franchisees contributed 2%

---

2. *See discussion by Stacy Dutton at Kidder Peabody's equity research department, quoted in* Reuters *news report, November 9, 1993.*

and 3.75% of sales per year respectively for national and local advertising campaigns. In 1994 royalties from these agreements amounted to $17.4 million, and initial franchise fees for new stores were $13 million. The company also earned interest income from franchise developers, since it provided a line of credit to assist them in new store development. This source of revenue grew rapidly in 1994 to $11.6 million. Other revenue sources included income from leasing some of its stores to franchise operators, and fees for software services provided to developers.

Area developer financing was provided to qualifying developers to assist them in expanding their operations. Under these arrangements, Boston Chicken provided the developer with a revolving line of credit that became available once at least 75% of the developer's equity capital had been spent on developing stores. The agreement provided limits on the amount that the developer could draw over time, primarily as a function of developers' equity capital. Once the drawing period expired, the loan converted to an amortizing four- to five-year term loan, with a variable interest rate set at 1% over the Bank of America Illinois "reference rate." Some loans also included a conversion option, permitting Boston Chicken to convert the loan into equity in the developer after two years, usually at a 12–15% premium over the equity price at the loan's inception.

Communications Infrastructure

The company invested $8–10 million to build computer software that provided support for its network of stores, and linked headquarters to developer stores. This software used information entered at the checkout counter to advise store managers when to put on another rack of chickens or to heat up another tray of mashed potatoes. It made appropriate adjustments for the day of the week, the season, and customer preferences at a particular store in making its recommendations. The software also provided information on employee work schedules to match daily peaks in customer purchases, automatically reordered food supplies from approved vendors, and updated the store's financial performance on an hourly basis.

New Market Development

New store site selection was critical to the company's future success. In 1995 it employed more than 180 real estate and construction professionals to ensure that the pace of development was sustained and that site standards were maintained. Given these resources, the company was optimistic that it could open at least 325 new stores per year in the foreseeable future.

Operating Improvements

In 1994, the company implemented a number of plans to improve operating efficiency and reduce store-level costs. These included long-term agreements with key suppliers, the introduction of flagship stores, expanded menus, in-store computer feedback from customers, and drive-thru lanes. Long-term agreements with suppliers provided opportunities to lock in prices for key inputs. For example, in October 1994 the firm reached a five-year cost-plus agreement with Hudson Foods to purchase the entire capacity from two Hudson poultry processing plants.

Flagship stores included a retail store and a kitchen facility with enough space and equipment to perform the initial stages of food preparation, such as washing and chopping vegetables, for up to 20 "satellite" stores. Prepared food was then sent to satellite stores, which completed the cooking process and served the products. This concept increased the quality and freshness of the side items, because a flagship had more frequent delivery of fresh ingredients. It also led to greater consistency in food taste, facilitated increased innovation in menu items (since there were fewer production people to train), and utilized facilities more effectively.

In fall 1994, the company added vegetable pot pies, Caesar salad, and cinnamon apples to its menu to satisfy customer demand for more variety in food offerings. Rotisserie-roasted turkey, ham, and meat loaf entrees were added in mid-1995. Stores offering these new products showed double-digit sales gains without any significant new advertising campaign. A new line of deli-type sandwiches featuring turkey, ham, and meat loaf on fresh-baked bread was also added to boost lunch sales. In 1995 the firm invested $20 million in Progressive Bagels (PBCI), a retailer of fresh gourmet bagels. Under this agreement, Boston Chicken provided an eight-year senior secured loan to Progressive Bagels, as well as providing administrative, real estate, and systems support services. Management argued that this investment provided the firm with the opportunity to learn more about the potential of morning service, which could further increase store productivity. By late 1995, this investment was increased to $80 million, and PBCI had grown to 53 stores (from a base of 20 units), with plans to open 200–225 stores in 1996. Finally, in an attempt to increase sales in the traditionally weak fourth quarter, the company began offering whole hams and turkeys for Thanksgiving and Christmas meals. As a result of these expanded product offerings, Boston Chicken decided to change its name to Boston Market.

In 1995 the company began using technology to keep in better touch with store customers. Touch-activated computer terminals were added to some stores, enabling customers to rate the quality of food and service. Blaine Hurst, the former Ernst & Young partner who headed Boston Chicken's computer operations, pointed out "if I can save half a percentage point on food costs, that's a lot of money. But if I can know almost instantaneously that customers don't like the drink selection and I can have that changed within a week—that's worth a lot more money."

Finally, to improve convenience for customers, the company decided to add drive-thru lanes to its stores. By late 1994, 62 stores in 18 states had drive-thru windows. In some cases, as much as 30 percent of store sales came from these windows. The company's market research indicates that as many as two-thirds of these customers would not have visited the stores had this convenience not been available. Drive-thrus were planned for a further 65 stores in 1995, and ultimately 70% of the stores were expected to be converted to drive-thru.

EXPECTED FUTURE PERFORMANCE

In late 1995, most restaurant analysts were bullish about Boston Chicken's future performance. For example, Michael Moe of Lehman Brothers noted: "Boston Chicken is truly the leader in the home meal replacement market. . . . Dual-income families are searching for an affordable alternative to preparing meals at home. Boston Chicken satisfies this need by preparing food that customers view as high quality, healthy and convenient. This home meal replacement is a hit with value-minded consumers. The bagel industry is another hot area of opportunity for Boston Chicken. Presently the bagel industry is one of the hottest growth areas in America."[3] Moe rated the stock to be a strong buy, and projected that EPS would be $0.63 in 1995, $0.90 in 1996, and would continue to grow by 45% per year from 1997 to 2001.

However, not everyone was impressed. Roger Lipton of Lipton Financial Services contended that Boston Chicken's franchisees had actually lost money. Lipton Financial Services was an affiliate of Axiom Capital Management, which had shorted the stock. He estimated that sales at a franchised store had to average $23,000 a week (net of promotional discounts) to cover labor, cost of sales, and other expenses. Actual average weekly sales, Lipton claimed, were only $18,900 per store, implying that franchisees were losing money. Lipton pointed out that "the quality of earnings is very low, since all of Boston Chicken's income comes from fees, royalties, and interest payments from franchisees, most of whom were financed by the franchiser."[4]

Management responded to concerns about the economics of franchisees by reporting that average weekly store sales were $23,388 for the third quarter of 1995, versus $22,227 for the second quarter, and that EBITDA store margins were running at about 15–16%. On December 1, 1995, the stock closed at $33.75, up more than 100% over the beginning of the year price (versus a 56% increase for the S&P 500).[5] But uncertainty about the company persisted. Short interest positions in the stock were at an all-time high of 10 million shares, more than 20% of the shares outstanding and double the short interest position at the beginning of 1995.

QUESTIONS

1. Assess Boston Chicken's business strategy. What are its critical success factors and risks?

2. How is the company reporting on its performance and risks? What are the key assumptions behind these policies? Do you think that its accounting policies reflect the risks?

3. What adjustments, if any, would you make to the firm's accounting policies?

4. What questions would you ask management about the company's performance?

5. How is Boston Chicken performing?

6. What assumptions is the market making about the company's future performance and risks? Do you agree with those assessments?

EXHIBIT I

Boston Chicken, Inc., Abridged 1994 Annual Report

FINANCIAL HIGHLIGHTS

	Fiscal Years Ended	
(dollars in thousands, except per share data)	December 25, 1994	December 26, 1993
Systemwide store revenue	$383,691	$152,056
Company revenue	96,151	42,530
Net income	16,173	1,647
Net income per share	$0.38	$0.06
Shareholders' equity	$259,815	$94,906
Weighted average number of shares outstanding	42,861	32,667

3. Michael Moe, Lehman Brothers, October 25, 1995.

4. "Inside Wall Street," Business Week, June 12, 1995.

5. The equity beta for Boston Chicken was 1.50, and at December 1, 1995 the 30-year U.S. Government Treasuries yielded 6.04%.

MANAGEMENT'S DISCUSSION AND ANALYSIS

General

The total number of stores in the Boston Market system increased from 34 at the year ended December 29, 1991 to 534 at the year ended December 25, 1994. This rapid expansion significantly affects the comparability of results of operations form year to year as well as the Company's liquidity and capital resources. The following table sets forth information regarding store development activity for the years indicated.

	Stores at Beginning of Year	Net Stores Opened in Year	Net Stores Transferred in Year[a]	Stores at End of Year
Year Ended December 27, 1992:				
Company-operated	5	15	(1)	19
Financed area developers	0	3	0	3
Non-financed area developers and other	29	31	1	61
Total	34	49	0	83
Year Ended December 26, 1993:				
Company-operated	19	28	(9)	38
Financed area developers	3	66	9	78
Non-financed area developers and other	61	40	0	101
Total	83	134	0	217
Year Ended December 25, 1994:				
Company-operated	38	49	(46)	41
Financed area developers	78	168	68	314
Non-financed area developers and other	101	100	(22)	179
Total	217	317	0	534

[a]*Stores transferred during the year primarily reflect the Company's practice of opening new Company-operating stores to seed development in targeted markets prior to execution of area development agreements relating to such markets. At the time such agreements are executed, the Company typically sells Company-operating stores located in the market to the area developer in that market. Stores transferred also reflect the purchase and/or sale of Boston Market stores in markets with multiple area developers in order to facilitate consolidation of such markets.*

Results of Operations

Fiscal Year 1994 Compared to Fiscal Year 1993

Revenue

Total revenue increased $53.7 million (126%) from $42.5 million for 1993 to $96.2 million for 1994. Royalty and franchise-related fees increased $42.5 million (335%) to $55.2 million for 1994, from $12.7 million for 1993. This increase was primarily due to an increase in royalties attributable to the larger base of franchise stores operating systemwide, from 179 stores at December 16, 1993 to 493 stores at December 5, 1994, an increase in franchise fees related to the increase in the number of stores that commenced operation as franchised stores during the year, and higher interest income generated on increased loans made to certain area developers. Additional factors contributing to the increase in revenue from royalty and franchise-related fees include an increase in lease income due to a higher number of store sites which the Company owns and leases to area developers, and recognition of software license and maintenance fees for store-level computer software systems developed by the Company for use by franchisees. No software-related fees were earned in 1993.

Revenue from Company-operated stores increased $11.1 million (37%) from $29.8 million for 1993 to $40.9 million for 1994. This increase was due to a higher average number of Company-operated stores open during the year. The Company had 38 Company-operated stores at December 26, 1993, compared to 41 at December 25, 1994. During 1994, the Company sold 54 Company-operated stores which it had opened to seed new markets.

Cost of Products Sold

Cost of products sold increased $4.6 million (41%), to $15.9 million for 1994 compared with $11.3 million for 1993. This increase was primarily due to an increase in the number of Company-operated stores open during the periods. Management does not believe that the cost of products sold as a percentage of store revenue at Company-operated stores is indicative of cost of products sold as a percentage of store revenue at franchise stores due to the Company's practice of opening new stores primarily to seed new markets. These newer stores, which constitute the majority of the Company-operated store base, tend to have higher food and paper costs as a result of increased food usage for free tasting, inefficiencies resulting from employee inexperience, and a lack of store-specific operating history to assist in forecasting daily food production needs.

Salaries and Benefits

Salaries and benefits increased $7.2 million (47%), from $15.4 million in 1993 to $22.6 million in 1994. The increase resulted from an increase in the number of employees at the Company's support center necessary to support systemwide expansion and an increase in the number of employees at Company-operated stores due to a higher average number of Company-operated stores open during the year.

General and Administrative

General and administrative expenses increased $14.0 million (101%) to $27.9 million for 1994 from $13.9 million for 1993. The increase is attributable to the development of the Company's support center infrastructure necessary to support systemwide expansion and higher general and administrative expenses at Company-operated stores resulting from a higher average number of Company-operated stores open during the year. Included in general and administrative expenses were depreciation and amortization charges of $6.1 million in 1994 and $2.0 million in 1993. The increase in depreciation and amortization expense is primarily attributable to a substantially higher fixed asset base reflecting the Company's investment in its infrastructure.

Provision for Relocation

In September 1994, the Company consolidated its four Chicago-based support center facilities into a single facility and relocated to Golden, Colorado. The total cost of relocation was $5.1 million.

Other Expense

The Company incurred other expense of $4.2 million in 1994, compared with other expense of $0.3 million in 1993. This increase reflects higher interest expense, primarily attributable to the $130.0 million of convertible subordinated debt and short-term borrowings under its unsecured credit facility, partially offset by higher interest income.

Income Taxes

Included in income taxes in 1994 is a $3.5 million benefit reflecting the realization of deferred tax assets attributable to the increased level of operating income, offset by a current provision for income taxes.

Liquidity and Capital Resources

Liquidity

The Company's primary capital requirements are for store development, including providing partial financing for certain of its area developers, purchasing real estate which is then leased to its area developers, and opening Company-operated stores. The remainder of the Company's capital requirements related primarily to investments in corporate infrastructure, including property and equipment and software development, which are necessary to support the increase in the number of stores in operation systemwide. For the year ended December 25, 1994, the Company expended approximately $268.1 million on store development, including financing area developers, purchasing real estate and opening Company-operated stores. The Company also expended approximately $52.3 million on corporate infrastructure, including its new support center facility.

The Company has entered into secured loan agreements with certain of its area developers whereby the area developers may draw on a line of credit, with certain limitations, in order to provide partial funding for expansion of their operations. In connection with certain of these loans, after a specified moratorium period, the Company has the right to convert the loan which typically results in a controlling equity interest in the area developer. As of December 25, 1994, The Company had secured loan commitments aggregating approximately $332.5 million, of which approximately $201.3 million had been advanced. The Company anticipates fully funding its commitments pursuant to its loan agreements with these area developers, and anticipates increasing such loan commitments and entering into additional loan commitments with other area developers in targeted market areas. In connection with entering into new area development agreements, the Company intends to sell Company-operated stores located in any such areas to the respective area developer. The Company is currently negotiating such agreements for a number of metropolitan areas, including Kansas City, Minneapolis, Omaha, New York, and San Francisco/San Jose. The timing of such transactions will have significant effect on the size and timing of the Company's capital requirements.

In 1994, the Company sold 54 Company-operated stores to its area developers in the Philadelphia, Detroit, Denver, Colorado Springs, Phoenix, Tucson, Las Vegas, Albuquerque, Salt Lake City, Southern New Jersey, and Boston metropolitan areas. In addition to opening stores to seed development in new markets and subsequently selling such stores to the new area developer for such market, the Company purchases and resells Boston Market stores in markets with multiple area developers in order to facilitate consolidation of such markets. In connection with these consolidation activities, the Company has issued a total of 1,112,436 shares of common stock pursuant to its shelf registration statement for the acquisition of 32 Boston Market stores and paid cash for 2 Boston Market stores. Of the 34 stores purchased, 26 stores were subsequently sold. The Company believes that all of the shares issued in connection with these consolidation activities have been sold by the recipients pursuant to Rule 145 (d) under the Securities Act of 1933, as amended. The aggregate proceeds from the sale of Company-operated stores to seed new markets and from the sale of stores which were acquired to consolidate markets were approximately $62.3 million. There were no material gains recognized as a result of these sales.

In March 1995, the Company entered into a secured loan agreement providing $20 million of convertible debt financing to Progressive Bagel Concepts, Inc. ("PBCI"). The Company has agreed to increase the amount available to PBCI under the loan agreement subject to PBCI's ability to meet certain conditions.

Capital Resources

For the year ended December 25, 1994, the Company's primary sources of capital included $35.9 million generated from operating activities, $130.0 million from the issuance of 4½% convertible subordinated debentures maturing February 1, 2004 (the "Debentures"), and $125.7 million from the sale of shares of common stock. The Debentures are convertible at any time prior to maturity into shares of the Company's common stock at a conversion rate of $27.969 per share, subject to adjustment under certain conditions. Beginning February 1, 1996, the

Debentures may be reduced at the option of the Company, provided that until February 1, 1997, the Debentures cannot be redeemed unless the closing price of the Company's common stock equals or exceeds $39.16 per share for at least 20 out of 30 consecutive trading days. The Debentures are redeemable initially at 103.6% of their principal amount and at declining prices thereafter, plus accrued interest. Interest is payable semi-annually on February 1 and August 1 of each year.

In 1994, the Company entered into a $75.9 million master lease agreement to provide equipment financing for stores owned by certain of its area developers and certain Company-operated stores. The lease bears interest at LIBOR plus an applicable margin and, including renewal terms, expires in December 1998. As of December 25, 1994, the Company had utilized $66.1 million of the facility.

As of December 25, 1994, the Company had $25.3 million available in cash and cash equivalents, $75.0 million available under its unsecured revolving credit facility, and $8.9 million available under its master lease agreement.

The Company anticipates that it and its area developers will have need for additional financing during the 1995 fiscal year. The timing of the Company's capital requirements will be affected by the number of Company-operated and franchise stores opened, operational results of stores, the number of real estate sites purchased by the Company for Company use and for leasing by the Company to franchisees, and the amount and timing of borrowings under the loan agreements between the Company and certain of its existing or future area developers and by PBCI. As the Company's capital requirements increase, the Company will seek additional funds from future public or private offerings of debt or equity securities. There can be no assurance that the Company will be able to raise such capital on satisfactory terms when needed.

Seasonality

Historically, the Company has experienced lower average store revenue in the months of November, December, January, and February as a result of the holiday season and inclement weather. The Company's business in general, as well as the revenue of Company-operated stores, may be affected by a variety of other factors, including, but not limited to, general economic trends, competition, marketing programs, and special or unusual events. Such effects, however, may not be apparent in the Company's operating results during a period of significant expansion.

CONSOLIDATED BALANCE SHEETS

	1994	1993
Assets		
Current assets		
Cash	$25,304	$4,537
Accounts receivable, net	6,540	2,076
Due from affiliates	6,462	3,126
Notes receivable	16,906	1,512
Prepaid expenses & other current assets	2,282	1,843
Deferred income taxes	1,835	—
Total current assets	59,329	13,094
Property & equipment, net	163,314	51,331
Notes receivable	185,594	44,204
Deferred financing costs	8,346	358
Other assets	10,399	1,077
Total assets	$426,982	$110,064

(continued)

CONSOLIDATED BALANCE SHEETS *(continued)*

	1994	1993
Liabilities & Stockholders' Equity		
Current liabilities		
Accounts payable	$15,188	$6,216
Accrued expenses	6,587	1,835
Deferred franchise revenue	5,505	2,255
Total current liabilities	27,280	10,306
Deferred franchise revenue	5,815	3,139
Convertible subordinated debt	130,000	
Other noncurrent liabilities	1,061	1,713
Deferred income taxes	3,011	
Stockholders' Equity		
Common stock	447	347
Additional paid-in capital	252,298	103,662
Retained earnings (deficit)	7,070	(9,103)
	259,815	94,906
Total liabilities and stockholders' equity	$426,982	$110,064

CONSOLIDATED STATEMENTS OF OPERATIONS

	1994	1993	1992
Revenue			
Royalties & franchise-related fees	$55,235	$12,681	$2,627
Company-operated stores	40,916	29,849	5,656
Total revenues	96,151	42,530	8,283
Costs and expenses			
Cost of products sold	15,876	11,287	2,241
Salaries and benefits	22,637	15,437	7,110
General and administrative	27,930	13,879	5,241
Provision for relocation	5,097	—	—
Total costs and expenses	71,540	40,603	14,592
Income (loss) from operations	24,611	1,927	(6,309)
Other income (expense)			
Interest income (expense), net	(4,235)	(440)	270
Other income, net	74	160	189
Total other income (expense)	(4,161)	(280)	459
Income (loss) before income taxes	20,450	1,647	(5,850)
Income taxes	4,277	—	—
Net income (loss)	$16,173	$1,647	$(5,850)
Net income (loss) per share common and equivalent share	$0.38	$0.06	$(0.21)
Number of shares	42,861	32,667	28,495

CONSOLIDATED STATEMENTS OF CASH FLOWS (in thousands)

	Fiscal Years Ended		
	Dec. 25, 1994	Dec. 26, 1993	Dec. 27, 1992
Cash from operating activities			
Net income (loss)	$16,173	$1,647	$(5,850)
Adjustments to reconcile income (loss) to net cash provided by (used in) operating activities			
Depreciation and amortization	6,074	1,970	260
Deferred income taxes	4,277		
Vesting of common stock for services rendered			39
Gain on disposal of assets	(368)	(150)	(29)
Changes in assets and liabilities			
Accounts receivable and due from affiliates	(7,800)	(4,343)	(689)
Accounts payable and accrued expenses	13,724	6,247	1,102
Deferred franchise revenue	5,926	3,236	1,223
Other assets and liabilities	(2,088)	(561)	332
Net cash from (used) in operations	35,198	8,046	(3,612)
Cash from investing activities			
Purchase of plant, property & equipment	(163,622)	(49,151)	(8,453)
Proceeds from sale of assets	62,342	6,161	385
Acquisition of other assets	(12,790)	(1,093)	(273)
Issuance of notes receivable	(225,282)	(45,690)	(773)
Repayment of notes receivable	68,498	747	—
Net cash used in investing activities	(270,854)	(89,026)	(9,114)
Cash from financing activities			
Proceeds from issue common stock	125,703	66,150	19,843
Proceeds from convertible subordinate notes	130,000	9,658	
Borrowings under credit facility	96,130	32,275	
Repayments under credit facility	(96,130)	(32,275)	
Payment of capital lease obligation	—	—	(300)
Net cash from financing activities	255,703	75,808	19,543
Net increase (decrease) in cash	20,767	(5,172)	6,817
Cash, beginning of year	4,537	9,709	2,892
Cash, end of year	$25,304	$4,537	$9,709
Supplemental cash flow information			
Interest paid	$3,395	$226	$29
Noncash transactions			
Conversion of convt. subord. notes into common stock	$—	$10,072	$—
Issuance of commons stock for assets	$19,931	—	$—

The accompanying notes to the consolidated financial statements are an integral part of these statements.

Boston Chicken, Inc.

OTHER INFORMATION

	1994	1993	1992	1991
Store Information				
Company operated	41	38	19	5
Finance area developers	314	78	3	0
Nonfinanced area developers	179	101	61	29
Total	534	217	83	34
Systematic store revenue	383.7	152.1	42.7	20.8
Quarterly Data Revenue				
1st quarter	23,449			
2nd quarter	20,360			
3rd quarter	25,186			
4th quarter	27,165			
Net Income				
1st quarter	2,561			
2nd quarter	3,383			
3rd quarter	4,679			
4th quarter	5,550			

NOTES TO CONSOLIDATED FINANCIAL STATEMENTS

1. Description of Business

Boston Chicken, Inc., and Subsidiary (the "Company") operate and franchise food service stores that specialize in complete meals featuring home style entrees, fresh vegetables, salads, and other side items. At December 26, 1993, there were 217 stores systemwide, consisting of 38 Company-operated stores and 179 franchise stores. At December 25, 1994, there were 534 stores systemwide, consisting of 41 Company-operated stores and 493 franchise stores. In 1992, 1993, and 1994, in connection with its practice of opening new stores to seed development in targeted markets, the Company sold 1, 13, and 54 Company-operated stores, respectively, to newly formed area developers or franchisees of the Company. During 1994, in connection with its practice of acquiring stores in markets with multiple area developers in order to facilitate consolidation of such markets, the Company purchased 34 stores and resold 26 of them.

2. Summary of Significant Accounting Policies

Principles of Consolidation

The accompanying consolidated financial statements include the accounts of the Company and its subsidiary. All material intercompany accounts and transactions have been eliminated in consolidation.

Fiscal Year

The Company's fiscal year is the 52/53-week period ending on the last Sunday in December. Fiscal years 1992, 1993, and 1994 each contained 52 weeks, or thirteen four-week periods. The first quarter consists of four periods and each of the remaining three quarters consists of three periods, with the first, second, and third quarters ending 16 weeks, 28 weeks, and 40 weeks, respectively, into the fiscal year.

Cash and Cash Equivalents

Cash and cash equivalents consist of cash on hand and on deposit, and highly liquid instruments purchased with maturities of three months or less.

Inventories

Inventories, which are classified in prepaid expenses and other current assets, are stated at the lower of cost (first-in, first-out) or market and consist of food, paper products, and supplies.

Property and Equipment

Property and equipment is stated at cost, less accumulated depreciation and amortization. The provision for depreciation and amortization has been calculated using the straight-line method. The following represent the useful lives over which the assets are depreciated and amortized:

Buildings and improvements	15–30 years
Leasehold improvements	15 years
Furniture, fixtures, equipment and computer software	6–8 years
Pre-opening costs	1 year

Property and equipment additions include acquisitions of property and equipment, costs incurred in the development and construction of new stores, major improvements to existing stores, and costs incurred in the development and purchase of computer software. Pre-opening costs consist primarily of salaries and other direct expenses relating to the set-up, initial stocking, training, and general management activities incurred prior to the opening of new stores. Expenditures for maintenance and repairs are charged to expense as incurred. Development costs for franchised stores are expensed when the store opens.

Deferred Financing Costs

Deferred financing costs are amortized over the period of the related financing, which ranges from two to ten years.

Revenue Recognition

Revenue from Company-operated stores is recognized in the period related food and beverage products are sold. Revenue derived from initial franchise fees and area development fees is recognized when the franchise store opens. Royalties are recognized in the same period related franchise store revenue is generated. The components of royalties and franchise-related fees are comprised of the following:

(in thousands of dollars)	Dec. 25, 1994	Dec. 26, 1993	Dec. 27, 1992
Royalties	$17,421	$5,464	$1,491
Initial franchise and area development	13,057	5,230	1,136
Interest income from area developer financing (See Note 8)	11,632	1,130	—
Lease income	5,361	253	—
Software fees	6,480	—	—
Other	1,284	604	—
Total royalties and franchise-related fees	$55,235	$12,681	$2,627

Subject to the provisions of the applicable franchise agreements, the Company is committed and obligated to allow franchisees to utilize the Company's trademarks, copyrights, recipes, operating procedures, and other elements of the Boston Market system in the operation of franchised Boston Market stores.

Per Share Data

Net income (loss) per common share is computed by dividing net income (loss), adjusted in 1993 for interest related to the conversion of 7% convertible subordinated notes (see Note 9), by the weighted average number of common shares and dilutive common stock equivalent shares outstanding during the year.

Common and equivalent shares include any common stock, options, and warrants issued within one year prior to the effective date of the Company's initial public offering, with a price below the initial public offering price. These have been included as common stock equivalents outstanding, reduced by the number of shares of common stock which could be purchased with the proceeds from the assumed exercise of the options and warrants, including tax benefits assumed to be realized.

Employee Benefit Plan

The Company has a 401(k) plan for which employee participation is discretionary and to which the Company makes no contribution.

Reclassification

Certain amounts shown in the 1992 and 1993 financial statements have been reclassified to conform with the current presentation.

3. Debt

The Company has entered into a revolving credit agreement on an unsecured basis providing for borrowings of up to $75 million through June 30, 1997. Borrowings under the agreement may be either floating rate loans with interest at the bank's reference rate of eurodollar loans with interest at the eurodollar rate, plus an applicable margin. In addition, a commitment fee of .25% of the average daily unused portion of the loan is required. The agreement contains various covenants including restricting other borrowings, prohibiting cash dividends, and requiring the Company to maintain interest coverage and cash flow ratios and a minimum net worth. As of December 25, 1994, no borrowings were outstanding.

In February, 1994, the Company issued $130 million of 4.5% convertible subordinated debentures maturing February 1, 2004. Interest is payable semi-annually on February 1 and August 1 of each year. The debentures are convertible at any time prior to maturity into shares of common stock at a conversion rate of $27.969 per share, subject to adjustment under certain conditions. Beginning February 1, 1996, the debentures may be redeemed at the option of the Company, provided that through February 1, 1997, the debentures cannot be redeemed unless the closing price of the common stock equals or exceeds $39.16 per share for at least 20 out of 30 consecutive trading days. The debentures are redeemable initially at 103.6% of their principal amount and at declining prices thereafter, plus accrued interest.

4. Income Taxes

As of December 25, 1994, the Company has cumulative Federal and state net tax operating loss carryforwards available to reduce future taxable income of approximately $30.5 million which begin to expire in 2003. The Company has recognized the benefit of the loss carryforwards for financial reporting, but not for income tax purposes. Certain ownership changes which have occurred will result in an annual limitation of the Company's utilization of its net operating losses.

At December 28, 1992, the first day of fiscal 1993, the Company adopted SFAS No. 109 "Accounting for Income Taxes" ("SFAS 109"). Upon adoption of SFAS 109 there was no cumulative effect on the Company's financial statements because the Company's deferred tax assets exceeded its deferred tax liabilities and a valuation allowance was recorded against the net deferred tax assets due to uncertainty regarding realization of the related tax benefits.

The primary components that comprise the deferred tax assets and liabilities at December 26, 1993, and December 25, 1994, are as follows:

(in thousands of dollars)	Dec. 25, 1994	Dec. 26, 1993
Deferred tax assets:		
Accounts payable and accrued expenses	$794	$78
Deferred franchise revenue	3,469	1,992
Other noncurrent liabilities	262	623
Net operating losses	11,639	4,844
Other	173	52
Total deferred tax assets	16,337	3,742
Less valuation reserve	—	(3,847)
Net deferred taxes	16,337	3,742
Deferred tax liabilities		
Due from are developers	—	(814)
Property and equipment	(17,047)	(2,807)
Other assets	(466)	(121)
Total deferred tax liabilities	(17,513)	(3,742)
Net deferred tax liability	$(1,176)	$—

The decrease in the valuation allowance from December 26, 1993 to December 25, 1994 was $3,847,000 and the decrease in the valuation allowance from December 27, 1992 to December 26, 1993 was $180,000, which was net of a $446,000 increase related to the tax benefit from the exercise of stock options.

The provision for income taxes for the fiscal year ended December 25, 1994, consists of $4,277,000 of deferred income taxes, which is net of an income tax benefit of $3,102,000 pertaining to the exercise of stock options.

The difference between the Company's 1993 and 1994 actual tax provision and the tax provision by applying the statutory Federal income tax rate is attributable to the following:

(in thousands of dollars)	Fiscal Years Ended	
	Dec. 25, 1994	Dec. 26, 1993
Income tax expense at statutory rate	$6,953	$560
State taxes, net of Federal benefit	818	66
Other	26	—
Change in valuation allowance	(3,520)	(626)
Provision for income taxes	$4,277	$—

5. Marketing and Advertising Funds

The Company administers a National Advertising Fund to which Company-operated stores and franchisees make contributions based on individual franchise agreements (currently 2% of base revenue). Collected amounts are spent primarily on developing marketing and advertising materials for use systemwide. Such amounts are not segregated from the cash resources of the Company, but the National Advertising Fund is accounted for separately and not included in the financial statements of the Company.

The Company maintains Local Advertising Funds that provide comprehensive advertising and sales promotion support for the Boston Market stores in particular markets. Periodic contributions are made by both Company-operated and franchise stores (currently 3% to 3.75% of base revenue). The Company disburses funds and accounts for all transactions related to such Local Advertising Funds. Such amounts are not segregated from the cash resources of the Company, but are accounted for separately and are not included in the financial statements of the Company.

The National Advertising Fund and certain Local Advertising Funds had accumulated deficits at December 26, 1993, and December 25, 1994, which were funded by advances from the Company. Such advances are reflected in Due from affiliates, net.

6. Area Developer Financing

The Company currently offers partial financing to certain area developers for use in expansion of their operations. Only developers which are developing a significant portion of an area of dominant influence ("ADI") or metropolitan area of a major city and which meet all of the Company's requirements are eligible for such financing. Certain of these financing arrangements permit the Company to obtain an equity interest in the developer at a predetermined price after a moratorium (generally two years) on conversion of the loan into equity. The maximum loan amount is generally established to give the Company majority ownership of the developer upon conversion (or option exercise, as described further below) provided the Company exercises its right to participate in any intervening financing of the developer.

Area developer financing generally requires the developer to expend at least 75% of its equity capital toward developing stores prior to drawing on the revolving loan account, with draws permitted during a two- or three-year draw period in a pre-determined amount, generally equal to two to four times the amount of the developer's equity capital. Upon expiration of the draw period, the loan converts to an amortizing term loan payable over four to five years in periodic installments, sometimes with a final balloon payment. Interest is generally set at 1% over the applicable "reference rate" of Bank of America Illinois from time to time and is payable each period. The loan is secured by a pledge of substantially all of the assets of the area developer and any franchisees under its area development agreement and generally by a pledge of equity of the owners of the developer.

(a) Loan Conversion Option

For loans with a conversion option, all or any portion of the loan amount may be converted at the Company's election (at any time after default of the loan or generally after the second anniversary of the loan and generally up to the later of full repayment of the loan or a specified date in the agreement) into equity in the developer at the conversion price set forth in such loan agreement, generally at a 12% to 15% premium over the per equity unit price paid by the developer for the equity investment made concurrently with the execution of the loan agreement or subsequent amendments thereto. To the extent such loan is not fully drawn or has been drawn and repaid, the Company has a corresponding option to acquire at the loan conversion price the amount of additional equity it could have acquired by conversion of the loan, had it been fully drawn.

There can be no assurance the Company will or will not convert any loan amount or exercise its option at such time as it may be permitted to do so and, if it does convert, that such conversion will constitute a majority interest in the area developer. Absent a default under any such agreement, the Company currently cannot exercise these conversion or option rights.

(b) Commitment to Extend Area Developer Financing

The following table summarizes credit commitments for area developer financing, certain of which are conditional upon additional equity contributions being made by area developers:

(In thousands of dollars, except number of area developers)	Dec. 25, 1994	Dec. 26, 1993
Number of area developers receiving financing	13	5
Loan commitments	$332,531	$51,041
Unused loans	(131,265)	(7,243)
Loans outstanding (included in Notes Receivable)	$201,266	$43,798
Allowance for loan losses	$ —	$ —

The principal maturities on the aforementioned notes receivable are as follows:

(In thousands of dollars)	
1995	$16,288
1996	4,456
1997	13,132
1998	12,132
1999	15,417
Thereafter	139,841
	$201,266

(c) Credit Risk and Allowance for Loan Losses

The allowance for credit losses is maintained at a level that in management's judgment is adequate to provide for estimated possible loan losses. The amount of the allowance is based on management's review of each area developer's financial condition, store performance, store opening schedules, and other factors, as well as prevailing economic conditions. Based upon this review and analysis, no allowance was required as of December 26, 1993 and December 25, 1994.

7. Relocation

In September 1994, the Company consolidated its four Chicago-based support center facilities into a single facility and relocated to Golden, Colorado. The cost of the relocation, including moving personnel and facilities, severance payments, and the write-off of vacated leasehold improvements was $5.1 million.

8. Subsequent Events

In March 1995, the Company entered into a convertible secured loan agreement providing $20 million of financing to Progressive Bagel Concepts, Inc. ("PBCI"). The Company has agreed to provide PBCI additional convertible secured loans subject to PBCI's ability to meet certain conditions.

In March 1995, PBCI entered into stock purchase agreements with the Company to purchase $19.5 million of common stock. The number of shares to be issued will be based upon the market value of the stock two days prior to the closing date. The Company has granted PBCI registration rights and has provided a price guarantee equal to the per share purchase price on any shares sold within a specified number of days of the registration becoming effective.

REPORT OF INDEPENDENT PUBLIC ACCOUNTANTS

To the Board of Directors and Stockholders of Boston Chicken, Inc.:

We have audited the accompanying consolidated balance sheets of Boston Chicken, Inc. (a Delaware corporation) and Subsidiary as of December 25, 1994 and December 26, 1993, and the related consolidated statements of operations, stockholders' equity, and cash flows for the fiscal years ended December 25, 1994, December 26, 1993, and December 27, 1992. These financial statements are the responsibility of the Company's management. Our responsibility is to express an opinion on these financial statements based on our audits.

We conducted our audits in accordance with generally accepted auditing standards. Those standards require that we plan and perform the audit to obtain reasonable assurance about whether the financial statements are free of material misstatements. An audit includes examining, on a test basis, evidence supporting the amounts and disclosures in the financial statements. An audit also includes assessing the accounting principles used and significant estimates made by management, as well as evaluating the overall financial statement presentation. We believe that our audits provide a reasonable basis for our opinion.

In our opinion, the financial statements referred to above present fairly, in all material respects, the financial position of Boston Chicken, Inc. and Subsidiary as of December 25, 1994 and December 26, 1993, and the results of their operations and their cash flows for the fiscal years ended December 25, 1994, December 26, 1993, and December 27, 1992, in conformity with generally accepted accounting principles.

(Arthur Andersen LLP)

Denver, Colorado

January 31, 1995 (except with respect to the matters discussed in Note 12, as to which the date is March 24, 1995)

EXHIBIT 2

Boston Chicken Inc., Summary of 1994–1995 Quarterly Results

	1st Quarter	2nd Quarter	3rd Quarter	4th Quarter
1995				
Revenue ($000)	$40,107	$34,800	$38,671	
Net Income ($000)	7,116	7,420	8,814	
EPS	$0.15	$0.15	$0.14	
1994				
Revenue ($000)	$23,449	$20,360	$25,186	$27,165
Net Income ($000)	2,561[a]	3,383[a]	4,679[a]	5,550
EPS	$0.06	$0.08	$0.11	$0.12

[a]Pre-tax provisions for relocation were $4,708,000 in the second quarter of 1994, and $389,000 in the third quarter of 1994.

The City of New York

In July 1996 Moody's Investors Service, Inc., was reviewing the ratings for the general obligation bonds of the City of New York. With a population of approximately 7.3 million, New York was the largest city in the United States and an international business and cultural center. Its key industries included banking, securities, life insurance, communications, publishing, printing, fashion-design, apparel manufacture, retailing, and construction. In addition, the City was the leading tourist destination in the United States.

New York's economy was closely linked to national economic events. Thus, in the early 1990s, it experienced a decline in employment and real gross product. Growth picked up in the period 1992 to 1994, but slowed after 1995. The City's general obligation bonds were rated Baa1, the lowest rated investment grade bonds.

Moody's review included an analysis of the challenges facing U.S. municipalities generally, as well as an examination of the financial performance of New York. At the completion of review, Moody's had to decide whether to upgrade, downgrade, or maintain the City's current rating.

MUNICIPALITIES

Municipal governments typically provided a range of services to local communities, including legislative, executive and judicial functions. They also offered a range of other services, such as primary and secondary education, public safety (police and fire), public works (streets, sewers, and sanitation), public welfare, public transportation, airports, utilities (water and power), colleges, hospitals, corrections facilities, community development, and parks and recreation facilities. To fund these activities, municipal governments received support from state and federal governments, property and other forms of taxes, charges for various services, and utility revenues.

Municipal governments grew dramatically after World War II, from 2.8 million employees in 1945 to 7.4 million in 1970 and 10 million in 1987. This level

Professor Paul M. Healy prepared this case as the basis for class discussion rather than to illustrate either effective or ineffective handling of an administrative situation. The case has benefited from the comments of Jack Miller and Elizabeth Krahmer.

of employment exceeded that for the combined state and federal civilian governments.

During the 1990s municipalities faced a number of financial challenges, including deteriorating infrastructure, stagnant revenues accompanied by increasing cost structures, unfunded mandates from federal and state governments to provide additional services, pressures to increase the quality of public services provided (without increasing costs), and competition between municipalities to attract new businesses.

Much of the infrastructure for older U.S. cities, such as New York, was provided during the Depression. For example, the public works projects of the New Deal provided for the construction of municipal roads, bridges, and some public buildings. The 1970s saw a shift from maintenance and replacement of this infrastructure to increased social services. As a result, infrastructure deteriorated and by the early 1990s often required replacement.

A second financial challenge facing older U.S. municipalities arose from stagnant revenue bases and increased cost structures. Many municipalities in the Northeast and the Midwest had stable or declining populations, and had seen key businesses move to less costly areas of the country. As a result, their revenue base was stagnant. Compounding this problem, their costs had escalated during the 1980s and early 1990s. For example, medical costs increased at rates significantly higher than inflation during this period. This increased significantly the cost of medical benefits for municipal employees, as well as the cost of providing health services to older and poorer residents through public hospital systems.

A third factor affecting municipal governments had been the increase in unfunded State and Federal government mandates to provide additional services. For example, state and federal governments required local governments to accept increased responsibility for undertaking such services as police and safety, mass transit, housing for the indigent, and special education, without necessarily providing the full funding for these services.

The 1980s and 1990s also saw increased product and service quality in many areas of the private sector. For example, there have been significant product improvements in the computer and auto industries, faster customer response times due to overnight delivery, faxes, and email, as well as opportunities for home shopping and banking. Taxpayers frequently expected the same types of quality improvements in public services, leading to a growing expectations gap between taxpayers and public service providers about the quality and cost of services. As a result, there was widespread pressure on local governments to improve productivity and to make existing resources stretch further.

Finally, there was increased competition among local governments to attract new businesses to their community. In many cases, local governments offered tax incentives and commitments to provide infrastructure to companies considering locating in their communities. For example, in late September 1993, after months of negotiations with at least 30 states and municipalities which were willing to provide attractive location packages, Mercedes-Benz announced that it had decided on Tuscaloosa, Alabama as the site of its new $300 million plant. The plant, which was expected to open in 1997, would employ 1,500 and manufacture 60,000 sport utility vehicles per year. The city of Tuscaloosa committed as much as $30 million for land acquisition and site preparation; Mercedes would be allowed to buy this package for $100, implying that the deal cost local taxpayers roughly $20,000 per new job.

FINANCIAL REPORTING BY MUNICIPALITIES

Financial reporting standards for municipalities were developed by the Government Accounting Standards Board (GASB), as well as by the Financial Accounting Standards Board (FASB) and municipal laws. There were a number of differences between financial reporting for municipalities and reporting by for-profit organizations. Some of these differences were differences in terminology. For example, the income statement was called the Statement of Revenues and Expenditures and Changes in Fund Balances, and owners equity was termed the "fund balance" in government organizations. However, there were also substantive differences, including the use of fund accounting and modifications to accrual accounting.

Fund Accounting

Fund accounting required separate funds reports to be maintained to account and report for many of the different activities of government. For example, separate statements were typically created for the local public hospital, for new capital projects, for debt service, for public employee pension funds, and for general government operations. Each of these activities was viewed as a separate entity or "fund" and received its own allocation of resources. For many funds these resources are restricted, and could only be used for specific purposes. Separate financial reports are therefore prepared for each fund account so that users can monitor whether the resources allocated to the funds were used in the way intended.

For municipalities there are three major classes of funds: governmental funds, proprietary funds, and fiduciary funds.

Governmental funds included the general fund (where resources were unrestricted), special revenue funds (which were restricted to outlays for specific purposes other than major capital projects), capital project funds (where funds were restricted to use for capital expenditures), and debt service funds (used to accumulate funds to pay interest and principal on outstanding debt).

Proprietary funds were for activities that were intended to be operated like a business. They included enterprise funds (such as hospitals and water and sewer operations) which provided goods and services to outside parties and which are intended to be self-supporting. Proprietary funds were also created for operations that provided goods or services for other parts of the government.

Fiduciary funds were assets held by a government unit in trust. They typically included pension funds for government employees.

Financial statements for municipalities presented separate results for all three classes of funds. Also, separate group accounts were reported for debt obligations and fixed assets.

Modifications to Accrual Accounting

For proprietary funds, the traditional accrual accounting system was used. However, for governmental funds several modifications to accrual accounting were made. These modifications (for revenue recognition, accrual of interest, and depreciation), made governmental fund accounting closer to a cash basis of accounting than accrual accounting.

The first key difference between governmental accounting and traditional accrual accounting was that revenues for governmental funds were reported when they became measureable and available, rather than when they were earned. For example, property taxes were recognized as revenue when levied rather than when they were earned. A second major difference was that interest on long-term debt was not recorded until it became due, rather than when it was accrued. Thus, if quarterly interest payments on municipal bonds outstanding were due on January 31, a municipality with a December 31 year-end would not accrue interest owed to bondholders for the months of November and December. Finally, while depreciation was recorded for business-like activities (proprietary funds), for governmental funds new capital outlays were effectively expensed. As a result, the balance sheet for the principal government fund, the general fund, typically included only current assets and liabilities.

THE CITY OF NEW YORK'S FINANCES

New York City had a checkered financial recent history. In February 1975, the New York Urban Development Corporation was unable to repay a $100 million short-term note to Chase Manhattan Bank. This triggered a crisis that resulted in the City being shut out of the credit market. Its bleak prospects eventually forced bankers, unions and government to work together to reach an agreement. City management took on three sacred cows (low transit fares, CUNY tuition, and subsidized housing); a special agency, the Municipal Assistance Corporation of the City of New York (MAC), was created as a vehicle to issue new municipal debt; State legislators agreed to provide a 28 percent increase in intergovernmental aid; the banks deferred debt and interest payments and provided additional financing; and municipal employees accepted short-term pay cuts and layoffs (many through attrition) and agreed that their pension fund would invest in new MAC debt.

Subsequent analysis attributed the City's financial collapse to a dramatic increase in short-term debt (from $747 million to $4.5 billion in only six years). The New York State Charter Revision Commission explained that:

Since 1970–71 every expense budget has been balanced with an array of gimmicks—revenue accruals, capitalization of expenses, raiding reserves, appropriation of illusory fund balances, suspension of payments, carry-forward of deficits and questionable receivables, and finally, the creation of a public benefit corporation whose purpose was to borrow funds to bail out the expense budget.[1]

As a result of the management and budgetary changes discussed above, by 1981 the City had balanced its budget again, and has since recovered from the financial crisis.

Exhibit 1 presents General Fund Revenues and Expenditures for the City during the period 1992 to 1996, the 1996 budget, footnotes, and management discussion of performance. Revenues were generated from a variety of sources, including real estate taxes, sales taxes, income taxes, as well as funding from the federal and state governments. As reported in **Exhibit 2**, in 1996 real estate tax rates for the City were 10.37 percent of assessed property values, and 1.88 percent of their market values. This difference reflects the City's practice of assessing property at less than its full market value.[2] The ratio of the assessed value of property to its market value (called the Special Equalization Ratio) had declined steadily from 29.7 percent in 1993 to 22.1 percent in 1996.

Sales taxes arose from the City's 4 percent sales tax as well as the State's 4.25 percent retail sales tax. In addition, the City levied a personal income tax on City residents and on earnings made in the City for non-residents, and a corporate income tax on companies doing business in the city. Other revenues were generated by fees paid to

---

1. See R. Herzlinger, "Public Sector Accounting," Prentice Hall, Englewood Cliffs, NJ, 1996, p. 316.

2. Revenues from real estate taxes are limited by the State Constitution, which requires real estate revenues to be no more than 2.5% of the average market value of real estate for the most recent five years.

the City for issuing licenses, permits and franchises; interest income; tuition fees from city-run colleges and universities; and rents collected from city-owned property and airports. In 1995, the City included in Other Revenues $200 million from the recovery of prior year FICA overpayments for Social Security and Medicare, as well as $120 million from the sale of upstate jails to the State. Other Revenues in 1996 included one-time receipts of $170 million from the New York City Health and Hospitals Corporation, and $28 million from the New York City Housing Financing Agency.

Most of the federal and state funding provided to the City was in the form of categorical grants, which were earmarked for specific activities. These include expenditures for welfare, education, higher education, health and mental health, community development, job training programs, housing, and criminal justice. The City also received a modest amount of unrestricted federal and state aid, which could be used for general-purpose expenditures. However, this support had been declining.

The City's major General Fund Expenditures were for social services, education, public safety, debt service, health, and pensions. As reported in Exhibit 1, the difference between General Fund revenues and expenditures, the General Fund surplus, has been $5 million for the three years 1994–1996. However, this surplus did not tell the whole story, since the City was required to balance its budget each year. The reported surplus therefore includes discretionary transfers and expenditures used to cover a deficit or to eliminate any surplus. Operating surpluses before discretionary transfers and expenditures were $570 million, $371 million, $72 million, $71 million, and $229 million in the period 1991 to 1996.

New York's financial plan for the period 1997 to 2000, presented in **Exhibit 3**, shows a steadily growing gap between General Fund revenues and expenditures. By 2000 this gap was projected to be $3.4 billion. To meet this deficit the City has embarked on a series of programs to contain costs and increase revenues. The new programs were expected to provide revenues and cost savings by reducing entitlements, by restructuring City government through consolidating and privatizing operations, by increasing federal and state aid, and by selling assets. In addition, for 1997 the City projected a savings of $150 million in pension fund costs from changing the actuarial assumption on investment earnings.

Other studies, however, suggest that the City's problems may be more serious than official projections. For example, a May 1996 report by the City Comptroller identifies between $1.176 billion and $1.546 billion of potential risks for the 1997 forecasts. These included uncertainties about $100 million of assumed state aid, $160 million in proposed revisions to Medicaid benefits, $40 million from changes in entitlement programs, $319 million in airport-related payments which had been the subject of ongoing unsuccessful negotiation, and as much as $400 million from unidentified cuts in education. These concerns were echoed in staff reports from the OSDC and the Control Board. The OSDC report, published in May 1996, concluded that the City had a structural imbalance, and only succeeds in balancing the 1997 budget by including $1.4 billion of one-time items. The study points out that the City's structural problems did not appear to have diminished by workforce reductions of more than 20,000 employees, the lowering of public assistance and Medicaid costs, and the scaling back of tax reduction proposals.

In addition to its 1996 operating outlays of $32 billion, the City made capital outlays of $3.8 billion. These were financed through the issuance of bonds by the City and City agencies, as well as by state and federal grants. **Exhibit 4** provides a breakdown of Capital Expenditures for the period 1992 to 1996, as well as long-term projections of capital outlays required to maintain and improve the City's infrastructure. These included outlays for mass transit facilities, sewers, bridges and tunnels, and investments to improve the City's operating productivity. The four year Capital Commitment Plan for the period 1997 to 2000 projected that in 1997 the city would make commitments for capital projects of $4.3 billion, and will have capital expenditures of $3.7 billion.

As required by its charter, the City reported on the condition of fixed assets, and recommended maintenance expenditures and capital outlays needed to ensure assets were in a good state of repair. The report suggested that the City was letting its fixed assets deteriorate. Actual maintenance outlays in the last five years have been only 33 percent of recommended levels, and the four year Capital Commitment Plan projected a continuance of this pattern for the period 1997 to 2000. In addition, budgeted capital expenditures in the Capital Plan were only 63 percent of those recommended.

Bond Rating Review

As shown in **Exhibit 5**, at December 31, 1996 the City had $30.3 billion of debt outstanding. This included debt for the City itself, MAC, and City-guaranteed debt. On a per capita basis the City's debt had increased from $2,202 in 1989 to $3,901 in 1995, outpacing the growth in pretax personal income of City residents.

The New York State Constitution required that the City's debt outstanding be less than 10 percent of the average market value of taxable real estate for the last five years, and that debt raised to fund low-rent housing, low-income nursing homes, and urban renewal be less than 2 percent of taxable real estate for the pervious five years. The City's projections indicated that by 1998 its debt outstanding will exceed the general debt limit. As a result the City was proposing State legislation to create the new Infrastructure Finance Authority. The Infrastructure Finance Authority would be permitted to issue debt that would not be subject to the constitutional limit.

Throughout 1996, the City's $25.9 billion of general obligation bonds had been rated Baa1 and A– by Moody's and Fitch Investors Service respectively. However, Standard & Poor's had downgraded their rating from A– to BBB+, and Moody's and Fitch were also contemplating a downgrade. Additional information on Moody's ratings as well as the relation between yields and ratings are presented in Exhibit 6. During 1996 the City issued $5.3 billion of general obligation bonds, using $2.7 billion to refinance outstanding bonds. Yields on 30 year City debt peaked in 1995 at 6.65% and declined to 6.18% by March 1996. The City's debt traded 53 basis points over the Bond Buyer 20 Bond Index in July 1995, but this spread had declined to 48 basis points by June 1996.

QUESTIONS

1. Who are the key constituents participating in municipal governments? What challenges do they create for New York City?

2. What are the key performance indicators that you would consider in reviewing the performance of The City of New York for Moody's municipal bond ratings? How has The City performed on these dimensions? What concerns, if any, do you have about its recent performance?

3. Given your analysis in question 1, what is your assessment of the reasonableness of the assumptions underlying The City's projections made in its four-year plan?

4. Would you recommend downrating The City's General Obligation bonds?

EXHIBIT I

The City of New York Condensed Financial Statements—General Fund Revenues and Expenditures, 1992–96

(in millions)	Adopted Budget 1996	1996	1995	Actual 1994	1993	1992
General Fund Revenues						
Taxes (net of refunds):						
Real estate	$7,274	$7,100	$7,474	$7,773	$7,886	$7,818
Sales and use	3,097	3,111	3,013	2,855	2,739	2,621
Income	6,502	6,808	6,015	6,281	5,751	5,389
Other	1,029	1,095	1,184	1,206	1,204	1,221
	17,902	18,114	17,686	18,115	17,580	17,049
Federal, State and Other Aid:						
Categorical	9,891	10,880	10,733	10,143	9,535	8,880
Unrestricted	549	621	603	667	707	826
	10,440	11,501	11,336	10,810	10,242	9,706
Other than Taxes and Aid:						
Charges for services	1,253	1,312	1,298	1,277	1,304	1,195
Other revenues	1,578	1,118	1,244	1,127	961	1,039
OTB transfers	30	26	27	24	29	33
	2,861	2,456	2,569	2,428	2,294	2,267
Total Revenues	31,203	32,071	31,591	31,353	30,116	29,022
General Fund Expenditures						
General government	$811	$855	$853	$875	$862	$853
Public safety and judicial	4,226	4,446	4,121	3,846	3,759	3,586
Board of Education	7,286	7,835	7,863	7,561	7,213	6,626
City University	363	348	348	353	571	459
Social services	7,522	7,901	8,112	8,030	7,430	7,108
Environmental protection	1,096	1,138	1,120	1,156	1,094	989
Transportation services	667	732	933	981	1,023	1,044
Parks, recreation, cultural	239	244	240	238	229	202
Housing	399	455	527	590	516	541
Health (including HHC)	1,544	1,829	1,737	1,620	1,452	1,276
Libraries	176	253	168	172	146	129
Pensions	1,555	1,356	1,273	1,274	1,427	1,370
Judgments and claims	279	309	251	271	231	232
Fringe and other benefits	1,227	1,581	1,444	1,552	1,492	1,378
Other	948	210	307	375	267	257
Transfers for debt service	2,865	2,574	2,289	2,454	2,440	2,968
Total Expenditures	31,203	32,066	31,586	31,348	30,152	29,018
Surplus (deficit)	0	5	5	5	(36)	4

Source: The City of New York, Comprehensive Annual Financial Report of the Comptroller for the Fiscal Year Ended June 30, 1996.

The City of New York

EXHIBIT 2

Real Estate Tax Levies, Values, and Tax Collections, The City of New York

Comparison of Real Estate Tax Levies, Tax Limits, and Tax Rates

Fiscal Year	Total Levy	Operating Limit[a]	Rate Per $100 of Full Valuation	Average Tax Rate per $100 of Assessed Valuation
1993	$8,392.5	$11,945.0	$1.60	$10.59
1994	8,113.2	13,853.8	1.30	10.37
1995	7,889.8	13,446.5	1.14	10.37
1996	7,871.4	8,633.4	1.88	10.37
1997	7,835.1	7,857.3	2.46	10.37

[a]The State Constitution limits the amount of revenue which the City can raise from the real estate tax for operating purposes ("the operating limit") to 2.5% of the average full value of taxable real estate in the City for the current and the last four years less interest on temporary debt and the aggregate amount of business improvement district charges subject to the 2.5% tax limitation. The most recent calculation of the operating limit does not fully reflect the current downturn in the real estate market, which was expected to lower the operating limit in the future.

Billable Assessed and Full Value of Taxable Real Estate

Fiscal Year	Billable Assessed Valuation of Taxable Real Estate (in millions)	÷	Special Equalization Ratio	=	Full Valuation (in millions)
1993	$79,370.6		0.2965		$267,691.6
1994	78,364.6		0.2627		298,304.4
1995	76,202.4		0.2384		319,641.1
1996	76,029.4		0.2209		344,180.3
1997	75,668.5		0.2069		365,724.8

Real Estate Tax Collections and Delinquencies

Fiscal Year	Tax Levy (in millions)	Tax Collections as Percentage of Tax Levy	Delinquent at Fiscal Year End (in millions)	Delinquency as Percentage of Tax Levy
1990	$6,872.4	94.7%	$230.2	3.35%
1991	7,681.3	93.7	315.7	4.11
1992	8,318.8	93.1	370.2	4.45
1993	8,392.5	92.5	411.2	4.90
1994	8,113.2	92.7	403.4	4.97
1995	7,889.8	93.5	381.6	4.84
1996	7,871.4	93.4	288.9	3.67

EXHIBIT 3

The City of New York Financial Plan, 1997–2000

(in millions)	Fiscal Years			
	1997	1998	1999	2000
Revenues				
Taxes:				
General property tax	$7,088	$7,244	$7,469	$7,752
Other taxes	10,407	10,837	11,352	11,897
Tax audit revenue	659	659	659	659
Tax reduction program	(25)	(188)	(366)	(432)
Miscellaneous revenues	4,468	3,549	3,117	2,894
Unrestricted intergovernmental aid	523	510	509	513
Anticipated state actions	50	–	–	–
Other categorical grants	293	275	281	280
Interfund revenues	260	260	258	256
Less: Intracity revenues	(647)	(647)	(646)	(644)
Disallowances against categorical grants	(15)	(15)	(15)	(15)
Total City Funds	$23,061	$22,484	$22,618	$23,160
Federal categorical grants	3,771	3,600	3,586	3,582
State categorical grants	6,149	6,071	6,106	6,087
Total Revenues	$32,981	$32,155	$32,310	32,829
Expenditures				
Personal service	$16,237	$16,813	$17,612	$18,182
Other than personal service	14,128	14,064	14,256	14,271
Debt service	2,735	3,015	3,124	3,241
MAC debt service funding	328	394	423	370
General reserve	200	200	200	200
Total Expenditures	$33,628	$34,486	$35,615	$36,894
Less: Intracity Expenses	(647)	(647)	(646)	(644)
Net Total Expenditures	$32,981	$33,839	$34,969	$36,250
Deficit	$0	$1,684	$2,959	$3,421

EXHIBIT 4

The City of New York Actual and Planned Capital Outlays, 1992–2000

Actual Capital Outlays (in millions)

	1996	1995	1994	1993	1992
Education	$812	$881	$727	$758	$686
Environmental protection	1,135	819	768	934	1,046
Transportation	554	444	423	341	364
Transit authority	218	150	221	250	330
Housing	246	292	387	431	639
All other	831	1,108	817	903	828
Total Expenditures	$3,796	$3,694	$3,343	$3,617	$3,893

Capital Commitment Plan, 1997–2000 (in millions)

	1997	1998	1999	2000
Education	$713	$859	$799	$1,392
Environmental protection	1,385	1,270	1,488	518
Transportation	760	643	671	590
Transit authority	497	231	231	231
Housing	311	267	317	382
Sanitation	185	604	167	361
City operations/Facilities	1,321	630	650	587
Economic and port development	71	46	35	44
Reserve for unattained commitments	(449)	(107)	(300)	(244)
Total Commitments	$4,793	$4,443	$4,058	$3,861
Total Expenditures	$4,255	$3,958	$4,114	$4,179

MANAGEMENT DISCUSSION OF CAPITAL PROJECTS

Capital expenditures increased by $102 million to $3.8 billion in fiscal year 1996, or 2.8% more than in fiscal year 1995 and approximately 2.5% less than just four years ago. Expenditures on the infrastructure component of the Capital Budget were $2.1 billion in fiscal year 1996, $873 million more than in fiscal year 1995. Expenditures for environmental protection (excluding sanitation) accounted for 48.6% of the total spent on infrastructure in fiscal year 1996. Expenditures for mass transit in fiscal year 1996 accounted for 10.6% of the total expenditures on infrastructure. The amount expended on the City's water distribution and sewage collection system in fiscal year 1996 was $1.0 billion.

In October 1990, the City completed a project to inventory the major portions of its physical plant. The first citywide and individual agency report was published in fiscal year 1991, which has been updated yearly. It provides the City with a comprehensive assessment of the condition of its major assets, the projected costs necessary to restore these assets to a state of good repair and schedules detailing the maintenance required to maintain the assets' structural integrity. The City estimates costs for repairs, replacements, and major maintenance for fiscal years 1997 through 2000 to be $4.3 billion.

EXHIBIT 5

Combined Net City Debt

(in millions)	1996	1995	1994	1993	1992
Net City debt	$25,052	$23,258	$21,531	$19,424	$17,916
Net MAC debt	3,936	4,033	4,215	4,470	4,657
Net Samurai debt	200	200	200	200	—
Total City, MAC and Samurai Debt	29,188	27,491	25,946	24,094	22,573
City guaranteed debt	1,155	1,104	1,114	733	745
Combined Net City Debt	$30,343	$28,595	$27,060	$24,827	$23,318

City, MAC, and City-Guaranteed Proprietary Corporation Debt Service

Fiscal Years	Principal on City Long-term Debt	Interest on City Long-term Debt	City-Guaranteed Debt	Required MAC Funding	Total
1966	$22,718	$150,987	$22,560	$425,310	$621,575
1997	1,220,995	1,493,357	110,015	570,498	3,394,865
1998	1,206,764	1,401,147	116,997	583,535	3,308,443
1999	1,133,395	1,329,846	125,751	602,079	3,191,071
2000	1,072,079	1,271,698	125,749	537,438	3,006,964
2001	1,072,637	1,218,150	125,634	537,621	2,954,042
2002–2147	19,111,773	11,693,985	1,644,505	3,766,678	36,216,941
Total	$24,840,361	$18,559,170	$2,271,211	$7,023,159	$52,693,901

City, MAC, and City-Guaranteed Proprietary Corporation Debt

Fiscal Year	Debt Per Capita	Debt Per Capita as % of Personal Income Per Capita	Debt as % of Assessed Value of Taxable Property	Debt as % of Full Value of Taxable Property
1989	$2,202	9.96%	25.4%	4.6%
1990	2,490	10.49	26.0	4.5
1991	2,917	11.93	28.0	4.5
1992	3,192	12.14	28.5	4.1
1993	3,389	12.51	31.3	3.9
1994	3,691	n.a.	35.2	4.4
1995	3,901	n.a.	36.9	4.1

EXHIBIT 6

Moody's Investor Service, Inc.—Bond Ratings

Rating	Description of Rating	Average Yield, December 20, 1995
Aaa	Best quality or "gilt edge," with the smallest degree of investment risk. Interest payments are protected by large or exceptionally stable margin and principal is secure. Protective elements can be visualized and are most unlikely to impair strong position of such issues.	5.38%
Aa	High quality by all standards. Together with the Aaa group they comprise high grade bonds. They are rated lower than the best bonds because margins of protection may not be as large, fluctuation of protective elements may be of greater amplitude, or risks appear somewhat larger than in Aaa securities.	5.50%
A	Upper medium grade obligations. Security to principal and interest is considered adequate, but susceptibility to impairment some time in the future.	5.55%
Baa	Medium grade obligations, i.e., they are neither highly protected nor poorly secured. Interest payments and principal security appear adequate for the present but certain protective elements may be lacking or unreliable over any great length of time. Such bonds lack outstanding investment characteristics and have speculative characteristics.	5.70%
Ba	Judged to have speculative elements; their future cannot be considered as well assured. Often the protection of interest and principal payments may be very moderate, and not well safeguarded during good and bad times over the future. Uncertainty of position characterizes bonds in this class.	n.a.
B	Lack characteristics of desirable investment. Assurance of interest and principal payments or maintenance of other terms of the contract over any long period of time may be small.	n.a.
Caa	Poor standing. Such issues may be in default or there may be present elements of danger with respect to principal or interest.	n.a.
Ca	Speculative in a high degree. Such issues are often in default or have other marked shortcomings.	n.a.
C	Lowest rated class of bonds. Issues so rated have extremely poor prospects of ever attaining any real investment standing.	n.a.

Source: Moody's Bond Record. Moody's Investors Service, New York.

Comdisco, Inc.: Financial Statement Analysis (A)

Comdisco Inc., the world's leading independent lessor of IBM computers, would seem like a company Wall Street ought to love. Annual revenues are up fourfold since 1978, to an estimated $600 million in the fiscal year that ended September 30. Earnings per share have grown at an even more torrid tempo, and return on shareholders' equity is running at an estimated 35%. Yet at a recent price of $37, the stock was selling at 15 times projected earnings in fiscal 1984—a tepid multiple for a company whose earnings could grow at a 30% clip over the next five years.

* * *

Just about the only thing wrong with Comdisco is the tainted reputation that computer-leasing companies acquired as a result of the well-known bankruptcies of OPM Leasing and Itel. Securities analysts, though see no similarities between Comdisco and those fiascos. OPM Leasing turned out to be a spectacularly fraudulent operation, and Itel's downfall resulted in large part from overly optimistic accounting assumptions, coupled with a large inventory of obsolete equipment. Comdisco's accounting couldn't be more conservative, analysts say. They add that the company has managed, through the use of ingenious leasing arrangements, to eliminate almost all exposure to equipment obsolescence. Comdisco, asserts John Keefe of Drexel Burnham Lambert, has practically nothing to fear from any future IBM decision.[1]

The quotes above appeared in the Personal Investing Section of *Fortune* magazine in October 1983.

BUSINESS HISTORY AND OPERATIONS

Comdisco, Inc. is a Chicago-based company founded in 1969 by its current chairman of the board and president, Kenneth Pontikes. The company originally began as an IBM computer dealer. As demand for computer leasing started to grow during the late 1970s, the company started emphasizing leasing operations. By 1982, leasing old and new IBM computer equipment constituted the primary business activity of the company, and Comdisco had become the largest computer leasing company. Comdisco's customers

---

1. Reprinted with permission from Fortune, *October 31, 1983.*

were primarily large corporations. In 1982, the company had business relationships with 70% of the Fortune 500 companies including 49 of the 50 largest U.S. companies.

The computer remarketing industry had many participants: small independent operators, larger private organizations, and leasing subsidiaries of conglomerates. Comdisco was one of the few independent public corporations in the industry. The firms in the industry were primarily of two types: broker/dealers or third party lessors. The broker/dealers obtained for customers computer equipment from either a vendor or current user; third party lessors provided lease financing. Comdisco engaged in both these activities.

Comdisco achieved its dominance in the computer leasing industry through a strategy of full-service leasing. Under this strategy, the company offered its customers a number of services which were not offered by competitors. Comdisco's subsidiaries, Comdisco Technical Services, Inc. and Comdisco Transport, Inc., specialized in equipment refurbishment, delivery, installation, de-installation, and technical planning and site preparation. Comdisco Maintenance Services, another subsidiary, offered a low-cost alternative to IBM's maintenance service. Comdisco Disaster Recovery Services, Inc. was established to provide another valuable service to the company's customers: contingent data processing capacity to be used when a customer's own data center had unavoidable failures. Through this service, Comdisco's customers had access to four fully operational data centers as a backup to their own data centers, to be used in a natural disaster or accident.

Comdisco's broad customer base provided the company with a number of competitive advantages. First, taking advantage of its access to 10,000 important users IBM equipment in the U.S. the company created a proprietary data base of their computing needs. This data base provided Comdisco's sales force with current and timely information on potential customers and their requirements. Second, being IBM leading dealer, Comdisco maintained large inventories of a broad range of IBM equipment. Comdisco's personnel closely monitored IBM's new products and pricing policies. This product knowledge combined with large inventories enabled the company to assist customers with their computer acquisition plans and to offer quick deliveries. Finally, using its data base, the company could help its customers sell their old hardware when they acquired new equipment from Comdisco.

While the above strategy enabled Comdisco to establish its dominance over others in the computer leasing industry, the company was still potentially vulnerable to competition from IBM itself since IBM equipment accounted for most of Comdisco's revenues. In 1981, IBM formed a financing subsidiary, IBM Credit Corporation, to provide customer financing. Shortly after that, IBM announced its intention to enter into computer leasing and established a joint venture for this purpose with Merrill Lynch and Metropolitan Life Insurance. A number of industry analysts felt that this might result in increased competition for companies like Comdisco.

Comdisco's management, however, felt that IBM's recent moves did not pose a threat to the company's competitive position because IBM's entry into leasing would enhance the tarnished image of the computer leasing business, a net benefit to the industry. They also believed that, as IBM began to emphasize outright sale of its equipment over short-term rentals, many of IBM's customers might be forced to look for other lessors like Comdisco who offered short-term leases. This was likely to provide additional business opportunities which would offset any loss of long-term lease business to IBM.

While equipment leasing to computer users was Comdisco's primary activity, the company also offered tax-oriented leases to investors who were primarily interested in the tax benefits associated with leasing. In recent years, the financial services income from these tax advantaged transactions accounted for a growing portion of the company's profits.

ACCOUNTING POLICIES FOR LEASING

Comdisco offered computer equipment to its customers through a variety of lease arrangements. Using the terminology of the Financial Accounting Standards Board's Statement No. 13, Comdisco's leases can be classified into one of three types: sales-type leases, direct financing leases, or operating leases.

Classification

Both sales-type and direct financing leases transferred substantially all the benefits and risks inherent in the ownership of the leased property to the lessee. A sales-type lease usually gave rise to a dealer's profit or loss for Comdisco. Therefore, in a sales-type lease, the fair value of the leased equipment (normal selling price) at the inception of the lease differed from the cost or carrying amount. In contrast, in a direct financing lease, the primary service that Comdisco offered was the financing of the equipment's acquisition by the lessee. In such a lease, the fair value of the equipment was equal to the cost or carrying amount. Comdisco earned only a financing income (interest) and no dealer's profit. An operating lease was a simple rental of the equipment, and Comdisco retained ownership of the equipment throughout the lease term.

Under FASB's guidelines, the accounting classification of a lease was based on whether or not it satisfied certain conditions:

1. The lease transfers ownership of the equipment to the lessee by the end of the lease term.
2. The lease contains an option allowing the lessee to purchase the property at a bargain price.
3. The lease term is equal to 75% or more of the estimated economic life of the property.
4. The present value of the rental is equal to 90% or more of the fair market value of the leased property.
5. Collectibility of the payments from the lessee is reasonably predictable.
6. No important uncertainties surround the amount of cost yet to be incurred by the lessor.

A lease meeting *at least one* of the first four conditions and *both* of the last two conditions was classified as a sales-type lease or direct financing lease. Such a lease was treated as a sales-type lease if the fair value of the leased equipment was different from its carrying amount; otherwise it was classified as a direct financing lease. A lease that did not meet the combination of conditions just described was classified as an operating lease.

The accounting treatment in Comdisco's financial statements for the above three types of leases was as follows:

Operating Lease   Lease revenue consisted of monthly rentals; the cost of equipment was recorded as leased equipment. The difference between the cost and the estimated residual value at the end of the lease term was depreciated on a straight-line basis over the lease term. Salesmen's commissions and other initial direct costs were capitalized as deferred charges and were amortized on a straight-line basis.

Sales-Type Lease   At the inception of the lease, the present value of rentals was treated as sales revenue. Equipment cost less the present value of the residual was recorded as cost of sales. The present value of rentals and of the residual was recorded on the balance sheet as net investment in sales-type lease. As each lease payment was received, the net investment was reduced and interest income was recognized.

Direct Financing Lease   At the inception of the lease, the cost of the leased equipment was recorded as net investment in the direct financing lease. As each lease payment was received, the net investment was reduced by the corresponding amount. The difference between the sum of the lease payments and the cost of the leased equipment was unearned profit from the direct financing lease, and it was recognized monthly so as to produce a constant rate of return on the net investment.

In addition to the leases where Comdisco was a lessor, it was also often a lessee: the company acquired equipment from computer vendors and others through leasing arrangements. If such a lease met at least one of the first four conditions listed discussed earlier, it was classified by Comdisco as a capital lease; otherwise it was classified as an operating lease. The accounting treatment of the leases where Comdisco was a lessee was as follows:

Operating Lease   Monthly rentals were treated as rental expense.

Capital Lease   At the inception of the lease, the present value of lease rentals was recorded as a capital lease asset. An equal amount was also recognized as a liability an obligation under the capital lease. The capital lease asset was depreciated over the lease term. When a lease payment was made, the obligation under capital lease was reduced and interest expense on the lease obligation was recognized.

NONRECOURSE DISCOUNTING OF LEASE PAYMENTS

In order to finance its investment in leased assets, Comdisco often assigned the stream of lease payments to a financial institution at a fixed interest rate on a nonrecourse basis. In return, Comdisco received from the financial institution a loan equal to the present value of the lease payment stream. The financial institution received the lease payments from the lessee as repayments of the loan. In the event of default by a lessee, the financial institution had a first lien on the underlying leased equipment, with no further recourse against the company.

For operating leases, proceeds from discounting were recorded on the balance sheet as discounted lease rentals liability. As lessees made payments to the financial institutions, discounted lease rentals were reduced by the interest rate method. For sales-type leases and direct financing leases, proceeds from discounting were not included in discounted lease rentals. Instead, future rentals were eliminated from the net investment in sales-type or direct financing leases, and any gain or loss on the financing was immediately recognized in the income statement.

TAX ADVANTAGED TRANSACTIONS

In addition to leasing equipment to computer users, Comdisco undertook leasing transactions with investors who were interested in tax shelters. While the specific terms and conditions of these tax advantaged transactions varied, a typical transaction was as follows:

1. After the inception of the initial user lease and independent of it, Comdisco sold all the leased equipment to a third-party investor. This sale usually occurred three to nine months after the commencement of the initial user lease. The sales price equaled the then current fair market value of the equipment. The payment from the investor to Comdisco consisted of: (a) cash and a negotiable interest-bearing promissory note due within two years for 10–22% of the sales

price (the "equity payment") and (b) an installment note for the balance payable over an 84 month period.

2. Simultaneously with the sale, Comdisco leased the equipment back from the investors for 84 months. The lease payments under the leaseback obligation were equal to the installment payments receivable by Comdisco from the investor (1b.).

3. As part of the leaseback arrangement, during the 61st through 84th months of the leaseback period, the investor shared in the re-lease proceeds that the company received from subleasing the equipment to a user. Upon the expiration of the leaseback period, the investor had the exclusive right to the equipment.

The net result of the above transaction was that Comdisco gave up the depreciation tax benefit, a portion of the rental revenues for months 61–84, and 100% of the equipment value after the 84th month. In return, the company received the non-refundable equity payment (1a.).

If the equipment sold to the investor was originally under an operating lease, the equity payment was recorded by Comdisco as financial services revenue in the period in which the tax advantaged transaction occurred. From the fourth quarter of 1983, the company began to allocate as cost of financial services a portion of the net book value of the equipment at lease termination. For sales-type and direct financing leases, the equity payment was first applied to reduce a portion of the residual value of the equipment shown in the balance sheet (as investment in sales-type and direct financing leases). This is because the company's ability to recover the residual value was decreased due to the rental sharing under the tax advantaged transaction. The excess of the equity payment over the residual value reduction was recorded as financial services revenue in the period in which the tax advantaged transaction occurred.

RECENT PERFORMANCE

During the ten years ending in 1982, Comdisco's sales and profits grew rapidly. During fiscal 1982 the company reported $29.4 million profits on revenues of $471.6 million, representing an 88% increase in profits and 56% increase in sales during the year. (See Exhibit 3 for an abridged version of the 1982 annual report.) The company continued its strong growth performance in fiscal 1983. The company's profits and revenues in the first nine months of the fiscal year were $36.1 million and $401.4 million, respectively. (See Exhibit 2 for the company's interim report for this period.)

In Comdisco's second quarterly report for 1983, Kenneth Pontikes, Comdisco's Chairman of the Board and President, commented on the company's future:

> [These] new activities, along with the continued growth of the company's lease and customer base, enhance the company's long term growth prospects. The company's history of outstanding performance and the recent issuance of $250,000,000 of convertible subordinated debentures, which further strengthened the company's capital base, provide it with the flexibility required for continued growth in today's marketplace.

The company's shares, listed on The New York Stock Exchange, reflected this optimistic outlook: their price appreciated from about $9 in January 1982 to $37 by the end of September 1983. Exhibit 1 shows the movement of Comdisco's stock price and Standard & Poor's 500 index from January 1982 to September 1983. Comdisco's stock price increased by more than 300% during this period compared to roughly 40% increase in Standard & Poor's 500 index. However, as the *Fortune* magazine comments indicate, many analysts considered Comdisco's stock to be still undervalued and expected it to continue to outperform the market.

QUESTIONS

1. Evaluate Comdisco's business activities and the company's strategy.

2. Using the information in Comdisco's financial statements and footnotes, fill in the following to the extent possible (use plug figures if necessary):

Account	Balance as of 9/30/81	Increases during fiscal '82	Decreases during fiscal '82	Balance as of 9/30/82
Obligations under capital leases	_____ +	_____ −	_____ =	_____
	−	−	−	−
Discounted lease rentals	_____ +	_____ −	_____ =	_____
	−	−	−	−
Net investment in sales-type and direct financing leases	_____ +	_____ −	_____ =	_____
	−	−	−	−

Identify the business transactions that would have given rise to the changes identified in the above accounts.

3. Analyze the relative contribution of rentals, sales of computer equipment, and financial services to Comdisco's reported profits during fiscal years 1981 and 1982 and the first nine months of fiscal year 1983. What are the reasons for the differences in the profit margins of these three activities? Which activity is contributing most to Comdisco's profits?

4. Evaluate the quality of Comdisco's disclosure in its annual report regarding the company's lease accounting policies. Do you think the disclosure is adequate to evaluate the company's performance?

EXHIBIT I

Movement of Comdisco's Stock and S&P 500 Index, January 1982–September 1983

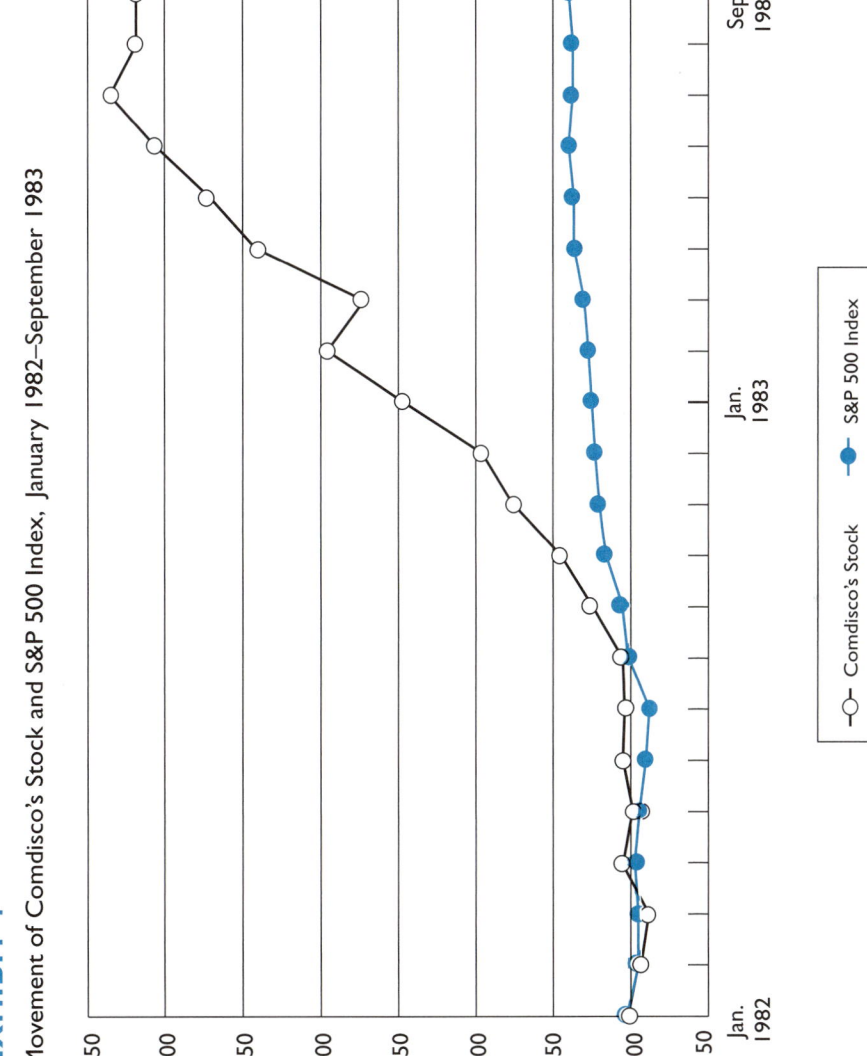

EXHIBIT 2

Quarterly Report — Third Quarter Ended June 30, 1983

To Our Stockholders

I am pleased to report net earnings of $13,199,000 or $.45 per share for the third quarter of fiscal 1983. These results represent increases of 127% and 96%, respectively, over the three months ended June 30, 1982 when net earnings were $5,824,000 or $.23 per share. Earnings improved as a result of increased profitability of financial services activities, increased leasing of computer equipment and a lower effective tax rate. Total revenue for the quarter ended June 30, 1983 was $127,455,000 compared to $94,691,000 for the prior year period. The increase in total revenue was primarily due to the continued growth of the Company's lease base. In the third quarter of fiscal 1983, the Company entered into 850 new leases with total revenue of $266.1 million during the initial lease terms. These figures compare to 605 new leases and $180.4 million of revenue for the year earlier period.

Net earnings for the nine months ended June 30, 1983 were $36,064,000, or $1.25 per share, representing increases of 69% and 51%, respectively, over the prior year period. Total revenue for the first nine months of fiscal 1983 amounted to $401,367,000 compared to $334,189,000 for the nine months ended June 30, 1982. The Company's impressive results for the first nine months of fiscal 1983 were primarily due to its active participation in the peripheral equipment and 3081 and 3083 processor markets, which have resulted in increased computer equipment sales, leasing and financial services activities. In addition, deliveries by IBM of the 3081 and 3083 processors have stimulated both sale and leasing of displaced IBM 3033 processors.

On July 21, 1983, the Board of Directors declared a cash dividend of $.04 per share to be paid on September 9, 1983 to stockholders of record as of August 19, 1983. This is the twenty-seventh consecutive quarterly cash dividend declared since the Company commenced paying cash dividends in 1977.

In April 1983, the Company announced its Corporate Lease Line Program, an expanded leasing program designed to meet the growing demand for lease financing of office and industrial equipment. The Corporate Lease Line Program expands the Company's array of complementary services and capitalizes on its expertise in providing customers with innovative and cost effective financing options.

During the third quarter of fiscal 1983, the Company began operations of a newly established, wholly owned subsidiary, Comdisco Resources, Inc. ("CRI"). Initially CRI will be primarily engaged, through joint ventures with established partners, in the acquisition of mineral and royalty rights in producing domestic oil and gas properties and the acquisition of onshore leasehold interests, primarily for resale to others for oil and gas exploration and development. For fiscal 1983 and 1984, investments of approximately $32.0 million and $13.0 million, respectively, have been budgeted by CRI.

These new activities, along with the continued growth of the Company's lease and customer base, enhance the Company's long term growth prospects. The Company's history of outstanding financial performance and the recent issuance of $250,000,000 of convertible subordinated debentures, which further strengthened the Company's capital base, provide it with the flexibility required for continued growth in today's marketplace.

Kenneth N. Pontikes
Chairman of the Board and President
August 10, 1983

CONSOLIDATED STATEMENTS OF EARNINGS AND RETAINED EARNINGS
For the Three and Nine Months Ended June 30, 1983 and 1982 (unaudited)

(in thousands except per share data)	Three Months Ended June 30		Nine Months Ended June 30	
	1983	1982	**1983**	1982
Revenue				
Rental	**$70,056**	$53,462	**$193,520**	$148,434
Sale of computer equipment	**29,159**	24,113	**129,626**	110,108
Financial services	**15,493**	12,890	**50,073**	62,040
Other	**12,747**	4,226	**28,148**	13,607
Total Revenue	**127,455**	94,691	**401,367**	334,189
Cost and Expenses				
Equipment depreciation, amortization and rental	**56,647**	40,378	**152,586**	115,325
Cost of computer equipment	**26,112**	21,318	**114,631**	99,659
Financial services	**1,524**	1,065	**3,614**	6,641
Selling, general and administrative	**13,938**	10,722	**43,060**	38,074
Interest	**14,035**	12,016	**38,112**	34,560
Total costs and expenses	**112,256**	85,499	**352,003**	294,259
Earnings before income taxes	**15,199**	9,192	**49,364**	39,930
Income taxes	**2,000**	3,368	**13,300**	18,568
Net earnings	**$13,199**	5,824	**36,064**	21,362
Retained earnings at beginning of period	**$92,445**	$58,223	**$71,268**	$43,359
Net earnings	**13,199**	5,824	**36,064**	21,362
Dividends paid	**(1,150)**	(394)	**(2,838)**	(1,068)
Retained earnings at end of period	**$104,494**	$63,653	**$104,494**	$63,653
Net earnings per common and common equivalent share	**.45**	.23	**1.25**	.83
Cash dividends per common share	**.04**	.03	**.11**	.09
Common and common equivalent shares outstanding	**29,611**	29,118	**29,234**	28,918

CONSOLIDATED BALANCE SHEET
June 30, 1983 and 1982 (unaudited) and September 30, 1982 (unaudited)

(in thousands except number of shares)	June 30 1983	1982	September 30 1982
Assets			
Cash and marketable securities (at cost which approximates market)	$175,215	$4,586	$39,762
Receivables	66,430	38,854	45,055
Inventory of computer equipment	48,914	38,716	35,382
Investment in sales-type and direct financing leases	63,735	28,541	23,682
Leased and other equipment	703,759	532,969	534,611
Less: accumulated depreciation and amortization	263,401	174,408	192,714
Net equipment	440,358	358,561	341,897
Other assets and deferred charges	55,925	43,446	50,901
	$850,577	$512,704	$536,679
Liabilities and Stockholders' Equity			
Note payable	$—	$2,650	$2,385
Subordinated debentures	262,250	62,250	62,250
Accounts payable	29,001	26,982	19,110
Obligations under capital leases	14,669	20,122	18,636
Income taxes	42,817	31,585	36,197
Other liabilities	45,139	39,219	45,265
Discounted lease rentals	280,976	247,899	261,780
	674,852	430,707	445,623
Stockholders' equity:			
Common stock $.10 par value Authorized 50,000,000 shares; issued 28,768,366 and 11,757,418 shares at June 30, 1983 and 1982, respectively (11,769,043 at September 30, 1982)	2,877	1,176	1,177
Additional paid-in capital	68,718	17,657	18,965
Deferred translation adjustment	(364)	(489)	(354)
Retained earnings	104,494	63,653	71,268
Total stockholders' equity	175,725	81,997	91,056
	$850,577	$512,704	$536,679

CONSOLIDATED STATEMENTS OF CHANGES IN FINANCIAL POSITION
For the Nine Months Ended June 30, 1983 and 1982 (unaudited)

(in thousands)	1983	1982
Source of Funds		
Total provided by operations	$123,798	$133,285
Issuance of common stock upon conversion of 13% convertible debentures, net	52,465	—
Proceeds from issuance of subordinated debentures	245,250	—
Discounted lease rentals	141,002	92,535
Other	305	2,624
	562,820	228,444
Application of Funds		
Increase in leased equipment and inventory	238,304	175,193
Decrease in note payable	2,385	795
Redemption of convertible debentures	50,000	—
Reduction of discounted lease rentals and obligations under capital leases	126,332	45,611
Other assets and deferred charges	7,508	11,039
Other	2,838	1,068
	427,367	233,706
Increase (decrease) in cash and marketable securities	135,453	(5,262)
Cash and marketable securities at beginning of period	39,762	9,848
Cash and marketable securities at end of period	$175,215	$4,586

Notes to Consolidated Financial Statements

June 30, 1983 and 1982 (unaudited)

1. Principles of Reporting

The accompanying consolidated financial statements include the accounts of the Company and its wholly-owned subsidiaries after elimination of intercompany accounts and transactions. In the opinion of management, the accompanying consolidated financial statements contain all adjustments necessary for a fair presentation. The Company has a fiscal year that ends September 30.

The balance sheet at September 30, 1982 has been derived from the audited financial statements at that date.

2. Subordinated Debentures

On November 4, 1982, the Board of Directors announced the redemption of all of the Company's 13% Convertible Subordinated Debentures Due 2001 (the "Convertible Debentures") at a redemption price of $1,117 for each $1,000 principal amount of Convertible Debenture, plus accrued and unpaid interest to December 6, 1982. The Convertible Debentures were convertible into shares of common stock of the Company, at the option of the Convertible Debenture holder, at a conversion price of $9.75 per share. Common stock issued upon conversion of $49,839,000 principal amount of the convertible Debentures totaled 5,111,360 shares.

On May 4, 1983, the Company completed the sale of $250,000,000 principal amount of its 8% Convertible Subordinated Debentures Due May 1, 2003 (the "Debentures"). The Debentures are convertible into common stock of the Company at the rate of $36.50 per share. An aggregate of 6,849,315 shares has been reserved for issuance upon conversion of the Debentures. Temporarily, the net proceeds from the Debentures, which amounted to approximately $245,250,000, have been invested in short-term instruments and used to finance an increase in the Company's lease portfolio pending receipt of cash upon discounting of the related lease receivables.

3. Income Taxes

The rates used in computing the provision for federal income taxes at June 30, 1983 and 1982 vary from the statutory tax rate primarily due to investment tax credits generated in the respective years and Domestic International Sales Corporation (DISC) tax benefits. During the third quarter of fiscal 1983, the Company generated substantial investment tax credits resulting from the increase in leasing activity. Accordingly, the Company estimates that the annual effective tax rate will be approximately 27% for fiscal 1983 compared to the estimated rates of 33% and 40% used in the first six months of fiscal 1983 and the first nine months of fiscal 1982, respectively. The reduction in the estimated income tax rate resulted in an increase of approximately $2,100,000 in net earnings or $.07 per share in the third quarter of fiscal 1983. The effective tax rate for the quarter and nine months ended June 30, 1982 varies from the estimated annual rate due to a reinstatement of deferred income taxes resulting from the sale of investment tax credits which had been used to reduce deferred income taxes at September 30, 1981.

4. Common Stock

All references in the financial statements and notes to the number of common shares and per share data have been adjusted for the two-for-one stock split distributed in March 1983.

EXHIBIT 3

Annual Report for Fiscal Year 1982—(edited by the casewriter)

To Our Stockholders

In fiscal 1982 Comdisco continued its outstanding performance with record earnings and revenues. Net earnings of $29.4 million, or $2.27 per share, represented increases of 88% and 68%, respectively, over fiscal 1981, while total revenue increased 56% to $471.6 million. These results were achieved despite the recessionary economic environment. The compound annual growth rate in net earnings over the last five years is an exceptional 43%. The primary factors contributing to the record earnings in fiscal 1982 were the increased volume and profitability of financial services activity, the growth of the Company's lease and customer bases, and the ability of the Company to capitalize on the active market for IBM 3033 processors and disk storage devices.

The higher level of financial services activity was the result of tax-advantaged leasing transactions associated with the Company's lease portfolio of used equipment and also the arrangement of "tax benefit transfers" that were structured under the Economic Recovery Tax Act of 1981. Late in fiscal 1982, Congress passed the Tax Equity and Fiscal Responsibility Act of 1982, which included legislation that will eventually eliminate "tax benefit transfers." This will cause the arrangement of traditional leveraged leases to re-emerge as a primary financial services activity of the Company.

The growth of Comdisco's lease base continued on a strong trend in fiscal 1982 as more users committed themselves to the leasing of equipment. The Company significantly increased its activity in the leasing of peripheral equipment. During fiscal 1982 the Company entered into 2,259 new leases with total revenue of $701.6 million during the initial term of these leases. This compares to 1,620 leases and $338.8 million in revenue during fiscal 1981.

The initial deliveries by IBM of its 3081 processor stimulated activity in all Comdisco's businesses. The Company participated in the lease placement of 3081 processors, and in the remarketing of the displaced 3033 processors. The Company's increased marketing efforts led to a 31% increase in its customers, which include most of the largest corporations in the United States. In fiscal 1981 Comdisco set up

a "mid-range" marketing force that has successfully expanded the Company's customer base among medium-sized corporations. Comdisco's foreign subsidiaries continued to increase their marketing presence and also produced record results in the twelve months ended September 30, 1982. Fiscal 1982 also saw the continued refinement of Comdisco's computerized marketing data base that tracks user information for virtually all large IBM systems installed in the United States.

Two of Comdisco's newer subsidiaries, Comdisco Disaster Recovery Services and Comdisco Technical Services, made significant progress in fiscal 1982. The addition of the Texas Disaster Recovery Center by December 31, 1982 will bring the number of centers to four, providing further evidence that Comdisco Disaster Recovery Services can provide its customers with the most comprehensive disaster back-up services available. Comdisco Technical Services expanded its equipment installation and facilities planning operations and showed increased profitability.

Probably as significant as the record earnings results achieved in fiscal 1982, was the strengthening of Comdisco's financial position. Total assets increased 33% to $536.7 million, while stockholders' equity increased 55% to $9.1 million. The announcement in early November 1982 of the redemption of the Company's $50 million convertible debentures is anticipated to increase stockholders' equity to approximately $140 million and will reduce the Company's interest expense by $6.5 million per year. In addition, the Company had nearly $40 million in cash and marketable securities at September 30, 1982 while borrowing under various revolving credit agreements was zero. Because of its improved financial position, Comdisco is ideally situated to capitalize on opportunities in its traditional marketplace as well as those that arise in other areas.

In September 1982 Raymond F. Sebastian, formerly President of Comdisco Financial Services (CFS), was appointed to the position of Senior Vice President/Corporate Development of Comdisco and will devote full time to the analysis of various investment opportunities available to the Company. He was replaced as President of CFS by Basil R. Twist, Jr. who, with

Mr. Sebastian, has formulated the strategies that have made CFS so successful since its formation in 1976. Michael J. O'Connell has resigned as Executive Vice President of Comdisco effective January 1, 1983 to pursue other endeavors, but will continue as a Director. Mr. O'Connell has been with Comdisco since 1971 and has made valuable contributions to the Company's success.

In March 1982 Comdisco split its common stock 3-for-2 and paid dividends in fiscal 1982 totaling $.23 per share, an increase of 28% over the prior year, as adjusted. More importantly, return on average stockholders' equity has averaged 34.0% over the last five years. This has occurred over a period of time in which most of the Company's borrowings, other than discounted lease rentals, have been eliminated.

Comdisco begins fiscal 1983 in a strong capital position with high liquidity, a strong, competitive market position and a comprehensive array of complementary services for its customers. The Company provides leasing and other cost-effective services which continue to be attractive despite the current economic outlook. The delivery of more IBM 3081 processors will also increase opportunities for Comdisco in its marketplace.

Perhaps more so than many companies, Comdisco relies on the determination, skill and creative energies of its employees for its past and future success. This is another factor that gives me much optimism for Comdisco's continued success. With the on-going dedication of Comdisco's employees and the support of the Company's customers and stockholders, I am confident that Comdisco's superior growth rates in earnings and revenue can be maintained.

Kenneth N. Pontikes
Chairman of the Board and President

November 11, 1982

Management's Discussion and Analysis of Financial Condition and Result of Operations

Summary

The Company continued to achieve outstanding growth during fiscal 1982 as total revenue and net earnings increased 56% and 88%, respectively, compared to fiscal 1981. Increases in revenue and net earnings were accomplished despite the recessionary economic climate. Total revenue for fiscal 1982 and 1981 was $471.6 million and $301.5 million respectively. Net earnings increased from $15.6 million, or $1.35 a share, in fiscal 1981 to a record of $29.4 million, or $2.27 a share in fiscal 1982. The primary factors contributing to the record earnings were the increased volume and profitability of financial services activity, the growth of the Company's lease and customer base, and the ability of the Company to capitalize on the active market for 3033 processors and disk storage devices.

Revenue

Total revenue for fiscal 1982 reflected increases in all activities. In fiscal 1981, total revenue increased 19% over fiscal 1980 total revenue, as a result of higher revenue from all activities other than sale of computer equipment. For the five year period ended September 30, 1982, the Company has achieved an annual compound growth rate of 25% for total revenue.

The growth of the Company's lease base continued on a strong trend during fiscal 1982. This growth has been achieved as a result of the increased demand for leasing, broader penetration of the market, and the increase of activity levels created by initial product deliveries by IBM. Leasing offers computer users flexibility through short term commitments and conserves capital in a weak economy. As a result of this growth, rental revenue of $206.6 million in fiscal 1982 and $131.6 million in fiscal 1981 represented increases of 57% and 62%, respectively, over the preceding year.

Revenue from the sale of computer equipment increased during fiscal 1982 as a result of the active market for the IBM 3033 processor. The market for 3033 processors was stimulated by initial deliveries of IBM's 3081 processor and by the impact of IBM purchase price reductions on the 3033, which improved its price/performance ratio. Revenue from the sale of computer equipment declined

16% in fiscal 1981 compared to fiscal 1980, primarily due to computer users' increased preference for leasing.

Financial services revenue totaled $73.9 million in fiscal 1982 in comparison to $30.8 million in fiscal 1981. The increase in financial services revenue was primarily the result of tax-advantaged computer leasing transactions associated with a portion of the Company's lease portfolio of used equipment and also tax benefit transfers that were structured under the Economic Recovery Tax Act of 1981. Fiscal 1981 financial services revenue increased 119% over fiscal 1980 due to higher revenue from tax leveraged leases with third-party investors.

Cost and Expenses

Total costs and expenses of $417.8 million for fiscal 1982 increased 49% over total costs and expenses of $280.2 million in fiscal 1981. Fiscal 1981 total costs and expenses were 15% higher than fiscal 1980. The increases were the result of the growth in the Company's lease portfolio and customer base and the continuing expansion in marketing of the Company's services.

Selling, general and administrative expenses were $51.8 million in fiscal 1982, $28.5 million in fiscal 1981 and $19.3 million in fiscal 1980. The increases were primarily due to costs associated with the Company's expanding marketing activities, including higher commissions and administrative expenses.

The increases in interest expense in fiscal 1982 and fiscal 1981 were due to increased discounted lease rentals as a result of the growth in the Company's leasing activity. Interest expense on discounted leases, which is a non-cash expense, is the largest component of total interest expense (69% and 46% of total interest expense in fiscal 1982 and 1981, respectively). The Company finances leases by assigning the noncancellable rentals to financial institutions on a nonrecourse basis at a fixed interest rate and receives from the lender the present value of the rental payments (the discounted amount). As rental payments are made directly to the lender, the Company recognizes interest expense.

Income Taxes

Income taxes as a percentage of earnings before income taxes were 45.4% in fiscal 1982 compared to 26.8% in fiscal 1981 and 20.8% in

fiscal 1980. Note 7 of Notes to Consolidated Financial Statements provides details about the Company's income tax provisions and effective tax rates. The higher effective tax rate in fiscal 1982 was attributable to lower investment tax credits due to the sale of such benefits by the Company as permitted under the Economic Recovery Tax Act of 1981 (the "Act"). The Act liberalized the leasing provisions of the tax law and made it possible for corporations which cannot use all their current year tax deductions and credits to transfer them to other corporations. The tax benefit transfers completed by the Company in fiscal 1982 provided cash flow benefits which otherwise would not have been available until future years.

International Operations

The Company operated principally in three geographic areas during fiscal 1982 and 1981; United States, Europe and Canada. The Company has subsidiaries in Belgium, Germany, Switzerland, the Netherlands, France, the United Kingdom and Canada. These subsidiaries offer services similar to those offered in the United States.

A more favorable environment in fiscal 1982 resulted in an increase in revenue from international operations of 42% from $55.9 million in fiscal 1981 to $79.6 million in fiscal 1982. The prior year's results had been depressed as a result of computer users deferring action pending shipment of new products. International revenues represented 17% of the Company's total revenue in fiscal 1982, and 18% in fiscal 1981.

Market and Dividend Information

The Company's common stock is traded on the New York Stock Exchange under the symbol CDO. The following table shows the quarterly price range and dividends paid for fiscal years 1982 and 1981, adjusted to reflect the three-for-two and five-for-four common stock splits effected in March 1982 and 1981, respectively.

	1982			1981		
Qtr.	High	Low	Div.	High	Low	Div.
1st	$18.00	$11.75	$.05	$13.27	$7.87	$.04
2nd	18.00	13.50	.06	15.50	11.50	.05
3rd	19.25	15.50	.06	16.09	13.17	.05
4th	23.00	15.00	.06	15.33	10.67	.05

At September 30, 1982, there were approximately 2,900 record holders of common stock.

Financial Position

During fiscal 1982, the Company's financial position and liquidity improved significantly, with cash and marketable securities amounting to $39.8 million at September 30, 1982 compared to $9.8 million at September 30, 1981. These improvements were due to an increased earnings level and continued emphasis on effective asset management. Major sources and uses of funds are set forth in the Consolidated Statements of Changes in Financial Position.

At September 30, 1982, the Company had $45 million of available borrowing capacity under various lines of credit from commercial banks. During fiscal 1982, the Company entered into agreements for the purpose of issuing commercial paper which may be used from time to time to meet some of the Company's short term debt requirements. These facilities ensure the availability of significant funds to finance additional growth.

The trend of computer users toward leasing rather than purchasing computer equipment is expected to continue due to economic conditions, IBM pricing policies, and new product announcements. The major portion of funds required by the Company to finance the purchase of equipment acquired for leasing is generated by assigning the noncancellable rentals to various financial institutions at fixed interest rates on a nonrecourse basis.

In June 1981, the Company sold $50 million of 13% convertible subordinated debentures.

The proceeds of the lower cost, fixed-rate long term debt were used to replace bank borrowings. The Company had no short term debt at September 30, 1982.

Total notes and debentures as a percentage of total capital (the sum of notes and debentures payable, discounted lease rentals and stockholders' equity) has declined in each of the last three fiscal years, to 16% at September 30, 1982, compared to 29% at September 30, 1980. Improved earnings have contributed to the high returns on average stockholders' equity. This key financial measure of performance reached 39.2% in fiscal 1982, compared with 30.6% in fiscal 1981. The Company's strong financial position and history of earnings growth provide a solid base for obtaining the necessary financial resources to finance additional growth and for investment opportunities.

Ratios

The following table presents ratios which illustrate the changes and trends for the last three fiscal years:

	1982	1981	1980
Return on average stockholders' equity	39.2%	30.6%	18.0%
Return on average assets	6.2%	4.9%	3.5%
Earnings before income taxes (as a percentage of revenue)	11.4%	7.1%	3.5%
Net earnings (as a percentage of revenue)	6.2%	5.2%	2.8%

Comdisco, Inc. (A)

FIVE YEAR SELECTED FINANCIAL DATA

Years Ended Sept. 30,	1982	1981	1980	1979	1978
Consolidated Summary of Earnings (in thousands):					
Revenue					
Rental	$206,592	$131,571	$80,979	$60,947	$42,524
Sale of computer equipment	166,705	125,384	149,708	149,983	103,995
Financial services	73,879	30,837	14,079	9,991	4,046
Other	24,454	13,746	8,348	4,355	2,717
Total Revenue	471,630	301,538	253,114	225,276	153,282
Cost and expenses					
Equipment depreciation, amortization and rental	160,523	99,413	68,328	47,698	32,260
Cost of computer equipment	149,654	111,784	134,595	128,470	93,176
Financial services	8,617	6,784	4,878	5,108	1,768
Selling, general and administrative	51,785	28,529	19,341	16,176	9,246
Interest	47,242	33,657	16,988	13,319	10,360
Total cost and expenses	417,821	280,167	244,130	210,771	146,810
Earnings before income taxes	53,809	21,371	8,984	14,505	6,472
Income taxes	24,432	5,730	1,870	3,900	1,550
Net earnings	$29,377	$15,641	$7,114	$10,605	$4,922
Common and Common Equivalent Share Data					
Net earnings	$2.27	$1.35	$.65	$1.07	$.53
Stockholders' equity	$7.74	$5.17	$3.95	$3.50	$1.77
Average shares outstanding (in thousands)	14,487	12,270	11,051	9,929	9,222
Cash dividends paid	$.23	$.18	$.15	$.12	$.06
Financial Position (in thousands):					
Total assets	$536,679	$404,507	$229,170	$173,950	$144,223
Total long-term debt	83,271	84,945	29,055	25,573	25,447
Discounted lease rentals	261,780	197,672	85,612	74,569	61,703
Stockholders' equity	91,056	58,746	43,565	35,508	14,994

Common and common equivalent share data have been adjusted to reflect a three-for-two stock split effected in February 1978, a two-for-one common stock split effected July 1978, a three-for-two common stock split effected in February 1979, a five-for-four common stock split effected in March 1981, and a three-for-two common stock split effected in March 1982.

Comdisco, Inc. (A)

CONSOLIDATED BALANCE SHEETS
(in thousands except number of shares)

September 30,	1982	1981
Assets		
Cash and marketable securities (at cost of $3,909 in 1982 and $1,883 in 1981 which approximates market)	$39,762	$9,848
Receivables:		
Accounts and notes (Net of allowance for doubtful accounts of $628 in 1982 and $528 in 1981)	41,368	28,379
Other	3,687	3,827
Inventory of computer equipment	35,382	25,036
Net investment in sales-type and direct financing leases	23,682	17,890
Leased and other equipment:		
Leased computer equipment	502,494	374,044
Capitalized leases–computer equipment	24,158	23,225
Buildings, furniture and other	7,959	4,184
Total equipment	534,611	401,453
Less: accumulated depreciation and amortization	192,714	115,073
Net equipment	341,897	286,380
Other assets and deferred charges	50,901	33,147
	$536,679	$404,507
Liabilities and Stockholders' Equity		
Note payable to bank	$2,385	$3,445
Convertible subordinated debentures	50,000	50,000
Subordinated debentures	12,250	12,250
Accounts payable	19,110	27,492
Obligations under capital leases	18,636	19,250
Income taxes:		
Current	6,076	—
Deferred	30,121	13,017
Other liabilities	45,265	22,635
Discounted lease rentals	261,780	197,672
	445,623	345,761
Stockholders' equity:		
Common stock $.10 par value. Authorized 50,000,000 shares in 1982 and 15,000,000 shares in 1981; issued 11,769,043 shares (7,571,151 in 1981)	1,177	757
Additional paid-in capital	18,965	14,630
Deferred translation adjustment	(354)	—
Retained earnings	71,268	43,359
Total stockholders' equity	91,056	58,746
	$536,679	$404,507

See accompanying notes to consolidated financial statements.

CONSOLIDATED STATEMENTS OF EARNINGS
(in thousands except per share data)

Years Ended September 30,	1982	1981	1980
Revenue			
Rental	$206,592	$131,571	$80,979
Sale of computer equipment	166,705	125,384	149,708
Financial services	73,879	30,837	14,079
Other	24,454	13,746	8,348
Total revenue	471,630	301,538	253,114
Cost and Expenses			
Equipment depreciation, amortization and rental	160,523	99,413	68,328
Cost of computer equipment	149,654	111,784	134,595
Financial services	8,617	6,784	4,878
Selling, general and administrative	51,785	28,529	19,341
Interest	47,242	33,657	16,988
Total costs and expenses	417,821	280,167	244,130
Earnings before income taxes	53,809	21,371	8,984
Income taxes	24,432	5,730	1,870
Net Earnings	$29,377	$15,641	$7,114
Net Earnings Per Common and Common Equivalent Share	$2.27	$1.35	$.65

See accompanying notes to consolidated financial statements.

Comdisco, Inc. (A)

CONSOLIDATED STATEMENTS OF STOCKHOLDERS' EQUITY
(in thousands)

Years Ended September 30, 1982, 1981, and 1980

	Common Stock, $.10 par Value	Additional Paid-in Capital	Retained Earnings	Deferred Translation Adjustment
Balance at September 30, 1979	$541	$12,405	$22,562	$—
Net earnings	—	—	7,114	—
Dividends paid	—	—	(865)	—
Stock options exercised	46	639	—	—
Income tax benefits resulting from exercise of non-qualified stock options	—	1,123	—	—
Balance at September 30, 1980	587	14,167	28,811	—
Net earnings	—	—	15,641	—
Dividends paid	—	—	(1,093)	—
Stock split	148	(148)	—	—
Stock options exercised	22	611	—	—
Balance at September 30, 1981	757	14,630	43,359	—
Cumulative amount as of September 30, 1981	—	—	—	(232)
Net earnings	—	—	29,377	—
Dividends paid	—	—	(1,468)	—
Stock split	391	(400)	—	—
Stock options exercised	14	835	—	—
Common stock issued	15	2,648	—	—
Translation adjustment	—	—	—	(122)
Income tax benefits resulting from exercise of non-qualified stock options	—	1,252	—	—
Balance at September 30, 1982	$1,177	$18,965	$71,268	$(354)

See accompanying notes to consolidated financial statements.

CONSOLIDATED STATEMENTS OF CHANGES IN FINANCIAL POSITION
(in thousands)

Years Ended September 30,	1982	1981	1980
Source of Funds			
From operations:			
Net earnings	$29,377	$15,641	$7,114
Noncash charges (credits) to operations:			
Depreciation and amortization	133,902	77,528	46,212
Increase in receivables	(12,849)	(5,531)	(12,278)
Investment in sales-type and direct financing leases	(5,792)	(11,732)	323
Income taxes	23,180	5,730	747
Increase in accounts payable and accrued liabilities	14,248	18,611	11,322
Other, net	474	(1,233)	2,490
Total provided from operations	182,540	99,014	55,930
Proceeds from issuance of subordinated debentures	—	48,560	—
Increase (decrease) in notes payable	(1,060)	(33,460)	25,339
Obligations under capital leases	5,663	14,249	2,885
Discounted lease rentals	145,626	183,557	62,786
Other	4,201	924	766
	336,970	312,844	147,706
Application of Funds			
Increase in leased equipment and inventory	190,180	202,002	75,361
Reduction of discounted lease rentals and obligations under capital leases	87,795	75,781	55,916
Purchase of subordinated debentures	—	2,162	—
Capitalized leases—computer equipment	5,663	14,249	2,885
Other assets and deferred charges	21,950	12,343	13,555
Cash dividends	1,468	1,093	865
	307,056	307,630	148,582
Increase (decrease) in cash and marketable securities	29,914	5,214	(876)
Cash and marketable securities at beginning of year	9,848	4,634	5,510
Cash and marketable securities at end of year	$39,762	$9,848	$4,634

See accompanying notes to consolidated financial statements.

NOTES TO CONSOLIDATED FINANCIAL STATEMENTS

1. Summary of Significant Accounting Policies

Principles of Consolidation: The accompanying consolidated financial statements include the accounts of the Company and its wholly-owned subsidiaries after elimination of intercompany accounts and transactions.

Revenue Recognition: Leases are accounted for either as sales-type, direct financing or operating leases. Lease terms generally range from four months to five years. Revenue from sales-type leases is recorded upon acceptance of the equipment by the customer and is reflected as sale of computer equipment. Revenue from direct financing leases is recorded over the term of the lease as interest income calculated using the interest method. Rental revenue from operating leases is recognized in equal monthly amounts over the term of the lease.

Revenue from the sale of computer equipment and the related cost of equipment is reflected in earnings at the time of acceptance of the equipment by the customer.

Revenue from the sale of equipment subject to operating leases is recognized at the closing of the transactions and is included as sale of computer equipment in fiscal 1981 and 1980. In addition to this revenue, the Company is also entitled to the use of such equipment subsequent to the lease expiration date for periods ranging generally from 6 months to 4 years. Revenue, if any, from the re-leasing of such equipment during this period is recognized upon acceptance of the equipment by the customer and is reflected as other revenue.

Under the provisions of the Economic Recovery Tax Act of 1981, the Company sold the tax benefits (investment tax credits and cost recovery allowances) on new equipment purchased for the Company's lease portfolio. The proceeds from the sale of tax benefits are recorded as financial services revenue. Also included as financial services revenue are fees for arranging tax benefit transfer agreements with third parties.

Fees from the sale of equipment included in the Company's lease portfolio of used equipment are recognized at the closing of the transactions and included as financial services revenue. Such transactions, which are structured as tax advantaged leases, entitle the

Company to the use of such equipment for periods ranging generally from one to six years subsequent to the initial lease expiration date.

The Company, through its CFS subsidiary, has entered into certain computer equipment transactions in which it has leased equipment (the "Lease") and in turn has subleased such equipment (the "Sublease"). In substantially all of these transactions, the Lease term exceeds the Sublease term. Monthly Sublease rentals are greater than the monthly Lease rentals; however, the present value of the total Sublease rentals ("Sublease Proceeds") may be less than the present value of the total Lease rentals ("Lease Obligations") due to the difference in lease terms. Rentals from the sublease are discounted by the Company with a financial institution on a nonrecourse basis. An escrow account is established to fund the Company's obligations under the lease for the period after the expiration of the Sublease. In the event the Sublease Proceeds exceed the Lease Obligations, the Company recognizes profit. When Lease Obligations exceed the Sublease Proceeds, no profit is recognized and the next excess Lease Obligation is deferred to be recovered from the Company's right to future rentals during the remaining term of the Lease. At September 30, 1982 and 1981, $21,258,000 and $10,148,000, respectively, of costs were deferred in connection with such transactions and are included in the balance sheet caption "Other assets and deferred charges." The Company recognized $3,113,000, $4,286,000, and $1,890,000 of interest income on investments held in escrow during the years ended September 30, 1982, 1981, and 1980, respectively.

Inventory of Computer Equipment: Inventory of computer equipment is stated at the lower of cost or market.

Equipment, Depreciation and Amortization: Leased equipment owned by the Company is generally recorded at cost. Depreciation and amortization of leased equipment are computed on the straight-line method for financial reporting purposes to estimated fair market value at lease termination (see Note 2).

Deferred Lease Costs: Salesmen's commissions and other direct expenses related to operating leases are deferred and amortized over the lease term.

Income Taxes and Investment Tax Credits: Deferred income taxes have been provided for income and expenses which are recognized in different periods for income tax purpose than for financial reporting purposes. Investment tax credits are accounted for on a flow-through basis.

Profit Sharing Plan: The Company has a profit sharing plan covering all employees. Company contributions to the plan are based on a percentage of employees' compensation, as defined. Profit sharing payments are based on amounts accumulated on an individual employees basis. Profit sharing expense for the years ended September 30, 1982, 1981 and 1980 amounted to $590,000, $489,000 and $178,000, respectively.

Earnings Per Share: Earnings per common and common equivalent share are computed based on the weighted average number of common and common equivalent shares outstanding during each period including the assumed conversion of the 13% convertible subordinated debentures, after elimination of the related interest expense (net of tax), and after giving retroactive effect to the three-for-two stock split effected in March 1982 (see Note 9). Dilutive stock options included in the number of common and common equivalent shares are based on the treasury stock method. The number of common and common equivalent shares used in the computation of earnings per share for the years ended September 30, 1982, 1981 and 1980 were 14,486,738, 12,269,703 and 11,050,277, respectively.

Foreign Currency Translation: Fiscal 1982 consolidated financial statements have been prepared in accordance with Financial Accounting Standards Board Statement No. 52, "Foreign Currency Translation," the provisions of which were adopted by the Company on a prospective basis as of October 1, 1981. Previous consolidated financial statements have been prepared in accordance with Statement No. 8, "Accounting for the Translation of Foreign Currency Transactions and Foreign Currency Financial Statements." The effect of the change was not material.

2. Depreciable Lives

Effective October 1, 1980 the Company extended its estimates of depreciable lives of certain IBM peripheral equipment. Effective January 1, 1981 the Company extended its estimates of depreciable lives and salvage values of certain IBM peripheral equipment. Previously, this equipment was depreciated to zero by September 30, 1983. The changes in estimates were made based on revised market conditions and reflect current estimates of the equipment's useful lives and salvage values. The effect of the changes on recorded leased equipment at the effective dates of the changes was an increase in net earnings of $4,488,000 (net of income taxes of $4,142,000), or $.37 per share, for the year ended September 30, 1981.

3. Investment in Sales-Type and Direct Financing Leases

The following table lists the components of the net investment in sales-type and direct financing leases as of September 30:

	1982	1981
	(in thousands)	
Minimum lease payments receivable	$24,142	$18,504
Estimated residual values of leased property	12,324	9,160
Less unearned income	12,784	9,774
Net investment in sales-type and direct financing leases	$23,682	$17,890

Future minimum lease payments to be received under the above lease agreements are as follows:

Years ending September 30	Sales-type and direct financing leases
	(in thousands)
1983	$7,306
1984	7,416
1985	5,534
1986	2,637
1987	1,249
	$24,142

The Company finances most sales-type and direct financing leases by assigning the non-cancellable rentals on a non-recourse basis. The proceeds from the assignment reduce the investment in sales-type and direct financing leases. Any gain or loss on the assignment is recognized at the time of such assignment.

4. Capitalized Leases

Capitalized leases—computer equipment
at September 30 is comprised of the following:

	1982	1981
	(in thousands)	
Capitalized leases – computer equipment	$24,158	$23,225
Less accumulated amortization	15,354	12,099
Net capitalized leases – computer equipment	$8,804	$11,126

At September 30, 1982, the Company, as lessee, was obligated to pay rentals under capitalized leases. The related equipment has been subleased and accounted for either as operating leases or as direct financing leases. The following table summarizes minimum rentals payable by the Company as lessee under capitalized leases:

Years ending September 30,	Capitalized Leases
	(in thousands)
1983	$8,196
1984	6,987
1985	4,801
1986	2,618
1987	1,810
Later years	521
Total minimum lease payments	24,933
Less imputed interest (9% to 17%)	6,297
Present value of net minimum lease payments	$18,636

Total minimum lease payments for capitalized leases have not been reduced by minimum non-cancellable sublease rentals of $16,094,000 due the Company in the future.

5. Bank Borrowings and Compensating Balances

The Company has a revolving credit agreement which entitles the Company to borrow up to $25,000,000 on an unsecured basis. The agreement, which expires March 31, 1983, carries an interest cost of prime rate (13.5% at September 30, 1982) and includes a fee of 3/8% per annum of the average daily unused amount. If the Company or the bank elects not to renew the agreement, the loan becomes a two-year term loan payable in equal quarterly installments with an interest cost of prime rate plus 1%. Under the agreement, the Company is required to maintain a defined debt to net worth ratio and dividend payments cannot exceed 20% of consolidated net earnings subsequent to September 30, 1980. At September 30, 1982, approximately $4,280,000 of retained earnings were available for payment of dividends.

In accordance with the terms of the agreement, the Company is required to maintain average cash balances with the bank equal to 5% of the $25,000,000 loan commitment. The amount of unused available borrowings under the agreement was $25,000,000 at September 30, 1982.

At September 30, 1982, the Company had additional unused lines of credit totaling $20,000,000 under which borrowings would bear interest at the prime rate. Under the agreements, the Company is required to maintain compensating balances equal to 5% of the outstanding borrowings.

6. Note Payable to Bank and Subordinated Debentures

Note Payable to Bank: The note payable to bank at September 30, 1982 and 1981 was an 11 3/4% term note payable in quarterly installments through December, 1984.

13% Convertible Subordinated Debentures: In June 1981, the Company issued $50,000,000 of 13% convertible subordinated debentures ("Convertible Debentures") due in 2001. Issue costs of $1,440,000 relating to the Convertible Debenture may be converted into shares of common stock of the Company, prior to maturity, at the option of the convertible Debenture holder at a conversion price of $19.50 per share.

The Convertible Debentures are redeemable in full or in part at the option of the company beginning in 1981 at an amount equal to 113.0% of the principal amount of the Convertible Debentures, the premium on redemption declining 1.3% per annum commencing in 1982 through 1991, and redeemable thereafter at par.

11 1/2% Subordinated Debentures: At September 30, 1982, $12,250,000 of 11 1/2% subordinated debentures (the "Debentures") due December 1, 1992, were outstanding. Annual sinking fund payments of $1,350,000 (9% of the aggregate original principal amount) commence December 1, 1982, and are calculated to retire 90% of the issue prior to maturity. During fiscal

1981, the Company, in connection with future sinking fund requirements, acquired $2,750,000 principal amount of the outstanding debentures which resulted in a gain of $318,000 (net of income taxes of $270,000).

Both the Debentures and the Convertible Debentures are subordinated to all senior indebtedness as defined in the indenture agreements. At September 30, 1982, the Company's senior indebtedness was approximately $2,473,000.

The annual maturities and sinking fund requirements of the note payable and subordinated debentures for the next five years are as follows:

Year Ending September 30	Aggregate Maturities
	(in thousands)
1983	$1,060
1984	1,060
1985	1,565
1986	1,350
1987	1,350

7. Income Taxes

The following data relate to the provision for income taxes for the years ended September 30:

	1982	1981	1980
Provision in lieu of income taxes	$1,252	—	$1,123
Current::			
Federal	5,000	—	—
State	1,076	—	—
	6,076	—	—
Deferred:			
Federal	16,281	4,216	147
State	273	553	220
Foreign	550	961	380
	17,104	5,730	747
Total tax provision	$24,432	$5,730	$1,870
Earnings before income taxes			
Domestic	$51,166	$18,992	$8,203
Foreign	2,643	2,379	781
Total	$53,809	$21,371	$8,984

Income tax benefits of $1,252,000 and $1,123,00 resulting from the exercise of non-qualified stock options were utilized to reduce the current Federal tax provision in fiscal 1982 and 1980, respectively.

The reasons for the difference between the U.S. Federal income tax rate of 46% and the effective income tax rate were as follows:

	Percentage of Pretax Earnings		
Years ended September 30	1982	1981	1980
U.S. Federal income tax	46.0%	46.0%	46.0%
Increase (reduction) resulting from:			
Domestic International Sales Corporation tax benefit	(.1)	(1.2)	(6.8)
Reduction of deferred income taxes applicable to investment tax credit carryforward	—	(20.4)	(20.1)
Investment tax credit	(2.0)	—	—
State income taxes, net of U.S. tax benefit	1.4	1.2	1.1
Other – net	.1	1.2	.6
	45.4%	26.8%	20.8%

The Company has not provided for income taxes on the unremitted earnings of the Domestic International Sales Corporation (DISC) subsidiary aggregating $4,253,000 through September 30, 1982, since the Company intends to postpone indefinitely the remittance of such earnings.

Deferred income taxes provided for timing differences were as follows:

Years ended September 30	1982	1981	1980
	(in thousands)		
Sale of tax benefits	$38,661	—	—
Difference between depreciation for tax purposes and financial statement purposes	(18,125)	6,311	570
Deferred compensation expense	754	(754)	—
Deferred leasing income	2,934	(2,093)	—
Deferred leasing costs	1,518	1,164	793
Portion of undistributed earnings in DISC	(178)	(454)	231
Difference between leases accounted for as sales-type leases for financial statement purposes and operating leases for tax purposes	(23,601)	194	2,915
Reinstatement (reduction) of deferred income taxes applicable to:			
Investment tax credit carryforward	12,021	(4,356)	(1,803)
Tax net operating loss realization (carryforward)	—	2,323	(650)
Income tax benefit resulting from exercise of non-qualified stock options	—	1,903	(1,123)
Other – net	3,120	1,492	(186)
	$17,104	$5,730	$747

8. Discounted Lease Rentals

Leased equipment owned by the Company is financed by assigning the noncancellable rentals to various lenders at fixed interest rates on a nonrecourse basis. The proceeds from the assignment of the lease rentals (discounted lease rentals) represent payments due under the lease discounted to their present value at the interest rate charged by the lender, generally ranging from 10% to 19%. The difference between monthly rentals due under discounted leases and the amortization of related discounted lease rentals represents interest expense. This expense amounted to $32,527,000, $15,468,000, and $8,380,000 in 1982, 1981, and 1980, respectively. In the event of default by the lessee, the lender has a first lien against the underlying leased equipment, with no further recourse against the Company.

9. Common Stock and Additional Paid-in Capital

On January 27, 1982, the Board of Directors declared a three-for-two split of the Company's common stock. This distribution was subject to the stockholders approval, which was obtained, amending the Certificate of Incorporation increasing the number of authorized shares from 15,000,000 to 50,000,000 with the par value remaining at $.10 per share. On January 28, 1981, the Board of Directors of the Company declared a five-for-four split of the Company's common stock. All references in the financial statements and notes to the number of shares of common stock and per share amounts have been adjusted for the aforementioned stock splits.

On November 18, 1981, the Board of Directors approved the Settlement Agreement (the "Agreement") between the Company and participants in the Residual Incentive Compensation Plan (the "Plan") related to vested residual computer interests. The Plan provided in part for the allocation of a percentage interest in the residual value of computer equipment to the participants. The Agreement was approved by the stockholders on March 15, 1982, and pursuant to the terms of the Agreement, the Company distributed to participants in

accordance with the terms of the Plan, the aggregate sum of $3,000,000 plus 150,000 shares of the Company's common stock.

Dividends on Common Stock: Common stock dividends paid were $.23 per share in 1982 compared with $.18 in 1981 and $.15 in 1980. Certain officers and directors of the Company and their affiliates, owning an aggregate of 5,028,645 shares (43%) of the outstanding common stock at September 30, 1982, have waived their rights to any cash dividends through February 1, 1983 and did not receive any of the previously mentioned cash dividends.

At September 30, 1982, the Company had reserved the following number of common shares for future issuance:

1979 Stock Option Plan	334,438
1981 Stock Option Plan	750,000
Employee Stock Purchase Plan	147,358
Conversion of Convertible Subordinated Debentures	2,564,103
	3,795,899

10. Stock Options and Stock Purchase Plan

On November 18, 1981, the Board of Directors amended the Company's 1979 Stock Option Plan (the "1979 Plan") to qualify the plan as an incentive stock option plan in accordance with the provisions of the Economic Recovery Tax Act of 1981. All outstanding stock options, which retained their original option price, are eligible for treatment as incentive stock options subject to certain limitations as defined in the amended 1979 Plan.

On January 27, 1982, the stockholders approved the 1981 Stock Option Plan (the "1981 Plan"). An aggregate of 750,000 shares were reserved for issuance pursuant to the exercise of options under the 1981 plan.

The Comdisco, Inc. Employee Stock Purchase Plan (the "Stock Plan") was adopted by the Board of Directors on November 17, 1981. An aggregate of 150,000 shares was reserved for issuance under the Stock Plan.

The changes in the number of shares under the option plans during 1982, 1981, and 1980 were as follows:

	1982	1981	1980
(in thousands except option price range)			
Number of shares:			
Shares under option			
beginning of the year	512	861	1,119
Options granted	169	—	612
Options exercised	(188)	(349)	(870)
Shares under option end			
of year	493	512	861
Aggregate option price:			
Shares under option			
beginning of year	$2,533	$3,257	$480
Options granted	3,284	—	3,187
Options exercised	(850)	(724)	(410)
Shares under option end			
of the year	$4,967	$2,533	$3,257
Options exercisable at			
end of year	58	164	12
Aggregate option price of			
exercisable options			
outstanding at end of year	$295	$722	$19
Options available for future			
grant at end of year	591	11	11
Option price range	$4.90–	$1.35–	$.12–
	$19.38	$7.00	$7.00

11. Operating Leases

The following table summarizes the Company's future rentals receivable and payable under noncancellable operating leases existing at September 30, 1982 for computer equipment and rentals payable for non-computer equipment and office space:

	Computer equipment			
Years ending Sept. 30	Rents receivable on equipment		Rents payable on subleased equipment	Other rents payable
	Owned	Subleased		
1983	$180,581	$21,704	$25,497	$2,033
1984	107,125	13,269	12,197	1,735
1985	43,115	5,799	5,002	1,600
1986	7,237	1,742	792	1,033
1987	352	544	—	233
Later years	11	—	—	77

Total rental income and related expense for the years ended September 30, 1982, 1981, and 1980 applicable to computer sublease activities are as follows:

Years ending September 30	Rental income	Rental expense
	(in thousands)	
1982	$23,633	$27,455
1981	24,152	22,415
1980	22,614	22,455

12. Commitments and Contingent Liabilities

At September 30, 1982, the Company was obligated under the following commitments: (1) to purchase computer equipment in the approximate aggregate amount of $31,768,000, (2) to sell computer equipment in the approximate aggregate amount of $20,926,000, and (3) to lease computer equipment to others with an aggregate initial term rental of approximately $55,107,000.

The Company has arranged for approximately $74,000,000 of letters of credit, primarily as guarantees for certain of the Company's sublease obligations and for future purchases of IBM equipment. The cost of such letters of credit range between 1/2% and 3/4% per annum of the amount outstanding.

ACCOUNTANTS' REPORT

The Stockholders and Board of Directors Comdisco, Inc.:

We have examined the consolidated balance sheets of Comdisco, Inc. and subsidiaries as of September 30, 1982 and 1981 and the related consolidated statements of earnings, stockholders' equity and changes in financial position for each of the years in the three year period ended September 30, 1982. Our examinations were made in accordance with generally accepted auditing standards and, accordingly, included such tests of the accounting records and such other auditing procedures as we considered necessary in the circumstance.

In our opinion, the aforementioned consolidated financial statements present fairly the financial position of Comdisco, Inc. and subsidiaries at September 30, 1982 and 1981 and the results of their operations and the changes in their financial position for each of the years in the three-year period ended September 30, 1982, in conformity with generally accepted accounting principles applied on a consistent basis.

Peat, Marwick, Mitchell & Co.
Chicago, Illinois
November 9, 1982

QUARTERLY FINANCIAL DATA

Summarized Quarterly Financial data for the fiscal years ended September 30, 1982 and 1981, is as follows:

(in thousands of dollars except per share amounts)

Quarter ended	December 31		March 31		June 30		September 30	
	1981	1980	1982	1981	1982	1981	1982	1981
Total revenue'	$121,189	$78,833	$118,309	$64,450	$94,691	$75,722	$137,441	$82,533
Net earnings	9,604	3,285	5,934	3,146	5,824	4,075	8,015	5,135
Net earnings per common and common equivalent share	$.73	$.29	$.47	$.27	$.46	$.35	$.61	$.42

Comdisco, Inc.: Financial Statement Analysis (B)

A published report implying that the accounting practices of computer leasing giant Comdisco, Inc. could result in overstated earnings has provoked strong rebuttals from the leasing industry while rattling the skeleton of the OPM Leasing Services, Inc. scandal.

The report appeared last week in Barron's financial weekly and suggested that internal and external forces are mixing to create a potential disaster scenario for Comdisco as well as other third-party lessors. Meanwhile, the report stated, company officers, including founder and chairman Kenneth Pontikes, have gone on a Comdisco stock-selling spree in the past two years, getting rich in the process.

After publication of the report, Comdisco's stock lost nearly 37% of its paper value in one frenzied day of trading last Monday, falling from $38 to $24 per share.[1]

The October 17, 1983 issue of *Computerworld* magazine carried the above report on Comdisco, Inc.

BUSINESS HISTORY AND OPERATIONS[2]

Comdisco, Inc. is a Chicago based company founded in 1969 by its current chairman of the board and president, Kenneth Pontikes. The company originally began as an IBM computer dealer. As demand for computer leasing started to grow during the late 1970s, the company started emphasizing leasing operations. By 1982, leasing old and new IBM computer equipment constituted the primary business activity of the company, and Comdisco had become the largest computer leasing company.

Comdisco's customers were primarily large corporations. In 1982, the company had business relationships with 49 of the 50 largest U.S. companies and with 70% of the Fortune 500 companies.

The computer remarketing industry had many participants: small independent operators, larger private organizations, and leasing subsidiaries of conglomerates. Comdisco was one of the few independent public corporations in the industry. The firms in the industry were primarily of two types: broker/dealers or third party lessors.

1. *Reprinted with permission from* Computerworld, *October 17, 1983.*

2. *This section can be skipped by those who read Comdisco, Inc.: Financial Statement Analysis (A) case (9-186-299).*

The broker/dealers obtained for a customer computer equipment from either a vendor or current user; third party lessors provided lease financing. Comdisco engaged in both these activities.

Comdisco achieved its dominance in the computer leasing industry through a strategy of full-service leasing. Under this strategy, the company offered its customers a number of services which were not offered by its competitors. Comdisco's subsidiaries, Comdisco Technical Services, Inc. and Comdisco Transport, Inc., specialized in equipment refurbishment, delivery, installation, de-installation, and technical planning and site preparation. Comdisco Maintenance Services, another subsidiary of the Company, offered a low cost alternative to IBM's maintenance service. Comdisco Disaster Recovery Services, Inc. was established by the company to provide another valuable service to its customers: contingent data processing capacity to be used when a customer's own data center had unavoidable failures. Through this service, Comdisco's customers had access to four fully operational data centers located as a backup to their own data centers, to be used in case the customer's own facilities were adversely affected by a natural disaster or accident.

Comdisco's large customer base provided the company with a number of competitive advantages. First, taking advantage of its access to many large users of IBM equipment, the company created a proprietary data base on the computing needs of 10,000 large IBM users in the United States. This data base provided Comdisco's sales force with current and timely information on potential customers and their requirements. Second, being the largest dealer in IBM equipment, Comdisco was able to maintain larger inventories of a broad range of IBM equipment. Comdisco's personnel closely monitored IBM's new products and pricing policies. The product knowledge and large inventories helped the company assist its customers with their computer acquisition plans and offer quick deliveries. Finally, using its large customer base, the company was able to help its customers to sell their old hardware when they acquired new equipment from Comdisco.

While the above strategy enabled Comdisco to establish its dominance over others in the computer leasing industry, the company was still potentially vulnerable to competition from IBM itself since IBM equipment accounted for most of Comdisco's revenues. In 1981, IBM formed a financing subsidiary, IBM Credit Corporation, to provide customer financing. Shortly after that, IBM announced its intention to enter into computer leasing and established a joint venture for this purpose with Merrill Lynch and Metropolitan Life Insurance. A number of industry analysts felt that this might result in increased competition for companies like Comdisco.

Comdisco's management, however, felt that IBM's recent moves did not pose a threat to the company's competitive position. They felt that IBM entry into leasing would enhance the image of the computer leasing business, a net benefit to the industry. They also believed that, as IBM began to emphasize outright sale of its equipment over short-term rentals, many of IBM's traditional customers might be forced to look for other lessors like Comdisco who offered short-term leases. This was likely to provide additional business opportunities which would offset any loss of long-term lease business to IBM.

While equipment leasing to computer users was Comdisco's primary activity, the company also offered tax-oriented leases to investors who were primarily interested in the tax benefits associated with leasing. In recent years, the financial services income from the tax advantaged transactions accounted for a growing portion of the company's revenues.

TAX ADVANTAGED TRANSACTIONS

In addition to the leasing the equipment to computer users, Comdisco undertook leasing transactions with investors who were interested in tax shelters. While the specific terms and conditions of these tax advantaged transactions varied, a typical transaction was as follows:

1. After the inception of the initial user lease and independent of it, Comdisco sold all the leased equipment to a third party investor. This sale usually occurred three to nine months after the commencement of the initial user lease. The sales price equaled the then current fair market value of the equipment. The payment from the investor to Comdisco consisted of: (a) cash and a negotiable interest-bearing promissory note due within two years for 10–22% of the sales price (the "equity payment") and (b) an installment note for the balance payable over an 84 month period.
2. Simultaneously with the sale, Comdisco leased the equipment back from the investors for 84 months. The lease payments under the leaseback obligation were equal to the installment payments receivable by Comdisco from the investor (1(b)).
3. As part of the leaseback arrangement, during the 61st through 84th months of the leaseback period, the investor shared in the re-lease proceeds that the company received from subleasing the equipment to a user. Upon the expiration of the leaseback period, the investor had the exclusive right to the equipment.

The net result of the above transaction was that Comdisco gave up the depreciation tax benefit, a portion of the rental revenues for months 61–84, and 100% of the equipment value after the 84th month. In return, the company received the non-refundable equity payment (1(a)).

If the equipment sold to the investor was originally under an operating lease, the equity payment was recorded by Comdisco as financial services revenue in the period in which the tax advantaged transaction occurred. From the fourth quarter of 1983, the company began to allocate as cost of financial services a portion of the net book value of the equipment at lease termination. For sales-type and direct financing leases, the equity payment was first applied to reduce a portion of the residual value of the equipment shown in the balance sheet (as investment in sales-type and direct financing leases). This is because the company's ability to recover the residual value was decreased due to the rental sharing under the tax advantaged transaction. The excess of the equity payment over the residual value reduction was recorded as financial services revenue in the period in which the tax advantaged transaction occurred.

THE *BARRON'S* ARTICLE

The October 10, 1983 issue of *Barron's*, a widely circulated financial weekly, carried an article on Comdisco, "Something Doesn't Compute: A Hard Look at Comdisco's Accounting." The article, excerpts from which are given in Exhibit 2, focused on four areas: the company's accounting, competition from IBM Credit Corporation, the company's tax advantaged leasing program, and the sale of company stock by insiders. The article attracted considerable attention on Wall Street, leading to hectic trading of the company's stock. The company's stock price dropped from $38.250 to $22.875 by the end of the week, representing a loss of about $453.5 million in the market value of the company (see Exhibit 1 for data on Comdisco's stock price).

In response to these events, Kenneth Pontikes, president of Comdisco, issued a letter to shareholders on October 12, 1983. The letter addressed the issues raised in the *Barron's* article and attempted to rebut the charges (see Exhibit 3). Pontikes concluded:

[Finally,] it is important for you, our stockholders, to understand completely that Comdisco is stronger financially than it has ever been; that we have greater opportunities before us than at any time in our history; and that management is dedicated to retaining stockholder confidence and enhancing stockholder wealth.

Shortly after the above developments, Comdisco released its annual report for fiscal 1983 (Exhibit 4).

QUESTIONS

1. Evaluate *Barron's* criticism of Comdisco's accounting and the company's response. Do you agree with the company or *Barron's*?

2. Compare the level of disclosure in Comdisco's annual reports in the (A) and (B) cases. Do you think the company's poor disclosure prior to 1983 made it vulnerable to the attack by *Barron's*? Would the market reaction to the *Barron's* article have been different if the company had a better disclosure policy?

3. Do you think Comdisco's stock in November 1983 was a "buy"?

EXHIBIT I

Movement of Comdisco's Stock Price and S&P 500 Index, January 1982–November 1983

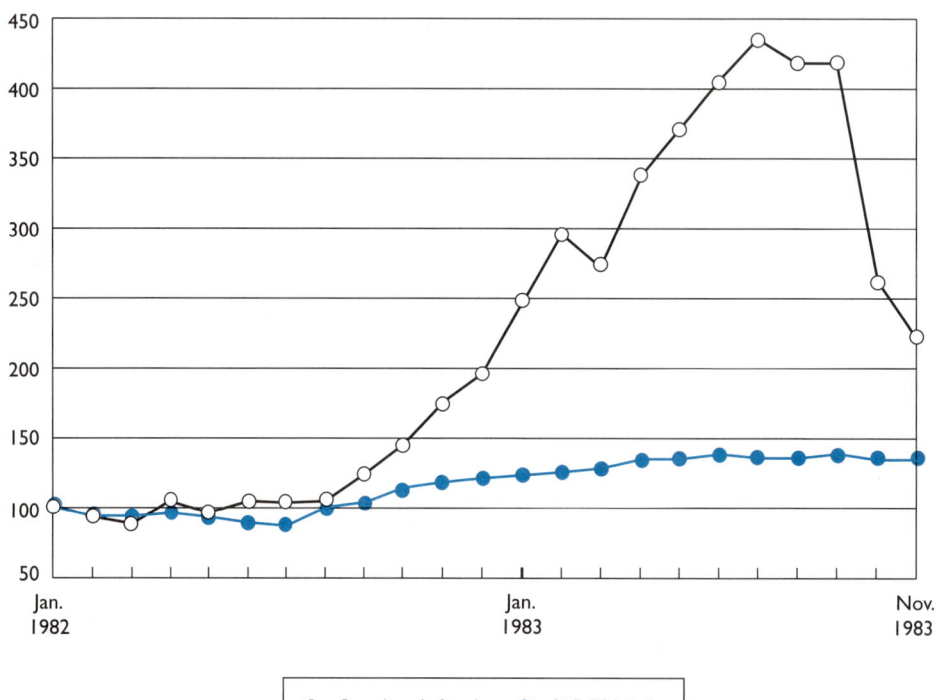

EXHIBIT 2

"Something Doesn't Compute—Hard Look at Comdisco Accounting Practices"[3]

Rhonda Brammer—*Barron's,* October 10, 1983

Twenty years ago, Ken Pontikes sold computer tapes and tab cards for IBM. He was paid $5,000 a year. When he lit out on his own five years later—starting up a one-man brokerage business in computers—his whole idea, he says "was to make a nice living." That start-up operation today is Chicago-based Comdisco, the biggest computer leasing company in the country. And yes, the 43-year-old Pontikes is making a living. His compensation was $2.4 million last year. So far this year, he's reported stock sales of $2.6 million. And his stake in the company, at the current market price, is worth $200 million plus.

His company could now be ranked an old-timer in the volatile computer leasing business, but its meteoric stock market rise is a recent phenomenon. In 1977, for example, shares could be had for a fraction of a dollar. As late as 1982, investors could have bought the stock under 7. Those same shares now sell at 38, just four points shy of their all-time high.

The spectacular rise in the stock reflects the transformation of the company itself, from a computer brokerage business—one that basically matched up computer buyers and sellers for a fee—into a complex financial service operation. Today, Comdisco not only buys and leases computers, but also "re-sells" the leased equipment in intricately structured tax shelters. The marketing men of a decade ago have been joined by a cadre of lawyers and accountants—tough, shrewd professionals, paid handsomely to keep one step ahead of the IRS. It's a new emphasis that has done wonders for the bottom line. Since 1980, sales have almost doubled, hitting $472 million in the 1982 fiscal year ended September. More important—thanks to the tax shelters—over the like stretch earnings expanded more than fourfold, to $29 million.

But past is not necessarily prologue. And Comdisco may be running into trouble on several fronts. First, sources close to the IRS say that computer-leasing tax shelters are the object of wrathful scrutiny these days. The very guidelines around which Comdisco structures deals are being rewritten.

Second, IBM is moving into territory where Comdisco had been undisputed king. The IBM Credit Corp. is pushing its way into third-party leasing with partners none other than Merrill Lynch and Metropolitan Life Insurance. By next year, say industry observers, the Armonk giant will rank No. 1. And with its enormous supplies of cheap capital, IBM already is offering surprisingly aggressive rates. This ominous trend threatens to put an increasing squeeze on the profit margins of computer leasing outfits like Comdisco. To compete they may well have no choice but to take calculated—and dangerous—financial risks.

Finally, there's some controversial accounting. Comdisco's method of accounting for "fees" from tax-advantaged leases is a matter unresolved by the accounting profession—and a potentially explosive issue. Right now, Comdisco has significant latitude in the level of profits it reports and the amount of residual values it carries on the balance sheet. The details are complex, but essentially Comdisco often records what it calls "fees" from tax-advantaged transactions as straight profit—without offsetting such "fees" against the company's investment in the equipment. It thereby keeps on its books a significant investment, recorded in "leased computer equipment" or "net investment in sales and direct financing leases"—an investment it hopes to recoup from the residual value when the equipment is re-leased.

And if there are no residual values when the equipment comes off lease? Well, based on information supplied by the company's financial department, if *all* equipment was considered to have zero residual value, Comdisco's entire net worth, as of the end of fiscal 1982, would vanish.

Obviously, the way residual values are treated affects earnings, too. When Comdisco reasons that it will recoup its net investment after the equipment is released, it books the "fee" from the sale of the tax shelter as pure profit. If, instead, it subtracted its investment in equipment from this fee—recovered the investment and

---

took it off the balance sheet—earnings would be a mere fraction of the substantial sums currently reported.

This method of accounting is thus disturbing on several scores. First, it's possible the residual values simply aren't there. Comdisco insists its assumptions are conservative—and they may well be—but all leasing companies have made such assertions, even the defunct ones. If there's a miscalculation, and the equipment should come off lease and suddenly be worthless, that means Comdisco would face a write-off.

Not to be overlooked, either, is the matter of when profits are recognized by Comdisco. Why should a company be allowed to report earnings today when it won't see the cash for four or five years, if ever? And finally, at the very least, financial statements might reasonably be expected to disclose net investment and assumed residual values, as well as detailed descriptions of how "fees" are booked.

None of this, however, is to say that Comdisco's accounting breaks the rules. Quite the contrary. "The accounting profession hasn't addressed the issue on this type of transaction," John Vosicky, Comdisco's vice president of accounting and financial controls, correctly points out. "One could argue that you could take the entire fee into income right away—on everything. Another could argue you reduce your investment completely, and you don't recognize anything until that investment is covered."

***

To better understand the accounting, consider a typical transaction, which in itself is no simple matter. The "tax-advantaged" leases, in order to get by the IRS, often involve layers of companies. And the shuffling of papers in sale-leaseback transactions can, in short order, obscure the economic realities of the deals.

But here are the basics.

Comdisco finds a user who wants to lease a computer for say, five years, and buys a machine for $100. Comdisco then takes the lease to the bank, and borrows the discounted value of the payments. A typical present value for the lease payments might be $85.

This borrowing from the bank appears on Comdisco's balance sheet as "discounted lease rentals," but the contract is so structured that the risk is essentially transferred to the bank. "These are hell-or-high water agreements," insists one Comdisco executive. If anything goes wrong—

if the user fails to make his payments—all the bank can do is confiscate the equipment. It has no recourse to Comdisco. So at this point, Comdisco's investment has effectively been reduced from $100 to $15.

Then comes the "tax advantaged" part of the deal. Comdisco sells the computer to an investor who is looking for a tax shelter. And here things start to get tricky.

Comdisco collects, say, $17 in cash, from the investor and then agrees to take a seven-year note for the remaining $83 of the purchase price of the equipment. At the same time, it signs a seven-year leaseback with the investor, so the rental payments the investor gets are spread over seven years. It's neatly arranged so the rental payments of this leaseback are precisely enough to cover the payments on the seven-year note. Put another way, Comdisco pays the investor rent, and the investor turns right around and pays this rent back to Comdisco as interest and principal on the note. It's a wash—a paper transaction. It's a nifty tax deal that has no effect on the actual user of the equipment, who continues to make his payments to the bank, which, in turn, reduces Comdisco's discounted lease receivables.

So has Comdisco made money? Well, it has paid $100 for a computer and borrowed $85 from the bank, to be paid off in five years by the user's rental payments. That leaves a $15 net investment. But it's also received $17 cash from the investor, and then shuffled papers so that an $83 note from the investor is exactly offset by lease payables of $83. Comdisco also retains the right to share the proceeds of re-leasing the computer in years six and seven with the investor. The bottom line is this: the $17 in cash offsets the $15 net investment. Comdisco is $2 richer.

So the income statement shows $2?

Not likely. All those high-paid lawyers and accountants on staff argue the $17 cash payment is a "fee"—for, among other things, putting the deal together. Clearly the $17 is theirs; they don't have to give it back. So in many cases Comdisco takes the entire fee as profit. It shows earnings of $17, even though it has only $2 in the cash register.

Where's the other $15? The difference between the reported profits and the actual cash sits quietly on the balance sheet—in "leased computer equipment" or sometimes in "net investment in sales-type and direct finance leases." That's the amount Comdisco hopes to recover from re-leasing the computer in years six and seven. But by booking the entire $17, it has effectively taken this assumed residual value into earnings on day one.

Now if in years six and seven, Comdisco re-leases the computer for, say $20, it can report a $5 profit. If the re-leasing brings in only $15, Comdisco has broken even. It has simply replaced the $15 paper asset on the balance sheet with a more spendable $15 in cash. But what if re-leasing brings in only $5? That presents a nasty problem—indeed, that means that Comdisco is looking at a $10 write-off.

***

Nor is the way "fees" are treated an idle, theoretical matter. It is vitally important to Comdisco's bottom line. For such fees comprise the bulk of the company's "financial services" revenues. And although revenues from computer sales and rentals are two to three times greater, the company's big profit center is clearly financial services. Peter Labe, an analyst at Smith Barney, a firm that has done investment banking for Comdisco, claims in a recent report that financial services "account for the bulk of corporate profits."

Comdisco doesn't dispute it. "No question," says Comdisco's Vosicky, "a large percentage of the profits are attributed to tax-advantaged transactions."

About 80–90%?

"I wouldn't say 90%," says Vosicky. "It depends on how you want to slice the pie." Profitability, he points out, depends on the allocation of general and administrative expenses. And Comdisco financials do not break out this information.

"I think it would be correct to say," continues Vosicky, "that the primary reason for the earnings increase is because of tax-advantaged transactions or financial services."

The bulk of the increase rather than the bulk of earnings?

"Yes."

In other words, the big leap in pretax earnings from $21 million in 1981 to $53 million in 1982 is primarily because of the tax-advantaged deals?

"Yes. I think that would be fair to say."

And if all fees had been reduced by the amount of investment in the equipment, how much less would financial services revenues have been in 1982?

"A lot of that revenue came from safe harbor leasing transactions where we don't have any investment. . . ."

But if the investment in equipment on all the other leases in 1982 was netted out, how much would financial services be reduced?

"It would probably be cut in half," replies Vosicky. "I would think at least cut in half."

And so this year, with no safe harbor leases, netting out all the investment in equipment would cause an even greater drop in financial services?

"Yet, it would."

Insofar as Comdisco reports profits now from the equipment leased—and leaves residual value on the books to be recovered later—it increases its exposure to obsolescence. And as of September 1982, the date of the most recent balance sheet with full footnotes, that exposure was considerable, at least in comparison with the company's net worth.

***

EXHIBIT 3

Letter to Shareholders

October 12, 1983

Dear Stockholders:

As I'm sure most of you know by now, the October 10, 1983 issue of Barron's includes an article about our Company. I believe the article and its subsequent impact on the price of the Company's stock entitle our stockholders to a clarification of the facts underlying the key issues raised. The article emphasizes four main areas: (1) The Company's accounting; (2) competition from IBM Credit Corporation; (3) our tax advantaged investment program; and (4) sales by insiders.

Accounting

The article raises questions concerning the Company's accounting policy with respect to the investment risk taken on leased equipment and implies that our policy with respect to payments from tax advantaged leases could result in an overstatement of income. Under the Company's depreciation policy, our leased equipment portfolio as of June 30, 1983 will be depreciated to a net book value at lease termination of $112,000,000. The estimated fair market value of this equipment at lease termination (as provided by independent forecasts from International Data Corporation, a highly regarded equipment valuation expert) was in excess of $279,000,000, a coverage ratio of nearly 2.5 to 1. The facts demonstrate that the Company's policies are conservative, and have created a potential significant source of future earnings. The specific financial implications of our policies are as follows:

(1) Equipment Values

While generally accepted accounting principles require varied accounting treatments for different types of leases, the central issue is the same for all of the Company's leases: Is the Company's depreciation policy reasonable, thus eliminating the likelihood of a future write-off? The answer is that our depreciation policy is reasonable, and, in fact, produced book values of leased equipment which are substantially less than the values estimated by independent industry experts, as shown by the table below:

Total Lease Portfolio at June 30, 1983 (000's omitted)

Lease Type	Net Book Value at Lease Termination	Estimated Fair Market Value at Lease Termination[*]	IBM List Price
Operating leases	$92,000	$208,000	$876,000
Sales type and direct financing leases	20,000	63,000	847,000
Other	—	8,000	60,000
	$112,000	$279,000	$1,783,000

[*]Source: International Data Corporation.

As shown above, fair market value estimates prepared by International Data Corporation provide a substantial margin over the Company's net book value at lease termination. This is still true even if the equipment is sold under a tax advantaged transaction. Since most tax advantaged transactions are structured so that the equipment will have a zero net book value by the time any tax advantaged investor shares in the fair market value proceeds, this sharing will not have a significant effect on the margin of fair market value available to the Company over the net book value at lease termination.

Another method of evaluating our depreciation policy is to review the operating lease portfolio (which comprises 82% of the total lease portfolio) by comparing, by year of termination, net book value at lease termination to estimated fair market value at lease termination. The following table illustrates this comparison:

Operating Lease Portfolio at June 30, 1983 (000's omitted)

Fiscal Year of Termination	Net Book Value at Lease Termination	Estimated Fair Market Value at Lease Termination	Estimated Excess Fair Market Value
1983	$16,000	$22,000	$6,000
1984	30,000	53,000	23,000
1985	19,000	50,000	31,000
1986	14,000	46,000	32,000
1987	13,000	37,000	24,000
	$92,000	$208,000	$116,000

Our auditors, Peat, Marwick, Mitchell & Co., review and agree with the Company's depreciation policies.

Referring to the foregoing table, it should be noted that 71% of the Company's operating lease book value is represented by leases which terminate by September 30, 1985. This short time period increases the reliability of residual value estimates. Equally as important, the Company has historically realized more from the remarketing of leased computer equipment than the value carried on its books, resulting in additional profit at the point of remarketing.

(2) Revenue Recognition
The sale of leased equipment in a tax advantaged transaction is separate from the underlying user lease transaction and results in payments to the Company from the investor. Revenue is recognized from these transactions in accordance with one of two basic methods:

(a) For all equipment where the underlying user lease term is five years or longer, and generally for all 308X mainframe transactions, these investor payments are first applied to reduce the Company's investment in the equipment. Any excess over the investment is recorded in the period in which the tax advantaged transaction occurs. During fiscal 1982 and the nine months ended June 30, 1983, the Company generated $83,160,000 of such payments. The Company's investment in the equipment was reduced by $43,890,000 and the difference, $39,270,000, was recorded as financial services during this period.

(b) For equipment where the underlying user lease term is less than five years (except for 308X mainframe transactions) these investor payments are recognized in the period in which the tax advantaged lease transaction occurs. This accounting treatment is appropriate since the Company's depreciation policy results in net book values at the end of the initial user lease term (typically 2–3 years) that already is less than fair market value estimates. To further reduce the Company's net book value for such equipment would materially understate current income and overstate future income by reducing or eliminating depreciation charges against future rental income.

Competition from IBM Credit Corporation

IBM has been Comdisco's single largest competitor for the entire 14 years Comdisco has been in business. Through its direct lease and rental programs, IBM has always been the dominant force in the computer leasing industry. IBM's increasing emphasis on generating equipment sales, however, is reflected in its withdrawal from the direct leasing business, which has resulted in a greatly expanding third party leasing market.

IBM Credit Corporation's (ICC) entry into the third party leasing business merely replaces part of the parent company's participation in leasing. ICC is participating in the third party market as a broker in much the same way as Comdisco. Comdisco has access to the same debt and equity markets as ICC, and on terms that will at most be only marginally less attractive to Comdisco than to ICC.

Tax Advantaged Investment Program

Our tax advantaged transactions have been carefully structured and documented. These transactions are bona fide investments with real economic substance and profit potential to the investor. They provide a valuable and effective way for individuals to provide capital for and participate in the equipment leasing industry. We take great pride in our reputation for providing a high quality computer leasing investment.

Like any tax advantaged investment, these transactions have certain tax risks, such as the possibility of IRS challenge and the risk of an adverse change in federal tax laws. We have made every effort to minimize these risks. Our nationally recognized tax counsel have provided their opinion that these transactions qualify as true leases for federal tax purposes under current law. We constantly monitor proposed federal tax changes, and we know of no imminent changes in federal tax laws or regulations affecting tax advantaged "wraparound" leases of computer equipment.

While these transactions have contributed substantially to Comdisco's profitability in recent years, our continued success in the computer equipment marketplace is not dependent on our ability to offer this specific form of transaction to investors. Nor does Comdisco's success depend on continuation of the status quo with respect to federal tax policy. We have employed and continue to employ a variety of transaction structures and have a history of adapting quickly to changes in the federal tax law and the marketplace. In fact, previous changes in federal tax laws and in the marketplace have often created significant opportunities for Comdisco.

Management Stockholdings

Management currently holds approximately 8,950,000 shares or 31% of the outstanding shares of the Company. These shares represent an ownership interest of approximately $240,000,000, based on the closing price on the New York Stock Exchange as of October 11, 1983. Over the years, sales of common stock have been made periodically by management. Tax liabilities created as a result of the exercise of stock options and sales by a retired senior executive who still owns approximately 650,000 shares account for a significant portion of these sales. The remaining sales are not significant when compared to current insider holdings.

Conclusion

In 1969, when we started Comdisco, we committed ourselves to building our business based on the principle of serving our customers with the highest degree of integrity and professionalism. Fortunately, over the years we have attracted talented individuals who share that commitment and who continue to value the principles of service, integrity and professionalism just as we did in 1969. We feel that our reputation and the trust that we have developed with our customers, our equity and debt investors, and our stockholders are our most valuable assets. We have not, and will not, compromise these principles in the conduct of our business.

Finally, it is important for you, our stockholders, to understand completely that Comdisco is stronger financially that it has ever been; that we have greater opportunities before us than at any time in our history; and that management is dedicated to retaining stockholder confidence and enhancing stockholder wealth.

Sincerely,

Kenneth N. Pontikes
(President)

EXHIBIT 4

Annual Report for Fiscal Year 1983 (edited by case writer)

To Our Stockholders

I am pleased to report that in fiscal 1983 your Company continued its outstanding growth and performance. Net earnings for fiscal 1983 of $51.8 million, or $1.78 per share, represented increases of 76% and 56%, respectively, over fiscal 1982 results. Total revenue increased 15% to $543.2 million. Your Company's continued success in the lease placement of IBM computer equipment, particularly 308X mainframes and 3380 disc storage devices, and in financial services activities were the primary reasons for the record results achieved. Dividends were increased 36% in fiscal 1983 from $.11 to $.15 per share, as adjusted for the 2-for-1 stock split distributed in March, 1983.

Leasing Activity. Leasing activity increased dramatically in fiscal 1983 as Comdisco entered into 3,470 new leases with total rentals in excess of $1 billion during the initial lease terms. This compares to 2,259 leases and over $700 million in total rentals for leases entered into during fiscal 1982. Comdisco leased to its customers 3380 disk storage devices and 3380 disk controllers with an initial cost in excess of $200 million in fiscal 1983. In addition the Company leased 308X mainframes having an aggregate purchase price of $289 million.

The large volume of 308X mainframe lease transactions did not correspondingly increase the Company's total revenue since these leases are required to be accounted for as direct financing leases. Under direct financing lease accounting only the net margins are recorded as revenue, not the gross rentals as under operating lease accounting (see Understanding Comdisco's Accounting for detailed explanation).

Pursuant to the Economic Recovery Tax Act of 1981, Comdisco elected in fiscal 1982 to sell tax benefits, including investment tax credits, to other corporations, and recorded the proceeds as financial services revenue. These "tax benefit transfers" increased both total revenue and earnings before taxes, but the corresponding reduction in investment tax credits increased the effective income tax rate to 45.4%. In fiscal 1983 the large volume of 308X mainframe and 3380 disk storage equipment purchased for its leasing activity increased the amount of investment tax credit available to Comdisco. Because of changes in tax laws in late 1982 effectively eliminating tax benefit transfers, it was no longer attractive for Comdisco to enter into these transactions, so these investment tax credits were utilized for its own account. Investment tax credits of $22 million were earned in fiscal 1983, including $12 million in the fourth quarter, reducing the effective income tax rate to 12%.

Financial Services Activity. In fiscal 1982, proceeds from tax benefit transfers were recorded as financial services revenue. As I mentioned earlier, these tax benefit transfers had the effect of increasing revenue and income tax expense. In fiscal 1983, most of the financial services revenue was generated by the sale of leased equipment in the Company's tax advantaged transactions (see Understanding Comdisco's Accounting). In tax advantaged transactions, Comdisco retains any available investment tax credit. Equipment with a fair market value of $430.2 million was sold under tax advantaged transactions in fiscal 1983 compared to $253.0 million of equipment for the prior year.

Marketplace Perspective. In fiscal 1984, the data processing industry is expected to continue its annual growth rate of 15–25%. IBM Corporation continues to be the dominant factor in the computer leasing industry through its direct lease and rental programs.

However, in recent years IBM has been emphasizing the sale of its equipment, with less emphasis on direct leasing. This is reflected in IBM's pricing strategy which favors the purchase of equipment. For example, during fiscal 1983, IBM reduced lessee purchase option credits to make its leasing program even less attractive. In addition, IBM will eliminate, as of January 1, 1984 its practice of passing through investment tax credits to its lessees. IBM's reduced emphasis on direct leasing has led to increased user demand for third party lease financing, resulting in higher growth in the third party computer leasing marketplace. Your Company is successfully participating in this expanding market.

IBM Credit Corporation has entered the third party leasing market, replacing part of IBM's participation in this market. However, we do not expect this development to adversely affect our competitive position. We believe IBM Credit Corporation to be a reasonable competitor which will not take unacceptable risks nor assume unrealistic residual values. Also, Comdisco has access to the same debt and equity markets as IBM Credit Corporation. Finally, and of critical importance, users of computer equipment need to remarket existing equipment when new equipment is acquired. Because IBM Credit Corporation does not remarket displaced equipment, Comdisco still retains an advantage by virtue of its ability to remarket used equipment. No company is better situated to handle all of its customers' need than Comdisco.

Activity in 308X mainframe and 3380 disk drives remains very strong, with your Company continuing to increase its market share. Comdisco's success in an expanding, competitive marketplace is directly attributable to its superior remarketing and lease financing capabilities.

Financial Condition and Liquidity. In fiscal 1983 Comdisco converted its $50 million of 13% convertible debentures into common stock and subsequently issued $250 million of 8% convertible debentures. As a result of these and other factors, Comdisco is in a stronger financial position than it has ever been. Stockholders' equity increased 110% to $91.5 million during fiscal 1983. At September 30, 1983 total assets were nearly $1 billion and cash and marketable securities exceeded $230 million. The continued improvement in your Company's financial condition was recognized by Moody's Investors Service, which raised Comdisco's bond rating for its convertible debentures to BA2 in fiscal 1983.

Personnel Changes. In fiscal 1983, the number of employees increased to 504, enhancing your Company's commitment to full customer service and helping to support continued growth. In November 1983, Raymond F. Sebastian was promoted to Executive Vice President from Senior Vice President-Corporate Development. Mr. Sebastian, an officer of Comdisco for eight years, will continue to oversee corporate development and take on additional administrative duties. In October 1983 Nicholas M. DiBari resigned his positions as Senior Vice President-Marketing and as a Director, for personal reasons. Mr. DiBari made valuable contributions to Comdisco's marketing structure and philosophy. Robert A. Bardagy has replaced Mr. DiBari as Senior Vice President-Marketing and as a Director. For the past six years, Mr. Bardagy has

been responsible for the Company's market making and trading programs.

Other Activities. In fiscal 1983, the Company announced its Corporate Lease Line Program. The Corporate Lease Line Program allows the Company's customers to lease almost all types of capital equipment at attractive lease rates with very little administrative burden. The Company has the ability to administer the program based on the customer's requirements. This program is expected to make a substantial contribution to fiscal 1984 results. Comdisco Disaster Recovery Services has increased its capabilities to meet the growing demands for its services. The contributions of Comdisco Technical Services and Comdisco Maintenance Services assist the Company in providing the whole array of services required by a data processing operation. The Company's international operations continue to contribute significantly to our profitability. Finally, our ability to capitalize on opportunities both inside and outside of our basic industry has never been greater.

A recent misunderstanding of Comdisco has led to lower market prices for our common stock. Accordingly, we expanded this Annual Report to describe our key operations and our accounting policies in greater detail. By any measurement, there are few publicly-held companies that can match Comdisco's performance since its inception in 1969. For the last five years the Company's compound growth rate for net earnings was an outstanding 60%, while net earnings per share and total revenue had growth rates of 46% and 29%, respectively. In fiscal 1983 return on average equity was 37%, with a 5-year average return of 33%. Comdisco's record speaks for itself.

I am proud of Comdisco's performance in fiscal 1983 and even prouder of the efforts and devotion of our employees. Without their outstanding efforts, we would not have achieved the success we have enjoyed. The support of our lenders, customers and you, our shareholders, is particularly gratifying. The first quarter of fiscal 1984 started out as our most active quarter ever, and I am confident that fiscal 1984 will prove to be Comdisco's most successful year to date.

Kenneth N. Pontikes
Chairman of the Board and President
November 28, 1983

Leasing's Four Fundamental Values

Initially, Comdisco was a computer equipment dealer, buying and selling equipment for its own account. Exceptional marketing capability helped make Comdisco the largest dealer in the industry by 1976.

By the late 1970's, market conditions had shifted and demand for computer leasing increased dramatically. Based on its exceptional marketing capability, Comdisco's emerging leasing operation quickly grew to become the Company's most significant business activity. Both dealer activity and the leasing operation—supported by unmatched remarketing capabilities—now contribute to Comdisco's overall success.

Today, Comdisco's fundamental business, the foundation on which its exceptional pattern of financial performance is based, is leasing—primarily the leasing of new and used IBM computer equipment. And, as business and institutions world-wide become more and more information driven, the demand for data processing systems will continue to grow.

Leasing is widely recognized as the most attractive alternative to purchasing multi-million dollar computer systems. Over the years, Comdisco has achieved leadership in the field, having built a lease portfolio of IBM equipment currently valued at approximately $1 billion.

The leasing business also creates values that enable Comdisco to capitalize on other related sources of revenue and earnings. At the core of Comdisco's business, there are four such fundamental values.

Initial User Lease—Value One

When Comdisco leases its new or used computer equipment to a customer, the customer's rental payments during the original lease term are the primary source of revenue. In fiscal 1983, for example, the Company entered into 3,470 leases having total lease payments of over $1 billion during the initial lease terms.

Lease contracts cannot be canceled, and the customer has full responsibility for maintenance and other expenses. Most leases have terms of two to five years.

These leases also allow Comdisco to finance its leasing growth through "nonrecourse debt." Typically, Comdisco takes an existing lease to a bank and assigns the stream of lease payments to the bank. In return, the bank gives Comdisco cash that is equal to the present value of the lease payment stream at market interest rates. The debt is nonrecourse because the bank looks to the lease payments to repay the loan. This nonrecourse debt for operating leases is recorded as "Discounted Lease Rentals" on Comdisco's Balance Sheet. Interest rates are fixed in this transaction, eliminating Comdisco's exposure to rate fluctuations. Comdisco retains ownership of the computer equipment.

Comdisco's continued success in computer leasing is supported by a variety of factors discussed in greater detail on the following pages of this Annual Report. Among them are a customer relationship with 70% of the *Fortune 500* companies, a proprietary data base containing information on all major data processing installations, a seasoned sales team with offices in key markets throughout the U.S., Canada and Europe, and a complete line of customer support services.

Remarketing Capacity—Value Two

Data processing technology is among the most dynamic in the history of world commerce. The marketplace has a virtually insatiable appetite for increased capacity and a constant stream of new technological advancements.

With change as one of the few constants in the industry, Comdisco's unmatched capacity to remarket equipment is a fundamental component in the Company's formula for success. Indeed, leasing customers place a significant value on Comdisco's market making ability. As new products enter the marketplace, customers know that Comdisco has a unique capacity to remarket existing equipment, making it financially feasible to upgrade systems to a competitive, state-of-the-art level.

Comdisco's ability to capitalize on re-lease values and residual values is directly related to exceptional market penetration, its proprietary data base of marketing information, its professional sales force, and the Company's expertise in computer equipment and that equipment's life cycle.

Tax Benefits—Value Three

Tax benefits are an integral part of any leasing operation. Substantial tax benefits—particularly in the form of investment tax credits and accelerated depreciation deductions—are generated through Comdisco's acquisition of computer equipment.

Comdisco has a number of valuable alternatives concerning these tax benefits. Comdisco can claim the investment tax credits, thus reducing its own income tax. The Company can also choose to pass the investment tax credit through to the lessee in exchange for higher rentals. Or, as a third option, leveraged lease transactions with third party investors can also be arranged. This option has the effect of passing on all benefits of ownership, including tax and residual values. The compensation leasing companies typically receive is a lump sum payment and a share in the residual value of the leased equipment.

The capacity of the Company's basic leasing business, which generates significant tax benefits, allows Comdisco to capitalize on certain favorable tax laws. Such laws can be traced to the Congress' longstanding desire to provide industry with incentives for capital spending. Both investment tax credits and accelerated depreciation deductions are the product of laws that reflect this Congressional intent. Comdisco generates value by structuring transactions which permit the full utilization of the tax benefits associated with its equipment portfolio. Comdisco has demonstrated its ability to profitably structure transactions in response to changes in tax laws. As long as Congress continues to encourage capital spending, the Company's control of equipment will enable it to continue structuring attractive tax-oriented transactions.

For example, in 1981 Congress devised "Safe Harbor Leasing" of equipment as a method for transferring tax benefits from one corporation to another. Called "tax benefit transfers," compensation for tax benefits was paid in a single lump sum at the beginning of the lease. Tax

benefit transfers were, in effect, simply the sale of investment tax credits and depreciation benefits. In 1982, as part of the Tax Equity and Fiscal Responsibility Act of 1982 (TEFRA), Congress effectively eliminated Safe Harbor Leasing. In doing so, Congress did not change its desire to stimulate capital investment through tax incentives, as evidenced by the fact that in 1984 a new type of tax-oriented lease, the finance lease, will be permitted.

Despite the effective elimination of Safe Harbor Leasing, Comdisco continues to be in a position to generate value from significant investment tax credits and ownership rights to substantial amounts of equipment. While the laws have changed, the Congressional philosophy underlying tax-oriented leasing has not.

Tax Advantaged Transactions—Value Four

The fourth fundamental value of Comdisco's leasing activity is the tax advantaged transaction. In this alternative, Comdisco may sell equipment that is under an initial user lease to an independent third party. This is a completely separate transaction having no effect on the equipment user. The buyer is typically an individual or corporate investor who wants to share in the financial rewards of leasing—re-lease values, residual values and tax benefits.

When Comdisco sells computer equipment in a tax advantaged transaction, it receives an equity payment from the buyer in an amount equal to between 10% and 22% of the equipment's fair market value. In return for this equity payment, the new owner receives: (a) the accelerated depreciation benefits on the equipment, (b) a portion of the lease rentals in the sixth and seventh years after the sale is made, and (c) 100% of the equipment's value after the seventh year.

The utilization of tax benefits, either by the Company for its own account or by an investor as a result of a tax advantaged transaction, results in a lower effective cost to the equipment user, which is in accordance with Congress' objective to stimulate capital expenditures.

These four values form the core of Comdisco's business—leasing activity, computer remarketing, tax benefits and tax advantaged transactions. Understanding these values is key to understanding Comdisco's growth potential and how the Company effectively minimizes the business risk in its operations.

Understanding Comdisco's Accounting

Lease Accounting

Comdisco accounts for its lease transactions in accordance with the rules set forth in Accounting for Leases (FASB 13) prescribed by the Financial Accounting Standards Board. FASB 13 contains guidelines for classifying lease transactions as one of the following three types:

- sales-type lease
- direct financing lease
- operating lease

A lease is classified and accounted for as sales-type or direct financing by Comdisco if it meets any one of the following criteria:

a. The lease transfers ownership of the property to the lessee (Comdisco's customer) by the end of the lease term;
b. The lease contains an option allowing the lessee to purchase the property at a bargain price;
c. The lease term is equal to 75% or more of the estimated economic life of the property; or
d. The present value of the rentals is equal to 90% or more of the fair market value of the leased property, less any related investment tax credit retained by Comdisco.

The majority of Comdisco's sales-type and direct financing leases are classified as such because they meet criterion d above.

If the leased equipment is new or purchased from the lessee (purchase/lease-back) and meets one or more of the preceding criteria, the lease is recorded as a direct financing lease; otherwise, the lease is recorded as a sales-type lease. All other leases which do not meet one or more of the preceding criteria are classified and accounted for as operating leases. Operating leases are generally shorter term leases (2–4 years).

Sales-Type Lease. A sales-type lease is recorded in the income statement as "Sale of computer equipment," along with other sales. The amount recorded as a sale is the present value of the lease payments. The cost of the equipment less the present value of estimated residual value at lease termination, if any, is recorded in the income statement as "Cost of computer equipment."

Direct Financing Lease. It is Comdisco's policy to finance all of its direct financing leases on a nonrecourse basis. Therefore, the net margin for a direct financing lease is recorded as "other revenue." The net margin represents the sum of the proceeds from the financing of the lease plus the present value of estimated residual value at lease termination, if any, less the equipment cost.

The present value of the residual values of sales-type and direct financing leases and the present value of the noncancellable lease rentals, prior to their financing, are included in the balance sheets as "Net investment in sales-type and direct financing leases."

Operating Lease. Revenue under an operating lease is recorded as payments accrue, that is, on a monthly basis over the term of the lease. The depreciation expense is also recorded on a monthly basis and the equipment cost is recorded on the Company's balance sheet as "Leased computer equipment."

To summarize, the revenue recognition effects of the three different types of leases is as follows:

- For a sales-type lease, the present value of the lease rentals is recorded as "Sale of computer equipment" at the closing of the transaction.
- For a direct financing lease, the net margin is recorded as "Other revenue."
- For an operating lease, the monthly rentals are recorded as "Rental revenue" over the term of the lease.

Effect of Direct Financing Leases. In fiscal 1983 a substantial portion of leases written by Comdisco were recorded as direct financing leases. Because only the net margins on these leases are recorded, the total leasing volume that Comdisco transacted in fiscal 1983 is understated when compared to prior years when many fewer direct financing leases were recorded. The following table sets forth the cumulative increase in rental revenue that would have been recorded in recent fiscal years if Comdisco had recorded all direct financing leases as operating leases:

a. Column A represents rentals reported in the Company's income statement for the respective years.

	Rental Revenue (in thousands)		
Fiscal Year	As Reported (A)	Increase (B)	Pro Forma
1979	$60,947	$9,634	$70,581
1980	80,979	14,612	95,591
1981	131,571	24,220	155,791
1982	206,592	65,284	271,876
1983	266,628	179,528	446,156

b. Column B represents rentals due under direct financing leases that are not recorded as rental revenue because of the accounting treatment afforded direct financing leases.

As a result, the actual increase in the volume of leasing is not apparent from a review of the Company's income statement.

Residual Values. Residual value is an estimate of the value of the equipment that is expected to be realized at the end of the lease term for sales-type and direct financing leases. Comdisco records the present value of a conservative estimate of residual value.

Depreciation. All of Comdisco's leased equipment under operating leases is depreciated to zero within five years, with a higher rate applicable to the period covered by the initial user lease. Operating leases are depreciated to Comdisco's estimate of fair market value at lease termination. These conservative estimates are supported by forecasts prepared by International Data Corporation (IDC), a recognized expert in residual value projections for computer equipment. In fact, at September 30, 1983 IDC's fair market value projections are 242% of the equipment's net book value at lease termination. As a result of this conservative depreciation policy, the Company has constantly realized substantially more proceeds on the sale or re-lease of its equipment than its recorded book value.

The following table projects the runoff of the Company's September 30, 1983 operating lease portfolio. The table compares the net book value of the equipment to its estimated fair market value in the fiscal year in which the existing leases terminate. Fair market value represents IDC estimates of the equipment value at lease termination.

Comdisco, Inc.—Operating Lease Portfolio Runoff as of September 30, 1983

	Fair Market Value Comparison to Net Book Value (in thousands)		
Fiscal Year of Termination	Net Book Value at Termination	Estimated Fair Market Value at Termination	Estimated Fair Excess Fair Market Value over Net Book Value
1984	$34,725	$70,234	$35,509
1985	15,665	43,682	28,017
1986	18,869	48,868	29,999
1987	13,820	36,525	22,705
1988	1,170	4,191	3,021
Total	$84,249	$203,500	$119,251

Tax Advantaged Transaction

While the specific terms and conditions of tax advantaged transactions vary, the following is a general description of a typical tax advantaged transaction:

1. At a date after the inception of the initial user lease and independent thereof, the Company may sell all or some of the leased equipment to a third party investor ("investor"). If the equipment is sold to an investor, the sale generally occurs three to nine months after the commencement of the initial user lease. The sales price equals the then current fair market value of the equipment and is paid in the form of:

    (a) cash and a negotiable, interest-bearing promissory note (due within two years) for 10–22% of the sales price (the "equity payment"), and

    (b) an installment note for the balance (90–78% of the sales price) payable over an 84-month period.

2. Simultaneously with the sale, the Company leases such equipment back from the investor for 84 months. The lease payments payable under the leaseback obligation generally are equal to the installment payments receivable under the installment note described in 1(b) above.

3. As part of the leaseback arrangement, during the 61st through 84th month of the leaseback period, the investor also shares in the re-lease proceeds that the company receives from subleasing the equipment. Upon the expiration of the leaseback period, the investor has the exclusive right to the equipment.

In summary, the Company has given up the accelerated depreciation benefits on the equipment for tax purposes, a portion of the rentals for months 61–84 and 100% of the equipment value after the 84th month in exchange for the non-refundable equity payment. This equity payment is the only portion of the tax advantaged transaction that is recorded by the Company.

Revenue Recognition. Revenue is recognized, according to the lease classification, in the following manner:

1. For equipment subject to operating leases, the equity payment is recognized as financial services revenue in the period in which the tax advantaged transaction occurs. The Company allocates as a cost a percentage of the net book value at the expiration of the

initial user lease to the revenue from the tax advantaged transaction because of its decreased right to re-lease rentals. In all cases, the equipment sold under tax advantaged transactions is fully depreciated prior to the time the investor is entitled to share in re-lease rentals.

2. For sales-type and direct financing leases, the Company may record on its balance sheet an estimated residual value at the inception of the initial user lease. The equity payment is first applied to remove a portion of that residual value. The residual value is decreased because the Company's ability to recover such residual value is reduced by the rental sharing under the tax advantaged transaction. Any excess of the equity payment over the reduction of residual value is recorded as financial services revenue in the period in which the tax advantaged transaction occurs.

Lease accounting and tax advantaged transactions represent two of the more complex areas of Comdisco's accounting. See the footnotes to the Consolidated Financial Statements for additional information.

Management's Discussion and Analysis of Financial Condition and Results of Operations

Summary

Fiscal 1983 was the third consecutive year of record revenue and earnings for the Company. Total revenue for fiscal 1983 and 1982 was $543.2 million and $471.6 million, respectively. Net earnings increased from $29.4 million, or $1.14 per share, in fiscal 1982 to $51.8 million, or $1.78 per share, in fiscal 1983. The Company's continued success in the lease placement of IBM computer equipment, particularly 308X mainframes and 3380 disk storage devices, and in financial services activities were the primary reasons for the record results achieved.

Revenue

Total revenue increased 15% over the prior fiscal year. The increase in total revenue in fiscal 1983 was not as dramatic as the increase in fiscal 1982 despite the substantial increase in the number of lease transactions in fiscal 1983, primarily

because of the different mix in lease transactions entered into in fiscal 1983. The lease classification, as determined by FASB Statement No. 13, "Accounting for Leases," has a significant effect on the manner in which revenue is recorded. During fiscal 1983, there was an active market for 308X mainframes, which were recorded as direct financing leases. In fiscal 1982, there was an active market for 308X mainframes, which were recorded as direct financing leases. In fiscal 1982, a larger percentage of leases were accounted for as operating leases. Under operating lease accounting, the gross rental is recognized in equal monthly amounts over the lease term as rental revenue. Since the Company finances most of its direct financing leases on a nonrecourse basis, the net margins are recorded as other revenue. The net margin represents the sum of the present value of the lease rentals, plus the present value of estimated residual value at lease termination, if any, less the equipment.

The growth of the Company's leasing activity continued on a strong upward trend in fiscal 1983. During fiscal 1983, the Company entered into 3,467 new leases with rental payments of $1.1 billion during the initial lease terms. This compared to 2,259 new leases and $702 million of rental payments during the initial lease term or the prior fiscal year. Rental revenue from equipment subject to operating leases increased 29% in comparison to the year earlier. The increase in operating leases in fiscal 1983 was primarily due to the high volume of lease placements of IBM's newest disk storage device, the 3380.

Revenue from the sale of computer equipment increased during fiscal 1983, primarily as a result of an active international market for 308X mainframes.

Financial services revenue for fiscal 1983 totaled $65.6 million, in comparison to $73.9 million in fiscal 1982 and $30.8 million in fiscal 1981. While the total financial services activity increased in volume during 1983, such increase is not reflected in financial services revenue in comparison to 1982. Pursuant to the Economic Recovery Tax Act of 1981, the Company elected in fiscal 1982 to sell tax benefits, including investment tax credits, to other corporations and recorded the proceeds as financial services revenue. In fiscal 1983, most of the financial services revenue was generated by the sales of leased equipment through the Company's tax advantaged transactions with the Company retaining any available investment tax credits on the equipment. In essence, in fiscal 1983, the investment tax credits associated with leasing were reflected in the reduced income tax rate, while in fiscal 1982, the sale of such benefits was reflected in higher financial services revenue. Financial services revenue for fiscal 1983 and 1982 includes $6.0 million and $13.8 million, respectively, of net revenue generated by arranging leases between third parties.

Other revenue for fiscal 1983 totaled $39.8 million in comparison to $24.5 million in fiscal 1982 and $13.7 million in fiscal 1981. The increase in fiscal 1983 is primarily due to higher revenue from direct financing leases, interest income earned on short term investments and higher revenues from the Company's disaster recovery services.

Cost and Expenses

Total costs and expenses of $484.3 million for fiscal 1983 increased 16% over total costs and expenses of $417.8 million in fiscal 1982. Fiscal 1982 total costs and expenses were 49% higher than fiscal 1981. The increases were the result of the growth in the Company's leasing activities and the continuing expansion in the marketing of its services.

Interest expense for fiscal 1983 totaled $53.7 million in comparison to $47.2 million in fiscal 1982 and $33.7 million in fiscal 1981. The primary component is the interest expense associated with the discounting of operating leases. This represented 67%, 69%, and 46% of total interest expense in fiscal 1983, 1982, and 1981, respectively. The Company finances leases by assigning the noncancellable rentals to financial institutions on a nonrecourse basis at fixed interest rates and receives from the lender the present value of the rental payments (the discounted amount). For operating leases, the Company recognizes interest expense over the term of the lease.

The redemption of the Company's 13% Convertible Debentures Due 2001 reduced the Company's interest expense by approximately $5.3 million in fiscal 1983. Interest expense on the 8% convertible debentures issued May 1, 1983 totaled $8.2 million. The increases in interest expense in fiscal 1982 and fiscal 1981 were due to increased discounted lease rentals as a result of the growth in the Company's leased equipment portfolio.

Income Taxes

Income taxes as a percentage of earnings before income taxes were 11.9% in fiscal 1983 compared to 45.4% in fiscal 1982 and 26.8% in fiscal 1981. The higher effective tax rate in fiscal 1982 was attributable to lower investment tax credits due to the sale of such benefits by the Company as permitted under the Economic Recovery Tax Act of 1981. No significant tax benefit transfer leases were originated by the Company in fiscal 1983 and the Company retained the investment tax credits for its account, thereby reducing the effective tax rate to 11.9% in fiscal 1983. Note 10 of Notes to Consolidated Financial Statements provides details about the Company's income tax provisions and effective tax rates.

International Operations

The Company operates principally in three geographic areas: the United States, Europe and Canada. The Company has subsidiaries in

Belgium, West Germany, Switzerland, the Netherlands, France, Sweden, Denmark, the United Kingdom and Canada. These subsidiaries offer services similar to those offered in the United States. A strong demand for IBM 308X processors, principally in Europe, resulted in an increase in revenue from international operations of 25% from $79.4 million in fiscal 1982 to $98.9 million in fiscal 1983. International revenues represented 18% of the Company's total revenue in fiscal 1983 and 17% in fiscal 1982.

Market and Dividend Information

The Company's common stock is traded on the New York Stock Exchange under the symbol CDO. The quarterly price range and dividends paid for fiscal year 1983 and 1982, adjusted to reflect the two-for-one and three-for-two common stock splits effected in March 1983 and March 1982, respectively, are shown below:

	1983			1982		
Qtr.	High	Low	Dvds.	High	Low	Dvd.
First	$18.38	$10.56	$.03	$9.00	$5.88	$.02
Second	27.13	16.56	.04	9.00	6.75	.03
Third	37.88	22.75	.04	9.63	7.75	.03
Fourth	42.00	34.25	.04	11.50	7.50	.03

At September 30, 1983, there were approximately 5,000 record holders of common stock.

Financial Condition

The Company's stockholders' equity increased substantially during fiscal 1983 as a result of the Company's record earnings and the conversion of $50,000,000 of 13% convertible subordinated debentures. Cash and marketable securities totaled $232.6 million at September 30, 1983. In May 1983 the Company sold $250,000,000 of 8% convertible subordinated debentures, the primary reason for the increase in cash and marketable securities. The proceeds of the offering were used to finance the increase in the Company's leasing activities and to invest in short-term marketable securities.

At September 30, 1983, the Company had $40 million of available borrowing capacity under various lines of credit from commercial banks and no short term debt.

The Company's current financial resources and estimated cash flow from operations will be adequate to fund anticipated requirements for fiscal 1984. The major portion of funds required by the Company to finance its leasing operations is provided by assigning the noncancellable rentals to various financial institutions at fixed interest rates on a nonrecourse basis. The Company's liquidity is aided by the maturation of its lease portfolio, since the remarketing of its leased equipment generates substantial funds. For example, the successful remarketing of equipment under leases which expire in fiscal 1984 is estimated to generate funds in excess of $50 million.

Total notes and debentures as a percentage of total capital (the sum of notes and debentures payable, discounted lease rentals and stockholders' equity) was 32%, 16%, and 20% at September 30, 1983, 1982, and 1981, respectively.

Ratios

The following table presents ratios which illustrate the changes and trends in earnings for the last three fiscal years:

	1983	1982	1981
Return on average stockholders' equity	36.7%	39.2%	30.6%
Return on average assets	6.9%	6.2%	4.9%
Earnings before income taxes (as a percentage of revenue)	10.8%	11.4%	7.1%
Net earnings (as a percentage of revenue)	9.5%	6.2%	5.2%

FIVE YEAR SELECTED FINANCIAL DATA

Years ended September 30,	1983	1982	1981	1980	1979
Consolidated Summary of earnings					
(in thousands)					
Revenue					
Rental	**$266,628**	$206,592	$131,571	$80,979	$60,947
Sale of computer equipment	**171,138**	166,705	125,384	149,708	149,983
Financial services	**65,635**	73,879	30,837	14,079	9,991
Other	**39,779**	24,454	13,746	8,348	4,355
Total revenue	**543,180**	471,630	301,538	253,114	225,276
Cost and expenses					
Equipment depreciation, amortization and rental	**214,439**	160,523	99,413	68,328	47,698
Cost of computer equipment	**151,573**	149,654	111,784	134,595	128,470
Selling, general and administrative	**64,655**	60,402	35,313	24,219	21,284
Interest	**53,673**	47,242	33,657	16,988	13,319
Total costs and expenses	**484,340**	417,821	280,167	244,130	210,771
Earnings before income taxes	**58,840**	53,809	21,371	8,984	14,505
Income taxes	**7,000**	24,432	5,730	1,870	3,900
Net earnings	**$51,840**	$29,377	$15,641	$7,114	$10,605
Common and Common Equivalent Share Data					
Net earnings	**$1.78**	$1.14	$.68	$.33	$.54
Stockholders' equity	**6.65**	3.87	2.59	1.98	1.75
Average of common and common equivalent shares (in thousands)	**29,502**	28,973	24,539	22,102	19,858
Cash dividends paid	**.15**	.11	.09	.07	.06
Stock splits	**2 for 1**	3 for 2	5 for 4	—	3 for 2
Financial Position (in thousands)					
Total assets	**$975,004**	$536,679	$404,507	$229,170	$173,950
Total long-term debt	**276,437**	83,271	84,945	29,055	25,573
Discounted lease rentals	**356,547**	261,780	197,672	85,612	74,569
Stockholders' equity	**191,487**	91,056	58,746	43,565	35,508
Leasing Data					
Number of new leases	**3,467**	2,259	1,620	1,083	616
Total firm rents, initial lease term (in thousands)	**$1,055,000**	$702,000	$339,000	$183,000	$126,000

CONSOLIDATED BALANCE SHEETS
(in thousands except number of shares)

Years Ended September 30,	1983	1982
Cash and marketable securities (at cost of $205,053 in 1983 and $3,909 in 1982, which approximates market)	$232,560	$39,762
Receivables:		
Accounts and notes (net of allowance for doubtful accounts of $1,215 in 1983 and $628 in 1982)	74,830	41,368
Other	9,014	3,687
Inventory of computer equipment	59,681	35,382
Net investment in sales-type and direct financing leases	96,097	23,682
Leased computer equipment:		
Owned	671,697	502,494
Capitalized leases	24,353	24,158
Total	696,050	526,652
Less accumulated depreciation and amortization	280,917	190,817
Net	415,133	335,835
Buildings, furniture and other (at cost less accumulated depreciation of $2,764 in 1983 and $1,897 in 1982)	9,068	6,062
Other assets and deferred charges	78,621	50,901
	$975,004	$536,679
Liabilities and Stockholders' Equity		
Note payable to bank	—	$2,385
Convertible subordinated debentures	250,000	50,000
Subordinated debentures	12,250	12,250
Accounts payable	58,963	19,110
Obligations under capital leases	14,187	18,636
Obligations under capital leases income taxes:		
Current	7,242	6,076
Deferred	18,121	30,121
Other liabilities	66,207	45,265
Discounted lease rentals	356,547	261,780
	783,517	445,623
Stockholders' equity:		
Common stock $.10 par value. Authorized 50,000,000 shares: issues outstanding 28,808,571 shares in 1983 (11,769,043 in 1982)	2,881	1,177
Additional paid-in capital	69,927	18,965
Deferred translation adjustment	(439)	(354)
Retained earnings	119,118	71,268
Total Stockholders' equity	191,487	91,056
	$975,004	$536,679

CONSOLIDATED STATEMENTS OF EARNINGS

Years Ended September 30,	1983	1982	1981
Revenue			
Rental	**$266,628**	$206,592	$131,571
Sale of computer equipment	**171,138**	166,705	125,384
Financial services	**65,635**	73,879	30,837
Other	**39,779**	24,454	13,746
Total revenue	**543,180**	471,630	301,538
Cost and expenses			
Equipment depreciation, amortization and rental	**214,439**	160,523	99,413
Cost of computer equipment	**151,573**	149,654	111,784
Selling, general and administrative	**64,655**	60,402	35,313
Interest	**53,673**	47,242	33,657
Total costs and expenses	**484,340**	417,821	280,167
Earnings before income taxes	**58,840**	53,809	21,371
Income taxes	**7,000**	24,432	5,730
Net Earnings	**$51,840**	$29,377	$15,641
Net Earnings per Common and Common			
Equivalent Share	**$1.78**	$1.14	$.68

CONSOLIDATED STATEMENT OF STOCKHOLDERS' EQUITY
(in thousands)

Years Ended September 30, 1983, 1982 and 1981	Common stock $.10 par value	Additional paid-in capital	Retained earnings	Deferred translation adjustment
Balance at September 30, 1980	$587	$14,167	$28,811	$—
Net earnings	—	—	15,641	—
Dividends paid	—	—	(1,093)	—
Stock split	148	(148)	—	—
Stock options exercised	22	611	—	—
Balance at September 30, 1981	757	14,630	43,359	—
Cumulative amount as of September 30, 1981	—	—	—	(232)
Net earnings	—	—	29,377	—
Dividends paid	—	—	(1,468)	—
Stock split	391	(400)	—	—
Stock options exercised	14	835	—	—
Common stock issued	15	2,648	—	—
Translation adjustment	—	—	—	(122)
Income tax benefits resulting from exercise of non-qualified stock options	—	1,252	—	—
Balance at September 30, 1982	1,177	18,965	71,268	(354)
Net earnings	—	—	51,840	—
Dividends paid	—	—	(3,990)	—
Issuance of common stock upon conversion of 13% convertible debentures	256	51,782	—	—
Stock split	1,435	(1,435)	—	—
Stock options exercised	13	582	—	—
Employee Stock Purchase Plan	—	33	—	—
Translation adjustment	—	—	—	(85)
Balance at September 30, 1983	**$2,881**	**$69,927**	**$119,118**	**$(439)**

Comdisco Inc. (B)

CONSOLIDATED STATEMENTS OF CHANGES IN FINANCIAL POSITION
(in thousands)

Years Ended September 30,	1983	1982	1981
Source of Funds			
From operations:			
Net earnings	$51,840	$29,377	$15,641
Noncash changes (credits) to operations:			
Depreciation and amortization	180,676	133,902	77,528
Increase in receivables	(38,789)	(12,849)	(5,531)
Investment in sales-type and direct financing leases	(72,415)	(5,792)	(11,732)
Income taxes	(10,834)	23,180	5,730
Increase in accounts payable and accrued liabilities	60,795	14,248	18,611
Other, net	5,636	474	(1,233)
Total provided from operations	176,909	182,540	99,014
Proceeds from issuance of subordinated debentures	245,250	—	48,560
Issuance of common stock upon conversion of 13% convertible debentures, net	53,365	—	—
Obligations under capital leases	1,984	5,663	14,249
Discounted lease rentals	257,096	145,626	183,557
Other	543	4,201	924
	735,147	338,030	346,304
Application of Funds			
Increase in leased equipment and inventory	282,341	190,180	202,002
Decrease in notes payable	2,385	1,060	33,460
Redemption of convertible debentures	50,000	—	—
Reduction of discounted lease rentals and obligations under capital leases	168,762	87,795	75,781
Purchase of subordinated debentures	—	—	2,162
Capitalized leases—computer equipment	1,984	5,663	14,249
Other assets and deferred charges	32,887	21,950	12,343
Cash dividends	3,990	1,468	1,093
	542,349	308,116	341,090
Increase in cash and marketable securities	192,798	29,914	5,214
Cash and marketable securities at beginning of year	39,762	9,848	4,634
Cash and marketable securities at end of year	$232,560	$39,762	$9,848

NOTES TO CONSOLIDATED FINANCIAL STATEMENTS

1. Summary of Significant Accounting Policies

Principles of Consolidation: The accompanying consolidated financial statements include the accounts of the Company and its wholly-owned subsidiaries after elimination of inter-company accounts and transactions.

Inventory of Computer Equipment: Inventory of computer equipment is stated at the lower of cost or market.

Initial Direct Costs: Salesmen's commissions and other initial direct costs related to operating leases are deferred and amortized over the lease term.

Investment in Sales-Type and Direct Finance Leases: At lease commencement, the Company records the total lease rentals, estimated residual value of the leased equipment and unearned lease income as investment in sales-type and direct financing leases.

A. *Sales-Type Leases*

Revenue from sales-type leases is recorded as sale of computer equipment upon acceptance of the equipment by the customer. The amount of the sale is the present value of the lease payment. The carrying value of the equipment less the present value of the estimated residual value at lease termination, if any, is charged to cost of computer equipment. Unearned lease income represents the lease rentals plus the estimated residual value of the equipment less the present value of these amounts.

B. *Direct Financing Leases*

The total lease rentals plus the estimated residual value of lease termination, if any, less the equipment cost is recorded as unearned lease income.

The Company finances most sales-type and direct financing leases by assigning the noncancellable rentals on a nonrecourse basis. The proceeds from the assignment eliminate the total lease rentals receivable and related unearned income on sales-type and direct financing leases. Any gain or loss on the financing is recognized at the time of such financing. For leases which are not financed, unearned lease income is recognized as other revenue using the interest method over the lease term.

Leased Computer Equipment: Leased computer equipment under operating leases is recorded at cost. During the initial lease term, computer equipment is depreciated to the Company's estimate of fair market value at expiration of the initial lease term. Equipment sold under tax advantaged transactions is fully depreciated within five years. Equipment not sold under tax advantaged transactions is fully depreciated over the next lease term or five years from the date of acquisition, whichever is longer.

Financial Service Transactions: At a date after the inception of an initial user lease and independent thereof, the Company may sell some or all of the equipment to a third party investor. The sales price equals the then current fair market value of the equipment and is paid in the form of cash and a negotiable, interest-bearing promissory note (due within two years) for 10–22% of the sales price (the "equity payment"), and an installment note for the balance (90–78% of the sales price) payable over an 84 to 96 month period. Simultaneously with the sale, the Company leases such equipment back from the investor for 84 to 96 months. The lease payments payable under the leaseback obligation generally are equal to the installment payments receivable under the installment note. As part of the leaseback arrangement, from the 61st month of the leaseback period until the expiration of the leaseback, the investor shares in the release proceeds that the Company receives from subleasing the equipment. Upon the expiration of the leaseback period, the investor has the exclusive right to the equipment.

For equipment subject to sales-type and direct financing leases, the equity payment is first applied to remove a portion of the residual value of the equipment at the expiration of the initial user lease. The residual value is decreased because the Company's right to the full residual has been reduced by the tax advantaged transaction. Any excess of the equity payment over the reduction of residual value is recorded as financial services revenue in the period in which the tax advantaged transaction occurs.

For equipment subject to operating leases, the equity payment is recognized as financial services revenue in the period in which the tax advantaged transaction occurs. Against this revenue, the Company allocates as a cost a percentage of the net book value remaining at termination of the initial user lease. The balance of the net book value remaining at initial lease termination will be fully depreciated within five years from the date of equipment purchase.

In fiscal 1982 and the first quarter of fiscal 1983, the Company sold the tax benefits (investment tax credit and cost recovery allowances) on certain new equipment purchased for the Company's lease portfolio, under the provisions of the Economic Recovery Tax Act of 1981. The proceeds from the sale of tax benefits are recorded as financial services revenue. Also included in financial services revenue are fees for arranging lease transactions between third parties.

Income Taxes and Investment Tax Credit: Deferred income taxes are provided for income and expenses which are recognized in different periods for income tax purposes than for financial reporting purposes. Investment tax credits are accounted for on a flow-through basis.

Earnings Per Share: Earnings per common and common equivalent share are computed based on the weighted average number of common and common equivalent shares outstanding during each period including the effect of conversion of the 13% convertible subordinated debentures, after elimination of the related interest expense (net of tax), and after giving retroactive effect to the two-for-one stock split effected in March 1983. (See Note 11.) Dilutive stock options included in the number of common and common equivalent shares are based on the treasury stock method. The number of common and common equivalent shares used in the computation of earnings per share for the years ended September 30, 1983, 1982, and 1981 were 29,501,678, 28,973,476, and 24,539,406, respectively.

2. Investment in Sales-Type and Direct Financing Leases

The following table lists the components of the net investment in sales-type and direct financing leases as of September 30:

	1983	1982
Minimum lease payments	**$88,718**	$24,142
Estimated residual values of leased equipment	**29,863**	12,324
Net investment in equipment pending sale to third parties	**7,305**	—
Less unearned income	**29,789**	12,784
Net investment in sales-type and direct financing leases	**$96,097**	$23,682

Future minimum lease payments to be received as of September 30, 1983 are as follows:

Years ending September 30	Minimum lease payments receivable
	(in thousands)
1984	$24,844
1985	22,910
1986	20,696
1987	14,706
1988	5,562
	$88,718

3. Leased Computer Equipment

Leased computer equipment at September 30, 1983 is comprised of the following:

Year lease commenced	Equipment cost	Accumulated depreciation	Net book value
1979	$20,357	$16,598	$3,759
1980	41,718	29,167	12,551
1981	146,118	96,179	49,939
1982	182,301	85,348	96,953
1983	281,203	35,518	245,685
	$671,697	$262,810	$408,887

An analysis of the operating lease portfolio by year the equipment was first available from the manufacturer follows below. This does not represent the year of purchase by the Company. The Company's depreciation policy generally depreciates computer equipment to zero within five years of the date of purchase.

Year of delivery	Net book value
1970	$1,816
1973	8,244
1974	21,319
1975	58,656
1976	9,290
1978	58,556
1979	88,338
1980	42,543
1981	31,637
1982	88,488
	$408,887

4. Operating Leases

Rental revenue from operating leases is recognized in equal monthly amounts over the term of the lease. The following table summarizes the Company's future rentals receivable and payable under noncancellable operating leases existing at September 30, 1983 for computer equipment and rents payable for non-computer equipment and office space:

Computer equipment				
Year ending September 30	Rents receivable on equipment		Rents payable on subleased equipment	Other rents payable
	Owned	Subleased		
	(in thousands)			
1984	$213,012	$28,334	$28,023	$2,430
1985	135,624	17,723	14,118	1,787
1986	63,488	7,309	4,340	831
1987	20,378	2,399	883	435
1988	1,345	275	60	250
	$433,847	$56,040	$47,424	$5,733

Total rental income and related expense for the years ended September 30, 1983, 1982, and 1981 applicable to computer sublease activities were as follows:

Years ended September 30	Rental income	Rental expense
	(in thousands)	
1983	$29,316	$33,694
1982	23,633	27,455
1981	24,152	22,415

5. Discounted Lease Rentals

Leased equipment owned by the Company is financed by assigning the noncancellable rentals to various lenders at fixed interest rates on a nonrecourse basis. The proceeds from the assignment of the lease rentals represent payments due under the lease discounted to their present value at the interest rate charged by the lender. The proceeds from the financing of equipment subject to sales-type and direct financing leases reduce the investment in sales-type and direct financing leases (see Note 1). The proceeds from the financing of equipment subject to operating leases is recorded on the balance sheet as

Discounted Lease Rentals. Interest expense under financings is computed under the interest method and amounted to $36,173,000, $32,527,000 and $15,468,000 in 1983, 1982 and 1981, respectively. In the event of default by the lessee, the lender has a first lien against the underlying leased equipment, with no further recourse against the Company.

The annual maturities of discounted lease rentals for the next five years are as follows:

Year ending September 30	Aggregate maturities
	(in thousands)
1984	$164,193
1985	113,318
1986	56,099
1987	20,528
1988	2,409
	$356,547

6. Capitalized Leases—Computer Equipment

The Company, as lessee, leases computer equipment from other parties which may be recorded as capitalized leases pursuant to FASB Statement No. 13. If the lease qualifies as a capital lease, the Company records as an asset the lesser of the fair market value of the equipment or the present value of the minimum lease payments. The Company amortizes the asset in a manner consistent with its normal depreciation policy for leased equipment.

Capitalized leases—computer equipment at September 30, is comprised of the following:

	1983	1982
	(in thousands)	
Capitalized leases— computer equipment	$24,353	$24,158
Less accumulated computer amortization	18,107	15,354
Net capitalized leases— computer equipment	$6,246	$8,804

At September 30, 1983, the Company, as lessee, was obligated to pay rentals under those capitalized leases. The following table summarizes minimum rentals payable by the Company as lessee under capitalized leases:

Years ending September 30	Minimum rentals payable
	(in thousands)
1984	$7,527
1985	5,244
1986	2,807
1987	1,810
1988	521
Total minimum lease payments	17,909
Less imputed interest (9% to 17%)	3,722
Obligations under capital leases (present value of net minimum lease payments)	$14,187

The Company has subleased equipment under capitalized leases to others resulting in non-cancellable sublease rental income of $10,532,000 due to the Company in the future.

7. Other Assets and Deferred Charges

During the third quarter of fiscal 1983, the Company began operations of a newly established, wholly owned subsidiary, Comdisco Resources, Inc. ("CRI"). CRI is primarily engaged, through joint ventures with established partners, in the acquisition of mineral and royalty rights in producing domestic oil and gas properties and in the acquisition of onshore leasehold interests primarily for resale to others for oil and gas exploration and development. At September 30, 1983, included in other assets and deferred charges are $22,959,000 of investments representing primarily onshore leasehold interests in unproved properties held for resale to others. For fiscal 1984, approximately $17,800,000 and $9,000,000, respectively, has been budgeted for investment in proved producing domestic oil and gas properties and unproved onshore leasehold interests for resale to others for oil and gas exploration and development.

The Company, through its CFS subsidiary, has entered into certain computer equipment transactions in which it has leased equipment and in turn has subleased such equipment. In substantially all of these transactions, the lease term exceeds the sublease term. At September 30, 1983 and 1982, $19,336,000 and $21,258,000, respectively, of costs (representing the present value of the excess of lease payments over the initial sublease payments) were deferred in connection with such transactions and are included in other assets and deferred charges. These deferred costs will be recovered from remarketing the equipment after the expiration of the initial sublease. At September 30, 1983, the Company has firm noncancellable rentals under binding contracts totaling $9,102,000 as a result of remarketing a portion of this portfolio. All of these noncancellable rentals will be used to reduce the investment in the period such rentals are received.

8. Bank Borrowings and Compensating Balances

The Company has a revolving credit agreement which entitles it to borrow up to $15,000,000 on an unsecured basis. The agreement, which expires March 31, 1984, carries an interest cost of prime rate (11.0% at September 30, 1983) and includes a fee of 3/8% per annum of the average daily unused amount. If either the Company or the bank elects not to renew the agreement, the loan becomes a two-year term loan payable in equal quarterly installments with an interest cost of prime rate plus 1%. Under the agreement, the Company is required to maintain a defined debt to net worth ratio and dividend payments cannot exceed 20% of consolidated net earnings subsequent to September 30, 1980. At September 30, 1983, approximately $10,658,000 of retained earnings were available for payments of dividends.

In accordance with the terms of the agreement, the Company is required to maintain average cash balances with the bank equal to 5% of the $15,000,000 loan commitment. The amount of unused available borrowings under the agreement was $15,000,000 at September 30, 1983.

At September 30, 1983, the Company had an additional unused line of credit totaling $25,000,000 which bears interest at the prime rate. Under the agreement, the Company is required to maintain compensating balances equal to 5% of the outstanding borrowings.

9. Subordinated Debentures

8% Convertible Subordinated Debentures: In May 1983, the Company issued $250,000,000 of 8% convertible subordinated debentures ("Convertible Debentures") due in 2003. Issue costs of approximately $5,000,000 were deferred and are being amortized over 20 years. Each $1,000 principal amount may be converted into shares of common stock of the Company, prior to maturity, at the option of the Convertible Debenture holder at a conversion price of $36.50 per share.

The Convertible Debentures are not redeemable prior to November 1, 1984 unless the average closing price of the common stock is $51.10 for the twenty consecutive trading days ending on the fifth day preceding the date of notice of redemption. Thereafter, they are redeemable in full or in part at the option of the Company at an amount equal to 108.0% of the principal amount, with the premium on redemption declining 8% per annum commencing in 1984 through 1993, and redeemable thereafter at par.

13% Convertible Subordinated Debentures: On November 4, 1982, the Board of Directors announced the redemption of all of the Company's 13% Convertible Subordinated Debentures Due 2001 at a redemption price of $1,117 for each $1,000 principal amount, plus accrued and unpaid interest to December 6, 1982. Common stock issued upon conversion of $49,839,000 principal amount totaled 5,111,360 shares.

11 1/2% Subordinated Debentures: At September 30, 1983, $12,250,000 of 11 1/2% subordinated debentures due December 1, 1992 were outstanding. Annual sinking fund payments of $1,350,000 (9% of the aggregate original

principal amount) commenced December 1, 1982 and are calculated to retire 90% of the issue prior to maturity. During fiscal 1981, the Company, in connection with future sinking fund requirements, acquired $2,750,000 principal amount of the outstanding debentures which resulted in a gain of $318,000 (net of income taxes of $270,000).

The annual maturities and sinking fund requirements of all the subordinated debentures for the next five years are as follows:

Years ending September 30	Aggregate maturities
	(in thousands)
1984	$—
1985	1,300
1986	1,350
1987	1,350
1988	1,350

10. Income Taxes

The following data related to the provision for income taxes for the years ended September 30:

	1983	1982	1981
Current:			
Federal	$13,000	$6,252	$—
State	6,000	1,076	—
	19,000	7,328	—
Deferred:			
Federal	(12,200)	16,281	4,216
State	(2,200)	273	553
Foreign	2,400	550	961
	(12,000)	17,104	5,730
Total tax provision	$7,000	$24,432	$5,730
Earnings before income taxes:			
Domestic	$51,869	$51,166	$18,992
Foreign	6,971	2,643	2,379
Total	$58,840	$53,809	$21,371

Income tax benefits of $900,000 resulting from the redemption of the 13% convertible debentures in fiscal 1983 and $1,252,000 resulting from the exercise of non-qualified stock options in fiscal 1982 were utilized to reduce the current Federal tax liability.

The reasons for the difference between the U.S. Federal income tax rate of 46% and the effective income tax rate were as follows:

Comdisco Inc. (B)

	Percentage of Pretax Earnings		
	1983	1982	1981
U.S. Federal income tax	**46.0%**	46.0%	46.0%
Increase (reduction) resulting from:			
Domestic International Sales Corporation tax benefit	—	(.1)	(1.2)
Reduction of deferred income taxes applicable to investment tax credit carrryforward	—	—	(20.4)
Investment tax credit	**(37.9)**	(2.0)	—
State income taxes, net of U.S. tax benefit	**3.5**	1.4	1.2
Other – net	**.3**	(.1)	1.2
	11.9%	45.4%	26.8%

The Company has not provided for income taxes on the unremitted earnings of the Domestic International Sales Corporation (DISC) subsidiary aggregating $4,253,000 through September 30, 1983, since the Company intends to postpone indefinitely the remittance of such earnings.

Deferred income taxes provided for timing differences were as follows:

	1983	1982	1981
Sale of tax benefits	**$(6,172)**	$38,661	$—
Difference between depreciation for tax purposes and financial statement purposes	**(6,305)**	(18,125)	6,311
Deferred compensation expense	**1,264**	754	(754)
Deferred leasing income	**7,445**	2,934	(2,093)
Deferred leasing costs	**19**	1,518	1,164
Interest income on escrow account bonds not included in book income	**(7,972)**	—	—
Portion of undistributed earnings in DISC	—	(178)	(454)
Difference between leases accounted for as sales-type leases for financial statement purposes and operating leases for tax purposes	**211**	(23,601)	194
Reinstatement (reduction) of deferred income taxes applicable to:			
Investment tax credit carryforward	—	12,021	(4,356)
Tax net operating loss realization	—	—	2,323
Income tax benefit resulting from exercise of non-qualified stock options	—	—	1,903
Other – net	**(490)**	3,120	1,492
	$(12,000)	$17,104	$5,730

The Internal Revenue Service is examining the tax returns for the years 1980, 1981, and 1982. However, no final adjustments have been proposed and no provision for additional taxes is deemed necessary. The Company has settled all tax years through fiscal 1979.

11. Common Stock and Additional Paid-In Capital

On January 20, 1983, the Board of Directors declared a two-for-one split of the Company's common stock effective March 1983. On January 27, 1982 the Board of Directors declared a three-for-two split of the Company's common stock. On January 20, 1981 the Board of Directors of the Company declared a five-for-four split of the Company's common stock. All references in the financial statements and notes to the number of shares of common stock and per share amounts have been adjusted for the aforementioned stock splits.

On November 18, 1981, the Board of Directors approved the Settlement Agreement (the "Agreement") between the Company and participants in the Residual Incentive Compensation Plan (the "Plan") related to vested residual computer interests. The Plan provided in part for the allocation of a percentage interest in the residual value of computer equipment to the participants. The Agreement was approved by the stockholders on March 15, 1982 and, pursuant to the terms of the Agreement, the Company distributed to participants in accordance with the terms of the Plan the aggregate sum of $3,000,000 plus 300,000 shares of the Company's common stock.

Dividends on Common Stock: Common stock dividends paid were $.15 per share in 1983 compared with $.11 in 1982 and $.09 in 1981. Agreements with officers and directors who own approximately 29% (8,358,759 shares) of the outstanding common stock regarding waiver of their rights to certain cash dividends payable prior to February 1, 1983, have expired and have not been renewed.

At September 30, 1983, the Company has reserved the following number of common shares for future issuance:

1979 Stock Option Plan	542,851
1981 Stock Option Plan	1,474,200
Employees Stock Purchase Plan	196,430
Conversion of 8% Convertible Debentures	6,849,315
	9,062,796

12. Employee Benefit Plans

1979 Stock Option Plan: On November 18, 1981, the Board of Directors amended the Company's 1979 Stock Option Plan (the "1979 Plan") to qualify the plan as an incentive stock option plan in accordance with the provisions of the Economic Recovery Tax Act of 1981. All outstanding stock options, which retained their original option price, are eligible for treatment as incentive stock options subject to certain limitations as defined in the amended 1979 Plan.

1981 Stock Option Plan: On January 27, 1982, the stockholders approved the 1981 Stock Option Plan (the "1981 Plan") and 1,500,000 shares were reserved for issuance pursuant to the exercise of options under the 1981 Plan.

Employee Stock Purchase Plan: The Comdisco, Inc. Employee Stock Purchase Plan (the "Plan") was adopted by the Board of Directors on

November 17, 1981 and 200,000 shares were reserved for issuance under the Plan.

The changes in the number of shares under the option plans during 1983, 1982 and 1981 were as follows:

	1983	1982	1981
Number of shares: (in thousands except option price range)			
Shares under option beginning of year	986	1,024	1,722
Options granted	308	338	—
Options exercised	(133)	(376)	(698)
Shares under option end of year	1,161	986	1,024
Aggregate option price:			
Shares under option beginning of year	$4,967	$2,533	$3,257
Options granted	6,739	3,284	—
Option exercised	(596)	(850)	(724)
Shares under option end of year	$11,110	$4,967	$2,533
Options exercisable at end of year	238	116	328
Aggregate option price of exercisable options outstanding at end of year	$1,247	$295	$722
Options available for future grant at end of year	874	1,182	22
Option price range	$2.45	$2.45	$.68
	$21.88	$9.69	$3.50

Profit Sharing Plan: The Company has a profit sharing plan covering all employees. Company contributions to the plan are based on a percentage of employees' compensation, as defined. Profit sharing payments are based on amounts accumulated on an individual employee basis. Profit sharing expense for the years ended September 30, 1983, 1982, and 1981 amounted to $834,000, $590,000, and $489,000, respectively.

13. Commitments and Contingent Liabilities

At September 30, 1983, the Company was obligated under the following commitments: (1) to purchase computer equipment in the approximate aggregate amount of $58,782,000, (2) to sell computer equipment in the approximate aggregate amount of $9,370,000, and (3) to lease computer equipment to others with an aggregate initial term rental of approximately $86,133,000.

The Company has arranged for approximately $68,683,000 of letters of credit, primarily as guarantees for certain of the Company's sublease obligations and for future purchases of IBM equipment. The cost of such letters of credit range between 1/2% and 3/4% per annum on the amount outstanding.

ACCOUNTANT REPORT

The Stockholders and Board of Directors, Comdisco, Inc.:

We have examined the consolidated balance sheet of Comdisco, Inc. and subsidiaries as of September 30, 1983 and 1982 and the related consolidated statements of earnings, stockholders' equity and changes in financial position for each of the years in the three-year period ended September 30, 1983. Our examinations were made in accordance with generally accepted auditing standards and, accordingly, included such tests of the accounting records and such other auditing procedures as we considered necessary in the circumstances.

In our opinion, the aforementioned consolidated financial statements present fairly the financial position of Comdisco Inc. and subsidiaries at September 30, 1983 and 1982 and the results of their operations and the changes in their financial position for each of the years in the three-year period ended September 30, 1983, in conformity with generally accepted accounting principles applied on a consistent basis.

Peat, Marwick, Mitchell & Co.
Chicago, Illinois
November 9, 1983

QUARTERLY FINANCIAL DATA

Summarized quarterly financial data for fiscal years ended September 30, 1983 and 1982 is as follows:

(in thousands of dollars except for per share amounts)

Quarter Ended	December 31 1982	1981	March 31 1983	1982	June 30 1983	1982	September 30 1983	1982
Total revenue	$141,011	$121,189	$132,901	$118,309	$127,455	$94,691	$141,813	$137,441
Net earnings	12,531	9,604	10,334	5,934	13,199	5,824	15,776	8,015
Net earnings per common and common equivalent share	$.45	$.37	$.35	$.24	$.45	$.23	$.53	$.31

In the fourth quarter of fiscal 1983, the Company generated substantial investment tax credits, which resulted in an annual effective tax rate of 11.9%. This reduction in the income tax rate resulted in an increase of approximately $7,430,000 in net earnings ($.25 per share) for the fourth quarter of fiscal 1983.

Computer Associates International, Inc.: Governance and Investor Communication Challenge

In the first six months of 2002, Computer Associates announced the appointment of six new members to its board of directors. The changes in board composition followed a period in which the company had made significant changes to its business model and its financial reporting. Commenting on the four new director changes announced on July 16, 2002, Sanjay Kumar, CA's CEO, noted:

Our business model, which was implemented in October 2000, is delivering sustainable competitive advantage and—as evidenced by today's announcements, the April additions of Jay Lorsch, a noted governance expert from Harvard, and Walter Schuetze, the former chief accountant to the Securities and Exchange Commission, and last year's addition of lead independent director Lewis Ranieri—we have continued to make excellent progress in attracting highly qualified independent directors to CA's board.

Despite management's belief that the company had made good progress in improving its business model and governance, there remained considerable skepticism about CA in the stock market. The company's stock price dropped by about 60% during the first half of 2002 (see **Exhibit 1** for a comparison of the stock's performance versus that of the S&P 500). Investors were confused about the company's new accounting and were skeptical of the "pro forma" numbers the company was disclosing as a way to help investors assess the impact of the accounting change. In addition, Sam Wyly, a Texas entrepreneur who had sold his company, Sterling Software, to CA in 2001, was continuing his efforts to challenge management through a protracted proxy fight.

Kumar was convinced that the business and accounting changes that the company made were absolutely the right things to have done. He was pleased to see that the new business model the company had implemented was producing exactly the type of results he had hoped to achieve. And he thought the company was doing its best to communicate with Wall Street. He was, therefore, surprised by the skepticism with which investors viewed the company and its financial reports.

Professors Paul Healy and Krishna Palepu prepared this case. HBS cases are developed solely as the basis for class discussion. Cases are not intended to serve as endorsements, sources of primary data, or illustrations of effective or ineffective management.

As Kumar prepared for the upcoming board meeting, he wondered how the company should respond to the skepticism in the market and how the company's new board could help him restore investor confidence.

COMPUTER ASSOCIATES

Charles Wang founded Computer Associates in 1976 as a joint venture with Swiss-owned Computer Associates (CA) to sell software in the United States. The company's first product, a file organizer for IBM storage systems, was highly successful, and in 1980 Wang bought out his Swiss partners.[1] Wang sought to provide CA customers with higher-quality products than they could buy from IBM and to develop a strong distribution network to sell these products.

During the 1980s and 1990s, Wang recognized the importance of increasing the range of software products that could be offered and supported through CA's extensive distribution and service network. Acquisitions of existing software which reduced the risk of in-house development and moved products to market sooner, became CA's favorite means of growth (see **Exhibit 2** for a list of major acquisitions). To integrate its acquisitions, CA would interview and subsequently rank all new employees and then either assign them new positions or let them go.

Wang stepped down as CEO in 2000 to become chairman, and Kumar, who had joined the company through the acquisition of UCCEL in 1987 and had been CA's president since 1994, became CEO.

By 2002 CA had become the third-largest independent software company in the world (after Microsoft and Oracle). The company had expanded beyond mainframe utilities into PC software, database and banking applications, and network software. For the year ended March 31, 2002, CA reported annual sales of $3 billion, operating cash flow of $1.3 billion, and ending assets of $12.2 billion. (Financial statements and selected footnote information for the year ended March 31, 2002 are presented in **Exhibit 3**.)

CA's Old Business Model and Accounting

Under a typical licensing arrangement, customers agreed to pay a license fee to CA for the right to use software for a period of three to ten years. CA based license fees on either the aggregate capacity of all machines that used the software, or on the processing power of individual licensed machines. The license fees also reflected the number of years of the license—the longer the license period, the higher the fee. However, the incremental fee for additional years of licensing declined over time at a rate of roughly 30% per year to reflect obsolescence. Despite the fact that licenses were for multiple years, current financial reporting rules required CA to report the licensing fee as revenue once a customer had signed a contract, the software had been delivered, and collection of fees was reasonably assured.

CA also charged customers an annual maintenance fee of roughly 10–20% of the initial license fee. Annual renewal rates for CA maintenance contracts typically exceeded 85%. Maintenance fees, whether bundled with product licenses or priced separately, were required to be recognized ratably over the maintenance period.

1. For more information on Computer Associates International, please see Amy Hutton, "Computer Associates International," HBS No. 102-061 (Boston: Harvard Business School Publishing, 2002).

Unlike other independent software firms, CA provided its customers with the option of financing the initial license fee. As a result, CA's financial statements looked very different from those of its major competitors. Its balance sheet included sizable receivables—on March 31, 1999, 60% of its assets were short- or long-term receivables. Its income statement included effective interest from financing its customers—for 1999, effective interest amounted to $408 million, 9% of total licensing revenues. Also, its cash inflows were steadier, since revenues were collected over time rather than at the time of sale.

Problems with the Old Business Model

Despite being the standard for the software industry, the old business model had generated a number of problems. The primary problem was that customers had learned that pressure on sales representatives for CA (as well as for other software firms) to meet quarterly sales targets intensified toward the end of each quarter. By waiting until the last week of the quarter to sign a license agreement, savvy customers were able to negotiate attractive licensing-fee discounts. Consequently, CA recorded a significant portion of its sales for a given quarter in the last week of the quarter.

This selling pattern was primarily driven by the incentives of CA's sales representatives and top management. Sales representatives were compensated on a commission basis, with commissions computed quarterly as a percentage of the present value of the annual license fees for contracts sold. Sales representatives' financial incentives were therefore tied to quarterly sales targets, and pressure to meet these targets intensified as the quarter end approached. CA's top management faced similar pressures, in their case to meet Wall Street quarterly revenue and earnings expectations. Management pressure to increase sales each quarter reinforced the incentives of sales representatives, particularly since the full effect of multiyear licenses was recorded as revenue when the contract was signed and the software delivered.

Sales representatives would therefore agree to deep discounts on licenses signed in the last week of the quarter. Discounts were particularly significant for the later years of a contract, when obsolescence risk was high and the present-value implications for sales representatives' commissions were small. Top management went along with the discounting to boost reported revenues and earnings. Because the incremental costs of software production were negligible, reducing license fees for the later contract years could be argued to still be profitable for shareholders, since even minimal revenues in those years contributed toward recovering the costs of software development.

However, there were a number of negative consequences to the pattern in sales over the quarter. First, it made it very difficult for firms in the software industry to maintain margins. There was constant pressure to lower prices. For example, it was difficult for sales representatives to deny discounts offered to customers negotiating contracts in the last week of the quarter to other customers who negotiated new contracts the following quarter. More importantly, customers who had succeeded in negotiating attractive discounts on licenses in the later years of a contract used these low rates as a base for negotiating subsequent license fees when the contract was up for renewal.

The sales pattern also made it difficult for CA to forecast revenues and earnings for any given quarter. Since most of the quarter's sales arose in the last week, management found it difficult to warn analysts and investors of any drop in revenues until after the quarter was actually over. As a result, it was difficult for analysts to forecast earnings, leading to wide stock price swings at the time of earnings announcements. CA was particularly sensitive to this problem—in July 2000 the company saw its stock price fall by 42% when it announced a quarterly earnings shortfall that was partially caused by delays in "several large contracts, previously expected to close in the final days of the quarter."[2]

Finally, the current business model had several other negative implications for CA. Sales representatives tended to focus heavily on clients who were considering buying or renewing their long-term licenses. However, once a license agreement was signed, they had little incentive to follow up during the contract period, which often ran several years; their time was better spent focusing on new customers or customers whose licenses were about to expire. As a result, there was considerable customer dissatisfaction with CA. This dissatisfaction, coupled with reluctance by customers to experiment with new software that required another multiyear license, reduced opportunities for follow-up sales of new software products to existing customers.

Change in CA's Business Model

In October 2000, CA announced changes in its business model, including reducing software license lives, changing the method of compensating sales representatives, and revamping customer support.

By reducing software license lives from seven years to a minimum of one month and a maximum of three years, CA's management anticipated that sales representatives would have to meet regularly with customers and offer good service. This would be needed to ensure that customers renewed existing contracts but could also be used as an opportunity to sell new software products. Under the new arrangement, customers could experiment with new products for a minimum of one month. If they did not find them valuable, they could simply fail to renew them the following month. Also, shorter contracts were expected to reduce the opportunity for sales representatives to agree to discounts on license fees as they had in the sixth and seventh years of a long-term contract. CA was confident that the shorter contract lives would not adversely affect its economics because the renewal rates historically had been very high.

Under the new sales representative compensation arrangement, sales representatives were given monthly sales quotas. Commission rates were made variable, with the highest rates reserved for sales of new products to new customers, lower rates for sales of new products to existing customers, and the lowest rate being the extension of a license for an existing customer. In addition, sales representatives' training focused on improving customer service and satisfaction, and 20% of commissions were assigned on the basis of customer satisfaction. To make sure that the sales representatives did not oppose the business model change, or worse still, leave the organization, CA's management promised that their total compensation under the new scheme would not be lower than their current compensation.

Finally, CA revamped its customer service organization by unifying all post-sales customer groups under a common organizational structure. In addition, the company hired 625 new staff for its customer relations organization, so that customers could have a single point of contact for all their needs.

2. Laura Johannes, "Computer Associates Says Latest Results Will Be Hurt by Delays in Big Contracts," The Wall Street Journal, July 5, 2000, p. A14.

Change in CA's Revenue Recognition

At the same time that it changed its business model, CA changed its method of reporting revenues. Instead of recognizing the present value of multiyear license fees in the year the contract was signed and software delivered, the company began to recognize revenues ratably over the life of the contract.

CA's management argued that the accounting change would benefit both customers and shareholders:

> Ratable recognition will help CA move away from the end-of-quarter customer "dance" that leaves both CA and our customers unhappy—a situation that is obviously inconsistent with a business model that stresses partnership. It is well known in the software industry that the majority of deals are signed at the end of the quarter, as vendors try to make their quarterly numbers. This end-of-quarter flurry of deals—the proverbial "hockey stick effect"—creates an unnecessarily adversarial relationship between customers and vendors in which both parties rush to sign any deal rather than the right deal.
>
> Ratable recognition provides shareholders with greater transparency and lower volatility in quarterly revenue and earnings. Because a majority of our contracts have historically been closed in the last few days of the quarter, CA, like other software companies, has had difficulty providing guidance on quarterly earnings.[3]

However, since CA could not retroactively change its method of accounting, the reporting change posed a short-term challenge for investors in comparing the company's performance over time. Under the new method, license-fee revenues for 2001 were only $3.7 billion versus $5.6 billion for 2000, in part because 2001 revenues included only the license fees for that year and not the multiyear effect of new licensing contracts shown in 2000. As a result, CA reported a loss of $591 million in 2001, compared with a profit of $696 million in 2000.

MANAGEMENT AND BOARD THINKING ABOUT THE CHANGES

Kumar, the CEO, summed up CA's perspective on the new business model:

> The new business model is one of our most important steps in unlocking the value of CA for our customers, shareholders, and employees. We are taking the lead in adopting a model that improves our ability to partner with our customers to realize value and that creates the transparency and consistency in financial results desired by investors. Our employees are highly energized by the changes we are making.

Citing a study by the consulting firm McKinsey & Company, Kumar stated that "given all the benefits the new business model offers, we expect to see more software companies following our lead."

The company's board was fully involved in the company's business model and accounting change. While the board members strongly supported both moves, they expressed concern that investors might not fully understand the potential benefits of

3. Source:"How our new business model delivers value to customers, shareholders, and employees," company document, copyright 2001, Computer Associates International, Inc.

the proposed changes. Of particular concern to the board was the potential problem investors might face in comparing the company's past and future performance, given the change in accounting policy. The board's concern was reinforced by advice from investment bankers who indicated that time-series comparability of reported numbers was of critical importance to investors.

To help investors compare performance across years, CA provided "pro forma, pro rata" revenues and earnings for the current year (2001) and the year before (2000) under the new accounting method and under the assumption that it had always owned two companies acquired in 1999 and 2000. This information was presented in the management discussion and analysis section of the company's annual report. Thus, unlike the pro forma information provided by many companies in their press releases, this information was subject to attestation by the company's auditor, KPMG. (Pro forma information is presented in **Exhibit 4**.) Pro forma total revenues were $5.8 billion and $5.6 billion for 2002 and 2001, and earnings were $1,542 million and $951 million, respectively.

CA also used the pro forma numbers in its communication with analysts and Wall Street, in its press releases, and in the information provided on the company's Web site. The company felt that this approach would make it easier for investors to understand the benefits of the change in business model and not misinterpret the decline in reported revenues and profits in the current year as a result of the changed generally accepted accounting principles (GAAP) accounting statements.

Reactions to the Business and Accounting Changes

Reactions to CA's business and accounting changes were mixed. An article in *Fortune* was positive about the changes:

> The most immediate result is higher profit margins, because software companies no longer have to make concessions on price. It should also mean an end to those nasty earnings misses, as substantially more revenue gets locked in at the beginning of the quarter rather than the end. . . . And negotiations for big deals should go a lot smoother. At the last minute, the software company can tell haggling customers to take a hike (or at least to come back next quarter). "Assuming there's a real need on the customer's part, they'll have to get the deal done in the normal course of business rather than waiting until the 11th hour of the next quarter," says John Barr of Robertson Stephens. Adds Jack Ciesielski, publisher of The Analysts Accounting Observer: "Its just a cleaner, more realistic way of recognizing revenue. They're looking at having more numbers we can trust."[4]

IDC also supported the moves, citing the improved incentives between CA and its customers and the opportunities for the company to sell new products to its existing customers. In a bulletin, IDC concluded:

> Computer Associates (CA) has taken a market-leading position with respect to software payments, moving from an annuity model to one in which it will accept payments for software licenses on a month to month basis and recognize revenue the same way, regardless of how customers buy the software. . . . The move should also take the bumps out of CA's revenue stream by removing incentives for customers to wait till the end of a quarter or year to close a deal in the hopes

---

4. Herb Greenberg, "Against the grain: Software makers get freed by an accounting change," Fortune, June 1, 2001.

of throttling CA salespeople into providing bigger discounts. Additionally, CA is better positioned to get access to new and competitive accounts, as well as emerging partners that need to finance nascent business models.[5]

However, not all the responses were as supportive. On April 29, 2001, *The New York Times* published a piece on CA titled "A Software Company Runs Out of Tricks; The Past May Haunt Computer Associates." Among other things, the article challenged CA's pro forma financial information:

As measured by standard accounting rules, Computer Associates' sales have fallen almost two-thirds over the last six months. To cover that, the company has begun presenting its financial results in a way that confuses even the Wall Street analysts who follow it.

On April 16, Computer Associates reported another banner quarter. "New Business Model Rules; Q4 Rocks," it said proudly in a news release outlining its results for the three months ended March 31. The company appeared untouched by the slowdown in technology spending that hurt other big software companies like Oracle.

Computer Associates said that on a "pro forma, pro rata" basis, its revenues had risen to $1.44 billion for the quarter, from $1.39 billion in the period a year earlier. Profits were 47 cents a share, it said, up from 39 cents a share.

But the last line of the April 16 news release told a different story. There, Computer Associates reported its revenue and income according to "generally accepted accounting principles," the standard that companies are required to use in filings with the Securities and Exchange Commission [SEC] to calculate results. By those rules, revenue fell almost 60%, to $732 million, from $1.91 billion. After earning a profit of $1.13 a share, or about $700 million, last year, the company lost 29 cents a share, or about $175 million, this year.[6]

Analysts and investors, who viewed the company's accounting change and pro forma disclosure with suspicion, cited several concerns. First, they wondered whether the new revenue recognition policy meant that the company's previous policy was overly aggressive. Did the company overstate its revenues and earnings in previous years? This was especially troubling because top management was awarded close to $1 billion in stock compensation based on the past reported performance. Second, were the pro forma disclosures, which showed significantly better results than those reported under the current accounting policy, meant to divert investors' attention from the company's poor performance? Third, were the new business model and accounting changes really motivated by the reasons stated by management or merely to hide that the company was no longer in a position to achieve dramatic growth acquisitions as in the past?

PROXY FIGHT AND CORPORATE GOVERNANCE CHANGES

Close on the heels of the accounting and business model controversy, the company found itself in the middle of a proxy fight. In June 2001, Wyly, a Texas entrepreneur who had sold his company, Sterling Software, to CA a year earlier for $3.91 billion,

5. Steve McHale and Kevin Restivo, International Data Corporation Document #23533, November 2000.

6. Alex Berenson, "A Software Company Runs Out of Tricks: The Past May Haunt Computer Associates," The New York Times, April 29, 2001, section 3, p. 1.

launched a proxy fight requesting CA's shareholders to vote out CA's current management team and the board. Wyly was attempting to capitalize on the controversy surrounding the company's accounting and investors' prior concerns regarding CA's top management compensation and corporate governance. Wyly alleged that "the company has abused and alienated customers, employees and shareholders alike. Management's use of accounting gimmicks and its excessive compensation for lackluster performance have strained credibility with the financial community."[7]

After a bruising fight, CA's management won the proxy fight in August 2001 after promising shareholders that it would make the board more independent and share more strategic information with investors. Specifically, the company promised to add two independent directors to its board, in addition to the two independent directors it had added just after the proxy fight began. The company also promised to share with shareholders information on customer satisfaction from its own surveys, disclose specific growth targets, and generally pursue friendlier investor relations strategy. In return, all 10 incumbent directors won more than 75% of the votes cast in the proxy fight.

Subsequent to the proxy fight, the company initiated a number of significant board and corporate governance changes. In March 2002 the company announced the appointment of two new directors, Schuetze and Lorsch. Schuetze was a charter member of the Financial Accounting Standards Board, a member of the Financial Accounting Standards Advisory Council, and a member and chair of the Accounting Standards Executive Committee of the American Institute of Certified Public Accountants. He had been the chief accountant to the SEC from January 1992 to March 1995 and the chief accountant of the commission's division of enforcement from November 1997 until February 2000. Lorsch was a Harvard Business School professor and a renowned governance expert.

In May 2002, the company adopted a set of new governance policies. Under these policies, the company appointed one of its directors and the former vice chairman of Salomon Brothers, Ranieri, as the "lead independent director." Schuetze was appointed as the chairman of the company's audit committee. Other governance changes adopted included an annual board evaluation of the company's CEO, adoption of New York Stock Exchange (NYSE) guidelines for deciding which directors qualified as independent, reducing the number of insiders on the board to three (out of a total of 12 directors), and limiting the terms of the independent directors.

In July 2002, CA named four new directors: Kenneth Cron, CEO of Vivendi Universal Games, a division of Vivendi Universal; Robert E. La Blanc, former vice chairman of Continental Telecom Corporation and a former general partner of Salomon Brothers Inc.; Alex Serge Vieux, an international technology and software entrepreneur; and Thomas H. Wyman, the former chairman and CEO of CBS, Inc.[8] These four directors replaced Willem F.P. de Vogel, a private investor and director since 1991; Shirley Strum Kenny, president of the State University of New York at Stony Brook and director since 1994; Richard Grasso, the chairman of the NYSE and director since 1994; and Roel Pieper, an executive in the high-tech field. The first three of these were retiring as a result of the new director term-limit policy that the company had adopted; Pieper stepped down as a result of other business commitments. In addition to the newly appointed six board members, the company had five other continuing members. (A list of the other members of CA's board, their length of tenure, and their affiliations is shown in **Exhibit 5**.)

---

7. Stephanie Kirchaessner, "Texan seeks to oust CA board," Financial Times, June 22, 2001.

8. Jerry Guidera, "Computer Associates Names Directors Before Proxy Battle," The Wall Street Journal, July 17, 2002.

The Investor Communication Challenge

As Kumar reviewed the events of the last 15 months, he was pleased with the progress that had been made. He was convinced that the company's new business model was not only the right model for the company and its customers but one that all software companies were likely to adopt sooner or later. Internal data clearly showed that the new business model was producing all the benefits that he had hoped to achieve. As intended, there was a significant decline in end-of-quarter contract-closing frenzy, with all its associated dysfunctional financial and organizational consequences that the company had had to deal with prior to the business model change. New sales contracts were shorter and more profitable. Internal surveys indicated that customer satisfaction was increasing as sales representatives were interacting more frequently with customers, both to renew existing contracts and to explore the sale of new products to existing customers. The new approach to revenue recognition was not only conservative but also made revenues and earnings more predictable.

However, the company still faced a significant challenge in convincing investors and Wall Street analysts that the new business model and accounting were beneficial. Despite all the efforts that Kumar and his chief financial officer, Ira Zar, had made during the past year, investors and analysts still seemed to be skeptical. Further, the decision to release the pro forma, pro rata numbers, intended to help investors compare performance over time, seemed to have created suspicion and confusion.

Investor concerns intensified when the company announced in February 2002 that the SEC was investigating its past accounting practices.[9] Short sellers, capitalizing on this investigation, spread rumors the company had adopted the new accounting method to disguise past accounting abuses that had overstated revenues and earnings. Even though the company strongly denied these allegations, investor confidence was clearly damaged. Wyly, the company's dissident investor, announced yet another challenge to the company's management by filing a slate of five nominees to replace incumbent directors at a vote at the company's annual shareholder meeting on August 28, 2002.

Kumar felt that the recent dramatic changes made to the company's board and governance would be a strong foundation on which to rebuild investor trust and confidence. He wondered what changes, if any, the company should make to its investor communication strategy as part of this effort. Should the company rethink its decision to release the pro forma, pro rata numbers? If these numbers were not reported, should they be replaced with some other information? Given all the supplementary information that the company was already reporting, would more disclosure help or hurt? How could the company convince investors that the business and accounting changes were truly in their long-term interest? What role should the board play in crafting this strategy?

QUESTIONS

1. What was CA trying to accomplish by the change in business model? How did the changes accomplish these goals? What risks does the new model create?

2. How does the change in accounting fit with the new business model?

3. Do you agree with the company's decision to produce pro forma earnings numbers?

4. What action plan would you recommend for Sanjay Kumar?

---

9. Alex Berenson, "Computer Associates Says U.S. is Seeking Data on Accounting," The New York Times, May 2002, p. 4.

Computer Associates International, Inc.

EXHIBIT 1

Stock Performance of Computer Associates International, Inc.

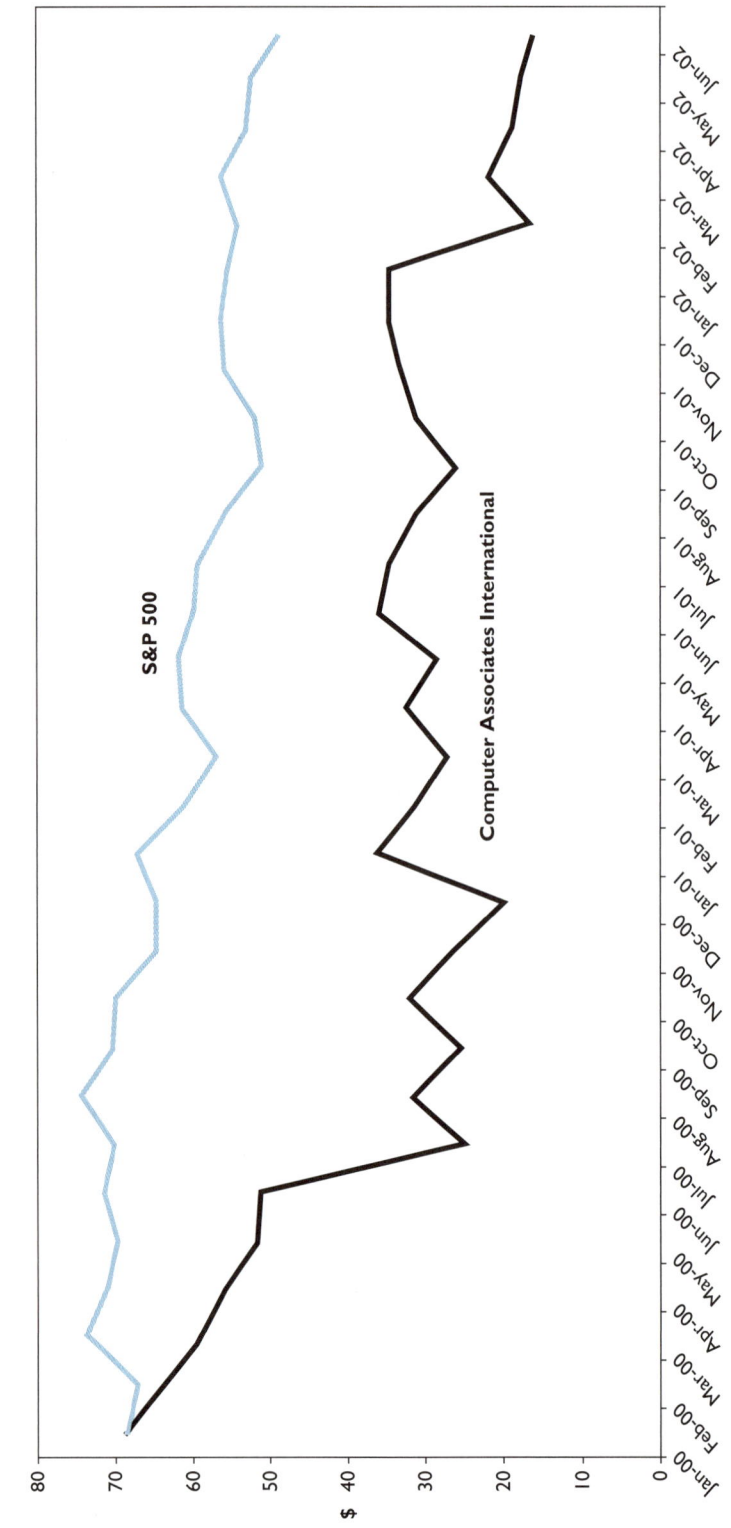

S&P 500

Computer Associates International

$

80
70
60
50
40
30
20
10
0

Jan-00
Feb-00
Mar-00
Apr-00
May-00
Jun-00
Jul-00
Aug-00
Sep-00
Oct-00
Nov-00
Dec-00
Jan-01
Feb-01
Mar-01
Apr-01
May-01
Jun-01
Jul-01
Aug-01
Sep-01
Oct-01
Nov-01
Dec-01
Jan-02
Feb-02
Mar-02
Apr-02
May-02
Jun-02

Source: Datastream International.

Computer Associates International, Inc.

EXHIBIT 2

Major Acquisitions by Computer Associates International, Inc.

Acquisition Date	Acquisition Cost	Company Acquired	Products Acquired
1982		Capex Software	MVS operating systems
1984		Supercalc	Spreadsheet software
1987	$780 m	UCCEL	Utilities software
1989	$320 m	Cullinet	Database and banking applications
1994	$309 m	ASK	Network software
1995	$1.7b	Legent	Systems software Client/server solutions
1996	$1.2b	Cheyenne Software	Network solutions
1999	$3.5b	PLATINUM Technology International Inc.	Portals, business intelligence, application development, and infrastructure management
2000	$4.0b	Sterling Software	Business software

Source: CA web site, http://ca.com/about/history.htm, and press releases from *The Wall Street Journal* and *Financial Times*.

EXHIBIT 3

Financial Statements and Selected Footnotes, Computer Associates International, Inc. and Subsidiaries, Consolidated Balance Sheets

	Year Ended March 31,	
(dollars in millions)	2002	2001
ASSETS		
CURRENT ASSETS		
Cash and cash equivalents	$1,093	$763
Marketable securities	87	87
Trade and installment accounts receivable, net	1,825	1,788
Deferred income taxes	0	106
Other current assets	56	65
TOTAL CURRENT ASSETS	3,061	2,809
INSTALLMENT ACCOUNTS RECEIVABLE, due after one year, net	1,566	2,883
PROPERTY AND EQUIPMENT		
Land and buildings	531	524
Equipment, furniture and improvements	857	839
	1,388	1,363
Accumulated depreciation and amortization	670	569
TOTAL PROPERTY AND EQUIPMENT, net	718	794
PURCHASED SOFTWARE PRODUCTS, net of accumulated amortization of $2,648 and $2,193, respectively	1,836	2,328
GOODWILL AND OTHER INTANGIBLE ASSETS, net of accumulated amortization of $1,524 and $1,023, respectively	4,835	5,400
OTHER ASSETS	210	222
TOTAL ASSETS	$12,226	$14,436
LIABILITIES AND STOCKHOLDERS' EQUITY		
CURRENT LIABILITIES		
Loans payable and current portion of long-term debt	$508	$816
Accounts payable	208	272
Salaries, wages and commissions	236	196
Accrued expenses and other current liabilities	474	613
Deferred subscription revenue (collected)—current	577	166
Taxes payable, other than income taxes payable	116	132
Federal, state and foreign income taxes payable	195	257
Deferred income taxes	7	0
TOTAL CURRENT LIABILITIES	2,321	2,452
LONG-TERM DEBT, net of current portion	3,334	3,629
DEFERRED INCOME TAXES	1,267	1,900
DEFERRED SUBSCRIPTION REVENUE (COLLECTED)—NONCURRENT	208	127
DEFERRED MAINTENANCE REVENUE	456	538
OTHER NONCURRENT LIABILITIES	23	10

(continued)

Financial Statements and Selected Footnotes, Computer Associates International, Inc. and Subsidiaries, Consolidated Balance Sheets (*continued*)

(dollars in millions)	Year Ended March 31,	
	2002	2001
STOCKHOLDERS' EQUITY		
Common stock, $.10 par value, 1,100,000,000 shares authorized		
630,920,576 shares issued	63	63
Additional paid-in capital	3,878	3,936
Retained earnings	2,335	3,483
Accumulated other comprehensive loss	(361)	(388)
Treasury stock, at cost—53,739,842 shares for 2002		
and 55,223,485 shares for 2001	(1,298)	(1,314)
TOTAL STOCKHOLDERS' EQUITY	4,617	5,780
TOTAL LIABILITIES AND STOCKHOLDERS' EQUITY	$12,226	$14,436

Computer Associates International, Inc.

Computer Associates International, Inc. and Subsidiaries, Consolidated Statement of Operations (*continued*)

(in millions except per share amounts)	Year Ended March 31,		
	2002	2001	2000
REVENUE			
Subscription revenue	$827	$59	$–
Software fees and other	432	1,881	4,179
Maintenance	958	1,087	877
Financing fees	444	638	529
Professional services	303	525	509
TOTAL REVENUE	2,964	4,190	6,094
OPERATING EXPENSES:			
Amortization of capitalized software costs	487	492	271
Cost of professional services	283	463	446
Selling, general and administrative	1,790	2,120	1,462
Product development and enhancements	678	695	568
Commissions and royalties	275	308	300
Depreciation and amortization	609	618	323
Purchased research and development	–	–	795
1995 Stock Plan	–	(184)	–
TOTAL OPERATING EXPENSES	4,122	4,512	4,165
(Loss) income before other expenses	(1,158)	(322)	1,929
Interest expense, net	227	344	339
(Loss) income before income taxes	(1,385)	(666)	1,590
Income taxes	(283)	(75)	894
NET (LOSS) INCOME	(1,102)	(591)	696
BASIC (LOSS) EARNINGS PER SHARE	($1.91)	($1.02)	$1.29
Basic weighted-average shares used in computation	577	582	539
DILUTED (LOSS) EARNINGS PER SHARE	($1.91)	($1.02)	$1.25
Diluted weighted-average shares used in computation	577	582	557

Computer Associates International, Inc. and Subsidiaries, Consolidated Statement of Cash Flows (*continued*)

	Year Ended March 31,		
(in millions)	2001	2000	1999
Operating Activities:			
Net (loss) income	($1,102)	($591)	$696
Adjustments to reconcile net (loss) income to net cash provided by operating activities:			
Depreciation and amortization	1,096	1,110	594
Provision for deferred income taxes	(544)	(350)	412
Charge for purchased research and development	0	0	795
Compensation expense (gain) related to stock and pension plans	24	(146)	30
Decrease (increase) in noncurrent installment accounts receivable, net	1,316	828	(1,039)
Increase in deferred subscription revenue (collected)—noncurrent	81	127	0
(Decrease) increase in deferred maintenance revenue	(81)	(3)	113
Foreign currency transaction loss—before taxes	6	14	5
Impairment charge	59	0	50
Gain on sale of property and equipment	0	0	(5)
Changes in other operating assets and liabilities, net of effect of acquisitions:			
(Increase) decrease in trade and installment receivables, net—current	(45)	253	83
Increase in deferred subscription revenue (collected)—current	415	166	0
Other changes in operating assets and liabilities	26	(25)	(168)
NET CASH PROVIDED BY OPERATING ACTIVITIES	1,251	1,383	1,566
INVESTING ACTIVITIES:			
Acquisitions, primarily purchased software, marketing rights and intangibles, net of cash acquired	(2)	(174)	(3,049)
Settlements of purchase accounting liabilities	(59)	(367)	(429)
Purchases of property and equipment	(25)	(89)	(198)
Proceeds from sale of property and equipment	0	5	12
Disposition of businesses	0	158	0
Purchases of marketable securities	(38)	(48)	(95)
Sales of marketable securities	36	40	189
Increase in capitalized development costs and other	(53)	(49)	(36)
NET CASH USED IN INVESTING ACTIVITIES	(141)	(524)	(3,606)
FINANCING ACTIVITIES:			
Dividends paid	(46)	(47)	(43)
Purchases of treasury stock	(95)	(449)	0
Proceeds from borrowings	3,387	1,049	3,672
Repayments of borrowings	(3,967)	(1,981)	(776)
Purchase of a call spread option	(95)	0	0
Exercise of common stock options and other	0	0	96
NET CASH (USED IN) PROVIDED BY FINANCING ACTIVITIES	(40)	(50)	2,949
INCREASE (DECREASE) IN CASH AND CASH EQUIVALENTS BEFORE EFFECT OF EXCHANGE RATE CHANGES ON CASH	334	(519)	909
Effect of exchange rate changes on cash	(4)	(25)	(1)
INCREASE (DECREASE) IN CASH AND CASH EQUIVALENTS	330	(544)	908
CASH AND CASH EQUIVALENTS—BEGINNING OF YEAR	763	1,307	399
CASH AND CASH EQUIVALENTS—END OF YEAR	$1,093	0	$1,307

Computer Associates International, Inc. and Subsidiaries, Selected Notes to Consolidated Financial Statement (*continued*)

NOTE 1—SIGNIFICANT ACCOUNTING POLICIES

Basis of Revenue Recognition: The Company derives revenue from licensing software products and providing post-contract customer support (hereafter referred to as "maintenance") and professional services, such as consulting and education services. The Company licenses its software products to end users primarily through the Company's direct sales force.

The Company licenses to customers the right to use its software products pursuant to software license agreements (hereafter referred to as a "license arrangement"). The license arrangement generally restricts the customer's right to use the Company's enterprise software products as specified in the license arrangement. The license arrangements' original terms generally range from one to ten years for license arrangements prior to December 2000 and one to five years for license arrangements beginning in December 2000. In addition, customers can subscribe to software arrangements under month-to-month licenses beginning in December 2000. The timing and amount of license revenue recognized during an accounting period is determined by the nature of the contractual provisions included in the license arrangement with customers.

Beginning in December 2000, the Company began executing software license arrangements that include flexible contractual provisions that, among other things, allow customers to receive unspecified future software products within designated product lines. Under these arrangements (referred to as the "new Business Model"), the Company is required to recognize revenue attributable to the software products ratably over the term of the license arrangement commencing upon delivery of the currently available software products.

The Company recognizes revenue pursuant to the requirements of the American Institute of Certified Public Accountants ("AICPA") Statement of Position No. 97-2 "Software Revenue Recognition" ("SOP 97-2"), issued in October 1997, as amended by AICPA Statement of Position No. 98-4 and No. 98-9. SOP 97-2 was effective for the Company April 1, 1998. Amendment 98-4 deferred for one year to April 1, 1999, the effective date of certain SOP 97-2 provisions pertaining to multiple-element arrangements. SOP 98-9 amended SOP 97-2 and requires recognition of revenue under the "residual method" when certain criteria are met and was effective for the Company April 1, 1999. These statements set forth GAAP for recognizing revenue on software transactions and establish four criteria necessary in order to recognize revenue—persuasive evidence of an arrangement exists, delivery has occurred, the fee is fixed or determinable and collectibility is probable. Under the residual method, revenue is recognized in a multiple element arrangement when company-specific objective evidence of fair value exists for all of the undelivered elements in the arrangement, but does not exist for one or more of the delivered elements in the arrangement. At the outset of the arrangement with the customer, the Company defers revenue for the fair value of its undelivered elements (e.g., maintenance, consulting, education services) and recognizes revenue for the remainder of the arrangement fee attributable to the elements initially delivered in the arrangement when the criteria in SOP 97-2 have been met. For license arrangements prior to December 2000 (referred to as the "old Business Model"), once the four criteria in SOP 97-2 were met, revenue was recognized up-front for such delivered elements. Under the new Business Model, once the four criteria are met, revenue attributable to license and maintenance fees is recognized ratably over the arrangement term as the terms of such arrangements provide for flexible contractual provisions, such as "unspecified future deliverables."

Subscription Revenue: Subscription revenue represents the ratable recognition of revenue by the Company attributable to license arrangements under the new Business Model.

Deferred subscription revenue, in general, represents the aggregate portion of all undiscounted contractual and committed license and maintenance fees pursuant to all new Business Model arrangements that has not yet been recognized as revenue on a ratable basis over the life of the license arrangement.

Beginning in fiscal year 2002, the Company has disaggregated the total deferred subscription revenue into two components, the amount of cash collected in excess of the amount recognized as revenue and the amount that has not yet been collected that has not been recognized as revenue. Each appear within the Company's Consolidated Balance Sheets as "Deferred subscription revenue (collected)," and as "Deferred subscription revenue," a component of installment accounts receivable, respectively. The components of installment accounts receivables are detailed in Note 5. Each of these components is further classified as either current or non-current. Balances applicable to fiscal year 2001 have been reclassified for comparability purposes.

Software Fees and Other: Prior to December 2000, the Company executed software license arrangements that included contractual provisions that resulted in the recognition of revenue attributable to the software products upon delivery of the software products, provided that the arrangement fee was fixed or determinable, collectibility of the fee was probable and persuasive evidence of an arrangement existed.

The Company has a standard business practice of entering into long term installment contracts with customers. The Company has a history of enforcing the contract terms and successfully collecting under such arrangements, and therefore considers such fees fixed or determinable.

The Company also enters into license arrangements with distribution partners whereby revenue is recognized upon sell-through to the end user by the distribution partner.

Maintenance: For arrangements executed under the old Business Model, maintenance was bundled for a portion of the term of the license arrangement. Under these arrangements, the fair value of the maintenance, which was based on optional annual renewal rates stated in the arrangement, initially was deferred and subsequently amortized into revenue over the initial contractual term of the arrangement. Maintenance renewals have been recognized ratably over the term of the renewal arrangement. The Company has recently experienced maintenance renewal rates on such contracts of approximately 80%.

The "Deferred maintenance revenue" line item on the Company's Consolidated Balance Sheets principally represents payments received in advance of services rendered as of the balance sheet dates.

For arrangements executed under the new Business Model, maintenance is bundled for the entire term of the license arrangement. Under these arrangements, maintenance revenue is included in subscription revenue and is recognized ratably over the term of the license arrangement, along with the license fee, commencing upon delivery of the currently available software products.

Financing Fees: Accounts receivable resulting from old Business Model product sales with extended payment terms are discounted to present value at prevailing market rates. In subsequent periods, the receivable is increased to the amount due and payable by the customer through the accretion of financing revenue on the unpaid receivables due in future years.

Professional Services: Professional services revenue is derived from the Company's consulting services and educational programs. The fair value of the professional services, which is based on fees charged to customers when the related services are sold separately or under time and materials contracts, initially is deferred and subsequently recognized as revenue when the services are performed. For professional services rendered pursuant to a fixed-price contract, revenue is recognized on the percentage-of-completion method.

Source: Computer Associates International, Inc., 10-K Statement, March 31, 2002.

EXHIBIT 4

Computer Associates International, Inc. Pro Forma Results of Operations

To provide comparable financial results, management's discussion and analysis is supplemented with separate pro forma financial information. This pro forma information is presented in order to give effect to the purchase of PLATINUM and Sterling under the assumption that the Company, PLATINUM and Sterling operated under the new Business Model since their inception. Pro forma operating results are calculated by adjusting prior period revenue recorded under the old Business Model to revenue recognized on a ratable basis under the new Business Model, exclusive of acquisition amortization and special items. Reconciliations of GAAP results to pro forma operating results are provided below. While these results may not be indicative of operations had these acquisitions actually occurred on that date and had the Company historically been operating under the new Business Model, the Company believes they provide a basis for comparison at the outset of the transition to the new Business Model. Professional services revenue and total expenses are identical under both the new and old Business Models; therefore, management's discussion and analysis of these captions has not been repeated under the pro forma results of operations. The following pro forma measures may not be comparable to similarly titled measures reported by other companies.

(in millions, except per share amts)	Fiscal Year Ended March 31, 2002			Fiscal Year Ended March 31, 2001		
	GAAP Results	Adjustments	Pro Forma Operating Results	GAAP Results	Adjustments	Pro Forma Operating Results
Revenue[8]	$2,964	$2,837[1]	$5,801	$4,190	$1,368[2]	$5,558
Total expenses[8]	4,349	(1,015)[3]	3,334	4,856	(820)[4]	4,036
Pretax (loss) income	(1,385)	3,852[5]	2,467	(666)	2,188[5]	1,522
Income tax (benefit) provision	(283)	1,208[6]	925	(75)	646[6]	571
Net loss	(1,102)		N/A	(591)		N/A
Net operating income	N/A		1,542	N/A		951
Diluted EPS	($1.91)		N/A	($1.02)		N/A
Shares used	577		N/A	582		N/A
Diluted operating EPS	N/A		$2.61	N/A		$1.61
Shares used	577	14[7]	591	582	10[7]	592

(1) Represents amortization of revenue recognized at contract signing from direct product sales in prior fiscal years for CA ($2,513), Sterling ($161) and PLATINUM ($163) as if revenue had been ratably recognized since their inception.

(2) Represents amortization of revenue recognized at contract signing from direct product sales in prior fiscal years for CA ($2,317), Sterling ($228) and PLATINUM ($252) as if revenue had been ratably recognized since their inception, offset by revenue recognized up-front ($1,429) under the old Business Model.

(3) Represents the elimination of acquisition amortization ($956) and a charge associated with the impairment of assets for sale ($59).

(4) Represents the elimination of acquisition amortization ($973), a gain associated with the 1995 Stock Plan ($184) and a charge related to the Inacom bankruptcy ($31).

(5) Represents the effect on pre-tax loss resulting from the adjustments to revenue and expenses reflected in footnotes (1), (2), (3), and (4).

(6) Represents the tax effect of adjustments. The assumed effective tax rate approximated 37.5%.

(7) Represents the inclusion of common stock equivalents since they are no longer antidilutive.

(8) Prior period adjusted to conform with current period presentation. See Note 1 of the Consolidated Financial Statements for additional information.

Total pro forma revenue for the fiscal year ended March 31, 2002 was $5.801 billion, an increase of 4%, or $243 million, over the prior year pro forma revenue of $5.558 billion. The increase was attributable to the ratable recognition of revenue on contracts transacted during the prior fiscal year, partially offset by a reduction in professional services revenue ($222 million), which was primarily the result of the divestiture of FSG in the third quarter of fiscal year 2001, which generated $94 million of revenue in that fiscal year and the Company's decision to reduce professional services associated with non-CA products. North America and international pro forma revenue represented 64% and 36%, respectively, of overall pro forma revenue in both fiscal years 2002 and 2001. The international pro forma revenue was unfavorably impacted by the effect of exchange rates on the U.S. dollar versus foreign currencies.

On a pro forma basis, pre-tax income excluding acquisition amortization and special charges was $2.467 billion for fiscal year 2002, an increase of 62%, or $945 million, over prior year's pre-tax income of $1.522 billion, exclusive of acquisition amortization and special items. Pro forma net income, excluding acquisition amortization and special items, was $1.542 billion for the fiscal year ended March 31, 2002, an increase of $591 million, or 62%, over fiscal year 2001. The increase was largely attributable to the Company's emphasis on overall cost control measures related to a reduction in the Company's headcount of approximately 3,000 over the prior fiscal year. The Company's consolidated annual effective tax rate, excluding acquisition amortization and special items, was assumed to be 37.5% for both fiscal years 2002 and 2001.

Source: Computer Associates 10-K Statement, March 31, 2002.

EXHIBIT 5

Continuing Members of Board of Directors, Computer Associates International, Inc.

Name	Age	Director Share	Share Ownership
Russell M. Artzt (1)	52	1980	0.6%
Executive Vice President—Research and Development since April 1987 and the Senior Development Officer of the Company since 1976			
Alfonse M. D'Amato (2) (4)	61	1999	
Partner in Park Strategies LLP, a business consulting firm, since January 1999. United States Senator from January 1981 until January 1999. During his tenure, he served as Chairman of the Senate Committee on Banking, Housing and Urban Affairs, and Chairman of the Commission on Security and Cooperation in Europe. He is also a director of Avis Rent-a-Car, Inc. and NRT Incorporated.			
Lewis Ranieri (1) (3)	54	2001	
Founder and prime originator of Hyperion Partners L.P. and Hyperion Partners II L.P. (collectively "Hyperion"). He is also Vice Chairman and Director of Hyperion Capital Management, Inc. and chairman or director of various Hyperion entities. Since June 26, 2001, Mr. Ranieri has served as a director of the Company. From July 1968 to December 1987, he was Vice Chairman of Salomon Brothers, Inc. He also serves as Chairman and Chief Executive Officer of Ranieri & Co., Inc., a private investment corporation. He is also a director of Delphi Financial Group, Inc., Reckson Associates Realty Corp., and Transworld Healthcare, Inc.			
Sanjay Kumar (1)	37	1994	1.1%
President and Chief Operating Officer since January 1994. He was Executive Vice President-Operations from January 1993 to December 1993, Senior Vice President-Planning from April 1989 to December 1992, Vice President-Planning from November 1988 to March 1989. He joined the Company with the acquisition of UCCEL in August 1987.			
Charles B. Wang (1)	54	1976	6.4%
Chief Executive Officer of the Company since 1976 and Chairman of the Board since April 1980. He is also a director of Symbol Technologies, Inc.			

(1) Member Executive Committee.

(2) Member Audit Committee.

(3) Member Stock Option and Compensation Committee.

(4) Member Nominating Committee.

Source: Computer Associates International, Inc., Proxy Statement, 2001.

DICOM Group plc and Captiva Software Corp.

In early 2005, John Ventura, a software analyst at a money management firm, received a request from Annette Defoe, the firm's Global Technology Fund portfolio manager, for help in evaluating the investment potential of leading firms in the information capture software market. Defoe was impressed by the sector's recent stock performance, and asked Ventura to analyze the two largest firms in the market, DICOM Group plc and Captiva Software Corp. to assess whether they would satisfy his objective of investing in technology firms with superior growth and profitability prospects.

INFORMATION CAPTURE MARKET[1]

Information capture arose as businesses demanded the ability to scan paper documents, and to index, store, and archive the resulting images. By 2004, the market had evolved as providers were able to "collect paper documents, forms and e-documents, transform them into accurate, retrievable information, and deliver them into business applications and databases."[2]

The steady worldwide market growth in 2003 and 2004 was driven by a number of factors. Customers had become used to the convenience of data access on the internet and were demanding comparable electronic access to documents for a variety of uses. In addition, despite predictions to the contrary, paper use by businesses was increasing, leading to increased demand for information capture. Other factors that played into the strong market conditions included new regulatory requirements for maintaining documents (e.g., Sarbanes-Oxley), increased company security needs for preserving paper records highlighted by the experience of companies affected by 9/11, opportunities to improve productivity by automating document processing, and government initiatives to make documents available online.

Market research firms projected that the information capture market would experience growth of 7–8% through 2006. For example, in a 2003 report, Strategy Partners valued worldwide industry sales at $772 million (£480 million) in 2002,

Professor Paul M. Healy prepared this case. This case was developed from published sources. HBS cases are developed solely as the basis for class discussion. Cases are not intended to serve as endorsements, sources of primary data, or illustrations of effective or ineffective management.

1. Background information on the information capture industry is drawn from the 2004 annual reports of DICOM Group plc and Captiva Software Corp.

2. DICOM Group plc 2004 Annual Report, p. 15.

and forecasted compound annual growth of 7.1% for Europe and 7.8% for North America through 2006.[3]

DICOM GROUP PLC

DICOM was formed in Switzerland by Otto and Martin Schmid in 1991. The company initially focused on distributing professional document scanners and information capture software. In 1993 Christoph Löslein joined the firm and founded a subsidiary in Germany. The firm subsequently expanded into the remainder of Europe and into South East Asia. It also began providing technical and professional services through its distribution network. In 1996 it listed on the London Stock Exchange.

The 2000 acquisition of Kofax Image Products, a US-based information capture software company for $56 million, broadened DICOM from a pure distribution and services business into information capture software development. The new company expanded the software business through a combination of internal R&D through its Kofax subsidiary (£7.9 million in 2004 and £7.3 million in 2003) and strategic acquisitions of new technologies. By 2004, its software products were able to handle information capture from structured documents (where the geographic location of specific information was already know), semi-structured documents such as forms and invoices (where the location of information could be narrowed down to a general region), and unstructured documents such as correspondence, Web pages, PDF files, and paper contracts (where the location of information could not be easily predicted).

The firm's selling model, in part reflecting its history, differed by geographic region. In Europe and Asia, DICOM Group's sales force sold hardware (primarily scanners), Kofax capture software, as well as capture services to resellers and integrators, who then provided content management and other office automation solutions to end users. In the US, the company operated under the Kofax name, and its Kofax sales force sold only Kofax software (and no hardware) to resellers.

From 2000 to 2004, DICOM grew steadily from an annual turnover of £99 million to £156 million. As shown in **Table A**, the company's turnover in 2004 was

TABLE A

DICOM Turnover and Operating Profits by Business Segment and Geographic Market for the Year Ended June 31, 2004 (in £ million)

	Turnover	Operating profit before goodwill amortization	Operating profit
Business Segments			
Information capture	119,532	11,844	8,623
Samsung General Agency	36,665	1,078	1,078
Geographic Markets			
Europe	120,459	6,824	5,504
North America	30,309	6,865	5,067
Australasia	4,426	(767)	(870)

Source: DICOM Group plc 2004 Annual Report, p. 53.

3. Ibid., p. 16.

concentrated in Europe in the information capture market. Its only other source of turnover was from Samsung General Agency, a partnership with Samsung to market LCD computer displays, and LCD and plasma screens and TVs in Switzerland.

Financial statements for DICOM for the years ended June 31, 2003 and 2004, prepared in accordance with the U.K. accounting standards, are shown in **Exhibit 1**. In discussing the results for the 2004 year, the firm's Chairman, Otto Schmid, noted that "the weakness of the US dollar (on average 9% lower than in the previous financial year) has adversely affected the reported sterling results of our US operations where over half of the Group's operating profits are generated."[4] In local currency, Information Capture (IC) sales grew by 5% for 2004, led by 14% growth in DICOM's own product sales. The company's stock performance from July 1, 2002 to February 28, 2005 is presented in **Exhibit 2** and stock market information is shown in **Exhibit 3**.

CAPTIVA SOFTWARE CORP.

Captiva Software was formed in late July 1998 as a result of the merger of two firms that developed and distributed form-processing software applications, FormWare Corp. (located in Park City, Utah) and Wheb Systems Inc. (from San Diego). Captiva was in turn acquired by ActionPoint in 2002, which took its name and business. The new firm was located in San Diego and listed on NASDAQ.

Like DICOM, Captiva used its own research ($9.7 million spent in 2004 and $9 million in 2003) and strategic acquisitions to provide its customers with software products that covered capture from structured, semi-structured, and unstructured documents. The company sold scanners, its own software and maintenance services to a diverse set of end users in the insurance, financial services, technology, government, and manufacturing industries (61% of sale). In addition, 39% of its revenues came from sales through resellers. Eighty percent of sales were generated in the domestic U.S. market.

Financial statements for Captiva for the years ended December 31, 2003 and 2004, prepared in accordance with U.S. Accounting Standards, are shown in **Exhibit 4**. Results for 2004 were affected by the February acquisition of ADP Context for $5.5 million. The acquisition increased sales for the year by roughly 9% and net income by 17%. Management anticipated that the firm would be able to continue its strong growth by leveraging its existing customer base, increasing sales from resellers, expanding into new geographic markets, targeting smaller companies, and broadening product offerings through research and strategic acquisitions.[5] The company's stock performance from July 1, 2002 to February 28, 2005 (when the stock was valued at $83.90 per share) is presented in **Exhibit 2** and stock market information is shown in **Exhibit 3**.

CONCLUSION

Ventura sat down to prepare the key financial ratios and cash flow data for the two companies. He recalled that since they followed different accounting standards, it might be worth assessing their effect on reported performance. **Exhibit 5** summarizes

4. DICOM Group Annual Report, p. 6.
5. Captiva Software Corp. 2004 10-K, p. 3.

the accounting methods used by the two companies. After reviewing their business strategies and financial performance Ventura had to decide whether it was worth recommending one, both or neither stock to Defoe for her Global Technology Fund.

QUESTIONS

1. What are the key business success factors and risks for DICOM and Captiva?

2. Do the financial statements for the two firms enable you to compare their performance? If not, what changes need to be made to ensure comparability?

3. What financial ratios would you use to judge the performance of DICOM and Captiva? How do they compare on these dimensions?

4. Which company do you rate as the better investment prospect? Why?

EXHIBIT I

Financial Statements for DICOM Group plc for the Years Ended June 30, 2003 and 2004

CONSOLIDATED PROFIT AND LOSS ACCOUNT

	Year to June 30, 2004 (£000)	Year to June 30, 2003 (£000)
Turnover	156,197	156,432
Cost of sales	(93,291)	(97,386)
Gross Profit	62,906	59,046
Operating expenses	(53,205)	(50,119)
Operating profit before goodwill amortization	12,922	11,796
Goodwill amortization	(3,221)	(2,869)
Operating profit	9,701	8,927
Share of results of associated undertakings	91	41
Loss on disposal of fixed asset investment	(2,218)	–
Net interest receivable/payable and similar charges	183	(167)
Interest receivable	376	247
Interest payable	(193)	(414)
Profit on ordinary activities before taxation	7,757	8,801
Taxation	(3,885)	(3,407)
Profit on ordinary activities after taxation	3,872	5,394
Minority interests	24	58
Profit attributable to ordinary shareholders	3,896	5,452
Earnings per ordinary share:		
Basic	18.7p	26.2p
Diluted	18.2p	26.0p
Dividend per ordinary share	5.55p	4.83p

Source: DICOM Group plc annual reports.

(continued)

Financial Statements for DICOM Group plc for the Years Ended June 30, 2003 and 2004 (*continued*)

BALANCE SHEETS

	Group at June 30, 2004 (£000)	Group at June 30, 2003 (£000)
Fixed assets		
Intangible assets	41,432	43,785
Tangible assets	5,135	4,978
Investments	398	9,303
	46,965	58,066
Current assets		
Stocks	10,864	11,050
Debtors	33,791	34,409
Trade	23,925	23,000
Deferred tax asset	488	—
Other	9,378	11,409
Investments	126	110
Cash at bank and in hand	23,273	6,758
	68,054	52,327
Creditors		
Amounts falling due within one year	(38,615)	(37,448)
Bank and other interest-bearing loans	(1,641)	(3,525)
Trade	(13,481)	(12,022)
Other	(23,493)	(21,901)
Net current assets	29,439	14,879
Total assets less current liabilities	76,404	72,945
Amounts falling due after more than one year	(4,628)	(2,732)
Long-term loans	(738)	(1,098)
Other	(3,890)	(1,634)
Provisions for deferred taxation	(631)	(699)
Net assets	71,145	69,514
Capital and reserves		
Called up share capital	2,112	2,088
Share premium account	52,730	51,868
Merger reserve	1,717	1,717
ESOP shares	(503)	(502)
Profit and loss account	15,147	14,331
Shareholders funds—Equity	71,203	69,502
Minority Interests—Equity	(58)	12
	71,145	69,514

Source: DICOM Group plc annual reports.

(*continued*)

Financial Statements for DICOM Group plc for the Years Ended June 30, 2003 and 2004 (*continued*)

CASH FLOW STATEMENT

	Year to June 30, 2004 (£000)	Year to June 30, 2003 (£000)
Reconciliation of operating profit to operating cash flows:		
Operating profit	9,701	8,927
Depreciation and amortization	5,948	5,034
Profit on sale of subsidiary undertaking	—	(170)
Profit/loss on sale of tangible fixed assets	7	2
Decrease/(increase) in stocks	285	(107)
Increase in debtors	(1,684)	(555)
Increase in creditors	4,702	2,410
Foreign exchange differences	(316)	(88)
Net cash inflow from operating activities	18,643	15,453
Returns on investments and servicing of finance:		
Interest paid	(235)	(402)
Interest received	391	264
Dividend paid to minorities	—	(25)
Net cash inflow (outflow) for returns on investments and services of finance	156	(163)
Capital expenditure and financial investments:		
Purchase of tangible fixed assets	(2,608)	(2,184)
Sale/(Purchase) of fixed assets investments	269	(439)
Disposal of fixed assets investment	4,906	—
Sale of tangible fixed assets	82	31
Net cash inflow (outflow) for capital expenditure and financial investments	2,649	(2,592)
Acquisitions and disposals:		
Purchase of subsidiary undertakings	(1,091)	(9,954)
Net overdraft acquired with subsidiary	(149)	(48)
Disposal of subsidiaries	3,064	1,604
Net cash disposed with subsidiary	—	(718)
Net cash inflow/(outflow) for acquisitions	1,824	(9,116)
Management of liquid resources:		
Investment in short-term deposits	(13,001)	(849)
Net cash outflow from management of liquid resources	(13,001)	(849)
Financing:		
Issue of ordinary shares (net of issue costs)	886	147
Debt due within a year:		
Loan repayment	(1,972)	—
Loan taken out	—	1,723
Debt due beyond one year:		
Loan repayment	(301)	(33)
Capital element of finance leases repayment	(293)	(371)
	(2,566)	1,319
Net cash (outflow/inflow from financing)	(1,680)	1,466

Source: DICOM Group plc annual reports.

EXHIBIT 2

Stock Performance of DICOM Group plc, Captiva Software Corp., and World Software and Computer Services Index from July 1, 2002 to February 28, 2005

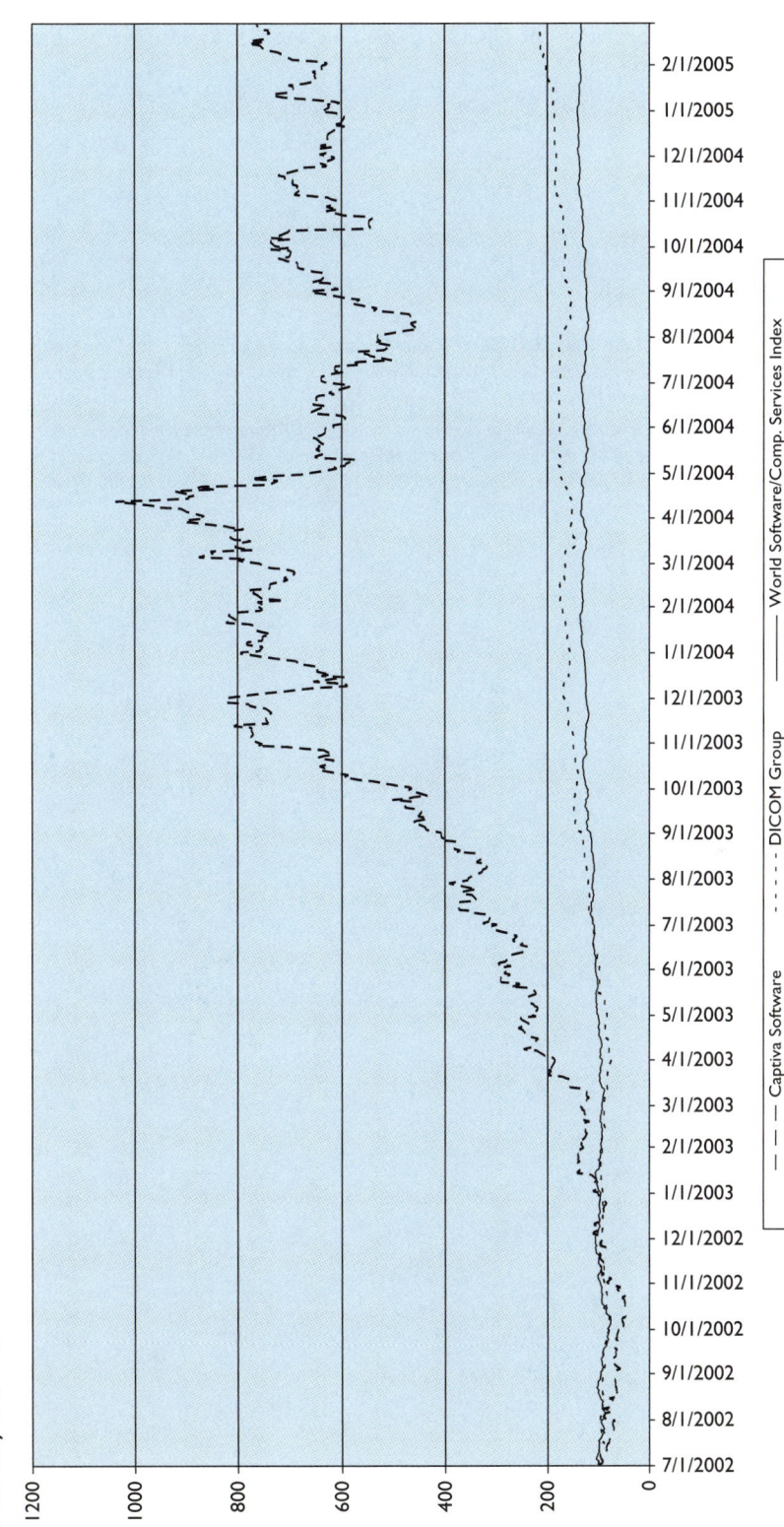

Source: Datastream International.

DICOM Group plc and Captiva Software Corp.

EXHIBIT 3

Stock market information for DICOM Group plc and Captiva Software Corp. on February 28, 2005

	DICOM Group plc	Captiva Software Corp.
Stock price	£9.45	$12.16
Price-earnings multiple	30.6	36.1
Price to book equity multiple	2.7	4.0
Estimated cost of equity[1]	6.8%	6.1%

Sources: Datastream International, DICOM Group plc and Captiva Software Corp., the web site for Bank of England (http://www.bankofengland.co.uk/), and the web site for the U.S. Federal Reserve Board (http://www.federalreserve.gov/releases/h15/data.htm).

[1] For DICOM, the cost of equity is estimated as the yield on 10-year UK government bonds on February 28, 2005 (4.7%) plus the company's beta (0.46) multiplied by a market risk premium of 4.5%. For Captiva, the cost of equity is estimated as the yield on 10-year U.S. Treasuries on February 28, 2005 (4.2%) plus the company's beta (0.42) multiplied by the risk premium of 4.5%.

EXHIBIT 4

Financial Statements for Captiva Software Corp. for the Years ended December 31, 2003 and 2004 (amounts in $000, except per share figures)

CONSOLIDATED BALANCE SHEETS

	2004	2003
ASSETS		
Current assets:		
Cash and cash equivalents	$27,273	$16,038
Accounts receivable, net	13,612	10,780
Prepaid expenses and other current assets	3,301	3,314
Total current assets	44,186	30,132
Property and equipment, net	1,355	924
Other assets	1,558	2,354
Goodwill	10,244	6,082
Intangible assets, net	3,197	3,762
Total assets	$60,540	$43,254
LIABILITIES AND STOCKHOLDERS' EQUITY		
Current liabilities:		
Accounts payable	$1,462	$891
Accrued compensation and related liabilities	3,372	2,793
Other liabilities	4,508	3,166
Line of credit	—	—
Deferred revenue	13,296	11,264
Total current liabilities	22,638	18,114
Deferred revenue	496	519
Other liabilities	359	235
Total liabilities	23,493	18,868
Stockholders' equity		
Preferred stock, $0.001 par value, 2,000 shares authorized, none issued and outstanding	—	—
Common stock, $0.01 par value, 25,000 shares authorized, 12,294 and 10,790 issued and outstanding at December 31, 2004, 2003, and 2003 respectively	123	108
Additional paid-in capital	32,549	24,171
Retained earnings	4,179	38
Accumulated other comprehensive income	196	69
Total stockholders' equity	37,047	24,386
Total liabilities and stockholders' equity	$60,540	$43,254

Source: Captiva Software Corp. 10-K reports.

(continued)

DICOM Group plc and Captiva Software Corp.

Financial Statements for Captiva Software Corp. for the Years ended December 31, 2003 and 2004 (amounts in $000, except per share figures) (*continued*)

CONSOLIDATED STATEMENT OF OPERATIONS

	2004	2003
Net revenues:		
Software	$33,804	$27,006
Services	27,480	22,724
Hardware and other	6,728	7,415
Total revenues	68,012	57,145
Cost of revenues:		
Software	4,660	2,631
Services	10,222	9,936
Hardware and other	5,429	5,969
Amortization of purchased intangibles	2,573	2,095
Total cost of revenues	22,884	20,631
Gross profit	45,128	36,514
Operating expenses:		
Research and development	9,706	8,979
Sales and marketing	21,477	17,816
General administrative	7,034	6,102
Merger-related restructuring costs	(181)	(58)
Write-off of in-process research and development	66	—
Write-off of withdrawn stock offering	205	—
Total operating expenses	38,307	32,839
Income from operations	6,821	3,675
Other income:		
Interest and other income, net	264	74
Income before taxes	7,085	3,749
Provision for income taxes	2,944	1,162
Net income	$4,141	$2,587
Earnings per share:		
Basic	$0.36	$0.27
Diluted	$0.31	$0.23

Source: Captiva Software Corp. 10-K reports.

(*continued*)

Financial Statements for Captiva Software Corp. for the Years ended December 31, 2003 and 2004 (amounts in $000, except per share figures) (*continued*)

CONSOLIDATED STATEMENTS OF CASH FLOW

	2004	2003
Cash flows from operating activities		
Net income	$4,141	$2,587
Adjustments to reconcile net income to net cash provided by operating activities		
Depreciation and amortization	3,166	2,702
Tax benefit from stock option exercises	3,519	3,641
Deferred income taxes	(720)	(2,177)
Write-off of in-process research and development	66	—
Changes in operating assets and liabilities, net of effect of acquisitions		
Accounts receivable, net	(1,453)	984
Prepaid expenses and other assets	802	(921)
Accounts payable	571	192
Deferred revenue	544	456
Accrued compensation and related liabilities	579	(121)
Other liabilities	1,320	(1,441)
Net cash provided by operating activities	12,535	5,902
Cash flows from investing activities:		
Purchases of property and equipment	(888)	(517)
Cash paid to acquire Context, including direct acquisition costs	(5,459)	—
Net cash used in investing activities	(6,347)	(517)
Cash flows from financing activities		
Repayment of borrowings under credit agreement	—	(2,145)
Proceeds from issuance of common stock	4,872	5,050
Net cash provided by financing activities	4,872	2,905
Effect of exchange rate changes on cash	175	295
Net increase in cash and cash equivalents	11,235	8,585
Cash and cash equivalents at beginning of year	16,038	7,453
Cash and cash equivalents at end of year	$27,273	$16,038

Source: Captiva Software Corp. 10-K reports.

DICOM Group plc and Captiva Software Corp.

EXHIBIT 5

Accounting Methods Used by DICOM Group plc and Captiva Software Corp. for 2003–2004 Financial Statements

Accounting item	DICOM Group plc	Captiva Software Corp.
Depreciation	Recorded on a straight-line basis over 2–5 years.	Recorded on straight-line basis over 3–5 years.
Software development costs	Expensed in period of outlay.	Expensed in period of outlay. Rules require capitalization of costs once technological feasibility reached, but no costs have been capitalized.
Goodwill	Amortized on a straight-line basis over 3–20 years. Amortization is non-deductible expense for tax purposes. Regular tests for impairment conducted.	Not amortized, but tested annually for impairment.
Intangible assets	Not reported.	Amortized on a straight-line basis over 3–4 years for completed technology, 3–5 years for customer contracts and relationships, and 5 years for patents and trademarks.
Deferred taxes	Deferred tax obligation reported in full for timing differences between financial reporting and tax accounting using tax rate expected to apply when differences are expected to reverse. Deferred tax assets are recognized if it is more likely than not that they will be recovered.	Accounted for under the asset and liability method, based on differences between financial reporting and tax bases of assets and liabilities using enacted tax rates that will be in effect when differences are expected to reverse. Valuation allowances are created to reduce deferred tax assets to amounts expected to be realized.
Stock-based compensation	Method of recording options not reported, but probably recorded on intrinsic value method, which results in no expense.	Recorded using intrinsic value method, which results in no expense. If the fair value method had been used, net income would have been reduced by $2,857 and $1,291 in 2004 and 2003, respectively.

(continued)

Accounting Methods Used by DICOM Group plc and Captiva Software Corp. for 2003–2004 Financial Statements (*continued*)

Accounting item	DICOM Group plc	Captiva Software Corp.
Turnover/revenue recognition	Turnover from software licenses is recognized upon shipment. Fee income from installation, consulting and training are recognized over the period when the services are provided. Fees from maintenance and support contracts are billed in advance and recognized monthly, spread evenly over the period covered by the fee. Turnover from hardware products is recognized upon shipment.	Software revenues recorded on three bases: (a) licensing revenues are recognized when software is shipped; (b) subscription revenues are recognized ratably over the term of the arrangement, and (c) royalty revenues are recorded when resellers ship products incorporating software provided resellers obligations are non-cancelable and not subject to acceptance rights or return. Service revenues from software maintenance and support contracts are recognized on a straight-line basis over the support period, usually 12 months. Revenues from hardware sales, typically purchased from third-party vendors and resold to Captiva customers for use with company software, are recognized on delivery. Deferred revenues primarily arise from undelivered maintenance and support services.

Source: DICOM Group plc 2004 annual report and Captiva Software Corp. 2004 10-K report.

Hewlett-Packard–Compaq: The Merger Decision

For the past two-and-a-half years, the HP Board of Directors and management team have been evaluating the best strategic move for HP. Together, we debated the hard questions, we looked at all the alternatives and we became convinced that a merger with Compaq is the single best way to create shareowner value and return HP to industry leadership.

— HP CEO Carleton Fiorina, HP 2001 Annual Report

We profoundly disagree with management's assertion that HP needs to make this large and very risky acquisition. To undertake the proposed merger is to make a big, long-term, bet-the-company move. It worsens the HP stockholders' portfolio of businesses. It does not solve key strategic problems. It creates enormous immediate risk and intermediate-term incremental challenges, and it comes at a very high price.

— HP Dissident Board Member Walter Hewlett, 2001 Proxy Statement

On March 19, 2002, amid boos from the audience at a special meeting for shareholders, Carleton (Carly) Fiorina, president and CEO of Hewlett-Packard (HP), announced the shareholders' approval of the acquisition of rival Compaq Computer by a "slim but sufficient" 51.4% margin. The controversial $24 billion deal marked the largest merger in the history of the computer industry. At its core, the merger was designed to create a global technology powerhouse that could provide end-to-end products and services increasingly demanded by lucrative enterprise (large-scale business) customers. In so doing, the merger would position the combined company to challenge industry leader IBM.

The March 19 meeting capped off a bitter six-month proxy fight that pitted HP heir and dissident HP board member Walter Hewlett, who opposed the merger, against HP's new CEO and its remaining board members, who favored the acquisition. When HP first announced its intention to acquire Compaq on September 4, 2001,[1] the news sent HP's and Compaq's stock prices down approximately 19% and

Professor Krishna Palepu and Research Associate Jonathan Barnett prepared this case. This case was developed from published sources. HBS cases are developed solely as the basis for class discussion. Cases are not intended to serve as endorsements, sources of primary data, or illustrations of effective or ineffective management.

1. HP and Compaq issued a joint press release announcing their intention to merge late in the evening on September 3, 2001. September 4, 2001, was the first trading day that reflected the merger news.

10%, respectively. Some seven months later, on the day of the March 19 meeting, shares of HP and Compaq continued to trail preannouncement levels by 19% and 10%, respectively. The slim approval margin coupled with the severity of the market's reaction left many wondering whether the deal was a good one.

INDUSTRY BACKGROUND

The computer hardware industry in 2001 was highly competitive and marked by frequent product introductions, continuous improvement in product price/performance characteristics, and fierce competition. In the face of continuous change, participants were either able to quickly tailor their product and service offerings in a way that allowed them to operate profitably, or they were acquired or dissolved. IBM and Dell were examples of firms that succeeded by pursuing divergent strategies. IBM pursued a full-service provider model and was well entrenched in high-growth, high-margin businesses. Dell pursued a focus strategy, centered principally on lower-margin segments of the industry—personal computers (PCs) and servers. Compaq, once the industry leader in PCs, faced significant challenges as it tried to regain its position in the industry through a series of acquisitions that proved somewhat difficult to digest.

IBM

IBM introduced its first computer in 1952. Throughout the 1960s and 1970s, IBM's combined strength in research and development (R&D) and marketing earned it market share near 80%. In 1981, the IBM PC was introduced, giving rise to a PC industry based on Microsoft's Windows operating system and Intel's computer chips (collectively referred to as the "Wintel" standard). Because Wintel standards were open and available to all PC manufacturers, many PC clone manufacturers entered to compete with IBM. Compaq initially, and Dell later on, became the PC industry leader, posing significant challenges for IBM. As a result of rapid advances in computing power, PCs were increasingly able to handle complex computing tasks, challenging the role of high-priced mainframe computers, which were the mainstay of IBM. As a result, after earning $6.6 billion in 1984, IBM began to erode in performance. In 1992, IBM lost $5 billion, and in 1993 losses grew to nearly $8 billion, making it the worst year in IBM's history. That same year, CEO John Akers was replaced by Louis Gerstner, the first outsider to run the company.

Gerstner set a new course for IBM that centered on offering customers "integrated solutions"—comprehensive, end-to-end solutions consisting of hardware, software, and services. This was a marked difference from the predominant industry model, which emphasized selling individual components and left the integration task to customers. In offering integrated solutions, Gerstner sought to recapture lost PC margins by bundling PCs with higher-growth, higher-margin offerings, led by software and high value-added services. Moreover, in response to what Gerstner described as a new era in computing—deemed network-centric computing and exemplified by the Internet—IBM shifted its hardware focus away from low-margin PCs toward more profitable servers and storage, which enabled networks to function.

Gerstner believed the transition to a networked world would create considerable demand for highly profitable services, and he moved quickly to establish IBM's position in the then-nascent services market. In 1995, IBM formed IBM Global Services (IGS), a single, global team that delivered seamless, integrated solutions to customers worldwide.[2] In 1996, IBM merged its consulting practice into IGS, making IGS the world's largest information technology (IT) services provider. This decision reflected a shift in IBM's services philosophy from merely offering services as an after-sales activity such as maintenance to a broader, and more profitable, approach of assisting customers in every facet of their ongoing business operations.

Between 1995 and 2001, IGS revenue and employee count increased at a compound annual rate of 9.5%. Much of this growth was the result of an expanded portfolio of offerings that included many more e-business services as a result of the powerful effect of the Internet on commerce. By 2001, IGS had become the world's largest consultancy, systems integrator, and strategic outsourcing leader. In 2001, IGS revenue topped $35 billion, with a backlog of $102 billion, and surpassed IBM's hardware revenue for the first time. That same year, IGS accounted for 41% of IBM's total worldwide revenue, 47% of pretax profit, and with 148,300 employees, nearly half of the company's workforce. In 2001, IBM not only led the industry in IT services, but it was also the number one or two company in total software—including high-growth Web software, servers, high-end disk storage, and maintenance.[3]

IBM's integrated solutions strategy offered customers the benefits of a one-stop shopping experience with packaged solutions offered at a predictable price. Though the strategy met with initial success, it involved one potential challenge. Since IBM manufactured much of the hardware that could form a part of the solution its IT consulting and services arm might advocate to a client, customers might be concerned about a potential conflict of interest. As a result, some customers still preferred to work with independent consultants, such as Accenture, that could both recommend best-of-breed solutions and implement them.

Dell Computer

Dell Computer was principally focused on selling built-to-order, competitively priced PCs and servers. Dell was founded on a simple, yet powerful, concept: "by selling computer systems directly to customers, Dell could best understand their needs and efficiently provide the most effective computing solutions to meet those needs."[4] In the words of Michael Dell, "the competitive advantages of the direct business model entailed great prices on the latest relevant technology, outstanding reliability and superb service."[5] In addition, high levels of customer satisfaction engendered loyalty and led to repeat purchases.

Dell's early business model consisted of buying component parts wholesale, manufacturing IBM computer clones, and selling them by mail order to customers who did not want to pay the higher prices charged by computer stores. In addition to eliminating the retail markup, the direct-to-customer model circumvented the need to maintain months of aging and costly inventory, which was particularly advantageous given increasingly shorter component product life cycles. In the absence of inventory stockpiles, Dell was able to introduce the latest technology more quickly than companies with slow-moving, indirect distribution channels. Moreover, with Dell's focus on computers based on open standards, customers got the benefit of extensive research and development from an entire industry, rather than from a single company. As a

---

2. "IBM Global Services: A Brief History," IBM Corporate Archives, May 2002.

3. "IBM Global Services: A Brief History," IBM Corporate Archives, May 2002.

4. "Dell at a Glance—Company Facts," Dell Computer Corporation.

5. Dell Computer Corporation 2001 Annual Report.

result of these advantages, Dell was able to sell PCs at about 40% of the price of a comparable IBM machine.[6] The business model was an instant success, and by 1992, just eight years after its founding, Dell was included among the *Fortune* 500 list of the world's largest companies. The following year, Dell joined ranks as one of the top five computer system makers worldwide.

Because the Internet promised to further reduce operating expenses by better coordinating customer and component parts orders, Dell moved quickly to launch www.Dell.com in 1994. As the new system was phased in, component inventory was nearly eliminated, and as the system proved viable, Dell moved quickly to refine it. In 1996, Dell began selling PCs through its web site and added online technical support in 1999. By 2001, nearly half of the company's $32 billion in revenue came from Internet-based sales.

Dell's Internet-based direct model not only improved profitability and preserved the advantages of the mail-order model, it offered the added advantage of allowing Dell to move closer to its customers, to better understand their needs, and to tailor the organization to better serve them. Whereas Dell's initial success stemmed from its ability to offer significant price discounts because it sold direct, Dell's success after implementing the new model stemmed from the close relationships it built with its major customers. Indeed, Dell exploited the direct model to lock customers in.

Dell used its abundant profits and cash flow to fuel growth primarily in major corporate accounts. In 1996, Dell began a major push into the network-server market, followed by the introduction of workstations in 1997 and storage products in 1998. In 2000, Dell broadened its high-end network servers and Internet-related services offerings and formed a division for its storage operations.

In 2001, Dell was ranked first in global PC market share. Dell also held the number one ranking in worldwide workstation shipments and was ranked first in the U.S. for standard Wintel architecture-based servers. Despite a challenging industry environment, in fiscal 2001, Dell set company records in unit shipments, revenue, net profit, earnings per share, and cash flow per share. It was also ranked number one in service and customer satisfaction in nearly every industry survey, including receiving the "Reader's Choice" award for service and reliability from *PC Magazine* for the ninth consecutive year.[7] Dell was also extraordinarily profitable. For fiscal years 2001, 2000, 1999, and 1998, Dell's return on invested capital was 355%, 243%, 195%, and 186%, respectively.

Compaq Computer

Compaq Computer was founded in 1982 to manufacture and sell portable IBM-compatible computers. The company sold its first computer in January of 1983 and by year-end had recorded $111 million in sales—the greatest first-year sales record in the history of American business.[8] Compaq's early success was due, in part, to its emphasis on leading-edge technology—what it referred to as "high performance PC technology"—and this edge continued to fuel sales records in subsequent years.[9] In 1987, Compaq was the first company to surpass $1 billion in sales in the first five years of operations, and in 1988 it became the first company to surpass $2 billion in six years.[10]

6. As reported by Hoover's Online.

7. Dell Computer 2001 Annual Report.

8. "Chronology of Computer History," http://www.cyberstreet.com/hcs/museum/chron.htm.

9. Compaq Computer 1988 Annual Report.

10. Compaq Computer 1987 Annual Report.

To sell its products, Compaq leveraged the dealer and supplier network built around the IBM PC. Rather than create a large sales force, Compaq gave exclusive rights to dealers for sales and service of its products and by 1990 had networks in 152 countries. In the wake of the 1991 U.S. recession and in response to aggressive price competition, Compaq adopted a price trendsetter strategy in 1992. To that end, Compaq cut its gross profit margins in half and instituted a price war. IBM responded by introducing aggressively priced PCs; however, by 1994 Compaq surpassed IBM to become the world leader in PC sales.

While Compaq's dealer network supported its rapid growth, it also added a layer of expense that put Compaq at a cost disadvantage to Dell. In 1997, amid heightened PC price competition and diminishing margins, Compaq responded with a two-pronged strategy: emulate Dell by introducing a direct Internet sales channel, and emulate IBM by transforming itself into a full-line provider.

Compaq's direct channel dramatically reduced its own inventory and that in the dealer channel and improved the PC division's cost structure. However, fearing the alienation of its dealers and, in turn, a potential loss of market share to competitors, Compaq continued to ship its products through the retail channel. As long as Compaq continued to fill orders through its dealers, it could only narrow, but not eliminate, the cost advantage of vendors that shipped direct. Furthermore, as long as dealers controlled the customer interface, Compaq was prevented from developing closer relations with customers, such as those fostered by Dell.

In emulating IBM, Compaq sought to shift its business mix away from PCs and toward more profitable higher-end computers and services. To implement this strategy, Compaq acquired Tandem Computer in 1997 and Digital Equipment Corporation in 1998. Tandem enabled Compaq to offer high-end, mission-critical business computing. Digital added minicomputers, a midrange server line, an enterprise sales force, and a field service operation consisting primarily of engineers and maintenance technicians.

Compaq's acquisition of Digital significantly impacted 1998 operating results. Consolidated revenue increased 26.8% to $31.2 billion, almost entirely due to the addition of Digital. However, Compaq ended the year with a net loss of $2.7 billion because of both large write-offs of purchased in-process R&D and merger integration expenses. Compaq expected to report better profit results in subsequent years as it reaped the benefits from the Digital acquisition. However, despite earlier reassurances, on April 9, 1999, Compaq announced that first-quarter earnings would be less than half of Wall Street's consensus estimate as a result of heightened competition and lower-than-expected sales. The news stunned the investment community and caused many to question Compaq's ability to effectively compete while integrating the two companies. The announcement, which created both a credibility problem and loss of investor confidence, triggered a 22% decline in Compaq's stock price. In swift response, Compaq's board ousted its CEO.

In July 1999, Compaq's board announced that its chief information officer, Michael Capellas, would assume the CEO position. "It's hard to describe 1999 as anything but a tough year for Compaq, its employees and its stockholders," recounted Capellas in his first letter to shareholders. "In a strong technology market, our performance was . . . disappointing. Our commercial PC business was hampered by a selling and distribution model that was no longer profitable. We lacked focus. Neither our customers nor our employees clearly understood who Compaq was or where we were going. In this environment, we needed to make some significant changes, and we did."[11]

_____

11. *Compaq Computer 1999 Annual Report.*

Compaq's 1999 revenues reflected the first full year of operations that included both the Tandem and Digital acquisitions. For the year, consolidated revenue increased 24%, gross margins declined to 22.7% due to aggressive PC price competition, and operating expenses increased 26%. Factoring in a one-time gain from the spin-off of Alta Vista, an Internet search engine acquired in the Digital deal, Compaq finished the year with $569 million in net earnings. Compaq shares ended the year down 36%. In 2000, Capellas made the Internet Compaq's primary focus. That year, Compaq began to deliver improved execution. Sales increased 10% to $42 billion, gross margins increased 0.8% to 23.5%, and operating expenses as a percentage of sales declined 3% to 18%.

In 2001, the U.S. economy in general, and the technology sector in particular, softened considerably, due in part to the collapse of the dot-com sector. A dramatic slowdown in business investment was compounded by the September 11 terrorist attacks and tipped the U.S. into its first recession in a decade. Further exacerbating matters was the fact that the economic slowdown was global in scope and included both consumer and business spending. The market downturn took a heavy toll on the high-tech sector, and for the first time in nearly a decade, the information technology industry contracted.

For the year, Compaq's consolidated revenue fell 21% to $33.6 billion. Revenue was negatively impacted by price competition in PCs and low-end servers and by promotions aimed at reducing channel inventory. As a result, gross margins declined 2%. In this environment, Compaq continued to cut costs, lowering operating expenses by 6%. Cost-reduction efforts were not enough, however, to counterbalance declining sales and margins. Compaq ended the year with a $785 million net loss, of which $587 million was attributed to the Access (PC) business (see **Exhibit 1** for a detailed description of Compaq's segments and recent segment performance). In an attempt to further shift emphasis from hardware to services, Compaq bid for consulting firm Proxicom but lost out. Compaq shares lost more than 35% for the year. Despite ongoing efforts to transform Compaq from a PC company into a full-service enterprise computing company, Compaq still faced significant strategic and financial challenges.

One Wall Street analyst commented on Compaq's continued challenges as follows: "Compaq needs to dramatically reduce its cost structure, or it may never be able to fend off Dell in the PC and industry standard server markets. [T]he company also needs to further strengthen its high-end server strategy and its customer perception. Further, to build a true service-centric model, Compaq needs to increase its exposure to value-added professional services, as opposed to slower-growing maintenance services."[12]

HEWLETT-PACKARD

Founded in 1939 in a garage by Stanford University engineers William Hewlett and David Packard, Hewlett-Packard had since grown to become one of the world's leading providers of computing and imaging solutions and services. With 87,000 employees, operations in 120 countries, and revenue of nearly $45 billion in fiscal 2001, HP competed in nearly every major IT product segment.

As reported in the company's annual report, HP sought to be the category leader with respect to each of the specific products and categories in which it competed, and it actively expanded into new and adjacent markets.[13] As of October 31, 2001, HP's

12. Bill Shope, "Compaq Computer," *ABN-AMRO Inc., December 19, 2001*.

13. *Hewlett-Packard 2001 10-K.*

three major business segments included Imaging and Printing Systems, Computing Systems, and Information Technology Services (IT Services).[14]

HP's Imaging and Printing Systems division marketed a broad array of products ranging from low-end printers and supplies to commercial printing solutions. In 2001, the Imaging and Printing Systems division was ranked number one in the $25 billion global printer market, with 40% market share. In 2001, 2000, and 1999, the division accounted for 43%, 41%, and 43% of HP's revenue and 106%, 65%, and 64% of HP's earnings from operations, respectively.

HP's Computing Systems division marketed systems targeting the consumer, commercial (small and midsized businesses), and enterprise segments. With global market shares of 7% and 13%, respectively, HP was ranked fourth in both the $153 billion PC market and in the $50 billion server market. In 2001, 2000, and 1999, the Computing Systems division accounted for 40%, 42%, and 41% of HP's revenue, respectively. The division reduced HP's overall operating income as a result of a loss in 2001, and it accounted for 23% of operating income in 2000 and 1999.

HP's IT Services division marketed design and installation services, hardware-related support and maintenance services, and increasingly consulting and outsourcing services. IT Services was HP's fastest-growing segment, and in 2001 the division was ranked eighth in the $666 billion global services market. In 2001, 2000, and 1999, the IT Services segment accounted for 17%, 14%, and 14% of HP's revenue and 18%, 15%, and 16% of HP's earnings from operations, respectively.

(**Exhibit 2** further describes HP's three business units and summarizes recent segment performance. **Exhibit 3** provides market share estimates for HP and its competitors in the segments in which it competed.)

Late 1990s: Stalled Growth Necessitates Change

In 1998, HP Labs upheld its reputation as a prodigious source of innovation with the introduction of 20 new printing and imaging products—the largest rollout in the company's history. Despite the company's being armed with a suite of new products and against the backdrop of an IT infrastructure-spending boom that began the preceding year, HP's sales growth declined to a 15-year low. Notwithstanding cost-reduction initiatives that included "difficult but necessary" voluntary-severance programs and manufacturing consolidations, "unacceptably high expense growth" contributed to a decline in earnings from operations and net earnings of 11% and 6%, respectively.[15]

While HP management pointed to a weakened macroeconomic environment and competitive price pressures in PCs and printers to help explain its slumping sales, industry observers cited management's inability to keep pace with changing market conditions as a key contributor. Specifically, critics chastised HP management for failing to follow Dell's lead in adopting a low-cost, Internet-based direct sales channel to offset its reliance on the retail channel.[16] HP similarly trailed IBM in establishing itself as a leading provider of both Internet-related products and integrated solutions. In response to criticism and in an effort to improve efficiency, in 1998 HP began to take the steps needed to offer customers the ability to buy PCs online. Despite these efforts, HP's sales continued to decline in 1999. In March, after 33 years of service and under mounting pressure for change, CEO Platt announced his retirement.

---

14. HP utilized an October 31 fiscal year-end.

15. Hewlett-Packard 1998 Annual Report.

16. All told, HP channel partners included approximately 20,000 retail outlets.

Reinventing HP to Lead in the Internet Age

In July 1999, HP's board appointed a new outside president and CEO, Carly Fiorina, with a mandate for radical change—to reinvent HP to lead in the Internet age. A self-described "change CEO," Fiorina had a reputation for being a salesperson extraordinaire at AT&T and Lucent. She also had the requisite expertise in the Internet domain and had previously overseen the large-scale spin-off of Lucent from AT&T. For all of these reasons, Fiorina was selected by the board to be part of HP's answer to stalled growth.[17]

Little more than three months after taking the helm and in her first letter to shareholders, Fiorina promised balanced revenue and earnings growth, targeting 12–15% growth in 2000. Fiorina also identified the following six strategic priorities that would reposition HP for sustainable growth:[18]

1. Accelerating growth in existing businesses
2. Streamlining the existing decentralized operating model to fuel growth opportunities
3. Implementing a "total customer experience" approach—with the aim of turning the customer experience into a source of competitive advantage
4. Taking advantage of HP's strong balance sheet and cash generation capability to fund new growth initiatives
5. Leveraging HP's market position to drive the adoption of next-generation appliances, e-services, and infrastructure in high-growth markets
6. Creating e-services ecosystems and placing HP at the center by exploiting HP's reputation for being the best partner in the industry

Much as Gerstner had reasoned earlier, Fiorina believed that advances in technology, increased competition, and changing customer requirements were rapidly transforming the structure and economics of the IT industry. Indeed, Fiorina's decision to join HP was based, in part, on her belief in HP's ability to respond to these changes by transforming itself into a leading provider of integrated solutions: "It was clear to me when I came here in July 1999 that customers would deal with fewer players and this would lead to a structural shift. It was clear HP could lead: It was global, it had the scope and scale to do sustained R&D, and it had a powerful brand with positive associations."[19]

Guided by the company's new strategic objectives, Fiorina quickly set out to transform HP into a Web services powerhouse that provided all the equipment and related services corporations would need to do business on the Internet. To that end, Fiorina confronted HP's fragmented empire, which she described as "fat and slow," and revamped HP's organizational structure, collapsing 83 independent product lines (and 83 separate sales forces) into 17 product categories. Fiorina also created a more effective selling organization by establishing three front-end sales forces, for consumer products, corporate products, and HP consulting services. They would market and sell products made by three back-end groups—printers, computers, and technology consulting services.

---

17. In March 1999, HP announced it would split into two companies, spinning off its flagship and smaller Test and Measurement division as Agilent Technologies, while keeping the HP name on its vast computer products operations. HP's executive search criteria included identifying an individual who had previously overseen a similar spin-off.

18. Hewlett-Packard 1999 Annual Report, Letter to Shareholders.

19. HP 2000 Annual Report.

Not content to stop there, Fiorina scrapped HP's profit-sharing plan in favor of a double-barreled pay-for-performance incentive program tied to revenue and profit growth. She also supercharged innovation by implementing a new incentive program that would double the number of patents filed in the following year. Fiorina's reach extended to HP's culture as well. As she explained in her 2000 letter to shareholders, for decades the HP Way served as a guiding set of principles that shaped actions and differentiated HP as a place to build a career. In recent years, however, the intent of those principles became clouded and was used to justify behavior such as conflict avoidance, excessive focus on consensus, and weak performance management. In 2000, HP management defined what new ways of working together would be required going forward and captured these requirements in The Rules of the Garage, which preserved and built on the beliefs and core values inherent in the HP Way.

Amid these changes, HP posted four quarters of improving top-line performance in 2000 and achieved 15% revenue growth. Leading sales growth contributors included a refreshed server product line and significant organic growth in consulting services. Indeed, during 2000 HP backed its commitment to its services business with the hiring of 1,700 consultants. Management announced it would continue to grow services organically as well as to consider other ways to capitalize on this increasingly important area. While meeting its revenue growth target, HP missed its earnings target, delivering just 6% growth in net earnings.[20] HP's share price declined 31% for the year.

In 2001, HP had to contend with the dramatic slowdown in business and consumer spending that marked the 2001 U.S. recession. However, HP management failed to heed signs that tech buying started to wane in the fall of 2000. While the company assured Wall Street that it would make its first-quarter numbers, results were 25% below the Street's expectations. News of the earnings shortfall caused a 14% decline in HP's stock price and cast doubt over Fiorina's credibility.

Fiorina responded with a renewed effort to improve HP's cost structure. To that end, HP asked 80,000 employees—nearly the entire workforce—to take a pay cut and laid off close to 8,000 workers. Further efforts to streamline HP's operating model included outsourcing PC manufacturing, relocating low-end printer manu-facturing to the Asia Pacific region, and rolling out a Build-to-Customer-Order program that offered consumers and enterprise customers the ability to configure and purchase notebook PCs directly from HP over the Internet.

Despite management's efforts, HP's 2001 net earnings declined 89% on an 8% decline in revenue. Revenue from the Printing and Computer divisions declined due to both a decrease in sales unit volume and pervasive price competition. As a result, earnings from HP's Printing and Services divisions helped offset the Computer division's $450 million loss. IT Services revenue increased 6% due, in part, to the division's winning several substantial outsourcing agreements with customers includ-ing Nokia, Sara Lee, Halliburton, and Qwest Communications. HP's Services division also established key alliances with Accenture and the Management Consulting Services practice of PricewaterhouseCoopers.[21]

---

20. *In 2000, HP's net earnings (after tax) from continuing operations before extraordinary items and cumulative effect of changes in accounting principles increased 14.7%, in line with sales. However, after factoring in income from discontinued operations, HP's net income increased just 6%. Based on these results, Fiorina claimed she fulfilled her promise of deliver-ing balanced growth in revenue and earnings yet also claimed failure in meeting profitability targets.*

21. *Hewlett-Packard 2001 Annual Report.*

Growth in HP's profitable Services division coupled with ongoing cost-reduction initiatives were not enough to overcome investors' concerns about how HP would fare in both the current recession and beyond in the emerging tech landscape. This concern was reflected in HP's stock price, which declined 35% for the year. Faced with the first worldwide recession since 1975 and the worst annual decline in U.S. spending on IT since 1958, Fiorina's quest for profitable growth would ultimately lead her to consider potential acquisitions, including that of Compaq (see **Exhibit 4** for ratios used to evaluate the profitability and operating, investment, and financial management of IBM, Dell, Compaq, and HP).

THE MERGER

The merger of HP and Compaq is the best way to strengthen our businesses and improve our market position, deliver more of what our customers need, enhance opportunities for our employees and increase the value of our share-owners' investments.

— HP CEO Carly Fiorina, 2001 Letter to Shareholders

In early 2001, faced with a myriad of challenges, Fiorina hired consulting firm McKinsey & Co. to help evaluate strategic options for the future growth of the company. The options the company faced included a go-it-alone plan, one that would split the company up, and one that would grow IT Services by buying tech-services companies. HP previously attempted to expand its services business in late 2000 when it approached PricewaterhouseCoopers to discuss acquiring its consulting practice for a price in the vicinity of $17 billion to $18 billion; however, talks ended without an agreement.[22]

Also in early 2001, Fiorina contacted Compaq CEO Capellas to determine his interest in licensing HP's UNIX operating system, HP-UX. After several days of deliberation, Capellas contacted Fiorina to suggest that the synergies between HP and Compaq went beyond HP-UX and, in turn, raised the idea of a possible business combination.

After further discussion, Fiorina and Capellas determined that there was sufficient interest to seek authorization from their respective boards to further consider the combination (see **Exhibit 5** for background information for each of HP's board members). That authorization was granted, and, in turn, Compaq retained consulting firm Accenture to assist in assessing the attractiveness of the merger. Thereafter, HP, assisted by McKinsey, and Compaq, assisted by Accenture, separately conducted a comprehensive business due diligence investigation of the operations of the other.

HP and Compaq also engaged investment banks Goldman Sachs and Salomon Smith Barney, respectively, to advise their directors regarding the financial aspects of the business combination. Goldman's initial feedback to HP: the stock would take a 10–15% hit right off the bat because of the massive risk of merging two $40 billion behemoths with such a big stake in the low-margin PC business, adding, "Are you sure you want to do this?"[23]

22. Subsequently, in July 2002, IBM purchased PricewaterhouseCoopers' consulting arm for $3.5 billion.
23. "Carly's Last Stand?" BusinessWeek, December 24, 2001.

Over the next several months, representatives from HP, Compaq, McKinsey, Accenture, Goldman, and Salomon met repeatedly to discuss the business combination. In August, McKinsey delivered a report to HP's board detailing how HP could make the merger work. McKinsey concluded that most botched tech mergers involved companies trying to buy their way into new businesses they knew little about. This deal, on the other hand, could be more like successful mergers in other industries where similar companies combined, such as Exxon and Mobil.[24]

On September 3, the boards of HP and Compaq convened separately to consider the terms of a proposed merger agreement that had been negotiated by their respective management teams. Backed by the strategic analyses of McKinsey and Accenture, advisors from Goldman and Salomon presented their financial analyses, each concluding that the exchange ratio provided for in the merger agreement was, at the time of the meeting, fair to HP and Compaq shareholders (see **Exhibits 6** and **7** for Goldman's exchange ratio and contribution analysis). Based in part on this finding, both boards voted unanimously to approve the merger agreement and resolved to recommend that their shareholders vote for the merger. Indeed, the merger decision hinged on majority shareholder approval on the part of both companies. That night, the boards executed the merger agreement and issued a joint press release announcing their decision.

As set forth in the merger agreement, HP would acquire all of the outstanding stock of Compaq in exchange for 0.6325 shares of HP common stock for each outstanding share of Compaq stock and the assumption of options based on the same exchange ratio. The estimated purchase price of $24 billion was derived using an average market price per share of HP common stock of $20.92, which was based on an average of the closing prices for a range of trading days (August 30, August 31, September 4, and September 5, 2001) around the announcement date (September 3, 2001) of the proposed merger.[25]

Management's Reasons for the Merger

HP management contended that while the marketplace was changing, with customers increasingly demanding full-line end-to-end hardware and service providers, neither HP nor Compaq was in that position alone. However, together they could replicate IBM's model. "We get a time at bat against IBM every single time," claimed Fiorina.[26] Indeed, HP would not only enjoy top market share in printers, PCs, and storage, it would also have the second-largest server business and the third-largest tech-services organization.

In a proxy statement provided to shareholders, HP management identified several potential benefits from the merger:[27]

1. Personal Systems: Improved Economics and Innovation

HP and Compaq needed to improve the economics of their PC businesses to effectively compete with industry leader Dell. Management predicted that the combined company would have a lower cost structure due to economies of scale. HP would

24. Ibid.
25. HP 2001 Annual Report, Note 6. Acquisitions and Divestitures.
26. The Financial Times (London), May 1, 2002.
27. Hewlett-Packard S-4 Report, January 14, 2002.

also be able to leverage Compaq's progress in developing a direct sales channel, yielding a more flexible distribution model.

2. Complementary Leadership in Key Markets

Compaq's strength in industry standard servers coupled with HP's Linux and UNIX offerings would result in an industry-leading product line spanning the entire server category. In addition, Compaq led in overall storage. By adding HP's strength in high-end storage, the combined company would be the industry leader in both the enterprise storage segment and the fastest-growing sub-segment—storage area networks. The combined company would also be better positioned to provide integrated solutions that met the needs of customers as a result of having a broader portfolio of products and services. In doubling HP's sales force, the merger would also allow HP to increase account coverage and better compete for important customer engagements around the world.

3. IT Services: Strengthened Business Provides Critical Mass in Key Growth Market

Management believed the merger would significantly strengthen HP and Compaq's combined services business for several reasons. First, the combined services business would have 65,000 IT architects operating in 160 countries, which would provide the critical mass needed to accelerate growth in this key market. The merger would also expand the support business, an important driver of customer loyalty, and would provide a larger customer base to sell to. The combined support business would, in turn, deliver a larger stream of predictable revenue with double-digit profits. Management also believed that the merger would result in a leading position in managed services—the fastest-growing service segment—mission-critical services (servers and solutions), and multivendor support.

4. Financial Benefits

According to plan, the merger would yield $2.5 billion in annual cost savings by mid-2004. These cost savings would significantly improve overall profitability and were estimated to have a net present value in the range of $5 to $9 per share (see **Exhibit 8** for management's post-merger consolidated and segment-level operating targets and related assumptions). Over time, and as a result of the improved profitability, the merger would enable HP to increase investment in the imaging and printing business, currently the company's primary cash generator.

Walter Hewlett's Opposition to the Merger[28]

Background to the Dissent

Despite backing by the CEOs of HP and Compaq, their respective boards, consultants McKinsey and Accenture, and financial advisors Goldman and Salomon, the proposed deal faced significant and powerful opposition. The most notable critic of the proposed merger was Walter Hewlett, 14-year HP director and son of HP cofounder William Hewlett.

In addition to his role as director, Hewlett was cotrustee of the William R. Hewlett Revocable Trust (the Trust) and chairman of the William and Flora Hewlett Foundation (the Foundation), which collectively owned 72.8 million shares—or 5.9%—of HP common stock. In this capacity, Hewlett was not only a powerfully symbolic HP figurehead, he was also HP's second-largest shareholder and an important voting constituent.

Hewlett first learned of Fiorina's discussions about a combination with Compaq at an HP board meeting in May 2001. For the next three months, during subsequent

---

28. Content from this section was derived from the Hewlett-Packard Schedule 14-A Proxy Statement, December 27, 2001.

board meetings, Hewlett considered the merits of the transaction and voiced concerns centered on a growing conviction that the merger would destroy shareholder value. As a shareholder and director, Hewlett firmly believed in the board's fiduciary duty to pursue shareholder value and to guide HP to profitable growth.

Despite Hewlett's opposition, Fiorina continued to pursue the merger. On August 31, three days before the HP board would vote on the merger, Larry Sonsini, HP's legal counsel, told the board that the merger agreement required unanimous approval. In response, Hewlett made it clear that this requirement put him in an uncomfortable position, as he was not convinced that the merger was in the best interest of HP.

Sonsini asked to speak with Hewlett outside the presence of the rest of the board and told him that HP would proceed with the merger whether or not he voted in favor of it. However, if Hewlett voted against the merger, the agreement could not be signed without renegotiation, which might result in HP's having to pay a higher price. Sonsini further advised Hewlett that even if he voted for the merger as a board member, he could subsequently vote against it as a stockholder.

Hewlett believed it was his duty to negotiate the lowest possible price for Compaq if the merger was to be submitted to a shareholder vote. Since the merger would be approved without his vote, Hewlett decided to vote for the merger as a director and to give shareholders the chance to make their own decision. On September 3, during the telephone call in which the proposed merger was approved by HP's board, Hewlett informed the board that he might not support the merger as a stockholder, adding that if the shareholder vote were to occur that day, he would vote against it.

Hewlett's concerns about the transaction seemed to be confirmed by the stock market's negative reaction to the proposed merger. On November 5, 2001, two months after the initial announcement, HP's share price trailed the preannouncement level by 27%, representing an aggregate loss of $12.3 billion of market value. During the same time, an index of comparable companies increased 9.9%.[29] Hewlett viewed the market's reaction as a sign of significant shareholder dissatisfaction.

After the proposed merger was announced, the Hewlett Foundation's independent stock committee asked the Foundation's chief investment officer, Laurence Hoagland, to analyze the merger. Hoagland was previously CEO of Stanford Management Company, which oversaw Stanford University's investment portfolio.

Separately, Hewlett and cotrustee Edwin Van Bronkhorst—former HP CFO—engaged Friedman Fleischer & Lowe, LLC (FFL), a San Francisco investment bank, to evaluate the merger on behalf of the Trust. Hoagland and FFL separately determined that the merger was not in the best interest of the Foundation or the Trust, and, in turn, both entities decided to vote their shares against the merger.

Armed with two independent analyses that supported the market's reaction, Hewlett decided to make his views known publicly in an effort to terminate the transaction and the uncertainty surrounding HP's future. On November 6, 2001, Hewlett announced that the Foundation, the Trust, Hewlett's sisters Eleanor and Mary, and he would vote against the merger. Later that same day, David Woodley Packard, son of HP cofounder David Packard, announced that he too would vote against the merger. News of the opposition on the parts of Hewlett and Packard sent HP shares soaring 17%. The market's reaction reinforced Hewlett's belief that the merger was not beneficial for HP.

---

29. The index of comparable companies consisted of Accenture Ltd., Apple Computer, Computer Sciences Corporation, Dell Computer, Electronic Data Systems, EMC Corporation, Gateway Inc., IBM, KPMG International, Network Appliance, and Sun Microsystems. These are the same companies used by Goldman in its "Selected Companies Analysis" in connection with rendering its fairness opinion to HP.

Within weeks, HP's largest shareholder, The David and Lucille Packard Foundation (the Packard Foundation), which owned 10.4% of HP common stock, conducted its own independent analysis. The Packard Foundation's board consisted of five Packard family members and seven additional members including a former CEO and a former COO of HP. To assist it in determining how to vote its shares, the Packard Foundation's board retained consulting firm Booz-Allen & Hamilton (BAH). On December 7, the Packard Foundation announced that it too would vote against the merger. Shares of HP and Compaq closed down 2% and 14%, respectively.

Despite the market's reaction and opposition by the Hewlett and Packard families, Fiorina was determined to take the merger to a vote. In response, and acting on behalf of the Trust, Hewlett initiated a proxy war and began to take the steps needed to solicit votes against the merger.

Hewlett's Reasons for Voting Against the Merger

Hewlett concurred with Fiorina that the marketplace was changing. However, he believed acquiring Compaq was not the solution. Rather than merge, Hewlett favored strengthening HP's profitable printing business and shedding all noncore businesses.

In a proxy statement issued by Hewlett to HP shareholders, Hewlett offered the following four reasons for voting against the merger:[30]

1. HP's Business Portfolio Will Be Worse

The proposed merger would dilute HP stockholders' interest in the profitable imaging and printing business and increase their exposure to an unprofitable PC business. Further, the imaging and printing segment had at least 10% normalized operating profit margins, and the market was expected to grow at over 10% per year. Conversely, the PC segment was unprofitable, and that market was expected to shrink for the next several years and then grow at less than half the rate of the imaging and printing market (see **Exhibits 9** and **10** for HP and Compaq's combined *pro forma* business mix and margin analysis).

2. The Integration Risk of the Proposed Merger Is Substantial

No significant combination involving a computer company had ever met expectations. The odds were against success in this merger, particularly since HP management had no experience with a merger of this magnitude. Further, HP management described the transaction challenge as "a massive integration effort . . . in the midst of reinvention." The complexity of putting two companies together in a difficult economy, when each was undergoing its own transition, presented daunting and unacceptable challenges. Moreover, even if the cost synergies were achieved, it was likely that merger-related revenue losses would offset or exceed them. Analysts estimated revenue losses could be as high as 15% in 2002 and 17% in 2003. These estimates were substantially greater than HP's forecast of 5%.

3. The Financial Impact on HP Stockholders Has Been and Will Be Negative

The market had twice made it clear that the proposed combination would destroy value for HP shareholders—once when HP's stock price dramatically declined after the proposed merger was announced, and again when HP's stock price dramatically increased after the Hewlett and Packard families made their opposition known (see **Exhibits 11** and **12** for stock price reaction on key event dates).

---

30. *Hewlett-Packard Schedule 14-A Proxy Statement, December 27, 2001.*

In addition, since the announcement of the merger, Wall Street estimates for the future financial performance of Compaq became available and were significantly lower than the estimates considered by the HP board at the time it approved the merger. This meant that HP stockholders were getting too little of the combined company relative to HP's contribution to earnings. On the announced terms of the merger, HP stockholders would own 64.4% of the combined company and HP would contribute 66.5% of the combined company's net income in calendar 2002. But based on First Call's revised earnings estimate, which was 33% lower than the estimate cited in HP's solicitation materials, HP would contribute 87.1% and 76.7% of the combined earnings in calendar years 2002 and 2003. Compared with an exchange ratio resulting in HP stockholders owning 80% of the combined company, the existing terms of the merger resulted in the transfer of $13.7 billion in value from HP stockholders to Compaq stockholders. Based on the revised estimate, HP would pay 82.6 times Compaq's 2002 earnings, rather than the agreed upon 22.2 price-earnings multiple.

Furthermore, despite management's assertions that a key asset of the combined company would be a stronger balance sheet, the credit agencies disagreed. Shortly after the transaction was announced, Moody's downgraded HP's long-term debt by two notches from Aa3 to A2, and Standard & Poor's put HP on CreditWatch with a negative outlook. S&P explained its decision as follows:

> If the merger is completed, Compaq's ratings would be reviewed for upgrade reflecting its acquisition by a stronger credit. The CreditWatch negative placement of HP is based on the acquisition of a lower-rated company with a similar-size revenue base and S&P's concerns about integration and business disruption risks inherent in a merger of this size in the highly competitive and rapidly evolving technology market.
>
> Thus, the merged balance sheet would be worse than that of HP on a stand-alone basis, resulting in a lower credit rating, greater equity risk, and a higher cost of capital. In contrast, Compaq's stockholders were getting a great deal at HP stockholders' expense. Compaq would get a business lifeline to the profitable imaging and printing business, a better credit rating, and the security of greater earnings coverage for its PC losses.

4. HP's Strategic Position Will Not Materially Improve

The proposed merger would not materially improve HP's strategic position for several reasons. First, the proposed merger would dramatically increase HP's market position in unattractive lower-end commodity businesses, such as PCs and low-end servers. Regarding PCs, though the combined company would have a 60–70% share of the retail consumer PC market, neither company had a profitable PC business model. Further, neither company had successfully transitioned to a direct distribution model to become more cost competitive with Dell. Compaq had made some progress in the U.S. and almost none in the rest of the world. Analysts estimated that approximately 3% of HP's sales and 20–30% of Compaq's sales were direct. Analysts also estimated it would take several years for Compaq to become competitive with Dell. The combination of two unprofitable businesses, in an increasingly competitive market, that - individually made little progress in developing a direct distribution model, was unlikely to become a source of profit in a combined company.

Regarding servers, the proposed merger would not materially improve HP's market position in midrange and high-end servers or in high-end services, all of which had higher profit margins than PCs. Compaq's server market share was primarily in the low end of the market, where margins were lower and under increasing pressure from Dell. Entry-level servers accounted for 76% of Compaq's 2000 server revenue, and average selling prices for entry-level servers had fallen 52% from 1997 to the third quarter of 2001. In the midrange and high-end server markets, the combined company's market share would still trail IBM's by a considerable margin. And in terms of storage, Compaq's storage business was attractive, but it was also relatively small and did not justify taking the risks of the proposed merger.

HP's strategic position would also not improve because the deal would divert management's attention and financial resources from HP's preeminent imaging and printing business. In this fast-moving market, HP could not afford to wait for its other businesses to become profitable. Diversion of management attention during the integration process and underinvestment in imaging and printing could have a significantly adverse impact on HP's leadership position.

The merger would also do little to increase HP's consulting and outsourcing capabilities, which had higher profit margins than its existing hardware support and maintenance services. HP management acknowledged that high-growth consulting and outsourcing capabilities were needed to compete with IBM in selling high-value-added, end-to-end solutions. However, Compaq's service business, like that of HP, was focused on the lower-growth, lower-margin hardware support and maintenance segments.

Opinions of Capital Market Intermediaries

As a result of the voting decisions made by the Hewlett and Packard family members, approximately 16% of HP's outstanding common stock was positioned against the merger. Of the remaining voting shares, 25% were held by retail investors, and 57% were held by institutional investors.

Needing only a majority vote, Fiorina and Capellas conducted an intensive coast-to-coast road show courting institutional investors, and in an effort to enhance their credibility, they engaged Institutional Shareholder Services (ISS) to evaluate the deal. ISS billed itself as "a leading independent provider of proxy voting services for institutional investors."[31] On March 5, 2002, ISS advised institutional shareholders to vote for the merger. ISS Vice President Patrick McGurn explained, "My initial reaction was in line with Walter's. My gut instinct was, they've got to be kidding. But after 20 meetings and incalculable hours pouring over management's plan for weaving the two companies together, we had a high enough confidence level to say the risk was manageable."[32]

The views of other independent intermediaries were varied. Analysts in favor of the merger felt that the combination was the best available option for two firms that were struggling to compete and cited the proposed cost savings as one of the primary benefits. "There's enormous opportunity for synergies," said Deutsche Banc Alex Brown analyst George Elling, who expected HP shares to be worth $40 if the companies executed as planned.[33] "Without this merger, HP wouldn't have the sales horsepower to compete with Sun or IBM," added analyst John Jones of JB Ventures.[34] Jones also noted that the tech giant would have not one but two cash cows—HP's $9

---

31. As described on ISS's web site (www.issproxy.com/about/index.asp), ISS's core business consisted of analyzing proxies and issuing informed research and objective vote recommendations. ISS also operated an institutional business that served the corporate market with a variety of governance tools assisting management with executive and director compensation modeling, capital structure planning, and understanding corporate governance best practices.
32. "HP and Compaq: What's an Investor to do?" BusinessWeek, March 18, 2002.
33. George Elling, "Hewlett-Packard," Deutsche Banc Alex Brown, September 19, 2001.
34. "HP and Compaq: What's an Investor to do?" BusinessWeek, March 18, 2002.

billion ink-cartridge business, plus a computer-repair business double the size of HP's. This, in turn, would allow HP to fund more than $4 billion in R&D, up from the $2.6 billion it currently spent.

Critics of the deal included UBS Warburg analysts Don Young and Anthony Torna. Adamant in their opposition, Young and Torna downgraded both companies from buy to hold and reduced their 12-month price target for HP from $37.50 to $18.00.[35] "We do not like this deal," asserted the analysts, adding, "we do not find the strategic rationale of this merger to be attractive."[36] Young and Torna shared Hewlett's concern that the deal would dilute investors' exposure to HP's profitable imaging business while significantly increasing investors' exposure to the commodity PC business: "Our prior positive view of HP was solely based on the value in the imaging business as we believe HP's server business is poorly positioned and its PC business is late to endorse direct distribution."[37] They also questioned the strategic benefits of combining HP's and Compaq's service businesses. "When one looks at the quality of services, the unattractive maintenance business dominates HP's [and Compaq's] mix while outsourcing/consulting/systems integration dominates that of IBM . . . . This is not another IBM! This deal does not result in HP becoming a stronger challenger to IBM in the enterprise space," concluded Young and Torna. Indeed, to become a stronger challenger, HP would likely need a follow-on acquisition (see **Exhibit 13** for a services comparison of HP, Compaq, and IBM).[38]

Echoing similar sentiments, J.P. Morgan H&Q analyst Daniel Kunstler commented, "Hewlett Packard's and Compaq's heritage is in the computing business but they've lost their competitive advantage and they want to get it back through services . . . that goal is their pipe dream . . . . In terms of creating better value for shareholders, they are better off not doing this deal."[39]

Critics also questioned the risk involved in taking on Compaq's PC business. Though Compaq had made strides toward becoming more efficient through outsourcing production, streamlining distribution, and selling more on the Web, its PC unit still lost $587 million in 2001. If Fiorina aimed to turn a 3% operating profit, Compaq would need to extend its own efficiency gains and teach HP to do the same. Yet, to the extent that HP and Compaq continued to rely on the retail channel, Dell's leaner model would continue to have a low-cost edge. "Dell's advantage is large and increasing," claimed CEO Michael Dell.[40]

A final concern was the difficulty in integrating two large-scale businesses. Critics echoed Hewlett's observation that large technology mergers had a history of failure. However, Fiorina was well aware of the challenge. In an effort to improve the odds of successfully integrating the two companies, Fiorina and Capellas formed integration teams, ultimately involving more than 1,000 staff who spent an estimated 1.3 million man-hours planning in minute detail. These plans, made far in advance, eventually helped convince ISS to support the deal.

On balance, Banc of America analyst Joel Wagonfeld concluded that the trade-offs in whether to merge or not included faster revenue growth and a higher net

---

35. On March 18, 2002, the day before the HP shareholder vote, the closing stock prices for HP and Compaq were $19.25 and $10.36, respectively.

36. Don Young and Anthony Torna, "Hewlett-Packard," UBS Warburg Research Note, September 6, 2001.

37. Ibid.

38. Don Young and Anthony Torna, "Hewlett-Packard," UBS Warburg Research Note, September 6, 2001.

39. "A New Computing Giant?" The New York Times, September 5, 2001.

40. "HP and Compaq: What's an Investor to do?" BusinessWeek, March 18, 2002.

Hewlett-Packard–Compaq

income margin in the next few years for a stand-alone HP, versus faster growth in earnings and market-leading positions as a combined entity (see **Exhibit 14**).[41]

THE SHAREHOLDERS VOTE

The 51.4% shareholder approval margin reflected a high level of uncertainty concerning the merits of the merger. It also prompted a lawsuit brought by Hewlett alleging that HP improperly pressured the asset management arm of Deutsche Banc to reverse its voting decision at the last minute. Deutsche Banc controlled 1.3% of the company's shares and originally decided to vote more than 25 million shares against the merger. However, on the day of the vote, the bank changed course and voted 17 million votes in favor of the deal.

While the narrow victory allowed HP's management to proceed with the merger, many observers wondered whether the move would truly help or hurt the company's strategic and financial position in the long run. The acrimony surrounding the deal also raised important questions related to corporate governance—including the appropriate roles of management, the board, and various advisors and intermediaries—in the complex world of mergers and acquisitions.

QUESTIONS

1. What are the strategic challenges that HP is facing?

2. Is the proposed merger likely to address these challenges?

3. How do you interpret the market's reaction to the proposed deal?

4. If you were a shareholder of HP, how would you vote on the deal?

41. Joel Wagonfeld, "The Hewlett-Packard/Compaq Merger," Banc of America Securities, October 2001.

EXHIBIT I

Compaq Segment Descriptions

Enterprise Computing

Enterprise Computing designed, developed, manufactured and marketed advanced computing and telecommunications products and solutions for enterprise customers worldwide. The segment consisted of three global business units: Industry Standard Servers, Business Critical Solutions and Enterprise Storage. Enterprise Computing accounted for approximately 32%, 34%, and 34% of Compaq's revenues in 2001, 2000, and 1999, respectively. In 2001, Compaq's Enterprise division shared the number one ranking with EMC Corporation in the $50 billion storage market, with 17% market share. Compaq's Enterprise division also held the number three ranking in the $50 billion server market, with 13% market share.

Access

The Access segment delivered products and solutions designed to provide home and business users with anytime, anywhere access to information, communication and entertainment. For the business customer, the Access segment offered a broad range of commercial computing devices, services and solutions, including desktop, notebook, and workstation computers and a full line of Compaq branded monitor and networking products. For the consumer customer, the Access segment offered products and technologies that worked together to help the home or home office user to simplify their lives, connect their world and have fun including desktop and notebook Internet PCs and a line of monitors and printers sold under the Compaq brand. In addition, the Access segment offered a line of personal devices and solutions marketed under the iPaq brand, targeting the convergence of business and home computing. These include entertainment and communications products, home networking products, desktop computers, microportable projectors and devices used to access the Internet. The Access segment accounted for approximately 45%, 49%, and 47% of Compaq's revenue in 2001, 2000, and 1999, respectively. In 2001, Compaq's Access division held the number two ranking in the $153 billion PC market, with 11% market share. The Access division was also ranked eighteenth in the $25 billion printer market, with .7% market share.

Compaq Global Services

The Compaq Global Services segment helped customers manage the complexities and risks of multi-vendor/multi-technology information technology environments in over 200 countries. Global Services' solutions were optimized for the highest levels of performance, availability and security, and the division was the industry leader in delivering enterprise solutions based on Microsoft Corporation's technologies. Compaq's Global Services segment consisted of four global business units: Customer Support, Systems Integration, Managed Services and Financial Services. Customer Support offerings included lifecycle support services, business-critical services and high availability support services for multi-vendor, multi-technology hardware and software products. Lifecycle support services consisted of installation, user assistance, maintenance, upgrading, replacement and disposition services available through a product's end of life. Systems Integration meant designing, configuring and installing a variety of computers and other information technology devices, often from different vendors and performing different functions, to provide a unitary system within a user environment. Systems Integration offerings included end-to-end information systems consulting, technical and application design services, systems integration, Internet and network architecture, project management services and e-business solutions. Managed Services offerings included outsourcing and resource management services, as well as business continuity and recovery services. Financial Services offerings included customized enterprise financing solutions that encompassed computers, networks and technology upgrades, as well as asset management services for large and multinational business customers. Asset management services involved the tracking, recovery, reconditioning and disposition of equipment. Compaq Global Services accounted for approximately 23%, 18%, and 19% of Compaq's revenue in 2001, 2000, and 1999, respectively. In 2001, Compaq's Global Services division was ranked ninth in the $666 billion services market, with 1% market share.

Source: Compaq 2001 10-K Report.

(continued)

Compaq Segment Descriptions (*continued*)

Compaq Segment Performance for the Years Ended December 31
(in millions)

	2001	2000[a]	1999[a]	1998[a]
Enterprise Computing				
Revenue	$10,699	$14,253	$12,947	NR[b]
Annual growth rate	−25%	10%	NA[b]	
Percent of total segment revenue	31.89%	33.76%	33.67%	
Operating Income	163	1,656	674	NR
Annual growth rate	−90%	146%	NA	
Percent of total operating income	25.51%	62.68%	71.25%	
Compaq Global Services				
Revenue	$7,789	$7,483	$7,413	NR
Annual growth rate	4%	1%	NA	
Percent of total segment revenue	23.21%	17.72%	19.28%	
Operating Income	1,062	884	998	NR
Annual growth rate	20%	−11%	NA	
Percent of total operating income	166.20%	33.46%	105.50%	
Access				
Revenue	$15,193	$20,624	$18,128	NR
Annual growth rate	−26%	14%	NA	
Percent of total segment revenue	45.28%	48.85%	47.15%	
Operating Income (loss)	(587)	145	(437)	NR
Annual growth rate	−505%	−133%	NA	
Percent of total operating income	NM[b]	5.49%	NM	
Segment Eliminations and other				
Revenue	($127)	($138)	($41)	NR
Annual growth rate	−8%	237%	NA	
Operating Income (loss)	1	(43)	(289)	NR
Annual growth rate	−102%	−85%	NA	
Consolidated Segment Totals				
Revenue	$33,554	$42,222	$38,447	NR
Annual growth rate	−21%	10%	NA	
Operating Income	639	2,642	946	NR
Annual growth rate	−76%	179%	NA	

Source: Compaq 2001 10-K Report.

[a]*Segment results reflect changes made during 2001 in the organization of Compaq's businesses and its expense alloca-tion methodology. In 2001, Compaq combined its commercial personal computing business with its consumer business to form the Access segment. In addition, the results of Compaq's financing business, which were previously reflected in the Other segment category, were included in the Compaq Global Services segment in 2001. Further, Compaq allocated certain ex-penses, such as information management, facilities and marketing costs, to the segments during 2001. The effect of this change in expense allocation was to lower segment operating profit by the amount of the allocated costs. Segment finan-cial data for the fiscal years ended December 31, 2000 and 1999 has been restated to reflect these organizational changes. Finally, segment data in prior years was reported on a geographic versus business unit basis and is therefore not reported (NR) here. In turn, growth rates were not available (NA) in 1999.*

[b]*NR—Not Reported, NA—Not Applicable, NM—Not Meaningful.*

EXHIBIT 2

Hewlett-Packard Segment Descriptions

Imaging and Printing Systems

HP's portfolio of printing and imaging offerings ranged from low-end printers and supplies to commercial printing solutions. Imaging and Printing Systems provided laser and inkjet printers, copiers, scanners, all-in-one devices, personal color copiers and faxes, digital senders, wide-and-large format printers, print servers, network-management software, digital photography products, imaging and printing supplies, imaging and software solutions, and related professional and consulting services.

Computing Systems

Computing Systems provided a broad range of computing systems for the enterprise, commercial, and consumer markets. The products and solutions ranged from mission-critical systems and software to personal computers for the business and home. Major product lines included UNIX and PC servers, desktop and mobile personal computers, workstations, software solutions, and storage solutions.

IT Services

IT Services provided consulting, education, design, and installation services, ongoing support and maintenance, proactive services like mission-critical support, outsourcing, and utility-computing capabilities. Financing capabilities included leasing, automatic technology-refreshment services, solution financing, and venture financing.

Source: Hewlett-Packard 2001 10-K Report.

(*continued*)

Hewlett-Packard Segment Descriptions (*continued*)

Hewlett-Packard Segment Performance for Years Ended October 31

(in millions)	2001	2000	1999	1998	1997
Imaging and Printing Systems[a]					
Total net revenue	$19,447	$20,476	$18,550	$16,709	$15,986
Annual growth rate	−5.0%	10.4%	11.0%	4.5%	NA
Percent of total segment revenue	43.4%	41.0%	42.6%	41.3%	43.9%
Earnings (loss) from operations	$1,987	$2,746	$2,355	$2,043	$2,037
Annual growth rate	−27.6%	16.6%	15.3%	0.3%	NA
Percent of total operating earnings	105.7%	64.8%	63.8%	62.6%	59.8%
Computing Systems[a]					
Total net revenue	$17,771	$21,095	$17,814	$17,315	$15,500
Annual growth rate	−15.8%	18.4%	2.9%	11.7%	NA
Percent of total segment revenue	39.7%	42.2%	40.9%	42.8%	42.6%
Earnings (loss) from operations	−$450	$960	$850	$480	$581
Annual growth rate	−146.9%	12.9%	77.1%	−17.4%	NA
Percent of total operating earnings	NM	22.7%	23.0%	14.7%	17.1%
IT Services					
Total net revenue	$7,599	$7,129	$6,255	$5,685	$4,804
Annual growth rate	6.6%	14.0%	10.0%	18.3%	NA
Percent of total segment revenue	17.0%	14.3%	14.4%	14.0%	13.2%
Earnings (loss) from operations	$342	$634	$575	$748	$797
Annual growth rate	−46.1%	10.3%	−23.1%	−6.1%	NA
Percent of total operating earnings	18.2%	15.0%	15.6%	22.9%	23.4%
All Other[b]					
Total net revenue	NR[c]	$1,299	$886	$773	$84
Annual growth rate	NA[c]	46.6%	14.6%	820.2%	NA
Percent of total segment revenue	NA	2.6%	2.0%	1.9%	0.2%
Earnings (loss) from operations	NR	−$103	−$71	−$5	−$11
Annual growth rate	NA	45.1%	1320.0%	−54.5%	NA
Percent of total operating earnings	NA	NM[c]	NM	NM	NM
Total Segments					
Total net revenue	$44,817	$49,999	$43,505	$40,482	$36,374
Annual growth rate	−10.4%	14.9%	7.5%	11.3%	NA
Earnings (loss) from operations	$1,879	$4,237	$3,689	$3,266	$3,404
Annual growth rate	−55.7%	14.9%	13.0%	−4.1%	NA

Source: Hewlett-Packard's 1997–2001 annual reports and casewriter's estimates.

[a]*In the second and third quarters of fiscal 2000, HP made certain strategic changes to its organizational structure. These changes included the movement of its appliances business from the Computing Systems segment to a separate operating segment, and the movement of the majority of its services business related to imaging and printing from the Imaging and Printing Systems segment to its IT Services segment. The appliances operating segment is included in "All Other" since it did not meet the materiality threshold for a reportable segment. Segment financial data for the fiscal years ended October 31, 1999 and 1998 has been restated to reflect these organizational changes.*

[b]*HP's immaterial operating segments were aggregated to form an "all other" category.*

[c]*NR—Not Reported, NA—Not Applicable, NM—Not Meaningful.*

EXHIBIT 3

Hewlett-Packard 2000–2001 Market Share Estimates by Business Segment

Segments:	Information Technology Services	Personal Computers	Servers	Printers
2001 Estimated worldwide market size in billions:	$666[a]	$153	$50	$25
Market share rank:				
Rank: 1	IBM	Dell	IBM	**Hewlett-Packard**
Market share:	5%	14.1%	26.5%	40.4%
Rank: 2	EDS	**Compaq**	Sun Microsystems	Epson
Market share:	2.9%	11.3%	16.7%	14.5%
Rank: 3	Fujitsu	IBM	**Compaq**	Canon
Market share:	2%	8.1%	13.4%	8.9%
Rank: 4	Computer Sciences	**Hewlett-Packard**	**Hewlett-Packard**	Xerox
Market share:	1.60%	6.9%	12.9%	8.4%
Rank: 5	Accenture	NEC	Dell	Lexmark
Market share:	1.50%	5.0%	6.8%	7.4%
Rank: 8	**Hewlett-Packard**	—	—	—
Market share:	1.10%			
Rank: 9	**Compaq**	—	—	—
Market share:	1%			
Rank: 18	—	—	—	**Compaq**
Market share:				0.7%

Source: Compiled from Gartner Dataquest (as reported in *The New York Times*, September 5, 2001).

[a]*Actual market size in 2000.*

EXHIBIT 4

FY 2001 BAV Ratios for Hewlett-Packard, Compaq Computer, IBM, and Dell Computer[a]

DECOMPOSING PROFITABILITY: DUPONT ALTERNATIVE	Hewlett-Packard	Compaq[b]	IBM	Dell
NOPAT/Sales	1.0%	−2.3%	9.2%	6.8%
× Sales/Net Assets	2.98	3.11	1.89	18.94
= Operating ROA	**3.1%**	**−7.3%**	**17.4%**	**129.3%**
Spread	−2.8%	−7.3%	16.7%	129.3%
× Net Financial Leverage	0.07	−0.11	1.21	−0.68
= Financial Leverage Gain	−0.2%	0.8%	20.1%	−88.3%
ROE (Operating ROA + Spread * Net Financial Leverage)	**2.9%**	**−6.5%**	**37.4%**	**41.0%**

EVALUATING OPERATING MANAGEMENT	Hewlett-Packard	Compaq[b]	IBM	Dell
Key Growth Rates:				
Annual Sales Growth	−7.5%	−20.5%	−2.9%	26.2%
Annual Net Income Growth	−89.0%	−238.0%	−4.6%	30.7%
Key Profitability Ratios:				
Sales/Sales	100.0%	100.0%	100.0%	100.0%
Cost of Sales/Sales	73.5%	78.8%	63.0%	79.8%
Gross Margin	**26.5%**	**21.2%**	**37.0%**	**20.2%**
SG&A/Sales	16.1%	15.9%	20.0%	10.0%
Other Operating Expenses/Sales	6.8%	7.6%	6.2%	1.8%
Investment Income/Sales	−1.0%	0.0%	0.0%	1.7%
Other Income, Net of Other Expense/Sales	−1.0%	0.0%	2.2%	0.0%
Minority Interest/Sales	0.0%	0.0%	0.0%	0.0%
EBIT Margin	**1.7%**	**−2.3%**	**13.0%**	**10.0%**
Net Interest Expense (Income)/Sales	0.1%	0.0%	0.3%	0.0%
Pre-Tax Income Margin	**1.6%**	**−2.3%**	**12.8%**	**10.0%**
Taxes/Sales	0.2%	−0.6%	3.8%	3.0%
Unusual Gains, Net of Unusual Losses (after tax)/Sales	−0.5%	−0.7%	0.0%	−0.2%
Net Income Margin	**0.9%**	**−2.3%**	**9.0%**	**6.8%**
EBITDA Margin	4.7%	1.8%	18.6%	10.8%
NOPAT Margin	1.0%	−2.3%	9.2%	6.8%
Recurring NOPAT Margin	2.4%	−1.7%	7.6%	7.0%

EVALUATING INVESTMENT MANAGMENT	Hewlett-Packard	Compaq[b]	IBM	Dell
Working Capital Management:				
Operating Working Capital/Sales	12.4%	5.1%	13.1%	25.2%
Operating Working Capital Turnover	8.08	19.69	7.63	−19.41%
Accounts Receivable Turnover	5.28	4.00	2.79	12.23
Inventory Turnover	5.83	12.24	11.35	65.08
Accounts Payable Turnover	6.58	6.25	6.60	7.19
Days' Receivables	69.15	91.29	130.61	29.85
Days' Inventory	62.58	29.83	32.16	5.61
Days' Payables	55.44	58.43	55.29	50.75

(continued)

FY 2001 BAV Ratios for Hewlett-Packard, Compaq Computer, IBM, and Dell Computer[a] (*continued*)

Long-Term Asset Management:

Net Long-Term Assets Turnover	4.73	3.69	2.51	9.58
Net Long-Term Assets/Sales	21.1%	27.1%	39.9%	10.4%
PP&E Turnover	10.05	9.78	5.14	41.68
Depreciation & Amortization/Sales	3.0%	4.1%	5.6%	0.8%

EVALUATING FINANCIAL MANAGEMENT	Hewlett-Packard	Compaq[b]	IBM	Dell
Short-Term Liquidity:				
Current Ratio	1.53	1.31	1.13	1.48
Quick Ratio	0.83	0.95	0.95	1.30
Cash Ratio	0.26	0.22	0.10	0.80
Operating Cash Flow Ratio	0.17	0.12	0.14	0.05
Debt and Long-Term Solvency:				
Liabilities-to-Equity	1.39	1.06	3.15	1.16
Debt-to-Equity	0.35	0.11	1.39	0.10
Net-Debt-to-Equity	0.07	−0.11	1.21	−0.68
Debt-to-Capital	0.26	0.10	0.58	0.09
Net-Debt-to-Net Capital	0.06	−0.12	0.55	−2.15
Interest Coverage Ratio:				
Interest Coverage	3.08		47.02	
Payout Ratio:				
Dividend Payout Ratio	152.2%	−21.5%	12.5%	n/a
Sustainable Growth Rate:	−1.5%	−7.9%	32.8%	41.0%

Source: Business Analysis and Valuation (BAV) Model version 2.31, HBS Courseware #103-701.

NA = not available; n/a = not applicable.

[a]*Ratios involving balance sheet items are based on the beginning balance sheet.*

[b]*Please note that Compaq's ratios may be misleading, since net income was negative in 2001.*

EXHIBIT 5

Hewlett-Packard 2001 Board of Directors

Philip M. Condit
Director since 1998
Age 58

Mr. Condit has been Chairman of The Boeing Company since February 1997, its Chief Executive Officer since April 1996 and a member of its board since 1992. He served as President of The Boeing Company from August 1992 until becoming Chairman.

Patricia C. Dunn
Director since 1998
Age 47

Ms. Dunn has been Global Chief Executive of Barclays Global Investors since 1998 and its Co-Chairman since October 1995. Ms. Dunn oversees the activities and strategy of BGI, the world's largest institutional investment manager, having joined the firm's predecessor organization, Wells Fargo Investment Advisors in 1978.

Carleton S. Fiorina
Director since 1999
Age 46

Ms. Fiorina became Chairman of the Board in September 2000 and was named President, Chief Executive Officer and director of HP in July 1999. From October 1997 until she joined HP, Ms. Fiorina was Group President of the Global Services Provider Business of Lucent Technologies, Inc., a communications systems and technology company. From October 1996 to October 1997, she was President of Lucent Technologies' Consumer Products Business, and from January to October 1996 she was Executive Vice President, Corporate Operations. Ms. Fiorina is a member of the Board of Directors of Cisco Systems, Inc., and also serves on the U.S. China Board of Trade.

Sam Ginn
Director since 1996
Age 63

Mr. Ginn served as Chairman of Vodafone AirTouch Plc from 1999, following the merger of Vodafone and AirTouch, until his retirement in May 2000. He was Chairman of the Board and Chief Executive Officer of AirTouch from December 1993 to June 1999. Mr. Ginn is also a director of Chevron Corporation.

Richard A. Hackborn
Director since 1992
Age 63

Mr. Hackborn served as Chairman of the Board from January 2000 to September 2000. He was HP's Executive Vice President, Computer Products Organization from 1990 until his retirement in 1993 after a 33-year career with HP. He is a director of the William and Flora Hewlett Foundation and the Boise Art Museum.

Walter B. Hewlett
Director since 1987
Age 56

Mr. Hewlett has been an independent software developer involved with computer applications in the humanities for more than five years. In 1997, Mr. Hewlett was elected to the Board of Overseers of Harvard University. In 1994, Mr. Hewlett participated in the formation of Vermont Telephone Company of Springfield, Vermont and currently serves as its Chairman. Mr. Hewlett founded the Center for Computer Assisted Research in the Humanities in 1984, for which he serves as a director. Mr. Hewlett has been a trustee of The William and Flora Hewlett Foundation since its founding in 1966 and currently serves as its Chairman. Mr. Hewlett has served as a director of Agilent Technologies, Inc. since 1999. He is the son of the late HP co-founder Mr. William R. Hewlett.

George A. Keyworth II
Director since 1986
Age 61

Dr. Keyworth has been Chairman and Senior Fellow with the Progress & Freedom Foundation, a public policy research institute, since 1995. He is a director of General Atomics, Vapotronics, Inc., and Bravo Labs. Dr. Keyworth holds various honorary degrees and is an honorary professor at Fudan University in Shanghai, People's Republic of China.

(continued)

Hewlett-Packard 2001 Board of Directors (*continued*)

Robert E. Knowling, Jr. Director since 2000 Age 45	Mr. Knowling was President and Chief Executive Officer of Covad Communications Company, a national broadband service provider of high-speed Internet and network access using DSL technology, from July 1998 through November 2000. He also served as Chairman of Covad from September 1999 to November 2000. From 1997 through July 1998, Mr. Knowling served as the Executive Vice President of Operations and Technologies at US WEST Communications, Inc. From November 1994 through March 1996, he served as Vice President of Network Operations for Ameritech Corporation. Mr. Knowling is a director of Ariba, Inc., Heidrick & Struggles International, Inc. and the Juvenile Diabetes Foundation International. He also serves as a member of the advisory board for both Northwestern University's Kellogg Graduate School of Management and the University of Michigan Graduate School of Business.
Robert P. Wayman Director since 1993 Age 55	Mr. Wayman has served as an Executive Vice President responsible for finance and administration since December 1992 and Chief Financial Officer since 1984. Mr. Wayman is a director of CNF Transportation, Inc., Sybase Inc., and Portal Software, Inc. He also serves as a member of the Kellogg Advisory Board to Northwestern University School of Business and is Chairman of the Private Sector Council.

Source: Hewlett-Packard 2001 Proxy, February 27, 2001.

EXHIBIT 6

Goldman Contribution Analysis

The following is an excerpt from Hewlett-Packard's January 14, 2002, Proxy Statement:

Contribution Analysis:

Goldman Sachs performed a contribution analysis in which the company analyzed and compared:

- The relative contributions to be made by each of HP and Compaq on a percentage basis to the revenue, operating income, profit before taxes and net income of the combined company on a pro forma basis assuming the completion of the merger; and
- The relative ownership of the combined company implied from their relative contributions, on a percentage basis, by the shareowners of HP and the shareowners of Compaq on a pro forma basis assuming the completion of the merger.

The relative percentage contributions made by each company are shown in the table below under the caption "Percentage Contribution to the Combined Company." The contribution analyses that Goldman Sachs performed did not take into account any revenue gains or losses or expense synergies expected by HP management to be achieved by the combined company following the completion of the merger.

In connection with its contribution analysis, Goldman Sachs also used the relative percentage contributions of HP and Compaq to the revenue, operating income, profit before taxes and net income of the combined company to derive a range of implied exchange ratios for the merger of between .524 and 1.000 in comparison to the actual exchange ratio for the merger of .6325. The results of this analysis are presented in the table below under the caption "Implied Exchange Ratio."

For comparative purposes, Goldman Sachs calculated the relative implied ownership of the combined company using the exchange ratio in the merger of .6325 of a share of HP common stock for each share of Compaq common stock. The results of the relative implied ownership are presented in the table below under the caption "Percentage Contribution to the Combined Company."

	Percentage Contribution to the Combined Company		Implied Exchange Ratio
	Hewlett-Packard	Compaq	
Revenue			
CY2001	55.7%	44.3%	0.994
CY2002	55.5%	44.5%	1.000
Operating Income			
CY2001	58.3%	41.7%	0.895
CY2002	59.9%	40.1%	0.840
Profit Before Tax			
CY2001	65.0%	35.0%	0.619
CY2002	63.6%	36.4%	0.658
Net Income			
CY2001	67.8%	32.3%	0.547
CY2002	66.5%	33.5%	0.582
FY2003	68.8%	31.2%	0.524
FY2004	68.2%	31.8%	0.537

	Percentage Contribution to the Combined Company		Actual Exchange Ratio
	Hewlett-Packard	Compaq	
	64.4%	35.6%	0.6325

Source: Hewlett-Packard, January 14, 2002.

EXHIBIT 7

Goldman Sachs Historical Exchange Ratio Analysis
The following is an excerpt from Hewlett-Packard's January 14, 2002, Proxy Statement:

Historical Exchange Ratio Analysis:

Goldman Sachs performed a historical exchange ratio analysis in which the company compared:

- a series of implied exchange ratios for the merger derived from historical trading prices of HP common stock and Compaq common stock over certain specified periods of time beginning August 31, 2001, the last trading day prior to the public announcement of the merger; and
- the exchange ratio in the merger of .6325 of a share of HP common stock for each share of Compaq common stock.

Goldman Sachs calculated the implied exchange ratios by dividing the closing prices per share of Compaq common stock for the relevant period of time, by the closing prices per share of HP common stock for the same period. The results of Goldman Sach's implied exchange ratio analysis are presented in the table below under the caption "Implied Exchange Ratio."

In connection with its historical exchange ratio analysis, Goldman Sachs also calculated the extent to which the exchange ratio in the merger of .6325 of a share of HP common stock for each share of Compaq common stock exceeded, on a percentage basis, each of the implied exchange ratios derived from historical trading prices. The results of this analysis are presented in the table below under the caption "Premium to Implied Exchange Ratio."

Historical Period	Implied Exchange Ratio	Premium to Implied Exchange Ratio
As of August 31, 2001	0.532	18.9%
20-day average	0.568	11.3%
60-day average	0.558	13.4%
120-day average	0.578	9.5%
360-trading-day average	0.571	10.8%
1-year average	0.597	6.0%
3-month high	0.627	0.9%
3-month low	0.494	28.1%

Source: Hewlett-Packard Proxy, January 14, 2002.

EXHIBIT 8

HP and Compaq Combined Fiscal 2003 Margin Targets and Sources of Cost Savings

Consolidated results:

Operating margin:	8–10%
EBIT margin:	9%

Segment Operating Margins:

Enterprise division:	9.2% vs. HP's fiscal 2001–3.2% margin
Access division:	3% vs. HP's fiscal 2001–4.2% margin
Services division:	13.7% vs. HP's fiscal 2001–4.5% margin

Anticipated cost savings by 2004:

Source:	Amount:
Administrative/IT costs	$625 million
Cost of Goods Sold	$600 million
Sales management	$475 million
R&D efficiencies	$425 million
Indirect purchasing	$250 million
Marketing efficiencies	$125 million
Total savings	$2.5 billion

HP management further estimated that these cost savings had a net present value in the range of $5–$9 per share.

Management's estimates were based on the following assumptions:

P/E multiples	15–25X
Discount rate[a]	15%
Tax rate	26%
Weighted average contribution margin	12%
Reduction in revenue	4.9%

Source: Compiled from Hewlett-Packard Form S-4, January 14, 2002; Thomson Financial Datastream; and casewriter's estimates.

[a] On September 4, 2001, the announcement date of the merger, the 5-year and 10-year Treasury rates were 4.63% and 4.99%, respectively. On this same date, the betas for HP and Compaq were 1.32 and 1.45, respectively.

EXHIBIT 9

Pro Forma Business Segment Mix as a Percentage of Revenue—Hewlett-Packard, Compaq, and IBM ($ millions)

| | FY2001E | | 2001E | | 2001E | | 2001E | |
	HP	Percent	Compaq	Percent	HP & Compaq	Percent	IBM	Percent
PCs	$9,158	21%	$14,873	43%	$24,031	31%	$14,087	16%
Servers:								
UNIX	3,226	7%	2,651	8%	5,877	7%	NA	NA
Industry Standard	1,775	4%	6,926	20%	8,701	11%	NA	NA
Servers total:	5,001	11%	9,577	28%	14,578	19%	11,720	13%
Storage	2,627	6%	2,048	6%	4,675	6%	2,980	3%
Software	868	2%	0	0%	868	1%	12,768	4%
Total Computing	17,654	40%	26,498	77%	44,152	56%	49,788	55%
Services	7,625	17%	7,897	23%	15,522	20%	35,462	39%
Technology	0	0%	0	0%	0	0%	8,233	9%
Printing	18,954	43%	0	0%	18,954	24%	0	0%
Other	1,157	3%	0	0%	1,157	1%	4,989	6%
Elim	−1,084	−2%	−147	0%	−1,231	−2%	0	0%
Total	$44,306	100%	$34,248	100%	$78,554	100%	$90,239	100%

Source: Compiled from UBS Warburg, September 6, 2001.

EXHIBIT 10

Combined Hewlett-Packard–Compaq Product Line Margin Analysis

| | | Operating Margin Model | |
	% of Revenues	Low	High
PCs	31%	1%	4%
Servers:			
UNIX	7%	0%	8%
Industry Standard	11%	5%	8%
Storage	6%	5%	8%
Software	1%	−5%	10%
Services	20%	5%	9%
Printing	24%	11%	14%
Other/elim.	−1%	0%	0%
Total	100%	5%	8%

Source: Compiled from UBS Warburg, September 6, 2001, and casewriters' estimates.

EXHIBIT 11

Relative Stock Price Performance—HP, Compaq, Dell, and IBM—August 1, 2001 through October 1, 2001

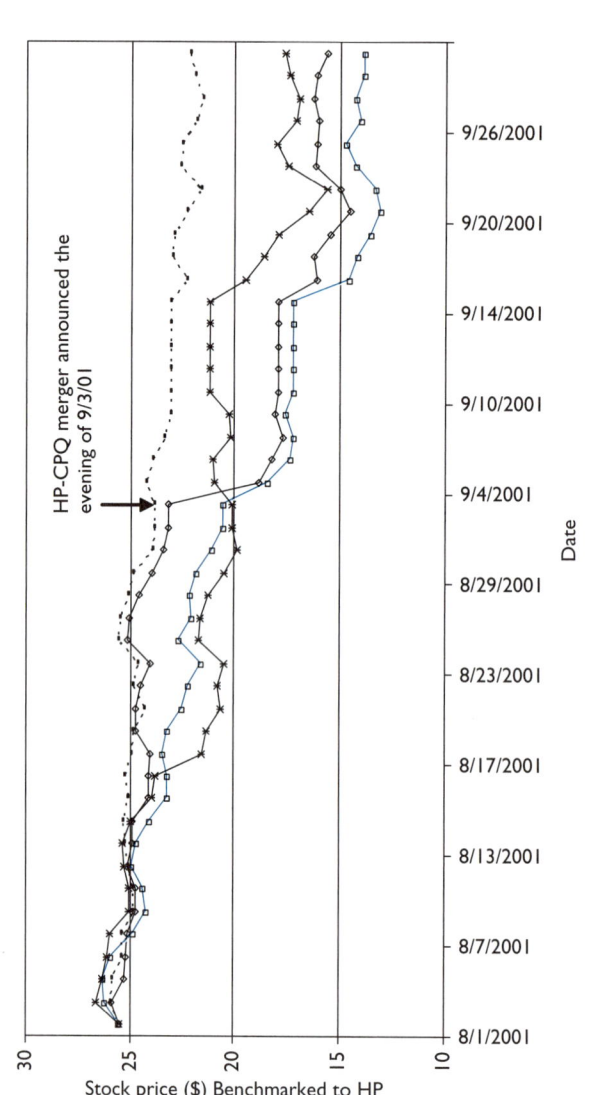

Source: Compustat.

EXHIBIT 12
Hewlett-Packard and Compaq Stock Price Reactions on Key Event Dates

Event	Event Date	HP Stock Price Day Before	HP Stock Price Day of Event	Percentage Change	Compaq Stock Price Day Before	Compaq Stock Price Day Of Event	Percentage Change
Initial merger announcement	4-Sep-01	23.21	18.87	−18.70%	12.35	11.08	−10.28%
Walter Hewlett announces that his family members, the Foundation, and the Trust will vote against the merger.[a]	6-Nov-01	16.89	19.81	17.29%	8.99	8.50	−5.45%
The Packard Foundation announces it will vote against the merger.	7-Dec-01	23.52	23.00	−2.21%	11.32	9.70	−14.31%
ISS advises institutional investors to vote in favor of the merger.	5-Mar-02	20.6	20.18	−2.04%	10.58	10.98	3.78%
HP shareholders narrowly approve merger vote.	19-Mar-02	19.25	18.80	−2.34%	10.36	11.14	7.53%

Source: Compiled from Thomson Financial Datastream and casewriter estimates.

[a]*David Woodley Packard announced later that day that he too would vote against the merger.*

Hewlett-Packard–Compaq

EXHIBIT 13

2000 Services Comparison—Hewlett-Packard, Compaq, Hewlett-Packard and Compaq, and IBM ($ millions)

| | FY2000 | | FY2000 | | FY2000 | | FY2000 | |
	HP[a]	Percent	Compaq[a]	Percent	HP & Compaq[a]	Percent	IBM	Percent
Outsourcing	$642	12%	$675	11%	$1,317	12%	$13,597	41%
Business Innovation and Integration	1,010	19%	1,687	27%	2,697	24%	12,757	38%
ebiz integration								
Sell and support								
Strategy								
ERP								
Infrastructure								
Maintenance and Training	3,598	69%	3,779	62%	7,377	65%	6,796	21%
Total Services	$5,250	100%	$6,141	100%	$11,391	101%	$33,150	100%
% of Revenues	11%		15%		13%		38%	

Source: Compiled from UBS Warburg, September 6, 2001, and casewriters' estimates.

[a]*Excludes financing operations.*

EXHIBIT 14

Hewlett-Packard vs. Hewlett-Packard and Compaq—Anticipated Trade-offs

On its own, HP could grow faster in the next few years . . .

	2001	2002	2003	2004	Growth Rate
Annual Revenue ($bn)					
HP/Compaq	$77.80	75.7	81	86.4	3.60%
HP	44.2	46.6	51.5	54.5	7.30%

And net income margins would be higher . . .

	2001	2002	2003	2004	
Net Income Margin					
HP/Compaq	2.3%	3.6%	5.3%	6.5%	
HP	3.4%	4.9%	6.1%	6.3%	

However, in buying Compaq, HP can expand profits faster . . .

	2001	2002	2003	2004	Growth Rate
Net Income ($bn)					
HP/Compaq	$1.80	2.7	4.3	5.6	45.90%
HP	1.5	2.3	3.1	3.4	32.10%

And set itself up for leadership in key markets . . .

Product/ Service	HP and Compaq	Market share/Rank	Industrywide Gross Profit Margins	Industrywide Annual Growth Rate
Printers[a]	$19.40	39.0%/1	31%	7.0%
PCs	24.5	21.1%/1	1%	0.0%
Servers	12.5	26.7%/2	21%	3.1%
Storage	6.4	26.3%/1	37%	3.0%
Services	15.4	2.6%/3	20%	11.4%

Source: Compiled from Gartner Inc., IDC, Credit Suisse First Boston, and company reports.

[a]Includes ink cartridges and accessories.

Hewlett-Packard–Compaq

The Home Depot, Inc.

The difference between a company with a concept and one without is the difference between a stock that sells for 20 times earnings and one that sells for 10 times earnings. The Home Depot is definitely a concept stock, and it has the multiple to prove it—27–28 times likely earnings in the current fiscal year ending this month. On the face of it, The Home Depot might seem like a tough one for the concept-mongers to work with. It's a chain of hardware stores. But, as we noted in our last visit to the company in the spring of '83, these hardware stores are huge warehouse outlets—60,000 to 80,000 feet in space. You can fit an awful lot of saws in these and still have plenty of room left over to knock together a very decent concept.

And in truth, the warehouse notion is the hottest thing in retailing these days. The Home Depot buys in quantum quantities, which means that its suppliers are eager to keep within its good graces and hence provide it with a lot of extra service. The company, as it happens, is masterful in promotion and pricing. The last time we counted, it had 22 stores, all of them located where the sun shines all the time.

Growth has been sizzling. Revenues, a mere $22 million in fiscal '80, shot past the quarter billion mark three years later. As to earnings, they have climbed from two cents in fiscal '80 to an estimated 60 cents in the fiscal year coming to an end [in January 1985].

Its many boosters in the Street, moreover, anticipate more of the same as far as the bullish eye can see. They're confidently estimating 30% growth in the new fiscal year as well. Could be. But while we share their esteem for the company's merchandising skills and imagination, we're as bemused now as we were the first time we looked at The Home Depot by its rich multiple. Maybe a little more now than then.[1]

The above report appeared on January 21, 1985, in "Up & Down Wall Street," a regular column in *Barron's* financial weekly.

This case was prepared by Professor Krishna Palepu as the basis for class discussion rather than to illustrate either effective or ineffective handling of an administrative situation.

1. *Reprinted with permission from* Barron's, *January 21, 1985.*

COMPANY BACKGROUND

Bernard Marcus and Arthur Blank founded The Home Depot in 1978 to bring the warehouse retailing concept to the home center industry. The company operated retail "do-it-yourself" (DIY) warehouse stores which sold a wide assortment of building materials and home improvement products. Sales, which were on a cash-and-carry basis, were concentrated in the home remodeling market. The company targeted as its customers individual homeowners and small contractors.

The Home Depot's strategy had several important elements. The company offered low and competitive prices, a feature central to the warehouse retailing concept. The Home Depot's stores, usually in suburbs, were also the warehouses, with inventory stacked over merchandise displayed on industrial racks. The warehouse format of the stores kept the overhead low and allowed the company to pass the savings to customers. Costs were further reduced by emphasizing higher volume and lower margins with a high inventory turnover. While offering low prices, The Home Depot was careful not to sacrifice the depth of merchandise and the quality of products offered for sale.

To ensure that the right products were stocked at all times, each Home Depot store carried approximately $4,500,000 of inventory, at retail, consisting of approximately 25,000 separate stock-keeping units. All these items were kept on the sales floor of the store, thus increasing convenience to the customer and minimizing out-of-stock occurrences. The company also assured its customers that the products sold by it were of the best quality. The Home Depot offered nationally advertised brands as well as lesser known brands carefully chosen by the company's merchandise managers. Every product sold by The Home Depot was guaranteed by either the manufacturer or by the company itself.

The Home Depot complemented the above merchandising strategy with excellent sales assistance. Since the great majority of the company's customers were individual homeowners with no prior experience in their home improvement projects, The Home Depot considered its employees' technical knowledge and service orientation to be very important to its marketing success. The company pursued a number of policies to address this need. Approximately 90% of the company's employees were on a full-time basis. To attract and retain a strong sales force, the company maintained salary and wage levels above those of its competitors. All the floor sales personnel attended special training sessions to gain thorough knowledge of the company's home improvement products and their basic applications. This training enabled them to answer shoppers' questions and help customers in choosing equipment and material appropriate for their projects. Often, the expert advice the sales personnel provided created a bond that resulted in continuous contact with the customer throughout the duration of the customer's project.

Finally, to attract customers, The Home Depot pursued an aggressive advertising program utilizing newspapers, television, radio, and direct mail catalogues. The company's advertising stressed promotional pricing, the broad assortment and depth of its merchandise, and the assistance provided by its sales personnel. The company also sponsored in-store demonstrations of do-it-yourself techniques and product uses. To increase customers' shopping convenience, The Home Depot's stores were open seven days a week, including weekday evenings.

Fortune magazine commented on The Home Depot's strategy as follows:

> *Warehouse stores typically offer shoppers deep discounts with minimal service and back-to-basics ambiance. The Home Depot's outlets have all the charm of a freight yard and predictably low prices. But they also offer unusually helpful*

customer service. Although warehouse retailing looks simple, it is not: As discounting cuts into gross profit margins, the merchant must carefully control buying, merchandising, and inventory costs. Throwing in service, which is expensive and hard to systematize, makes the job even tougher. In the do-it-yourself (DIY) segment of the industry—which includes old-style hardware stores, building supply warehouses, and the everything-under-one-roof home centers—The Home Depot is the only company that has successfully brought off the union of low prices and high service.[2]

The Home Depot's strategy was successful in fueling an impressive growth in the company's operations. The first three Home Depot stores, opened in Atlanta in 1979, were a quick success. From this modest beginning, the company grew rapidly and went public in 1981. The company's stock initially traded over-the-counter and was listed on the New York Stock Exchange in April 1984. Several new stores were opened in markets throughout the sunbelt and the number of stores operated by The Home Depot grew from 3 in 1979 to 50 by the end of fiscal 1985. As a result, sales grew from $7 million in 1979 to $700 million in 1985. Exhibit 1 provides a summary of the growth in the company's operations. The company's stock price performance during 1985 is summarized in Exhibit 2.

INDUSTRY AND COMPETITION

The home improvement industry was large and growing during the 1980s. The industry sales totaled approximately $80 billion in 1985 and strong industry growth was expected to continue, especially in the do-it-yourself (DIY) segment, which had grown at a compounded annual rate of 14% over the last 15 years. With the number of two-wage-earner households growing, there was an increase in families' average disposable income, making it possible to increase the frequency and magnitude of home improvement projects. Further, many homeowners were undertaking these projects by themselves rather than hiring a contractor. Research conducted by the Do-It-Yourself Institute, an industry trade group, showed that DIY activities had become America's second most popular leisure-time activity after watching television.

The success of warehouse retailing pioneered by The Home Depot attracted a number of other companies into the industry. Among the store chains currently operating in the industry were Builders Square (a division of K Mart), Mr. HOW (a division of Service Merchandise), The Home Club (a division of Zayre Corp.), Payless Cashways (a division of W.R. Grace), and Hechinger Co. Most of these store chains were relatively new and not yet achieving significant profitability.

Among The Home Depot's competitors, the most successful was Hechinger, which had operated hardware stores for a long time and recently entered the do-it-yourself segment of the industry. Using a strategy quite different from The Home Depot's, Hechinger ran gleaming upscale stores and aimed at high profit margins. As of the end of fiscal 1985, the company operated 55 stores, located primarily in southeastern states. Hechinger announced that it planned to expand its sales by 20 to 25% a year by adding 10 to 14 stores a year. A summary of Hechinger's recent financial performance is presented in Exhibit 3.

---

2. *Reprinted with permission from* Fortune, *February 1988, p. 73.*

THE HOME DEPOT'S FUTURE

While The Home Depot had achieved rapid growth every year since its inception, fiscal 1985 was probably the most important in the company's seven-year history. During 1985 the company implemented its most ambitious expansion plan to date by adding 20 new stores in eight new markets. Nine of these stores were acquired from Bowater, a competing store chain which was in financial difficulty. As The Home Depot engaged in major expansion, its revenues rose 62% from $432 million in fiscal 1984 to $700 million in 1985. However, the company's earnings declined in 1985 from the record levels achieved during the previous fiscal year. In fiscal 1985, The Home Depot earned $8.2 million, or $0.33 per share, as compared with $14.1 million or $0.56 per share in fiscal 1984.

Bernard Marcus, The Home Depot's chairman and chief executive officer, commented on the company's performance as follows:

> *Fiscal 1985 was a year of rapid expansion and continued growth for The Home Depot. Feeling the time was ripe for us to enhance our share of the do-it-yourself market, we seized the opportunity to make a significant investment in our long-term future. At the same time, we recognized that our short-term profit growth would be affected.*

The Home Depot's 1985 annual report (Exhibit 4) provided more details on the firm's financial performance during the year.

As fiscal 1985 came to a close, The Home Depot faced some critical issues. The competition in the do-it-yourself industry was heating up. The fight for market dominance was expected to result in pressure on margins, and industry analysts expected only the strongest and most capable firms in the industry to survive. Also, The Home Depot had announced plans for further expansion that included the opening of nine new stores in 1986. The company estimated that site acquisition and construction would cost about $6.6 million for each new store, and investment in inventory (net of vendor financing) would require an additional $1.8 million per store. The company needed significant additional financing to implement these plans.

Home Depot relied on external financing—both debt and equity—to fund its growth in 1984 and 1985. However, the significant drop in its stock price in 1985 made further equity financing less attractive. While the company could borrow from its line of credit, it had to make sure that it could satisfy the interest coverage requirements (see Note 3 in Exhibit 4 for a discussion of debt covenant restrictions). Clearly, generating more cash from its own operations would be the best way for Home Depot to invest in its growth on a sustainable basis.

QUESTIONS

1. Evaluate Home Depot's business strategy. Do you think it is a viable strategy in the long run?

2. Analyze Home Depot's financial performance during the fiscal years 1983–1985. Compare Home Depot's performance in this period with Hechinger's performance. (You may use the ratios and the cash flow analysis in Exhibit 3 in this summary.)

3. How productive were Home Depot's stores in the fiscal years 1983–1985? (You may use the statistics in Exhibit 1 in this analysis.)

4. Home Depot's stock price dropped by 23 percent between January 1985 and February 1986, making it difficult for the company to rely on equity capital to finance its growth. Covenants on existing debt (discussed in Note 3 of Exhibit 4) restrict the magnitude of the company's future borrowing. Given these constraints, what specific actions should Home Depot take with respect to its current operations and growth strategy? How can the company improve its operating performance? Should the company change its strategy? If so, how?

EXHIBIT 1

Summary of Performance During Fiscal Years 1981–1985

NET SALES
$ in millions
81: 51.5, 82: 117.6, 83: 256.2, 84: 432.8, 85: 700.7

NET EARNINGS
$ in millions
81: 1.4, 82: 5.3, 83: 10.3, 84: 14.1, 85: 8.2

STOCKHOLDERS' EQUITY
$ in millions
81: 5.2, 82: 18.4, 83: 65.3, 84: 80.2, 85: 89.1

TOTAL ASSETS
$ in millions
81: 16.9, 82: 33.0, 83: 105.2, 84: 249.4, 85: 380.2

CUSTOMER COUNT
millions
81: 1.9, 82: 4.2, 83: 8.5, 84: 14.3, 85: 23.3

SQUARE FOOTAGE
millions
81: .6, 82: .7, 83: 1.4, 84: 2.4, 85: 4.0

NUMBER OF MARKETS
81: 2, 82: 5, 83: 7, 84: 11, 85: 15

NUMBER OF STORES
81: 8, 82: 10, 83: 19, 84: 31, 85: 50

NUMBER OF EMPLOYEES AT YEAR END
thousands
81: .7, 82: 1.1, 83: 2.4, 84: 4.0, 85: 5.4

EXHIBIT 2

The Home Depot's Common Stock Price and Standard & Poor's 500 Composite Index from January 1985 to February 1986

Date	Home Depot Stock Price	S&P 500 Composite Index
1/2/85	$17.125	165.4
2/1/85	16.375	178.6
3/1/85	19.000	183.2
4/1/85	17.000	181.3
5/1/85	18.000	178.4
6/3/85	16.125	189.3
7/1/85	13.000	192.4
8/1/85	12.625	192.1
9/2/85	11.875	197.9
10/1/85	11.375	185.1
11/1/85	10.750	191.5
12/2/85	11.000	200.5
1/2/86	12.625	209.6
2/3/86	13.125	214.0
Cumulative Return:	−23.4%	29.4%

The Home Depot's $\beta = 1.3$ (Value Line estimate).

EXHIBIT 3

Summary of Financial Performance of Hechinger Company

Part I—Hechinger's Financial Ratios

	Year Ending		
	February 1, 1986	February 2, 1985	January 28, 1984
Profit Before Taxes/Sales (%)	7.80	9.40	9.80
× Sales/Average Assets	1.48	1.72	2.02
× Average Assets/Average Equity	2.21	2.12	1.79
× (1 − Average Tax Rate)	0.62	0.55	0.54
= Return on Equity (%)	15.80	18.90	19.10
× (1 − Dividend Payout Ratio)	0.93	0.95	0.95
= Sustainable Growth Rate (%)	14.70	18.00	18.10
Gross Profit/Sales (%)	29.30	30.10	32.10
Selling, General and Administrative Expenses/Sales (%)	21.60	21.10	22.90
Interest Expenses/Sales (%)	2.10	1.30	0.70
Interest Income/Sales (%)	2.20	1.70	1.30
Inventory Turnover	4.50	4.50	4.40
Average Collection Period* (Days)	32.00	33.00	35.00
Average Accounts Payables Period** (Days)	58.00	61.00	63.00

Assumed 365 days in the fiscal year.

**Payables also include accrued wages and expenses. Purchases are computed as cost of sales plus increase in inventory during the year. Assumed 365 days in the fiscal year.*

Part II: Hechinger's Cash Flow

	Year Ending		
(Dollars In Thousands)	February 1, 1986	February 2, 1985	January 28, 1984
Cash Provided from Operations			
Net Earnings	$23,111	$20,923	$16,243
Items not requiring the use of cash or marketable securities			
Depreciation and amortization	6,594	4,622	3,429
Deferred income taxes	1,375	2,040	1,515
Deferred rent expense	2,321	2,064	1,463
	33,401	**29,649**	**22,650**
Cash Invested in Operations			
Accounts receivable	4,657	7,905	7,954
Merchandise inventories	17,998	8,045	20,596
Other current assets	4,891	3,760	1,304
Accounts payable and accrued expenses	(6,620)	(12,099)	(9,767)
Taxes on income—current	285	3,031	(575)
	21,211	**10,642**	**19,512**
Net Cash Provided from Operations	**12,190**	**19,007**	**3,138**
Cash Used for Investment Activities			
Expenditures for property, furniture and equipment, net of disposals, and other assets	**(36,037)**	**(25,531)**	**(16,346)**
Cash Used to Pay Dividends to Shareholders	**(1,550)**	**(1,091)**	**(868)**
Cash Provided from Financing Activities			
Proceeds from public offering of 8 $\frac{1}{2}$% Converted Subordinated Debentures, net of expenses	—	85,010	—
Proceeds from public offering of common stock net of expenses	28,969	—	13,439
Proceeds from sale and leaseback transactions under operating leases	—	8,338	6,874
Increase (decrease) in long-term debt	—	(4,750)	6,366
Decrease in short-term debt	—	—	(318)
Exercise of stock options including income tax benefit	180	674	611
Decrease in capital lease obligations	(311)	(280)	(254)
	28,838	**88,992**	**26,718**
Increase in Cash and Marketable Securities	**$3,441**	**$81,377**	**$12,642**

The Home Depot, Inc.

EXHIBIT 4

Abridged Annual Report for Fiscal Year 1985

A Letter to Our Shareholders

Fiscal 1985 was a year of rapid expansion and continued growth for The Home Depot. Feeling the time was ripe for us to enhance our share of the do-it-yourself market, we seized the opportunity to make a significant investment in our long-term future. At the same time, we recognized that our short-term profit growth would be affected.

The Home Depot intends to be the dominant factor in every market we serve. The key to our success has been that upon entering a new market, we make a substantial commitment—opening multiple stores, providing excellent customer service, creating highly visible promotions, and growing the entire market. We turn the novice into a do-it-yourselfer and enable the expert to do more for less money.

From shortly before the end of fiscal 1984 to the close of fiscal 1985, The Home Depot entered eight new markets—Dallas, Houston, Jacksonville, San Diego, Los Angeles, Shreveport, Baton Rouge and Mobile—in a period of approximately 13 months. In that time, the number of Home Depot stores rose dramatically, from 22 to 50, including 9 stores acquired in the Bowater acquisition which had not been in our original plan. Twenty of these stores were opened during the past fiscal year alone. During this time span, we have become the only national warehouse retailing chain serving markets across the Sunbelt.

This expansion program required a tremendous investment of capital expenditures and inventory, as well as in personnel. As a result, our net earnings declined from record levels achieved during the previous fiscal year. In fiscal 1985, The Home Depot earned $8,219,000, or $.33 per share, as compared with $14,122,000, or $.56 per share, in fiscal 1984. However, as The Home Depot engaged in this major thrust forward, it also increased its market share and market presence as revenues rose 62% from $432,779,000 in fiscal 1984 to $700,729,000 in fiscal 1985.

Despite our significant investments, we still continue to be in a very strong financial condition. In December, The Home Depot replaced a prior $100 million bank credit line with an eight-year decreasing revolving credit agreement of $200 million. In addition, we are pursuing sale-and-leaseback negotiations for an aggregate of approximately $50 million for ten of our stores. These sources of additional funds, along with internally generated cash flow, will provide us with an ample financial foundation to continue to underwrite our growth over the next several years.

We are also quite proud that The Home Depot achieved its substantial gain in sales and market share in what turned out to be a very difficult year for our industry and retailing in general. The do-it-yourself "warehouse" industry, which we pioneered only a few short years ago, has recently attracted many competitors, some of whom have already fallen by the wayside, having mistaken our dramatic success as a path towards easy profits. Now the industry is faced with a situation when only the strongest and most capable will survive. As this process continues, we expect to encounter additional cost competition in the fight for market dominance. However, with our strengths—both financial and our successful ability to develop a loyal customer base—we are confident that The Home Depot will emerge an even stronger company.

We have never doubted The Home Depot's ability to be a leader in our business. We have the market dominance, the superior retailing concepts and the necessary foundation of experienced management. Further, we have the determination to maintain our position.

Looking at some of our markets individually, clearly our most difficult environment has been in Houston, where the oil-related economy is undergoing painful contractions combined with particularly fierce industry competition. This has caused our newly-opened stores to operate at a sub par level. In Dallas/Fort Worth, the stores we acquired at the end of fiscal 1984 have not yet generated the profits we expect. Such difficult market conditions demand a flexible reaction both in merchandising and operations. Recognizing the future potential of both of these markets, our management team is addressing the issues and feels confident that the final outcome will be positive.

In the other markets entered this year, the situation has been considerably more positive. There, our stores are experiencing growth much closer to our historical patterns.

In support of our California and Arizona operations, a west coast division was inaugurated to facilitate a timely response to the demands of that marketplace. With management personnel in place, this division is now responsible for the merchandising and operations of all stores in the western states.

Other highlights of the past year's activities include the progress we have made in expanding our management team, and the computer systems we installed into our operations to enhance our efficiency.

During the year, we completed the store price look-up phase of our management information system. This facilitates tracking individual items' sales through our registers, resulting in a more concise method of inventory reorder and margin management with the information now available.

During the coming year we will be testing a perpetual inventory tie-in with our price look-up system, eliminating pricing of our merchandise at the store level. The latter is being tested in several stores presently and hopefully will be expanded to include all of our stores by year end. This will have a significant effect on labor productivity at the store level.

The Home Depot is always looking for ways in which to do things better, priding ourselves on our flexibility and ability to innovate and to react to changing conditions. Whether it is a matter of developing state-of-the-art computer systems, reevaluating our store layouts or adapting to fast-changing markets and new types of merchandising, flexibility has always been a Home Depot characteristic.

In fiscal 1986, The Home Depot will continue to expand, but at a much more moderate pace. We plan to open nine new stores. These stores will be in existing markets except for the two locations in the new market of San Jose, California.

When we open stores in existing markets, sharing advertising costs and operational expenses, we achieve a faster return than stores in new markets. With this in mind, in January 1986, we withdrew from the Detroit market and delayed the opening of stores in San Francisco. These stores were targeted for a substantial initial loss in earnings that would have been necessary to achieve market

dominance. From our standpoint, these new markets would have had the combined effect of diluting our personnel and negatively affecting our earnings.

It has always been Home Depot's philosophy to maintain orderly growth and achieve market dominance as we expand to new markets. Indeed, growth for growth's sake has never been and never will be our objective. We intend to invest prudently and expand aggressively in our business and our markets only when such expenditures meet our criteria for long-term profitability.

We are quite optimistic about our company's future—both for fiscal 1986 and for the years to follow. Essential to this optimism is the fact that The Home Depot has consistently proven that we can grow the market in every geographical area we enter. Simply, this means that we do not have to take business away from hardware stores and other existing home-improvement outlets, but rather, to create new do-it-yourselfers out of those who have never done their own home improvements.

Our philosophy is to educate our customers on how to be do-it-yourselfers. Our customers have come to expect The Home Depot's knowledgeable sales staff to guide them through any project they care to undertake, whether it be installing kitchen cabinets, constructing a deck, or building an entire house. Our sales staff knows how to complete each project, what tools and material to include, and how to sell our customers everything they need.

The Home Depot traditionally holds clinics for its customers in such skills as electrical wiring, carpentry, and plumbing, to name a few. Upon the successful completion of such clinics, our customers are confident in themselves and in The Home Depot. This confidence allows them to attempt increasingly advanced and complex home improvements.

Concerning our facilities, Home Depot's warehouse retailing concept allows us to carry a truly fantastic selection of merchandise and offer it at the lowest possible prices. Each of our stores ranges from about 65,000 to over 100,000 square feet of selling space, with an additional 4,000 to 10,000 square feet of outdoor selling area. In these large stores, we are able to stock all the materials and tools needed to build a house from scratch, and to landscape its grounds. With each store functioning as its own warehouse, with a capacity of over 25,000 different items, we are able to keep our prices at a minimum while providing the greatest selection of building materials and name brand merchandise.

For the majority of Americans, their home is their most valuable asset. It is an asset that consistently appreciates. It is also an asset in need of ongoing care and maintenance. By becoming do-it-yourselfers, homeowners can significantly enhance the value of their homes. We at The Home Depot have found that by successfully delivering this message, we have created loyal and satisfied customers. And by maintaining leadership in our markets, we have established

a sound basis on which to build a future of growth with profitability.

The Home Depot management and staff are dedicated to the proposition that we are—and will remain—America's leading do-it-yourself retailer.

Bernard Marcus
Chairman and
Chief Executive Officer

Arthur M. Blank
President and
Chief Operating Officer

CONSOLIDATED STATEMENTS OF EARNINGS

	Fiscal Year Ended		
	February 2, 1986 (52 weeks)	February 3, 1985 (53 weeks)	January 29, 1984 (52 weeks)
Net Sales (note 2)	$700,729,000	$432,779,000	$256,184,000
Cost of Merchandise Sold	519,272,000	318,460,000	186,170,000
Gross Profit	181,457,000	114,319,000	70,014,000
Operating Expenses:			
Selling and store operating expenses	134,354,000	74,447,000	43,514,000
Preopening expenses	7,521,000	1,917,000	2,456,000
General and administrative expenses	20,555,000	12,817,000	7,376,000
Total Operating Expenses	162,430,000	89,181,000	53,346,000
Operating Income	19,027,000	25,138,000	16,668,000
Other Income (Expense):			
Net gain on disposition of property and equipment (note 7)	1,317,000	—	—
Interest income	1,481,000	5,236,000	2,422,000
Interest expense (note 3)	(10,206,000)	(4,122,000)	(104,000)
	(7,408,000)	1,114,000	2,318,000
Earnings Before Income Taxes	11,619,000	26,252,000	18,986,000
Income Taxes (note 4)	3,400,000	12,130,000	8,725,000
Net Earnings	$8,219,000	$14,122,000	$10,261,000
Earnings per Common and Common Equivalent Share (note 5)	$.33	$.56	$.41
Weighted Average Number of Common and Common Equivalent Shares	25,247,000	25,302,000	24,834,000

CONSOLIDATED BALANCE SHEETS

	February 2, 1986	February 3, 1985
Assets:		
Current Assets:		
Cash, including time deposits of $43,374,000 in 1985	**$9,671,000**	$52,062,000
Accounts receivable, net (note 7)	**21,505,000**	9,365,000
Refundable income taxes	**3,659,000**	—
Merchandise inventories	**152,700,000**	84,046,000
Prepaid expenses	**2,526,000**	1,939,000
Total current assets	**190,061,000**	147,412,000
Property and Equipment, at Cost (note 3):		
Land	**44,396,000**	30,044,000
Buildings	**38,005,000**	3,728,000
Furniture, fixtures, and equipment	**34,786,000**	18,162,000
Leasehold improvements	**23,748,000**	11,743,000
Construction in progress	**27,694,000**	14,039,000
	168,629,000	77,716,000
Less accumulated depreciation and amortization	**7,813,000**	4,139,000
Net property and equipment	**160,816,000**	73,577,000
Cost in Excess of the Fair Value of Net Assets		
Acquired, net of accumulated amortization		
of $730,000 in 1985 and $93,000 in 1984 (note 2)	**24,561,000**	25,198,000
Other	**4,755,000**	3,177,000
	$380,193,000	$249,364,000
Liabilities and Stockholders' Equity		
Current Liabilities:		
Accounts payable	**$53,881,000**	$32,356,000
Accrued salaries and related expenses	**5,397,000**	3,819,000
Other accrued expenses	**13,950,000**	10,214,000
Income taxes payable (note 4)	**—**	626,000
Current portion of long-term debt (note 3)	**10,382,000**	287,000
Total current liabilities	**83,610,000**	47,302,000
Long-Term Debt, Excluding Current		
Installments (note 3):		
Convertible subordinated debentures	**100,250,000**	100,250,000
Other long-term debt	**99,693,000**	17,692,000
	$199,943,000	$117,942,000
Other Liabilities	**861,000**	1,320,000
Deferred Income Taxes (note 4)	**6,687,000**	2,586,000
Stockholders' Equity (note 5)		
Common stock, par value $.05. Authorized:		
50,000,000 shares; issued and outstanding—		
25,150,063 shares at February 2, 1986 and		
25,055,188 shares at February 3, 1985	**1,258,000**	1,253,000
Paid-in capital	**48,900,000**	48,246,000
Retained earnings	**38,934,000**	30,715,000
Total stockholders' equity	**89,092,000**	80,214,000
Commitments and Contingencies		
(notes 5, 6 and 8)	**$380,193,000**	$249,364,000

The Home Depot, Inc.

CONSOLIDATED STATEMENTS OF CHANGES IN FINANCIAL POSITION

	Fiscal Year Ended		
	February 2, 1986	February 3, 1985	January 29, 1984
Sources of Working Capital:			
Net earnings	$8,219,000	$14,122,000	$10,261,000
Items which do not use working capital:			
Depreciation and amortization of property and equipment	4,376,000	2,275,000	903,000
Deferred income taxes	3,612,000	1,508,000	713,000
Amortization of cost in excess of the fair value of net assets required	637,000	93,000	—
Net gain on disposition of property and equipment	(1,317,000)	—	—
Other	180,000	77,000	59,000
Working Capital Provided by Operations	15,707,000	18,075,000	11,936,000
Proceeds from disposition of property and equipment	9,469,000	861,000	3,000
Proceeds from long-term borrowings	92,400,000	120,350,000	4,200,000
Proceeds from sale of common stock, net	659,000	814,000	36,663,000
	$118,235,000	$140,100,000	$52,802,000
Uses of Working Capital:			
Additions to property and equipment	$99,767,000	$50,769,000	$16,081,000
Current installments and repayments of long-term debt	10,399,000	6,792,000	52,000
Acquisition of Bowater Home Center, Inc., net of working capital of $9,227,000 (note 2):			
Property and equipment	—	4,815,000	—
Cost in excess of the fair value of net assets acquired	—	25,291,000	—
Other assets, net of liabilities	—	(913,000)	—
Other, net	1,728,000	2,554,000	252,000
Increase in working capital	6,341,000	50,792,000	36,417,000
	$118,235,000	$140,100,000	$52,802,000
Changes in Components of Working Capital:			
Increase (decrease) in current assets:			
Cash	(42,391,000)	$29,894,000	$13,917,000
Receivables, net	15,799,000	7,170,000	1,567,000
Merchandise inventories	68,654,000	25,334,000	41,137,000
Prepaid expenses	587,000	1,206,000	227,000
	42,649,000	63,604,000	56,848,000
Increase (decrease) in current liabilities:			
Accounts payable	21,525,000	10,505,000	17,150,000
Accrued salaries and related expenses	1,578,000	(93,000)	2,524,000
Other accrued expenses	3,736,000	2,824,000	341,000
Income taxes payable	(626,000)	(657,000)	406,000
Current portion of long-term debt	10,095,000	233,000	10,000
	36,308,000	12,812,000	20,431,000
Increase in Working Capital	$6,341,000	$50,792,000	$36,417,000

SELECTED FINANCIAL DATA

	Fiscal Year Ended				
	February 2, 1985	February 3, 1985[1]	January 29, 1984	January 30, 1983	January 31, 1982
Selected Consolidated Statement of Earnings Data:					
Net sales	**$700,729,000**	$432,779,000	$256,184,000	$117,645,000	$51,542,000
Gross Profit	**181,457,000**	114,319,000	70,014,000	33,358,000	14,735,000
Earnings before income taxes and extraordinary item	**11,619,000**	26,252,000	18,986,000	9,870,000	1,963,000
Earnings before extraordinary item	**8,219,000**	14,122,000	10,261,000	5,315,000	1,211,000
Extraordinary item-reduction of income taxes arising from carryforward of prior years operating losses	**—**	—	—	—	234,000
Net earnings	**$8,219,000**	$14,122,000	$10,261,000	$5,315,000	$1,445,000
Per Common and Common Equivalent Share:					
Earnings before extraordinary item	$.33	$.56	$.41	$.24	$.06
Extraordinary item	—	—	—	—	.01
Net earnings	$ .33	$.56	$.41	$.24	$.07
Weighted average number of common and common equivalent shares	25,247,000	25,302,000	24,834,000	22,233,000	21,050,000
Selected Consolidated Balance Sheet Data:					
Working Capital	**$106,451,000**	$100,110,000	$49,318,000	$12,901,000	$5,502,000
Total assets	**380,193,000**	249,364,000	105,230,000	33,014,000	16,906,000
Long-term debt	**199,943,000**	117,942,000	4,384,000	236,000	3,738,000
Stockholders' equity	**89,092,000**	80,214,000	65,278,000	18,354,000	5,024,000

(1) 53-week fiscal year, all others were 52-week fiscal years.

The Home Depot, Inc.

Management Discussion and Analysis of Results of Operations and Financial Condition

The data below reflect the percentage relationship between sales and major categories in the Consolidated Statements of Earnings and selected sales data of the percentage change in the dollar amounts of each of the items.

	Fiscal Year[a]			Percentage Increase (Decrease) of Dollar Amounts	
	1985	1984	1983	1985 v 1984	1984 v 1983
Selected Consolidated Statements of Earnings Data:					
Net sales	**100.0%**	100.0%	100.0%	**61.9%**	68.9%
Gross profit	**25.9**	26.4	27.3	**58.7**	63.3
Cost and expenses:					
Selling and store operating	**19.2**	17.2	17.0	**80.5**	71.1
Preopening	**1.1**	.4	.9	**292.3**	(21.9)
General and administrative	**2.9**	3.0	2.9	**60.4**	73.8
Net gain on disposition of property and equipment	**(.2)**	—	—	**—**	—
Interest income	**(.2)**	(1.2)	(.9)	**(71.7)**	116.2
Interest expense	**1.4**	.9	—	**147.6**	3,863.5
	24.2	20.3	19.9	**92.9**	72.6
Earnings before income taxes	**1.7**	6.1	7.4	**(55.7)**	38.3
Income taxes	**.5**	2.8	3.4	**(72.0)**	39.0
Net earnings	**1.2%**	3.3%	4.0%	**(41.8%)**	37.6%
Selected Consolidated Sales Data:					
Number of customer transactions	**23,324,000**	14,256,000	8,479.000	**63.6%**	68.1%
Average amount of sale per transaction	**$30.04**	$30.36	$30.21	**(1.1)**	.5
Weighted average weekly sales per operating store	**$342,500**	$365,500	$360,300	**(6.3)**	1.4

[a]Fiscal years 1985, 1984, and 1983 refer to the fiscal years ended February 2, 1986, February 3, 1985, and January 29, 1984, respectively. Fiscal 1984 consisted of 53 weeks while 1985 and 1983 each consisted of 52 weeks.

Results of Operations

For an understanding of the significant factors that influenced the Company's performance during the past three fiscal years, the following discussion should be read in conjunction with the consolidated financial statements appearing elsewhere in this annual report.

Fiscal Year Ended February 2, 1986 Compared to February 3, 1985

Net sales in fiscal year 1985 increased 62% from $432,779,000 to $700,729,000. The growth is attributable to several factors. First, the Company opened 20 new stores during 1985 and closed one store. Second, second-year sales increases were realized from the three new stores opened in 1984 and from the nine former Bowater Home Center stores acquired during 1984. Third, comparable store sales increases of 2.3% were achieved despite comparing the 52-week 1985 fiscal year to the sales of the 53-week 1984 fiscal year, due in part to the number of customer transactions increasing by 64%. Finally, the weighted average weekly sales per operating store declined 6% in 1985 due to the significant increase in the ratio of the number of new stores to total stores in operation—new stores have a lower sales rate than mature stores until they establish market share.

Gross profit in 1985 increased 59% from $114,319,000 to $181,457,000. This increase was due to the increased sales and was partially offset by a reduction in the gross profit margin from 26.4% to 25.9%. The reduction is primarily due to lower margins achieved while establishing market presence in new markets.

Cost and expenses increased 93% during 1985 and, as a percent of sales, increased from 20.3% to 24.2%. The increase in selling and store operating, preopening expenses and net interest expense is due to the opening of 20 new stores, the costs associated with the former Bowater Home Center stores, and the related cost of building market share. The large percentage of new stores which have lower sales but fixed occupancy and certain minimum operating expenses tends to cause the percentage of selling and store operating costs to increase as a percentage of sales. The net gain on disposition of property and equipment is discussed fully in note 7 to the financial statements.

Earnings before income taxes decreased 56% from $26,252,000 to $11,619,000 resulting from the increase in operating expenses to support the Company's expansion program. The Company's effective income tax rate declined from 46.2% to 29.3% resulting from an increase in investment and other tax credits as a percentage of the total tax provision. As a percentage of sales, earnings decreased from 3.3% in 1984 to 1.2% in 1985 due to the increase in operating expenses as discussed above.

Fiscal Year Ended February 3, 1985 Compared to January 29, 1984

Net sales in fiscal 1984 increased 69% from $256,184,000 to $432,779,000. The growth was attributable to several factors. First, the company opened three new stores during fiscal 1984. Second, the Company had sales of $9,755,000 from the nine former Bowater Home Center stores acquired on December 3, 1984. Third, second-year sales increases were realized from the nine stores opened during fiscal 1983. Fourth, comparable store sales increases of 14% were due in part to 53 weeks in fiscal 1984 compared to 52 weeks in fiscal 1983 and in part to the number of customer transactions increasing by 63%. Finally, excluding the sales of the former Bowater Home Center stores, the weighted average weekly sales per operating store increased 6% to $383,500 in fiscal 1984.

Gross profit in fiscal 1984 increased 63% from $70,014,000 to $114,319,000. This net increase was due to the increased sales and was partially offset by a reduction in the gross profit margin from 27.3% to 26.4%. The reduction in the gross profit percentage is largely the result of the purchase of a high proportion of promoted merchandise by customers in the second quarter.

Costs and expenses increased 73% during fiscal 1984. As a percent of sales, costs and expenses increased from 19.9% to 20.3% due to increased selling, store operating, general and administrative expenses. This planned increase was in preparation of the Company's future expansion. Interest expense increased significantly as a result of the issuance of substantial debt during fiscal 1984 to fund the Company's expansion. These increases were partially offset by reduced preopening expenses and increased interest income resulting from temporary investment of the proceeds of the debt financing.

Earnings before income taxes increased 38% from $18,986,000 to $26,252,000 resulting from the factors discussed above. Such pretax earnings, however, were reduced by a loss from the Bowater stores of approximately $1,900,000 from date of acquisition (December 1984) to year end. The Company's effective income tax rate increased slightly from 46.0% to 46.2% resulting principally from less investment and other tax credits as a percentage of the total tax provision. As a percentage of sales, earnings decreased from 4.0% in fiscal 1983 to 3.3% in fiscal 1984. The decline is a result of the company's reduced gross profit percentage and increases in the operating expenses discussed above.

Impact of Inflation and Changing Prices

Although the Company cannot accurately determine the precise effect of inflation on its operations, it does not believe inflation has had a material effect on sales or results of operations. The Company has complied with the reporting requirements of the Financial Accounting Standards Board Statement No. 33 in note 10 to the financial statements. Due to the experimental techniques, subjective estimates and assumptions, and the incomplete presentation required by this accounting pronouncement, the Company questions the value of the required reporting.

The Home Depot, Inc.

Liquidity and Capital Resources

Cash flow generated from existing store operations provided the Company with a significant source of liquidity since sales are on a cash-and-carry basis. In addition, a significant portion of the Company's inventory is financed under vendor credit terms. The Company has supplemented its operating cash flow from time to time with bank credit and equity and debt financing. During fiscal 1985, $88,000,000 of working capital was provided by the revolving bank credit line, $4,400,000 from industrial revenue bonds, and approximately $15,707,000 from operations. In addition, during fiscal 1985, the Company entered into a new credit agreement for a $200,000,000 revolving credit facility with a group of banks.

The Company has announced plans to open nine new stores during fiscal 1986, two in the new market of northern California and the balance in existing markets. The cost of this store expansion program will depend upon, among other factors, the extent to which the Company is able to lease second-use store space as opposed to acquiring leases or sites and having stores constructed to its own specifications. The Company estimates that approximately $6,600,000 per store will be required to acquire sites and construct facilities to the Company's specifications and that approximately $1,700,000 will be required to open a store in leased space plus any additional costs of acquiring the lease. These estimates include costs for site acquisition, construction expenditures, fixtures and equipment, and in-store minicomputers and point-of-sale terminals. In addition, each new store will require approximately $1,800,000 to finance inventories, net of vendor financing. The Company believes it has the ability to finance these expenditures through existing cash resources, current bank lines of credit which include a $200,000,000 eight-year revolving credit agreement, funds generated from operations, and other forms of financing, including but not limited to various forms of real estate financing and unsecured borrowings.

NOTES TO CONSOLIDATED FINANCIAL STATEMENTS

1. Summary of Significant Accounting Policies

Fiscal Year

The Company's fiscal year ends on the Sunday closest to the last day of January and usually consists of 52 weeks. Every five or six years, however, there is a 53-week year. The fiscal year ended February 2, 1986 (1985) consisted of 52 weeks, the year ended February 3, 1985 (1984) consisted of 53 weeks and the year ended January 29, 1984 (1983) consisted of 52 weeks.

Principles of Consolidation

The consolidated financial statements include the accounts of the Company and its wholly owned subsidiary. All significant intercompany transactions have been eliminated in consolidation. Certain reclassifications were made to the 1984 balance sheet to conform to current year presentation.

Merchandise Inventories

Inventories are stated at the lower of cost (first-in, first-out) or market, as determined by the retail inventory method.

Depreciation and Amortization

The Company's buildings, furniture, fixtures, and equipment are depreciated using the straight-line method over the estimated useful lives of the assets. Improvements to leased premises are amortized on the straight-line method over the life of the lease or the useful life of the improvement, whichever is shorter.

Investment Tax Credit

Investment tax credits are recorded as a reduction of Federal income taxes in the year the credits are realized.

Store Preopening Costs

Non-capital expenditures associated with opening new stores are charged to expense as incurred.

Earnings Per Common and Common Equivalent Share

Earnings per common and common equivalent share are based on the weighted average number of shares and equivalents outstanding. Common equivalent shares used in the calculation of earnings per share represent shares granted under the Company's employee stock option plan and employee stock purchase plan.

Shares issuable upon conversion of the 8 1/2% convertible subordinated debentures are also common stock equivalents. Shares issuable upon conversion of the 9% convertible subordinated debentures would only be included in the computation of fully diluted earnings per share. However, neither shares issuable upon conversion of the 8 1/2% nor the 9% convertible debentures were dilutive in any year presented, and thus neither were considered in the earnings per share computations.

2. Acquisition

On December 3, 1984 the Company acquired the outstanding capital stock of Bowater Home Center, Inc. (Bowater) for approximately $38,420,000 including costs incurred in connection with the acquisition. Bowater operated nine retail home center stores primarily in the Dallas, Texas metropolitan area. The acquisition was accounted for by the purchase method and, accordingly, results of operations have been included with those of the Company from the date of acquisition. Cost in excess of the fair value of net assets acquired amounted to approximately $25,291,000, which is being amortized over forty years from date of acquisition using the straight-line method.

The following table summarizes, on a pro forma, unaudited basis, the estimated combined results of operations of the Company and Bowater for the years ended February 3, 1985 and January 29, 1984, as though the acquisition were made at the beginning of fiscal year 1983. This pro forma information does not purport to be indicative of the results of operations which would have actually been obtained if the acquisition had been effective on the dates indicated.

| | Fiscal Year ended | |
	February 3, 1985	January 29, 1984*
	(Unaudited)	
Net sales	$482,752,000	$274,660,000
	Fiscal Year ended	
Net earnings	9,009,000	6,913,000
Earnings per common and common equivalent share	.36	.28

* Includes the operations and pro forma adjustments from the date of inception of Bowater's operations in August, 1983.

3. Long-Term Debt and Lines of Credit

Long-Term debt consists of the following:	February 2, 1986	February 3, 1985
8 1/2% convertible subordinated debentures, due July 1, 2009, convertible into shares of common stock of the Company at a conversion price of $26.50 per share. The debentures are redeemable by the Company at a premium from July 1, 1986 to July 1, 1995, will retire 70% of the issue prior to maturity. Interest is payable semi-annually.	$86,250,000	$86,250,000
9% convertible subordinated debentures, due December 15, 1999, convertible into shares of common stock of the Company at a conversion price of $16.90 per share. The debentures are redeemable by the Company at a premium from December 15, 1986 to December 15, 1994. An annual mandatory sinking fund of $2,000,000 per year is required from 1994 to 1998. Interest is payable semi-annually.	14,000,000	14,000,000
Total convertible subordinated debentures	100,250,000	100,250,000
Revolving credit agreement. Interest may be fixed for any portion outstanding for up to 180 days, at the Company's option, based on a CD rate plus 3/4%, the LIBOR rate plus 1/2% or at the prime rate.	88,000,000	—
*Variable Rate Industrial Revenue Bond (see note 7)	10,100,000	10,100,000
*Variable Rate Industrial Revenue Bond, secured by a letter of credit, payable in sinking fund installments from December 1, 1991 through December 1, 2010	4,400,000	—
9 5/8% Industrial Revenue Bond, secured by a letter of credit, payable on December 1, 1993, with interest payable semi-annually	4,200,000	4,200,000

(continued)

Long-Term Debt and Lines of Credit *(continued)*

*Variable Rate Industrial Revenue Bond, secured by land, payable in annual installments of $233,000 with interest payable semi-annually	**3,267,000**	3,500,000
Other	**108,000**	179,000
Total long-term debt	**210,325,000**	118,229,000
Less current portion	**10,382,000**	287,000
Long-term debt, excluding current portion	**$199,943,000**	$117,942,000

*The interest rates on the variable rate industrial revenue bonds are related to various short-term municipal money market composite rates.

Maturities of long-term debt are approximately $10,382,000 for fiscal 1986 and $234,000 for each of the next four subsequent years.

During the fiscal year ended February 2, 1986, the Company entered into a new unsecured revolving line of credit for a maximum of $200,000,000, subject to certain limitations, of which $88,000,000 is outstanding at year-end. Commitment amounts under the agreement decrease by $15,000,000 on July 31, 1990, by $20,000,000 each six months from that date through January 31, 1993, by $35,000,000 on July 31, 1993 and with the remaining $50,000,000 commitment expiring on January 31, 1994. Maximum borrowings outstanding within the commitment limits may not exceed specified percentages of inventories, land and buildings, and fixtures and equipment, all as defined in the Agreement. Under certain conditions, the commitments may be extended and/or increased. An annual commitment fee of 1/4% to 3/8% is required to be paid on the unused portion of the revolving line of credit. Interest rates specified may be increased by a maximum of 3/8 of 1% based on specified ratios of interest rate coverage and debt to equity.

Under the revolving credit agreement, the Company is required, among other things, to maintain during fiscal year 1985 a minimum tangible net worth (defined to include the convertible subordinated debentures) of $150,000,000 (increasing annually to $213,165,000 by January 3, 1989), a debt to tangible net worth ratio of no more than 2 to 1, a current ratio of not less than 1.5 to 1, and a ratio of earnings before interest expense and income taxes to interest expense, net, of not less than 2 to 1. The Company was in compliance with all restrictive covenants as of February 2, 1986. The restrictive covenants related to the letter of credit agreements securing the industrial revenue bonds and the convertible subordinated debentures are no more restrictive than those under the revolving line of credit agreement.

Interest expense in the accompanying consolidated statements of earnings is net of interest capitalized of $3,429,000 in fiscal 1985 and $1,462,000 in fiscal 1984.

4. Income Taxes

The provision for income taxes consists of the following:

	February 1, 1986	Fiscal Year Ended February 3, 1985	January 29, 1984
Current:			
Federal	**$(578,000)**	$9,083,000	$6,916,000
State	**366,000**	1,539,000	1,096,000
	(212,000)	10,622,000	8,012,000
Deferred:			
Federal	**3,306,000**	1,464,000	713,000
State	**306,000**	44,000	—
	3,612,000	1,508,000	713,000
Total	**$3,400,000**	$12,130,000	$8,725,000

The Home Depot, Inc.

The effective tax rates for fiscal 1985, 1984, and 1983 were 29.3%, 46.2%, and 46.0%, respectively. A reconciliation of income tax expense at Federal statutory rates to actual tax expense for the applicable fiscal years follows:

| | | Fiscal Year Ended | |
	February 2, 1986	February 3, 1985	January 29, 1984
Income taxes at Federal statutory rate, net of surtax exemption	$5,345,000	$12,076,000	$8,734,000
State income taxes, net of Federal income tax benefit	363,000	855,000	592,000
Investment and targeted jobs tax credits	(2,308,000)	(800,000)	(747,000)
Other, net	—	(1,000)	146,000
	$3,400,000	$12,130,000	$8,725,000

Deferred income taxes arise from differences in the timing of reporting income for financial statement and income tax purposes. The sources of these differences and the tax effect of each are as follows:

| | | Fiscal Year Ended | |
	February 2, 1986	February 3, 1985	January 29, 1984
Accelerated depreciation	$2,526,000	$1,159,000	$713,000
Interest capitalization	855,000	349,000	—
Other, net	231,000	—	—
	$3,612,000	$1,508,000	$713,000

5. Leases

The Company leases certain retail locations, office, and warehouse and distribution space, equipment, and vehicles under operating leases. All leases will expire within the next 25 years; however, it can be expected that in the normal course of business, leases will be renewed or replaced. Total rent expense, net of minor sublease income for the fiscal years ended February 2, 1986, February 3, 1985, and January 29, 1984 amounted to approximately $12,737,000, $6,718,000, and $4,233,000, respectively. Under the building leases, real estate taxes, insurance, maintenance, and operating expenses applicable to the leased property are obligations of the Company. Certain of the store leases provide for contingent rentals based on percentages of sales in excess of specified minimums. Contingent rentals for fiscal years ended February 2, 1986, February 3, 1985, and January 29, 1984 were approximately $650,000, $545,000, and $111,000.

The approximate future minimum lease payments under operating leases at February 2, 1986 are as follows:

Fiscal Year	
1986	$16,093,000
1987	16,668,000
1988	16,345,000
1989	16,086,000
1990	16,129,000
Thereafter	171,455,000
	$252,776,000

7. Disposition of Property and Equipment

During the fourth quarter of fiscal year 1985, the Company disposed of certain properties and equipment at a net gain of $1,317,000. The properties represented real estate located in Detroit, Houston and Tucson, and the equipment represented the trade-in of cash registers of current generation point of sale equipment. Under the terms of the Detroit real estate sale, the purchaser will either assume the bond obligations of the Company of $10,100,000 after February 2, 1986 or pay the Company the funds disbursed under the bonds in order for the Company to prepay the total amount outstanding. Included in accounts receivable at February 2, 1986 is $13,800,000 related to these transactions.

8. Commitments and Contingencies

At February 2, 1986, the Company was contingently liable for approximately $5,300,000 under outstanding letters of credit issued in connection with purchase commitments.

The Company has litigation arising from the normal course of business. In management's opinion, this litigation will not materially affect the Company's financial condition.

9. Quarterly Financial Data (Unaudited)

The following is a summary of the unaudited quarterly results of operations for fiscal years ended February 2, 1986 and February 3, 1985:

	Net Sales	Gross Profit	Net Earnings	Net Earnings per Common and Common Equivalent Share
Fiscal year ended February 2, 1986:				
First Quarter	**$145,048,000**	**$36,380,000**	**$1,945,000**	**$.08**
Second Quarter	**174,239,000**	**45,572,000**	**2,499,000**	**.10**
Third Quarter	**177,718,000**	**46,764,000**	**1,188,000**	**.05**
Fourth Quarter	**203,724,000**	**52,741,000**	**2,587,000**	**.10**
	$700,729,000	**$181,457,000**	**$8,219,000**	**$.33**
Fiscal year ended February 3, 1985:				
First Quarter	$95,872,000	$25,026,000	$3,437,000	$.14
Second Quarter	119,068,000	29,185,000	3,808,000	.15
Third Quarter	100,459,000	27,658,000	3,280,000	.13
Fourth Quarter	117,380,000	32,450,000	3,597,000	.14
	$432,779,000	$114,319,000	$14,122,000	$.56

The Home Depot, Inc.

AUDITORS' REPORT

The Board of Directors and Stockholders,
The Home Depot, Inc.:

We have examined the consolidated balance sheets of The Home Depot, Inc. and subsidiary as of February 2, 1986 and February 3, 1985 and the related consolidated statements of earnings, stockholders' equity, and changes in financial position for each of the years in the three-year period ended February 2, 1986. Our examinations were made in accordance with generally accepted auditing standards, and, accordingly, included such tests of the accounting records and such other auditing procedures as we considered necessary in the circumstances.

In our opinion, the aforementioned consolidated financial statements present fairly the financial position of The Home Depot, Inc. and subsidiary at February 2, 1986 and February 3, 1985, and the results of their operations and the changes in their financial position for each of the years in the three-year period ended February 2, 1986, in conformity with generally accepted accounting principles applied on a consistent basis.

PEAT, MARWICK, MITCHELL & CO.
Atlanta, Georgia
March 24, 1986

Korea Stock Exchange, 1998

In July 1998, Hong In-Kie, chairman and CEO of the Korea Stock Exchange, was
pondering how best to attract a significant amount of long-term capital into the
Korean stock market. Hong, a graduate of Harvard Business School AMP '85,
avid mountain climber, church leader, and accomplished tenor, was aware that there
were stiff challenges ahead. At the pinnacle of a successful career as a bureaucrat and
as ex-president of a large conglomerate in one of the world's most dynamic
economies, he had a unique birds-eye view of Korean society and the economy.

During the past 30 years, the Korean economy had grown at 8.6% annually. At the
end of 1996, Korea became the eleventh largest economy in the world and a member of the Organization for Economic Cooperation and Development (OECD). Used
to hosannas as a worldwide leader in areas as diverse as shipbuilding, construction,
semiconductors and automobiles, Korea found itself in the unenviable position of
having practically depleted its foreign exchange reserves by November of 1997 and
having had to seek assistance from the International Monetary Fund (IMF). As a
result of the economic crisis, the Korea Composite Stock Price Index (KOSPI) closed
at 376.31 by the end of 1997—down 42.2% from the closing index of 651.22 in
1996 (see **Exhibit 1** for selected economic data).

Hong described the current situation as follows: "It is like a movie unfolding every
day, and we are all watching and on stage at the same time. Events are occurring so
fast that the headlines in the evening version of the paper and the morning version
of the same paper are often substantially different." Hong was convinced that finding a way to spur the development of the stock market was a crucial part of the
change needed to shepherd Korea out of its current economic predicament.

KOREAN ECONOMIC SYSTEM

Prior to the 1997 economic crisis, the Korean economy was viewed by many, both
inside and outside the country, as a dramatic success story. While there were many
facets to the export-oriented economic strategy of Korea, two features stood out: a
bank-centered financial system that financed the rapid industrial growth, and the
chaebol system that created globally competitive enterprises.

Bank-Centered Financial System

Unlike the U.S. and the U.K. economies' reliance on the stock market, the Korean economy relied heavily on the banking system for channeling savings to industrial investments. In this respect, Korea followed the example of Germany and Japan in the development of its financial system. Many commentators, both in Korea and abroad, believed that the bank-centered financial system facilitated long-term investments, largely due to the close relationships between industrial enterprises and financiers. Because stock market investors typically had no long-term relationship with the firms in which they invested, the U.S-style stock market system was alleged to lead to "myopic management."

Even though Korean banks operated in the private sector, the national government had significant influence on the banking industry. Through ownership and the appointment of bank directors, the Korean government could influence banks' lending decisions to further its economic development plans. For example, in the 1970s, government policies favored the development of heavy industries, such as construction, machinery, and shipbuilding. The government encouraged companies to expand business in these industries and provided favorable capital related to that expansion through banks.

The Chaebol System—Business Groups

The Korean economy was dominated by multibusiness organizations known as chaebols. The largest chaebols, such as Samsung, Daewoo, Hyundai, LG, and the SK Group, operated in a wide variety of industries, such as construction, shipbuilding, automobiles, consumer electronics, computing, telecommunication, and financial services. The 30 largest chaebols accounted for 51.8% of the total industrial output of Korea in 1996. The top 4 chaebols—Hyundai, Samsung, LG, and Daewoo—accounted for 31.2% of the total industrial output of Korea in 1996.

Historically, government policy favored the growth of chaebols. These policies included granting industrial licenses, distributing foreign borrowings, and providing favored access to bank financing.[1] The promotion of chaebols was seen by the Korean government as a way to create domestic industry that could compete in global markets. Indeed, Korean chaebols played a very critical role in the export-led growth of the Korean economy. By 1996, the top 7 trading companies of chaebols accounted for 47.7% of Korea's total exports.[2]

The chaebol organizational structure conferred several advantages in the early growth stage of the Korean economy, by enabling entrepreneurs to overcome the problem of underdeveloped product, labor, and financial markets. At this stage, many of the institutions that underpin the functioning of advanced markets were either missing or absent in Korea.

In advanced markets, intermediary institutions and legal structures address potential information and incentive problems. These institutions permit individual entrepreneurs to raise capital, access management talent, earn customer acceptance, and require all parties to play by the same rules of the game. Entrepreneurs and investors can be sure of the stable legal environment in advanced markets to protect property

---

1. In the early 1970s, the interest rate on foreign borrowing was 5–6%, whereas the interest rate on domestic bank debt was 25–30%. The interest rate for borrowing from non-banks was higher than that from banks. The privilege of using foreign borrowing and bank loans significantly contributed to the accumulation of chaebols' growth.

2. Top 7 trading companies included affiliates of Hyundai, Samsung, LG, Daewoo, SK, Ssangyong, and Hyosung.

rights, giving entrepreneurs the confidence that they will reap the fruits of their entrepreneurial activity. In this context found in advanced markets, it is less likely that the entrepreneur will benefit significantly by being associated with a large corporate entity. Hence, the costs of business diversification are likely to exceed any potential benefits.

In an emerging market like Korea, in contrast, there were a variety of market failures, caused by information and incentive problems. For example, the financial markets were characterized by a lack of adequate disclosure and weak corporate governance and control. Intermediaries such as financial analysts, mutual funds, investment bankers, venture capitalists, and the financial press were either absent or not fully evolved. Finally, securities regulations were generally weak, and their enforcement was uncertain. Similar problems abounded in product markets and labor markets, once again because of the absence of intermediaries.

The absence of intermediary institutions made it costly for individual entrepreneurs to acquire necessary inputs like finance, technology, and management talent. Market and legal imperfections also made it costly to establish quality brand images in product markets and to establish contractual relationships with joint venture partners. As a result, an enterprise could often be more profitably pursued as part of a large diversified business group, such as a chaebol, which acted as an intermediary between individual entrepreneurs and imperfect markets.

For example, affiliates of chaebols also enjoyed preferential access to financing from domestic banks because of their strong connections with bankers and government officials. Also, established companies in a chaebol often provided cross-guarantees on loans to new affiliates, making it easier for new ventures to raise financing from domestic and foreign lenders.

Korean chaebols such as Samsung and Daewoo were also able to use their size and scope to invest in world-class brand names. These brand names enabled new companies promoted by these leading chaebols, even in unrelated fields, to gain instant credibility in export markets and with technology partners.

Chaebols were the preferred employers for students at prestigious Korean universities. Because of their size and scope, chaebols could offer job security in an economy with no safety nets. Further, chaebols such as Samsung and the SK Group made extensive investment in the training and development of their employees, in effect creating their own "business schools." Due to their size, they could hire professors from top business schools in the world to lead their in-house training programs. Because Korea did not have many world-class business schools, the in-house "business schools" of chaebols were in a unique position to develop management talent.

As a result of the above advantages, chaebols were uniquely positioned to launch new ventures in the Korean economy. Chaebols relied extensively on domestic and foreign debt to finance their rapid growth. Reliance on domestic debt arose as a result of the bank-centered nature of the financial system. Further, with a view to retaining control of Korean businesses in Korean hands, government policy restricted foreign direct investment in Korean chaebols. While foreign investors could invest through the stock market, foreign money tended to be invested in Korean companies through banks and other financial institutions.[3]

---

3. The details of the institutional investor market in Korea can be found in "The growing financial market importance of institutional investors: the case of Korea," by Yu-Kyung Kim, OECD Proceedings: Institutional Investors in the New Financial Landscape, 1998.

One of the key characteristics of chaebols was family ownership. Family control was enhanced through equity cross-holdings. The average family ownership in the top 30 chaebols was 10.6%, and the average ownership through cross-holding equity ownership among member firms was 32.8% in 1995. Cross-holdings increased the founder family's control on large business groups.[4] Traditionally, the voting rights of institutional investors, such as securities firms and insurance companies, was limited by the law, and minority shareholders were not active.[5] As a result, the founder or founder's family could effectively control the business group with relatively small direct ownership. The family typically controlled top management positions.[6]

By 1996, prior to the economic crisis, the median debt-to-equity ratio of the top 30 Korean chaebols stood at 420% (see **Exhibit 2**). While each company in a chaebol borrowed money independently, bankers often demanded and received cross-guarantees from the other firms in the chaebol. Since Korean financial accounting rules did not require the disclosure of these cross-guarantees, it was difficult for outsiders to assess the true debt commitments of a given Korean company.

THE "IMF" CRISIS

The Korean economic crisis in 1997 was part of a broader Asian financial crisis that first started in Thailand, when the baht weakened as foreign investors lost confidence in the Thai economy. Amid the Asian currency crisis, foreign financial institutions, concerned about potential financial distress for Korean firms, started calling in their loans rapidly. Foreign portfolio investors also began to sell their investments and repatriate the sales proceeds for fear of the depreciation of the Korean won.[7]

The outflow of foreign portfolio investment funds continued for four consecutive months, from August to November, bringing Korea close to depleting its foreign exchange reserves. On November 21, the Korean government requested the IMF's assistance to avoid a potential default on its obligations. After frenzied negotiations, the IMF agreed to provide Korea with US$55 billion or more in a bailout package. **Exhibit 3** shows the chronology of events surrounding the crisis. The rapid change in the value of the Korean won during 1997 and 1998 is shown in **Exhibit 4**.

The Search for a Solution

Many observers, both inside and outside Korea, were stunned by the rapid change of investor sentiment. The darling of foreign investors and economists until then, Korea found itself in the middle of an economic crisis that threatened to wipe out the fruits of hard work of a whole generation. As a sense of gloom enveloped the country, a heated debate focused on the search for the root causes of the crisis.

The nexus of the banking system and the chaebols, once viewed as the means to rapid economic growth, came under increased attack. Influential policymakers,

---

4. *Cross holdings could take many forms. Companies A and B could own equity in each other. Alternatively, A might own part of B, B part of C, and C part of A. These arrangements typically meant that a smaller amount of equity ownership in one company was sufficient to ensure control of it than in situations where there were no cross-holdings.*

5. *Under these regulations, institutional investors were restricted to so-called "shadow voting," which essentially meant that they voted with the management. After the recent crisis, this practice was abolished.*

6. *In 1995, among the top 30 chaebols, only one chaebol—KIA Motors—had a CEO who was not related to the founder's family.*

7. *1997 Fact Book published by Korea Stock Exchange.*

including those at the IMF, believed that the chaebols, with their close connections to politicians and government officials, could get loans without much resistance from banks. As a result, the vaunted "relationship financing" model, meant to facilitate long-term investments, was now viewed more as facilitating "crony capitalism." A consensus began to emerge that, with easy access to financing, a lack of supervision by banks, and the government's emphasis on job creation, chaebols focused excessively on growth and expansion, and ignored profitability.

On December 19, 1997, in the middle of a serious economic crisis, Kim Dae-Jung was elected President of Korea. Soon after entering office, President Kim noted that big business groups, together with government officials in power in the past, must take responsibility for having brought the economy to near-collapse. He proclaimed that it was the collusion between the government and business, the government's control of finance, and widespread corruption that had battered the economy. Kim said, "Unless chaebols implement reform, they would face the recall of existing debts or the suspension of fresh credit. Only profitable enterprises and exporting companies will be regarded as 'patriotic' firms eligible for government supports."[8]

As a condition for IMF bailout loans, receiving countries must adhere to the economic programs prescribed by the IMF. Michel Camdessus, IMF managing director, stated: "The program comprises strengthened fiscal and monetary policies, far-reaching financial reforms, and further liberalization of trade and capital flows, as well as improvement in the structure and governance of Korean corporations." The IMF's program for Korea was heavily influenced by the conclusion that it was time for Korea to significantly restructure its financial and industrial sectors (see **Exhibit 5** for details of the IMF-supported program of economic reform).

Some Koreans were positive about the IMF program because they felt that it could serve as an opportunity to sharpen Korea's international competitiveness, even though it was to be carried out by the force of outsiders. There were, however, others who expressed concern that the rapid changes proposed under the program were not only unrealistic but could lead to significant layoffs and social instability. In fact, the common reference to the economic crisis as the "IMF crisis" reflected the ambivalence in the Korean reaction to both the causes and the remedies being debated.

ECONOMIC RESTRUCTURING[9]

To implement the IMF program and to restore international confidence in Korea, the newly elected government of President Kim Dae-Jung began to aggressively pursue financial sector reforms and a total restructuring of chaebols. To this end, the Financial Supervisory Commission (FSC) was established on April 1, 1998, under the prime minister's jurisdiction to supervise all financial institutions, including banks, securities firms, and insurance companies. The restructuring process of the financial industry and the corporate sector was administrated by the FSC. The FSC pursued a strategy of sequential restructuring. Banks were to be restructured first. Corporate sector restructuring would be accelerated through bank reform.

---

8. Lee Chang-sup, "Kim rules out new currency crisis," Korea Times, September 28, 1998.

9. This section is based on the reports published by Ministry of Finance and Economy (MOFE) and Financial Supervisory Commission (FSC) in Korea.

Bank Restructuring

The FSC requested 12 banks that fell short of the 8% capital adequacy ratio set by the Bank for International Settlement (BIS) (as of December 1997) to submit rehabilitation plans. Bank appraisal committees and accounting firms assessed the size of nonperforming loans through asset due diligence reviews and made full provisions and write-offs based on the actual size of non-performing loans. Based on this review, the FSC conditionally approved the bail-out of 7 banks, and ordered the closure of 5 nonviable banks. Conditionally approved banks were asked to submit implementation plans which included changes in management, cost reductions, and recapitalization plans, such as mergers, joint ventures, or rights issues.

Five banks, which were classified as nonviable, were to be acquired by healthy banks. To protect acquiring banks from spilled-over problem loans, several measures were taken: only good assets would be sold with a 6-month put option; government would inject fresh capital to enhance the acquiring bank's capital adequacy to pre-acquisition level; the acquiring bank's bad assets would be purchased by Korea Asset Management Corporation, funded by public resources; and deposit guarantees would be honored until the completion of all restructuring in order to prevent any bank runs.

One example of bank restructuring was a merger between Commercial Bank of Korea and the Hanil Bank. On July 31, 1998, following the guidelines of the FSC, two banks announced a one-to-one merger. The newly merged bank proposed that in order for the merged bank to succeed, the following actions would be taken: (1) an accountable management system through drastic management improvement; (2) early resolution of nonperforming loans through injection from public resources; (3) capital injection from international investors.[10]

A key issue in the normalization of the Korean financial sector was to develop a plan to clear nonperforming loans. At the end of March 1998, the nonperforming loans of financial institutions were estimated to be about 120 trillion won, which is about 23.3% of Korean financial institutions' entire credit portfolio. The Korean government estimated that the total market value of the non-performing loans would be equal to 50% of their book value. The realized losses borne by financial institutions were therefore estimated to be approximately 60 trillion won.

To finance these losses, the Korean government planned to raise 50 trillion won through government bonds. From this amount, 41 trillion won would be used to purchase non-performing loans, and to recapitalize the affected financial institutions; the remaining 9 trillion won would be reserved for the potential new demand for increased deposit protection. The government expected financial institutions to issue new equity worth 20 trillion won, which accounted for as much as one-third of total current capitalization in the Korean stock market.

Corporate Restructuring

In the short term, the Korean government's focus with respect to corporate restructuring was to shut down nonviable enterprises and to improve the financial condition of the rest. In the long term, the objective was to improve the management and governance of the corporate sector in general and of the chaebols in particular. To achieve these objectives, the FSC delineated five principles of corporate restructuring: (1) improving the financial structure, (2) eliminating the practice of mutual guarantees of loans among affiliated firms, (4) focusing on "core" business sectors, (4) increasing transparency,

---

10. Joint press conference upon announcement of the merger between the Commercial Bank of Korea and the Hanil Bank.

(5) improving corporate governance (e.g., increasing major shareholders' and management's accountability).

In order to direct the restructuring process, the FSC classified all Korean companies into three categories. Companies classified as "viable" would receive full support from financial institutions; those that were classified as "subject to exit" would be sold off or shut down on a timely basis; and those that were classified as "subject to restructuring" would benefit from proactive support toward restructuring from financial institutions. In June 1998, 55 corporations, which represented 17% of the total number of corporations subject to the assessment, were classified as nonviable and ordered to exit. Of these 55 companies, 20 were affiliated companies of the top 5 chaebols (Hyundai, Samsung, LG, Daewoo, and SK), and 32 were affiliates of the top 6 to 64 business groups.

One of the senior officials at FSC stated; "To reduce excessive reliance on debt financing, the government set a target for reducing Korean companies' debt to equity (D/E) ratio from the current level of approximately 500% to a level of 200% by the end of 1999. To meet this requirement, Korean companies had to raise more equity or sell off some of their assets."

Korean chaebols were directed by the FSC to formulate restructuring plans with a view to identifying core businesses on which they would focus, and to close down or divest the rest. To improve transparency and governance of individual companies in a chaebol, new guidelines curtailed the role of the central corporate office and prohibited cross-guarantees. The top 5 chaebols were cajoled into the so-called "Big Deal" swaps of business units in order to boost national competitiveness by cutting out some domestic competition. To expedite the pace of corporate restructuring, government submitted several legislative articles to the coming session of the National Assembly. These articles allowed tax benefits for restructuring, simplified the mergers and acquisitions process, and permitted corporate spin-offs and carve-outs.

Attracting Foreign Capital

Recognizing the importance of foreign capital for the successful restructuring of Korean banks and chaebols, President Kim Dae-Jung proclaimed his intention to make Korea a haven for foreign investors. Foreign investors were essential in several ways. First, since all major Korean companies were looking to sell assets and raise new capital, the only viable buyers were foreign investors. Second, foreign investors brought with them world-class management and governance practices to Korea.

To attract foreign capital, the government proposed several new policies. Under the new policy, foreign firms were allowed to freely establish mutual funds in Korea. At the same time, restrictions on foreign investors were also reduced. Earlier, foreign investors needed the approval of the board of directors of a company to buy more than 10% of its outstanding shares. On May 25, 1998, under the new rules, the 10% limit was completely abolished. The government also granted special privileges to domestic companies that attracted foreign investment or sold their assets to foreigners.

While these moves were somewhat effective in increasing foreign investors' interest in Korea, several hurdles remained. Deals for foreign direct investment could not be consummated because of widespread disagreement in valuation estimates of Korean sellers and foreign buyers. These valuation difficulties were exacerbated by the poor quality of accounting information. Further, foreign buyers were uncertain about the ease with which they could lay off employees. Despite the recent agreement between government, industry, and labor unions to cooperate in the restructuring process, the possibility of widespread layoffs, especially by foreign owners, could be received with hostility.

The popular sentiment toward foreign direct investment was also ambiguous. On the one hand, the Korean government undertook a process of educating Koreans that attracting international investors was critical to economic rebuilding. On the other hand, there was a popular feeling against foreign investment, partly due to the 40-year Japanese ruling of the country that ended in 1945. As a result, while many American franchises such as McDonald's and KFC have prospered in Korea, symbolic gestures against foreign investment abounded. When Microsoft attempted to buy a Korean word processing software company in financial distress, there was a fund-raising campaign to save the company and keep it in Korean hands. Even if the amount of foreign investment involved in this deal was only about US$20 million, it was symbolic.

Foreign investors were also wary of the risks involved in investing in Korean companies through the stock market. Even in advanced capital markets, investing in stocks involved taking additional risks relative to investing in bonds or bank deposits. Unlike debt-holders, shareholders were not promised a fixed payoff. Further, when insiders had a controlling stake, they could take actions that were potentially harmful to minority shareholders. In advanced markets, these potential risks faced by public shareholders were mitigated through a variety of mechanisms such as credible financial reporting, minority shareholder protection laws, the threat of hostile takeovers, scrutiny by an aggressive analyst community, and the supervision of management by an independent board of directors.

In Korea, as of early 1998, many of these institutional mechanisms that protected shareholders and reduced their risks were either absent, underdeveloped, or poorly enforced. Relative to international standards, accounting rules and disclosure regulations were lax; there was a wide-spread belief that external auditors were either unwilling or unable to exercise independence; it was rare for shareholders to sue corporate managers or auditors successfully; boards were viewed as being too close to corporate managers; there was no effective threat of a hostile takeover or a proxy fight to replace a company's management; and the financial analysts themselves often worked for brokerage houses owned by large chaebols. The net result of these institutional voids was a perception among investors, both domestic and foreign, that investing in Korean stocks was very risky.

DEVELOPING THE CAPITAL MARKETS

As chairman and CEO of the Korea Stock Exchange, Hong In-Kie was committed to leading the development of the Korean capital markets to a truly world-class level. He believed that the long-term prosperity of Korea depended critically on the success of this initiative.

Traditionally, the stock market played a relatively small role in the Korean financial system. The first significant boost to the Korean stock market came in 1976 when the Securities and Exchange Law underwent extensive revision. The main objective of the amendment was to ensure more effective supervision of the securities industry and to reinforce investor protection.

Throughout the latter half of the 1970s, the Korean securities market experienced an unprecedented rush of public offerings. The number of listed corporations, which stood at only 66 in 1972, jumped to 356 by the end of 1978. At the end of 1997, the number of listed companies was 776. During the period from 1972 to 1997, the traded value of listed stocks jumped more than two thousand-fold from 71 billion won to 162.3 trillion won, and the total market capitalization increased from 246 billion won to 71 trillion won (see **Exhibit 6** and **Exhibit 7**).

Even though the absolute amount of both the traded value of stocks and market capitalization has increased over time, the relative magnitude of market capitalization to GDP declined in recent years. In 1994 and 1995, the market value to GDP ratio was greater than 40%, but it declined to 30% in 1996 and to 17% in 1997 (see **Exhibit 8**). The significance of equity as a source of financing also decreased over the last decade: The proportion of financing from the stock market relative to all sources of external finance declined from 23% in 1989 to 7.87% in 1997 (see **Exhibit 9** and **Exhibit 10**).

The KOSPI composite index (100 as of January 4, 1980) rose from 532 on January 1, 1988, to 1007 as of April 1, 1989. Many small investors were counting capital gains in excess of 100%, in a little over a year. However, this 1988–1989 upturn in the Korea Stock Exchange was not sustainable. The composite index has since dived and climbed like a roller coaster. On August 21, 1992, the composite index bottomed out at 460. Many small investors became seriously disillusioned with the stock market in 1992. They blamed the government for their losses. Indeed, for political reasons, the government had repeatedly intervened to prop up share prices by infusing large inflows of cash from various stabilization funds. Hardly anyone approached the market from a long-term perspective focusing on the fundamental financial soundness of the company, managerial acumen, or on dividend performance.[11]

Recent Developments

After Hong In-Kie became the CEO of the stock exchange in 1993, he initiated several efforts to modernize it. In 1996, the stock exchange moved to a new skyscraper with a fully computerized trading floor and a strict computerized surveillance system to monitor trading activity. Under Hong's leadership, the Korea Stock Exchange introduced derivative products for the first time—KOSPI 200 stock index futures contracts in May 1996 and KOSPI 200 stock index option contracts in July 1997. While Hong was proud of these innovations and the investments in improving the "physical infrastructure" of the exchange, he was aware that the exchange would not become truly world-class without significant improvements in supporting "institutional infrastructure." Hong noted with satisfaction some recent developments in this direction.

Recognizing the fact that the lack of transparency was one of the weaknesses that contributed to the current crisis, the Korean government proposed major changes in accounting rules. New regulations required the 30 largest conglomerates to prepare certified financial statements which would cover all the affiliated companies on a combined basis beginning in the 1999 fiscal year. The objective of this requirement was to improve the transparency of large conglomerates. There was also a move to make a fundamental change in Korean Generally Accepted Accounting Principles by adopting the more stringent International Accounting Standards.

There was also a change in the process through which accounting standards were set. Earlier, the Korea Securities and Exchange Commissions (KSEC) used to set accounting standards. When a new accounting standard was proposed, the KSEC would form a temporary board to review that standard. Board members included auditors, accounting professors, and government officials. Starting in April 1998, the KSEC became a part of the Financial Supervisory Board, and the FSC took over the supervision of accounting standard setting.

---

11. James M. West, "Korea Stock Exchange," *Korea Herald, August 30, 1998.*

To improve shareholder rights, the Korean government took a number of steps. For example, in April 1998, to improve minority shareholders' rights, the current requirement of 1% ownership to bring suits against management was eased to 0.05%; the requirement of 1% ownership to request the dismissal of a director or an auditor for an illegal act was relaxed to 0.5%; the minimum share-ownership required to examine corporate books was reduced from 3% to 1%.

New regulations also attempted to ease restrictions that had previously made hostile takeovers of Korean companies very difficult. Earlier, a company or an individual could not acquire more than 25% of the outstanding shares of another company unless an open tender offer to purchase more than 50% of the outstanding shares was made. However, in February 1998, this provision was abolished. Also, restrictions on institutional investors' voting rights were eliminated.

Public shareholders were also becoming more vocal in demanding management accountability. In May 1998, for the first time, foreign shareholders were beginning to have a voice on the management of Korean companies. The New York-based hedge fund Tiger Management, with the coalition of other foreign funds, staged a successful revolt at SK Telecom, the country's leading cellular phone operator. These outsider shareholders forced the phone company to stop subsidizing its sister companies in the SK Group. SK Telecom, for instance, backed a $50 million loan to its sibling SK Securities, which recently suffered heavy losses in derivatives trading. To guard against such maneuvers in the future, minority shareholders demanded—and got—three outside directors on the board of SK Telecom and an independent auditor.[12]

Management accountability was also being championed by nongovernmental organizations such as The People's Solidarity for Participatory Democracy (PSPD). The organization was founded in September 1994 and headed by professor Chang Ha-sung at Korea University. In July 1998, PSPD successfully won a legal judgment against the management of the Korea First Bank for failure to exercise due diligence in its lending to a failed company—Hanbo Steel. The court order required four ex-top managers of Korea First Bank to pay about US$30 million with their personal wealth to the bank (not to the plaintiffs) to make up for the losses caused by their negligence. The Korean press hailed it as the first case where plaintiffs won in a suit against management, based on management's failure to perform due diligence.

Future Challenges

Hong In-Kie was convinced that a lot of progress was made in the past few months. There was evidence that foreign investors were beginning to come back. Korea was also winning praise from the IMF for following closely its prescriptions. However, he was also aware that much more needed to be done.

Although the new accounting regulations were aimed at improving the quality of information available to investors to monitor corporate managers, there was much skepticism about the rules that had been mandated. The editor of a major Korean newspaper commented, "It's fine for the government and the international investors to demand transparency. However, it's important to realize that the different facets of Korean society are closely tied together—the government, business, and the banks. The entire system will have to be made transparent, not just a part of it."

---

12. *Starting in 1999, it is a listing requirement for all Korea Stock Exchange listed firms to have at least 25% of their board members composed of outside directors.*

Hong also noted that, without effective auditing, financial reports were unlikely to be viewed by investors as reliable. One of the senior partners at a Big Five accounting firm in the United States echoed this sentiment: "Foreign investors know that the quality of audits in Korea is suspect; they will not be satisfied unless the financial statements of their Korean companies are signed by reputed international accounting firms."

The recent victory of minority shareholders represented the coming of major changes in Korean financial markets. However, this development was viewed with mixed feelings by several observers. Given the absence of sophistication about financial markets by the average Korean citizen, there was a concern that minority shareholder rights would be pushed forward without adequate attention paid to minority shareholder responsibilities. Would the prospect of shareholder lawsuits and second-guessing management decisions by courts hamper the restructuring process?

There was also a debate in Korea and other emerging markets on the appropriate speed of opening capital markets to foreign investors, given the experience of the past few months. One of the major concerns was the instability of the stock market due to speculative hot money. There was a concern that rapid outflow would significantly damage not only the stock market but also the foreign exchange rate. In order to prevent this, many emerging countries imposed regulations on foreign investment and intervened in the stock market.

Hong believed that full liberalization of the stock market was the fundamental solution. He stated, "Government regulations, as in the case of Malaysia, or government interventions in the stock market, as in the case of Hong Kong, do not guarantee the long-term development of a stock market. While in the rest of the world the acronym PKO may stand for Peace Keeping Operation, the same term in Asian securities markets is known as Price Keeping Operation—a derogatory term for intervention by the government. As the underlying philosophy of the government is based on democracy and a market economy, stock market participants must not rely on government to implement artificial market-boosting measures. In the short term, the stock market may have difficulty in breaking out of the doldrums, but as the market finds itself free from any sort of intervention, it will grow into a more independent, transparent, predictable, accountable, and self-sustaining market. Korea is following closely the IMF prescription towards a fully open market. The earlier we can get to the open market, the better." However, he wondered whether Korea had the institutional infrastructure necessary to support an open stock market.

As he pondered over these issues, Hong knew that the stakes were high. A senior editor of one of Korea's leading newspapers summed up the situation, "The newly elected president asked for a year to resolve matters. It has been six months already. If things don't improve, Korean people may not remain patient much longer." Due to the efforts made by government and business, there was a sign of increase in the foreign investment in Korean stocks (see **Exhibit 11**). However, it has not reached the level that meets Hong's expectation. Hong wondered which of several possible directions the Korean stock market should pursue to attract foreign investment.

QUESTIONS

1. What are the merits and demerits of a stock versus a bank system financing?

2. To prevent another bad loan problem in the future, what changes should be made in South Korean banks?

3. Is it a good idea for South Korea to rely more on the stock market as a source of corporate finance? Is it a good idea from the perspective of the chaebols?

4. How long do you think it will take South Korea to develop a vibrant stock market? What are the impediments? Are the changes contemplated adequate for the development of a vibrant stock market? What other steps would you recommend?

EXHIBIT 1

Selected Economic Indicators

	1995	1996	1997	1998 (Estimate)
Korea Composite Stock Price Index (year-end)	882.94	651.22	376.31	
Real GDP growth (percent change)	8.8	5.5	−0.4	−4.0 to −5.5
Consumer prices (percent change)	7.4	4.8	7.7	10.0
Central government balance (% of GDP)	3.0	2.4	−0.9	−2.4
External debt (billion US$)	82.6	90.5	91.8	89.7

Source: International Monetary Fund.

Korea Stock Exchange

EXHIBIT 2

Top 30 Chaebols' Financial Data as of 1996 (excluding financial and insurance industry)

(unit: billion won)		Assets	Owners' Equity	Debt-to-Equity	Return on Equity
1	Hyundai	52,821	9,842	437%	5.69%
2	Samsung	50,705	13,809	267%	1.71%
3	LG	37,068	8,302	346%	5.64%
4	Daewoo	34,197	7,817	337%	5.90%
5	Sunkyung	22,743	4,703	384%	12.73%
6	Ssangyong	15,802	3,102	409%	−1.90%
7	Hanjin	13,907	2,118	557%	−10.49%
8	Kia	14,121	2,289	517%	−4.70%
9	Hanwha	10,592	1,244	751%	−11.01%
10	Lotte	7,753	2,654	192%	5.34%
11	Kumho	7,399	1,281	478%	−0.58%
12	Halla	6,627	306	2066%	12.89%
13	Dong-Ah	6,289	1,383	355%	4.64%
14	Doosan	6,369	808	688%	−23.33%
15	Daelim	5,849	1,118	423%	6.35%
16	Hansol	4,214	1,075	292%	1.10%
17	Hyosung	4,131	879	370%	7.16%
18	Dongkuk Steel	3,698	1,161	219%	4.75%
19	Jinro	3,826	99	3765%	−169.06%
20	Kolon	3,840	919	318%	4.80%
21	Kohap	3,653	529	591%	7.34%
22	Dongbu	3,423	946	262%	3.00%
23	Tongyang	2,631	646	307%	0.05%
24	Haitai	3,398	448	658%	5.89%
25	New Core	2,796	211	1225%	15.99%
26	Anam	2,638	456	479%	10.22%
27	Hanil	2,599	384	577%	−40.00%
28	Keopyung	2,296	513	348%	−0.04%
29	Miwon	2,233	432	417%	−7.42%
30	Shinho	2,139	362	491%	−2.93%
	Mean	11,325	2,328	617%	−5.01%
	Median	5,032	1,011	420%	3.82%

Source: Korea Fair Trade Commissions.

EXHIBIT 3

Chronological Highlights of the Korean Economic Crisis

	Events
August 20, 1997	The IMF approves a US$4 billion stand-by credit for Thailand, and disburses US$1.6 billion.
October 8, 1997	The IMF announces support for Indonesia's intention to seek support from the IMF and other multilateral institutions.
November 21, 1997	The IMF welcomes Korea's request for IMF assistance.
December 4, 1997	The IMF approves a US$21 billion stand-by credit for Korea, and disburses US$5.6 billion.
December 11, 1997	Korean government increased foreigners' stock ownership ceiling from 26% to 50%.
December 12, 1997	Korean government allowed foreigner investment on short-term financial instrument in domestic market.
December 31, 1997	The Korea Composite Stock Price Index closed the year at 376.31, down 42.2% from the closing index of 651.22 in 1996. Total market capitalization was reduced to about 71 trillion won.
April 1, 1998	Financial Supervisory Commission(FSC) was established to supervise all financial institutions, including banks, securities firms, and insurance companies.
April 9, 1998	Foreign Exchange Equalization Bonds of US$4 billion were issued successfully and the Korean government shifted its focus from escaping from the currency crisis to financial and corporate sector restructuring.
May 25, 1998	The ceiling on foreigners' stock investment was abolished, fully liberalizing the Korean stock market to foreign investors.
June 10, 1998	President Kim Dae-Jung addressed the U.S. Chamber of Commerce in Washington, D.C. He promised that Korea would become one of the best countries for international investors to freely and safely do business. Foreign Investment Promotion Act is designed to make Korea hospitable to foreign investors by providing financial concessions and administrative support.
June 18, 1998	The creditor banks of 313 corporations subjected to the assessment announced 55 corporations as financially nonviable corporations and ordered them to liquidate their businesses.
June 29, 1998	Financial Supervisory Committee (FSC) ordered 5 banks to shut down their operations and merge with other banks. FSC requested 7 banks, classified as conditional approval, to submit restructuring implementation plans.
July 24, 1998	Minority shareholders won, for the first time in history, a lawsuit against management for mismanagement of a bank.
July 31, 1998	Two conditionally approved banks, the Commercial Bank of Korea and the Hanil Bank, announced one-to-one merger.

EXHIBIT 4

Bilateral U.S. Dollar—Korean Won Exchange Rate

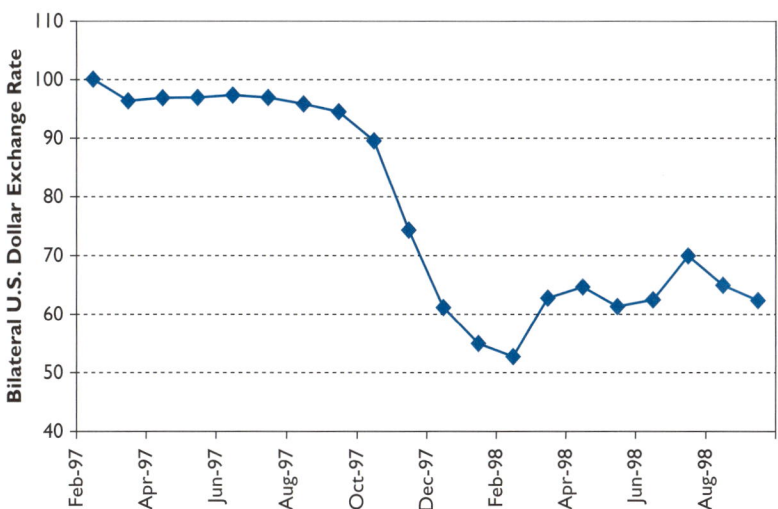

Source: Bank of Korea.

EXHIBIT 5

The IMF-supported Program of Economic Reform

Financial sector restructuring	Comprehensive financial sector restructuring that introduced a clear and firm exit policy for financial institutions, strong market and supervisory discipline, and independence for the central bank.
	Abolishment of regulations prohibiting a foreigner from becoming a director of a commercial bank.
	Requirement that all merchant banks meet their capital adequacy ratios.
Transparency and corporate sector restructuring	Efforts to dismantle the nontransparent and inefficient ties among the government, banks, and businesses, including measures to upgrade accounting, auditing, and disclosure standards. Require that corporate financial statements be published, every half year, on a consolidated basis and certified by external auditors according to the international accounting standards.
	Submission of legislation fully liberalizing hostile takeovers of Korea corporations by domestic companies and foreigners.
	Amendment of the Bankruptcy Law to accelerate the corporate bankruptcy procedure.
	Phase out the system of cross-guarantees within conglomerates.
Foreign investment	Full liberalization measures to open up the Korean money, bond, and equity markets to capital inflows, and to liberalize foreign direct investment.
	Permission for foreign banks' securities companies to establish subsidiaries in Korea.
Labor market reform	Amendment of layoff-related laws which facilitate the redeployment of labor.
	Increase in the government's financial support for the unemployed.
	Expansion in the number of companies whose employees are eligible for unemployment insurance and raising the minimum unemployment subsidy.
Trade policy	Trade liberalization measures, including setting a timetable in line with WTO commitments to eliminate trade-related subsidies and the import diversification program, as well as streamlining and improving transparency of import certification procedures.

Source: Adapted from reports published by Financial Supervisory Commissions.

EXHIBIT 6

10-Year History of Korea Composite Stock Price Index (KOSPI)

Source: *Fact Book* published by Korea Stock Exchange.

EXHIBIT 7

Stock Trading Value (unit: billion won)

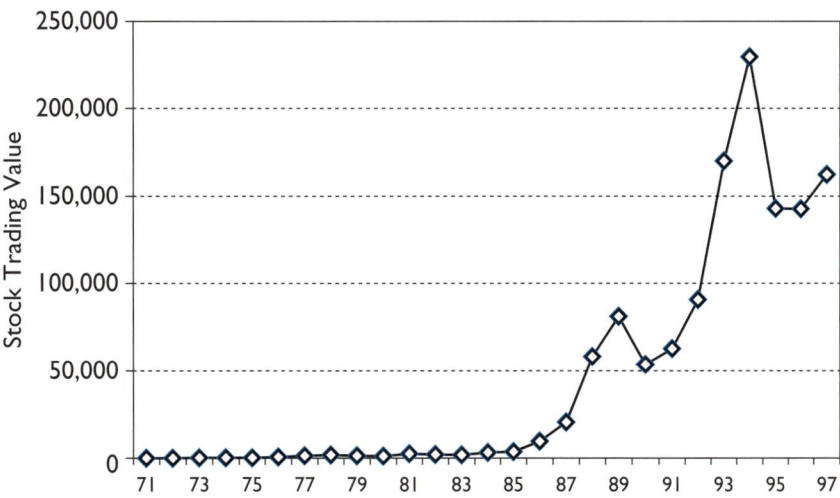

Source: *Fact Book* published by Korea Stock Exchange.

EXHIBIT 8

Market Capitalization Divided by GDP

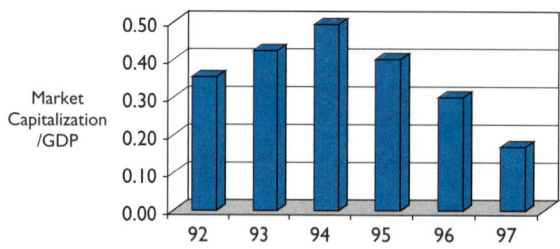

Source: *Fact Book* published by Korea Stock Exchange.

EXHIBIT 9

Financing of Korean Corporations (unit: billion won)

	Through Financial Institutions		Through Capital Markets					
	Bank	Non-Bank	CP	Stock	Bonds	Foreign[a]	Others[b]	Total
1989	5,698	7,963	5,131	8,310	4,932	−185	4,292	36,140
1990	7,995	11,477	1,902	5,987	10,931	3,247	6,517	48,056
1991	11,487	12,686	−2,211	5,555	14,065	2,501	8,002	52,085
1992	8,313	11,599	4,183	7,177	6,616	2,527	9,737	50,152
1993	8,440	11,718	9,017	8,619	9,218	−1,298	9,857	55,571
1994	18,367	20,981	4,405	13,198	13,568	4,037	10,423	84,978
1995	14,991	16,884	16,096	14,445	14,958	5,568	11,656	94,597
1996	18,571	18,424	20,691	13,342	20,265	12,063	13,542	116,899
1997	15,116	28,399	4,773	8,974	27,422	7,162	22,127	113,973

Source: Bank of Korea.

[a]*Foreign implies funds borrowed from overseas capital markets.*

[b]*Others include letters of credit, loans from government, reserve for retirement allowances, etc.*

EXHIBIT 10

Financing of Korean Corporations (in %)

	Through Financial Institutions	Through Bond/CP Markets	Through Stock Markets	Foreign	Others	Total
1989	37.80%	27.84%	22.99%	−0.51%	11.87%	100.00%
1990	40.52%	26.70%	12.46%	6.76%	13.56%	100.00%
1991	46.41%	22.76%	10.66%	4.80%	15.36%	100.00%
1992	39.70%	21.53%	14.31%	5.04%	19.42%	100.00%
1993	36.27%	32.81%	15.51%	−2.34%	17.74%	100.00%
1994	46.30%	21.15%	15.53%	4.75%	12.27%	100.00%
1995	33.69%	32.83%	15.27%	5.89%	12.32%	100.00%
1996	31.65%	35.04%	11.41%	10.32%	11.58%	100.00%
1997	38.18%	28.25%	7.87%	6.28%	19.41%	100.00%

Source: Bank of Korea.

EXHIBIT 11

Foreign Investment in Korean Stock (unit: US$ billion)

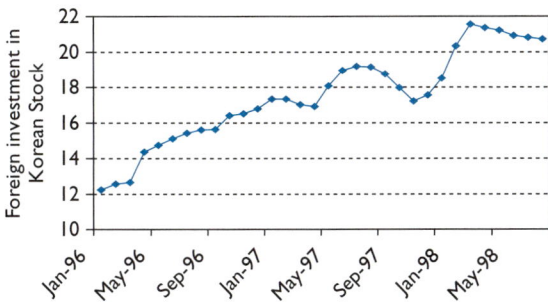

Source: Korea Stock Exchange.

Manufactured Homes, Inc.

This Winston-Salem company sells affordable Southern comfort: fully furnished and carpeted mobile homes for as little as $10,000. Robert Sauls, the 59-year-old founder and chairman, was an orphaned boy who never finished high school. Through acquisitions, Sauls has built the retailer into the industry's largest, with annual sales ballooning to about $180 million in four years. The company sells the homes, built primarily by Fleetwood Enterprises and Redman Industries, to rural blue-collar workers in the Southeast. "Our people buy in good times and bad," says Sauls. If he can raise the capital, he foresees a doubling of sales in four to five years. The stock recently sold at 6.5 times estimated 1988 earnings.

Jane Edwards, Director of Research at a small Boston-based investment management firm specializing in growth stocks, noted the above review of Manufactured Homes in the February 15, 1988 issue of *Fortune* magazine's *Companies To Watch* column. She knew that attractive growth stocks are hard to find and wondered whether Manufactured Homes would be a good addition to her firm's growth stock portfolio. She checked the recent performance of Manufactured Homes' common stock and noted that the stock performed favorably relative to the stock market (see Exhibit 1). Jane Edwards asked her assistant Peter Herman to gather additional information on the company and to write a report analyzing the company's recent financial statements.

COMPANY BACKGROUND AND MARKETING FOCUS

Herman's preliminary research on Manufactured Homes indicated that the company was founded in 1975 with two retail outlets for mobile homes. The company grew rapidly and by March 31, 1987, had a network of 120 retail outlets located in seven southeastern states. Eighty-five percent of the company's retail centers were located in North Carolina, South Carolina, Alabama, Georgia, and Florida, with the remaining sales centers in Virginia and West Virginia. The company went public in 1983 and was listed on the American Stock Exchange in January 1987.

This case was prepared by Professor Krishna Palepu as a basis for classroom discussion rather than to illustrate effective or ineffective handling of an administrative situation.

The southeastern U.S. was the country's fastest-growing market for mobile homes due to suitable climate, the easy availability of vacant land for mobile-home parks, and the region's demographics. Potential customers for manufactured homes included individuals seeking a single-family primary residence but lacking the ability to purchase conventional housing, retirees, and those wanting a second home for vacation purposes.

The company targeted individuals in the low income category, which was a segment of the manufactured homes market in the company's seven state operating area. The company's customers were typically between the ages of 18 and 40, blue-collar workers in manufacturing, service, and agricultural industries, and earned approximately $20,000 per year. Many of them were seeking single-family accommodations for their families and turned to manufactured homes because conventional low-cost housing was becoming increasingly less affordable.

Manufactured homes came in a wide variety of styles, including both single and multi-sectional units. They typically had a living room, a kitchen and dining area, and bedrooms and baths, with a wide variety in the size, number and layout of rooms among the various models. The single-sectional homes ranged in size from 588 to 1008 square feet and retailed at prices between $10,000 and $25,000, with the majority selling below $17,000. The multi-sectional homes were 960 to 2016 square feet and sold at prices ranging from $17,000 to $40,000. Single-sectional homes represented most of the company's sales. While approximately 30% of all unit sales in the industry in 1986 were multi-sectional homes, they represented only about 20% of Manufactured Homes' unit volume.

The company believed that its focus on the lower end of the market had two advantages. First, since its customers were seeking to fulfill an essential housing need, sales were less affected by changes in general economic conditions. Second, the company's repossession rates were significantly lower than those of the industry since its customers were likely to work very hard to keep their primary residences even when times were bad.

REVENUES

Most of Manufactured Homes' sales were credit sales where the customer paid a down payment of 5 to 10% of the sales price and entered into an installment sales contract with the company to pay the remaining amount over periods ranging from 84 to 180 months. The company generally sold the majority of its retail installment contracts to unrelated financial institutions on a recourse basis. Under this agreement, Manufactured Homes was responsible for payments to the financial institution if the customer failed to make the payments specified in the installment contract.

While the installment sale interest rate that Manufactured Homes charged its customers was limited by competitive conditions, it was typically higher than market interest rates. Therefore, the financial institutions to whom these contracts were sold on a recourse basis, usually paid the company the stated principal amount of the contract and a portion of the differential between the stated interest rate and the market rate. (The remainder of the interest rate differential was retained by the financial institutions as a security against credit losses and was paid to the company in proportion to customer payments received. The reserve required varied up to seven percent of the aggregate amount financed, including principal and interest.) The company therefore had two sources of revenue: the sale of homes (sales revenue), and the interest rate "spread" (finance participation income).

Peter Herman noted that Financial Accounting Board's Statement 77 (FASB-77) governs the accounting treatment for installment sales receivables that are transferred by a company to a third party on a recourse basis. Transfers of receivables that are subject to recourse must be reported as sales if the following three conditions are satisfied:

1. The seller unequivocally surrenders the receivable to the buyer.
2. The seller's remaining obligations to the buyer under the recourse provision must be subject to reasonable estimation on the date of the transfer of the receivable. For this purpose, the seller should be able to estimate:

    (a) The amount of bad debts and related costs of collection and repossession, and

    (b) The amount of prepayments.

    If the seller cannot make these estimates reasonably well, a transfer of the receivable cannot be reported as a sale.
3. The seller cannot be required to repurchase the receivable from the buyer except in accordance with the recourse provision.

If any of the above conditions is not satisfied, the seller of the receivable must report the proceeds from the transfer as a loan against the receivable.

FINANCIAL PERFORMANCE

Manufactured Homes' revenues increased rapidly in recent years, from $11 million in 1983 to $120 million in 1986. In the company's 1986 annual report, Robert Sauls, the CEO, forecasted the company's growth to continue and expected the 1987 revenues to be $140–145 million. Herman noted that the company's sales for the first nine months of 1987 exceeded this forecast. The company's latest 10-Q statement reported $148 million revenues for the nine months ended September 30, 1987.

Based on the performance in the first nine months of 1987, the *Value Line Investment Survey* forecasted that Manufactured Homes would achieve $180 million revenues and $6 million net income (or $1.65 per share) in 1987, and $210 million revenues and $7.5 million net income (or $2.00 per share) in 1988. *Value Line* commented on the company's near term prospects as follows:[1]

> *We look forward for [per] share net [income] to advance 20% in 1988, despite a difficult selling environment. Industrywide shipments for the company's core Carolina markets were down in the December quarter and are likely to remain soft in the year ahead. We think, however, that Manufactured Homes will nevertheless find growth opportunities. True, the number of retail centers probably won't increase much this year. On the other hand, the rapid expansion of retail centers over the past five years has put in place a large number of dealerships that have plenty of opportunity for increasing volume.*
>
> *Management is seeking to average 100 units per store as these sales locations mature. At the end of 1986, stores were selling 47 units per year on average, and that figure rose 20% for the first nine months of 1987. Although the market will be very competitive this year, we think the company's special attention to the low-end of the market, to which many large competitors pay less attention, will give Manufactured Homes a solid niche position. Adding in the reduced tax rate, we think full year [per] share net [income] may well reach the $2.00 mark.*

---

1. Reprinted with permission from Value Line Investment Survey, February 26, 1988.

Volume buying gives this retailer an edge. Because Manufactured Homes buys in bulk, it can negotiate lower prices from the manufacturers it deals with. And by passing the savings on to customers, the company is able to underprice smaller, "mom and pop" outlets. Furthermore, because of its size, the company is able to more efficiently handle inventory financing and mortgage assistance for its customers.

Before making a final recommendation to Edwards, Herman wanted to take a detailed look at Manufactured Homes' financial statements for the fiscal year 1986 (Exhibit 2) and the interim statements for the first nine months of 1987 (Exhibit 3).

QUESTIONS

1. Identify the accounting policies of Manufactured Homes which have the most significant impact on the company's financial statements. What are the key assumptions behind these policies? Do you think that these assumptions are justified?

2. Evaluate the company's financial and operating performance during 1986 and the first nine months of 1987.

3. Given the company's business strategy, accounting policies, and recent performance, what is your assessment of its current condition and future potential?

EXHIBIT 1

Performance of Manufactured Homes' Common Stock and S&P 500 Stock Index Relative to Their Levels on January 2, 1987

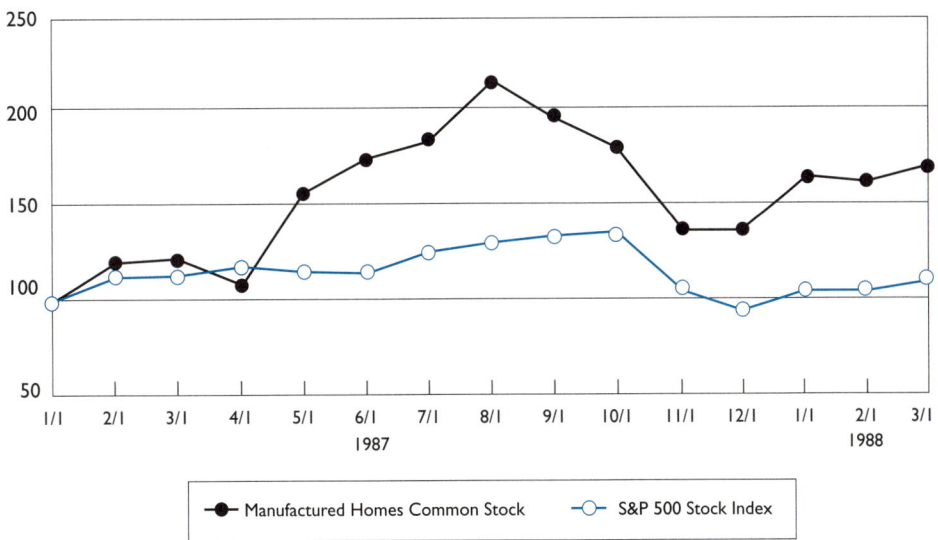

	Manufactured Homes' Stock Price	S&P 500
January 2, 1987	$9.000	246.45
March 1, 1988	14.875	267.82
Value Line estimated ß	1.05	1.0

EXHIBIT 2

Annual Report for the Year Ended December 31, 1986

Chairman's Letter to Stockholders

The year 1986 was a period of significant accomplishment for your company which served to strengthen our leadership position in the manufactured homes industry. The results achieved were the culmination of a corporate development plan set in motion years ago. For the fourth consecutive year revenues reached record levels, $120 million compared with $80 million in 1985. We are now one of the largest retailers of manufactured, single-family homes in the nation.

As part of our long-term efforts to increase market share, we added 39 retail outlets, bringing the total to 114 at year end. We now have retail outlets in seven states that combined represent approximately 40 percent of the total U.S. market for manufactured homes.

We continue to be primarily a sales and marketing company with manufacturing and retail financing on a limited basis to support the company's growth plan.

We completed a major financing in April 1986 and a second financing in February 1987, both managed by Wertheim Schroder and Company, that totaled $43 million. A portion of the proceeds was used to pay down variable rate debt associated with inventory financing with fixed rate debt and save money in the process. The remainder of the proceeds is to be used for general corporate purposes.

We were pleased at the recognition we received for the growth we have achieved over the last four years as both *Business Week* and *INC. Magazine* included our company in their lists of the fastest growing companies in America. Some describe our growth as explosive. We, however, consider these accomplishments a direct result of a well-structured and carefully executed corporate development plan. Our plans for growth are founded on the basic premise that expansion not exceed our ability to manage our affairs.

From $11 million in revenues in 1983 and a position of near obscurity in the industry, our progress has led us to a position of leadership in the industry. While we are extremely pleased with our revenue performance, we are also mindful that we must operate profitably. Net earnings per share for 1986 were only 53 cents. The sharp decline in 1986 earnings is directly

related to a fourth quarter net loss of $1,347,642. Charges against earnings in the fourth quarter for losses on credit sales and other charges totaling more than three million dollars, coupled with the cost of strengthening your company's position in the marketplace, created a temporary setback in earnings while establishing a basis for a strong 1987.

A strategic plan can only be confirmed as correct when tested by adversity; and last year was something of an acid test for our industry. During 1986, many retailers, in hopes of gaining greater market share, or in some cases hoping for survival, engaged in excessive price cutting. In addition, financial institutions in response to concern over the economy in some geographic areas tightened their policies. We not only dealt with the problems that confronted us but turned some into opportunities.

Over the years management has made it a practice to monitor the various retailers of the manufactured homes in our operating area. First, we wanted to understand our competition; and second, we were looking for acquisition candidates. From a large list of companies, we singled out those that best met our standards of performance. We wanted only those firms with superior management and sales teams. We were able to acquire two of these firms on favorable terms and left management in place.

As a result we succeeded in not only enlarging our market penetration in our traditional states of North Carolina, South Carolina, Georgia, Florida and Alabama, but were able to enter new markets with nine retail outlets in Virginia and West Virginia and six additional outlets in Alabama.

Our independent dealer network continues to grow, and now numbers 26 in five states. The independent dealer program offers important advantages and opportunities. Because of the advantages we bring to these small dealers, we continue to receive more requests to join our team.

During the last half of 1986 we sacrificed short-term results to increase market share. We attained that share and as expected it cost us dearly. Selling, general and administrative expense increased from an average of $4.5 million in the first and second quarters to $6 million in the third quarter and to $8 million in the fourth quarter.

As we look to 1987, it is with the knowledge that we are working from a solid foundation. Our financial position is strong. Our debt service requirements are manageable without impairing future earnings performance. Our retail network continues to mature, and sales by location will increase.

Our goal in 1987 is to maintain our market share and show a substantial increase in profit margins. Your Board of Directors has shown confidence in our ability to perform by authorizing me to give you a conservative estimate of our 1987 revenues. Our first quarter revenues are expected to be $32 million with earnings per share of 24 cents. If current economic conditions continue, we expect 1987 revenues to be $140–145 million. The expected significant increase in margins should make this a great year.

I am grateful for the confidence and support of our employees, financial institutions, suppliers and customers; and to you, our shareholders, I would like to say a special "Thanks!"

Robert M. Sauls
Chairman of the Board, President and Chief Executive Officer

Operating Philosophy

We are convinced that a company is no better than the people selected to manage its affairs. Quality of product and service are vital to any successful enterprise; but again without quality managers and line employees, the business will not succeed. Manufactured Homes has consistently sought and employed only the highest quality individuals at every level within the organization.

It is our practice to provide our employees, at all levels with suitable working conditions and remuneration. We ask only that they perform to the highest level of ability and be innovative in terms of how we can best operate our business.

We believe that the results of the past four years speak for themselves in terms of the invaluable contributions made by our management team and employees.

Industry Profile

The manufactured homes industry is fragmented. At this time there are approximately 10,000 manufactured home retailers throughout the nation, most of which fall into the category of "mom and pop" operations. The industry is presently undergoing a period of transition and consolidation. More and more of the smaller firms, lacking volume buying power and adequate capitalization, are disappearing or becoming a part of a larger company like Manufactured Homes.

The industry has always been competitive but has become more so in recent years. The continuing increases in the average price of conventional housing have forced low income families to seek other alternatives. And more and more are turning to manufactured homes, which have much more to offer than an apartment with the added advantage of equal to lower monthly payments.

In the past, the manufactured home industry suffered from consumer misconceptions created in large part by the use of the term "mobile home." While manufactured homes can be transported from place to place, only five percent are ever relocated once in place. In addition, 60 percent of all homes sold are placed on private property.

Furthermore, the features offered in today's homes are equal to that found in conventional housing but at far less cost.

Industry estimates indicate there are 12 million people living in 6 million manufactured homes. Because of the quality and price advantage, this number is expected to increase on a year-to-year basis for the foreseeable future.

As competition for market share increases, companies like Manufactured Homes will benefit if for no other reason than the financial advantages volume buying affords. This is the primary reason so many independent dealers are actively seeking a working relationship with our company. The same can be said of those companies willing to be acquired.

Retail Operations

During 1986 we sold 6,239 new and used homes, a 61 percent increase over the previous year. These sales generated $113 million in revenues or 46 percent above the previous year. With our enlarged retail network in place, we anticipate that sales will again reach record levels in 1987.

The potential market for manufactured homes includes individuals seeking a single-family residence, but lacking the ability to purchase conventional housing. In addition, these homes are sold to retirees and those wanting a second home for vacation purposes. The latter two groups are increasing in great numbers as our population grows older. However, for our company we have concentrated on a single portion of the marketplace, those individuals in the low income category. This market segment is in great numbers in our seven-state operating area as well as other parts of the nation.

Manufactured Homes had its beginning 11 years ago in Winston-Salem, North Carolina. We began with one retail outlet. Our initial growth took place in North Carolina and eventually South Carolina. These two states accounted for 90 percent of sales in 1985. To continue to market only in these two states eventually could have resulted in corporate stagnation. In 1983, the year we became a publicly-held company, we began to formulate what might be best termed as a geographic expansion plan. The real question was, in which states could we operate most effectively and profitably.

Our initial planning went beyond the southeastern states, which remain the largest single regional source of manufactured home sales. We looked at a number of states including Texas which, at the time, was the number one state in manufactured home sales. After careful evaluation, we concluded that our interests and those of our stockholders would best be served in the southeastern portion of the United States. Texas was the most tempting, but it was obvious to management that the reward was not worth the risk; and as time has proven, Texas has become a graveyard for many manufactured home retail companies.

Like many other retail businesses, presence in the marketplace is critical. After determining to concentrate in the seven states management selected, North Carolina, South Carolina, Georgia, Alabama, Florida, Virginia and West Virginia, we moved aggressively to open new retail outlets and acquire others. In 1983, we had 13 retail outlets; in 1984, the number was 32 and as of March 31, 1987 it's 120.

One of the major keys to success for our company is the insistence that our retail people listen to the customers in terms of interior design and features. When we sense a major trend developing, we go to our suppliers seeking what eventually becomes an entire new line of homes.

We also provide important incentives for our retail managers and sales force. Our base salaries are among the finest in the industry, and we add to that a bonus incentive plan tied

directly to margin performance. When times require, we can deal with competitive pricing, but our goal is to maximize sales without sacrificing margins.

Manufacturing

We acquired a manufacturing facility but not as a means of competing with the major manufacturers. In fact, last year we were the largest single retailer of Fleetwood and Redman homes, two of the nation's largest builders of manufactured homes. We acquired the facility to safeguard the company during periods when demand for homes outpaced supply. It also provides the opportunity to manufacture especially designed homes in smaller numbers, thereby eliminating the major commitment that would be required by unaffiliated suppliers.

The firm we acquired was Craftsman Homes, and we continue to manufacture under this brand name. When we acquired the company in 1985, it was producing one home per day. That operation is now producing ten floors per day. Large numbers of our customers have been asking for more entertainment features in the home. With our manufacturing capabilities, we have responded with a home we call the Entertainment Center, and sales have been most rewarding.

We have no immediate need nor intention to enlarge this facility. As it stands, manufacturing can make important contributions, but we can also put this operation on hold without damage to either revenues or earnings.

Financial Considerations

Believing that interest rates will eventually return to the double digit range, we have been successful in replacing our variable rate debt with fixed rate debt. In April 1986, we completed an $18 million private placement of 9% convertible subordinated notes, due 2001. The notes are convertible into common stock at $17.50 per share. The notes were purchased by Prudential Insurance Company of America and Equity-Linked Investors.

In February 1987, we completed a private placement of $25 million of unsecured senior notes in two series. Series A notes, due 1990, were issued in the amount of $15 million at an interest rate of 8.64%. Series B notes, due 1992, were issued in the amount of $10 million at an interest rate of 9.42%. The entire placement was managed by Wertheim Schroder and Co. and purchased by Prudential Insurance Company of America, and we are gratified with the trust they have placed in the future of Manufactured Homes.

There are four key elements that bear on our financial performance related to the sale of homes. These elements are repossessions, recourse financing, loan losses and finance participation.

In almost all cases mortgages executed by the Company are sold to financial institutions. At this moment all of the elements mentioned come into play. The recourse financing provision requires that the Company reassume ownership of the home when the buyer becomes in default of mortgage payments. We knew this when the company was started 11 years ago, and the actions required to deal with this situation are a part of each year's operating plan.

The possibility of repossessions is another reason for selecting the low income segment of the marketplace. Families in this category will make extreme sacrifices to save their homes. We experience one of the lowest repossession rates in the industry. Of the homes returned, we move quickly to renovate and refurbish them and have them resold, normally within 60 to 90 days, at a price equal to or greater than the loan payoff.

We also make provisions for those instances when loan losses do occur. Based on our historical experience, we now maintain a financial reserve equal to 1.7 percent of total net contingent liability for credit sales. Our annual loan loss provisions have consistently exceeded actual losses by more than 20 percent, even though homes which have been sold for four or more years are seldom repossessed. Finance participation is an important source of income for the Company. Simply, funds derived from finance participation is the "spread" between the finance charges included in the mortgage agreement initiated by the Company and those required by the financial institution. A portion of the "spread" is paid in cash to the Company and the remainder over the life of the mortgage contract. The portion retained by the financial institution is accounted for by discounting to present value based on the time period, normally 120 to 180 months, required to actually collect the funds.

Financial Services Subsidiary

Plans for our finance operations, MANH Financial Services Corp., are similar in nature to that for our manufacturing division. The company did not enter this business segment to compete with the financial institutions that have historically provided our mortgage banking requirements. This new entity will be employed primarily to facilitate financing agreements with our banks.

Financial Services does have mortgage lending capabilities that will only be employed at those times when our conventional banking arrangements are unable to act on a timely basis. Again, like our manufacturing operations, management has no intention of expanding Financial Services. As it exists now, it provides the Company with the flexibility required to deal quickly with mortgage finance transactions.

Selected Financial Data

Years Ended December 31,	1986	1985	1984	1983	1982
Operating Results:					
Revenues	$120,264,954	$79,525,988	$36,195,802	$10,986,036	$7,477,966
Earnings (loss) before cumulative effect of change in accounting principle[1]	2,033,425	3,718,325	2,694,529	536,881	(59,570)
Earning (loss) per share	.53	.98	.77	.21	(.03)
Net Earnings (loss)	2,033,425	3,213,754	2,694,529	536,881	(59,570)
Net earnings (loss) per share	.53	.85	.77	.21	(.03)
Financial Position at Year-End:					
Total assets	$81,377,803	$50,944,924	$17,660,984	$6,836,087	$5,025,130
Long-term debt	18,609,987	1,082,543	400,000	—	491,280
Stockholders' equity	14,167,119	11,052,759	7,633,005	4,938,654	733,195
Working capital	15,111,883	4,820,912	4,819,203	3,699,184	(147,124)

Manufactured Homes, Inc.

Quarterly Financial Data (unaudited)

Quarter	First	Second	Third	Fourth	Total
1986[2]:					
Revenues	$23,324,633	$29,724,418	$33,295,241	$33,920,662	$120,264,954
Net earnings (loss)	641,702	1,562,205	1,177,160	(1,347,642)	2,033,425
Net earnings (loss) per share	.17	.40	.30	(.36)	.53
Average shares and equivalents	3,850,277	3,944,518	3,922,406	3,733,968	3,864,161
1985:					
Revenues	$10,965,457	$22,103,134	$24,083,556	$22,373,841	$79,525,988
Earnings before cumulative effect of change in accounting principle[1]	741,395	1,312,511	1,112,714	551,705	3,718,325
Earnings per share	.21	.34	.29	.14	.98
Net earnings	236,824	1,312,511	1,112,714	551,705	3,213,754
Net earnings per share	.08	.34	.29	.14	.85
Proforma amounts:					
Net earnings	741,395	1,312,511	1,112,714	551,705	3,718,325
Net earnings per share	.21	.34	.29	.14	.98
Average shares and equivalents	3,488,968	3,820,016	3,870,857	3,838,486	3,802,693

[1] See Note 2 of notes to consolidated financial statements for information regarding a change in accounting principle for finance participation income in 1985.

[2] During the fourth quarter of 1986, the Company provided approximately $3,000,000 for losses on credit sales, primarily due to industry conditions, which are causing unusually high costs relating to the repossession of homes. In addition, the Company incurred abnormal costs in the fourth quarter of approximately $300,000 relating primarily to the write-off of previously recognized finance participation income. The aggregate provision for these items amounted to approximately $3,300,000 in the fourth quarter. The Company cannot determine the extent to which these fourth quarter provisions may be applicable to the first, second, and third quarter of 1986.

Common Stock Prices and Dividend Information

The Company's common stock is traded on the American Stock Exchange under the symbol MNH.

Quarter	1986		1985	
	High	Low	High	Low
First	15 3/4	10	8 3/4	4 3/8
Second	16 1/2	12 1/4	13 1/4	8 1/4
Third	15	9 3/4	15 3/8	10 1/2
Fourth	12	8 7/8	14	8 3/4

The Company has never paid a cash dividend and does not intend to for the foreseeable future. The weighted average number of shares outstanding for 1986 was 3,660,048 shares, for 1985 and 1984, 3,488,968 shares, for 1983, 2,588,518 shares, and for 1982, 2,100,000 shares. The approximate number of stockholders at March 1987 was 2,000.

MANAGEMENT DISCUSSION AND ANALYSIS

Results of Operations

1986 Versus 1985

The Company's net sales in 1986 were $106,095,667 compared with $68,674,779 in 1985, an increase of $37,420,888 or 54%.

The Company's program of managed sales growth resulted in greater penetration due to:

	1986	1985	Increase
An increase of 44% in the number of company-owned and operated sales centers	92	64	28
A 100% expansion of the MANH Independent Retailer network	22	11	11
A total increase of 52% in sales centers for the year	114	75	39

The total number of new and used homes sold in 1986 was 6,239, a 61% increase over the 3,866 homes sold in 1985. New home sales for both years were 87% of total home sales.

A manufactured home sales center usually experiences a five-year growth and development period. The Manufactured Homes (AMEX Symbol: MNH) sales center should develop a sales production level of at least 100 new homes per year at maturity, although this average annual sales volume can vary widely by geographic location. The Company in 1986 averaged 47 new sales per sales center versus 45 in 1985. The average reflects the rapid expansion of new sales centers. Approximately 47% of the average potential capacity per sales center had been achieved, leaving significant growth potential within the Company's current sales center network without the need for significantly increasing the number of sales centers.

New home sales were 80% single-wides in 1986, as compared with 84% in 1985. This reflects a shift to more double-wides resulting from the acquisition of two subsidiaries. In addition, a number of our customers are able to purchase double-wide homes since interest rates are lower. However, the primary emphasis of MNH's marketing plan continues to be towards the less expensive, single-wide home which fits the economic capability of a significant percentage of

potential customers within the MNH market area of the five southeastern states, plus Virginia and West Virginia.

The average MNH selling price of new homes by Company sales centers for 1986 was $17,300 versus $17,400 in 1985. The gross profit margins were unchanged for 1985.

Craftsman Manufactured Homes, Inc., a wholly owned subsidiary of MNH, expanded its production capability from one production line to two. Revenues in 1986 were in excess of $15,746,000 of which $7,489,000 were direct sales to non-affiliated dealers with $8,257,000 being sold to Company sales centers for resale. The Company purchased the manufacturing facility in September 1985. The Craftsman manufacturing subsidiary sold 481 homes directly to dealers not associated with MNH in 1986 as compared with 130 homes in 1985.

Repossessions and Early Pay-offs

Manufactured housing, as an industry, has been significantly impacted by the slow economic growth of the economy coupled with an extended period of low interest rates. These factors are reflected by a year-to-year decrease in 1986 of 15% in manufactured homes sold throughout the Company's market area.

Lower interest rates have resulted in two noticeable shifts within the housing industry: (1) certain owners may select conventional homes over manufactured homes; and (2) an intensive marketing effort by financial institutions for mortgage refinancing has resulted in many home owners refinancing their mortgages at lower interest rates, which for MNH usually means a mortgage prepayment.

The Company's experience relative to prepayments of home mortgages, until 1986, had been minor. However, late in 1986, prepayments became a recognized concern. Prepayment of mortgages caused management to reevaluate certain assumptions resulting in a significant increase in the reserve for credit losses related to mortgage prepayments in order to address the prospects of mortgage interest rates continuing to remain at present levels of 8 1/2 to 9 1/2 percent.

Repossessions of homes result primarily from customers' inability to meet their mortgage payment commitment. Approximately 70% of all MNH credit sales are with recourse, which means the Company will buy back from the financial institution holding a customer's mortgage those homes repossessed by the mortgage holder which were originally sold by MNH subsidiaries.

The Company's experience related to repossessions has shown very little change during the past ten years. However, during the fourth quarter of 1986, approximately $2,000,000 of repossession expense and interest chargebacks were experienced and charged off. Therefore, a charge to earnings, for both prepayments and repossessions, was made and the reserve for credit losses was increased to $3,000,000 at December 31, 1986.

One of the causes of the $2,000,000 charge was the refusal of some unrelated financial institutions to refinance the repossession that occurred in their portfolio, and a second cause was that the Company had to finance them through MANH Financial Services thereby having an immediate charge in finance participation on the pay-off and not recognizing the finance participation income of the resale.

During the first three quarters of 1986, the provision for credit losses was approximately 1% of net sales. Due to the recent fourth quarter charges, management will increase the provision for losses for 1987 to 1 1/2% of net sales as a precautionary measure against future repossession and early pay-off.

Finance Participation

Finance participation was $12,084,108 in 1986 versus $9,715,558 in 1985, a 24.4% increase. As a percentage of net sales, it was 11.4% in 1986 compared with 14.1% in 1985. Several factors caused the percentage of decrease in realized finance participation: (1) increased cash sales; (2) increased non-recourse sales where no finance participation is received; (3) contributions of manufacturing to the sales volume where no finance participation is received; and (4) a decrease in the interest rate spread earned by the Company when the sales contracts are sold to financial institutions. The decreased "spread" was the most important factor in 1986 as two major financial institutions changed their "retail rate" and reduced the "spread" received by the Company by 33%.

Finance participation is an important part of the Company's revenue. This source of revenue is monitored closely and alternative sources of financing are considered for customer mortgage funding on an ongoing basis.

Insurance

The Company earns commissions for writing homeowner insurance policies at the time of sale of the home and from renewal premiums. Income from insurance sales was $721,758 in 1986 compared with $413,282 in 1985, a 75% increase.

Selling, General and Administrative

The Company's selling, general, and administrative expense (SG&A) has historically ranged around 17% of revenue. This range varies according to the Company's growth pattern and marketing emphasis.

In 1986, the significant factors affecting the Company's SG&A expense, which was 19% of revenue, were that: (1) the Company initiated a second production line at its manufacturing plant; (2) acquired two additional subsidiaries—Piggy Bank Homes of Alabama and Jeff Brown Homes in Virginia and West Virginia, in mid-September 1986; (3) initiated two additional operating subsidiaries—AAA Mobile Homes (formerly part of MNH), and MANH Independent Retailers Corp. (formerly spread among several subsidiaries for operational purposes); (4) opened 13 new company sales centers; added 11 independent dealers to the retail network; and (5) and formed MANH Financial Services Corp. as of October 1986. This expansion and realignment of subsidiaries, which occurred mostly during the fourth quarter, were part of an overall marketing strategy to more effectively penetrate the Company's market. The significant increase in sales over 1985 of 54% resulted from staffing an additional 13 company-owned sales centers, with special emphasis on bonus programs to sell aged inventory and homes received in trade for new sales, as well as improving the percentage of homes which were sold with recourse. This aggressive marketing program was designed to achieve momentum for a strong 1987, but increased SG&A expense significantly at the same time.

Several other cost factors effecting SG&A expense were: (1) An increase in liability insurance rates on policy renewals during 1986 at an annual rate 40% higher than in 1985, or approximately an additional $350,000; and (2) the cost incurred during the year related to the completion of a 15-month standardization of accounting procedures and data processing enhancement program which centralized the Company's management information with on-line capability to each subsidiary. This is a significant step forward in better data management and timely preparation of financial information.

Interest Expense

Interest expense increased $1,543,352 to $3,367,940 in 1986 from $1,824,588 in 1985, or 85%. The increase resulted from a $12,536,000 increase in total inventory and approximately an $8,000,000 increase in total receivables directly related to the expansion of 39 sales centers in 1986.

Income Taxes

The Company's effective income tax rate was 49.8% in 1986 compared to 47.2% in 1985. This increase resulted primarily from the elimination of investment tax credits under the Tax Reform Act of 1986.

Organization

Each of the Company's nine subsidiaries are profit centers. Each subsidiary has its own chief executive officer with total profit and loss responsibility. The Company's long-range plan for growth is by strategic acquisitions, expanding market share, and developing management talent through a newly organized salesperson training program, all to meet the need of providing low-cost housing to the American consumer.

Manufacturing

Craftsman Manufactured Homes, Inc., the MNH manufacturing subsidiary, commenced operations in September 1985. It has grown from virtually a start-up operation to a sales volume in excess of $15,000,000 in 1986. Approximately 57% of the 1,119 homes manufactured were sold to and through Company related sales centers. The balance of the homes were sold to non-related independent retailers. The Craftsman plant operates two production lines with a plant capacity of approximately 3,500 floors (multi-section homes require more than one floor) per year.

Financial Services

MANH Financial Services Corp. was organized on October 14, 1986 to facilitate the marketing of new, repossessed and pre-owned homes. Two major retail financial sources curtailed the purchase of conditional sales contracts which resulted in slow response to contract applications and therefore lost sales. The Company responded with the formation of MANH Financial Services Corp. to operate on a limited basis. The growth of this subsidiary will depend largely on whether or not the unrelated financial institutions continue to service the Company's growth.

1985 Versus 1984

The Company's net sales for 1985 were $68,674,779 compared to $30,480,571 for 1984, an increase of 125%. The majority of this increase was due to the addition of eight retail sales centers during the first quarter and the acquisition of Country Squire Mobile Homes, Inc. on March 22, 1985, with 20 retail sales centers. The Company also opened seven retail sales centers in the second quarter, six in the third quarter, and two in the fourth quarter. Volume increases in sales centers which were in operation at the end of 1984 also occurred while the average sales price per unit remained fairly constant from 1984 to 1985. The Company's purchase of a manufacturing facility on September 4, 1985, contributed approximately 7% of the 1985 sales increase.

Finance participation income for 1985 was $9,715,558 compared to $5,221,279, an increase of 86%. This was less than the percentage increase in sales due to three factors: (1) The election to discount the unreceived portion of finance participation income to its present value; (2) Country Squire earned significantly less finance participation income than the other retail groups, primarily because of non-recourse sales; and, (3) the inclusion of manufacturing sales which do not earn finance participation income. Insurance commissions, interest and other revenues increased proportionally in relation to the increase in sales.

Cost of sales as a percentage increased approximately 2% in 1985. This increase was due to the substantial increase in sales to independent retailers which traditionally have lower margins, and a slight decrease in margins at Company-owned sales centers. Selling, general and administrative expenses increased in 1985 as a result of increased sales volume and reflect the increase in number of sales centers and additional personnel to support our continued growth. Provision for losses on credit sales remained relatively constant as a percentage of net sales from 1984 to 1985. Interest rates were generally lower in 1985; however, total interest cost increased significantly due to increased inventories to support the added sales centers.

Liquidity and Capital Resources

The Company, in April 1986, sold $18,000,000 of 9% convertible subordinated notes due May 15, 2001. The proceeds were used primarily to reduce floor plan notes payable and to significantly improve the Company's liquidity. During 1986, the Company purchased Jeff Brown Homes, Inc. with nine sales centers and Piggy Bank Homes of Alabama, Inc. with six sales centers, added 13 Company-owned sales centers, formed a finance company subsidiary with an initial capitalization of $500,000, expanded the principal offices of its wholly-owned subsidiary, Tri-County Homes, Inc., and opened a second production line at its manufacturing facility, using funds generated from the sale of the subordinated notes and from operations.

At December 31, 1986, the Company had available $1,000,000 in a bank line of credit and $8,000,000 in unused floor plan lines of credit.

On February 13, 1987, the Company old $25,000,000 of unsecured senior notes due in 1990 and 1992 bearing interest at a blended rate of 8.95%. The proceeds have been partially used to reduce floor plan notes payable.

Although working capital increased significantly in 1986, operations used working capital of $2,956,041 compared to providing working capital of $2,847,026 in 1985 and $2,599,953 in 1984. The use of working capital by operations in 1986 was principally due to the interest rate spread applicable to finance participation and significant reductions in deferred income taxes applicable to the provision for credit losses and finance participation income.

The Tax Reform Act of 1986 will benefit the Company through a reduction of the corporate income tax rate. However, beginning January 1, 1987, the Act will require the Company to accelerate the payment of Federal income taxes. However, the Company believes that funds to be generated by operations, combined with credit lines currently available, will be sufficient to satisfy capital needs for current operations.

CONSOLIDATED BALANCE SHEETS

December 31,	1986	1985
ASSETS		
Current Assets:		
Cash and cash equivalents:		
Cash and temporary investments	$2,486,024	$2,968,837
Contract proceeds receivable from financial institutions (Note 9)	11,496,078	5,189,535
Total cash and cash equivalents	13,982,102	8,158,372
Finance participation receivable – current portion (Note 2)	2,691,497	2,486,001
Deferred finance participation income	(801,511)	(523,038)
Net finance participation receivable	1,889,986	1,962,963
Other receivables (Note 4)	3,746,863	2,057,674
Refundable income taxes (Note 11)	778,971	—
Inventories (Notes 5 and 9)	38,163,712	25,628,156
Prepaid expenses	538,419	408,124
Deferred income taxes (Note 11)	761,262	436,496
Total current assets	59,861,315	38,651,785
Finance participation receivable – noncurrent portion (Note 2)	16,128,799	10,269,713
Deferred finance participation income	(3,923,178)	(2,968,629)
Net finance participation receivable	12,205,621	7,301,084
Property, plant and equipment at cost (Notes 6 and 10)	7,504,272	5,467,164
Accumulated depreciation and amortization	(2,410,812)	(1,555,427)
Net property, plant and equipment	5,093,460	3,911,737
Excess of costs over net assets of acquired companies less amortization (Note 3)	2,107,874	973,860
Other assets	2,109,533	106,458
	$81,377,803	$50,944,924

CONSOLIDATED STATEMENTS OF CHANGES IN FINANCIAL POSITION

	1986	1985
LIABILITIES AND STOCKHOLDER'S EQUITY		
Current Liabilities:		
Notes payable	$1,099,971	$—
Long-term debt – current installments (Note 10)	810,901	1,100,624
Floor plan notes payable (Note 9)	35,207,386	27,468,153
Accounts payable	4,899,250	2,210,560
Income taxes (Note 11)	—	1,828,234
Accrued expenses and other liabilities (Note 8)	2,731,924	1,223,302
Total current liabilities	44,749,432	33,830,873
Long-term debt – noncurrent installments (Note 10)	18,609,987	1,082,543
Reserve for losses on credit sales (Note 7)	3,000,000	1,863,992
Deferred income taxes (Note 11)	851,265	3,114,757
Total liabilities	67,210,684	39,892,165

(continued)

Manufactured Homes, Inc.

CONSOLIDATED STATEMENTS OF CHANGES IN FINANCIAL POSITION (*continued*)

	1986	1985
Stockholders' equity (Notes 10 and 12):		
Common stock – $.50 par value per share;		
authorize 10,000,000 shares; issued and outstanding		
3,733,968 shares in 1986 and 3,488,968 shares in 1985	1,866,984	1,744,484
Additional paid-in capital	3,508,351	2,549,916
Retained earnings	8,791,784	6,758,359
Total stockholders' equity	14,167,119	11,052,759
Commitments and contingent liabilities (Notes 3 and 13)		
	$81,377,803	$50,944,924

CONSOLIDATED STATEMENTS OF EARNINGS

Years Ended December 31,	1986	1985	1984
Revenues:			
Net sales	$106,095,667	$68,674,779	$30,480,571
Finance participation income	12,084,108	9,715,558	5,221,279
Insurance commissions	721,758	413,282	231,618
Interest	338,447	163,663	123,564
Other	1,024,974	558,706	138,770
Total revenues	120,264,954	79,525,988	36,195,802
Costs and expenses:			
Cost of sales	86,212,901	56,222,412	24,324,851
Selling, general and administrative	22,852,093	13,639,942	5,895,891
Provision for losses on credit sales (Note 7)	3,777,900	793,497	253,004
Interest	3,367,940	1,824,588	570,527
Total costs and expenses	116,210,834	72,480,439	31,044,273
Earnings before income taxes	4,054,120	7,045,549	5,151,529
Income taxes (Note 11)	2,020,695	3,327,224	2,457,000
Earnings before cumulative effect of change in accounting principle (Note 2)	2,033,425	3,718,325	2,694,529
Cumulative effect on prior years of change in accounting principle for finance participation (Notes 2 and 11)	—	(504,571)	—
Net earnings	$2,033,425	$3,213,754	$2,694,529
Earnings per share:			
Before cumulative effect of change in accounting principle	.53	$.98	$.77
Cumulative effect on prior years of change in accounting principle for finance participation	—	(.13)	—
Net earnings per share – primary	$.53	$.85	$.77
Net earnings per share – fully diluted	$.53	$.84	$.77
Proforma amounts assuming retroactive application of the change in accounting principle (Note 2):			
Net earnings	$2,033,425	$3,718,325	$2,365,334
Net earnings per share – primary	$.53	$.98	$.68

Manufactured Homes, Inc.

CONSOLIDATED STATEMENTS OF CHANGES IN FINANCIAL POSITION

Year Ended December 31,	1986	1985	1984
Working capital was provided by			
Operations:			
Net earnings	$2,033,425	$3,213,754	$2,694,529
Adjustments for items not requiring (providing) working capital:			
Depreciation and amortization	946,858	556,236	210,699
Noncurrent deferred income taxes	(2,197,061)	78,637	1,412,812
Provision for losses on credit sales, net of actual charges	699,343	(217,402)	134,614
Issuance of nonqualified stock options	142,000	206,000	—
Finance participation income	(12,084,108)	(9,715,558)	(5,221,279)
Collections, current and deferred finance participation income portion of finance participation receivable	7,503,502	8,725,359	3,316,397
Other	—	—	52,181
Working capital provided (used) by operations	(2,956,041)	2,847,026	2,599,953
Proceeds from long-term debt	18,396,000	1,651,822	400,000
Exercise of stock options	938,935	—	—
Decrease in other assets	—	4,024	—
	16,378,894	4,502,872	2,999,953
Working capital was used for			
Net assets, exclusive of working capital of $806,363 in 1985 and deficits in working capital of $1,109,080 in 1986 and $140,604 in 1984, of acquired companies (Note 3)	1,285,935	422,179	1,220,198
Additions to property, plant and equipment	1,917,489	2,756,178	580,259
Current installments and repayment of long-term debt	1,071,308	1,322,806	70,423
Additions to other assets and excess costs	1,813,191	—	9,054
	6,087,923	4,501,163	1,879,934
Increase in working capital	$10,290,971	$1,709	$1,120,019
Changes in working capital, by component			
Cash and cash equivalents	$5,823,730	$6,136,129	$579,418
Finance participation receivable – current portion	(72,977)	1,193,013	569,838
Other receivables	1,689,189	1,715,543	233,696
Refundable income taxes	778,971	—	—
Inventories	12,535,556	17,448,795	5,616,654
Prepaid expenses	130,295	371,403	25,918
Deferred income taxes	324,766	102,710	203,000
Notes payable	(1,099,971)	—	—
Long-term debt – current installments	289,723	(900,624)	(200,000)
Floor plan notes payable	(7,739,233)	(22,962,163)	(3,986,435)
Accounts payable	(2,688,690)	(1,896,668)	(219,293)
Income taxes	1,828,234	(620,489)	(1,207,745)
Accrued expenses and other liabilities	(1,508,622)	(585,940)	(495,032)
Increase in working capital	$10,290,971	$1,709	$1,120,019

Manufactured Homes, Inc.

NOTES TO CONSOLIDATED FINANCIAL STATEMENTS

December 31, 1986, 1985, and 1984

Note 1
Summary of Significant Accounting Policies

Principles of Consolidation and Nature of Business

The consolidated financial statements include the accounts of Manufactured Homes, Inc. and all subsidiaries, each wholly-owned, and hereafter referred to collectively as the "Company." All significant intercompany items are eliminated.

The Company is engaged principally in the retail sale of new and used manufactured single-family homes.

Inventories

Inventories are stated at the lower of cost or market, with cost being determined using the specific unit method for new and used manufactured homes and average cost for materials and supplies.

Property, Plant and Equipment

Depreciation of property, plant and equipment is provided principally by the straight-line method over the estimated useful lives of the respective assets. Amortization of leasehold improvements is provided by the straight-line method over the shorter of the lease terms or the estimated useful lives of the improvements.

Income Taxes

Deferred income taxes are recognized for income and expense items that are reported in different periods for financial reporting and income tax purposes.

Income Recognition

A sale is recognized when payment is received or, in the case of credit sales, when a down payment (generally 10% of the sales price) is received and the Company and the customer enter into an installment contract. Installment contracts are normally payable over periods ranging from 120 to 180 months. Credit sales represent the majority of the Company's sales.

Under existing financing arrangements, the majority of installment contracts are sold, with recourse to unrelated financial institutions at an agreed upon rate which is below the contractual interest rate of the installment contract. At the time of sale, the Company receives immediate payment for the stated principal amount of the installment contract and a portion of the finance participation resulting from the interest rate differential. The remainder of the interest rate differential is retained by the financial institution as security against credit losses and is paid to the Company in proportion to customer payments received by the financial institution. The Company accounts for these transactions as sales in accordance with Statement of Financial Accounting Standards No. 77, "Reporting by Transferors for Transfers of Receivables with Recourse," and recognizes finance participation income equal to the difference between the contractual interest rates of the installment contracts and the agreed upon rates to the financial institutions; the portion retained by the financial institutions is discounted for estimated time of collection and carried at its present value (see Note 2).

Reserve for Losses on Credit Sales

Estimated losses arising from the recourse provisions of the Company's financing arrangements with unrelated financial institutions are provided for currently based on historical loss experience and current economic conditions and consist of estimated future rebates of finance participation income due to prepayment or repossession, estimated future losses on installment contracts repurchased from financial institutions and estimated future losses on installment contracts transferred to new purchasers in lieu of repossession. Actual losses are charged to the reserve when incurred.

Excess of Costs over Net Assets of Acquired Companies

The excess of costs over net assets of acquired companies is being amortized over 30 years on the straight-line method.

Earnings per Share

Primary earnings per share are based on the weighted average number of common and common equivalent shares outstanding. Such average shares are as follows:

Years Ended December 31,	1986	1985	1984
Outstanding shares	3,660,048	3,488,968	3,488,968
Equivalent shares	204,113	313,725	—
	3,864,161	3,802,693	3,488,968

The equivalent shares in 1986 and 1985 represent the shares issuable upon exercise of stock options and warrants after the assumed repurchase of common shares with the related proceeds at the average price during the period. Common equivalent shares were not considered in 1984 as the resulting dilution was insignificant.

Fully diluted earnings per share are based on the weighted average number of common and common equivalent shares outstanding plus the common shares issuable upon the assumed conversion of the convertible subordinated notes and elimination of the applicable interest expense less related income tax benefit. In determining equivalent shares, the assumed repurchase of common shares is at the higher of the average or period-end price.

Note 2
Accounting Change

Prior to 1985, the Company recognized finance participation income without discounting for the estimated time of collection of the portion retained by the unrelated financial institutions as security against credit losses. However, in 1985 the Company adopted the practice whereby the portion of finance participation income retained by the financial institutions is recorded at its present value based upon estimated time of collection. The Company believes the new method is preferable since it more accurately reflects the value of the finance participation receivable at the date the installment contracts are sold to the financial institutions.

As a result of this change, earnings in 1985, before the cumulative effect of the change on prior years, were decreased by $538,466 ($.14 per share). Net earnings were further decreased by $504,571 ($.13 per share), which represents the cumulative effect of the change on prior years. Proforma net earnings and earnings per share amounts reflecting retroactive application of the change are shown in the consolidated statements of earnings.

Note 3
Acquisitions

On January 6, 1984, Manufactured Homes, Inc. acquired the outstanding common stock of Tri-County Homes, Inc., a retailer of manufactured housing located in eastern North Carolina. The purchase agreement required cash payments of $400,000 and potential earn-out payments of $600,000, all earned at December 31, 1984. The acquisition has been accounted for as a purchase

and, accordingly, the operations of Tri-County are included in the consolidated financial statements of Manufactured Homes, Inc. beginning in 1984. Effective March 22, 1985, Manufactured Homes, Inc. acquired the outstanding common stock of Country Squire Mobile Homes, Inc., a retailer of manufactured housing located principally in South Carolina. The purchase agreement required cash payments of $873,000 and includes potential earn-out payments of $1,960,000 over the period 1985 to 1990. The potential earn-out is based on a percentage of Country Squire's pre-tax earnings as defined. At December 31, 1986, $642,947 ($396,000 in 1986 and $246,947 in 1985) of the potential earn-out had been earned and recorded as an adjustment of the purchase price. The acquisition has been accounted for as a purchase and, accordingly, the operations of Country Squire are included in the consolidated financial statements of Manufactured Homes, Inc. since March 22, 1985. The following unaudited proforma data presents the results of operations of the Company and Country Squire as if the acquisition had occurred at January 1, 1984.

Years ended December 31,	1985	1984
Total revenues	$87,729,677	$59,696,534
Net earnings	3,090,464	2,812,632
Net earnings per share:		
Primary	$ .81	$ .81
Fully diluted	$ .80	$ .81

In September 1986, Manufactured Homes, Inc. acquired the outstanding common stock of two companies engaged in the retail sale of manufactured homes. The purchase agreements required aggregate cash payments of $151,000 and potential earn-out payments of $874,000 over the period 1987 to 1992. The potential earn-outs are based on a percentage of the respective companies' pre-tax earnings as defined. The acquisitions have been accounted for as purchases and, accordingly, their operations, which are not material, are included in the consolidated financial statements of Manufactured Homes, Inc., since September 1986. At date of acquisition, one company had operating loss carryforwards of $612,049 and to the extent utilized, the income tax reductions will be accounted for as adjustments of the purchase price. At December 31, 1986, $324,510 (tax benefit of $159,226) of the carryforwards had been utilized.

The net assets, exclusive of working capital of $806,363 in 1985 and deficits in working capital of $1,109,080 in 1986 and $140,604 in 1984, of the acquired companies were as follows:

Years Ended December 31,	1986	1985	1984
Finance participation receivable	$323,931	$1,337,147	$1,172,853
Property, plant and equipment	169,092	747,092	131,367
Other assets	493,089	23,403	61,016
Long-term debt	(202,752)	(353,527)	(70,423)
Reserve for losses on credit sales	(436,665)	(1,675,000)	(74,615)
Other liabilities	—	(679,524)	—
Excess of costs over net assets of acquired companies	939,240	1,022,588	—
	$1,285,935	$422,179	$1,220,198

Note 4
Other Receivables

Other receivables consist of the following:

December 31,	1986	1985
Manufacturers' volume bonuses	$1,979,021	$1,557,029
Sundry	1,767,842	500,645
	$3,746,863	$2,057,674

Note 5
Inventories

Inventories consist of the following:

December 31,	1986	1985
New manufactured homes	$31,920,134	$22,766,030
Used manufactured homes	4,971,040	2,068,099
Materials and supplies	1,272,538	794,027
	$38,163,712	$25,628,156

Note 6
Property, Plant and Equipment

The cost and estimated useful lives of the major classifications of property, plant and equipment are as follows:

December 31,	Estimated Useful Life	1986	1985
Land	—	$735,329	$620,083
Buildings	15–20 years	1,660,321	849,427
Manufactured homes-office units	5–7 years	1,048,571	1,013,543
Leasehold improvements	3–5 years	615,319	566,638
Furniture & equipment	3–10 years	1,921,101	1,108,123
Vehicles	3–5 years	1,485,222	1,124,154
Signs	3–7 years	38,409	185,196
		$7,504,272	$5,467,164

Note 7
Reserve for Losses on Credit Sales

An analysis of the reserve for losses on credit sales follows:

Years Ended December 31,	1986	1985	1984
Balance at beginning of year	$1,863,992	$406,394	$197,165
Amount at date of acquisition applicable to acquired companies, less actual charges of $69,236 in 1986 and $604,403 in 1985	367,429	1,070,597	74,615
Provision for losses	3,777,900	793,497	253,004
Actual charges	(3,009,321)	(406,496)	(118,390)
Balance at end of year	$3,000,000	$1,863,992	$406,394

Note 8
Accrued Expenses and Other Liabilities

A summary of accrued expenses and other liabilities follows:

December 31,	1986	1985
Payroll and related costs	$1,580,235	$697,287
Other	1,151,689	526,015
	$2,731,924	$1,223,302

Note 9
Floor Plan Notes Payable

A substantial portion of the Company's new manufactured home inventories are financed through floor plan arrangements with certain unrelated financial institutions. A summary of floor plan notes payable follows:

December 31,	Rate	Floor Plan Lines	1986	1985
General Electric				
Credit Corporation	Prime + 1.75 (9.25%)	$27,052,000	**$22,601,520**	$17,183,988
ITT Diversified				
Credit Corporation	Prime + 2.00 (9.50%)	7,200,000	**5,869,438**	5,224,373
CIT Financial Services	Prime + 2.00 (9.50%)	4,000,000	**3,958,932**	1,761,854
Whirlpool Acceptance				
Corporation	Prime + 1.50 (9.00%)	1,500,000	**1,210,586**	—
U.S. Home Acceptance	Prime (7.50%)	1,000,000	**36,680**	815,066
Citicorp Acceptance				
Company, Inc.	Prime + 2.00 (9.50%)	975,000	**—**	1,706,728
Others	Various	1,850,000	**1,530,230**	776,144
		$43,577,000	**$35,207,386**	$27,468,153

The floor plan liability at December 31, 1986 is collateralized by inventories and contract proceeds receivable from financial institutions. The floor plan arrangements generally require periodic partial repayments with the unpaid balance due upon sale of the related collateral.

    The weighted average interest rate paid on the outstanding floor plan liability was 10.9%, 11.0%, and 14.7% for 1986, 1985, and 1984, respectively. The maximum amount outstanding at any month end during each year was $35,207,386 for 1986, $27,468,153 for 1985, and $4,508,319 for 1984, with a weighted average balance outstanding for each year of approximately $25,500,000, $16,000,000, and $3,750,000, respectively.

Note 10
Long-Term Debt

A summary of long-term debt follows:

December 31,	1986	1985
9% convertible subordinated notes payable, due in annual installments		
of $1,800,000 beginning May 15, 1992 through May 15, 2001	**$18,000,000**	—
Note payable, due in monthly installments of $66,667 through		
October 1, 1987, interest at prime rate (7 1/2% at December 31, 1986)		
and collateralized by property, plant and equipment with a depreciated		
cost of $1,160,640	**666,670**	1,466,667
Obligation payable in January 1988, interest at the prime rate (7 1/2% at		
December 31, 1986) and collateralized by the common stock of		
Country Squire Mobile Homes, Inc. (Note 3)	**396,000**	—
Obligation payable in annual installments of $200,000 through		
April 15, 1987, repaid in 1986	**—**	400,000
Various notes payable, due in monthly installments, including interest		
at rates ranging from 8% to 18%	**358,218**	316,500
	19,420,888	2,183,167
Less current installments	**810,901**	1,100,624
Long-term debt-noncurrent installments	**$18,609,987**	$1,082,543

The aggregate annual maturities of the long-term debt for the five years following December 31, 1986 are: 1987, $810,901; 1988, $508,497; 1989, $53,498; 1990, $33,255; 1991, $14,737.

Pursuant to an agreement dated April 25, 1986 (the "1986 Agreement"), the Company sold its Convertible Subordinated Notes due May 15, 2001, in the amount of $18,000,000 to two lenders. The proceeds from these notes have been used principally to reduce floor plan notes payable. The notes are convertible into shares of the Company's common stock at the conversion price of $17.50 per share. The conversion price is subject to adjustment in the event of stock dividends, stock splits, payment of extraordinary distributions, granting of options or sale of additional shares of common stock. The notes are subject to prepayment at the option of the Company between October 28, 1986 and May 15, 1996 at 100% of par if for a specified period preceding the written notice of prepayment the closing market price per share of the Company's common stock is equal to or greater than a percentage of the conversion price. Such percentage decreases from 200% through May 15, 1989 to 110% at May 15, 2001. The 1986 Agreement contains various restrictive covenants which include, among other things, maintenance of a minimum level of working capital as defined, maintenance of a minimum level of net earnings available for fixed charges as defined, consolidated current assets as defined, equal or greater than senior debt, payment of cash dividends and the creation of additional indebtedness.

Subsequent to December 31, 1986 and pursuant to an agreement dated February 13, 1987 (the "1987 Agreement"), the Company sold the Prudential Insurance Company of America Series A and Series B Senior notes in the aggregate of $25,000,000. The Series A notes in the amount of $15,000,000 bear interest at the rate of 8.64% and are due February 15, 1990. The Series B notes in the amount of $10,000,000 bear interest at the rate of 9.42% and are due February 15, 1992. The proceeds from these notes have been used partially to reduce floor plan notes payable and the remainder added to corporate funds. The 1987 Agreement also contains restrictive financial covenants. The 1987 Agreement financial covenants were changed to reflect more accurately the Company's current financial structure.

Concurrent with the execution of the 1987 Agreement, the financial covenants contained in the 1986 Agreement were amended to conform to the covenants in the 1987 Agreement. At December 31, 1986, the Company was in compliance with the various restrictive covenants in the 1986 Agreement with the exception of the net earnings available for fixed charges covenant. The Company was in compliance with all of the restrictive covenants in the 1986 Agreement, as amended. Retained earnings available for the payment of cash dividends amounted to $1,516,712 at December 31, 1986.

Note 11
Income Taxes

Income taxes are reflected in the consolidated statements of earnings as follows:

Years ended December 31,	1986	1985	1984
Before cumulative effect of change in accounting principle	$2,020,695	$3,327,224	$2,457,000
Cumulative effect on prior years of change in accounting principle	—	(449,989)	—
	$2,020,695	$2,877,235	$2,457,000

Components of income tax expense (benefit) are as follows:

Years ended December 31,	1986	1985	1984
Current:			
State	$550,653	$342,085	$166,000
Federal	3,942,668	2,366,685	1,075,000
	4,493,321	2,708,770	1,241,000
Deferred:			
State	(305,198)	20,529	143,000
Federal	(2,167,428)	147,936	1,073,000
	(2,472,626)	168,465	1,216,000
	$2,020,695	$2,877,235	$2,457,000

A reconciliation of the statutory Federals income tax rate with the Company's actual income tax rate follows:

Years ended December 31,	1986	1985	1984
Statutory Federal income tax rate	46.0%	46.0%	46.0%
State income tax rate less applicable Federal income tax benefit	3.2	3.2	3.2
Investment and jobs tax credit	—	(1.2)	(.4)
Nontaxable items – net	1.1	(.2)	.2
Other – net	(.5)	(.6)	(1.3)
Actual income tax rate	49.8%	47.2%	47.7%

The sources of deferred income tax expenses (benefits) and their tax effects are as follows:

Years ended December 31,	1986	1985	1984
Provision for losses on credit sales	$(1,622,079)	$743,032	$705,000
Finance participation income	(778,939)	(521,030)	453,000
Operating loss and tax credit carryforwards	—	—	244,000
Manufacturers' volume bonuses	(105,058)	(32,062)	(203,000)
Depreciation	103,519	50,415	17,000
Accrued compensation	63,027	(101,434)	—
Allowance for doubtful account	—	29,544	—
Other – net	(133,096)	—	—
	$(2,472,626)	$168,465	$1,216,000

The operating loss and tax credit carryforwards in 1984 represent the reinstatement of deferred tax credit recognized in previous years for financial reporting purposes.

The Tax Reform act of 1986 will benefit the Company through a reduction of the statutory Federal income tax rate.

Note 12
Common Stock

In connection with a public offering of common stock in 1983, the Company sold to the primary underwriter warrants to purchase 142,500 shares of common stock at a price equal to 120% of the public offering price. The warrants are exercisable for a four-year period beginning in 1984 at $3.84 per share. On June 14, 1983, the Board of Directors approved an Incentive Stock Option Plan and reserved 608,900 shares of the Company's authorized common stock for award to officers, directors and key employees. Under the Plan, options are granted at the discretion of a committee appointed by the Board of Directors and may be either incentive stock options or nonqualified stock options. Incentive options must be at a price equal to or greater than fair market value at date of grant. Nonqualified options may be at a price lower than fair market value at date of grant. The Plan expires June 13, 1993.

Activity and price information regarding the plan follows:

	Shares	Option Price Range
Balance December 31, 1983	104,750	$2.40–$3.20
Granted	119,250	$2.40–$3.75
Canceled	(20,500)	$3.20
Balance December 31, 1984	203,500	$2.40–$3.75
Granted	297,600	$4.06–$11.25
Canceled	(5,250)	$2.40–$3.75
Balance December 31, 1985	495,850	$2.40–$11.25
Granted	32,300	$11.00–$17.50
Exercised	(245,000)	$2.40–$4.06
Canceled	(18,250)	$2.70–$10.38
Balance December 31, 1986	264,900	$2.40–$17.50

At December 31, 1986, options for 17,000 shares were currently exercisable. The remaining options become exercisable through the expiration date of the Plan. The excess, if any, of the fair market value at date of grant over the exercise price of nonqualified options is considered compensation and is charged to operations as earned. For 1986 and 1985, the charge to operations was $142,000 and $206,000, respectively. No options were granted at prices lower than fair market value prior to 1985.

At December 31, 1986, 1,534,971 shares of the Company's authorized common stock were reserved for issuance as follows: 142,500 shares for the outstanding warrants, 363,900 shares for the Incentive Stock Option Plan, and 1,028,571 shares for the convertible subordinated notes.

Note 13
Commitments and Contingent Liabilities

The Company leases office space, the majority of its retail sales centers and certain equipment under noncancellable operating leases that expire over the next five years. Total rental expense under such leases amounted to $1,335,809 in 1986, $888,719 in 1985, and $433,759 in 1984. Approximately 10%, 18%, and 22%, respectively, of such amounts were paid to the Company's majority stockholder and the officers of certain subsidiaries.

Future minimum payments under noncancellable operating leases as of December 31, 1986 follow:

Year Ending December 31,	Minimum Payments
1987	$1,298,346
1988	787,572
1989	498,572
1990	312,510
1991	192,912
	$3,089,912

At December 31, 1986 the Company was contingently liable as guarantor on approximately $180 million (net) of installment sales contracts sold to financial institutions on a recourse basis. [Case writer's note: This contingent liability was $150 million at December 31, 1985, $116 million at December 31, 1984, and $45 million at December 31, 1983.]

Note 14
Supplementary Income Statement Information

Advertising costs amounted to $1,569,658, $1,021,978, and $311,285 in 1986, 1985, and 1984, respectively. Maintenance and repairs, depreciation and amortization of intangible assets, preoperating costs and similar deferrals, taxes, other than payroll and income taxes, and royalties did not exceed 1% of revenues in 1986, 1985, or 1984.

REPORT OF INDEPENDENT CERTIFIED PUBLIC ACCOUNTANTS

THE BOARD OF DIRECTORS AND STOCKHOLDERS MANUFACTURED HOMES, INC.:

We have examined the consolidated balance sheets of Manufactured Homes, Inc. and subsidiaries as of December 31, 1986 and 1985 and the related consolidated statements of earnings, stockholders' equity and changes in financial position for each of the years in the three-year period ended December 31, 1986. Our examinations were made in accordance with generally accepted auditing standards and, accordingly, included such tests of the accounting records and such other auditing procedures as we considered necessary in the circumstances.

In our opinion, the aforementioned consolidated financial statements present fairly the financial position of Manufactured Homes, Inc. and subsidiaries at December 31, 1986 and 1985 and the results of their operations and the changes in their financial position for each of the years in the three-year period ended December 31, 1986, in conformity with generally accepted accounting principles consistently applied during the period except for the change, with which we concur, in the method of recording the uncollected portion of finance participation income as explained in Note 2 to the consolidated financial statements.

PEAT, MARWICK, MITCHELL & CO.
Charlotte, North Carolina
March 10, 1987

Manufactured Homes, Inc.

Manufactured Homes, Inc.

EXHIBIT 3

CONSOLIDATED BALANCE SHEETS (unaudited)

	September 30, 1987	December 31, 1986
ASSETS		
Current Assets:		
Cash and cash equivalents:		
Cash and temporary investments (includes)		
$5,212,849 of restricted cash in 1987	$9,311,240	$2,486,024
Contract proceeds receivable from financial institutions	17,435,191	11,496,098
Total cash and cash equivalents	26,746,431	13,982,102
Finance participation receivable – current portion	4,572,042	2,691,497
Deferred finance participation income	(1,208,275)	(801,511)
Net finance participation receivable	3,363,767	1,889,986
Installment sales contracts held for resale (less unearned interest of $3,648,675)	2,382,573	—
Other receivables	6,343,052	3,746,863
Refundable income taxes	—	778,971
Inventories	41,638,452	38,163,712
Prepaid expenses	587,749	538,419
Deferred income taxes	1,000,262	761,262
Total current assets	82,062,286	59,861,315
Finance participation receivable – noncurrent portion	25,020,194	16,128,799
Deferred finance participation income	(5,984,910)	(3,923,178)
Net finance participation receivable	19,035,284	12,205,621
Property, plant and equipment, at cost	9,248,065	7,504,272
Accumulated depreciation and amortization	(3,166,445)	(2,410,812)
Net property, plant and equipment	6,081,620	5,093,460
Deferred income taxes	1,847,735	—
Excess of costs over net assets of acquired companies, less amortization	2,130,099	2,107,874
Other assets	1,446,657	2,109,533
	$112,603,681	$81,377,803
LIABILITIES AND STOCKHOLDERS' EQUITY		
Current liabilities:		
Notes payable	$—	$1,099,971
Long-term debt – current installments	90,038	810,901
Floor plan notes payable	28,306,796	35,207,386
Accounts payable	8,181,736	4,899,250
Income taxes	2,469,015	—
Accrued expenses and other liabilities	5,351,963	2,731,924
Total current liabilities	44,399,548	44,749,432
Long-term debt – noncurrent installments	43,000,000	18,609,987
Reserve for losses on credit sales	4,850,000	3,000,000
Deferred income taxes	—	851,265
Total liabilities	92,249,548	67,210,684

(continued)

CONSOLIDATED BALANCE SHEETS (unaudited) *(continued)*

	September 30, 1987	December 31, 1986
Stockholder's equity:		
Common stock – $.50 par value per share; authorized 10,000 shares; issued and outstanding 3,777,168 shares in 1987 and 3,733,968 in 1986	1,888,584	1,866,984
Additional paid-in capital	3,830,314	3,508,351
Retained earnings	14,635,235	8,791,784
Total stockholders' equity	20,354,133	14,167,119
	$112,603,681	$81,377,803

CONSOLIDATED STATEMENT OF EARNINGS (unaudited)

	Three Months Ended September 30,		Nine Months Ended September 30,	
	1987	1986	1987	1986
Revenues:				
Net sales	$44,590,244	$29,464,161	$126,599,392	$76,396,868
Finance participation income	8,439,473	3,277,085	18,895,975	8,629,223
Insurance commissions	291,868	180,870	976,128	465,577
Interest	373,415	98,327	925,116	230,602
Other	534,916	121,378	786,971	221,448
Total revenues	54,229,916	33,141,821	148,183,582	85,943,718
Costs and expenses:				
Cost of sales	36,325,647	23,741,484	101,997,757	61,554,367
Selling, general and administrative	10,806,534	5,905,930	27,973,865	14,823,385
Provision for losses on credit sales	1,096,027	294,716	3,203,913	772,417
Interest	1,568,906	877,531	4,416,596	2,303,482
Total costs and expenses	49,797,114	30,819,661	137,592,131	79,453,651
Earnings before income taxes	4,432,802	2,322,160	10,591,451	6,490,067
Income taxes	2,038,000	1,145,000	4,748,000	3,109,000
Net earnings	$2,394,302	$1,177,160	$5,843,451	$3,381,067
Net earnings per share:				
Primary	$.60	$.30	$1.48	$.87
Fully diluted	$.53	$.28	$1.31	$.83

Manufactured Homes, Inc.

CONSOLIDATED STATEMENTS OF CHANGES IN FINANCIAL POSITION (unaudited)

	Nine Months Ended September 30	
	1987	1986
Working capital was provided by:		
Operations:		
Net earnings	$5,843,451	$3,381,067
Adjustments for items not requiring (providing)		
working capital:	921,388	664,769
Depreciation and amortization		
Noncurrent deferred income taxes	(2,699,000)	(345,000)
Provision for losses on credit sales, net of actual changes	1,850,000	(318,539)
Issuance of nonqualified stock options	39,000	106,500
Finance participation income	(18,895,975)	(8,629,223)
Collections and net change in noncurrent portion		
of finance participation receivable	12,066,312	5,019,381
Working capital used by operations	(874,824)	(121,045)
Proceeds from long-term debt	25,000,000	18,000,000
Exercise of stock options	304,563	1,060,805
Decrease in other assets	662,876	—
	25,092,615	18,939,760
Working capital was used for:		
Net assets, exclusive of working capital,		
of acquired companies:		
Finance participation receivable	—	349,749
Property and equipment	—	212,716
Other assets	—	509,514
Long-term debt	—	(257,571)
Reserve for losses on credit sales	—	(436,664)
Deferred income taxes	—	78,486
Excess of costs over net assets of acquired companies	—	867,849
	—	1,324,079
Additions to property, plant and equipment	1,851,773	1,365,703
Current installments and repayment of long-term debt	609,987	1,015,876
Additions to other assets and excess costs	80,000	879,665
	2,541,760	4,585,323
Increase in working capital	$22,550,855	$14,354,437
Changes in working capital, by component:		
Cash and cash equivalents	$12,764,329	$6,425,144
Finance participation receivable – current portion	1,473,781	239,967
Installment sales contracts held for resale	2,382,573	—
Other receivables	2,596,189	2,818,093
Refundable income taxes	(778,971)	—
Inventories	3,474,740	6,923,301
Prepaid expenses	49,330	59,791
Deferred income taxes	239,000	52,001
Notes payable	1,099,971	(1,391,500)
Long-term debt – current installments	720,863	167,046
Floor plan notes payable	6,900,590	1,424,866
Accounts payable	3,282,486)	(2,811,331)
Income taxes	(2,469,015)	1,820,226
Accrued expenses and other liabilities	(2,620,039)	(1,373,167)
Increase in working capital	$22,550,855	$14,354,437

Notes to Consolidated Financial Statements

1. Pursuant to an agreement dated February 13, 1987, the Company sold to Prudential Insurance Company of America Series A and Series B Senior notes in the aggregate of $25,000,000. The Series A notes in the amount of $15,000,000 bear interest at the rate of 8.64% and are due February 15, 1990. The Series B notes in the amount of $10,000,000 bear interest at the rate of 9.42% and are due February 15, 1992. The proceeds from these notes have been used partially to reduce floor plan notes payable and to fund the Company's finance subsidiary with the remainder added to working capital.

2. On August 18, 1987, the Company's finance subsidiary sold, with recourse, a portfolio of retail installment sales contracts with a principal balance of approximately $8,300,000 to an unrelated financial institution. As a result, the Company recognized, in the third quarter, finance participation income, net of discounts and estimated future servicing costs, of $1,688,690. The terms of the sale required the Company to provide to the unrelated financial institution as security against credit losses, an irrevocable reducing letter of credit in the amount of $3,000,000 secured by a six-month renewable certificate of deposit equal in amount to the letter of credit. At September 30, 1987, approximately $2,200,000 of the proceeds from the sale was held in an escrow account pending receipt, from the appropriate state agencies, of the titles to certain of the new and pre-owned homes securing the retail installment sales contracts in accordance with the terms of the sale.

3. Primary earnings per share are based on the weighted average number of common and common equivalent shares outstanding. Such average shares are as follows:

	Three Months Ended September 30,		Nine Months Ended September 30,	
	1987	1986	1987	1986
Outstanding shares	3,773,894	3,726,427	3,758,245	3,635,137
Equivalent shares	205,159	195,979	187,848	272,150
	3,979,053	3,922,406	3,946,093	3,907,287

The equivalent shares represent shares issuable upon exercise of stock options and warrants after the assumed repurchase of common shares with the related proceeds at the average price during the period.

Fully diluted earnings per share are based on the weighted average number of common and common equivalent shares outstanding plus the common shares issuable upon the assumed conversion of the convertible subordinated notes and elimination of the applicable interest expense less related income tax benefit. In determining equivalent shares, the assumed repurchase of common shares is at the higher of the average or period-end price.

4. Certain amounts in the 1986 financial statements have been reclassified to conform to the presentation adopted in 1987.

5. In the opinion of management, all adjustments which are necessary for a fair presentation of operating results are reflected in the accompanying interim financial statements. All such adjustments are considered to be of a normal recurring nature.

MANAGEMENT'S DISCUSSION AND ANALYSIS OF FINANCIAL CONDITION AND RESULTS OF OPERATIONS

Results of Operations

The Company's net sales for the three-month period ended September 30, 1987 were $44,590,244 compared to $29,464,161 for the comparable period of 1986, an increase of 51%. Net sales for the nine month period ended September 30, 1987 were $126,599,392 compared to $76,396,868 for the comparable period of 1986, an increase of 66%. These increases are due primarily to the acquisitions in September 1986 of Jeff Brown Homes, Inc., with nine retail sales centers, and Piggy Bank Homes of Alabama, Inc., with six retail sales centers, and the opening of 24 additional retail centers between September 30, 1986 and September 30, 1987. In addition, the average number of homes sold per retail sales center for the three month and the nine-month periods ended September 30, 1987 increased by 28% and 20% respectively, over the corresponding periods of 1986.

Finance participation income for both the three month and the nine month periods ended September 30, 1987 was greater as a percentage of net sales than in the comparable periods of 1986 due primarily to improved financing terms from third-party finance sources and the sale in August 1987 of a portfolio of retail installment sales contracts with a principal balance of approximately $8,300,000, which resulted in finance participation income of $1,688,690 net of discounts and estimated future servicing costs. This portfolio consisted of retail installment sales contracts originated during 1987 and the fourth quarter of 1986. Insurance commissions increased as a percentage of net sales due to added emphasis being placed on this revenue source. Interest income increased significantly due to an improved cash position in 1987 and the interest earned on retail installment sales contracts while held in the Company's finance subsidiary. Other income increased primarily due to a gain of $400,000 recognized in September 1987 on the cancellation of a lease on one of the Company's sales centers.

Cost of sales increased as a percentage of net sales for the three-month period ended September 30, 1987 as compared to the corresponding period of 1986 primarily as a result of extremely competitive market conditions. For the nine month period ended September 30, 1987, cost of sales as a percentage of net sales was unchanged from the comparable period of 1986. Selling, general and administrative expenses were higher, as a percentage of total revenues, for both the three month and nine month periods ended September 30, 1987 as a result of expenses incurred for the following activities: the acquisitions in September 1986 of Piggy Bank Homes of Alabama, Inc. and Jeff Brown Homes, Inc.; the segregation and expanded operations of MANH Independent Retailers Corp. and AAA Mobile Homes, Inc. as separate subsidiaries of the Company; the increased number of retail sales centers; and the establishment in October 1986 of the Company's finance subsidiary.

The provision for losses on credit sales, as a percentage of total revenues, increased significantly for both the three month and nine month periods ended September 30, 1987 as compared to the corresponding periods of 1986, primarily as a result of industry-wide problems which became evident in the second half of 1986 and which caused the Company to incur increased costs relating to the prepayment of retail installment sales contracts, the repossession of homes and the resale of repossessed homes.

Interest rates were generally lower in 1987; however, total interest expense increased significantly in 1987 due to increased borrowings to support additional retail sales centers and to fund the activities of the Company's finance subsidiary.

Manufactured Homes, Inc.

Liquidity and Capital Resources

Liquidity and capital resources were greater at September 30, 1987 than at September 30, 1986 due to the sale in February 1987 of $25,000,000 of unsecured senior notes due in 1990 and 1992 bearing interest at a blended rate of 8.95% and to increased floor plan lines of credit. At September 30, 1987, the Company had available $3,000,000 in a bank line of credit and approximately $18,500,000 in unused floor plan lines of credit. In addition, the Company filed a registration statement with the Securities and Exchange Commission on September 22, 1987 for the proposed sale by the Company of 1,200,000 shares of its previously unissued common stock. Due to recent events in the financial market place, the status of this proposed sale is now uncertain.

The Tax Reform Act of 1986 is benefiting the Company through a reduction of the corporate income tax rate. However, beginning January 1, 1987, the Act required the Company to change from the reserve method to the direct write-off method for providing for losses on credit sales, which is requiring the Company to accelerate the payment of federal income taxes. However, the Company believes that funds to be generated by operations, combined with financial resources and credit lines currently available, will be sufficient to satisfy capital needs for current operations.

Oracle Systems Corporation

In August 1990 Lawrence J. Ellison, CEO of Oracle Systems Corporation, was facing increasing pressure from analysts about the method the company used to recognize revenue in its financial reports. Analysts' major concerns were clearly articulated by a senior technology analyst at Hambrecht & Quist, Inc. in San Francisco:

> Under Oracle's current set of accounting rules, Oracle can recognize any revenue they believe will be shipped within the next twelve months. . . . Many other software firms have moved to booking only the revenue that has been shipped.

Given its aggressive revenue-recognition policy and relatively high amount of accounts receivable, many analysts argued that Oracle's stock was a risky buy. As a result, the company's stock price had plummeted from a high of $56 in March to around $27 in mid-August. This poor stock performance concerned Larry Ellison for two reasons. First, he worried that the firm might become a takeover candidate, and second that the low price made it expensive for the firm to raise new equity capital to finance its future growth.[1]

ORACLE'S BUSINESS AND PERFORMANCE

Since its formation in California in June 1977, Oracle Systems Corporation has grown rapidly to become the world's largest supplier of database management software. Its principal product is the ORACLE relational database management system, which runs on a broad range of computers, including mainframes, minicomputers, microcomputers, and personal computers. The company also develops and distributes a wide array of products to interface with its database system, including applications in financial reporting, manufacturing management, computer aided systems engineering, computer network communications, and office automation. Finally, Oracle offers extensive maintenance, consulting, training, and systems integration services to support its products.

Oracle's leadership in developing software for database management has enabled it to achieve impressive financial growth. As reported in Exhibit 1, the company's sales grew from $282 million in 1988 to $971 million two years later. Larry Ellison was proud of this rapid growth and committed to its continuance. He often referred to Genghis Khan as his inspiration in crushing competitors and achieving growth.

---

1. Cholthicha Srivisal and Professor Paul M. Healy prepared this case at the MIT Sloan School of Management. The case is intended solely as the basis for class discussion and is not intended to serve as an endorsement, source of primary data, or illustration of effective or ineffective management.

The primary factors underlying Oracle's strong performance have been its successes in R&D and its committed sales force. The firm's R&D triumphs are proudly noted in the 1990 annual report:

In 1979, we delivered ORACLE, the world's first relational database management system and the first product based on SQL. In 1983, ORACLE was the first database management system to run on mainframes, minicomputers, and PCs. In 1986, ORACLE was the first database management system with distributed capability, making access to data on a network of computers as easy as access on a single computer.

We continued our tradition of technology leadership in 1990, with three key achievements in the area of client-server computing. First, we delivered software that allows client programs to automatically adapt to the different graphical user interfaces on PCs, Macintoshes, and workstations. Second, we delivered our complete family of accounting applications running as client programs networked to an ORACLE database server. Third, the ORACLE database server set performance records of over 400 transactions per second on mainframes, 200 transactions per second on minicomputers, and 20 transactions per second on PCs.

Oracle's sales force has also been responsible for its success. The sales force is compensated on the basis of sales, giving it a strong incentive to aggressively court large corporate customers. In some cases salespeople even have been known to offer extended payment terms to a potentially valuable customer to close a sale.

Oracle's growth slowed in early 1990. In March the firm announced a 54 percent jump in quarterly revenues (relative to 1989's results)—but only a 1 percent rise in earnings (see Exhibit 2 for quarterly results for 1989 and 1990). Management explained that several factors contributed to this poor performance. First, the company had recently redrawn its sales territories and, as a result, for several months salespeople had become unsure of their new responsibilities, leaving some customers dissatisfied. Second, there were problems with a number of new products, such as Oracle Financials, which were released before all major bugs could be fixed. However, the stock market was unimpressed by these explanations, and the firm's stock price dropped by 31 percent with the earnings announcement.

REVENUE RECOGNITION

The deterioration in its financial performance prompted analysts to question Oracle's method of recognizing revenues. For example, one analyst commented:

Oracle's accounting practices might have played a role in the low net income results. The top line went up over 50%, though the net bottom line did not do so well, because Oracle's running more cash than it should be as a result of financial mismanagement. The company's aggressive revenue-recognition policy and relatively high amount of accounts receivables make the stock risky.

Oracle's major revenues come from licensing software products to end users, and from sublicensing agreements with original equipment manufacturers (OEMs) and software value-added relicensors (VARs). Initial license fees for the ORACLE database management system range from $199 to over $5,500 on micro- and personal computers, and from $5,100 to approximately $342,000 on mini- and mainframe computers. License fees for Oracle Financial and Oracle Government Financial products range from $20,000 to $513,000, depending on the platform and number of users. A customer may obtain additional licenses at the same site at a discount. Oracle recognizes revenues from these licenses when a contract has been signed with a financially sound customer, even though shipment of products has not occurred.

OEM agreements are negotiated on a case-by-case basis. However, under a typical contract Oracle receives an initial nonrefundable fee (payable either upon signing the contract or within 30 days of signing) and sublicense fees based on the number of copies distributed. Under VAR agreements the company charges a development license fee on top of the initial nonrefundable fee, and it receives sublicense fees based on the number of copies distributed. Sublicense fees are usually a percentage of Oracle's list price. The initial nonrefundable payments and development license fees under these arrangements are recorded as revenue when the contracts are signed. Sublicense fees are recorded when they are received from the OEM or VAR.

Oracle also receives revenues from maintenance agreements under which it provides technical support and telephone consultation on the use of the products and problem resolution, system updates for software products, and user documentation. Maintenance fees generally run for one year and are payable at the end of the maintenance period. They range from 7.5 percent to 22 percent of the current list price of the appropriate license. These fees are recorded as unearned revenue when the maintenance contract is signed and are reflected as revenue ratably over the contract period.

The major questions about Oracle's revenue recognition concern the way the firm recognizes revenues on license fees. There is no currently accepted standard for accounting for these types of revenues.[2] However, Oracle tends to be one of the more aggressive reporters. The firm's days receivable exceeds 160 days, substantially higher than the average of 62 days receivable for other software developers (see Exhibit 3 for a summary of days receivable for other major software developers in 1989 and 1990). As a result, some analysts argue that the firm should recognize revenue when software is delivered rather than when a contract is signed, consistent with the accounting treatment for the sale of products. In addition, the collectibility of license fees is considered questionable by some analysts, who have urged the firm to recognize revenue only when there is a reasonable basis for estimating the degree of collectibility of a receivable. Estimates by Oracle's controller indicate that if Oracle were to change to a more conservative revenue recognition policy, the firm's days receivable would fall to about 120 days.

MANAGEMENT'S CONCERNS

Oracle's management was concerned about analysts' opinions and the downturn in the firm's stock. The company had lost credibility with investors and customers due to its recent poor performance and its controversial accounting policies.

One of the items on the agenda at the upcoming board meeting was to consider proposals for changing the firm's revenue recognition method and for dealing with its communication challenge. Ellison knew that his opinion on this question would be influential. As he saw it, the company had three alternatives. One was to modify the recognition of license fees so that revenue would be recognized only when substantially all the company's contractual obligations had been performed. However, he

---

2. *The Financial Accounting Standards Board was considering the issue of revenue recognition for software developers at this time. It was widely expected that the Board would make a pronouncement on the topic early in 1991.*

worried that such a change would have a negative impact on the firm's bottom line and further depress the stock price. A second possibility was to wait until the FASB announced its position on software revenue recognition before making any changes. Finally, the company could make no change and vigorously defend its current accounting method. Ellison carefully considered which alternative made the most sense for the firm.

QUESTIONS

1. What factors might have led analysts to question Oracle Systems' method of revenue recognition in mid-1990? Are these legitimate concerns?

2. Estimate the earnings impact for Oracle from recognizing revenue at delivery, rather than when a contract is signed.

3. What accounting or communication changes would you recommend to Oracle's Board of Directors?

EXHIBIT I

Oracle Systems Corporation—Consolidated Financial Statements

CONSOLIDATED BALANCE SHEETS
As of May 31, 1990 and 1989 (in $000, except per share data)

	1990	1989
ASSETS		
CURRENT ASSETS:		
Cash and cash equivalents	$44,848	$44,848
Short-term investments	4,980	4,500
Receivables		
Trade, net of allowance for doubtful accounts of $28,445 in 1990 and $16,829 in 1989	468,071	261,989
Other	28,899	16,175
Prepaid expenses and supplies	22,459	9,376
Total current assets	569,257	336,933
PROPERTY, net	171,945	94,455
COMPUTER SOFTWARE DEVELOPMENT COSTS, net of accumulated amortization of $14,365 in 1990 and $6,180 in 1989	33,396	13,942
OTHER ASSETS	12,649	14,879
TOTAL ASSETS	$787,247	$460,209
LIABILITIES AND STOCKHOLDERS' EQUITY		
CURRENT LIABILITIES:		
Notes payable to banks	$31,236	$9,747
Current maturities of long-term debt	11,265	13,587
Accounts payable	64,922	51,582
Income taxes payable	18,254	14,836
Accrued compensation and related benefits	61,164	39,063
Customer advances and unearned revenues	42,121	15,403
Other accrued liabilities	32,417	23,400
Sales tax payable	22,193	8,608
Deferred income taxes	—	2,107
Total current liabilities	283,572	178,333
LONG-TERM DEBT	89,129	33,506
OTHER LONG-TERM LIABILITIES	4,936	5,702
DEFERRED INCOME TAXES	22,025	12,114
STOCKHOLDERS' EQUITY:		
Common stock, $.01 par value-authorized, 200,000,000 shares; outstanding: 131,138,302 shares in 1990 and 126,933,288 shares in 1989	388	346
Additional paid-in capital	118,715	84,931
Retained earnings	267,475	150,065
Accumulated foreign currency translation adjustments	1,007	(4,788)
Total stockholders' equity	387,585	230,554
TOTAL LIABILITIES AND STOCKHOLDERS' EQUITY	$787,247	$460,209

CONSOLIDATED STATEMENTS OF INCOME

For the Years Ended May 31, 1990 to 1988 (in $000, except per share data)

	1990	1989	1988
REVENUES			
Licenses	$689,898	$417,825	$205,435
Services	280,946	165,848	76,678
Total revenues	970,844	583,673	282,113
OPERATING EXPENSES			
Sales and marketing	465,074	272,812	124,148
Cost of services	160,426	100,987	51,241
Research and development	88,291	52,570	25,708
General and administrative	67,258	34,344	17,121
Total operating expenses	781,049	460,713	218,218
OPERATING INCOME	189,795	122,960	63,895
OTHER INCOME (EXPENSE):			
Interest income	3,772	2,724	2,472
Interest expense	(12,096)	(4,318)	(1,540)
Other income (expense)	(8,811)	(1,121)	152
Total other income (expense)	(17,135)	(2,715)	1,084
INCOME BEFORE PROVISION FOR INCOME TAXES	172,660	120,245	64,979
PROVISION FOR INCOME TAXES	55,250	38,479	22,093
NET INCOME	$117,410	$81,766	$42,886
EARNINGS PER SHARE	$.86	$.61	$.32
NUMBER OF COMMON AND COMMON EQUIVALENT SHARES OUTSTANDING	136,826	135,066	132,950

CONSOLIDATED STATEMENTS OF CASH FLOWS

For the Years Ended May 31, 1990 to 1988 (in $000)

	1990	1989	1988
CASH FLOWS FROM OPERATING ACTIVITIES			
Net income	$117,410	$81,766	$42,886
Adjustments to reconcile net income to net cash provided by operating activities:			
Depreciation and amortization	44,078	23,156	12,973
Provision for doubtful accounts	16,625	9,211	4,839
Increase in receivables	(227,046)	(149,900)	(74,777)
Increase in prepaid expenses & supplies	(12,834)	(5,684)	(1,458)
Increase in accounts payable	12,491	25,236	12,854
Increase income taxes payable	3,002	6,821	7,940
Increase in other accrued liabilities	42,166	38,057	21,420
Increase in customer advances and unearned revenues	25,786	6,496	5,682
Increase (decrease) in deferred taxes	7,728	(10,857)	8,170
Increase (decrease) in other non-current liabilities	(766)	1,938	—
Net cash provided by operating activities	28,640	26,240	40,529
CASH FLOWS FROM INVESTING ACTIVITIES			
Increase in short-term investments	(480)	2,998	(7,498)
Capital expenditures	(89,275)	(68,428)	(30,959)
Capitalization of computer software development costs	(27,639)	(10,526)	(4,447)
Increase in other assets	(1,116)	(2,084)	(481)
Purchase of a business	—	(6,650)	—
Net cash used for investing activities	(118,510)	(84,690)	(43,385)
CASH FLOWS FROM FINANCING ACTIVITIES			
Notes payable to banks	21,156	10,305	(169)
Proceeds from issuance of long-term debt	68,530	37,539	1,445
Payments of long-term debt	(34,239)	(6,205)	(3,638)
Proceeds from common stock issued	18,460	11,060	4,712
Tax benefits from stock options	15,366	10,593	3,992
Net cash provided by financing activities	89,273	63,292	6,342
EFFECT OF EXCHANGE RATE CHANGES ON CASH	552	(1,061)	69
NET INCREASE (DECREASE) IN CASH	(45)	3,781	3,555
CASH: BEGINNING OF YEAR	44,893	41,112	37,557
Cash: end of year	$44,848	$44,893	$41,112

EXCERPTS FROM NOTES TO CONSOLIDATED FINANCIAL STATEMENTS

1. Organization and Significant Accounting Policies

Organization

Oracle Systems Corporation (the Company) develops and markets computer software products used for database management, applications development, decision support, programmer tools, computer network communication, end user applications, and office automation. The Company offers maintenance, consulting, and training services in support of its clients' use of its software products.

Basis of Financial Statements

The consolidated financial statements include the Company and its subsidiaries. All transactions and balances between the companies are eliminated.

Business Combination

In November 1988, the Company's subsidiary, Oracle Complex Systems Corporation, acquired all of the outstanding shares of Falcon Systems, Inc., a systems integrator, for $13,714,000 in cash and $4,600,000 in notes which become due November 1, 1991. The acquisition was accounted for as a purchase and the excess of the cost over the fair value of assets acquired was $5,648,000, which is being amortized over 5 years on a straight-line method. Pro forma results of operations, assuming the acquisition had taken place June 1, 1987, would not differ materially from the Company's actual results of operations.

Software Development Costs

Effective June 1, 1986, the Company began capitalizing internally generated software development costs in compliance with Statement of Financial Accounting Standards No. 86, "Accounting for the Costs of Computer Software to be Sold, Leased or Otherwise Marketed." Capitalization of computer software development costs begins upon the establishment of technological feasibility for the product. Capitalized software development costs amounted to $27,639,000, $10,526,000, and $4,447,000 in fiscal 1990, 1989, and 1988, respectively.

Amortization of capitalized computer software development costs begins when the products are available for general release to customers, and is computed product by product as the greater of: (a) the ratio of current gross revenues for a product to the total of current and anticipated future gross revenues for the product, or (b) the straight-line method over the remaining estimated economic life of the product. Currently, estimated economic lives of 24 months are used in the calculation of amortization of these capitalized costs. Amortization amounted to $8,185,000, $3,504,000, and $2,345,000 for fiscal years ended May 31, 1990, 1989, and 1988, respectively, and is included in sales and marketing expenses.

Statements of Cash Flows

The Company paid income taxes in the amount of $33,731,000, $29,006,000, and $711,000 and interest expense of $8,026,000, $4,274,000 and $1,540,000 during the fiscal years ended 1990, 1989, and 1988, respectively. The Company purchased equipment under capital lease obligations in the amount of $17,616,000, $4,692,000, and $4,108,000 in fiscal 1990, 1989, and 1988, respectively.

Revenue Recognition

The Company generates several types of revenue including the following:

License and Sublicense fees. The Company licenses ORACLE products to end users under license agreements. The Company also has entered into agreements whereby the Company licenses Oracle products and receives license and sublicense fees from original equipment manufacturers (OEMs) and software value-added relicensors (VARs). The minimum amount of license and sublicense fees specified in the agreements is recognized either upon shipment of the product or at the time such agreements are effective (which in most instances is the date of the agreement) if the customer is creditworthy and the terms of the agreement are such that the amounts are due within one year and are nonrefundable, and the agreements are noncancellable. The Company recognizes revenue at such time as it has substantially performed all of its contractual obligations. Additional sublicense fees are subsequently recognized as revenue at the time such fees are reported to the Company by the OEMs and VARs.

Maintenance Agreements. Maintenance agreements generally call for the Company to provide technical support and certain systems updates to customers. Revenue related to providing technical support is recognized proportionately over the maintenance period, which in most instances is one year, while the revenue related to systems updates is recognized at the beginning of each maintenance period.

Consulting, Training, and Other Services. The Company provides consulting services to its customers; revenue from such services is generally recognized under the percentage of completion method.

2. Short-Term Debt

Short term debt (in $000) consists of:	Year Ended May 31	
	1990	1989
Unsecured revolving lines of credit	$18,198	$5,955
Other	13,038	3,792
Total	$31,236	$9,747

At May 31, 1990, the Company had short-term unsecured revolving lines of credit with two banks providing for borrowings aggregating $42,000,000, of which $18,198,000 was outstanding. These lines expire in September 1990 ($2,000,000), November 1990 ($10,000,000), and January 1991 ($30,000,000). Interest on these borrowings is based on varying rates pegged to the banks' prime rate, cost of funds, or LIBOR. The Company also had other unsecured short-term indebtedness to banks of $13,038,000 at May 31, 1990, payable upon demand. The average interest rate on short-term borrowings was 9.4% at May 31, 1990.

The Company is required to maintain certain financial ratios under the line of credit agreements. The Company was in compliance with these financial covenants at May 31, 1990.

3. Long-Term Debt

At May 31, 1990, the Company had long-term unsecured revolving lines of credit with four banks providing for borrowings aggregating $135,000,000, of which $61,460,000 was outstanding. Of the $61,460,000 outstanding, $58,210,000 was classified as long-term debt and $3,250,000 was classified as current maturities of long-term debt. These lines of credit expire in December 1991 ($60,000,000), March 1992 ($15,000,000), July 1992 ($20,000,000), January 1991 ($20,000,000), and March 1991 ($20,000,000). The Company has the option to convert $20,000,000 of its line expiring in January of 1991 and $8,000,000 of that expiring in March of 1991 into two term loans which would mature in 1993. Interest on these borrowings vary based on the banks' cost of funds rates. At May 31, 1990 the interest rate on outstanding domestic and foreign currency borrowings ranged from 8.6% to 15.6%. The aggregate amount available under these lines of credit at May 31, 1990 was $73,540,000.

Under the line-of-credit agreements, the Company is required to maintain certain financial ratios. At May 31, 1990 the Company was in compliance with these financial covenants.

Subsequent to May 31, 1990, the Company obtained two additional unsecured revolving lines of credit, one which expires May 1992 ($20,000,000) and one which expires January 1991 ($20,000,000).

4. Stockholders' Equity

Stock Option Plan

The Company's stock option plan provides for the issuance of incentives stock options to employees of the Company and nonqualified options to employees, directors, consultants, and independent contractors of the Company. Under the terms of this plan, options to purchase up to 23,335,624 shares of Common Stock may be granted at not less than fair market value, are immediately exercisable, become vested as established by the Board (generally ratably over four to five years), and generally expire ten years from the date of grant. The Company has the right to repurchase shares issued upon the exercise of unvested options at the exercise price paid by the stockholder should the stockholder leave the Company prior to the scheduled vesting date. At May 31, 1990, 271,300 shares of Common Stock outstanding were subject to such repurchase rights. Options to purchase 5,005,720 common shares were vested at May 31, 1990.

Non-Plan Options

In addition to the above option plan, nonqualified stock options to purchase a total of 5,712,000 common shares have been granted to employees and directors of the Company. These options were granted at the fair market value as determined by the Board of Directors, became exercisable immediately, vest either immediately (for directors) or ratably over a period of up to five years (for individuals other than directors) and generally expire ten years from the date of grant. The Company has the right to repurchase shares issued upon the exercise of unvested options at the exercise price paid by the stockholder should the stockholder leave the Company prior to the scheduled vesting date. Options to purchase 160,000 common shares were vested as of May 31, 1990.

As of May 31, 1990, the Company had reserved 11,135,194 shares of Common Stock for exercise of options.

Stock Purchase Plan

In October 1987, the Company adopted an Employee Stock Purchase Plan and reserved 8,000,000 shares of Common Stock for issuance thereunder. Under this plan, the Company's employees may purchase shares of Common Stock at a price per share that is 85% of the lesser of the fair market value as of the beginning or the end of the semi-annual option period. Through May 31, 1990, 2,326,772 shares have been issued and 5,673,228 shares are reserved for future issuances under this plan.

REPORT OF INDEPENDENT PUBLIC ACCOUNTANTS

To Oracle Systems Corporation:

We have audited the accompanying consolidated balance sheets of Oracle Systems Corporation (a Delaware corporation) and subsidiaries as of May 31, 1990 and 1989 and the related consolidated statements of income, stockholders' equity, and cash flows for each of the three years in the period ended May 31, 1990. These financial statements are the responsibility of the company's management. Our responsibility is to express an opinion on these financial statements based on our audits. We conducted our audits in accordance with generally accepted auditing standards. Those standards require that we plan and perform the audit to obtain reasonable assurance about whether the financial statements are free of material misstatement. An audit includes examining, on a test basis, evidence supporting the amounts and disclosures in the financial statements. An audit also includes assessing the accounting principles used and significant estimates made by management, as well as evaluating the overall financial statement presentation. We believe that our audits provide a reasonable basis for our opinion.

In our opinion, the financial statements referred to above present fairly, in all material respects, the financial position of Oracle Systems Corporation and subsidiaries as of May 31, 1990 and 1989 and the results of their operations and their cash flows for each of the three years in the period ended May 31, 1990, in conformity with generally accepted accounting principles.

Our audits were made for the purpose of forming an opinion on the basic financial statements taken as a whole. The schedules listed under Item 14(a)2. are presented for purposes of complying with the Securities and Exchange Commission's rules and are not part of the basic financial statements. These schedules have been subjected to the auditing procedures applied in the audit of the basic financial statements and, in our opinion, fairly state in all material respects the financial data required to be set forth therein in relation to the basic financial statements taken as a whole.

ARTHUR ANDERSEN & CO.
SAN JOSE, CALIFORNIA
JULY 9, 1990

EXHIBIT 2

Oracle Systems Corporation—Review of Quarterly Results in Fiscal 1989 and 1990 (in $000 except per share data)

	Fiscal 1990 Quarter Ended			
	Aug. 31 1989	Nov. 30 1989	Feb. 28 1990	May 31 1990
Revenues	$175,490	$209,023	$236,165	$350,166
Net income	11,679	28,491	24,282	52,958
Earnings per share[a]	$.09	$.21	$.18	$.39

	Fiscal 1989 Quarter Ended			
	Aug. 31 1988	Nov. 30 1988	Feb. 28 1989	May 31 1989
Revenues	$90,639	$123,745	$153,354	$215,935
Net income	7,067	17,189	23,964	33,546
Earnings per share[a]	$.05	.13	$.18	$.25

[a]Adjusted to reflect the two-for-one stock splits in the third quarter of fiscal 1988 and the first quarter of fiscal 1990.

EXHIBIT 3

Days' Receivable for Selected Companies in the Software Industry for 1989–1990

Company	1989	1990
Borland International Corp.	49	45
Lotus Development Corp.	64	64
Microsoft Corp.	51	56
Novell Corp.	85	81
Average	62	62

Pre-Paid Legal Services, Inc.

Pre-Paid Legal plans are designed to help middle-income Americans have affordable access to quality legal assistance.

— Pre-Paid Legal Services Corporate Vision

Harland C. Stonecipher founded the Pre-Paid Legal Services, Inc. (PPLS) in 1972 after an expensive encounter with lawyers stemming from an automobile accident. PPLS sold legal expense insurance that provided for partial payment of legal fees in connection with the defense of certain civil and criminal actions. The company went public in 1979 and grew rapidly throughout the 1980s as an increasing number of Americans subscribed to legal service insurance (see Exhibit 1). In 1998 the company had membership revenues of $110 million, earnings of $30.2 million, and end-of-year book equity of $101.1 million. In May 1999 it began trading on the New York Stock Exchange and in August 1999 its market capitalization reached $738 million, an increase of 101% over the previous year.

Despite its strong financial performance, opinions about the future of Pre-Paid Legal Services (PPLS) varied widely among U.S. equity analysts in the period late-1997 to mid-1999. The company was highly recommended by a number of analysts, but there was also persistent short selling of the stock.[1] Short sellers' primary concern about the company was outlined in a *Fortune* article in late 1997. The business publication alleged that the company was using an inappropriate method of accounting for sales commissions. As a result of this uncertainty, the company's stock price fluctuated widely from a high of $40.50 to a low of $13.50 between late 1997 and mid-1999 (see Exhibit 2).

Professor Paul Healy and Teaching Fellow Jacob Cohen J.D. prepared this case. HBS cases are developed solely as the basis for class discussion. Cases are not intended to serve as endorsements, sources of primary data, or illustrations of effective or ineffective management. This is an abridged version of "Pre-Paid Legal Services, Inc. (A)," HBS No. 100-029 and "Pre-Paid Legal Services, Inc. (B)," HBS No. 100-030, prepared by Professor Paul Healy and Teaching Fellow Jacob Cohen J.D.

1. *Short sellers borrow stock certificates from a brokerage firm and sell the stocks on the open market. If the stock price declines, short sellers can buy back stock, cover their loan from the brokerage firm, and earn a profit. Of course, if the price increases, short sellers make a loss.*

BUSINESS DESCRIPTION[2]

PPLS offered its customers (termed members) a wide range of legal insurance. The most popular plan, The Family Plan, accounted for 94% of all memberships in 1998. This plan provided reimbursement for a broad range of legal expenses incurred by members and their spouses, including will and testament preparation, document review and letter writing, and some of the legal costs associated with employment-related trial defense, traffic violations, and Internal Revenue Service audits.[3] The Family Plan specified limits on the number of hours of attorney time that a member was entitled to receive for many of these services. It also provided a 25% discount on attorney rates for the purchase of any legal services over and above those provided under the insurance contract.

PPLS's membership premiums in 1998 averaged $19.08 per month (or $229 per year). Premiums were typically paid on a monthly basis either by automatic charges to the member's credit card or through employee payroll deductions. The premiums were generally guaranteed renewable and non-cancelable except for fraud, nonpayment of premiums, or upon written request by a member. The annual membership persistency rate in 1998 was high; approximately 75% of members at the beginning of the year and new members during the year continued to be enrolled in the program at the end of the year. At March 31, 1999, PPLS had 648,475 active members, and membership had been increasing at about 40% per year.

PPLS marketed its memberships through a multi-level program that encouraged buyers to become salespeople. Members that sought to become sales associates paid the company a fee, typically $65, to cover the cost of training materials, training meetings, and home office support services. Registered sales associates sold the company's services to their friends and business associates. The most successful even recruited and developed their own sales force. In 1998 PPLS generated 76% of its annual sales from the roughly 150,000 members registered as sales associates. The remaining 24% of sales were generated through arrangements with insurance and service companies with established sales forces, such as CNA and Primerica Financial Services.

Sales associates were compensated on a commission basis (see Exhibit 3). Prior to 1995, associates that signed-up a new member received a commission of 70% of the first year premium, and a 16% commission for subsequent year renewals. First year commissions were paid in advance whereas renewal commissions were paid as premiums were received. For example, if a new member signed up at a premium of $229 per year, the associate responsible for the sale received a first year commission of $160 (0.70*$229) at sign-up. If the member renewed in subsequent years, the sales associate received a monthly commission of $3.04 (0.16*$19).

After 1995 PPLS modified its commission formula to a flat 25% commission for both initial year and subsequent renewal memberships. To retain and attract sales associates, PPLS advanced the sales associate three years of commission on every new membership sold. If a membership lapsed before the advances had been recovered, PPLS deducted 50% of any unearned advances from future commissions to the relevant associate. For example, if a new member signed up at a premium of $229,

---

2. The material in this section is from Pre-Paid Legal Services, Inc.'s 1998 10-K Statement.

3. Legal services specifically excluded from coverage included domestic matters, bankruptcy, deliberate criminal acts, alcohol or drug-related matters, business matters, and pre-existing conditions.

the associate received a commission advance of $171.75 (25%*3*$229). If one year later the member cancelled the policy, PPLS sought to recover $57.25, equal to 50% of the second and third year commissions (50% of $229*2*0.25).

PPLS had historically offered two forms of legal services, each with very different implications for managing legal claim costs. The first form of service, termed open panel, allowed members to use their own attorney to provide legal services available under their policy. Member's attorneys were reimbursed for their services using a payment schedule that reflected "usual, reasonable and customary fees" for a particular service and geographic area.

The second form of service, closed panel memberships, required members to access legal services through a network of independent attorneys that were under contract with PPLS. These provider attorneys were paid a fixed monthly fee on a per capita basis to provide services to plan members living within the state in which the attorney was licensed to practice. PPLS contracted with one large, highly rated legal firm in each of its 36 major markets. Provider attorneys are typically rated "AV" by Martindale-Hubbell, its highest rating. They were selected after a detailed review by PPLS management.

Average costs of membership benefits in 1998 were 33% of membership premiums and management reported that these costs were expected to remain at around 35% in the future.

FINANCIAL PERFORMANCE

PPLS reported record financial performance in period 1997 and 1998 (see Exhibit 4 for summary financial data and Exhibit 5 for 1998 financial statements and excerpted footnotes.). Membership revenues during this period grew by an average of 59% per year, net income grew by 71% per year, and operating cash flows grew 500% per year. The firm's financial performance for the first six months of 1999 continued to be impressive. Membership revenues grew by 20%, earnings by 54%, and operating cash flows by 138% (from $2.4 million to $5.7 million).

As a result of the company's growth performance, a number of equity analysts that followed the stock recommended it to their clients. For example, David Strasser of Salomon Brothers issued strong buy recommendations for PPLS in August 1997 and commented on the stock as follows:

We reiterate our Strong Buy recommendation on the shares of Pre-Paid Legal Services, Inc. . . . We have recently increased our one-year price to $34 from $26. We did this for several reasons. First, the company continues to demonstrate consistent earnings growth, in line with Wall Street estimates, which gives us greater visibility of our projected 36% growth rate. . . . We are also encouraged by the company's ability to generate positive operating cash flow while still growing revenues 53%. This positive cash flow is indicative of the seasoned membership base that generates cash in spite of the company's policy of paying commission advances to its associates for new sales. We continue to believe that the company will announce an alliance with a major insurance company to sell the company's products. This would essentially double the size of the company's productive sales force and increase overall visibility of the prepaid legal product.[4]

4. Analyst Report, David Strasser, Salomon Brothers, August 1997.

ACCOUNTING DISPUTE

Despite its strong financial performance, in late 1997 PPLS was a target of short selling. On November 24, 1997, *Fortune* published an article titled "Will Pre-Paid Keep Growing?" The article cited short seller Robert Olstein of Olstein's Financial Alert Fund, who explained that his concern arose because "PPLS's accounting for commissions is unrealistic and not in accordance with economic reality."[5] The *Fortune* article noted that:

> *Rather than record the commissions as an instant hit to earnings, Pre-Paid spreads them out over a three-year period. Such deferrals, the shorts argue, make today's earnings growth look stronger than it really is. In the first half of this year, for example, if the company had swallowed commissions when they were paid, it would have shown little if any earnings growth—certainly not a level of growth to justify the stock's trading at nearly 40 times earnings.*
>
> *Plus, trouble could emerge if the company's cancellation rate on its policies increases and it can't somehow recover the commissions it has already paid. Pre-Paid shrugs this off, arguing that its historic cancellation rate is a manageable 24%. And, Harp (PPLS's CEO) boasts, "I can predict this business more precisely than anybody you want to mention."*
>
> *Maybe so, but the company's own figures, disclosed in SEC filings, show that the rate is on an upward trend. The fillings also state that Pre-Paid's cancellation rate will rise if newly written policies make up a greater portion of its business, and the company warns (deep in its 10-K annual report) that it experienced a "significant increase" in sales of new contracts last year. Unless this shift is offset by "other factors," the 10-K says, financial performance could be severely hurt. In other words, Olstein contends, Pre-Paid may face a big write-off at some point.*

MANAGEMENT RESPONSE

PPLS argued that its policy of accounting for commissions resulted in a commission expense that was more consistent with the collection of the premiums generated by the sale of such contracts. Exhibit 6 shows management's discussion of commissions and membership persistency in the firm's 10-K statement. In addition, between October 1998 and June 1999 management acquired 1,384,440 of the firm's shares on the open market at an average price of $28 per share.[6]

Nonetheless, concern over the company's accounting persisted. In late June 1999, short sales were 6.5% of outstanding shares, more than four times the level of typical companies.[7] The company's stock traded at $26.63, well off its yearly high of $39.25 and the all-time high of $40.50.

Rick Nelson, an analyst at Furman Selz, summed up the market sentiment this way: "insiders feel they've got a company that's trading well off its high where the

---

5. Herb Greenberg, "Will Pre-Paid Keep Growing? A Company's HMO-Style Approach to Legal Services Has Won It Plenty of Fans—And a Soaring Price. But Shortsellers Say The Numbers Don't Add Up," Fortune, November 24, 1997.

6. Quicken.com, Insider Trading in Pre-Paid Legal Services.

7. "Uncovered Short Positions Rise on Big Board and Amex," The New York Times, June 22, 1999.

operating fundamentals are going gangbusters. But the shorts have caught on the notion that from a cash flow standpoint, the company just can't handle the growth, and that their business model itself will come back to haunt them."[8]

QUESTIONS

1. How does PPLS create value for its customers? What are the critical risks that it has to manage well?

2. How did the pre-1995 commission formula work? Why do you think the company changed its policy?

3. Based on the post-1995 commission formula and information in the case on pricing and commission rates, calculate the cash inflows for premiums and cash outflows for commissions for years 1 to 3 that would arise from the sign-up of 1000 new members at the beginning of year 1. Assume that (a) actual member renewal rates are 75 percent for both years 2 and 3 and (b) 25 percent of recoverable commission advances in each of years 2 and 3 prove uncollectable.

4. How does Pre-Paid Legal account for the transactions described in question 3?

5. Do you agree with *Fortune's* criticism of PPLS's method of reporting for commissions? Why or why not?

6. What actions could PPLS's management take to reduce the unease among key investors about the firm's accounting and its business model?

EXHIBIT 1

Number of subscribers to legal service plans in the US in the period 1981 to 1997

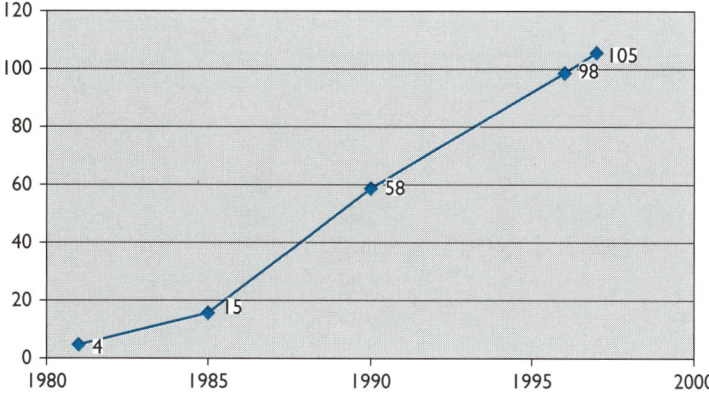

Source: Prepaid Legal Annual Report, 1998.

The above estimates were developed by The National Resources Center for Consumer LegaServices (NRC) and reported by PPLS in its 1998 10-K Report. NRC estimates included free member plans sponsored by

8. Ian Mount, "The Long and Short of It," SmartMoney.com, May 25, 1999.

labor unions, the American Association for Retired Persons, the National Education Association and military services, as well as employer-paid plans. PPLS estimated that 10% of the total legal insurance market was covered by plans comparable to those provided by PPLS. The other major companies servicing this market were Hyatt Legal Services, ARAG Group, LawPhone, National Legal Plan, and the Signature Group. The NRC estimated that in 1997 the market share of these firms (and PPLS) was 79%. The market share of PPLS alone was estimated at 15%.

EXHIBIT 2

Stock Performance for Pre-Paid Legal Services Inc. versus Dow Jones Industrial Average in the period August 1997 to July 1999.

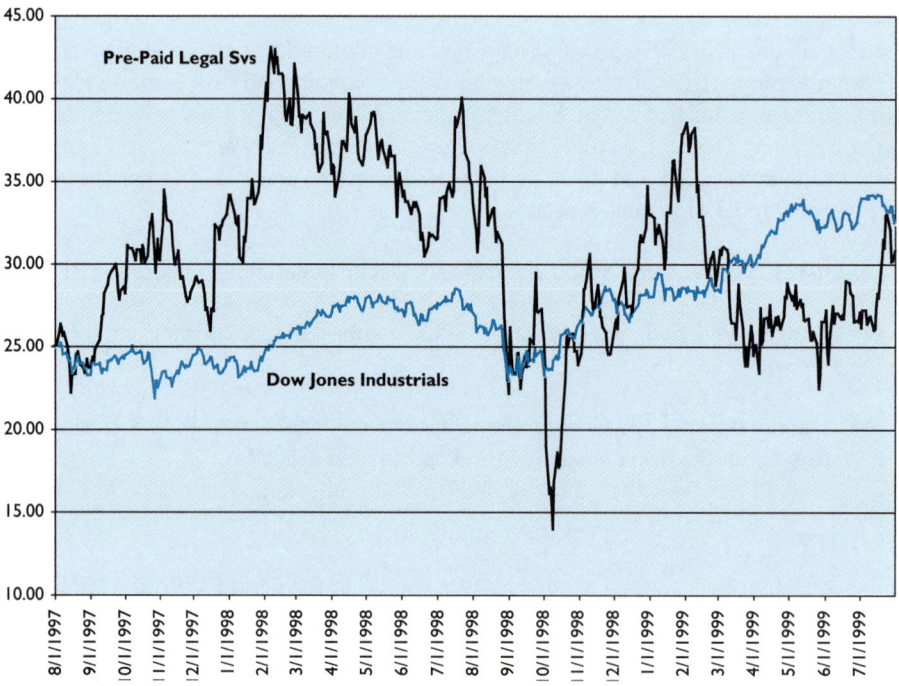

Source: Datastream International.

EXHIBIT 3
Summary of Commission Rates and Timing of Payment for PPLS

Plan	First Year Commission	Subsequent Year Commissions
Pre-1995		
Commission rate	70% of subscription	16% of subscription
Timing of payment	At customer sign-up	Monthly
1995		
Commission rate	25% of subscription	25% of subscription
Timing of payment	Advance of three years worth of commissions at customer sign-up	None for first three years, then monthly

EXHIBIT 4
Summary Financial Information for Pre-Paid Legal Services (for year ended December 31)

(in $000)	1998	1997	1996	1995
Membership revenues	$110,003	$76,688	$50,582	$31,290
Net Income	30,210	18,790	12,470	7,312
Cash from operations	$9,895	$7,733	$942	$548
Total assets	$167,903	$91,912	$57,532	$35,629
Book value of equity	101,304	70,511	45,474	29,740
New Memberships sold	391,827	283,723	194,483	109,922
Period end Memberships in force	603,017	425,381	294,151	203,535
Commission advances – current	$21,224	$15,705	$9,108	$3,923
Noncurrent commission advances, net	60,661	38,038	21,744	8,548

Source: Annual Reports, 1995–98.

EXHIBIT 5

Financial Statements and Selected Footnotes for Pre-Paid Legal Services, December 31, 1998

BALANCE SHEET

(In Thousands of Dollars)	December 31, 1998	December 31, 1997
ASSETS		
Current assets:		
Cash and cash equivalents	$8,604	$27,722
Available-for-sale investments, at fair value	2,368	0
Held-to-maturity investments	0	4,242
Accrued Membership income	3,595	2,399
Inventories	2,588	2,116
Prepaid product commissions	1,384	2,136
Amount due from coinsurer	12,498	0
Membership commission advances – current portion	21,224	15,705
Total current assets	52,261	54,320
Available-for-sale investments, at fair value	36,207	0
Held-to-maturity investments	0	650
Investments pledged	2,922	2,772
Membership commission advances, net	60,661	38,038
Property and equipment, net	7,678	5,226
Production costs, net	1,373	1,008
Other	6,801	3,702
Total assets	$167,903	$105,716
LIABILITIES AND STOCKHOLDERS' EQUITY		
Current liabilities:		
Membership benefits	$3,808	$2,649
Deferred product sales revenue	3,932	4,737
Accident and health reserves	12,498	0
Life insurance reserves	970	0
Current portion of capital lease obligation	487	142
Accounts payable and accrued expenses	9,386	12,009
Total current liabilities	31,081	19,537
Deferred income taxes	27,148	16,471
Life insurance reserves	7,711	0
Capital lease obligation, net of current portion	659	238
Total liabilities	66,599	36,246
Stockholders' equity:		
Preferred stock, $1 par value; authorized 400 shares; 3 issued and outstanding as follows: $3.00 Cumulative Convertible Preferred Stock, 3 shares authorized, issued and outstanding at December 31, 1998 and 1997, respectively; liquidation value of $55.00 at December 31, 1998	3	3
Special preferred stock, $1 par value; authorized 500 shares, issued and outstanding in one series designated as follows: $1.00 Non-Cumulative Special Preferred Stock, 18 and 23 shares authorized, issued and outstanding at December 31, 1998 and 1997, respectively; liquidation value of $240 and $304 at December 31, 1998 and 1997, respectively	18	23

(continued)

BALANCE SHEET (*continued*)

(In Thousands of Dollars)	December 31, 1998	December 31, 1997
Common stock, $.01 par value; 100,000 shares authorized; 24,321 and 24,151 issued at December 31, 1998 and 1997, respectively	243	242
Capital in excess of par value	55,241	52,051
Retained earnings	49,528	19,328
Accumulated other comprehensive income:		
Unrealized gains (losses) on investments	(24)	0
Less: Treasury stock at cost; 797 and 747 shares held at December 31, 1998 and 1997, respectively	(3,705)	(2,177)
Total stockholders' equity	101,304	69,470
Total liabilities and stockholders' equity	167,903	105,716

Source: This data was extracted from Pre-Paid Legal Services Inc.'s 10-K Statement and downloaded from the SEC's EDGAR database using PricewaterhouseCoopers Global Technology Centre Edgarscan. Please read the on-line disclaimer at http://edgarscan.pwcglobal.com/EdgarScan/edgarscan_disclaimer.html.

INCOME STATEMENT

(In Thousands of Dollars except for per share measures)	December 31, 1998	December 31, 1997	December 31, 1996
Revenues:			
Membership premiums	$110,003	$76,688	$50,582
Product sales	27,779	41,070	26,425
Associate services	17,255	12,143	5,646
Interest income	2,576	1,689	1,303
Other	2,840	1,814	1,678
	160,453	133,404	85,634
Costs and expenses:			
Membership benefits	36,103	25,132	16,871
Product costs	17,967	27,017	20,568
Commissions	24,261	16,717	11,476
General and administrative	21,902	20,311	15,150
Associate services and direct marketing	14,738	11,431	4,544
Depreciation	2,944	2,026	533
Premium taxes	1,206	866	372
	119,121	103,500	69,514
Income before income taxes	41,332	29,904	16,120
Provision for income taxes	11,122	12,381	5,857
Net income	30,210	17,523	10,263
Less dividends on preferred shares	10	13	15
Net income applicable to common stockholders.	$30,200	17,510	10,248
Basic earnings per common share	$1.29	$0.76	$0.46
Diluted earnings per common share	$1.26	$0.74	$0.44
Comprehensive Income			
Net income	$30,210	$17,523	$10,263
Other comprehensive income (loss):			
Unrealized gains (losses) on investments:			
Unrealized holding gains (losses) arising			
during period	(24)	0	0
Other comprehensive income	(24)	0	0
Comprehensive income	$30,186	$17,523	$10,263

CASH FLOW STATEMENT

(In Thousands of Dollars)	December 31, 1998	December 31, 1997	December 31, 1996
Cash flows from operating activities:			
Net income	$30,210	$17,523	$10,263
Adjustments to reconcile net income to net cash provided by operating activities:			
Provision for stock grant, stock transfer and associate stock			
Options	0	644	1,122
Provision for deferred income taxes	11,122	12,293	5,857
Depreciation and amortization	2,944	2,026	533
Net changes in asset and liability accounts, net of effects of purchase of UFL:			
Increase in accrued Membership income	(1,196)	(689)	(672)
Increase in commission advances	(28,142)	(22,891)	(18,381)
Increase in other assets	(304)	(678)	(1,360)
Increase in inventories	(472)	(489)	(1,270)
Decrease (increase) in prepaid product commissions	752	(513)	(622)
(Decrease) increase in deferred revenue	(805)	771	1,390
Increase in Membership benefits	1,159	787	315
(Decrease) increase in accounts payable and accrued expenses	(5,373)	5,688	1,914
Net cash provided by (used in) operating activities	9,895	14,472	(911)
Cash flows from investing activities:			
Acquisition of UFL, net of cash acquired	(18,995)	0	0
Additions to property and equipment and production costs	(4,926)	(3,619)	(1,592)
Purchases of held-to-maturity investments	(36,116)	(3,035)	(1,374)
Proceeds from sales of held-to-maturity investments	23,718	0	0
Maturities of held-to-maturity investments	4,892	400	111,000
Net cash used in investing activities	(31,427)	(6,254)	(2,855)
Cash flows from financing activities:			
Proceeds from sale of common and preferred stock	3,186	3,229	4,904
Increase in capital lease obligations	766	248	84
Purchase of treasury stock	(1,528)	0	0
Dividends paid on preferred stock	(10)	(13)	(15)
Net cash provided by financing activities	2,414	3,464	4,973
Net (decrease) increase in cash and cash equivalents	(19,118)	11,682	1,207
Cash and cash equivalents at beginning of year	27,722	16,040	14,833
Cash and cash equivalents at end of year	$8,604	$27,722	$16,040

(continued)

CASH FLOW STATEMENT (*continued*)

(In Thousands of Dollars)	December 31, 1998	December 31, 1997	December 31, 1996
Supplemental disclosure of cash flow information:			
Cash paid for interest	47	36	28
Purchases of property and equipment under capital leases	1,104	445	63
Assets acquired in acquisition of UFL	44,598		
Liabilities assumed in acquisition of UFL	23,929		

Source: This data was extracted from Pre-Paid Legal Services Inc.'s 10-K Statement and downloaded from the SEC's EDGAR database using PricewaterhouseCoopers Global Technology Centre Edgarscan. Please read the on-line disclaimer at http://edgarscan.pwcglobal.com/EdgarScan/edgarscan_disclaimer.html.

SELECTED FOOTNOTE INFORMATION

Note 1 – Nature of Operations and Summary of Significant Accounting Policies

Estimates

The preparation of financial statements in conformity with generally accepted accounting principles requires management to make estimates and assumptions that affect the reported amounts of assets and liabilities and disclosure of contingent assets and liabilities at the date of the financial statements and the reported amounts of revenues and expenses during the reporting period. Actual results could differ from those estimates.

Commissions

Effective March 1, 1995, the Company implemented a level membership commission schedule of approximately 25% of annual premium revenue for all Membership years. This commission schedule results in the Company incurring commission expense related to the sale of its legal expense plans on a basis consistent with the collection of the premiums generated by the sale of such Memberships. The Company currently advances the equivalent of three years of commissions on new Membership sales. In January 1997, the Company implemented a new policy whereby associates receive only earned commissions on the first three Memberships submitted unless the associate successfully completes a training program which includes an intensive one-day training seminar, produces three Memberships and recruits one associate within 15 business days from their training date. Prior to March 1, 1995, first year commissions payable on the sale of a Membership, and earned in the first Membership year, were approximately 70% of annual Membership premiums while renewal commissions (payable as earned after the first Membership year) were approximately 16% of annual premiums.

Revenue Recognition

Membership premiums are recognized in income when due in accordance with Membership terms which generally require the holder of the Membership to remit premiums on a monthly basis. Memberships are canceled for nonpayment of premium after ninety days. Premiums due but not collected at the end of an accounting period are recorded as accrued Membership income; a provision for uncollectible premiums, if any, is recorded currently. Revenues from Associates' training program fees and sales of marketing supplies are recognized as income when cash is received. Revenues for product sales are recognized when products are shipped or services provided.

Commission Advances

Commission advances represent the unearned portion of commissions advanced to Associates on sales of Memberships. Commissions are earned as premiums are collected, usually on a monthly basis. The Company reduces Commission advances as premiums are paid and commissions earned. Unearned commission advances on lapsed Memberships are recovered through collection of premiums on an associate's active Memberships. At December 31, 1998 and 1997, the Company had an allowance of $4.0 million and $3.7 million, respectively, to provide for estimated uncollectible balances. The Company charges interest at the prime rate on unearned commission advances relating to Memberships that canceled subsequent to the advance being made.

Membership Benefit Liability

The Membership benefit liability represents claims reported but not paid and actuarially estimated claims incurred but not reported on open panel Memberships and per capita amounts due provider attorneys on closed panel Memberships. The Company calculates the benefit liability costs on open panel Memberships based on completion factors that consider historical claims experience based on the dates that claims are incurred, reported to the Company and subsequently paid. Processing costs related to these claims are accrued based on an estimate of expenses to process such claims.

Life Insurance Reserves

Incurred but not reported claim estimates are actuarially estimated based on life insurance in-force and estimated claims occurrences.

Source: This data was extracted from Pre-Paid Legal Services Inc.'s 10-K Statement and downloaded from the SEC's EDGAR database using PricewaterhouseCoopers Global Technology Centre Edgarscan. Please read the on-line disclaimer at http://edgarscan.pwcglobal.com/EdgarScan/edgarscan_disclaimer.html.

EXHIBIT 6

Management Discussion of Commissions and Membership Persistency, excerpted from Management's Discussion and Analysis of Financial Condition and Results, Pre-Paid Legal Services 10-K, December 31, 1998.

Commissions

Beginning with new Memberships written after March 1, 1995, the Company implemented a level commission schedule which results in the Company incurring commission expense related to the sale of its legal expense plans on a basis more consistent with the collection of the premiums generated by the sale of such Memberships. Prior to March 1, 1995, the Company had incurred much higher commissions (approximately 70%) during the first year of the Membership with substantially lower commissions (approximately 16%) in all subsequent years. The level commission structure results in the Company incurring commissions at the rate of approximately 25% per year for all Membership years.

Prior to January 1997 the Company advanced commissions at the time of sale of all new Memberships. In January 1997, the Company implemented a policy whereby the associate receives only earned commissions on the first three sales unless the associate has successfully completed the new training program that was implemented at the same time. For all sales beginning with the fourth Membership or all sales made by an associate successfully completing the new training program, the Company currently advances commissions at the time of sale of a new Membership. The amount of cash potentially advanced upon the sale of a new Membership, prior to the recoupment of any charge-backs (described below), represents an amount equal to up to three years commission earnings. Although the average number of marketing associates receiving an advance commission payment on a new Membership is 11, the overall initial advance may be paid to more than twenty different individuals, each at a different level within the overall commission structure. This commission advance immediately increases an associate's account with the Company and represents prepaid commissions on active Memberships.

Should a Membership lapse before the advances have been recovered for each commission level, the Company immediately generates a "charge-back" to the applicable sales associate to recapture 50% of any unearned advance. This charge-back is immediately deducted from any future advances that would otherwise be payable to the associate for additional new Memberships. The Company historically has been able to immediately recover the majority of such charge-backs. Any remaining unrecovered advance on a Membership that has lapsed represents a receivable from the associate and is reflected as commission advances and is categorized as current or non-current based on the expected recovery period. Additionally, even though a commission advance may have been fully recovered on a particular Membership, no additional commission earnings from any Membership will be paid to an associate until all previous advances on all Memberships, both active and lapsed, have been recovered. During 1998, 22% of all associates submitting new Memberships accounted for 75% of all such new Memberships produced thereby further enhancing the recovery of commission advances.

The Company's commission advance policy exposes the Company to the risk of uncollectible commission advances particularly for associates who do not receive commissions on a large number of Memberships or who experience below average Membership persistency. The Company closely monitors such commission advances to ensure maximum recoverability and maintains a recoverability reserve which at December 31, 1998 and 1997, was $4.0 million and $3.7 million, respectively.

Associates also receive compensation when associates sponsored by them or other associates that they have sponsored in their organization successfully complete the new training program implemented by the Company on January 4, 1997. In order to successfully qualify, the new associate going through the training program must produce 3 new Memberships and recruit 1 new associate within 15 days of receiving the training.

Membership Persistency

One of the major factors affecting the Company's profitability and cash flow is Membership persistency, which represents the ability of the Company to retain a Membership, and therefore receive premiums,

Pre-Paid Legal Services, Inc.

once it has been written. The Company monitors its overall Membership persistency rate, as well as the persistency rates with respect to Memberships sold by individual associates and agents and persistency rates with respect to Membership sales by geographic region and payment method. The Company's Membership persistency rate measures the number of Memberships in force at the end of a year as a percentage of the total of (i) Memberships in force at the beginning of such year, plus (ii) new Memberships sold during such year. From 1981 through the year ended December 31,1998, the Company's annual Membership persistency rates, using the foregoing method, have averaged approximately 75%. The annual Membership persistency rates were 73.8%, 73.6%, and 73.9% for 1998, 1997, and 1996, respectively. The Company's overall Membership persistency rate varies based on, among other factors, the relative age of total Memberships in force. The Company's overall Membership persistency rate could be lower when the Memberships in force include a higher proportion of newer Memberships. During the last three years, the Company has experienced significant increases in new Membership sales and, as a result, the percentage of newer Memberships in its total Memberships in force has increased. Unless offset by other factors, this increase could result in a decline in the Company's overall Membership persistency rate as determined by the formula described above, but does not necessarily indicate that the new Memberships written are less persistent, only that the ratio of new Memberships to total Memberships is higher than it averaged during the 1981 through 1998 period. The Company's financial condition and results of operations may be materially adversely affected if the persistency rates of existing and new Memberships are materially lower than the Company's historical experience.

Source: This data was extracted from Pre-Paid Legal Services Inc.'s 10-K Statement and downloaded from the SEC's EDGAR database using PricewaterhouseCoopers Global Technology Centre Edgarscan. Please read the on-line disclaimer at http://edgarscan.pwcglobal.com/EdgarScan/edgarscan_disclaimer.html.

Prudential Securities

In December 2000, after nearly 20 years as a full-service investment bank, Prudential Securities announced that it would exit the investment banking business and focus exclusively on providing brokerage services to its institutional and retail clients. John Strangfeld, head of the investments division of Prudential Financial, which included Prudential Securities, explained the decision as follows:

Our firm had been a survivor for many years but had never really been a winner. We had a strategy that looked like everyone else's, trying to serve both the issuer and the investor, and we had experienced very erratic results. We were faced with three options: carry on with the existing strategy of looking like a smaller-scale version of everyone else, choose a different path, or divest. Our decision was to choose a different path that played to our strengths, and that resulted in a sustainable, differentiated strategy that was better aligned with the needs and aspirations of Prudential Financial. In essence, we decided to cast our lot entirely with the investor. This change eliminated many of the conflicts of interest that you normally see when firms try to serve both the issuer and the investor. It meant we could tell our clients and our employees that Prudential Financial stands for one thing: the investor. All of our energy and resources, as well as every ounce of capital, would be devoted to the investor.

Prudential's decision to change direction raised a number of important questions about both its new and former strategies. Why had the company found it so difficult to build prestige in the investment banking industry? Had the initial decision to enter the industry been flawed? Or, had it simply failed to execute on the strategy? Looking ahead, would the new strategy be effective in creating value? If so, what challenges would the company face in its implementation, and how should it manage those challenges?

INVESTMENT BANKING INDUSTRY

Investment banks serve as intermediaries between issuers (buyers of capital) and investors (providers of capital) by matching issuers and investors, providing advice on a fair price for the transaction, and committing to create a liquid market in the new

Professors Boris Groysberg and Paul Healy and Doctoral Candidate Amanda Cowen prepared this case. HBS cases are developed solely as the basis for class discussion. Cases are not intended to serve as endorsements, sources of primary data, or illustrations of effective or ineffective management.

security following the issue. "Full-service" investment banks offer clients a wide range of services including:

- **Corporate finance:** Banks regularly assist corporations and governments in raising capital through the public or private sale of financial securities (debt or equity). In a private placement, the investment bank's primary role is to locate suitable investors and to negotiate the terms of the financing. In a public offering, the investment bank may also be responsible for underwriting the offering. The bank commits to purchase the securities from the client at a predetermined price and resells them to investors, reducing price uncertainty for the issuer. In return, the investment bank generates a spread between the issue price and the resale price and receives banking fees for its involvement in the issue. Often an investment bank will not buy an entire offering but will coordinate a group of firms, called an underwriting syndicate, to participate in the purchase and distribution of the new securities. The lead manager (the bank that organized the syndicate) and the comanagers (the other firms that assume a large portion of the underwriting risk) receive the dominant share of the banking fees from a new issue (see **Exhibit 1**).
- **Sales and trading (also known as brokerage):** Sales reps develop relationships with clients and provide them with investment advice. These services can lead clients to decide to buy or sell securities, generating commission revenues for the bank. Reps at large firms typically specialize in dealing with small individual (or retail) investors, institutional clients (e.g., pension funds, mutual funds, etc.), or wealthy individuals. Purchases and sales of securities on clients' behalf are executed by traders. Timely execution is clients' top priority along with the ability to handle large trades. Often a bank provides liquidity for investors by purchasing or selling a given security at publicly quoted prices. The bank profits from serving in this market-maker role by capturing the spread between the price at which they buy a security and the (higher) price at which they will sell it. Traders may also engage in proprietary trading, executing transactions on behalf of the firm itself, in hopes of profiting from predicted changes in securities prices.
- **Investment research:** Analysts in the research department are responsible for following particular companies and issuing periodic reports on them. These reports include the latest company and industry developments, along with forecasts of a company's earnings per share and stock price, and stock recommendations on whether to buy, hold, or sell a stock. Research reports are used by sales reps or by analysts themselves to provide investment advice to the firm's clients. Analyst reports are also used to create demand for investment banking deals. In the late 1990s analysts at some banks contributed actively to investment banking business by spotting up-and-coming companies that needed capital and by appearing at road shows to market new offerings. Unlike the other key functions at investment banks, research departments do not generate any direct revenues—they are cost centers that support and are funded by other departments in the bank.
- **Mergers and acquisitions advisory:** Professionals in the mergers and acquisitions group advise clients on the purchase or sale of assets or entire companies. In return for these advisory services, the banks receive fees, typically a percentage of the transaction size, if the merger is consummated.
- **Asset management:** Banks also offer clients a range of investment products, such as mutual funds. Portfolio managers oversee the funds and decide how investor capital will be used. Investment managers assist clients in deciding which funds and other financial products best meet their goals. The firm receives fees for these services that are a fixed percentage of assets under management.

The largest investment banks provide all of these services to their clients. However, many firms only offer a subset. For example, The Blackstone Group primarily focuses on M&A advisory business, Sanford C. Bernstein provides investment research and sales and trading services but does not underwrite securities, and Red Chip Review only provides research services.

INVESTMENT BANKING AT PRUDENTIAL INSURANCE COMPANY

Prudential Insurance Company was founded by John Dryden in 1875 to provide life insurance to working class families. The company was named after the Prudential Assurance Company of Great Britain, a pioneer in industrial insurance on the other side of the Atlantic. The company quickly developed a reputation for financial stability, inspiring its well-recognized symbol—"The Rock."

During the 1970s, Donald MacNaughton, Prudential's CEO, encouraged employees to think of Prudential's business as selling, not just providing, insurance. This approach led Prudential to expand into auto and homeowners insurance. MacNaughton believed that Prudential's continued prosperity could only be assured if it leveraged its selling capabilities and found new ways to serve policyholders.[1] Insurance was certainly one component of a customer's financial needs, but there were many others. MacNaughton and his successors worried that, unless Prudential could broaden its product offerings, other financial services firms could capture a portion of its customer base by offering a broad array of financial services through a single distribution network.

The Acquisition of the Bache Group Inc.

In early 1981, the Bache Group was looking for help. For two years, management had been trying to fend off a hostile takeover attempt by First City Financial, a Canadian financial services company owned by the Belzberg family. The family had acquired over 20% of the company despite defensive maneuvers by Bache management, and most insiders considered the takeover virtually inevitable.[2] However, Bache's CEO, Harry Jacobs, had one last plan—in February 1981 he launched a search for another potential acquirer.

Garnett Keith, a senior vice president, was the first person at Prudential to be contacted about the acquisition: "I received a phone call from Bob Baylis at First Boston, and he asked me if Prudential would like to acquire Bache. And I said well, not likely, but let me talk to the chairman. So I went and talked to Bob Beck, and he thought about it and was quite enthusiastic."

At the time, Bache was primarily a retail brokerage firm, although not a very prestigious one. An analyst recruited to the firm recalled his first weeks on the job:

> Bache was headquartered at 100 Gold Street, which was one of the seediest, most disgusting buildings in Manhattan. The furniture looked awful, and the orange carpeting was worn down to its last few threads. It was not a place to which you'd want to bring anyone you were trying to impress. Bache had a poor reputation among institutional investors, and it had no investment banking that

---

1. *The Prudential Insurance Company,* The Power of a Story *(New York: Harcourt Inc., 2001), pp. 49–51.*

2. *"Prudential Offers $385 Million for Bache,"* Dow Jones Newswires, *March 19, 1981, available from Factiva, www.factiva.com.*

anyone could see. It did have a large retail sales force, but it often seemed in bad spirits, was not terribly successful, and was not well respected. During my first few months at Bache I recall moments when I found myself staring at my rotary-dial telephone and feeling as if I was back in the nineteenth century.

Despite Bache's marginal position in the industry, Beck saw the acquisition as a way to jump-start Prudential's "financial supermarket" strategy. The goal was to turn Prudential into a one-stop shop for all of a customer's financial service needs. Beck understood that the quality of Bache's products (especially its equity research) would have to be improved, but he also envisioned a day when insurance agents would sell mutual funds and brokers would sell life insurance. Keith explained why Beck was so confident that Prudential could effectively harness these synergies:

Bob Beck was a consummate marketing executive. He had run Prudential's agency organization and was very confident in his ability to manage people selling product on commission. What he saw in Bache was another commission-driven sales organization that additional products could be put through. At the time, Bache clearly had mediocre products and therefore was not able to attract and hold top talent. Beck felt that Prudential could upgrade Bache's product and then could attract and hold a better-quality financial advisor, which is what really drives business.

Others, like Fred Fraenkel, a former research director at the firm, were more skeptical and harbored doubts as to whether Prudential understood the complexities of the financial services industry:

Prudential was a really large mutual insurance company that had tens of millions of lives insured. It was based in Newark and run by insurance company executives whose motto was "perpetual and invulnerable." That had little to do with returns or profitability or cost or policyholders. "You give me money, you're going to die, I'm going to pay your policy face amount." What assures that? That we're perpetual and invulnerable. So they had a view of the world that didn't really have anything to do with what went on in the rest of the financial services continuum.

In March 1981, Prudential Insurance Company of America offered $385 million to acquire Bache Group Inc. The deal was consummated the following year. Although Bache had a small investment banking operation, there were no plans to grow that business. Keith explained why:

The investment side of the Prudential organization was quite concerned that if we owned something that had even a fledgling investment banking operation, it was going to foul up our relationships with the bulge-bracket investment banks that were necessary to keep our cash flow invested. Through the whole acquisition process, less was more. Less investment banking made it more attractive to Prudential. The last thing we wanted was investment banking activity over at Bache that could potentially ruin a much more important cash investment process at Prudential, the parent. Investment banking was a concern, not an attraction.

New Management at Bache

Shortly after the acquisition, Prudential began looking for someone to lead the new concern, now called Prudential-Bache Securities, or Pru-Bache for short. In 1983,

George Ball was hired. At the time, Ball was second-in-command at E.F. Hutton, a highly successful retail brokerage firm. Fraenkel described him as an exceptional motivator:

> *He was the son of the superintendent of schools of Milburn, New Jersey, a speed reader, a very high-IQ person, a very dynamic person, who had spent his career in a meteoric rise through E.F. Hutton on the retail side of the firm. The thing he was unbelievably good at was personnel management. E.F. Hutton was like Bache, it had several thousand brokers, and he knew every broker's name, and he knew every broker's wife's name, and he knew every kid of every broker and what school they were at. George was a memory-system person; he had "mental compartments" where he could literally memorize thousands of items and recall them instantly. He would ask people personal questions and everyone felt they were his best friend. He was probably one of the best cheerleader-managers that I've ever been around.*

Ball's first priority was to develop the institutional side of the business—to build a research department and a sales and trading organization that could service large institutional investors. He believed these important capabilities could then be leveraged to develop other businesses. To lead the effort he looked to his former colleagues. Mike Shea, currently president of Prudential's equity group, remembered:

> *The first big move was the joining of Greg Smith, Fred Fraenkel, and Ed Yardeni from E.F. Hutton. They came in as the strategy trio. And their mission was to begin the formation of a true institutional business. A lot of institutional sales-people followed from E.F. Hutton and a couple of other places to Pru in the early '80s because they wanted to be involved in the business with them. So that was really the very beginning; that was the genesis.*

The "strategy trio" had some success in accomplishing their goals. Pru-Bache began to service institutional clients and started to leverage their new capabilities to better service retail clients as well. Soon the focus turned to investment banking.

Project '89: The Genesis of Investment Banking

Bache had always had a small investment banking operation. In the years immediately following the merger, little was done to improve this business because of the potential impact on the Prudential Insurance Company's Wall Street relationships. Insurance companies have huge cash reserves (because premiums are paid in advance of policy benefits), and Prudential relied on the large investment banks to profitably invest its cash. The decision to expand Pru-Bache's investment banking business was approved by Prudential's chairman, Beck; however, where the idea originated was less clear. Ball recalled that it was Keith who originally wanted to use Pru-Bache to "internalize some of the investment banking fees that were being paid to the bulge-bracket firms." Keith remembered things differently:

> *The idea to build investment banking definitely came from George Ball. He pitched to Bob Beck that we simply had to have better product, product that was more lucrative because we were both the distributor and the originator, the investment banker. He argued that we needed that extra revenue to share with our financial advisors in order to attract the better financial advisors that we wanted to hire.*

What is certain is that in 1987 Ball officially launched Project '89. Project '89 was seen by many as Pru-Bache's attempt to achieve bulge-bracket status by 1989.[3] The amount of money invested in the project (close to $200 million) and the rhetoric used to attract new professionals certainly suggested that was the aim.[4] However, not everyone agreed that this was the stated goal. Keith, who was present at the executive committee meetings during this time, recalled Beck's signing off on a very different project:

> *George convinced Bob Beck that he should be allowed to build a better investment banking organization. And what he sold Bob Beck was to be the "best of the rest"—that he knew he'd get his head kicked in if he took on Goldman Sachs, Morgan Stanley, and First Boston, but he needed to be at least as good as PaineWebber. So the franchise and the funding George got from the Prudential board with Bob Beck's blessing was to upgrade Bache's investment banking activity to equal the "best of the rest."*

Prior to Project '89, Pru-Bache's investment banking business ranked well behind those of the bulge firms. Furthermore, the current investment banking professionals were not terribly impressive. Therefore, from the outset it was decided that a serious effort to develop investment banking would require new blood. As *Investment Dealer's Digest* put it, ultimately "Project '89 was about hiring, and about spending top dollar to do so."[5] Pru-Bache hired aggressively in all of its divisions; 30 senior investment bankers were hired in the first five months of the project. These professionals were brought in to develop the firm's relationships with *Fortune* 500 companies in hopes that associations with big companies would translate into large fees and increased visibility.[6]

Most of Pru-Bache's new hires were recruited from elite firms, since those were the firms it hoped to compete against. The compensation packages offered during Project '89 became legendary. Not only were the salaries and bonuses higher than those paid by many bulge firms, but they were usually guaranteed—not tied to individual or firm performance.[7] A research analyst at a bulge-bracket firm, approached by the firm during Project '89, commented on Prudential's recruiting efforts:

> *Honestly, they didn't have a lot to offer me. Pru-Bache was a firm with a terrible reputation. It had an investment bank that was in the building stage but had no real presence and no track record. So what they had to offer was, essentially, money. From my perspective, this simply wasn't a big enough incentive to move. At that time, I was an Institutional Investor-ranked analyst. The research director at my firm did not want to lose me. When he heard about Prudential's offer, he matched it and I stayed put.*

---

3. "Bulge-bracket" firms were the largest and most prestigious investment banks in the industry. The original members of the bulge were Morgan Stanley; First Boston; Kuhn, Loeb & Co.; and Dillon, Read & Co. During the 1970s, Salomon Brothers and Goldman Sachs entered the elite underwriting bracket, while Dillion, Read's market share slipped, eventually pushing it out of the bulge. Kuhn, Loeb & Co. also appeared to be in trouble, until 1978, when it merged with Lehman Brothers. By the early 1980s, Merrill Lynch had climbed into the bulge several years after its acquisition of White Weld, an investment bank. However, many attributed Merrill's success to the fact that it had built its investment banking business around its strong retail distribution network, which gave the firm an edge in issuing securities for clients.

4. Jessica Sommar, "Rock Slide," Investment Dealer's Digest, April 1, 1991, pp. 20–27.

5. Ibid., p. 21.

6. Ibid., p. 22.

7. Ibid., p. 22.

At first, Project '89 appeared to yield positive results (see **Exhibit 2**). Prudential-Bache represented Rupert Murdoch in his bid for the *Herald & Weekly* in Australia. It also completed the Reliance Electric Company management buyout, quite possibly the largest leveraged buyout divestiture ever done at the time. The research department began to move up in the *Institutional Investor* rankings (see **Exhibit 3**). Many of Pru-Bache's divisions posted profits.

The '87 Crash and the Demise of Project '89

On October 19, 1987, the stock market plummeted more than 500 points, losing over 20% of its value in a single day. The crash had a serious impact on all banks, but the fledgling Pru-Bache was especially hard hit. Investment banking deals disappeared. Retail commissions also dried up due to falling investor confidence. The following year, Prudential Insurance cut funding for Project '89. Recruiting activities stopped, and over 25% of Pru-Bache's banking professionals were let go. In 1988, there was a bright spot when the firm completed the Diamandis management buyout of the CBS magazine division. Unfortunately, the market correction of 1989 followed soon after. Pru-Bache posted losses of $50 million in 1989 and $250 million in 1990.[8] In early 1991, George Ball resigned.

As with everything regarding Project '89, there was some controversy over just what caused its failure. Clearly the stock market crashes were part of the reason—revenues dried up while Pru-Bache's compensation commitments were fixed. However, others maintained that it was Prudential Insurance Company that effectively killed the project by reneging on its financial commitment before all the necessary personnel were in place.[9] In fact, many have noted instances in which Prudential failed to support Pru-Bache. Although the insurance company did a great deal of investing, it directed very little of its business to Pru-Bache, preferring instead to deal with the bulge firms. Prudential also limited the types of deals that Pru-Bache could pursue. For example, the firm was not allowed to participate in hostile takeovers, which it defined as "if the target company said 'no' at any time during negotiations." This was problematic given that, according to one banker, "target companies routinely said 'no' the first time out as a standard negotiating tactic."[10] Ball commented on Pru-Bache's relationship with its parent:

> *Prudential was very helpful in terms of providing the appearance of more than adequate capital for any transaction. It was not helpful in terms of cross-marketing or relationship sharing. There were a good deal of restrictions placed upon the investment bank that made it almost impossible for any of the expected synergies to be achieved. In point of fact, I think that people at Prudential went out of their way to drive business outside of the Prudential family, rather than saying that "if you've got equal competence and there are no apparent conflicts, let at least part of the business be done inside." Some people at Prudential Insurance Company would relatively subtly, but nonetheless overtly, give companies a signal that they might be better off using Goldman Sachs or Morgan Stanley than Prudential Securities.*

---

8. *Ibid., pp. 21–24.*

9. *Ibid., p. 24.*

10. *Ibid., p. 25.*

Others involved in Project '89 believed that it was doomed from the start. They argued that the decision to recruit professionals from the bulge-bracket firms was fundamentally flawed, because clients ultimately cared about the reputation and track record of the firm, not the banker (see **Exhibit 4**). Even Ball believed there was some validity to this argument:

> We hired three people to build up the investment banking business in the mid-'80s quite rapidly, hiring people who were managing directors and had very good records at bulge-bracket firms thinking that they could transfer at least some part of their relationship business to Pru-Bache, and that turned out to be a relatively fallacious assumption. The franchise of a Goldman Sachs or a Morgan Stanley is what made these people outstanding investment banking producers, and torn away from that franchise they could carry relatively little of their business with them. That was my fault for misassessing that, or at least letting people move as quickly as they did without testing the premise better.

Keith agreed: "Franchise matters a huge amount in investment banking. The same investment banker may generate a billion dollars in revenue at Goldman Sachs and generate $400 million a year at Prudential-Bache. So you can't afford to match the Goldman Sachs compensation package because he isn't going to generate the revenues to let you pay him."

A comment by Steve Balog, a former Pru-Bache research analyst, also suggested that the timeline for Project '89 was simply too aggressive:

> In order to successfully build an investment bank, you've got to say: "This is a 30-year plan. And you know what? All of us that are sitting around here talking about it today, we're all going to be gone. We're going to be gone halfway through, but this is the plan. We're going to establish this institution as a premiere player in the industry, but it's going to be beyond us. So if any of us are thinking we're going to be a hero in doing this—forget it! It takes too long—longer than many of us have the tolerance, or patience, or even years left for."

Wick Simmons's Tenure at Prudential Securities

Following Ball's departure, Hardwick "Wick" Simmons was hired as CEO of the recently renamed Prudential Securities. Simmons was a descendant of one of America's oldest banking families. He joined the firm from Shearson, where he was one of the most likable top executives. In fact, many believed that Simmons was selected for the Prudential job precisely because of his affable personality, optimism, and integrity.[11] These characteristics turned out to be quite important, since Simmons spent the first few years of his tenure dealing with the fallout from Project '89.

When Simmons arrived at Prudential, morale was low. Prudential Insurance had already fired nearly 75% of the investment banking staff and closed other businesses down altogether. Those that remained doubted that the firm could ever become a real player in the industry. There were rumors that Prudential Securities would be sold. One employee remembered: "Every morning we would all come in and open *The [Wall Street] Journal* and go to the index to see if Prudential was mentioned or not. We'd hold our breath and pray that it wasn't there. But very often it was and, with few exceptions, the news was bad."

11. Suzanna Andrews, "The Strange, Charmed Life of Wick Simmons," Institutional Investor, January 1, 1995, available from Factiva, www.factiva.com.

To make matters worse, Prudential Securities faced a barrage of lawsuits and regulatory inquiries over limited partnerships it had sold to clients in the late 1980s, which ultimately cost the firm $1.4 billion in fines and settlements.

Despite these problems, the firm's operations were profitable, and Simmons worked to rebuild its capabilities. He hired and trained professionals from outside the industry, rather than from the bulge firms, and emphasized client service and regulatory compliance. On the investment banking side, Prudential Securities stopped targeting *Fortune* 500 firms and instead pursued smaller clients in a limited number of industries.

By the late-1990s, the partnership scandal behind them, Prudential Securities began to have some success. In the first two months of 1996, the firm managed six equity issues that totaled over $400 million. By 1997, the firm was ranked 12th in initial public offering market share, and the investment banking division was expected to generate $150 million in revenues. The new strategy seemed to be working. Medium-sized companies, often overlooked by bulge-bracket firms, appreciated the attention and service they received from Prudential Securities. "With Prudential, you always feel like you're their No. 1 client," commented the president of an auto financing firm.[12] The firm was especially successful in the real estate and telecommunications industries and had plans to continue to develop its other focal industries: consumer goods, energy, specialty finance, health care, and technology. To further this strategy, in 1999, Prudential bought Vector Securities International, Inc., an investment bank that specialized in health care, and Volpe Brown Whelan & Co., a technology investment bank.

Some of Prudential's progress was attributable to the stock market boom of the late 1990s; it was common for second-tier investment banks to gain market share during this time. Nevertheless, Prudential Securities' leadership was hopeful that these gains could be leveraged in the future to help the firm establish a larger presence in the industry.

CHANGES IN THE INVESTMENT BANKING INDUSTRY

In the late 1990s, a number of important changes threatened to change the nature of competition and the way business was done in the investment banking industry. These included industry consolidation and increased concern about conflicts of interest between banking firms and investors.

Industry consolidation   Historically, commercial banks, banks that accept deposits and make loans, had been prohibited from engaging in investment banking activities. This legislation, called the Glass-Stegall Act, was passed in 1933 and was intended to protect depositors from bank collapses like those that preceded the Great Depression. This legislation was relaxed through the 1990s and was officially repealed in 1999. Large commercial banks, such as Citibank and Chase Manhattan, quickly entered the industry. These firms spent billions building investment banking operations internally, hiring bankers from their competitors, or acquiring small- to medium-sized investment banks. Citicorp acquired Salomon Smith Barney in a $140 billion merger with Travelers in 1998. It subsequently extended its global reach by acquiring County NatWest in Australia and London's Schroders and entering into a joint venture with Nikko Securities. In 2000, Chase & Co. merged with J.P. Morgan to create a $32 billion bank. Further

---

12. Jon Birger, "The Rock is on a Roll: Prudential Wins Back Investment Business," Crain's New York Business, October 27, 1997, available from Factiva, www.factiva.com.

consolidation in the late 1990s included commercial bank acquisitions of boutique firms that specialized in the technology sector: Bank of America (BAC) acquired Montgomery Securities, and Deutsche Bank bought Bankers Trust (including BT Alex. Brown).[13] Many argued the ability of these newly formed firms to also offer commercial financing could give them a competitive edge over traditional firms.[14]

Consolidation was also spurred on by increasing price competition. Customers gained power in the industry and were much more price sensitive; many believed the financial services market was increasingly becoming a commodity business. As a result, existing players looked to grow to take advantage of economies of scale in marketing, sales, and technology. To leverage their reputation and gain cost advantages, many established firms sought to expand and diversify their product offering through acquisition. For example, in an attempt to create a global financial services firm with both institutional and retail capabilities, Morgan Stanley and Dean Witter merged in 1997. CSFB acquired Donaldson, Lufkin & Jenrette in November of 2000 in a $12.4 billion stock and cash deal. UBS completed its $12 billion takeover of PaineWebber in the same month with the objective of growing its private-client business in the United States.[15]

Conflicts of interest   While the investment banking business boomed in the late 1990s, some institutional and retail investors felt that the quality of the service they received had deteriorated. Many noted that analysts, in an effort to attract clients and earn large bonuses, had been overly optimistic about stocks that their firms had underwritten.[16] Helene Sorin, an institutional equity sales director, commented: "By the time you got into the summer of 2000, clients were very unhappy with advice from their financial advisors. They were disappointed with the quality of advice, the portfolio performance, and the importance of the issuer relative to the investor. Investors, whether they were institutional or retail, began saying, 'I don't like what we're getting from the Street.' "

In 2001, Eliot Spitzer, the attorney general of New York, launched an investigation into investment research at several bulge-bracket firms. He was determined to uncover whether conflicts of interest had tainted the forecasts and recommendations of equity analysts. Investment banks worked to defend their reputations, but it seemed clear that regulatory reforms would soon follow. Some firms found opportunities created by the climate of distrust. For example, Sanford C. Bernstein, a firm long regarded for its investment research, enjoyed a surge in popularity because it did not engage in underwriting activities. Many argued that this model could prove feasible for other firms and help to improve the quality of research available to investors.[17]

PRUDENTIAL'S EXIT FROM INVESTMENT BANKING

In 2000, Simmons retired. Strangfeld became the new CEO and soon after a vice chairman at Prudential Financial. The issue of exiting investment banking had been under consideration at Prudential Financial, and it was only months after Simmons's departure that Strangfeld announced the decision to exit.

---

13. John Sterlicchi, "The Big Investment Banks Get Bigger," Upside Today, April 23, 2001.

14. Justin Schack, "The New Battle for the Bulge," Institutional Investor, August 2001, pp. 35–43.

15. John Sterlicchi, "The Big Investment Banks Get Bigger."

16. Robert O'Harrow Jr., "The Era of the Superstar Analyst May Be Over," The Washington Post on the Web, May 22, 2002.

17. Emily Thornton, "Research Should Pay its Own Way," BusinessWeek on the Web, June 3, 2002.

Strangfeld's decision was influenced by several factors. First, after years as a mutual company, The Prudential Insurance Company was planning to go public in 2001. In order to ensure an attractive valuation and a successful offering, it was important to communicate to the financial markets the positioning and fit of all of Prudential's businesses. Strangfeld believed it was important that Prudential Securities adopt a strategy that not only fit with the goals of its parent company but was also differentiated from its competitors. He believed that some of the company's disappointing performance over the years was attributable to its "me too" strategy (see **Exhibits 2, 3,** and **5**). There were also economic reasons to support exiting investment banking at the end of 2000. The markets had started to soften, and Strangfeld knew that a mid-tier company would find it even more difficult to - compete as the demand for investment banking services declined.

The exit decision was more than simply a maneuver to jettison an underperforming business; it lay at the heart of a new investor-focused strategy—one Strangfeld believed Prudential Securities was uniquely positioned to pursue. The credibility of research analysts was beginning to be called into question, and Strangfeld thought that a brokerage firm unencumbered by investment banking conflicts would be attractive to investors. Although the firm would continue to serve both institutional and retail clients, Strangfeld believed the new strategy would be especially compelling for retail customers, who had begun to doubt the firm's investment management skills as the value of their portfolios fell. Prudential planned to use its network of over 4,000 financial advisors as more than just "stock jockeys" plugging the tip of the day. This network would be used to provide financial planning services as well as investment management advice to the retail market.

The new strategy was certainly consistent with that of The Prudential Insurance Company; from its inception it had helped individual investors and families plan and invest for the future. It was also a differentiated strategy—without a large sales network it would be difficult for others to profitably follow Prudential's lead. Many of the firms that did have a sizable sales network were deeply entrenched in investment banking (e.g., Merrill Lynch); it was unlikely that they would choose to exit. Nevertheless, there were several challenges to implementing this new strategy. One of the most critical was how to attract and retain good research analysts, since high-quality research lay at the heart of Prudential's new approach. Steve Buell, director of global equity research, commented:

> We must attract analysts who are investment-oriented, client-focused, highly competitive folks that continually challenge themselves and are bold enough to publish provocative points of view. As a firm, we must stand by these analysts when they are confronted by company executives that are unhappy with their point of view. When the market recovers from its current slump and investment banking activity returns to the Street, our competitors may try to hire our analysts because of their growing success and their enhanced reputation for independence and integrity. It will be our challenge to give these analysts a work environment that offers both independence and a competitive level of compensation.

Another challenge was how the firm would explain its new direction to existing clients, many of whom relied on Prudential Securities for investment banking services. Despite these challenges, Strangfeld had no regrets about his decision:

In hindsight, discontinuing investment banking was an even better idea than we had realized, because we have experienced a severe economic downturn. To go through this as a 17th-ranked investment bank would have been something close to a financial debacle. Our decision became even more appealing as all the conflicts between investment research and underwriting hit the front page. We really feel that we got ahead of the curve, and we stayed there.

We have increasing conviction about the wisdom of where we're going. The absence of conflicts in research is clearly a virtue in today's marketplace, and I think our client base respects us for it. The firm also has a differentiated strategy. We have not had the defections of people or the defections of clients that some people thought we would.

However, the decision to exit investment banking raised several important questions for Prudential Securities. First, could the company deliver on its promise to provide investors with impartial research? If so, what changes would it need to make in the way that it hired and rewarded its analysts? Second, how would investors respond to the reversal in many recommendations made by Prudential analysts as they began providing more impartial research? Finally, how would Prudential fund investment research in the future? Would brokerage fees alone be sufficient to cover the costs of both investment research and trade execution?

The exit also raised critical questions for other firms in the industry. At the same time that Prudential was deciding to exit investment banking, Citigroup and J.P. Morgan Chase were aggressively building financial powerhouses that combined commercial banking, investment banking, and insurance. Was Prudential exiting too soon? What implications, if any, did Prudential's experience in combining insurance and investment banking have for the new financial service conglomerates?

QUESTIONS

1. Why did Prudential think that it was a good idea to buy Bache?

2. In 1987, Prudential decided to develop the investment banking side of its business. Why did it pursue this strategy? What were the risks from pursuing this strategy?

3. Why was it so difficult for Pru-Bache to achieve its goal of becoming a bulge investment bank?

4. Which of the three options that Strangfeld is considering would you recommend him to pursue?

Prudential Securities

EXHIBIT I

Equity Underwriting

Graph A: Gross Spreads in Equity Underwriting

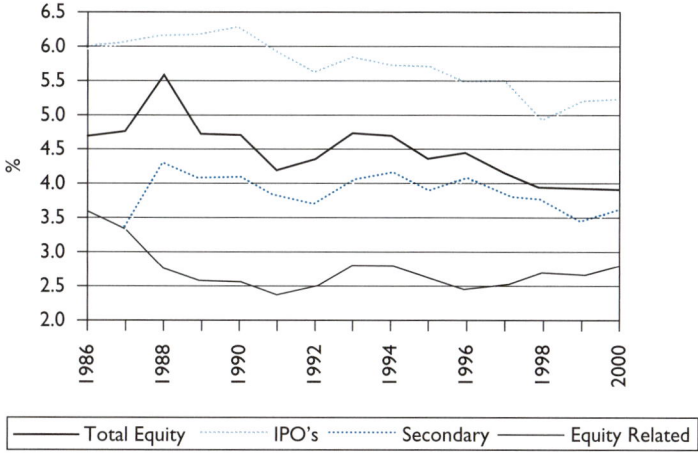

Source: "The Brokerage Industry," UBS Warburg research report, April 11, 2003, p. 25.

Graph B: Allocation of Gross Spreads in Equity Underwriting

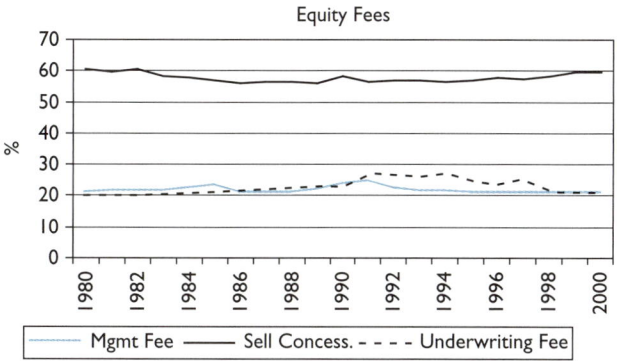

The gross spread is the difference between the share price received by the issuer and the share price at which the offering is first sold to the public. The gross spread is allocated in three pieces. One piece, called the management fee, is the portion of the gross spread that goes directly to the lead underwriter. A second piece, called the underwriting fee, goes to the deal's managers. The lead and comanager(s) must then decide amongst themselves how to divide up this piece. The remaining piece, the selling concession, is allocated among all firms that participated in a deal (lead manager, comanagers, and other syndicate members). Again, how to divide up this piece of the pie is dependent upon negotiation amongst all firms. In practice, however, the lead manager often captures about half of the selling concession. This is in addition to the management fee and some portion of the underwriting fee.

Source: Thomson Financial securities data.

EXHIBIT 2

League Tables History: Prudential Securities' Market Share, 1980–2000

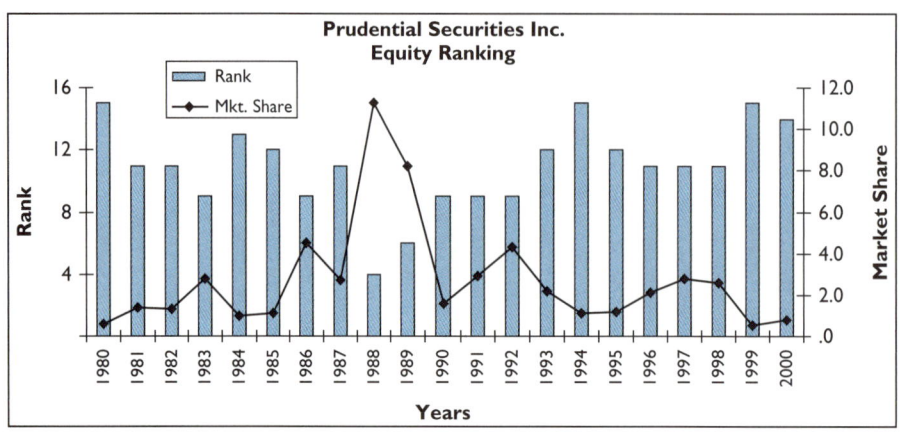

Source: Thomson Financial DATABASE: U.S. Common Stock (C).

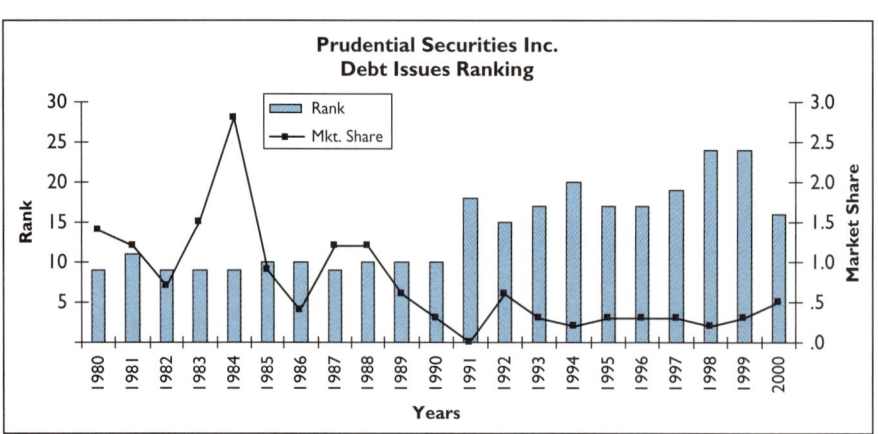

Source: Thomson Financial DATABASES: All U.S. Public Debt, exc. Taxable Municipals (CD, D).

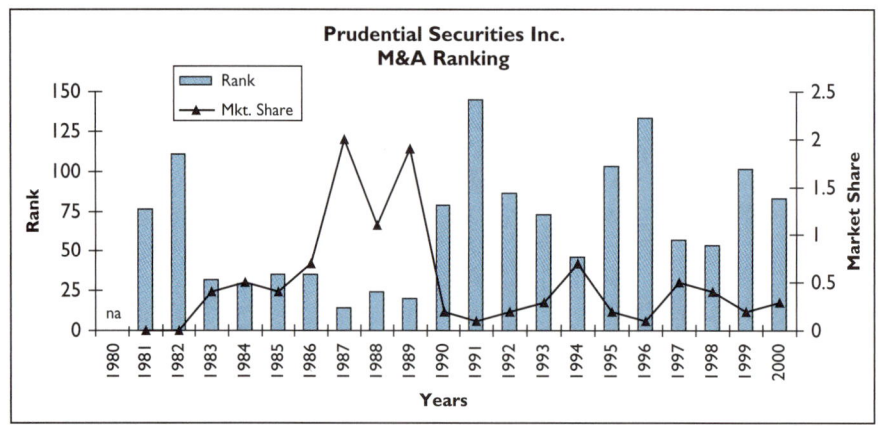

Source: Thomson Financial DATABASES: Special Merger Sectors (Aus/NZ) (MA, OMA, IMA).

EXHIBIT 3

Performance of Prudential Securities' Research Department

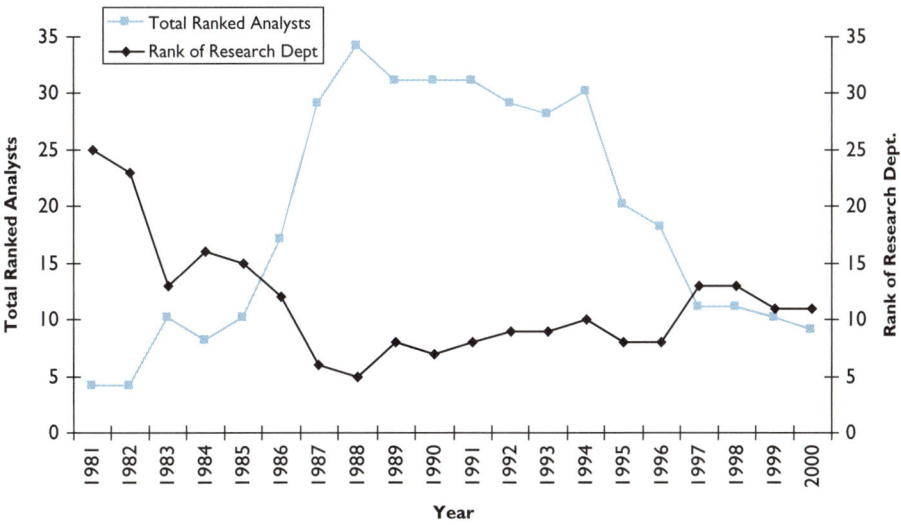

Source: *Institutional Investor*, from October 1981 through October 2000.

EXHIBIT 4

Client Responses on Criteria for Selecting Investment Banks and Customer

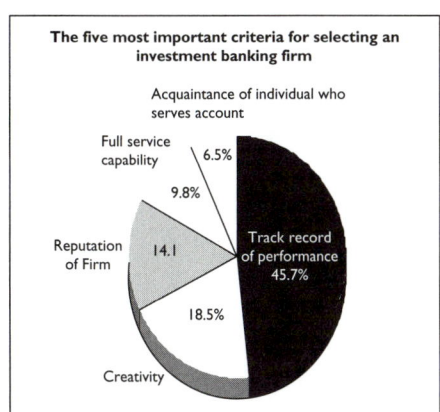
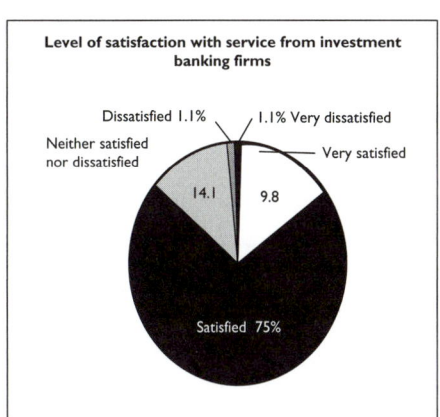

Source: "What CFOs Really Think about Investment Bankers," Staff Reports, *Investment Dealer's Digest*, February 6, 1995, pp. 16–20.

EXHIBIT 5

Client Satisfaction Ratings of Investment Banks

CFOs' opinion of investment banking firms in terms of client orientation (Percentage saying "very good" or "excellent")

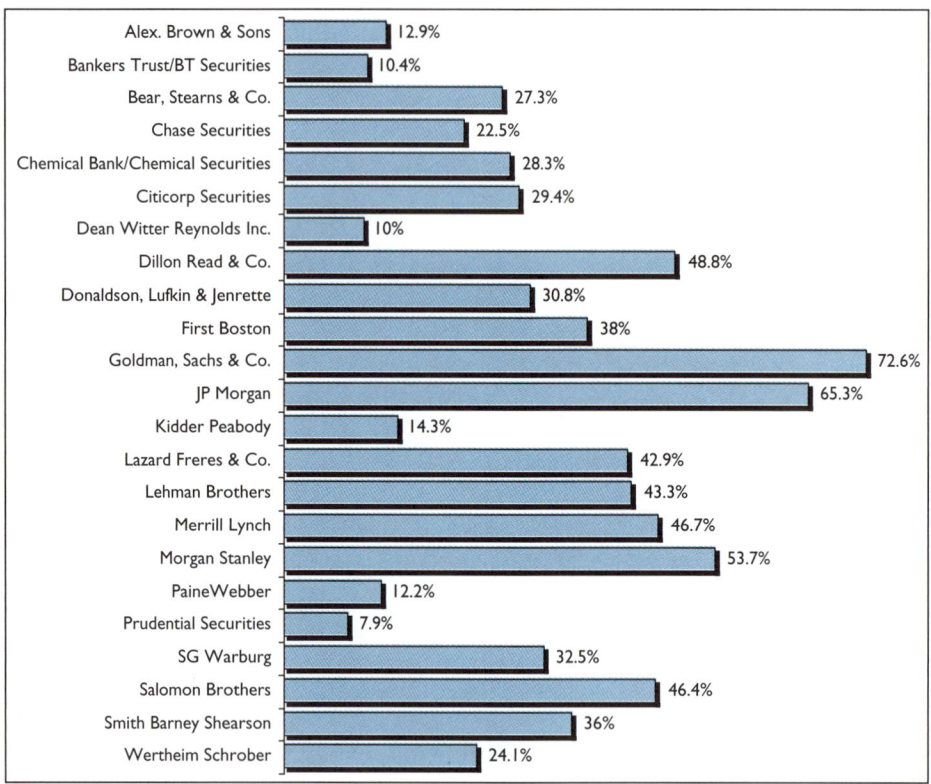

(continued)

EXHIBIT 5 *(continued)*

CFO's opinion of investment banking firms in terms of expertise (Percentage saying "very good" or "excellent")

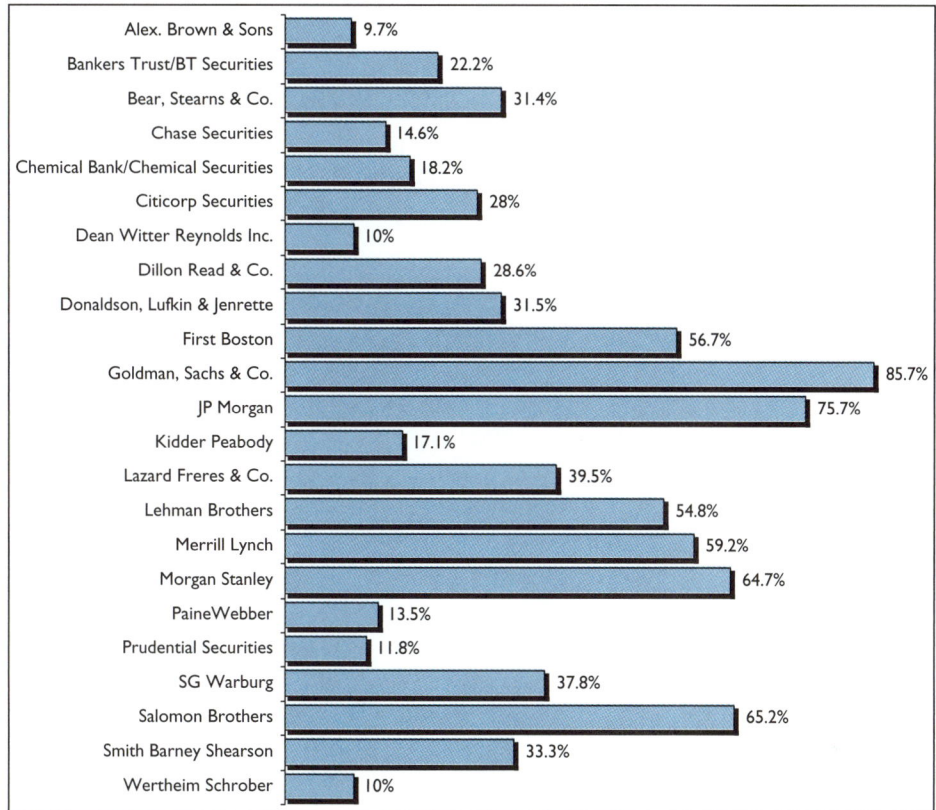

Firm	Percentage
Alex. Brown & Sons	9.7%
Bankers Trust/BT Securities	22.2%
Bear, Stearns & Co.	31.4%
Chase Securities	14.6%
Chemical Bank/Chemical Securities	18.2%
Citicorp Securities	28%
Dean Witter Reynolds Inc.	10%
Dillon Read & Co.	28.6%
Donaldson, Lufkin & Jenrette	31.5%
First Boston	56.7%
Goldman, Sachs & Co.	85.7%
JP Morgan	75.7%
Kidder Peabody	17.1%
Lazard Freres & Co.	39.5%
Lehman Brothers	54.8%
Merrill Lynch	59.2%
Morgan Stanley	64.7%
PaineWebber	13.5%
Prudential Securities	11.8%
SG Warburg	37.8%
Salomon Brothers	65.2%
Smith Barney Shearson	33.3%
Wertheim Schrober	10%

Source: "What CFOs Really Think about Investment Bankers," Staff Reports, *Investment Dealer's Digest*, February 6, 1995, pp. 16–20.

10 Uncommon Values®: Optimizing the Stock-Selection Process

On April 30, 2004, Steve Hash, research director at Lehman Brothers, prepared to initiate the firm's "10 Uncommon Values" stock-picking process for the year. Each year for 54 years, Lehman's research department had identified 10 stocks that it expected to generate superior returns for investors in the succeeding 12 months. These stocks and an analyst's summary report on each were published in a booklet entitled *10 Uncommon Values*.

The performance of the stocks selected for 10 Uncommon Values had historically been strong—a portfolio that acquired the recommended stocks and held them for one year would have outperformed the Standard & Poor's (S&P) 500 in 39 of the preceding 54 years. But between 2000 and 2002 the recommendations had performed poorly, generating an average return of −22.5% versus the S&P 500's −11.7% return.

The process of picking stocks for 10 Uncommon Values began with each analyst selecting one stock among those he or she covered. An investment committee then selected the 10 best bets among analysts' recommendations. Changes had been made over the years. The size of the investment committee had fluctuated from as many as nine members to as few as three. The selection process had also changed: the amount of time devoted to reviewing analysts' recommendations had ranged from as long as 30 minutes per analyst to as little as 10 minutes. Finally, the ramifications for analysts whose recommendations were selected had changed. Between 1988 and 1993 they had been awarded cash bonuses, but since 1994 there had been no direct remuneration. Hash wondered how these changes had affected the integrity and effectiveness of the selection process, particularly in light of the list's recent subpar performance. Additional research was needed, he decided, before settling on the methodology to be used by the 2004 committee.

SELL-SIDE ANALYSTS[1]

Sell-side security analysts who work for companies like Lehman Brothers have been described as Wall Street's "financial detectives" and "wizards of odds." They are responsible for scrutinizing the performance of public companies and making investment

1. Sell-side analysts work for investment banks. They provide investment advice to retail and institutional investors. By contrast, buy-side analysts work for money-management firms; these analysts also scrutinize companies and provide investment advice, but their recommendations are solely for the use of money managers at their own firms.

recommendations to their clients. Analysts' work requires an understanding of industry trends, including the impact of macroeconomic and political factors on the industry and its firms. Analysts evaluate the financial implications of firms' strategic choices, review the appropriateness of their accounting, evaluate their financial performance, build statistical and economic models to forecast future earnings and stock prices, and make recommendations on firms' investment potential. This work is summarized and interpreted in written reports that are updated regularly and distributed to clients. A typical analyst follows 10–18 companies in a single industry or related industries, and may write between 30 and 50 reports a year. Finally, analysts build relationships with clients, particularly institutional clients, to sell their research ideas. It is not unusual for analysts to have more than 700 institutional clients—that is, individuals who receive their research reports and seek their advice. On average, an analyst makes more than 250 contacts a month with clients. The breadth of expertise that analysts are called on to embody prompted one research director to remark that "the successful analyst today is expected to be a legal expert, an economist, an accountant, and an authority on the stock market—as well as an industry specialist. The job is almost impossible."

Analysts' Information Networks

To collect the information they need on the companies they cover, analysts develop broad networks of relationships. Analysts talk to consultants, customers, suppliers, and competitors; they also participate in periodic company briefings, attend industry conferences, read industry publications and company statements, and make regular visits to company offices. Industry experts estimate that analysts spend roughly 40% of their time on these activities. Many analysts also seek extra insight into their companies and industries through irregular channels. For example, Michael Culp, a restaurant-and-lodging analyst and later a successful research director, visited fast-food outlets from time to time to assess customer satisfaction and then presented his findings in the form of "The Michael Culp Edible Meals Index." An analyst who covered games gained insight by visiting a toy store, where he found that the retailer was sharply discounting certain games.

Analysts also regularly interact with traders, institutional sales reps, and portfolio/investment strategists at their own firms. These relationships generate valuable proprietary information.

Traders   Traders pass on news from the trading floor about large-volume trades and information about stocks that clients are considering buying or selling. This information is useful for analysts' short-term action reports. Analysts in turn alert traders to management, dividend, or legal changes and interpret earnings reports and their impact on the short- and long-term performance of a company's stock. Analysts also inform traders about possible future changes in clients' holdings of a particular stock.

Traders frequently attend the research department's morning meetings, where they can discuss events that are likely to have a significant impact on a stock. Some firms also schedule formal meetings and/or appoint a liaison between analysts and traders. Finally, certain firms formalize relationships between traders and analysts by assigning traders to specific industries and by scheduling regular meetings to coordinate the actions of traders and analysts in the same industry.[2]

---

2. Paul Strauss, "The new dialogue between analysts and traders," Institutional Investor, October 1977, pp . 134–138.

The Institutional Sales Force   Sales representatives promote analysts' work by communicating their buy and sell recommendations to clients and keeping them updated on changes in research fundamentals. They also keep analysts informed about their clients' decisions. In the absence of a strong sales force, an analyst would have to spend far more time marketing his or her research, thus shortchanging research-related activities. Consequently, investment banks usually team up analysts with institutional sales reps.

Portfolio/Investment Strategists   Portfolio strategists provide information on economic factors, such as the strength of the economy, and technical indicators like the direction of stock prices and trading volume. They also advise clients on when to rebalance their portfolios, to increase or decrease risk and to change exposure to particular stocks or sectors, as the market outlook changes. Equity analysts integrate such information into their own research reports to provide comprehensive analysis of company and industry fundamentals and company portfolio strategy, a combination highly valued by institutional clients.

Finally, analysts build strong relations with clients, particularly institutional clients, to sell their research ideas. It is not unusual for analysts to have more than 700 institutional clients, that is, people who receive their research reports and seek their advice. On average, an analyst makes more than 250 contacts a month with clients.

Rankings of Analysts

Every year since 1972, the trade journal *Institutional Investor* has ranked sell-side analysts. The top analysts in each sector win inclusion in its All-American Research Team. Institutional clients evaluate analysts on six criteria: (1) earnings estimates, (2) servicing initiatives, (3) accessibility and responsiveness, (4) stock selection, (5) industry knowledge, and (6) written reports. Analysts in a given sector are ranked by weighting the votes they receive in accordance with the size of the respondent's firm. In each industry/sector, there are four awards: first place, second place, third place, and runner-up.

Ranking by *Institutional Investor* is a stamp of approval that wins an analyst credibility, power, visibility, and better compensation. At the major investment banks, *Institutional Investor*'s leading analyst in a given industry or sector can earn $2 million to $5 million per year.

FUNDING ANALYST RESEARCH

Investment banks do not sell investment research directly to their clients. Instead, clients pay for research indirectly through markups on other services that rely on research. Prior to 1975, funding came from fixed commissions on trading. Clients paid a regulated commission fee that compensated investment banks for both research and execution of trades. The 1975 deregulation of commissions changed the funding model for firms and led commission rates to decline (see **Exhibit 1**). As clients demanded lower commissions, new funding sources were needed to cover the costs of research. At investment banks like Lehman Brothers, these sources included fees from underwriting and money management as well as retail and institutional trading.

These changes in funding were accompanied by changes in the role of financial analysts in their firms and in the market. By the mid-1990s, analysts were expected to generate revenues for their firms by helping with underwritings, acquisitions, divestitures, and the firm's own money-management activities.[3] These changes made it increasingly challenging for analysts to maintain the integrity of their research. Barry Tarasoff, director of research at Wertheim Schroeder, commented that, as a result of the new funding models, "the toughest part of the job is to maintain the integrity of the research—and unless the organization understands the importance of that integrity at the highest level, it's doubly hard."[4]

Following the crash in technology stocks in 2000 and scandals at companies like Enron and Worldcom, the New York State Attorney General's office, headed by Elliott Spitzer, investigated whether financial analysts had contributed to the financial market problems by failing to provide independent research. The investigation uncovered evidence that some leading analysts publicly touted firms that were potential clients of their investment banks, though privately they questioned the firms' viability. As a result, ten of the largest U.S. investment banks agreed in April 2003 to implement a series of reforms and to pay penalties for prior indiscretions. The reforms included new operating procedures to separate research from investment banking both physically and financially, refocusing analysts' compensation on stock-picking ability. These reforms prompted investment banks to revert to the model of funding research through commissions from institutional equity and retail trading.

LEHMAN BROTHERS AND 10 UNCOMMON VALUES

Founded in 1850, Lehman Brothers offers a full range of global investment-banking services, including fixed-income and equities sales, trading and research, merger and acquisition advising, public finance, and private-client investment advisory services. Lehman Brothers was acquired by American Express in 1984. Ten years later, in response to deteriorating performance in investment banking, American Express decided to refocus on its core business and to spin off Lehman Brothers. Once again a stand-alone firm, Lehman sought to regain its position as one of Wall Street's premier investment banks. It cut costs; focused on high-margin businesses like equity origination, mergers and acquisitions (M&A), and high-yield; expanded globally; reaffirmed its commitment to high-quality research; and entered into a strategic alliance to provide Fidelity Investments' retail and institutional brokerage clients access to Lehman's lead-managed initial public and equity offerings, as well as its equity and debt research. In 2003, Lehman was rated ninth in global equity underwriting volume, seventh in global high-yield underwriting volume, and ninth in global announced mergers-and-acquisitions volume. Its research department had risen from eighth place in 1998 to become the highest-ranked department on Wall Street (see **Exhibits 2a** and **2b**).

Unlike managers at some investment banks who believed that star analysts' skills are innate, research managers at Lehman believed they could transform high-potential analysts into stars through training, mentorship, and incentives. The firm developed a 13-week training program, aimed explicitly at developing stars, whose sessions covered every aspect of the job from stock picking to dealing with the press, salespeople, retail brokers, clients, and company management. The department also emphasized

---

3. Jeffrey M. Laderman, Chuck Hawkins, and Irene Recio, "How much should you trust your analyst?" BusinessWeek, July 23, 1990.

4. Barbara Donnelly, "Tough Times for Research Directors," The Wall Street Journal, May 28, 1991, p. C1.

informal mentorship and a team-oriented culture. In fact, the research department was described in sports metaphors as a basketball team (not a baseball or a football team) where the players interact, the coaches are on the sidelines with a game plan, and the same coaches run practices to prepare players for each game.

The Roots of 10 Uncommon Values

Lehman Brothers emphasized equity research as a means of providing value for its clients and shareholders, and in 1949 was the first firm to create a top-10 stock list. According to Jack Rivkin, a former global head of research, the top-10 list was created primarily to increase demand for the firm's brokerage services. "The reason it was done in July, in the middle of the summer, was because July is typically a dead period for the brokers," Rivkin explained. "So someone decided, 'Let's figure out what we can do during the summer doldrums to generate some business.'" As **Exhibit 3** shows, 10 Uncommon Values generally succeeded in increasing trading volume in the recommended stocks around the time of the report's publication.

Over the years, 10 Uncommon Values developed a reputation for adding value to Lehman Brothers' clients. On average, during the year following publication of each 10 Uncommon Values report, the selected stocks earned 14.2%, versus only 8.1% for the S&P 500 Index. Of the 10 stocks, 6.6 appreciated in value and 3.4 declined. Adjusted for risk, the recommended stocks enjoyed average abnormal returns in the year subsequent to selection of 6.2%. However, as **Exhibit 4** illustrates, much of this return was realized on the date the report was published.

The Stock-Selection Process

Essentially the same process had been used to select stocks for 10 Uncommon Values for 54 years. At the end of April Lehman's senior research analysts (currently 92 people) were asked to present their best fundamental investment idea to the Investment Policy Committee (IPC). As background, analysts were given forecasts about the performance of the market as a whole by experts at the firm. Fred Fraenkel, Lehman's former head of global equity research, explained:

> *The first thing we did was to make the analyst aware of what our experts on top-down philosophies were thinking. The economists, strategists, and quantitative analysts' views were made known. We would put together what we were thinking would happen to the economy, to the market, and to different parts of the market quantitatively over the next year. If somebody wanted to put in a recommendation that went against all of those things, it was fine. But they had to be able to explain it.*

Each analyst prepared a written report on his or her stock recommendation. This report consisted of the investment thesis, its rationale, risk and valuation analysis, and conclusions. It also included descriptions of the company's products and cost structure, the sector's outlook (growth, competitive threats), earnings models, valuation comparisons, and the company's historical stock performance versus the S&P 500 Index. All analysts used the same template. The reports on the selected stocks were later published. (See **Exhibit 5** for a list of 10 Uncommon Values stocks selected between 2000 and 2002 and **Exhibit 6** for a sample report.)

The IPC then reviewed the analysts' reports and met with each analyst to review his or her idea and to test its merits by challenging its underlying assumptions.

Joe Murphy, formerly Lehman's associate head of production, and currently senior vice president and head of research product development at Keefe, Bruyette & Woods, described a typical IPC meeting:

> We liked to get the analyst's submissions two or three days in advance in order to familiarize ourselves with their theses. We were moving a lot of people through a very narrow time frame. The submission requirements were that you give us the material you used to make your argument, including text, models, and a technical chart. Knowing the story in advance helped move the process along more smoothly and also prompted much more probing questions, which there were a whole lot of. The diversity of backgrounds of the members of the committee kept the presenting analysts on their toes.
>
> The members of the committee analyze and debate the underlying fundamentals of each company and its industry, each company's competitive position, and the potential catalysts that might lead to superior stock-price appreciation in the coming year with each individual analyst. The committee also considered macroeconomic trends and technical analysis as part of this stock-selection process.
>
> Analysts had to select a stock, write a report using the committee's standardized template, and prepare a presentation to the committee. For some analysts this process took as long as two days; others managed to complete it in as little as three hours. Most analysts viewed the process positively but some were skeptical. In particular, analysts from underperforming industries considered it a waste of time. If the IPC concluded that the industry's fundamentals were bad, even a great stock had a low chance of being selected. Some analysts complained that the process required too much time and preparation, especially when the stock had no chance of being selected.
>
> After the interviews, the committee debated the merits of each idea and selected its 10 favorites. Murphy described this process:
>
> After full consideration, each member votes for what he or she considers the 10 best investment ideas for the coming year. The votes are equally weighed; those common stocks with the most votes are the ones that make up the 10 Uncommon Values portfolio. Finally, we would review the list and decide: do we want this to be a more diversified portfolio, or are we putting all of our eggs in one basket? So there was some horse trading on "Is this a good idea? Is that a good idea?" That's when we would get the economists and the strategists involved. We would also get the technical analysts' input. How do the chosen companies look on a technical basis from now to June of the following year? So it was a tremendously involved process.

Scott Collins, senior vice president of equity and product development and a member of the IPC, commented: "Uncommon value to us in this list means that there is something about the stock, the company, that we think is unrecognized on the Street. So, you know, even though the list is pretty varied in terms of the types of names, in terms of the types of stock ideas, each one has something about them that we think is misunderstood or mispriced."[5]

The final list of recommendations was published at the end of June; the investment cycle began on July 1 and ended on June 30 of the following year. The selected stocks remained in the 10 Uncommon Values portfolio for the rest of the year regardless

---

5. *Sean Callebs, "Lehman VP Discusses S&P Portfolio Selections," CNNfn, Take It Personally, July 1, 1997.*

of subsequent developments. In tracking performance, Lehman assumed that an equal-weighted portfolio of the 10 stocks was acquired on July 1 and held for one year. Murphy explained:

> *One of the more difficult parts of the process was getting the analysts to change their frame of reference for valuing a stock from the then-typical 12-to-18-month time horizon to June 30 of the following year. We priced the stock on the first business day of July, and we wanted to know where the stock would be on June 30 of the following year. For this exercise, we didn't care if the stock fell off a cliff the following day.*

Internal Benefits

To capitalize on the domestic success of 10 Uncommon Values, Lehman launched a European version, 10 Uncommon EuroValues, in 1999, and plans were afoot to implement Asia Pacific and Latin American versions. Several analysts and research management believed that the process positively influenced analysts' standards for identifying a good stock recommendation. Others regarded the process as a useful training tool, especially for younger analysts. One committee member pointed out that the committee asked the same questions that analysts might be asked during presentations to clients. Some analysts even believed that committee members were deliberately hypercritical of analysts' ideas. Some analysts valued the grilling as a low-risk way to test their best ideas, but others objected that the committee had too many different perspectives. "You never know what you will be asked," one analyst said. "It became more and more difficult to prepare for these meetings. How much diversity do you actually need?"

VARIATIONS IN THE STOCK-SELECTION PROCESS

Numerous changes were made over the years in the size and composition of the IPC, the decision-making and voting processes, and the rewards to analysts whose recommendations were selected.

Fluctuations in Committee Size

The size of the investment committee fluctuated between three and nine members between 1977 and 2002. (See **Exhibit 7** for committee characteristics and stock-selection performance in those years.) In general, committee size increased over time. The committee grew fastest in the late 1990s, from six members in 1998 to seven in 1999, eight in 2000, and nine in 2002.

Variation in Committee Composition

The composition and aggregate experience of the committee also varied over the years. In some years the committee was composed exclusively of members of the research department. At other times, representatives of other departments were added to diversify the group: participants had included the chief U.S. strategist, the director and/or associate director of U.S. equity research, the head of U.S. equity product management, the core equity portfolio manager for Lehman Brothers Bank, the head of institutional sales, and the head of trading. Murphy explained that diversity generated fresh perspectives in the questions raised during the review process.

The participation of such senior-level personnel represented a significant financial investment on the part of Lehman Brothers. The time commitment of each committee member was estimated at 30–35 hours per year, and their time was highly valued. The director of research earned around $2 million, and other senior managers earned between $900,000 and $1.7 million. An average analyst made about $600,000 a year.

Variation in the Decision-Making Process

Insiders described three distinct decision-making processes. In one version, committee members listened to all the analysts' presentations without deliberating until the committee's final meeting in June. At that meeting, the members reviewed their notes from analysts' presentations, debated the merits of each, and identified the top 10. In the second method the committee deliberated briefly after each analyst's presentation, immediately eliminating some stocks from consideration. In June the committee met again to choose the best 10 from the 20–25 surviving stocks. The third method involved two rounds of selection. During the "lightning round," analysts presented ten-minute "elevator pitches." The committee chose 20 stocks, whose sponsor analysts were invited to make longer presentations; the committee then made its final decision.

Variation in Time Invested

Over the years, the time devoted to selecting the top 10 stocks had varied considerably (see **Exhibit 7**). Steve Balog, Lehman's former head of U.S. equity research, described the approach used in the late 1980s and early 1990s:

> It was as if the analysts were doing a stock pitch to a client—a quick three-minute stock pitch. You then asked them questions and the analysts would leave. After the analyst left the room, you'd ask everyone what they thought. If it wasn't bad, we'd put the stock over to the side as a "possible." Others were a clear reject for several reasons—weak logic; growth idea, not value idea; not cheap enough; not likely to work within the year—a bunch of reasons to reject a name. So then you get down to 20 names or so that are possible out of the 50-plus. And out of those, maybe you would bring the analyst in to hear some more, and then you would decide on your 10 names. Another five would be runners-up or silver medalists.

According to Fraenkel, the 20 or so follow-up meetings lasted roughly 45 minutes each. Then the committee met to tally its selections. There tended, Fraenkel recalled, to be broad consensus on the first six or seven selections. "Then we'd tussle over the last three or four. The whole process took two months. Once we'd selected the stocks, we needed to create brochures and write-ups on each company. We had to be ready for a press release."

As the number of research analysts grew, the IPC had to meet with more analysts each year. (See **Exhibit 8** for the tally of Lehman Brothers U.S. equity analysts and U.S. companies covered in the period 1984–2002.) The pressure of time forced the committee to allocate less time to each analyst. In 2003, the IPC devoted about 15 minutes to each analyst, including deliberations. It was suggested that the committee begin meeting in March rather than April. But doing so would require that the researchers' analyses cover a longer period: rather than forecasting the stock's performance over 12 months, they would need to generate analyses for 15–16 months.

Variation in Commitment

Changes in top management's commitment to 10 Uncommon Values have coincided with changes in research directors. From 1977 to 1982, management's commitment to research, and to the 10 Uncommon Values process, was high. Lehman's acquisition by American Express in 1983 caused turmoil in the research department of the merged company, and commitment to the screening process suffered. From 1987 to 1992, however, when Jack Rivkin was head of research and then head of equity, the stock-selection process was closely scrutinized. Paul Williams, who replaced Rivkin, had no equity experience and put little emphasis on 10 Uncommon Values. Following its spinoff from American Express in 1994, Lehman pursued firmwide cost-cutting, causing high turnover among equity analysts. Over a 15-month period, 30 of 72 equity analysts departed, along with the heads of global equity research and U.S. equity research. For two years, the 10 Uncommon Values process was not a priority. But in 1996, Lehman decided to rebuild its research department. In 1997 Joe Gregory and Steve Hash, global and U.S. research heads respectively, were given a mandate to make the equity research department the best on Wall Street. Over the ensuing six years, they placed strong emphasis on 10 Uncommon Values. "We really did the process with a lot of rigor. First, we tried to eliminate the worst ideas," Hash remarked. "After that, coming up with the best 10 ideas was easier."

Variation in Analyst Rewards

Between 1988 and 1993, Lehman Brothers rewarded analysts whose recommendations were selected. Steve Balog described the compensation:

> *You got a special bonus if you had a stock get into the 10 Uncommon Values and a smaller bonus for the five silver-medalist names. The amount was significant, perhaps 5–10% of one's total compensation. It wasn't gonna' allow you to retire but it could get you a good chunk of a Lexus. The amount felt like enough to get broad participation—allow greed to overcome the fear that one's idea torpedoes that year's list and you would be the department goat.*

Analysts whose stocks were selected typically received cash bonuses of about $50,000 in the early 1990s. The five silver medalists, or runners-up, received about $25,000 each.

Financial awards were discontinued in 1994, but many in the firm believe that analysts have continued to take the process seriously. "It became its own folklore—they wanted to be on the list," one committee member explained. "They would come back and be upset if the stocks weren't on the list."

Variation in the Committee Voting Process

The investment committee's voting process also varied slightly over the years. Some years committee members voted by secret ballot, and the stocks that received the most votes were automatically selected. Other years voting was transparent, and members often debated the two or three stocks that made it into the top 10 by the narrowest margins to make sure that the last two to three seeds went to deserving stocks. In most years, the committee members publicly voted for their best 10 stocks.

SUMMARY

Steve Hash asked himself several questions. What was the value of 10 Uncommon Values to Lehman Brothers and its clients? How much time and effort should the firm invest in the process of selecting stocks for the report? How many members should the IPC have, and how should they be selected? And should analysts whose stocks were selected be compensated?

QUESTIONS

1. Quantify the annual short-term costs and benefits of running Ten Uncommon Values for Lehman Brothers. Does the process create short-term financial value for the firm? What other intangible costs and benefits arise from the process?

2. Does Ten Uncommon Values create value for Lehman's clients?

3. Is there any evidence that specific features of the Ten Uncommon Values (e.g., the use of incentive compensation for analysts, committee size, management commitment to the process) have an impact on the committee's performance?

4. Under the Global Settlement, the leading investment banks agreed to create an Investment Committee to evaluate all changes in research recommendations. What impact, if any, is this agreement likely to have on (a) Lehman's Ten Uncommon Values process and (b) the quality of investment research at the leading banks?

EXHIBIT I

Average Commission per Share (in cents), 1997–2002

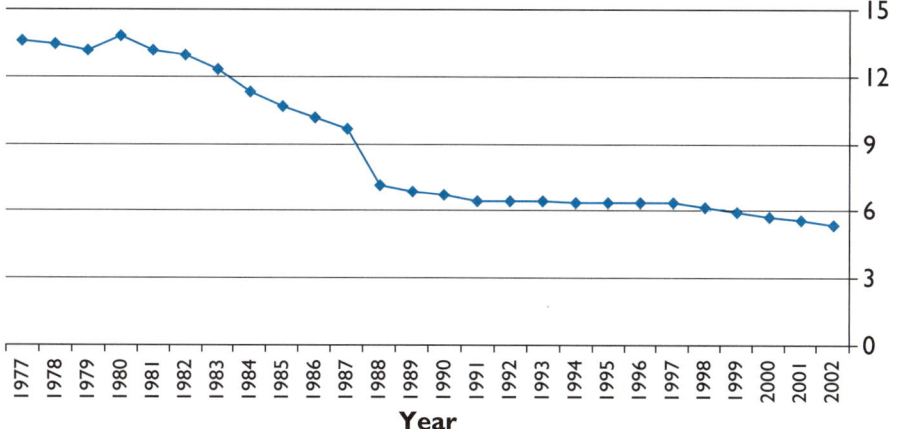

Source: Compiled from Greenwich Associates, "Commission Rates and Concentration of Business," 1977–2002.

EXHIBIT 2a

Ranking of Lehman Brothers' Research Department by *Institutional Investor*, 1998–2003

	1998	1999	2000	2001	2002	2003
Rank of Department	8	8	8	5	2	1

EXHIBIT 2b

Lehman Brothers' Listed Trading Market Share (%) and Number of Ranked Analysts, 1998–2003

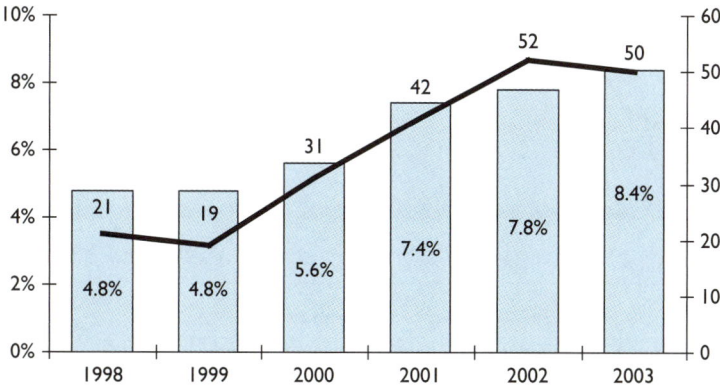

Source: Company documents.

EXHIBIT 3

Average Daily Trading Volume for a 10 Uncommon Values® Stock in Period Surrounding
Report Publication, 1999–2003

Year	Average Daily Trading Volume for a Stock Selected for 10 Uncommon Values® in Days Surrounding Report Publication (t = 0, day of publication)		
	Days t − 1 to t + 1	Days t − 10 to t − 2	Days t + 2 to t + 10
1999	10,131,243	7,998,768	8,876,183
2000	7,883,309	5,169,609	5,054,633
2001	11,537,403	11,271,615	9,594,369
2002	6,542,515	5,094,030	6,095,831
2003	13,083,986	12,999,080	11,700,118
Average	9,835,691	8,506,620	8,264,227

Source: Casewriter.

EXHIBIT 4

Mean and Cumulative Abnormal Returns Around Publication of Lehman Brothers
10 Uncommon Values®, 1963–2002[a]

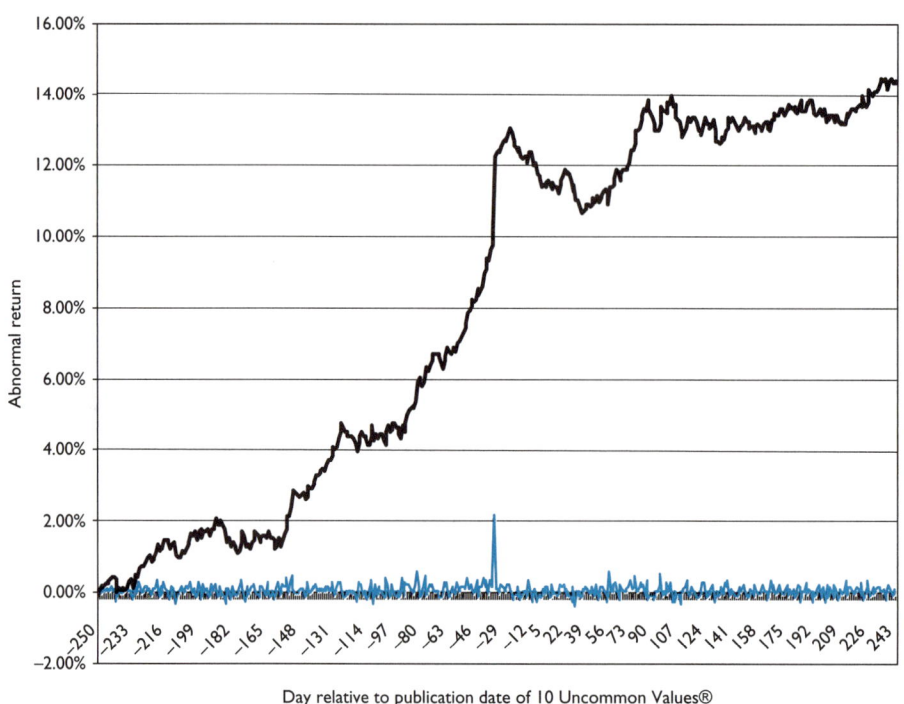

Day relative to publication date of 10 Uncommon Values®

— Abnormal Returns   ▬ Cumulative Abnormal Returns

Source: Casewriter calculations.

[a]*Abnormal returns are returns for the 10 Uncommon Values® stocks net of returns on benchmark stocks with comparable market capitalizations and book-to-market ratios.*

EXHIBIT 5
Beginning and Ending Per-Share Values of 10 Uncommon Values® Stocks, 2000–2002

2000	6/27/00	6/27/01
Agilent Technologies Inc.	$75.4375	$29.8500
BEA Systems Inc.	38.9375	30.9600
Cedant Corp.	12.8750	19.7500
Gemstar-TV Guide International Inc.[a,b]	49.8750	38.0000
Hewlett-Packard Co.[a]	116.6250	26.4500
Juniper Networks Inc.	126.4375	30.2200
Lilly (Eli) & Company	84.7500	74.0200
Micron Technology Inc.	90.0000	39.7400
Nortel Networks Corp.	68.0625	8.4200
Tellabs Inc.	62.6875	16.6300

2001	6/27/01	6/26/02
Alcoa Inc.	$38.46	$31.35
Bed Bath & Beyond Inc.	29.05	36.92
Cisco Systems, Inc.	17.93	13.43
Comcast Corporation	42.50	22.72
Concord EFC, Inc.[a]	54.04	30.10
Harley-Davidson, Inc.	48.03	50.00
Liberty Media Corporation[c]	16.00	8.50
Mirant Corporation	33.90	7.05
Washington Mutual Inc.	36.81	37.65
Waste Management, Inc.	29.70	27.12

2002	6/26/02	6/24/03
American International Group	$66.24	$56.89
Apollo Group Inc.	38.62	63.19
Bed Bath & Beyond Inc.	36.92	39.50
Capital One Financial Corporation	56.80	49.50
HealthSouth Corporation	12.35	0.42
KLA-Tencor Corporation	43.61	45.91
McKesson Corporation	33.30	35.35
Pfizer Inc.	35.00	35.40
Wendy's International Inc.	39.57	29.68
Weyerhaeuser Company	63.61	53.11

Source: "10 Uncommon Values in Common Stocks," Lehman Brothers, June 2003.

[a]Adjusted for a stock dividend or split.
[b]Formerly Gemstar International Group. Gemstar and TV Guide completed their merger on July 11, 2000.
[c]Formerly AT&T-Liberty Media, with the ticker symbol LMG/A.

10 Uncommon Values

EXHIBIT 6

Example of a Stock-Selection Template Completed by an Analyst

10 Uncommon Values
in Common Stocks

Education Services

Apollo Group, Inc. (APOL)

Gary E. Bisbee, CFA 1.212.526.3047 glbisbee@lehmon.com	2 Buy		FY Aug		Price Performance (%)			
						Abs Pref	Rel to S&P 500	Rel to Nasdaq
	Price (6/26/02):	38.62	EPS 02/03:	0.87/1.08				
	Target:	43	P/E 02/03:	44.2/35.6	1-Month	9.3	19.4	23.2
	52-Week Range:	39–22	BVPS:	3.58	3-Month	12.2	26.7	33.9
	Shares Out (MM):	176.0	Dividend:	Nil	6-Month	27.8	43.1	54.9

Note: EPS figure are calendarized.

Investment Thesis

Conclusion: In our view, Apollo Group's business model is uniquely positioned within a thriving industry to outperform the market during the current uncertain economic and a subsequent rebound.

Rationale: We believe that Apollo's low-execution-risk internal rollout strategy provides strong growth, high revenue and earnings visibility, and superior ROIC and free cash flow generation. In our view, drivers of Apollo's future growth will be consistent execution on its proven growth model and positive industry dynamics, which are driving higher enrollments.

Catalysts: The shares should benefit from upside earnings surprises, as Apollo has exceeded consensus by a cumulative $0.24 (17.9%) over the past 11 quarters. We expect this trend to continue, as evidenced by our fiscal 2003 EPS estimate of $1.03, which is $0.04 ahead of consensus.

Valuation Analysis: At 37 times estimated fiscal 2003 EPS. Apollo trades slightly below its five-year average forward multiple of 40. We believe Apollo's defensible competitive positioning, low execution-risk model, unmatched financial flexibility (providing downside protection), and ability to outperform in the face of a difficult economy will prompt investors to maintain a premium multiple on the shares for the foreseeable future.

Company Description

Products: Through the University of Phoenix (including University of Phoenix Online), Apollo offers undergraduate and graduate degree programs in a variety of fields, including business, education, IT, and nursing. The programs are tailored to the needs of working adults, including curricula focused on job-related skills, convenient scheduling, and small class size.

Top Line: Apollo's three-pronged strategy entails opening four to six new campuses per year, continuing to grow the existing base of campuses by opening additional learning centers and introducing new Educational programs, and aggressively growing University of Phoenix Online. We expect this strategy to drive 30% and 23% top-line growth in fiscal 2002 and 2003, respectively.

Cost Structure: Apollo has significant operating leverage as it scales enrollments. We estimate 300 and 70 basis points of operating margin expansion for fiscal 2002 and 2003, respectively.

Bottom Line: We expect EPS growth of 38% and 24% for fiscal 2002 and 2003, respectively, with upside surprises likely.

Industry Outlook

Growth: Positive demographic, economic, and social trends are expected to drive post-secondary enrollments to an all-time high of 17.7 million in 2011 (up 16% from 15.3 million in 2001). In addition to 5% annual price increases, continued market share gains should drive for-profit revenue growth of 15% annually through 2005.

Competitive Landscape: With 6,400 Title IV–eligible institutions serving the market, past-secondary education is very competitive. New competition is mitigated, howere, by a challenging regulatory environment, an effective barrier to entry. With its focus on working adults, Apollo has a defensible market position in an underserved, high-growth segment of the post-secondary universe.

Competitive Threats: Apollo is likely to face stiffer competition, as its success in tailoring programs and delivery options for the huge and underserved working adult market (and the growth this success has produced) has not gone unnoticed by the competition.

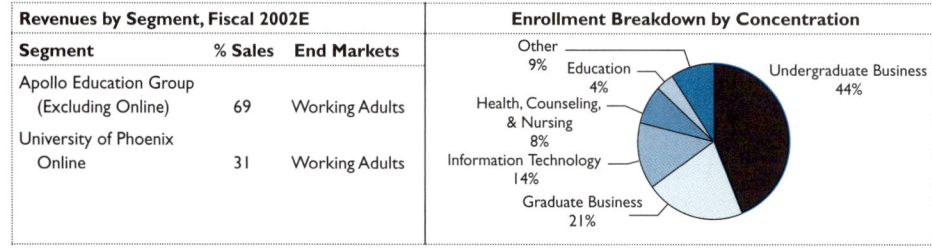

Revenues by Segment, Fiscal 2002E		
Segment	**% Sales**	**End Markets**
Apollo Education Group (Excluding Online)	69	Working Adults
University of Phoenix Online	31	Working Adults

Enrollment Breakdown by Concentration

Other 9%
Education 4%
Undergraduate Business 44%
Health, Counseling, & Nursing 8%
Information Technology 14%
Graduate Business 21%

Apollo Group, Inc.—Earnings Model, 2001–2003E ($ Millions)

	FY01A	1Q02A	2Q02A	3Q02E	4Q02E	FY02E	FY03E
Revenue	769	228	223	276	275	1,002	1,229
Instructional Costs and services	410	117	119	130	138	503	605
Selling and Promotional	150	45	47	51	58	200	250
General and Administrative	48	15	13	15	15	58	72
Depreciation and Amortization	33	9	9	10	8	35	42
EBITDA	194	60	52	91	71	275	344
Operating Income	161	51	44	81	64	240	302
Interest/Other Income	14	3	3	3	3	12	14
Pretax Income	175	54	46	84	67	252	316
Tax	67	21	18	33	26	99	125
Net Income	108	33	28	51	41	152	192
EPS	0.60	0.18	0.15	0.27	0.22	0.83	1.03
Average Shares Out (MM)	174.0	174.9	175.4	176.0	176.1	175.6	176.7
Year-over-Year Percentage Change							
Revenue	26.1%	28.9%	36.6%	29.0%	27.6%	30.2%	22.7%
Operating Income	41.1%	32.2%	81.5%	53.3%	40.6%	48.8%	26.1%
Net Income	51.4%	32.7%	71.8%	43.5%	29.8%	41.4%	25.7%
EPS	45.5%	28.0%	67.9%	40.0%	26.8%	37.6%	24.1%
Profitability Measurements							
Gross Margin	46.7%	48.8%	46.6%	53.0%	49.8%	49.8%	50.8%
Operating Margin	20.9%	22.5%	19.6%	29.2%	23.3%	23.9%	24.6%
Selling & Promotional/Sales	19.5%	19.9%	21.1%	18.3%	21.0%	20.0%	20.4%
G&A/Sales	6.2%	6.4%	6.0%	5.5%	5.6%	5.8%	5.8%

Valuation Comparison

Company	Ticker	Rating	Price 6/26/02	52-Week Range	Mkt Cap ($B)	EPS 2002E	EPS 2003E	P/E 2002E	P/E 2003E	5-Year Proj. CAGR
Apollo Group	APOL	2	38.62	40–22	6.8	0.87	1.08	44.2	35.6	25%
Career Education Corp	CECO	1	45.07	48–21	2.1	1.28	1.61	35.1	28.0	25%
Corinthian Colleges	COCO	NR	31.15	34–12	1.4	0.93	1.10	33.5	28.3	23%
DeVry Inc.	DV	3	23.64	41–22	1.7	0.98	1.18	24.0	20.0	19%
Education Management Corp.	EDMC	2	42.74	46–23	1.5	1.34	1.60	31.8	26.7	22%
ITT Educational Services	ESI	NR	22.54	27–12	1.1	0.86	1.02	26.2	22.1	20%
Strayer Education Inc.	STRA	NR	64.16	67–37	0.9	1.76	2.12	36.5	30.3	20%

Note: EPS Figures are calendarized.

Source: Company reports, First Call estimates, and Lehman Brothers estimates.

Lehman Brothers Inc. makes a market in the securities of Apollo Group, Inc., Career Education Corporation, and Education Management Corporation.

Key to Investment Rankings: This is a guide to expected total return (price performance plus dividend) relative to the total return of the stock's local market over the next 12 months. 1 = Strong Buy (expected to outperform the market by 15 or more percentage points); 2 = Buy (expected to outperform the market by 5–15 percentage points); 3 = Market Perform (expected to perform in line with the market, plus or minus 5 percentage points); 4 = Market Underperform (expected to underperform the market by 5–15 percentage points); 5 = Sell (expected to underperform the market by 15 or more percentage points).

Source: "10 Uncommon Values in Common Stocks," Lehman Brothers, June 2002, pp. 9–10.

EXHIBIT 7

10 Uncommon Values® Investment Committee Characteristics and Stock-Selection Performance, 1977–2002

Year	Financial Incentive	Committee Size	Average Minutes per Analyst[a]	Firm Commitment	Abnormal Return (over-the-market return)[b]
1977	No	3	30	High	10.97%
1978	No	3	30	High	0.45%
1979	No	3	30	High	12.93%
1980	No	3	30	High	−25.34%
1981	No	4	30	High	15.84%
1982	No	4	30	High	45.92%
1983	No	4	20	Low	−0.17%
1984	No	4	20	Low	9.81%
1985	No	4	20	Low	3.26%
1986	No	5	20	Low	−15.03%
1987	No	6	10	High	−2.38%
1988	Yes	6	10	High	8.54%
1989	Yes	6	10	High	−4.60%
1990	Yes	7	10	High	1.42%
1991	Yes	7	10	High	−8.17%
1992	Yes	5	10	High	17.21%
1993	Yes	6	10	High	16.05%
1994	No	6	20	Low	−9.31%
1995	No	6	20	Low	4.96%
1996	No	6	20	High	15.96%
1997	No	6	20	High	20.14%
1998	No	6	20	High	38.73%
1999	No	7	20	High	5.58%
2000	No	8	15	High	−1.09%
2001	No	8	15	High	−4.54%
2002	No	9	15	High	−17.53%

Source: Company records and casewriter calculations.

[a]Presentation and evaluation minutes.

[b]The average annual buy-and-hold return for 10 Uncommon Values® stocks, net of returns on benchmark stocks with comparable market capitalizations and book-to-market ratios.

EXHIBIT 8

Number of Lehman Brothers U.S. Equity Analysts and U.S. Companies Covered, 1984–2002

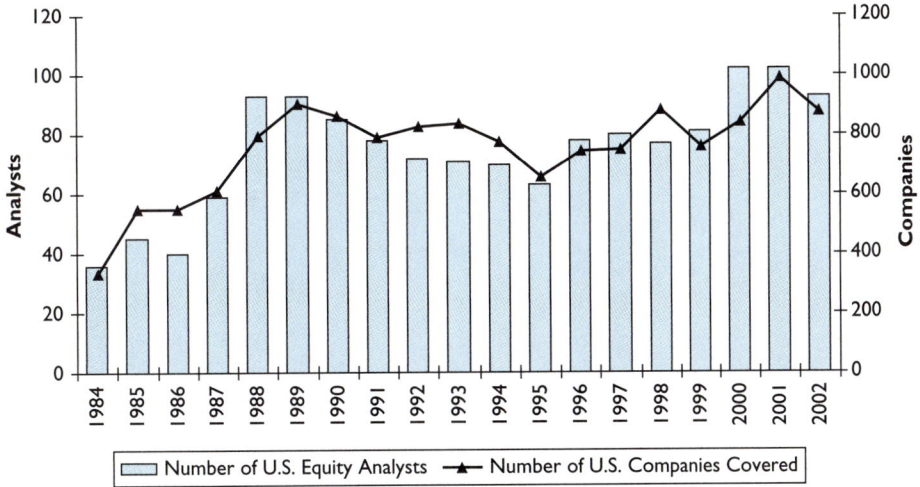

Source: Thomson Research, a Thomson Financial product.

10 Uncommon Values

Teva Pharmaceutical Industries, Ltd

In Israel we have a 1970s song based on a poem from 1953 by Amir Gilboa about Theodor Herzl [the most important early advocate for the establishment of Israel]. It has a line in it about Herzl: "Suddenly a man rises in the morning, feels he is a people, and starts walking." That is exactly what Hurvitz did. Suddenly he woke up in the morning, feels he is a giant world class company, and starts walking. No one, aside from Herzl, has accomplished anything as remotely as impressive in this country as Hurvitz. It was impossible, a million to one odds at best, and he still did it. He woke up one morning and started walking.

—Ori Hershkovitz, equity analyst at Tel Aviv-based Leader & Company

The markets had not been kind to Teva Pharmaceutical during the first half of 2006. The stock had plunged nearly 30% from January 1 to June 30, erasing billions of dollars from the company's market capitalization. Even good news, such as reports in July of Teva's wildly successful introduction of generic Zocor—the largest blockbuster drug ever to go off-patent—had failed to boost the stock significantly. Since nearly every retirement fund and mutual fund in Israel invested in Teva, this drop had been felt throughout the population, effectively amounting to every Israeli family losing NIS 3000 or $675.[1]

The largest public company in the country's nearly 60-year history, Teva was more than the world's leading producer of generic pharmaceuticals. It represented the gold standard of business in Israel. As the country's first true multinational, it had eschewed the traditional conglomerate model, choosing instead a highly focused approach embraced by later generations of successful Israeli companies. With revenues growing from $91 million in 1985 to an estimated $8.5 billion in 2006, the company had bred a class of professional managers and scientists not before seen in the country. It had served as a bridge from Israeli science to the market and had been an important source of talent and capital for the growing biotechnology sector. It had also helped to catalyze the country's domestic capital markets by being one of the early companies to list on the Tel Aviv Stock Exchange in 1968.[2]

Professors Tarun Khanna and Krishna Palepu and Doctoral Student Claudine Madras prepared this case. HBS cases are developed solely as the basis for class discussion. Cases are not intended to serve as endorsements, sources of primary data, or illustrations of effective or ineffective management.

1. "Plummeting Teva stocks affect every household," Yedioth Ahronot, June 25, 2006.

2. Alternately, the company could be viewed as listing in 1951, accounting for an antecedent company.

Chairman Eli Hurvitz was viewed as a titan in Israel and Teva as the realization of his vision. He had led the company as chief executive through its growth years from the mid-1970s through his retirement in that capacity in 2002. He had been a central actor in the development of Israel's economy as a whole, and in 2002, was awarded the Israel Prize by the government, the most prestigious civilian award in the country.

By 2005, Teva's $7.4 billion acquisition of Ivax had catapulted the company to the top position among global generics into what one reporter dubbed "Generics answer to Big Pharma."[3] Less than one year later, Teva filled 20% more prescriptions than Pfizer, the world's largest pharmaceutical company. It had a portfolio and pipeline twice the size of its next closest competitors.[4] With a 20% of the U.S. market, it was by far the largest player in the world's largest market. Also, with the Ivax acquisition, Teva had gained the broadest geographic reach in the industry. One of the top players in Western Europe, it also had a significant operations in the fast growing markets of Eastern Europe and Latin America, and had a presence in over 50 countries globally.

Teva's historical place in Israel's economic growth was assured; however, its future was less clear. While Teva may have been Generics answer to Big Pharma, Big Pharma had finally and resoundingly answered back. Novartis, one of the world's largest pharmaceuticals companies and the only one with a consistently strong presence in generics over the last two decades, had spent $10 billion on generics acquisitions since 2001. Novartis' generics unit, Sandoz, was now the second largest generics company in the world with the resources of a much larger firm at their disposal. Other innovative firms were aggressively fighting patent challenges both legally and through alliances with generics companies or moving to revive their own generics arms.

Low cost firms from India, Eastern Europe and elsewhere were also upping their game, emulating strategies that Teva itself pioneered over the last decade. Partly as a consequence, the pricing of generics in the U.S. market, the core of Teva's business for twenty years, had declined between 15% and 30% over the past three years.[5] However, the U.S. and worldwide markets continued to grow as aging population and rising expenditures created pressure for lower cost options.

Could the company maintain its annual growth rate of 33% of the last five years and, if so, how? Teva could maintain its focus on the U.S. generics market, with major blockbusters set to lose their patent protection over the medium term, taking advantage of the glut to grow its share during the inevitable consolidation. Alternately, the company could focus on the global generics market, either the large potential markets that were slowing opening up to generics, such as Germany, France and Japan, or the newer markets, such as Latin America or Asia. Finally, Teva could continue to move up the value chain from low-cost generics into more specialized products such as drugs with complex delivery systems or "biosimilar" versions of large-molecule drugs, and, ultimately, into innovative drugs which carried both significantly higher risks and returns. In the meantime, Teva also needed to guard against the innovative firms and low-cost players to make sure that, as the incumbent, it did not allow creeping complacency to become fatal. The industry had changed significantly over the past five years; and the Israeli market leader needed to change with it.

---

3. "Teva/Ivax: Generics' Answer to Big Pharma," In Vivo, September 2005.

4. Dan Suesskind, personal communication; Ranbaxy company documents.

5. Casewriter estimates based on published financial reports and IMS data.

THE GENERIC PHARMACEUTICALS INDUSTRY

Generic pharmaceuticals refer to "bioequivalent" versions of their innovative counterparts. Most often in tablet and capsule form but also available in syringes, inhalers and other delivery devices, generics effectively duplicated the active compounds developed by the original drug maker. These drugs were subject to the same regulatory standards and could only be manufactured and sold if the original drugs were not protected by patents. From a medical perspective, these drugs were largely identical to the innovative versions and to each other.

Generics were typically priced significantly lower than their original versions because the drug makers did not need to recoup the massive costs of the initial research and development associated with drug discovery nor support the massive sales and marketing costs associated with introducing a new drug. See Exhibit 1 a comparison of the cost structures between innovative firms and generics firms. While the innovative and generics industries had both grown worldwide at around 9 to 10 annually since 2000 (see Exhibit 2) the innovative side was expected to slow to 5–8% as major drugs lost their patent protection without a large immediate pipeline to replace them, while generics growth was expected to speed up to as much as 16% in major markets. Daniel Vasella, the CEO of Novartis, predicted that sales of generics would double to $100 billion worldwide by 2010 from the $52 billion in 2005.[6] In contrast, the size of the worldwide pharmaceutical industry was approximately $600 billion in 2006.

Generic Markets

United States   The United States, by far the world's largest generics market, was the first major country to embrace unbranded generics with the establishment of the Hatch-Waxman Act in 1984. This act dramatically and immediately opened up the market, with generics penetration as a percentage of the total number of prescriptions increasing from 13% in 1983 to higher than 50% in 2006 with prices close to 11% of the innovative products on a per-dose basis.[7]

The act contained two important provisions. First, it introduced the Abbreviated New Drug Application (ANDA) process which allowed generic drugs to shortcut the lengthy drug approval processes required by the Food and Drug Administration. Second, through its "Paragraph IV" provision, it allowed generics companies to challenge innovative drugs long before patent expiration, which generics companies often used to challenge follow-on patents filed by innovative companies to extend the effective lifetime of a drug. Crucially, it established a 180-day exclusivity period for the first company to submit an ANDA under a paragraph IV challenge, providing incentives for generics competition. This exclusivity period set up a highly coveted duopoly for the first six months after generics introduction, and resulted in a vicious escalation in the legal battles between innovative companies and their generics counterparts.

During the traditional 180-day exclusivity period, during which a generic drug faced competition only from its patented counterpart, the generic could be expected

---

6. *"Mixing Medicines: Betting $10 Billion on Generics, Novartis Seeks to Inject Growth,"* Wall Street Journal, May 4, 2006.

7. Remarks by Lester M. Crawford. Acting Commissioner of Food and Drugs to the Generics Pharmaceutical Association, 26 February 2005, and WR Hambrecht estimates.

to capture up to 75% of the market by volume of prescriptions with discounts of 20–40% off the original drug price.[8] Gross margins during this period were typically near 70–90%, close to the innovator's margins of 90–95%. After the 180-day period expired and other generics competition entered the market, the pricing of the 180-day generic drug decreased significantly, although the company often maintained a higher market share than the new generic entrants. In a typical scenario, the pricing would decline to 90% off the innovative price, while the market share of the 180-day holder would decrease from 70–75% to 30–40%, with the corresponding sharp decline in margins. These numbers differed across products and with the number of competitors entering the market.

Europe   The market for generics in the rest of the world varied greatly across countries. The European Union, very slowly moving towards internal harmonization, was still far from achieving that aim. The United Kingdom and the Netherlands, the most competitive markets in the region, most resembled the U.S. in their market structures. Pharmacists were free to substitute generic drugs for innovative versions at their discretion unless explicitly overruled by the physician, and prices were largely market-driven. As a result, generic penetration was also high (in 2004, 49% of total prescriptions for both the U.K. and the Netherlands) as governments, the public, physicians and pharmacists generally accepted generics substitution.[9]

Most countries, however, restricted the use of generics following systems referred as "physician-driven" or "branded generics" markets. Germany and France represented this end of the regulatory spectrum: pharmacists did not have the latitude to substitute generics at their discretion and generics companies branded and marketed their drugs directly to physicians in the same manner as innovative companies. As a result, generics companies operating in these markets had to support much larger sales forces and marketing activities than in pharmacist-driven markets. Furthermore, prices for both innovative and generic drug tended to be government regulated; therefore, discounts associated with generic drugs generally were much lower than in liberalized markets. These markets had lower penetration rates than pharmacist-driven markets (see Exhibit 3), but were still some of the largest markets globally both in size and potential (see Exhibit 4).

Asia, Latin America, and Rest of World   Japan, the largest pharmaceuticals market outside of North America and Germany, was also heavily regulated and had a generics penetration of approximately 10%.[10] Japan and other East Asian markets also had various structural barriers to generics substitution, including a perception by patients and most physicians of inferior quality of the products. Physicians also generated a portion of their income from pharmaceuticals, given their role as both a prescriber and dispenser of drugs, and thus had little incentive to substitute the lower priced generics. Over time, however, penetration in Japan, like all the large markets, was expected to increase as aging populations and rising health care costs.

Developing markets, such as Latin America, Eastern Europe, Russia, India, and China were also growing as demand increased for reliable generics as middle classes emerged, governments moved to provide higher quality care, and lower overall absolute wealth led to a strong preference for the less costly generic drugs. For example, in Poland,

8. *Dr Joseph Aleksandrowicz, personal communication.*

9. *Source: European Generics Association, http://www.leaddiscovery.co.uk/datamonitor_shots/*
BEST%20Nov%2016th% 20Generics%20Sample%20Pages%202.pdf.

10. *Eran Ezra, personal communication.*

Lithuania, and Hungary, generics penetration by volume in 2004 was 87%, 73%, and 50%, respectively.[11] Many of these markets were physician-driven, requiring all the corresponding sales and marketing activities, and were heavily government regulated. See Exhibit 5 for select developing market indicators of both developing and developed countries.

Industry Players

From the early 1980s until the early 2000s, the industry was dominated largely by local companies. In the United States, Teva, Mylan Laboratories, Watson Pharmaceuticals and Barr Laboratories had been the largest players in a highly fragmented industry, while a variety of companies operated in Europe, such as Germany's Ratiopharm and the U.K.'s Generics Ltd (since acquired by Merck KGaA). Starting in the mid-1990s, the industry began to consolidate slowly and then a decade later, it experienced two competitive seismic shifts: the entrance of new types of competitors and the introduction of aggressive tactics by the innovative firms. In 2005 Novartis acquired two generics companies, Hexal (Germany) and Eon (U.S.), and merged them into its generics arm, Sandoz, catapulting it temporarily into the top position in the generics industry. More significant than the relative size of the firm, this acquisition marked the first serious effort by an innovative company to compete in generics after a wave of failed attempts in the 1990s. Pfizer had also recently picked up activity with its Greenstone unit and others had recently signaled that they were reassessing the sector.

Several philosophies regarding international expansion prevailed. One philosophy held that local market share was far more important than global share given the highly localized nature of pricing and regulations. According to one observer, Sandoz had focused on developing a top three presence in specific markets, namely Germany, much of the rest of Western Europe (with the notable exceptions of the United Kingdom, Ireland, and Italy) and the United States.[12] This approach was similar to that followed historically by Teva, but contrasted with that of Ivax, another global generics firm since acquired by Teva, which had expanded into a broad number of markets, but often with smaller market shares.

Aside from Sandoz, low-cost players began to emerge from newly competitive markets such as India (Ranbaxy, Dr. Reddy's Laboratories, Orchid, among others), Eastern Europe (Pliva, Aegis, and Gedeon Richter) and Iceland (Actavis). Indian firm Ranbaxy was one leader of this generation. The Indian market had long been heavily protected and the government had *de facto* allowed local firms to circumvent international patent laws to manufacture drugs domestically, a practice which ended in 2005 with India's commitments as a full member of the World Trade Organization. With fierce domestic competition and very low consumer ability to pay, India had among the least expensive pharmaceutical prices in the world. For example, the country had over one hundred brands of generic ciprofloxacin priced at an average of 63 cents for 10 tablets of 500 mg each, compared to $51 for generic ciprofloxacin in the U.S.[13] However, a large component of the price differences between generics in the Indian and US markets was attributable to additional costs

11. European Generics Association, http://www.leaddiscovery.co.uk/datamonitor_shots/ BEST%20Nov%2016th% 20Generics%20Sample%20Pages%202.pdf.

12. Dr Joseph Aleksandrowicz, personal communication.

13. "Emerging Giants," BusinessWeek, July 21, 2006.

which would have to be borne by all participants, such as obtaining federal approval and maintaining quality standards, as well as the pharmacy markup.

Ranbaxy had grown up in this environment and had used its advantages to compete abroad. By 2005, the company generated 80% of its $1.2 billion revenues outside the country, with Davinder Brar, the former Ranbaxy CEO, often credited with creating India's first major multinational. In mid-2006, it also had the second largest generics pipeline in the US after Teva, with 59 generics applications pending with the US FDA at the end of 2005.[14] With this pipeline, as well as its low-cost production and presence in 23 of the top 25 markets globally, Ranbaxy had set itself the goal of surpassing Teva globally by 2012.[15] However, it was still smaller on an absolute scale, and revenue was increasing at a rate of 19% over the past five years versus 33% for Teva. See Exhibit 6 for competitor information.

A second trend also affected profitability. Innovative giants such as Merck, Pfizer and Eli Lilly increasingly released their own "authorized generic" version of their product during the 180-exclusivity period, often by licensing production rights to a competitor generics company. This practice cut into the revenues of the first-filer by an estimated 50–60%.[16] While varying significantly across products, a representative generic drug which may have held 75% market share and 30% discount off the original price without authorized generic competition might have its share reduced to 50% and discounts rise to 60%. In 2004 and 2005, several high-profile antitrust cases emerged from these practices involving both Teva and Mylan as plaintiffs; however, given no signs of dampened competition in the industry—in fact, the opposite had occurred—no one expected the practice to be regulated or subside. Since 2003, every major drug with revenues over $1 billion going off patent had an authorized generic introduced onto the market.[17] As a result, generics companies could depend less on 180-day exclusivities for profitability and many looked to other means of protecting their margins, such as entering profit-sharing alliances with innovative firms or with each other and focusing on niche drugs which attracted less competition.

Generic Products

Generics could be roughly divided into three categories of products: commodity generics, niche or "specialty" generics and biosimilars.

Commodity Generics   Commodity generics, typically in tablet or capsule form, were generic versions of the small molecule pharmaceuticals that made up the bulk of innovative firms' traditional businesses and consequently comprised the largest segment of generics. Examples ranged from generic versions of antibiotics Cipro and Zithromax to painkiller Oxycontin to cholesterol-lowering drugs Pravachol and Zocor. The margins on these drugs were typically the lowest of the three categories for the drugs not sold during a 180-day exclusivity period, although varied based on the number of competitors. For example, Eli Lilly's Prozac, one of the most successful antidepressant drugs in history, had both a very large branded market and was a relatively simple compound to synthesize. As a result, once the

14. Ranbaxy web site, accessed August 28, 2006.

15. "Emerging Giants," BusinessWeek, July 21, 2006.

16. Teva internal communication (Dan Suesskind, August 28, 2006).

17. Fenwick and West, November, 2005.

patent and the 180-exclusivity period had expired, eighteen competitors entered the market, collapsing prices and erasing profits.[18]

Niche Generics   Generic drugs could qualify as niche drugs because either their active molecules were difficult to synthesize or their delivery mechanism was non-standard. Respiratory drugs, for example, had patented inhalers and had to be branded and prescribed by physicians even in normally pharmacist-driven markets. Niche drugs could attract as few as one or even no generic version, depending on the difficulty and size of market. As expected, generic companies realized higher gross margins on these products than on commodity generics, while the capital required was greater than for commodity generics but less than for the next segment of drugs, biosimilars.

Biosimilars   The market for biosimilars was a multibillion dollar but largely undeveloped segment. Biosimilars were the generic versions of the so-called "biotech" drugs pioneered by companies such as Amgen and Genentech. The active compounds in these drugs were highly complex proteins or other large molecules that were far harder to replicate than traditional pharmaceuticals. While the worldwide market for biotech drugs was only $29 billion in 2002, it was expected to grow to $112 billion by 2012, a 12% annual growth rate, and take on increasing importance over the long term as the innovation in small-molecule drugs diminished and was replaced by this class of products.[19] Because of the complexity of the original drugs, the regulatory pathway for biosimilars was still undetermined in the U.S. and just appearing in Europe. However, the expected rewards were high as the prices of these drugs were expected to be discounted by only 10–20% off the branded prices, and the margins correspondingly closer to innovative drugs than commodity generics.

Some estimated that the market could support only three to four companies competing in this sector because the capital and expertise required created significant barriers to entry. Predicted one industry analyst, "the companies that will be successful in [biosimilars] will be those that really have the resources to roll out a product launch. The biggest three that pharma needs to be worried about are Sandoz, Teva and Barr."[20] As of mid-2006, only Sandoz had launched a major biosimilar, a human growth hormone, in Australia and Europe, and both Teva and Barr had acquired companies to enter the field, with Sicor and Pliva (still pending), respectively.

Exhibit 7 shows several stylized scenarios of revenues and margins of drugs in these different categories.

TEVA'S EARLY HISTORY

Teva's roots can be traced back to 1901 as Salomon, Levine and Elstein (SLE), a wholesale drug distributor based in Jerusalem to serve the local population and wave of immigrants from Europe during the first four decades of the twentieth century. During the 1930s, refugees from Nazi Germany came to British-Mandate Palestine and set up several small drug manufacturing plants, including one called Teva ("nature" in Hebrew). These early immigrants tended to be highly educated,

---

18. Rouhi, "Generic Tide is Rising," *Chemical and Engineering News*, vol. 80, no. 38, CENEAR 80 38, pp. 37–51.

19. *Medical and Healthcare Marketplace Guide*, 2004.

20. http://news.monstersandcritics.com/health/article_1193475.php/Analysis_Biosimilars_to_make_big_splash.

and many had been scientists, physicians and engineers in their home country. Because Germany was the birthplace of the pharmaceuticals industry and arguably had the top universities and scientific research institutions at the time, they brought many specialized skills required to set up pharmaceuticals cottage businesses in their new country.

In 1945, the newly created Arab League declared a general boycott against domestic and foreign businesses operating in the Jewish portion of Palestine, which subsequently transferred over to all businesses dealing with Israel upon the establishment of the country in 1948. This boycott contributed to an economic structure in which foreign direct investment comprised less than 5% of all investment in Israel through the 1970s.[21] For the nascent pharmaceuticals industry, the absence of any large foreign pharmaceuticals company spurred a domestic industry of about twenty family-owned drug distributors and manufacturers each with annual revenues of approximately $1 million.[22] Together these family firms produced both the scale and, more significantly, the full portfolio of products required to serve the population of approximately 2 million people by the late 1950s. This full portfolio resulted in a community of Israeli chemists with a broad set of synthesis skills, experienced in supplying drugs at a lower cost to serve the relatively poor home market. Also, since the patent-holding foreign firms would not conduct business directly in Israel, domestic firms could invoke the threat of "compulsory licensing" to pressure the patent holders into licensing the pharmaceuticals for use in the domestic market.[23] Compulsory licensing provisions were common in the legal codes of most countries, and could be invoked in certain situations in which good faith attempts to obtain a license under negotiated commercial terms failed for non-commercial reasons. While compulsory licensing was rarely invoked by these local pharmaceuticals companies, the threat increased their leverage to obtain voluntary licenses from the patent holders.

In the 1950s, SLE purchased Assia, a small manufacturing pharmaceuticals company. In 1962, Eli Hurvitz, a young employee of Assia, began the drive for consolidation of the fragmented industry. Hurvitz, born in Jerusalem in 1932, had started at Assia as a young economist in 1954. He had served as a private in the Israeli Defense Forces during the 1948 war of independence and then obtained a degree in economics from Hebrew University. Hurvitz finished his active military service as member of a generation of young Israelis highly dedicated to developing the new country. Dan Suesskind, the longtime chief financial officer of Teva, reflected many years later, "As far as I know, Eli Hurvitz is the only soldier I know who came out of the military a private and was promoted to brigadier general during the reserves. He devoted many years to service and his life to the country."

By 1962, both Hurvitz and Nachman Salomon, the head of the combined company, became convinced of the need to consolidate the industry. Salomon put Hurvitz in charge of negotiating the acquisitions. In 1963, after much discussion, they completed their first acquisition, of a company called Zori. "How did we choose them? Because at the time, they spoke Hebrew, and everyone else spoke German. We could actually talk to them!" Hurvitz commented. He remembered on his first major lesson in business:

> *With these private, family-owned companies, they were not ready to dilute their ownership and lose control. We had to show them that mergers produce synergies,*

---

21. *meria.idc.ac.il/journal/2002/issue3/jv6n3a3.html as accessed on November 14, 2005.*

22. *Eli Hurvitz, personal communication, November 2005.*

23. *Dan Suesskind, personal communication.*

that they make money. We needed one example to prove that the result was not small at all but an order of magnitude. Only then could we convince the rest of them.

In 1968, he completed his second acquisition, this time of Teva, which had been publicly listed on the Tel Aviv Stock Exchange since 1951. The combined company officially changed its name to Teva Pharmaceutical in 1976. That year, Hurvitz became the chief executive of the merged entity, now the largest pharmaceuticals company in Israel with revenues of $28 million.

The Billion Dollar Theory

By the early 1980s, having recently acquired Ikapharm, the second-largest remaining pharmaceuticals company in Israel after Teva, Hurvitz recognized that the company had grown as far as it could within its home market.[24] He hired Dr. Joseph Aleksandrowicz to head the strategic planning process for the company, which he continued to do until 1995. Aleksandrowicz recalled, "In the early 1980s, no company in Israel had any organized strategic planning. It was unheard of in the country at the time. Businesses were run more informally. Our production was best and FDA approved, we had marketing, computers, finance, and excellent, devoted people. But no one was used to creating a strategy."

Aleksandrowicz organized a two year intensive program for the executive team, bringing in professors from leading American business schools to educate the leaders of the $50 million company. It was during one of these sessions in the mid-1980s that Hurvitz issued a challenge that became dubbed "The Billion Dollar Theory." Said one participant at the meeting, "Eli said to us: 'We have all the capabilities of a full-sized company. If we were operating in a large western market, we could be a billion dollar company, instead of the $50 million organization we are today. Now,' he asked us, 'how do we make that happen?' "

Hurvitz himself recalled the conversation:

I remember in one planning meeting, I went around to each member of the executive team, asking what their growth goals were for the next year, five years. I heard 10%, 15% at the most. Everyone was thinking incrementally, 'how can I take my current business and grow it?' I realized with that type of thinking, we would never grow to our potential. I had to break out of that thinking.

With the Billion Dollar Theory to guide them, the executive team recognized that they would have to expand beyond their current presence primarily in Israel and become the first Israeli company to enter a large, Western market. Dr. Aleksandrowicz recalled that, in addition to new markets, two other issues occupied the group:

One big issue was corporate structure: should we be a focused company or a conglomerate? In the end, we decided to be focused rather than diversified. This was also extremely unusual for Israel at the time. The second issue was where to focus: should we be a chemicals company or a pharmaceuticals company? We decided on pharma, since it had more profits, we could collaborate with

---

24. During the late 1960s, Teva had expanded briefly overseas to West Africa and Kenya, reflecting a period of close ties between the governments of these countries and the companies recognition then of the need for expansion. However, these markets proved limited in size and increasingly politically problematic and eventually Teva exited the region.

the scientific institutions in Israel, such as the Weizmann Institute, Hebrew University of Jerusalem, or the Technion, and we could export around the world. If if if . . . there were so many ifs in this direction! This path was so much riskier, but it also had a higher payoff if we were successful.

At the time, the company was partly owned by Koor Industries, the largest Israeli conglomerate controlled by the Histradrut, the powerful domestic trade union rooted in the socialist beginnings of the country. The board members from Koor in particular resisted this move as too risky for a company that employed so many people and served the basic health needs of much of the population. Hurvitz remembered:

At the time, we had a $60 million market capitalization and it would cost us $20 to $25 million to enter the U.S. market. Now the decision seems obvious, but those numbers made it impossible to pass through the board. So I made them a pledge: I will not ever take a risk so big that it would jeopardize the company. I will risk quarterly or yearly profits, but never the company. I have always followed that. I managed the company for one hundred quarters, not afraid to bet a year but never the company.

Expanding Abroad

The executive team chose the U.S. market first, a difficult decision for a country and company with closer cultural and trade ties to Europe. However, Europe was a still patchwork of regulation and price controls, while the U.S. could be treated as a single market on the verge of uniform liberalization and market-based pricing. Teva entered the U.S. through a joint venture with WR Grace, a major American conglomerate, which gave them access to capital and contacts within the market. Chief Financial Officer Dan Suesskind said, "When we got together with W.R. Grace we said to them, 'We are willing to contribute to the partnership what ever we have, but money we don't ship over the ocean, of this they have enough in the U.S.' That's how we got to this arrangement."

Professor Elon Kohlberg, member of the board of the Teva's North America business, noted:

Here comes Teva, a nothing company from a tiny country . . . and somehow, Hurvitz manages to structure a deal where Grace puts in over 90% of the capital for 50% of the joint venture. Who else could negotiate that kind of deal? . . . Grace was so much bigger than us at the time, and yet Mr. Grace himself used to come to the office just to spend time with Eli. He viewed him as an equal. That was part of the genius of Hurvitz.

In late 1985, the Teva And Grace (TAG) joint venture acquired Lemmon, a $20 million U.S. arm of Nattermann, a German company. From there, Teva entered the U.S. market and, just as in the Zori deal in Israel, once it had established a foothold, sales and market share steadily grew. Hurvitz built an internal team focused on acquisitions that earned a reputation in the industry for its systematic approach and successful outcomes. Teva became the most active acquirer in the industry, sometimes paying less than one times sales for a target company and rigorously executing the integration.

By 1993, the company had reached $502 million in revenues, halfway to its billion dollar goal, and North America had overtaken Israel as the largest contributor to the business. Teva continued to expand throughout the 1990s and 2000s, fueled by a series of acquisitions in North America and Europe (see Exhibit 8), and passed the billion dollar revenue mark in 2000. By 2002, when Hurvitz retired as CEO, the company was one of the top three providers of generic drugs in the U.S., Canada, the U.K., the Netherlands, France, and Hungary, in addition to being the market leader in Israel.

Developing Their Competitive Advantage

Over time, together with Mylan Laboratories, Teva became one of the largest supplier to the growing segment of national pharmacy chains in the United States, with Mylan and Geneva (the U.S. generics arm of Novartis prior to Sandoz). At the time the industry was dominated by wholesalers and distributors which had long focused on serving mom-and-pop pharmacies. Teva filled a vacuum for these national chains, enabling them to reduce their own internal costs by sourcing much of their formulary from a single company without use of a middleman. Teva provided not only a broad scope of products, but also inventory management, volume-based discounts and pricing bundles, services less valuable to the mom-and-pops but very important to the cost-conscious chains. Teva also kept its focus on low prices, acknowledging the commodity-like nature of the industry. Hurvitz reflected,

> *Throughout the 1980s, everyone kept saying, "the Chinese are coming!" Everyone was terrified of this situation back then. So, we had to neutralize price as an issue for us. We spent a lot of time on our manufacturing and business model to ensure this, and always, always guaranteed the lowest price to our customers. If our competitors lowered prices after the contract was signed, we would give our customers credit. We were willing to forego part of our income in the short term for the long term. We knew back then that he who keeps market share will be the one who makes money in this industry.*

This philosophy stayed with Teva in the subsequent years. According to Hershkovitz, "No one takes market share from Teva, no one. In the past, they have slashed their prices like nobody's business. This is a rule for the Indian companies: if you go into a Teva drug, you lose money, as simple as that."

Teva also focused on rigorous execution as a means of gaining advantage, including filing ANDA applications earlier and more thoroughly than its competitors, backward integrating into active pharmaceutical ingredients, and efficiently managing its supply chain. As a result, Teva was able to sustain a large pipeline of paragraph IV challenges as well as a broad portfolio of commodity generics, an elusive balance for its competitors.

Developing an Innovative Business

In the early 1980s, Teva decided to enter the innovative drug market, a moved dubbed as "sheer *chutzpah*"[25] by Eli Hurvitz. By 2006, Teva's strong relationship with Israeli academic institutions yielded 150 to 180 proposals for new drugs per year. They had launched three drugs: two in partnership with Weizmann, including their blockbuster drug, Copaxone, in 1996, which became the leading treatment for multiple sclerosis. Teva relied on these external institutions for drug discovery, in contrast to Pfizer or other companies producing innovative drugs who had large internal basic research divisions. As a result, Dr. Irit Pinchasi, the VP of global innovative R&D, estimated that Teva's estimated that Teva's drug development cost for Copaxone amounted to

---

25. *"Nerve, gall or supreme self-confidence,"* Merriam-Webster Dictionary, *accessed August 30, 2006.*

approximately four to six times less than the $1 billion typically required to bring an innovative drug to market.[26]

Becoming the Global Leader in the Early 2000s

In 2002, Israel Makov succeeded Hurvitz as CEO, who, at 70 years old, remained in place as chairman. This event marked the first leadership handover within the company since 1976. From 2002 through 2006, Teva grew from $2.52 billion in revenues in 2002 to an estimated $8.5 billion in 2006. In 2003, Teva executed its first multi-billion dollar acquisition of Sicor which, at $3.4 billion, was eight times the deal size of their previous largest acquisition. Sicor offered not only additional scale, but also expansion into new customers, products and technologies, selling injectable liquid products directly to hospitals rather than more traditional tablets to pharmacies. Some hailed the acquisition as an opportunity to expand and diversify away from commodity generics, particularly into biosimilars and the lucrative injectables business. Others cautioned that businesses were too different and that the opportunity cost of choosing Sicor over other businesses had been high. Said one observer, "Focus had been the key to Teva's success over the years, during periods when other companies fell down trying to do too much. Sicor changed too many variables at once."

Two years later, in 2005, Teva acquired Ivax for $7.4 billion, a move viewed positively by analysts for a variety of reasons. Some saw it as a tactical acquisition to gain access to Ivax' very strong first-to-file paragraph IV pipeline in the U.S., which included generic Zocor and Zoloft (two of the largest blockbusters in history) at a time when Teva's own pipeline had softened. Others viewed the acquisition as more strategic, with Ivax's strong positions in global markets where Teva had little presence, particularly Latin America and Eastern Europe, as well as their innovative pipeline and niche generics in therapeutic areas new to Teva. Still others viewed the innovative and niche businesses positively, but were cautious of overexpansion into many small physician-driven markets.

TEVA IN 2006

Profits, Products, and Markets

In 2006, Teva's profits could be roughly divided into six sources: U.S. 180-day exclusivities, remaining U.S. commodity generics, Europe and Japan generics, rest of world generics markets, niche products and innovative pharmaceuticals. See Exhibit 9 for an approximate breakdown of revenue within these categories.

U.S. 180-Day Exclusivities   The combined Ivax-Teva pipeline in 2006 was the largest in the industry. As of August 9, 2006, the company had 46 first-to-file Paragraph IV applications, covering drugs with $35 billion in branded revenues. From January through August 31, 2006, Teva had launched four drugs with exclusivities, including generic Zocor in June, the largest generics launch in the history of the industry covering branded sales of $4.4 billion. From January 1, 2004 through May, 2006, Teva had filed 24 Paragraph IV challenges versus eight for Sandoz.[27]

---

26. "Not just generics and Copaxone," Globes, 10 April 2006.

27. Wall Street Journal, May 4, 2006.

However, this market was tightening as more companies vied for a fixed number of exclusivities.

U.S. Commodity Generics   By the middle of 2006, Teva controlled approximately 18% of the base U.S. generics market by number of prescriptions, with Mylan and Sandoz, the next closest companies controlling 11% and 10% respectively (see Exhibit 10). Its total pipeline as of August 9, 2006, including the 180-day drugs, was 148 drugs products with branded sales of over $84 billion.[28] This segment formed the core of Teva's business, and some analysts expressed concern regarding the systemic price erosion in the U.S. market.

Europe and Japan Generics   Prior to the Ivax acquisition, Teva had focused on the pharmacist-driven markets in the U.K. and the Netherlands, as well as several other larger markets which showed signs of potentially moving to a pharmacy-driven model. It had maintained either low or no presence in the markets that remained dominated by physician-driven regulation, most notably Germany and Japan.

Europe comprised approximately 30% of Teva's 2005 revenues, with 60% in the U.S. and the balance split between Israel and the rest of the world (see Exhibit 11). Ivax gave Teva presence in the growing markets of the Czech Republic, Poland, Russia, and Slovakia (see Exhibit 12). Within Europe, Hungary, UK and the Netherlands comprised approximately 75% of Teva's revenues, reflecting Teva's strength in pharmacist-driven markets and the legacy of Biogal, their acquisition in Hungary. Germany and France, the two largest physician-driven markets together comprised slightly more than half of the remaining European revenues. Analysts differed on how Teva should approach these and other physician-driven markets. On the one hand, Teva could wait for them to adapt into a market structure closer to the pharmacy-driven model in which Teva excelled. On the other hand, Sandoz, Actavis and other companies were already aggressively expanding into continental Europe, establishing dominant positions that could become difficult to disrupt in the future.

In 2005, Sandoz and Dr. Reddy's Laboratories acquired the second and fourth largest companies in Germany, Hexal and Betapharm, respectively. The first and third largest German generic companies, Ratiopharm and STADA were still independent with 2005 revenues of approximately $2 billion and $1 billion.[29] Teva's Germany presence, in contrast, was much smaller. During the first quarter of 2006, Teva reported German revenues of only €9 million, and no immediate intentions of executing any acquisitions to strengthen their position.[30] When asked about Teva's go-slow strategy in Germany, Hurvitz responded:

We had a different short term strategy in Germany than in the U.S. We haven't entered Germany yet and, if the system stays the same, we are not as good as others at detailing [pharmaceuticals sales to physicians] there. Only if we come with something new will we be able to enter in an important way into the German market. If the system remains as it is today, and as long as you have to invest a large margin in detailing, there are better people than us. We are niche players right now until the market changes.

28. Q2 earnings call, August 8, 2006 and Hurvitz, personal communication.
29. Both companies are private, turnover is estimated and converted from euro to dollar.
30. Teva, company documents, IMS data.

In Japan, as well as South Korea and other Asian markets, Teva—like most other generics companies from outside the region—had adopted a wait-and-see strategy and had little presence.

Rest of World Generics   Aside from Europe, Japan and North America, Ivax brought the leading presence in Latin America, which had contributed approximately 25% to Ivax' 2004 profits and was growing quickly. Overall, including Latin America, sales had been $258 million in 1Q06, up 104% from 1Q05, which in turn had increased at a 38% annual rate since 1Q02.

Niche Products and Biosimilars   After the Ivax acquisition, Teva reorganized its internal operations and set up a separate specialty division to focus on niche products (such as hospital and respiratory drugs) and biosimilars. Teva expected $400 million in revenues from their respiratory franchise in 2006, growing to $1 to 2 billion by 2010.[31] It had not launched any significant biosimilars products in 2006, but expected this segment to be a high growth area. However, some questioned whether Teva had focused too heavily on the U.S. market, which was bogged down in a regulatory impasse that was estimated to take possibly as long as five years to resolve. In contrast, Sandoz had focused more on Europe, working closely with the European regulatory authorities and at least one marketed drug.

Nonacquisitive expansion into other specialty areas presented few opportunities for growth since most areas were heavily occupied by other companies and rewarded concentration of expertise.

Innovative Pharmaceuticals   Copaxone had been Teva's first innovative drug, and had become the top treatment for multiple sclerosis in the world with worldwide total sales of $1.2 billion in 2005. It continued to grow at an annualized rate of 22% in 2006, compared to a combined rate of 13.5% for its competitors,[32] and had become an important contributor to Teva's overall profits. The cost structure for Copaxone differed from a typical innovative drug. In addition to lower research and development costs, sales and marketing expenses, typically two to three times the cost of R&D at large innovative firms, were lower for Copaxone, given the limited population of prescribing physicians. Furthermore, Teva had partnered with Sanofi-Aventis through 2008 to manage the sales and marketing of the drug, thus off-loading much of these costs from Teva. Most analysts estimated that Sanofi-Aventis passed on between 50–60% of the revenues back to Teva.

Azilect, a treatment for Parkinson's disease, had been released to the market in mid 2006. Dan Suesskind noted the importance of bringing this second drug to market: "At least [Azilect] showed that Copaxone was not a one-off. Having two marketed drugs is almost more important than having a pipeline." Teva also had a pipeline in other therapeutic areas with estimated potential sales of $6 billion by 2015.[33] Outside analysts estimated that this number could, in fact, be much higher and that, given the superior economics of innovative products, the relative proportion of innovative to generic drugs in Teva's revenue mix would steadily increase during the next decade. Others wondered whether four or five different therapeutic areas[34] was too much for Teva's limited research budget and limited experience bringing drugs to market.

31. Q2 earnings call, August 8, 2006.
32. Teva company documents, IMS data.
33. Teva company documents.
34. Central Nervous System, immunology, oncology, hematology, and respiratory.

Supply Chain

In the generics industry, the challenge in managing an efficient supply chain lay in gaining scale benefits and low cost while simultaneously supporting large-scale product rollouts, a broad product line, no product defects and high service levels to customers, all in multiple markets. Teva, initially limiting its markets to the U.S. and Israel and only slowing adding in new markets, had maintained a rigorously low-cost culture and achieved greater scale benefits than any of its competitors.

Said Eli Shohet, vice president responsible for the Ivax integration and the Central and Eastern Europe region:

> The bottom line is that we have scale advantages that cannot be matched by other companies at this time. Compare Ivax before the merger and Teva. In Teva, we have two plants in Israel that are currently capable of eight billion tablets and one in Canada with the same scale. One batch at Teva would have required five to six runs at Ivax, all in different locations. This is so much more expensive, and this is how most companies are set up. With our size, we can also source raw materials on a much larger scale than our competitors. You cannot just look at labor costs. First of all, they are not the only input and second of all, we are much more productive and capital intensive. And for labor intensive processes, we have operations in India.

Teva reconfigured its supply chain every several years since the early 1990s and after every major acquisition. The most recent integration with Ivax had been particularly challenging, as Ivax and Teva organized their worldwide operations very differently. Reflected Shohet,

> The culture of the two companies is the same, but the business model different. Since 1995, Teva has operated as a global company. We localize the management and marketing in each region while having a global backend in R&D, manufacturing and APIs [active pharmaceutical ingredients]. The Ivax business model was an international company. It operated as a series of independent companies with very little cross-border interaction.

The backbone of Teva's supply chain was managed through several centers of excellence located globally to take advantage of differences in local labor skills and costs, tax provisions, and intellectual property regulations. The supply chain started with active pharmaceutical ingredient (API) production, a step which many of Teva's competitors at least partially outsourced, often to Teva. Teva's API division had sold $1.1 billion of ingredients in 2005, approximately evenly divided between internal and external use, and was one of the world's largest third party suppliers of APIs. Once the APIs were produced, they were sent to pharmaceutical manufacturing facilities. The two largest of these facilities were in Israel which primarily supplied the U.S. and Israeli market and had a capacity of 16 billion tablets, and in Hungary which primarily served Europe. Teva estimated that it would produce 36 billion tablets in 2006. Overall Teva reported unit costs reducing by 30% in the past five years due primarily to scale effects (see Exhibit 13).[35] Once the tablets were produced and packaged appropriately, they were shipped to their various markets and distributed locally. See Exhibit 14 and Exhibit 15 for maps of their global operations and Israeli operations.

---

35. *Teva company documents.*

Given the security risk associated with Israel's political situation, redundancies in the supply chain and extensive disaster planning had been conducted to mitigate disruptions associated with war or terrorism within the country.

Research and Development

In 2006, Teva reported R&D expenses at an annualized rate of $500 million or approximately 6% of sales. In addition, Teva held significant equity stakes in several Israeli startups. Allocating resources between innovative and generics areas was one of the company's main challenges. The lead time for innovative drug development was 10 to 15 years, while generics development was three to five years, and the act of selecting and executing projects required very different skills and information. Reflected Dr. Ben-Zion Weiner, the head of Teva's research and development group:

> It is interesting how these two animals live under the same roof. On the one hand, we have low risk products in generics, and then we have Copaxone and Azilect. The same person manages both and is responsible for dividing the resources. This is a very tricky decision making process. How do you trade off, say, investing in low risk 10 generics drugs versus one high potential innovative drug? This is a big part of our challenge.

Within the generics R&D division, Weiner's group had worked to create "an ANDA factory." Over the past decade, Teva had filed and won the greatest number of 180-day exclusivities in the industry, earning a reputation for quick ANDA filings and aggressive patent litigation. "Of course," said Dr. Weiner, "fifteen years ago, we were the entrepreneurs in this area. Since then, we have been studied by others and the gap has shrunk."

The innovative R&D group, on the other hand, had a different set of challenges. Said Weiner, "We are so small compared to the big guys. The consolidated research and development budget of the top 10 innovative firms is $45 billion. What can we do with a budget of [a few hundred million] against that? And that's just the top 10, the total budget of the industry is much bigger."

In this context, the Teva team decided to leave the original research to external institutions, and to build research franchises in areas that did not require mass marketing to the general public and family doctors. With the addition of Ivax' research arm and existing pipeline, Pinchasi estimated that, by 2010, Teva would have a sufficient pipeline theoretically to launch one new innovative drug per year, in comparison to five per year of leading pharmaceuticals companies such as Pfizer.[36] Said Hershkovitz, "[Teva's innovative R&D group] is running way, way under the radar right now. They are currently running over 10 phase 2 trials, in addition to their phase 3 trials. And every month it seems as if we discover another clinical trial that they are involved in through equity in a startup."

Mergers and Acquisitions

Since 1985 Teva had executed 14 transactions together worth over $12 billion, more than any other generics company, including Sandoz. It had built a reputation for successful mergers and fair treatment of employees, in part arising from the small community within Israel in which the consequences of treating employees poorly could be severe, and more importantly, because it reflected deeply held values of Eli Hurvitz.

---

36. "Not just generics and Copaxone," Globes, April 10, 2006.

With the current glut of companies within the industry in generics, many acknowledged the need for consolidation. In the U.S., the top four firms controlled less than 50% of the market, the next six together controlled 20%, and none of the more than 40 firms in the remaining tail controlled more than 2%.[37] As Hurvitz stated,

> *The market needs consolidation, globally. This is very much needed. America is getting somewhat stable but still has a long way to go. Every competitive market has similar structure in its stable state—you have one big company, the next big company, maybe a third one and then a lot of smaller players. The more commoditized the market, the more this is true. And in this industry, the smaller players are the price leaders. . . . Mathematically we have a problem: we are already large. Today we are 20% of the [U.S.] market. How far can we go?*

The industry had seen a sharp increase in the number of transactions completed in 2005, with a wide range of multiples paid (see Exhibit 16).

Financing Growth and Ownership Structure

Over the years, Teva had financed its growth through a combination of bank loans, retained earnings, and paid-in share capital from issues on both the Tel Aviv Stock Exchange and the NASDAQ, on which it first registered shares (in the form of American Depository Shares) in 1982.

Teva's ownership structure had evolved significantly in the past fifteen years. During the 1980s, approximately 75% of Teva was controlled by a combination of the founding families (22%), Koor Industries (25%), the directors and officers (14%) and W.R. Grace (14%). In 1989, Koor ownership was purchased by a consortium of Teva and two Israeli banks, which subsequently sold their 19% stake to a holding company controlled by the controversial media mogul Robert Maxwell. Maxwell's stake was gradually ramped down, and by 1994, control had been dispersed to institutional investors, with no one entity controlling more than 5% of the company. In 2006, the percent of shares held by insiders and 5% owners was 7% while institutional and mutual funds accounted for 60% of the company ownership.

Culture

The Teva team had experienced very low turnover in its history. Much of the executive team that was present when the company first expanded to the U.S. was still at the company in 2006. As the company expanded into multiple countries and developed specialized and innovative units, the challenges grew to maintain the aggressively low cost culture that had enabled Teva to reach its current position.

Other companies, particularly Novartis, were tackling the same issue although from different corporate roots. Sandoz had achieved operating margins of only 7.3% in 2005 compared to 25% for Teva, and some employees commented on the issues with running a generics division within an innovative company, "In Novartis, if you sell the [branded] product one month later or not it doesn't make a big difference, because there is no other company to sell it," says Bedri Toker, Sandoz's top executive in Turkey, "But as a generic company I have to be first because there are many companies that can sell the same product. . . . The way of thinking is very different." Roche, another large innovative firm, had also considered entering the generics business three times over the last decade, but decided against it based on their belief that pure generics companies

---

37. *Teva investor lunch, August 9, primary: IMS June data.*

would always be able to underprice Roche. Hurvitz held similar views, saying, "It is very easy to manage a generic company when you are poor. It becomes very complicated when you are rich. It is impossible for a rich company to act poor. As long as we remember this equation, and we do not become bureaucrats, and as long as we fight the fat culture, we will succeed."

Roche, like the other companies, also decided that is was too difficult to manage patent creation and challenging under one corporate umbrella.[38] This issue arose for both Novartis and Teva. Sandoz could not challenge any Novartis patents, and filed far fewer Paragraph IV challenges than Teva. On Teva's side, as they released more innovative drugs to the market, they anticipated greater challenges by other generics firms to these drugs. Responded Dr. Pinchasi to how they will manage these dual missions: "That will be interesting, no? We're now trying to learn what you have to do to make things hard for generic drug makers . . . After all, we know better than anyone how to challenge patents, but there's no guarantee we'll succeed. Yes, there are quite a few companies that would like to turn the tables on us, and challenge our patents."[39]

Many were watching whether either Sandoz or Teva could manage both businesses effectively under one corporate umbrella, particularly as they came from different roots but both sought growth in similar areas: generics sales in global markets, biosimilars and niche innovative drugs.

SUMMARY

The past few decades had been a tremendous success for the underdog from the Middle East competing against richer, Western companies. However, the company was now the reigning incumbent in an increasingly competitive industry. New low-cost players were coming in behind them, having learned from Teva's success and hungry to capture a share of the growing market. The innovative firms had also finally woken up, with one hand vigorously protecting their hard-earned patents and, with the other, encroaching on the generics market. In front of Teva lay the complex world of global markets for generics, as well as the innovative drug market, both of which were large and growing but did not necessarily play to Teva's historical strengths. How should Teva grow in the next ten years? Should it focus on consolidating the U.S. and other substitution-oriented generics markets, on further expanding into the global branded generics markets, or on gradually turning itself into a more specialized generics or even an innovative firm? Alternatively, did it need to focus on all three areas to succeed, and if so, could it manage such diverse goals under one roof?

QUESTIONS

1. The generics drug industry has a relatively low average profitability, but Teva has been able to consistently report significant profitability. What are the reasons for Teva's superior performance in its industry?

2. How sustainable is Teva's superior performance going forward? What are the potential threats? Do you think Teva can deal with these threats effectively?

38. Wall Street Journal, May 4, 2006.
39. "Not just generics and Copaxone," Globes, April 10, 2006.

3. What are potential sources of Teva's future growth? What are some of the challenges the company faces in pursuing its future growth? In your view, will Teva be able to deal with these challenges successfully and maintain its growth? If not, why not?

EXHIBIT 1

Innovative and Generics Cost Structure Comparison (2005)

	TEVA	Barr	Sandoz	Watson	Mylan	Big Pharma[a]	Generics[b]
Nest sales	100%	100%	100%	100%	100%	100%	100%
Gross profit	47%	70%	51%	48%	56%	75%	51%
R&D expenses	7%	12%	9%	6%	7%	14%	7%
SG&A	15%	29%	26%	10%	14%	33%	16%
Op income	25%	32%	13%	13%	25%	28%	19%
Industry sales growth[c]						5%	16%

Source: Bank of America Securities, Company 20F and 10K filings.

[a]*Bank of America Securities, 2003.*

[b]*Average of Teva, Watson, Mylan, and Sandoz.*

[c]*From European and Chemical news (see footnote from text).*

Teva Pharmaceutical Industries, Ltd

EXHIBIT 2
Pharmaceuticals Industry Revenue and Growth

Pharmaceuticals Industry Revenues

Revenues ($bn)	2000	2001	2002	2003	2004	2005	CGR (%)
Worldwide	362	395.1	431.3	470.8	513.9	561	9.2
North America	152	171.1	192.7	216.9	244.2	274.9	12.6
Europe	79.6	85.3	91.3	97.8	104.8	112.2	7.1
Eastern and Central Europe	7.2	7.9	8.6	9.4	10.3	11.2	9.2
Japan	57.9	59.7	61.5	63.4	65.3	67.3	3.1
East Asia and China	18.1	20.5	23.2	26.3	29.8	33.7	13.2
India	3.6	3.9	4.3	4.7	5.1	5.6	9.2
Latin America	25.3	27.6	30.1	33	36	39.3	9.2
Rest of World	18.3	19.1	19.6	19.3	18.4	16.8	−1.7

Generics Industry

Revenues ($, mm)	1998	1999	2000	2001	2002	2003	Past CGR (%)	Estimated Future CAGR[a]
Worldwide	27,180	29,750	32,600	35,900	39,400	43,300	9.8	10.0
United States	11,150	12,300	13,550	15,000	16,500	18,200	10.3	12.6
Western Europe	6,250	7,100	8,100	9,300	10,600	12,100	14.1	10.5
Japan	4,860	5,100	5,350	5,600	5,900	6,200	5.0	4.8
Rest of World	4,920	5,250	5,600	6,000	6,400	6,800	6.7	9.5

Region Share of Pharma Market (2003)	
North America	50.9
Europe	25.4
Japan	11.7
Africa, Asia, Australia	7.9
Latin America	4.1

Distrib'n of Sales of New Meds[b]	
United States	62%
Europe	21%
Japan	7%
Rest of World	10%

Source: *Medical and Healthcare Marketplace Guide*, 2004.

[a]Novartis estimates.

[b]Launched between 1997 and 2001.

EXHIBIT 3

Generics Penetration in Selected Markets (2004)

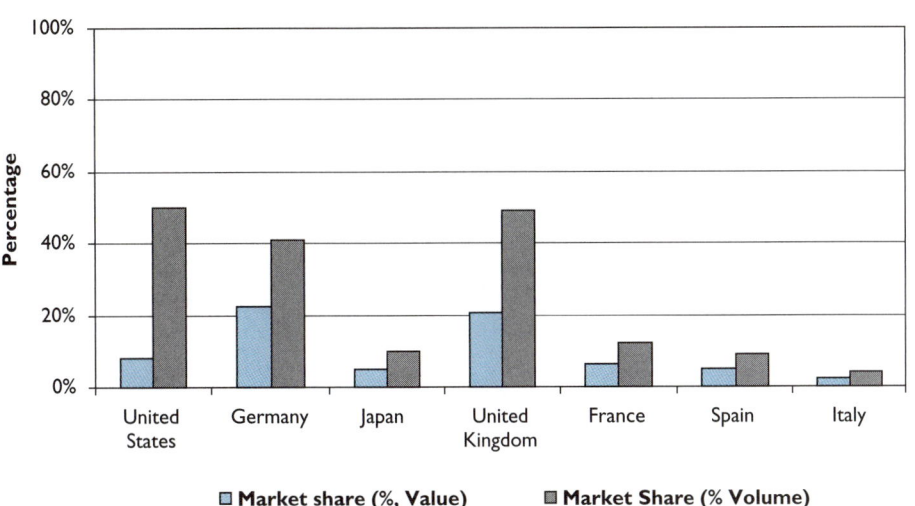

☐ **Market share (%, Value)**   ■ **Market Share (% Volume)**

Source: European Generics Association.

EXHIBIT 4

Estimated Size and Growth of the Largest Generics Markets 2004–2008

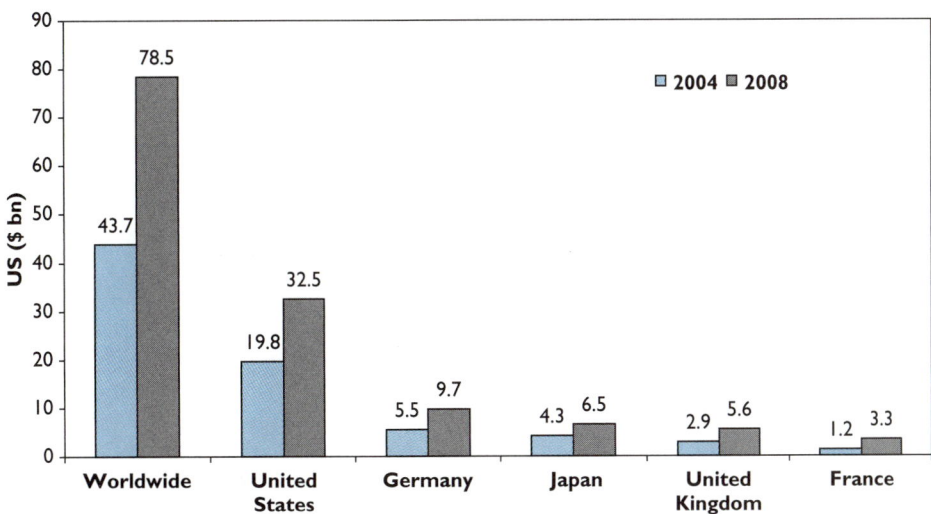

Source: IMS, Datamonitor, secondary source (Ranbaxy).

Teva Pharmaceutical Industries, Ltd

EXHIBIT 5
Selected Market Indicators

	Population, Total (mm)[a]	Population Growth (annual %)	GDP (current US$, $bn)[a]	GDP Growth (annual %)[a]	GNI/Cap, (current US$)[a]	% GDP Spend on Healthcare (2002)[b]	Life Expectancy at Birth[b]	Physicians Total	Physicians per 1,000 Pop.	Pharmacists Total No.[b]	Pharmacists per 1,000 Pop.	Healthcare Expenditures/ cap ($)[b]	% of Healthcare Spent on Pharma[c]
Low and Middle Income Countries													
Argentina	39	0.97	153	8.98	3,720	8.9	74	108,800	3.01	15,300	0.42	305	
Brazil	186	1.32	604	4.90	3,090	7.6	69	198,153	1.15	51,317	0.30	212	
China	1,316	0.70	1,932	10.10	1,290	5.6	71	1,364,000	1.06	359,000	0.28	61	
Hungary	10	−0.20	101	4.65	8,270	8.4	73	32,877	3.33	5,125	0.52	684	31.00
India	1,103	1.51	691	6.90	620	4.8	62	645,825	0.60	592,577	0.56	27	
Israel	7	2.08	117	4.44	17,380	8.9	80	24,577	3.82	4,480	0.70	1,514	
Mexico	107	1.34	676	4.36	6,770	6.2	74	195,897	1.98	3,189	0.03	372	
Poland	39	−0.01	242	5.44	6,090	6.5	75	95,272	2.47	25,397	0.66	354	
Russia	143	−0.29	581	7.14	3,410	5.6	65	609,043	4.25	11,404	0.08	167	
South Korea	48	0.57	680	4.64	13,980	5.6	76	75,045	1.57	50,623	1.08	705	
Turkey	73	1.44	303	8.93	3,750	7.6	70	96,000	1.35	22,500	0.32	257	
Developed Countries													
Canada	32	0.87	978	2.90	28,390	9.9	80	66,583	2.14	20,765	0.67	2,669	16.20
France	60	0.35	2,047	2.32	30,090	10.1	80	203,487	3.37	63,909	1.06	2,981	21.00
Germany	83	0.12	2,741	1.57	30,120	11.1	79	277,885	3.37	47,956	0.58	3,204	14.30
Italy	58	0.13	1,678	1.22	26,120	8.4	81	241,000	4.20	66,119	1.15	2,139	22.30
Japan	128	0.19	4,623	2.70	37,180	7.9	82	251,889	1.98	154,428	1.21	2,662	
Netherlands	16	0.49	579	1.44	31,700	9.8	79	50,854	3.15	3,134	0.19	3,088	10.10
United Kingdom	60	0.31	2,124	3.14	33,940	8.0	79	133,641	2.30	29,726	0.51	2,428	
United States	298	0.92	11,712	4.20	41,400	15.2	77	730,801	2.56	249,642	0.88	5,711	12.40

Source: World Heath Organization, World Bank.

Teva Pharmaceutical Industries, Ltd

EXHIBIT 6

Competitor Information (need IMS, updated info here)

Annual, 2005	Teva	Barr	Sandoz[a]	Mylan	Watson	Ranbaxy	Ratiopharm[b]
Annual Sales ($ mil)	5,250.40	1,047.40	4,694.00	1,253.40	1,646.20	1,117.00	~ $2,000
Estimated U.S. generics revenues[c]	2,170.00	tbd	tbd	tbd	tbd	328.00	NA
Operating income	1312.9	330	342.00			41.9	NP
Employees	14,000	1,900	13,397	3,000	3,844	9,000	5,300
Market Cap ($ mil.)	26,191.30	6,403.70	NA	4,626.50	3,247.60	3,249.00	Not public
Strategic position							
Total Rx market share in U.S.[d]	18.0%	4.0%	10.0%	11.0%	9.0%	2.0%	NA
Number of U.S. Rx (June 2006, '000)[d]	391	82	212	236	195	49	NA
Rx growth in U.S.[d]	17.4%	-2.9%	11.7%	8.3%	7.6%	27.2%	NA
Number of products in the U.S.	326	75	—	140	125		—
FDA approvals[c]	43	16	—	22			—
FDA applications (pipeline)[d]	201	35	—	41	35	59	—
Para IV applications[d]	47	10	—	10	1		—
Profitability							
Gross Profit Margin	51.86%	76.72%	—	53.40%	50.82%		—
Operating Profit Margin	25.01%	31.51%	7.30%	13.21%	8.40%	3.75%	—
Return on Equity	17.70%	18.90%	—	21.70%	6.60%		—
Return on Assets	10.30%	16.70%	—	9.00%	4.50%		—
Growth							
12-Month Revenue Growth	9.40%	4.90%	—	-1.70%	0.30%		—
12-Month Net Income Growth	223.20%	74.90%	—	-31.30%	-8.70%		—
36-Month Revenue Growth	29.50%	7.30%	—	-0.30%	10.60%		—
36-Month Net Income Growth	24.00%	12.00%	—	-14.70%	-9.70%		—

Source: Company 10K, 20F, Hoovers, WR Hambrecht.

[a]Data unavailable.
[b]Private company, data not published.
[c]Casewriter estimates.
[d]IMS, June 2006.

Teva Pharmaceutical Industries, Ltd

EXHIBIT 7

Representative Revenues and Margins for Different Categories of Pharmaceuticals

	Patent-Protected Innovative Blockbuster	Commodity Version of Blockbuster in U.S. (and Other Substitute Markets) with 180-Day Exclusivity	Commodity Generic in Substitute Markets without Exclusivity	Commodity Generic in Branded Market	Niche Drug ($1 Bn Baseline)	Biosimilar Version of Biotech $1 Bn Blockbuster
Approximate 12-month revenue	1,000	120	10	175	490	400
Approximate gross margin	930	60	4	140	392	340
Approximate operating profit	300	50	3	35	196	120
Assumptions:						
Market share by volume	100%	50% first 6 mos then 35%	10%	25%[a]	70%	50%
Discount	0%	60% first 6 mos then 90%	90%	30%	30%	20%

Source: Casewriter estimates.

EXHIBIT 8
Teva Acquisitions from 1985 to 2005

Date	Company Acquired	Location	Deal Value (USD, M)	Value/Sales
Jul-05	Ivax	United States	7,367	3.65
Aug-04	Dorom	Italy	85	2.33
Oct-03	Sicor	United States	3,401	6.49
Jun-02	Honeywell Fine Chemicals	Italy	168	N/A
Feb-02	Bayer Classics	France	86	N/A
Dec-99	Novopharm	Canada	258	N/A
Aug-99	Copley	United States	220	1.77
May-98	Pharmachemie	Netherlands	87	N/A
Aug-96	APS/Berk	United Kingdom	53	0.81
Jan-96	Biocraft Labs	United States	296	2.12
Nov-95	Biogal	Hungary	25	0.36
Mar-92	Procintex and GRY-Pharm	Italy, Germany	23	N/A
1988	Abic	Israel	27	N/A
1985	Lemmon	United States	21	N/A

Source: Windhover's Strategic Intelligence Systems, Company 20F, Thomson Financial, Securities Data.

EXHIBIT 9
Teva Estimated Revenue Breakdown, 2003–2005

	2005	2004	2003
Net Sales	5,250	4,799	3,276
Copaxone (@55%)	647	515	396
API	524	501	371
Other	23	22	20
Generics in U.S.	2,166	2,173	1,399
Generics in Europe	—	—	—
Generics in ROW	1,890	1,589	1,091
Generics in EU and ROW	1,890	1,589	1,091
Total generics sales	4,056	3,761	2,489
Number of generics prescriptions in U.S.	252	220	tbd

Source: Company 20F and casewriter estimates.

EXHIBIT 10

Teva Total Generics Prescriptions

Total Prescriptions in U.S. (June 2006)					
All Pharmaceutical Companies			Generics Only		
Company		Growth	Company	Share	Growth
Teva USA	393,014	17.3	Teva USA	390,845	18%	17.4
Pfizer	314,200	−9.1	Mylan	236,033	11%	8.3
Novartis (without Sandoz)	292,317	8.4	Sandoz	212,020	10%	11.7
Mylan	239,045	7.8	Watson	195,053	9%	7.6
Watson	195,060	7.6	Mallinckrodt	103,874	5%	23.9
Merck	137,545	9.9	Actavis	89,020	4%	−1.2
GlaxoSmithKline	128,982	−3.0	Barr	82,034	4%	−2.9
AstraZeneca	114,789	8.3	Par	71,767	3%	−2.8
Mallinckrodt	103,874	23.9	Qualitest	70,888	3%	−7.2
Actavis	89,022	−1.2	Ranbaxy	49,335	2%	27.2

Source: Teva, primary: IMS, June 2006.

EXHIBIT 11

Teva's Revenues by Geography (1987 to 2005) (U.S. $ in thousands)

	1987	1988	1989	1990	1991	1992	1993	1994	1995	1996	1997	1998	1999	2000	2001	2002	2003	2004	2005[a]
North America	46	62	83	97	105	138	229	281	293	460	552	516	604	1,031	1,288	1,611	2,055	3,059	3,146
% total	*33%*	*29%*	*31%*	*33%*	*33%*	*35%*	*46%*	*48%*	*44%*	*48%*	*49%*	*46%*	*47%*	*59%*	*62%*	*64%*	*63%*	*64%*	*60%*
Europe and CIS	13	14	18	23	27	37	42	53	78	162	220	286	384	399	457	600	861	1,245	1,529
% total	*9%*	*7%*	*7%*	*8%*	*9%*	*9%*	*8%*	*9%*	*12%*	*17%*	*20%*	*26%*	*30%*	*23%*	*22%*	*24%*	*26%*	*26%*	*29%*
Israel	74	124	152	159	170	194	202	226	263	281	284	253	240	245	241	232	257	285	307
% total	*53%*	*59%*	*57%*	*54%*	*53%*	*49%*	*40%*	*38%*	*39%*	*29%*	*25%*	*23%*	*19%*	*14%*	*12%*	*9%*	*8%*	*6%*	*6%*
Other countries	7	11	16	17	19	28	29	28	34	50	60	61	54	76	91	76	103	210	268
% total	*5%*	*5%*	*6%*	*6%*	*6%*	*7%*	*6%*	*5%*	*5%*	*5%*	*5%*	*5%*	*4%*	*4%*	*4%*	*3%*	*3%*	*4%*	*5%*
Total	**140**	**211**	**268**	**295**	**321**	**396**	**502**	**588**	**668**	**954**	**1,117**	**1,116**	**1,282**	**1,750**	**2,077**	**2,519**	**3,276**	**4,799**	**5,250**

Source: Teva annual reports, 20K.

Notes: 1987 converted at 1.5387 NIS = $1.

Starting in 1996, Europe turned into Western Europe plus Hungary.

Teva Pharmaceutical Industries, Ltd

EXHIBIT 12

Teva and Ivax Geographic Mix, 2004

Teva[a]		Ivax[b]	
North America	3,059	United States	860
% total	64%	% total	46%
Europe and CIS	1,245	Europe	704
% total	26%	% total	37%
Israel	285	Latin America	316
% total	6%	% total	17%
Other countries	210	Other countries	0
% total	4%	% total	0%
Total	**4,799**	**Total**	**1,880**

Source: WR Hambrecht.

[a]Teva 2004, 20F.
[b]WR Hambrecht estimates.

EXHIBIT 13

Teva Cost and Output Trends (1998 to 2005)

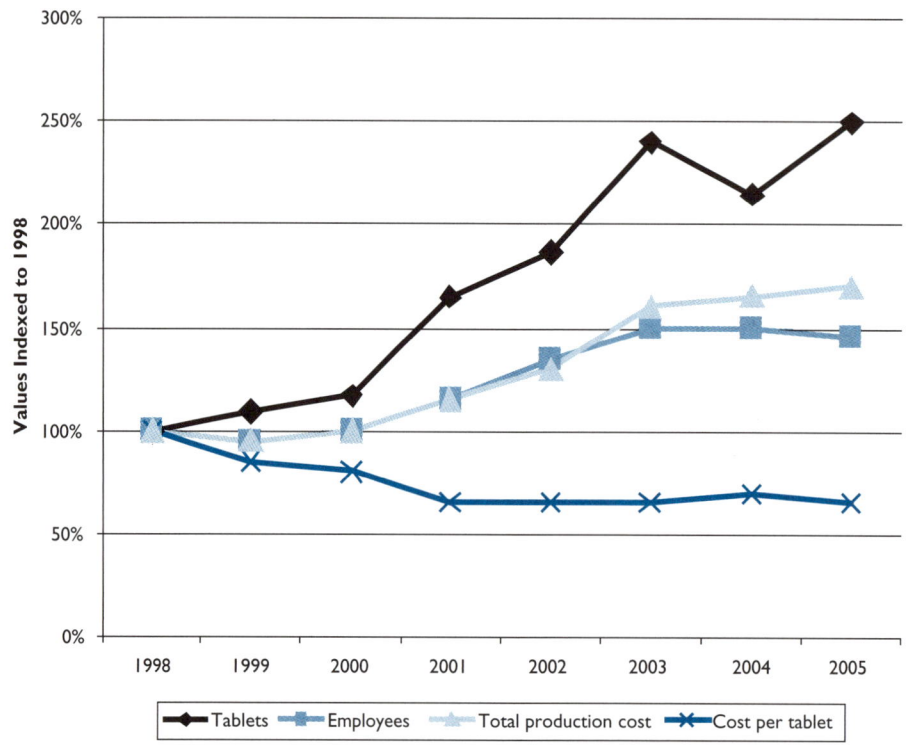

Source: Teva.

EXHIBIT 14

Teva Post-Ivax Global Operations

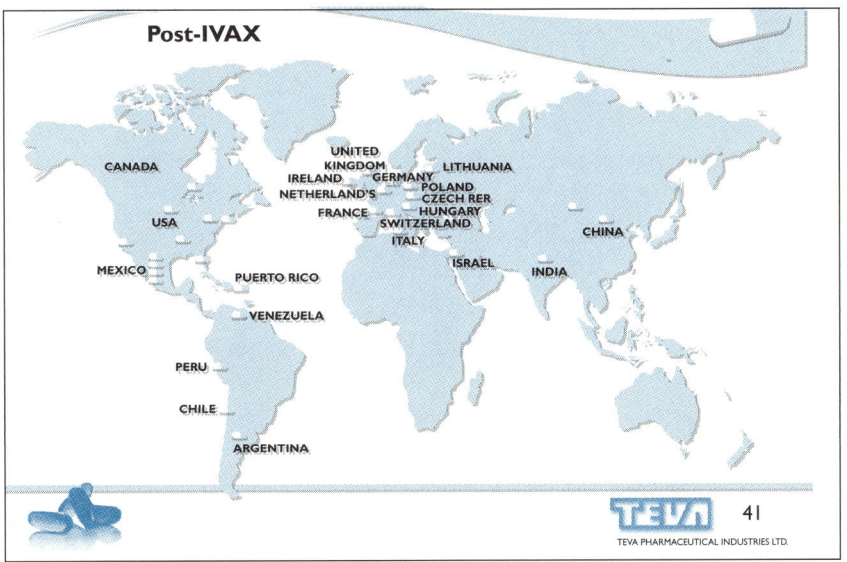

Source: Teva company documents.

EXHIBIT 15

Teva Israel Production

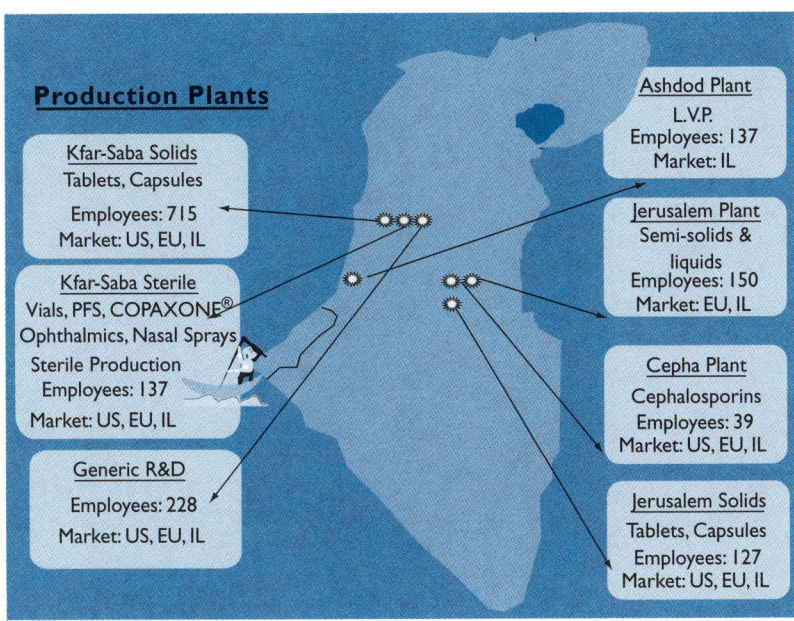

Source: Teva company documents.

EXHIBIT 16

Major Recent Deals in the Generics Industry (2001 to 2006)

Date	Acquiror	Company Acquired	Deal Value (USD, M)	Value/ Sales
4/24/2006	Ranbaxy Laboratories Ltd	Ethimed NV	np	np
3/4/2006	Dr Reddys Laboratories Ltd	Betapharm Arzneimittel GmbH	571	np
1/26/2006	Teva Pharma Inds Ltd	IVAX Corp	7,367	3.65
12/19/2005	Actavis Group hf	Alpharma Inc-Generics Business	810	np
8/4/2005	RoundTable Healthcare Partners	CorePharma LLC	np	np
7/26/2005	Novartis AG	Eon Labs Inc	933	6.67
7/21/2005	Novartis AG	Eon Labs Inc	1,700	5.84
6/6/2005	Novartis AG	Hexal AG	5,685	np
8/16/2004	Sandoz GmbH	Sabex Inc	565	np
6/30/2004	Sandoz GmbH	Durascan Medical Products A/S	60	2.00
6/10/2004	Pharmaceutical Resources Inc	Kali Laboratories Inc	145	np
1/22/2004	Teva Pharma Inds Ltd	SICOR Inc	3,401	6.49
1/5/2004	Ranbaxy Laboratories Ltd	RPG Aventis	np	np
3/10/2003	STADA Arzneimittel AG	Schein Pharm Holdings UK Ltd	19	1.64
4/1/2002	Dr Reddys Laboratories Ltd	BMS Laboratories Ltd	13	1.13
10/24/2001	Barr Laboratories Inc	Duramed Pharmaceuticals Inc	594	6.31
4/24/2006	Ranbaxy Laboratories Ltd	Ethimed NV	np	np
3/4/2006	Dr Reddys Laboratories Ltd	Betapharm Arzneimittel GmbH	571	np

Source: Thomson Financial, Securities Data.

INDEX

Note: In each entry, the first number is the chapter number; the numbers following the hyphen (-) are the range of pages on which the entry appears. Bold type is used to indicate the numbers of rules. Italic type indicates the page numbers of charts and tables. An "n" after a page number indicates that the entry is an author's note.

AUTHOR INDEX

IMPORTANT FORMULAS

Ratio Analysis

(1) ROE = Operating ROA + Spread × Net financial leverage
    (Operating margin × Asset turnover) + Spread × Net financial leverage

$$\text{ROE} = \frac{\text{Net income}}{\text{Equity}}$$

$$\text{Operating ROA} = \frac{\text{Net operating profit after tax}}{\text{Operating working capital} + \text{Net long-term assets}}$$

$$\text{Spread} = \text{Operating ROA} - \frac{\text{Net interest expense after tax}}{\text{Debt} - (\text{Cash} + \text{Short-term investments})}$$

$$\text{Net financial leverage} = \frac{\text{Interest-bearing debt} - (\text{Cash} + \text{Short-term investments})}{\text{Equity}}$$

$$\text{Operating margin} = \frac{\text{Net operating profit after tax}}{\text{Sales}}$$

$$\text{Asset turnover} = \frac{\text{Sales}}{\text{Assets} - (\text{Cash} + \text{Short-term investments})}$$

(2) Sustainable growth rate = ROE × (1 − Dividend payout rate)

$$\text{Dividend payout rate} = \frac{\text{Dividends}}{\text{Net income}}$$

Equity Valuation

(1) $\text{Equity value} = BVE_0 + \dfrac{NI_1 - r_e \cdot BVE_0}{(1 + r_e)} + \dfrac{NI_2 - r_e \cdot BVE_1}{(1 + r_e)^2}$

$\qquad + \dfrac{NI_3 - r_e \cdot BVE_2}{(1 + r_e)^3} + \cdots$

where BVE_t = book value of equity at the end of year t
$\qquad NI_t$ = net income available to common shareholders for year t
$\qquad r_e$ = cost of equity capital